CA

D0851922

Following Chapter 18

Services Marketing
People, Technology, Strategy

Fourth Edition

Christopher Lovelock
Lovelock Associates

Prentice Hall

Upper Saddle River, New Jersey 07458

Acquisitions Editor: Leah Johnson
Editorial Assistant: Rebecca Calvert
Assistant Editor: Anthony Palmiotto
Managing Editor (Editorial): Bruce Kaplan
Editor-in-Chief: Jim Boyd
Marketing Manager: Shannon Moore
Marketing Assistant: Kathleen Mulligan
Permissions Coordinator: Suzanne Grappi
Managing Editor (Production): John Roberts
Production Manager: Arnold Vila
Associate Director, Manufacturing: Vincent Scelta
Design Manager: Patricia Smythe
Cover Design: Marjory Dressler
Cover Illustration: Marjory Dressler
Composition: Impressions Book and Journal Services, Inc.

Library of Congress Cataloging-in-Publication Data
Lovelock, Christopher H.
  Services marketing / Christopher Lovelock.—4th ed.
      p. cm.
  Includes bibliographical references and index.
  ISBN 0-13-017392-4
  1. Professions—Marketing. 2. Service industries—Marketing. I. Title.
HF5415.122 .L68 2000
658.8—dc21   00-035959

Credits and acknowledgments for materials borrowed from other sources and reproduced, with permission, in this textbook appear on page 694.

Printed in the United States of America
10 9 8 7 6 5 4 3 2 1
ISBN 0-13-017392-4

To my brothers, Roger and Jeremy,
and my sister, Rachel, with love

Contents

Preface

Preparing the fourth edition of *Services Marketing: People, Technology, Strategy* has been an exciting challenge. Seventeen years have passed since the first edition appeared in 1984. I'm struck by how much the nature of research, teaching, and management practice in the field has changed during that time. In response, the book has changed greatly, too. The second edition, which appeared in 1991, and the third, published in 1996, both represented significant revisions, necessarily incorporating new concepts and examples and dispensing with those that were becoming dated—as any good textbook revision should. But the fourth, published at a time of extraordinarily rapid change in the global economy, represents the most substantial revision of all.

Services marketing, once a tiny academic field championed by just a handful of pioneering professors, has become a thriving area of activity. Paralleling growing research efforts in both academia and business, students are increasingly interested in taking courses that focus on different aspects of managing service organizations, including marketing. This makes a lot of sense from a career standpoint because most business school graduates will be going to work in service industries, and managers report that manufacturing-based models of business practice are not always useful to them.

What's New in the Fourth Edition?

Responding to continuing rapid changes in technology and the environment of the service sector, as well as to new research findings and reviewer suggestions, the content of the fourth edition represents a major revision. It comprises 18 chapters, 10 readings , and 10 cases of varying lengths and levels of difficulty. Key changes from the third edition—described in more detail later in this preface—include:

- four new chapters, plus substantial revisions to each of the others
- seven new readings
- five new cases and updates or revisions to three more
- more substantive coverage of consumer behavior, people management issues, business-to-business services, and Internet-based services
- improved approaches to pedagogy, designed to enhance student learning
- revised and enlarged supplements, including an excellent instructor's manual and more than 200 PowerPoint color transparencies.

Target Audiences and Courses

Unlike the third edition, which was targeted at both MBA and undergraduate audiences, the new fourth edition is designed primarily for use in MBA and Executive MBA courses. However, reflecting AACSB requirements for use of separate texts in MBA and undergraduate courses taught at the same institution, *Services Marketing*, Fourth Edition, is designed to be conceptually consistent with my simpler and shorter undergraduate text, Christopher Lovelock and Lauren Wright, *Principles of Service Marketing and Management* (Prentice Hall, 1999). My hope is that the availability of these two compatible texts will make life easier for instructors who need to teach service courses at two different levels. Both books also meet AACSB guidelines concerning inclusion of international content.

As the fourth edition's new subtitle suggests, *Services Marketing: People, Technology, Strategy* presents an integrated approach to studying services that places marketing issues within a broader general management context. Whatever a manager's specific job may be, he or she has to understand and acknowledge the close ties that link the marketing, operations, and human resource functions. With that perspective in mind, this book has been designed so instructors can make selective use of chapters, readings, and cases to teach courses of different lengths and formats in either services marketing or service management.

Books are necessarily printed in a linear sequence. However, *Services Marketing* has been designed to give instructors the flexibility to depart from the printed order if they wish. For instance, the reading on "Service Markets and the Internet" can be assigned near the beginning of the course if instructors wish to give early emphasis to information technology. Similarly, chapter 18, "Technology and Service Strategy," and chapter 15, "Managing People in Service Organizations," can easily be moved up in the course sequence.

Distinguishing Features of the Book

Key features of this highly readable book include its strong managerial orientation and strategic focus, use of conceptual frameworks that have been classroom tested for relevance to both MBA students and executive seminar participants, incorporation of key academic research findings, use of interesting examples to link theory to practice, and inclusion of carefully selected readings and cases to accompany the text chapters.

Services Marketing, Fourth Edition, is designed to complement the materials found in traditional marketing principles texts. It avoids sweeping and often misleading generalizations about services, recognizing explicitly that the differences between specific categories of services (based on the nature of the underlying service process) may be as important to student understanding as the broader differences between goods marketing and services marketing. It also draws a distinction between the marketing of services and the marketing of goods *through service.*

The book shows how different technologies—and information technology in particular—are changing the nature of service delivery and can offer innovative ways for service providers and customers to relate to each other (the people side of the business). Both text and readings make widespread use of recent research in such areas as service encounters, customer expectations and satisfaction, loyalty and relationship marketing, service quality, service recovery, managing demand and capacity, productivity improvement in services, pricing and yield management, new service development, technology, and service leadership.

The service sector of the economy can best be characterized by its diversity. No single conceptual model suffices to cover marketing-relevant issues among organizations ranging from huge international corporations (in fields such as airlines, banking, insurance, telecommunications, hotel chains, and freight transportation) to locally owned and operated small businesses such as restaurants, laundries, taxis, optometrists, and many business-to-business services. So

Services Marketing offers a carefully designed "toolbox" for service managers, teaching students how different concepts, frameworks, and analytical procedures can best be used to examine and resolve the varied challenges faced by managers in different situations. Once introduced, many of these tools reappear in subsequent chapters.

Throughout the book, I stress the importance for service marketers of understanding the operational processes underlying service creation and delivery. These processes are grouped into four categories, each of which has distinctive implications for the nature of service encounters, the roles played by customers and service personnel, the strategic application of information technology to delivery systems, and management practice.

New Chapter Content in the Fourth Edition

Changes and enhancements to the chapters include the following:

- A substantial revision and updating of all text materials, including addition of numerous references from the period 1997–2000.
- Use of the new 8Ps framework of integrated service management, which adds Productivity and Quality as linked concepts and modifies several of the elements of the traditional 7Ps framework (for instance, describing service delivery systems in terms of "Place, Cyberspace, and Time" instead of the outdated "Place" terminology).
- Addition of four new chapters, each focusing on a critical topic in services marketing that is also linked to other areas throughout the text:
  - Customer Behavior in Service Settings (chapter 4)
  - Creating Delivery Systems in Place, Cyberspace, and Time (chapter 11)
  - Managing Customer Waiting Lines and Reservations (chapter 14)
  - Technology and Service Strategy (chapter 18)
- A significant rewrite of material relating to human resource management (see chapter 15, "Managing People in Service Organizations").
- A major rewrite of material on strategy and organization (see chapter 16, "Organizing for Service Leadership").
- Deeper analysis of customer-oriented issues relating to demand and capacity management.
- A restructured and resequenced discussion of positioning, service product strategies, new service development, and service delivery.
- More coverage of business-to-business services.
- An enhanced treatment of service pricing, designed to capture student interest and including such topics as activity-based costing, yield management, and introduction of new types of service fees.
- A more balanced treatment of marketing communication, describing its role in educating service customers in addition to promoting sales.
- Coverage of technology issues and Internet/Web applications throughout the book, supplemented by a reading, case material, and in-depth treatment in chapter 18 of how technological change impacts services.
- Discussion of ethical issues facing service managers, raised as appropriate in specific and relevant contexts.
- A substantial revision of chapter 17, "International and Global Strategies in Service Management." Important concepts are clarified with interesting, accessible examples from the United States, Canada, and around the world.
- Better integration between chapters to tighten the linkages between chapters and also facilitate their use in alternative sequences.
- Specific referrals within the chapter text to relevant readings and cases.

New Readings and Cases

Complementing the chapters is a selection of readings and cases. These materials offer instructors an opportunity to expose students to the ideas, insights, and research findings of leading academic thinkers and to stimulate classroom discussion of real-world service issues. Specifically, the fourth edition features:

- Ten excellent readings of which three are carried over from the third edition. The seven new readings, copyrighted between 1997 and 2001, are drawn from *Harvard Business Review, International Journal of Service Industry Management, Journal of Service Research,* and *Sloan Management Review.* They also include three new articles specially commissioned for this book from leading academic experts.
- Ten challenging and exciting cases from a cross section of service industries, including business-to-business and professional services as well as consumer services. Five of these cases are new, one has been revised, and two updated; only two are unchanged from the third edition. Five of these cases bear 2000 or 2001 copyright dates. (Note: Additional cases, including some old favorites from the third edition, will be featured in downloadable form on a Prentice Hall Web site.)

New and Improved Pedagogical Aids

In response to adopter requests, the following pedagogical enhancements have been added to the text:

- An introduction to each chapter highlights key issues and questions to be addressed.
- Three types of boxed inserts are included in many of the chapters:
  - *Management Memo* (suggestions for good practice)
  - *Research Insights* (summaries of interesting published research)
  - *Service Perspectives* (in-depth examples that illustrate key concepts)
- New and improved graphics, including reproductions of ads, are included to enhance both visual appeal and student learning.
- Review Questions and Application Exercises have been added at the end of each chapter.
- A short and accessible note for students on "Studying and Learning from Cases" (revised from the third edition), precedes the cases, which are now gathered together at the end of the book.
- The six-part *Instructors Resource Manual for Services Marketing 4/E* includes:
  1. Detailed course design and teaching hints, plus sample course outlines.
  2. Chapter-by-chapter teaching suggestions plus discussion of learning objectives and sample responses to study questions and exercises.
  3. An overview of each reading, with suggestions for how to use it and the best chapter(s) with which to assign it.
  4. A description of 16 suggested student exercises and 5 comprehensive projects (designed for either individual or team use).
  5. Detailed teaching notes for each of the 10 cases, plus suggestions for possible chapters with which they might be paired.
  6. Full-page black-and-white reproductions of the more than 200 PowerPoint slides, created specifically for use with this book. Attractive color versions of each slide are also available.

Acknowledgments

Over the years, many colleagues in both the academic and business worlds have provided me with valuable insights into the management and marketing of services, through their writings and in conference or seminar discussions. High on the list was my good friend, the late Eric Langeard, a European pioneer in services marketing who, sadly, died in 1998. I have also benefited enormously from in-class and after-class discussions with MBAs and executive program participants.

Although it's impossible to mention everyone who has influenced my thinking, I particularly want to express my appreciation to the following individuals: John Bateson of Gemini Consulting; Leonard Berry of Texas A&M University; Mary Jo Bitner, Steven Brown, and David Bowen of Arizona State University; Richard Chase of the University of Southern California; Pierre Eiglier of Université d'Aix-Marseille III; Liam Glynn of University College, Dublin; Christian Grönroos of the Swedish School of Economics in Finland; Evert Gummesson of Stockholm University; James Heskett, Theodore Levitt, Earl Sasser, and Len Schlesinger, all currently or formerly of Harvard Business School; Jean-Claude Larréché of INSEAD; David Maister of Maister Associates; Richard Munn of the Information Technology Services Marketing Association; "Parsu" Parasuraman of the University of Miami; Fred Reichheld of Bain & Co.; Roland Rust of Vanderbilt University; Benjamin Schneider of the University of Maryland; Charles Weinberg of the University of British Columbia; George Yip of the University of Cambridge; and Valarie Zeithaml of the University of North Carolina.

Special thanks are due, in particular, to the insights received from the co-authors with whom I have worked closely in recent years on international adaptations of *Services Marketing*: Denis Lapert of Reims Management School; Barbara Lewis of the Manchester School of Management; Paul Patterson of the University of New South Wales; Sandra Vandermerwe of Imperial College, London; Rhett Walker of the Royal Melbourne Institute of Technology; and Jochen Wirtz of the National University of Singapore. Appreciative thanks are due, too, to Lauren Wright of California State University, Chico, with whom I worked to create and write *Principles of Service Marketing and Management*.

Four individuals graciously agreed to contribute original articles to the readings contained in this book. I'm delighted to acknowledge the participation of John Deighton of Harvard Business School, Ray Fisk of the University of New Orleans, Steve Grove of Clemson University, and Javier Reynoso of ITESM, Monterrey, Mexico. I thank, too, those authors (listed on pages xvii–xviii) of the previously published cases and readings, as well as the copyright holders for permission to reprint these and other materials.

I am also pleased to acknowledge the insightful and helpful comments of the reviewers: Dawn Iacobucci, Northwestern University; Douglas J. Dalrymple, Indiana University; Surendra N. Singh, Oklahoma State University; and Tom J. Brown, Oklahoma State University. They challenged my thinking and, through their critiques and suggestions, encouraged me to include many substantial changes in the fourth edition.

It takes more than an author to create a book and its supplements. Warm thanks are due to my son, Tim, who helped to design and prepare many of the PowerPoint graphics developed as teaching aids. And, of course, I'm very appreciative of all the hard work put in by the editorial, production, and marketing staff in helping to transform my sometimes messy manuscript into a handsome published text. They include supplements editor Anthony Palmiotto, editorial assistant Rebecca Calvert, design manager Pat Smythe, managing editor for production John Roberts, senior marketing manager Shannon Moore, and at Impressions, Mary Boss. Finally, a big thank you to Leah Johnson, my editor, for her enthusiasm and support.

—Christopher Lovelock

About the Author and Contributors

 *Christopher Lovelock,* one of the pioneers of service marketing, divides his professional life among writing, teaching, and consulting. Based in New England, he gives seminars and workshops in the United States and around the world. He has also lived and worked in Britain, Canada, France, and Switzerland. His past academic career includes 11 years on the faculty of the Harvard Business School; 2 years as a visiting professor at the International Institute for Management Development (IMD) in Switzerland, and short-term appointments at Berkeley, Stanford, the Sloan School at MIT, Theseus Institute, and INSEAD. Christopher is author of 60 articles, over 100 teaching cases, and 20 books. He is a recipient of the *Journal of Marketing*'s Alpha Kappa Psi Award, the American Marketing Association's Award for Career Contributions to the Services Discipline, and many awards for outstanding cases. He holds MA and BCom degrees from the University of Edinburgh, an MBA from Harvard, and a PhD from Stanford.

Leonard L. Berry is Distinguished Professor of Marketing at Texas A&M University, where he holds the J. C. Penney Chair of Retailing Studies and is director of the Center for Retailing Studies.

Mary Jo Bitner is the AT&T Professor of Services Marketing and Management at Arizona State University and research director for its Center for Services Marketing and Management.

Martin Bless was formerly a research associate at the International Institute for Management Development (IMD), Switzerland.

Bernard J. Booms is a professor at Washington State University.

Richard B. Chase is Justin B. Dart Professor of Operations Management and director of the Center for Service Excellence at the University of Southern California.

John Deighton is professor of business administration at the Harvard Business School and co-editor of the *Journal of Interactive Marketing*.

Raymond P. Fisk is professor and chair of marketing at the University of New Orleans.

Stephen J. Grove is professor of marketing at Clemson University.

James L. Heskett is the UPS Foundation Professor of Business Logistics emeritus at the Harvard Business School.

Raija Jarvinen teaches at the University of Tampere, Finland.

Thomas O. Jones was formerly a professor at the Harvard Business School.

Sheryl E. Kimes is a professor at Cornell University.

Jean-Claude Larréché is the Alfred H. Heineken Professor of Marketing at INSEAD, France.

Uolevi Lehtinen teaches at the University of Tampere, Finland.

Gary W. Loveman, formerly at Harvard, is executive vice president of Harrah's Entertainment, Inc.

Harvey Mintzberg is the Cleghorn Professor of Management Studies at McGill University, Canada, and a professor of organization at INSEAD, France.

Louise A. Mohr is an associate professor at Georgia State University.

Ivor Morgan is a professor at Babson College.

Das Narayandas is an associate professor at the Harvard Business School.

A. Parasuraman is a professor at the University of Miami, where he holds the James W. McLamore Chair of Marketing; he is also editor of the *Journal of the Academy of Marketing Science.*

Delphine Parmenter is a research associate at INSEAD, France.

Reg Price is a director of R Cubed, Auckland, New Zealand.

Javier Reynoso is head of the services management research group at ITESM, Mexico.

G. Lynn Shostack is managing director of Joyce International, Inc.

W. Earl Sasser, Jr., is UPS Foundation Professor of Service Management at the Harvard Business School.

Leonard A. Schlesinger was formerly a professor at the Harvard Business School.

Ludo Van der Heyden is the Wendel/CGIP Professor for the Large Family Firm at INSEAD, France, where he holds the Solvay Chair for Technical Innovation.

Ismo Vuorinen teaches at the University of Tampere, Finland.

PART I

Understanding Services

CHAPTER 1

Distinctive Aspects of Service Management

Ours is a service economy and it has been one for some time.

KARL ALBRECHT AND RON ZEMKE[1]

As consumers, we use services every day. Businesses and other organizations also use a wide array of services, usually purchasing on a much larger scale than do individuals or households. Turning on a light, listening to the radio, talking on the telephone, riding a bus, having a pizza delivered, mailing a letter, getting a haircut, refueling a car, writing a check, renting a video, or sending clothes to the cleaners are all examples of service consumption at the individual level. The institution at which you are studying is itself a complex service organization. In addition to educational services, the facilities at today's colleges and universities usually comprise libraries and cafeterias, counseling services and placement offices, a bookstore, copy services, telephones and Internet connections, and maybe even a bank. If you are studying at a residential university, additional services are likely to include dormitories, health care, indoor and outdoor sports and athletic facilities, a theater, and even perhaps a post office and a bank.

Unfortunately, customers—including you, perhaps—are not always happy with the quality and value of the services they receive. People complain about late deliveries, rude or incompetent personnel, inconvenient service hours, poor performance, needlessly complicated procedures, and a host of other problems. They grumble about the difficulty of finding sales assistants to help them in shops, express frustration about mistakes on their credit card bills or bank statements, shake their heads over the complexity of new self-service equipment, mutter about poor value, and sigh as they are forced to wait for service or stand in line almost everywhere they go.

Suppliers of services often seem to have a very different set of concerns. Many complain about how difficult it is to make a profit, how hard it is to find skilled and motivated employees, or how difficult to please customers have become. Some firms seem to believe that the surest route to financial success lies in cutting costs and eliminating what they believe to be unnecessary frills. A few even give the impression that they could run a much more efficient operation if it weren't for all the stupid customers who keep making unreasonable demands and messing things up!

Happily, in almost every field of endeavor there are service suppliers who know how to please their customers while also running a productive, profitable operation, staffed by pleasant and competent employees. In this book, you'll be introduced to innovative organizations, both large and small, from the Americas, Europe, and around the world. By studying the evolution and recent strategies of such organizations—as well as learning from the failures of others—you will start to draw important insights about the most effective ways to manage and market the different types of services found in today's economy.

In this chapter, we present an overview of today's dynamic service economy and explore the following questions:

1. How significant is the service sector in the economies of different countries?
2. What characteristics make services different from goods, and what are the implications for service marketers?
3. Why is it important to examine services marketing in the broader framework of integrated service management?
4. What are the major changes occurring in the service sector, and how are these changes affecting the nature of service competition?
5. Why do service businesses need to integrate the marketing, operations, and human resource functions?

Services in the Modern Economy

Around the world, the service sector of the economy is going through a period of almost revolutionary change in which established ways of doing business continue to be shunted aside. At the beginning of a new millennium, we are seeing the manner in which we live and work being transformed by new developments in services. Innovators continually launch new ways to satisfy our existing needs and to meet needs that we did not even know we had (how many of us, 10 years ago, anticipated a personal need for e-mail?). The same is true of services directed at corporate users.

Although many new service ventures fail, a few succeed—sometimes spectacularly. Many long-established firms are also failing or being merged out of existence, but others progress by continually rethinking the way they do business, looking for innovative ways to serve customers better, and taking advantage of new developments in technology. Consider the following examples:

● *Aramark,* which describes itself as being the "world leader in managed services," has experienced rapid growth as a result of the global trend toward outsourcing of services. It provides companies and public agencies with a wide array of services that its customers used to perform for themselves, including food services, plant operations, facilities maintenance, meeting planning, uniform rental, and laundry. Aramark's customers include businesses, college campuses, schools, hospitals, major league sports teams, convention centers, and even prisons.
● *Southwest Airlines* is the most consistently profitable airline in America. It has successfully positioned itself as a low-cost, no-frills carrier on domestic routes. Underlying its success are punctual, frequent flights that offer excellent value for customers; a low-cost operations strategy that runs counter to established industry traditions; and human resource policies

that have created an extraordinarily loyal and hardworking group of employees. Airlines from around the world have studied Southwest's marketing, operations, and human resource strategies, but none has yet been able to achieve its finely tuned balance.

- *Charles Schwab,* America's largest discount broker, got its start in 1975 when fixed commission rates were abolished in the United States. Its low prices attracted lots of investors away from full-service brokers. The company has always been quick to take advantage of new developments in information technology. Growth was fueled by early investments in automation, which allowed Schwab to expand its offerings through a primarily telephone-based channel. In 1995, it introduced software that allowed clients to trade through their own computers. With the growth of the Internet and the advent of other online brokers, Schwab actively sought to move the core of its business online. By 2000, approximately half its accounts were trading through the Internet.

- *Intrawest Corporation* has spread from its Canadian base in Vancouver, British Columbia, to become one of the largest operators of ski resorts in North America. Its properties include Whistler-Blackholm, British Columbia; Mammoth, California; Copper Mountain, Colorado; and Killington, Vermont. Intrawest's expertise includes a multistep strategy of enhancing the skiing experience, building an appealing resort community that will encourage people to stay longer, and expansion into year-round activities at each resort.

- *Aggreko* describes itself as "the world's power rental leader." Headquartered in the United Kingdom, it rents mobile electricity generators and temperature control equipment from 70 depots in 20 countries. Much of the firm's business comes from planned backup operations or special events—such as the Olympics—but it is also poised to respond rapidly to emergency situations, such as natural disasters that knock out normal power supplies. Speed, flexibility, reliability, and environmental sensitivity are among its strengths. Its customer base is dominated by large companies and government agencies.

- *Encyclopaedia Britannica* has been known to generations of students and their families for its massive, 32-volume set of leather-bound books, recently priced at $1,250 (and also available on CD-ROM). But in October 1999, the company adopted a radical new strategy, offering the entire contents of the encyclopaedia *free* on its Web site, www.britannica.com, which also includes current news and features from many other sources. In its new role as a provider of free Internet-based information services, the company hopes to make money by selling advertising on its site.

What Is a Service?

The group of services described earlier is remarkably diverse yet represents only a fraction of the many different industries found in the service sector. Because of this diversity, services have traditionally been difficult to define. Complicating matters further is the fact that the way in which services are created and delivered to customers is often hard to grasp because many inputs and outputs are intangible. Most people have little difficulty defining manufacturing or mining or agriculture, but defining *service* can elude them. Here are two approaches that capture the essence:

- A service is an act or performance offered by one party to another. Although the process may be tied to a physical product, the performance is essentially intangible and does not normally result in ownership of any of the factors of production.
- Services are economic activities that create value and provide benefits for customers at specific times and places as a result of bringing about a desired change in—or on behalf of—the recipient of the service.

More amusingly, services have also been described as "something that may be bought and sold, but which cannot be dropped on your foot."[2]

Understanding the Service Sector

Services make up the bulk of today's economy, not only in the United States and Canada, where they account for 73 percent and 67 percent of the gross domestic product (GDP), respectively, but also in developed industrial nations throughout the world.[3] In most countries, the service sector of the economy is very diverse, comprising a wide array of different industries that sell to individual consumers and business customers as well as to government agencies and nonprofit organizations. Figure 1.1 shows how service industries contribute to the U.S. economy, relative to manufacturing, government (itself mostly services), agriculture, mining, and construction.

From one continent to another, national economies are in a continuing state of evolution. Consider Europe. As shown in Table 1.1, the changes in the composition of the economy in some European nations have been dramatic over the past three decades, reflecting a combination of economic growth (in which most of the new value added has come from services) and, in some cases, an absolute decline in traditional economic activities such as agriculture, mining,

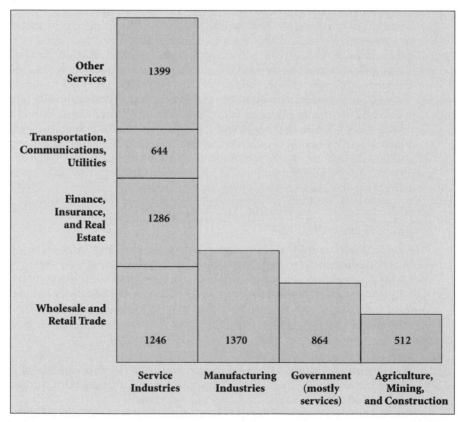

FIGURE 1.1 Contribution of Service Industries to the U.S. Economy: Gross Domestic Product by Industry, 1997 (in billions of 1992 constant dollars)

Source: U.S. Bureau of Economic Analysis, *Survey of Current Business,* September 1999, Table B3, p. D–28.

TABLE 1.1	*Size of the Service Sector in Selected European Countries*		
Value Added by Services as a Percentage of Gross Domestic Product in 1994, 1980, and 1960[a]			
	1994	1980	1960
Ireland	83	n.a.	52
France	70	62	50
Netherlands	70	n.a.	45
Denmark	69	65	58
Sweden	68	62	53
United Kingdom	66	55	54
Austria	64	56	42
Finland	63	51	48
Hungary	60	n.a.	n.a.
Italy	60	55	47
Czech Republic	55	30[b]	n.a.

Source: *The Economist, Pocket Europe in Figures* (London: Profile Books, 1997)

[a]Caution should be used in interpreting and comparing these data because they are based on national government statistics whose collection procedures and classification criteria may not be consistent across countries or even across time within the same country.

[b]Data for Czechoslovakia before partition.

and manufacturing. Ireland shows the strongest growth in the value added by services as a percentage of the GDP, thanks to a remarkable economic growth rate that has given people more spending power; increased tourism (embracing a variety of service-based industries); and attraction of foreign investment in such areas as financial services, telecommunications, and customer call centers.

Service industries also account for most of the growth in new jobs. Unless you are already predestined for a career in a family manufacturing or agricultural business, the probability is high that you will spend most of your working life in companies (or public agencies and nonprofit organizations) that create and deliver services. Perhaps you will even create your own service business!

As a national economy develops, the relative share of employment among agriculture, industry (including manufacturing and mining), and services changes dramatically. Figure 1.2 shows how the evolution to a service-dominated employment base is likely to take place over time as per capita income rises. The combination of increased productivity and automation in agriculture and industry on the one hand and the rapid increase in the demand for both new and traditional services on the other jointly result in a rapid increase in the percentage of a country's labor force that is employed in services. Although many people still perceive the world's second-largest economy, Japan, to be manufacturing dominated, that is no longer the case from the point of view of employment. Japan remains behind the United States in the percentage of its labor force in service employment, but the shift toward services has been rapid in recent years.

It comes as a surprise to most people to learn that the dominance of the service sector is not limited to highly developed nations. For instance, World Bank statistics show that the service sector accounts for more than half the gross national product (GNP) and employs more than half the labor force in many Latin American and Caribbean nations, too.[4] Most of these coun-

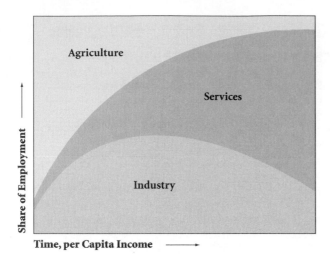

Share of Employment

Time, per Capita Income →

FIGURE 1.2 Changing Structure of Employment As an Economy Develops
Source: International Monetary Fund, *World Economic Outlook* (Washington, DC: International Monetary Fund, May 1997).

tries have a large underground economy that is not captured in official statistics. In Mexico, it has been estimated that as much as 40 percent of trade and commerce is "informal."[5] Significant service output is created by undocumented work in domestic jobs (e.g., cook, housekeeper, or gardener) or small, cash-based enterprises such as restaurants, laundries, boarding houses, and taxi companies. Parallel situations are believed to prevail to varying degrees in many Asian and European countries, although perhaps not to the same extent.

Service organizations range in size from huge international corporations based on such enterprises as airlines, banking, insurance, telecommunications, hotel chains, and freight transportation to a vast array of locally owned and operated small businesses, including restaurants, laundries, taxi companies, optometrists, and numerous business-to-business services. Franchised service outlets—in fields ranging from fast foods to bookkeeping—combine the marketing characteristics of a large chain that offers a standardized product with local ownership and operation of a specific facility. Some firms that create a time-sensitive physical product, such as printing or photographic processing, are now describing themselves as service businesses because much of the value added is created by speed, customization, and convenient locations. Regis McKenna has written, "Companies best equipped for the twenty-first century will consider investment in real time systems as essential to maintaining their competitive edge and keeping their customers."[6]

Governments and nonprofit organizations are also in the business of providing services, although the extent of such involvement may vary widely from one country to another, reflecting both tradition and political values. In many countries, colleges, hospitals, and museums are in public ownership or operate on a not-for-profit basis, but for-profit versions of each type of institution also exist. As we'll see later in this chapter, many countries are experiencing a significant shift from public to private ownership in industries ranging from airlines to electricity and from railroads to telecommunications.

There's a hidden service sector, too, within many large corporations that are classified by government statisticians as being in manufacturing, agricultural, or natural resources industries. So-called *internal services* cover a wide array of activities, potentially including recruitment, publications, legal and accounting services, payroll administration, office cleaning, landscape maintenance, freight transport, and many other tasks. To a growing extent, organizations are choosing to outsource those internal services that can be performed more efficiently by a specialist subcontractor.[7] Internal services are also being spun out as separate service operations offered in the wider marketplace. As such tasks are outsourced, they become part of the competitive marketplace and are therefore more easily identifiable as contributing to the services component of the economy.[8] Even when such services are not outsourced, however, managers of the departments that supply them would do well to think in terms of providing good service to their internal customers.

New approaches to classifying service industries seek to separate the manufacturing and service components of work performed within manufacturing industries to give a more accurate portrayal of today's economy. They also include a host of new service activities that weren't even thought of 20 to 30 years ago (see Management Memo 1.1).

MANAGEMENT MEMO 1.1

Introducing NAICS: A New Way to Classify the Economies of North America

The North American Industrial Classification System—developed jointly by the statistical agencies of Canada, Mexico, and the United States—offers a new approach to classifying industries in the economic statistics of the three North American Free Trade Agreement (NAFTA) countries. It will replace previous national systems, such as the 60-year-old Standard Industrial Classification (SIC) formerly used in the United States and is already in use in Canada.

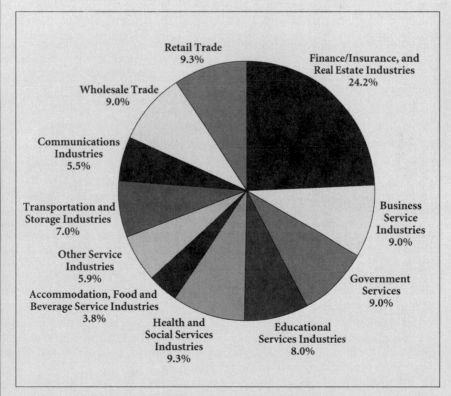

FIGURE 1.3   Composition of Canada's Service Economy by NAICS Industry Sectors, February 2000

Source: "Gross Domestic Product at Factor Cost Seasonally Adjusted at Annual Rates," *CANSIM* Matrix 4680. Ottawa: Statistics Canada, May 2000, www.statcan.ca/english/econoind.

NAICS (pronounced *nakes*) includes many new service industries that have emerged in recent decades and also reclassifies as services so-called auxiliary establishments that provide services (such as accounting, catering, and transportation) within manufacturing companies. Every sector of the economy has been restructured and redefined. NAICS includes 358 new industries that the SIC did not identify, 390 that are revised from their SIC counterparts, and 422 that continue substantially unchanged. These industries are grouped into 20 sectors (as opposed to just 10 SIC divisions) and reorganize data on both manufacturing and service industries.

Among the new sectors devoted to services are Information, which recognizes the emergence and uniqueness of businesses in the information economy; Health Care and Social Assistance; Professional, Scientific, and Professional Services; Arts, Entertainment, and Recreation, which includes most businesses engaged in meeting consumers' cultural, leisure, or entertainment interests; Educational Services; and Accommodation and Food Services. Examples of new NAICS industry classifications that were not previously broken out separately are

Casino Hotels	HMO Medical Centers
Continuing Care Retirement Communities	Industrial Design Services
Diagnostic Imaging Centers	Investment Banking and Securities Dealing
Diet and Weight Reducing Centers	Management Consulting Services
Environmental Consulting	Satellite Telecommunications
Golf Courses and Country Clubs	Telemarketing Bureaus
Hazardous Waste Collection	Temporary Help Services

NAICS uses a consistent principle for classification: Businesses that use similar production processes are grouped together. Its goal is to make economic statistics more useful and to capture developments that encompass applications of high technology (e.g., cellular telecommunications), new businesses that previously did not exist (e.g., environmental consulting), and changes in the way business is done (e.g., warehouse clubs). Figure 1.3 displays the composition of Canada's service economy (67 percent of GDP) by NAICS industry sectors.

Source: Economic Classification Policy Committee, "NAICS—North American Industry Classification System: New Data for a New Economy." (Washington, D.C.: Bureau of the Census, October 1998); www.census.gov/naics.

Marketing Services versus Physical Goods

The dynamic environment of services today places a premium on effective marketing. Among the keys to competing effectively in this new and challenging environment are skills in marketing strategy and execution—areas in which many service firms have traditionally been weak.

Marketing can be described in several ways. It can be seen as a strategic thrust pursued by top management, as a set of functional activities performed by line managers (such as product policy, pricing, delivery, and communications), or as a customer-driven orientation for the entire organization. This book seeks to integrate all three perspectives. It also recognizes that the services marketing function is much broader than the activities and output of the traditional marketing department, requiring close cooperation between marketers and those managers responsible for operations and human resources.[9]

Although it's still very important to run an efficient operation, that orientation no longer suffices for success. Employees must be customer service oriented as well as concerned about efficiency. The service product must be tailored to customer needs, priced realistically, distributed through convenient channels, and actively promoted to customers. Today, many new market entrants are positioning their services to appeal to specific market segments through their pricing, communication efforts, and service delivery, rather than trying to be all things to all people.

But are the marketing concepts and practices that have been developed in manufacturing companies directly transferable to service organizations? The answer is often no, because marketing management tasks in the service sector tend to differ from those in the manufacturing sector in several important respects. Let's explore why.

All *products*—a term that we use in this book to describe the core output of any type of industry—deliver benefits to the customers who purchase and use them. *Goods* can be described as physical objects or devices, whereas *services* are actions or performances.[10] Early research into services sought to differentiate them from goods, focusing particularly on four generic differences, referred to as *intangibility, heterogeneity* (or *variability*), *perishability of output,* and *simultaneity of production and consumption.*[11] Although these characteristics are still cited, they oversimplify the real-world environment. Worse, they simply don't apply to all services. More practical insights are provided in Table 1.2, which lists nine basic differences that can help us to distinguish the tasks associated with services marketing and management from those commonly involved with marketing physical goods. This table also highlights some key managerial implications that will form the basis for much of our analysis and discussion in this and later chapters.

It's important to note that in identifying these differences, we're still dealing with generalizations that do not apply equally to all services. (In chapter 2, we classify services into distinct categories, each of which presents somewhat different challenges for marketers and other managers.) Let's examine each characteristic in more detail and highlight a few fundamental marketing implications.

No Customer Ownership of Services

Perhaps the key distinction between goods and services lies in the fact that customers usually derive value from services without obtaining ownership of any tangible elements (exceptions include food services and installation of spare parts during delivery of repair and maintenance services). In many instances, service marketers offer customers the opportunity to rent the use of a physical object such as a rental car or hotel room, to hire the labor and expertise of people whose skills range from brain surgery to knowing how to clean your home quickly and effectively, or to rent (as a loan) a sum of money.

A key implication for marketers concerns pricing. When the firm rents out usage of its physical, human, or intangible assets, time becomes an important denominator; in particular, determining the relevant costs requires time-based calculations. Another important issue concerns which criteria drive customer choice behavior for a rental, which tends to be short term in nature. Marketing a car rental service to a customer, for instance, is very different from attempting to sell a car at an automobile dealership to that same person, who may intend keeping it for at least three to five years. People usually rent cars for a period of 1 to 14 days when they are away from home. In most instances, they reserve a particular class or category of vehicle (such as compact, intermediate, or full-size) rather than a specific brand and model. Instead of worrying about such physical characteristics as colors and upholstery, customers focus on such elements as the location and appearance of pickup and delivery facilities, hours when facilities are open, extent of insurance coverage, cleanliness and maintenance of vehicles, provision of free shuttle buses at airports, availability of 24-hour reservations service, and quality of service provided by customer-contact personnel.

Service Products As Intangible Performances

Although services often include tangible elements—such as sleeping in a hotel bed, working out at a health club, having your teeth cleaned at the dentist, or getting damaged equipment repaired—the service performance itself is basically an intangible. In services, the benefits come

TABLE 1.2 *Management Implication of Some Basic Differences between Goods and Services*	
How Services Differ from Goods	**Some Key Implications**
Customers do not obtain ownership of services	Need to think of temporary rentals rather than permanent sales How best to price such rentals? Customer criteria are different for renting an object instead of purchasing it
Service products are intangible performances	Consider how to create and communicate tangible evidence Understand how to stage the performance and manage each step
Greater involvement of customers in the production process	Customer behavior and competence can help or hinder productivity Customers may need to be managed as partial employees Consider opportunities for self-service Location and opening hours of service "factories" must be convenient for customers Design of service factory must be appealing and user-friendly
Other people may form part of the product	Behavior and demeanor of employees and other customers must be managed, because it affects customer satisfaction Recruit service personnel who possess (or can be trained) to have both technical skills and human skills; keep them motivated May be unwise to mix different market segments at the same time and location.
More variability in operational inputs and outputs	Quality control—particularly consistency—is more difficult to achieve Productivity may be improved by standardization Replacing employees by automation may reduce variability
Many services are difficult for customers to evaluate	Need to develop trust between customer and firm Educating customers will help them make smarter choices
Absence of inventories after production	Once produced, services cannot usually be stored, so firms must develop strategies to manage demand levels Manage capacity levels to match predicted fluctuations in demand Profitability of capacity-constrained service businesses is often a function of getting the right business at the right time at the right price
Time factor is relatively more important	Must understand customers' time constraints and priorities Recognize that spending time is often seen by customers as a burden Look for ways to compete on fast service delivery; minimize waiting Expand service hours; consider 24/7 service
Delivery systems may involve both electronic and physical channels	Consider opportunities for electronic delivery of any information-based service elements Recognize opportunities for instantaneous delivery of service worldwide Where services are delivered through physical channels, need to combine service factory, retail outlet, and point of consumption

from the nature of the performance, which requires a different marketing emphasis from marketing tangible goods, including a need to employ tangible images and metaphors to demonstrate the competencies of the service firm and to illustrate the benefits resulting from service delivery.

An interesting way to distinguish between goods and services is to place them on a scale from tangible-dominant to intangible-dominant (illustrated below in Figure 1.4).[12] Kotler proposes five categories of market offer:[13]

- Pure tangible good (such as soap or salt)
- Tangible good with accompanying services (for example, cars or computers)
- Hybrid (e.g., a restaurant) combining roughly equal parts of good and services
- Major service with accompanying minor goods and services (e.g., air travel)
- Pure service (such as babysitting or psychotherapy)

Sasser, Olsen, and Wyckoff suggest that an acid test of whether a product is a good or a service is to determine whether more than half the value comes from the service elements.[14] At a restaurant, for example, the cost of the food itself may account for as little as 20 to 30 percent of the price of the meal; the balance of the value added comes from food preparation; cooking; table service; extras such as parking, coatroom, and toilets; and the restaurant environment itself.

The notion of service as a performance that cannot be touched, wrapped, or taken away leads to the use of a theatrical metaphor for service management that likens service delivery to

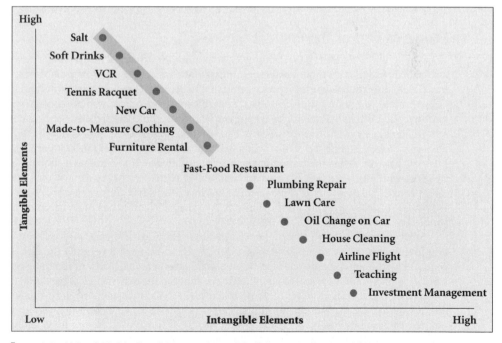

FIGURE 1.4   Value Added by Tangible versus Intangible Elements in Goods and Services

the staging of a play, with service personnel as the actors and customers as the audience. The reading "Service Theater: An Analytical Framework for Services Marketing" by Stephen Grove and Raymond Fisk (pp. 83 to 92) describes both the theoretical constructs and practical implications of what is often referred to as *dramaturgy*.

Customer Involvement in the Production Process

Performing a service involves assembling and delivering the output of a mix of physical facilities and mental or physical labor. Many services require customers to participate in creating the service product (exceptions include a wide array of services in which production is left entirely to the service provider, such as office cleaning, weather forecasting, car repair, and life insurance). Customer involvement in helping to create the service product can take the form of self-service—as in using a laundromat or withdrawing money from an automated teller machine (ATM)—or cooperation with service personnel in settings such as hairdressers, hotels, colleges, or hospitals. Under such circumstances, customers can be thought of as partial employees, and service firms have much to gain from trying to train their customers so as to make them more competent and productive.[15]

Changing the nature of the production process often affects the role that customers are asked to play in that process. In your own role as a service consumer, you know that although your main interest is in the final output, the way in which you are treated during service delivery can also have an important impact on your satisfaction. When customers are required to visit the service delivery site, that facility should be sited in a convenient location and open at times that suit customers' needs. Customers are more likely to return if they find that buildings and equipment are designed in ways that make them user-friendly and reasonably attractive to visit.

People as Part of the Product

In many "high-contact services, customers not only come into contact with service personnel but also rub shoulders with other customers (literally so, if they ride a bus or train during the rush hour). By contrast, low-contact services are often delivered at arm's length, with human contact being limited to resolution of problems. The difference between one high-contact service and another often lies in the quality of employees who serve the customers. It can be a challenging task to manage service encounters between customers and service personnel in ways that will create a satisfactory experience. Similarly, the type of customers who patronize a particular service business helps to define the nature of the service experience. If you attend a sporting event, the behavior of the fans can be a big plus and add to the excitement of the game if they are enthusiastic but well behaved. But if some of them become rowdy and abusive, it can detract from the enjoyment of other spectators at the stadium. For good or ill, other customers become part of the product in many services.

Service firms need to devote special care to selecting, training, and motivating those employees who will be serving customers directly. In addition to possessing the technical skills required by the job, they also need to possess good interpersonal skills. At the same time, firms have to manage and shape customer behavior so that the misbehavior of a few doesn't spoil the experience for everybody else. In some instances, service marketers need to think carefully about whether it is a good idea to mix several segments together in the same service facility. If you were a tired business traveler, how would you feel if you arrived at your hotel late at night to find it overrun by noisy conventioneers having a wonderful time drinking and singing?

Greater Variability in Operational Inputs and Outputs

The presence of employees and other customers in the operational system makes it difficult to standardize and control variability in both service inputs and outputs. Manufactured goods can be produced under controlled conditions that have been designed to optimize both productivity and quality and then checked for conformance with quality standards long before they reach the customer. The same is true for services performed while the customer is absent, such as processing bank checks, repairing cars, or cleaning offices at night. But for those services that are consumed as they are produced, final "assembly" must take place under real-time conditions, which may vary from customer to customer and even from one time of the day to another. As a result, mistakes and shortcomings are both more likely and harder to conceal. These factors make it difficult for service organizations to improve productivity, control quality, and offer a consistent product. As a former packaged goods marketer observed some years ago after moving to a new position at Holiday Inn:

> We can't control the quality of our product as well as a Procter and Gamble control engineer on a production line can. . . . When you buy a box of Tide, you can reasonably be 99 and 44/100ths percent sure that this stuff will work to get your clothes clean. When you buy a Holiday Inn room, you're sure at some lesser percentage that it will work to give you a good night's sleep without any hassle, or people banging on the walls and all the bad things that can happen in a hotel.[16]

However, not all variations in service delivery are necessarily negative, and modern service businesses are coming to recognize the value of customizing at least some aspects of the service offering to the needs and expectations of individual customers. In fields such as health care, it's essential.[17] On the other hand, replacement of service workers by automation may hold the key to cheaper and more consistent performances.

Difficulty of Customer Evaluation

Most physical goods tend to be relatively high in *search properties,* the characteristics of the product that a customer can determine prior to purchasing it, such as color, style, shape, price, fit, feel, hardness, and smell. Other goods and some services, by contrast, may emphasize *experience properties* that can be discerned only after purchase or during consumption, such as taste, wearability, ease of handling, quietness, and personal treatment. Finally, there are *credence properties*—characteristics that customers find hard to evaluate even after consumption. Examples of services in which credence properties predominate include surgery, professional services such as accountancy, and many technical repairs.[18]

Service marketers can help customers overcome some of the unease that they feel before purchasing a service by helping them to match their needs to specific service features and educating them as to what to expect both during and after service delivery. A firm that develops a reputation for considerate and ethical treatment of its customers will gain the trust of its existing customers and benefit from positive word-of-mouth referrals.

No Inventories for Services after Production

Because a service is a deed or performance, rather than a tangible item that the customer keeps, it is, in a sense, perishable and cannot be physically stocked for sale after production is completed. Of course, the necessary facilities, equipment, and labor can be held in readiness to create the service, but these simply represent productive capacity, not the product itself. Having unused capacity in a service business is rather like running water into a sink without a plug. The flow is wasted unless customers (or possessions requiring service) are present to receive it. When demand exceeds capacity, customers may be sent away disappointed unless they are prepared to wait.

An important task for service marketers, therefore, is to find ways of smoothing demand levels to match capacity through price incentives, promotions, or other means. There may also be opportunities for the firm to stretch or shrink its capacity to serve—in the form of employees, physical space, and equipment—so as to match predicted fluctuations in demand; in this instance, good forecasting is important. When service firms speak of their *inventory,* they are referring to their future capacity to deliver service—such as hotel rooms not yet reserved for next Tuesday night. If profit maximization is an important goal, then marketers should be careful to target the right segments at the right times, focusing on selling during peak periods to those segments who are the least price sensitive.

Importance of the Time Factor

Many services are delivered in real time. Customers have to be physically present to receive service from organizations such as airlines, hospitals, hairdressers, and restaurants. People are willing to spend only a limited amount of time at the service "factory"—particularly if it involves just waiting in line—so service must be delivered with acceptable speed. Customers place a value on their time, and sometimes people are willing to pay more for faster service. Increasingly, busy customers expect service to be available at times when it suits them—rather than when it suits the service company. In response, more and more firms are offering extended hours and even going to 24/7 service (available 24 hours a day, seven days a week).

In other instances, the focus is on elapsed time. Even when customers place an order for a service to be undertaken in their absence, they have expectations about how long a particular task should take to complete—whether it is repairing a machine, completing a research report, cleaning a suit, or preparing a legal document. In general, today's customers are increasingly time sensitive, and speed is often seen as a key element in good service. Service marketers need to understand customers' time constraints and priorities, which may vary from one market segment to another. They need to look for ways to compete on speed and to minimize time wasted waiting for service. Under competitive pressure to deliver service more quickly, operations managers in progressive organizations are continually looking for ways to streamline processes without compromising the quality of work performed.

Different Distribution Channels

Unlike manufacturers, which produce their products in one location and require physical distribution channels to move goods from factory to customers, many service businesses use electronic channels (as in broadcasting or electronic funds transfer). Alternatively, they may choose to combine the service factory, retail outlet, and point of consumption at a single location, thus requiring them to get involved in site selection, building design and maintenance, and management of customer contact personnel. Sometimes, as in banking, firms offer customers a choice of distribution channels, ranging from visiting the bank in person to conducting home banking on the Internet.

As a result of advances in computers and telecommunications—especially the growth of the Internet—electronic delivery of services is expanding rapidly. Any service element that is information based has the potential for instantaneous delivery anywhere in the world where there is compatible equipment to receive it. Thanks to e-mail and Web sites, even small businesses have the option to offer their services inexpensively across vast geographic distances. A firm that could not survive serving a narrow market segment in a limited geographic area now has the option to greatly increase its market potential within that same tightly defined segment.

An Integrated Approach to Service Management

This book is not just about services marketing. Throughout the chapters, you'll also find continuing reference to two other important functions: service operations and human resource management. Imagine yourself as the manager of a small hotel or think big, if you like, and picture yourself as the chief executive of a major bank. In both instances, you need to be concerned on a day-to-day basis that your customers are satisfied, that your operational systems are running smoothly and efficiently, and that your employees are not only working productively but are also doing a good job either of serving customers directly or of helping other employees to deliver good service. Even if you see yourself as a middle manager, with specific responsibilities in either marketing or operations or human resources, your success in the job will often involve understanding of these other functions and periodic meetings with colleagues working in these areas. In short, integration of activities between functions is the name of the game. If there are problems in any one of these three areas, then it may signal financial problems ahead.

The Eight Components of Integrated Service Management

When discussing strategies to market manufactured goods, marketers usually address four basic strategic elements: product, price, place (or distribution), and promotion (or communication). Collectively, these categories are often referred to as the 4 Ps of the marketing mix.[19] However, the distinctive nature of service performances, especially such aspects as customer involvement in production and the importance of the time factor, requires that other strategic elements be included. To capture the nature of this challenge, we will be using the 8 Ps model of *integrated service management,* which highlights the strategic decision variables facing managers of service organizations.[20]

Our visual metaphor for the 8 Ps is the racing eight, a lightweight boat (or "shell") powered by eight rowers, made famous by the Oxford and Cambridge boat race that has taken place annually on the River Thames near London for almost one hundred and fifty years. Today, similar races involving many different teams are a staple of rowing competitions around the world as well as a featured sport in the Summer Olympics. Speed not only comes from the rowers' physical strength but also reflects their harmony and cohesion. To achieve optimal effectiveness, each of the eight rowers must pull on his or her oar in unison with the others, following the direction of the coxswain, who is seated in the stern. A similar synergy and integration between each of the 8 Ps is required for success in any competitive service business (Figure 1.5). The coxswain—who steers the boat, sets the pace, motivates the crew, and keeps a close eye on competing boats in the race—is a metaphor for management.

Product Elements. Managers must select the features of both the core product (either a good or service) and the bundle of supplementary service elements surrounding it, with reference to the benefits desired by customers and how well competing products perform. In short, they must be attentive to all aspects of the service performance that have the potential to create value for customers.

Place, Cyberspace, and Time. Delivering product elements to customers involves decisions on the place and time of delivery as well as on the methods and channels employed. Delivery may involve physical or electronic distribution channels (or both), depending on the nature of

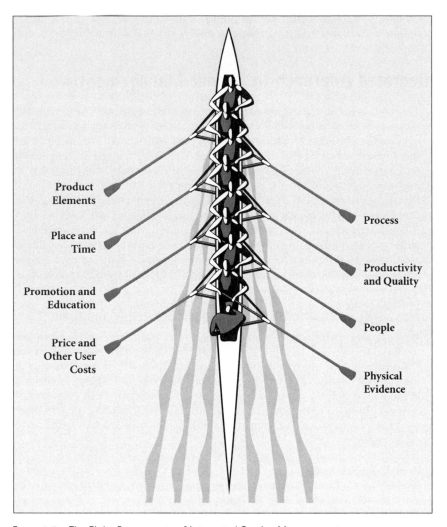

Product
Elements

Place and
Time

Promotion and
Education

Price and
Other User
Costs

Process

Productivity
and Quality

People

Physical
Evidence

FIGURE 1.5   The Eight Components of Integrated Service Management

the service being provided. Use of messaging services and the Internet allows information-based services to be delivered in cyberspace for retrieval by telephone or computer wherever and whenever it suits the customer. Firms may deliver service directly to customers or through intermediary organizations, such as retail outlets that receive a fee or percentage of the selling price to perform certain tasks associated with sales, service, and customer contact. Speed and convenience of place and time for the customer are becoming important determinants in service delivery strategy.

Process. Creating and delivering product elements to customers requires the design and implementation of effective processes that describe the method and sequence of actions in which service operating systems work. Badly designed processes are likely to annoy customers when the latter experience slow, bureaucratic, and ineffective service delivery. Similarly, poor processes make it difficult for frontline staff to do their jobs well, result in low productivity, and increase the likelihood of service failures.

Productivity and Quality. These elements, often treated separately, should be treated strategically as interrelated. No service firm can afford to address either element in isolation. *Productivity* relates to how inputs are transformed into outputs that are valued by customers, whereas *quality* refers to the degree to which a service satisfies customers by meeting their needs, wants, and expectations. Improving productivity is essential to keep costs under control, but managers must beware of making inappropriate cuts in service levels that are resented by customers (and perhaps by employees, too). Service quality, as defined by customers, is essential for product differentiation and building customer loyalty. However, investing in quality improvement without understanding the tradeoff between incremental costs and incremental revenues may hurt profitability.

People. Many services depend on direct, personal interaction between customers and a firm's employees (such as getting a haircut or eating at a restaurant). The nature of these interactions strongly influences the customer's perceptions of service quality.[21] Customers will often judge the quality of the service they receive based on their assessment of the people providing that service. They may also make judgments about other customers they encounter. Successful service firms devote significant effort to recruiting, training, and motivating their personnel. Firms often seek to manage customer behavior, too.

Promotion and Education. No marketing program can succeed without effective communications. This component plays three vital roles: providing needed information and advice, persuading target customers of the merits of a specific product, and encouraging them to take action at specific times. In services marketing, much communication is educational in nature, especially for new customers. Companies may need to teach these customers about the benefits of the service, as well as where and when to obtain it, and provide instructions on how to participate in service processes. Communications can be delivered by individuals, such as salespeople and trainers, or through such media as TV, radio, newspapers, magazines, posters, brochures, and Web sites. Promotional activities may serve to marshal arguments in favor of selecting a particular brand or use incentives to catch customers' attention and motivate them to act.

Physical Evidence. The appearance of buildings, landscaping, vehicles, interior furnishing, equipment, staff members, signs, printed materials, and other visible cues all provide tangible evidence of a firm's service quality. Service firms need to manage physical evidence carefully, because it can have a profound impact on customers' impressions. In services with few tangible elements, such as insurance, advertising is often employed to create meaningful symbols. For instance, an umbrella may symbolize protection, and a fortress, security.

Price and Other User Costs. This component addresses management of the expenditures and other outlays incurred by customers in obtaining benefits from the service product. Responsibilities are not limited to the traditional pricing tasks of establishing the selling price to customers, setting trade margins, and establishing credit terms. Service managers also recognize and, where practical, seek to minimize other burdens that customers may bear in purchasing and using a service, including time, mental and physical effort, and unpleasant sensory experiences, such as noises and smells.

Linking Services Marketing, Operations, and Human Resources

As shown by the component elements of the 8 Ps model, marketing cannot operate successfully in isolation from other functions in a service business. Three management functions play central and interrelated roles in meeting customer needs: marketing, operations, and human resources. Figure 1.6 illustrates this interdependency. In following chapters, we raise the question of how marketers should relate to and involve their colleagues from other functions in planning and implementing marketing strategies.

Service firms must understand the implications of the eight components of integrated service management to develop effective strategies. Firms whose managers succeed in developing integrated strategies will have a better chance of surviving and prospering. Those that fail to grasp these implications, by contrast, are likely to be outmaneuvered by competitors that are more adept at responding to the dramatic changes affecting the service economy.

You can expect to see the 8 Ps framework used throughout this book. Although any given chapter is likely to emphasize just one (or a few) of the eight components, you should always keep in mind the importance of integrating the component(s) under discussion with each of the others when formulating an overall strategy.

Marketing Services versus Marketing Goods through Service

With the growth of the service economy and the increasing emphasis on adding value-enhancing services to manufactured goods, the lines between services and manufacturing sometimes become a bit blurred. As Theodore Levitt, one of the world's best-known marketing experts, commented almost thirty years ago: "There are not such things as service industries. There are only industries whose service components are greater or less than those of other industries. Everybody is in service."[22] More recently, Roland Rust, editor of the *Journal of Service*

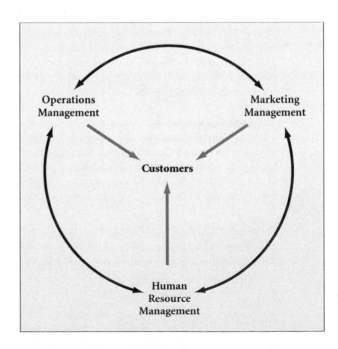

FIGURE 1.6   Interdependence of Marketing, Operations, and Human Resources

Research, suggested that manufacturing firms had got this message when he observed that "most goods businesses now view themselves primarily as services."[23] However, it's important to clarify the difference between situations in which a service itself is the core product and those in which manufacturers are adopting servicelike strategies to help them market the physical goods that they produce.

In this book, we draw a distinction between *marketing of services*—where a service is the core product—and *marketing goods through service.* In the latter case, a manufacturing or natural resource firm may base its marketing strategy on a philosophy of serving customers well and seek to add supplementary service elements that add value to the core product, but that core product still remains a physical good—of which the customer takes ownership—and not an intangible performance. Many of the services that accompany physical products at the time of sale are not charged for separately but bundled in with the price of the product itself. Purchasers of a luxury car such as the Lexus receive an exceptional level of service from the dealer, based on the firm's detailed understanding of the benefits that customers seek from owning and driving a prestige brand of car. They also receive excellent warranty coverage. But the Lexus is still a manufactured product, and we still need to distinguish between marketing that product at the time of sale and subsequently marketing services that customers will pay for to maintain their car in good working order.

Creating Value in a Context of Values

By now it should be clear to you that managers need to be concerned about giving good value to customers and treating them fairly in decisions involving all elements of the 8 Ps. *Value* can be defined as the worth of a specific action or object relative to an individual's (or organization's) needs at a particular point in time, less the costs involved in obtaining those benefits.

Firms create value by offering the types of services that customers need, accurately presenting their capabilities, and delivering them in a pleasing and convenient fashion at an acceptable price. In return, firms receive value from their customers, primarily in the form of the money paid by the latter to purchase and use the services in question. Such transfers of value illustrate one of the most fundamental concepts in marketing, that of *exchange,* which takes place when one party obtains value from another in return for something else of value. These exchanges aren't limited to buying and selling. An exchange of value also takes place when employees go to work for an organization. The employer gets the benefit of the worker's efforts; in turn, the employee receives wages, benefits, and possibly such valued experiences as training, on-the-job experience, and working with friendly colleagues.

As a customer yourself, you regularly make decisions on whether to invest time, money, and effort to obtain a service that promises the specific benefits you seek. Perhaps the service in question solves an immediate need, such as getting a haircut, eating a pizza, repairing your bike or car, or passing a couple of hours at a movie theater or another entertainment facility. Alternatively, as with getting an education, you may be prepared to take a long-term perspective before the payoff is realized. But if, after the fact, you find you've had to pay more than you expected or received fewer benefits than anticipated, you're likely to feel cheated. At a minimum, you'll be muttering darkly about poor value (more likely, your discontent will be loudly and colorfully expressed!). If you feel you were badly treated during service delivery, although the service itself provided the desired benefits, you may conclude that this poor treatment diminished the value received. Alternatively, perhaps you or people you know have worked for a company that treated its employees poorly, even to the extent of not computing wages fairly or failing to deliver promised job-related benefits. That's not the best way for management to build employees' commitment to the firm or dedication to serving customers, is it? In fact, customers are quick to pick up on bad vibes from unhappy service workers.

No firm that seeks long-term relationships with either customers or employees can afford to mistreat them or to provide poor value on an ongoing basis. At a minimum, it's bad business; at worst, it's unethical. Sooner or later, shortchanging or mistreating customers and employees is likely to rebound to the firm's disadvantage. Unfortunately, not all firms, employees, or even customers have the other parties' best interests at heart. The potential for abusive behavior is perhaps higher in services than in manufacturing, reflecting the difficulty of evaluating many services in advance (and even after the fact), the need to involve customers in service production in many instances, and the face-to-face encounters that customers may have with service personnel and other customers.[24]

Hence, companies need a set of morally and legally defensible values to guide their actions and to shape their dealings with both employees and customers. A useful way of thinking about values is as underlying beliefs about how life should be lived, how people should be treated (and behave), and how business should be conducted. To the extent possible, managers would be wise to use their firm's values as a reference point when recruiting and motivating employees. They should also clarify the firm's values and expectations in dealing with prospective customers, as well as making an effort to attract and retain customers who share and appreciate those same values.

Businesses and business schools are devoting more attention today to discussions of what constitutes ethical behavior. However, there's nothing new in the notion of ethical conduct of business affairs or in the recognition of the merit of good values. More than thirty years ago, Siegmund Warburg of the investment banking house of S.G. Warburg (now SBC Warburg) remarked that a company's reputation for "integrity, generosity, and thorough service is its most important asset, more important than any financial item. However, the reputation of a firm is like a very delicate living organism which can easily be damaged and which has to be taken care of incessantly, being mainly a matter of human behavior and human standards."[25]

What's new today is the greater scrutiny given to a firm's business ethics and the presence of tougher legislation designed to protect both customers and employees from abusive treatment. In this book, we will periodically raise ethical issues as they relate to different aspects of service management. Don't be surprised to find occasional questions relating to ethical practice as well as relevant examples. We'll also look at the responsibility of customers to behave in considerate ways toward suppliers and other customers. In particular, in chapter 3 we discuss how managers should deal with customers who behave in unethical or abusive ways.

The Evolving Environment of Services

The growth of the service sector went largely unnoticed for many years. Government statistics recorded its advance, but economists, consultants, and politicians continued to act as though manufacturing were still king of the national economy. The journalist George F. Will surprised people when he observed in 1983 that "McDonald's has more employees than U.S. Steel. Golden Arches, not blast furnaces symbolize the American economy."[26] (U.S. Steel has since been replaced by a diversified company called USX.) Unfortunately, Will's comment gave many people the erroneous impression that the service sector was built around low-paid, hamburger-flipping jobs. In practice, of course, service jobs cover a huge spectrum of positions in both consumer services and business-to-business services, with knowledge-based jobs in particular being very well compensated. Even as service industries grew, however, many practitioners remained wedded to an outdated view of marketing, regarding it as little more than advertising and public relations. Academics, too, were slow to respond to the changing business environment, but eventually scholars began challenging the notion of applying traditional marketing concepts to the burgeoning service sector (see Research Insights 1.1 for a summary of how the academic field of services marketing has evolved).

RESEARCH INSIGHTS 1.1

The Evolution of Services Marketing as an Academic Field

Services marketing is still a relatively new field of study. The early years of marketing as an academic discipline (in the late nineteenth and early twentieth centuries) initially focused on selling agricultural products and then expanded to include the selling of manufactured products. The accepted wisdom was that marketing involved physical goods only. Services such as accounting, banking, insurance, and transportation were seen by academics merely as aids to distribution and selling and not as products to be marketed in their own right. Most marketing scholars ignored the shift to a service-dominated economy; Berry and Parasuraman note that for many years it was seen as risky to a younger academic's career to undertake research in an area that older professors saw as unimportant.

Brown, Fisk, and Bitner concur, observing that "new ideas and concepts gain acceptance slowly" in academia. They divide the evolution of services marketing thought into three stages: Crawling Out (pre-1980), Scurrying About (1980–1985), and Walking Tall (since 1986). Early research focused on such topics as differences between goods and services, descriptions of the service sector and its importance, defining service characteristics, the distinctive nature of marketing channels for services, the service production process, and how marketing strategy needs to be different for services.

Two developments stimulated academic interest in services marketing in the early 1980s. One was the deregulation of service industries—such as transportation, financial services, health care, and telecommunications—which led to intensified competition and greatly increased the need for marketing. The second was a series of service marketing conferences sponsored by the American Marketing Association that brought together marketing academics and practitioners from both sides of the Atlantic. Key issues and concepts addressed during this period included classification of services, service characteristics, service quality, service encounters, relationship marketing, internal marketing, consumer evaluation processes for services, the challenge of marketing intangibles, designing services, human resource and operations management issues relating to services marketing, and service mapping (flowcharting).

From the mid-1980s onwards, there was a huge growth in publications as well as increasing empirical and theoretical rigor in research. International conferences stimulated cross-fertilization of research and global diffusion of findings. Academic centers for services marketing were created and played a key role in sponsoring seminars and research. The field became more multidisciplinary (e.g., inputs from social psychology research) and more cross-functional (linking marketing to operations and human resource management). Key topics included service quality and customer satisfaction, managing service encounters, the customer's role in service production and delivery, the role of tangibles and physical environments in customer evaluations, and technology in service design. Studies of customer retention and relationship marketing emphasized the need to retain as well as attract customers. Researchers also described the role of service guarantees, documented recovery strategies for service failures, and stressed the importance of understanding the long-term value of a customer and documenting financial losses from customer defections. Finally, internal marketing focused on the notions that everyone in the organization has a customer and that internal customers must be sold on the service and happy in their jobs before they can serve external customers well.

Source: Leonard L. Berry and A. Parasuraman, "Building a New Academic Field—The Case of Services Marketing," *Journal of Retailing* 69 (spring 1993): 13–60; Stephen W. Brown, Raymond P. Fisk, and Mary Jo Bitner, "The Development and Emergence of Services Marketing Thought," *Journal of Retailing* 69 (spring 1993): 61–103.

In many industries, including airlines, banking, telecommunications, and other utilities, government regulations both protected existing players and constrained their ability to develop new markets. During the 1970s and 1980s, however, innovative newcomers offering new standards of service began to succeed in unprotected markets that established competitors had long taken for granted. Other firms anticipated changing consumer needs by creating new service concepts.

During the past 20 years, the pace of change has accelerated. Many barriers to competition have been swept away, allowing the entry of eager newcomers, ranging from tiny start-up operations that provide maintenance of telecommunications lines and equipment inside the customer's home or office (a task once restricted to a monopoly provider) to well-financed multinational firms importing service concepts that were previously developed and tested in other countries. Established businesses often find it hard to maintain customer loyalty in the face of competitors offering new product features; improved performance; price cutting; clever promotions; and introduction of more convenient, technology-driven delivery systems.

Many factors underlie the transformation of services management. Depending on the industry and the country in which the service firm does business, the underlying causes of such changes may include any of the forces presented in Figure 1.7. Like the factors underlying any revolution, some of the origins of today's service sector revolution go back a number of years, whereas others reflect a chain of relatively recent events that continues to unfold. In the balance of this chapter, we look at each of these dynamics in more detail.

Government Policies

Actions by governmental agencies at regional, national, and supranational levels continue to shape the structure of the service economy and the terms under which competition takes place. Traditionally, many service industries were highly regulated. Government agencies mandated price levels, placed geographic constraints on distribution strategies, and in some instances even defined the product attributes. Since the late 1970s, there has been a trend in the United States and Europe toward complete or partial deregulation in several major service industries. Meanwhile in Latin America, democratization and new political initiatives are creating economies that are much less regulated than in the past. Reduced government regulation has already eliminated or minimized many constraints on competitive activity in such industries as airfreight, airlines, railroads, trucking, banking, securities, insurance, and telecommunications. Barriers to entry by new firms have been dropped in many instances, geographic restrictions on service delivery have been reduced, there is more freedom to compete on price, and existing firms have been able to expand into new markets or new lines of business.

But reduced regulation is not an unmixed blessing. Fears have been expressed that if successful firms become too large—through a combination of internal growth and acquisitions—the level of competition may eventually decline. Conversely, lifting of restrictions on pricing may benefit customers in the short run as competition lowers prices but leaves insufficient profits for needed future investments. For instance, fierce price competition among U.S. domestic airlines led to huge financial losses within the industry during the early 1990s, bankrupting several firms. This made it difficult for unprofitable carriers to invest in new aircraft and raised troublesome questions about service quality and safety.[27] Profitable foreign airlines, such as British Airways and Singapore Airlines, gained market share by offering better service on international routes.

Another important action taken by the governments of many countries has been privatization of what were once government-owned services. The term *privatization* was first widely used in the United Kingdom to describe the policy of transforming government organizations into investor-owned companies. Privatization has been moving rapidly ahead in many other

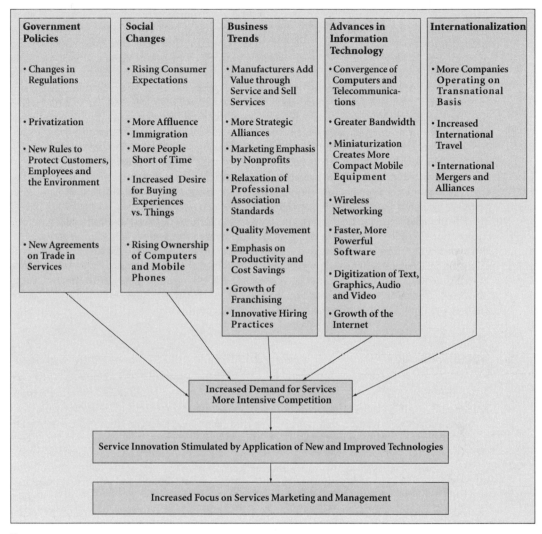

FIGURE 1.7   Factors Stimulating the Transformation of the Service Economy

European countries, too, as well as in Canada, Australia, New Zealand, and more recently in some Asian and Latin American nations. The transformation of such operations as national airlines, telecommunication services, and utilities into private-enterprise services has led to restructuring, cost cutting, and a more market-focused posture. When privatization is combined with a relaxing of regulatory barriers to allow entry of new competitors, the marketing implications can be dramatic, with foreign competitors moving into markets that were previously closed to outside investment. Thus, French companies specializing in water treatment have purchased and modernized many of the privatized water utilities in the United Kingdom, and U.S. companies have invested in a number of that country's regional electrical utilities. In turn, British Telecommunications has responded vigorously to new competition at home and made numerous investments around the world, including a strategic alliance with AT&T for delivery of global services to international companies.

Privatization can also apply to regional or local government departments. At the local level, for instance, services such as rubbish removal and cleaning have been shifted from the public sector to private firms. Not everyone is convinced, however, that such changes are beneficial to all segments of the population. When services are provided by public agencies, there are often cross-subsidies designed to achieve broader social goals. With privatization, there are fears that the search for efficiency and profits will lead to cuts in service and price increases. The result may be to deny less-affluent segments the services they need at prices they can afford. Hence, many argue for continued regulation of prices and terms of service in key industries such as health care, telecommunications, water, electricity, and passenger rail transportation.

Not all regulatory changes represent a relaxation of government rules. In many countries, steps continue to be taken to strengthen consumer protection laws, to safeguard employees, to improve health and safety, and to protect the environment. These new rules often require service firms to change their marketing strategies, their operational procedures, and their human resource policies.

Finally, national governments have long controlled trade in both goods and services. International trade in services is being stimulated by decisions to loosen trading restrictions through negotiations of the World Trade Organization (WTO). And individual countries are choosing to enter into free-trade agreements with some of their neighbors. Examples include NAFTA, concluded between Canada, Mexico, and the United States; Mercosur and Pacto Andino in South America: and, of course, the evolution of the European Union (EU), which currently comprises 15 member countries.

Social Changes

The demand for consumer services—and the way in which people use them—has been strongly influenced by a host of social changes. More people are living alone than before, and more households contain two working adults, including telecommuters and others who work from in-home offices. One result is that more people find themselves short on time and are obliged to hire firms or individuals to perform tasks that used to be performed by a household member. Examples range from child care to housecleaning and from laundry to food preparation. Per capita income has risen significantly in real terms for many segments of the population (although not all have benefited from this trend). Increasing affluence gives people more disposable income, and there has been an observed trend from purchasing new physical possessions to buying services and experiences. In fact, some writers have begun speaking of the "experience economy." Pine and Gilmore suggest that offering memorable experiences is a way to create value and add differentiation.[28]

A combination of changing lifestyles, higher incomes, and declining prices for many high-technology products has meant that more and more people are buying computers, thus enabling them to use the Internet to send and receive e-mail and access Web sites from around the world. Meantime, the rapid growth in use of mobile phones and other wireless equipment means that customers are more connected than ever before and no longer out of touch once they leave their homes or offices.

Another important social trend has been increased immigration into countries such as the United States, Canada, and Australia. These countries are becoming much more multicultural than previously, posing opportunities—and even requirements—for service features designed to meet the needs of nontraditional segments now living within the domestic market. For instance, many immigrants, even if they have learned to speak the language of their new country, prefer to do business in their native languages and appreciate those service organizations that accommodate this preference by offering communications in multiple languages.

Business Trends

Significant changes have taken place during the past quarter-century in how business firms operate. For instance, service profit centers within manufacturing firms are transforming many well-known companies in fields such as computers, motor vehicles, and electrical and mechanical equipment. Supplementary services once designed to help sell equipment—including consultation, credit, transportation and delivery, installation, training, and maintenance—are now offered as profit-seeking services in their own right, even to customers who have chosen to purchase competing equipment. Several large manufacturers (including General Electric, Ford, and DaimlerChrysler) have become important players in the global financial services industry as a result of developing credit-financing and leasing divisions. Similarly, many manufacturers now base much of their competitive appeal on the capabilities of their worldwide consultation, maintenance, repair, and problem-solving services. In fact, service profit centers often contribute a substantial proportion of the revenues earned by such well-known manufacturers as IBM, Hewlett-Packard, and Xerox.

Meantime, the financial pressures confronting public and nonprofit organizations have forced them not only to develop more efficient operations but also to pay more attention to customer needs and competitive activities. In their search for new sources of income, many "nonbusiness" organizations are developing a stronger marketing orientation, which often involves rethinking their product lines; adding profit-seeking services such as shops, retail catalogs, restaurants, and consultancy; becoming more selective about the market segments they target; and adopting more realistic pricing policies.[29]

Many professional associations have been forced by government or legal pressure to remove or relax long-standing bans on advertising and promotional activities. Among the types of professionals affected by such rulings are accountants, architects, doctors, lawyers, and optometrists, whose practices now engage in much more vigorous competitive activity than previously. The freedom to engage in advertising, promotion, and overt selling activities is, after all, essential in bringing innovative services, price cuts, and new delivery systems to the attention of prospective customers. On the other hand, critics worry that the huge surge in legal advertising, especially in the United States, simply encourages people to file more and more lawsuits, many of them frivolous.

With increasing, often price-based competition has come greater pressure for firms to improve productivity. Demands by investors for better returns on their investments have also fueled the search for new ways to increase profits by reducing the costs of service delivery. Historically, the service sector has lagged behind the manufacturing sector in productivity improvement, although there are encouraging signs that some services are beginning to catch up, especially when allowance is also made for simultaneous improvements in quality. Using technology to replace labor (or to permit customer self-service) is one cost-cutting route that has been followed in many industries. Reengineering of processes often results in speeding up operations by cutting out unnecessary steps. However, managers need to be aware of the risk that cost-cutting measures, driven by finance and operations personnel without regard for customer needs, may lead to a perceived deterioration in quality and convenience.

In fact, customer discontent with the quality of service has been ongoing. In the case of manufactured products, complaints have often concerned poor service at the retail point of purchase and with difficulties in solving problems, obtaining refunds, or getting repairs made after the sale. By contrast, service industries such as banks, hotels, car hire firms, restaurants, and telephone companies have been criticized as much for human failings on the part of their employees as for failures on the technical aspects of service. Recognition that improving quality is good for business and necessary for effective competition has led to a radical change in thinking. Traditional notions of quality (based on conformance to standards defined by operations managers) have been replaced by the new imperative of letting quality be customer driven, which has had enormous implications for the importance of service marketing and the role of customer research in both the service and manufacturing sectors.[30] Numerous firms have invested in research to determine what their customers want on every dimension of service, in quality improvement programs designed to deliver what customers want, and in ongoing measurement of how satisfied their customers are with the quality of service received. However, maintaining quality levels over time continues to be difficult.

Franchising has become widespread in many service industries, not only for consumer services but also for business-to-business services. It involves the licensing of independent entrepreneurs to produce and sell a branded service according to tightly specified procedures and has become a popular way to finance the expansion of multisite service chains that deliver a consistent service concept. Large franchise chains are replacing (or absorbing) a wide array of small, independent service businesses in fields as diverse as bookkeeping, car hire, dry cleaning, haircutting, photocopying, plumbing, quick-service restaurants, and real estate agency services. Among the requirements for success are creation of mass-media advertising campaigns to promote brand names nationwide (and even worldwide), standardization of service operations, formalized training programs, an ongoing search for new products, continued emphasis on improving efficiency, and dual marketing programs directed at customers and franchisees, respectively.

Finally, changes have occurred in service firms' hiring practices. Traditionally, many service industries were very inbred. Managers tended to spend their entire careers working within a single industry, even within a single organization. Each industry was seen as unique, and outsiders were suspect. Relatively few managers possessed graduate degrees in business, such as an MBA, although they might have held an industry-specific diploma in a field such as hotel management or health care administration. In recent years, however, competition and enlightened self-interest have led companies to recruit more highly educated managers who are willing to question traditional ways of doing business and able to bring new ideas from previous work experience in another industry. Some of the best service companies are known for being very selective in hiring employees, seeking individuals who will share the firm's strong service quality culture and be able to relate to customers well. And within many firms, intensive training programs are now exposing employees at all levels to new tools and concepts.

Advances in Information Technology

New technologies are radically altering the ways in which many service organizations do business with their customers—as well as what goes on behind the scenes. Perhaps the most powerful force for change today comes from the integration of computers and telecommunications. Digitization allows text, graphics, video, and audio to be manipulated, stored, and transmitted in the digital language of computers. Faster and more powerful software enables firms to create relational databases that combine information about customers with details of all their transactions and then to mine these databases for insights into new trends, new approaches to segmentation, and new marketing opportunities. Greater bandwidth, made possible by innovations such as fiber-optic cables, allows fast transmission of vast amounts of information so that customer-contact personnel can interact almost instantly with a central data base, no matter where they happen to be located. The creation of wireless networks and the miniaturization of electronic equipment—from cell phones to laptops and scanners—allow sales and customer service personnel to keep in touch while on the move. Companies operating information-based services, such as financial service firms, have seen the nature and scope of their businesses totally transformed by the advent of national (or even global) electronic delivery systems.

Most recently, the development of the Internet and its best known component, the World Wide Web, has provided not only an important new medium of communication between service organizations and their customers but also the potential for creating radically new business models, including what one leading technology firm has christened "e-services" (Figure 1.8). Properly designed and configured, such services offer unprecedented speed and reach. Existing service providers ignore the Internet at their peril.[31] For instance, by taking advantage of the Internet, Amazon.com has become a global operation in just a few short years, marketing its huge array of books and music through its Web site and using modern business logistics to ship purchases quickly to customers all over the world.

Technological change affects many other types of services, too, from airfreight to hotels to retail stores. Express package firms such as TNT, DHL, Federal Express, or United Parcel Service (UPS), for instance, recognize that the ability to provide real-time information about customers' packages has become as important to success as the physical movement of those packages. Technology does more than enable creation of new or improved services. It may also facilitate reengineering of such activities as delivery of information, order taking, and payment; enhance a firm's ability to maintain more consistent service standards; permit creation of centralized customer service departments; allow replacement of personnel by machines for repetitive tasks; and lead to greater involvement of customers in operations through self-service technology.

FIGURE 1.8   Hewlett-Packard Promotes "E-Services."

Internationalization and Globalization

The internationalization of service companies is readily apparent to any tourist or business executive traveling abroad. More and more services are being delivered through national or even global chains. Brand names such as Air Canada, Burger King, Citibank, Hertz, Kinko's, and Mandarin Hotels have spread far from their original national roots. In some instances, such chains are entirely company owned; in other instances, the creator of the original concept has entered into partnerships with outside investors. Airlines and airfreight companies that were formerly just domestic in scope today have extensive foreign-route networks. Numerous financial service firms, advertising agencies, hotel chains, fast-food restaurants, car hire agencies, and accounting firms now operate on several continents. Some of this growth has been internally generated, but much has also come about through acquisitions of other companies. A strategy of international expansion may be driven by a search for new markets or by the need to respond to existing customers who are traveling abroad in ever greater numbers. A similar situation prevails in business-to-business services. When companies set up operations in other countries, they often prefer to deal with just a few international suppliers rather than numerous local firms.

The net effect of such developments is to increase competition and to encourage the transfer of innovation in both products and processes from country to country. Developing a strategy for competing effectively across numerous different countries is becoming a major marketing priority for many service firms. Franchising offers a way to enable a service concept developed in one nation to be delivered around the world through distribution systems owned by local investors. International takeovers have been routine. For example, both Federal Express and UPS have expanded into numerous countries by purchasing local courier firms.

Many well-known service companies around the world are U.S.-owned; examples include Citicorp, McDonald's, and Andersen Consulting. The upscale Four Seasons hotel chain is Canadian. In turn, North Americans are often surprised to learn that Burger King and Holiday Inn are both owned by British companies, whereas Motel 6 and Red Roof Inns are owned by France's Groupe Accor. An alternative to mergers and takeovers is strategic alliances, whereby several firms working in the same or complementary industries in different countries join forces to expand the geographic reach and product scope. Examples include the airline and telecommunication industries.

Managing in a Continually Changing Environment

It has been said that the only person in the world who appreciates a change is a wet baby. Large companies are especially threatened by disruptive change.[32] But the willingness and ability of managers in service firms to respond to the dramatic developments affecting the service economy will determine whether their own organizations survive and prosper or go down to defeat at the hands of more agile and adaptive competitors. The implications of the changes outlined previously are several. On the positive side, demand for many services is likely to grow. But the opening up of the service economy means that there will be greater competition for that demand. In turn, more competition will stimulate innovation, not least through the application of new and improved technologies. Both singly and in combination, these developments will require managers of service organizations to focus more sharply on marketing strategy.

None of the industries in the service sector find themselves untouched by at least some of the factors described earlier. In many industries, notably transportation and financial services, several elements are converging—like a gale, a new moon, and heavy rains—to produce a flood tide that will wreck organizations whose management seeks to maintain the status quo. Other managers with more foresight recognize, like Shakespeare's Brutus, that a tide taken at the flood can lead to fortune. But where does this tide lead, and what does it imply for the role of marketing in the service sector? As we'll see in later chapters, some service organizations have succeeded by taking advantage of the changing environment to create new offerings or enhance their competitive positions.

Conclusion

Why study services? Because modern economies are driven by service businesses, both large and small. Services are responsible for the creation of a substantial majority of new jobs, both skilled and unskilled, around the world. The service sector includes a tremendous variety of different industries, including many activities provided by public and nonprofit organizations. It accounts for over half the economy in most developing countries and for 70 percent or more in many highly developed economies.

As we've shown in this chapter, services differ from manufacturing organizations in many important respects and require a distinctive approach to marketing and other management functions. As a result, managers who want their enterprises to succeed cannot continue to rely solely on tools and concepts developed in the manufacturing sector. In the remainder of this book, we'll discuss in more detail the unique challenges and opportunities faced by service businesses. It's our hope that you'll use the material from this text to enhance your future experiences not only as a service employee or manager but also as a customer of many different types of service businesses!

REVIEW QUESTIONS

1. Review the definitions of service on pages 3–4. Do you agree that services are necessarily economic activities?
2. Business schools have traditionally placed more emphasis on manufacturing industries than on service industries in their courses. Why do you think this is so? Does it matter?
3. Why is time so important in services?
4. What are the marketing implications of freer competition in service industries that used to be heavily regulated?
5. Is the risk of unethical business practices greater or lesser in service businesses than in manufacturing firms. Why (or why not)?
6. Why do marketing, operations, and human resources have to be more closely linked in services than in manufacturing? Give examples.

APPLICATION EXERCISES

1. Give examples of how, during the past 10 years, computer and telecommunications technology has changed some of the services that you use.
2. Choose a service company with which you are familiar and show how each of the 8 Ps of integrated service management applies.
3. Visit the Web sites of the following national statistical bureaus: U.S. Bureau of Economic Analysis (www.bea.gov) and Statistics Canada (www.statcan.ca) and obtain data on the latest trends in services as a percentage of gross domestic product and as the percentage of employment accounted for by services; then break down these two statistics by type of industry and in terms of service exports and imports.

ENDNOTES

1. Karl Albrecht and Ron Zemke, *Service America!* (Homewood, IL: Dow Jones Irwin, 1985), 1
2. Evert Gummesson, "Lip Service: A Neglected Area in Services Marketing," *Journal of Consumer Services* 1, no. 1 (1987): (citing an unknown source). For an extended list of definitions, see Christian Grönroos, *Service Management and Marketing* (Lexington MA: Lexington Books, 1990), 26–27.
3. U.S. Bureau of Economic Analysis, *Survey of Current Business,* September 1999, table B3, p. D-28 (www.bea.doc.gov); CANSIM, "Gross Domestic Product at Factor Cost, Seasonally Adjusted at Annual Rates, October 1999," *Canadian Statistics* (Ottawa: Statistics Canada, January 2000) (www.statcan.ca).
4. World Bank, *El mundo del trabajo en una economía integrada* (Washington, DC: World Bank, 1995).
5. Javier Reynoso, "The Evolution of Services Management in Developing Countries: Insights from Latin America," in *New and Evolving Paradigms: The Emerging Future of Marketing,* ed. Tony Meenaghan (Dublin, Ireland: American Marketing Association and University College Dublin, 1997), 112–121.
6. Regis McKenna, *Real Time* (Boston: Harvard Business School Press, 1997), 11.
7. See, for instance, the discussion of outsourcing information-based services in James Brian Quinn, *Intelligent Enterprise* (New York: The Free Press, 1992), 71–97.
8. "North American Industry Classification System," Bureau of the Census (www. census.gov/naics), 1998.
9. A number of books have addressed these themes. They include Karl Albrecht and Ron Zemke, *Service America!* (Homewood, IL: Dow-Jones Irwin 1985); Sandra Vandermerwe, *From Tin Soldiers to Russian Dolls: Creating Added Value through Services* (Oxford: Butterworth-Heinemann, 1993); Christopher Lovelock, *Product Plus: How Product + Service = Competitive Advantage* (New York: McGraw-Hill, 1994); Benjamin Schneider and David E. Bowen, *Winning the Service Game* (Boston: Harvard Business School Press, 1995); James L. Heskett, W. Earl Sasser Jr., and Leonard A. Schlesinger, *The Service Profit Chain* (New York: The Free Press, 1997); and Leonard L. Berry, *Discovering the Soul of Service* (New York: The Free Press, 1999).
10. Leonard L. Berry, "Services Marketing Is Different," *Business,* May–June 1980.
11. Summaries of such research are provided by Valarie A. Zeithaml, A. Parasuraman, and Leonard L. Berry, "Problems and Strategies in Services Marketing," *Journal of Marketing* 49 (spring 1985): 33–46; and by Scott Edgett and Stephen Parkinson, "Marketing for Service Industries: A Review," *The Service Industries Journal* 13 (July 1993): 19–39.
12. G. Lynn Shostack, "Breaking Free from Product Marketing," *Journal of Marketing* (April 1977): 73–80.
13. Philip Kotler, *Marketing Management: Analysis, Planning and Control,* 9th ed. (Upper Saddle River, NJ: Prentice Hall, 1997), 467.
14. W. Earl Sasser, R. Paul Olsen, and D. Daryl Wyckoff, *Management of Service Operations: Text, Cases, and Readings* (Boston: Allyn & Bacon, 1978).
15. Bonnie Farber Canziani, "Leveraging Customer Competency in Service Firms," *International Journal of Service Industry Management* 8, no. 1 (1997): 5–25.
16. Gary Knisely, "Greater Marketing Emphasis by Holiday Inns Breaks Mold," *Advertising Age,* January 15, 1979.
17. Curtis P. McLaughlin, "Why Variation Reduction Is Not Everything: A New Paradigm for Service Operations," *International Journal of Service Industry Management* 7, no. 3 (1996): 17–31.
18. This section is based on Valarie A. Zeithaml, "How Consumer Evaluation Processes Differ between Goods and Services," in *Marketing of Services,* ed. J. A. Donnelly and W. R. George (Chicago: American Marketing Association, 1981), 186–190.
19. The 4 Ps classification of marketing decision variables was created by E. Jerome McCarthy, *Basic Marketing: A Managerial Approach* (Homewood, IL: Richard D. Irwin, Inc., 1960).
20. Our 8 Ps model of service management expands on a framework with seven elements—the original 4 Ps plus participants, physical evidence, and process—proposed by Bernard H. Booms and Mary J. Bitner, "Marketing Strategies and Organization Structures for Service Firms," in *Marketing of Services,* ed. J. H. Donnelly and W. R. George (Chicago: American Marketing Association, 1981), 47–51.
21. For a review of the literature on this topic, see Michael D. Hartline and O. C. Ferrell, "The Management of Customer Contact Service Employees," *Journal of Marketing* 60, no. 4 (October 1996): 52–70.
22. Theodore Levitt, *Marketing for Business Growth* (New York, McGraw-Hill, 1974), 5.

23. Roland Rust, "What is the Domain of Service Research?" (editorial), *Journal of Service Research* 1(November 1998): 107.
24. K. Douglas Hoffman and John E. G. Bateson, "Ethical Issues in Services Marketing," chap. 6 in *Essentials of Services Marketing* (New York: The Dryden Press, 1997), 100–120.
25. Siegmund Warburg , cited in a presentation by Derek Higgs, London, September 1997.
26. George F. Will, *Newsweek,* 1983.
27. Timothy K. Smith, "Why Air Travel Doesn't Work," *Fortune,* April 3, 1995, 42–56; Bill Saporito, "Going Nowhere Fast," *Fortune,* April 3, 1995, 58–59.
28. B. Joseph Pine II and James H. Gilmore, *The Experience Economy* (Boston: Harvard Business School Press, 1999).
29. See Christopher H. Lovelock and Charles B. Weinberg, *Public and Nonprofit Marketing,* 2d ed. (Redwood City, CA.: The Scientific Press/Boyd and Davis, 1989); and Philip Kotler and Alan Andreasen, *Strategic Marketing for Nonprofit Organizations,* 5th ed. (Upper Saddle River, NJ: Prentice-Hall, 1996).
30. Valarie A. Zeithaml, A. Parasuraman, and Leonard L. Berry, *Delivering Quality Service* (New York: The Free Press, 1990).
31. See, for instance, Larry Downes and Chunka Mui, *Unleashing the Killer App* (Boston: Harvard Business School Press, 1998); and Mary Modahl, *Now or Never* (New York: Harper Business, 2000).
32. Clayton M. Christiansen and Michael Overdorf, "Meeting the Challenge of Disruptive Change," *Harvard Business Review,* 78, March–April 2000, 66–77.

CHAPTER 2

Customer Involvement in Service Processes

Several kinds of statements about behavior are commonly made. When we tell an anecdote or pass along a bit of gossip, we report a single event—what someone did upon such and such an occasion. . . . These accounts have their uses. They broaden the experience of those who have not had firsthand access to similar data. But they are only the beginnings of a science. The next step is the discovery of some sort of uniformity.

B. F. SKINNER

The service sector is amazingly varied, and the array of transactions that you might make during the course of a typical week represents only a small sample of the innumerable services directed at individual consumers. As a review of the listings in your local Yellow Pages (or commercial telephone directory) will show, there are is a huge array of business-to-business services, too.

It's surprising how many managers consider the particular service industry in which they work to be unique—or at least sharply different from the rest. Certainly, some distinctions can be drawn, but it would be a mistake to assume that any one of the services that you use, for instance, has nothing in common with any of the others. In fact, the more service managers can identify meaningful parallels to their own firms' situations, the better their chances of beating the competition by applying good ideas from other businesses that share relevant characteristics. One hallmark of innovative service firms is that their managers have been willing to look outside their own industries for effective strategies that they can adapt for use in their own organizations.

In this chapter, our focus will be on developing useful ways of grouping services into categories that share managerially relevant characteristics, particularly as these relate to marketing strategy. We emphasize the *process* element of the 8 Ps as we explore the following questions:

1. What is the value of classification in services marketing?
2. In what managerially relevant ways do services differ from one another?

3. What are the underlying processes by which services are created and delivered?
4. How does the nature of a customer's involvement with a service vary according to the underlying process?
5. Why do different service processes require different approaches to marketing strategy?

How Do Services Differ from One Another?

In chapter 1, we looked at some of the ways in which services might differ from goods. Now we turn our attention to examining differences between services and show that important insights can be gained by looking for similarities between seemingly different service industries. We'll start our search for useful categorization schemes by outlining the scientific basis for classification, continue by examining how goods have traditionally been classified, and then consider the implications of classification schemes focused specifically on services.

The Value of Classification Schemes

The academic discipline of management studies is based on the notion that insights can be gained through theory and research that will lead to more effective management practices. As noted by Shelby Hunt, a respected researcher in marketing, "the purpose of theory is to increase scientific understanding through a systematized structure capable of both *explaining* and *predicting* phenomena." Classification schemes, he adds, "play fundamental roles in the development of a discipline, since they are the primary means for *organizing* phenomena into classes or groups that are amenable to systematic investigation and theory development."[1]

Marketing practitioners have long recognized the value of developing distinctive strategies for different types of goods. One of the earliest and most famous classification schemes in marketing divides goods into convenience, shopping, and specialty categories according to how frequently consumers buy them and how much effort they are prepared to put into comparing alternatives and locating the right product to match their needs.[2] This scheme helps managers obtain a better understanding of consumer expectations and behavior and provides insights into the management of retail distribution systems. This same classification can also be applied to retail service institutions. For instance, a bank ATM is a convenience service, a package holiday is a shopping service, and obtaining a skilled lawyer to try a difficult legal case is an example of a specialty service. In each instance, the task of finding the desired service has been made somewhat easier today by the Internet, which enables customers to use search engines and Web sites to identify and evaluate alternative suppliers with much less effort than previously.

Another major classification is that of durable and nondurable goods. Durability is closely associated with purchase frequency, which has important implications for development of both distribution and communications strategy. Although service performances are intangible, the durability of benefits serves to determine repurchase frequency. For example, the benefits of a haircut or hairstyling eventually start to disappear as the person's hair grows longer, thus requiring another visit to the barber or stylist a month or so after the last one. By contrast, most workers and students need to buy lunch every day they go to work or school (unless they pack a brown-bag meal at home), dentists recommend that you get your teeth cleaned every six months, and homeowners usually find that their house exteriors need to be repainted only every 5 to 10 years, depending on the climate.

Yet another classification is consumer goods (those purchased for personal or household use) versus industrial goods (those purchased by companies and other organizations). This classification relates not only to the types of goods purchased—although there is some overlap—

but also to methods for evaluating competing alternatives, purchasing procedures, the size of purchase orders, and actual usage behavior. Once again, this classification is transferable to services. For example, you may be the only one involved in a decision about which Internet provider to select for use with your own computer. But a corporate decision about choice of online services for use by employees may involve managers and technical specialists from several departments. Business-to-business services, as the name suggests, comprise a large group of services targeted at corporate customers and may range from executive recruiting to security and from payroll management to office cleaning.

Although these goods-based classification schemes are helpful, they don't go far enough in highlighting the key strategic issues facing service managers. We need to classify services into marketing-relevant groups, looking for points of similarity between different industries. The insights from these classifications should be helpful to managers in enabling them to focus on marketing strategies that fully apply to specific service situations.

Core Products versus Supplementary Services

Many service products consist of a bundle, as it were, that includes a variety of service elements and even some physical goods. It's important to distinguish between the core product that the customer buys and the set of supplementary services that often accompany that product. For instance, the core product of the lodging industry is a bed for the night, whether that bed is located in a youth hostel or in a luxury room at a five-star hotel. Youth hostels don't offer many additional services beyond reservations, basic meals, and simple washing facilities. By contrast, as shown in Figure 2.1, a luxury hotel will offer many additional services to enhance its guests'

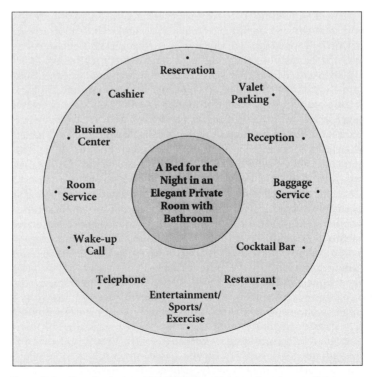

FIGURE 2.1   Core Product and Supplementary Services for a Luxury Hotel

visits. Some of these services will be offered free and others will carry a charge, but they are all subordinate to the core service of overnight sleeping accommodation that defines the lodging industry.

When we speak of services in this chapter, we are referring to the core service that the customer is buying—such as taking an airline flight, attending a concert, hiring an accounting firm to prepare an audit of a company's accounts, or purchasing a homeowners insurance policy. Most core services are also accompanied by a cluster of supplementary services that are intended to add value to the core. Examples include meals and baggage service on an airline flight, refreshments at a concert, professional advice from an experienced auditor, or a helpful booklet from an insurance company with suggestions on how to protect your home. Our classification schemes in this chapter refer to the core product, but supplementary services can themselves be classified, too. We offer an in-depth discussion of the nature and role of supplementary services in chapter 8.

How Might Services Be Classified?

The traditional way of grouping services is by industry. Service managers may say, "We're in the transportation business" (or hospitality, banking, telecommunications, or repair and maintenance). These groupings help us to define the core products offered by the firm and to understand both customer needs and competition. However, they may not capture the true nature of each business within the industry, because service delivery can differ widely even within a single category. For example, food can be provided to customers in settings ranging from a quick-service restaurant with no seats at an airport to an exclusive Paris restaurant bearing the coveted Michelin three-star rating.

Numerous proposals have been made for classifying services.[3] Among the meaningful ways in which services can be grouped or classified are those listed in Table 2.1 and discussed in the following paragraphs.

The Degree of Tangibility or Intangibility of Service Processes. Does the service entail something physical and tangible (such as sleeping in a hotel bed or dry cleaning your clothes), or do its processes involve a greater amount of intangibility (such as teaching or telephoning)? Different service processes not only shape the nature of the service delivery system but also affect the role of employees and the experience of customers.

Who or What Is the Direct Recipient of the Service Process? Some services, such as haircutting or public transportation, are directed at customers in person. In other situations, customers seek services (such as dry cleaning) to restore or improve objects that belong to them but remain uninvolved themselves in the process of service delivery and do not consume the benefits until later. The nature of the service encounter between service suppliers and their cus-

TABLE 2.1 *Selected Ways of Classifying Services*
• Degree of tangibility of service processes
• Who or what is the direct recipient of the service process?
• The place and time of service delivery
• Customization versus standardization
• Nature of the relationship with customers
• Extent to which demand and supply are in balance
• Extent to which facilities, equipment, and people are part of the service experience

tomers varies widely according to the extent to which customers themselves are integrally involved in the service process. Consider a simple experience such as mailing a letter, which involves putting on the stamp and dropping the envelope in mailbox. Here, it's the letter that is being transported, not you, and your own involvement with the service is quickly over. Services to the person of the customer tend to be somewhat more complex. Consider the task of getting your hair washed and cut, which may involve the need to make an advance reservation; wait at the store for your turn; describe to the haircutter what you want; get yourself wrapped in a protective sheet; and cooperate with the cutter during washing, cutting, and drying—tasks that may involve more than one employee and a move from one chair to another.

The Place and Time of Service Delivery. When designing delivery systems, service marketers must ask themselves whether customers need to visit the service organization at its own sites or whether service should come to the customer (for instance, you can go to a pizza parlor or telephone for home delivery). Or perhaps the interaction can occur through physical channels such as postal delivery (as with sending a package by mail or courier) or electronic channels (as with Internet-based services that allow you to transact in cyberspace). These managerial decisions involve consideration of the nature of the service itself, where customers are located (both home and workplace may be relevant), their preferences relating to time of purchase and use, and the relative costs of different alternatives.

Customization versus Standardization. Services can be classified according to the degree of customization or standardization involved in service delivery. An important marketing decision is whether all customers should receive the same service or whether service features (and the underlying processes) should be adapted to meet individual requirements. Cable television subscriptions, for instance, come in several standard options. A bus service is standardized with a fixed route and timetable (unlike a taxi), but passengers can choose when to ride and where to get on and off. An eye examination by an optometrist will follow standardized procedures but must end with a customized diagnosis if a prescription for corrective lenses is needed.

Nature of the Relationship with Customers. Some services involve a formal relationship in which each customer is known to the organization (or at least to its computer) and all transactions are individually recorded and attributed (for example, the use of a bank account or a patient's eye history at an optometrist). But in other services, unidentified customers undertake fleeting transactions and then disappear from the organization's sight (for instance, a phone company will have no record of who made a call from a pay phone unless a charge card is used). As we shall see in chapter 6, some services lend themselves naturally to a membership-style relationship in which customers must apply to join the "club" and their subsequent performance is monitored over time (as in insurance or college enrollment.) Other services, such as buses, hairdressers, dry cleaners, and restaurants, need to undertake proactive efforts to create an ongoing relationship. Although a bus company does not normally record an individual passenger's rides, it can keep records of all monthly pass holders so that it can mail out passes every month; it could include a newsletter describing service improvements or route and timetable changes. Sometimes companies create special club membership or frequent-user programs to reward loyal users. For instance, both the hairdresser and the cleaner could record customers' names and addresses and periodically make them special offers.

Extent to Which Demand and Supply Are in Balance. Some service industries face steady demand for their services, whereas others encounter significant fluctuations. In chapter 13, we address the problem faced by marketers when the demand for service fluctuates widely over time. In such situations, either capacity must be adjusted to accommodate the level of demand or marketing strategies must be implemented to predict, manage, and smooth demand levels to bring them into balance with capacity. Many factors account for demand variations, and we discuss them in detail later in this book.

Extent to Which Facilities, Equipment, and People Are Part of the Service Experience. Customers' service experiences are shaped, in part, by the extent to which they are exposed to tangible elements in the service delivery system. Think about all the physical evidence that a patient might encounter at a hospital: first, the building exteriors and parking lots, then interior lobbies and waiting areas, patients' rooms with beds and other furnishings, meal service, and treatment areas with medical equipment. In the course of even a brief stay, the patient might encounter medical personnel, such as doctors and nurses; a variety of nonmedical employees, such as food service personnel; cleaners and orderlies; and other patients. By contrast, it is rare for a telephone customer to encounter physical equipment, other than the phone handset, or to deal with company personnel.

Implications of Different Classifications

The service classification schemes that we've just discussed can help managers better answer the following questions: What does our service operation actually do? What sorts of processes are involved in creating the core product that we offer to customers? And speaking of customers, where do they fit in our operation? The answers will differ depending on the nature of the underlying service process required to create and deliver a particular service. So now we turn to the most fundamental of the 8 Ps of integrated service management: the processes by which service products are created and delivered. Our focus will be on the core service product, but you should note that supplementary services also require delivery and that the process employed may differ from that used for the core product.

Service as a Process

Marketers don't usually need to know the specifics of how physical goods are manufactured—that's the responsibility of the people who run the factory. However, the situation is different in services. Because customers are often involved in service production, marketers do need to understand the nature of the processes to which their customers may be exposed. A *process* is a particular method of operation or a series of actions, typically involving multiple steps that often need to take place in a defined sequence. Think about the steps that a customer might go through in visiting a hair salon: phoning in advance to make an appointment, arriving at the shop, waiting, having a shampoo, discussing options with the hairdresser, having her hair cut and styled, tipping the cutter, paying at the reception desk, and finally leaving the store.

Service processes range from relatively simple procedures involving only a few steps—such as filling a car's tank with fuel—to highly complex activities such as transporting passengers on an international flight. Later, we show how these processes can be represented in diagrams known as *flowcharts* that help us to understand what is going on (and perhaps how a specific process might be improved).

Categorizing Service Processes

A process implies taking an input and transforming it into output.[4] But if that's the case, then what is each service organization actually processing, and how does it perform this task? Two broad categories of things get processed in services: people and objects. In many cases, ranging from passenger transportation to education, customers themselves are the principal input to the service process (as in a haircut or an airline flight); in other instances, the key input is an object such as a malfunctioning computer that needs repair or a piece of financial data that needs to be associated with a particular account. In some services, as in all manufacturing, the process is physical: Something tangible takes place. But in information-based services, the process can be intangible.

By looking at service processes from a purely operational perspective, we see that they can be categorized into four broad groups. Figure 2.2 shows a four-way classification scheme based on tangible actions to people's bodies or physical possessions and intangible actions to people's minds or their intangible assets. Each of these four categories involves fundamentally different forms of processes, with vital implications for marketing, operations, and human resource man-

What is the Nature of the Service Act?	Who or What is the Direct Recipient of the Service?	
	People	**Possessions**
Tangible Actions	***People processing*** (services directed at people's bodies): Passenger transportation Health care Lodging Beauty salons Physical therapy Fitness center Restaurant/bars Barbers Funeral services	***Possession processing*** (services directed at physical possessions): Freight transportation Repair and maintenance Warehousing/storage Office cleaning services Retail distribution Laundry and dry cleaning Refueling Landscaping/gardening Disposal/recycling
Intangible Actions	***Mental stimulus processing*** (services directed at people's minds): Advertising /PR Arts and entertainment Broadcasting/cable Management consulting Education Information services Music concerts Psychotherapy Religion Voice telephone	***Information processing*** (services directed at intangible assets): Accounting Banking Data processing Data transmission Insurance Legal services Programming Research Securities investment Software consulting

FIGURE 2.2   Understanding the Nature of the Service Act

agers. We will refer to the categories as *people processing, possession processing, mental stimulus processing,* and *information processing.* Although the industries within each category may appear, at first sight, to be very different, analysis will show that they do, in fact, share important process-related characteristics. As a result, managers in one industry may be able to obtain useful insights from studying another one and then create valued innovations for their own organizations.

1. *People processing involves tangible actions to people's bodies.* Examples of people-processing services include passenger transportation, hairdressing, and dental work. Customers need to be physically present throughout service delivery to receive the desired benefits of such services.
2. *Possession processing includes tangible actions to goods and other physical possessions belonging to the customer.* Examples of possession-processing include airfreight, lawn mowing, and cleaning services. In these instances the object requiring processing must be present, but the customer need not be.
3. *Mental stimulus processing refers to intangible actions directed at people's minds.* Services in the mental stimulus–processing category include entertainment, spectator sports events, theater performances, and education. In such instances, customers must be present mentally but can be located either at the same location where the service is being created—such as a lecture hall or sports stadium—or in a remote location connected by broadcast signals or telecommunication linkages.
4. *Information processing describes intangible actions directed at a customer's assets.* Examples of information-processing services include insurance, banking, and consulting. In this category, little direct involvement with the customer may be needed once the request for service has been initiated, and even that can be undertaken remotely by mail, phone, or Internet.

Let's examine why these four different types of processes often have distinctive implications for marketing, operations, and human resource strategies.

People Processing. From ancient times, people have sought out services directed at themselves (for example, being transported, fed, lodged, restored to health, or made more beautiful). To receive these types of services, customers must physically enter the service system. Because they are an integral part of the process, they cannot obtain the benefits they desire by dealing at arm's length with service suppliers. They must enter the *service factory,* which is a physical location—sometimes mobile, such as a taxi, ferry, or aircraft—where people or machines (or both) create and deliver service benefits to customers. Sometimes, of course, service providers are willing to come to customers, bringing the necessary tools of their trade with them to create the desired benefits at the customers' preferred locations. Examples include doctors who are willing to make house calls (all too rare, nowadays) and hairdressing or beauty services for infirm residents of nursing homes.

If customers want the benefits that a people-processing service has to offer, they must be prepared to spend time actively cooperating with the service operation. The level of involvement required of customers may entail anything from boarding a city bus for a 5-minute ride to undergoing a lengthy course of unpleasant treatments at a hospital. In between these extremes are activities such as ordering and eating a meal; having one's hair washed, cut, and styled; and spending a couple of nights in a hotel room. The output from these services (after a period of time that can vary from minutes to months) is a customer who has reached her destination or satisfied his hunger or is now sporting clean and stylishly cut hair or has had a couple of good nights' sleep away from home or is now enjoying much better health.

It's important for managers to think about process and output in terms of what happens to the customer (or other object being processed) because it helps them to identify what benefits are being created. Reflecting on the service process itself helps to identify some of the nonfinancial burdens—such as spending time, mental and physical effort, and even experiencing fear and pain—that customers incur in obtaining these benefits.

Possession Processing. Often, customers ask a service organization to provide treatment to some physical possession—which could be anything from a house to a hedge, a car to a computer, or a dress to a dog. Many such activities are quasi-manufacturing operations and don't always involve simultaneous production and consumption. Examples include cleaning, maintaining, storing, improving, or repairing physical objects—both live and inanimate—that belong to the customer in order to extend their usefulness. Additional possession-processing services include transport and storage of goods; wholesale and retail distribution; and installation, removal, and disposal of equipment—in short, the entire value-adding chain of activities that may take place during the lifetime of the object in question.

Customers are less physically involved with this type of service than with people-processing services. Consider the difference between passenger and parcel transportation.

In the first instance, you have to go along for the ride to obtain the benefit of getting from one location to another. But with parcel service, you hand the package to a clerk at a post office counter (or request that a courier collect it from your home or office) and simply wait for it to be delivered. In most possession-processing services, the customer's involvement is usually limited to dropping off the item that needs treatment, requesting the service, explaining the problem, and later returning to pick up the item and pay the bill. If the object to be processed is something that is difficult or impossible to move, such as landscaping, installed appliances, heavy equipment, or part of a building, then the service factory must come to the customer, with service personnel bringing the tools and materials necessary to complete the job on site.

In other instances, the service process might involve applying insecticide in a house to get rid of ants, trimming a hedge at an office park, repairing a car, installing software in a computer, cleaning a jacket, or giving an injection to the family dog. The output in each instance should be a satisfactory solution to a customer's problem or some tangible enhancement of the item in question. Completing the promised work on time is also key to customer satisfaction.

Mental Stimulus Processing. Services that interact with people's minds include education, news and information, professional advice, psychotherapy, entertainment, and certain religious practices. Anything touching people's minds has the power to shape attitudes and influence behavior. So if customers are in a position of dependency or there is potential for manipulation, strong ethical standards and careful oversight are required.

Receiving these services requires an investment of time on the customer's part. However, recipients don't necessarily have to be physically present in a service factory—just mentally in communication with the information being presented. There's an interesting contrast here with people-processing services. Although passengers can sleep through a flight and still obtain the benefit of arriving at their desired destination, a student who falls asleep in class will not be any wiser at the end than at the beginning!

Services such as entertainment and education are often created in one place and transmitted by television or radio to individual customers in distant locations. However, they can also be delivered live and in person to groups of customers at originating locations such as theaters or lecture halls. We need to recognize that watching a live concert on television in one's home is not the same experience as watching it in a concert hall in the company of hundreds or even thousands of other people. In the latter instance, managers of concert halls find themselves facing many of the same challenges as their colleagues in people-processing services. Similarly, the experience of participating in a discussion-based class through interactive cable television lacks the intimacy of people debating each other in the same room.

Because the core content of all services in this category is information based (whether it's music, voice, or visual images), it can easily be converted to digital bits or analog signals, recorded for posterity, and transformed into a manufactured product, such as a compact disc, videotape, or audiocassette, which may then be packaged and marketed much like any other physical good. These services can thus be inventoried because they can be consumed at a later date than they were produced. The performance can also be replayed multiple times. For instance, in the course of a year, a Spanish instructional videotape in a language lab might be used over and over again by hundreds of different students.

Information Processing. Information processing, one of the buzzwords of our age, has been revolutionized by computers. But not all information is processed by machines; professionals in a wide variety of fields use their brains, too. Information is the most intangible form of service output, but it may be transformed into more enduring, tangible forms as letters, reports, books, tapes, or disks. Among the services that are highly dependent on effective collection and processing of information are financial services and professional services such as accounting, law, marketing research, management consulting, and medical diagnosis.

The extent of customer involvement in both information- and mental stimulus–processing services is often determined more by tradition and a personal desire to meet the supplier face-to-face than by the needs of the operational process. Strictly speaking, personal contact is quite unnecessary in industries such as banking or insurance. Why should managers subject their firm to all the complexities of managing a people-processing service when they could deliver the same core product at a distance? As a customer, why go to the service factory when there's no compelling need to do so?

Habit and tradition often lie at the root of existing service delivery systems and service usage patterns. Professionals and their clients may say they prefer to meet face-to-face because they feel they learn more about each other's needs, capabilities, and personalities that way. However, experience shows that successful personal relationships built on trust can be created and maintained purely through telephone or e-mail contact. As technology improves and people continue to become more comfortable with videophones or the Internet, we can expect to see a continuing shift to arm's-length transactions.

Variations in Customer Involvement

By charting processes in visual form, we can also see clearly how different the customer's involvement with the service organization can be for each of the four processes in their purest forms. Figure 2.3 displays a simple flowchart for each of the following scenarios: staying at a motel, getting a VCR repaired, obtaining a weather forecast and obtaining health insurance. Imagine that you are the customer in each instance and think about the extent and nature of your involvement in service delivery in each instance.

1. *Staying at a motel (people processing).* It's late evening. You are driving on a long trip and are getting tired. You see a motel with a vacancy sign and price displayed and decide it is time to stop for the night. You park in the lot, noting that the grounds are clean and the buildings seem freshly painted, and enter the office where a friendly clerk checks you in and gives you the key to your room. You walk across the forecourt to the room with your bag and let yourself in. After undressing and using the bathroom, you go to bed. Following a good night's sleep, you rise the next morning, shower, dress, pack, and then walk to the office where you return your key to a different clerk, pay, and leave the motel.

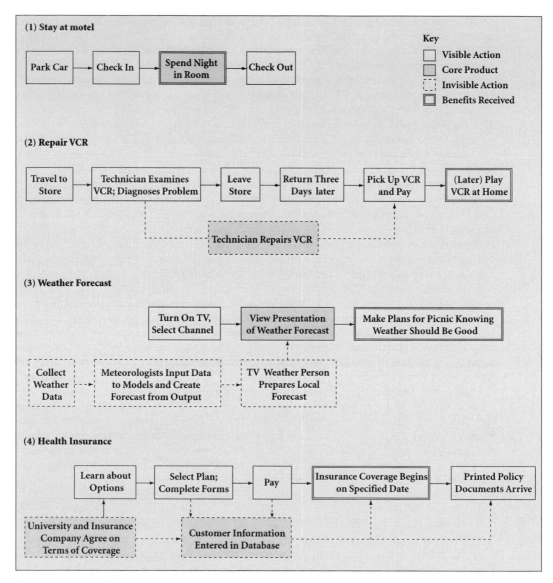

FIGURE 2.3   Simple Flowcharts for Delivery of Different Types of Services

2. *Repairing a VCR (possession processing).* When you play videotapes on your VCR, the picture quality on the television screen is poor. Fed up with the situation, you search the yellow pages to find an appliance repair store in your area. At the store, the technician checks your machine in the front office and declares that it needs to be adjusted and cleaned. The estimated price seems reasonable, so you agree to the work and are told the VCR will be ready in three days' time. The technician disappears into the back office with your machine, and you leave the store. On the appointed day, you return to pick up the VCR and pay. Back home, you plug in the VCR, insert a tape, and find that the picture is now much improved.

3. *Weather forecasting (mental stimulus processing).* You want to arrange a picnic trip to the lake this weekend, two days from now, but one of your friends says she has heard there is the possibility of a big storm. Back home that evening, you check the weather forecast on television. The meteorologist shows animated charts indicating the probable path of the storm over the next 48 hours and declares that the latest computer projections from the National Weather Service suggest it is likely to pass well to the south of your area. Armed with this information, you call your friends to tell them that the picnic is on.

4. *Health Insurance (information processing).* Your university mails you a package of information before the beginning of the new semester. This package includes a brochure from the student health service describing the several different health insurance options available to students. Although you consider yourself very healthy, except for seasonal allergies, you remember the unfortunate experience of a friend who recently incurred heavy hospital bills for a badly broken leg; uninsured, he was forced to liquidate his modest savings and sell his nice new car to pay the bills. So at the time of registration, you select an option that will cover the cost of hospital treatment, plus visits to the student health center; you fill in a printed form that includes some standard questions about your medical history and then sign it. The cost of the insurance is added to your term bill. Subsequently, you receive written confirmation of your coverage in the mail. Now you no longer have to worry about the risk of unexpected medical expenses.

As you can see from these simple flowcharts, your role as customer varies sharply from one process to another. The first two examples involve physical processes. At the motel, you are actively involved in the service, which is delivered in real time over a period of perhaps eight hours. For a fee, you rent the use of a bedroom, bathroom, and other physical facilities for the night. When you leave, you can't take the service elements with you, but if the bed had been uncomfortable, you might have felt tired and physically sore for some time afterwards. Your role at the VCR store, however, was limited to a few minutes explaining the symptoms, leaving the machine there, and returning several days later to pick it up. You have to trust the technician's competence and honesty in executing the service in your absence, because you are not involved in actual production of the service. You enjoy the benefits later when using the repaired VCR.

The other two services that were described involve intangible actions and a relatively passive role for you as customer. The production of the weather forecast is undertaken by the National Weather Service or other professional weather-forecasting organization. Weather data inputs collected by a variety of sophisticated instruments in satellites, aircraft, and on the earth's surface are entered into a computer, enabling projections of future weather conditions in different locations to be made. Subsequently, the television station's meteorologist examines the model's forecasts, interprets them for the local area, and presents both a description of current conditions and a prediction for the next several days during the news program. All you have to do is to tune the television to the chosen station, pay attention to what is being presented, and use that information to make your own future plans. There is no specific fee to be paid for the forecast, because you have already invested in the cost of buying a television and an aerial for reception of local transmissions, but it does take a few minutes of your time. If you had been using the television for entertainment purposes, however, you might have spent several hours watching different programs.

In the case of the health insurance, all that is required is for you to review the options, select the one that best meets your needs, complete and sign the form, and pay your term bill. The actual production of the insurance coverage takes place at the insurance company, based on detailed analysis of past data involving the extent and cost of medical treatments for students of your age group and modified by anticipated trends in health care costs during the coming year. The fee that you pay for this group coverage will be determined by negotiation between the university and the insurance company. Your protection is maintained automatically for the duration of the coverage. No further action is required on your part unless you need to make claim. The benefit is peace of mind, knowing that you will be taken care of if something goes wrong and that your financial assets will be protected.

Different Processes Pose Distinctive Management Challenges

The challenges and tasks facing managers who work in each of the four different service categories that we've just described are likely vary to some extent. The process classification scheme is central to understanding these differences and developing effective service strategies. Not only does it offer insights into the nature of service benefits in each instance, but it also provides an understanding of the behavior that is required of the customer. There are also implications for developing channel strategy, designing and locating the service delivery system, and using information technology to best advantage.

Identifying Service Benefits

Managers need to recognize that operational processes, however important, are basically just a means to an end. The key is to understand the specific benefits that customers hope to obtain from the service provider. Many firms bundle together lots of different activities as part of their effort to provide good service. But innovation in service delivery requires that a constant spotlight be maintained on the processes underlying delivery of the core product—a bed for the night in the lodging industry, fast transportation of people in the airline industry, or cleaning and pressing clothes in the laundry industry.

New technology often allows service organizations to deliver the same (or improved) benefits to customers via distinctly different processes. Sometimes customers are delighted to receive service through faster, simpler, more convenient procedures. However, operations managers need to beware of imposing new processes, in the name of efficiency, on customers who prefer the existing approach (particularly when the new approach relies on technology and equipment to replace personal service by employees). By working with marketing personnel, operations specialists will improve their chances of designing new processes that deliver the benefits desired by customers in user-friendly ways.

As we saw in the four flowcharts, the timing and duration of the benefits derived from the service may differ markedly. Renting a motel room is a real-time service in which the customer is an active participant; if the customers sleeps well, the benefits are realized throughout the night and even extend into the following day. By contrast, the customer does not participate in the actual repair of the VCR; moreover, the benefits of this repair are not realized until the machine returns home and is put to use again. Once repaired, the machine may continue to offer the benefits of a better-quality picture for years before it requires further servicing. The customer is mentally but not physically involved in watching the weather forecast on television, transmitted in real time from a studio but created in advance of the program; it provides the customer with the immediate benefit of information to make a quick decision. Finally, the customer's involvement in health care insurance is limited to filling out an application and paying the policy fee; however, the benefits—in the form of peace of mind—will be felt as long as the policy remains in effect. A healthy, honest customer would hope not to need to make a claim on the insurance because that would mean that something unpleasant had happened.

Design of the Service Factory

Every service has customers (or hopes to find some), but not every service interacts with them in the same way. Customer involvement in the core activity may vary sharply for each of the four categories of service process. Nothing can alter the fact that people-processing services require the customer to be physically present within the service factory. If you're currently in Minneapolis and want to be in Amsterdam tomorrow, you simply can't avoid boarding an international flight and spending time in a jet high above the Atlantic. If you want your hair cut, you can't delegate this activity to somebody else's head—you have to sit in the barber's chair yourself. If you have the misfortune to break your leg, you will personally have to submit to the unpleasantness of having the bone x-rayed, reset by an orthopedic surgeon, and then encased in a protective cast for several weeks.

When customers visit a service factory, their satisfaction will be influenced by such factors as:

- Encounters with service personnel
- Appearance and features of service facilities—both exterior and interior
- Interactions with self-service equipment
- Characteristics and behavior of other customers

Where customers are required to be physically present throughout service delivery, the process must be designed around them from the moment they arrive at the service factory. Customers may initially need parking (or other assistance in traveling to and from the service facility). The longer they remain on site, the more they are likely to need other services, including hospitality basics such as food, beverages, and toilets. In many instances, they will have to play active roles in creation and delivery of the service. Well-managed service firms teach their customers how to participate effectively in service operations.

Service delivery sites that customers need to visit must be located and designed with their convenience in mind. If the service factory is noisy, smelly, confusingly laid out, and sited in an inconvenient location, then customers are likely to be turned off. Marketing managers need to work closely with their counterparts in operations to design facilities that are both pleasing to customers and efficient to operate. The exterior of a building creates important first impressions, whereas the interior can be thought of as the stage on which the service performance is delivered. The longer customers remain in the factory and the more they expect to spend, the more important it is to offer facilities that are comfortable and attractive.

Marketers need to work with human resource managers, too. Here the task is to ensure that those employees who are in contact with customers present an acceptable appearance and have both the personal and technical skills needed to perform well. Unfortunately, service staff often lack the skills needed to provide satisfactory service for their customers. At the same time, customers may need some basic training or guidance on how to work cooperatively with service personnel to achieve the best results. In situations where customers are expected to do some of the work themselves—as in self-service—then facilities and equipment must be designed for ease of use.

Alternative Channels for Service Delivery

Unlike the situation in people-processing services, managers responsible for possession-processing, mental stimulus–processing, and information-processing services need not oblige their customers to visit a service factory. Instead, they may be able to offer a choice between one of several alternative delivery channels. Possibilities include (1) letting customers come to a user-friendly factory, (2) limiting contact to a small retail office that is separate from the main factory (or back office), (3) coming to the customer's home or office, and (4) conducting business from a distance.

Let's take cleaning and pressing of clothes—a possession-processing service—as an example. One approach is to do your laundry at home. If you lack the necessary machines, then you can pay to use a laundromat, which is essentially a self-service cleaning factory. If you prefer to leave the task of laundry and dry cleaning to professionals, as many people choose to do with their best clothes, then you can go to a retail store that serves as a drop-off location for dirty clothes and pickup point for newly cleaned items. Sometimes, cleaning is conducted in a space behind the store; at other times, the clothing is transported to an industrial site some distance away. Home pickup and delivery is available in some cities, but this service tends to be expensive because of the extra costs involved. Some people can afford to pay a housekeeper or maid to come to their home and do their laundry and ironing for them (usually in conjunction with other household tasks).

Both physical and electronic channels allow customers and suppliers to conduct service transactions at arm's length. For instance, instead of shopping at a shopping center, you can study a printed catalog and order by telephone for parcel delivery, or you can try shopping on the Internet, entering your orders electronically after reviewing your choices on a Web site display. Information-based items, such as software or research reports, can even be downloaded immediately to your own computer.

Today's managers need to be creative because the combination of information technology and modern package transportation services such as Federal Express offers many opportunities to rethink the place and time of service delivery. Some manufacturers of small pieces of equipment allow customers to bypass retail dealers when a product needs repair. Instead, a courier will come to pick up the defective item (even supplying appropriate packaging if necessary), ship it to a repair site, and return the item a few days later when the problem has been fixed. Electronic distribution channels offer even more convenience, because transportation time can be eliminated. For instance, by using telecommunication links, engineers in a central facility (which could be located on the other side of the world) may be able to diagnose problems in defective computers and software at distant customer locations and transmit electronic signals to correct the defects.

Rethinking service delivery procedures for all but people-processing services may allow a firm to get customers out of the factory and transform a high-contact service into a low-contact one. When the nature of the process makes it possible to deliver service from afar, then the design and location of the factory can focus on purely operational priorities. Some industry observers are predicting that within the next two decades, the traditional bank branch will cease to exist and we will be conducting most of our banking transactions via ATMs, telephones, or personal computers (not everybody agrees with this prediction!). The chances of success in such an endeavor are enhanced when the new procedures are user-friendly, less expensive, and offer customers greater convenience.

Making the Most of Information Technology

It's clear that information-based services (a term that covers both mental stimulus–processing and information-processing services) have the most to gain from advances in information technology because telecommunications and the Internet allow the operation to be physically separated from its customers, without even the need for physical shipments.[5] A growing number of banks are now adding Internet capability so that customers can access their accounts and conduct certain transactions from their home or office computers. One of the challenges, however, is to persuade customers to switch their banking behavior to the Web from more traditional channels.

Many examples of using technology to transform the nature of the core product and its delivery system are based on radio and television. From studio symphony performances to electronic churches to call-in gardening advice programs, broadcasting—and now interactive cable—have created new ways to bring advice, entertainment, culture, and spiritual enlightenment to widely scattered audiences. In many countries, education is offered through electronic channels as an alternative to the traditional mode of face-to-face presentations in a physical classroom. Virtual universities are springing up, such as the University of Phoenix in the United States. One of the oldest and largest efforts of this nature is the Open University (OU) in Great Britain. The OU has been offering degree programs to students nationwide through the electronic campus of British Broadcasting Service (BBC) television and radio for over thirty years. Anyone can watch or hear the programs, of course, but registered students also receive printed course material through the mail and communicate with tutors by mail, e-mail, or telephone.

Distance education is now taking place in Africa, where only 3 percent of 18- to 25-year-olds enroll in college and few have any business experience. In 1997, the World Bank launched the African Virtual University, which enables students in 16 African countries to take courses and seminars taught by professors from universities around the world.[6] Instructors deliver lectures in front of cameras in their own classrooms and the video is routed via fiber optics, integrated services digital network (ISDN) lines, or satellite to an uplink in Washington, D.C., from where it is transmitted by satellite to various locations in Africa. A student in one country, say, Ghana, can talk with the instructor in real time via standard telephone lines, while students in Kenya, Tanzania, and Zimbabwe listen to the dialog.

As we pointed out earlier in this chapter, a distinction needs to be made between marketing the core product and the provision of supplementary services to enhance that core product. Much of the discussion surrounding use of the Internet concerns supplementary services that are based on the transfer of information relating to the product, as opposed to downloading the core product itself. Modern telecommunications and computer technologies allow customers to connect their own computers (or other input-output devices) with the service provider's system in another location. In response, more and more companies are designing Web sites to allow customers to review information on the goods and services offered for sale, place orders or reservations, and even make payment.

Today, the Web is having an increasingly significant impact on distribution strategy for a broad array of industries.[7] However, in many cases, these Web sites are an example of marketing goods through service rather than marketing a core service product. Figure 2.4 displays examples of both types of Web site. In the case of Charles Schwab, the core product—financial services—can be delivered via the Web. In the case of L.L. Bean, however, the Web site offers only such supplementary services—information about the physical products sold by the company and the ability to order and pay for goods online. Actual delivery of the core product—outdoor clothing, camping gear, and sporting equipment—requires the use of physical channels. To transport orders to customers, L.L. Bean has outsourced shipping and delivery services to a major logistics supplier, Federal Express.

Balancing Supply and Demand

Sharp fluctuations in demand are a bane in the lives of many managers. But manufacturing firms can stock supplies of their product as a hedge against fluctuations in demand. This strategy enables them to enjoy the economies derived from operating factories at steady production levels. Few service businesses can do this easily. For example, the potential income from an empty seat on an airliner is lost forever once that flight takes off. Hotel room nights are equally perishable in this sense. And the productive capacity of a car repair garage is wasted if no cars come in for servicing on a day when the garage is open. Conversely, when demand for service exceeds supply, the excess business may be lost. If someone can't get a seat on one flight, another carrier gets the business or the trip is canceled. In other situations, customers may be forced to wait in a queue until sufficient productive capacity is available to serve them.

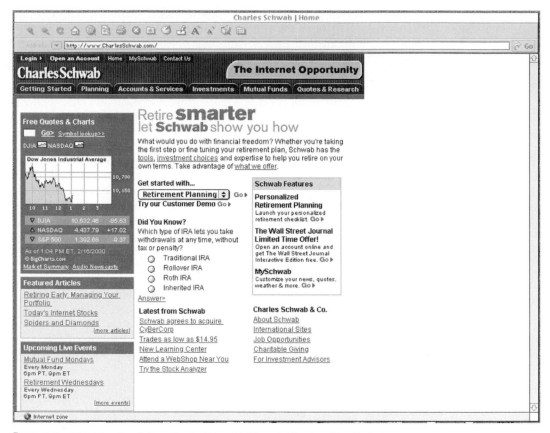

FIGURE 2.4   Web Sites Can Deliver Charles Schwab's Financial Services Directly But ...

In general, services that process people and physical objects are more likely to face capacity limitations than those that are information based. Radio and television transmissions, for instance, can reach any number of homes within their receiving area or cable distribution network. In recent years, information processing and transmission capacity has been vastly increased by greater computer power, digital switching, and the replacement of coaxial cables by fiber-optic ones. Although the surge in demand for Internet services is now causing capacity problems on many telecommunication lines, this problem will eventually be resolved through installation of broadband communication capability. Early 1998 saw the introduction of the first transatlantic cable network to cater principally to Internet service. The next generation of cables, due to be deployed between 2000 and 2005, is expected to increase transmission capacity ten-fold.[8]

However, technology has not found similar ways to increase the capacity of those service operations that process people and their physical possessions without big jumps in costs. So managing demand becomes essential to improving productivity in those types of services that involve tangible actions. Either customers must be given incentives to use the service outside peak periods, or capacity must be allocated in advance through reservations. For example, a golf course may employ both of these strategies by discounting greens fees during off-peak hours and requiring reservations for the busier tee times.

. . . L. L. Bean's Goods Require a Physical Channel to Reach the Customer.

The problem for people-processing services is that customers will wait in line only so long—they have other things to do and may soon become bored, tired, and impatient. One strategy for reducing or eliminating the need for waiting is to institute a reservation system, but the times offered should be honored if this course of action is chosen. By contrast, physical possessions rarely suffer if they have to wait (unless they are highly perishable). More relevant to customers is the cost and inconvenience associated with delays in waiting to recover the item being serviced. Customers may be inconvenienced if their clothes or cars are not ready when promised. The issue of demand and capacity management is so central to productive use of assets (and thus profitability) that we'll devote significant coverage to the topic in chapters 13 and 14.

People as Part of the Product

The more involved customers become in the service delivery process, the more they tend to see service personnel (the people element of the 8 Ps). In many people-processing services, customers meet lots of employees and often interact with them for extended periods of time. They are also more likely to run into other customers—after all, many service facilities achieve their operating economies by serving large numbers of customers simultaneously. A bus, college class, restaurant meal, and hairdressing salon all tend to serve many customers simultaneously. When other people become a part of the service experience, they can enhance it or detract from it. Thus, good comments in class from other students can enhance the value of a course. But lazy customers who fail to clear their table at McDonald's spoil things for the next customers to arrive. A poor attitude and appearance on the part of a flight attendant may discourage a passenger from flying on that airline in the future. Direct involvement in service production means that customers evaluate the quality of employees' appearance and social skills as well as their technical skills. And because customers also make judgments about other customers, managers find themselves trying to manage customer behavior, too. Service businesses of this type tend to be harder to manage because of the human element. As a manager, how would you get everyone to clear their table after eating at a quick-service restaurant? How would you make the staff at different retail service stores more friendly? How would you ensure that all flight attendants were pleasant to passengers?

Avoiding Overgeneralization

Having gained some of the insights that can be drawn from categorizing services into different groups, you should now be in a better position to understand some of the differences between services. In chapter 1, we introduced nine distinctive characteristics of services, cautioning that not all of them applied to every service. In Table 2.2 we see how well these characteristics apply to services in each of the four process-based service categories.

What this table shows is that when we focus on core product processes, seven of the nine characteristics apply best to what we have called people processing—tangible actions delivered to the customer in person. But, intangibility of performances and ability to use electronic delivery channels apply better to the two information-based categories—mental stimulus processing and information processing. Further, customer involvement in production doesn't always apply to possession processing and information processing services.

In the past, the first eight characteristics applied quite well to many services in the possession-processing and information-based categories because the traditional delivery model used to require customers to visit a local service factory to obtain them. Banking and educational services were formerly restricted to an operating model that assumed person-to-person delivery at a specific site. With the growth of remote, technology-driven delivery systems, a very different set of services is starting to emerge, created at a center that could be located almost anywhere and delivered either through physical channels using fast business logistics services or through electronic channels operating in cyberspace. Marketing managers would be wise to recognize that these new, information-based service configurations present their own distinctive marketing challenges and opportunities. We will be considering the impact of electronic delivery channels throughout the book and devote chapter 16 to the technology of service delivery. For further insights into the ways in which information technology is reshaping traditional marketing perspectives, see the reading "Service Markets in the Age of the Internet" by John Deighton on pp. 444 to 454.

Conclusion

Although not all services are the same, many do share important characteristics in common. Rather than restricting our insights to broad distinctions between goods and services, it's more useful to identify different categories of services and to study the marketing, operations, and human resource challenges facing service industries within each of these groups

TABLE 2.2 Applicability of Distinctive Characteristics of Services to Different Types of Service Processes

Distinctive Characteristics	People Processing	Possession Processing	Mental Stimulus Processing	Information Processing
Customers do not obtain ownership of services	Yes, but they do own output of food service	Yes, but they do own spare parts installed with repairs	Yes	Yes, but output can take recorded or printed form (e.g., consulting report)
Service products are intangible performances	Yes, but tangible elements may affect comfort and satisfaction	Yes, but may be tangible output (e.g., clean clothes)	Yes	Yes
Customer involvement in the production process	Yes, but this may be passive rather than active	Not usually	Yes, but may be just passive mental involvement at a remote site	Sometimes
Other people may form part of the product	Yes	Sometimes	Sometimes	Sometimes
More variability in operational inputs and outputs	Yes—hard to standardize because of personal involvement	Can often be standardized	Can often be standardized	Can often be standardized
Many services are difficult for customers to evaluate	Varies—depends on familiarity	Varies—depends on familiarity and visibility of results	Varies—may be easy to make value judgments	Varies
Absence of inventories after production	Yes	Yes	Can be recorded for later delivery or replay	Yes, unless it takes printed or recorded form
Time factor is relatively more important	Yes (service is delivered in real time with customer present)	Yes, if results are needed fast (focus on elapsed time)	Yes, but may be opportunities to timeshift through recording	Yes, if results are needed fast (focus on elapsed time)
Delivery system may involve both electronic and physical channels	Physical channels only (for core product)	Physical channels only (for core product)	Either	Either

The four-way classification scheme discussed in depth in this chapter focuses on different types of service processes. Some services require direct physical contact with customers (hairdressing and passenger transport); others center on contact with people's minds (education and entertainment). Some involve processing of physical objects (cleaning and freight transport); others process information (accounting and insurance.) As you can now appreciate, the processes that underlie the creation and delivery of any service have a major impact on marketing and human resources. That is why process is a key element of the 8 Ps of integrated service management. Process design (or redesign) is not just a task for the operations department. Both managers and employees must understand underlying processes—particularly those in which customers are actively involved—to run a service business that is both efficient, effective, and user-friendly.

REVIEW QUESTIONS

1. Review each of the different ways in which services can be classified. How would you explain the usefulness of each framework to managers?
2. Give examples of durable and nondurable benefits in services and describe the implications
3. In what ways does design of the service factory affect (a) customer satisfaction with the service and (b) employee productivity?
4. Which of the supplementary services featured in Fig. 2.1 can be delivered electronically?
5. What do you see as the major ethical issues facing those responsible for creating and delivering mental stimulus–processing services?

APPLICATION EXERCISES

1. Make a list of at least 10 services that you have used during the past week. Then categorize them by type of process.
2. Note down the different types of service factory that you visit in the course of a typical month and how many times you visit each type.
3. In which instances could you avoid visiting the service factory and instead obtain service from a distance?
4. How have other customers affected your own service experiences—either positively or negatively?
5. Identify a large-scale distance education program (it could be professional education—as in medicine, law, or architecture—or a virtual university) and document its activities. To what extent are physical channels used to supplement the use of electronic channels?

ENDNOTES

1. Shelby D. Hunt, *Marketing Theory: Conceptual Foundations of Research in Marketing* (Columbus, OH: Grid, Inc., 1976), 117–118.
2. Melvin T. Copeland, "The Relation of Consumers' Buying Habits to Marketing Methods," *Harvard Business Review* 1 (April 1923): 282–289.
3. See, for example, Christopher H. Lovelock, "Classifying Services to Gain Strategic Marketing Insights," *Journal of Marketing* 47 (Summer 1983): 9–20; Christian Grönroos, *Service Management and Marketing* (Lexington, MA: Lexington Books, 1990), 31–34; John Bowen, "Development of a Taxonomy of Services to Gain Strategic Marketing Insights," *Journal of the Academy of Marketing*

Science 18 (winter 1990): 43–49; Rhian Silvestro, Lyn Fitzgerald, Robert Johnston, and Christopher Voss, "Towards a Classification of Service Processes," *International Journal of Service Industry Management* 3, no. 3 (1992): 62–75, and Hans Kasper, Wouter De Vries, and Piet Van Helsdingen, *Services Marketing Management: An International Perspective* (Chichester, UK: John Wiley & Sons, 1999), 43–70.

4. These classifications are derived from Lovelock, "Classifying Services to Gain Strategic Marketing Insights," and represent an extension and adaptation of a framework in T. P. Hill, "On Goods and Services," *Review of Income and Wealth* 23 (December 1977): 315–338. For an operations-based discussion of service processes, see "Dealing with Inherent Variability: The Difference between Manufacturing and Service?" *International Journal of Production Management* 7, no. 4 (1987): 13–22.

5. For a classification of technology-based services, see Pratibha A. Dabholkar, "Technology-Based Service Delivery," in *Advances in Services Marketing and Management,* Volume 3, 1994, ed. T. A. Schwartz, D. E. Bowen, and S. W. Brown (Greenwich, CT: JAI Press, 1994), 241–271.

6. David A. Light, "Pioneering Distance Education in Africa," *Harvard Business Review* 77 (September– October 1999): 26.

7. Leyland Pitt, Pierre Berthon, and Jean-Paul Berthon, "Changing Channels: The Impact of the Internet on Distribution Strategy," *Business Horizons,* March–April 1999, 19–28.

8. Alan Cane, "Transatlantic Internet Cable Goes into Service," *Financial Times,* March 5, 1998, 4.

CHAPTER 3

Managing Service Encounters

All the world's a stage, and all the men and women merely players; They have their exits and their entrances, and one man in his time plays many parts.

WILLIAM SHAKESPEARE, *AS YOU LIKE IT*

Some of the services that people use require active contact with the organization, including visits to its facilities and face-to-face interactions with employees. Examples include restaurants and airlines. In other cases, customers never go near the organization's offices and need to contact an employee only when something goes wrong—in which case they most likely speak to someone by telephone. Public utilities like electricity and cable television fall into this category.

This chapter introduces the notion of a spectrum of customer contact with the service organization that ranges from high to low. An important theme of this book is that high-contact encounters between customers and service organizations differ sharply from low-contact ones. We'll show how the extent of customer contact affects the nature of the service encounter as well as strategies for achieving productivity and quality improvements.

The four process-based service categories discussed in chapter 2 prescribe the minimum level of customer contact needed to obtain service in each instance. However, many service organizations currently provide far higher levels of contact than is theoretically necessary to deliver the service in question. Sometimes these high contact levels reflect customer preferences for person-to-person service from providers. But in many instances they result from a management decision to continue relying on traditional approaches instead of reengineering existing service processes to create innovative, lower-contact approaches.

In this chapter, we consider how the nature and extent of service encounters shape customer experiences and how firms should manage encounters to create satisfied customers and desirable outcomes for the business itself. We explore such questions as the following:

1. How does reducing (or increasing) the level of customer contact impact decisions relating to service design and delivery strategies?
2. What is the distinction between backstage and frontstage operations?
3. What are critical incidents, and what is their significance for customer satisfaction and dissatisfaction?
4. What insights can be gained from viewing service delivery as a form of theater?
5. When customers behave badly, what problems do they cause for the firm, its employees, and other customers?
6. What is the potential role of customers as coproducers of services?

Customers and the Service Operation

Where does the customer fit within a service organization? In service businesses, customers tend to be more involved in the production of the service than is usually the case in manufacturing. Suppliers of people-processing services usually expect their customers to come to what Theodore Levitt has called "factories in the field"—sites where service production, delivery, and consumption are all rolled into one.[1] In other instances, as was shown in chapter 2, service personnel can come to the customer or the firm can deal at arm's length with its customers through either physical or electronic channels.

Customers who are actively involved in the service operation can have a significant impact on the organization's productivity. Sometimes they are expected to cooperate closely with full-time service employees; at other times they may be given the option of undertaking self-service. In both such instances, the customer becomes deeply involved in the service operation—a very different environment than is normally found in manufacturing (especially consumer goods production).

Technology and Customer Contact

Developments in technology often offer radically new ways for a business to create and deliver its services, particularly those core and supplementary services that are information based.[2] But it's not always easy to graft a new, technology-based model of service delivery onto a traditional operation with an established culture and a clientele that has long been used to doing things in a certain way. Some organizations believe it may be easier to create an entirely new operation that is largely independent of the parent. For instance, in an effort to attract new business and take advantage of cost-saving advances in Internet technology, First USA Bank created a separate Internet subsidiary with an unusual sounding name. WingspanBank.com was launched in mid-1999 with the slogan "If your bank could start over, this is what it would be." A similar strategy was used 10 years earlier by Britain's Midland Bank (now HSBC Bank) when it launched the world's first all-telephone bank under the name First Direct. This was the first bank to operate 24 hours a day, seven days a week, and attracted worldwide attention within the banking industry.[3] (The planning and development of the bank is described in the case study "First Direct: Branchless Banking" on pp. 639 to 652.)

Clearly, customers who undertake home banking by computer or by phone have a different type of relationship with their bank than do those who continue to visit a traditional retail bank branch. The former benefit from place and time convenience, dealing with bank personnel from a distance by using a computer or telephone (supplied by the customers or their employers) rather than entering a service factory. Their only physical encounters are with ATMs, which can be found in numerous convenient locations and do not necessarily belong to the bank with which customers have their account. If someone has a problem, then a first option is to send an e-mail or to telephone a 24-hour customer service center. Customers' impressions of First Direct's operation, therefore, reflect how fast the phone is answered (standards require 75 percent of all calls to be answered in 20 seconds or less), the courtesy and professionalism of the employee's voice, and the speed with which the desired transactions can be completed. Customers' impressions of WingspanBank.com are likely to be determined in significant degree by the appearance and ease of use of the bank's Web site. To obtain assistance, customers can send e-mails, use 24/7 free telephone service, or even send a letter by regular mail. However, despite WingspanBank.com's claim on its Web site that "You can forget about banker's hours," as of early 2000, some telephone-based service transactions (such as applying for a home equity loan) could only be conducted during certain hours from Monday through Saturday.[4]

Visiting a branch involves different and more time-consuming contacts. Customers can visit a branch only during opening hours and may have to travel some distance to get there. They are exposed to the exterior and interior of the building; may have to spend time waiting in a queue with other customers; and deal face-to-face with an employee who, in many banks, will be hiding behind a security grill or glass screen. Many people enjoy the social interaction of visiting a retail outlet, especially if they know the staff members who serve them and don't trust machines. A recent U.S. study found that 73 percent of respondents preferred to bank in a staffed branch, and 64 percent said that they would rather not use technology at all for certain types of transactions.[5] However, given the huge size of the U.S. market for financial services, that still leaves tens of millions of customers who prefer the technology option. And the proportion of such customers can be expected to grow as younger, more technology-oriented customers enter the market and at least some of the technophobes evolve, with education and experience, toward greater acceptance of technology.

Variability is a fact of life in situations where customers differ widely and service personnel interact with those customers on a one-on-one basis. [6] The longer and more actively that customers are involved in the process of service delivery, the greater the likelihood that each customer's experience will be somewhat different from that of other customers (and from previous experiences by the same customer). Not all variations are bad; in fact, many customers seek a tailored approach that recognizes them as individuals with distinctive needs. The challenge is for employees to be flexible, treating each person as an individual rather than as a clone of the last customer.[7]

Many service problems revolve around unsatisfactory incidents between customers and service personnel. In an effort to simplify service delivery, improve productivity, and reduce some of the threats to service quality, some firms are using technology to minimize or even eliminate contact between customers and employees. Thus, face-to-face encounters are giving way to telephone encounters. Meantime, personal service is being replaced by self-service, often through the medium of computers or easy-to-use machines. And Web sites are beginning to replace or supplement voice telephone contacts for many types of service transactions.

Service Encounters: Differing Levels of Customer Contact

A *service encounter* is a period of time during which customers interact directly with a service.[8] In some instances, the entire service experience can be reduced to a single encounter, involving ordering, payment, and execution of service delivery on the spot. In other cases, the customer's experience comprises a sequence of encounters, an extended process that may be spread out over a period of time, involve a variety of employees, and even take place in different locations (think about flying on a passenger airline). Although some researchers use the term *encounter* simply to describe personal interactions between customers and employees,[9] realistically we also need to think about encounters involving interactions between customers and self-service equipment. As the level of customer contact with the service operation increases, service encounters are likely to be longer and more frequent. In Figure 3.1 we've grouped services into three levels of customer contact, representing the extent of interaction with service personnel, physical service elements, or both. Notice the different locations on the chart of traditional retail banking, telephone banking, and home banking by Web site.

High-contact services tend to be those in which customers visit the service facility in person. Customers are actively involved with the service organization and its personnel throughout service delivery (e.g., hairdressing or medical services). All people-processing services (other than those delivered at home) are high contact. Services from the other three process-based categories may also involve high levels of customer contact when, for reasons of tradition, preference, or lack of other alternatives, customers go to the service site and remain there until service delivery is completed. Examples of services that have traditionally been high contact but that technology allows to be low contact today include retail banking, purchase of retail goods, and higher education.

Medium-contact services entail less involvement with service providers. They involve situations in which customers visit the service provider's facilities (or are visited at home or at a

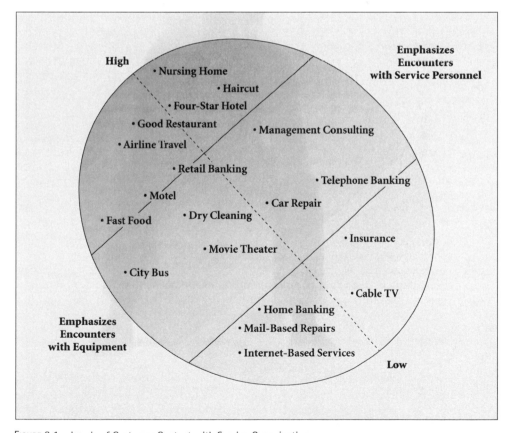

FIGURE 3.1   Levels of Customer Contact with Service Organizations

third-party location by that provider) but either do not remain throughout service delivery or else have only modest contact with service personnel. The purpose of such contacts is often limited to (1) establishing a relationship and defining a service need (e.g., management consulting, insurance, or personal financial advising, where clients make an initial visit to the firm's office but then have relatively limited interactions with the provider during service production), (2) dropping off and picking up a physical possession that is being serviced, or (3) trying to resolve a problem.

Low-contact services involve very little, if any, physical contact between customers and service providers. Instead, contact takes place at arm's length through the medium of electronic or physical distribution channels—a fast-growing trend in today's convenience-oriented society. Both mental stimulus processing (e.g., radio and television) and information-processing services

FIGURE 3.2   Unconventional Advertising for an Unconventional Bank

(e.g., insurance) fall naturally into this category. Also included are possession-processing services in which the item requiring service can be shipped to the service site or subjected to remote fixes delivered electronically to the customers' premises from a distant location (increasingly common for resolving software problems). Finally, many high- and medium-contact services are being transformed into low-contact services as customers engage in home shopping, conduct their insurance and banking transactions by telephone, or research and purchase products through the World Wide Web. Advertising for Web-based services often promotes speed and convenience. For instance, WingspanBank.com contrasts the old and new approaches: "In the 60 seconds it takes to find a parking spot at your old bank, you can get an answer on your loan application . . . leave your car in the garage. Your new bank's in the den" (see Figure 3.2).

Service as a System

The level of contact that a service business intends to have with its customers is a major factor in defining the total service system, which includes three overlapping subsystems: *service operations* (where inputs are processed and the elements of the service product are created), *service delivery* (where final assembly of these elements takes place and the product is delivered to the customer), and *service marketing,* which embraces all points of contact with customers, including advertising, billing, and market research (see Figure 3.3).

Parts of this system are visible (or otherwise apparent) to customers; other parts are hidden in what is sometimes referred to as the *technical core,* and the customer may not even know of their existence.[10] Some writers use the terms *front office* and *back office* in referring to the visible and invisible parts of the operation. Others talk about *front stage* and *backstage,* using the analogy of theater to dramatize the notion that service is a performance.[11] We like this dramaturgical analogy and will be using it throughout the book. For a detailed discussion of dramaturgy, please see the reading by Stephen Grove and Raymond Fisk, "Service Theater: An Analytical Framework for Services Marketing," which appears on pp. 83 to 92.

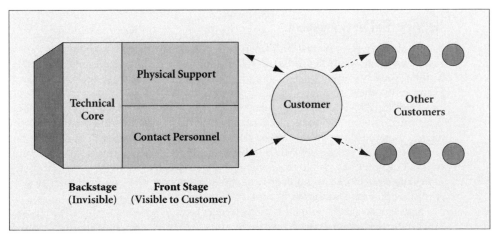

FIGURE 3.3   The Service Business as a System
Source: Adapted from Eric Langeard, John E. G. Bateson, Christopher Lovelock, and Pierre Eiglier, *Services Marketing: New Insights from Consumers and Managers* (Cambridge, MA: Marketing Science Institute, 1981).

Service Operations System

Like a play in a theater, the visible components of service operations can be divided into those relating to the actors (or service personnel) and those relating to the stage set (or physical facilities, equipment, and other tangibles). What goes on backstage is of little interest to customers. Like any audience, they evaluate the production on those elements that they actually experience during service delivery and, of course, on the perceived service outcome. Naturally, if the backstage personnel and systems (e.g., billing, ordering, and account keeping) fail to perform their support tasks properly in ways that affect the quality of frontstage activities, customers will notice. For instance, restaurant patrons will be disappointed if they order fish from the menu but are told it is unavailable (in reality, someone forgot to go to the fish market that morning) or find that their food is overcooked (actually caused by improperly set oven controls). Other examples of backstage failures include receiving an incorrect hotel bill due to a keying error, not receiving your course grades because of a computer failure in the college registrar's office, or being delayed on a flight because the aircraft has had to be taken out of service for engine repairs.

The proportion of the overall service operation that is visible to customers varies according to the level of customer contact. Because high-contact services directly involve the physical person of the customer, either customers must enter the service factory (although there may still be many backstage activities that they don't see), or service workers and their tools must leave their backstage and come to the customer's chosen location. Examples include roadside car repair by automobile clubs or physical fitness trainers who work with clients at their homes or offices. Medium-contact services, by contrast, require a less substantial involvement of the customer in service delivery. Consequently, the visible component of the service operations system is smaller. Low-contact services usually have a strategy of minimizing customer contact with the service provider, so most of the service operations system is confined to a remotely located backstage; frontstage elements are normally limited to post and telecommunications contacts. Think for a moment about the telephone company that you use. Do you have any idea where its exchange is located? If you have a credit card, it's likely that your transactions are processed far from where you live.

Service Delivery System

Service delivery is concerned with where, when, and how the service product is delivered to the customer. As shown earlier in Figure 3.3, this subsystem embraces not only the visible elements of the service operating system—buildings, equipment, and personnel—but may also entail exposure to other customers.

Traditionally, service providers had direct interactions with their customers. But to achieve goals ranging from cost reduction and productivity improvement to greater customer convenience, many services that don't need the customers to be physically present in the factory now seek to reduce direct contact. Midland Bank's creation of First Direct is a prime example of this trend. As a result, the visible component of the service operations system is shrinking in many industries as electronic technology or redesigned physical flows are used to drive service delivery from higher to lower levels of contact.

Self-service delivery often offers customers greater convenience than face-to-face contact. Machines such as automated gasoline pumps, ATMs, or coin-operated food and drink dispensers can be installed in numerous locations and made accessible 24 hours a day, seven days a week. Cafeteria service allows customers to see menu items before making their selection. Self-guided museum tours allow visitors to enjoy an exhibition at their own pace. But there are potential disadvantages, too. The shift from personal service to self-service sometimes disturbs customers. So a strategy of replacing employees by machines or other self-service procedures may require an information campaign to educate customers and promote the benefits of the new approach. It also helps to design user-friendly equipment, including free telephone access to an employee who can answer questions and solve problems. Of course, not all self-service is installed in remote locations. Cafeterias and self-guided museum tours are examples of customers taking on tasks that would otherwise have to be assigned to service personnel. Later in this chapter, we'll discuss the role of the customer as a coproducer of service in collaboration with the service provider.

Using the theatrical analogy, the distinction between high contact and low contact can be likened to the differences between live theater on a stage and a drama created for radio. That's because customers of low-contact services normally never see the factory where the work is performed; at most, they will talk with a service provider (or problem solver) by telephone. Without buildings and furnishings or even the appearance of employees to provide tangible clues, customers must make judgments about service quality based on ease of telephone access, followed by the voice and responsiveness of a telephone-based customer service representative.

When service is delivered through impersonal electronic channels, such as self-service machines, automated telephone calls to a central computer, or the customer's own computer, there is very little traditional theater left to the performance. Some firms compensate for this by giving their machines names; playing recorded music; or installing moving color graphics on video screens, adding sounds, and creating computer-based interactive capabilities to give the experience a more human feeling. A few Web sites are even designed to look like displays in shop windows.

Responsibility for designing and managing service delivery systems has traditionally fallen to operations managers. But marketing needs to be involved, too, because understanding customer needs and concerns is important to ensure that the delivery system works well. What's more, if we're dealing with a service facility where customers may interact with each other—

SERVICE PERSPECTIVES 3.1

What Options Do You Use to Obtain Bank Services?

Not everyone is comfortable with the trend toward lower-contact services, which is why some firms give their customers a choice. For instance, some retail banks now offer an array of service delivery options. Consider this spectrum of alternatives. Which options do you currently use at your bank? Which would you like to use in the future? And which are currently available?

1. Visit the bank in person and conduct transactions with a bank clerk.
2. Use postal service to send deposits or request new checkbooks.
3. Use an ATM.
4. Conduct transactions by telephone with a customer service representative.
5. Use the keys on a telephone to interact with the bank in response to voice commands (or a telephone screen display).
6. Conduct home banking through your own computer, using a modem and special software.
7. Conduct transactions by computer through the World Wide Web.

In each instance, what factors explain your preference? Do they relate to the type of transactions you conduct or to a situational element such as the weather or time of day? Are you influenced by your feelings of liking (or disliking) human contact in a banking context? Or is there some other explanation? What advice would you give to your bank for how to serve you better?

such as a hotel, aircraft, or post office—their behavior has to be managed discreetly so that they will act in ways that are compatible with the firm's strategy, including the comfort and safety of other customers. Finally, for marketing reasons, it may be important to offer customers a choice of delivery systems (see Service Perspectives 3.1).

The Dramaturgy of Service Delivery

As we've pointed out earlier, the theater is a good metaphor for services because service delivery consists of a series of processes that customers experience as a performance. It is a particularly useful approach for high-contact service providers (such as physicians, educators, restaurants, and hotels) and for businesses that serve many people simultaneously rather than providing individualized service (for example, professional sports, hospitals, and entertainment.) Figure 3.4 shows the relative importance of theatrical dimensions for different types of service businesses. As you can see, watch repair services have very few frontstage theatrical components compared with services such as airlines and spectator sports.

Service facilities contain the stage on which the drama unfolds. Sometimes the setting changes from one act to another (for example, when airline passengers move from the entrance to the terminal to the check-in stations and then on to the boarding lounge and finally step inside the aircraft). The stage may have minimal props, as in a typical post office, which tends to be rather utilitarian, or elaborate scenery, as in some modern resort hotels. Many service dramas are tightly scripted, as in the way that service is delivered in a formal restaurant setting, whereas others are improvisational in nature.

Some services are more ritualized than others. In highly structured environments, such as the practice of dentistry in an office, how the actors (in this case, receptionists, dental hygienists, technicians, and dentists) move relative to the stage (the dentist's office), items of scenery (furniture and equipment), and other actors may be defined in a manner analogous to theatrical blocking.

Not all service providers require customers to attend performances at the company's theater. In many instances, the customer's own facilities provide the stage where actors perform with their props. For example, outside accountants are often hired to provide specialized ser-

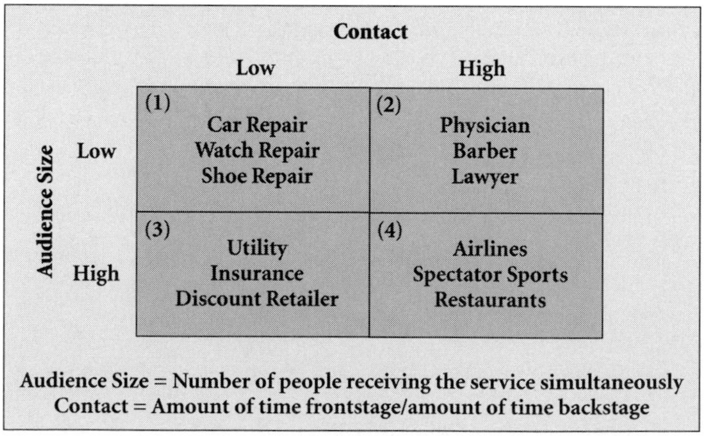

		Contact	
		Low	High
Audience Size	**Low**	**(1)** Car Repair Watch Repair Shoe Repair	**(2)** Physician Barber Lawyer
	High	**(3)** Utility Insurance Discount Retailer	**(4)** Airlines Spectator Sports Restaurants

Audience Size = Number of people receiving the service simultaneously
Contact = Amount of time frontstage/amount of time backstage

FIGURE 3.4   Relative Importance of Theatrical Dimensions
Source: Stephen J. Grove and Raymond P. Fisk, "The Dramaturgy of Services Exchange: An Analytical Framework for Services Marketing," in *Emerging Perspectives on Services Marketing,* ed. L. L. Berry, G. L. Shostack, and G. D. Upah (Chicago: The American Marketing Association, 1983), 45–49.

vices at a client's site. (Although this may be convenient for the client, it isn't always very appealing for the visiting accountants, who sometimes find themselves housed in rat-infested basements or inventorying frozen food for hours in a cold storage locker!)[12] Telecommunication linkages offer an alternative performance environment, allowing customers to be involved in the drama from a remote location—a delivery option long awaited by those traveling accountants, who would probably much prefer to work for their clients from the comfort of their own offices via modems and computers.

Frontstage personnel are members of a cast, playing roles as actors in a drama and supported by a backstage production team. In some instances, they are expected to wear special costumes when on stage (like the protective clothing—traditionally white—worn by dental professionals, the fanciful uniforms often worn by hotel doormen, or the more utilitarian brown ones worn by UPS drivers). When service employees wear distinctive apparel, they stand out from personnel at other firms. In this respect, uniform designs can be seen as a form of packaging that provides physical evidence of brand identity.[13] In many service companies, the choice of uniform design and colors is carefully integrated with other corporate design elements. Many frontstage employees must conform to both a dress code and grooming standards (such as Disney's rule that employees can't wear beards). Depending on the nature of their work, employees may be required to learn and repeat specific lines ranging from announcements in several languages to a singsong sales spiel (just think of the last telemarketer you spoke with) to a parting salutation of "Have a nice day!" And just as in theater, companies often use scripting to define actors' behavior as well as their lines. Eye contact, smiles, and handshakes may be required in addition to a spoken greeting. Other rules of conduct may include bans on smoking, eating and drinking, or gum chewing while on duty.

Role and Script Theories

Role and script theories offer some interesting insights for service providers. If we view service delivery as a theatrical experience, then both employees and customers act out their parts in the performance according to predetermined roles. Grove and Fisk define a *role* as "a set of behavior patterns learned through experience and communication, to be performed by an individual in a certain social interaction in order to attain maximum effectiveness in goal accomplishment."[14] Roles have also been defined as combinations of social cues, or expectations of society, that guide behavior in a specific setting or context.[15] In service encounters, employees and customers each have roles to play. The satisfaction of both parties depends on *role congruence,* or the extent to which each person acts out his or her prescribed role during a service encounter. Employees must perform their roles to customer expectations or risk dissatisfying or losing customers altogether. And customers, too, must play by the rules, or they risk causing problems for the firm, its employees, and even other customers.

Scripts are sequences of behavior that both employees and customers are expected to learn and follow during service delivery. Scripts are learned through experience, education, and communication with others.[16] Much like a movie script, a service script provides detailed actions that customers and employees are expected to perform. The more experience a customer has with a service company, the more familiar the script becomes. Any deviations from this known script may frustrate both customers and employees and can lead to high levels of dissatisfaction. If a company decides to change a service script (for example, by using technology to turn a high-contact service into a low-contact one), service personnel and customers should be educated about the new script and the benefits it provides.

Some scripts are highly routinized and allow service employees to move through their duties quickly and efficiently (such as flight attendants' scripts for economy class). This approach helps to overcome two of the inherent challenges facing service firms—how to reduce variability and ensure uniform quality. The risk is that frequent repetition may lead to mindless service delivery that ignores customers' needs.

Not all services involve tightly scripted performances. For providers of highly customized services—such as doctors, educators, hairstylists, or consultants—the service script is flexible and may vary by situation and by customer. When customers are new to a service, they may not know what to expect and be fearful of behaving incorrectly. Organizations should be ready to educate new customers about their roles in service delivery because inappropriate behaviors can disrupt service delivery and make other customers feel embarrassed and uncomfortable. An interesting use of script training, described by Clark and Salalman, concerns the ways in which executive search firms coach job candidates for meetings with prospective employers.[17]

Defining customer and employee scripts is a good way to start the flowcharting process. These scripts provide a full description of the service encounter and can help identify potential or existing problems in a specific service process. Table 3.1 shows a script for teeth cleaning and a simple dental examination involving three players—the patient, the receptionist, and the dental hygienist. Each has a specific role to play. In this instance, the script is driven primarily by the need to execute a technical task both proficiently and safely (note the mask and gloves). The core service task of examining and cleaning teeth can be accomplished satisfactorily only if the patient cooperates in an experience that is at best uncomfortable and at worst even painful. Several script elements refer to information flows. Confirming and honoring appointments avoids delays for customers and ensures effective use of dental professionals' time. Obtaining patient histories and documenting analysis and treatment is vital for maintaining complete dental records and also for accurate billing. Payment on receipt of treatment improves cash flow and avoids the problem of bad debts. Adding greetings, thank yous, and good-byes displays friendly good manners and helps to humanize what most people see as a slightly unpleasant experience.

Examining existing scripts may suggest ways to modify the nature of customer and employee roles with a view to improving service delivery, increasing productivity, and enhancing the nature of the customer's experience. As service delivery procedures evolve in response to new technology or other factors, revised scripts may need to be developed.

Service Marketing System

Other elements, too, may contribute to the customer's overall view of a service business. These include communication efforts by the advertising and sales departments, telephone calls and letters from service personnel, billings from the accounting department, random exposures to service personnel and facilities, news stories and editorials in the mass media, word-of-mouth comments from current or former customers, and even participation in market research studies.

Collectively, the components just cited—plus those in the service delivery subsystem—add up to what we term the *service marketing system*. In essence, this represents all the different ways in which the customer may encounter or learn about the organization in question. Because services are experiential, each of these elements offers clues about the nature and quality of the service product. Inconsistency between different elements may weaken the organization's credibility in the customers' eyes. Figure 3.5 depicts the service marketing system for a high-contact service.

As you know from your own experience, the scope and structure of the service marketing system often vary sharply from one type of organization to another. Figure 3.6 shows how the picture changes when we are dealing with a low-contact service, such as a credit card account. The significance of this approach to conceptualizing service creation and delivery is that it represents a customer's view, looking at the service business from the outside, as opposed to an internally focused operations perspective.

TABLE 3.1 *Script for Teeth Cleaning and Simple Dental Examination*

Patient	Receptionist 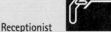	Dental Hygienist 
1. Phone for appointment	2. Confirm needs and set date	
3. Arrive at dental office	4. Greet patient; verify purpose; direct to waiting room; notify hygienist of arrival	5. Review notes on patient
6. Sit in waiting room		7. Greet patient and lead way to treatment room
8. Enter room; sit in dental chair		9. Verify medical and dental history; ask about any issues since previous visit
		10. Place protective covers over patient's clothes
		11. Lower dental chair; put on own protective face mask, gloves, and glasses
		12. Inspect patient's teeth (option to ask questions)
		13. Place suction device in patient's mouth
		14. Use high-speed equipment and hand tools to clean teeth in sequence
		15. Remove suction device; complete cleaning process
		16. Raise chair to sitting position; ask patient to rinse
17. Rinse mouth		18. Remove and dispose of mask and gloves; remove glasses
		19. Complete notes on treatment; return patient file to receptionist
		20. Remove covers from patient
		21. Give patient free toothbrush; offer advice on personal dental care for future
22. Rise from chair		23. Thank patient and say good-bye
24. Leave treatment room	25. Greet patient; confirm treatment received; present bill	
26. Pay bill	27. Give receipt; agree on date for next appointment; document agreed-on date	
28. Take appointment card	29. Thank patient and say good-bye	
30. Leave dental office		

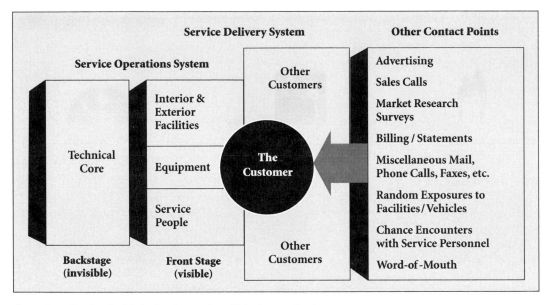

FIGURE 3.5   The Service Marketing System for a High-Contact Service

Physical Evidence

Because many service performances are inherently intangible, they are often hard to evaluate. As a result, customers often look for tangible clues as to the nature of the service. Sometimes, encounters are random rather than planned. For instance, what impression would it create on you to see a damaged vehicle belonging to an express delivery service broken down by the side of the road? Or to observe a poorly groomed flight attendant traveling to (or from) the airport and wearing a uniform that is frayed and dirty? Or to visit a friend in a hospital where the

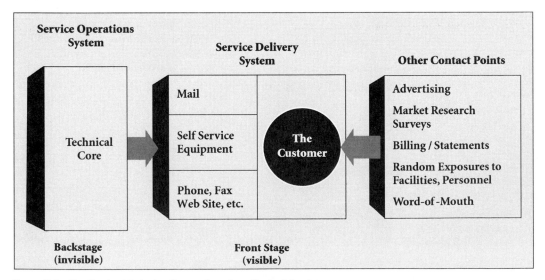

FIGURE 3.6   The Service Marketing System for a Low-Contact Service

---

TABLE 3.2 *Tangible Elements and Communication Components in the Service Marketing System*

1. Service personnel. Contacts with customers may be face-to-face, by telecommunications (telephone, fax, telegram, telex, electronic mail), or by mail and express delivery services.

   These personnel may include
   - Sales representatives
   - Customer service staff
   - Accounting/billing staff
   - Operations staff who do not normally provide direct service to customers (e.g., engineers, janitors)
   - Designated intermediaries whom customers perceive as directly representing the service firm
2. Service facilities and equipment
   - Building exteriors, parking areas, landscaping
   - Building interiors and furnishings
   - Vehicles
   - Self-service equipment operated by customers
   - Other equipment
3. Nonpersonal communications
   - Form letters
   - Brochures/catalogs/instruction manuals/Web sites
   - Advertising
   - Signage
   - News stories/editorials in the mass media
4. Other people
   - Fellow customers encountered during service delivery
   - Word-of-mouth comments from friends, acquaintances, or even strangers

---

grounds and buildings are beautifully maintained; the interior decor is cheerful rather than institutional; and the friendly staff wears smart, spotlessly clean uniforms?

Because service performances are intangible, physical evidence gives clues as to the quality of service and in some cases will strongly influence how customers (especially inexperienced ones) evaluate the service. Hence, managers need to think carefully about the nature of the physical evidence provided to customers by the service marketing system. We'll be addressing this element of the 8 Ps in more depth in chapters 8 and 10, but Table 3.2 provides an initial checklist of the main tangible and communication elements to which customers might be exposed. Of course, the number of elements that are visible will vary depending on whether service delivery involves high or low customer contact. In low-contact services, additional physical evidence may be communicated through advertising; using video footage on television; printed illustrations in newspapers, magazines, or brochures; or pictures on Web sites.

Managing Service Encounters for Satisfactory Outcomes

Many services (especially those classified as high contact) involve numerous encounters between customers and service employees, either in person or by phone. Service encounters may also take place between customers and physical facilities or equipment. In low-contact services, customers are having more and more encounters with automated machines that are designed to replace human personnel.

To highlight the risks and opportunities associated with service encounters, Richard Normann, a Paris-based Swedish consultant, borrowed a metaphor from bullfighting. Normann writes:

> [W]e could say that the perceived quality is realized at the moment of truth, when the service provider and the service customer confront one another in the arena. At that moment they are very much on their own. . . . It is the skill, the motivation, and the tools employed by the firm's representative and the expectations and behavior of the client which together will create the service delivery process.[18]

In bullfighting, what is at stake is the life of either the bull or the matador (or possibly both). The moment of truth is the instant at which the latter deftly slays the bull with his sword—hardly a very comfortable analogy for a service organization intent on building long-term relationships with its customers! Normann's point, of course, is that it's the life of the relationship that is at stake. Contrary to bullfighting, the goal of relationship marketing—which is discussed in depth in chapter 5—is to prevent one unfortunate (mis)encounter from destroying what is already, or has the potential to become, a mutually valued, long-term relationship.

Jan Carlzon, the former chief executive of Scandinavian Airlines System (SAS), used the moment-of-truth metaphor as a reference point for transforming SAS from an operations-driven business into a customer-driven airline. Carlzon made the following comments about his airline:

> Last year, each of our 10 million customers came into contact with approximately five SAS employees, and this contact lasted an average of 15 seconds each time. Thus, SAS is "created" 50 million times a year, 15 seconds at a time. These 50 million "moments of truth" are the moments that ultimately determine whether SAS will succeed or fail as a company. They are the moments when we must prove to our customers that SAS is their best alternative.[19]

Managing People in Service Encounters

The quote from Carlzon immediately makes apparent the link between marketing and human resource management in service organizations. With its own people as part of the product, no service business can afford to divorce its customer-contact employees from the firm's marketing strategy. Increasingly, high-contact employees in what have traditionally been service delivery jobs with no sales content are now expected to play a selling role, too. This role shift requires them to be both producers and marketers of a service. As a result, waiters, bank clerks, and even auditors in accounting firms are being asked to promote new services, encourage customers to purchase additional items, or refer them to sales specialists.

Making matters even more complex for managers is the fact that primary responsibility for their company's success often rests with relatively junior personnel in such customer-contact positions as bus driver, shop assistant, telephone-based customer service representative, receptionist in a professional service firm (e.g., architects, lawyers, or management consultants), or car rental agent. These individuals, who are often young and inexperienced and less well educated than their customers, need both technical and interpersonal skills to succeed. Not only must they be able to perform the technical aspects of the job quickly and accurately, but they must also be able to do so while relating well to customers.[20] In chapter 16, we consider how careful recruitment, training, and ongoing mentoring of employees can contribute to improvements in both productivity and quality.

To cope effectively with all of these challenges, managers should brief employees on what the firm is trying to achieve in the marketplace. However, there are limits to the ability of policy manuals and other control procedures to ensure that employees consistently deliver good service. Service employees also need training, authority, and management support to ensure that their important but often brief encounters with customers result in satisfactory outcomes. The case is sometimes made for flattening the organization chart and turning it upside down, thereby placing customer-contact personnel on the upper level of an inverted pyramid.[21] This implies that instead of striving to control employee behavior, managers should be acting as coaches and role models to help the latter provide better service to customers.

Critical Incidents in Service Encounters

Critical incidents are specific encounters between customers and service employees that are especially satisfying or dissatisfying for one or both parties. The critical incident technique (CIT) is a methodology for collecting and categorizing such incidents in service encounters. Conducting such an analysis offers an opportunity to determine which types of incidents during service delivery are likely to be particularly significant in determining whether or not customers are satisfied.

The Customer's Perspective. Findings from a CIT study can be very helpful in pinpointing opportunities for future improvements in service delivery processes. Determining the most likely failure points in service encounters, where there is a risk of significantly upsetting customers, is the first step in taking corrective action to avoid such incidents. Similarly, CIT findings concerning the nature of incidents that customers seem to find very satisfying may enable managers to train their employees to replicate such positive experiences in the future.

Negative critical incidents that are satisfactorily resolved have great potential for enhancing loyalty because they demonstrate to customers that the organization really cares about them. But the reverse is also true. In a study by Susan Keveaney of 838 critical incidents that led customers to switch to a competitor, dissatisfactory service encounters (cited by 34 percent of respondents) ranked second to core service failures (cited by 44 percent) as a reason for switching. Other key reasons were high, deceptive, or unfair pricing (30 percent); inconvenience in terms of time, location, or delays (21 percent); and poor response to service failures (17 percent). Many respondents described a decision to switch suppliers as resulting from interrelated incidents, such as a service failure followed by an unsatisfactory response to resolving the problem.[22] These findings underscore the importance of the dictum "Service is Everybody's Business," regardless of an employee's job or departmental affiliation.

A European replication of this research studied 875 critical incidents across six different industries—job agencies, health care, education, housing societies, restaurants, and public transportation.[23] It employed the same broad classification of incidents but, not surprisingly, noted substantial differences between industries in the types of incidents reported within each category. Further analysis distinguished between the timing of incidents; although about three-quarters of both positive and negative incidents occurred during service consumption; approximately 14 percent of each type occurred before consumption; and about 10 percent, after consumption. Preconsumption incidents are important because they are associated with first impressions. A bad preconsumption incident may lead the customer to terminate the encounter without even trying the core service; a positive incident gets the customer off to an excellent start. Positive postconsumption incidents either put icing on the cake of an overall good experience or help the firm to recover from problems during service delivery. In contrast, negative postconsumption experiences either spoil what had, until then, been a satisfactory encounter or add insult to the injury of earlier problems during service delivery.

The findings reported in Research Insights 3.1 come from a study of critical incidents described by customers who had had particularly satisfying or dissatisfying experiences when

RESEARCH INSIGHTS 3.1

Studying Critical Incidents in the Airline, Hotel and Restaurant Businesses

In a study of critical incidents, a sample of customers was asked to think of a time when they had a particularly satisfying or dissatisfying interaction with an employee of an airline, hotel, or restaurant and then answer the following questions:

- When did the incident happen?
- What specific circumstances led up to this situation?
- Exactly what did the employee say or do?
- What resulted that made you feel the interaction was satisfying (dissatisfying)?

A total of 699 incidents were recorded, split roughly equally between satisfying and unsatisfying incidents. They were then categorized into three groups: (1) employee response to service failures, (2) employee responses to requests for customized service, and (3) unprompted and unsolicited employee actions.

When employees responded to critical incidents involving a service failure, analysis showed that the outcomes were twice as likely to be dissatisfactory for customers as satisfactory. The reverse was true when customers asked employees to adapt the service in some way to meet a special need or request. In the third grouping, relating to unexpected events and employee behavior, satisfactory and unsatisfactory outcomes were equally matched. Exhibit 3.A displays reports on specific incidents, as described in the customers' own words.

Source: Mary Jo Bitner, Bernard H. Booms, and Mary Stanfield Tetreault, "The Service Encounter: Diagnosing Favorable and Unfavorable Incidents," *Journal of Marketing* 54 (January 1990): 71–84.

EXHIBIT 3.A   *Customer Reports on Critical Incidents Involving Service Employees*

GROUP 1 SAMPLE INCIDENTS: EMPLOYEE RESPONSE TO SERVICE DELIVERY FAILURES

INCIDENT

Satisfactory	Dissatisfactory
A. Response to Unavailable Service	
They lost my room reservation, but the manager gave me the V.I.P. suite for the same price.	We had made advance reservations at the hotel. When we arrived, we found we had no room—no explanation, no apologies, and no assistance in finding another hotel.
B. Response to Unreasonably Slow Service	
Even though I didn't make any complaint about the hour-and-a-half wait, the waitress kept apologizing and said that the bill was on the house.	The airline employees continually gave us erroneous information; a one-hour delay turned into a six-hour wait.
C. Response to Other Core Service Failures	
My shrimp cocktail was half frozen. The waitress apologized and didn't charge me for any of my dinner.	One of my suitcases was all dented and looked as though it had been dropped from 30,000 feet. When I tried to make a claim for my damaged luggage, the employee insinuated that I was lying and trying to rip them off.

EXHIBIT 3.A *Continued*

GROUP 2 SAMPLE INCIDENTS: EMPLOYEE RESPONSE TO CUSTOMER NEEDS AND REQUESTS

Satisfactory	Dissatisfactory

A. Response to "Special Needs" Customers

The flight attendant helped me calm and care for my airsick child.	My young son, flying alone, was to be assisted by the stewardess from start to finish. At the Albany airport she left him alone in the airport with no one to escort him to his connecting flight.

B. Response to Customer Preferences

The front desk clerk called around and found me tickets to the Mariners' opening game.	The waitress refused to move me from a window table on a hot day because there was nothing left in her section.
It was snowing outside—my car broke down. I checked 10 hotels and there were no rooms. Finally, one understood my situation and offered to rent me a bed and set it up in one of their small banquet rooms.	The airline wouldn't let me bring my scuba gear on board coming back from Hawaii even though I brought it over as carry-on luggage.

C. Response to Admitted Customer Error

I lost my glasses on the plane; the stewardess found them, and they were delivered to my hotel free of charge.	We missed our flight because of car trouble. The service clerk wouldn't help us find a flight on an alternative airline.

D. Response to Potentially Disruptive Others

The manager kept his eye on an obnoxious guy at the bar to make sure that he didn't bother us.	The hotel staff wouldn't deal with the noisy people partying in the hall at 3 A.M.

GROUP 3 SAMPLE INCIDENTS: UMPROMPTED AND UNSOLICITED EMPLOYEE ACTIONS

Satisfactory	Dissatisfactory

A. Attention Paid to Customer

The waiter treated me like royalty. He really showed he cared about me.	The lady at the front desk acted as if we were bothering her. She was watching TV and paying more attention to the TV than the hotel guests.

B. Truly Out-of-the-Ordinary Employee Behavior

We always travel with our teddy bears. When we got back to our room at the hotel we saw that the maid had arranged our bears very comfortably in a chair. The bears were holding hands.	I needed a few more minutes to decide on a dinner. The waitress said, "If you would read the menu and not the road map, you would know what you want to order."

EXHIBIT 3.A *Continued*	

GROUP 3 SAMPLE INCIDENTS: UMPROMPTED AND UNSOLICITED EMPLOYEE ACTIONS

INCIDENT

Satisfactory	Dissatisfactory
C. Employee Behaviors in the Context of Cultural Norms	
The busboy ran after us to return a $50 bill my boyfriend had dropped under the table.	The waiter at this expensive restaurant treated us like dirt because we were only high school kids on a prom date.
D. Gestalt Evaluation	
The whole experience was so pleasant . . . everything went smoothly and perfectly.	The flight was a nightmare. A one-hour layover went to three and one half hours. The air conditioning didn't work. The pilots and stewardesses were fighting because of an impending flight attendant strike. The landing was extremely rough. To top it all off, when the plane stopped, the pilots and stewardesses were the first ones off.
E. Performance Under Adverse Circumstances	
The counter agent was obviously under stress, but kept his cool and acted very professionally.	

Adapted from Mary Jo Bitner, Bernard H. Booms, and Mary Stanfield Tetrault, "The Service Encounter: Diagnosing Favorable and Unfavorable Incidents," *Journal of Marketing* 54 (January 1990): 71–84.

using airline, hotel, or restaurant services. Note the 12 different types of incidents and examples of the language used by customers to describe both positive and negative interactions with service employees.

The Employee's Perspective. Customer-employee contact is a two-way street. Understanding the employee's view of the situation is really important, because thoughtless or poorly behaved customers can often cause needless problems for service personnel who are trying hard to serve them well. Continuing dissatisfaction with a succession of negative incidents can even drive good employees to quit their jobs.

Another CIT study (by the same researchers who conducted the study described in Research Insights 3.1) examined hundreds of critical incidents from an employee perspective. [24] (See the reading "Critical Service Encounters: The Employee's Viewpoint," by Mary Jo Bitner, Bernard Booms, and Lois A. Mohr, on pp. 93 to 107.) The results showed that more than 20 percent of all incidents that employees found unsatisfactory could be attributed to problem customers, whose bad behavior included drunkenness, verbal and physical abuse, breaking laws or company policies, and failing to cooperate with service personnel. It's simply not true that the customer is always right.

The Problem of Customer Misbehavior

Customers who act in uncooperative or abusive ways are a problem for any company, but they have more potential for mischief in service businesses, particularly those in which the customer comes to the service factory. If misbehaving customers come face-to-face with service personnel and other customers, their behavior can put employees at risk and spoil other people's service experiences. When customers visit the service factory, that offers potential for theft and vandalism. And customers who act inappropriately can interfere with a firm's efforts to improve productivity and quality.

Addressing the Challenge of Jaycustomers

Visitors to North America from other English-speaking countries are often puzzled by the term *jaywalker,* that distinctively American word used to describe people who cross streets at unauthorized places or in a dangerous manner.[25] The prefix *jay-* comes from a nineteenth-century slang term for a stupid person. We can create a whole vocabulary of derogatory terms by adding the prefix *jay-* to existing nouns and verbs. How about *jaycustomer,* for example, to denote someone who *jayuses* a service or *jayconsumes* a physical product (and then *jaydisposes* of it afterwards)? We define a jaycustomer as one who acts in a thoughtless or abusive way, causing problems for the firm, its employees, and other customers.

Every service encounters its share of jaycustomers. But opinions on this topic seem to polarize around two opposing views of the situation. One is denial: The customer is always right. The other view sees the marketplace of customers as positively overpopulated with nasty people (and even nastier corporate purchasers) who simply cannot be trusted to behave in ways that self-respecting suppliers should expect and require. The first viewpoint has received wide publicity in gung-ho management books and in motivational presentations to captive groups of employees. But the second view often appears to be the more widely held among cynical managers who have been burned at some point in their professional lives. As with so many opposing viewpoints in life, there are important grains of truth in both perspectives.

Six Types of Jaycustomers

Jaycustomers are undesirable. At worst, a firm needs to control or prevent their abusive behavior. At best, it would like to avoid attracting them in the first place. Because defining the problem is the first step in resolving it, let's start by considering the different types (or segments) of jaycustomers who prey on suppliers of both goods and services. We've identified six broad categories and given them generic names, but many customer-contact personnel have come up with their own special terms of endearment for these charming people. As you reflect on these categories, you may, perhaps, be stimulated to add a few more of your own.

The Thief. This jaycustomer has no intention of paying and sets out to steal goods and services (or to pay less than full price by such devices as switching price tickets or contesting bills on baseless grounds). Shoplifting is a major problem in retail stores. What retailers euphemistically call "shrinkage" is estimated to cost them enormous amounts of money in annual revenues. Many services lend themselves to clever schemes for avoiding payment. For those with a technical bent, it is sometimes possible to bypass electricity meters, access telephone lines free of charge, or circumvent normal cable television feeds. Riding free on public transportation, sneaking into movie theaters, or not paying for restaurant meals are also popular pastimes. And we mustn't forget the use of fraudulent forms of payment such as stolen credit cards or checks that are intended to bounce. The challenge for managers is to devise schemes to protect their firms against thieves while avoiding the temptation to employ Gestapo-like tactics against the great bulk of honest customers.

While working as a graduate student in California, I was once asked by the regional manager of Greyhound Bus Lines in San Francisco if I could help him to obtain a book that described how to steal a wide variety of goods and services without getting caught. Wittily—if unwisely—titled *Steal This Book,* the volume included a whole chapter on how to ride free on long-distance buses—hence the manager's interest.[26] I found the book invitingly displayed at the Stanford University bookstore. Sure enough, it included a veritable encyclopedia of tips on how to rip off capitalist-pig, Establishment-run enterprises (this was in the 1970s). Greyhound was indeed featured, complete with a host of ideas for riding free and avoiding detection. Feeling a little foolish at ignoring the invitation on the cover, I took the priceless volume to the young woman at the cash register, wondering if this was the first time that anyone had actually paid for it. Today, its updated contents are probably somewhere on the Internet.

The man from Greyhound had the right idea. Finding out how people steal your product is the first step in taking preventive measures to stop thieves or corrective measures to catch them and, where appropriate, to prosecute. But managers should try not to alienate their honest customers by degrading the latter's own service experiences. And provision must be made for honest but absent-minded customers who forget to pay. Many stores now attach electronic tags to their merchandise that can be removed only at a cashier's station. If the customer passes a point near the exit doors with merchandise that still bears a tag, it sets off an alarm, thus offering a clear choice between returning to the register or making a break for it.

The Rule Breaker. Just as highways need safety regulations (including "Don't Jaywalk" laws against jaywalking), many service businesses find it necessary to establish rules of behavior for employees and customers to guide them safely through the various steps of the service encounter. Some of these rules are imposed by government agencies for reasons of health and safety. Air travel is perhaps the best example; in few other environments outside prison are healthy, mentally competent, adult customers quite so constrained (albeit with good reason). In addition to enforcing government regulations, suppliers often lay down their own set of rules to facilitate the smooth functioning of the operation, avoid unreasonable demands being placed on employees, prevent misuse of products and facilities, protect themselves legally, and discourage individual customers from behaving in ways that would detract from the quality of the service experience. On top of formal rules are the unwritten norms of social behavior in any given culture to which customers are expected to adhere without being told.

There are risks attached to making lots of rules. They can make an organization appear bureaucratic and overbearing. And they can transform employees, whose orientation should be service to customers, into police officers who see (or are told to see) their most important task as enforcing all the rules. A third problem is that there are always going to be some customers who break the rules anyway—either because they haven't bothered to take note of them or just on principle.

How should a firm deal with rule breakers? Much depends on which rules have been broken. In the case of legally enforceable ones—theft, bad debts, or trying to take guns on aircraft—the courses of action need to be laid down explicitly, as much to protect employees as to punish or discourage wrongdoing by customers. Company rules are a little more ambiguous. Are they really necessary in the first place? If not, get rid of them. Do they deal with health and safety? If so, advance education and reminders will reduce the need for taking corrective action. The same is true for rules designed to protect the comfort and enjoyment of all customers using the same facility. And then there are unwritten social norms such as "Thou shalt not jump the queue" (although this is a much stronger cultural expectation in the United States or Canada than in many countries, as any visitor to Paris Disneyland can attest!). Other customers can often be relied on to help service personnel enforce rules that affect everybody else or even to take the initiative in doing so. The fewer the rules, the more explicit the important ones can be.

The Belligerent. You've probably seen him (or her) in a store, at the airport, in a hotel or restaurant, red in the face and shouting angrily or perhaps icily calm and mouthing off insults, threats, and obscenities.[27] Things don't always work as they should: Machines break down, service is clumsy, customers are ignored, a flight is delayed, an order is delivered incorrectly, staff are unhelpful, a promise is broken. Or perhaps the customer in question is expressing resentment at being told to abide by the rules. Service personnel are often abused even when they are not to blame. If an employee lacks authority to resolve the problem, that may make the belligerent madder still, even to the point of physical attack. Drunkenness and drug abuse add extra layers of complication (see Service Perspectives 3.2). Organizations that care about their employees go to great efforts to develop skills in dealing with these difficult situations. Training exercises that involve role-playing help employees to develop the self-confidence and assertiveness that they need to stand up to upset customers. Employees also need to learn how to defuse anger, calm anxiety, and comfort distress (particularly when there is good reason for the customer to be upset with the organization's performance).

What is an employee to do when an aggressive customer brushes off attempts to defuse the situation? In a public environment, one priority should be to move the person away from other customers. Sometimes supervisors may have to arbitrate disputes between customers and staff members; at other times, they need to stand behind the employee's actions. If an employee has been physically assaulted by a customer, then it may be necessary to summon security officers or the police. Some firms try to conceal such events, fearing bad publicity, but others feel obliged to make a public stand on behalf of their employees, even in small ways, such as the Body Shop manager who ordered an ill-tempered customer out of the store, telling her: "I won't stand for your rudeness to my staff."

Telephone rudeness poses a different challenge. Service personnel have been known to hang up on angry customers, but that action doesn't resolve the problem. Bank customers, for instance, tend to get upset when learning that checks have been returned because they are overdrawn (they've broken the rules) or that a request for a loan has been denied. One suggested approach for handling customers who continue to berate a telephone-based employee is for the latter to say firmly: "This conversation isn't getting us anywhere. Why don't I call you back in a few minutes when you've had time to digest the information?" In many cases, a breathing space for reflection is exactly what's needed.

The Family Feuders. A subcategory of belligerents are those who get into arguments (or worse) with other customers, often members of their own family. Employee intervention may calm the situation or further exacerbate it. Sometimes the trick is to get other customers on your side. Some situations require detailed analysis and a carefully measured response. Others, like customers who start a food fight in a nice restaurant (yes, such things do happen), require almost instantaneous response. Where necessary, service managers need to be prepared to think on their feet and act fast.

The Vandal. It's astonishing the level of physical abuse to which service facilities and equipment can be subjected. Soft drinks are poured into a bank's cash machines; graffiti are scrawled on both interior and exterior surfaces; cigarettes burn holes in carpets, tablecloths, and bedcovers; bus seats are slashed and hotel furniture broken; telephone handsets are torn off; customers' cars are vandalized; glass is smashed; and fabrics are torn. The list is endless. Not all of the damage is done by customers, of course. Much exterior vandalism is done by bored youths. And disgruntled employees have been known to commit sabotage. But much of the problem does originate with wrongly behaved, paying customers. Alcohol and drugs are sometimes the cause, psychological problems may contribute, and plain carelessness also plays a role. And there are occasions when unhappy customers, feeling mistreated by the service provider, try to get their own back. Finally, there are those charming people with a constant urge to carve their name on something so that posterity may remember their visit.

SERVICE PERSPECTIVES 3.2

Air Rage: The Growing Problem of Unruly Passengers

Joining the term *road rage*—coined in 1988 to describe angry, aggressive drivers who threaten other road users—is a newer term, *air rage*. Perpetrators of air rage are violent, unruly passengers who endanger flight attendants, pilots, and other passengers.

Incidents of air rage are perpetrated by only a tiny fraction of all airline passengers—reportedly about five thousand times a year—but each incident in the air may affect the comfort and safety of hundreds of other people. Incidents at airports, by contrast, can be more easily isolated.

Acts of violence may be committed against employees or the aircraft itself. On a flight from Orlando (Florida) to London in May 1999, a drunken passenger smashed a video screen and began ramming a window, telling fellow passengers they were about to "get sucked out and die." The crew strapped him down, and the aircraft made an unscheduled landing in Bangor (Maine), where the unruly passenger was arrested by U.S. marshals. Another unscheduled stop in Bangor the following month involved a drug smuggler on board a flight from Jamaica to the Netherlands. When a balloon filled with cocaine ruptured in his stomach, he went berserk, pounding a bathroom door to pieces and grabbing a female passenger by the throat.

On a flight from London to Spain, a passenger who was already drunk at the time of boarding was angered when a flight attendant told him not to smoke in the lavatory and refused to serve him another drink; later, he smashed her over the head with a duty-free vodka bottle before being restrained by other passengers (she required 18 stitches to close the wound). Other dangerous incidents have included throwing hot coffee at flight attendants, headbutting a copilot, trying to break into the cockpit, throwing a flight attendant across three rows of seats, and attempting to open an emergency door in flight.

In testimony before the U.S. Congress, an airline captain speaking for the Air Line Pilots Association declared that "passenger interference is the most pervasive security problem facing airlines." A growing number of carriers are taking air-rage perpetrators to court. Northwest Airlines permanently blacklisted three violent travelers from flying on its aircraft. And in 1998, British Airways began handing out warning cards to any passenger getting dangerously out of control.

What causes air rage? Researchers suggest that air travel has become increasingly stressful as a result of crowding and longer flights; the airlines themselves may have contributed to the problem by squeezing rows of seats more tightly together and failing to explain delays. Findings suggest that risk factors for air-travel stress include anxiety and an anger-prone personality; they also show that traveling on unfamiliar routes is more stressful than traveling on a familiar one. Another factor is believed to be restrictions on smoking.

Airlines are training their employees not only in how to handle violent individuals but also in how to spot problem passengers before they start causing serious problems. Some carriers offer travelers specific suggestions on how to relax during long flights. And a few European airlines are considering offering nicotine patches to passengers who are desperate for a smoke but are no longer allowed to light up.

Source: Based on information in Daniel Eisenberg, "Acting Up in the Air," *Time*, December 21, 1998; Carol Smith, "Air Travel Stress Can Make Life Miserable," *Seattle Post Intelligencer,* syndicated article, August 1999; and "Air Rage Capital: Bangor Becomes Nation's Flight Problem Drop Point," *The Baltimore Sun,* syndicated article, September, 1999.

The best cure is prevention. Improved security can discourage some vandals. Good lighting helps, as does open design of public areas. Consultants can suggest pleasing yet vandal-resistant surfaces, protective coverings for equipment, and rugged furnishings. Better education of customers on how to use equipment properly (rather than fighting with it) and warnings about fragile objects can reduce the likelihood of abuse or careless handling. And then there are economic sanctions: security deposits or signed agreements in which customers agree to pay for any damage that they cause.

And what should managers do if prevention fails and damage is done? If the perpetrator is caught, they should first clarify whether there are any extenuating circumstances (accidents do happen). Sanctions for deliberate damage can range from a warning to prosecution. As far as the physical damage itself is concerned, fix it swiftly (within any constraints imposed by legal or insurance considerations). The general manager of a bus company had the right idea when he said: "If one of our buses is vandalized, whether it's a broken window, a slashed seat, or graffiti on the ceiling, we take it out of service immediately, so nobody sees it. Otherwise you just give the same idea to five other characters who were too dumb to think of it in the first place!"

The Deadbeat. Leaving aside those individuals who never intended to pay in the first place (our term for them is *thief*), there are many reasons why customers end up as delinquent accounts who fail to pay what is due for the service they have received. But once again, prevention is better than cure. A growing number of service businesses insist on prepayment, any form of ticket sale being a good example. Direct-marketing organizations ask for your credit card number as they take your order. The next best thing is to present the customer with a bill immediately on completion of service. If the bill is to be sent by mail, send it fast, while the service is still fresh in the customer's mind.

Not every apparent delinquent is a hopeless deadbeat. Perhaps there's good reason for the delay; perhaps acceptable payment arrangements can be worked out. A key question is whether such a personalized approach can be cost justified, relative to the results obtained by purchasing the services of a collection agency. There may be other considerations, too. If the client's problems are only temporary ones, what is the long-term value of maintaining the relationship? Will it create positive goodwill and word of mouth to help the customer work things out? These decisions are judgment calls, but if creating and maintaining long-term relationships is the firm's goal, they bear exploration.

The Customer as Coproducer

In some service environments, you (and other customers) play a relatively passive role, waiting to be served. So long as you can state your needs clearly and pay promptly when billed, you play a minimal role in the process of service delivery (think about leaving clothes at a laundry). In other instances, however, you are expected to be actively involved in the production process— one of the distinctive features of service management that we noted in chapter 1. This involvement may take two forms. Sometimes, you are given the tools and equipment to serve yourself (as when you take your clothes to a laundromat); in others, such as health improvement, you work jointly with health professionals as coproducers of the service from which you wish to benefit. Table 3.3 illustrates the differing levels of participation required of customers across an array of service businesses.

TABLE 3.3 *Levels of Customer Participation across Different Services*		
Low (Customer Presence Required during Service Delivery)	Moderate (Customer Inputs Required for Service Creation)	High (Customer Coproduces the Service Product)
Products are standardized	Client inputs customize a standard service	Active client participation guides the customized service
Service is provided regardless of any individual purchase	Provision of service requires customer purchase	Service cannot be created apart from the customer's purchase and active participation
Payment may be the only required customer input	Customer inputs (information, materials) are necessary for an adequate outcome, but the service firm provides the service	Customer inputs are mandatory and coproduces the outcome
Examples:		
End consumer		
Bus travel	Hair cut	Marriage counseling
Motel stay	Annual physical exam	Personal training
Movie theater	Full-service restaurant	Weight-reduction program
Business-to-business customer		
Uniform cleaning service	Agency-created advertising campaign	Management consulting
Pest control	Payroll service	Executive management seminar
Interior greenery maintenance	Independent freight transportation	Install wide area network (WAN)

Source: Adapted from Mary Jo Bitner, William T. Faranda, Amy R. Hubbert, and Valarie A. Zeithaml, "Customer Contributions and Roles in Service Delivery," *International Journal of Service Industry Management* 8, no. 3 (1997): 193–205.

Service Firms as Teachers

The more work that customers are expected to do, the greater their need for information about how to perform for best results. In such situations, the firm should take responsibility for educating inexperienced customers. Lack of knowledge can lead to frustration with the process, unsatisfactory results, and even put the customer at risk—think about the unpleasant things that might happen to a customer who smokes a cigarette and spills gasoline while refueling a car at a self-service pump! This situation explains why education often needs to be accorded a key role in marketing communications strategy for service businesses.

The necessary education can be provided in many different ways. Brochures and posted instructions are two widely used approaches. Automated machines often contain detailed operating instructions and diagrams (unfortunately, these are sometimes intelligible only to the engineers who wrote them). Thoughtful banks place a telephone beside their ATMs so that customers can call a real person for help and advice at any time if they are confused about the on-screen instructions. Advertising for new services often contains significant educational content. In many businesses, customers look to employees for advice and assistance and are frustrated if they can't obtain it. Service providers, ranging from sales assistants and customer service representatives to flight attendants and nurses, must themselves be trained to help them improve their teaching skills. As a last resort, people may turn to other customers and ask for help.

Schneider and Bowen suggest giving customers a realistic *service preview* in advance of service delivery to provide them with a clear picture of the role they will play in service coproduction.[28] For example, a company might show a video presentation to help customers understand their role in the service encounter. This technique is used by some dentists to help patients understand the surgical processes they are about to experience and indicate how they should cooperate to help make things go as smoothly as possible—certainly a sensible goal for all parties involved!

Increasing Productivity and Quality When Customers Are Coproducers

The greater customers' involvement in service production, the greater their potential to influence the processes in which they are engaged. Thanks to the Internet, today's customers have access to information that was formerly available only to skilled researchers and experienced professionals. Knowledge creates competence. The challenge for companies is to find ways of harnessing customer competencies.[29] Some researchers argue that firms should view customers as partial employees "who can influence the productivity and quality of service processes and outputs."[30] This perspective requires a change in management mindset, as Schneider and Bowen make clear:

> If you think of customers as partial employees, you begin to think very differently about what you hope customers will bring to the service encounter. Now they must bring not only expectations and needs but also relevant service production competencies that will enable them to fill the role of partial employees. The service management challenge deepens accordingly.[31]

They go on to suggest that customers who are offered an opportunity to participate at an active level are more likely to be satisfied—regardless of whether or not they actually choose the more active role—because it is gratifying to be offered a choice. If they choose active involvement, they may need and appreciate assistance in mastering their roles, as suggested in Management Memo 3.1.

MANAGEMENT MEMO 3.1

Managing Customers as Human Resources

Managing customers as partial employees requires using the same human resource logic as in managing a firm's paid employees and should follow these five steps:

1. Conduct a job analysis of customers' present roles in the business and compare it against the roles that the firm would like them to play.
2. Determine if existing customers possess an awareness of how they are expected to perform and have the skills needed to perform as required.
3. Educate customers in advance and provide on-the-job training as needed.
4. Motivate customers by ensuring that they are rewarded for performing well (for instance: satisfaction from better quality and more customized output, enjoyment of participating in the actual process, and a belief that their own productivity speeds the process and keeps costs down).
5. Regularly appraise customers' performance. If this is unsatisfactory, either retrain them or seek to change their role and the procedures in which they are involved. Alternatively, consider "terminating" these customers (nicely, of course!) and look for new ones.

Source: Adapted from Benjamin E. Schneider and David E. Bowen, *Winning the Service Game* (Boston: Harvard Business School Press, 1995), 85–100.

Effective human resource management starts with recruitment and selection. The same approach should hold true for partial employees. So, if coproduction requires specific skills, firms should target their marketing efforts to recruit new customers who have the competency to perform the necessary tasks.[32] After all, many colleges do the same in their student selection process!

Conclusion

Service encounters cover a spectrum from high-contact to low-contact; their position on this spectrum is often determined by the nature of the operational processes used to create and deliver the service in question. With the growing trend to deliver information-based services through electronic channels, rather than asking the customer to come to the service factory, many service encounters are shifting to a lower-contact mode than previously, with important implications for the nature of the customer's experience.

Service businesses can be divided into three overlapping systems. The operations system consists of the personnel, facilities, and equipment required to run the service operation and create the service product; only part of this system, described here as frontstage, is visible to the customer. The delivery system incorporates the visible operations elements and the customers who, in self-service operations, take an active role in helping create the service product—as opposed to being passively waited on. Finally, the marketing system includes not only the delivery system, which is essentially composed of the product and distribution elements of the traditional marketing mix, but also additional components such as billing and payment systems, exposure to advertising and sales people, and word-of-mouth comments from other people.

In all types of services, understanding and managing service encounters between customers and service personnel is central to creating satisfied customers who are willing to enter into long-term relationships with the service provider. The higher the level of contact, the more we can apply theatrical analogies to the process of staging service delivery, in which employees and customers play roles and often follow well-defined scripts. In high-contact services, customers are exposed to many more tangible clues and experiences than they are in medium- and low-contact situations. Critical incidents occur when some aspect of the service encounter is particularly satisfactory or unsatisfactory.

In some instances, including self-service, customers play an active role in the process of creating and delivering services, effectively working as partial employees whose performance will affect the productivity and quality of output. Under these circumstances, service managers must be sure to educate and train customers so that they have the skills needed to perform well.

REVIEW QUESTIONS

1. As a senior bank executive, what actions would you take to encourage more customers to bank by phone, post, Internet, or ATM rather than visiting a branch?

2. What are the backstage elements of (a) an insurance company, (b) a car repair facility, (c) a hotel, (d) an airline, (e) a university, (f) a funeral home, (g) a consulting firm, and (h) a television station? Under what circumstances would it be appropriate to allow customers to see some of these backstage elements, and how would you do it?

3. What roles are played by frontstage service personnel in low-contact organizations? Are these roles more or less important to customer satisfaction than in high-contact services?

4. Why is it valuable for service operations managers to try to see their business through the eyes of their customers?
5. Use the list in Table 3.1 to develop a profile of the service marketing system for a variety of services—hospital, airline, consulting engineer or legal service, college, hotel, dry cleaner, credit union, automobile service center, or post office. (You can base your profiles on your own experience or interview other customers.)
6. What is the difference between a moment of truth, a service encounter, and a critical incident?
7. Review Exhibit 3-A (pp. 70–72). As a manager, how would you try to prevent future recurrence of each of the 12 dissatisfactory incidents? (Hint: Consider the underlying cause of the problem and possible reasons for the inappropriate response that upset the customer.)
8. Are customers playing partial employee roles more or less likely to be taken advantage of by unscrupulous service providers? Why (or why not?)

APPLICATION EXERCISES

1. Which types of service businesses does the theater metaphor fit best? Why? Illustrate your argument with an evaluation of the theatrical dimensions of some specific service businesses in your local area.
2. Develop two different customer scripts, one for a standardized service and one for a customized service (your choice). What are the key differences between the two?
3. Define the term *partial employee* and describe three recent situations in which you were engaged in such a role.

ENDNOTES

1. Theodore Levitt, "Your Factories in the Field: Customer Service and Service Industries," chap. 3 in *Marketing for Business Growth* (New York: McGraw-Hill, 1973), 51–70.
2. Robert J. Petersen, Sridar Balasubramanian, and Bart J. Bronnenberg, "Exploring the Implications of the Internet for Consumer Marketing," *Journal of the Academy of Marketing Sciences* 25, no. 4 (1997): 329–346.
3. Saul Hansell, "500,000 Clients, No Branches," *New York Times,* September 3, 1995, sec. 3, p.1.
4. WingspanBank.com Web site (www.WingspanBank.com), April 2000.
5. Eleena de Lisser, "Customers Thwart Banks' Plans to Cut Branches," *Wall Street Journal,* May 16, 1997, B1, B5.
6. Curtis P. McLaughlin, "Why Variation Reduction Is Not Everything: A New Paradigm for Service Operations," *International Journal of Service Industry Management* 7, no. 3 (1996): 17–39.
7. Lance A. Bettencourt and Kevin Gwinner, "Customization of the Service Experience: The Role of the Frontline Employee," *International Journal of Service Industry Management* 7, no. 2 (1996): 2–21.
8. Lynn Shostack, "Planning the Service Encounter," in *The Service Encounter,* ed. J. A. Czepiel, M. R. Solomon, and C. F. Surprenant (Lexington, MA: Lexington Books, 1985), 243–254.
9. Carole F. Surprenant and Michael R. Solomon, "Predictability and Personalization in the Service Encounter," *Journal of Marketing* 51 (winter 1987): 73–80.
10. Richard B. Chase, "Where Does the Customer Fit in a Service Organization?" *Harvard Business Review* 56 (November–December 1978): 137–42.
11. Stephen J. Grove, Raymond P. Fisk, and Mary Jo Bitner, "Dramatizing the Service Experience: A Managerial Approach," in *Advances in Services Marketing and Management,* ed. T. A. Schwartz, D. E. Bowen, and S. W. Brown (Greenwich CT: JAI Press, 1992), 1:91–122. See also B. Joseph Pine II and James H. Gilmore, *The Experience Economy* (Boston: Harvard Business School Press, 1999).

12. Elizabeth MacDonald, "Oh, the Horrors of Being a Visiting Accountant," *Wall Street Journal*, March 10, 1997, B1.
13. Michael R. Solomon, "Packaging the Service Provider," *The Service Industries Journal* 6 (July 1986).
14. Stephen J. Grove and Raymond P. Fisk, "The Dramaturgy of Services Exchange: An Analytical Framework for Services Marketing," in Emerging Perspectives on Services Marketing, ed. L. L. Berry, G. L. Shostack, and G. D. Upah (Chicago:: The American Marketing Association, 1983), 45–49.
15. Michael R. Solomon, Carol Surprenant, John A. Czepiel, and Evelyn G. Gutman, "A Role Theory Perspective on Dyadic Interactions: The Service Encounter," *Journal of Marketing* 49 (Winter 1985): 99–111.
16. See R. P. Abelson, "Script Processing in Attitude Formation and Decision-Making," in *Cognitive and Social Behavior*, ed. J. S. Carrol and J. W. Payne (Hillsdale, NJ: Erlbaum, 1976), 33–45; and Ronald H. Humphrey and Blake E. Ashforth, "Cognitive Scripts and Prototypes in Service Encounters," in *Advances in Service Marketing and Management*, ed. T. A. Schwartz, D. E. Bowen, and S. W. Brown (Greenwich, CT: JAI Press, 1994), 3:175–199.
17. Timothy Clark and Graeme Salalman, "Creating the Right Impression: Towards a Dramaturgy of Management Consultants," *The Service Industries Journal* 18 (January 1998): 18–38.
18. Normann first used the term "moments of truth" in a Swedish study in 1978; subsequently it appeared in English in Richard Normann, *Service Management: Strategy and Leadership in Service Businesses*, 2d ed. (Chichester, UK: John Wiley & Sons, 1991), 16–17.
19. Jan Carlzon, *Moments of Truth* (Cambridge, MA: Ballinger Publishing Co., 1987), 3.
20. Jørn Flohr Nielsen and Viggo Host, "The Path to Service Encounter Performance in Public and Private 'Bureaucracies'," *The Service Industries Journal*, 20, January 2000, 40–60.
21. Sandra Vandermerwe, *From Tin Soldiers to Russian Dolls: Creating Added Value through Service* (Oxford, UK: Butterworth-Heinemann, 1993), 81.
22. Susan M. Keaveney, "Customer Switching Behavior in Service Industries: An Exploratory Study," *Journal of Marketing* 59 (April 1995): 71–82.
23. Inge Wels-Lips, Marleen van der Ven, and Rik Pieters, "Critical Service Dimensions: An Empirical Investigation across Six Industries," *International Journal of Service Industry Management* 9, no. 3 (1998): 286–309.
24. Mary Jo Bitner, Bernard Booms, and Lois A. Mohr, "Critical Service Encounters: The Employee's View," *Journal of Marketing* 58 (October 1994): 95–106.
25. This section is adapted from Christopher Lovelock, *Product Plus* (New York: McGraw-Hill, 1994), chap.15.
26. Abbie Hoffman, *Steal This Book* (San Francisco: Grove Press, 1972).
27. For an amusing and explicit depiction of various types of belligerent customers, see Ron Zemke and Kristin Anderson, "The Customers from Hell," *Training* 26 (February 1990): 25–31; reprinted in John E. G. Bateson and K. Douglas Hoffman, *Managing Services Marketing*, 4th ed. (Fort Worth, TX: The Dryden Press, 1999), 61–62.
28. Benjamin Schneider and David E. Bowen, *Winning the Service Game* (Boston: Harvard Business School Press, 1995), 92.
29. C. K. Prahalad and Venkatram Ramaswamy, "Co-opting Customer Competence," *Harvard Business Review* 78 (January–February 2000): 79–90.
30. David E. Bowen, "Managing Customers as Human Resources in Service Organizations," *Human Resources Management*, 25, no. 3 (1986): 371–383.
31. Schneider and Bowen, *Winning the Service Game*, 85.
32. Bonnie Farber Canziani, "Leveraging Customer Competency in Service Firms," *International Journal of Service Industry Management*, 8, no. 1 (1997): 5–25.

Service Theater:
An Analytical Framework
for Services Marketing

Stephen J. Grove
Raymond P. Fisk

The theater metaphor is a useful framework for describing and analyzing service performances. Employees serving customers may be thought of as actors and customers as the audience that experiences the performance. The marketing implications of this metaphor are discussed for airline travel and electronic performances in cyberspace.

Introduction

The significant differences between services and physical goods have spawned numerous prescriptions for the successful design and delivery of service products. A keen understanding of the nature of services is an important first step toward achieving service excellence. Various models have been developed to help practitioners and scholars comprehend the complex character of the service experience. One early model suggests expanding the traditional marketing-mix elements of product, price, promotion, and place to include three additional Ps (i.e., participants, physical evidence, and process of service assembly) among a services marketing mix (Booms and Bitner 1981). A second model depicts the service experience as an elaborate production system of technology, management, resources, and personnel that is driven by a business mission and is responsive to customer expectations (Grönroos 1991). In a third model, services are described as a "servuction system" (a hybrid of service and production) that includes physical areas that are visible and invisible to the service customer, an inanimate environment, contact personnel, and customer interaction. (Langeard et al. 1981)

Although these models generate valuable insights regarding service experiences, none describes the complex nature of services, demonstrates their common characteristics, captures their interactive essence, and facilitates communication about their enactment in a lucid and simple fashion. Based on observations derived from the sociology and theater literatures, we propose a simple yet comprehensive framework for understanding service experiences. We contend that service experiences are theater and encompass many of the same features and principles as theatrical performances. This article explores service theater as a comprehensive framework for understanding, analyzing, and discussing service experiences. First, we examine the social and physical context of service experiences. Second, the theatrical nature of service experiences is explained. Third, airlines services are described as an example of service theater. Fourth, the service metaphor is extended to the realm of cyberspace.

The Social and Physical Context of Service Experiences

At any moment of any day, you may be involved in a service experience. A *service experience* occurs whenever a customer and a service organization interact. A visit to the dentist's office, a night's stay in a hotel, a session surfing the World Wide Web, or a meal in a restaurant are all examples of service experiences. Listening to a rock concert, mailing a letter, or purchasing a pair of shoes are service experiences as well. While not always the case, a service experience frequently occurs in an organization's physical environment and involves the presence of other customers. The service provided by an ocean liner, for example, encompasses the

Portions of this article are based on our earlier publication, "The Dramaturgy of Services Exchange: An Analytical Framework for Services Marketing" published by the American Marketing Association in 1983.

vessel and the passengers. The layout of the ship, its decor and comfort, its features and furnishings, and other environmental aspects affect the cruise experience. In addition, the people sharing space on the ocean liner affect one another by their number, character, and actions.

Most services are the result of one or more workers performing various tasks. To illustrate, consider the number of employees involved in making a hospital stay a success. Physicians and orderlies, nurses and their aides, porters and desk clerks, and a host of others all play a part in fashioning the patient's experience. Overall, the physical setting, the service workers and their tasks, and the other customers combine to influence the nature of the service experience.

Due to intangibility and the simultaneity of production and consumption of services, customers often have difficulty assessing the quality of the services they receive (Zeithaml 1981). Hence, the social milieu (i.e., the interaction with the workers and other customers) and the service's physical environment (i.e., the nature of the facilities and equipment) provide important cues to the excellence of the service rendered. Based on this observation, astute service organizations are wise to "tangibilize" their service offering by managing these aspects of the customers' experience (Berry 1981; Lovelock 1994; Shostack 1977). Because the staging of a theatrical performance involves many of the same considerations that are important for fashioning a successful service experience (i.e., expressive physical cues, performers and their actions, and audience participation), we suggest that it is plausible to approach services as theater.

The Theatrical Nature of Service Experiences[1]

Describing human behavior as theater is not new, but systematically applying a theater metaphor to service experiences is unique. Much of the basis for applying theater to services can be linked to observations anchored in the sociological school of thought known as *dramaturgy* as well as to an appreciation of theater as a performing art. Dramaturgy depicts social interaction in the terms and concepts of a theatrical production. The contemporary dramaturgical perspective is significantly based on the work of Erving Goffman and his book *The Presentation of Self in Everyday Life* (1959). Goffman examined the structure of social

interaction when people are in the presence of others and how a definition of the behavioral situation is created and maintained, even in the face of potential disruptions. Although Goffman contends that people use theatrical devices and insights to accomplish these goals, we propose that service organizations can use similar tools to create successful service experiences for their customers. After all, just as theater is described as "an experience—a shared indivisible event that includes both those who perform and those who observe" (Wilson 1991, 3), services can be characterized in the same way. Several of the concepts that Goffman offers and others have found in the theater literature are relevant for framing services as theater. Among these are performance, performance teams, regions and region behavior, and impression management.

Performance

Performance describes an *actor's* activity when there is continuous contact with an *audience*. By their nature, performances are designed to have some impact on an audience. Performances can be characterized as sincere or cynical. Sincere performances occur when an actor essentially becomes the role that he is playing. Cynical performances occur when an actor views a performance only as a means to an end. To create and communicate a believable performance, actors often employ various expressive devices, such as aspects of the setting, their personal appearance, and their behavioral manner.

The *setting* is comprised of the decor, furnishings, and physical layout at the performance's location, while the actor's *personal appearance* and *manner* are reflected in their dress, facial expression, gestures, demographic profile, and personality. When consistent with each other, the setting and the actor's personal profile create an important set of cues for the audience. With this in mind, it's not surprising that actors may conceal or underplay aspects of the expressive devices that may be incompatible with the desired performance. The reality portrayed in a service performance is fragile and is easily upset by even minor contradictions.

Service experiences are performances. They reflect the efforts of a service organization and its workers (actors) to satisfy customer (audience) needs. Those needs might be a stylish haircut, transportation from Chicago to Toronto, care for a pet poodle, or

---

[1]Much of this discussion relies on the insight of Erving Gofman and his book, *The Presentation of Self in Everyday Life*, published by Doubleday and Company in 1959.

safe storage of a person's life savings. In each of these cases, to create and sustain customer perceptions of excellence, service personnel must adhere to the principles of a successful performance. They must (1) believe in the importance of customer satisfaction (i.e., be sincere), (2) consider the communicative capability of the service setting and workers' personal profiles (i.e., attend to the expressive devices), and (3) work hard to avoid contradicting the image of excellence they seek (i.e., present a consistent front). Consider the example of Ritz Carlton, where each of these performance-related directives is fastidiously followed. The result is a well-designed service delivery system that has garnered the esteemed Malcolm Baldrige Award and is a widely recognized image of excellence.

Performance Teams

Most theatrical productions require the coordinated effort of several actors to create an audience's experience. *Performance teams* are sets of actors who cooperate to create a single impression to which the audience responds. Although each member contributes in her own way, it is the combined effort of the entire team that fashions an audience's experience. In a sense, the importance of the performance is the common bond that holds a team together. Those participating in any theatrical production must respect each other's role if the performance is to be perceived as credible. When actors criticize their teammates, fail to cooperate, or neglect the effort to portray a unified front, a performance may be shattered.

Service organizations face similar consideration in the process of service delivery. Most service experiences are the result of several workers cooperating as a team. These workers may operate in full view of the customer, that is, the *cast,* or be among those who are instrumental to the service delivery yet are seldom seen. Even providing simple services such as changing automobile oil or laundering clothes requires that all employees recognize the importance of the performance promised to the customer.

A single employee can ruin the service experience for the customer by failing to enact his tasks correctly, ridiculing others' efforts, or failing to project the desired image. When the service process goes well, it is usually the result of a team effort that is unnoticed by the customer. When service fails, it is frequently because a team member did not play her assigned part. This issue takes on greater complexity as the size of the cast and support personnel increases. For instance, compare the difficulty of ensuring a successful team effort for a hotel versus a full-service car wash. The complex nature of a hotel service requires more workers, which makes creating and sustaining teamwork more difficult.

The Setting: Regions and Region Behavior

The setting where a performance occurs is an important source of information for the audience and a critical component of any theatrical production. The setting is comprised of front and back regions. The front region, or *frontstage,* is in full view of the audience and is the part of the setting that carries significant communicative capability. The frontstage and the cast members who perform there must meet the audience's approval. Attention to detail, careful planning of the physical cues, well-rehearsed scripts, and choreographed movements by the actors are all important. The back region, or *backstage,* is hidden from the audience's view and is where the preparation and support for the frontstage performance occurs. Here, actors drop their front and step out of character. In the backstage, actors may rehearse their parts, memorize their scripts, perfect their teamwork, or work through flaws in their parts. Also found backstage are various workers and equipment that contribute to the frontstage performance, but they are usually unnoticed by the audience. In a theatrical production, these include wardrobe personnel, stage crews, lighting, and sound equipment.

Normally, the two regions are kept separate owing to the risk of the audience discovering behavior and physical cues contradictory to a credible performance. Beyond observing imperfection in performances, the audience could be exposed to improper behavior and unappealing physical evidence. Cursing, slovenly demeanor, complaining, unkempt equipment, and dirty conditions might be seen. To protect against such mishaps, careful attention is often given to keeping the passageway between the two regions closed.

The typical service experience occurs in a setting marked by distinct front- and backstage areas, too. The service setting, sometimes referred to as the *servicescape* (Bitner 1992), is comprised of a front region designed to appeal to customers and to facilitate service delivery and a back region housing the operational support system of the service. The frontstage involves various props, decor, and furnishings that define the service for the customer and frame the performance. Lighting, music, air temperature, and aroma play a role here, too. For example, a restaurant can present itself as an Italian eatery, a

Chinese take-out, or a French bistro by the selection of frontstage devices. However, if the backstage equipment, support staff, and management in the kitchen area go awry, all may be lost. If a diner stumbles into a food preparation area on his way to the restroom, the appearance of the chef, the backstage work conditions, the behavior of the staff, or other disruptive cues may shatter the perception of excellence. For that reason, most restaurants do not allow patrons to enter their back regions.

Actors and Impression Management

At the heart of any theatrical performance are the actors whose presence and behavior fashion the show for the audience. Some performances are better than others due to the casting and the abilities of the actors involved. The actors' task is to present or contribute to a believable performance. In general, it is the actors that the audience views as the key determinant of a show's quality. Hence, actors in a theatrical production engage in *impression management,* or the creation and maintenance of a credible show. Impression management relies on actors' abilities to convey their roles effectively. Beyond learning their parts, actors' interpretations of their roles through such things as facial expression, gestures, and vocal inflections have much to do with a play's effect on the audience (Wilson 1991). Impression management also involves the various performers (and backstage personnel, too) adhering to defensive practices that are designed to guard against mistakes. Specifically, the actors must demonstrate loyalty, discipline, and circumspection regarding the performance.

Loyalty means that the actors must accept the importance of the performance and avoid disclosing secrets regarding its enactment to the audience or others not directly involved in the production. *Discipline* means that they are obliged to learn their parts and guard against unwittingly committing gestures or mistakes that might destroy a performance. Finally, *circumspection* means that the actors need to plan in advance how best to stage the show. If an actor reveals inside information, he is being disloyal. If he allows his personal problems to interfere with his stage responsibilities, he lacks discipline. If he fails to consider what it takes to be credible in his role, he is not circumspect. For a successful performance to occur, none of these can happen, or the impression will be damaged.

Service experiences rely on the impression-management expertise of the workers in much the same way that stage performances do. From the customers' point of view, the employees *are* the service. (Schneider and Bowen 1995; Surprenant and Solomon 1987; Tansik 1990), and their attitudes and behavior have a significant impact (Hartline and Ferrel 1996). What the workers do (their technical skills) and how they do it (their functional skills) are critical to customers' evaluations of service excellence (Grönroos 1990). The dentist, hotel clerk, and educator are assessed on how well they perform regarding the outcome of their effort (e.g., a filled cavity, properly assigned room, and information learned, respectively) and the manner in which it was done (e.g., the concern shown, the courtesy displayed, the responsiveness demonstrated).

In each service, the workers must strive to manage an impression of excellence through their adherence to defensive practices. They must (1) keep potentially destructive information undisclosed (e.g., the risk of abnormal pain from the dental drill), (2) guard against the intrusion of personal strife (e.g., resist the urge to share financial problems with the hotel guest), and (3) ensure a well-devised service delivery through forethought (e.g., anticipate students' questions regarding lecture material). These considerations can be addressed by service organizations in the hiring, training, and monitoring of their workers. The significance of impression management and the various ways an impression might be destroyed are important issues to stress in service organizations and in theatrical productions. It is not surprising that some have advocated that service training should include an acting class (Billingsley 1998; Grove, Fisk, and Knowles 1996).

Audience

Every theatrical performance is designed to appeal to a particular audience. Stated differently, if any performance is to be fully appreciated, it must conform to the audience's desires and expectations. Great performances are sometimes lost on the wrong audience. Individuals expecting to see a comedy are often disappointed with a drama. Even with the right audience, adaptations or adjustments by the actors are sometimes needed to keep the audience entertained. Hence, a successful performance requires attracting and reaching the appropriate audience. The right audience has a vested interest in seeing the show unfold smoothly. Specifically, the audience can be expected to engage in so-called protective practices which allow the show to go on when minor mishaps occur. After all, the audience attends a performance to see the entire show. If an actor misses a line or is out of place on stage or if a stage prop is missing, the audience will typically allow such miscues in the interest of enjoying the entire production. At the same time, those responsible for a stage production must ensure that some audience members do not disrupt others through their verbal or physical actions. Someone talking too loudly or crowding another's personal space can ruin the performance for other audience members.

Many services are delivered to multiple customers sharing the same servicescape, such as hotels, hospitals, schools, airlines, and restaurants. For a service experience to be successful, "recruiting the right customers is as important as recruiting the right personnel" (Gummesson 1993, 1999). Similar to the case of a stage production, the wrong customers (audience) for a service designed for others are likely to be dissatisfied (Lovelock 1994). The young couple who enter a restaurant expecting full-service, romantic dining only to find buffet-style, family dining will be disappointed. Most services are not likely to exclude paying customers simply because they do not fit the desired target audience profile. Also, antidiscrimination laws often prohibit attempts to exclude customer groups. Consequently, efforts at maintaining customer compatibility (Martin and Pranter 1989), policing the customers (Lovelock 1981), and recognizing how customers affect each other (Grove and Fisk 1997) ensure that everyone's service experience is positive.

Like theatrical productions, service providers can expect that the customers will overlook small flaws or minor problems during the process of service delivery in the interest of enjoying the service in its entirety. For that reason the dirty utensil, the hotel room that is missing a towel, or the taxi that's five minutes late are usually overlooked. Although any of these may be a failed "moment of truth" (Carlzon 1987), each is seldom significant enough by itself to destroy the overall quality of the service experience.

As a final note, successful service strategy begins with knowing the customers. Disney stresses the critical role of "guestology" (the study of the customers it services) as a key reason for its success. Disney conducts over two hundred external surveys a year; tracks demographic profiles, price sensitivity, and evaluation of attractions by guests; monitors the tens of thousands of letters and comment cards it receives; and practices management by walking around. By doing so, Disney gathers critical information that enables the design of a service experience that delights its guests (Johnson 1991).

Airline Service: An Application of Service Theater

This section develops a theatrical explanation of airline services as an illustration of the service theater concepts we have developed. Throughout the example, the service actors (airport and airline employees), service setting (airport facilities and airplane cabin), service audience (passengers), and service performance (enactment of the airline service) are interwoven to create a successful service experience. The example is developed around the theatrical device of the three-act play. Act 1 is the airport departure. Act 2 is the airline flight. Act 3 is the destination arrival.

Act 1: Airport Departure

Act 1 begins as airline passengers arrive at the front door of the airport. A porter might approach a passenger at the curb and offer to check her bags, or the passenger may decide to proceed inside the airport to the ticket counter. The ticket counter is the first frontstage area controlled by the airline. The passengers may note the cleanliness of the area and the state of the computer terminals and information displays. A performance team of ticket counter staff must work together to check in each passenger and the passenger's baggage. Every passenger's identity must be verified, his or her ticket and seating assignment must be confirmed, security questions must be asked, and any baggage must be tagged for its destination. The counter personnel are likely to exhibit efficiency, courtesy, and composure as they deal with one passenger after another. The uniforms they wear and the scripts they follow enhance their professionalism.

Once the baggage is checked, it disappears into the backstage region of the airport. The passenger is then instructed to proceed to a second frontstage area, the departure gate, where a smaller performance team of two or three airline staff prepares passengers for departure. The decor and comfort of the waiting area, the size and mix of passengers waiting to board the plane, and the efficiency with which the process unfolds will all impact passenger experiences. The staff is expected to display the same professionalism as their ticket-counter peers as they process passengers, handle ticket or seating problems, and announce airline boarding procedures and times. Like the waiting area, the staff's actions and demeanor are aspects of the unfolding service performance.

Every airline develops its own version of boarding procedures, which must be clearly conveyed to passengers to ensure efficiency. As an example, when a recent British Airways flight to London was called to board, the U.S. passengers formed a rather haphazard line of people two to three people across. One of the British Airways uniformed staff looked at the line in dismay and announced over the loudspeaker that "no one is going to go to London until you form a *proper* line." The Americans looked at each other in puzzlement and then realized that a "proper line" must be a single-file line. By contrast, Southwest Airlines has developed a nearly legendary reputation for the speed and efficiency of its boarding procedures by issuing a numbered plastic tag at check-in but no seat assignment. Based on these numbers, passengers on Southwest are boarded in groups, and they are expected to take the first seat available.

Act 2: The Airline Flight

Act 2 is the main act of the airline service and begins as passengers enter the airplane cabin. New performance teams of airline pilots and cabin personnel are the key players in act 2. The frontstage area is the cabin itself, and the backstage areas are the cockpit and the baggage compartment. A crew member, smartly attired and neatly groomed, greets the passengers as they board the plane and directs them to their seats. Once passengers have taken their seats and buckled their seat belts, the airplane will begin to pull away from the gate and taxi toward the runway. Already the passengers will be forming impressions of act 2 based on many different cues. The comfort of the seats, the amount of leg room, the air quality, the clarity of the public address system, and the colors and patterns of the cabin furnishings and carpet are consciously and unconsciously scanned. Even the number and mix of other passengers are noticed. Along the way, passengers are instructed about safety procedures. Most airlines follow a standard script to recite the safety procedures, yet others improvise. For example, it is common for a crew member on Southwest Airlines to sing the safety instructions to the passengers.

After the plane takes off, the cabin crew begins food and beverage service, and in-flight entertainment may commence. Each of these provides further cues to help passengers form impressions of the service. Meanwhile, the captain will greet the passengers over the loudspeaker and comment on flying conditions, flight time, visible landmarks along the flight, and weather at the destination. The pilot usually closes with a comment that the crew will do everything they can to make the flight

pleasant and comfortable. It is noteworthy that the cabin crew usually introduces themselves to passengers, whereas the land-based crews almost never introduce themselves. The gestures and expressions of the flight attendants, the affability ascribed to the pilot by virtue of his voice, and the helpfulness of the crew in general furnish additional information that fashions the flight experience for the service's audience. Other passengers in the service audience can also strongly influence each passenger's evaluation of the flight. Babies crying, children kicking the back of seats, or drunks trying to start a conversation can play a very negative role in the evaluation of the service despite the best efforts of the airline crew.

Although standard flight procedures or scripts must be followed, flight crews must sometimes go to extra lengths to make passengers comfortable. Several years ago, one of the authors boarded a Delta Air Lines flight the morning after a major airline crash. Safety anxieties were on the minds of passengers that morning as they nervously buckled their seat belts while the plane prepared to depart. Fortunately, the pilot and crew were well aware that the passengers might be unusually tense. As the plane made its last turn onto the runway and began its acceleration for liftoff, the sounds of the *William Tell* Overture burst from the loudspeakers. The unexpected but well-known music broke the anxiety among the travelers, and the plane hurtled into the air with a cabin full of passengers laughing uproariously.

Act 3: Destination Arrival

Act 3 begins as passengers line up to exit the airplane cabin and enter the airport facilities at their destination. The airplane crew and the workers at the destination must cooperate to move the passengers out of the cabin and on their way. Attempts are made to open the cabin doors quickly and speed travelers into the terminal. The cabin crew will often take advantage of one last opportunity to demonstrate efficiency through the manner by which they dispatch this task. They also attempt to convey a personal touch by bidding the passengers farewell and thanking them for flying their airline. However, most of the activity in this act of the service performance is self-service or occurs backstage as the airline's baggage crew unloads the plane and delivers the baggage to the baggage claim area. Occasionally, passengers may catch a glimpse of baggage handlers tossing luggage onto trams to be whisked away to the terminal as they wait to deplane. This normally backstage activity then becomes a frontstage spectacle that may have significant consequences for impressions of service excellence. The horror of observing a carefully packed suitcase containing breakable souvenirs haphazardly hurled into a heap of bags has caused many travelers considerable distress.

Most airlines have at least one person directing passengers to their connecting flights, to airport exits, or to the baggage claim area once they surge into the terminal. Aided by computer devices, experience with exasperated voyagers, and a personality that can withstand the pressure akin to that faced by a traffic officer, this service performer is likely to be the final face that the passenger puts on the service personnel. The clarity of his directions, the urgency he conveys, and the courtesy he displays can confirm the excellence of the service experience. If the passenger must find her way to the baggage claim, one last scene of the airline's service performance remains to be played: the speed of baggage delivery. It is an aspect of the airline's service that often goes unappreciated when the backstage personnel and systems operate efficiently, but it is a significant source of dissatisfaction if bags are slow to arrive or are lost in transit. Once the airline passengers locate their baggage and exit the airport, the airline service experience is completed.

Throughout the three-act service experience depicted here, various actors and their roles, setting conditions and regions, audience participation and circumstances, and performance attributes play significant parts in the passengers' impression of service excellence. Conceiving the entire service as theater provides a common framework that links and organizes the many factors that contribute to a service experience. Regardless of the service considered, the metaphor of theater can be applied.

Service Theater in Cyberspace

As the twentieth century drew to a close, a remarkable phenomenon occurred: the emergence and widespread adoption of electronic commerce (e-commerce). *Cyberspace* is a term used to describe the artificial reality created by computers and the Internet that makes e-commerce possible. Today, a vast array of products are bought and sold through the medium of cyberspace. Whether purchasing an automobile, financial advice, a tanning bed, or tax preparation, cyberspace brings the seller and buyer together in a manner far removed from typical retailing. Cyberspace also makes it possible for organizations to disseminate all sorts of information pertaining to their operations. Business

location, availability of merchandise, hours of operation, prices, installation instructions, and more can be communicated quickly and efficiently through cyberspace. In essence, cyberspace provides a means for organizations to provide a service (whether it is the retailing of a product or provision of information). All of the service theater concepts discussed in the previous sections pertain to cyberspace just as they do for marketing services in physical space. Although the boundaries between the various components of service theater may become blurred in the seamless world of cyberspace, they are nevertheless present and pliable.

In cyberspace the service performance is electronic. Unlike most services that are delivered in physical space, a cyberspace performance can be carefully automated and tightly scripted. Like its physical-space counterpart, much of what transpires during a cyberspace performance is dictated by the stage on which it occurs. However, the setting and the service stage in cyberspace are inherently more limited in terms of physical size than those found in physical space. The user's computer screen and the narrow bandwidth feeding it constitute a cyberspace service's frontstage. These frontstage dimensions combine to create a special challenge for cyberspace service marketers, forcing them to work hard to grab their audience's attention and to provide their audience with provocative reasons to "remain seated" during the performance's enactment. After all, cyberspace customers can switch performances with the mere click of a button! Yet what a cyberspace service may lack in frontstage dimensions, it can compensate for greatly with its backstage operation. Because of the interconnected nature of the Internet, the backstage in cyberspace may be much larger than is typical in physical space. The cyberspace backstage can range from one computer server and the support staff who operate it to a large network of servers and support staff across a multisite organization that collectively sustain the service performance 24 hours a day, seven days a week. Delivering an excellent cyberspace service experience to its audience requires an organization to choreograph and direct a performance that takes advantage of the backstage domain. Failure to do so may result in the audience's quick exit, perhaps to another service's performance. In cyberspace, there is no distance or travel time between service theaters. Further, because there are so many free services in cyberspace, there are virtually no switching costs to barricade the exit doors. Only a riveting performance will prevent switching.

Obviously, the design of the frontstage, the ease of its navigation, and the story it tells must be compelling.

In cyberspace, the service actors are often masked by the performance itself. In one sense, the Web site that provides the service portrays the actors as well as the performance. Essentially, the automated nature of the Web site makes it difficult to distinguish the cyberspace performance from the actors' roles. The two are frequently seamless. Across most cyberspace services, the actions of the service actor—the behaviors that create and deliver the service—are captured by and hidden in the text and texture of the Web site itself. Although they are impossible to discern separately from the Web site, they are there nonetheless. As the technology for delivering services in cyberspace improves, it may be feasible to simulate the appearance of human actors on the Web site and produce an anthropomorphic presence that more closely reflects service interaction in physical space. For those few cyberspace services that currently provide access to a live human being via their electronic link, that is, someone who can respond to questions or inquiries, the service actor is simply a participant in a remote servicescape (Bitner 1992). In such cases, his or her performance must exhibit all of the same considerations as any service actor that is invisible yet interactive with the customer (e.g., telephone receptionists or catalogue sales personnel).

Finally, the audience that participates in cyberspace's service theater is in control of most of the action. The audience can choose the time that the "curtain will go up" and the location of the service performance itself. Hence, cyberspace organizations must design their performances so that their audience can begin the service at its convenience and depart when it wishes. The backstage support and the frontstage design must facilitate the audience's entrance into, movement about, and exit from the cyberspace setting. A further, interesting aspect is that once the audience has gained access to the service organization, it commonly chooses the story line of a service performance in cyberspace. Due to the interactive nature of an Internet Web site such as Amazon.com or Yahoo!, each customer may select a set of pages uniquely suited to his or her interests. Amazon.com tries to encourage this behavior by greeting each repeat visitor with a customized page that includes suggested books and other items based on the pattern of previous purchases. This self-directed component of the service performance ostensibly provides a greater opportunity for a satisfying outcome to the service performance, but only if care is taken to design the various theatrical dimensions of the cyberspace service with the audience in mind. The performance must be simple but provocative; the staging must be inviting yet beguiling; and the actors must be caring and creative in meeting the audience's needs. Otherwise, the cyberspace service experience bytes.

Summary and Conclusion

The preceding passages demonstrate the correspondence between theatrical concepts rooted in dramaturgy or stage productions and those that are important for managing the service experience. From our perspective, both theater and services are involved in a large-scale effort to manage impressions. If service organizations explore the theatrical nature of services in their industry, they are likely to discover that the concepts discussed here (and other theatrical elements) may have profound significance.

To some, viewing and framing services as theater may hint at artificiality and manipulation. In reality, when a theatrical approach to services is successfully developed, the opposite is probable. Organizations and their personnel begin to see that they are in the business of creating experiences and recognize that this effort involves all of the trappings that are commonly found in theatrical productions. Hence, there is no room for insincerity. Poor performances—ones that are not credible—are not tolerated. No one can slouch in his or her responsibility, whether it is frontstage or backstage, because everyone plays a part in the overall production. The ultimate goal is a performance that engages the customer in an experience that suspends beliefs of organizational disinterest, commercialism, impersonality, and disregard. A theatrical approach attempts this through a unified and well-executed portrayal designed to create and sustain impressions that reflect the audience's desires. This cannot happen unless the service organization accepts the premise that services are theater in their own right and works hard to ensure an excellent performance.

If customers discover that a service organization has presented a false front, they are likely to take their patronage elsewhere. Hence, service marketers must convey the significance of service theater and stress authenticity throughout the service organization. In most cases, service organizations must guard against the temptation to display canned performances. Many performances are rigidly scripted with little room for actors to improvise. Managers should learn the importance of adapting to customer needs and wants and pursuing flexible strategies in fashioning the service experience. Rather than follow a fixed script, the service worker should be empowered to tailor the performance to the audience. Service managers should also appreciate the need for appropriateness. Absurd, ludicrous, or uncaring performances are likely to yield very negative customer reviews and may result in a service performance that closes early, whereas pertinent, seemly, and caring performances are likely to be held over by popular demand. In short, service performances must respond to the desires of the service audience.

In summary, service theater provides a unifying framework for describing and communicating the service experience. To that end, we have identified the many ways service organizations share characteristics and practices that are similar to theater or a dramaturgical depiction of human behavior. Whether it is a vendor selling Lucky Dogs on Bourbon Street in New Orleans, the combined efforts of the cast members at Disney World, the telephone receptionist taking customers' orders at L.L. Bean, or the cyberspace service offered by Amazon.com, a theatrical performance is occurring. Different service experiences are likely to reflect theatrical elements to varying degrees, yet from the customer's perspective, a show is always unfolding. For example, although the appearance of L.L. Bean's setting or actors is unlikely to carry much importance for its audience's experience, the actors' demeanor and defensive practices and the service's backstage operations are sure to have a significant impact. In contrast, the Lucky Dog vendor has a different set of theatrical elements to address. The frontstage, that is, the vending cart, and the merchant's appearance are quite important to the audience's enjoyment of the service. Organizations must determine which theatrical elements are of greatest significance for forming the customers' impressions and experience.

As a conceptual tool, therefore, service theater demonstrates the implicit and explicit relationships among the service organization, its customers, its employees, and its physical or cyberspace properties. As with any metaphor, the description of services in theatrical terms facilitates communication and analysis of the phenomenon and can be used to generate researchable propositions. It is our contention that applying the theater metaphor to services provides a holistic framework and vocabulary for understanding and managing service experiences.

REFERENCES

Berry, Leonard L. 1981. "Perspectives on the Retailing of Services." In *Theory in Retailing: Traditional and Nontraditional Sources,* edited by Ronald W. Stampfl and Elizabeth C. Hirschman. Chicago: American Marketing Association.

Billingsley, Kevin. 1998. "Service Providers Can Learn A Lot in Acting 101." *Marketing News* 32 (23): 13–14.

Bitner, Mary Jo. 1992. "Servicescapes: The Impact of Physical Surroundings on Customers and Employees." *Journal of Marketing* 56 (April): 57–71.

Booms, Bernard H., and Mary Jo Bitner. 1981. "Marketing Strategies and Organizational Structures for Service Firms." In *Marketing of Services,* edited by James H. Donnelly and William R. George. Chicago: American Marketing Association.

Carlzon, Jan. 1987. *Moments of Truth.* New York: Ballinger.

Goffman, Erving. 1959. *The Presentation of Self in Everyday Life.* Garden City, NY: Doubleday.

Grönroos, Christian. 1990. *Services Marketing and Management.* Lexington, MA: Lexington Books.

Grove, Stephen J., and Raymond P. Fisk. 1983. "The Dramaturgy of Services Exchange: An Analytical Framework for Services Marketing." In *Emerging Perspectives on Services Marketing,* edited by Leonard L. Berry, G. Lynn Shostack, and Gregory D. Upah. Chicago: American Marketing Association.

———. 1997. "The Impact of Other Customers on Service Experiences: A Critical Incident Examination of 'Getting Along.'" *Journal of Retailing* 73(1): 63–85.

Grove, Stephen J., Raymond P. Fisk, and Patricia A. Knowles. 1996. "Developing the Impression Management Skills of the Service Actor." Paper presented at the Frontiers in Services Marketing Conference, Nashville, Tennessee.

Gummesson, Evert. 1993. *Quality Management in Service Organizations.* St. Johns University, NY: International Service Quality Association.

Hartline, Michael D., and O. C. Ferrell. 1996. "The Management of Customer-Contact Service Employees: An Empirical Investigation." *Journal of Marketing* 60 (October): 52–70.

Johnson, Rick. 1991. "A Strategy for Service—Disney Style." *Journal of Business Strategy.* (September/October: 38–43.

Langeard, Eric, John E. G. Bateson, Christopher H. Lovelock, and Pierre Eiglier, eds. 1981. *Marketing of Services: New Insights from Consumers and Managers.* Cambridge, MA: Marketing Science Institute.

Lovelock, Christopher H. 1981. "Why Marketing Management Needs to be Different for Services." In *Marketing of Services,* edited by James H. Donnelly and William R. George. Chicago: American Marketing Association.

————. 1994. *Product Plus: How Product + Service = Competitive Advantage.* New York: McGraw-Hill.

Martin, Charles L., and Charles A. Pranter. 1989. "Compatibility Management: Customer-to-Customer Relationships in Service Environments." *Journal of Services Marketing.* 3 (summer): 6–15.

Schneider, Benjamin, and David E. Bowen. 1995. *Winning the Service Game.* Boston: Harvard Business School Press.

Shostack, G. Lynn. 1977. "Breaking Free from Product Marketing." *Journal of Marketing* 41 (April): 73–80.

Surprenant, Carol F., and Michael R. Solomon. 1987. "Predictability and Personalization in Service Encounter." *Journal of Marketing* 51 (April): 86–96.

Tansik, David A. 1990. "Managing Human Resource Issues for High-Contract Service Personnel." In *Service Management Effectiveness: Balancing Strategy Organization and Human Resources, Operations, and Marketing,* edited by David Bowen, Richard B. Chase, Thomas G. Cummings, and associates. San Francisco: Jossey-Bass.

Wilson, Edwin. 1991. *The Theater Experience.* 5th ed. New York: McGraw-Hill.

Zeithaml, Valarie A. 1981. "How Consumer Evaluation Processes Differ between Goods and Services." In *Marketing of Services,* edited by James H. Donnelly and William R. George. Chicago: American Marketing Association.

Critical Service Encounters: The Employee's Viewpoint

Mary Jo Bitner
Bernard H. Booms
Lois A. Mohr

In service settings, customer satisfaction is often influenced by interactions with contact employees. Previous research identified the sources of satisfaction and dissatisfaction in service encounters from the customer's point of view; this study explores these sources in service encounters from the contact employee's point of view. Drawing on insights from role, script, and attribution theories, 774 critical service encounters reported by hotel, restaurant, and airline employees are analyzed. The findings have implications for business practice in managing service encounters, employee empowerment and training, and managing customers.

The worldwide quality movement that has swept the manufacturing sector over the last decade is beginning to take shape in the service sector (*Business Week* 1991; Crosby 1991). According to some, the shift to a quality focus is essential to the competitive survival of service businesses, just as it has become essential in manufacturing (Heskett et al. 1994; Schlesinger and Heskett 1991).

Service quality researchers have suggested that "the proof of service [quality] is in its flawless performance" (Berry and Parasuraman 1991, p. 15), a concept akin to the notion of "zero defects" in manufacturing. Others have noted that "breakthrough" service managers pursue the goal of 100% defect-free service (Heskett, Sasser, and Hart 1990). From the customer's point of view, the most immediate evidence of service occurs in the service encounter or the "moment of truth" when the customer interacts with the firm. Thus, one central goal in the pursuit of "zero defects" in service is to work toward 100% flawless performance in service encounters. Here, flawless performance is not meant to imply rigid standardization, but rather 100% satisfying performance from the customer's point of view. The cost of not achieving flawless performance is the "cost of quality," which includes the costs associated with redoing the service or compensating for poor service, lost customers, negative word of mouth, and decreased employee morale.

Although more firms are realizing the importance of service quality and customer satisfaction, it is not always clear how to achieve these goals. Situations arise in which quality is low and the problem is recognized by both the firm (i.e., employees) and the customer, but there may be disagreement on the causes of the problem and the appropriate solutions. In service encounters such disagreements, sure to diminish customer satisfaction, underscore the importance of understanding the types of events and behaviors that cause customers to be satisfied or dissatisfied. Because the service encounter involves at least two people, it is important to understand the encounter from multiple perspectives. Armed with such understanding, firms are better able to design process and educate both employees and customers to achieve quality in service encounters.

Previous research in the context of the restaurant, hotel, and airline industries identified categories of events and behaviors that underlie critical service encounters from the customer's point of view (Bitner, Booms, and Tetreault 1990; hereafter BBT). The primary purpose of this study is to examine the contact employee's perspective of critical service encounters and to understand, in the context of the same three industries, the kinds of events and behaviors that employees believe underlie customer satisfaction. The employee perspective is then compared with BBT to gain insight into any disparities in perspectives. A second purpose of the study is to evaluate the usefulness of the classification scheme developed by BBT (1990).

Reprinted with permission from *Journal of Marketing*, Vol. 58, (October 1994), 95–106.

If the scheme is conceptually robust, it should hold for different respondent groups.

The research is guided by the following questions:

- From the contact employee's point of view, what kinds of events lead to satisfying service encounters for the customer? What causes these events to be remembered favorably?
- From the contact employee's point of view, what kinds of events lead to dissatisfying service encounters for the customer? What causes these events to be remembered with distaste?
- Do customers and employees report the same kinds of events and behaviors leading to satisfaction and dissatisfaction in service encounters?

Before presenting the empirical study, we discuss relevant research and theory.

Customer and Contact Employee Viewpoints

Frontline personnel are a critical source of information about customers. There are two basic ways that customer knowledge obtained by contact employees is used to improve service: (1) Such knowledge is used by the contact employees themselves to facilitate their interactions with customers and (2) It is used by the firm for making decisions. First, employees often modify their behavior from moment to moment on the basis of feedback they receive while serving customers. Schneider (1980) argues that people who choose to work in service occupations generally have a strong desire to give good service. To the extent that this is true, contact personnel can be expected to look frequently for cues that tell them how their service is received by customers. The more accurate their perceptions are, the more likely their behavioral adjustments are to improve customer satisfaction.

Second, because contact personnel have frequent contact with customers, they serve a boundary-spanning role in the firm. As a result, they often have better understanding of customer needs and problems than others in the firm. Researchers have theorized and found some evidence that open communication between frontline personnel and managers is important for achieving service quality (Parasuraman, Berry, and Zeithaml 1990; Zeithaml, Berry, and Parasuraman 1988). Schneider and Bowen (1984) argue that firms should use information gathered from contact personnel in making

strategic decisions, especially decisions regarding new service development and service modifications.

It seems reasonable to conclude that accurate employee understanding of customers enables both the employee and the firm to adjust appropriately to customer needs. However, previous research correlating customer and employee views of service is sparse and offers mixed conclusions. Schneider and Bowen (1985) and Schneider, Parkington, and Buxton (1980) found high correlations ($r = .63$ and $r = .67$, respectively) between employee and customer attitudes about overall service quality in a bank setting. Their results are contradicted, however, in a study by Brown and Swartz (1989). These researchers gathered data on patient experiences with their physicians and compared them with the physicians' perceptions of their patients' experiences. The differences they found were rather large and inversely related to overall patient satisfaction.

Another study of 1300 customers and 900 customer service professionals conducted by Development Dimensions International found differences in perceptions between the two groups (*Services Marketing Newsletter* 1989). Customer service professionals in that study consistently rated the importance of particular service skills and competencies and their actual performance higher than customers rated the same skills and competencies. Similarly, Langeard and colleagues (1981) found that field managers at two banks tended to overestimate (compared with customer ratings) the importance of six broad service delivery dimensions. Other studies have found differences when comparing customer and employee evaluations of business situations using scenarios and role playing in product failure contexts (Folkes and Kotsos 1986), a complaint context (Resnik and Harmon 1983), and the context of retailer responses to customer problems (Dornoff and Dwyer 1981).

We would therefore expect, on the basis of these studies, to find similarities in employee and customer views of the service encounter, but we would expect significant differences as well. Role, script, and attribution theories provide conceptual bases for these expectations.

Theoretical Explanations

Role and Script Theories

Similarities in how customers and employees view service encounters are most likely when the two parties share common role expectations and the service script is well defined (Mohr and Bitner

1991; Solomon et al. 1985). A *role* is the behavior associated with a socially defined position (Solomon et al. 1985), and *role expectations* are the standards for role behavior (Biddle 1986). In many routine service encounters, particularly for experienced employees and customers, the roles are well defined and both the customer and employee know what to expect from each other.

In addition, many types of service encounters, such as seating customers in a restaurant, are repeated frequently throughout a person's life, resulting in strong, standardized, and well-rehearsed scripts (i.e., structures that describe appropriate sequences of role behaviors)(Schank and Abelson 1977). When service encounters have strong scripts, the employee and customer are likely to share expectations about the events that will occur and the order of occurrence. They are less likely to share ideas about subscripts, which are prescriptions for handling what Schank and Abelson describe as "obstacles and errors," two types of interferences that may occur in otherwise predictable scripts.

Role and script theory, combined with the routine nature of many service encounters, suggests that customers and employees are likely to share a common perspective on service experiences. It is also clear that differences in perspective may arise when roles are less defined, a participant is unfamiliar with expected behaviors, or interferences require the enactment of complex or less routine subscripts.

Attribution Theory

Dissimilarities in viewpoint may arise when service encounter partners have conflicting views of the underlying causes behind the events, that is, when their attributions differ. Research shows that there are many biases in the attribution process (Fiske and Taylor 1984). Most clearly relevant for the perceptions of service providers and customers is the self-serving attribution bias. This is the tendency for people to take credit for success (i.e., to give internal attributions for their successes, a self-enhancing bias) and deny responsibility for failure (i.e., to blame failure on external causes, a self-protecting bias). Given these biases we would expect employees to blame the system or the customer for service failures, whereas the customer would be more likely to blame the system or the employee. The result would be different views of the causes of service dissatisfaction. It is less clear that this bias would operate in the case of a service encounter success. Although the desire for self-

enhancement might lead both the employee and customer to give themselves credit for the success, the fact that the customer is paying the firm for a service would probably preclude the bias on the customer's side. Overall, then, the self-serving attribution bias leads to the expectation that the perspectives of the employee and customer will differ more in service success situations.

Both empirical research and theory suggest that similarities as well as differences in perspective are likely to occur between service encounter participants. Role and script theories suggest that in relatively routine situations such as the ones studied, there will be strong similarities in perspective. However, attribution biases suggest that there will also be significant differences in viewpoint. We explore to what extent the perspectives of contact personnel and those of customers are different. And, to the degree that they are different, the data provide insight into the nature of these disparities.

Method and Analysis

Data Collection

Data were collected using the critical incident technique (CIT), a systematic procedure for recording events and behaviors that are observed to lead to success or failure on a specific task (Ronan and Latham 1974), in this case, satisfying the customer. (For more detailed discussions of the method, see BBT; Flanagan 1954; Wilson-Pessano 1988). Using the CIT, data are collected through structured open-ended questions, and the results are content analyzed. Respondents are asked to report specific events from the recent past (within 6 to 12 months). These accounts provide rich details of firsthand experiences in which customers have been satisfied or dissatisfied. Because respondents are asked about specific events rather than generalities, interpretation, or conclusions, this procedure meets criteria established by Ericsson and Simon (1980) for providing valuable, reliable information about cognitive processes. Researchers have concluded that when used appropriately (Flanagan 1954; Wilson-Pessano 1988), the critical incident method is reliable in terms of stability of the categories identified across judges, valid with respect to the content identified, and relevant in that the behaviors illuminated have proven to be important to the success or failure of the task in question (Ronan and Latham 1974; White and Locke 1981).

Hotel, restaurant, and airline employees were interviewed and asked to recall critical service encounters that caused satisfaction or dissatisfaction for customers of their firms. Thirty-seven trained student interviewers collected the data— 781 total incidents. Each one recruited a minimum of ten employees from among the same three industries studied in BBT, asking each employee to describe one incident that was satisfactory and one that was dissatisfactory from the customer's point of view.

Because all the interviewers were employed in the hospitality sector, they recruited fellow employees and employees of establishments with which they were familiar. They were instructed not to interview fellow students. The refusal rate was negligible. The incident sample represented 58 hotels, 152 restaurants, and 4 airlines. On average, the employees providing the incidents had 5.5 years of working experience in their respective industries. The employees ranged in age from 16 to 65 (mean age 27) and were 55% female and 45% male. The instructions to the employees being interviewed were as follows:

Put yourself in the shoes of customers of your firm. In other words, try to see your firm through your customer's eyes.

Think of a recent time when a customer of your firm had a particularly satisfying (dissatisfying) interaction with yourself or a fellow employee. Describe the situation and exactly what happened.

They were then asked the following questions:

1. When did the incident happen?
2. What specific circumstances led up to this situation?
3. Exactly what did you or your fellow employee say or do?
4. What resulted that made you feel the interaction was satisfying (dissatisfying) from the customer's point of view?
5. What should you or your fellow employee have said or done? (for dissatisfying incident only)

To be used in the analysis, an incident was required to (1) involve employee-customer interaction, (2) be very satisfying or dissatisfying from the customer's point of view, (3) be a discrete episode, and (4) have sufficient detail to be visualized by the interviewer. Seven incidents failed to meet these criteria, leaving 774 incidents (397 satisfactory and 377 dissatisfactory).

Classification of Incidents

The incident classification system developed by BBT was used as a starting point for sorting the data with the assumption that, to the degree that customers and employees remember satisfying and dissatisfying encounters in the same way, the same classification system should be appropriate. Incidents that could not be classified within the original scheme would then provide evidence for differences in perspective.

One researcher trained in the classification scheme coded the incidents. Any that did not fit into the scheme were put aside. This researcher and a second then worked together on categorizing this group of 86 incidents (11% of the total). These incidents were read and sorted, combined, and re-sorted until a consistent coding scheme was developed that combined similar incidents into distinct, meaningful categories. When the new categories were labeled and the two researchers achieved consensus on assignment of the incidents, the new categories (one major group with four subcategories) were added to the original classification system.

A set of complete coding instructions was then written (see Appendix A). They included general instructions for coders, operational definitions of each category, and decision rules for assigning incidents to categories. These are procedures recommended by Perreault and Leigh (1989) for improving the reliability of judgment-based data. The coding instructions were used to train a third researcher who had not participated in the categorization decisions. This researcher then coded the 774 employee incidents, providing an interjudge reliability check on the classification system. Discrepancies between the first and third researchers' assignments were resolved by the second researcher.

The interjudge agreement between the first and third researchers was 84% for the satisfying incidents and 85% for the dissatisfying incidents. These figures are respectably high, especially considering that the classification system in this study contains 16 categories. The percentage agreement statistic probably underestimates interjudge reliability in this case because this statistic is influenced by the number of coding categories (i.e., the more categories, the lower the percentage agreement is likely to be) (Perreault and Leigh 1989). For this reason, two other measures of interjudge reliability were calculated. Cohen's κ, which corrects for the likelihood of chance agreement between judges, was found to be .816 for the satisfying and .823 for the dissatisfying incidents. Perreault and Leigh (1989) argue, however, that κ is an overly conservative measure of reliability because it assumes an a priori knowledge of the likely distribution of responses across categories. To correct for this they designed an alternative index of reliability, I_r, appropriate for marketing data. Rather than contrasting interjudge agreement with an estimate of chance agreement, I_r is based on a model of the level of agreement that might be expected given a true (population) level of reliability. Furthermore, the index focuses on the reliability of the whole coding process, not just on the agreement between judges. I_r was found to be .911 and .914 for the satisfying and dissatisfying incidents, respectively.

Results and Discussion

The categories of events and behaviors that employees believe underlie their customers' satisfaction and dissatisfaction in service encounters are identified and discussed first. Then the results are compared with customer perceptions using the BBT data.

Classification of Employee-Reported Incidents

The critical incident classification system based on incidents gathered from customers (BBT) consists of three major groups of employee behaviors that account for all satisfactory and dissatisfactory incidents: (1) employee response to service delivery system failures, (2) employee response to customer needs and requests, and (3) unprompted and unsolicited employee actions. Of the 774 employee incidents, 668 were classified into one of these three groups and the 12 categories within them. The incidents were very familiar in detail to those provided by customers. (See BBT for detailed descriptions of the groups and categories and sample incidents.)

Eighty-six encounters (11% of the total) did not fit any of the predetermined groups. These incidents were categorized into one major group labeled "problem customer behavior," and they were added to the categorization scheme as "Group 4." In these cases, the coders could not attribute the satisfaction and dissatisfaction to an action or attitude of the employee—instead, the root cause was the customer. Such customers were basically uncooperative, that is, unwilling to cooperate with the service provider, other customers, industry regulations, and/or laws. These situations created problems for the employees, and rarely were they

able to deal with them in such a way as to bring about customer satisfaction; only 3 of these incidents were satisfactory.

Within the problem customer behavior group, four categories emerged (Table 1 provides examples of incidents from the four new categories):

1. *Drunkenness*—The employee perceives the customer to be clearly intoxicated and creating problems such as harassing other customers nearby, giving the employee a hard time, or disrupting the atmosphere of the establishment;
2. *Verbal and physical abuse*—The customer verbally and/or physically abuses either the employee or other customers;
3. *Breaking company policies or laws*—The customer refuses to comply with policies or laws, and the employee attempts to enforce compliance; and
4. *Uncooperative customers*—The customer is generally rude and uncooperative or unreasonably demanding. From the employee's perspective, the customer is unwilling to be satisfied, no matter what is done for him or her.

The Employee's View of Satisfactory Versus Dissatisfactory Encounters

Here we examine the frequencies and proportions of employee accounts in the four groups and 16 categories as shown in Table 2. It should be noted that the frequencies and proportions shown in the table reflect numbers of reported events. The actual frequency of occurrence of the type of event represented by a particular group or category cannot be inferred from the data. Nor can greater importance be inferred by greater frequencies in a particular category (Wilson-Pessano 1988). The data are shown in full in Table 2; however, our discussion focuses on the four major groups. To facilitate understanding, the employee-reported incidents are summarized and ranked according to the percentage of incidents in the four major incident groups:

Distribution of Dissatisfactory Incidents

Rank Order	Group #	Percentage
1	Group 1—Response to failures	51.7
2	Group 4—Problem customers	22.0
3	Group 2—Response to requests	16.4
4	Group 3—Unprompted action	9.8

TABLE 1	*Group Four Sample Incidents: Problem Customers*

Incident	
Dissatisfactory	**Satisfactory**

A. Drunkenness

An intoxicated man began pinching the female flight attendants. One attendant told him to stop, but he continued and then hit another passenger. The copilot was called and asked the man to sit down and leave the others alone, but the passenger refused. The copilot then "decked" the man, knocking him into his seat.	A person who became intoxicated on a flight started speaking loudly, annoying the other passengers. The flight attendant asked the passenger if he would be driving when the plane landed and offered him coffee. He accepted the coffee and became quieter and friendlier.

B. Verbal and Physical Abuse

While a family of three was waiting to order dinner, the father began hitting his child. Another customer complained about this to the manager who then, in a friendly and sympathetic way, asked the family to leave. The father knocked all the plates and glasses off the table before leaving.	None

C. Breaking Company Policies or Laws

Five guests were in a hotel room two hours past checkout time. Because they would not answer the phone calls or let the staff into the room, hotel security staff finally broke in. They found the guests using drugs and called the police.	None

D. Uncooperative Customer

When a man was shown to his table in the nonview dining area of the restaurant, he became extremely angry and demanded a window table. The restaurant was very busy, but the hostess told him he could get a window seat in a half hour. He refused to wait and took his previously reserved table, but he complained all the way through dinner and left without tipping.	None

Distribution of Satisfactory Incidents

Rank Order	Group #	Percentage
1	Group 2—Response to requests	49.4
2	Group 1—Response to failures	27.5
3	Group 3—Unprompted action	22.4
4	Group 4—Problem customers	.8

When employees were asked to report incidents resulting in customer dissatisfaction, they tended to describe problems with external causes such as the delivery system or inappropriate customer behaviors. By far the largest number of dissatisfactory incidents were categorized in Group 1 (response to delivery system failures), with the next largest proportion falling into Group 4 (problem customers). These results are not unexpected given what attribution theory suggests. When things go

TABLE 2 *Group and Category Classification by Type of Incident Outcome (Employees Only)*

	Type of Incident Outcome					
	Satisfactory		Dissatisfactory		Row Total	
Group and Category	No.	%	No.	%	No.	%
Group 1. Employee Response to Service Delivery System Failures						
A. To unavailable service	31	7.8	37	9.8	68	8.8
B. To unreasonably slow service	23	6.0	48	12.7	71	9.2
C. To other core service failures	55	13.9	110	29.2	165	21.3
Subtotal, Group 1	109	27.5	195	51.7	304	39.3
Group 2. Employee Response to Customer Needs and Requests						
A. To "special needs" customers	80	20.2	14	3.7	94	12.1
B. To customer preferences	99	24.9	43	11.4	142	18.3
C. To admitted customer error	11	2.8	0	0.0	11	1.4
D. To potentially disruptive others	6	1.5	5	1.3	11	1.4
Subtotal, Group 2	196	49.4	62	16.4	258	33.3
Group 3. Unprompted and Unsolicited Employee Actions						
A. Attention paid to customer	43	10.8	6	1.6	49	6.3
B. Truly out-of-the-ordinary employee behavior	25	6.3	28	7.4	53	6.8
C. Employee behaviors in the context of cultural norms	7	1.8	3	.8	10	1.3
D. Gestalt evaluation	0	0.0	0	0.0	0	0.0
E. Performance under adverse circumstances	14	3.5	0	0.0	14	1.8
Subtotal, Group 3	89	22.4	37	9.8	126	16.3
Group 4. Problematic Customer Behavior						
A. Drunkenness	3	.8	16	4.2	19	2.5
B. Verbal and Physical Abuse	0	0.0	9	2.4	9	1.2
C. Breaking company policies or laws	0	0.0	16	4.2	16	2.1
D. Uncooperative customer	0	0.0	42	11.1	42	5.4
Subtotal, Group 4	3	.8	83	22.0	86	11.1
Column Total	397	51.3	377	48.7	774	100%

wrong, people are more likely to blame external, situational factors than to attribute the failure to their own shortcomings. A modest number of dissatisfactory incidents were found in Group 2. In many of these cases, the employees implied that they were unable to satisfy customer needs due to constraints placed on them by laws or their own organization's rules and procedures, again placing the blame on an external source. The smallest percentage of dissatisfactory incidents were classified in Group 3, which reflects spontaneous negative employee behaviors (e.g., rudeness, lack of attention). Again, this is consistent with the bias toward not blaming oneself for failures.

The largest proportion of satisfactory incidents, from the employee's point of view, occurred in response to customer needs and requests (Group 2). Almost half of particularly satisfying customer encounters reported by employees resulted from their ability to adjust the system to accommodate customer needs and requests. Success is attributed in these cases to the employee's own ability and willingness to adjust. The next largest proportion of satisfactory incidents were categorized in Group 1. This is an interesting set of incidents, because each one began as a failure but ended as a success because of the ability of the employee to recover. Employees clearly remember their ability to recover in failure situations as a significant cause for ultimate customer satisfaction. A relatively modest (when compared with the customer view) number of satisfactory incidents were categorized as unprompted and unsolicited employee actions (Group 3). Perhaps employees do not view their own behaviors as "spontaneous," but they instead remember them in association with a specific external cause (e.g., a customer need, a service failure). Finally, there were virtually no satisfactory incidents categorized in the problem customer group (Group 4). This makes sense, because it is difficult to imagine a very problematic customer leaving the encounter feeling satisfied except under highly unusual circumstances.

Comparing Customer and Employee Views

Table 3 combines data from the current study with the original BBT data for purposes of comparison. Because the employees and customers in these two studies all described different incidents, conclusions from employee-customer comparisons are exploratory, and the explanations are somewhat speculative. Although we rely on role and attribution theories to explain the differences we observed, it is possible that these differences could be due to sampling variations or differences in the incident pool from which the two groups drew. However, given the care taken in collecting the data to avoid systematic biases, that both studies were conducted in the same city using the same

TABLE 3 *Comparison of Employee and Customer Responses: Incident Classification by Type of Incident Outcome*

| | Type of Incident Outcome | | | | | |
| | Satisfactory | | Dissatisfactory | | Row Total | |
Groups	No.	%	No.	%	No.	%
Group 1. Employee Response to Service Delivery System Failures						
Employee Data	109	27.5	195	51.7	304	39.3
Customer Data	81	23.3	151	42.9	232	33.2
Group 2. Employee Response to Customer Needs and Requests						
Employee Data	196	49.4	62	16.4	258	33.3
Customer Data	114	32.9	55	15.6	169	24.2
Group 3. Unprompted and Unsolicited Employee Actions						
Employee Data	89	22.4	37	9.8	126	16.3
Customer Data	152	43.8	146	41.5	298	42.6
Group 4. Problematic Customer Behavior						
Employee Data	3	.8	83	22.0	86	11.1
Customer Data	0	0.0	0	0.0	0	0.0
Column Total						
Employee Data	397	51.3	377	48.7	774	100%
Customer Data	347	49.6	352	50.4	699	100%

three industries, and that many of the same firms were the source of incidents in both studies, we have confidence in our theoretical explanations of the results.

A large majority of the employee incidents from the current study could be categorized in the original three groups and 12 categories, suggesting strong similarities in the way employees and customers report the sources of satisfaction and dissatisfaction in service encounters. Recall that these are relatively routine service encounters and in both studies the respondents were experienced service participants. Even so, the addition of a fourth group and the significant differences in frequencies and proportions of incidents found in the groups suggest that there are dissimilarities in what they report as well. Hierarchical log-linear analysis of Table 3 shows a significant three-way interaction between group (1, 2, 3, or 4), type of outcome (satisfactory or dissatisfactory), and incident source (employee or customer) (L.R. χ^2 change = 8.17; p = .04). There is also a significant two-way interaction between group and incident source (L.R. χ^2 change = 263.31; p < .0001). Because of the significant three-way interaction, the results are discussed separately for satisfactory and dissatisfactory incidents.

Within the dissatisfactory incident classifications, customers and employees have relatively similar proportions in Groups 1 and 2. The significant interaction is caused by Group 3, which is dominated by customer incidents, and Group 4, which contains incidents reported by employees only. These results are very consistent with expectations based on attribution biases. Employees are highly unlikely to describe customer dissatisfaction as being caused by their own predispositions, attitudes, or spontaneous behaviors. Customers, on the other hand, will be likely to blame the employee rather than anything they themselves might have contributed. This is clearly reflected in the observation that customers report no dissatisfactory incidents caused by their own problem behaviors (Group 4). The differences in how customers and employees report satisfactory encounters are provocative as well, albeit less extreme. Again, this is consistent with attribution theory, which predicts larger differences in perceptions in failure than in success situations. Within the satisfactory incidents, Groups 1 and 4 are equally represented for both customers and employees. The significant interaction is the result of Group 2 being dominated by employee incidents and Group 3 being dominated by customer incidents.

Implications for Researchers

Generalizability of the Service Encounter Classification Scheme

The importance and usefulness of robust classification schemes for theory development and practical application have been discussed by social scientists (e.g., McKelvey 1982) and marketing scholars (e.g., Hunt 1991; Lovelock 1983). Yet we have few such frameworks in marketing, primarily because the classification schemes that have been proposed have rarely been subjected to empirical validation across times and contexts.

This study represents one contribution in a program of research designed to test the validity and generalizability of a scheme for categorizing sources of service encounter satisfaction and dissatisfaction (BBT). If the scheme holds in different settings (e.g., different industry contexts, or in internal as well as external encounters) and across different respondents (e.g., customers versus providers, customers in different cultures), then the scheme can be viewed as more robust and of greater theoretical as well as practical value. Other studies have reported that the three major groups of behaviors identified by BBT are also found in a retail context (Kelley, Hoffman, and Davis 1993) and a study of 16 consumer services (Gremler and Bitner 1992). Through replication, the framework becomes more valuable in identifying generalizable "service behaviors."

The results of our research indicate that all the categories found in the original customer-prospective study were also found when employees were asked to report except "problem customers." The addition of this new group provides a more complete classification that can be further examined in other contexts.

Problem Customers

A primary contribution of this research effort is the empirically based finding that unsatisfactory service encounters may be due to inappropriate customer behaviors—the notion that sometimes customers are wrong. Others have suggested the existence of problem customers (e.g., Lovelock 1994; Schrage 1992; Zemke and Anderson 1990). Lovelock, for example, suggests the term "jaycustomers" to label customers who "misconsume" in a manner similar to jaywalkers who cross streets in unauthorized places. Our research provides empirical evidence that these difficult customer types do exist and in fact can be the source of their own dissatisfaction.

Although no one really believes customers are always right, firms have policies that pretend this is so, and managers urge and demand that customer contact employees treat customers as if they are always right. Needless to say, such avoidance leads to stresses and strains for managers and frontline personnel alike and potentially bigger problems for firms. (See Hochschild 1983 for a discussion of personal and organizational impacts of nonauthentic ways of dealing with customers.) With a better understanding of problem customers can come better methods of eliminating or dealing with the underlying causes of the problems.

This area is ripe with important research questions, such as the following: What types of problems do customers cause? What are the most frequent problems? What types of customers tend to be problem customers? Under what circumstances do customers create either more or fewer problems? And, from a management viewpoint, what can be done to identify problem customers, and how can and should employees deal with them?

This initial research represents a start at addressing some of these questions and the beginnings of a typology of problem customer behaviors. The categories of behaviors discovered are not surprising given the nature of the industries studied. Each service involves the possible serving of food and drink—including alcoholic beverages. In each service the customers are in close physical proximity for extended periods of time. Restaurant, airline, and hotel customers are many times in tight public spaces that put them cheek to jowl with other customers. Personal social interactions are carried out in front of other customers who are most often strangers. And, as mentioned previously, the types of encounters studied here are all relatively routine and commonly experienced. Finally, customers frequently have transaction-based encounters with the service personnel rather than long-term relationship-based encounters. It is assumed that these circumstances influenced the nature of the subcategories of problems identified in Group 4. Thus, although we believe that the major problem customer group will surface whenever employees are asked to relate instances of dissatisfactory encounters, further research is needed to identify other subcategories within the group and relate problem types to serve industry conditions, circumstances, and customer segments.

Although we have identified problem customers by exploring the sources of customer dissatisfaction, there may be other types of "wrong customers." For example, even when customers do not misbehave, they may not be good relationship customers for the organization because they do not meet the target market profile, they are not profitable in the long term, or in some cases may not be compatible with the service provider in terms of personality or work style (Lovelock 1994; Zeithaml and Bitner 1996). It is beyond the scope of this article to discuss the full conceptualization of wrong customers, but it may be fruitful for researchers in the future to incorporate the misbehaving customers we have identified into this more extensive conceptual scheme.

Theory Implications

Role and script theories suggest that customers and employees in routine, well-understood service transactions will share parallel views of their roles and the expected sequence of events and behaviors. The types of service encounters studied here and in the original study do represent frequently encountered and routine services. Shared views of the encounter should result in common notions of the sources of customer satisfaction and dissatisfaction. The fact that 89% of the employee incidents could be classified in the original classification scheme suggests that customers and employees do indeed report incidents with most of the same sources of satisfaction and dissatisfaction.

An interesting issue for further research is whether the overall strong similarity of views between customers and employees would result if the industries studied were ones less routine and well practiced.

Results of the study indicate that though employees and customers do report many of the same sources of customer satisfaction and dissatisfaction, there are also significant differences. These disparities show up in the distribution of incidents across the major groups, and the differences were most dramatic for the dissatisfactory service encounters. The self-serving attribution bias suggests explanations for why some of these differences were observed.

Managerial Implications

Using the Classification Scheme

One purpose of this study was to evaluate the soundness of the classification scheme developed by BBT in a distinctive context. Through the addition of the problem customer grouping, the framework is now more complete, and the scheme itself can provide a starting point for a company or industry to begin identifying with greater specificity the events and behaviors peculiar to its own setting. For example, the framework has been used for proprietary purposes in medical and travel agent contexts. In these cases, the companies began with the existing groups in the classification scheme and fleshed out the categories with useful specifics that could be employed in service training or service redesign.

The Customer Is Not Always Right

In the industries studied here, problem customers were the source of 22% of the dissatisfactory incidents. This group may be even larger in industries in which the customer has greater input into the service delivery process (e.g., health care, education, legal services).

Several implications are suggested by the problem customer group. First, managers must acknowledge that the customer is not always right, nor will he or she always behave in acceptable ways. Contact employees who have been on the job any period of time know this, but frequently they are being told that the "customer is king" and are not given the appropriate training and tools to deal with problem customers. Employees need appropriate coping and problem-solving skills to handle customers as well as their own personal feelings in these situations. Employees can also be taught to recognize characteristics of situations (e.g., unexpected peaks in demand, inordinate delays) and anticipate the moods of their customers so that some potential problem situations can be avoided completely or alleviated before they accelerate.

To provide employees with the appropriate training and skills for working with problem customers, the organization must clarify its position regarding such customers. A basic problem customer strategy might be conceptualized as ranging along a continuum from "refuse to serve them" to "satisfy them at all costs." For example, some car rental companies have attempted to refuse customers with bad driving histories by checking records in advance and rejecting bad-risk drivers (Dahl 1992). In a different context, some Madison Avenue ad agencies say that "some accounts are so difficult to work with that they simply cannot—or will not—service them" (Bird 1993). Although organizations have intuitively recognized that not all customer segments are right for the firm and that each individual customer is not right all the time, some are beginning to acknowledge these facts

more explicitly and are attempting to quantify the impact of problem or "wrong" customers on profitability and organizational stress.

Beyond the need to develop employee skills, there is the need for "training" customers so that they will know what to expect and appropriate behaviors in given situations. For example, some upscale resorts that offer highly discounted rates in nonpeak seasons find that their discount customers, who may not be accustomed to the "rules of behavior," appreciate information on what to wear and other expected behaviors while at the resort. In other more complex and less familiar service situations (e.g., professional services), customers may truly appreciate knowing more about their role in the service process and the behaviors and information that are needed from them to make the service succeed (Bloom 1984). It has been suggested that by treating customers as "partial employees" they can learn to contribute to the service in ways that will enhance their own satisfaction (Bowen 1986).

Employees as Sources of Customer Data

Previous research has suggested that contact employees are good sources of information on customer attitudes (Schneider and Bowen 1985; Schneider, Parkington and Buxton 1980). Our study confirms these findings insofar as employees of hotels, restaurants, and airlines report all the same categories of customer satisfaction and dissatisfaction reported by customers in the same industries. However, we would caution against relying too much on contact employee interpretations of customer satisfaction for two reasons. First, although they report the same basic categories, the proportions of incidents found in the categories are significantly different from those reported by customers. Second, in some industries in which service encounters are less routine, contact employees may not be as accurate in their assessment of customer expectations and satisfaction (see Brown and Swartz 1989).

Employee Desire for Knowledge and Control

It is apparent in reading the incidents that contact employees *want* to provide good service and are very proud of their abilities to do so. This pride comes through in the large percentage of satisfactory incidents found in Group 2, in which employees' own skills, abilities, and willingness to accommodate customer needs were the sources of customer satisfaction. Balancing out this sense of pride are a large number of frustrating incidents in which employees believe they cannot for some reason recover from a service failure or adjust the system to accommodate a customer need. These reasons usually stem from lack of basic knowledge of the system and its constraints, inability to provide a logical explanation to the customer, cumbersome bureaucratic procedures, poorly designed systems or procedures, or the lack of authority to do anything.

Reliability Is Critical

The data show that a majority of the dissatisfactory incidents reported by employees resulted from inadequate responses to service delivery system failures. This result, together with other research reporting service reliability as the single most important dimension used by consumers to judge service quality (Parasuraman, Zeithaml, and Berry 1988, 1990), implies a need for service process and system analysis to determine the root causes of system failures (Kingman-Brundage 1989; Shostack 1984, 1987). Systems can then be redesigned and processes implemented to ensure higher reliability from the customer's point of view. The best way to ensure satisfaction, however, is not to have a failure in the first place.

Conclusion

The research suggests that many frontline employees do have a true customer orientation and do identify with and understand customer needs in service encounter situations. They have respect for customers and a desire to deliver excellent service. Oftentimes the inability to do so is governed by inadequate or poorly designed systems, poor or nonexistent recovery strategies, or lack of knowledge. When employees have the skills and tools to deliver high-quality service, they are proud of their ability to do so.

We also learned from employees that customers can be the source of their own dissatisfaction through inappropriate behavior or being unreasonably demanding. We suspect that this new group of dissatisfactory incidents caused by problem customers would surface in any service industry and that its existence represents a strategic challenge for the organization as well as an operational, real-time challenge for service employees. In a time when "customer is king" is the stated philosophy of most forward-thinking organizations, acknowledgment that wrong customers exist, coupled with creative thinking about customer roles and man-

agement of customer expectations, may considerably deepen understanding of and ability to cultivate customer relationships.

Appendix A
Instructions for Coders
Overview

1. You will be provided with a set of written critical service encounter events. Each "story" or "event" is recorded on a standardized questionnaire. Two types of questionnaires were used, one for satisfying interactions and one for dissatisfying interactions.
2. Each service encounter questionnaire reflects the events and behaviors associated with an encounter that is memorable because it is either particularly satisfying or particularly dissatisfying. The respondents were employees of restaurants, airlines and hotels. However, they were asked to take the customer's point of view in responding to the questions. Thus, the data reflect employees' remembrances of times when customers had particularly dis/satisfying encounters with their firms.
3. You will be asked to categorize each incident into one of 16 categories, based on the key factor that triggered the dis/satisfying incident. Sorting rules and definitions of categories are detailed below.
4. It is suggested that you read through each entire service encounter before you attempt to categorize it. If an incident does not appear to fit within any of the 16 categories, put it aside. In addition, do not attempt to categorize incidents that do not meet the basic criteria. An incident must: (A) include employee-customer interaction, (B) be very satisfying or dissatisfying from the customer's point of view, (C) be a discrete episode, and (D) have sufficient detail to be visualized by the interviewer.

Coding Rules

Each incident should be categorized within one category only. Once you have read the incident, you should begin asking the following questions in order to determine the appropriate category. Definitions of the categories are attached.

1. Is there a service delivery system failure? That is, is there an initial failure of the core service that causes the employee to respond in some way? Is it the employee's response that causes the event

to be remembered as highly satisfactory or dissatisfactory?

If the answer is *yes,* place the incident in Group 1. Then ask, what type of failure? (A) unavailable service; (B) unreasonably slow service; (C) other core service failures.

If the answer is *no,* go on to question 2.

2. Is there an explicit or implicit request or need for accommodation or extra service(s)? That is, is the customer asking (either explicitly or implicitly) that the system be somehow adjusted to accommodate him/her? Is it the employee's response that causes the event to be remembered as highly satisfactory or dissatisfactory?

If the answer is *yes,* place the incident in Group 2. Then ask what type of need/request is triggering the incident: (A) "special needs" customer; (B) customer preferences; (C) admitted customer error; (D) potentially disruptive other customers.

If the answer is *no,* go on to question 3.

3. Is there an unprompted and unsolicited action on the part of the employee that causes the dis/satisfaction? (Since this follows rules 1 and 2, it obviously implies that there is no service failure and non explicit/implicit request.)

If the answer is *yes,* place the incident in Group 3. Then, ask what type of unprompted and unsolicited action took place; (A) attention paid to customer; (B) truly out-of-the-ordinary action; (C) employee behaviors in the context of cultural norms; (D) gestalt evaluation; (E) exemplary performance under adverse circumstances.

If the answer is *no,* go to question 4.

4. Does the dis/satisfaction stem from the actions/attitudes/behaviors of a "problem customer"? That is, rather than the dis/satisfaction being attributable to an action or attitude of the employee, is the root cause actually the customer?

If the answer is *yes,* place the incident in Group 4. Then, ask what type of behavior is causing the problem: (A) drunkenness; (B) verbal/physical abuse; (C) breaking/resisting company policies or laws; (D) uncooperative customer.

If the answer is *no,* put the incident aside.

CIT Classification System—Definitions

Group 1. Employee response to service delivery system failure (failure in the core service, e.g., the hotel room, the restaurant meal service, the flight, system failures).

A. Response to unavailable service (services that should be available are lacking or absent, e.g., lost hotel room reservation, overbooked airplane, unavailable reserved window table).
B. Response to unreasonably slow service (services or employee performances are perceived as inordinately slow). (Note: When service is both slow and unavailable, use the *triggering* event.)
C. Response to other core service failures (e.g., hotel room not clean, restaurant meal cold or improperly cooked, damaged baggage).

Group 2. Employee response to customer needs and requests (when the customer requires the employee to adapt the service delivery system to suit his/her unique needs, contains either an explicit or inferred request for customized [from the customer's point of view] service).

A. Response to "special needs" customers (customers with medical, dietary, psychological, language, or sociological difficulties; children; elderly customers).
B. Response to customer preferences (when the customer makes "special" requests due to personal preferences; this includes times when the customer requests a level of service customization clearly beyond the scope of or in violation of policies or norms).
C. Response to admitted customer error (triggering event is a customer error that strains the service encounter, e.g., lost tickets, incorrect order, missed reservations).
D. Response to potentially disruptive others (when other customers exhibit behaviors that potentially strain the encounter, e.g., intoxication, rudeness, deviance).

Group 3. Unprompted and unsolicited employee actions (events and behaviors that are truly unexpected from the customer's point of view, not triggered by a service failure, and show no evidence of the customer having a special need or making a special request).

A. Attention paid to customer (e.g., making the customer feel special or pampered, ignoring or being impatient with the customer).

B. Truly out-of-the-ordinary employee behavior (particularly extraordinary actions or expressions of courtesy, or profanity, inappropriate touching, violations of basic etiquette, rudeness).

C. Employee behaviors in the context of cultural norms (norms such as equality, honesty, fairness, discrimination, theft, lying, or refraining from the above when such behavior was expected).

D. Gestalt evaluation (no single feature stands out, instead "everything went right" or "everything went wrong").

E. Exemplary performance under adverse circumstances (when the customer is particularly impressed or displeased with the way an employee handles a stressful situation).

Group 4. Problematic customer behavior (customer is unwilling to cooperate with laws, regulations, or the service provider; this includes rudeness, abusiveness, or a general unwillingness to indicate satisfaction with the service regardless of the employee's efforts).

A. Drunkenness (in the employee's perception, the customer is clearly intoxicated and creating problems, and the employee has to handle the situation).

B. Verbal and physical abuse (the customer verbally and/or physically abuses either the employee or other customers, and the employee has to handle the situation).

C. Breaking/resisting company policies or laws (the customer refuses to comply with policies [e.g., showing airplane ticket to the flight attendant before boarding] or laws [e.g., use of illegal drugs in the hotel room], and the employee has to enforce compliance).

D. Uncooperative customer (customer is generally rude and uncooperative or extremely demanding; any efforts to compensate for a perceived service failure are rejected; customer may appear unwilling to be satisfied; and the employee has to handle the situation).

REFERENCES

Berry, Leonard L. and A. Parasuraman (1991), *Marketing Services*. New York: The Free Press.

Biddle, B.J. (1986), "Recent Developments in Role Theory," *Annual Review of Sociology*, 12, 67–92.

Bird, Laura (1993), "The Clients That Exasperate Madison Avenue," *Wall Street Journal* (November 2), B1.

Bitner, Mary Jo, Bernard H. Booms, and Mary Stanfield Tetreault (1990), "The Service Encounter: Diagnosing Favorable and Unfavorable Incidents," *Journal of Marketing*, 54 (January), 71–84.

Bloom, Paul N. (1984), "Effective Marketing for Professional Services," *Harvard Business Review* (September/October), 102–10.

Bowen, David E. (1986), "Managing Customers as Human Resources in Service Organizations," *Human Resource Management*, 25 (3), 371–83.

Brown, Stephen W. and Teresa A. Swartz, (1989) "A Gap Analysis of Professional Service Quality," *Journal of Marketing*, 53 (April), 92–98.

Business Week (1991), Special Issue on Quality.

Crosby, Lawrence A. (1991), "Expanding the Role of CSM in Total Quality," *International Journal of Service Industry Management*, 2(2), 5–19.

Dahl, Jonathan (1992), "Rental Counters Reject Drivers Without Good Records," *Wall Street Journal* (October 23), B1.

Dornoff, Ronald J. and F. Robert Dwyer (1981), "Perceptual Differences in Market Transactions Revisited: A Waning Source of Consumer Frustration," *The Journal of Consumer Affairs*, 15 (Summer), 146–57.

Ericsson, K. Anders and Herbert A. Simon (1980), "Verbal Reports as Data," *Psychological Review*, 87 (May), 215–50.

Fiske, Susan T. and Shelley E. Taylor (1984), *Social Cognition*. Reading, MA: Addison-Wesley.

Flanagan, John C. (1954), "The Critical Incident Technique," *Psychological Bulletin*, 51 (July), 327–58.

Folkes, Valerie S. and Barbara Kotsos (1986), "Buyers' and Sellers' Explanations for Product Failure: Who Done It?" *Journal of Marketing*, 50 (April), 74–80.

Gremler, Dwayne and Mary Jo Bitner (1992), "Classifying Service Encounter Satisfaction Across Industries," in *Marketing Theory and Applications*, Chris T. Allen et al., eds. Chicago: American Marketing Association, 11–18.

Heskett, James L., Thomas O. Jones, Gary W. Loveman, W. Earl Sasser, Jr., and Leonard A. Schlesinger (1994), "Putting the Service-Profit Chain to Work," *Harvard Business Review* (March/April), 164–72.

Heskett, James L., W. Earl Sasser, Jr., and Christopher W. L. Hart (1990), *Service Breakthroughs*. New York: The Free Press.

Hochschild, Arlie Russell (1983), *The Managed Heart*. Berkeley, CA: University of California Press.

Hunt, Shelby (1991), *Modern Marketing Theory*, Cincinnati, OH: South-Western Publishing Company.

Kelley, Scott W., K. Douglas Hoffman, and Mark A. Davis (1993), "A Typology of Retail Failures and Recoveries," *Journal of Retailing*, 69 (4), 429–52.

Kingman-Brundage, Jane (1989), "The ABCs of Service System Blueprinting," in *Designing a Winning Service Strategy,* Mary Jo Bitner and Lawrence A. Crosby, eds. Chicago: American Marketing Association, 30–33.

Langeard, Eric, John E. G. Bateson, Christopher H. Lovelock and Pierre Eiglier (1981), *Services Marketing: New Insights from Consumers and Managers.* Cambridge, MA: Marketing Science Institute.

Lovelock, Christopher (1983), "Classifying Services to Gain Strategic Marketing Insights," *Journal of Marketing,* 47 (Summer), 9–20.

———— (1994), *Product Plus.* New York: McGraw-Hill.

McKelvey, Bill (1982), *Organizational Systematics: Taxonomy, Evolution, Classification.* Berkeley, CA: University of California Press.

Mohr, Lois A. and Mary Jo Bitner (1991), "Mutual Understanding Between Customers and Employees in Service Encounters," in *Advances in Consumer Research,* Vol. 18, Rebecca H. Holman and Michael R. Solomon, eds. Provo, UT: Association for Consumer Research, 611–17.

Parasuraman, A., Leonard L. Berry, and Valarie A. Zeithaml (1991), "Refinement and Reassessment of the SERVQUAL Scale," *Journal of Retailing,* 67 (4), 420–50.

Parasuraman, A., Valarie Zeithaml, and Leonard L. Berry (1988), "SERVQUAL: A Multiple-Item Scale for Measuring Consumer Perceptions of Service Quality," *Journal of Retailing,* 64 (Spring), 12–40.

———— (1990), "An Empirical Examination of Relationships in an Extended Service Quality Model," Report No. 90-122. Cambridge, MA: Marketing Science Institute.

Perreault, William D., Jr. and Laurence E. Leigh (1989), "Reliability of Nominal Data Based on Qualitative Judgments," *Journal of Marketing Research,* 26 (May), 135–48.

Resnik, Alan J. and Robert R. Harmon (1983), "Consumer Complaints and Managerial Response: A Holistic Approach," *Journal of Marketing,* 47 (Winter), 86–97.

Ronan, William W. and Gary P. Latham (1974), "The Reliability and Validity of the Critical Incident Technique: A Closer Look," *Studies in Personnel Psychology,* 6 (Spring), 53–64.

Schank, Roger C. and Robert P. Abelson (1977), *Scripts, Plans, Goals and Understanding.* New York: John Wiley and Sons, Inc.

Schlesinger, Leonard A. and James L. Heskett (1991), "The Service-Driven Service Company," *Harvard Business Review* (September/October), 71–81.

Schneider, Benjamin (1980), "The Service Organization: Climate Is Crucial," *Organizational Dynamics* (Autumn), 52–65.

Schneider, Benjamin, and David E. Bowen (1984), "New Services Design, Development and Implementation and the Employee," in *Developing New Services.* William R. George and Claudia Marshall, eds. Chicago: American Marketing Association, 82–101.

———— (1985), "Employee and Customer Perceptions of Service in Banks: Replication and Extension," *Journal of Applied Psychology,* 70(3), 423–33.

Schneider, Benjamin, John J. Parkington, and Virginia M. Buxton (1980), "Employee and Customer Perceptions of Service in Banks," *Administrative Science Quarterly,* 25 (June), 252–67.

Schrage, Michael (1992), "Fire Your Customers," *Wall Street Journal* (March 16), A8.

Services Marketing Newsletter (1989), "Recent Study Shows Gap Between Customers and Service Employees on Customer Service Perceptions," 5 (Summer), 1.

Shostack, G. Lynn (1984), "Designing Services That Deliver," *Harvard Business Review* (January/February), 133–39.

———— (1987), "Service Positioning Through Structural Change," *Journal of Marketing,* 51 (January), 34–43.

Solomon, Michael R., Carol Surprenant, John A. Czepiel, and Evelyn G. Gutman (1985), "A Role Theory Perspective on Dyadic Interactions: The Service Encounter," *Journal of Marketing,* 49 (Winter), 99–111.

White, Frank M. and Edwin A. Locke (1981), "Perceived Determinants of High and Low Productivity in Three Occupational Groups: A Critical Incident Study," *Journal of Management Studies,* 18 (4), 375–87.

Wilson-Pessano, Sandra R. (1988), "Defining Professional Competence: The Critical Incident Technique 40 Years Later," American Institutes for Research, invited address to the Annual Meeting of the American Educational Research Association, New Orleans.

Zeithaml, Valarie A., Leonard L. Berry, and A. Parasuraman (1988), "Communication and Control Processes in the Delivery of Service Quality," *Journal of Marketing,* 52 (April), 35–48.

Zeithaml, Valarie A., and Mary Jo Bitner (1996), *Services Marketing.* New York: McGraw-Hill.

Zemke, Ron and Kristin Anderson (1990), "Customers From Hell," *Training* (February), 25–33.

PART II

Focus on Customers and Managing Relationships

CHAPTER 4

Customer Behavior in Service Settings

The facts will eventually test all our theories, and they form, after all, the only impartial jury to which we can appeal.

Louis Agassiz

Understanding customer behavior lies at the heart of marketing. Why do customers buy one product and not another? Who or what influences their decisions and their brand preferences? Against what criteria do they evaluate possible alternatives? Why do they buy one type of service when a different type might have provided a better solution to their needs? And what drives these needs in the first place? Although buying patterns tend to be different between household consumers and corporate purchasers, many of these basic questions remain the same.

Once a customer has actually purchased a service, marketers need to examine how and when they use it. How does the customer interact with service facilities, service personnel, and even other customers, especially in the case of high-contact services? Finally, of course, marketers are interested in whether the experience of receiving the service and its benefits has met the customer's expectations.

In this chapter, we analyze the nature of service consumption and consider how individual consumers evaluate and purchase services. We explore such questions as the following:

1. Why are services generally harder to evaluate—both before and after consumption—than most goods?

2. How do service characteristics such as the intangibility of service performances and variability in service inputs and outputs affect consumer evaluation processes?
3. What is the nature of the purchase process for services?
4. What is the difference between core and supplementary service elements, as well as between hygiene factors and enhancing factors?
5. What is the best way to go about constructing a simple flowchart that shows a service process from the customer's perspective?

The Nature of Service Consumption

The term *consumption* is often equated in the economic literature with consumer and corporate expenditures (as in "household consumption of goods and services rose 1.2 percent in the current quarter"). In reality, the word means "the act or process of using something up." It's easy to understand how packaged goods are consumed. A soft drink is drunk, cornflakes are eaten, detergent is poured into the washing machine, and heating fuel is burned. By contrast, durables, such as appliances, garden furniture, computers, or cars, are designed to last a number of years. Their useful life can be extended through maintenance, repair, and even upgrades, but eventually they break, wear out, rust, rot, or become obsolete.

This notion of physical consumption or deterioration doesn't apply to most services. Exceptions exist as regards food and beverage services, but they are a special case. Certainly, the factors of production necessary to create services eventually need replacement. Employees leave or retire; fuel is consumed to heat, cool, or light service facilities or to operate service vehicles; furnishings suffer from wear and tear; machines break down or become obsolete; and buildings may eventually have to be reconstructed or even demolished. A key task for operations management is to ensure that all of these elements remain in good working order—through either maintenance, repair, or replacement—so that the quality of the service performance is not compromised. Grönroos captures the distinction between goods consumption and service consumption by describing the former as *output* consumption and the latter as *process* consumption.[1]

Is it even appropriate to use the term *consumer* to describe a service customer? In chapter 1, we noted that customers didn't normally obtain ownership of services. They merely acquire the right to a performance that makes use of the service firm's assets. Perhaps the single most important element that is consumed in service delivery is *time,* which is an irreplaceable resource for both customers and providers. In many instances, service organizations rent out use of their physical or intangible assets—buildings, vehicles, machines, instruments, rooms, seats, beds, and telecommunication bandwidth. Banks rent money to customers in the form of loans. Firms also let customers rent the labor and expertise of their employees. But there's an opportunity cost involved: The asset becomes unavailable for alternative uses. Similarly, customers who *spend time* using a service cannot devote that time to another purpose.

Understanding User Costs for Services

To obtain the benefits of a service performance, customers must be prepared to offer something in exchange. There are some transactions, often associated with the public sector, that require no direct financial payment—using a public library, for instance. And occasionally, a firm will give away a service free of charge as a promotion or image builder. But most services do carry a price. From a customer's standpoint, the monetary price charged by the supplier may be just the first of many costs associated with purchase and delivery of a service. Let's take a look at what's involved (as we do so, you might find it useful to review your own experiences in different service contexts).

Purchase Price plus Other Financial Expenditures. Customers often incur additional financial costs over and above the purchase price. Necessary incidental expenses may include travel to the service site, parking, and purchase of other facilitating goods or services ranging from meals to babysitting. The combined total of all these expenses (including the price of the service itself) represents the financial costs of service. However, there's more to come, because the costs of service go beyond financial outlays (see Figure 4.1).

Nonfinancial Outlays and Burdens. In most service consumption situations, customers also incur a variety of nonfinancial costs, representing the time, effort, and discomfort associated with search, purchase, and use. Customer involvement in production (which is particularly important in people-processing services and in self-service) means that customers incur such burdens as mental and physical effort and exposure to unwanted sensory experiences—such as noise, heat, and smells. Services that are hard to evaluate in advance may also create psychological burdens, such as anxiety. Nonfinancial user costs can be grouped into four distinct categories:

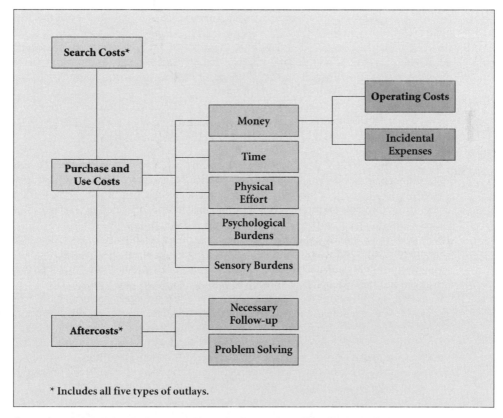

FIGURE 4.1   Determining the Total User Costs of a Service: More Than Meets the Eye?

1. *Time expenditures* are inherent in service delivery. There's an opportunity cost to customers for the time they are involved in the service delivery process because they could spend that time in other ways. They could even be working to earn additional income. Internet users are often frustrated by the amount of time they waste trying to access a Web site (not for nothing do people jest about the World Wide Wait!).

2. *Physical effort* (such as fatigue, discomfort, and occasionally even injury) may be incurred in obtaining services, especially if customers must come to the service factory and if delivery entails self-service.

3. *Psychological burdens* such as mental effort, feelings of inadequacy, or fear are sometimes attached to evaluating service alternatives, making a selection, and then using a particular service.

4. *Sensory burdens* relate to unpleasant sensations affecting any of the five senses. In a service environment they may include putting up with noise, unpleasant smells, drafts, excessive heat or cold, uncomfortable seating, visually unappealing environments, and even nasty tastes.

Customers sometimes refer to physical, psychological, and sensory burdens collectively as "effort" or "hassle."

As shown in Figure 4.1, the total costs of purchasing and using a service also include those associated with search activities. When you were looking at colleges or business schools, how much money, time, and effort did you spend before deciding where to apply? How much time and effort would you put into comparing alternative barbers or hairdressers if the one you currently patronize were to close?

There may be additional outlays after the initial service is completed. A doctor may prescribe a course of physical therapy and drugs that the patient must continue for several months. A much-resented postpurchase cost is when service failures force customers to waste time, money, and effort trying to resolve the problem.

Understanding Customer Needs and Expectations

Customers buy goods and services to meet specific needs, and they evaluate the outcomes of their purchases based on what they expect to receive. Needs are deeply rooted in people's unconscious minds and concern long-term existence and identity issues. When people feel a need, they are motivated to take action to fulfill it. Abraham Maslow identified five categories of human needs—physiological, safety, love, esteem, and self-actualization—and proposed that basic needs such as food and shelter must be met before others can be fulfilled.[2] Although poverty, malnutrition, and lack of housing remain pressing issues around the world, including North America, physiological needs have long ceased to be the sole issue for most residents of advanced industrialized countries such as the United States and Canada. Greater prosperity means that increasing numbers of individuals are seeking to satisfy social and self-actualization needs, which create demand for more sophisticated goods and services. For instance, travel and leisure services have been a major beneficiary of increased disposable income, leading many firms to develop a variety of enticing vacation packages. However, as customer needs and preferences continue to evolve, the leisure industry needs to adapt its offerings accordingly. Service Perspectives 4.1 describes how the once successful Club Med operation fell on hard times and had to undergo radical surgery to renew its appeal in a changing marketplace.

In North America, as in other highly developed regions, evidence shows that many consumers are reaching the point where they have most of the physical goods they want and are now turning to services to fill new or still unmet needs. Increased spending on more elaborate

SERVICE PERSPECTIVES 4.1

Pressures on Club Med to Evolve in Response to Changing Customer Needs

When Gilbert Trigano launched Club Med in the 1950s, the concept of holiday villages offering limitless food and innumerable sporting activities in splendid natural surroundings at a single price was unique. It also reflected a significant change in social behavior. Trigano recognized the emergence of a new, younger segment among French and other European consumers that was influenced by growing affluence and U.S. values rather than traditional formality. The Club Med concept provided an attractive form of escapism with its informality and friendly customer service from an enthusiastic staff. The atmosphere attracted a crowd that was primarily young, affluent, educated, and single. These people enjoyed sports, travel, and exotic locations. It was a burgeoning market.

By the late 1960s, Club Med, with its communal lifestyle—which included shared huts, group activities, and large dining tables designed to break down social barriers between guests—had captured the spirit of the times. In the 1970s and 1980s, as standards of living and status-seeking behavior continued to grow, leisure (in all its aspects) became a much more important part of people's lives. Club Med opened villages around the world and epitomized the ultimate leisure experience: a relatively expensive holiday, either at the beach or (later) at winter ski villages in the mountains.

Yet 10 years later, problems began to emerge. The group's financial situation weakened, and there was widespread criticism that the Club Med concept had become outmoded. Younger people, critics claimed, were now more individualistic and no longer keen on the kinds of sybaritic, group activities for which Club Med was renowned. Finding young, new customers was becoming harder and harder. Meantime, the club's most loyal customers had grown older and considered new criteria for leisure opportunities. Rather than seeking ways to have fun as swinging singles, these guests were concerned about what to do with their children on vacation and how to achieve a healthy lifestyle, including nutritious food, low-impact exercises, and other ways to restore physical and emotional well-being. By 1990, the conspicuous consumption of the 1980s was giving way to more emphasis on value for money. The emergence of low-price, all-inclusive holiday package tours was eroding Club Med's traditional customer base, yet the club had not lowered its own prices in response.

After huge losses in 1996, the Trigano family was ousted from the daily running of the company, and Philippe Bourguignon—who had turned Disneyland Paris around—was brought in to revive the club. In his words, "Club Med has tried to be everything for everyone. But you have to make choices." His plan was to enhance value for money, attract a younger clientele, and extend the vacation season by providing services such as entertainment, sports, and cafés throughout the year rather than simply during an annual holiday. His approach was aimed at meeting the needs of two very different kinds of segments—the younger, value-conscious market that Club Med had not yet succeeded in winning over and the mature group of customers who had been the backbone of Club Med's past success but whose loyalty was now at risk.

To meet the needs of the former group, Bourguignon immediately closed several loss-making villages and converted a number of others into lower-priced camps, rebranded as Club Aquarius. Plans were also made to transform the traditional Club Med concept by catering more to the creature-comfort requirements of older, existing customers.

Source: Based, in part, on articles in the *Financial Times,* February 24, 1997, and October 7, 1997.

vacations, sports, entertainment, restaurant meals, and other service experiences are assuming greater priority, even at the expense of spending slightly less on physical goods. According to Daniel Bethamy of American Express, consumers want "memorable experiences, not gadgets."[3] This shift in consumer behavior and attitudes provides opportunities for those service companies that understand and meet changing needs, continuing to adapt their offerings over time as needs evolve. The notion of service experiences also extends to business and industrial situations; consider the example of modern trade shows where exhibitors, including manufacturers, set out to engage the customer's interest through interactive presentations and even entertainment.[4]

Customers' expectations about what constitutes good service vary from one business to another. For example, although accounting and veterinary surgery are both professional services, the experience of meeting an accountant to talk about your tax returns tends to be very different from visiting a vet to get treatment for your sick pet. Expectations are also likely to vary in relation to differently positioned service providers in the same industry. Although travelers expect no-frills service for a short domestic flight on a discount carrier, they would undoubtedly be very dissatisfied with that same level of service on a full-service airline flying from Los Angeles to Sydney or from Toronto to Paris, even in economy class. Consequently, it's very important for marketers to understand customer expectations of their own firm's service offerings.

How Are Expectations Formed?

When individual customers or corporate purchasing departments evaluate the quality of a service, they may be judging it against some internal standard that existed prior to the service experience.[5] Perceived service quality results from customers comparing the service they perceive they have received against what they expected to receive. People's expectations about services tend to be strongly influenced by their own prior experience as customers—with a particular service provider, with competing services in the same industry, or with related services in different industries. If they have no relevant prior experience, customers may base their prepurchase expectations on factors such as word-of-mouth comments, news stories, or the firm's marketing efforts.

Over time, certain norms develop for what to expect from service providers within a given industry. These norms are reinforced by both customer experience and supplier-controlled factors such as advertising, pricing, and the physical appearance of the service facility and its employees. For example, Americans don't expect to be greeted by a doorman and a valet at a Motel 6, but they certainly do at a Ritz-Carlton hotel, where service levels are known to be much higher. Customer expectations may also vary from one industry to another, reflecting industry reputations and past experience. In many countries, people have lower expectations of government service providers than they do of private companies. Expectations may even vary within different demographic groups (for example, between men and women, older and younger consumers, or blue- versus white-collar workers.)

To make things more complicated, expectations also differ from country to country. For instance, although it may be acceptable and unsurprising for a train to arrive several hours late in some countries, rail schedules are so precise in Switzerland that the margin for error is measured in seconds. Research Insights 4.1 compares U.S. and German expectations of banking.

The Components of Customer Expectations

Customer expectations embrace several different elements, including desired service, adequate service, predicted service, and a zone of tolerance that falls between the desired and adequate service levels.[6] The model shown in Figure 4.2 shows how expectations for desired service and adequate service are formed.

RESEARCH INSIGHTS 4.1

Comparing U.S. and German Expectations of Banking Services

A cross-cultural study tested the conventional wisdom that the United States is a more customer-centered and service-oriented society than Germany. Researchers from both countries worked together to design a self-administered questionnaire that asked respondents to rate 26 different expectations about excellent service quality and to evaluate their own banks on these factors. Overall, Americans had higher expectations for banking services than did Germans. One of the biggest differences between the two groups was that Americans expected significantly more access to technologically based services such as telephone banking. (This difference might be partly explained by the high price of telephone service in Germany, where local calls are still relatively expensive, whereas they are free in the United States, being included in the monthly subscription charge.)

U.S. customers ranked trust and friendliness as the two most important attributes of high-quality banking services, whereas Germans wanted competent investment advice and timely service delivery. Still, the two groups did agree on some things. Four of the five top-ranked expectations were the same for both countries, and both groups agreed that bank size, receiving promotional information by mail, and corporate social responsibility were low in importance.

Almost all customers, regardless of nationality, had higher expectations for service quality than their banks actually delivered. And in both countries, women had slightly higher expectations than men. However, the gap between expectations and performance was generally greater for Americans than for Germans. Even though Americans expected and received better banking service than their German counterparts, they reported a higher level of dissatisfaction. In this case, better service performance did not lead to increased perceptions of service quality—perhaps because it created even higher expectations!

Source: Terrence Witkowski and Joachim Kellner, "How Germans and Americans Rate Their Banking Services," *Marketing News,* October 7, 1996, 7.

Desired and Adequate Service Levels. *Desired service* is the type of service customers hope to receive. It is a wished-for level of service—a combination of what customers believe can be and should be delivered in the context of their personal needs. However, most customers are realistic and understand that companies can't always deliver the level of service they would prefer; hence, they also have a threshold level of expectations, termed *adequate service,* which is defined as the minimum level of service customers will accept without being dissatisfied. Among the factors that set this expectation are situational factors affecting service performance and the level of service that might be anticipated from alternative suppliers. The levels of both desired and adequate service expectations may reflect explicit and implicit promises by the provider, word-of-mouth comments, and the customer's past experience (if any) with this organization.[7]

Predicted Service. The level of service customers actually anticipate receiving is known as *predicted service* and directly affects how they define adequate service on any given occasion. If good service is predicted, the adequate level will be higher than if poorer service is predicted. Customer predictions of service may be situation specific. For example, from past experience, customers visiting a museum on a summer day may expect to see larger crowds if the weather is poor than if the sun is shining. So a 10-minute wait to buy tickets on a cool, rainy day in summer might not fall below their adequate service level.

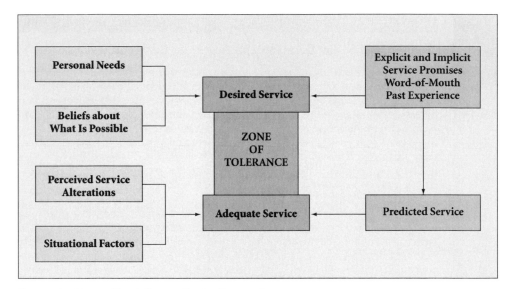

FIGURE 4.2   Factors That Influence Service Expectations
Source: Adapted from Valarie A. Zeithaml, Leonard A. Berry, and A. Parasuraman, "The Nature and Determinants of Customer Expectations of Service," *Journal of the Academy of Marketing Science* 21, no. 1 (1993): 1–12.

Zone of Tolerance. As discussed in chapter 1, the inherent nature of services makes consistent service delivery difficult across employees in the same company and even by the same service employee from one day to another. The extent to which customers are willing to accept this variation is called the *zone of tolerance* (refer back to Figure 4.2). A performance that falls below the adequate service level will cause frustration and dissatisfaction, whereas one that exceeds the desired service level will both please and surprise customers, creating what is sometimes referred to as *customer delight.* Another way of looking at the zone of tolerance is to think of it as the range of service within which customers don't pay explicit attention to service performance.[8] By contrast, when service falls outside the range, customers will react either positively or negatively.

The zone of tolerance can increase or decrease for individual customers depending on factors such as competition, price, or importance of specific service attributes. These factors most often affect adequate service levels (which may move up or down in response to situational factors), whereas desired service levels tend to move up very slowly in response to accumulated customer experiences. Consider a small-business owner who needs some advice from her accountant. Her ideal level of professional service may be a thoughtful response by the next business day. But if she makes the request at the time of year when all accountants are busy preparing corporate and individual tax returns, she will probably know from experience not to expect a fast response. Although her ideal service level probably won't change, her zone of tolerance for response time may be much broader because she has a lower adequate service threshold.

How Customers Evaluate Service Performances

Service performances—especially those that are contain few tangible clues—can be difficult to evaluate. As a result, there is a greater risk of making a purchase that proves to be disappointing. Customers who have purchased a physical good that subsequently proves to be a poor choice can often recover easily from their mistake (for instance, they can return a defective CD player, exchange clothing that is the wrong size, or have a car repaired under warranty). These options are not as readily available with services, although recovery is easier for some types of service than others. Consider the four categories of service introduced in chapter 2. In the case of possession-processing services, repeating the performance may be an acceptable option. For example, a cleaning service can reclean an office if a customer complains about the quality of the job. By contrast, people-processing services that are performed on people's bodies may be hard to reverse. After all, a bad haircut must be grown out, and the consequences of a faulty surgical operation or a poorly done tattoo may last forever!

Mental stimulus–processing services such as education, live entertainment, or sporting events can also be difficult to replace if quality does not meet customers' expectations. Theatergoers cannot realistically ask for their money back if actors perform their roles poorly or the script is bad, and neither can sports fans expect refunds if their favorite team plays badly (instead, they use other methods to let the players know of their dissatisfaction!). Similarly, universities don't usually compensate students for poor-quality classroom experiences. Even if a college were willing to let dissatisfied students repeat classes free of charge with a different instructor, those students would still incur significant extra time and mental effort.

Finally, information-based services can present challenges for customers when service quality is unsatisfactory. Banking or accounting errors may not be noticed until later, by which time damage may have been done to a customer's reputation (for instance a check was returned rather than paid or a faulty tax return was filed). Customers who receive a consulting recommendation or medical opinion that makes them dubious have the option of seeking a second opinion, but that will involve extra money, time, and worry.

A Continuum of Product Attributes

One of the basic differences between goods and services (discussed in chapter 1) is that services are harder for customers to evaluate. All products can be placed on a continuum ranging from "easy to evaluate" to "difficult to evaluate" depending on whether they are high in search attributes, experience attributes, or credence attributes.[9] These three attribute categories provide a useful framework for understanding how consumers evaluate different types of market offerings. As shown in Figure 4.3, most physical goods are located toward the left of the spectrum, with services to the middle or right.

Search Attributes. Physical goods tend to emphasize those attributes that allow customers to evaluate a product before purchasing it. Features such as style, color, texture, taste, and sound allow prospective consumers to try out, taste-test, or test-drive the product prior to purchase. These tangible attributes help customers understand and evaluate what they will get in exchange for their money and reduces the sense of uncertainty or risk associated with the purchase occasion. Goods such as clothing, furniture, cars, electronic equipment, and foods are high in search attributes.

Experience Attributes. These are properties that can't be evaluated prior to purchase. Customers must experience these features to know what they are getting. Holidays, live entertainment performances, sporting events, and restaurants fall into this category. Although people can examine brochures, scroll through Web sites that explain the features of a holiday destination, view travel films, or read reviews by travel experts, they can't really evaluate or feel the dramatic beauty associated with (for example) hiking in the Canadian Rockies or the magic of scuba diving in the Caribbean until they actually experience these activities. And neither can customers always rely on information from friends, family, or other personal sources when eval-

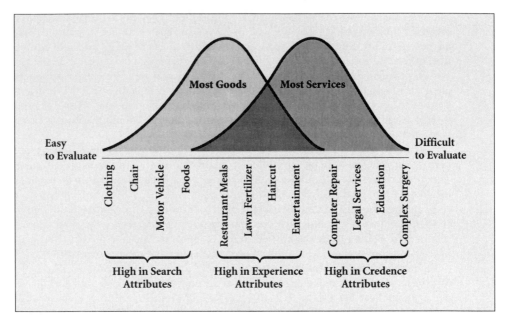

FIGURE 4.3   How Product Characteristics Affect Ease of Evaluation
Source: Adapted from Valarie A. Zeithaml, "How Consumer Evaluation Processes Differ Between Goods and Services," in *Marketing of Services,* ed. J. H. Donnelly and W. R. George (Chicago: American Marketing Association, 1981).

uating these or other types of services. Consider your own experiences in following up recommendations from friends to see a particular film. Although you probably walked into the theater with high expectations, you would have felt disappointed after viewing the film if it did not live up to your expectations. Different people may interpret or respond to the same stimuli in different ways.

Credence Attributes. Product characteristics that customers find impossible to evaluate confidently even after purchase and consumption are known as *credence attributes* because the customer is forced to trust that certain benefits have been delivered even though it may be hard to document them. For example, relatively few people possess enough knowledge about financial markets to assess whether their stockbroker got the best possible returns on their invested funds. Patients can't usually evaluate how well their dentists have performed complex dental procedures. And most college students must simply have faith that their professors are providing them with a worthwhile educational experience!

In summary, most services tend to be located from the center to the right of the continuum, reflecting two of the basic differences between goods and services that we discussed in chapter 1: intangibility of service performances and variability of inputs and outputs (which often leads to quality control problems). These characteristics present special challenges for service marketers, requiring them to find ways to reassure customers and reduce the perceived risks associated with buying and using services whose performance and value can't easily be predicted.

Strategic Responses to the Intangibility of Service Performances

Marketers whose products are high in experience characteristics often try to provide more search attributes for their customers. One approach is to offer a free trial. Some providers of online computer services have adopted this strategy. For example, America Online (AOL) offers potential users a free software diskette and the chance to try its services without charge for a certain number of hours. This reduces customers' concerns about entering into a paid contract without first being able to test the service. AOL hopes that consumers will be hooked on its Web services by the end of the free trial period.

Advertising is another way to help customers visualize service benefits when there are few inherent search attributes. For instance, the only tangible thing that holders of a credit card get directly from the company is a small plastic card, followed at monthly intervals by an account statement. But that's hardly the essence of the service provided. Think about the credit card advertisements you've seen recently. Did they promote the card itself, or did they feature exciting products that you could purchase and exotic places to which you could travel by using your card? Such advertisements stimulate consumer interest by showing physical evidence of the benefits of credit card use.

Providers of services that are high in credence characteristics have an even greater challenge. Their benefits may be so intangible that customers can't evaluate the quality of what they've received even *after* the service has been purchased and consumed. In this case, marketers often try to provide tangible cues to customers about their services. For example, some high-contact services design their facilities to provide customers with physical evidence of service quality. Professionals such as doctors, architects, and lawyers often display their degrees and other certifications for the same reason—they want customers to see the credentials that qualify them to provide expert service. Many professional firms have developed Web sites to inform prospective clients about their services, highlight their expertise, and even showpiece successful past engagements.

Variability and Quality Control Problems

The continuum of product attributes in Figure 4.3 also has implications for another distinguishing service characteristic—the degree of customer involvement in the production process. Quality is relatively easier to control in a manufacturing environment than in most services because the elements of production can be more closely monitored and failures spotted before the product is sold to the customer. However, quality control for services that fall in the experience and credence ranges is more difficult because production often involves customer involvement.

Customers' evaluations of such services often involve clues provided by the physical setting of the business, employees, and even other customers. For example, your experience in purchasing a haircut combines the following factors: your impression of the barbershop or hair salon, how well you can describe what you want to the barber or hairstylist, this individual's ability to understand and deliver what you've requested, and the appearance of other customers and workers in the shop. Barbers and hairdressers will tell you, if asked, that it is difficult for them to do a good job if customers don't cooperate during service delivery.

Many credence products are pure services that possess few (or no) tangible features so that customers must rely on the expertise of a professional service provider to deliver a satisfactory offering. In such instances, it's important that providers be able to interact with customers effectively and educate them as to the nature of both the process and the outcome. Sometimes, as in medicine, this outcome is uncertain. Doctors with good personal skills often excel at explaining to patients the range of possible outcomes from a particular course of treatment, thus minimizing unpleasant surprises (and even reducing the risk of subsequent malpractice suits).

Misunderstanding the nature of the service can also lead to disappointment. Consider the case of an architectural firm that designs a building that, it believes, closely matches the features desired by a client. And yet the customer is disappointed by the completed structure and feels that the architect has delivered a poor-quality product. What has gone wrong? Possible explanations may include the client's inability to clarify exactly what was needed or to interpret from the plans what the architect was proposing. Alternatively, the builder may not have executed the plans accurately or may have cut costs in places that affected the building's appearance and structural integrity. What should an architect do to prevent such situations from occurring? A first step is to ensure good two-way communications with customers, thereby helping them to articulate their needs and priorities and subsequently review and comment on the proposed architectural design. Increasingly, computer technology is being used to create simulations for clients. For instance, virtual reality enables a client to walk around both the interior and exterior of a proposed building and to experience visually the impact of changes in dimensions, layout, building materials, and design. They can even see how the building will appear when the sun is in different positions or with different landscaping.

Service providers must work hard to keep the quality of their products consistent over time. This is more difficult when production involves direct interaction with service employees, whose performances are likely to vary from one day to another. But customers don't want variations in service quality, as Michael Flatley, the Irish founder, director, and former lead dancer of *Lord of the Dance* knows. In a television interview not long before his retirement from dancing, he observed: "The people who drive hundreds of miles to see this show . . . they don't want to know I'm almost 39 . . . they don't want to know my legs are sore . . . they don't want to know I go home and put my feet in ice. They just want to know that what they're seeing is the best show ever—tonight, not tomorrow night!"[10] Flatley's insistence on providing the best performance possible every time has produced results—his company achieves sold-out performances around the world, and audiences often show their appreciation by giving the dancers a standing ovation. He himself has moved from dancing to producing the shows.

How Perceived Quality Relates to Satisfaction

Although the terms *quality* and *satisfaction* are sometimes used interchangeably, researchers stress the need for greater precision. Zeithaml and Bitner, for example, portray satisfaction as a broader concept, arguing that perceived service quality is but one component of customer satisfaction, which also reflects price-quality tradeoffs and personal and situational factors.[11]

Satisfaction can be defined as an attitude—like judgment following a purchase act or a series of consumer-product interactions.[12] Most studies are based on the theory that the confirmation or disconfirmation of preconsumption product standards is the essential determinant of satisfaction. So, in a service context, the model argues that customers have certain service standards in mind prior to consumption (their expectations), observe service performance and compare it with their standards, and then form satisfaction judgments based on this comparison. The resulting judgment is labeled *negative disconfirmation* if the service is worse than expected, *positive disconfirmation* if better than expected, and simple *confirmation* if as expected.[13] When there is substantial positive disconfirmation plus pleasure and an element of surprise, then customers are likely to be delighted (for a discussion of customer delight, see Research Insights 4.2).

Why is satisfaction important to service managers? There's evidence of strategic links between the level of customer satisfaction and a firm's overall performance. As Fournier and Mick declare, "Customer satisfaction is central to the marketing concept. . . . [I]t is now com-

RESEARCH INSIGHTS 4.2

Customer Delight: Going beyond Satisfaction

Managers of companies that are known for their commitment to quality have declared that satisfaction is not enough, making comments such as "we must take quality beyond customer satisfaction to customer delight" and "sheer survival means companies have to deliver more than customer satisfaction." Their views reflect findings that there is often a low correlation between satisfaction and customer loyalty.

But what is *delight?* Is it more than just a very high level of satisfaction? One view is that achieving delight requires focusing on what is currently unknown or unexpected by the customer. In short, it's more than just avoiding problems—the so-called zero-defects strategy.

Seeking to answer such questions, researchers from Vanderbilt University in the United States and the University of Auckland in New Zealand undertook a detailed literature review and then performed two exploratory studies of consumers who were patronizing specific services.

In the first study, patrons of a recreational wildlife theme park were approached as they entered the facility and asked if they would participate in an attitude survey of the park. As they were about to leave the park, they were given a questionnaire to complete and promised a small discount coupon for the park's gift shop as an incentive. Of the 124 visitors who were approached, 90 provided questionnaires with valid responses. The second survey involved single-ticket purchasers for a symphony concert in a large city. In this case, the incentive took the form of complimentary tickets to a future performance. Of 150 concert goers who were approached, 104 provided usable surveys.

The subjects were asked how the experience compared to their expectations (from much better to much worse), how satisfied they were with the park/symphony compared to their expectations of satisfaction (from much more satisfied to much less satisfied), how frequently during their visit they felt each of a variety of specific emotions (such as surprised, happy, and delighted), how satisfied they were with their decision to visit the park/symphony, and how likely they were to return.

Detailed analysis of the resulting data showed that delight was a function of three components:

1. Unexpectedly high levels of performance
2. Arousal (e.g., surprise, excitement)
3. Positive affect (e.g., pleasure, joy, or happiness)

Satisfaction, by contrast, proved to be a function of only disconfirmed expectations (better than expected) and positive affect. The authors concluded that their tentative conceptual framework lent support to the managerial belief that achieving customer delight is a separate goal from simply achieving satisfaction. But they cautioned: "If delight is a function of surprisingly unexpected pleasure, is it possible for delight to be manifest in truly mundane services and products, such as newspaper delivery or trash collecting?" They argued that consumers must have sufficient involvement in a service for aroused emotion to be part of the consumption experience and that there must be a sufficient range of very pleasing performances so that the potential to surprise the customer actually exists.

Source: Richard L. Oliver, Roland T. Rust, and Sajeev Varki, "Customer Delight: Foundations, Findings, and Managerial Insight," *Journal of Retailing* 73 (fall 1997): 311–336.

mon to find mission statements designed around the satisfaction notion, marketing plans and incentive programs that target satisfaction as a goal, and consumer communications that trumpet awards for satisfaction achievements in the marketplace."[14]These two researchers believe that satisfaction is an active, dynamic process that evolves over time and shouldn't be construed only from the perspective of a single transaction. Their findings suggest that the (dis)satisfactions of other relevant household members often contribute to an individual consumer's (dis)satisfaction. (Although there's a lack of formal research into customer satisfaction with business services, we can hypothesize that similar patterns of influence would be found among the different individuals who collectively make purchasing decisions for a company.)

Customer satisfaction is not an end in itself. Instead, it's the means to achieving a number of key business goals (Figure 4.4). First, satisfaction is inextricably linked to customer loyalty and relationship commitment. Second, highly satisfied (delighted) customers spread positive word of mouth and in effect become walking, talking advertisements for an organization whose service has pleased them, thus lowering the cost of attracting new customers. First Direct, the all-telephone bank introduced in chapter 3 (and featured as a case study on pp. 639 to 652), has gained huge numbers of new customers from recommendations by its existing account holders. Recommendations are particularly important for providers of services that are high in credence attributes, such as professional service firms. The quality of legal, accounting, consulting, and engineering services, for example, is hard to evaluate in advance of purchase, so positive comments by a satisfied client reduce the risk for a new purchaser. Third, highly satisfied customers may be more forgiving. Someone who has enjoyed good service delivery many times in the past is more likely to believe that a service failure is a deviation from the norm. Hence, it may take more than one unsatisfactory incident for strongly loyal customers to change their perceptions and consider switching to an alternative supplier. In this respect, high satisfaction acts like an insurance policy against the impact of a single failure. Finally, delighted customers are less susceptible to competitive offerings. We return to this topic in chapter 13, where we take a closer look at service quality issues.

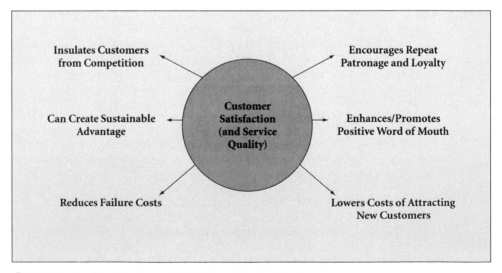

FIGURE 4.4   Benefits of Customer Satisfaction and Service Quality
Source: C. H. Lovelock, P. G. Patterson, and R. H. Waller, *Services Marketing: Australia and New Zealand* (Sydney: Prentice Hall, 1998), 119.

The Purchase Process for Services

When customers decide to buy a service to meet an unfilled need, they go through what is often a complex purchase process. This process has three separate stages—the prepurchase stage, the service encounter stage, and the postpurchase stage, each containing two or more steps (see Figure 4.5). We now describe each of these stages.

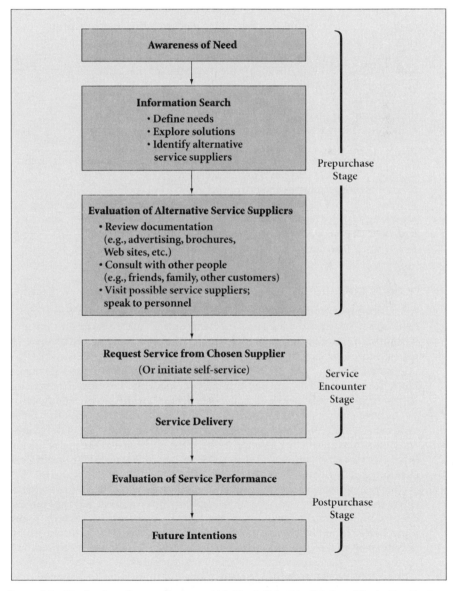

FIGURE 4.5   The Purchase Process: Customer Activities in Selecting, Using, and Evaluating Service

Prepurchase Stage

The decision to buy and use a service is made in the prepurchase stage. Individual needs and expectations are very important here because they influence what alternatives customers will consider. If the purchase is routine and relatively low risk, customers may move quickly to selecting and using a specific service provider. But when more is at stake or a service is about to be used for the first time, they may conduct an intensive information search (contrast how you approached the process of applying to college or graduate school versus buying a pizza or a hamburger!). The next step is to identify potential suppliers and then weigh the benefits and risks of each option before making a final decision.

This element of perceived risk is especially relevant for services that are high in experience or credence attributes and thus difficult to evaluate prior to purchase and consumption. First-time users are especially likely to face greater uncertainty. Risk perceptions reflect customers' judgments of the probability of a negative outcome. The worse the possible outcome and the more likely it is to occur, the higher the perception of risk. Different types of perceived risks are outlined in Table 4.1.

When customers feel uncomfortable with risks, they can use a variety of methods to reduce them during the prepurchase stage. In fact, you've probably tried some of the following risk-reduction strategies yourself before deciding to purchase a service:

- Seeking information from respected personal sources (family, friends, peers)
- Relying on a firm that has a good reputation
- Looking for guarantees and warranties
- Visiting service facilities or trying aspects of the service before purchasing
- Asking knowledgeable employees about competing services
- Examining tangible cues or other physical evidence
- Using the Internet to compare service offerings

Service Encounter Stage

After deciding to purchase a specific service, customers experience one or more contacts with their chosen service provider. These moments of truth in the service encounter often begin with submitting an application, requesting a reservation, or placing an order. As we saw in chapter 3, contacts may take the form of personal exchanges between customers and service employees or impersonal interactions with machines or computers. In high-contact services, such as restaurants, health care, hotels, and public transportation, customers may experience a variety of elements during service delivery, each of which has the potential to provide clues to service quality.

Service environments include all of the tangible characteristics to which customers are exposed. The appearance of building exteriors and interiors; the nature of furnishings and equipment; the presence or absence of dirt, odor, or noise; and the appearance and behavior of other customers can all serve to shape expectations and perceptions of service quality. We discuss these topics in more depth in chapter 11.

Service personnel are the most important factor in most high-contact service encounters, where they have direct, face-to-face interactions with customers, but they can also affect service delivery in low-contact situations, as in telephone-based service delivery. Knowledgeable customers often expect employees to follow specific scripts during the service encounter; excessive deviations from these scripts can lead to dissatisfaction. Handling service encounters effectively on the part of the employee usually combines learned skills with the right type of personality. Careful recruitment, training, compensation, and motivation are essential inputs. We discuss the necessary human resource strategies in chapter 15.

TABLE 4.1	Perceived Risks in Purchasing and Using Services
Type of Risk	Examples of Customer Concerns
Functional risk (unsatisfactory performance outcomes)	● Will this training course give me the skill I need to get a better job? ● Will this credit card be accepted wherever and whenever I want to make a purchase? ● Will the dry cleaner be able to remove the stains from this jacket?
Financial risk (monetary loss, unexpected costs)	● Will I lose money if I make the investment recommended by my stockbroker? ● Will I incur lots of unanticipated expenses if I go on this vacation? ● Will repairing my car cost more than the original estimate?
Temporal risk (wasting time, consequences of delays)	● Will I have to wait in line before entering the exhibition? ● Will service at this restaurant be so slow that I will be late for my afternoon meeting? ● Will the renovations to our bathroom be completed before our friends come to stay with us?
Physical risk (personal injury or damage to possessions)	● Will I get hurt if I go skiing at this resort? ● Will the contents of this package get damaged in the mail? ● Will I fall sick if I travel abroad on vacation?
Psychological risk (personal fears and emotions)	● How can I be sure this aircraft won't crash? ● Will the consultant make me feel stupid? ● Will the doctor's diagnosis upset me?
Social risk (how others think and react)	● What will my friends think of me if they learn I stayed at this cheap motel? ● Will my relatives approve of the restaurant I have chosen for the family reunion dinner? ● Will my business colleagues disapprove of my selection of an unknown law firm?
Sensory risk (unwanted impacts on any of the five senses)	● Will I get a view of the parking lot from my room, rather than the beach? ● Will the bed be uncomfortable? ● Will I be kept awake by noise from the guests in the room next door? ● Will my room smell of stale cigarette smoke? ● Will the coffee at breakfast taste disgusting?

Support services are made up of the materials and equipment plus all of the backstage processes that allow frontstage employees to do their work properly. This element is critical, because many customer-contact employees can't perform their jobs well without receiving internal services from support personnel. As an old service-firm axiom goes: "If you aren't servicing the customer, you are servicing someone who is."[15]

When customers use a people-processing service, they often find themselves in close proximity to other customers. Waiting rooms at a medical clinic may be filled with other patients; trains, buses, or aircraft are usually carrying many passengers at once, requiring travelers to sit next to strangers. Similarly, restaurants serve many patrons simultaneously, and a successful play or film will attract a large audience (in fact, the absence of an audience is a bad sign!). Unfortunately, as we noted in chapter 3, some of these other customers occasionally behave badly, thus detracting from the service experience. Managers need to anticipate such incidents and have contingency plans in place for how to deal with the different types of problems that might occur.

Postpurchase Stage

During the postpurchase stage, customers continue a process they began in the service encounter stage—evaluating service quality and their satisfaction or dissatisfaction with the service experience. The outcome of this process will affect their future intentions, such as whether to remain loyal to the provider that delivered service and whether to pass on positive or negative recommendations to family members and other associates.

Customers evaluate service quality by comparing what they expected with what they perceive they received. If their expectations are met or exceeded, they believe they have received high-quality service. If the price-quality relationship is acceptable and other situational and personal factors are positive, then these customers are likely to be satisfied. As a result, they are more likely to make repeat purchases and become loyal customers. However, if the service experience does not meet customers' expectations, they may complain about poor service quality, suffer in silence, or switch providers in the future.

Evaluating the Service Offering

Because the consumer evaluation and purchase processes are more complex for services, it's especially important that service managers understand how customers view the totality of the service offering (sometimes referred to as the *service package.*) One of the best and most customer-oriented definitions of a service offering comes from FedEx. Early in the company's history, its senior managers decided to define service very simply as "all actions and reactions that customers perceive they have purchased." This statement views service through the customers' eyes. Hence, it can be applied to any business and clarifies that service is a bundle consisting of the core product plus a cluster of supplementary services.

Increasing Customers' Perceptions of Value

Whatever the business, companies have to think in terms of performing well on all actions and reactions that customers perceive they are purchasing. And they need to be clear about which of these various interactions constitutes the core product and which represent supplementary service elements. The core product, as noted in chapter 2, provides the central benefit that addresses specific customer needs. It defines the fundamental nature of a company's business— lodging, transportation, cleaning, and so forth. Supplementary service elements supply additional benefits to enhance the core product and differentiate it from competitors' offerings. In FedEx's case, the core product is time-definite shipping and delivery of packages. For small-business users, supplementary services may include requests for pickup, information, free packaging in the form of envelopes and small boxes, pickup (or collection from a drop box), insurance, delivery, access to a Web site for tracing the progress of packages and confirming shipment, problem solving, and billing.

In most businesses—both service and manufacturing—the core product tends to become a commodity as competition increases and the industry matures. In natural resources, such as oil, minerals, or agricultural produce, the product may begin life as a commodity. It's very difficult to protect innovative products from imitation by competitors (brand names and proprietary software are among the few aspects of service design that can be legally protected). Even in manufacturing, where inventions can be patented, it's becoming increasingly difficult to sustain product leadership. Just think about how quickly innovative new high-technology products are cloned and protective patents are circumvented!

Competing on Supplementary Service Elements

Every business that aspires to market leadership should be working to enhance existing products and to develop new ones. But achieving significant innovation in the core product is nearly always time-consuming and expensive, sometimes requiring enormous research investments. In mature product categories, such innovation only occurs infrequently. Think for a moment: What was the most recent successful *major* innovation in airline travel, financial services, hotels, dry cleaning services, or package holidays? And when did each take place?

Because significant innovation in core products seems to be an infrequent event in many industries, much of the action takes place among supplementary service elements. That's where most companies in mature industries should focus their strategic thinking for the short and medium term because supplementary services offer the best opportunity for increasing customers' perceptions of value. This idea is not a new one by any means. Almost thirty years ago, Ted Levitt observed, "We live in an age in which our thinking about what a product or service is must be quite different from what it was before. It is not so much the basic, generic, central thing we are thinking about that counts, but the whole cluster of satisfactions with which we surround it."[16] After all, customers expect companies to do a competent job on the core product— whether it's a manufactured good such as a microwave oven or a service such as cleaning a company's offices at the end of the business day. If a supplier can't perform effectively on the core task, sooner or later it will fail.

Hygiene Factors and Enhancing Factors

In a mature industry, meaningful differentiation and added value usually come from a bundle of supplementary service elements. Performing on the core product is a matter of do or die. Banks that lose their customers' money, airlines whose aircraft never arrive at their intended destinations, and architectural firms that design buildings so flawed that they subsequently collapse will soon go out of business. But there are some differences in the relative role and importance of the various supplementary services that surround (or might surround) the core product. These supplementary services can usefully be portrayed in terms of what are called *hygiene factors* and *enhancing factors.*[17] The latter, sometimes referred to as *satisfiers,* can be further divided into parity and superiority elements.

Hygiene Factors. Supplementary services characterized as hygiene factors are service elements that customers take for granted. If they are absent—or present but performed below a certain threshold level of acceptability—customers will be dissatisfied. From a strategic standpoint, they can be viewed as "do-or-decline" factors. For instance, managers are starting to find that customers expect firms to provide needed information (by phone or otherwise), take orders promptly and accurately, provide intelligible bills, and accept responsibility for problem solving as a matter of course. (Inevitably, there are some variations by industry and by country in this respect.) If an organization can't perform well on these tasks—which are generic to almost all service industries—it will appear incompetent and uncaring to its customers, and the stage will be set for a steady decline. Hygiene factors for service businesses vary from industry to industry. But companies must provide these elements at a certain threshold level just to stay in business.

Enhancing Factors. Other supplementary services can be seen as optional service extras whose presence will create satisfaction but whose absence will not necessarily cause dissatisfaction. Enhancing factors can be divided into parity and superiority elements, depending on whether the service firm seeks just to match the average service level on each element provided by those competing suppliers who also offer it or whether the firm will try to offer enhancing service elements that are distinctively superior (or even unique) relative to competing offerings.

Some years ago, Qantas Airways surveyed 2,500 passengers to determine their essential needs in air travel. The research yielded a list of 22 needs.[18] In order of priority, they ranged from no lost baggage and no damaged baggage at the top of the list to assistance with customs/immigration and on-time departures at the bottom of the list. Naumann and Jackson describe how this same list later formed the basis for a series of focus groups in which participants were asked which attributes of air travel would cause them to be extremely dissatisfied and which would lead to great satisfaction.[19]

The results are shown in Table 4.2, which groups the 22 factors according to whether they are hygiene factors or enhancing factors. The theory underlying these two groupings is that although meeting customer expectations on each of the 14 hygiene factors will avoid *dis*satisfaction, it will not necessarily lead customers to feel more satisfied. High satisfaction can only be achieved when hygiene factors meet expectations and enhancing factors are delivered at a level that exceeds customer expectations. Merely looking at a list of needs and assuming that those ranked highest should receive priority action is not a good recipe for success. (Please note that although these research findings are useful for illustrative purposes, research undertaken today might yield a slightly different set of factors, reflecting changing passenger needs and expectations as well as new airline marketing initiatives such as frequent-flyer programs. We might also anticipate differences between the business and pleasure-traveler market segments.)

In short, service marketers must decide what the basis for their organization's competitive strategy will be. When targeting a specific market segment, managers need to determine through research on which elements superior performance will yield a meaningful competitive

---

TABLE 4.2   *Hygiene Factors and Enhancing Factors in Airline Travel*

Hygiene Factors	Enhancing Factors
● No lost baggage	● Comfortable seats
● No damaged baggage	● Prompt baggage delivery
● Clean toilets	● Ample leg room
● Courteous and efficient cabin crew	● Good quality meals
● Clean and tidy cabin	● Prompt reservation service
● Comfortable cabin temperature/humidity	● Assistance with connections
● Being kept informed of delays	● Transport to cities
● Accurate arrival information to relatives/friends	● Quick/friendly airport check-in
● Well-organized boarding	
● Self-service baggage trolleys	
● On-time arrival	
● Provision of pillows/rugs	
● Assistance with customs/immigration	
● On-time departures	

Source: Earl Naumann and Donald W. Jackson, Jr., "One More Time: How Do You Satify Customers?" *Business Horizons*, May–June, 1999, 71–76.

edge and on which others it will suffice simply to offer the industry standard of performance. In a highly competitive environment, innovation often centers on creating new enhancing factors that can help distinguish the firm's service from its competitors'.

An important issue here is how long it will take before a new enhancing factor is copied by the competition and reduced to the status of a hygiene factor. For instance, once it became clear in the United Kingdom that telephone banking was here to stay, other British banks sought, with varying degrees of success, to compete with First Direct by adding telephone-based delivery systems of their own and trying to match the level of service established by the original innovator. Meanwhile, forward-looking banks in many other countries, including the United States and Canada, monitored the British experience and soon began to develop their own versions of telephone banking. In consequence, bank customers have come to expect extended-hours customer service by phone. Similarly today, many banks are observing and studying WingspanBank.com, the Internet bank, to evaluate its performance and determine what they can learn from its experience.

Managers must decide where the opportunities lie for adding distinctive extras and when the focus should be on improving basic performance. Although some supplementary elements are industry specific, many others are not (e.g., telephone information and order taking, statements and billing, and food and beverage service). We cover the topic of supplementary service elements in more detail in chapter 8, where we examine their role in providing additional value for customers.

Understanding Customer Behavior at Different Points in the Service Experience

In order to design a service that meets or exceeds the expectations of its customers, service providers must have an idea not only of what customers want but also of what they actually experience during their service encounters. In the high-contact service environments typified by most people-processing services, most customers arrive at a service site with certain expectations. Their subsequent behavior, however, may be shaped by the nature of the physical environment, the employees they encounter, the sequence in which different activities take place, and the roles that they are expected to play. Recent research suggests that consumers' expectations are continuously updated during the course of a service encounter, with final evaluations of service quality being heavily based on these updated expectations rather than on the expectations held before the encounter began.[20]

Managers and service employees are often unaware of the full extent of a typical customer's service experience. One of the most effective ways to gain insights into customer behavior during service delivery is to create a description, in sequence, of the steps that customers and employees must go through in a given service environment. These steps can be shown visually using flowcharts. Simple flowcharts were introduced in chapter 2. Here, we examine service processes in more detail. By depicting each of the contacts between customers and a service provider, flowcharts can highlight problems and opportunities in the service delivery process as it affects those customers—what we call frontstage activities.

Developing a Flowchart

Flowcharting can usefully be applied to any type of service when management needs to gain a better understanding of how the service is currently being created and delivered.[21] It is relevant to both high-contact and low-contact service environments. (An alternative term, *service blue-*

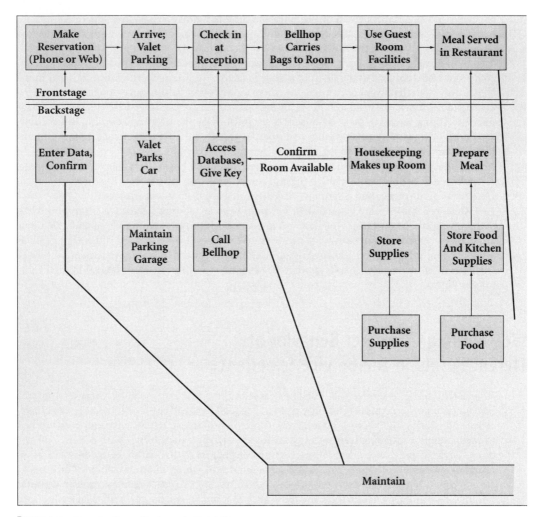

FIGURE 4.6   Flowcharting a Customer's Hotel Stay

printing, is often used when planning a new or revised process and prescribing in very specific detail how it should function.) The objectives of this exercise are threefold:

1. Understand each step in the process that constitutes the customer's overall experience with the service
2. Identify what encounters customers have with different service personnel, specific physical facilities, and equipment
3. Relate the customers' behavior and experience at each stage of the process to changes in their expectations and satisfaction.

Developing a flowchart begins by identifying each interaction that a particular type of customer has when using a specific service. Managers need to distinguish between the core product and the supplementary service elements; in fact, flowcharting is a very useful way of figuring out

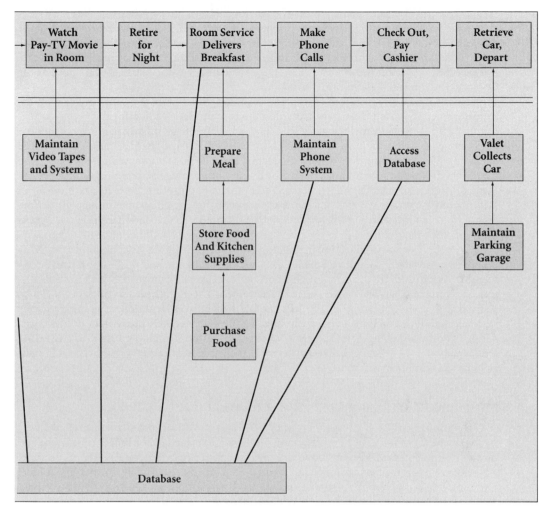

FIGURE 4.6   Flowcharting a Customer's Hotel Stay (*continued*)

what these supplementary elements actually are. The next step is to put all these interactions linearly into the sequence in which they occur. The service delivery process is like a river flowing through time: Some activities take place upstream, as it were, and others occur downstream. At each step, management needs to ask: What does the customer really want (perhaps the customer would like to speed up this step or even avoid it altogether)? And where is the potential for failure at this step?

Let's illustrate flowcharting with a simplified model of a service to which most readers can relate fairly easily: a stay at a hotel (Figure 4.6). As with many services, the customer's first encounter with a hotel involves a supplementary service rather than the core product (which is basically rental of a bedroom for a night's sleep). The initial step, for most business travelers, is to make a reservation. This action may be taken some time before the visit actually takes place.

On arrival, guests traveling by car will need to park the vehicle in the hotel's garage (perhaps a valet will do it for them). The next step is to check in at reception, after which guests may be escorted to their rooms by an employee who carries the bags. Already, four supplementary services have been delivered before a guest even reaches the room. Before retiring for the night—the core service—a guest may choose to use several more services, such as dinner at one of the hotel restaurants and watching a pay-TV movie. After rising, the guest may request that breakfast be sent up by room service and then make some phone calls, before checking out at the cashier's desk, and asking a valet to retrieve the car from the parking garage.

Figure 4.6 depicts the customer's experience, in simplified form, as a series of boxes on the frontstage portion of the flowchart. Note that the core product—a bed for the night—is surrounded by a variety of supplementary services. Some hotel guests might use more supplementary services than those shown in the flowchart; others might use fewer. A variety of activities are taking place backstage, too, behind the scenes; some of these are shown here. In fact, each step in the frontstage process is supported by a series of backstage activities, including assignment of staff; maintenance of facilities and equipment; and capture, storage, and transfer of information. As you review this flowchart, ask yourself: At what points might the poor performance by staff members or misbehavior by other customers spoil a guest's experience? And as the manager, what strategy would you plan for anticipating and handling such problems?

Many services are provided on an ongoing basis, such as utilities (telephone, gas, water, or electricity), Internet and cable or satellite TV, banking, insurance, and professional association membership. In such instances, a flowchart of service delivery might start to look quite repetitive. In retail banking, for instance, once the account has been opened, service delivery can be charted as a series of monthly cycles. Each month is slightly different, reflecting the frequency with which different services are used (for instance, how many checks are written or how many ATM withdrawals are made). Over time, changes in patterns might be observed, reflecting learning about new delivery systems and lifestyle changes that may require new types of financial services (for instance, a mortgage).

Intra-Encounter Changes in Expectations and Satisfaction

Although some service encounters are very brief and consist of just a few discrete delivery steps—such as a taxi ride or a simple haircut—others may extend over a longer time frame and involve multiple steps. A leisurely restaurant meal might stretch over a couple of hours or more, whereas a visit to a theme park might last all day. From arrival to departure, the one-night hotel visit described earlier probably lasts at least 12 to 14 hours, and the first step, the reservation, may have taken place days or even weeks prior to arrival.

As customers interact with representatives of the service firm, impersonal delivery systems such as Web sites, the physical environment of the service encounter, and—in high-contact environments—other customers, they are exposed to information that can influence both their expectations and their evaluations of the service. In chapter 3, we note how Carlzon uses the term *moments of truth* to highlight the importance of the impressions created by airline passengers' contacts with staff before, during, and after a flight. A key question for managers is whether customers' expectations change during the course of service delivery in the light of the perceived quality of sequential steps in the process. (You might want to reflect on whether your own impressions and expectations change during the course of an extended service performance.) Ideally, service firms should try to provide consistently high performance at each step in service delivery. But in reality, many service performances are inconsistent. It's commonly believed that first impressions are very important, but is that really the case? Should service providers strive to make a strongly positive initial impression as opposed to offering consistent but merely adequate performance throughout delivery or emphasizing a strong conclusion? The two laboratory studies reported in Research Insights 4.3 each seek to provide answers to such questions.

RESEARCH INSIGHTS 4.3

Learning from Laboratory Studies

A laboratory study is one that simulates real-world events in a controlled setting. In the two studies discussed here, groups of business students were given information that simulated different service experiences.

One study explored how respondents judged hypothetical service encounters in three different service categories—a weekend car rental, an international flight, and a retail purchase. Within each category, one of three scenarios was presented to participants. In the first, the initial service events were performed well, the core service was performed adequately, and the concluding steps were carried out poorly, thus creating a deteriorating trend; in the second, the situation was reversed to create an improving trend; and in the third, a consistently adequate service was delivered from start to finish. The findings showed that a weak start that built toward a strong finish received more favorable judgments than either a consistently adequate performance or a strong start accompanied by a decline in performance. The tentative conclusion to be drawn from this research is that managers who are not immediately able to raise all elements of the service encounter to a consistently high standard should begin by focusing on improving the concluding events in the process rather than the opening steps.

Another laboratory study simulated a visit to a restaurant. Respondents were presented with two scenarios in which they were going out to eat with a group of friends and were supplied with information at certain key steps during the service encounter. The findings showed that respondents continuously updated their expectations during service delivery and that these evolving expectations had a larger effect on their perceptions of service quality than did perceived service performance. A key managerial insight from this study is that it's very important for managers to shape and control customers' expectations as service delivery proceeds.

Although laboratory studies such as these have inherent limitations, their findings often challenge conventional wisdom and suggest the need for further research and experimentation under real-world conditions. Flowcharting a complex, extended service performance may suggest that certain steps deserve special management attention, not only for service improvement but also for proactive efforts to update customer expectations of the steps that will follow.

Source: David E. Hansen and Peter J. Danaher, "Inconsistent Performance during the Service Encounter," *Journal of Service Research* 1 (February 1999): 227–235; and Lawrence O. Hamer, Ben Shaw-Ching Liu, and D. Sudharshan, "The Effects of Intraencounter Changes in Expectations on Perceived Service Quality Models," *Journal of Service Research* 1 (February 1999): 275–289.

The Value of Flowcharting

In summary, flowcharting provides a means for managers to gain understanding of customer behavior in relation to underlying service processes; it is thus a necessary first step in exercising control over such procedures. Marketers find this technique particularly useful for defining the point(s) in the process at which the customer uses the core service and identifying the different supplementary services that make up the overall service package. [22] Suggestions for how to undertake flowcharting to obtain the best value from this technique are outlined in Management Memo 4.1. Managers must recognize that unless they fully understand the customer's own exposure to and involvement in a service environment, it is difficult to improve service quality and productivity. Speeding up processes and weeding out unnecessary steps to avoid wasted time and effort are often important ways to improve the perceived value of a service.

MANAGEMENT MEMO 4.1

Advice on Creating a Flowchart

Key Steps

1. Define the purpose of the flowchart clearly: What do you wish to learn (and why) about what type of service, involving what sorts of customers and under what types of usage conditions?
2. Compile a list of the activities that constitute the experience of relevant customers. Initially, keep these activities aggregated (e.g., do not decompose "board aircraft" into "hand boarding pass to agent, walk down jetway, enter aircraft, find seat, stow carry-on bag, sit down").
3. Chart each step in the customer's experience in the sequence in which it is normally encountered (alternative charts may be needed if sharply different sequences are encountered—they may be evidence of segments with differing needs or of alternative versions of the service).
4. Validate your description—solicit inputs from customers and be sure to involve relevant service personnel. (Each may have his/her understanding of the process—an open discussion may help to achieve consensus.)
5. Supplement the flowchart by a brief narrative describing the activities and their interrelationships. Be sure to identify the different players clearly.

General Advice

- Remember that there is no one, correct way to do a flowchart: Two differently structured descriptions may serve your purpose equally well.
- Note complaints by customers and personnel concerning problems at specific points in the process, because such problems provide good clues as to where you should go into greater detail, and disaggreggate broad steps such as "board aircraft" into more specific components. (The term granularity is often used to describe level of detail; the desired level is achieved when all questions have been answered.)
- If informational processes are an important issue, you may wish to show a parallel flow indicating points at which information is collected and records/databases are created, accessed, or updated.

Source: Adapted from Table 10.1 in Christopher Lovelock, *Product Plus: How Product + Service = Competitive Advantage* (New York: McGraw-Hill, 1994), 155.

When we come to discuss design of new services in chapter 8, we introduce a more detailed and structured version of the flowchart known as a *service blueprint*. Blueprinting includes setting service standards and charting the backstage activities that support each front stage activity. (These tasks are of particular value in examining service quality problems and in developing internal marketing programs designed to reach backstage personnel.)

Conclusion

Gaining a better understanding of how customers evaluate, select, use, and occasionally abuse services should lie at the heart of strategies for service design and delivery. In this chapter we discovered that several of the unique characteristics of services (especially intangibility and quality control problems) mean that customer evaluation processes often differ from those involved in evaluating physical goods and thus present unique challenges for services management, as do each of the other stages that customers go through in the purchase decision process.

Because the consumer evaluation and purchase processes for many services are often complex, it's especially important that service managers understand how customers view the service offering and the factors that determine customer expectations and satisfaction. We briefly examined the concept of core and supplemental elements, noting that the latter can be divided into hygiene factors (those that must be provided) and enhancing factors (optional extras). Achieving competitive advantage in the marketplace often centers on choosing which enhancing factors to offer and whether to match or exceed competitive performance on these optional supplementary elements.

Finally, the chapter demonstrated how to create a visual picture of the service delivery process from the customer's perspective. Flowcharts provide a step-by-step analysis of a typical customer's service encounters, indicating how a customer's experience of each step of frontstage service delivery relates to the many operational tasks performed backstage.

REVIEW QUESTIONS

1. Describe search, experience, and credence attributes and give examples of each.
2. Explain why services are often harder for customers to evaluate than physical goods.
3. How are customers' expectations formed? Explain the distinction between desired service and adequate service with reference to a recent service experience of your own.
4. What role do needs play in consumer purchase behavior?
5. Define the three stages in the purchase process for services.
6. Distinguish between the core product and supplementary service elements. Which of these provides the most opportunities for competitive advantage? Why?
7. Clarify the difference between hygiene factors and enhancing factors. What is the implication of each for competitive strategy?

APPLICATION EXERCISES

1. Choose a service that you are familiar with and create a simple flowchart of how you use it, commenting on the sequence, your expectations at each stage, and encounters with other people (staff and customers).
2. Keep a diary for a few days of the costs you incur in using at least five different services. Be sure to document monetary outlays, time expenditures, mental and physical effort, and sensory burdens for each service. What conclusions do you draw from analyzing your diary entries?

ENDNOTES

1. Christian Grönroos, "Service Reflections: Service Marketing Comes of Age," in *Handbook of Services Marketing and Management,* ed. T. Schwartz and D. Iacobucci (Thousand Oaks, CA: Sage Publications, Inc., 2000), 13–16.
2. Abraham H. Maslow, *Motivation and Personality* (New York: Harper and Brothers, 1954).
3. Stephanie Anderson Forest, Katie Kerwin, and Susan Jackson, "Presents That Won't Fit under the Christmas Tree," *Business Week,* December 1, 1997, 42.
4. B. Joseph Pine II and James H. Gilmore, "Welcome to the Experience Economy," *Harvard Business Review* 76 (July–August 1998): 97–108.

5. See Benjamin Schneider and David E. Bowen, *Winning the Service Game* (Boston: Harvard Business School Press, 1995); and Valarie A. Zeithaml, Leonard L. Berry, and A. Parasuraman, "The Nature and Determinants of Customer Expectations of Services," *Journal of the Academy of Marketing Science* 21 (1993): 1–12.

6. Valarie A. Zeithaml, Leonard L. Berry, and A. Parasuraman, "The Behavioral Consequences of Service Quality," *Journal of Marketing* 60 (1996): 35.

7. Cathy Johnson and Brian P. Mathews, "The Influence of Experience on Service Expectations," *International Journal of Service Industry Management* 8, no. 4 (1997): 46–61.

8. Robert Johnston, "The Zone of Tolerance: Exploring the Relationship between Service Transactions and Satisfaction with the Overall Service," *International Journal of Service Industry Management* 6, no. 5 (1995): 46–61.

9. Valarie A. Zeithaml, "How Consumer Evaluation Processes Differ between Goods and Services," in *Marketing of Services,* ed. J. H. Donnelly and W. R. George (Chicago: American Marketing Association, 1981).

10. Quoted from a television interview with Michael Flatley on the television news program *Dateline NBC,* October 13, 1997.

11. Valarie A. Zeithaml and Mary Jo Bitner, *Services Marketing: Integrating Customer Focus Across the Firm,* 2d ed. (Burr Ridge, IL: Irwin–McGraw-Hill, 2000), 74–75.

12. Youjae Yi, "A Critical Review of Customer Satisfaction," in *Review of Marketing 1990,* ed. V. A. Zeithaml (Chicago: American Marketing Association, 1990).

13. Richard L. Oliver, *Satisfaction: A Behavioral Perspective on the Consumer* (New York: McGraw-Hill, 1996).

14. Susan Fournier and David Glen Mick, "Rediscovering Satisfaction," *Journal of Marketing* 63 (October 1999): 5–23.

15. Bill Fromm and Len Schlesinger, *The Real Heroes of Business* (New York: Currency Doubleday, 1993), 241.

16. Theodore Levitt, "What's Your Product and What's Your Business?" chap. 2 in *Marketing for Business Growth* (New York: McGraw-Hill, 1973), 47.

17. See, for example, Barbara R. Lewis, "Service Quality: An Investigation of Customer Care in Major UK Organisations," *International Journal of Service Industry Management* 1, no. 2 (1990): 33–44; Robert Johnston, "The Determinants of Service Quality: Satisfiers and Dissatisfiers," *International Journal of Service Industry Management* 6, no. 5, 1995), 53–71; and Barbara R. Lewis, "Customer Care in Services," in *Understanding Services Management,* ed. W. J. Glynn and J. G. Barnes (Chichester, UK: John Wiley & Sons, 1995), 57–88.

18. Earl Naumann and Donald W. Jackson Jr., "One More Time: How Do You Satisfy Customers?" *Business Horizons,* May–June 1999, 71–76.

19. Lawrence O. Hamer, Ben Shaw-Ching Liu, and D. Sudharshan, "The Effects of Intraencounter Changes in Expectations on Perceived Service Quality Models," *Journal of Service Research* 1 (February 1999): 275–289.

20. For alternative approaches, see Christian Grönroos' description of the customer relationship life cycle in *Service Management and Marketing* (Lexington, MA: Lexington Books, 1990), 129–133; and Sandra Vandermerwe, "Jumping into the Customer's Activity Cycle," chap. 4 in *From Tin Soldiers to Russian Dolls* (Oxford: Butterworth Heinemann, 1993), 48–71.

21. A related tool for gaining understanding of service processes is structured analysis and design technique (SADT), which allows a service modeler to decompose a service process into successively more detailed levels to answer specific questions. For more details, see Carole Congram and Michael Epelman, "How to Describe Your Service: An Invitation to the Structured Analysis and Design Technique," *International Journal of Service Industry Management* 6, no. 2 (1995): 6–23.

CHAPTER 5

Targeting Customers, Managing Relationships, and Building Loyalty

The first step in managing a loyalty-based business system is finding and acquiring the right customers.

FREDERICK F. REICHHELD

The term *mass marketing* is used less and less these days. Instead, today's marketers are concerned with *focus* or *targeting* or *mass customization*. Underlying such terms is the notion of market segmentation. More and more firms are trying to decide which types of customers they can serve well rather than trying to be all things to all people. Managers in innovative firms constantly debate what improvements in product elements—or entirely new services—they need to offer to attract and retain customers from specific segments that are believed to present good opportunities for growth and profits. Once a firm has won customers whom it sees as desirable, the challenge shifts to building relationships: turning them into loyal customers who will do a growing volume of business with the firm in the future.

Few service businesses can survive by serving just a single segment, especially if they have a lot of productive capacity to fill over the course of the business year. In this chapter, we emphasize the importance of choosing to serve a mix—or portfolio—of several carefully chosen target segments and taking pains to build and maintain their loyalty through well-conceived relationship marketing strategies. We explore the following questions:

1. What segmentation variables are particularly relevant to service organizations?
2. Why do capacity-constrained firms need to target multiple market segments?
3. What do we mean by the concept of loyalty?

4. How can a firm calculate the financial value of a customer who remains loyal over a period of years?
5. What strategies are associated with the concept of relationship marketing?

Targeting the Right Customers

Who should we be serving? is a question that every service business needs to raise periodically. Customers often differ widely in terms of needs. They also differ in terms of the value that they can contribute to a company. Not all customers offer a good fit with the organization's capabilities, delivery technologies, and strategic direction. In short, companies should be selective about the market segments that they target.

Market segmentation is one of the most central concepts in the field of marketing, and there are many different traditional ways to segment a market. (If you have not previously taken a marketing course, you will find it useful to study the Marketing Review.) Effective market segmentation should group buyers in ways that result in similarity *within* each segment and dissimilarity *between* each segment on relevant characteristics.

The nature of services suggests that certain additional variables not commonly used in manufacturing strategies may offer advantageous approaches to segmentation, including

- Timing of service use (helpful for planning demand management strategies designed to fill available capacity at specific times)
- Level of skill and experience (especially relevant for situations in which customers will be working with a service provider as coproducers or performing self-service)
- Preferred language (important in planning marketing communications of any sort, especially face-to-face contact)
- Access to electronic delivery systems (e.g., the Internet) and attitudes toward use of new service technologies

In this chapter, we emphasize the importance in many industries of choosing to serve a mix—or portfolio—of several carefully chosen target segments and taking pains to build and maintain their loyalty. We also note that not all segments are worth serving and that it may not be realistic to try to retain them. One researcher makes this point nicely in a discussion of banking:

> A bank's population of customers undoubtedly contains individuals who either cannot be satisfied, given the service levels and pricing the bank is capable of offering, or will never be profitable, given their banking activity (their use of resources relative to the revenue they supply). Any bank would be wise to target and serve only those customers whose needs it can meet better than its competitors in a profitable manner. These are the customers who are most likely to remain with that bank for long periods, who will purchase multiple products and services, who will recommend that bank to their friends and relations, and who may be the source of superior returns to the bank's shareholders.[1]

Searching for Value, Not Just Numbers

Too many service firms still focus on the *number* of customers they serve—an important issue for operations and human resource planning—without giving sufficient attention to the *value* of each customer. Generally speaking, heavy users, who buy more frequently and in larger volumes, are more profitable than occasional users. Think about the activities that you do on a regular basis. Do you have a favorite restaurant or pizza parlor where you often eat with friends or

Identifying and Selecting Target Segments

Market segmentation is central to almost any professionally planned and executed marketing program. The concept of segmentation recognizes that customers and prospects within a market vary across a variety of dimensions and that not every segment constitutes a desirable target for the firm's marketing efforts.

Market Segments

A *market segment* is composed of a group of current and potential customers who share common characteristics, needs, purchasing behavior, or consumption patterns. Effective segmentation should group buyers into segments in ways that result in as much similarity as possible on the relevant characteristics within each segment but dissimilarity on those same characteristics between each segment. Two broad categories of variables are useful in describing the differences between segments. The first have to do with user characteristics; the second, with usage behavior

User characteristics may vary from one person to another, reflecting demographic characteristics (for instance, age, income, and education), geographic location, and psychographics (the attitudes, values, lifestyles, and opinions of decision makers and users). More recently, marketers have begun to speak of *Technographics*—a term recently trademarked by technology consulting firm Forrester Research—that groups customers according to their willingness and ability to use the latest technology. Another important segmentation variable is the specific benefits that individuals and corporate purchasers seek from consuming a particular good or service.

Usage behavior relates to how a product is purchased, delivered, and used. Among such variables are when and where purchase and consumption take place, the quantities consumed (heavy users are always of particular interest to marketers), frequency and purpose of use, the occasions under which consumption takes place (sometimes referred to as *occasion segmentation*), sensitivity to such marketing variables as advertising, pricing, speed and other service features, and availability of alternative delivery systems. Finally, there are problem customers whose misbehavior makes them very undesirable.

Target Segment

After evaluating different segments in the market, a firm should focus its marketing efforts by targeting one or more segments that fit well with the firm's capabilities and goals. Target segments are often defined on the basis of several variables. For instance, a hotel in a particular city might target prospective guests who shared such user characteristics as (1) traveling on business (demographic segmentation), (2) visiting clients within a defined area around the hotel (geographic segmentation), and (3) willing to pay a certain daily room rate (user response).

When researching the marketplace, service marketers should be looking for answers to such questions as

- In what useful ways can the market for our firm's service be segmented?
- What are the needs of the specific segments that we have identified?
- Which of these segments best fits our institutional mission and our current operational capabilities?
- What do customers in each segment see as our firm's competitive advantages and disadvantages? Are the latter correctable?
- In the light of this analysis, which specific segment(s) should we target?
- How should we differentiate our marketing efforts from those of the competition to attract and retain the types of customers that we want?
- What is the long-term financial value to us of a loyal customer in each of the segments that we currently serve (and those that we would like to serve)?
- How should our firm build long-term relationships with customers from the target segments? And what strategies are needed to create long-term loyalty?

family? Is there a movie theater that you patronize regularly? Do you ride a bus or train to work or college every weekday? Are you often to be seen at your local laundromat?

If you answered yes to any of these questions, then you are potentially a lot more interesting to the management of the organizations in question than a one-time visitor who is just passing through town. The revenue stream from your purchases—and those of others like you—may amount to quite a considerable sum over the course of the year. Sometimes your value as a frequent user is openly recognized and appreciated: You sense that the business is tailoring its service features, including service hours and prices, to attract people like you and doing its best to make you loyal. In other instances, however, you may feel that nobody knows or cares who you are. Your purchases may make you a valuable customer, but you certainly don't feel valued.

Matching customers to the firm's capabilities is vital. Managers must think carefully about how customer needs relate to such operational elements as speed and quality, the times when service is available, the firm's capacity to serve many customers simultaneously, and the physical features and appearance of service facilities. They also need to consider how well their service personnel can meet the expectations of specific types of customers in terms of both personal style and technical competence. Finally, they need to ask themselves, Can my company match or exceed competing services that are directed at the same types of customers?

Technographic Segmentation

Market segments have traditionally been defined using geographic, demographic, psychographic, or behavioral variables. Because of the dramatic increase in technology-related goods and services, some marketers are now suggesting a new segmentation variable that reflects customers' willingness and ability to use the latest technology.[2] Forrester Research has created a 10-category segmentation scheme called Technographics that is based on the interaction between three variables: attitude toward technology (optimistic versus pessimistic), financial situation (more affluent or less affluent), and application of technology (career, family, or entertainment). The resulting matrix comprises nine groups, each of which has been given a descriptive name; a tenth group called "sidelined citizens" is comprised of individuals with no interest at all in technology (see Figure 5.1). Some of the potential applications of this approach to segmentation are described in Research Insights 5.1.[3]

Segmentation Strategies for Effective Capacity Utilization

Capacity-constrained service businesses need to make the best use of their productive capacity. The problem for such businesses is to find enough customers to use their service at any given time and place. Managers should recognize the risks involved in trying to fill capacity with just any warm body. Instead, they should be asking themselves whether they have attracted the right sorts of customers at the right places, times, and prices. In people-processing services, where customers themselves become part of the product, conflicts may arise when people from distinctively different segments come together simultaneously in the same facility. Imagine the dismay among patrons at a bar that prides itself on providing a quiet and romantic environment when a group of rowdy individuals arrives, determined to raise hell.

Most businesses face fluctuations in demand over time, with predictable peak and off-peak periods. When customers from a firm's principal target segment are absent, marketers often seek to attract customers from other segments to fill capacity during periods of low demand. In general, there's less risk of customer conflicts when different segments patronize a facility at different times. In principle, if the off-peak business is financially profitable, can be handled effectively, and is not going to hurt the organization's image, then it's worth accepting. Little harm is probably done to an airline's positioning strategy if it uses its aircraft for charter flights when business demand is low. But if a hotel or restaurant gains a reputation for attracting a totally different type of customer in the off-season, there is a risk that this may negate its desired high-season image, particularly if a few high-season customers happen to visit during another season expecting to find the same types of customers and service levels as before. One solution is to be quite explicit about the different positioning strategies.

	CAREER	FAMILY	ENTERTAINMENT
OPTIMISTS	**Fast Forwards** These consumers are the biggest spenders, and they're early adopters of new technology for home, office, and personal use.	**New Age Nurturers** Also big spenders but focused on technology for home uses, such as a family PC.	**Mouse Potatoes** They like the online world for entertainment and are willing to spend for the latest in technology.
	Techno-strivers Use technology from cell phones and pagers to online services primarily to gain a career edge.	**Digital Hopefuls** Families with a limited budget but still interested in new technology; good candidates for the under-$1,000 PC.	**Gadget Grabbers** They also favor online entertainment but have less cash to spend on it.
PESSIMISTS	**Hand-shakers** Older consumers—typically managers—who don't touch their computers at work; they leave that to younger assistants.	**Traditionalists** Willing to use technology, but slow to upgrade; not convinced upgrades and other add-ons are worth paying for.	**Media Junkies** Seek entertainment and can't find much of it online; prefer TV and other, older media.
	Sidelined Citizens Not interested in technology.		

Data: Forrester Research Inc.

☐ More Affluent   ▨ Less Affluent

Figure 5.1 Segmenting Customers Relative to Technology Use
Source: Paul C. Judge, "Are Tech Buyers Different?" *Business Week,* January 26, 1998, 65.

RESEARCH INSIGHTS 5.1

Classifying Technology Users—From Mouse Potatoes to Media Junkies

As the consumer market for technology soars, companies selling products from cellular phones to Internet services are discovering that traditional segmentation tactics don't paint an accurate picture of who their customers are and what motivates them to buy. The failure of some highly publicized high-tech products has convinced many marketers that a new taxonomy is needed to describe what makes technology customers tick. They argue that although traditional consumer research may identify who bought a computer, it won't specify that four different people in a household use it—often for entirely different purposes. Market researchers have been scrambling to determine whether the purchase process is different for complex technology products—and how people actually use technology in their home and work environments.

Forrester Research has designed a study called Technographics to survey 131,000 consumers annually about their motivations, buying habits, and financial ability to buy technology goods and services. Already some big-name companies such as Sprint, Visa, Ford, and Bank of America have signed on. "Technology is not just changing the way consumers spend time," says Technographics client Gil Fuchsberg. "It's also changing the way nearly every company is making, selling and delivering products."

To help companies identify the right target customers, Forrester has defined 10 "technographical" categories ranging from the tech-crazy "fast forwards" to the disinterested "sidelined citizens." To get an idea of how this segmentation scheme works, consider the Williams family. Cindy, age 46, is an administrative secretary in Tulsa, Oklahoma. She and her husband Gary, age 44, have one computer they bought three years ago. They are not connected to the Web and don't use the computer much themselves. Their sons, ages 11 and 12, want an upgraded PC that is better for the computer-based games they love. Because of the Williams' status and income—two traditional segmentation variables—traditional consumer research results would identify them as promising technology buyers.

But Forrester maintains that these results would be misleading and that any high-tech firm marketing sophisticated products to the Williams family would be wasting its money. Technographics classifies the Williams as "traditionalists"—family-oriented buyers who could afford new technological gadgets but are unconvinced that they're worth buying. Why would the Williams be traditionalists? The age of their computer (three years old is ancient by tech standards) and the lack of an Internet connection are two big clues. Using this information, high-tech companies might decide to bypass the Williams in spite of their demographic fit because they are unlikely to be avid technology consumers.

Source: Excerpted from Paul C. Judge, "Are Tech Buyers Different?" *Business Week,* January 26, 1998, 64–68.

Customers As Part of the Service Experience

When service users share a common facility—such as a hotel, restaurant, retail store, or transport vehicle—the size and composition of the customer base has important implications for both the image of the service organization and the nature of the service experience. If you are a customer of a high-contact, shared service, you can quickly determine whether it is well or poorly patronized. You can also see what sorts of people are using the service—their appearance; age range; apparent income bracket; dress (formal or casual); and whether they appear to have come alone, in couples, or in groups. Also apparent (sometimes obtrusively so!) is how these other customers are behaving: Are they quiet or noisy, slow or active in their movements? Do they appear cheerful or glum, considerate toward others or rude?

As you know from your own experience, the way in which other customers behave can affect your own enjoyment of a service. If you like classical music and attend symphony concerts, you expect audience members to keep quiet during the performance, rather than spoiling the music by talking or coughing loudly. By contrast, a silent audience would be destroy the ambience of a rock concert or team sports event, where active audience participation usually adds to the excitement. There is a fine line, however, between spectator enthusiasm and abusive behavior by hooligan supporters of rival sports teams.

Because customers contribute strongly to the atmosphere of many high-contact services, a firm should seek to attract (and retain) customers from the most appropriate market segments. Managers also need to ensure that prospective customers are aware of what constitutes appropriate dress and behavior. For instance, if you were the owner of a restaurant that thrived on business from casually dressed students, you might not want to encourage patronage from middle-aged people in business suits. In contrast, a hotel that has succeeded in building up a clientele of business travelers should consider how they might react to the presence in the lobby or dining room of a large group of tourists on a packaged vacation. Some establishments, however, thrive on attracting a diverse mix of customers. This diversity becomes part of their culture and works well—so long as no one's behavior actively disturbs other people.

A uniform customer base is not always possible or even desirable for many service businesses. Two or more distinct market segments may each contribute importantly to the organization's success, yet they may not mix well. Ideally, potentially conflicting segments should be separated in place and time. Examples of place separation include seating airline passengers in first-class, business-class, and economy-class cabins (based on how much they are willing to pay for enhanced service features), placing convention participants on a different floor of a hotel from other guests, and assigning bank customers with substantial accounts a separate entrance and transaction area—even a special branch of their own—to offer more privacy. Separation of customers in time can be achieved through sequential rather than joint use of the same service facility by customers from different market segments—that way neither group encounters the other.

Can Firms Restrict Service to Target Customers Only?

Many marketers would probably like to be able to decline requests for service from prospective customers who do not fit the market position sought by their firm. There are ways to discourage unwanted persons from requesting services—for instance, by insisting on certain standards of dress—but outright refusal to admit someone to a service facility may be viewed as illegal or unethical if that person has the ability to pay and is not behaving in a disorderly manner.

One of marketing's roles is to inform prospective customers in advance about the specific nature of a service so they know what to expect. This increases the chances of a satisfactory fit between customers and the organization. Sometimes, however, friction develops between customers and staff—or between different customers—and employees may have to play police officer and either resolve the problem or ask the offending individuals to leave the premises. In fact, some businesses have employees assigned specifically to this role, like bouncers at a bar. Failure to take action quickly and efficiently may seriously damage the impression that other customers have of the service, thus destroying the chances of obtaining repeat business. Some firms will take action to ban a badly behaved customer from future use of their services.

Selecting the Appropriate Customer Portfolio

Artists and writers often prepare a portfolio of their work to show to prospective purchasers or employers. The term also describes the collection of financial instruments held by an investor or the array of loans advanced by a bank. In financial services, the goal of portfolio analysis is to determine the mix of investments (or loans) that is appropriate to one's needs, resources, and risk preference. In an investment portfolio, the contents should change over time in response to the performance of individual portfolio elements, as well as reflecting changes in the customer's situation or preferences.

Creating a Portfolio of Market Segments

We can apply the concept of portfolio to service businesses with an established base of customers. Different segments offer different values for a service firm. Like investments, some types of customers may be more profitable than others in the short term, but others may have greater potential for long-term growth. Similarly, the spending patterns of some customers may be stable over time, whereas others may be more cyclical, spending heavily in boom times but cutting back sharply in recessions. A wise firm may seek a mix of such customers to reduce the risks associated with cyclicality.

If managers know the annual value of each category of customers (revenues received minus the associated costs of serving them) as well as the proportions represented by each category within the customer base, they can project the ongoing value of all these customers in terms of future revenue streams. Models exist for projecting the future value of the *customer portfolio* (defined as the size and composition of the firm's complete set of customer relationships), based on historical data of customer acquisitions, classes of service purchased, service upgrades and downgrades, and terminations. These historical data can be adapted to reflect pricing and cost changes, promotional efforts, and market-related risks (including the anticipated impact of competitive actions or changes in market dynamics). A good example is subscriptions to cable or satellite television.[4]

Attracting, Retaining, Upgrading, and Terminating Customers

At a minimum, any firm should focus its advertising, sales, and promotional strategies to reach prospects from desired segments and seek to avoid customers who do not fit the desired profile. Unfortunately, marketers tend to overemphasize attraction of new customers. All too often, rewards and recognition for salespeople go to those who bring in new business. However, this is not necessarily the most profitable strategy. A widely circulated statement is that on average it costs a firm five to six times as much to attract a new customer as it does to implement retention strategies to hold on to an existing one.[5]

Well-managed firms understand the importance of working hard to retain and develop their existing customers and to devise compensation packages designed to encourage such behavior. Customer retention involves marketing and account management activities aimed at developing long-term, cost-effective links between customers and the organization for the mutual benefit of both parties. Service firms can use a variety of strategies to maintain and enhance relationships, including such basics as treating customers fairly, offering service augmentations, and treating each customer as though he or she were a segment of one—the essence of mass customization.[6] Offering service extras often plays a key role in building and sustaining relationships between vendors and purchasers of industrial goods.[7] As a relationship develops with a customer, marketing efforts may be used to encourage an increased volume of purchases, upgrading the type of service used, or adding new services. For instance, a telephone subscriber might start with a fairly basic level of service but then be encouraged to purchase additional features, such as caller ID, call waiting, and call forwarding.

Theodore Levitt has this to say about relationship management in professional firms:

It is not surprising that in professional partnerships, such as law, medicine, architecture, consulting, investment banking, and advertising, individuals are rated and rewarded by the client relationships they control. These relationships, like other assets, can appreciate or depreciate . . . Relationship management requires companywide programs for maintenance, investment, improvement, and even for replacement.[8]

As David Maister emphasizes, marketing is about getting *better* business, not just *more* business.[9] The caliber of a professional firm is measured by the type of clients it serves and the nature of the tasks on which it works. Volume alone is no measure of excellence, sustainability, or profitability. In professional services, such as consulting firms or legal partnerships, the mix of business attracted may play an important role in both defining the firm and providing a suitable mix of assignments for staff members at different levels in the organization. Figure 5.2 illustrates a portfolio of professional assignments matched to different skill levels within the firm.

Not all existing customer relationships are worth keeping. Some customers no longer fit the firm's strategy, either because that strategy has changed or because the nature of the customer's behavior and needs has changed. Careful analysis may show that many relationships are no longer profitable for the firm because they cost more to maintain than the revenues they generate. Just as investors need to dispose of poor investments and banks may have to write off bad loans, each service firm needs to regularly evaluate its customer portfolio and consider terminating unsuccessful relationships. Legal and ethical considerations, of course, will determine whether it is proper to take such actions.

Occasionally customers are fired outright (although concern for due process is still important). Certain relationships involve adherence to mutually agreed rules. Bank customers who

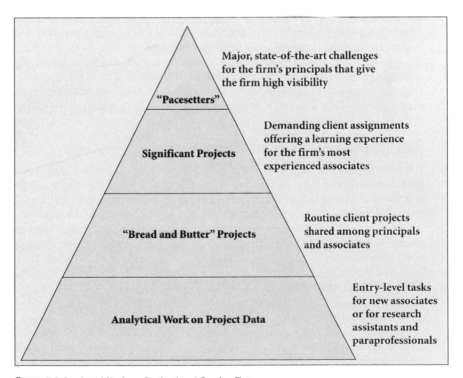

FIGURE 5.2 Product Mix for a Professional Service Firm

bounce too many checks, students who are caught cheating in exams, or country club members who consistently abuse the facilities or other people may be asked to leave or face expulsion. In other instances, termination may be somewhat less confrontational. Banks wishing to divest themselves of certain types of accounts that no longer fit with corporate priorities have been known to sell them to other banks (one example is credit cardholders who receive a letter in the mail telling them that their account has been transferred to another card issuer). Alternatively, a professional such as a doctor or lawyer may suggest to difficult or dissatisfied clients that they should consider switching to another provider whose expertise or style is more suited to their needs and expectations.

Creating and Maintaining Valued Relationships

What is a valued relationship? It's one in which the customer finds value because the benefits received from service delivery significantly exceed the associated costs of obtaining them. Research by Gwinner, Gremler, and Bitner suggests that relational benefits for individual consumers include greater confidence, social benefits, and special treatment (see Research Insights 5.2). Kumar emphasizes that relationships in a business-to-business service are largely dependent on the quality of the interactions between individuals at each of the partnering firms. "As relationships strengthen over a period of time," he observes, "the service provider's personnel often assume the role of outsourced departments and make critical decisions on behalf of their clients."[10]

For the firm, a valued relationship is one that is financially profitable over time and in which the benefits of serving a customer may extend beyond revenues to include such intangibles as the knowledge and pleasure obtained from working with that customer. Having a good working relationship between two parties implies that they relate positively to one another, as opposed to just conducting a series of almost anonymous transactions. In a healthy and mutually profitable relationship, both parties have an incentive to ensure that it extends for many years. And the seller, in particular, recognizes that it pays to take an investment perspective, justifying the initial costs of acquiring new customers and learning about their needs—which may even make the account unprofitable in its first year—by an expectation of future profits.

Relationships versus Transactions

A fundamental distinction in marketing exists between strategies intended to bring about a single transaction and those designed to create extended relationships with customers. The term *relationship marketing* has been widely used to describe the latter type of activity, but until recently it was only loosely defined. Research by Coviello, Brodie, and Munro suggests that there are, in fact, four distinct types of marketing: transactional marketing and three categories of what they call relational marketing: database marketing, interaction marketing, and network marketing.[11]

Transactional Marketing. A *transaction* is an event during which an exchange of value takes place between two parties. One transaction—or even a series of transactions—does not necessarily constitute a relationship, because relationships require mutual recognition and knowledge between the parties. When each transaction between a customer and a supplier is essentially discrete and anonymous, with no long-term record kept of a customer's purchasing history and little or no mutual recognition between the customer and the firm's employees, then no meaningful marketing relationship can be said to exist.

RESEARCH INSIGHTS 5.2

How Customers See Relational Benefits in Service Industries

What benefits do customers see themselves receiving from being in an extended relationship with a service firm? Researchers seeking answers to this question conducted two studies. The first consisted of in-depth interviews in respondents' own homes with 21 individuals from a broad cross-section of backgrounds. These interviews averaged 48 minutes in length. Respondents were asked to identify service providers that they used on a regular basis and invited to identify and discuss any benefits they received as a result of being a regular customer. Among some of the verbatim comments were the following:

- "I like him [hairstylist]. . . . He's really funny and always has lots of good jokes. He's kind of like a friend now."
- "I know what I'm getting—I know that if I go to a restaurant that I regularly go to, rather than taking a chance on all of the new restaurants, the food will be good."
- "I often get price breaks. The little bakery that I go to in the morning, every once in a while, they'll give me a free muffin and say, 'You're a good customer, it's on us today.' "
- "You can get better service than drop-in customers. . . . We continue to go to the same automobile repair shop because we have gotten to know the owner on a kind of personal basis, and he . . . can always work us in."
- "Once people feel comfortable, they don't want to switch to another dentist. They don't want to train or break a new dentist in."

After evaluating and categorizing the comments, the researchers designed a second study in which some survey questionnaires were distributed to a convenience sample of about four hundred people. The subjects were told to select a specific service provider with which they had a strong, established relationship. Then the questionnaire asked them to assess the extent to which they received each of 21 benefits (derived from analysis of the first study) as a result of their relationship with the specific provider they had identified. Finally, they were asked to assess the importance of these benefits for them.

A total of 299 usable surveys were returned. A factor analysis of the results showed that most of the benefits that customers derived from relationships could be grouped into three clusters. The first, and most important, group concerned what the researchers labeled confidence benefits, followed by social benefits and special treatment.

Confidence benefits included feelings by customers that in an established relationship there was less risk of something going wrong, confidence in correct performance, ability to trust the provider, lowered anxiety when purchasing, knowing what to expect, and receipt of the firm's highest level of service.

Social benefits embraced mutual recognition between customers and employees, being known by name, friendship with the service provider, and enjoyment of certain social aspects of the relationship.

Special treatment benefits included better prices, discounts or special deals that were unavailable to most customers, extra services, higher priority when there was a wait, and faster service than most customers.

Source: Kevin P. Gwinner, Dwayne D. Gremler, and Mary Jo Bitner, "Relational Benefits in Services Industries: The Customer's Perspective," *Journal of the Academy of Marketing Science* 26, no. 2 (1998): 101–114. Copyright © 1998 by Sage Publications, Inc. Reprinted by permission of Sage Publications.

With very few exceptions, consumers buying manufactured goods for household use do so at discrete intervals, paying for each purchase separately and rarely entering into a formal relationship with the original manufacturer—although they may have a relationship with the dealer or retail intermediary that sells them. The same is true for many services, ranging from passenger transport to food service or visits to a cinema, where each purchase and use is a discrete event.

Database Marketing. In this type of marketing, the focus is still on the market transaction but now includes information exchange. Marketers rely on information technology—possibly in the form of a database or the Internet—to form a relationship with targeted customers and retain their patronage over time. However, the nature of these relationships is often not a close one, with communication being driven and managed by the seller. Technology is used to (1) identify and build a database of current and potential customers, (2) deliver differentiated messages based on consumers' characteristics and preferences, and (3) track each relationship to monitor the cost of acquiring the consumer and the lifetime value of the resulting purchases.[12] Although technology can be used to personalize the relationship (as in word-processed letters that insert the customer's name), relations remain somewhat distant. Utility services such as electricity, gas, and cable television are good examples.

Interaction Marketing. A closer relationship exists in situations where there is face-to-face interaction between customers and representatives of the supplier (or "ear-to-ear" interaction by phone). Although the service itself remains important, value is added by people and social processes. Interactions may include negotiations and sharing of insights in both directions. This type of relationship has long existed in many local environments where buyer and seller know and trust each other, ranging from community banks to dentistry. It is also commonly found in many business-to-business services. Both the firm and the customer are prepared to invest resources (including time) to develop a mutually beneficial relationship. This investment may include time spent sharing and recording information. Consider the following observation concerning a large telecommunications operator that is trying to enter into a dialog with its small-business customers (taken from the case "BT: Telephone Account Management," reproduced on pp. 615 to 624).

BT found that customers demanded a continuing dialog focused on an understanding of their needs as opposed to a tactical contact aiming to sell them the "flavor of the month." Customers were also motivated by continuity of contact, wanting to deal with a specific person on a regular basis. They would spend up to 20 minutes disclosing information about their business and needs, but having invested that amount of time, they expected the relationship to be perpetuated.

One of the challenges posed by the growth of service companies is to maintain mutual interactions with customers even as technology allows a shift from high to low contact (as discussed in chapter 3) and face-to-face communications are replaced by mail, telecommunications, and the Internet.

Network Marketing. We often say that someone is a good networker because he or she is able to put individuals in touch with others who have a mutual interest. This type of marketing occurs primarily in a business-to-business context, where firms commit resources to develop positions in a network of relationships with customers, distributors, suppliers, the media, consultants, trade associations, government agencies, competitors, and even the customers of their customers. Suppliers often have a team of individuals who collaborate to provide effective service to a parallel team within the customer organization. However, the concept of networking is also relevant in consumer marketing environments where customers are encouraged to refer friends and acquaintances to the service provider. Individual customers may themselves have relationships with several different individuals or departments within a supplier firm.

The four types of marketing described previously are not necessarily mutually exclusive. A firm may have transactions with some customers who have neither the desire nor the need to make future purchases while it works hard to serve others whom it is encouraging to climb the loyalty ladder. Evert Gummesson identifies no fewer than 30 types of relationships within the broader context of total relationship marketing. He advocates *total relationship marketing,* described as

> [M]arketing based on relationships, networks, and interaction, recognizing that marketing is embedded in the total management of the networks of the selling organization, the market, and society. It is directed to long-term, win-win relationships with individual customers, and value is jointly created between the parties involved.[13]

Creating Membership Relationships

Although some services involve discrete transactions, in other instances purchasers receive service on a continuing basis. Even where the transactions are themselves discrete, there may still be an opportunity to create an ongoing relationship. The different nature of these situations offers an opportunity for categorizing services. First, we can ask, does the supplier enter into a formal membership relationship with customers, as with telephone subscriptions, banking, and the family doctor? Or is there no defined relationship? And second, is the service delivered on a continuous basis, as in insurance, broadcasting, and police protection? Or is each transaction recorded and charged separately? Table 5.1 shows the matrix resulting from this categorization, with examples in each category.

Membership relationships are formalized relationships between the firm and identifiable customers that may offer special benefits to both parties. Services involving discrete transactions

TABLE 5.1 *Relationships with Customers*		
	Type of Relationship between the Service Organization and Its Customers	
Nature of Service Delivery	Membership Relationship	No Formal Relationship
Continuous delivery of service	Insurance Cable TV subscription College enrollment Banking	Radio station Police protection Lighthouse Public highway
Discrete transactions	Long-distance calls from subscriber phone Theater series subscription Travel on commuter ticket Repair under warranty Health treatment for HMO member	Car rental Mail service Toll highway Pay phone Movie theater Public transportation Restaurant

can be transformed into membership relationships either by selling the service in bulk (for instance, a theater series subscription or a commuter ticket on public transport) or by offering extra benefits to customers who choose to register with the firm (loyalty programs for hotels, airlines, and car rental firms fall into this category). The advantage to the service organization of having membership relationships is that it knows who its current customers are and, usually, what use they make of the services offered. This can be valuable information for segmentation purposes if good records are kept and the data are readily accessible in a format that lends itself to computerized analysis. Knowing the identities and addresses of current customers enables the organization to make effective use of direct mail (including e-mail), telephone selling, and personal sales calls—all highly targeted methods of marketing communication. In turn, members can be given access to special numbers or even designated account managers to facilitate their communications with the firm.

When no formal relationship exists between supplier and customer, continuous delivery of the product is normally found only among those free services that economists term *public goods*—for instance, broadcasting, police protection, lighthouse services, and public roads—which are continuously available to all comers and financed from tax revenues.

The nature of service relationships has important implications for pricing. Whenever service is offered on an ongoing basis, there can be a single periodic charge covering all contracted services. Most insurance policies fall in this category, as do tuition and board fees at a residential college. The big advantage of this package approach is its simplicity. Some memberships, however, entail a series of separate and identifiable transactions, with the price paid being tied explicitly to the number and type of such transactions. Although more complex to administer, such an approach is fairer to customers (whose usage patterns may vary widely) and may discourage wasteful use of what are perceived as free services. In such instances, members may be offered advantages over casual users—for instance, discount rates (telephone subscribers pay less for long-distance calls made from their own phones than do pay-phone users) or advance notification and priority reservations (theater subscriptions). Some memberships offer certain services (such as rental of equipment or connection to a public utility system) for a base fee and then make incremental charges for each separate transaction above a defined minimum.

Membership relationships usually result in customer loyalty to a particular service supplier. (Sometimes, however, there is no choice, because the supplier has a monopoly, and unhappy customers may see themselves as hostages rather than voluntary patrons!) As a marketing strategy, many service businesses seek ways to develop formal, ongoing relations with customers in order to ensure repeat business or continuing financial support. Hotels, for instance, have developed frequent-guest programs offering priority reservations, upgraded rooms, and other rewards for return patrons. Many nonprofit organizations, such as museums, are creating membership programs to reinforce the links with some of their most active supporters, offering them extra benefits such as private showings and meetings with curators or artists as a reward for annual donations. The marketing task here is to determine how to build sales and revenues through such memberships while avoiding the risk of freezing out a large volume of desirable casual business.

Discrete transactions—when each usage involves a payment to the service supplier by an essentially anonymous consumer—are typical of services such as transport, restaurants, cinemas, and shoe repairs. The problem for marketers of such services is that they tend to be less informed about who their customers are and what use each customer makes of the service than their counterparts in membership-type organizations.

Managers in businesses that sell discrete transactions have to work a little harder to establish relationships. In small businesses such as hairdressers, frequent customers are (or should be) welcomed as regulars whose needs and preferences are remembered. Keeping formal records of customers' needs, preferences, and purchasing behavior is useful even in small firms because doing so helps employees avoid having to ask repetitive questions on each service occasion, allows them to personalize the service given to each customer, and also enables the firm to anticipate future needs.

In large companies with substantial customer bases, transactions can still be transformed into relationships by opening accounts, maintaining computerized customer records, and instituting account management programs that may involve a telephone number to call for assistance or even a designated account representative. Long-term contracts between suppliers and their customers take the nature of relationships to a higher level, transforming them into partnerships and strategic alliances.

The Search for Customer Loyalty

Loyalty is an old-fashioned word that has traditionally been used to describe fidelity and enthusiastic devotion to a country, cause, or individual. More recently, in a business context, it has been used to describe a customer's willingness to continue patronizing a firm over the long term, purchasing and using its goods and services on a repeated and preferably exclusive basis, and voluntarily recommending the firm's products to friends and associates. However, brand loyalty extends beyond behavior to include preference, liking, and future intentions. Richard Oliver has argued that consumers first become loyal in a cognitive sense, perceiving from brand attribute information that one brand is preferable to its alternatives.[14] At the second stage, affective loyalty, a consumer develops a liking toward the brand based on cumulatively satisfying usage occasions; such attitudes are not easily dislodged by counterarguments from competitors. In the third stage, conative loyalty, the consumer is committed to rebuy the same brand, which should lead to the fourth stage, action loyalty, resulting in repurchase.

"Few companies think of customers as annuities," says Frederick Reichheld, author of *The Loyalty Effect* and a major researcher in this field.[15] And yet that is precisely what a loyal customer can mean to a firm: a consistent source of revenues over a period of many years. However, this loyalty cannot be taken for granted. It will continue only as long as the customer feels that he or she is receiving better value (including superior quality relative to price) than could be obtained by switching to another supplier. If the original firm does something to disappoint the customer—or if a competitor starts to offer significantly better value—then there is a risk that the customer will defect.

Defector was a nasty word during the Cold War. It described disloyal people who sold out their own side and went over to the enemy. Even when they defected toward our side, rather than away from it, they were still suspect. Today, in a marketing context, the term *defection* is being used to describe the action of customers who drop off a company's radar screen and transfer their brand loyalty to another supplier. Reichheld and Sasser popularized the term *zero defections,* which they describe as keeping every customer the company can profitably serve (as we've already said, there are always some customers a firm is not sorry to lose!).[16] Not only does a rising defection rate indicate that something is already wrong with quality (or that competitors offer better value), but it may also signal the risk of a coming fall in profits. Large customers don't necessarily disappear overnight; they may signal their mounting disaffection by steadily reducing their purchases. Observant firms record customer purchase trends carefully and are quick to respond with service recovery strategies—the topic of chapter 6—in the event of customer complaints or other service failures.

There are many possible ways to disappoint customers through service quality failures. A major source of disappointment, especially in high-contact service situations, is poor performance by service employees. Reichheld and other researchers believe that there is an explicit link between customers' satisfaction with service on the one hand and employees' satisfaction with their jobs on the other. To the extent that service workers are capable, enjoy their jobs, and perceive themselves as well treated by their employer, they will be motivated to remain loyal to that firm for an extended period of time, rather than constantly switching jobs. Competent and loyal workers tend to be more productive than new hires, to know their customers well, and to be better able to deliver high-quality service. In short, employee loyalty can contribute to customer loyalty through a series of links that Heskett, Sasser, and Schlesinger refer to in their reading (reproduced on pp. 574 to 584) as the "service profit chain."[17]

Realizing the Full Profit Potential of a Customer Relationship

How much is a loyal customer worth in terms of profits? In 1990, Reichheld and Sasser analyzed the profit per customer in different service businesses, categorized by the number of years that a customer had been with the firm.[18] They found that the longer customers remained with a firm in each of these industries, the more profitable they became to serve. Annual profits per customer, which have been indexed over a five-year period for easier comparison, are summarized in Figure 5.3. The industries studied (with average profits from a first-year customer shown in parentheses) were as follows: credit cards ($30), industrial laundry ($144), industrial distribution ($45), and automobile servicing ($25).

Underlying this profit growth, say the two researchers, are four factors working to the supplier's advantage to create incremental profits. In order of magnitude at the end of seven years, these factors are

1. *Profit derived from increased purchases* (or, in a credit card or banking environment, higher account balances). Over time, business customers often grow larger and so need to purchase in greater quantities. Individuals may purchase more as their families grow or as they become more affluent. Both types of customers may decide to consolidate their purchases with a single supplier who provides high-quality service.

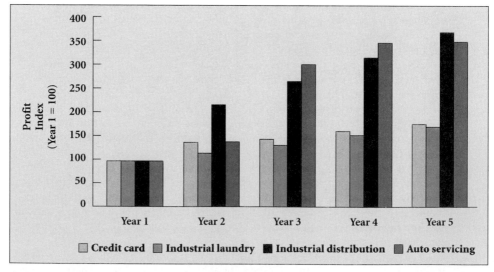

FIGURE 5.3 How Much Profit a Customer Generates over Time
Source: Based on data in Frederick J. Reichheld and W. Earl Sasser Jr., "Zero Defections: Quality Comes to Services," *Harvard Business Review* 73 (September–October 1995): 59–75.

2. *Profit from reduced operating costs.* As customers become more experienced, they make fewer demands on the supplier (for instance, less need for information and assistance); they may also make fewer mistakes when involved in operational processes, thus contributing to greater productivity.

3. *Profit from referrals to other customers.* Positive word-of-mouth recommendations are like free sales and advertising, saving the firm from having to invest as much money in these activities.

4. *Profit from price premium.* New customers often benefit from introductory promotional discounts, whereas long-term customers are more likely to pay regular prices. Moreover, when customers trust a supplier, they may be more willing to pay higher prices at peak periods or for express work.

Figure 5.4 shows the relative contribution of each of these different factors over a seven-year period, based on analysis of 19 different product categories (both goods and services). Reichheld argues that the economic benefits of customer loyalty noted earlier often explain why one firm is more profitable than a competitor. Further, the upfront costs of attracting these buyers can be amortized over many years.

However, it would be a mistake to assume that loyal customers are always more valuable than those making one-time transactions.[19] On the cost side, not all types of service incur heavy promotional expenditures to attract a new customer—sometimes it's more important to invest in a good retail location that will attract walk-in traffic. Unlike banks, insurance companies, and other membership organizations that require an application process and specific procedures to establish a new account, many service firms face no setup costs when a new customer first seeks to make a purchase. And on the revenue side, loyal customers may not necessarily spend more than one-time buyers; in some instances, they may even expect price discounts. The challenge for managers is to investigate the situation in their own organizations and determine profitability levels for different types of customer. (For insights on how to calculate customer value in any given business, see Management Memo 5.1.)

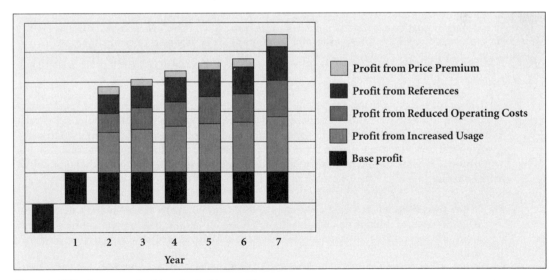

FIGURE 5.4 Why Customers Are More Profitable over Time
Source: Frederick J. Reichheld and W. Earl Sasser Jr., "Zero Defections: Quality Comes to Services," *Harvard Business Review* 73 (September–October 1995): 59–75. Copyright © 1990 by the President and Fellows of Harvard College.

MANAGEMENT MEMO 5.1

Calculating the Value of a Loyal Customer

Calculating customer value is an inexact science that is subject to a variety of assumptions. You may want to try varying these assumptions to see how it affects the final figures. Generally speaking, revenues per customer are easier to track on an individualized basis than are the associated costs of serving a customer, unless (a) no individual records are kept and/or (b) the accounts served are very large and all account-related costs are individually documented and assigned.

Acquisition Revenues Less Costs

If individual account records are kept, then the initial application fee paid and initial purchase (if relevant) should be found in these records. Costs, by contrast, may have to be based on average data. For instance, the marketing cost of acquiring a new client can be calculated by dividing the total marketing costs (advertising, promotions, selling, etc.) devoted toward acquiring new customers by the total number of new customers acquired during the same period. If each acquisition takes place over an extended period of time, you may want to build in a lagged effect between when marketing expenditures are incurred and when new customers come on board. The cost of credit checks—where relevant—must be divided by the number of new customers, not the total number of applicants, because some applicants will probably fail this hurdle. Account setup costs will also be an average figure in most organizations.

Annual Revenues and Costs

If annual sales, account fees, and service fees are documented on an individual-account basis, then account revenue streams (except referrals) can be easily identified. The first priority is to segment your customer base by the length of its relationship with your firm. Depending on the sophistication and precision of your firm's records, annual costs in each category may be directly assigned to an individual account holder or averaged for all account holders in that age category.

Value of Referrals

Computing the value of referrals requires a variety of assumptions. To get started, you may need to conduct surveys to determine (a) what percentage of new customers claim that they were

For profit-seeking firms, the potential profitability of a customer should be a key driver in marketing strategy. As Grant and Schlesinger declare, "Achieving the full profit potential of each customer relationship should be the fundamental goal of every business . . . Even using conservative estimates, the gap between most companies' current and full potential performance is enormous."[20] They suggest analysis of the following three gaps between actual and potential performance:

- What percentage of its target customers does a firm currently have—market share—and what percentage could it potentially obtain? (If there is a large gap between a firm's current share and its potential, then it may make sense to develop strategies to attract these new customers).
- What is the current purchasing behavior of customers in each target segment? And what would be the impact on sales and profits if they exhibited the ideal behavior profile of (1) buying all services offered by the firm, (2) using these to the exclusion of any purchases from competitors, and (3) paying full price? (In many instances, firms need to examine

influenced by a recommendation from another customer and (b) what other marketing activities also drew the firm to that individual's attention. From these two items, estimates can be made of what percentage of the credit for all new customers should be assigned to referrals. Additional research may be needed to clarify whether "older" customers are more likely to be effective recommenders than "younger" ones.

Net Present Value

Calculating net present value (NPV) from a future profit stream will require choice of an appropriate annual discount figure. (This could reflect estimates of future inflation rates.) It also requires assessment of how long the average relationship lasts. The NPV of a customer is then the sum of the anticipated annual profit on each customer for the projected relationship lifetime, suitably discounted each year into the future.

Acquisition		Year 1	Year 2	Year 3	Year n
Initial revenue	**Annual revenues**				
Application fee[a] _____	Annual account fee[a]				
Initial purchase[a] _____	Sales	_____	_____	_____	_____
	Service fees[a]	_____	_____	_____	_____
	Value of referrals[b]	_____	_____	_____	_____
Total revenues _____					
Initial costs	**Annual costs**				
Marketing _____	Account management	_____	_____	_____	_____
Credit check[a] _____	Cost of sales	_____	_____	_____	_____
Account set up[a] _____	Write-offs (e.g., bad debts)	_____	_____	_____	_____
Less total costs _____		_____	_____	_____	_____
Net profit (Loss) _____		_____	_____	_____	_____

[a]If applicable.

[b]Anticipated profits from each new customer referred (could be limited to the first year or expressed as the net present value of the estimated future stream of profits through year n); this value could be negative if an unhappy customer starts to spread negative word-of-mouth that causes existing customers to defect.

opportunities to cross-sell new services to existing customers. Meantime, frequent-user programs that are designed to reward loyalty can help to cement relationships more tightly. Getting customers to pay higher prices than they have been used to, however, may be more difficult unless competitors are also trying to reduce the availability of discount promotions.)

- How long, on average, do customers remain with the firm? What impact would it have if they remained customers for life? (As we showed earlier, the profitability of a customer often increases over time. Management's task is to identify the reasons why customers defect and then take corrective action.)

Many elements are involved in gaining market share, cross-selling other products and services to existing customers, and creating long-term loyalty. The process starts, as we suggested earlier, by identifying and targeting the right customers and then learning everything possible about their needs, including their preferences for different forms of service delivery. Consistently doing an outstanding job of satisfying these needs should lie at the heart of any service quality program, as described in chapter 13. The big challenge for service marketers lies not only in giving prospective customers a reason to do business with their firms but also in offering them incentives to remain as customers and even increase their purchases—yet without the firm having to give away all the potential profits in the process!

Reinforcing Loyalty by Rewarding Repeat Users

Customer loyalty programs seek to bond customers to a company (or to specific products) by offering additional incentives. Informal loyalty programs, sometimes found in small businesses, may take the form of periodically giving regular customers a small treat as a way of thanking them for their custom. In the past, many retailers participated in trading stamp programs, offering customers adhesive stamps, proportional in value to the amount of their purchase, that could be glued into a book and redeemed for gifts once a certain number had been obtained. However, such programs tended to reward size of purchase rather than frequency, did not identify precise purchasing patterns, and often had the disadvantage that the stamps themselves were issued by a trading stamp company independent of the participating retailers.

Within any competitive product category, managers recognize that few customers consistently buy only one brand, especially in situations where service delivery involves a discrete transaction (such as a car rental) rather than being continuous in nature (as with insurance coverage). In many instances, consumers are loyal to several brands while spurning others—sometimes described as "polygamous loyalty." This behavior should not be confused with variety seeking, which results in consumers flitting butterfly-like from brand to brand without any fixed allegiance at all. In such instances, the marketing goal becomes one of strengthening the customer's preference for one brand over the others.

To assess the potential of a loyalty program to alter normal patterns of behavior, Dowling and Uncles argue that marketers need to examine three psychological effects:

- *Brand loyalty versus deal loyalty.* To what extent are customers loyal to the core service (or brand) rather than to the loyalty program itself? Marketers should focus on loyalty programs that directly support the value proposition and positioning of the product in question, rather than just creating a point of differentiation.
- *How buyers value rewards.* Several elements combine to determine a loyalty program's value to customers: (1) the cash value of the redemption rewards (if customers had to purchase them); (2) the range of choice among rewards—for instance, a selection of gifts rather than just a single gift; (3) the aspirational value of the rewards—something exotic that the consumer would not normally purchase may have greater appeal than a cash-back offer; (4) whether the amount of usage required to obtain an award places it within the realm of possibility for any given consumer; (5) the ease of using the program and making claims for redemption; and (6) the psychological benefits of belonging to the program and accumulating points.
- *How soon customers obtain benefits from participating in the rewards program.* Deferred gratification tends to weaken the appeal of a loyalty program. One solution is to send customers periodic statements of their account status, indicating progress toward reaching a particular milestone and promoting the rewards that might be forthcoming when that point is reached.[21]

Frequent-Flyer Programs in the Airline Business

Among the most well-known programs for rewarding repeat users are those offered by most passenger airlines. The original frequent-flyer program was established by American Airlines in 1983. Targeted at business travelers (the individuals who fly the most), this promotion enabled passengers to claim travel awards based on the accumulated distance they had traveled on the airline. The number of miles flown became the basis of the scoring system that entitled customers to claim from a menu of free tickets in different classes of service. American Airlines was taken by surprise at the enormous popularity of this program. Other major airlines soon felt obliged to follow and quickly implemented similar schemes of their own. Each airline hoped that its own frequent-flyer program, branded with a distinctive name such as AAdvantage (American) or Mileage Plus (United), would induce a traveler to remain brand loyal, even to the extent of some inconvenience in scheduling. However, many business travelers, accustomed to flying on a variety of different airlines, enrolled in several programs, thereby limiting the effectiveness of these promotions for individual carriers.

To make their programs more appealing, the airlines signed cooperative agreements with regional and international carriers as well as with "partner" hotels and car rental firms, allowing customers to be credited with mileage accrued through a variety of travel-related activities. What had begun as a one-year promotion by American Airlines was soon transformed into a permanent—and quite expensive—part of the industry's marketing structure. (The costs of operating a frequent-flyer program today are estimated at between 3 and 6 percent of an airline's revenue.)

As time passed, airlines in the United States started to use double- and triple-mileage bonus awards as a tool for demand management (the topic of chapter 13), seeking to encourage travel on less popular routes. A common strategy was to award bonus miles for changing flights at an intermediate hub rather than taking a nonstop flight or for flying at off-peak hours or during the low season when many empty seats were available. To avoid giving away too many free seats at peak time, some airlines offered more generous redemption terms during off-peak periods; some even blacked out key vacation periods such as Christmas and New Year, making flights on certain days ineligible for free tickets.

Competitive strategies often involved bonus miles, too. Bonus wars broke out on certain routes. At the height of its mid-1980s battle with New York Air on the lucrative 230-mile (370-km) New York–Boston shuttle service, the PanAm Shuttle offered passengers 2,000 miles for a one-way trip and 5,000 miles for a return journey completed within a single day. Bonus miles also came to be awarded for travel in first or business class. And bonuses might also be awarded to encourage passengers to sample new services or to complete market research surveys. To record the mileage of passengers enrolled in their frequent-flyer programs, the airlines had to install elaborate tracking systems that captured details of each flight. They also had to create systems for recording and maintaining each member's current account status and to devise procedures for redeeming miles for free travel (some of these activities were often outsourced to independent contractors).

American Airlines was probably the first carrier to realize the value of its frequent-flyer database for learning more about the travel behavior of its best customers, enabling it to create highly targeted direct-mail lists, such as travelers who flew regularly between a certain pair of cities. The airline was also able to examine bookings for individual flights to see what percentage of seats was filled by frequent flyers, most of whom were probably traveling on business and therefore not as price sensitive as people travelling on vacation or pleasure trips. This information proved to have great value when countering competition from low-cost discount airlines, whose primary target segment was price-conscious pleasure travelers. Rather than reducing all fares on all flights between a pair of cities, American Airlines realized that it needed only to offer a limited number of discount fares, primarily on those flights known to be carrying significant numbers of nonbusiness passengers. Even on such flights, the airline would seek to limit availability of discount fares by such means as requiring an advance purchase or an extended stay in the destination city so that it would be difficult for business travelers to trade down from full fare to a discount ticket.

Rewarding Value of Use, Not Just Frequency, at British Airways

Many international carriers initially resisted creating frequent-flyer programs of their own. They were concerned not only about the expense but also that these programs required the airline to give award claimants free seats that could have been sold, during periods of high demand, to paying passengers. British Airways (BA) created its own program, known as the Executive Club, in 1992. Until that point, its response to the competitive pressure of these programs had been limited to giving its passengers miles in a U.S. carrier's awards program. But senior BA management wanted to capture the competitive leverage inherent in learning more about its best customers and building their loyalty to the brand.

Unlike some programs, in which customer usage is measured simply in miles, Executive Club members receive both air miles toward redemption of air-travel awards and points toward silver- or gold-tier status for travel on BA. Certain flights on BA's subsidiary airlines, including Deutsche BA and Air Liberté, also qualify for points and miles. With the creation of the "oneworld" airline alliance with American Airlines, Qantas, and other carriers, Executive Club members have been able to earn miles and points by flying these partner airlines, too.

As shown in Table 5-A, silver and gold cardholders are entitled to special benefits while they are actually traveling, such as priority reservations and a superior level of on-the-ground service. For instance, even if a cardholder is only traveling in economy class, he or she will be entitled to first-class standards of treatment at check-in and in the airport lounges. But whereas miles can be accumulated for up to five years (after which they expire), tier status is only valid for 15 months beyond the calendar year in which it was earned. In short, the right to special privileges must be re-earned every year. The objective of awarding tier status (which is not unique to BA) is to encourage passengers who have a choice of airline to concentrate their travel on British Airways, rather than belonging to several frequent-flyer programs and collecting mileage awards from all of them. Few passengers travel with such frequency that they will be able to obtain the benefits of gold-tier status (or its equivalent) on more than one airline. However, one of the rewards of that status may be the ability to use lounges and other amenities in airlines that belong to the same international alliance (such as oneworld or Star—the alliance that includes United Airlines, Air Canada, and Lufthansa).

The assignment of points also varies according to class of service: BA seeks to recognize higher ticket expenditures with proportionately higher awards. Longer trips earn more points than shorter ones (a domestic or short-haul European trip in economy class generates 15 points; a transatlantic trip, 60 points; and a trip from the United Kingdom to Australia or New Zealand, 100 points).

To reward purchase of higher-priced tickets, passengers earn points at double the economy rate if they travel in Club (business class), at triple the rate in First, and more than four times the economy rate if flying Concorde supersonic service between London and New York. Likewise, passengers get class-of-service mileage bonuses for both Club (+25 percent) and First (+50 percent). In contrast, certain deeply discounted fares do not qualify for points at all.

To encourage gold and silver cardholders to remain loyal, BA offers incentives for Executive Club members to retain their current tier status (or to move up from silver to gold). Silver cardholders receive a 25 percent bonus on all air miles, regardless of class of service, whereas gold cardholders receive a 100 percent bonus; in other words, it doesn't pay to spread the miles among several frequent-flyer programs! The airline also makes it slightly easier to retain existing tier status once this has been achieved. For instance, it takes an annual total of 700 points to qualify for silver status and 1,700 points for gold status, but once a traveler has reached that level, requalification requires only 500 points for silver or 1,200 points for gold.

Although the airline makes no promises on complimentary upgrades, members of BA's Executive Club are more likely to receive such an invitation than other passengers, with tier status being an important consideration. For obvious reasons, however, BA does not wish its most frequent travelers to feel that they can plan on buying a less expensive ticket and then automatically receive an upgrade!

TABLE 5.A   *Benefits Offered by British Airways to Its Most-Valued Passengers*

Benefit	Silver Cardholders	Gold Cardholders
Travel insurance	Competitively priced	Complimentary in some countries
Lounge access	Club departure lounges	First-class departure lounges and (if in economy) Arrivals Lounges in London
Immunization (U.K. only)	25% discount at any of BA's 40 travel clinics in the U.K.	Same
Check-in desk	Club (for economy travelers)	First (for economy or Club)
Reservations	Dedicated line, priority booking, and waitlisting	Dedicated line, priority reservations in Club, First, and Concorde; top-priority waitlisting in all classes
Advance notification of delays		When flight delays exceed 4 hours and customer has provided contact number
48-hour ticket dispatch (U.K. only)		If purchased through dedicated line
Special services assistance		Problem solving (beyond that accorded to other BA travelers)
Bonus air miles (U.S. only)	25%	100%
Bonus tickets award (U.S. members only)		Free companion ticket for round-trip transatlantic travel after every 60,000 miles flown on BA within a calendar year

Note: British Airways has branded its economy class as World Traveller on intercontinental routes and as Euro-Traveller in Europe. Similarly, business class is know as Club World and Club Europe.

In due course, many international airlines felt obliged to introduce their own frequent-flyer programs, offering miles (or kilometers) to compete with U.S. carriers and then with each other (see Service Perspectives 5.1 for a description of how British Airways has designed its Executive Club).

A number of other service businesses have sought to copy the airlines with loyalty programs of their own. Hotels, car rental firms, telephone companies, retailers, and even credit card issuers have been among those that seek to identify and reward their best customers. Although some provide their own rewards—such as free merchandise, class of vehicle upgrades, or free hotel rooms in vacation resorts—many firms denominate their awards in miles that can be credited to a selected frequent-flyer program. In short, air miles have become a form of promotional currency in the service sector.

Of course, rewards alone will not suffice to retain a firm's most desirable customers. If customers are dissatisfied with the quality of service they receive or believe that they can obtain better value from a less expensive service, they may quickly become disloyal. Neither BA nor any other service business that has instituted an awards program for frequent users can ever afford to lose sight of its broader goals of offering high service quality and good value relative to the price and other costs incurred by customers.

Conclusion

All marketers need to be concerned about who their customers are, but this concern takes on added dimensions for certain types of services. When customers have a high level of contact with the service organization and with one another, the customer portfolio helps to define the character of the organization, because customers themselves become a part of the product. Too diverse a portfolio may result in an ill-defined image, especially if all segments are present at the same time. Abusive customers may spoil the experience for others and hurt profitability in other ways, too. So marketers must be selective in targeting the desired customer segments, and guidelines must be established for customers' behavior while they are using the service.

For services that are capacity constrained, the marketer's task is not only to balance supply and demand but also to obtain the most desirable types of customers at a particular point in time. This may require targeting different segments at different times. For profit-seeking businesses, a key issue is which segments will yield the greatest net revenues. Public and nonprofit organizations, although they shouldn't ignore financial issues, need to consider which segments will help them best fulfill their nonfinancial objectives. In all instances, accurate market analysis and forecasting assume great importance in guiding marketing strategy.

Finally, marketers need to pay special attention to those customers who offer the firm the greatest value because they purchase its products with the greatest frequency and spend the most on premium services. Programs to reward frequent users—of which the most highly developed are the frequent-flyer clubs created by the airlines—not only serve to identify and provide rewards for high-value customers but also enable marketers to track the former's behavior in terms of where and when they use the service, what service classes or types of product they buy, and how much they spend. The greatest success is likely to go to organizations that can give their best customers incentives to remain loyal, rather than playing the field and spreading their patronage among many other suppliers.

REVIEW QUESTIONS

1. Explain what is meant by the term *customer portfolio*. How should a firm decide what is the most appropriate mix of customers to have?

2. What are the arguments for spending money to keep existing customers loyal? Evaluate the strengths and weaknesses of frequent-user programs in different service industries.

3. What criteria should a marketing manager use to decide which of several possible segments should be targeted by the firm?

4. Identify some of the measures that can be used to encourage long-term relationships with customers.

5. What does segmentation have to do with capacity utilization? For what types of services is this a relevant issue?

6. Select a people-processing service business and then pick two types of jaycustomer and develop strategies designed (a) to discourage these people from using your service in the first place if they have already begun to cause problems, (b) to prevent them from causing distress to other customers or to employees, (c) to minimize financial loss to your organization.

APPLICATION EXERCISES

1. Identify three service businesses that you patronize on a regular basis. Now for each business, complete the following sentence: "I am loyal to this business because _____." What conclusions do you draw about (a) yourself as a consumer and (b) the performance of each of the businesses?

2. Identify two service businesses that you used several times but have now ceased to patronize (or plan to stop patronizing soon) because you were dissatisfied. Complete this sentence: "I stopped using (or will soon stop using) this organization as a customer because _____." Again, what conclusions do you draw about yourself and the firms in question?

3. Interview two people who are currently participating in loyalty programs with one or more service businesses (note that some individuals may belong to more than one loyalty program in the same industry, such as two frequent-flyer programs). Ask (a) what motivated them to sign up in the first place, (b) whether participating in the program has changed their purchasing/usage behavior in any way, (c) whether it has made them less likely to use competing suppliers, (d) what they think of the rewards available, (e) whether membership in the program leads to any immediate benefits each time they use the service, (f) what they think of the rewards, and (g) whether they have yet been able to redeem any of these rewards. On the basis of these interviews, what can you conclude about the effectiveness of these two programs?

4. Based on the responses you received to question 3, what additional research would you like to conduct if you were the manager responsible for each of these programs (and why)?

ENDNOTES

1. Roger Hallowell, "The Relationships of Customer Satisfaction, Customer Loyalty, and Profitability: An Empirical Study," *International Journal of Service Industry Management* 7, no.4 (1996): 27–42.
2. See, for example, A. Parasuraman, "Technology Readiness Index [TRI]: A Multiple Item Scale to Measure Readiness to Embrace New Technologies." *Journal of Service Research*, 2, May 2000.
3. For more detailed coverage, see Mary Modahl, *Now or Never: How Companies Must Change Today to Win the Battle for Internet Consumers*. New York: Harper Business, 2000, especially pp. 3–78.
4. Charles B. Weinberg and Christopher H. Lovelock, "Pricing and Profits in Subscription Services Marketing: An Analytical Approach to Customer Valuation," in *Creativity in Services Marketing: What's New, What Works, What's Developing,* ed. M. Venkatesan, D. M. Schmalensee, and C. Marshall (Chicago: American Marketing Association, 1986), 129–133.
5. According to Paul S. Bender, *Design and Operation of Customer Service Systems* (New York: AMACOM, 1976), a lost customer reduces profits by $118 compared with a $20 cost to keep a customer satisfied.
6. Leonard L. Berry and A. Parasuraman, *Marketing Services: Competing through Quality* (New York: The Free Press, 1991). See especially chap. 8, 132–150.
7. Barbara Bund Jackson, "Build Relationships That Last," *Harvard Business Review* (November–December 1985): 120–128.
8. Theodore Levitt, *The Marketing Imagination*, rev. ed. (New York: The Free Press, 1986), 121.
9. David H. Maister, *True Professionalism* (New York: The Free Press, 1997); see especially chap. 20.
10. Piyush Kumar, "The Impact of Long-Term Client Relationships on the Performance of Business Service Firms," *Journal of Service Research* 2 (August 1999):6.
11. Nicole E. Coviello, Roderick J. Brodie, and Hugh J. Munro. "Understanding Contemporary Marketing: Development of a Classification Scheme," *Journal of Marketing Management,* 13, no. 6, 501–522.
12. J. R. Copulsky and M. J. Wolf, "Relationship Marketing: Positioning for the Future," *Journal of Business Strategy* 11, no. 4 (1990): 16–20.
13. Evert Gummesson, *Total Relationship Marketing* (Oxford: Butterworth-Heinemann, 1999), 24.

14. Richard L. Oliver, "Whence Consumer Loyalty?" *Journal of Marketing* 63 (special issue 1999): 33–44.
15. Frederick F. Reichheld, *The Loyalty Effect* (Boston: Harvard Business School Press, 1996).
16. Frederick F. Reichheld and W. Earl Sasser Jr., "Zero Defections: Quality Comes to Services," *Harvard Business Review* 73 (September–October 1995): 59–75.
17. James L. Heskett, W. Earl Sasser Jr., and Leonard A. Schlesinger, *The Service Profit Chain* (New York: The Free Press, 1997).
18. Reichheld and Sasser, "Zero Defections."
19. Grahame R. Dowling and Mark Uncles, "Do Customer Loyalty Programs Really Work?" *Sloan Management Review* (Summer 1997), 71–81.
20. Alan W. H. Grant and Leonard H. Schlesinger, "Realize Your Customer's Full Profit Potential," *Harvard Business Review* 73 (September–October, 1995): 59–75.
21. Dowling and Uncles, "Do Customer Loyalty Programs Really Work?" 74.

CHAPTER 6

Complaint Handling and Service Recovery

One of the surest signs of a bad or declining relationship is the absence of complaints from the customer. Nobody is ever that satisfied, especially not over an extended period of time.

THEODORE LEVITT

"Thank Heavens for Complainers" was the provocative title of an article about customer complaining behavior that also featured a successful manager exclaiming, "Thank goodness I've got a dissatisfied customer on the phone! The ones I worry about are the ones I never hear from."[1] Customers who do complain give a firm the chance to correct problems (including some that the firm may not even know it has), restore relationships with the complainer, and improve future satisfaction for all.

Although the first law of service productivity and quality might be "Do it right the first time," we can't ignore the fact that failures continue to occur, sometimes for reasons outside the organization's control. You've probably noticed from your own experience that the various moments of truth in service encounters are especially vulnerable to breakdowns. Such distinctive service characteristics as real-time performance, customer involvement, people as part of the product, and difficulty of evaluation greatly increase the chance of perceived service failures. How well a firm handles complaints and resolves problems may determine whether it builds customer loyalty or watches former customers take their business elsewhere.

In this chapter, we examine the nature and extent of consumer complaining behavior, evaluate the effectiveness of current service recovery practices, and explore the following questions:

1. What courses of action are open to a dissatisfied consumer?
2. What factors explain and influence complaining behavior?

3. How should managers design a service recovery system?
4. What techniques are available for identifying the root cause of specific problems?
5. Under what circumstances should firms offer service guarantees, and is it wise to make them unconditional?

Consumer Complaining Behavior

Chances are that you're not entirely satisfied with the quality of at least some of the services that you use. How do you respond when you have been disappointed? Do you complain informally to an employee, ask to speak to the manager, file a complaint with the head office of the firm that let you down, write to some regulatory authority, or telephone a consumer advocacy group? Or do you just grumble to your friends and family, mutter darkly to yourself, and take your business elsewhere next time you need that type of service?

If you don't normally tell a company (or outside agency) of your displeasure with unsatisfactory service or faulty goods, then you're not alone. Research around the world has exposed the sad fact that most people do not complain, especially if they don't think it will do any good. And even when they do communicate their dissatisfaction, managers may not hear about complaints made to customer-contact personnel.[2]

Customer Response to Service Failures

What options are open to customers when they experience a service failure? Figure 6.1 depicts the courses of action available. This model suggests at least four major courses of action:

- Do nothing.
- Complain in some form to the service firm.
- Take action through a third party (consumer advocacy group, consumer affairs or regulatory agencies, and civil or criminal courts).
- Abandon this supplier and discourage other people from using the service (negative word-of-mouth).

Following through the sequence of possible reactions, we can see a variety of end results, leaving the customer anything from furious to delighted. The risk of defection is high, especially when there are a variety of competing alternatives available. One study of customer switching behavior in service industries found that close to 60 percent of all respondents who reported changing suppliers did so because of a perceived failure: Twenty-five percent cited failures in the core service, 19 percent reported an unsatisfactory encounter with an employee, 10 percent reported by an unsatisfactory response to a prior service failure, and 4 percent described unethical behavior on the part of the provider.[3]

Managers need to be aware that the impact of a defection can go far beyond the loss of that person's future revenue stream. Angry customers often tell many other people about their problems. The Web has made life more difficult for companies that provide poor service, because unhappy customers can now reach thousands of people by posting complaints on bulletin boards or setting up Web sites to publicize their bad experiences with specific organizations.[4]

The TARP Study of Consumer Complaint Handling

The Technical Assistance Research Programs Institute (TARP) has studied consumer complaint handling in many countries. In 1986, it published a landmark study based on its own research and a detailed review of other studies from around the world. Its findings, which were widely

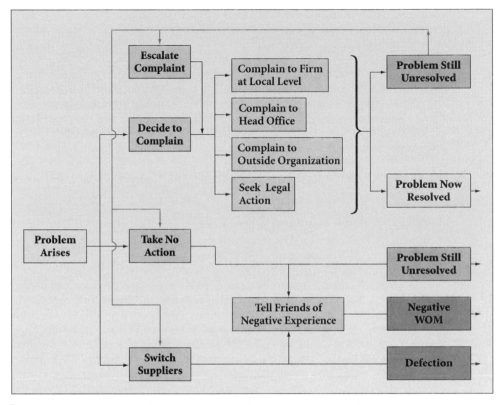

FIGURE 6.1   Courses of Action Open to a Dissatisfied Customer

publicized, prompted many managers to consider the impact of dissatisfied customers—especially those who never complained but simply defected to a competitor. Let's take a closer look at some specific findings.

What Percent of Problems Are Reported? From its own research and detailed literature studies, TARP found that when U.S. customers experienced problems concerning manufactured consumer products, only 25 to 30 percent of them actually complained. For grocery products or their packaging, the market research firm of A. C. Nielsen found a complaint rate of 30 percent. Even for problems with large-ticket durables, TARP determined that the complaint rate among dissatisfied customers was only 40 percent. Similar findings come from other countries. A Norwegian study found that the percentage of dissatisfied consumers who complained ranged from 9 percent for coffee to 68 percent for cars. A German study showed that only a small fraction of customers expressed dissatisfaction, but among this group the complaint rates ranged from 29 to 81 percent. And finally, a Japanese study found complaint rates of 17 percent among those experiencing a problem with services and 36 percent for those experiencing a problem with goods.

Where Do People Complain? Studies show that the majority of complaints are made at the place where the product was bought or the service received. Very few dissatisfied consumers complain directly to the manufacturers or to the head office. In fact, industry-specific studies conducted by TARP suggest that fewer than 5 percent of complaints about large-ticket durable goods or services ever reach corporate headquarters, presumably because retail intermediaries fail to pass them on.

Who Is Most Likely to Complain? In general, research findings suggest that consumers from high-income households are more likely to complain than those from lower-income ones and that younger people are more likely to complain than older ones. People who complain also tend to be more knowledgeable about the products in question and the procedures for complaining. Other factors that increase the likelihood of a complaint include problem severity, importance of the product to the customer, and whether financial loss is involved.

Why Don't Unhappy Customers Complain? TARP found three primary reasons why dissatisfied customers don't complain. In order of frequency, customers stated

- They didn't think it was worth the time or effort.
- They decided no one would be concerned about their problem or resolving it.
- They did not know where to go or what to do.

Unfortunately, this pessimism seems justified because a large percentage of people (40 to 60 percent in two studies) reported dissatisfaction with the outcome of their complaints. Another reason why people don't complain reflects culture or context. A study in Japan found that 21 percent of dissatisfied customers felt awkward or embarrassed about complaining. In some European countries, there is a strong guest-host relationship between service providers and customers (especially in the restaurant industry), and it's considered bad manners to tell customer-contact personnel that you are dissatisfied in any way with the service or the meal. Think about a couple of occasions when you were dissatisfied but did not complain. What were the reasons?

Impact on Repurchase Intentions. When complaints are satisfactorily resolved, there's a much better chance that the customers involved will remain brand loyal and continue to repurchase the items in question. TARP found that intentions to repurchase different types of products ranged from 69 to 80 percent among those complainers who were completely satisfied with the outcome of the complaint. This figure dropped to 17 to 32 percent (depending on the type of product) for complainers who felt that their complaint had not been settled to their satisfaction.

Variations in Dissatisfaction by Industry

Although significant improvements in complaint-handling practices occurred during the 1980s and early 1990s in some industries, many customers remain dissatisfied with the way in which their problems are resolved.

Further, there are discouraging signs that the situation is beginning to deteriorate again. A valuable measure of how well different industries in the United States are performing relative to the needs and expectations of the marketplace is provided by the American Customer Satisfaction Index (ACSI), which measures customers' overall evaluation of the total purchase and consumption experience, both actual and anticipated.[5] ACSI results show that manufactured products generally score higher than services. Figure 6.2 shows recent scores and how they have changed relative to the previous year.

As these data suggest, many service industries are still a long way from meeting their customers' expectations on service. (Of course, there can be considerable variation on performance between firms within the same industry.)

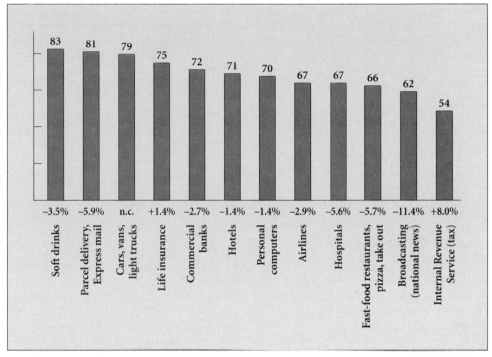

FIGURE 6.2　U.S. Customer Satisfaction Index Scores for Selected Industries in 1997, Showing Percent Change over 1996

Source: Based on data reported in Ronald B. Lieber and Linda Grant, "Now Are You Satisfied?" *Fortune,* February 16, 1998, 161–166.

Consumers in some countries, however, may be getting smarter and more aggressive about seeking satisfactory outcomes for their complaints. Recent findings from a large-scale study of consumer complaining behavior in Australia showed that among the industries studied, a majority of customers who had a serious problem did make the effort to complain.[6] The data in Table 6.1 shows considerable disparity from one service industry to another in both the incidence of unsatisfactory service and customers' likeliness to complain. As you review this table, ask yourself: Why were more Australians willing to complain about telephone service and other utilities than about restaurants and health services?

Other key findings from this study:

- Fifty-seven percent of respondents had experienced at least one problem with products or services within the past 12 months.
- On average, 73 percent of those respondents who had a serious problem took some action to have it corrected.
- Only 34 percent who took action were satisfied with the way the problem was resolved.
- Among those who were not happy with their complaint outcome, 89 percent reported they would not deal with the same firm again.
- Complaining households made an average of 3.4 contacts each in an effort to have their most serious problems resolved.

TABLE 6.1 *Service Problems and Complaining Behavior in Australia*		
Service Type	Percent of Respondents Experiencing a Problem in Past Year	Percent Taking Action about a Serious Problem
Computers	27	83
Government (e.g., social services)	26	76
Car and motorbike repairs, service	24	75
Small business	21	81
Investment advice	18	80
Housing (purchase and rental)	18	69
Banking	17	75
Public transport	15	52
Telephone	13	93
Restaurants and cafés	13	54
Health (medical, dental, etc.)	12	56
Professional services	11	68
Airlines and coaches	10	79
Accommodation	9	63
Insurance	9	74
Utilities (gas, water, electricity)	9	84
Entertainment and sport	6	59

Source: Society of Consumer Affairs Professionals, *SOCAP–TARP Study of Consumer Complaint Behavior in Australia* (Sydney: SOCAP, 1995).

- The further up the management hierarchy customers had to go to get the problem resolved, the more their satisfaction declined.
- On average a dissatisfied Australian customer told nine other people, whereas a satisfied customer told only half as many.

Factors Influencing Complaining Behavior

When consumers have an unsatisfactory service encounter, their initial (often unconscious) reaction is to assess what is at stake. In general, studies of consumer complaining behavior have identified two main purposes for complaining. First, consumers will complain to recover some economic loss, seeking either to get a refund or to have the service performed again (e.g., car repairs and dry cleaning services). They may take legal action if the problem remains unresolved. A second reason for complaining is to rebuild self-esteem. When service employees are rude, aggressive, deliberately intimidating, or apparently uncaring (such as when a sales assistant is discussing the weekend social activities with colleagues and pointedly ignores waiting customers), the customers' self-esteem, self-worth, or sense of fairness may be negatively affected. They may feel that they should be treated with more respect and become angry or emotional.

There are perceived costs to complaining. These may include the monetary cost of a stamp or phone call, time and effort in writing a detailed letter or making a verbal complaint, and the psychological cost of risking an unpleasant personal confrontation with a service provider—

especially if this involves someone whom the customer knows and may have to deal with again. Such costs may well deter a dissatisfied customer from complaining. Often, it is simply less stressful to defect to an alternative service supplier—especially when the switching costs are low or nonexistent. If you are unhappy with the service you receive from your travel agent, for example, what is there to prevent you from switching to a different agent next time? However, if you decide to switch doctors or dentists, you may have to ask to have all of your medical records transferred. This requires more effort and might make you feel uncomfortable.

Complaining represents a form of social interaction and is therefore likely to be influenced by role perceptions and social norms. One study found that for services where customers have "low power" (defined as the perceived ability to influence or control the transaction), they are less likely to voice complaints.[7] Professional service providers, such as doctors, dentists, lawyers, and architects, are a good example. Social norms tend to discourage customer criticism of such individuals, who are seen as experts about the service being offered. A clear implication is that professionals need to develop comfortable ways for customers to express legitimate complaints.

Complaints as Market Research Data

Responsive service organizations look at complaints as a stream of information that can be used to help monitor productivity and quality and highlight improvements needed to improve service design and execution. Complaints about slow service or bureaucratic procedures, for instance, may provide useful documentation of inefficient and unproductive processes. For complaints to be useful as research input, they should be funneled into a central collection point, recorded, categorized, and analyzed. Compiling this documentation requires a system for capturing complaints wherever they are made—without hindering timely resolution of each specific problem—and transmitting them to a central location where they can be recorded in a companywide complaint log (a detailed record of all customer complaints received by a service provider). Coordinating such activities is not a simple matter because there are many different entry points, including

- The firm's own employees at the front line, who may be in contact with customers face-to-face or by telecommunications
- Intermediary organizations acting on behalf of the original supplier
- Managers who normally work backstage but who are contacted by a customer seeking higher authority
- Suggestion or complaint cards mailed or placed in a special box
- Complaints to third parties—consumer advocate groups, legislative agencies, trade organizations, and other customers

The most useful roles for centralized complaint logs are (1) to provide a basis for follow-up and tracking all complaints to see that they have in fact been resolved, (2) to serve as an early warning indicator of perceived deterioration in one or more aspects of service, and (3) to indicate topics and issues that may require more detailed research. Firms that find ways of centralizing complaint data often discover that this information provides a valuable foundation for additional market research, using sample designs targeted at a broad cross-section of customers including those who—for cultural or other reasons—might be reluctant to initiate a complaint. Personal or telephone interviews also offer much better opportunities than mail or in-store surveys to dig deeper and probe for what lies behind certain responses. A skilled interviewer can solicit valuable information by asking customers questions such as

- Can you tell me why do you feel this way?
- Who (or what) caused this situation?
- How did customer contact employees respond?
- What action would you like to see the firm take to prevent a recurrence of such a situation?

Making It Easier for Customers to Complain

How can managers make it easier for unhappy customers to complain about service failures? Many companies have improved their complaint collection procedures by adding special toll-free phone lines, prominently displayed customer comment cards, and video or computer terminals for recording complaints. Some go even further, training their staff to ask customers if everything is satisfactory and to intervene if a customer is obviously discontented.[8] Of course, just collecting complaints doesn't necessarily help resolve them. In fact, accepting complaints and then ignoring them may make matters worse! Although friendly sympathy from an employee is a lot better than an irritable shrug, the challenge is to have a well-designed service recovery strategy that empowers employees to resolve problems quickly and satisfactorily.

Impact of Service Recovery Efforts on Customer Loyalty

TARP argues that complaint handling should be seen as a profit center, not a cost center, and has even created a formula to help companies relate the value of retaining a profitable customer to the overall costs of running an effective complaint handling unit. Putting U.S. industry data into this formula yielded some impressive returns on investment: from 50 to 170 percent for banking, 20 to 150 percent for gas utilities, over 100 percent for automotive service, and from 35 to an astonishing 400 percent for retailing.[9]

Underlying these return rates is a simple fact: When a dissatisfied customer defects, the firm loses more than just the value of the next transaction. It may also lose a long-term stream of profits from that customer and from anyone else who switches suppliers because of negative comments from an unhappy friend. So it pays to invest in service recovery efforts designed to protect those long-term profits.

Efforts to design service recovery procedures must take into account a firm's specific environment and the types of problems that customers are likely to encounter. Figure 6.3 displays the components of an effective service recovery system.

Service Recovery Following Customer Complaints

Service recovery is an umbrella term for systematic efforts by a firm to correct a problem following a service failure and to retain a customer's goodwill. Service recovery efforts play a crucial role in achieving (or restoring) customer satisfaction. In every organization, things may occur that have a negative impact on its relationships with customers. The true test of a firm's commitment to satisfaction and service quality isn't in the advertising promises or the decor and ambience of its offices but in the way it responds when things go wrong for the customer. (Unfortunately, firms don't always react in ways that match their advertised promises.) Effective service recovery requires thoughtful procedures for resolving problems and handling disgruntled customers. It is critical for firms to have effective recovery strategies, because even a single service problem can destroy a customer's confidence in a firm under the following conditions:

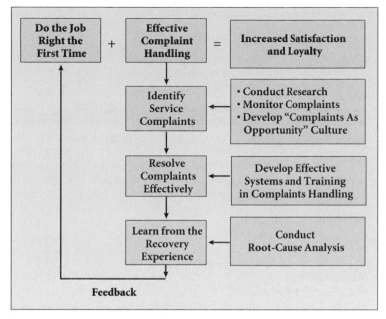

FIGURE 6.3   Components of an Effective Service Recovery System
Source: Christopher H. Lovelock, Paul G. Patterson, and Rhett H. Walker, *Services Marketing: Australia and New Zealand* (Sydney: Prentice Hall Australia, 1998), 455.

- The failure is totally outrageous (for instance, blatant dishonesty on the part of the supplier).
- The problem fits a pattern of failure rather than being an isolated incident.
- The recovery efforts are weak, serving to compound the original problem rather than correct it.[10]

Some complaints are made while service delivery is still taking place, whereas others are made after the fact. In both instances, how the complaint is handled may determine whether the customer remains with the firm or seeks new suppliers in the future. The advantage of getting real-time complaints is that there may still be a chance to correct the situation before service delivery is completed. The downside of real-time complaints (from an employee perspective) is that they can be demotivating. Dealing with them in real time can also interfere with service delivery. The real difficulty for employees is that they often lack the authority and the tools to resolve customer problems, especially when it comes to arranging alternatives at the company's expense or authorizing compensation on the spot. When complaints are made after the fact, the options for recovery are more limited. In this case, the firm can apologize, repeat the service to achieve the desired solution, or offer some other form of compensation.

Principles of Effective Problem Resolution

Recovering from service failures takes more than just pious expressions of determination to resolve any problems that may occur. It requires commitment, planning, and clear guidelines. Both managers and front-line employees must be prepared to deal with angry customers who are confrontational and sometimes behave in insulting ways toward service personnel who aren't at fault in any way. Service recovery efforts should be flexible, and employees should be empowered to use their judgment and communication skills to develop solutions that will satisfy complaining customers.[11]

The guidelines for effective problem resolution presented in Management Memo 6.1 are based on discussions with executives in many different industries. Of course, the service recovery process for a particular firm must take into account its specific environment and the types of problems that its customers are likely to encounter.

MANAGEMENT MEMO 6.1

Guidelines for Effective Problem Resolution

1. *Act fast.* If the complaint is made during service delivery, then time is of the essence to achieve a full recovery. When complaints are made after the fact, many companies have established policies of responding within 24 hours or sooner. Even when full resolution is likely to take longer, fast acknowledgment remains very important.

2. *Admit mistakes but don't be defensive.* Acting defensively may suggest that the organization has something to hide or is reluctant to fully explore the situation.

3. *Show that you understand the problem from each customer's point of view.* Seeing situations through the customers' eyes is the only way to understand what they think has gone wrong and why they are upset. Service personnel should avoid jumping to conclusions with their own interpretations.

4. *Don't argue with customers.* The goal should be to gather facts to reach a mutually acceptable solution, not to win a debate or prove that the customer is an idiot. Arguing gets in the way of listening and seldom diffuses anger.

5. *Acknowledge the customer's feelings,* either tacitly or explicitly (for example, "I can understand why you're upset"). This action helps to build rapport, the first step in rebuilding a bruised relationship.

6. *Give customers the benefit of the doubt.* Not all customers are truthful, and not all complaints are justified. But customers should be treated as though they have a valid complaint until clear evidence to the contrary emerges. If a lot of money is at stake (as in insurance claims or potential lawsuits), careful investigation is warranted; if the amount involved is small, it may not be worth haggling over a refund or other compensation. But it's still a good idea to check records to see if there is a past history of dubious complaints by the same customer.

7. *Clarify the steps needed to solve the problem.* When instant solutions aren't possible, telling customers how the organization plans to proceed shows that corrective action is being taken. It also sets expectations about the time involved (so firms should be careful not to overpromise).

8. *Keep customers informed of progress.* Nobody likes being left in the dark. Uncertainty breeds anxiety and stress. People tend to be more accepting of disruptions if they know what is going on and receive periodic progress reports.

9. *Consider compensation.* When customers do not receive the service outcomes that they paid for or have suffered serious inconvenience or loss of time and money because the service failed, either a monetary payment or an offer of equivalent service in kind is appropriate. This type of recovery strategy may also reduce the risk of legal action by an angry customer. Service guarantees often lay out in advance what such compensation will be, and the firm should ensure that all guarantees are met.

10. *Persevering to regain customer goodwill.* When customers have been disappointed, one of the biggest challenges is to restore their confidence and preserve the relationship for the future. Perseverance may be required to defuse customers' anger and to convince them that actions are being taken to avoid a recurrence of the problem. Truly exceptional recovery efforts can be extremely effective in building loyalty and referrals.

Well-managed companies seek to act quickly and perform well on each of the 10 guidelines discussed in the Management Memo. Research suggests that the slower the resolution of a service problem, the greater the compensation (or "atonement") needed to make customers satisfied with the outcome of the service recovery process.[12] Treating complaints with suspicion is likely to alienate customers. There's a real danger in assuming that all complainers are what we called jaycustomers in chapter 3. As the president of TARP notes, "Our research has found premeditated rip-offs represent 1 to 2 percent of the customer base in most organizations. However, most organizations defend themselves against unscrupulous customers by . . . treating the 98 percent of honest customers like crooks to catch the 2 percent who *are* crooks."[13]

One of the most challenging tasks facing service managers is to recover customers who have taken their business elsewhere after one or more particularly unsatisfactory service experiences. Strauss and Friege argue for a structured approach to winning back customers who have either given notice of their intent to terminate the relationship or have already been lost.[14]

Taking care of customers requires that the firm also take care of its own employees. Managers need to recognize that handling complaints about service failures and attempting service recovery can be stressful for employees, especially when they get treated abusively for problems over which they have no control. Compounding the stress are policies that impose inflexible, bureaucratic procedures rather than empower customer-contact personnel to handle recovery situations as they see fit. Bowen and Johnston argue that service firms need to develop "internal service recovery strategies" designed to help employees recover from the negative feelings that they may incur in being the target of employee anger and dissatisfaction.[15]

Similarly, management must ensure that the firm employs a sufficient number of well-trained and motivated employees to be able to provide good service in the first place plus prompt and effective recovery when things go wrong. Companies with a good reputation for customer care cannot afford to become complacent. Downsizing (a deliberate policy of reducing the number of employees to reduce costs) often involves a calculated gamble that replacing people by automated phone messages and Web sites will enable the firm to continue to respond satisfactorily to customers' problems. The telecommunications industry provides a cautionary tale of the risks of cutting back people-based service in favor of automated solutions, especially during a period of continuing mergers, acquisitions, and divestitures. Corporate customers from international airlines to the Chicago Board of Trade are among those whose telephone or Internet operations have been paralyzed by service failures that were subsequently compounded by the customer's inability to find anyone who could promptly resolve the problem.[16]

Service Guarantees

A small but growing number of companies offers customers an unconditional guarantee of satisfaction, promising that if service delivery fails to meet predefined standards, the customer is entitled to one or more forms of compensation—such as an easy-to-claim replacement, refund, or credit. Christopher Hart argues that these service guarantees are powerful tools for both promoting and achieving service quality for the following reasons:

1. Guarantees force firms to focus on what their customers want and expect in each element of the service.
2. Guarantees set clear standards, telling customers and employees alike what the company stands for. Payouts to compensate customers for poor service cause managers to take guarantees seriously because they highlight the financial costs of quality failures.

3. Guarantees require the development of systems for generating meaningful customer feed-back and acting on it.
4. Guarantees force service organizations to understand why they fail and encourage them to identify and overcome potential fail points.
5. Guarantees build marketing muscle by reducing the risk of the purchase decision and building long-term loyalty.[17]

Many firms have enthusiastically leapt on the service guarantees bandwagon without care-fully thinking through what is implied in making and keeping the promises of an unconditional service guarantee. Compare the following two examples of service guarantees (Table 6.2) and ask yourself whether you would like to be a customer of either organization.

Building Strategy around the Service Guarantee at Promus Hotel Corporation

Promus Hotel Corporation originally introduced its 100% Satisfaction Guarantee at Hampton Inn (see Figure 6.4) and has now extended it throughout Promus's entire hotel system, includ-ing Hampton Inn & Suites, Embassy Suites, and Homewood Suites, uniting all of the Promus brands with a single, common commitment to guest satisfaction.[18]

TABLE 6.2 *Examples of Three Guarantees*

Excerpt from the "Quality Standard Guarantees" of an Office Services Company

We guarantee 6-hour turnaround on documents of two pages or less . . . (does not include client subsequent changes or equipment failures). We guarantee that there will be a receptionist to greet you and your visitors during normal business hours . . . (short breaks of less than five minutes are not subject to this guarantee). You will not be obligated to pay rent for any day on which there is not a manager on site to assist you (lunch and reasonable breaks are expected and not subject to this guarantee).

Source: Reproduced in Eileen C. Shapiro, *Fad Surfing in the Boardroom* (Reading, MA: Addison-Wesley, 1995), 180.

U.S. Postal Service Express Mail Guarantee

Service Guarantee: Excludes all international shipments. Military shipments delayed due to Customs inspections are also excluded. If this shipment is mailed at a designated USPS Express Mail facility on or before the specified time for overnight delivery to the addressee, it will be delivered to the addressee or agent before the guaranteed time the next delivery day. Signature of the addressee, addressee's agent, or delivery employee is required upon delivery. If it is not delivered by the guaranteed time and the mailer makes a claim for a refund, the USPS will refund the postage unless: 1) delivery was attempted but could not be made, 2) this shipment was delayed by strike or work stoppage, or 3) detention was made for a law enforcement purpose.

Source: Printed on back of Express Mail receipt.

L.L. Bean's Guarantee

Our Guarantee. Our products are guaranteed to give 100% satisfaction in every way. Return anything purchased from us at any time if it proves otherwise. We will replace it, refund your purchase price or credit your credit card. We do not want you to have anything from L.L. Bean that is not completely satisfactory.

Source: Printed in all L.L. Bean catalogs and on the company's Web site, www.llbean.com/customerservice/, January 2000.

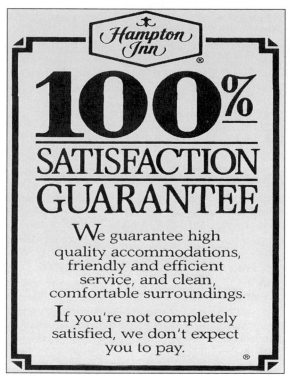

FIGURE 6.4   The Hampton Inn 100% Satisfaction Guarantee
Source: "Hampton Inn 100 percent Satisfaction Guarantee, Research Justifying the Guarantee," Promus Companies. Reprinted by permission.

As a business-building program, Promus views the 100% Satisfaction Guarantee as a great success. Its strategy of offering to refund the cost of the room for the day on which the guest expressed dissatisfaction has attracted new customers and also served as a powerful guest-retention device. People choose to stay at a Hampton Inn because they are confident they will be satisfied. At least as important, the guarantee has become a vital tool to help managers to identify new opportunities for quality improvement and to create the impetus to make those improvements. In this regard, the 100% Satisfaction Guarantee "turned up the pressure in the hose," as one manager put it, showing where leaks existed and providing the incentive to plug them. As a result, the guarantee has had an important impact on product consistency and service delivery across the Hampton Inn chain. Finally, studies of the 100% Satisfaction Guarantee's impact have shown a dramatically positive effect on financial performance.

However, fully implementing a 100% Satisfaction Guarantee is no easy task, as some of Promus's competitors who have tried to imitate its guarantee can attest. The story in Service Perspectives 6.1 is a pointed example.

Successful implementation of the 100% Satisfaction Guarantee requires that its underlying philosophy be embraced by every employee, from senior management to hourly workers. The challenge is to create a corporate culture based on a proactive commitment to consistently meet guests' expectations of 100 percent satisfaction. However, despite its proven benefits, the guarantee has faced both resistance and skepticism among hotel managers, not only at Hampton Inn but also as it was extended to Embassy Suites and Homewood Suites.

SERVICE PERSPECTIVES 6.1

How Unconditional Is Your Guarantee?

Christopher Hart tells this story of an incident at a hotel in a well-known chain during the summer of 1997 while accompanying his two cousins. Jeff and Roxy Hart were nearing the end of an extended holiday weekend. They needed to find an inexpensive place to stay. It was late in the day, and their flight left early the following morning. Jeff called Hampton Inn and found nothing available in the area. So he called (name deleted) Inn, which had rooms available, and booked one for $62.

"We found the hotel," said Chris, "noticing a huge banner draped from the bottom of the sign, advertising 'Rooms for $55.95, including breakfast.' We went inside."

After giving the front-desk clerk the basic information, Jeff was told that his room would be $69. "But the reservation agent I just booked the room with quoted me $62," said Jeff. "What's the story? And, by the way, what about the $55.95 price advertised on your sign? Can I get a room for that price?"

"Oh," replied the front-desk clerk. "That was a special promotion for the Spring. It's over now." (It was late June.)

Jeff responded, "But you're still advertising the price. It's illegal to advertise one price and charge another one."

"Let me get my manager," came the nervous response. Out came the manager. In the middle of the conversation in which Jeff was arguing the same points that he made with the front-desk clerk, Chris interjected, "By the way, I understand you offer a satisfaction guarantee. Right?"

"Not on the $55.95 rooms," came the reply from the manager.

"Well, what rooms is it on?"

"Only the good rooms."

"You mean you have bad rooms?"

"Well, we have some rooms that have not been renovated. Those are the ones we sell for $55.95. But we're sold out of them tonight."

Chris said, "Well, Jeff, you'd better get one of the more expensive rooms, because I'm not sure how satisfied you're going to be tomorrow."

The manager quickly added, "Did I mention that the guarantee doesn't apply on weekends?"

"No," barked Jeff, who had worked for 15 years conducting cost-benefit and compliance studies for the U.S. government, "and that's illegal, too!"

"Wait just a minute," said the manager, getting a puzzled look like something had just popped into his head. "Let me see something." He then buried his head into the computer, clicking away madly at the keyboard, creating the impression that he was working on our behalf. After an appropriate time, up popped his head, now with a big smile.

"One of the guests who originally reserved a $55.95 room, called and upgraded—but the upgrade wasn't recorded in the computer. I could let you have that room—but I can't guarantee your satisfaction."

"We'll take it," said Roxy, exhausted.

Designing the Guarantee. The first step in designing the guarantee at Hampton Inn was to answer a key question: What would guests want in a guarantee? Research revealed that they were most interested in the quality and cleanliness of their accommodation, friendly and efficient service, and a moderate price. They also wanted a guarantee that was simple and easy to invoke if warranted. In-depth guest interviews yielded an ideal customer-interaction flow and a map of 53 moments of truth critical to guests' satisfaction with their Hampton Inn stays. These moments of truth translated into concrete and controllable aspects of Hampton Inn's product and service delivery. Throughout the guarantee design process, an important new mind-set was reinforced: Listen to the guests, who knew best what satisfied them. Only the guests make the decision to return to a particular hotel or positively recommend a Promus hotel to others.

The vice president of marketing stated, "Designing the guarantee made us understand what made guests satisfied, rather than what *we thought* made them satisfied." It became imperative that everyone—from reservationists and front-line employees to general managers and personnel at corporate headquarters—listen carefully to guests, anticipate their needs to the greatest extent possible, and remedy problems quickly so that guests were satisfied with the solution. Viewing a hotel's function in this customer-centric way had a profound impact on the way Promus conducted business.

Concurrent with its guest-based qualitative research, Promus interviewed its most progressive and customer-oriented franchisees and hotel managers to understand their perceptions of the proposed guarantee. Even among those who fully supported the guarantee concept in principle, pressing concerns remained:

- Will guests try to cheat and rip us off?
- Will our employees give the store away?
- What will be the return on our efforts to increase the satisfaction of our customers?

Pilot Test. To prepare for the launch of the guarantee, a pilot test was conducted in 30 hotels that already had high customer satisfaction. Training was seen as critical. First, general managers were trained in the fundamentals of the guarantee—what it was and how it worked. Then the general managers trained their employees. Managers were taught to take a leadership role by actively demonstrating their support for the guarantee and helping their employees gain the confidence to handle guest concerns and problems. Finally, the guarantee was explained and promoted to guests.

Even at hotels that already had a high-satisfaction culture, Promus found that front-line employees were not always *fully empowered* to do whatever was needed to make a guest 100 percent satisfied. Further, employees did not always feel they were charged with explicit responsibility for guest satisfaction. They needed to understand that their job responsibilities would now extend beyond the functional roles for which they were initially hired (i.e., property maintenance, breakfast staff, front desk).

Managers and employees learned that the guarantee was not about giving money away—it was about making guests satisfied. They learned that satisfying guests by correcting problems had to be a priority. Employees were encouraged to creatively fix problems on the spot and rely on the guarantee as a safety net to catch guests who were still dissatisfied.

After learning the basic guarantee concepts and seeing the Hampton Inn 100% Satisfaction Guarantee, general managers were asked to form groups of 10 to 12. Their charge was to list the positive and negative aspects of the guarantee on a flipchart. Few groups could come up with more than one or two pages of positives, but the managers had little difficulty creating lists of negatives; one such list ran to 26 pages! Senior corporate managers went through each negative issue, addressing managers' concerns one by one. The concerns remained relatively consistent and centered on management control. There were also worries about guests abusing the guarantee and cheating—the sort of guests we nicknamed "jaycustomers" in chapter 3. (For a description of how Promus identifies guests who appear to be cheating, see Service Perspectives 6.2.)

Subsequent Experience. As part of the feedback loop for all Promus brands, the company provides reports every quarter, showing the top five reasons for guarantee invocations. Managers are helped to develop clear action plans for eliminating the sources of guarantee payouts at their hotels. Coupled with an awards program for employees who had undertaken exceptional acts of customer service, guest satisfaction has increased substantially at those hotels

> ### SERVICE PERSPECTIVES 6.2
>
> ### Tracking Down Guests Who Cheat
>
> As part of its guarantee tracking system, Promus has developed ways to identify guests who appeared to be cheating—using aliases or different satisfaction problems to invoke the guarantee repeatedly to get the cost of their room refunded. Guests showing high invocation trends receive personalized attention and follow-up from the Promus Guest Assistance Team. Wherever possible, senior managers will telephone these guests to ask them about their recent stays. The conversation might go as follows: "Hello, Mr. Jones. I'm the director of guest assistance at Promus Hotel corporation, and I see that you've had some difficulty with the last four properties you've visited. Since we take our guarantee very seriously, I thought I'd give you a call and find out what the problems were." The typical response is dead silence! Sometimes the silence is followed with questions of how headquarters could possibly know about their problems. These calls have their humorous moments as well. One individual, who had invoked the guarantee 17 times in what appeared to be a trip that took him across the United States and back, was asked innocuously, "Where do you like to stay when you travel?" "Hampton Inn," came the enthusiastic response. "But," said the Promus executive making the call, "our records show that the last 17 times you have stayed at a Hampton Inn, you have invoked the 100% Satisfaction Guarantee." "That's why I like them!" proclaimed the guest (who turned out to be a long-distance truck driver).

where the guarantee has been most strongly embraced. Further, once the sources of problems were systematically eliminated, payouts became less frequent. When this cycle of success occurred at a specific hotel, its staff became guarantee advocates who spread word of their success throughout the chain.

Over time, hotel managers have come to recognize two things. First, the number of people invoking the guarantee represents only a small percentage of all guests. Second, the percentage of cheaters in this group amounts to a ridiculously small number. As one manager admitted, "It occurred to me that I was managing my entire operation to accommodate the half of 1 percent of guests who actually invoke the guarantee. And out of that number, maybe only 5 percent were cheating. Viewed this way, I was focused on managing my business to only 0.025 percent of total revenues."

Experience has shown that guests are not typically looking for a refund—they just want to be satisfied with what they pay for. And because Promus's 100% Satisfaction Guarantee promises just that, it is a powerful vehicle for attracting and retaining guests. A 1996 survey found that

- Fifty-four percent of guests interviewed said they were more likely to consider Promus hotels because of the guarantee.
- Seventy-seven percent of guests interviewed said they would stay again at the same Promus hotel.
- Ninety-three percent of guests interviewed said they would stay at another Promus hotel.
- Fifty-nine percent of guests interviewed have already returned.

Developing Viable Guarantees

Among the reasons for Promus's success with its service guarantee are careful planning, listening to employee and manager concerns, an emphasis on training, and a willingness to delegate more authority to employees. The company has evaluated the possibility that customers would abuse its service guarantee—namely, making fraudulent claims so as to obtain a free night in a hotel—and determined that the incidence of such fraud is confined to a tiny fraction of its customers. Hence, customers are trusted when they register a complaint, and a refund is cheerfully given on the spot. However, the firm's management is not naive: There is careful tracking after the fact of all claims against the guarantee, and any suspicious-looking pattern of repeated claims is followed up.

Guaranteeing Specific Elements.

Guarantees need to be clear so that customers and employees can understand them easily. Sometimes, this means relating the terms of the guarantee to satisfaction with a specific activity rather than overall performance. For instance, the Irish Electricity Supply Board (ESB) offers 12 clearly stated service guarantees in its Customer Charter, relating to such elements as network repair, the main fuse, meter connection and accuracy, and scheduled appointments (when an employee visits the customer's premises). In each instance, the ESB has established a service standard, such as a promised speed of response, stating the payment that will be made to the customer if the company fails to meet its promised standards. The charter is written in simple language and tells customers what to do if they encounter any of the problems covered by the 12 guarantees. Compensation payments range from IR£ 20 to IR£ 100 ($26 to $130) depending on the nature of the problem and whether the customer is a household or a business.

Avoiding Inappropriate Use of Guarantees.

Is it always a good idea for a service firm to introduce a guarantee? The answer, according to Ostrom and Hart, is that managers should first think carefully about their firms' strengths and weaknesses in the context of the markets in which they compete.[19] Companies that already have a strong reputation for high-quality service may not need a guarantee; in fact, it might even be incongruent with their image to offer one. By contrast, firms whose service is currently poor must first work to improve quality to a level above that at which the guarantee might be invoked on a regular basis by most of their customers! Service organizations that suffer from high turnover, poor employee attitudes, and inability to recruit strong managers are also in no position to start offering guarantees. Similarly, firms whose service quality is truly uncontrollable (due to outside forces) would be foolish to consider guaranteeing any aspect of their service that was not amenable to improvement through internal strategies.

Because offering a guarantee is, in large measure, a marketing strategy, managers should ask themselves, Do the benefits outweigh the costs? The value of the extra business gained must be offset against the cost of paying compensation for failures covered by the guarantee plus the cost of investments to improve operational effectiveness and staff performance. However, in evaluating benefits, managers need to look at the long-term potential for greater operational productivity, increased staff pride and motivation, and the firm's ability to recruit and retain the best employees.

In a market where consumers see little financial, personal, or psychological risk associated with purchasing and using the service, we must question how much value would be added by instituting a guarantee. However, where perceived risks do exist but there is little perceived difference in service quality among competing offerings, then the first company to institute a guarantee may be able to obtain a first-mover advantage and create a valued differentiation for its services. But what should managers do if one or more competitors already has a guarantee in place? Doing nothing is a risk in that it may be seen as a de facto admission of inconsistent quality. There is also the possibility that the availability of a guarantee may eventually become a requirement in customers' purchase decision criteria. So the best response may be to attract customers' attention by launching a highly distinctive guarantee that not only goes beyond what the competition offers but will also be difficult for them to match or exceed in the short run.

Conclusion

Collecting customer feedback via complaints, suggestions, and compliments provides a means of increasing customer satisfaction. It's a terrific opportunity to get into the hearts and minds of customers. In all but the worst instances, complaining customers are indicating that they want to continue their relationship with the service firm. But they are also signaling that all is not well and that they expect the company to make things right.

Service firms need to develop effective strategies for recovering from service failures so that they can maintain customer goodwill. This is vital for the long-term success of the company. However, service personnel must also learn from their mistakes and try to ensure that problems are eliminated. After all, even the best recovery strategy isn't as good in the customer's eyes as being treated right the first time! Well-designed unconditional service guarantees have proved to be a powerful vehicle for identifying and justifying needed improvements as well for creating a culture in which staff members take proactive steps to ensure that guests will be satisfied.

REVIEW QUESTIONS

1. Explain the courses of action open to a dissatisfied consumer.
2. Describe the factors that may inhibit a dissatisfied consumer from complaining.
3. Concerning the TARP study results described in this chapter, what are the implications for managers?
4. Apply the four principles of service recovery at the managerial level to a service organization with which you are familiar. Describe how this organization follows/does not follow these guidelines. What impact do you see this as having on their customers' loyalty?
5. Evaluate the service guarantee introduced by Promus Hotels. What do you see as its main advantages and disadvantages?

APPLICATION EXERCISES

1. Think about the last time you experienced a less-than-satisfactory service experience. Did you complain? Why? If you did not complain, explain why not.
2. To whom would you personally feel most and least uncomfortable complaining? Why? How could the service providers in question reduce your discomfort to be sure of receiving important feedback from you and other customers?
3. When was the last time you were truly satisfied with an organization's response to your complaint? Describe in detail what happened and what made you satisfied.
4. Select three people and ask each of them to identify several occasions during the past year when they were dissatisfied with a service or a physical good purchased from a retailer. What action (if any) did they take in each case, and with what results? (If no action was taken, what were the reasons?)

ENDNOTES

1. Oren Harari, "Thank Heavens for Complainers," *Management Review,* March 1997, 25–29.
2. Technical Assistance Research Programs Institute (TARP), *Consumer Complaint Handling in America; An Update Study, Part II* (Washington, DC: TARP and U.S. Office of Consumer Affairs, April 1986).

3. Susan M. Keveaney, "Customer Switching Behavior in Service Industries: An Exploratory Study," *Journal of Marketing* 59 (April 1995): 71–82.

4. Bernd Stauss, "Global Word of Mouth," *Marketing Management,* fall 1997, 28–30.

5. Claes Fornell, Michael D. Johnson, Eugene W. Anderson, Jaesung Cha, and Barbara Everitt Bryant, "The American Customer Satisfaction Index: Nature, Purpose, and Findings," *Journal of Marketing* 60, no. 4 (October 1996): 7–18.

6. Society of Consumer Affairs Professionals (SOCAP), *SOCAP-TARP Study of Consumer Complaint Behaviour in Australia* (Sydney: SOCAP, 1995).

7. Cathy Goodwin and B. J. Verhage, "Role Perceptions of Services: A Cross-Cultural Comparison with Behavioral Implications," *Journal of Economic Psychology* 10 (1990): 543–558.

8. Christopher W. L. Hart, James L. Heskett, and W. Earl Sasser Jr., "The Profitable Art of Service Recovery," *Harvard Business Review* (July–August 1990): 148–156.

9. TARP, *Consumer Complaint Handling in America.*

10. Leonard L. Berry, *On Great Service: A Framework for Action* (New York: The Free Press, 1995), 94.

11. Barbara R. Lewis, "Customer Care in Services," in *Understanding Services Management,* ed. W. J. Glynn and J. G. Barnes (Chichester UK: Wiley, 1995), 57–89.

12. Christo Boshoff, "An Experimental Study of Service Recovery Options," *International Journal of Service Industry Management* 8, no. 2 (1997): 110–130.

13. John Goodman, quoted in "Improving Service Doesn't Always Require Big Investment," *The Service Edge,* July–August 1990, 3.

14. Bernd Strauss and Christian Friege, "Regaining Service Customers: Costs and Benefits of Regain Management," *Journal of Service Research* 1 (May 1999): 347–361.

15. David E. Bowen and Robert Johnston, "Internal Service Recovery: Developing a New Construct," *International Journal of Service Industry Management* 10, no. 2 (1999): 118–131.

16. Rebecca Blumenstein and Stephanie N. Mehta, "Lost in the Shuffle: As the Telecoms Merge and Cut Costs, Service Is Often a Casualty," *Wall Street Journal,* January 19, 2000, pp. A1, A6.

17. Christopher W. L. Hart, "The Power of Unconditional Service Guarantees," *Harvard Business Review* (July–August 1990): 54–62.

18. Information on Promus Hotel Corporation and the 100% Satisfaction Guarantee at Hampton Inn is drawn from Christopher W. Hart with Elizabeth Long, *Extraordinary Guarantees* (New York: AMACOM, 1997).

19. Amy L. Ostrom and Christopher Hart, "Service Guarantees: Research and Practice," in *Handbook of Services Marketing and Management,* ed. T. Schwartz and D. Iacobucci (Thousand Oaks, CA: Sage Publications, 2000), 299–316.

Listening to the Customer: The Concept of a Service-Quality Information System

Leonard L. Berry
A. Parasuraman

To improve service, companies must use multiple research approaches among different customer groups to ensure that they are hearing what customers are saying and responding to their suggestions.

The quality of listening has an impact on the quality of service. Firms intent on improving service need to listen continuously to three types of customers: external customers who have experienced the firm's service; competitors' customers who the firm would like to make its own; and internal customers (employees) who depend on internal services to provide their own services. Without the voices of these groups guiding investment in service improvement, all companies can hope for are marginal gains.

In this paper, we discuss the concept of a service-quality information system. We argue that companies need to establish ongoing listening systems using multiple methods among different customer groups. A single service-quality study is a snapshot taken at a point in time and from a particular angle. Deeper insight and more informed decision-making come from a continuing series of snapshots taken from various angles and through different lenses, which form the essence of systematic listening.

Systematic Listening

A service-quality information system uses multiple research approaches to systematically capture, organize, and disseminate service-quality information to support decision-making. Continuously generated data flow into databases that decision-makers can use on both a regular scheduled and as needed basis.

The use of multiple research approaches is necessary because each approach has limitations as well as strengths. Combining approaches enables a firm to tap the strengths of each and compensate for weaknesses. Continuous data collection and dissemination informs and educates decision-makers about the *patterns* of change—for example, customers' shifting service priorities and declining or improving performance in the company's or the competitors' service.

An effective service-quality information system offers a company's executives a larger view of service quality along with a composite of many smaller pictures. It teaches decision-makers which service attributes are important to customers and prospects, what parts of the firm's service system are working well or breaking down, and which service investments are paying off. A service-quality information system helps to focus service improvement planning and resource allocation. It can help sustain managers' motivation for service improvement by comparing the service performance of various units in the organization and linking compensation to these results. And it can be the basis for an effective first-line employee reward system by identifying the most effective service providers. (See Figure 1 for the principal benefits of a service-quality information system.)

The task of improving service in organizations is complex. It involves knowing what to do on multiple fronts, such as technology, service systems, employee selection, training and education, and reward systems. It involves knowing how to implement these actions and how to transform activity into sustainable improvement. Genuine service improvement requires an integrated strategy based on systematic listening. Unrelated, incomplete studies, outdated research, and findings about customers that are not shared provide insufficient support for improving service.

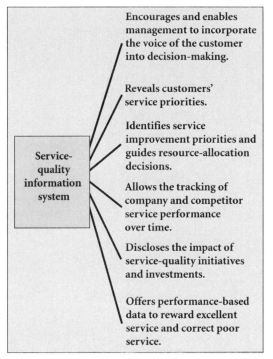

Figure 1 Principle Benefits of an Effective Service-Quality Information System

Source: L. Berry, *On Great Service: A Framework for Action*, New York: Free Press, 1995, p. 34.

Approaches to Service Research

A company can choose from many possible research approaches to build a service-quality information system (see Table 1). A firm would not use all approaches in the table in the same system; too much information obscures the most meaningful insights and may intimidate intended users. Conversely, incomplete information injects needless guessing into decision-making or, worse, paints a false picture. The nature of the service, the firm's service strategy, and the needs of the information users determine which service-quality research approaches to use.

An industrial equipment manufacturer might wish to use service reviews to benefit from unfiltered dialogue with multiple users, reach consensus on service support priorities, and solidify relationships. A restaurant, with a transaction-oriented business, would find service reviews far less efficient than other approaches. Because of the rela-

tionship nature of its business, a limousine service should consider new, declining and lost-customer surveys. It should identify any negatives that tarnish new customers' first impressions, or cause other customers to be less loyal or to defect, so it can take corrective measures. A taxi company probably wouldn't use these surveys because of a minimal relationship-marketing potential. A firm whose strategy emphasizes service reliability surely would want to capture and analyze customer service complaints to identify where the service system is breaking down. A company whose strategy depends on point-of-sale service excellence should consider mystery shopping research, which generates feedback on specific service providers.

Four research approaches summarized in the table apply to virtually all organizations and can be considered essential components of a service-quality information system: transactional surveys; customer complaint, comment, and inquiry capture; total market surveys; and employee surveys. These approaches ensure coverage of the three customer types (external customers, competitors' customers, internal customers), document failure-prone parts of the service systems, and provide both transaction-specific and overall service feedback.

Personal Involvement in Listening

A service-quality information system does not replace the need for managers to interact directly with customers. Becoming well informed about service quality requires more than reading or hearing the results of structured, quantitative studies. It also requires that decision-makers become personally involved in listening to the voices of their customers, which can include participating in or observing qualitative research, such as service reviews and focus groups. And it can include less formal interactions with customers, such as when airline executives query passengers on flights and retailers accompany customers through their stores to ask them what they see, like and dislike.

In 1993, the cash management division of First National Bank of Chicago changed its customer satisfaction surveys from mail questionnaires to telephone interviews. The change was prompted by poor response rates to the mail survey and customers' suggestions for improving survey effectiveness: conduct the surveys by phone because they are more efficient and have bank employees who can act on problems make the calls.

First Chicago recruited senior and middle managers to conduct three pre-scheduled twenty-

TABLE 1 *Research Approaches for Building Service-Quality Information Systems*

Type	Description	Purpose	Frequency**	Limitations
Transactional surveys*	Service satisfaction survey of customers following a service encounter.	Obtain customer feedback while service experience is still fresh; act on feedback quickly if negative patterns develop.	Continuous	Focuses on customers' most recent experience rather than their overall assessment. Non-customers are excluded.
Mystery shopping	Researchers become "customers" to experience and evaluate the quality of service delivered.	Measure individual employee service behaviours for use in coaching, training, performance evaluation, recognition and rewards; identify systemic strengths and weaknesses in customer-contact service.	Quarterly	Subjective evaluations: researchers may be more "judgmental" than customers would be; expense limits repetitions; potential to hurt employee morale if improperly used.
New, declining and lost-customer surveys	Surveys to determine why customers select the firm, reduce their buying or leave the firm.	Assess the role service quality and other issues play in customer patronage and loyalty.	Continuous	Firm must be able to identify and monitor service usage on a per customer basis.
Focus group interviews	Directed questioning of a small group, usually eight to twelve people. Questions focus on a specific topic. Can be used with customer, non-customer, or employee groups.	Provide a forum for participants to suggest service improvement ideas; offer fast, informal feedback on service issues.	As needed	Dynamics of group interview may prevent certain issues from surfacing. Focus groups are, in effect, brainstorming sessions; the information generated is not projectable to the population of interest. Focus group research is most valuable when coupled with projectable research.
Customer advisory panels	A group of customers recruited periodically to provide the firm with feedback and advice on service performance and other issues. Data are obtained in meetings, over the telephone, through mail questionnaires or via other means. Employee panels also can be formed.	Obtain in-depth, timely feedback and suggestions about service quality from experienced customers who cooperate because of the "membership" nature of the panel.	Quarterly	May not be projectable to entire customer base. Excludes non-customers. Panelists may assume role of "expert" and become less representative of customer base.

Service reviews	Periodic visits with customers (or a class of customers) to discuss and assess the service relationship. Should be a formal process with a common set of questions, capture of responses in a database, and follow-up communication with customers.	Identify customer expectations and perceptions of the company's service performance and improvement priorities in a face-to-face conversation. A view of the future, not just a study of the past. Opportunity to include multiple decision-makers and decision-influencers in the discussions.	Annually or semi-annually	Time consuming and expensive. Most appropriate for firms marketing complex services on an ongoing, relationship basis.
Customer complaint, comment, and inquiry capture*	System to retain, categorize, track and distribute customer complaints and other communications with the company.	Identify most common types of service failure for corrective action. Identify through customer communications opportunities to improve service or otherwise strengthen customer relationships.	Continuous	Dissatisfied customers frequently do not complain directly to the company. Analysis of customer complaints and comments offers only a partial picture of the state of service.
Total market surveys	Surveys that measure customers' overall assessment of a company's service. Research includes both external customers and competitors' customers, i.e., the total market.	Assess company's service performance compared to competitors; identify service-improvement priorities; track service improvement over time.	Semi-annually or quarterly	Measures customers' overall service assessments but does not capture assessments of specific service encounters.
Employee field reporting	Formal process for gathering, categorizing and distributing field employee intelligence about service issues.	Capture and share at the management level intelligence about customers' service expectations and perceptions gathered in the field.	Continuous to monthly	Some employees will be more conscientious and efficient reporters than others. Employees may be unwilling to provide negative information to management.

TABLE 1 *continued*

Type	Description	Purpose	Frequency**	Limitations
Employee surveys	Surveys concerning the service employees provide and receive, and the quality of their work lives.	Measure internal service quality; identify employee-perceived obstacles to improved service; track employee morale and attitudes. Employee surveys help answer "why" service performance is what it is.	Quarterly	The strength of employee surveys is also a weakness; employees view service delivery from their own vantage point, subject to their own biases. Employees can offer valuable insights into the root causes of service problems but are not always objective or correct in their interpretations.
Service operating data	A system to retain, categorize, track and distribute key service-performance operating data, such as service-response times, service failure rates and service delivery costs.	Monitor service performance indicators and take corrective action to improve performance as necessary. Relate operating performance data to customer and employee feedback.	Continuous	Operating performance data may not be relevant to customers' perceptions of service. Focus is on what is occurring but not why.

* Highlighted approaches normally would be part of any service-quality information system.

** Frequencies of use vary among companies.

minute phone interviews per month and write reports on each call for the database. Managers were trained to do the interviews and passed a certification test before surveying their first customer. They surveyed each employee of the client firm who had significant contact with the bank. Bank managers were responsible for "action items" that surfaced in the interviews. The bank's vice president of quality assurance, Aleta Holub, remarked, "We've really seen a cultural change from getting everyone a little closer to the customer."[1]

Directly hearing the voices of customers, noncustomers and employees adds richness, meaning and perspective to the interpretation of quantitative data. The First Chicago case illustrates the potential impact embedded in literally hearing the customer's voice, rather than hearing only a distilled or numeric representation of it. McQuarrie makes the point: "Everyone believes his or her own eyes and ears first. Key players hear about problems and needs directly from the most credible source— the customer. Learning is enhanced because of the vivid and compelling quality of first-hand knowledge.[2]

A well-designed and implemented service-quality information system raises the probability that a company will invest service improvement money in ways that actually improve service. It also continually underscores the need to improve service. Continually capturing and disseminating data reveal not only progress, but problems; not only strengths, but weaknesses. Quality service is a never-ending journey. An effective service-quality information system reminds everyone that more work needs to be done.

Developing an Effective Service–Quality Information System

The primary test of a service-equality information system is the extent to which it informs and guides service-improvement decision making. Another important test is the extent to which the system motivates both managerial and non-managerial employees to improve service. There are five guidelines for developing a system that can meet these tests:

1. Measure service expectations.
2. Emphasize information quality.
3. Capture customers' words.
4. Link service performance to business results.
5. Reach every employee.

The core success factors embedded are the coverage of external, competitors' and internal customers; the use of multiple measures; and ongoing measurement.

Measure Service Expectations

Measuring service performance per se is not as meaningful as measuring relative to customers' expectations. Customers' service expectations provide a frame of reference for their assessment of the service. Assume, for example, that a company measures only customers' perceptions of service performance using a 9-point scale. It receives an average perception score of 7.3 on the service attribute "Performs the service right the first time." How should managers interpret this score? Is it a good score? Without knowing what customers expect, this is a difficult question. There is no basis for gauging the rating. Managers' interpretation of the 7.3 perception score would likely be far different if customers' average expectation rating for this attribute were 8.2 rather than 7.0. As researchers Goodman et al. ask: "How satisfied is a satisfied customer? When is good, good enough? Unfortunately, companies that ask their customers how satisfied they are but fail to research customers' expectations cannot answer these questions."[3]

We collected service quality data from a computer manufacturer's customers (see Figure 2). We measured two levels of expectations: *desired service* (what the customer believes the service should be and can be) and *adequate service* (the minimal level of service acceptable to the customer). The top of the tolerance zone represents customers' average desired service-expectation score, the bottom, their average adequate service-expectation score. Service performance is superior if perception scores exceed the zone of tolerance, acceptable if perceptions are within the zone, and unacceptable if perceptions are below the zone.

Comparing the perceptions-only data with the combined perceptions-expectations data demonstrates the diagnostic value of measuring customers' expectations. Were the computer manufacturer to measure only customer perceptions, its management would have little guidance for investing service improvement resources. The perception scores are similar across the service dimensions. However, the inclusion of expectations data clearly shows that improving service reliability should take priority over improving tangibles. Although reliability and tangibles have identical perception scores,

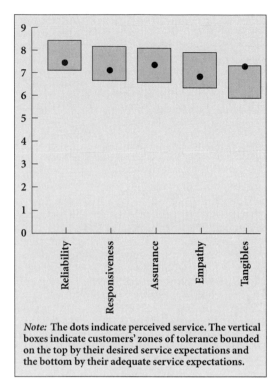

Note: The dots indicate perceived service. The vertical boxes indicate customers' zones of tolerance bounded on the top by their desired service expectations and the bottom by their adequate service expectations.

FIGURE 2 Service-Quality Ratings for a Computer Manufacturer

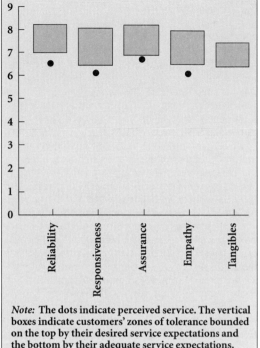

Note: The dots indicate perceived service. The vertical boxes indicate customers' zones of tolerance bounded on the top by their desired service expectations and the bottom by their adequate service expectations.

FIGURE 3 Service-Quality Ratings for a Retail Chain

customers' expectations for reliable service are much higher. Whereas customers' perceptions barely exceed adequate-level expectations for reliability, they exceed desired-level expectations for tangibles.

We also contrasted perceptions-only and perceptions-expectations data for a retail chain (see Figure 3). Without expectations data, management may conclude that the firm's service quality is acceptable because all perception scores are more than a full point above the scale's midpoint of 5. However, the addition of expectations scores suggests a much different conclusion, with service performance on four of the five dimensions not even meeting customers' minimum expectations.[4]

Documenting the value of measuring customer expectations in service-quality research is necessary because perceptions-only research is common. Measuring expectations adds complexity and possibly length to the survey process and can be more expensive. Moreover, accurately measuring expectations is not easy. The best way to do it and

whether it is even necessary are the subject of debate.[5] Advocates of perceptions-only measurement typically point out that service perception scores explain more variance in an overall service-quality measure than a combined expectations-perceptions measure. Perceptions ratings consistently explain more variance, most likely because pieces of the whole (perceptions of specific service attributes) are being regressed against the whole (an overall service perception measure). So why is it so critical to measure customer expectations of service? Because, as Figures 2 and 3 show, managers learn more about improving service when customer expectations provide a frame of reference for interpreting perception ratings.

Emphasize Information Quality

Quality of information—not quantity—is the objective in building a service-quality information system. The test of information quality is to ask if the information is:

- Relevant?
- Precise?
- Useful?
- In context?
- Credible?
- Understandable?
- Timely?

Relevant service-quality information focuses decision-makers' attention on the most important issues to meet and exceed external customer expectations, convert prospects, and enable employees to improve service. The more a service-quality information system focuses on the service priorities of the three customer types, the more likely managers will invest in the most appropriate initiatives that can make a positive difference.

Measuring the importance of service attributes is not the same as measuring customers' service expectations, although they are closely related. Customers' expectations are the comparison standards they use to judge the performance of various service attributes. However, the service attributes are not uniformly important to customers, and it is necessary to specifically measure their relative importance to monitor company and competitor performance on those attributes that drive customers' overall perceptions of service quality.

Information *precision* and *usefulness* go hand in hand. Information that is overly broad or general is not useful. Researcher Brian Lunde commented: "One of the worst criticisms that could be made by a line manager about a company's . . . information is that it is 'interesting.' 'Interesting' is code for 'useless.' The information simply must be specific enough that executives . . . can take action—make decisions, set priorities, launch programs, cancel projects."[6]

Information on what must be done to improve service is useful. Chase Manhattan Bank has determined empirically that the approval process is the primary driver of customers' quality perceptions for its mortgage loan service. Accordingly, Chase's service information system tracks its performance on the mortgage approval process compared to its principal competitors. However, Chase does not stop with overall perceptions of the mortgage approval process. It also investigates "sub-drivers" such as quick approval, communication, the appraisal process, amount of paperwork and unchanging loan amount. The information is sufficiently precise so managers know what to do and can assign implementation accountabilities. They review data patterns regularly at management meetings.[7]

An effective service-quality information system presents information dynamically. At any point in time, the system's output tells what is becoming more or less important—the *context*. Fresh data are more valuable when presented in the context of past data. The study of trend data reveals patterns, nuances and insights that one-time data cannot possibly reveal. Is the investment in new telephone technology paying off? Was it a good idea to redesign the account-opening procedures? Is the company's new investment in training reducing error rates? Has competitor advertising about service influenced customer expectations? Has the competitor's new store prototype given its service ratings a boost? Only trend data can answer these and myriad other questions. Ongoing research using common measures across study periods generates trend data that provide context and aid interpretation.

A service-quality information system will not motivate managerial and non-managerial employees unless the information is *credible*. Employees in low rated units may be embarrassed and financially hurt by the system's output and may question the information validity. Companies can improve information credibility by seeking input from operating units on the design of research approaches and the development of specific questions. Information sessions to explain research approaches to employees, with an opportunity for questions and answers, also can be useful. Clear explanations of the research method and sample size should accompany the dissemination of results. Multiple measures—a fundamental tenet of service-quality information systems—enhance information credibility when different measures point to similar conclusions. The use of an outside research firm for data collection can help convey impartiality.

Information quality also is determined by whether the information is *understandable* to intended users. Relevance, usefulness and credibility all are enhanced with easily understood research information. Unfamiliar statistical jargon and symbols confuse, intimidate and discourage users, leading to feigned use of the system and incorrect interpretations of its output. There should be a concerted effort to design a user-friendly system with uniform reports and clear presentation of data.

The *timeliness* of information influences its quality. All the other attributes of information quality are rendered impotent if information is not available when decision-makers need it. Companies should collect data to support their natural decision-making and planning cycles. Monthly transactional survey reports should be ready for the monthly management meeting, total market survey results should feed the annual planning and budgeting process, customer complaint analyses should be ready for the twice-a-month meetings of the service-improvement leadership team. The design of databases should accommodate trend-data retrieval for managers as needed. Companies should continually explore ways to accelerate data collection and dissemination. Firms might fax or e-mail questionnaires to respondents rather than use the postal service. Research results might be distributed internally on a company's intranet.

The information quality tests of relevance, precision, usefulness, context, credibility, understandability and timeliness are not absolutes. Improving information quality is a journey of trial and error, experience curve effects, user feedback and new knowledge. Building an effective system is a never-ending process of refinement. Larry Brandt, associate director of customer service at AMP, a manufacturer of electrical and electronic connectors, points out the necessity of continuous improvement: "We need to constantly evaluate what it is we're measuring, why we're doing it, and whether the results are worthwhile in the organization's big picture, or we run the risk of wasting time and effort.[8]

Capture Customers' Words

The best service-quality information systems are built with qualitative and quantitative databases, rather than strictly the latter. Quantified data are summaries; averages of customers' perceptions of a very specific service issue are still averages. Quantitative data bring many benefits to the service information table, including easy analysis, comparability from one period to the next, and potential projectability. What numbers don't offer are the tone, inflection, feeling, and "word pictures" from customers' voices. A service quality report showing that 4 per cent of the customer base is very dissatisfied and another 13 per cent is somewhat dissatisfied with the company's service may not get management's attention. However, if the report includes customers' verbatim comments, it may receive a very different reaction.

GTE Supply and Lexus customers illustrate the importance of capturing customers' words. GTE Supply purchases numerous products needed for the telephone operations of its customers, the local telephone companies. By implementing a systematic survey of customers' needs and opinions, GTE has improved service quality. The survey generates both quantitative and qualitative data for each customer. Current numerical quality ratings are compared to previous results to spot problems. In addition, the survey asks two open-ended questions: "Why do you say that?" (in response to a closed-ended overall quality question) and "What improvements, if any, could be made by Supply?" The company enters the customers' own words into a database and presents them to its managers along with the numerical data. GTE researchers James Drew and Tye Fussell remarked: "Tabulations of survey questions can highlight specific transaction characteristics in need of improvement from the customer's viewpoint. In contrast, open-ended comments are especially effective in motivating first-level managers and giving the tabulations substance and a human touch."[9]

Toyota introduced the Lexus line of luxury cars in the late 1980s, and by the early 1990s, the cars had vaulted to the top of the J.D. Power & Associates ratings in customer satisfaction. Soon after, another luxury carmaker retained Custom Research Inc. (CRI), a marketing research firm, to find out why Lexus owners were so satisfied. CRI conducted a series of focus groups to hear the Lexus story in the owners' words. Most of the Lexus drivers eagerly volunteered stories about the special care and attention they had received from their Lexus dealer. It became clear that although Lexus was manufacturing cars with few mechanical problems, the extra care shown in the sales and service process strongly influenced buyer satisfaction. Owners felt pampered and respected as valued Lexus customers. For example, one female owner mentioned several times during the focus group that she had never had a problem with her Lexus. However, on further probing she said, "Well, I suppose you could call the four times they had to replace the windshield a 'problem.' But frankly, they took care of it so well and always gave me a loaner car, so I never really considered it a 'problem' until you mentioned it now." CRI's research showed that the Lexus policy of always offering service customers a loaner car took almost all the pain out of the service experience. These insights from the focus groups helped explain the reasons behind the high J.D. Power satisfaction scores. And they gave CRI's client a view of the Lexus ownership experience not evident from the scores alone.

When customers express their views on videotape, the effect is even more compelling than printed verbatim comments. For company personnel, nothing beats seeing the intensity of customers' comments. Southwest Airlines shows contact employees videotapes of passengers complaining about service. Colleen Barrett, executive vice president for customers, states: "When we show the tape, you can hear a pin drop. It's fascinating to see the faces of employees while they're watching. When they realize the customer is talking about them, it's pretty chilling. That has far more impact than anything I can say."[10]

During the past few years, Levi Strauss & Co., one of the world's most successful companies, has been completely transforming its business processes, systems and facilities. Improving the speed and reliability distribution has been its principal objective. The team leading the transformation used videotaped interviews with customers to help convince the employees in such a successful company that change was essential. One big customer said, "We trust many of your competitors implicitly. We sample their deliveries. We open all Levi's deliveries." Another customer stated, "Your lead times are the worst. If you weren't Levi's, you'd be gone."[11]

Companies investing in service-quality information systems should consider using what McQuarrie calls "perennial questions."[12] A perennial question is open-ended and allows customers to speak directly about what concerns them most. Companies should ask it consistently and save responses in a database to ascertain data patterns. GTE Supply's question, "What improvements, if any, could be made by Supply?" is a perennial question. McQuarrie offers this example: "What things do we do particularly well or particularly poorly, relative to our competitors?" Examples of perennial questions directed to employees include:

- What is the biggest problem you face every day trying to deliver high-quality service to your customers?
- If you were president of the company and could make only one change to improve service quality, what change would you make?[13]

Combining customers' words with their numbers has synergy. The combination, when well executed, produces a high level of realism that not only informs but educates, not only guides but motivates.

Link Service Performance to Business Results

Intuitively, it makes sense that delivering quality service helps a company at the bottom line. Indeed, accumulating evidence suggests that excellent service enables a firm to strengthen customer loyalty and increase market share.[14] However, companies need not rely on outside evidence on this issue. Firms can develop their own evidence of the profit impact of service quality to make the investment more credible and fact-based for the planning and budgeting process.

A service-quality information system should include the impact of service performance on business results. An important benefit of new, declining, and lost-customer surveys is the measurement of market gains and damage linked to service quality. Surveys can reveal the number and percentage of new customers who selected the company for service-related reasons. Declining and lost-customer surveys can determine why customers are buying less or defecting, allowing estimates of revenue lost due to service. Calculating lost revenue because of service dissatisfaction, categorized by specific types of service dissatisfaction, is a dependable way to focus management attention on service improvement. By computing the average costs for reperforming botched services and multiplying them by frequency of occurrence, companies also can calculate the out-of-pocket costs of poor service. Combining lost revenue and out-of-pocket costs attributable to poor service generally will produce a sum far greater than management would assume without formal estimation.

Firms also can directly estimate the profit impact of effective service recovery by measuring complaining customers' satisfaction with the handling of their complaints and their repurchase intentions. Technical Assistance Research Programs (TARP) has conducted extensive studies documenting the much stronger repurchase intentions of complaining customers who are completely satisfied with the firm's response compared to dissatisfied customers (complainants and non-complainants) who remain dissatisfied. Firms can monitor the relationship between service recovery and business results by measuring dissatisfied customers' propensity to complain (the higher the better because of the opportunity to resolve the complaint), and by measuring complaining customers' satisfaction with the firm's response and their repurchase intentions. These data can be used to estimate the return on investment in service recovery, i.e., profits attributed to service recovery divided by the costs of service recovery.[15]

Another way to gauge the market impact of service quality is to measure customers' repurchase and other behavioral intentions in transactional and total market surveys. The surveys can ask respondents to rate how likely it is that they will, for example, recommend the firm, do more business with the firm in the next few years, or take some business to a competitor with better prices. Respondents' intentions can then be regressed against their perceptions of service quality to reveal associations between customers' service experiences and their future intentions concerning the firm. We have investigated empirically a battery of thirteen behavioral intention statements. Using factor analysis, the thirteen-item battery reconfigured into five dimensions (see Table 2).[16]

Our research shows strong relationships between service performance and customer loyalty and propensity to switch (see Figure 4). Customers whose service perceptions were below the zone of tolerance were less loyal and more likely to switch to a competitor than customers whose perceptions exceeded the zone. Customers exhibited some willingness to pay more for better service, particularly as service perceptions rose from inadequate to desired. Intentions to complain externally fell slightly across the zone.[17] (The internal response dimension is omitted from our analysis because it is based on a single item from the thirteen-item scale.)

Companies that measure customers' behavioral intentions (or actual behaviors) and monitor their sensitivity to changes in service performance gain valuable information on both why and how to invest in service improvement. Assessing the bottom-line impact of service performance will motivate managerial and non-managerial employees to implement needed changes. It will help a company move from just talking about service to improving service.

Reach Every Employee

A service-quality information system can be beneficial only if decision-makers use it. Accordingly, it must be more than a data collection system; it must also be a communications system. Determining who receives what information in what form and when is a principal design challenge. Chase Manhattan Bank vice president John Gregg commented: "I cannot stress enough the need to systematize the use of survey information, a key learning point for us in the last couple of years. It is not just how actionable the data are, but also the

---

TABLE 2 *Customers' Statements of Intention*

Behavioral-Intentions Dimension	Item Label	Item Wording*
Loyalty to company	1.	Say positive things about XYZ to other people.
	2.	Recommend XYZ to someone who seeks your advice.
	3.	Encourage friends and relatives to do business with XYZ.
	4.	Consider XYZ your first choice to buy ___ services.
	5.	Do more business with XYZ in the next few years.
Propensity to switch	6.	Do less business with XYZ in the next few years.
	7.	Take some of your business to a competitor that offers better prices.
Willingness to pay more	8.	Continue to do business with XYZ if its prices increase somewhat.
	9.	Pay a higher price than competitors charge for the benefits you currently receive from XYZ.
External response to problem	10.	Switch to a competitor if you experience a problem with XYZ's service.
	11.	Complain to other customers if you experience a problem with XYZ's service.
	12.	Complain to external agencies, such as the Better Business Bureau, if you experience a problem with XYZ's service.
Internal response to problem	13.	Complain to XYZ's employees if you experience a problem with XYZ's service.

*Each item was accompanied by a 7-point likelihood scale (1 = "Not At All Likely" and 7 = "Extremely Likely").

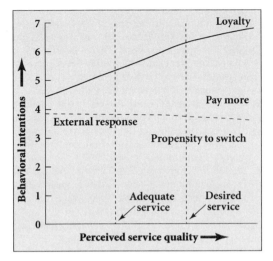

FIGURE 4 Relationship between Service Quality and Customers' Intentions for Computer Manufacturer

system for regularly reviewing the data and making decisions that determine effectiveness."[18]

All employees are decision-makers as they regularly make decisions that determine the effectiveness of their actions; therefore, a service-quality information system should disseminate relevant service information to everyone in the organization.

Front-line service providers, for example, should receive information about the expectations and perceptions of the external or internal customers they serve. These personnel might receive information different from what executives receive—and in different forms (for example, in training classes, newsletters and videos)—but they should be included in the system. Companies miss an important teaching, reinforcing, culture-building opportunity when they don't share relevant service information with employees lower in the hierarchy.

John Deere shares customer feedback with every employee. Its system is designed so that employees in different functions receive the information in an appropriate form, e.g., via e-mail, a hard copy of customer comments posted on bulletin boards, and specialized monthly reports. Les Teplicky, manager of after-market support at John Deere, stated: "You need senior management buy-in, good data collection, clear analysis—but all that won't matter unless every employee sees something in the information for them."[19]

Just as in the design of any product, knowing the needs of information users is critical to designing a service-quality information system. The system should revolve around what information different kinds of employees need to help them make good decisions and how and when to communicate the information. (See Table 3 for types of questions to include in both pre-design and post-

TABLE 3 *Questions for Service-Quality Information System Users*	
Pre-Design	**Post-Implementation**
• What would you like to know about the customers you serve?	• Are you receiving the information you need to help the company improve its service? (for managers)
• What type of information would help you improve service in our company?	• Are you receiving the information you need to best serve your customers? (for frontline employees)
• What type of information would you like to have about your own service performance? About your work unit? About the company? About the competition?	• What information on customer service would you like to receive that you currently do not receive? How would this additional information help you?
• If you presently receive information on customer service, what type of information is most valuable to you? Why? What is least valuable? Why?	• What customer service information that you receive is most valuable to you? Why? What is least valuable? Why?
• What are your preferred ways of receiving customer service information? How often would you like to receive this information?	• Do you receive customer service information on a timely basis? Please explain.
	• What could the company do to improve the usefulness of the customer service information it provides you?

implementation surveys of targeted information users.) Packaging the right information for each audience and presenting it effectively is key to the success of a service-quality information system. As Peter Drucker stated: "Knowledge is power. In post-capitalism, power comes from transmitting information to make it productive, not hiding it."[20]

When listening to customers becomes a habit in a company, when managers find it unthinkable to make service investment decisions unaided by relevant information, when employees eagerly await next month's service performance scores to gauge progress, when virtually all employees understand the service improvement priorities—then it is clear that the organization is systematically using information to improve service.

REFERENCES

1. Quoted in "First Chicago Shelves Paper Surveys, Asks Managers to Use the Telephone for Customer Satisfaction Research," *The Service Edge*, Vol. 8, March 1995, p. 4.

2. E.F. McQuarrie, "Taking a Road Trip," *Marketing Management*, Vol. 3, Spring 1995, p. 11.

3. I.A. Goodman, S.M. Broetzmann and C. Adamson, "Ineffective—That's the Problem with Customer Satisfaction Surveys," *Quality Progress*, Vol. 25, May 1992, p. 35.

4. For a detailed discussion of this study, see: A. Parasuraman, V.A. Zeithaml and L.L. Berry, "Alternative Scales for Measuring Service Quality: A Comparative Assessment Based on Psychometric and Diagnostic Criteria," *Journal of Retailing*, Vol. 70, Fall 1994, pp. 201–30.

5. See A. Parasuraman, V.A. Zeithaml and L.L. Berry, "Reassessment of Expectations as a Comparison Standard in Measuring Service Quality: Implications for Further Research," *Journal of Marketing*, Vol. 58, January 1994, pp. 111–24; J.J. Cronin and S.A. Taylor, "SERVPERF Versus SERVQUAL: Reconciling Performance-Based and Perceptions-Minus-Expectations Measurement of Service Quality," *Journal of Marketing*, Vol. 58, January 1994, pp. 125–31; and K.R. Teas, "Expectations as a Comparison Standard in Measuring Service Quality: An Assessment of a Reassessment," *Journal of Marketing*, Vol. 58, January 1994, pp. 132–39.

6. B.S. Lunde, "When Being Perfect is Not Enough," *Marketing Research*, Vol. 5, Winter 1993, p. 26.

7. J.P. Gregg, "Listening to the Voice of the Customer," Nashville, Tennessee: Frontiers in Services Conference, Presentation, October 1995.

8. Quoted in "Changes in Satisfaction Demands and Technology Alter the How's, What's, and Why's of Measurement," *The Service Edge*, Vol. 8, January 1995, p. 2.

9. J.H. Drew and T.R. Fussell, "Becoming Partners with Internal Customers," *Quality Progress*, Vol. 29, October 1996, p. 52.

10. Quoted in "Some Ways to Coddle Customers on a Budget," *The Service Edge*, Vol. 6, September 1993, p. 4.

11. D. Sheff, "Levi's Changes Everything," *Fast Company*, Vol. 2, June-July 1996, p. 67.

12. McQuarrie (1995), p. 12.

13. L.L. Berry, *On Great Service: A Framework for Action*, New York: Free Press, 1995, pp. 51–52.

14. See V.A. Zeithaml, L.L. Berry and A. Parasuraman, "The Behavioral Consequences of Service Quality," *Journal of Marketing*, Vol. 60, April 1996, pp. 31–46; and R.D. Buzzell and B.T. Gale, *The PIMS Principles*, New York: Free Press, 1987.

15. See *Consumer Complaint Handling in America: An Update Study*, Washington, D.C.: Technical Assistance Research Programs Institute, April 1986.

16. Zeithaml et al. (1996).

17. Ibid.

18. Personal correspondence.

19. Quoted in "Rallying the Troops," *On Achieving Excellence*, Vol. 11, February 1996, p. 2.

20. Interview with Peter F. Drucker, *Harvard Business Review*, Vol. 71, May-June 1993, p. 120.

PART III

Creating Value in a Competitive Market

CHAPTER 7

Positioning a Service in the Marketplace

To succeed in our overcommunicated society, a company must create a position in the prospect's mind, a position that takes into consideration not only a company's own strengths and weaknesses, but those of its clients as well.

AL REIS AND JACK TROUT

Ask a group of managers from different service businesses how they compete, and the chances are high that many will say simply, "On service." Press them a little further, and they may add words and phrases such as "value for money," "our people are the key," or "convenience."

None of this is very helpful to a marketing specialist who is trying to develop strategies to help an organization compete more effectively in the marketplace. At issue is what makes consumers or institutional buyers select—and remain loyal to—one service supplier over another. Terms such as *service* typically subsume a variety of specific characteristics, ranging from the speed with which a service is delivered to the quality of interactions between customers and service personnel and from avoiding errors to providing desirable extras that supplement the core service. Likewise, *convenience* could refer to a service that's delivered at a convenient location, available at convenient times, or easy to use. Without knowing which product features are of specific interest to customers, it's hard for managers to develop an appropriate competitive strategy for their firm and its products and harder still to evaluate a product's subsequent performance in the marketplace.

In a highly competitive environment, there's a risk that customers will perceive little real difference between competing alternatives and so make their choices based on which company offers the lowest price. Positioning strategy is concerned with creating and maintaining distinctive differences that will be noticed and valued by those customers with whom the firm would most like to develop a long-term relationship. Successful positioning requires managers to understand both their target customers' preferences and the characteristics of their competitors' offerings.

In this chapter, we place our emphasis on the *product elements, place,* and *price* components of the 8 Ps. We examine the need for focus in a competitive environment, review the issues involved in developing a positioning strategy, and explore the following questions:

1. What alternative focus strategies are available to service businesses?
2. Why is it necessary to distinguish between important and determinant attributes in consumer choice decisions?
3. What are the key concepts underlying competitive positioning strategy?
4. When is it appropriate to reposition an existing service offering?
5. How can positioning maps help managers better understand and respond to competitive dynamics?

The Search for Competitive Advantage

As competition intensifies in the service sector, it's becoming progressively more important for service organizations to differentiate their products in ways that are meaningful to customers. In highly developed economies, growth is slowing in such mature consumer service industries as banking, insurance, hospitality, and education. So corporate growth will have to be based on taking share from domestic competitors—or by expanding into international markets—which is one reason why so many service firms that once limited their activities to their home country are now expanding internationally (a strategy we explore in chapter 18). In each instance, firms should be selective in targeting customers and seek to be distinctive in the way they present themselves. A market niche that may seem too narrow to offer sufficient sales within one country may represent a substantial market when viewed from an international or even global perspective.

Competitive strategy can take many different routes. As George Day observes:

> The diversity of ways a business can achieve a competitive advantage quickly defeats any generalizations or facile prescriptions. . . . First and foremost, a business must set itself apart from its competition. To be successful, it must identify and promote itself as the best provider of attributes that are important to target customers.[1]

What this means is that managers need to think systematically about all facets of the service package and to emphasize improvements to those attributes that will be valued by customers in the target segment(s).

Four Focus Strategies

It's not usually realistic for a firm to try to appeal to all actual or potential buyers in a market because customers are too numerous, too widely scattered, and too varied in their needs, purchasing behavior, and consumption patterns. Different service firms also vary widely in their abilities to serve different types of customers. So rather than attempting to compete in an entire market, each company needs to focus its efforts on those customers it can serve best. In marketing terms, *focus* means providing a relatively narrow product mix for a particular market segment—a group of buyers who share common characteristics, needs, purchasing behavior, or consumption patterns. This concept is at the heart of virtually all successful service firms, which have identified the strategically important elements in their service operations and have concentrated their resources on them.

The extent of a company's focus can be described on two different dimensions, argues Robert Johnston—market focus and service focus. [2] *Market focus* is the extent to which a firm serves few or many markets, whereas *service focus* describes the extent to which a firm offers few or many services. These two dimensions define the four basic focus strategies shown in Figure 4.1.

A *fully focused* organization provides a very limited range of services (perhaps just a single core product) to a narrow and specific market segment. A *market-focused* company concentrates on a narrow market segment but has a wide range of services. *Service-focused* firms offer a narrow range of services to a fairly broad market. Finally, many service providers fall into the *unfocused* category because they try to serve broad markets and provide a wide range of services.

As you can see from Figure 7.1, focusing requires a company to identify the market segments that it can serve best with the services it offers. Marketers define a *market* as the set of all actual or potential buyers of a particular core product. However, it is usually unrealistic for a firm to try to appeal to all buyers in that market—or at least not to all buyers in the same way. For in most instances, buyers, whether they be individuals or corporations, are too numerous, too widely scattered, and too varied in their needs, purchasing behavior, and consumption patterns. Furthermore, different service firms vary widely in their abilities to serve different types of customers. Hence, rather than trying to compete in an entire market, perhaps against superior competitors, each firm should adopt a strategy of market segmentation, identifying those parts of the market that it can serve best. Firms that are in tune with customer requirements may choose to employ a needs-based segmentation approach, focusing on those customers whom research shows to value specific attributes.

Because each person or corporate purchaser has distinctive (even unique) characteristics and needs, any prospective buyer is potentially a separate target segment. Some personal and professional services are, indeed, customized to the needs of individual buyers. A dentist treats the needs of each patient on the basis of their specific dental condition, an architect may design a unique house for a wealthy client, and a bank may develop a sophisticated loan package tailored to the requirements of a large corporate customer. However, the majority of service businesses do not find such *microsegmentation* worthwhile in their industries. Instead, they look to achieve economies of scale by marketing to all customers within a specific market segment and

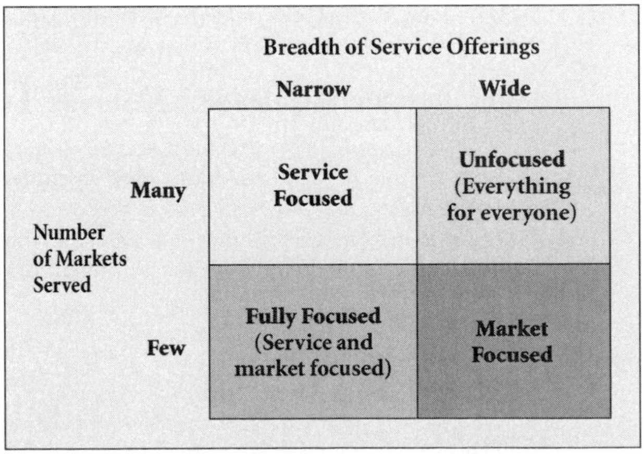

FIGURE 7.1. Basic Focus Strategies for Services
Source: Robert Johnston, "Achieving Focus in Service Organizations," *The Service Industries Journal* 16 (January 1996): 10–20.

		Breadth of Service Offerings	
		Narrow	Wide
Number of Markets Served	Many	Service Focused	Unfocused (Everything for everyone)
	Few	Fully Focused (Service and market focused)	Market Focused

serving each in a similar fashion. A strategy of *mass customization*—offering a service with some individualized product elements to a large number of customers at a relatively low price—may be achieved by offering a standardized core product but tailoring supplementary service elements to fit the requirements of individual buyers.[3] We have more to say about opportunities for customization of supplementary services in chapter 8.

Identifying and Selecting Target Segments

As discussed in chapter 5, a *market segment* is composed of a group of buyers who share common characteristics, needs, purchasing behavior, or consumption patterns. Effective segmentation should group buyers into segments in ways that result in as much similarity as possible on the relevant characteristics within each segment but highlight dissimilarity on those same characteristics between each segment.

A *target segment* is one that a firm has selected from among those in the broader market and may be defined on the basis of several variables. For instance, a department store in a particular city might target residents of the metropolitan area (geographic segmentation) who had incomes within a certain range (demographic segmentation), valued personal service from a knowledgeable staff, and were not highly price sensitive (both reflecting segmentation according to expressed attitudes and behavioral intentions). Because competing retailers in the city would probably be targeting the same customers, the department store would have to create a distinctive appeal (appropriate characteristics to highlight might include a wide array of merchandise categories, breadth of selection within each product category, and the availability of such supplementary services as advice and home delivery). Service firms that are developing strategies based on use of technology recognize that customers can also be segmented according to their degree of competence and comfort in using technology-based delivery systems.

An important marketing issue for any business is to accept that some market segments offer better opportunities than others. Target segments should be selected not only on the basis of their sales and profit potential but also with reference to the firm's ability to match or exceed competing offerings directed at the same segment.

To select target segments and to design effective positioning strategies, managers need insights into how the various components (or attributes) of a service are valued by current and prospective customers within different market segments. For instance, what level of quality and performance is required for each attribute? Are there significant differences between segments in the importance that customers attach to different attributes? How well do competing products meet customer requirements? Can an existing product be redesigned so that it better meets customer needs and is superior to competing offerings?

Using Research to Develop a Service Concept for a Specific Segment

How can a firm develop the right service concept for a particular target segment? Formal research is often needed to identify what attributes of a given service are important to specific market segments and how well prospective customers perceive competing organizations as performing against these attributes. But it's dangerous to overgeneralize. Strategists should recognize that the same individuals may set different priorities for attributes according to

- The purpose of using the service
- Who makes the decision
- The timing of use (time of day/week/season)
- Whether the individual is using the service alone or with a group
- The composition of that group

Consider the criteria that you might use when choosing a restaurant for lunch while on a holiday with friends or family versus selecting a restaurant for an expense-account business lunch at which you were meeting with a prospective client versus choosing somewhere to eat for a quick lunchtime meal with a coworker. Given a reasonable selection of alternatives, it's unlikely that you would choose the same type of restaurant in each instance, let alone the same one. It's also possible that if you left the decision to another person in the party, he or she would make a different choice.

Identifying who is making the decision to select a specific service is also important. In some cases, it's a single individual. In others, it may involve a decision-making unit of several participants. Consider a family trip to the movies. Different members of the household are likely to vary in their preferences for which film to see and how far they are willing to travel to a theater. The user is not always the decision maker. In the case of choosing a hospital for a particular treatment, the decision maker might be the end user (e.g., a patient) or—more likely—an intermediary (e.g., a doctor or even an insurance company). In the latter situation, a two-step model prevails. The marketer needs to determine, first, what attributes are important to the customer in choosing the intermediary and, second, what attributes are important to the intermediary in selecting the service provider. In many business-to-business services, the selection process for a major purchase may involve several different managers—sometimes referred to as the *buying center*—working together as a team. The selection criteria employed by each participant are likely to reflect the nature of their jobs within the company and whether or not the individuals will actually be using the product themselves.

Research into choice criteria often begins with focus group interviews, in which customers from specific segments are brought together in small groups for a semistructured discussion under the guidance of a professional group leader. Insights from these discussions can then be used to construct formal survey instruments, which might be administered to scientifically selected samples by mail, telephone, or other means.

Importance versus Determinance

Consumers usually make their choices between alternative service offerings on the basis of perceived differences between them. But the attributes that distinguish competing services from one another are not always the most important ones. For instance, many travelers rank safety as their number one consideration in air travel. They may avoid traveling by unknown carriers or on an airline that has a poor safety reputation, but after eliminating such alternatives from consideration, a traveler flying on major routes within North America or Europe (or between the two continents) is still likely to have several choices of carrier available that are perceived as equally safe. Hence, safety is not usually an attribute that influences the customer's choice at this point.

Determinant attributes (i.e., those that actually determine buyers' choices between competing alternatives) are often some way down the list of service characteristics that are important to purchasers, but they are the attributes on which customers see significant differences between competing alternatives. For example, convenience of departure and arrival times, availability of frequent-flyer miles and related loyalty privileges, quality of food and drinks service on board the aircraft, or the ease of making reservations, might be examples of determinant characteristics for business travelers when selecting an airline. For budget-conscious holiday makers, on the other hand, price might assume primary importance.

You may find it helpful to take a moment to think about your own selection criteria for different types of services. For instance, what are the most important considerations for you in choosing a restaurant or food-service outlet for an evening meal with friends of your own age? Make a note of the different criteria that you use and how important each one is to you. Now, apply these criteria to one or more recent restaurant visits in a situation where you had a choice of several competing alternatives and consider which attributes were determinant in making your selection between these different restaurants.

The marketing researchers' task, of course, is to survey customers in the target segment, identify the relative importance of different attributes, and then ask which ones have been determinant during recent decisions involving a choice of service suppliers. Researchers also need to be aware of how well each competing service is perceived by customers as performing on these attributes. Findings from such research form the necessary basis for developing a positioning (or repositioning) campaign.[4]

One further issue in evaluating service characteristics and establishing a positioning strategy is that some attributes are easily quantified whereas others are qualitative and highly judgmental. Price, for instance, is a straightforward quantitative measure. Punctuality of transport services can be expressed in terms of the percentage of trains, buses, or flights arriving within a specified number of minutes from the scheduled time. Both of these measures are easy to understand and therefore generalizable. But characteristics such as the quality of personal service or a hotel's degree of luxury are more qualitative and therefore subject to individual interpretation—although in the case of hotels, travelers may be prepared to trust the evaluations of independent rating services such as the Michelin guides, an automobile association, or (in many parts of the world) a government authority.

Creating a Competitive Position

Positioning is the process of establishing and maintaining a distinctive place in the market for an organization and/or its individual product offerings. Trout distills the essence of positioning into the following four principles:

1. A company must establish a position in the minds of its targeted customers.
2. The position should be singular, providing one simple and consistent message.
3. The position must set a company apart from its competitors.
4. A company cannot be all things to all people—it must focus its efforts.[5]

These principles apply to any type of organization that competes for customers. Thus, national postal services compete with private courier firms, public and nonprofit hospitals compete vigorously with each other and with private health care providers, and museums compete not only with other museums but also, at a generic level, with alternative forms of education, entertainment, and recreation. The marketplace for adult education courses is extremely competitive, consisting of both nonprofit and for-profit operations; to succeed, an educational institution needs a clear sense of mission and a distinctive position that sets it apart from the competition in ways that appeal to prospective students.

Understanding the concept of positioning is key to developing an effective competitive posture. This concept is certainly not limited to services—indeed, it had its origins in packaged goods marketing—but it offers valuable insights by forcing service managers to analyze their firm's existing offerings and to provide specific answers to the following questions:

● What does our firm currently stand for in the minds of current and prospective customers?
● What customers do we now serve, and which ones would we like to target for the future?
● What are the characteristics of our current service offerings (core products and their accompanying supplementary service elements), and at what market segments is each one targeted?

- In each instance, how do our service offerings differ from those of the competition?
- How well do customers in the chosen target market segments perceive each of our service offerings as meeting their needs?
- What changes do we need to make to our offerings to strengthen our competitive position within the market segment(s) of interest to our firm?

Sometimes firms have to make a significant change in an existing position. Such a strategy, known as *repositioning*, could mean revising service characteristics or redefining target market segments. At the firm level, repositioning may entail abandoning certain products and withdrawing completely from some market segments. For an example of a need to reposition due to legal and ethical considerations, see Service Perspectives 7.1.

Copy Positioning versus Product Positioning

In a competitive marketplace, a *position* reflects how consumers perceive the product's (or organization's) performance on specific attributes relative to that of one or more competitors. Customers' brand choices reflect which brands they know and remember as well as how each of these brands is positioned within each customer's mind. These positions are, of course, simply perceptual, but we need to remember that people make their decisions based on their individual perceptions of reality rather than on an expert's definition of that reality. It is worth noting that

SERVICE PERSPECTIVES 7.1

Unintended Consequences of Positioning at Domino's Pizza

Domino's Pizza, a large multinational chain with thousands of outlets, competes in an industry where the core product is basically a commodity. Although pizza parlors may argue that their product tastes better, competition is more likely to be based on value-added dimensions relating to service delivery. In fact, a firm that sells tough or tasteless food will probably not last long in a competitive marketplace. Some pizza parlors seek to add value by focusing on offering a pleasing restaurant environment, open at convenient hours at a convenient location, in which to eat the food. Others emphasize free home delivery, where customer needs include speedy delivery of a product that is still piping hot. For many years Domino's stressed speed, using the advertising slogan "30 Minutes or It's On Us" to position itself as the best performer on fast, reliable delivery. As a result, the company came to "own" the distinctive attribute of speed in the pizza delivery business. Whenever people thought of fast delivery, Domino's came to mind. According to Tom Monaghan, the company's president, the secret of the company's success and growth was "a fanatical focus on doing one thing well."

Unfortunately, the operational pressure to maintain speedy deliveries led to a series of highly publicized traffic accidents, including deaths and injuries to teenage delivery drivers. It was even alleged that one restaurant manager, seeking to minimize the loss of income resulting from late deliveries, had instituted a "King of the Lates" award for the driver with the most late deliveries during a given week.[6] In the face of lawsuits and mounting public outrage, Domino's withdrew its 30-minute guarantee and instituted a new slogan: "Delivering a Million Smiles a Day." To differentiate itself from the competition, the company introduced a new form of pizza bag "that thinks it's an oven." Transporting pizzas in a bag containing a state-of-the-art heating element enabled Domino's to position itself as the firm that delivered the hottest and freshest pizza to the customer's door; it then promoted its "Heatwave" pizza delivery system through a series of amusing television ads.[7]

staff members who are close to customers and have been trained to listen and to be observant may be able to infer customer perceptions with reasonable accuracy.

Many marketers associate positioning primarily with the communication elements of the marketing mix, notably advertising, promotions, and publicity. This view reflects the widespread use of advertising in packaged goods marketing to create images and associations for broadly similar branded products so as to give them a special distinction in the customer's mind—an approach sometimes known as *copy positioning*. A classic (although now tainted) example is the visual imagery of the rugged Western cowboy—the "Marlboro man"—created for a major cigarette brand. Note, however, that this imagery has nothing to do with the physical qualities of the tobacco; it is just a means of differentiating and adding glamour to what is essentially a commodity. Examples of how imagery may be used for positioning purposes in the service sector are found in the different color schemes and styles of consumer advertising employed by major oil companies, the distinctive "bullish" theme used periodically by Merrill Lynch (whose symbol is a bull), and the imagery associated with a specific brand name. For instance, research has shown that Virgin, one of Britain's best-known international brand names, is associated with fun, quality, trust, and innovation as well as being irreverent toward entrenched competitors and dedicated to service.[8] Some slogans promise a specific benefit, designed to make the company stand out from its competitors, such as T. Rowe Price's "Invest with Confidence," Lands' End's "Shopping online beats standing in line," Stanford Executive Programs' "Powerful Ideas, Innovative Practice," or Credit Suisse First Boston's "Global Vision. Euro Knowhow." However, as Dibb and Simkin point out:

> Evidence of strong branding in the service sector does not end with such catch phrases. [The leading organizations in different fields] already have a strong brand image in the sense that customers generally know exactly what they stand for. They are, already, clearly positioned in the customers' minds.[9]

Our primary concern in this chapter is the role of positioning in guiding marketing strategy development for services that compete on more than just imagery or vague promises. This entails decisions on substantive attributes that are known from research to be important to customers, relating to product performance, price, and service availability. To improve a product's appeal to a specific target segment, it may be necessary to change its performance on certain attributes, to reduce its price, or to alter the times and locations when it is available or the forms of delivery that are offered. In such instances, the primary task of communication—advertising, personal selling, and public relations—is to ensure that prospective customers accurately perceive the position of the service on dimensions that are important to them in making choices. Additional excitement and interest may be created by evoking certain images and associations in the advertising, but these are likely to play only a secondary role in customer choice decisions unless competing services are perceived as virtually identical on performance, price, and availability.

Positioning's Role in Marketing Strategy

Positioning plays a pivotal role in marketing strategy because it links market analysis and competitive analysis to internal corporate analysis. From these three, a position statement can be developed that enables the service organization to answer the questions What is our product (or service concept), what do we want it to become, and what actions must we take to get there? Table 7.1 summarizes the principal uses of positioning analysis as a diagnostic tool, providing input to decisions relating to product development, service delivery, pricing, and communication strategy.

TABLE 7.1 *Principal Uses of Positioning in Marketing Management*

1. Provide a useful diagnostic tool for defining and understanding the relationships between products and markets:
   - How does the product compare with competitive offerings on specific attributes?
   - How well does product performance meet consumer needs and expectations on specific performance criteria?
   - What is the predicted consumption level for a product with a given set of performance characteristics offered at a given price?
2. Identify market opportunities for
   a. Introducing new products
      - What segments to target?
      - What attributes to offer relative to the competition?
   b. Redesigning (repositioning) existing products
      - Appeal to the same segments or to new ones?
      - What attributes to add, drop, or change?
      - What attributes to emphasize in advertising?
   Eliminate products that
      - Do not satisfy consumer needs
      - Face excessive competition
3. Making other marketing mix decisions to preempt, or respond to, competitive moves:
   a. Distribution strategies
      - Where to offer the product (locations, types of outlet)?
      - When to make the product available?
   b. Pricing strategies
      - How much to charge?
      - What billing and payment procedures to employ?
   c. Communication strategies
      - What target audience(s) are most easily convinced that the product offers a competitive advantage on attributes that are important to them?
      - What message(s)? Which attributes should be emphasized and which competitors—if any—should be mentioned as the basis for comparison on those attributes?
      - Which communication channels—personal selling versus different advertising media? (Selected not only for their ability to convey the chosen message(s) to the target audience(s) but also for their ability to reinforce the desired image of the product.)

Developing a positioning strategy can take place at several different levels, depending on the nature of the business in question. Among multisite, multiproduct service businesses, a position might be established for the entire organization, for a given service outlet, or for a specific service offered at that outlet. It's particularly important that there be some consistency between the positions held by different services offered at the same location because the image of one may spill over onto the others. For instance, if a hospital has an excellent reputation for obstetrical services, this may enhance perceptions of its services in gynecology, pediatrics, surgery, and so forth.

Because of the intangible, experiential nature of many services, an explicit positioning strategy is valuable in helping prospective customers to get a mental fix on a product that would otherwise be rather amorphous. Failure to select a desired position in the marketplace—and to develop a marketing action plan designed to achieve and hold this position—may result in one of several possible outcomes, all undesirable:

1. The organization (or one of its products) is pushed into a position where it faces head-on competition from stronger competitors.
2. The organization (product) is pushed into a position that nobody else wants because there is little customer demand there.
3. The organization's (product's) position is so blurred that nobody knows what its distinctive competence really is.
4. The organization (product) has no position at all in the marketplace because nobody has ever heard of it.

Steps in Developing a Positioning Strategy

Competitive strategy is often narrowly focused at *direct competitors*—firms marketing products that offer customers a similar way of achieving the same benefits (e.g., in the case of education, another college offering similar classes). However, there may also be a serious threat from *generic competitors,* which offer customers a different way of achieving similar benefits (for instance, distance learning via broadcast programs or self-study through use of books, CDs, and videotapes both offer generic competition to conventional university classes).

The research and analysis that underlie development of an effective positioning strategy are designed to highlight both opportunities and threats to the firm in the competitive marketplace, including the activities of generic competitors. Figure 7.2 identifies the basic steps involved in identifying a suitable market position and developing a strategy to reach it.

Market analysis is needed to determine such factors as the overall level and trend of demand and the geographic location of this demand. Is demand increasing or decreasing for the benefits offered by this type of service? Are there regional or international variations in the level of demand? Alternative ways of segmenting the market should be considered and an appraisal made of the size and potential of different market segments. Research may be needed to gain a better understanding not only of customer needs and preferences within each of the different segments but also of how each perceives the competition.

Internal corporate analysis requires the organization to identify its resources (financial, human labor and know-how, and physical assets), any limitations or constraints, and the values and goals (profitability, growth, professional preferences, etc.) of its management. Using insights from this analysis, the organization should be able to select a limited number of target market segments that it is willing and able to serve with either new or existing services.

Competitive analysis, the identification and analysis of competitors, can provide a marketing strategist with a sense of their strengths and weaknesses, which, in turn, may suggest opportunities for differentiation. Relating these insights back to the internal corporate analysis should suggest which benefits should be offered to which target market segments. This analysis should consider both direct and indirect competition.

The outcome of integrating these three forms of analysis is a *position statement* that articulates the desired position of the organization in the marketplace (and, if desired, that of each of the component services that it offers). Armed with this understanding, marketers should be able to develop a specific plan of action. The cost of implementing this plan must, of course, be related to the expected payoff.

Anticipating Competitive Response

Before embarking on a specific plan of action, however, management should consider the possibility that one or more competitors might pursue the same market position. Perhaps another service organization has independently conducted the same positioning analysis and arrived at

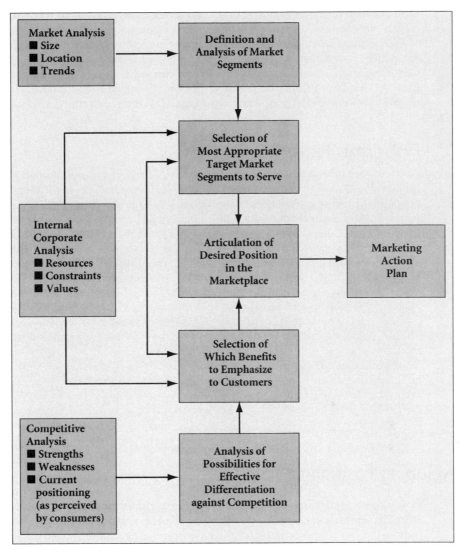

FIGURE 7.2.   Developing a Market-Positioning Strategy
Source: Developed from an earlier schematic by Michael R. Pearce.

similar conclusions? Or an existing competitor may feel threatened by the new strategy and take steps to reposition its own service so as to compete more effectively. Alternatively, a new entrant to the market may decide to play "follow the leader" yet be able to offer customers a higher service level on one or more attributes and/or a lower price.

The best way to anticipate possible competitive responses is to identify all current or potential competitors and to put oneself in their own management's shoes by conducting an internal corporate analysis for each of these competitors.[10] Coupling the insights from this analysis with data from existing market and competitive analysis (with one's own firm cast in the role of competitor) should provide a good sense of how competitors might be likely to act. If chances seem high that a stronger competitor will move to occupy the same niche with a superior service concept, then it would be wise to reconsider the situation.

Some firms develop sophisticated computer models to analyze the impact of alternative competitive moves. How would a price cut affect demand, market share, and profits? Based on past experience, how might customers in different segments respond to increases or decreases in the level of quality on specific service attributes? How long would it take before customers responded to a new advertising campaign designed to change perceptions?

Evolutionary Positioning

Positions are rarely static: They need to evolve over time in response to changing market structures, technology, competitive activity, and the evolution of the firm itself. Many types of business lend themselves to evolutionary repositioning by adding or deleting services and target segments. Some companies have shrunk their offerings and divested certain lines of business to be more focused. Others have expanded their offerings in the expectation of increasing sales to existing customers and attracting new ones. Thus, gas stations have added small retail stores offering extended hours of service, whereas supermarkets and other retail stores have added banking services. New developments in technology provide many opportunities for introducing not only new services but also new delivery systems for existing products. The reading by Lynn Shostack, "Service Positioning through Structural Change," (reproduced on pages 314 to 324) offers a number of strategic insights for narrowing or broadening the firm's existing product line and for deciding whether to make specific types of services more standardized or more customized.

Perceived quality of service emerged during the 1990s as an important strategic element in differentiating a firm from its competitors. The story in Service Perspectives 7.2 considers the example of Rentokil Initial, a provider of business-to-business services, which has profited from the growing trend toward outsourcing of services related to facilities maintenance.

Developing Positioning Maps

Developing a positioning map—a task sometimes referred to as *perceptual mapping*—is a useful way of representing consumers' perceptions of alternative products graphically. A map is usually confined to two attributes (although three-dimensional models can be used to portray three of these attributes). When more than three dimensions are needed to describe product performance in a given market, then a series of separate charts needs to be drawn for visual presentation purposes. A computer model, of course, can handle as many attributes as are relevant.[11]

Information about a product (or company's position relative to any one attribute) can be inferred from market data, derived from ratings by representative consumers, or both. If consumer perceptions of service characteristics differ sharply from "reality" as defined by management, then marketing efforts may be needed to change these perceptions.

As a generalization, graphic representations of product positions are much easier to grasp than tables of quantitative data or paragraphs of prose. They enable management to understand the nature of competitive threats and opportunities, they can highlight gaps between how customers (or prospects) see the organization and how management sees it, and they can help confirm or dispel beliefs that a service—or its parent organization—occupies a unique niche in the marketplace.

SERVICE PERSPECTIVES 7.2

Positioning a Brand across Multiple Services at Rentokil Initial

Rentokil Initial has evolved over a period of almost eighty years from its origins as a manufacturer of rat poison and a pesticide for killing wood-destroying beetles. From selling poisons and pesticides it shifted to pest control and extermination services and then broadened its base to include many other services related to facilities maintenance. Through organic growth and acquisition of over two hundred companies, it has grown to become the world's largest business services company. It sees its core competence as "the ability to carry out high quality services on other people's premises through a well-recruited, well-trained, and motivated staff." Cross-selling its existing customers—that is, promoting the use of an additional service to a customer who is already using the company for one or more services—became an important aspect of its strategy.

The company, which has been highly profitable, operates in more than forty countries, providing a range of services within each of the following categories: hygiene and cleaning, pest control, distribution and plant services, personnel services, and property services and security. According to its chief executive,

> We see ourselves very much as an industrial and commercial service company, with markets driven by outsourcing of blue-collar activities on the one hand, and on the other by the demand by employers for an improved and/or sustained environment for their employees.
>
> Our objective has been to create a virtuous circle. We provide a quality service in industrial and commercial activities under the same brand-name, so that a customer satisfied with one Rentokil Initial Service is potentially a satisfied customer for another. . . . Although it was considered somewhat odd at the time, one of the reasons we moved into [providing and maintaining] tropical plants [for building interiors] was in fact to put the brand in front of decision makers. Our service people maintaining the plants go in through the front door and are visible to the customer. This contrasts with pest control where no one really notices unless we fail. . . . The brand stands for honesty, reliability, consistency, integrity and technical leadership.[12]

The essence of Rentokil Initial's success lies in its ability to position each of its many business and commercial services in terms of the company's core brand values, which are highly relevant to the nature and quality of service that is delivered. In the case of acquisitions, the task of improving results often requires repositioning the attributes of the newly acquired service to reflect these brand values; related strategies include taking advantage of economies of scale, technical and people-management skills, and cross-selling possibilities. The brand image is reinforced through physical evidence in terms of distinctive uniforms, vehicle color schemes, and use of the corporate logo on all correspondence.

Using Positioning Maps to Plot Strategy: An Example from the Hotel Industry

The hotel business is highly competitive, especially during seasons when the supply of rooms exceeds demand. The famous hotelier, E. M. Statler, once declared that the three most important things for the success of a hotel were location, location, and location. Certainly, location is an important choice criterion among each of the principal market segments served by the industry: business travelers, tourists and vacationers, and convention participants. The preferred location will, of course, depend on guests' intended destinations in the local area. Some, for instance, may be visiting business clients in the financial district; others may be attending a trade show at the convention center; while tourists may be intent on sightseeing, shopping, and museum visits.

But both research and management experience show that location is not the only attribute that customers in each segment consider when selecting a hotel. Let's focus on the needs of the business traveler. Unlike tourists who must pay their own way, he or she is probably traveling on an expense account that may determine the level of hotel price that can be afforded. The attribute of price may serve to define different market segments, ranging from, say, chief executives whose firms may be willing to pay for them to stay in five-star hotels and business executives and senior professionals who are entitled to stay in four-star hotels to junior sales representatives whose expense accounts limit them to less luxurious types of accommodation. In short, there are different classes of hotel based on ability and willingness to pay for increasing levels of luxury and service as well as for factors such as a more desirable location.

Within each class of hotels, customers visiting a large city may find that they have several alternatives from among which to select a place to stay. The degree of luxury and comfort in physical amenities will be one choice criterion; research shows that business travelers are concerned not only with the comfort and facilities offered by their rooms (where they may wish to work as well as sleep) but also with other physical spaces, ranging from the reception area and restaurants to meeting rooms, swimming pools, and exercise facilities. The quality and range of services offered by hotel staff is another key criterion: Can a guest get 24-hour room service? Can clothes be laundered and pressed? Is there a knowledgeable concierge on duty? Are staff available to offer professional business services? There are other choice criteria, too, perhaps relating to the ambience of the hotel (modern architecture and decor are favored by some customers, but others may prefer old-world charm and antique furniture). Additional attributes include factors such as quietness, safety, cleanliness, and rewards programs for frequent guests.

Positioning the Palace. Let's look at an example, based on a real-world situation, of how developing a positioning map of their own and competing hotels helped managers of the Palace, a successful four-star hotel, develop a better understanding of future threats to their established market position in a large city that we will call Belleville.

Located on the edge of the booming financial district, the Palace was an elegant old hotel that had been extensively renovated and modernized a few years earlier. Its competitors included eight four-star establishments, and the Grand, one of the city's oldest hotels, which had a five-star rating. The Palace had been very profitable for its owners in recent years and boasted an above-average occupancy rate. For many months of the year, it was sold out on weekdays, reflecting its strong appeal to business travelers, who were very attractive to the hotel because of their willingness to pay a higher room rate than tourists or conventioneers. But the general manager and his staff saw problems on the horizon. Planning permission had recently been granted for four large new hotels in the city, and the Grand had just started a major renovation and expansion project, which included construction of a new wing. There was a risk that customers might see the Palace as falling behind.

To understand better the nature of the competitive threat, the hotel's management team worked with a consultant to prepare charts that displayed the Palace's position in the business traveler market both before and after the advent of new competition. Four attributes were selected for study: room price, level of physical luxury, level of personal service, and location. In this instance, management did not conduct new consumer research; instead, they inferred customer perceptions based on published information, data from past surveys, and reports from travel agents and knowledgeable hotel staff members who interacted frequently with customers. Information on competing hotels was not difficult to obtain because the locations were known, the physical structures were relatively easy to visit and evaluate, and the sales staff kept themselves informed on pricing policies and discounts. A convenient surrogate measure for service level was the ratio of rooms per employee, easily calculated from the published number of rooms and employment data provided to the city authorities. Data from surveys of travel agents conducted by the Palace provided additional insights on the quality of personal service at each competitor.

Scales were then created for each attribute. Devising one for price was simple, because the average price charged to business travelers for a standard single room at each hotel was already quantified. The rooms-per-employee ratio formed the basis for a service-level scale, with low ratios being equated with high service. This scale was then modified slightly in the light of what was known about the quality of service actually delivered by each major competitor. Level of physical luxury was more subjective and harder to quantify. The management team identified the hotel that members agreed was the most luxurious (the Grand) and then the four-star hotel that they viewed as having the least luxurious physical facilities (the Airport Plaza). All other four-star hotels were then rated on this attribute relative to these two benchmarks. Location was defined with reference to the stock exchange building in the heart of the financial district, because past research had shown that a majority of the Palace's business guests were visiting destinations in this area. The location scale plotted each hotel in terms of its distance from the stock exchange. The competitive set of 10 hotels lay within a four-mile, fan-shaped radius, extending from the exchange through the city's principal retail area (where the convention center was also located) to the inner suburbs and the nearby airport. Two positioning maps were created to portray the existing competitive situation. The first (Figure 7.3) showed the ten hotels on the dimensions of price and service level; the second (Figure 7.4) displayed them on location and degree of physical luxury.

A quick glance at Figure 7.3 shows a clear correlation between the attributes of price and service: Hotels offering higher levels of service are relatively more expensive. The shaded bar running from upper left to lower right highlights this relationship, which is not a surprising one (and can be expected to continue diagonally downwards for three-star and lesser-rated establishments). Further analysis shows that there appear to be three clusters of hotels within what is already an upscale market category. At the top end, the four-star Regency is close to the five-star Grand; in the middle, the Palace is clustered with four other hotels, and at the lower end, there is another cluster of three hotels. One surprising insight from this map is that the Palace appears to be charging significantly more (on a relative basis) than its service level would seem to justify. Because its occupancy rate is very high, guests are evidently willing to pay the going rate.

In Figure 7.4 we see how the Palace is positioned relative to the competition on location and degree of luxury. We would not expect these two variables to be related, and they do not appear to be so. A key insight here is that the Palace occupies a relatively empty portion of the map. It is the only hotel in the financial district—a fact that probably explains its ability to charge more than its service level (or degree of physical luxury) would seem to justify. There are two clusters of hotels in the vicinity of the shopping district and convention center: a relatively luxurious group of three, led by the Grand, and a second group of two offering a moderate level of luxury.

Anticipating New Competitors. What of the future? The Palace's management team next sought to anticipate the positions of the four new hotels being constructed in Belleville as well as the probable repositioning of the Grand. The construction sites were already known; two would be in the financial district, and two would be in the vicinity of the convention center, itself under expansion. Press releases distributed by the Grand had already declared its management's intentions: The "New Grand" would not only be larger, but the renovations would also be designed to make it even more luxurious, and there were plans to add new service features.

Predicting the positions of the four new hotels was not difficult for experts in the field, whereas customers might have had more difficulty in predicting each hotel's level of performance on different attributes, especially if they were unfamiliar with the chain that would be

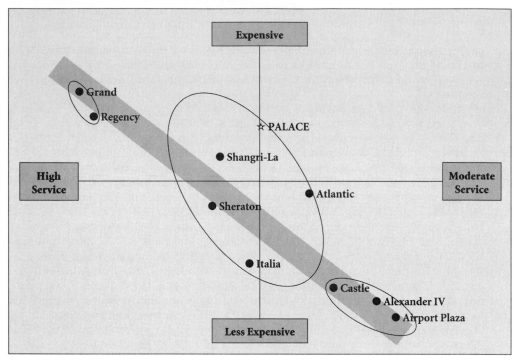

FIGURE 7.3 Belleville's Principal Business Hotels: Positioning Map of Service Level vs. Price Level

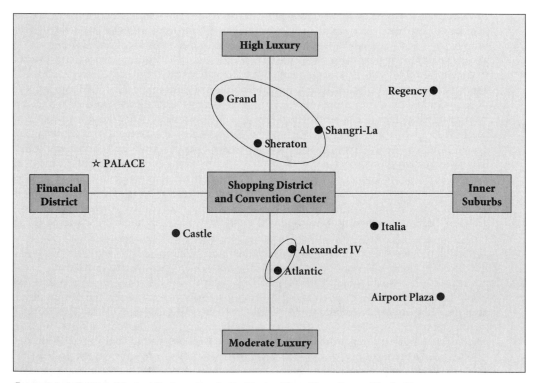

FIGURE 7.4 Belleville's Principal Business Hotels: Positioning Map of Location vs. Physical Luxury

operating the hotel in question. Preliminary details of the new hotels had already been released to city planners and the business community. The owners of two of the hotels had declared their intentions to seek five-star status, although this might take a few years to achieve. Three of the newcomers would be affiliated with international chains, and their strategies could be guessed by examining recent hotels opened in other cities by these same chains.

Pricing was also easy to project. New hotels use a formula for setting posted room prices (the prices typically charged to individuals staying on a weeknight in high season). This price is linked to the average construction cost per room at the rate of one dollar per night for every thousand dollars of construction costs. Thus, a 200-room hotel that costs $40 million to build (including land costs) would have an average room cost of $200,000 and would need to set a price of $200 per room night. Using this formula, Palace managers concluded that the four new hotels would have to charge significantly more than the Grand or Regency, in effect establishing what marketers call a *price umbrella* above existing price levels and thereby giving competitors the option of raising their own prices. To justify their high prices, the new hotels would have to offer customers very high standards of service and luxury. At the same time, the New Grand would need to raise its own prices to recover the costs of renovations, new construction, and enhanced service offerings (see Figure 7.5).

Assuming no changes by either the Palace or other existing hotels, the impact of the new competition in the market clearly posed a significant threat to the Palace, which would lose its unique locational advantage and in the future be just one of three hotels in the immediate vicinity of the financial district (Figure 7.6). The sales staff believed that many of the Palace's existing business customers would be attracted to the Continental and the Mandarin and willing to pay their higher rates to obtain the superior benefits offered. The other two newcomers were seen as more of a threat to the Shangri-La, Sheraton, and New Grand in the shopping district/convention center cluster. Meanwhile, the New Grand and the newcomers would create a high price/ high-service (and high-luxury) cluster at the top end of the market, leaving the Regency in what might prove to be a distinctive—and therefore defensible—space of its own. If you were a consultant to the Palace's general manager, what action would you recommend?

Changing Perceptions Through Advertising

Improving product features and correcting weaknesses can be expensive. Sometimes, however, weaknesses are perceptual rather than real. Ries and Trout describe the case of Long Island Trust, historically the leading bank in this large New York suburban area.[13] With the passage of legislation permitting unrestricted branch banking throughout New York State, many of the big banks from neighboring Manhattan began invading Long Island. Research showed that Long Island Trust was rated below banks such as Chase Manhattan and Citibank on such key selection criteria as having many branches, offering a full range of services, providing quality service, and having substantial capital. However, Long Island Trust ranked first on helping Long Island residents and the Long Island economy.

The bank's advertising agency developed a campaign promoting the Long Island position, playing to its perceived strengths rather than seeking to improve perceptions on attributes where it was perceived less favorably. The tenor of the campaign can be gauged from the following extract from a print ad:

> Why send your money to the city if you live on the Island? It makes sense to keep your money close to home. Not at a city bank but at Long Island Trust. Where it can work for Long Island. After all we concentrate on developing Long Island. Not Manhattan Island or some island off Kuwait.

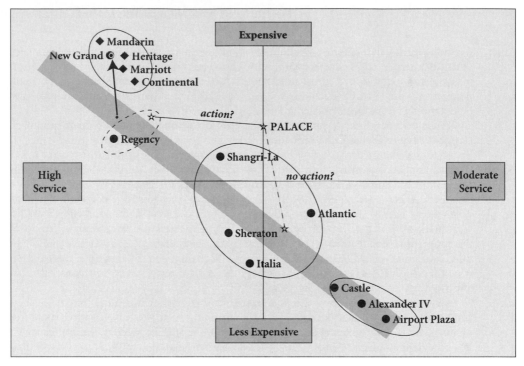

FIGURE 7.5   Belleville's Principal Business Hotels, Following New Construction: Positioning Map of Service Level vs. Price Level

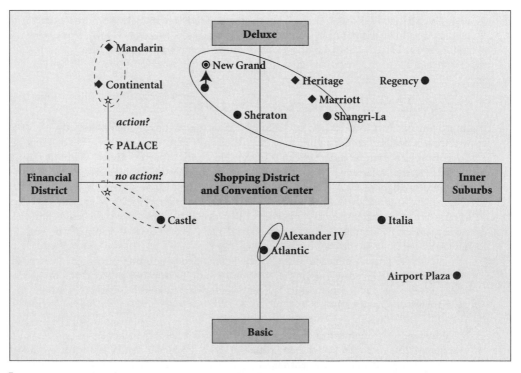

FIGURE 7.6   Belleville's Principal Business Hotels after New Construction: Positioning Map of Location vs. Physical Luxury

Other advertisements in the campaign promoted similar themes, such as "The city is a great place to visit, but would you want to bank there?"

When identical research was repeated 15 months later, Long Island Trust's position had improved on every attribute. The campaign had succeeded in reframing the terms of reference from a global to a local perspective. Although no significant changes had taken place in any of the attributes, the perceived strength of being a Long Island bank for Long Islanders had had a positive halo effect on all other attributes.

Researchers note that the presence of such halo effects—either positive or negative—make it more difficult to assess the specific strengths and weaknesses of competing services.[14] For instance, reported customer dissatisfaction with attribute A of a particular service may be real (and thus need corrective action) or could be the result of a negative halo effect caused by a high dissatisfaction with attribute B or even by a high overall dissatisfaction with the brand. One of the problems in consumer satisfaction research is that respondents often complete survey questionnaires quickly, without thoughtful consideration of each of the different dimensions on which they are rating a service firm's performance. In-depth personal interviews may offer a more reliable way to probe customers' evaluations but are, of course, considerably more expensive to administer.

A positioning strategy is, of course, only as good as the quality of the information used in constructing it. Often—as with Long Island Trust—more than two attributes need to be evaluated. (This would have required three 2-dimensional maps for presentation purposes.) As conditions change, research needs to be repeated and maps redrawn to reflect the dynamic nature of the marketplace. New market entrants and repositioning of existing competitors may mean that a formerly distinctive position has ceased to be so. Moreover, there may be occasions on which different maps need to be drawn for different market segments, if research shows that there are sharp variations in perceptions between segments. In the case of hotels, for instance, vacationers and conventioneers may have somewhat different priorities from business travelers and are probably less likely to be frequent guests of the same hotel.

Innovation in Positioning

Most companies focus on matching and beating their rivals, with the result that their strategies tend to emphasize the same basic dimensions of competition. However, one way to compete is to introduce new dimensions into the positioning equation that other firms cannot immediately match. Heskett frames the issue nicely: "The most successful service firms separate themselves from 'the pack' to achieve a distinctive position in relation to their competition. They differentiate themselves . . . by altering typical characteristics of their respective industries to their competitive advantage."[15]

In chapter 8, we look at opportunities for product innovation in services. In later chapters, we consider innovation in delivery systems.

Conclusion

Most service businesses face active competition. Marketers need to find ways of creating meaningful competitive advantages for their products. Ideally, they should be targeting segments that they can serve better than other providers. The concept of positioning is valuable because it forces explicit recognition of the different attributes comprising the overall service concept and emphasizes the need for marketers to understand which attributes determine customer choice behavior. Positioning maps provide a visual way of summarizing research data and display how different firms are perceived as performing relative to each other on key attributes. When combined with information on the preferences of different segments, including the level of demand that might be anticipated from such segments, positioning maps may suggest opportunities for creating new services or repositioning existing ones to take advantage of unserved market needs. If offering such a service is seen as compatible with the organization's resources and values, then the firm may be able to develop a profitable niche for itself in the market.

REVIEW QUESTIONS

1. Why should service firms focus their efforts? Describe the basic focus options and illustrate them with examples.
2. What is the distinction between important and determinant attributes in consumer choice decisions? What type of research would you need to conduct to decide which was which?
3. Describe what is meant by positioning strategy and the marketing concepts that underlie it.
4. Identify the circumstances under which it is appropriate to reposition an existing service offering.
5. How can positioning maps help managers better understand and respond to competitive dynamics?

APPLICATION EXERCISES

1. Choose an industry you are familiar with (like retail clothing stores, restaurants, television networks, or supermarkets) and create one or more perceptual maps showing the relative positions of different competitors in the industry, using for each map two attributes that you consider to represent key consumer choice criteria.
2. The travel agency business is losing business to online bookings offered to passengers by airline Web sites. Identify some possible focus options open to travel agencies wishing to develop new lines of business that would compensate for this loss of airline ticket sales.
3. What are your key criteria in choosing a restaurant for an evening meal with friends? Rank your criteria in order of importance. Now apply them to a recent decision you made on selecting a restaurant. Which criteria were determinant and why?
4. Imagine for a moment that you are a consultant to the Palace Hotel. Consider the options facing the hotel based on the four attributes appearing in the positioning charts (Figures 7.5 and 7.6). What actions do you recommend that the Palace should take in these circumstances? Justify your recommendations.

ENDNOTES

1. George S. Day, *Market Driven Strategy* (New York: The Free Press), 1990, 164.
2. Robert Johnston, "Achieving Focus in Service Organizations," *The Service Industries Journal* 16 (January 1996): 10–20.
3. Christopher W. L. Hart, "Mass Customization: Conceptual Underpinnings, Opportunities, and Limits," *International Journal of Service Industry Management* 6, no. 2 (1995): 36–45.
4. For further insights into multiattribute modeling, see William D. Wells and David Prensky, *Consumer Behavior* (New York: John Wiley & Sons, 1996), 321–325.
5. Jack Trout, *The New Positioning: The Latest on the World's #1 Business Strategy.* New York: McGraw-Hill, 1997.

6. Michael Kelly, "A Deadly Delivery Problem," the *Boston Globe,* July 19, 1989, 1, 6.

7. Details of Domino's Heatwave pizza bag were taken from the company's Web site at www.dominos.com, October 1999.

8. Richard Branson, "Why We Stretch the Virgin Brand," *Evening Standard* (London), August 4, 1997; Julia Flynn, Wendy Zellner, Larry Light, and Joseph Weber, "Then Came Branson," *Business Week,* October 26, 1998, 116–120.

9. Sally Dibb and Lyndon Simkin, "The Strength of Branding and Positioning in Services," *International Journal of Service Industry Management* 4, no. 1 (1993): 25–35.

10. For a detailed approach, see Michael E. Porter, "A Framework for Competitor Analysis," chap. 3 in *Competitive Strategy* (New York: The Free Press, 1980).

11. For examples of developing research data for perceptual mapping purposes, see Glen L. Urban and John M. Hauser, *Design and Marketing of New Products,* 2d ed. (Englewood Cliffs, NJ: Prentice Hall, 1993).

12. Sir Clive Thompson, "Rentokil Initial: Building a Strong Corporate Brand for Growth and Diversity," in *Brand Warriors,* ed. F. Gilmore (London: HarperCollinsBusiness,1997), 123–124.

13. Al Ries and Jack Trout, *Positioning: The Battle for Your Mind,* rev. ed. (New York: Warner Books, 1986).

14. Jochen Wirtz and John E. G. Bateson, "An Experimental Investigation of Halo Effects in Satisfaction Measures of Service Attributes," *International Journal of Service Industry Management* 6, no. 3 (1995): 84–102.

15. James L. Heskett, *Managing in the Service Economy* (Boston: Harvard Business School Press, 1984), 45.

CHAPTER 8

Creating the Service Product and Adding Value

Each and every one of you will make or break the promise that our brand makes to customers.
AN AMERICAN EXPRESS MANAGER SPEAKING TO HIS EMPLOYEES

All service organizations face choices concerning the types of products to offer and the operational procedures to employ in creating them. Chapter 7 noted that these choices are often driven primarily by market factors, with firms seeking to respond to the expressed needs of specific market segments and to differentiate the characteristics of their offerings against those of competitors. The availability of new delivery processes—such as the Internet for information-based services—allows firms to create new methods of delivering existing services that effectively change the nature of the service experience and create new benefits; the shift to Internet banking is a case in point. A more radical form of product innovation involves exploiting technological developments to satisfy latent needs that customers have not previously articulated or even recognized.

Service offerings typically consist of a core product bundled together with a variety of supplementary service elements. The core, as we saw in chapter 3, responds to the customer's need for a basic benefit—such as transportation to a specific location, resolution of a specific health problem, obtaining a professional solution to a problem, or repair of malfunctioning equipment. Supplementary services (discussed in depth later in this chapter) are those that facilitate and enhance use of the core service. They range from provision of needed information, advice, and documentation to problem solving and acts of hospitality.

Designing new services is a challenging task because it requires thinking about processes, people, and experiences as well as outputs and benefits. Processes can be depicted through blueprints that specify employee tasks and operational sequences as well as track the experience of the customer at each step in service delivery.

In this chapter, we consider the nature of service products, how to visualize them, and how to design them. Placing our emphasis on the *product elements* and *process* components of the 8 Ps, we explore such questions as

1. What are the key ingredients in a service product?
2. How can blueprinting a service process facilitate its production?
3. How might we categorize the supplementary services that surround core products?
4. What are some of the approaches that may be used in designing new services?
5. What is the role of branding for different service products?

Planning and Creating Services

What do we mean by a service product? In earlier chapters, we noted that a service is a performance rather than a thing. When customers purchase manufactured goods, they take title to physical objects. But service performances, being intangible and ephemeral, are experienced rather than owned. Even when there are physical elements to which the customer does take title—such as a cooked meal (which is promptly consumed), a gold filling in a tooth, a replacement part inside a car—a significant portion of the price paid by customers is for the value added by the accompanying service elements, including labor and expertise and the use of specialized equipment.

When customers are required by the nature of the service process to visit the service site—as in people-processing services—or choose to do so in other types of services (such as traditional retail bank branches), they may be asked to participate actively in the process of service creation and delivery. In situations where customers perform self-service, their experiences are often shaped by the nature and user-friendliness (or lack thereof!) of the supporting technology. In both instances, evaluations of the service product are likely to be much more closely interwoven with the nature of the delivery process than is the case for manufactured goods.

Key Steps in Service Planning

One of the challenges in services marketing is to ensure that the product management task maintains a strong customer focus at all times. Historically, operations management was often allowed to dominate this task, with the result that customer concerns were sometimes subjugated to operational convenience. On the other hand, marketers cannot work in isolation on new product development, especially when its delivery entails use of new technologies; they need to form a partnership with operations personnel and, in the case of high-contact services, with human resource managers as well. Figure 8.1 outlines the key steps involved in planning and creating services, emphasizing the need for managers to relate market opportunities to deployment of their firm's resources—physical, technological, and human.

The task begins at the corporate level with a statement of *objectives*. This statement leads into a detailed *market and competitive analysis* (addressing each of the markets in which the firm is currently involved or is thinking of entering). Paralleling this step is a *resource allocation analysis,* requiring definition and appraisal of the firm's current resources and how they are being allocated as well as identification of additional resources that might reasonably be obtained. This pair of steps can be thought of collectively as a form of strengths, weaknesses, opportunities, and threats (SWOT) analysis, identifying these factors on both the marketing and operational/human resources fronts. Each leads to a statement of assets.

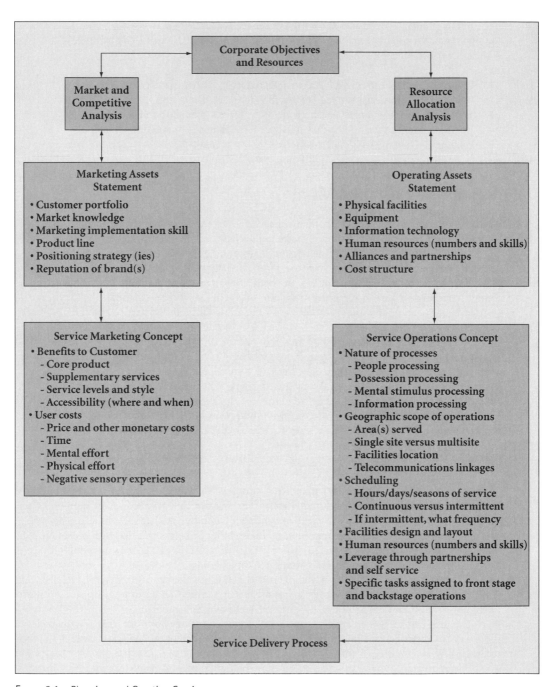

FIGURE 8.1   Planning and Creating Services

The *marketing assets statement* includes details of the firm's existing customer portfolio (such as its size, profile, and value), knowledge of the market and competitors, its current product line, the reputation of its brand(s), its marketing implementation skills, and its current positioning strategy(-ies). We saw in chapter 7 that a positioning statement can be developed for each service that the firm offers to one or more target market segments, indicating the characteristics that distinguish that service from competitive offerings.

The marketing opportunities revealed by this analysis must now be matched against an *operating assets statement.* Can the organization afford to allocate the physical facilities, equipment, information technology, and human resources needed to market existing service products more effectively; add enhancements designed to improve competitive appeal; or create new service offerings? Conversely, does an analysis of these operating assets suggest new opportunities to improve their utilization in the marketplace? If the firm lacks the resources needed for a new marketing initiative, could it leverage its existing assets by partnering with intermediaries or even with customers themselves? Finally, does an identified marketing opportunity promise sufficient profits to yield an acceptable return on the assets employed after deducting all relevant costs?

From a marketing perspective, the next step in transforming an opportunity into reality involves creating a *service marketing concept* to clarify the benefits offered to customers and the costs that they will incur in return. This marketing concept considers both core and supplementary services; the characteristics of these services in terms of both performance level and style; and where, when, and how customers will be able to have access to them. The related costs of service include not only money but also definition of the amount of time, mental hassle, physical effort, and negative sensory experiences likely to be incurred by customers in receiving service.

A parallel step is to establish a *service operations concept,* which stipulates the nature of the processes involved (including use of information technology) and how and when the different types of operating assets should be deployed to perform specific tasks. Hence, one must define the geographic scope and scheduling of operations, describe facilities design and layout, and identify the human resources required. The operations concept also addresses opportunities for leveraging the firm's own resources through use of intermediaries or the customers themselves. Finally, it clarifies which tasks and resources will be assigned to frontstage and which to backstage operations.

Defining the marketing and operations concepts is necessarily an interactive process because either or both may have to be modified to bring the two into the harmony needed to proceed with a given service offering. The planning task then moves on to a set of choices that management must make in configuring the service delivery process—the topic of chapter 11.

The Impact of Technology

Technological developments during the last 20 years have had a remarkable impact on the way in which services are produced and delivered. Innovations in core services range from new types of medical treatments to high-speed rail service and from satellite-based weather forecasting to addressable (that is, interactive) cable television systems. Many important changes relate to the use of information technology to improve supplementary services—a topic we will discuss later in this chapter. Developments in telecommunications and computer technology have also led to many innovations in how services are delivered, including increased use of telephone and Internet-based services. These innovations will be discussed in chapters 11 and 18.

Understanding the Service Offering

Most manufacturing and service businesses offer their customers a package of benefits, involving delivery of not only the core product but also a variety of service-related activities. Increasingly, these services provide the differentiation that separates successful firms from the also-rans. With both services and goods, the core product sooner or later becomes a commodity as competition increases and the industry matures. (If a firm can't do a decent job on the core elements, it's eventually going to go out of business!) Although managers continually need to consider opportunities to improve the core product, the search for competitive advantage in a mature industry often emphasizes performance on the supplementary services that are bundled with the core.

The Augmented Product

Marketing textbook authors have long been writing about the augmented product—also referred to as the *extended product* or the *product package*—in an effort to describe the supplementary elements that add value to manufactured goods. Several frameworks can be used to describe augmented products in a services context. Lynn Shostack developed a molecular model (Figure 8.2), which uses a chemical analogy to help marketers visualize and manage what she

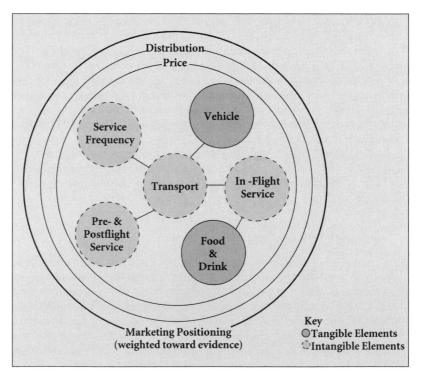

Figure 8.2   Shostack's Molecular Model: Passenger Airline Service
Source: G. Lynn Shostack, "Breaking Free from Product Marketing," *Journal of Marketing* 44 (April 1977): 73–80, published by the American Marketing Association. Reprinted with permission.

termed a "total market entity."[1] Her model can be applied to either goods or services. At the center is the core benefit, addressing the basic customer need, linked to a series of other service characteristics. She argues that as in chemical formulations, a change in one element may completely alter the nature of the entity. Surrounding the molecules are a series of bands representing price, distribution, and market positioning (communication messages).

The molecular model helps us to identify the tangible and intangible elements involved in service delivery. In an airline, for example, the intangible elements include transportation itself; service frequency; and preflight, in-flight, and postflight service. But the aircraft and the food and drinks that are served are all tangible. By highlighting such elements, marketers can determine whether their services are tangible dominant or intangible dominant. The more intangible elements exist, the more necessary it is to provide tangible clues about the features and quality of the service.

Eiglier and Langeard propose a model in which the core service is surrounded by a circle containing a series of supplementary services that are specific to that particular product.[2] Their approach, like Shostack's, emphasizes the interdependence of the various components. They distinguish between those elements needed to facilitate use of the core service (such as the reception desk at a hotel) and those that enhance the appeal of the core service (such as a fitness center and business services at a hotel).

Both models of the augmented product offer useful insights. Shostack wants us to determine which service elements are tangible and which are intangible to facilitate the formulation of product policy and communication programs. Eiglier and Langeard ask us to think about two issues: first, whether supplementary services are needed to facilitate use of the core service or simply to add extra appeal, and second, whether customers should be charged separately for each service element or whether all elements should be bundled under a single price tag. Further insight is provided by Grönroos, who clarifies the different roles played by supplementary services by describing them as either facilitating or supporting.[3]

Defining the Nature of the Service Offering

Product planners need to include three components in the design of the service offering. The most basic component is the *core product,* which addresses these questions: What is the buyer really purchasing, and what business are we in? The core product supplies the central problem-solving benefits that customers seek. Thus, transport solves the need to move a person or a physical object from one location to another, management consulting is expected to yield expert advice on the actions that a company should take, and repair services restore a damaged or malfunctioning machine or building to good working order.

The second component concerns the *core delivery process*—how the core product is delivered to the customer, the nature of the customer's role in that process, how long it lasts, and the prescribed level and style of service to be offered. In chapter 2, we discussed four core processes—people processing, possession processing, mental stimulus processing, and information processing—each of which has different implications for customer involvement; operational procedures; the degree of customer contact with service personnel, equipment, and facilities; and requirements for supplementary services.

The third component is the group of *supplementary services* that augment the core product, both facilitating its use and enhancing its value and appeal. Each of these supplementary elements, in turn, requires its own delivery system (which may or may not be tied to the core delivery process) and prescribed service level. These three components are captured in Figure 8.3, which presents the augmented product for hotel accommodation, a high contact people-processing service introduced earlier in flowchart form in Figure 4.6, p. 130–131. The bottom portion of Figure 8.3 shows a fourth design component, the *delivery sequence over time.* Note

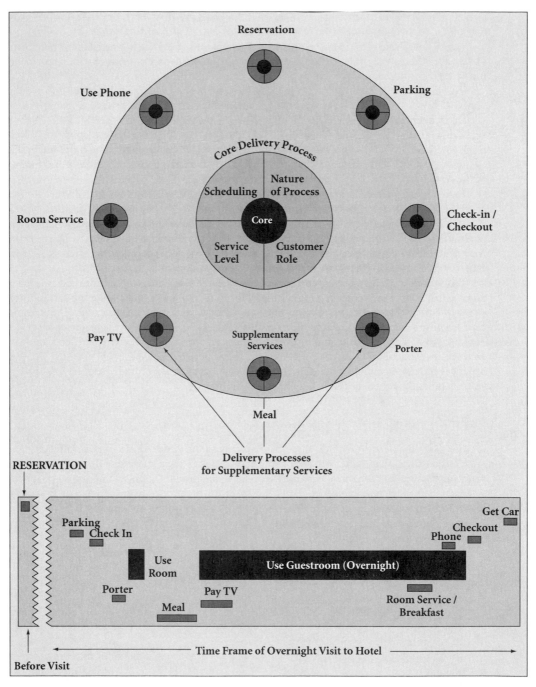

FIGURE 8.3 The Service Offering: Core Product, Supplementary Services, and Delivery Processes for an Overnight Hotel Stay

that neither the core service nor its supplementary elements are all delivered continuously throughout the duration of the service performance.

Introducing the temporal dimension is central to understanding the role that time plays not only in process scheduling but also as a potential cost of service for customers and as a resource allocation issue for the supplier. An important aspect of service planning is determining what is an appropriate amount of time for the customer to spend on different service elements. In some instances, research may show that customers from a given segment expect to budget a specific amount of time for a given activity that has value for them and would not wish to be rushed (for instance, eight hours for sleeping, an hour and a half for a business dinner, 20 minutes for breakfast). In other instances, such as making a reservation, checking in, payment, or waiting for a car to be retrieved from valet parking, customers may wish to minimize or even eliminate time spent on what they perceive as nonproductive activities.

Service Blueprinting

Service design is a complex task that can benefit from a more sophisticated version of flow-charting known as *blueprinting*. The design for a new building or a ship is usually captured in architectural drawings called blueprints because these reproductions have traditionally been printed on special paper where all the drawings and annotations appear in blue. The blueprints show what the product should look like and detail the specifications to which it should conform. In contrast to the physical architecture of a building, ship, or piece of equipment, service processes have a largely intangible structure. That makes them all the more difficult to visualize. The same is true of processes such as logistics, industrial engineering, decision theory, and computer systems analysis, each of which employs blueprint-like techniques to describe processes involving flows, sequences, relationships, and dependencies.[4]

Developing a Blueprint

Developing a service blueprint requires identifying all the key activities involved in service delivery and production and specifying the linkages between these activities.[5] (We introduced some of the relevant frameworks in chapter 4, when discussing a simpler version of blueprinting known as flowcharting; as noted in that chapter, any given activity can be refined by "drilling down" to obtain a higher level of detail—see Management Memo 4.1 on p. 134.

A central aspect of service blueprinting is to distinguish between what the customer experiences frontstage and the activities of employees and support processes backstage, where the customer cannot see them. Between the two lies what is called the *line of visibility*. Operationally oriented businesses are sometimes so focused on managing backstage activities that they neglect to consider the customer's view of frontstage activities. Accounting firms, for instance, often have elaborately documented procedures and standards for how to conduct an audit properly but may lack clear standards for when and how to host a meeting with clients or how to answer the telephone when they call.

Service blueprints clarify the interactions between customers and employees and how these are supported by additional activities and systems backstage. Because blueprints show the interrelationships between employee roles, operational processes, information technology, and customer interactions, they can facilitate the integration of marketing, operations, and human resource management within a firm. There is no single, required way to prepare a service blueprint, but it's recommended that a consistent approach be used within any one organization. To illustrate blueprinting later in this chapter, we adapt and simplify an approach proposed by Jane Kingman-Brundage.[6]

Blueprinting also gives managers the opportunity to identify potential *fail points* in the process that pose a significant risk of things going wrong and diminishing service quality. Knowledge of such fail points enables managers to design procedures to avoid their occurrence or to prepare contingency plans (or both). Points in the process where customers commonly have to wait can also be pinpointed. Standards can then be developed for execution of each activity, including times for completion of a task, maximum wait times in between tasks, and scripts to guide interactions between staff members and customers.

Blueprints of existing services may suggest product improvement opportunities resulting from reconfiguring delivery systems, adding or deleting specific elements, or repositioning the service to appeal to other segments. For example, Canadian Pacific Hotels (whose 27 properties include the Toronto York and the Banff Springs Hotel) decided to redesign its hotel services. It had already been successful with conventions, meetings, and group travel but wanted to build greater brand loyalty among business travelers. The company blueprinted the whole guest experience from pulling up at the hotel to getting the car keys from the valet. For each encounter, Canadian Pacific defined an expected service level based on customer feedback and created systems to monitor service performance. It also redesigned some aspects of its service processes to provide guests with more personalized service. The payoff for Canadian Pacific's redesign efforts was a 16 percent increase in its share of business travelers in a single year.

Blueprinting the Restaurant Experience

To illustrate blueprinting of a high-contact, people-processing service, we examine the experience of dinner for two at Chez Jean, an upscale restaurant that enhances its core food service with a variety of other supplementary services (Figure 8.4). A typical rule of thumb in full-service restaurants is that the cost of purchasing the food ingredients represents only about 20 to 30 percent of the price of the meal. The balance can be seen as the fee that the customer is willing to pay for renting a table and chairs in a pleasant setting, hiring the services of food preparation experts and their kitchen equipment, and providing serving staff to wait on them both inside and outside the dining room.

The key components of the blueprint, reading from top to bottom, are as follows:

1. Definition of standards for each frontstage activity (only a few examples are actually specified in the figure)
2. Physical and other evidence for frontstage activities (specified for all steps)
3. Principal customer actions (illustrated by pictures)
4. Line of interaction
5. Frontstage actions by customer-contact personnel
6. Line of visibility
7. Backstage actions by customer-contact personnel
8. Support processes involving other service personnel
9. Support processes involving information technology

Reading from left to right, the blueprint prescribes the sequence of actions over time. In earlier chapters and the Grove and Fisk reading (pp. 83), we saw that service performances could be likened to theater. To emphasize the involvement of human actors in service delivery, we have followed the practice adopted by some service organizations of using pictures to illustrate each of the 14 principal steps involving our two customers (there are other steps not shown), beginning with making a reservation and concluding with departure from the restaurant after the meal. Like many high-contact services involving discrete transactions—as opposed to the continuous delivery found in, say, utility or insurance services—the "restaurant drama" can be divided into three "acts" representing activities that take place before the core product is encountered, delivery of the core product (in this case, the meal), and subsequent activities while still involved with the service provider.

To emphasize the involvement of human actors in service delivery, we have adopted the practice used by some service organizations of using pictures to illustrate each of the 14 principal steps involving our two customers (there are other steps not shown), beginning with making a reservation and concluding with departure from the restaurant after the meal. Like many high-contact services involving discrete transactions—as opposed to the continuous delivery found in, say, utility or insurance services—the "restaurant drama" can be divided into three "acts" representing activities that take place before the core product is encountered, delivery of the core product (in this case, the meal), and subsequent activities while still involved with the service provider.

The "stage," or *servicescape,* includes both the exterior and interior of the restaurant. Frontstage actions take place in a very visual environment; restaurants are often quite theatrical in their use of physical evidence (such as furnishings, decor, uniforms, lighting, and table settings) and may also employ background music in their efforts to create a themed environment.

Act I. In this particular drama, the first act begins with making a reservation—an interaction that is conducted by telephone with an unseen employee. In theatrical terms, the telephone conversation might be likened to a radio drama, with impressions being created on the evidence of the respondent's voice, speed of response, and style of the conversation. The act concludes with being escorted to a table and seated. These five steps constitute our customers' initial experience of the restaurant performance, with each involving an interaction with an employee—by phone or face-to-face. By the time the customers reach their table in the dining room, they have been exposed to several supplementary services, including reservations, valet parking, coatroom, cocktails, and seating. They have also seen a sizable cast of characters, including five or more contact personnel and many other customers.

Standards can be set for each service activity but should be based on a good understanding of guest expectations. Below the line of visibility, the blueprint identifies key actions to ensure that each frontstage step is performed in a manner that meets or exceeds those expectations. These actions include recording reservations; handling customers' coats; delivery and preparation of food; maintenance of facilities and equipment; training and assignment of staff for each task; and use of information technology to access, input, store, and transfer relevant data.

Identifying Fail Points. Running a good restaurant is a complex business and much can go wrong. The most serious fail points, marked by a small ⒡ in a circle, are those that will result in failure to access or enjoy the core product. They involve the reservation (Could the customer get through by phone? Was a table available at the desired time and date? Was the reservation recorded accurately?) and seating (Was a table available when promised?). Because service delivery takes place over time, there is also the possibility of delays between specific actions, requiring the customers to wait. Common locations for such waits are identified by a ⚠ within a triangle. Excessive waits will annoy customers.

In practice, every step in the process has some potential for failures and delays. David Maister coined the term *OTSU* (opportunity to screw up) to highlight the importance of thinking about all the things that might go wrong in delivering a particular type of service.[7] OTSUs are funny when you talk about them. John Cleese made millions laugh with his portrayal of an inept hotel manager in the television series *Fawlty Towers.* And Chevy Chase has entertained movie audiences for years by playing a customer tortured by inept, rude, or downright cruel service employees. However, customers don't always see the funny side when the joke is on them.

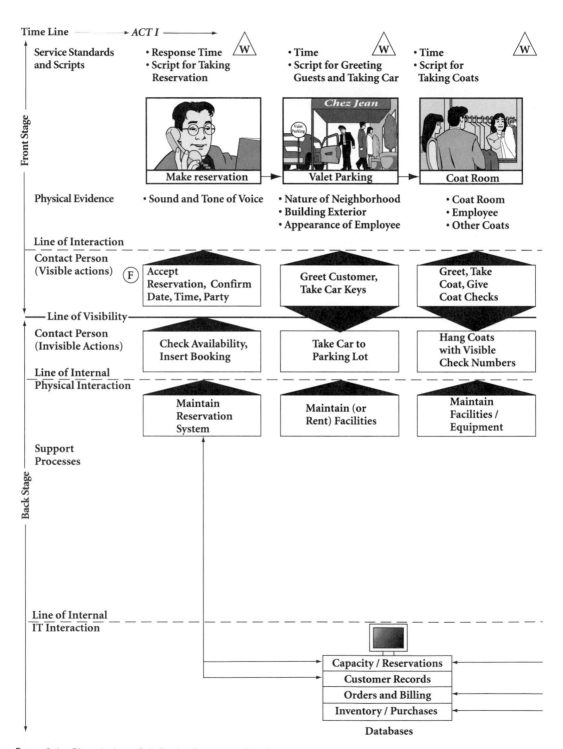

FIGURE 8.4 Blueprinting a Full-Service Restaurant Experience

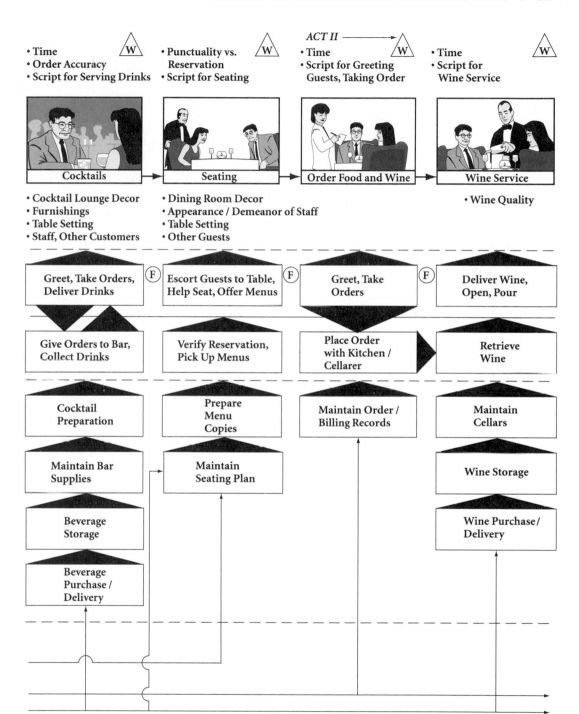

- Time
- Order Accuracy
- Script for Serving Drinks

- Punctuality vs. Reservation
- Script for Seating

ACT II
- Time
- Script for Greeting Guests, Taking Order

- Time
- Script for Wine Service

Cocktails → Seating → Order Food and Wine → Wine Service

- Cocktail Lounge Decor
- Furnishings
- Table Setting
- Staff, Other Customers

- Dining Room Decor
- Appearance / Demeanor of Staff
- Table Setting
- Other Guests

- Wine Quality

Greet, Take Orders, Deliver Drinks

Escort Guests to Table, Help Seat, Offer Menus

Greet, Take Orders

Deliver Wine, Open, Pour

Give Orders to Bar, Collect Drinks

Verify Reservation, Pick Up Menus

Place Order with Kitchen / Cellarer

Retrieve Wine

Cocktail Preparation

Prepare Menu Copies

Maintain Order / Billing Records

Maintain Cellars

Maintain Bar Supplies

Maintain Seating Plan

Wine Storage

Beverage Storage

Wine Purchase / Delivery

Beverage Purchase / Delivery

(F) Key Failure Points

(W) Risk of Excessive Wait (Standard should specify limits)

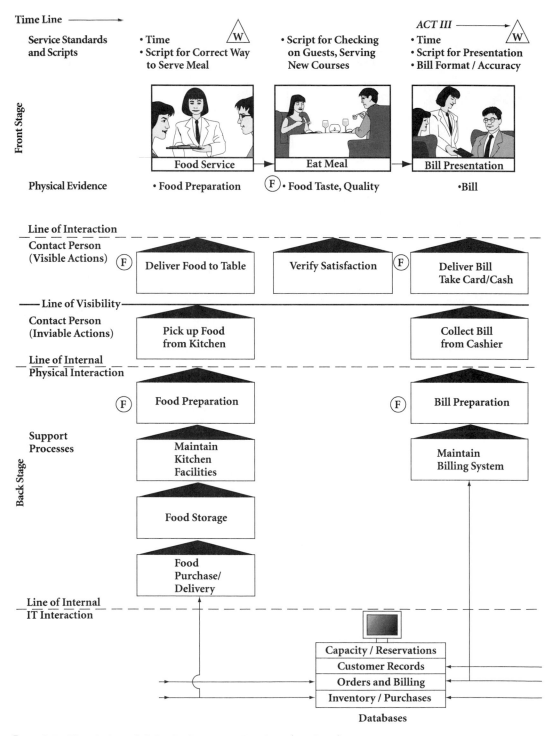

FIGURE 8.4   Blueprinting a Full-Service Restaurant Experience (*continued*)

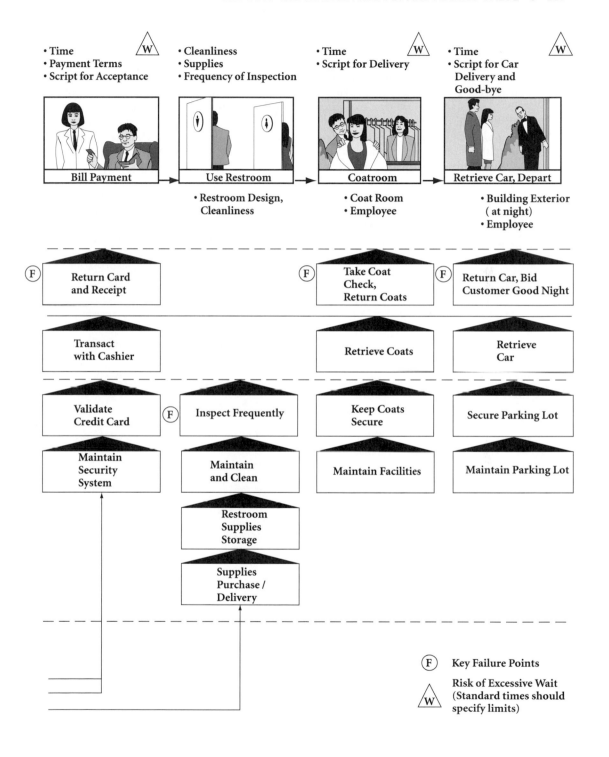

• Time
• Payment Terms
• Script for Acceptance

• Cleanliness
• Supplies
• Frequency of Inspection

• Time
• Script for Delivery

• Time
• Script for Car Delivery and Good-bye

Bill Payment → **Use Restroom** → **Coatroom** → **Retrieve Car, Depart**

• Restroom Design, Cleanliness

• Coat Room
• Employee

• Building Exterior (at night)
• Employee

Return Card and Receipt

Take Coat Check, Return Coats

Return Car, Bid Customer Good Night

Transact with Cashier

Retrieve Coats

Retrieve Car

Validate Credit Card

Inspect Frequently

Keep Coats Secure

Secure Parking Lot

Maintain Security System

Maintain and Clean

Maintain Facilities

Maintain Parking Lot

Restroom Supplies Storage

Supplies Purchase / Delivery

F Key Failure Points

W Risk of Excessive Wait (Standard times should specify limits)

It's only by identifying all the possible OTSUs associated with a particular task that service managers can put together a delivery system that is explicitly designed to avoid such problems.

Setting Service Standards. Through both formal research and on-the-job experience, service managers can learn the nature of customer expectations at each step in the process. As outlined in chapter 4, customers' expectations range across a spectrum—referred to as the zone of tolerance—from desired service (an ideal) to a threshold level of merely adequate service. Service providers should design standards for each step that are sufficiently high to satisfy and even delight customers; if that's not possible, then they will need to modify customer expectations. These standards may include time parameters, the script for a technically correct performance, and prescriptions for appropriate style and demeanor.

The opening scenes of a service drama are particularly important because customers' first impressions can affect their evaluations of quality during later stages of service delivery. Perceptions of their service experiences tend to be cumulative.[8] If a couple of things go badly wrong at the outset, customers may simply walk out. Even if they stay, they may now be looking for other things that aren't quite right. On the other hand, if the first steps go really well, their zones of tolerance may increase so that they are more willing to overlook minor mistakes later in the service performance. Research by Marriott Hotels indicates that four of the five top factors contributing to customer loyalty come into play during the first 10 minutes of service delivery.[9] And research into the design of doctor's offices and procedures suggests that unfavorable initial impressions can lead patients to cancel surgery or even change doctors (see Research Insights 8.1). However, performance standards should not be allowed to fall off toward the end of service

---

RESEARCH INSIGHTS 8.1

Cosmetic Surgeons' Offices Turn Off Patients

It appears that plastic surgeons could use some service marketing training along with their other courses in medical school. That's the diagnosis of two experts, Kate Altork and Douglas Dedo, who did a study of patients' reactions to doctors' offices. They found that many patients will cancel a surgery, change doctors, or refuse to consider future elective surgery if they feel uneasy in the doctor's office. The study results suggested that patients don't usually "doctor-jump" because they dislike the doctor but because they don't like the context of the service experience. The list of common patient dislikes includes graphic posters of moles and skin cancers decorating office walls, uncomfortable plastic identification bracelets for patients, claustrophobic examining rooms with no windows or current reading material, bathrooms that aren't clearly marked, and not enough wastebaskets and water coolers in the waiting room.

What do patients want? Most requests are surprisingly simple and involve creature comforts such as tissues, water coolers, telephones, plants, and bowls of candy in the waiting room and live flower arrangements in the lobby. Patients also want windows in the examining rooms and gowns that wrap around the entire body. They would like to sit on a real chair when they talk to a doctor instead of perching on a stool or examining table. Finally, preoperative patients prefer to be separated from postoperative patients because they are disturbed by sitting next to someone in the waiting room whose head is enclosed in bandages.

These study results suggest that cosmetic surgery patients would rather visit an office that looks more like a health spa than a hospital ward. By thinking like service marketers, savvy surgeons could use this information to create patient-friendly environments that will complement rather than counteract their technical expertise.

Source: Lisa Bannon, "Plastic Surgeons Are Told to Pay More Attention to Appearances," *Wall Street Journal,* March 15, 1997, p. B1. Reprinted with permission, through Copyright Clearance Center.

delivery. Other research findings point to the importance of a strong finish and suggest that a service encounter that is perceived to start poorly but then builds in quality will be better rated than one that starts well but declines to end poorly.[10]

Act II. Delivery of the Core Product. As the curtain rises on the second act, our customers are finally about to experience the core service they came for. For simplicity, we've condensed the meal into just four scenes. In practice, reviewing the menu and placing the order are two separate activities; meanwhile, meal service proceeds on a course-by-course basis. If you were actually running a restaurant yourself, you would need to go into greater detail to identify all of the steps involved in what is often a tightly scripted drama. Assuming all goes well, the two guests will have an excellent meal, nicely served in a pleasant atmosphere, and perhaps a fine wine to enhance it. But if the restaurant fails to satisfy customer expectations during Act II, it's going to be in serious trouble. Fail points abound. Is the menu information complete? Is it intelligible? Is everything listed on the menu actually available this evening? Will explanations and advice be given in a friendly and noncondescending manner for guests who have questions about specific menu items or are unsure about which wine to order?

After our guests decide on their meals, they place their order with the server, who must then pass on the details to personnel in the kitchen, bar, and billing desk. Mistakes in transmitting information are a frequent cause of quality failures in many organizations. Bad handwriting or unclear verbal requests can lead to delivery of the wrong items altogether—or of the right items incorrectly prepared. In subsequent scenes of Act II, our customers may evaluate not only the quality of food and drink—the most important dimension of all—but also how promptly it is served (not too promptly, for that would suggest frozen foods cooked by microwave) and the style of service. A technically correct performance by the server can still be spoiled by such human failures as disinterested, cold, ingratiating behavior or an overly casual manner.

Act III. The meal may be over, but much is still taking place both frontstage and backstage as the drama moves to its close. The core service has now been delivered, and we'll assume that our customers are happily digesting it. Act III should be short. The action in each of the remaining scenes should move smoothly, quickly, and pleasantly, with no shocking surprises at the end. We can hypothesize that in a North American environment, most customers' expectations would probably include the following:

- An accurate, intelligible bill is presented promptly as soon as the customer requests it.
- Payment is handled politely and expeditiously (with all major credit cards acceptable); the guests are thanked for their patronage and invited to come again.
- Customers visiting the restrooms find them clean and properly supplied.
- The right coats are promptly retrieved from the coatroom.
- The customer's car is brought promptly to the door in the same condition as when it was left; the attendant thanks them again and bids them a good evening.

But how often do failures intervene to ruin the customers' experience and spoil their good humor? Can you remember situations in which the experience of a nice meal in Act II was completely spoiled by one or more failures in Act III? My own informal research among participants in dozens of executive programs has found that the most commonly cited source of dissatisfaction with restaurants is an inability to get the bill quickly when the customers have finished their meal and are ready to leave! This seemingly minor failing, unrelated to the core product, can nevertheless leave a bad taste in a customer's mouth that taints the overall dining experience, even if everything else has gone well. When customers are on a tight time budget, making them

---

SERVICE PERSPECTIVES 8.1

In-and-Out Food Service

Restaurant Hospitality, a trade magazine for the restaurant industry, offers the following 10 suggestions for serving customers quickly without making them feel like they've been pushed out of the door. As you'll see, some of these tactics involve frontstage processes, whereas others take place backstage—but it is the interaction between frontstage and backstage that creates the desired service delivery.

1. Distinguish between patrons in a hurry and those who are not.
2. Design specials that are quick.
3. Guide hurried customers to those specials.
4. Place the quickest, highest-margin menu items either first or last on the menu.
5. Offer dishes that can be prepared ahead of time.
6. Warn customers when they order menu items that will take a lot of time to prepare.
7. Consider short-line buffets, roving carts, and more sandwiches.
8. Offer wrap-style sandwiches, which are a quickly prepared, filling meal.
9. Use equipment built for speed, like combination ovens.
10. Eliminate preparation steps that require cooks to stop cooking.

Adapted from Paul B. Hertneky, "Built for Speed," *Restaurant Hospitality,* January 1997, 58.

---

wait unnecessarily at any point in the process is akin to stealing their time. (For some solutions to this problem, see Service Perspectives 8.1.)

Our restaurant example was deliberately chosen to illustrate a high-contact, people-processing service with which all readers were likely to be familiar. But many possession-processing services (such as repair or maintenance) and information-processing services (such as insurance or accounting) involve far less contact with customers because much of the action takes place backstage. In these situations, a failure committed frontstage is likely to represent a higher proportion of the customer's service encounters with a company and may therefore be viewed even more seriously, because there are fewer subsequent opportunities to create a favorable impression.

Identifying and Classifying Supplementary Services

The more we examine different types of services, the more we find that most of them have many supplementary services in common.[11] Blueprinting (or flowcharting) offers an excellent way to understand the totality of the customer's service experience and identify the many different types of supplementary services accompanying a core product. In the restaurant example, supplementary services included reservation, valet parking, safekeeping of coats, cocktails, being escorted to a table, ordering from the menu, billing, payment, and use of toilets.

If you prepare flowcharts for a variety of services, you will soon notice that although core products may differ widely, common supplementary elements—from information to billing and from reservations/order taking to problem resolution—keep recurring. There are potentially dozens of different supplementary services, but almost all of them can be classified into one of the following eight clusters. We have listed them as either *facilitating* supplementary services that smooth delivery or are essential components (like payment) or *enhancing* supplementary services that may add extra value for customers.

Facilitating Supplementary Services	*Enhancing Supplementary Services*
Information	Consultation
Order taking	Hospitality
Billing	Safekeeping
Payment	Exceptions

In Figure 8.5, these eight clusters are displayed as petals surrounding the center of what we call the Flower of Service. We've shown them clockwise in the sequence in which they are likely to be encountered by customers (although this sequence may vary—for instance, payment may have to be made before service is delivered rather than afterwards). In a well-designed and well-managed service organization, the petals and core are fresh and well formed. A badly designed or poorly executed service is a like a flower with missing, wilted, or discolored petals. Even if the core is perfect, the overall impression of the flower is unattractive. Think about your own experiences as a customer (or when purchasing on behalf of an organization). When you were dissatisfied with a particular purchase, was it the core that was at fault, or was it a problem with one or more of the petals?

Not every core product is augmented by supplementary elements from all eight clusters. As we'll see, the nature of the product helps to determine which supplementary services must be offered and which might usefully be added to enhance value and make the organization easy to do business with. In general, people-processing services tend to be accompanied by more supplementary services than do the other three categories; similarly, high-contact services will have more than low-contact services.

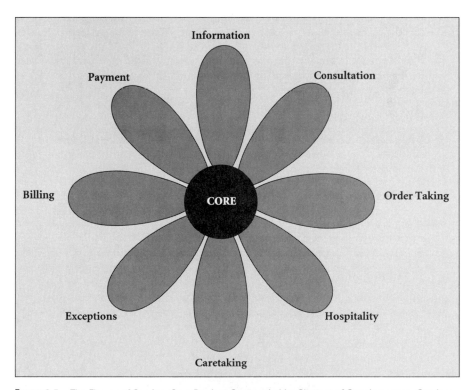

FIGURE 8.5   The Flower of Service: Core Product Surrounded by Clusters of Supplementary Services

A company's market-positioning strategy helps to determine which supplementary services should be included (see chapter 7). A strategy of adding benefits to increase customers' perceptions of quality will probably require more supplementary services (and also a higher level of performance on all such elements) than a strategy of competing on low prices. Firms that offer different grades of service—such as first class, business class, and economy class in an airline context—often differentiate them by adding extra supplementary services for each upgrade in service.

Information

To obtain full value from any good or service, customers need relevant information (Table 8.1). New customers and prospects are especially information hungry. Customers' needs may include directions to the site where the product is sold (or details about how to order it), service hours, prices, and usage instructions. Further information, sometimes required by law, could include conditions of sale and use, warnings, reminders, and notification of changes. Finally, customers may want documentation of what has already taken place, such as confirmation of reservations, receipts and tickets, and monthly summaries of account activity.

Companies should make sure the information they provide is both timely and accurate because incorrect information can annoy or inconvenience customers. Traditional ways of providing information to customers include using frontline employees (who are not always as well informed as customers might like), printed notices, brochures, and instruction books. Other information media include videotapes or software-driven tutorials, touch-screen video displays, and menu-driven recorded telephone messages. The most significant recent innovation has been corporate use of Web sites. Examples of useful applications range from train and airline schedules, hotel details, assistance in locating specific retail outlets such as restaurants and stores, and information on the services of professional firms. Many business logistics companies offer shippers the opportunity to track the movements of their packages—each of which has been assigned a unique identification number.

Order Taking

Once customers are ready to buy, a key supplementary element comes into play—accepting applications, orders, and reservations (Table 8.2). The process of order taking should be polite, fast, and accurate so that customers do not waste time and endure unnecessary mental or phys-

TABLE 8.1 *Examples of Information Elements*
Directions to service site
Schedules/service hours
Prices
Instructions on using core product/supplementary services
Reminders
Warnings
Conditions of sale/service
Notification of changes
Documentation
Confirmation of reservations
Summaries of account activity
Receipts and tickets

TABLE 8.2	*Examples of Order-Taking Elements*
Applications	
Membership in clubs or programs	
Subscription services (e.g., utilities)	
Prerequisite-based services (e.g., credit, college enrollment)	
Order entry	
On-site fulfillment	
Mail/telephone order for subsequent fulfillment	
Reservations and check-in	
Seats	Hire of vehicles or other equipment
Tables	Professional appointments
Rooms	Admissions to restricted facilities (e.g., exhibitions)

ical effort. Technology can be used to make order taking easier and faster for both customers and suppliers. The key lies in minimizing the time and effort required of both parties while also ensuring completeness and accuracy.

Banks, insurance companies, and utilities require prospective customers to go through an application process designed to gather relevant information and to screen out those who do not meet basic enrollment criteria (such as those with a bad credit record or serious health problems.) Universities also require prospective students to apply for admission. Reservations (including appointments and check-in) represent a special type of order taking that entitles customers to a specified unit of service—for example, an airline seat, a restaurant table, a hotel room, time with a qualified professional, or admission to a facility such as a theater or sports arena with designated seating. Accuracy in scheduling is vital—reserving seats for the wrong day is likely to be unpopular with customers.

Ticketless systems, based on telephone or Web site reservations, provide enormous cost savings for airlines because there is no travel agent commission—customers book directly—and the administrative effort is drastically reduced. A paper ticket at an airline may be handled 15 times, whereas an electronic ticket requires just one step. But some customers are disenchanted by the paperless process. Although they receive a confirmation number by phone when they make the reservations and need only to show identification at the airport to claim their seats, many people feel insecure without tangible proof that they have a seat on a particular flight.[12] And business travelers complain that needed receipts don't arrive until days or sometimes weeks after a trip, causing problems when claiming expenses from corporate accounting departments. Some airlines now offer to fax receipts and itineraries on request at the time a flight is booked.

Billing

Billing is common to almost all services (unless the service is provided free of charge). Inaccurate, illegible, or incomplete bills risk disappointing customers who may, up to that point, have been quite satisfied with their experience. Such failures add insult to injury if the customer is already dissatisfied. Billing should also be timely because this serves to stimulate faster payment. Procedures range from verbal statements to a machine-displayed price and from handwritten invoices to elaborate monthly statements of account activity and fees (Table 8.3). Perhaps the simplest approach is self-billing, when the customer tallies up the amount of an order and either encloses a check or signs a credit card payment authorization. In such

TABLE 8.3 *Examples of Billing Elements*	
Periodic statements of account activity	Machine display of amount due
Invoices for individual transactions	Self-billing (computed by customer)
Verbal statements of amount due	

instances, billing and payment are combined into a single act, although the seller may still need to check for accuracy.

More and more, billing is being computerized. Despite the potential for productivity improvements, computerized billing has its dark side, as when an innocent customer tries futilely to contest an inaccurate bill and is met by an escalating sequence of ever-larger bills (compounded interest and penalty charges), accompanied by increasingly threatening computer-generated letters.

Customers usually expect bills to be clear, informative, and itemized in ways that make it clear how the total was computed. Unexplained, arcane symbols that have all the meaning of hieroglyphics on an Egyptian monument (and are decipherable only by the high priests of accounting and data processing) do not create a favorable impression of the supplier. Neither does fuzzy printing or illegible handwriting. Laser printers, with their ability to switch fonts and typefaces, to box, and to highlight, can produce statements that are not only more legible but also organize information in more useful ways. Marketing research can help here by asking customers in advance what information they want and how they would like it to be organized.

American Express built its Corporate Card business by offering companies detailed documentation of the spending patterns of individual employees and departments on travel and entertainment. Intelligent thinking about customer needs led American Express to realize that well-organized information has value to a customer, beyond just the basic requirement of knowing how much to pay at the end of each month.

Busy customers hate to be kept waiting for a bill to be prepared in a hotel, restaurant, or rental car lot. Many hotels and rental car firms have now created express checkout options, taking customers' credit card details in advance and documenting charges later by mail. But accuracy is essential. Because customers use the express checkouts to save time, they certainly don't want to waste time later seeking corrections and refunds. An alternative express checkout procedure is used by some car rental companies. An agent meets customers as they return their cars, checks the mileage/kilometrage and fuel gauge readings, and then prints a bill on the spot using a portable wireless terminal. Many hotels push bills under guestroom doors on the morning of departure showing charges to date; others offer customers the option of previewing their bills before checkout on the television monitors in their rooms.

Payment

In most cases, a bill requires the customer to take action on payment (and such action may be very slow in coming!). One exception is bank statements, which detail charges that have already been deducted from the customer's account. Increasingly, customers expect ease and convenience of payment, including credit, when they make purchases in their own countries and while traveling abroad.

A variety of options exist to facilitate customer bill paying (Table 8.4). Self-service payment systems, for instance, require customers to insert coins, banknotes, tokens, or cards in machines. But equipment breakdowns destroy the whole purpose of such a system, so good maintenance and rapid-response troubleshooting are essential. Much payment still takes place through hand-to-hand transfers of cash and checks, but credit and debit cards are growing in importance as

TABLE 8.4	Examples of Payment Elements	
Self-service		
Exact change in machine	Insert token	
Cash in machine with change returned	Electronic funds transfer	
Insert prepayment card	Mail a check	
Insert credit/charge/debit card		
Direct to payee or intermediary		
Cash handling and change giving	Coupon redemption	
Check handling	Tokens, vouchers, etc.	
Credit/charge/debit card handling		
Automatic deduction from financial deposits (e.g. bank charges) control and verification		
Automated systems (e.g., machine-readable tickets operate entry gate)		
Personal systems (e.g., gate controllers, ticket inspectors)		

more and more establishments accept them. Other alternatives include tokens, vouchers, coupons, or prepaid tickets. Firms benefit from prompt payment because it reduces the amount of accounts receivable. To reinforce good behavior, COM Electric, a Massachusetts electrical utility, periodically sends thank-you notes to customers who have consistently paid on time.

To ensure that people actually pay what is due, some service businesses have instituted control systems, such as ticket checks before entering a movie theater or boarding a train. However, inspectors and security officers must be trained to combine politeness with firmness in performing their jobs so that honest customers do not feel harassed. But a visible presence often serves as a deterrent.

Consultation

Now we move to enhancing supplementary services, led by consultation. In contrast to information, which suggests a simple response to customers' questions (or printed information that anticipates their needs), consultation involves a dialog to probe customer requirements and then develop a tailored solution. Table 8.5 provides examples of several supplementary services in the consultation category. At its simplest, consultation consists of immediate advice from a knowledgeable service person in response to the request "What do you suggest?" (For example, you might ask the person who cuts your hair for advice on different hairstyles and products.) Effective consultation requires an understanding of each customer's current situation before suggesting a suitable course of action. Good customer records can be a great help in this respect, particularly if relevant data can be retrieved easily from a remote terminal.

Counseling represents a more subtle approach to consultation because it involves helping customers better understand their situations so that they can come up with their own solutions and action programs. This approach can be a particularly valuable supplement to services such as health treatment, when part of the challenge is to get customers to take a long-term view of their personal situation and to adopt more healthful behaviors, often involving some initial sacrifice. For example, diet centers such as Weight Watchers use counseling to help customers change behaviors so that weight loss can be sustained after the initial diet is completed.

Finally, there are more formalized efforts to provide management and technical consulting for corporate customers, such as the solution selling associated with marketing expensive indus-

TABLE 8.5	*Examples of Consultation Elements*
Advice	Tutoring/training in product usage
Auditing	Management or technical consultancy
Personal counseling	

trial equipment and services. The sales engineer researches the customer's situation and then offers objective advice about what particular package of equipment and systems will yield the best results for the customer. Some consulting services are offered free of charge in the hope of making a sale. However, in other instances the service is unbundled, and customers are expected to pay for it. Advice can also be offered through tutorials, group training programs, and public demonstrations.

Hospitality

Hospitality-related services should, ideally, reflect pleasure at meeting new customers and greeting old ones when they return. Well-managed businesses try, at least in small ways, to ensure that their employees treat customers as guests. Courtesy and consideration for customers' needs apply to both face-to-face encounters and telephone interactions (Table 8.6). Hospitality finds its full expression in face-to-face encounters. In some cases, it starts (and ends) with an offer of transport to and from the service site, as with courtesy shuttle buses. If customers must wait outdoors before the service can be delivered, then a thoughtful service provider will offer weather protection; if indoors, then a waiting area with seating and even entertainment (television, newspapers, or magazines) to pass the time should be made available. Recruiting employees who are naturally warm, welcoming, and considerate for customer-contact jobs helps to create a hospitable atmosphere.

The quality of the hospitality services offered by a firm can increase or decrease satisfaction with the core product. This is especially true for people-processing services where customers cannot easily leave the service facility. Private hospitals often seek to enhance their appeals by providing the level of room service, including meals, that might be expected in a good hotel. Some airlines seek to differentiate themselves from their competitors with better meals and more attentive cabin crew; Singapore Airlines is well recognized on both counts. Although in-flight hospitality is important, an airline journey doesn't really end until passengers reach their final destination. Air travelers have come to expect departure lounges, but British Airways (BA) came up with the novel idea of an arrivals lounge for its terminals at London's Heathrow and Gatwick airports to serve passengers arriving early in the morning after a long, overnight flight from the Americas, Asia, Africa, and Australia. It offers holders of first- and business-class tickets or a BA Executive Club gold card (awarded to the airline's most frequent flyers) the opportunity to use a special lounge where they can take a shower, change, have breakfast, and make

TABLE 8.6	*Examples of Hospitality Elements*
Greeting	Food and beverages
Toilets and washrooms	Bathroom kits
Transport	Security
Waiting facilities and amenities	
Lounges, waiting areas, seating	
Weather protection	
Magazines, entertainment, newspapers	

phone calls or send faxes before continuing to their final destination feeling a lot fresher. It's a nice competitive advantage, which BA has actively promoted. Other airlines have since felt obliged to copy it.

Safekeeping

While visiting a service site, customers often want assistance with their personal possessions. In fact, unless certain safekeeping services are provided (like safe and convenient parking for their cars), some customers may not come at all. The list of potential on-site safekeeping services is long. It includes provision of coatrooms; baggage transport, handling, and storage; safekeeping of valuables; and even child care and pet care (Table 8.7). Responsible businesses also worry about the safety of their customers. These days, many businesses pay close attention to safety and security issues for customers who are visiting their service facilities. Wells Fargo Bank mails a brochure with its bank statements containing information about using its ATMs safely. It seeks to educate its customers about how to protect both their ATM cards and themselves from theft and personal injury. And the bank makes sure that its machines are in brightly lit, highly visible locations to reduce any risks to its customers or their possessions.

Additional safekeeping services involve physical products that customers buy or rent. They may include packaging, pickup and delivery, assembly, installation, cleaning, and inspection. Some of these services may be offered free, whereas others carry a charge.

Exceptions

Exceptions involve supplementary services that fall outside the routine of normal service delivery (Table 8.8). Astute businesses anticipate exceptions and develop contingency plans and guidelines in advance. That way, employees will not appear helpless and surprised when customers ask for special assistance. Well-defined procedures make it easier for employees to respond promptly and effectively.

There are several different types of exceptions:

1. *Special requests.* There are many circumstances when a customer may request service that requires a departure from normal operating procedures. Advance requests often relate to personal needs, including care of children, dietary requirements, medical needs, religious

TABLE 8.7 *Examples of Safekeeping Elements*	
Caring for possessions customers bring with them	
Child care	Coatroom
Pet care	Baggage handling
Parking facilities for vehicles	Storage space
Valet parking	Safety deposit/security
Caring for goods purchased (or rented) by customers	
Packaging	Cleaning
Pickup	Refueling
Transportation	Preventive maintenance
Delivery	Repairs and renovation
Installation	Upgrade
Inspection and diagnosis	

TABLE 8.8	*Examples of Exceptions Elements*

Special requests in advance of service delivery

Children's needs	Religious observance
Dietary requirements	Deviations from standard operating procedures
Medical or disability needs	

Handling special communications

Complaints	Compliments
Suggestions	

Problem solving

Warranties and guarantees against product malfunction
Resolving difficulties that arise from using the product
Resolving difficulties caused by accidents, service failures, and problems with staff or other customers
Assisting customers who have suffered an accident or medical emergency

Restitution

Refunds	Compensation in kind for unsatisfactory goods and services
Free repair of defective goods	

observance, and personal disabilities. Such special requests are common in the travel and hospitality industries.

2. *Problem solving.* Situations arise when normal service delivery (or product performance) fails to run smoothly as a result of accidents, delays, equipment failures, or customers experiencing difficulty in using the product.

3. *Handling of complaints/suggestions/compliments.* This activity requires well-defined procedures. It should be easy for customers to express dissatisfaction, offer suggestions for improvement, or pass on compliments, and service providers should be able to make an appropriate response quickly.

4. *Restitution.* Many customers expect to be compensated for serious performance failures. Compensation may take the form of repairs under warranty, legal settlements, refunds, an offer of free service, or other forms of payment-in-kind.

Managers need to keep an eye on the level of exception requests. Too many requests may indicate that standard procedures need revamping. For instance, if a restaurant constantly receives requests for special vegetarian meals because there are none on the menu, this may indicate that it's time to revise the menu to include at least one such dish. A flexible approach to exceptions is generally a good idea because it reflects responsiveness to customer needs. On the other hand, too many exceptions may compromise safety, negatively impact other customers, and overburden employees.

Managerial Implications

The eight categories of supplementary services forming the Flower of Service collectively provide many options for enhancing the core product, whether it be a good or a service. Most supplementary services do (or should) represent responses to customer needs. As noted earlier, some are facilitating services–like information and reservations—that enable customers to use the core product more effectively. Others are extras that enhance the core or even reduce its nonfinancial costs (for example, meals, magazines, and entertainment are hospitality elements that help pass the time). Some elements—notably billing and payment—are, in effect, imposed by the service provider. But even if not actively desired by the customer, they still form part of the overall service experience. Any badly handled element may negatively affect customers' perceptions of service quality. The information and consultation petals illustrate the emphasis in this book on the need for education as well as promotion in communicating with service customers.

Not every core product will be surrounded by a large number of supplementary services from all eight petals. People-processing services tend to be the most demanding in terms of supplementary elements—especially hospitality—because they involve close (and often extended) interactions with customers. When customers do not visit the service factory, the need for hospitality may be limited to simple courtesies in letters and telecommunications. Possession-processing services sometimes place heavy demands on safekeeping elements, but there may be no need for this particular petal when providing information-processing services in which customers and suppliers deal entirely at arm's length. Financial services that are provided electronically are an exception to this, however—companies must ensure that their customers' intangible financial assets are carefully safeguarded in transactions that occur via phone or the Web.

Managers face many decisions concerning what types of supplementary services to offer, especially in relation to product policy and positioning issues. A study of Japanese, North American, and European firms serving business-to-business markets found that most companies simply added layer upon layer of services to their core offerings without knowing what customers really valued.[13] Managers surveyed in the study indicated that they did not understand which services should be offered to customers as a standard package accompanying the core and which could be offered as options for an extra charge. Without this knowledge, developing effective pricing policies can be tricky. There are no simple rules governing pricing decisions for core products and supplementary services. But managers should continually review their own policies and those of competitors to make sure they are in line with both market practice and customer needs. We'll discuss these and other pricing issues in more detail in chapter 9.

In summary, Tables 8.1 through 8.8 can serve as a checklist in the continuing search for new ways to augment existing core products and to design new offerings. The lists provided in these eight tables do not claim to be all-encompassing because some products may require specialized supplementary elements. In general, a firm that competes on a low-cost, no-frills basis will require fewer supplementary elements than would one marketing an expensive, high-value-added product. Alternative levels of supplementary services around a common core may offer the basis for a product line of differentiated offerings, similar to the various classes of travel offered by airlines. Regardless of which supplementary services a firm decides to offer, all of the elements in each petal should receive the care and attention needed to consistently meet defined service standards. That way, the resulting flower, as it were, will always have a fresh and appealing appearance—rather than looking wilted or disfigured by neglect.

Planning and Branding Service Products

In recent years, more and more service businesses have started talking about their *products*—a term previously associated with manufactured goods. Some will even speak of their "products and services," an expression also used by service-driven manufacturing firms. What is the distinction between these two terms in today's business environment?

A product implies a defined and consistent bundle of output and also the ability to differentiate one bundle of output from another. In a manufacturing context, the concept is easy to understand and visualize. Service firms can also differentiate their products in similar fashion to the various models offered by manufacturers. Quick-service restaurants are sometimes described as *quasi-manufacturing* operations because they produce a physical output combined with value-added service. At each site, they display a menu of their products, which are, of course, highly tangible—burger connoisseurs can easily distinguish Burger King's Whopper from a Whopper with Cheese as well as a Whopper from a Big Mac. The service comes from speedy delivery of a freshly prepared food item; the ability (in some instances) to order and pick up freshly cooked food from a drive-in location without leaving one's car; the availability within the restaurant of self-service drinks, condiments, and napkins; and the opportunity to sit down and eat one's meal at a table.

But providers of more intangible services also offer a menu of products, representing an assembly of carefully prescribed elements that are built around the core product and may bundle in certain value-added supplementary services. Additional supplementary services—often referred to collectively as *customer service*—may be available to facilitate delivery and use of the product as well as billing and payment. Let's look at some examples from hotels, airlines, and computer support services.

Product Lines and Brands

Most service organizations offer a line of products rather than just a single product. Some of these products are distinctly different from one another—as, for example, when a company operates several lines of business. Within a specific industry, a large firm may choose to offer several, differently positioned entries, each identified by a separate brand name. For instance, Marriott Corporation offers several different brands of hotels and resorts under the Marriott umbrella brand, including

- *Marriott Hotels* (big, full-service hotels in cities, offering large public areas and meeting facilities)
- *Marriott Resorts* (large, full-service hotels in resort areas, offering meeting facilities and access to extensive sporting and recreational amenities)
- *Courtyard by Marriott* (medium-sized hotels without conference facilities, targeted at business travelers who require comfortable rooms and business-related services but fewer hotel amenities)
- *Fairfield Inns* (inexpensive rooms with only limited hotel services)
- *Residence Inns* (offering a bedroom, living room, and kitchen at full-service hotel room prices; targeted at customers needing hotel amenities with more workspace and planning to stay at least several days).
- *SpringHill Suites* (moderately priced all-suites hotels targeted at both business and pleasure travelers; they offer separate working, sleeping, and eating areas, including a pantry with sink, microwave, and coffee maker)
- *TownePlace Suites* (suites with full kitchens designed for extended stays, offering residential comfort in a townhouse setting at reasonable prices)
- *Marriott Vacation Clubs International* (villa vacation resorts)

Each brand promises a distinct mix of benefits, targeted at a different customer segment. The offerings vary by service level (and thus price); there are also different room configurations available; certain brands are targeted at guests who will be making an extended stay; and finally, there are two resort brands that primarily target vacationers. In some instances, segmentation is situation based: The same individual may have different needs (and willingness to pay) under differing circumstances.

As an example of branding a high-tech, business-to-business product line, consider Sun Microsystems. The company offers a comprehensive hardware and software support program known as SunSpectrum Support. Four different levels of support are available, subbranded from platinum to bronze (they are displayed in menu form in Figure 8.6). The objective is to give buyers the flexibility to choose a level of support consistent with their own organization's needs (and willingness to pay), ranging from mission-critical support at the enterprise level to assistance with self-service support. Note the more extensive service hours available with the higher levels of support (24/7) as opposed to just daytime service on weekdays at the lower levels.

British Airways offers seven distinct air-travel products—sometimes referred to as *subbrands*. There are four intercontinental offerings—Concorde (supersonic deluxe service), First (deluxe subsonic service), Club World (business class), and World Traveller (economy class); two intra-European subbrands—Club Europe (business class) and Euro-Traveller (economy class); and within the United Kingdom, Shuttle, offering high-frequency service between London and major British cities. Each BA offering represents a specific service concept and a set of clearly stated product specifications for preflight, in-flight, and on-arrival service elements. BA's chief executive has said of Concorde, "The Concorde brand stands above all for speed, for

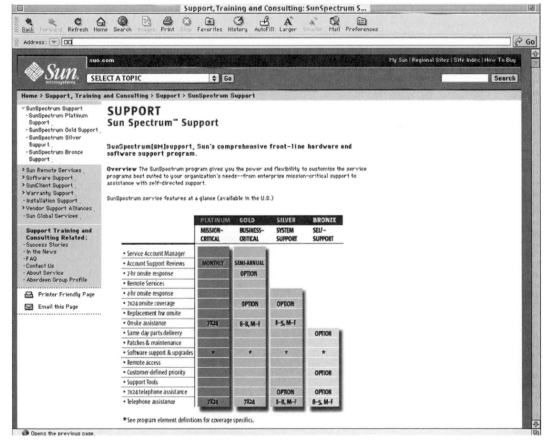

FIGURE 8.6 Four Levels of Support from Sun Microsystems
Source: www.sun.com/service/support/sunspectrum, January 2000.

getting from London to New York in three hours, twenty minutes. It represents a very exclusive means of travel, and in some ways it is also an exclusive club."[14]

To provide additional focus on product, pricing, and marketing communications, responsibility for managing and developing each service is assigned to an individual management team. Through internal training and external communications, staff and passengers alike are kept informed of the characteristics of each service. Except for Concorde, Super Shuttle, and nonjets, most aircraft in BA's fleet are configured in two or three classes. For instance, the airline's intercontinental fleet of 747s is equipped to serve First, Club World, and World Traveller passengers. On any given route, all passengers receive the same core product—say, a 10-hour flight from Los Angeles to London—but the nature and extent of most of the supplementary elements will differ widely, both on the ground and in the air. Passengers in First, for instance, not only benefit from better tangible elements—such as more comfortable seats that fold into beds, better food, and the use of an airport lounge before the flight—but also receive more personalized service from airline employees and benefit from faster service on the ground at check-in, passport control in London (special lines), and baggage retrieval (priority handling). The higher the service level, of course, the higher the price!

Offering a Branded Experience

Branding can be employed at both the corporate and product level by almost any service business. In a well-managed firm the corporate brand is not only easily recognized but also has meaning for customers: It stands for a particular way of doing business. Some firms choose to associate their corporate brand closely with individual product brands (subbrands). Subbrands that stand under the umbrella of a corporate brand should reflect the values of the latter. At the same time, the subbrand should communicate the particular experiences and benefits associated with a given service process. The Forum Corporation, a consulting and training firm, differentiates between (1) a random customer experience with high variability; (2) a generic branded experience in which most suppliers offer a consistently similar experience, differentiated only by the presence of the brand name (ATMs are a good example); and (3) what it calls a "Branded Customer Experience" in which the customer's experience is shaped in specific and meaningful ways. (See Management Memo 8.1 for Forum's recommendations on how to achieve this.)

MANAGEMENT MEMO 8.1

Moving Toward the Branded Customer Experience

Forum Corporation identifies six basic steps to develop and deliver the Branded Customer Experience:

1. Adopt new criteria beyond demographics to target profitable customers.
2. Achieve a superior understanding of what your targeted customers value.
3. Apply that understanding to shape a truly differentiated customer experience that will eclipse the competition.
4. Make everyone a brand manager. ("Each and every one of you will make or break the promise that our brand makes to customers.")
5. Make promises that you are sure your processes can exceed.
6. Measure and monitor. Anticipate what customers will value to sustain consistency of delivery in the future.

Source: Forum Issues #17 (Boston: The Forum Corporation, 1997).

Around the world, many financial service firms have created different brands to identify and distinguish an array of accounts and service packages, each of which offers distinctively different features. The objective is to transform a series of service elements and processes into a consistent and recognizable service experience, offering a definable and predictable output at a specified price. Unfortunately, there is often little discernible difference—other than name—between one bank's branded offering and another's.

An important role for service marketers is to become brand champions, familiar with and responsible for shaping every aspect of the customer's experience. When blueprinting a service process, one of the benefits of displaying pictures of customers' activities is that it highlights the need for consistent delivery standards, consistent physical and visual design standards, and scripts designed to present a consistent style. We can relate the notion of a branded service experience to the Flower of Service metaphor by emphasizing the need for consistency in the color and texture of each petal. Unfortunately, many service experiences remain very haphazard and create the impression of a flower stitched together with petals drawn from many different plants!

New Service Development

Competitive intensity and customer expectations are increasing in nearly all service industries. Thus, success lies not only in providing existing services well but also in creating new approaches to service. Because the outcome and process aspects of a service often combine to create the experience and benefits obtained by customers, both aspects must be addressed in new service development.

A Hierarchy of New Service Categories

The following list identifies seven categories of new services, ranging from major innovations to simple style changes.

1. *Major service innovations* are new core products for markets that have not been previously defined. These products usually include both new service characteristics and radical new processes. Examples include FedEx's introduction of overnight, nationwide, express package delivery in 1971; the advent of global news service from CNN; and eBay's launch of online auction services that embrace a vast number of categories.

2. *Major process innovations* consist of using new processes to deliver existing core products in new ways with additional benefits. For example, the University of Phoenix competes with other universities by delivering undergraduate and graduate degree programs in a non-traditional way. It has no permanent campus but offers courses either online or at night in rented facilities. Its students get most of the benefits of a college degree in half the time and at a much lower price than they would at other universities.[15] In recent years, the growth of the Internet has led to creation of many new start-up businesses employing new retailing models that exclude use of traditional stores but save customers time and travel. Often, these models add new, information-based benefits such as greater customization, the opportunity to visit chat rooms with fellow customers, and suggestions for additional products that match well with what has already been purchased.

3. *Product line extensions* are additions to current product lines by existing firms. The first company in a market to offer such a product may be seen as an innovator; the others are merely followers, often acting defensively. These new services may be targeted at existing customers to serve a broader array of needs or designed to attract new customers with different needs (or both). United Airlines is one of several major carriers to launch a separate low-cost operation (in its case, United Express) designed to compete with discount carriers

such as Southwest Airlines. Telephone companies have introduced numerous value-added services such as call waiting and call forwarding. Many banks now retail insurance products in the hope of increasing the number of profitable relationships with existing customers.

4. *Process line extensions* are less innovative than process innovations but often represent distinctive new ways of delivering existing products, either with the intent of offering more convenience and a different experience for existing customers or of attracting new customers who find the traditional approach unappealing. Most commonly, they involve adding a lower-contact distribution channel to an existing high-contact channel, such as creating telephone- or Internet-based banking service. Barnes and Noble, the leading bookstore chain in the United States, added a new Internet subsidiary, BarnesandNoble.com, to help it compete against Amazon.com. Such dual-track approaches are sometimes referred to as "clicks and mortar." Creating self-service options to complement delivery by service employees is another form of process line extension.

5. *Supplementary service innovations* take the form of adding new facilitating or enhancing service elements to an existing core service or of significantly improving an existing supplementary service. Kinko's now offers customers high-speed Internet access round-the-clock, seven days a week at most of its locations in the United States and Canada. Low-tech innovations for an existing service can be as simple as adding parking at a retail site or agreeing to accept credit cards for payment. Multiple improvements may have the effect of creating what customers perceive as an altogether new experience, even though it is built around the same core. Theme restaurants such as the Rainforest Café are examples of enhancing the core with new experiences. The cafés are designed to keep customers entertained with aquariums, live parrots, waterfalls, fiberglass monkeys, talking trees that spout environmentally related information, and regularly timed thunderstorms complete with lightning.[16]

6. *Service improvements* are the most common type of innovation. They involve modest changes in the performance of current products, including improvements to either the core product or to existing supplementary services.

7. *Style changes* represent the simplest type of innovation, typically involving no changes in either processes or performance. However, they are often highly visible, create excitement, and may serve to motivate employees. Examples include repainting retail branches and vehicles in new color schemes, outfitting service employees in new uniforms, introducing a new bank check design, or minor changes in service scripts for employees.

As the preceding typology suggests, service innovation can occur at many different levels; not every type of innovation has an impact on the characteristics of the service product or is

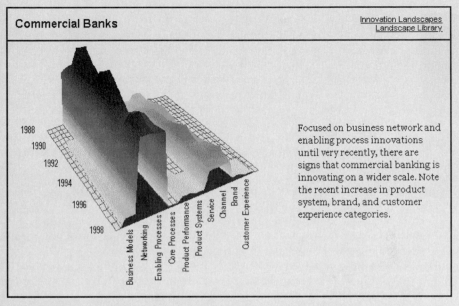

Commercial Banks

Focused on business network and enabling process innovations until very recently, there are signs that commercial banking is innovating on a wider scale. Note the recent increase in product system, brand, and customer experience categories.

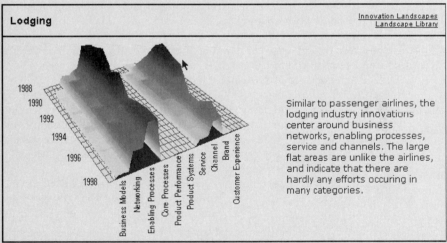

Lodging

Similar to passenger airlines, the lodging industry innovations center around business networks, enabling processes, service and channels. The large flat areas are unlike the airlines, and indicate that there are hardly any efforts occuring in many categories.

FIGURE 8.A   Innovation Landscapes Created by the Doblin Group
Source: www.doblin.com/Landscapes, January 2000.

innovative companies often stand out from the pack. Thus, Doblin notes that the airline industry has been moderately innovative in networking, enabling processes, and customer service, but a few carriers—notably Virgin, Southwest, and BA—have placed relatively more emphasis on innovations in the customer experience.

The innovation landscapes shown in the accompanying figure contrast a 10-year perspective (1988–1998) of innovation in the overall lodging industry with that among commercial banks. As an industry, the lodging industry landscape shows continuing high emphasis on enabling processes, recent growth in networking innovation, declining innovation in channels from a peak around 1990, and a continuing modest innovation in service but nothing in product performance or customer experience. By contrast, the commercial banking industry displays substantial innovation in networking and enabling processes; ongoing innovation in service and channels; and recent modest improvements to product performance, product systems, brand, and customer experience.

Commenting on the special case of Internet startups, Doblin comments:

"Normal" companies invest in product development first and then think about the secondary innovations that would boost its value. Startups like E*Trade and Quicken [both in financial services] are doing something quite different: they start at the fringes of the model, thinking first about business models and customer experiences, then move inwards to plan products, services, and processes.

Source: Doblin Group Web site, www.doblin.com/landscapes, 1999.

experienced by the customer. For a categorization of different types of business innovation, see Research Insights 8.2

Reengineering Service Processes

The design of service processes has implications not only for customers but also for the cost, speed, and productivity with which the desired outcome is achieved. Improving productivity in services often requires speeding up the overall process (or cycle time) because the cost of creating a service is usually related to how long it takes to deliver each step in the process, plus any dead time between each step. Reengineering involves analyzing and redesigning processes to achieve faster and better performance.[18] To reduce overall process time, analysts must identify each step, measure how long it takes, look for opportunities to speed it up (or even eliminate it altogether), and cut out dead time. Running tasks in parallel rather than in sequence is a well-established approach to speeding up processes (a simple household example would be to cook the vegetables for a meal while the main dish was in the oven rather than waiting to cook them until after the main dish was removed). Service companies can use blueprinting to diagram these aspects of service operations in a systematic way.

Examination of processes may also lead to creation of alternative delivery methods that are so radically different as to constitute entirely new service concepts. Options may include eliminating certain supplementary services, addition of new ones, instituting self-service procedures, and rethinking where and when service is delivered.

Figure 8.7 illustrates this principle with simple flowcharts of four alternative ways to deliver meal service, as compared with the full-service restaurant shown earlier in Figure 8.4. Take a look and contrast what happens frontstage in the cases of a fast-food restaurant, a drive-in restaurant, home delivery, and home catering. From the customer's perspective, what has been added to or deleted from the scenario as compared to service at Chez Jean? And in each instance, how do these changes affect backstage activities?

Physical Goods As a Source of New Service Ideas

Goods and services may be competitive substitutes when they offer the same key benefits. For example, if your lawn needs mowing, you could buy a lawn mower and do it yourself, or you could hire a lawn maintenance service to take care of the chore. Such decisions may be shaped by the customer's skills, physical capabilities, and time budget as well as such factors as cost

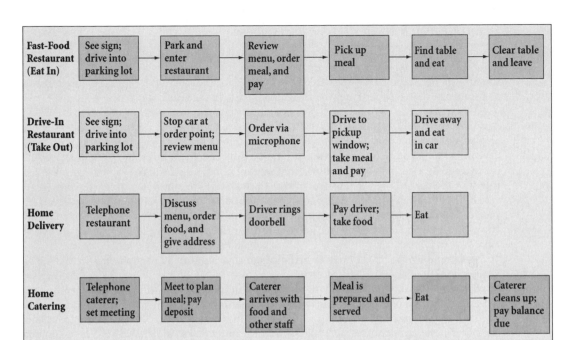

| Fast-Food Restaurant (Eat In) | See sign; drive into parking lot | Park and enter restaurant | Review menu, order meal, and pay | Pick up meal | Find table and eat | Clear table and leave |

| Drive-In Restaurant (Take Out) | See sign; drive into parking lot | Stop car at order point; review menu | Order via microphone | Drive to pickup window; take meal and pay | Drive away and eat in car |

| Home Delivery | Telephone restaurant | Discuss menu, order food, and give address | Driver rings doorbell | Pay driver; take food | Eat |

| Home Catering | Telephone caterer; set meeting | Meet to plan meal; pay deposit | Caterer arrives with food and other staff | Meal is prepared and served | Eat | Caterer cleans up; pay balance due |

FIGURE 8.7   Flowcharts for Meal Delivery Scenarios

comparisons between purchase and use, storage space for purchased products, and anticipated frequency of need. Many services can be built around providing an alternative to owning a physical good and doing the work oneself. Figure 8.8 shows four possible delivery alternatives each for car travel and word processing, respectively. Three of these alternatives present service opportunities. The alternatives are based on choosing between ownership and rental of the necessary physical goods and between performing self-service or hiring another person to perform the necessary tasks.

Any new physical product has the potential to create a need for related possession-processing services (particularly if the product is a high-value, durable item). Industrial equipment may require servicing throughout its life span, beginning with shipping and installation and continuing with maintenance, cleaning, consulting advice, problem solving, upgrading, repair, and ultimate disposal. Historically, such after-sales services have generated important revenue streams for many years after the initial sale for products such as trucks, factory machinery, locomotives, computers, and jet engines.

	Own a Physical Good	Rent the Use of a Physical Good
Perform the Work Oneself	• Drive own car • Type on own word processor	• Rent a car and drive it • Rent a word processor and type on it
Hire Someone to Do the Work	• Hire a chauffeur to drive car • Hire a typist to use word processor	• Hire a taxi or limousine • Send work out to a secretarial service

FIGURE 8.8   Services As Substitutes for Owning and/or Using Goods

Using Research to Design New Services

If a company is designing a new service from scratch, how can it figure out what features and price will create the best value for target customers? It's hard to know without asking these customers—hence, the need for research. Let's examine how the Marriott Corporation used market research experts to help with new service development in the hotel industry.

When Marriott was designing a new chain of hotels for business travelers (which eventually became known as Courtyard by Marriott), it hired marketing research experts to help establish an optimal design concept.[19] Because there are limits to how much service and how many amenities can be offered at any given price, Marriott needed to know how customers would make trade-offs to arrive at the most satisfactory compromise in terms of value for money. The intent of the research was to get respondents to trade off different hotel service features to see which ones they valued most. Marriott's goal was to determine if a niche existed between full-service hotels and inexpensive motels, especially in locations where demand was not high enough to justify a large full-service hotel. If such a niche existed, executives wanted to develop a product to fill that gap.

A sample of 601 consumers from four metropolitan areas participated in the study. Researchers used a sophisticated technique known as *conjoint analysis,* which asks survey respondents to make trade-offs between different groupings of attributes. The objective is to determine which mix of attributes at specific prices offers them the highest degree of utility. The 50 attributes in the Marriott study were divided into the following seven factors (or sets of attributes), each containing a variety of different features based on detailed studies of competing offerings:

1. *External factors*—building shape, landscaping, pool type and location, and hotel size
2. *Room features*—room size and decor, climate control, location and type of bathroom, entertainment systems, and other amenities
3. *Food-related services*—type and location of restaurants, menus, room service, vending machines, guest shop, and in-room kitchen
4. *Lounge facilities*—location, atmosphere, and type of guests
5. *Services*—reservations, registration, checkout, airport limousine, bell desk (baggage service), message center, secretarial services, car rental, laundry, and valet
6. *Leisure facilities*—sauna, whirlpool, exercise room, racquetball and tennis courts, game room, and children's playground
7. *Security*—guards, smoke detectors, and 24-hour video camera

For each of these seven factors, respondents were presented with a series of stimulus cards displaying different levels of performance for each attribute. For instance, the "room features" stimulus card displayed nine attributes, each of which had three to five different levels. Thus, amenities ranged from "small bar of soap" to "large soap, shampoo packet, shoeshine mitt" to "large soap, bath gel, shower cap, sewing kit, shampoo, special soap" and then to the highest level, "large soap, bath gel, shower cap, sewing kit, special soap, toothpaste, etc."

In the second phase of the analysis, respondents were shown a number of alternative hotel profiles, each featuring different levels of performance on the various attributes contained in the seven factors. They were asked to indicate on a five-point scale how likely they would be to stay at a hotel with these features, given a specific room price per night (see Figure 8.9).

The research yielded detailed guidelines for the selection of almost two hundred features and service elements, representing those attributes that provided the highest utility for the customers in the target segments at prices they were willing to pay. An important aspect of the study was that it not only focused on what business travelers wanted but also identified what they liked but weren't prepared to pay for (there's a difference, after all, between wanting some-

ROOM PRICE PER NIGHT IS $44.85

BUILDING SIZE, BAR/LOUNGE
Large (600 rooms) 12-story hotel with:
- Quiet bar/lounge
- Enclosed central corridors and elevators
- All rooms have very large windows

LANDSCAPING/COURT
Building forms a spacious outdoor courtyard
- View from rooms of moderately landscaped courtyard with:
  —many trees and shrubs
  —the swimming pool plus a fountain
  —terraced areas for sunning, sitting, eating

FOOD
Small moderately priced lounge and restaurant for hotel guests/friends
- Limited breakfast with juices, fruit, Danish, cereal, bacon and eggs
- Lunch—soup and sandwiches only
- Evening meal—salad, soup, sandwiches, six hot entrees including steak

HOTEL/MOTEL ROOM QUALITY
Quality of room furnishings, carpet, etc. is similar to:
- Hyatt Regencies
- Westin "Plaza" Hotels

ROOM SIZE & FUNCTION
Room 1 foot longer than typical hotel/motel room
- Space for comfortable sofa-bed and 2 chairs
- Large desk
- Coffee table
- Coffee maker and small refrigerator

SERVICE STANDARDS
Full service including:
- Rapid check in/check out systems
- Reliable message service
- Valet (laundry pick up/deliver)
- Bellman
- Someone (concierge) arranges reservations, tickets, and generally at no cost
- Cleanliness, upkeep, management similar to:
  —Hyatts
  —Marriotts

LEISURE
- Combination indoor-outdoor pool
- Enclosed whirlpool (Jacuzzi)
- Well-equipped playroom/playground for kids

SECURITY
- Night guard on duty 7 P.M. to 7 A.M.
- Fire/water sprinklers throughout hotel

"X" the ONE box below which best describes how likely you are to stay in this hotel/motel at this price:

Would stay there almost all the time	Would stay there on a regular basis	Would stay there now and then	Would rarely stay there	Would not stay there
☐	☐	☐	☐	☐

Note: This full-profile description of a hotel offering is one of the 50 cards developed by a fractional factorial design of the seven facets each at the five levels (developed by the Marriott's development team). Each respondent received five cards following a blocking design.

FIGURE 8.9   Sample Hotel Offering
Note: This full-profile description of a hotel offering is 1 of the 50 cards developed by a fractional factorial design of the seven facets each at the five levels (developed by the Marriott's development team). Each respondent received five cards following a blocking design.
Source: Jerry Wind, Paul E. Green, Douglas Shifflet, and Marsha Scarbrough, "Courtyard by Marriott: Designing a Hotel Facility with Consumer-Based Marketing Models," Interfaces, January–February 1989, 25–47.

thing and being willing to pay for it!). Using these inputs, the design team was able to meet the specified price while retaining the features most desired by the target market.

Marriott was sufficiently encouraged by the findings to build three Courtyard by Marriott prototype hotels. After testing the concept under real-world conditions and making some refinements, the company subsequently developed a large chain whose advertising slogan became "Courtyard by Marriott—the hotel designed by business travelers." The new hotel concept filled a gap in the market with a product that represented the best balance between the price customers were prepared to pay and the physical and service features they most desired. The success of this project has led Marriott to develop additional customer-driven products, including Fairfield Inn and Spring Hill Suites, using the same research methodology.

Achieving Success in New Service Development

Most of the research into new-product success factors has been confined to industrial or business-to-business markets and has emphasized studies of the development process for new physical goods. Storey and Easingwood argue that in developing new services, the product core is of only secondary importance. It is the quality of the total service offering and the marketing support that goes with this, that are key. Underlying success in these areas, they emphasize, is market knowledge: "Without an understanding of the marketplace, knowledge about customers, and knowledge about competitors, it is very unlikely that a new product will be a success." [20]

Tax and Stuart contend that new services should be defined in terms of the extent of change required to the existing service system, relative to the interactions between participants (people), processes, and physical elements (e.g., facilities and equipment).[21] They propose a seven-step planning cycle to evaluate the feasibility and associated risks of integrating a new service development into a firm's existing service system.

Service firms are not immune to the high failure rates plaguing new manufactured products. In recent years, entrepreneurs have created thousands of new so-called dot-com companies to deliver Internet-based services, but a high proportion are expected to fail. To what extent can rigorously conducted and controlled development processes for new services enhance their success rate? A study by Edgett and Parkinson focussed on discriminating between successful and unsuccessful new financial services.[22] They found that the three factors contributing most to success were, in order of importance:

1. *Market synergy*—The new product fit well with the existing image of the firm, provided a superior advantage to competing products in terms of meeting customers' known needs, and received strong support during and after the launch from the firm and its branches; furthermore, the firm had a good understanding of its customers' purchase decision behavior.
2. *Organizational factors*—There were strong interfunctional cooperation and coordination; development personnel were fully aware of why they were involved and of the importance of new products to the company.
3. *Market research factors*—Detailed and scientifically designed market research studies were conducted early in the development process with a clear idea of the type of information to be obtained; a good definition of the product concept was developed before undertaking field surveys

Broadly similar findings were obtained from a survey of 78 marketing managers in financial service firms to determine what distinguished successful from unsuccessful products.[23] In this instance, the key factors underlying success were determined as *synergy* (the fit between the product and the firm in terms of needed expertise and resources being present) and *internal marketing* (the support given to staff prior to launch to help them understand the new product and its underlying systems, plus details about direct competitors). Unfortunately, however, many firms fail to use a systematic approach. For instance, a survey of 43 marketing managers from leading British firms in banking, telecommunications, insurance, transportation and media found that only half had a formal new service development strategy. Idea generation was only undertaken on an ad hoc basis; and idea screening, while more prevalent, failed to support the strategy.[24]

Courtyard by Marriott's success in a very different industry—a people-processing service with many tangible components—supports the notion that a highly structured development process will increase the chances of success for a complex service innovation. However, it's worth noting that there may be limits to the degree of structure that can and should be imposed. Edwardsson, Haglund, and Mattson reviewed new service development in telecommunications, transport, and financial services. They concluded that

> [C]omplex processes like the development of new services cannot be formally planned altogether. Creativity and innovation cannot only rely on planning and control. There must be some elements of improvisation, anarchy, and internal competition in the development of new services. . . . We believe that a contingency approach is needed and that creativity on the one hand and formal planning and control on the other can be balanced, with successful new services as the outcome.[25]

Finally, we should note the potential for redesigning existing services. Berry and Lampo suggest that "[S]ervice firms can be innovative with what exists just as they can be innovative with what does not."[26] Among their proposals for consideration are self-service, delivering the service to the customer's location, streamlining the pre-service activities, bundling services together, and redesigning tangible elements of the service experience.

Conclusion

Innovation is central to effective marketing, but major service innovations are relatively rare. More common is the use of new technologies to deliver existing services in new ways. In mature industries, the core service can become a commodity. The search for competitive advantage often centers on improvements to the value-creating supplementary services that surround this core. In this chapter, we grouped supplementary services into eight categories, circling the core like the petals of a flower.

A key insight from the Flower of Service concept is that different types of core products often share use of similar supplementary elements. As a result, customers may make comparisons across industries, especially when dissatisfied. For instance, "If my stockbroker can give me a clear documentation of my account activity, why can't the department store where I shop?" Or "If my favorite airline can take reservations accurately, why can't the French restaurant up the street?" Questions such as these suggest that managers should be studying businesses outside their own industries in a search for best-in-class performers on specific supplementary services.

Managers should be aware of the importance of selecting the right mix of supplementary service elements—no more and no less than needed—and creating synergy by ensuring that they are all internally consistent. Research can be helpful in defining what elements to include and at what level relative to a given price point. Creating a distinctive branded service experience for customers requires consistency at all stages of the service delivery process. The critical issue is not how many petals the flower has but ensuring that each petal is perfectly formed and adds luster to the core product in the eyes of target customers.

REVIEW QUESTIONS

1. Review the blueprint of the restaurant experience in this chapter (Figure 8.4) and then identify and categorize each of the supplementary services described.
2. Explain the role of supplementary services. Can they be applied to goods as well as services? If so, how might they relate to marketing strategy?
3. Explain the distinction between enhancing and facilitating supplementary services. Give several examples of each, relative to services that you have used recently.
4. How is branding used in services marketing? What is the distinction between a corporate brand such as Marriott and the names of its different inn and hotel chains?
5. What does British Airways gain from using such subbrand names as Club World or Euro Traveller? Why not just use business class and economy class?
6. What is the purpose of techniques such as conjoint analysis in designing new services?

APPLICATION EXERCISES

1. Identify some real-world examples of branding from financial services such as specific types of retail bank accounts or insurance policies and define their characteristics. How meaningful are these brands likely to be to customers?
2. Prepare detailed blueprints for the following services:
   • Repair of a damaged bicycle
   • Applying to college or graduate school
   • Renting a car
   • One or more of the four different food service alternatives presented in Figure 8.9
3. What service failures have you encountered during the past two weeks? Did they involve the core product or supplementary service elements? Identify possible causes and how such failures might be prevented in the future.

ENDNOTES

1. G. Lynn Shostack, "Breaking Free from Product Marketing," *Journal of Marketing* 44 (April 1977): 73–80.
2. Pierre Eiglier and Eric Langeard, "Services as Systems: Marketing Implications," in *Marketing Consumer Services: New Insights,* ed. P. Eiglier, E. Langeard, C. H. Lovelock, J. E. G. Bateson, and R. F. Young (Cambridge, MA: Marketing Science Institute, 1977), 83–103. Note: An earlier version of this article was published in French in *Révue Française de Gestion,* March–April 1977, 72–84.
3. Christian Grönroos, *Service Management and Marketing* (Lexington, MA: Lexington Books, 1990), 74.
4. See G. Lynn Shostack, "Understanding Services through Blueprinting" in *Advances in Services Marketing and Management, 1992,* ed. T. A. Schwartz, D. E. Bowen, and S. W. Brown (Greenwich, CT: JAI Press, 1992), 75–90.
5. G. Lynn Shostack, "Designing Services That Deliver," *Harvard Business Review* (January–February 1984): 133–139.
6. Jane Kingman-Brundage, "The ABCs of Service System Blueprinting," in *Designing a Winning Service Strategy,* ed. M. J. Bitner and L. A. Crosby (Chicago: American Marketing Association, 1989).
7. David Maister, now president of Maister Associates, coined the term *OTSU* while teaching at Harvard Business School in the 1980s.

8. See for example, Eric J. Arnould and Linda L. Price, "River Magic: Extraordinary Experience and the Extended Service Encounter," *Journal of Consumer Research* 20 (June 1993): 24–25; and Nick Johns and Phil Tyas, "Customer Perceptions of Service Operations: Gestalt, Incident or Mythology?" *The Service Industries Journal* 17 (July 1997): 474–488.

9. "How Marriott Makes a Great First Impression," *The Service Edge* 6 (May 1993): 5.

10. David E. Hansen and Peter J. Danaher, "Inconsistent Performance during the Service Encounter: What's a Good Start Worth?" *Journal of Service Research* 1 (February 1999): 227–235.

11. The Flower of Service concept presented in this section was first introduced in Christopher H. Lovelock, "Cultivating the Flower of Service: New Ways of Looking at Core and Supplementary Services," in *Marketing, Operations, and Human Resources: Insights into Services,* ed. P. Eiglier and E. Langeard (Aix-en-Provence, France: IAE, Université d'Aix-Marseille III, 1992), 296–316.

12. Calmetta Coleman, "Fliers Call Electronic Ticketing a Drag," *Wall Street Journal,* January 17, 1997, p. B1.

13. James C. Anderson and James A. Narus, "Capturing the Value of Supplementary Services," *Harvard Business Review* 73 (January–February 1995): 75–83.

14. Robert Ayling, "British Airways: Brand Leadership Results from Being True to Our Long-term Vision," in *Brand Warriors,* ed. F. Gilmore (London: HarperCollinsBusiness, 1997), 42.

15. See James Traub, "Drive-Thru U.," *New Yorker,* October 20 and 27, 1997; and Joshua Macht, "Virtual You," *Inc. Magazine,* January 1998, 84–87.

16. Chad Rubel, "New Menu for Restaurants: Talking Trees and Blackjack," *Marketing News,* July 29, 1996, 1.

17. Nicholas G. Carr, Visualizing Innovation," *Harvard Business Review* (September–October 1999), 16.

18. See, for example, Michael Hammer and James Champy, *Reengineering the Corporation* (New York: HarpcrBusiness, 1993).

19. Jerry Wind, Paul E. Green, Douglas Shifflet, and Marsha Scarbrough, "Courtyard by Marriott: Designing a Hotel Facility with Consumer-Based Marketing Models," *Interfaces,* January–February 1989, 25–47.

20. Chris D. Storey and Christopher J. Easingwood, "The Augmented Service Offering: A Conceptualization and Study of Its Impact on New Service Success," *Journal of Product Innovation Management* 15 (1998): 335–351.

21. Stephen S. Tax and Ian Stuart, "Designing and Implementing New Services: The Challenges of Integrating Service Systems," *Journal of Retailing* 73, no. 1 (1997): 105–134.

22. Scott Edgett and Steven Parkinson, "The Development of New Financial Services: Identifying Determinants of Success and Failure," *International Journal of Service Industry Management* 5, no. 4 (1994): 24–38.

23. Christopher Storey and Christopher Easingwood, "The Impact of the New Product Development Project on the Success of Financial Services," *Service Industries Journal* 13, no. 3 (July 1993): 40–54.

24. David Kelly and Chris Storey, "New Service Development: Initiation Strategies," *International Journal of Service Industry Management,* 11, no. 1, 2000, 45–62.

25. Bo Edvardsson, Lars Haglund, and Jan Mattsson, "Analysis, Planning, Improvisation and Control in the Development of New Services," *International Journal of Service Industry Management* 6, no. 2 (1995): 24–35 (at page 34). See also Bo Edvardsson and Jan Olsson, "Key Concepts for New Service Development," *The Service Industries Journal* 16 (April 1996): 140–164.

26. Leonard L. Berry and Sandra K. Lampo, "Teaching an Old Service New Tricks: The Promise of Service Redesign," *Journal of Service Research,* 2, February 2000, 265.

CHAPTER 9

Pricing Strategies for Services

What is a cynic? A man who knows the price of everything and the value of nothing.

OSCAR WILDE

Have you ever noticed what a wide variety of terms service organizations use to describe the prices they set? Universities talk about *tuition,* professional firms collect *fees,* and banks charge *interest* or add *service charges.* Some bridges, tunnels, and expressways impose *tolls.* Transport operators refer to *fares;* clubs, to *subscriptions;* and brokers, to *commissions.* Landlords seek *rents,* museums establish *admissions charges,* utilities set *tariffs,* insurance companies determine *premiums,* and hotels publicize their *room rates.* These diverse terms are a signal that many services take a different approach to pricing than manufacturing firms.

Pricing—a key component of the 8 Ps—is often seen as a dull task that has more to do with accounting and finance than it does with marketing. But in services, it's a real challenge that requires active participation from marketers who understand the needs and behavior of customers and from operations managers who recognize the importance of matching the demand for service to the capacity available to meet that demand.

In for-profit organizations, a key goal is to relate pricing policies to the firm's need to make a profit. Among the challenges is the fact that defining costs tends to be more difficult in a service business than in a manufacturing operation. Without a good understanding of costs, managers cannot be sure that the prices set are, in fact, sufficient to recover all costs. Low-cost competitors may have an advantage in being able to set prices lower and yet still make a profit. Another challenge is to relate the value that customers perceive in a service to the price they are willing to pay for it. This step requires an understanding of other costs that the customer may be incurring in purchase and use, including outlays of a nonfinancial nature, such as time and effort. Managers also need to recognize that the same service may not be valued in the same way by all customers, offering the potential to set different prices for different market segments.

Because services often combine multiple elements, firms may face a choice between several different ways in which to obtain income from their customers. Pricing strategies can become quite creative, offering customers a choice of how much to pay for different service configurations or even at different times. However, firms need to be careful lest pricing schedules become so complex and hard to compare that they simply confuse customers. A policy of deliberately creating confusing price schedules, including hiding certain costs that only become apparent to customers after usage, is likely to lead to accusations of unethical behavior.

In this chapter, we review the role of pricing in services marketing and explore the following questions:

1. How does the price paid for a service relate to other costs and burdens incurred by customers?
2. What factors shape pricing strategy in the service sector?
3. Under what circumstances do service pricing strategies raise ethical concerns?
4. What are the different types of financial costs incurred by service organizations?
5. What should be the basis for pricing a service?

Paying for Service: The Customer's Perspective

From a customer's standpoint, the monetary price charged by a supplier is not necessarily the only cost involved in purchasing and using a service. Earlier, in chapter 4, we introduced the concept of exchange, recognizing that marketing is concerned with exchanges of value between suppliers and customers. In purchasing a service (or other product), the customer expects to receive a set of benefits whose anticipated value exceeds the perceived costs of obtaining it. These expenditures are composed of both financial and nonfinancial outlays.

Identifying the Outlays Incurred by Customers

Among the financial costs of a service are not just the price paid to the supplier but also the expenses incurred by the customer in searching for, purchasing, and using the service. To give a simple example, the cost of an evening at the movies for a couple with young children can far exceed the price of two tickets because it may include such expenses as hiring a babysitter, travel, parking, food, and beverages. Clearly, segmentation plays a role here: Customers without children and those who live within walking distance of the theater will incur fewer expenses.

For customers, the nonfinancial costs of service reflect the time, effort, and discomfort associated with search, purchase, and use. Customer involvement in production (which is particularly important in people-processing services and in self-service) means that customers incur such burdens as mental and physical effort and exposure to unwanted sensory experiences—such as noise, heat, and smells. Services that are high on experience and credence attributes may also create psychological costs, such as anxiety. As noted in chapter 4, the nonfinancial costs of service can be grouped into four distinct categories:

1. Time expenditures
2. Physical effort (such as fatigue and discomfort)
3. Psychological burdens (such as mental effort and negative feelings)
4. Negative sensory burdens (unpleasant sensations affecting any of the five senses)

Understanding Net Value

When customers purchase a specific service, they are weighing the perceived benefits obtained from the service against the perceived costs they will incur. Consider your own experience. As a customer, you make judgments about the benefits you expect to receive in return for your anticipated investment of money, time, and effort. Although our focus in this chapter is mainly on the monetary aspects of pricing, you have probably noticed that people often pay a premium to save time, minimize unwanted effort, and obtain greater comfort. In other words, they are willing to pay higher prices (financial costs of service) to reduce the nonfinancial outlays.

Recognizing the different trade-offs that customers are willing to make between these various costs, service companies sometimes create several levels of service. For example, airlines and hotel chains often provide multiple classes of service, offering customers the option of paying more in exchange for additional benefits. The essential trade-off for people choosing to stay in a low-price motel such as Motel 6 is that they must renounce the greater physical comfort and many value-enhancing supplementary services to be found in, say, a three-star Holiday Inn that charges a higher price. Similarly, a company purchasing the "silver" level of hardware and software support from Sun Microsystems cannot count on the same speed of response, hours of service, and additional benefits offered to "platinum" customers.

Research findings suggest that customer definitions of value may be highly personal and idiosyncratic. Four broad expressions of value emerged from one study: (1) value is low price, (2) value is whatever I want in a product, (3) value is the quality I get for the price I pay, and (4) value is what I get for what I give.[1] In this book, we base our definition of value on this fourth category and use the term *net value,* which is defined as the sum of all the perceived benefits (gross value) minus the sum of all the perceived service outlays. The greater the positive difference between the two, the greater the net value. Economists use the term *consumer surplus* to define the difference between the price customers pay and the amount they would actually have been willing to pay to obtain the desired benefits (or *utility*) offered by a specific product.

If the perceived outlays are greater than the perceived benefits, then the service in question will possess negative net value. Customers will probably describe the service as having "poor value" and decide not to purchase it. You can think of calculations that customers make in their minds as being similar to weighing materials on an old-fashioned pair of scales, with product benefits in one tray and the costs associated with obtaining those benefits in the other tray (Figure 9.1). When customers evaluate competing services, they are basically comparing the relative net values. Think about your own decision processes.

Increasing Net Value by Reducing Nonfinancial Costs of Service

A marketer can increase the net value of a service either by adding benefits to the core product, enhancing supplementary services, or by reducing the financial costs associated with purchase and use of the product. In many instances, service firms also have the option to improve value by minimizing unwanted nonfinancial outlays for customers. Research may help determine how much such improvements are worth to customers in financial terms. Possible approaches include

- Reducing the amount of time involved in service purchase, delivery, and consumption
- Minimizing unwanted psychological burdens at each stage
- Eliminating unwanted physical effort that customers may incur, notably during the search and delivery processes
- Decreasing unpleasant sensory burdens by creating more attractive visual environments; reducing noise; installing more comfortable furniture and equipment; curtailing offensive smells; and ensuring that foods, drinks, or medicines taste nice

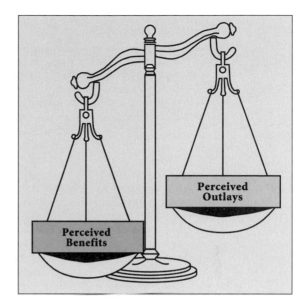

FIGURE 9.1   Net Value = (Benefits − Outlays)

Cutting these types of outlays significantly may even allow service firms to increase the monetary price while still offering what is perceived by customers as "good value."

Perceptions of net value may vary widely between customers and from one situation to another for the same customer. For example, how customers feel about the net value of a service may be sharply different after use than before use, reflecting the experiential qualities of many services. When customers use a service and find that it has cost more and delivered fewer benefits than expected, they are likely to speak angrily of poor value. In extreme cases, when they feel that the supplier misrepresented service features, benefits, expenditures, or outcomes, they may seek restitution or even press legal charges on the grounds of fraud. Good managers seek to provide full disclosure of all outlays associated with search, purchase, use, and postpurchase activities; in particular, they carefully scrutinize advertising claims and sales presentations to ensure that customers are not misled.

The Context of Service Pricing

Establishing pricing strategies for services poses some challenging problems for managers. (In this chapter, our discussion assumes a basic understanding of the financial costs— fixed, semi-variable, and variable—incurred by companies, as well as the notions of contribution and break-even analysis; if you haven't previously been exposed to these concepts or feel you could benefit from a refresher, you'll find it useful to study the Marketing Review.) Chapter 1 described key differences between goods and services marketing (refer back to Table 1.2, p. 10). Let's consider how some of these differences affect pricing strategy.

What Makes Service Pricing Different?

No Ownership of Services. It's usually harder for managers to calculate the financial costs involved in creating an intangible performance for a customer than it is to identify the labor, materials, machine time, storage, and shipping costs associated with producing a physical good whose ownership is transferred to the customer upon purchase. Yet without a good understand-

Understanding Costs, Contribution, and Break-Even Analysis

Fixed costs—sometimes referred to as *overheads*—are those economic costs that a supplier would continue to incur (at least in the short run) even if no services were sold. These costs are likely to include rent, depreciation, utilities, taxes, insurance, salaries and wages for managers and long-term employees, security, and interest payments.

Variable costs refer to the economic costs associated with serving an additional customer, such as making a bank transaction, selling a single seat in a bus or theater, serving an extra hotel guest for the night in a hotel, or doing one more repair job. In many services, such costs are very low; there is, for instance, very little labor or fuel cost involved in transporting an extra bus passenger. In a theater, the cost of seating an extra patron is probably minimal unless the ticket was sold through an independent agency that takes a fixed percentage of the price as its fee. Selling a hotel room for the night has slightly higher variable costs because the room will need to be cleaned and the linens sent to the laundry after a guest leaves. More significant variable costs are associated with such activities as serving food and beverages or installing a new part when undertaking repairs because they include provision of often costly physical products in addition to labor. Just because a firm has sold a service at a price that exceeds its variable cost doesn't mean that the firm is now profitable, for there are still fixed and semivariable costs to be recouped.

Semivariable costs fall in between fixed and variable costs. They represent expenses that rise or fall in stepwise fashion as the volume of business increases or decreases. Examples include adding an extra flight to meet increased demand on a specific air route or hiring a part-time employee to work in a restaurant on busy weekends.

Contribution is the difference between the variable cost of selling an extra unit of service and the money received from the buyer of that service. It goes to cover fixed and semivariable costs before creating profits.

Determining and allocating economic costs can be a challenging task in some service operations because of the difficulty of deciding how to assign fixed costs in a multiservice facility, such as a hospital. For instance, there are certain fixed costs associated with running the emergency unit in a hospital. But beyond that, there are fixed costs for running the hospital of which it is a part. How much of the hospital's fixed costs should be allocated to the casualty department? A hospital manager might use one of several approaches to calculate the EU's share of overheads. These could include (1) the percentage of total floor space that it occupies, (2) the percentage of employee hours or payroll that it accounts for, or (3) the percentage of total patient-contact hours involved. Each method is likely to yield a totally different fixed-cost allocation: One method might show the emergency unit to be very profitable, another might make it seem a break-even operation, and a third suggest that the EU was making a big loss.

Break-even analysis. Managers need to know at what sales volume a service will become profitable. This is called the *break-even point*. The necessary analysis involves dividing the total fixed and semivariable costs by the contribution obtained on each unit of service. For instance, if a 100-room hotel needs to cover fixed and semivariable costs of $2 million a year and the average contribution per room-night is $100, then the hotel will need to sell 20,000 room-nights per year out of a total annual capacity of 36,500. If prices are cut by an average of $20 per room-night (or variable costs rise by $20), then the contribution will drop to $80 and the hotel's break-even volume will rise to 25,000 room nights. The required sales volume needs to be related to *price sensitivity* (will customers be willing to pay this much?), *market size* (is the market large enough to support this level of patronage after taking competition into account?), and *maximum capacity* (the hotel in our example has a capacity of 36,500 room-nights per year, assuming no rooms are taken out of service for maintenance or renovation).

ing of costs, how can managers price at levels sufficient to yield a desired profit margin? Because of the labor and infrastructure needed to create performances, many service organizations have a much higher ratio of fixed costs to variable costs than is found in manufacturing firms.

Variability of Both Inputs and Outputs. It's not always easy to define a unit of service, raising questions as to what should be the basis for service pricing. Making matters even more complicated is the fact that apparently similar units of service may not cost the same to produce, and neither may they be of equal value to customers—especially if the variability extends to greater or lesser quality.

Many Services are Hard to Evaluate. The intangibility of service performances and the invisibility of the necessary backstage facilities and labor makes it harder for customers to see what they are getting for their money than when they purchase a physical good. Consider the homeowners who call a firm of electricians to request repair of a defective circuit. Two days later (if they are lucky) an electrician arrives. Carrying a small bag of tools, he disappears into the closet where the circuit board is located, soon locates the problem, replaces a defective circuit breaker, and presto! Everything works. A mere 20 minutes has elapsed. A few days later, the homeowners are horrified to receive a bill for $65, most of it for labor charges. Just think what the couple could have bought for that amount of money—new clothes, several compact discs, a nice dinner. What they fail to think of are all the fixed costs that the owner of the business needs to recoup: the office, telephone, insurance, vehicles, tools, fuel, and office support staff. The variable costs of the visit are also higher than they appear. To the 20 minutes spent at the house must be added 15 minutes of driving back and forth plus 5 minutes to unload (and later reload) needed tools and supplies from the van on arrival at the customer's house, thus effectively doubling the labor time devoted to this call. And the firm still has to add a margin to make a profit for the owner. But customers are often left feeling that they have been exploited.

Importance of the Time Factor. Another factor that influences service pricing concerns the way in which scheduling and the amount of time required to complete a service performance may affect customer perceptions of value. In many instances, customers are willing to pay more for a service delivered quickly than for one delivered more slowly (compare the cost of courier service against that of regular mail). Sometimes greater speed increases operating costs, too, reflecting the need to pay overtime wages or use more expensive equipment (a supersonic Concorde costs more to fly per passenger mile than a subsonic aircraft such as a Boeing 777 or an Airbus A-320). In other instances, achieving faster turnaround is simply a matter of giving priority to one customer's business over another's (clothes requiring express dry cleaning take the same amount of time to clean; time is saved for the customer by moving them to the front of the queue).

Availability of Both Electronic and Physical Distribution Channels. The use of different channels to deliver the same service—say, electronic rather than face-to-face banking—not only has different cost implications for the bank but also affects the nature of the service experience for the customer (and sometimes the total time required to conduct a transaction). Some people like the convenience of impersonal transactions; others, however, dislike self-service technology and prefer to deal with a real bank clerk. So a service transaction delivered through a particular channel may have value for one person but not for another.

Ethical Concerns

Services often invite performance and pricing abuses, especially credence services (see chapter 3) whose quality and benefits are hard to evaluate even after delivery.[2]

Exploiting Customer Ignorance. When customers don't know what they are getting from the service supplier, aren't present when the work is being performed, and lack the technical skills to know if a good job has been done, they are vulnerable to paying for work that wasn't done, wasn't necessary, or was not well executed. There's an implicit assumption among many customers that a higher-priced professional—say, a lawyer—must be more skilled than one who charges lower fees. Although price can serve as a surrogate for quality, it's sometimes hard to be sure if the extra value is really there.

Complexity and Unfairness. Pricing schedules for services are often quite complex. The quoted price may be only the first of several expenditures that customers will incur. Consider the credit card industry. Traditionally, the banks that issue these cards derived revenues from two sources: a small percentage of the value of each transaction (paid by the merchant) and high interest charges (often 18 to 20 percent) on balances that remained unpaid by the monthly date; the interest can be seen as the cost of renting a loan. However, as credit cards became more popular, costs started to rise for the banks on two fronts. First, more customers defaulted on their balances, leading to a big increase in bad debts. Secondly, as competition increased between banks, marketing expenses rose, and new categories of card were introduced. Gold and platinum cards offer more affluent customers features including free insurance on car rentals and other purchases plus loyalty rewards such as points redeemable for air miles for each dollar spent. On the revenue side, however, competition was leading banks to offer reduced interest rates, and more customers were paying off their monthly balance in full. So the banks sought additional revenue. Adding (or increasing) a variety of charges has generated substantial income; in 1998 credit card charges in the United States (other than interest) amounted to $18.9 billion.[3] Details of charges by one major bank for a platinum card that offers air miles, insurance protection, and other benefits are shown in the Service Perspectives 9.1. Ask yourself: Are these charges easy to understand, and are they fair and reasonable?

Complexity makes it easy (and perhaps more tempting) for firms to engage in unethical behavior. In the United States, the car rental industry has attracted some notoriety for advertising bargain rental prices and then telling customers on arrival that other fees such as collision insurance and personal insurance are compulsory; further, the staff sometimes fail to clarify certain small-print contract terms such as (say) a high-mileage charge that is added once the car exceeds a very low threshold of free miles. The hidden-extras phenomenon for car rentals in some Florida resort towns got so bad at one point that people were joking, "The car is free, the keys are extra!" A not uncommon practice when the car is returned is to charge fees for refueling a partially empty tank that far exceed what the driver would pay at the pump. When customers know that they are vulnerable to potential abuse, they become suspicious of both the firm and its employees. It's harder for customer service personnel to deliver friendly service under such conditions.

Assuming that the firm is honest, the best approach is a proactive one, spelling out all fees and expenses clearly in advance so that there are no surprises. A related approach is to develop a simple fee structure so that customers can more easily understand the financial implications of a specific usage situation.

Establishing Monetary Pricing Objectives

Any decision on pricing strategy must be based on a clear understanding of a company's pricing objectives. There are three basic categories of pricing objectives: revenue oriented, operations oriented, and patronage oriented (see Table 9.1).

SERVICE PERSPECTIVES 9.1

Charges, Fees and Terms for a Platinum Visa Card

Annual Fee	First year, free; thereafter $65
Finance charges on unpaid balances (annual percentage rates)	
Purchases	9.99% (minimum charge $0.50)
Cash advances	19.99% (minimum charge $0.50)
After failure to make two consecutive monthly payments (applies to all balances)	22.99%
Transaction charges for purchase of money order, wire transfer, or use of convenience checks	2% of transaction value (minimum $5, maximum $25)
Cash advance (use card to obtain money from an ATM or bank)	2% of cash advance value (minimum $10)
Other charges	
Late fee	$29
Returned check fee (payment)	$29
Overlimit fee	$25
Payment terms	Due by 10 A.M. on payment due date specified on monthly statement; failure to enclose coupon, pay by check or money order, or use envelope provided may result in up to a five-day delay in posting.

Source: First USA Bank, early 2000 (data taken from card member agreement and reverse of monthly statement).

Revenue-Oriented Objectives

Within certain limits, profit-seeking firms aim to maximize the surplus of income over expenditure. Perhaps top management is eager to reach a particular landmark financial target or seeks a specific percentage return on investment or has a stock market–oriented target of earning a certain amount per outstanding share. Revenue targets may be broken down by division or by type of service or even by geographic unit. Each of these practices requires setting prices based on an accurate knowledge of relevant costs. The more specific the documentation of profits, the greater the need for accurate costing. In some organizations, one service may be priced to yield a profit that is used to cross-subsidize other services. However, such cross-subsidies should be a deliberate choice, not an unplanned outcome of sloppy practice.

Managers responsible for public and nonprofit services, by contrast, are more likely to be concerned with breaking even or keeping the operating deficit within acceptable bounds; however, they cannot afford to ignore the revenue implications of pricing strategy, and neither can they lose track of how their costs are broken down and allocated.

TABLE 9.1 *Alternative Bases for Pricing*

Revenue Oriented

- Profit seeking
  - Make the largest possible surplus.
  - Achieve a specific target level, but do not seek to maximize profits.
- Cover costs
  - Cover fully allocated costs (including institutional overhead).
  - Cover costs of providing one particular service or manufacturing one particular product category (after deducting any specific grants and excluding institutional overhead).
  - Cover incremental costs of selling to one extra customer.

Capacity Oriented

- Vary prices over time to ensure that demand matches available supply at any specific time (thus making the best use of productive capacity).

Demand Oriented

- Maximize demand (when capacity is not a constraint), subject to achieving a certain minimum level of revenues.
- Recognize differing abilities to pay among the various market segments of interest to the organization and price accordingly.
- Offer methods of payment (including credit) that will enhance the likelihood of purchase.

Operations-Oriented Objectives

Capacity-constrained organizations seek to match demand and supply to ensure optimal use of their productive capacity at any given time. Hotels, for instance, seek to fill their rooms because an empty room is an unproductive asset. Similarly, professional firms want to keep their staff members occupied; theaters want to fill empty seats; and repair shops try to keep their facilities, machines, and workers busy. So when demand is low, such organizations may offer special discounts. When demand exceeds capacity, however, these organizations may try to increase profits and ration demand by raising prices.

Like the airlines, bus and rail operators have been able to increase the number of passengers during off-peak periods through strategies such as discounts for families, students, and senior citizens; reduced fares requiring advance purchase; and variations in fare by time of day, day of the week, and season. These sophisticated pricing strategies are a far cry from the rigid policy long followed by the national railroads in some countries of a simply charging a fixed rate per mile (or kilometer).

The problem with matching demand to supply through price is that prices need to be changed constantly, which may be confusing and even irritating to customers. Some firms are reluctant to engage in price discounting for fear that customers will equate this with a decline in quality. And when times are good, firms that raise prices sharply may be accused of price gouging. Occasionally, such greed is punished by discontented customers. For instance, anticipating a huge demand over the weekend of December 31, 1999, to January 2, 2000, from customers wishing to celebrate the arrival of the new millennium, numerous hotels and restaurants around the world raised their prices to astronomical levels. But many customers elected to stay home, and some establishments had so few advance reservations that they were forced to close for the weekend.

Patronage-Oriented Objectives

New services, in particular, often have trouble attracting customers. Yet to create the impression of a successful launch, it's important for the firm's image to be seen to be attracting a good volume of business from the right types of customers. Introductory price discounts may be used to stimulate trial, sometimes in combination with promotional activities such as contests and giveaways.

In some instances maximizing patronage, subject to achieving a certain minimum level of profits, may be more important than profit maximization. Getting a full house in a theater, sports stadium, or race track usually creates excitement that enhances the customer's experience. It also creates an image of success that serves to attract new patrons. Finally, advertisers and sponsors who pay to have their ads or brand logos associated with the event and displayed on internal screens, posters, vehicles, and uniforms or in brochures and handouts are eager to maximize their exposure to as large an audience as possible. They may withdraw their patronage from future events if the size (and sometimes type) of audience fails to match what has been promised.

Foundations of Pricing Strategy

Now let's turn to the issue of how firms should decide on specific financial prices that they charge for their services. The foundations underlying pricing strategy can be described as a tripod, with costs to the provider, competition, and value to the customer as the three legs (Figure 9.2).

The costs that a firm needs to recover usually impose a minimum price—a floor—for a specific service offering, and the perceived value of the offering to customers sets a maximum, or ceiling. The price charged by competitors for similar or substitute services typically determines where, within the floor-to-ceiling range, the price should actually be set. Let's look at each leg of the pricing tripod in more detail.

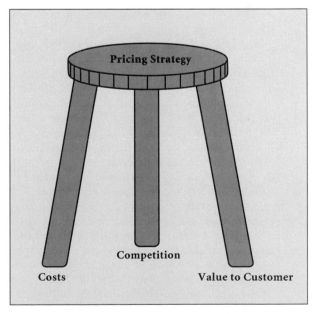

FIGURE 9.2 The Pricing Tripod

Cost-Based Pricing

This approach involves setting prices relative to financial costs. Companies seeking to make a profit must set a price sufficient to recover the full costs—variable, semivariable, and fixed—of producing and marketing a service and then add a sufficient margin to yield the desired level of profit at the predicted sales volume. Service businesses with high fixed costs include those with an expensive physical facility (such as a hotel, a hospital, a college, or a theater) or a fleet of vehicles (such as an airline, a bus line, or a trucking company) or a network (such as a telecommunications company, an Internet provider, a railroad, or a gas pipeline). On the other hand, the variable costs for such businesses of serving one extra customer may be minimal.

Under these conditions, managers may feel that they have tremendous pricing flexibility and be tempted to price very low to make an extra sale. Some firms promote *loss leaders,* which are products sold at less than full cost to attract customers who will then be tempted to buy profitable service offerings from the same organization. Managers need to keep track of the actual costs associated with loss leaders so that the amount of promotional subsidy is fully understood.

However, there can be no profit at the end of the year unless all relevant costs have been recovered. Many service businesses have gone bankrupt by ignoring this fact. Hence, firms that compete on the basis of low prices need to have a very good understanding of their cost structure and of the sales volume needed to break even at particular prices. Unlike public and nonprofit organizations, for-profit firms are rarely able to use government tax subsidies, donations, or income from endowments to cover all or part of their fixed costs.

Regulation and Pricing of Utility Services. Not all service firms are free to charge whatever price they choose. Most local utilities—telephone, water, cable television, electricity, and gas—are regulated by government agencies that have to approve changes in certain prices and terms of service. The pressure for better understanding of costs sometimes comes from industry regulators or politicians responding to complaints about excessively high prices. Traditionally, when a regulated company found its costs were rising and squeezing its profit margins, it would request a rate increase. Unless such a request were refused or the amount sharply reduced by the regulator, the company had little incentive to seek cost reductions. However, change came to the telecommunications business with the advent of deregulation in long-distance telephone service, itself stimulated by rapid changes in technology. With the entry of new competitors, customers could now choose between two or more long-distance carriers who used investments in new technology to bring down their costs. The result was intensive price competition on long-distance services (although not on local service, which in most cases remained a monopoly).

If a firm lacks the information needed to calculate the costs associated with serving different types of user, managers may just determine the total costs incurred during a certain period, divide them by actual unit sales, calculate an average cost per unit of service (e.g., kilowatt-hours or monthly phone-line rentals), and add a certain percentage for profit. However, as more sophisticated costing analysis came to be used in the telecommunications industry, it became clear that the prices charged to business users had been subsidizing household subscribers who were, in fact, much more expensive to serve than the phone companies had realized. The net result was a shift in regulatory policy to allow relatively larger price increases for households than for business users, who have even seen some cost reductions.

A parallel change is taking place in electricity service in some locations. In search of greater operating efficiencies, regulators have allowed many electrical utilities to split up their activities—notably generation of power, transmission, and local delivery—into separate companies, with customers being given the option of buying power from competing electricity generators. Subsequently, mergers have taken place within each of these three separate categories to achieve economies of scale. Nevertheless, many aspects of electricity pricing are still regulated by government agencies. Armed with better information on their costs, some utilities can now provide customers with more details of how the total price is computed. Figure 9.3 shows how one New England electrical distribution utility breaks down its charges on a homeowner's monthly bill (the categories have been reordered to illustrate the sequential process of supplying electricity). When prices change, consumers will be know in which category the change occurred.

Activity-Based Costing. In recent years, a growing number of organizations have reduced their dependence on traditional cost-accounting systems and developed activity-based cost management systems (ABC), which link resource expenses to the variety and complexity of products produced—not just to the physical volume. (An *activity* is a set of tasks that combine to compose the processes needed to create and deliver the service.) Each box displayed in a flow-chart or service blueprint (see chapters 4 and 8) constitutes an activity with which direct costs can be associated. There are also indirect administrative and support costs involved in managing any business. Managers need to move beyond seeing costs from just an accounting perspective to viewing them, more relevantly, as an integral part of the company's efforts to create value for its customers.[4]

Carù and Cugini clarify the limitations of traditional cost measurement systems to correlate the costs incurred with the value generated by any given activity:

Costs have nothing to do with value, which is established by the market and, in the final analysis, by the degree of customer acceptance. The customer is not interested a priori in the cost of a product . . . but in its value and price.

Management control which limits itself to cost monitoring without interesting itself in value is completely one-sided. . . . The problem of businesses is not so much that of cost control as it is the separation of value activities from other activities. The market only pays

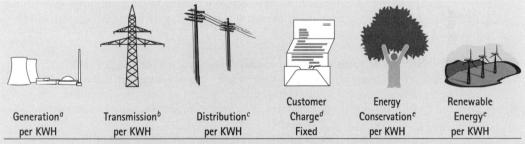

Generation[a] per KWH	Transmission[b] per KWH	Distribution[c] per KWH	Customer Charge[d] Fixed	Energy Conservation[e] per KWH	Renewable Energy[e] per KWH

Key: [a]Variable charge per kilowatt-hour (KWH) set by competitive bid—different power generators compete for contracts.

[b]Variable charge/KWH of moving electricity along high-voltage lines (possibly from other states or Canada); regulated by Federal Energy Regulatory Commission.

[c]Variable charge for delivery over local wires from substation; regulated by Massachusetts Department of Energy and Telecommunications (DTE).

[d]Fixed charge for providing service (e.g., meter reading, billing) regulated by DTE.

[e]Variable charges for energy efficiency/renewable energy activities mandated by legislation.

Note: Variable charges are segmented by purpose of use, with electricity used for water heating being measured on a separate meter and charged at a lower rate per KWH. Not shown above is a variable transition charge designed to allow the distribution company to continue to recover past investments in generating plants and power contracts.

FIGURE 9.3   Selected Components of a Massachusetts Homeowner's Electrical Bill

for the former. Businesses which carry out unnecessary activities are destined to find themselves being overtaken by competitors which have already eliminated these.[5]

Initially, the ABC approach was promoted as a more accurate way of calculating the costs of different manufactured products, especially when a single factory was responsible for multiple products. However, the type of analysis required can also yield more accurate cost information about service business activities and processes—and about the costs of creating specific types of services or serving specific customers. The net result is a management tool that can help companies to pinpoint the profitability of different market segments (or even individual customers), different service offerings, and different channels.[6]

It's essential to distinguish between those activities that are mandatory for operation within a particular industry or type of business and those that are discretionary. The traditional approach to cost control often results in a reduction of the value generated for customers because the activity that is being pruned back is, in fact, mandatory for providing a certain level and quality of service. For instance, many firms have created marketing problems for themselves by trying to save money by firing large numbers of customer service employees. However, this strategy has boomeranged in those situations where it results in a rapid decline in service that spurs discontented customers to take their business elsewhere. This is why service marketers need to work closely with colleagues in other functions to ensure that productivity initiatives do not compromise service quality. (For more details, see Management Memo 9.1).

Competition-Based Pricing

Firms marketing services that are relatively undifferentiated from competing offerings need to keep an eye on what competitors are charging and should to try to price accordingly. If customers see little or no difference between the services offered in the marketplace, they may just choose the cheapest. In such a situation, the firm with the lowest cost per unit of service enjoys an enviable marketing advantage. It has the option of either competing on price at levels that higher-cost competitors cannot afford to match or of charging the going market rate and earning larger profits than competing firms.

Price Leadership. In some industries, one firm may act as the price leader, with others taking their cue from this company. You can sometimes see this phenomenon at the local level when several gas stations compete within a short distance of one another or on opposite corners of a crossroads. As soon as one station raises or lowers its prices, each of the others will follow promptly.

During boom times in highly competitive industries such as airlines, hotels, and rental cars, other firms are often happy to go along with the leader—particularly if this supplier does not have the lowest costs—because prices are likely to be set at a level that allows good profits. During a downturn in the economy, however, such industries quickly find themselves with surplus productive capacity—unsold seats, empty rooms, or unrented cars. In an effort to attract more customers, one firm—often not the original leader—may cut prices. Because pricing is the easiest and fastest marketing variable to change, a price war may result overnight as competitors rush to match the other firm's bargain prices.

Price Bids and Negotiations. Industrial buyers sometimes request bids from competing service suppliers. Outsourcing contracts to provide food service, facilities maintenance, or freight transportation often use this approach to pricing. Under these conditions, each bidder not only

MANAGEMENT MEMO 9.1

Activity-Based Costing

Traditional cost systems provide useful data for pricing purposes when a single operation creates one homogeneous product for customers who behave in broadly similar ways. However, when service businesses experience considerable variability in both inputs and outputs, it's unrealistic to assign the same proportion of indirect and support costs to each unit of output. Customers, too, often vary in the demands they place on the firm.

Costs are not intrinsically fixed or variable, argue Cooper and Kaplan:

> Different products, brands, customers, and distribution channels make tremendously different demands on a company's resources. . . . ABC analysis enables managers to slice into the business many different ways—by product or group of similar products, by individual customer or client group, or by distribution channel—and gives them a close up view of whatever slice they are considering. ABC analysis also illuminates exactly what activities are associated with that part of the business and how those activities are linked to the generation of revenues and the consumption of resources.

> Instead of focusing on expense categories—such as labor or fuel—ABC analysis begins with identification of the different activities being performed and then determines the cost of each activity as it relates to each expense category. When managers segregate activities in this way, a cost hierarchy emerges, reflecting the level at which the cost is incurred. For instance, *unit-level activities* need to be performed for every unit of service produced (e.g., rotating the tires on a customer's car at a service garage), whereas *batch-level activities* are those that have to be performed for each batch or setup of work performed (e.g., periodically maintaining the equipment needed for tire rotation).

Other activities provide the *overall capability* that enables the company to produce a given type of service (e.g., conducting studies to establish and measure performance standards for tire rotation) or to support customers (e.g., performing account management) and product lines (e.g., creating and placing advertising) or to sustain facilities (e.g., building maintenance and insurance). Expenses are attached to each activity based on estimates by employees of how they divide their time between different tasks and what percentage of other resources (e.g., electricity consumption) is being consumed by each activity.

In short, the ABC hierarchy provides a structured way of thinking about the relationship between activities and the resources that they consume. A key question is whether each enumerated activity actually adds customer value to the services that the firm is selling.

Determining customer profitability is a key issue for many businesses. Traditional cost analysis tends to result in loading the same overhead costs on all customers, leading to the assumption that larger purchasers are more profitable. By contrast, ABC analysis can pinpoint differences in the costs of serving different customers, not only by identifying the types of activity associated with each customer but also by determining the amount of each activity demanded. For instance, a customer who buys in large volumes but who is extremely demanding in terms of the amount and level of support required may, in fact, prove to be less profitable than a small customer who requires little support.

Sources: Robin Cooper and Robert S. Kaplan, "Profit Priorities from Activity-Based Costing," *Harvard Business Review* (May–June, 1991); and Robert S. Kaplan, "Introduction to Activity-Based Costing," Note #9-197-076 (Boston: Harvard Business School Publishing, 1997).

needs to review costs and think about what the buyer might be willing to pay but must also try to estimate the level of bid that competitors are likely to submit. The more tightly specified the buyer's requirements, the less opportunity there is to differentiate one bidder's offer from another. The terms of the bid will specify whether the bids are to be sealed or not and whether the buyer is obligated to take the lowest bid (or for that matter, any bid). If the buyer feels that the bids are too high, it may change the specifications and invite a new round of bidding.

An alternative to bidding is negotiation, in which instance the firm may request proposals from several suppliers and then negotiate with a short list of those firms that seem the most qualified and have offered the most relevant or innovative approaches. Large consulting contracts, accounting audits, and engineering studies are often initiated through requests for proposals. In this type of situation, the buyer may conduct several rounds of negotiations, giving participating suppliers at least some information about competing offers as an incentive to lower their prices, conduct the work faster, or offer more features.

Value-Based Pricing

No customer will pay more for a service than he or she thinks it's worth. So marketers need to undertake ongoing research to determine how customers perceive service value. In some instances, value may vary according to the situation. For instance, people may be willing to pay more for repair services under emergency conditions (such as a car breakdown on an icy winter night).

Price is sometimes used as a means to communicate the quality and value of a service when customers find it hard to evaluate its capabilities in advance. In the absence of tangible clues, customers may associate higher prices with higher levels of performance on important service attributes.[7] Who is the better lawyer: the one who charges $60 an hour or the one who bills $200 per hour? If nothing else, a high fee suggests past success.

Service-pricing strategies are often unsuccessful because they lack any clear association between price and value.[8] Berry and Yadav propose three distinct but related strategies for capturing and communicating the value of a service: uncertainty reduction, relationship enhancement, and low-cost leadership.[9]

Pricing Strategies to Reduce Uncertainty. If customers are unsure about how much value they will receive from a particular service, they may remain with a supplier they already know or not purchase at all. There are three possible ways, singly or in combination, to reduce this uncertainty.

Service guarantees entitle customers to a refund if they are not completely satisfied (see the discussion of Hampton Inn's 100% Satisfaction Guarantee in chapter 6). When well designed and executed, service guarantees remove much of the advance risk associated with buying an intangible service—especially for services high in experience qualities, where customers can easily determine after the fact that service was, in fact, unsatisfactory.

Benefit-driven pricing involves pricing that aspect of the service that directly benefits customers (requiring marketers to research what aspects of the service the customers do and do not value.) For instance, prices for online information services are often based on log-on time, but what customers really value is the information that is browsed and retrieved. Poorly designed Web sites often waste customers' time because they are difficult to navigate and make it hard for users to find what they are looking for. The result is that pricing and value creation are out of sync. When ESA-IRS, a European online provider, implemented a new pricing strategy termed "pricing for information" and based on the information actually extracted, the company found that customers were more willing to use a time-consuming feature called ZOOM that allowed them to search several complex databases simultaneously with increased precision. They started staying online longer, and the use of ZOOM tripled as customers began to conduct more detailed searches. From then on, the company changed its marketing focus to selling information rather than selling time.

Flat-rate pricing involves quoting a fixed price in advance of service delivery to avoid any surprises. In essence, the risk is transferred from the customer to the supplier in the event that the service takes longer to deliver or involves more costs than anticipated. Flat-rate pricing can be effective in industries where service prices are unpredictable and suppliers are poor at controlling their costs and the speed at which they work. They are also effective in situations where competitors make low estimates to win business but subsequently claim that they were only giving an estimate—not making a firm pricing commitment.

Relationship Pricing. How does pricing strategy relate to developing and maintaining long-term customer relationships? Discounting to win new business is not the best approach if a firm is seeking to attract customers who will remain loyal—research indicates that those who are attracted by cut-price offers can easily be enticed away by another offer from a competitor.[10] More creative strategies focus on giving customers both price and nonprice incentives to consolidate their business with a single supplier.

A strategy of *discounting* prices for large purchases can often be profitable for both parties because the customer benefits from lower prices while the supplier may enjoy lower variable costs resulting from economies of scale. An alternative to volume discounting on a single service is for a firm to offer its customers discounts when two or more services are purchased together. The greater the number of different services a customer purchases from a single supplier, the closer the relationship is likely to be: On the one hand, both parties get to know each other better, and on the other hand, it's more inconvenient for the customer to shift its business.

Low-Cost Leadership. Low-priced services reduce the monetary burden for customers and appeal to customers who are on a tight financial budget. They may also lead purchasers to buy in larger volumes. One challenge when pricing low is to convince customers that they should not equate price with quality: They must feel they are getting good value. A second challenge is to ensure that economic costs are kept low enough to enable the firm to make a profit. Some service businesses have built their entire strategy around being the low-cost leader. A classic U.S. example of a focused pricing strategy in the airline business is that of Southwest Airlines, whose low fares often compete with the price of bus, train, or car travel. Southwest's low-cost operations strategy has been studied by airlines all over the world and now has many imitators, including WestJet in Canada.

Pricing and Demand

In most for-profit services, there is a relationship between price levels and demand levels, with demand tending to fall as price rises. This phenomenon has two important implications for service managers. First, assuming a good understanding of relevant costs, there is the need to determine how sensitive demand is to price and what net revenues will be generated at different price levels. Second, in a capacity-constrained business that experiences wide swings in demand over time, managers need to know how price can be used to manage the level demand relative to available capacity.

Price Elasticity

The concept of elasticity describes how sensitive demand is to changes in price. When price elasticity is at *unity,* sales of a service rise (or fall) by the same percentage that price falls (or rises). When a small change in price has a big impact on sales, demand for that product is said to be *price elastic.* But when a change in price has little effect on sales, demand is described as *price inelastic.* The concept is illustrated in the simple chart presented in Figure 9.4, which shows schedules for highly elastic demand (a small change in price results in a big change in the amount demanded) and highly inelastic demand (even big changes in price have little impact on the amount demanded).

Demand can often be segmented according to customers' sensitivity to price or service features. Most theaters and concert halls do not have a single, fixed admission price for performances. Instead, the price varies according to (1) the location of the seats, (2) the time of the performance, (3) the projected cost of staging the performance, and (4) the anticipated appeal of the performance.

To establish prices for different blocks of seats and to decide how many seats to offer within each price block (known as *scaling the house*), theater managers need to estimate the demand within each price category. Poor judgment may result in large numbers of empty seats in some price categories and immediate sellouts (and disappointed customers) in other categories. Management also needs to know theatergoers' preferences for scheduling of performances—matinees versus evenings, weekends versus weekdays, and possibly even seasonal variations. If afternoons are known to be a less popular time than evenings, then matinee performances should be priced lower in each seating category.

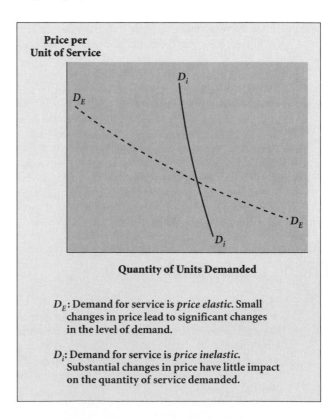

D_E: Demand for service is *price elastic.* Small changes in price lead to significant changes in the level of demand.

D_i: Demand for service is *price inelastic.* Substantial changes in price have little impact on the quantity of service demanded.

FIGURE 9.4   Illustrations of Price Elasticity

When establishing prices in theaters or other settings, managers must be clear about their goals. Do they want to manage demand to maximize attendance? Or do they seek profit maximization? Alternatively, can the objective be expressed as a combination of the two, for example, maximizing revenues, subject to a minimum attendance goal per performance of 70 percent of all seats sold? Perhaps the organization's mission statement also speaks to the goal of attracting less affluent segments, such as students and senior citizens, in which case management may wish to set aside some seats at a discount for people in those target segments. In a theater context, this social goal is sometimes addressed by offering unsold tickets at deeply discounted prices on the day of performance. A good reason for seeking to achieve frequent sellouts is that it encourages people to book and pay in advance (thus committing themselves) as opposed to waiting until the last minute—at which point they might change their minds.

Yield Management

Many service businesses are now focusing on yield management strategies—that is, maximizing the revenue yield that can be derived from available capacity at any given time (for an in-depth treatment of this topic, see the reading by Sheryl Kimes and Richard Chase, "The Strategic Levers of Yield Management," on pp. 325 to 335). Airlines, hotels, and car rental firms, in particular, have become adept at varying their prices in response to the price sensitivity of different market segments at different times of the day, week, or season. The challenge is to capture sufficient customers to fill the organization's perishable capacity without creating consumer surplus for customers who would have been willing to pay more.

The market is often very dynamic. For instance, the demand for both business and pleasure travel reflects current or anticipated economic conditions. Although business travelers do not always think of themselves as particularly price sensitive, many companies employ travel specialists who shop for the best travel bargains they can find within the constraints of an employee's travel needs. Tourists and other pleasure travelers, by contrast, are often very price sensitive; a special promotion, involving discounted fares and room rates, may even encourage people to undertake a trip that they would not otherwise have made.

How does a firm know what level of demand to expect at different prices in a highly dynamic market environment where the factors influencing demand are constantly changing? Advances in software and computing power have made it possible for firms to use very sophisticated mathematical models for use in yield management analysis. In the case of an airline, for example, these models integrate massive historical databases on past passenger travel with real-time information on current bookings to help analysts pinpoint how many passengers would want to travel between two cities at a particular fare on a flight leaving at a specified time and date.

Effective use of yield management models can improve a company's profitability significantly. Some firms are recognized as more sophisticated than others in their modeling and analytical capabilities. Not surprisingly, the exact nature of the models and their component variables is a closely guarded commercial secret. Service Perspectives 9.2 describes how American Airlines, one of the industry leaders in this somewhat esoteric field, uses yield management analysis to set fares for a specific flight.

Inherent in the American Airlines example is the concept of *price customization*—that is, charging different customers different prices for what is, in effect, the same product. As noted by Simon and Dolan,

> The basic idea of price customization is simple: Have people pay prices based on the value they put on the product. Obviously you can't just hang out a sign saying "Pay me what it's worth to you" or "It's $80 if you value it that much but only $40 if you don't." You have to find a way to segment customers by their valuations. In a sense, you have to "build a fence"

Pricing Seats on Flight AA 2015

Yield management programs require sophisticated software and powerful computers to crunch all the data that are fed into them. Managers, of course, are interested in the output that emerges from the computers rather than in the underlying science. Each flight on a given date is tracked separately. Let's look at American Airlines 2015, a popular flight from Chicago to Phoenix, Arizona, which departs daily at 5:30 P.M. on the 1,370-mile (2,200-km) journey.

The 125 seats in coach (economy class) are divided into seven fare categories, referred to by yield management specialists as "buckets." There is an enormous variation in ticket prices among these seats: Round-trip fares range from $238 for a bargain excursion ticket (with various restrictions and a cancellation penalty attached) all the way up to an unrestricted fare of $1,404. Seats are also available at an even higher price in the small first-class section. Scott McCartney tells how ongoing analysis by the computer program changes the allocation of seats between each of the seven buckets in economy class:

> In the weeks before each Chicago-Phoenix flight, American's yield management computers constantly adjust the number of seats in each bucket, taking into account tickets sold, historical ridership patterns, and connecting passengers likely to use the route as one leg of a longer trip.
>
> If advance bookings are slim, American adds seats to low-fare buckets. If business customers buy unrestricted fares earlier than expected, the yield management computer takes seats out of the discount buckets and preserves them for last-minute bookings that the database predicts will still show up.
>
> With 69 of 125 coach seats already sold four weeks before one recent departure of Flight 2015, American's computer began to limit the number of seats in lower-priced buckets. A week later, it totally shut off sales for the bottom three buckets, priced $300 or less. To a Chicago customer looking for a cheap seat, the flight was "sold out".
>
> One day before departure, with 130 passengers booked for the 125-seat flight, American still offered five seats at full fare because its computer database indicated 10 passengers were likely not to show up or take other flights. Flight 2015 departed full and no one was bumped.

Although AA 2015 for that date is now history, it has not been forgotten. The booking experience for this flight was saved in the memory of the yield management program to help the airline do an even better job of forecasting in the future.

Source: Scott McCartney, "Ticket Shock: Business Fares Increase Even as Leisure Travel Keeps Getting Cheaper," *Wall Street Journal,* November 3, 1997, pp. A1, A10. Printed with permission through Copyright Clearance Center.

---

between high-value customers and low-value customers so the "high" buyers can't take advantage of the low price.[11]

Successful yield management strategies require an understanding of the shape of the demand curve and an ability to relate the size and price-level of the different buckets to different value segments (see Figure 9.5).

Fencing Mechanisms. *Rate fences* are techniques for separating different value segments so that customers for whom the service offers high value are unable to take advantage of lower-price buckets. Fences can be either physical or nonphysical and represent qualifications of the individual, the service characteristics, or the timing of booking that must be met to receive a certain level of discount from the full price.[12] Physical fences include observable characteristics of

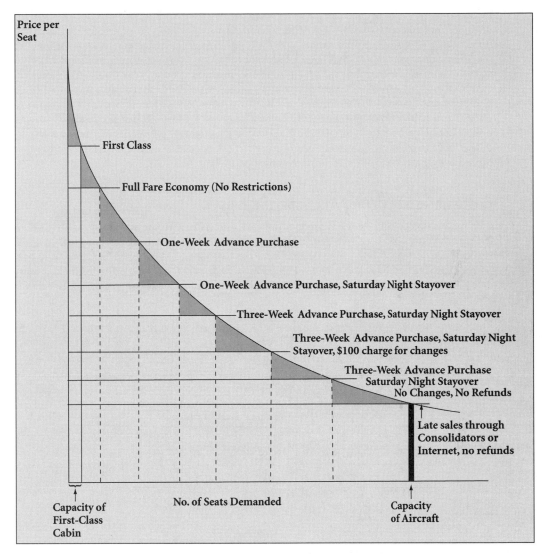

FIGURE 9.5   Relating Price Buckets and Fences to the Shape of the Demand Curve for a Specific Flight
Note: Shaded areas denote amount of consumer surplus (goal of segmented pricing is to minimize this).

the customer, such as child versus adult, and service characteristics such as class of travel, type of hotel room, or inclusion of certain amenities with a higher price (free breakfast at a hotel or a free golf cart at a golf course). Nonphysical fences include penalties for canceling or changing an inexpensive reservation, requirements for advance purchase, group membership or affiliation, and restrictions on time of use (an early-bird special in a restaurant available before 6:00 P.M. or a Saturday night stayover for an airline or hotel booking).

Implications for Ethical Behavior and Corporate Reputation.
Yield management shouldn't necessarily mean blind pursuit of short-term yield maximization. Overdependence on the output of computer models can easily lead to pricing strategies that are full of rules and

regulations, cancellation penalties, and a cynical strategy of overbooking without thought for disappointed customers who believed they had a firm reservation. To maintain goodwill and build relationships, a company should take the long-term perspective. So managers responsible for pricing decisions should build in strategies for retaining valued customer relationships, even to the extent of not charging the maximum feasible amount on a given transaction; after all, customer perceptions of price gouging do not build trust. There should also be thoughtfully planned contingencies for victims of overbooking, with service recovery efforts designed to restore goodwill following disappointment. Firms should guard against the risk that pricing policies may become too complex. Jokes abound about travel agents having nervous breakdowns because they get a different quote every time they call the airline for a fare and because there are so many exclusions, conditions, and special offers.

Customer-Led Pricing: Auctions and Bids

One method of pricing that is gaining popularity, especially with the advent of the Internet, is letting customers bid the price that they are prepared to pay. Priceline.com, launched in 1998, was the first service to sell airline tickets by letting customers bid the price that they were prepared to pay. It's estimated that half a million empty seats fly the skies of North America every day. Priceline.com offers the airlines a chance to dispose of these at bargain prices; but unlike

FIGURE 9.6   Priceline.com's Home Page, March 2000

consolidators (also known as "bucket shops"), it's left to the customer to make an offer. Would-be travelers visit Priceline.com's Web site (see Figure 9.6), where they insert their travel dates, destinations, and the price they are willing to pay. Priceline.com will respond within the hour if it can match the offer to an airline willing to sell seats at the offered price on that route and date (if Priceline.com can negotiate a lower price than offered, the company gets to keep the difference). However, customers must be prepared to take any flight on the given date and accept any routing, including changes at intermediate airports. The company calls this approach "buyer-driven commerce" and has since extended it to other services, including hotels, rental cars, and mortgages as well as new cars and, in some cities, groceries.[13]

Auctions have long been used as a way to sell physical goods, ranging from houses to military surplus materials. They have also gained popularity among nonprofit organizations as a fund-raising device, with many of the donated items consisting of services ranging from meals at fine restaurants to airline tickets, resort packages, nights at the opera, and even something as mundane (but useful) as housecleaning. Meanwhile, corporate purchasers increasingly use the speed and reach of the Internet to identify sellers of such time-sensitive service products as energy, telecommunications capacity, and advertising space and then bid competitively for the amount and type that they need.[14]

Putting Service Pricing Strategy into Practice

Although the main decision in pricing is usually seen as how much to charge, there are other decisions to be made, too. Table 9.2 summarizes the questions that service marketers need to ask themselves as they prepare to create and implement a well-thought-out pricing strategy. Let's look at each in turn.

How Much to Charge?

Realistic decisions on pricing are critical for financial solvency. The pricing tripod model, discussed earlier (Figure 9.2), provides a useful departure point. Let's revisit the three elements involved. The task begins with determining the relevant economic costs and then deciding whether, in a specific situation, the organization should try to cover just variable costs or recover a share of the indirect costs plus a margin for profit. Determining the costs to be recovered at different sales volumes— and, as appropriate, the margin—sets the relevant floor price.

The second task is to assess market sensitivity to different prices in terms of both the overall value of the service to prospective customers as well as their ability to pay. This step sets a ceiling price for any given market segment. It's vital to make an accurate prediction of what sales volume might be obtained at different price levels.

Competitive prices provide a third input. The greater the number of similar alternatives, the greater the pressure on the marketing manager to keep prices at or below those of the competition. The situation is particularly challenging when some competitors choose to compete on the basis of low price and have coupled this with an operating strategy designed to achieve low costs.

The wider the gap between the floor and ceiling prices, the more room there is for maneuver. If a ceiling price (the maximum that customers are willing to pay) is below the floor price (the lowest price the firm can afford to charge), the manager has two choices. One alternative is to recognize that the service is noncompetitive, in which case it should be discontinued. The other is to modify it in ways that differentiate it from the competition's offering and add value for prospective customers so that it now becomes competitive at a higher price. Public and non-profit organizations have a third option, which is to seek third-party funding—such as government subsidies or private donations—to cover some of the costs, thus allowing the service to be

TABLE 9.2	*Some Pricing Issues*

1. How much should be charged for this service?
   a. What costs are the organization attempting to recover? Is the organization trying to achieve a specific profit margin or return on investment by selling this service?
   b. How sensitive are customers to different prices?
   c. What prices are charged by competitors?
   d. What discount(s) should be offered from basic prices?
   e. Are psychological pricing points (e.g., $4.95 versus $5.00) customarily used?
2. What should be the basis of pricing?
   a. Execution of a specific task
   b. Admission to a service facility
   c. Units of time (hour, week, month, year)
   d. Percentage commission on the value of the transaction
   e. Physical resources consumed
   f. Geographic distance covered
   g. Weight or size of object serviced
   h. Should each service element be billed independently?
   i. Should a single price be charged for a bundled package?
3. Who should collect payment?
   a. The organization that provides the service
   b. A specialist intermediary (travel or ticket agent, bank, retailer, etc.)
   c. How should the intermediary be compensated for this work—flat fee or percentage commission?
4. Where should payment be made?
   a. The location at which the service is delivered
   b. A convenient retail outlet or financial intermediary (e.g., bank)
   c. The purchaser's home (by mail or phone)
5. When should payment be made?
   a. Before or after delivery of the service
   b. At which times of day
   c. On which days of the week
6. How should payment be made?
   a. Cash (exact change or not?)
   b. Token (where can these be purchased?)
   c. Stored value card
   d. Check (how to verify?)
   e. Electronic funds transfer
   f. Charge card (credit or debit)
   g. Credit account with service provider
   h. Vouchers
   i. Third-party payment (e.g., insurance company or government agency)?
7. How should prices be communicated to the target market?
   a. Through what communication medium? (advertising, signage, electronic display, sales people, customer service personnel)
   b. What message content (how much emphasis should be placed on price?)

sold at a lower price. This latter approach is commonly used to make services such as health, education, the arts, and urban transport more easily affordable to a broad cross-section of the population.

Finally, a specific figure must be set for the price that customers will be asked to pay. Should the firm price in round numbers or try to create the impression that prices are slightly lower than they really are? If competitors promote prices such as $5.95 and $9.95, a strategy of charging $6.00 or $10.00 may convey an image of prices somewhat higher than is really the case. On the other hand, rounded prices offer convenience and simplicity—benefits that may be appreciated by both consumers and salespeople because they help to speed up cash transactions. An ethical issue concerns the practice of promoting a price that excludes tax, service charges, and other extras. This is misleading if customers expect the quoted price to be inclusive.

What Should Be the Basis for Pricing?

Deciding the basis for pricing requires defining the unit of service consumption. Should it be based on completing a specific service task—such as repairing a piece of equipment, cleaning a jacket, or cutting a customer's hair? Should it be based on admission to a service performance—such as an educational program or a film, concert, or sports event? Should it be time based—for instance, using an hour of a lawyer's time, occupying a hotel room for a night, hiring a car for a week, subscribing to a satellite television service for a month, or paying for a semester's tuition at a university? Should it be tied to value, as when an insurance company scales its premiums to reflect the amount of coverage provided or a realtor takes a percentage commission of the selling price of a house?

Some service prices are tied to consumption of physical resources, such as food, drinks, water, or natural gas. For example, rather than charging customers an hourly rate for occupying a table and chairs, restaurants put a sizable markup on the food and drink items consumed. (Recognizing the fixed cost of table service—such as a clean tablecloth for each party—restaurants in some countries impose a fixed cover charge that is added to the cost of the meal; others may establish a minimum meal charge per person.) Transport firms have traditionally charged by distance, with freight companies using a combination of weight or cubic volume and distance to set their rates. Such a policy has the virtue of consistency and reflects calculation of an average cost per mile (or kilometer). However, it ignores relative market strength on different routes.

Simplicity may suggest a flat rate, as with postal charges for domestic letters below a certain weight, or a zone rate for packages that groups geographic distances into broad clusters. Long-distance phone calls reflect a combination of distance and time but, as with transportation, market analysis and competition have largely eliminated strictly distance-based formulas.

Changes in pricing strategy sometimes result in consumer opposition. Banks used to obtain most of their income from the spread between the interest rates they paid depositors and the rates they charged borrowers. However, these spreads have narrowed sharply due to competitive pressure. To generate income, banks are increasingly imposing transaction fees and other periodic charges. The issue of adding surcharges for ATM usage has generated numerous complaints from consumers (see Service Perspectives 9.3 for more details).

Price Bundling. As emphasized throughout this book, many services unite a core product with a variety of supplementary services. Meals and bar service on a cruise ship offer one example; baggage service on a train or aircraft is another. Should such service packages be priced as a

---

SERVICE PERSPECTIVES 9.3

ATM Surcharges

Banks used to charge their customers an extra dollar when they used a "foreign" ATM (that is, one belonging to another bank) on top of any service charges levied on their own customers, which might be as much as $1.25 per transaction when account balances fell below a certain level. In 1996, banks lobbied the two largest ATM networks—Visa's Plus and MasterCard's Cirrus—to withdraw their ban on any additional surcharges. They argued, successfully, that permitting surcharges would encourage placement of ATMs in useful but out-of-the-way places where volume would be lower. By 1999, 90 percent of all banks were surcharging at an average rate of $1.35; 100 percent of independent ATMs imposed charges, averaging $1.59 per transaction. The result was accusations of price gouging, leading to growing political pressure in the United States to limit or even ban surcharges. Banks responded by claiming that making ATMs available to noncustomers was a service that offered value and that people were clearly prepared to pay for this convenience. However, data showed ATM usage peaking in late 1999 as more people used their debit cards to obtain "cash back" at the register when making purchases at grocery stores, which don't charge fees for this service.

The big winners from surcharges appear to be several dozen small companies that install inexpensive ATMs that can only dispense cash and connect them to a national network. However, nonbank ATMs impose a double surcharge: first the $1+ fee for use of a foreign ATM *plus* an additional charge that may reach as high as $3 for a simple cash withdrawal. To make matters worse, nonbank ATMs often fail to disclose the extra surcharge; the first that users know about it is when they find it billed to their bank accounts.

On the other hand, many small-business owners like the nonbanks' approach to doing business. When the owner of a minimart was unable to persuade a bank to put an ATM in his store, he leased a machine from a company for about $300 a month. Customers pay an extra $1.50 surcharge for each transaction, of which $0.80 goes to the minimart owner. He claims that thanks to the machine, his store attracts more customers and sells more merchandise, netting him a profit of up to $50 a month after paying the leasing fee.

Sources: D. Foust, S. Browden, and G. Smith, "Mad as Hell at the Cash Machine," *Business Week,* September 15, 1997, 124; "High ATM Fees, Low Profiles," *Wall Street Journal,* December 4, 1997, p. B1; Mike McNamee, "Why ATM Outrage Is So Misplaced," *Business Week,* November 29, 1999, 44.

---

whole (referred to as a *bundle*), or should each element be priced separately? To the extent that people prefer to avoid making many small payments, bundled pricing may be preferable–and is certainly simpler to administer. But if customers dislike feeling that they have been charged for product elements they didn't use, itemized pricing may be preferable.

Some firms offer an array of choices. Telephone subscribers, for instance, can select from among several service options, ranging from paying a small monthly fee for basic service and then extra for each phone call made to paying a higher flat rate and getting a certain number of local, regional, or long-distance calls free. At the top of the scale is the option that provides business users with unlimited access to long-distance calls over a prescribed area. Bundled prices offer a service firm a certain guaranteed revenue from each customer while giving the latter a clear idea in advance of how much the bill will be. Unbundled pricing provides customers with flexibility in what they choose to acquire and pay for. However, customers may be angered if they discover that the actual price of what they consume, inflated by all the extras, is substantially higher than the advertised base price that attracted them in the first place. An ethical concern arises when pricing combinations are deliberately made so complex that customers have difficulty making careful evaluations to decide which alternative offers them the best deal.

Discounting. A strategy of discounting from established prices should be approached cautiously because it dilutes the average price received, reduces the contribution from each sale, and may attract customers whose only loyalty is to the firm that can offer the lowest price on the next transaction. As noted earlier, there is also a risk that customers who would have been willing to pay more now find themselves enjoying a bargain. Nevertheless, selective price discounting targeted at specific market segments may offer important opportunities to attract new customers and fill capacity that would otherwise go unused. MCI WorldCom's Friends & Family program offers customers discounts on calls they make to specific telephone numbers, providing the entire group signs up for service with MCI. A key objective is to enlist customers as sales agents and then to cement loyalty—group members have a vested interest in discouraging any member from canceling MCI service and using another supplier. Volume discounts are sometimes used to cement the loyalty of large corporate customers who might otherwise spread their purchases among several different suppliers. Another way to use discounting to build loyalty is by offering existing customers a discount off their next purchase.

Who Should Collect Payment?

As discussed in chapter 8, the petals of the Flower of Service include information, order taking, billing, and payment. Customers appreciate it when a firm makes it easy for them to obtain price information and make reservations; they also expect well-presented billing and convenient procedures for making payment. Sometimes firms delegate these tasks to intermediaries, such as travel agents who make hotel and transport bookings and collect payment from customers; ticket agents who sell seats for theaters, concert halls, and sports stadiums; and retailers who act as intermediaries for repair and maintenance work on physical goods. Although the original supplier pays a commission, the intermediary is usually able to offer customers greater convenience in terms of where, when, and how payment should be paid. Using intermediaries may also result in a net savings in administrative costs.

Where Should Payment Be Made?

Service delivery sites are not always conveniently located. Airports, theaters, and stadiums, for instance, are often situated some distance from where potential patrons live or work. When consumers purchase a service before using it, there are obvious benefits to using intermediaries that are more conveniently located or allowing payment by post. A growing number of organizations now accept telephone bookings and sales by credit card; callers simply give their card numbers and have the charge billed directly to their accounts. Finally, there is the option of card-based payments in cyberspace. Thanks to more robust encryption, the Web is starting to become an accepted medium for purchasing a wide array of goods and services.

When Should Payment Be Made?

Two basic options are to ask customers to pay in advance (as with an admission charge, airline ticket, or postage stamps) or to bill them once service delivery has been completed, as with restaurant bills and repair charges. Occasionally, a service provider may ask for an initial payment in advance of service delivery, with the balance being due later. This approach is quite common with expensive repair and maintenance jobs, when the firm—often a small business with limited working capital—must buy materials up front.

Asking customers to pay in advance means that the buyer is paying before the benefits are received. Shugan and Xie's research shows that service providers can improve profits by advance ticketing.[15] But prepayments may be advantageous to the customer as well as to the provider. Sometimes it's inconvenient to pay each time a regularly patronized service—such as the post or public transport—is used; to save time and effort, customers may prefer the convenience of buying a book of stamps or a monthly travel pass. Performing arts organizations with heavy up-front financing requirements offer discounted subscription tickets to bring in money before the season begins. And for obvious reasons, insurance services always require payment in advance!

How Should Payment Be Made?

As shown in Table 9.2, there are many different forms of payment. Cash may appear to be the simplest method, but it raises security problems and is inconvenient when exact change is required to operate machines. Tokens with a predefined value can simplify the process of paying road and bridge tolls or bus and metro fares. Accepting payment by check for all but the smallest purchases is now fairly widespread and offers customer benefits, although it may require controls to discourage bad checks, such as a hefty charge for returned checks ($15 to $20 on top of any bank charges is not uncommon at retail stores).

Credit cards can be used around the world, regardless of currency. Debit cards look like credit cards but act more like plastic checks because the sum charged is debited directly from the holder's account. As acceptance of credit and debit cards has become more universal, businesses that refuse to accept them increasingly find themselves at a competitive disadvantage. Many companies offer customers the convenience of a credit account (which generates a membership relationship between the customer and the firm).

Other payment procedures include directing the bill to a third party for payment and using vouchers as supplements to (or instead of) cash. Insurance companies that designate approved garages to inspect and repair customers' vehicles when they are involved in accidents. To make life easier for the customer, the garage bills the insurance company directly for the work performed, thus saving the customer the effort of paying personally, filing a claim, and waiting for reimbursement. Vouchers are sometimes provided by social service agencies to elderly or low-income people. Such a policy achieves the same benefits as discounting but avoids the need to publicize different prices and to require cashiers to check eligibility.

Now coming into broader usage are prepayment systems based on cards that store value on a magnetic strip or in a microchip embedded within the card. Telephone cards are one example. Service firms that want to accept payment in this form, however, must first install card readers. More sophisticated applications, such as the Mondex card, involve partnerships between banks, retailers, and telephone companies.[16] Working together, these partners offer a smart card that serves as an electronic wallet; customers can transfer funds to their cards from their bank accounts through the medium of a special telephone attachment. There is also provision to transfer funds from one card to another. Service marketers should remember that the simplicity and speed of payment may influence the customer's perception of overall quality.

Communicating Prices to the Target Markets

The final task, once each of the other issues has been addressed, is to decide how the organization's pricing policies can best be communicated to the target market(s). People need to know the price for some product offerings well in advance of purchase; they may also need to know how, where, and when that price is payable. This information must be presented in ways that are intelligible and unambiguous so that customers will not be misled and question the ethical standards of the firm.

Managers must decide whether or not to include information on pricing in advertising for the service. It may be appropriate to relate the price to the costs of competing products or to alternative ways of spending one's money. Certainly, salespeople and customer service representatives should be able to give prompt, accurate responses to customer queries about pricing, payment, and credit. Good signage at retail points of sale will save staff members from having to answer basic questions on prices.

Finally, when the price is presented in the form of an itemized bill, marketers should ensure that it is both accurate and intelligible. Hospital bills, which may run to several pages and contain dozens of items, have been much criticized for inaccuracy.[17] Telephone bills, too, can often be confusing; many companies have traditionally printed them on numerous small sheets of paper, crammed with technical jargon and laid out with related charges spread over different pages. Under pressure from government regulators, some phone companies have developed new and clearer formats, printed on larger sheets; the *Wall Street Journal* referred to it as the "Miracle of the Bells."[18]

Conclusion

Customers pay more to use a service than just the purchase price due to the supplier. For them, the costs of service also include related expenditures (such as travel to the service site) plus time, physical effort, psychological costs, and sensory costs. The value of a service reflects the benefits that it delivers to the customer minus all the associated costs. Customers are often willing to pay a higher price when the nonfinancial outlays are minimized.

Establishing a pricing strategy for a service business begins with clarification of objectives: Is the firm trying to go beyond just establishing the price itself? Issues such as convenience, security, credit, speed, simplicity, collection procedures, and automation may all play a role in improving customer satisfaction with service organizations. Technology has significant potential to facilitate creation of a cashless society, but in practice we are still some distance from that point.

In addition to all these decisions, pricing strategy must address the central issue of what price to charge for selling a given unit of service at a particular point in time (however that unit may be defined). It is essential that the monetary price charged should reflect good knowledge of the service provider's fixed and variable costs, competitors' pricing policies, and the value of the service to the customer.

REVIEW QUESTIONS

1. Of the various costs of service incurred by customers, which are likely to be the most significant in (a) traditional retail banking, (b) home banking, (c) going to the movies, (d) tax preparation services, (e) taking a taxi in an unfamiliar city, and (f) surgery?
2. Why is cost-based pricing particularly problematic in service industries?
3. In what ways does competition-based pricing work in favor of many service providers? In what circumstances does it not?
4. Explain the concept of yield management in a service setting. How might it be applied to (a) a professional firm (e.g. consulting), (b) a restaurant, and (c) a golf course?
5. Identify three aspects of pricing strategy that might raise ethical considerations. In each instance, how should such abuses be prevented?

APPLICATION EXERCISES

1. From a customer perspective, what serves to define value in the following services;
   (a) a nightclub, (b) a hairdressing salon, (c) a legal firm specializing in business and taxation law
2. Select a service organization of your choice and find out what its pricing policies and methods are. In what respects are they similar to or different from what has been discussed in this chapter?
3. Review recent bills that you have received from service businesses, such as those for telephone, car repair, cable television, a credit card, and so on. Evaluate each one against the following criteria: (a) general appearance and clarity of presentation, (b) easily understood terms of payment, (c) avoidance of confusing terms and definitions, (d) appropriate level of detail, (e) unanticipated ("hidden") charges, (f) accuracy, and (g) ease of access to customer service in case of problems or disputes.
4. Review the terms, fees, and interest rates on your credit cards (or a friend's). Compare them with that of the platinum Visa card featured in Service Perspectives 9.1 on p. 263. Other than making money, what is the bank trying to achieve in the platinum case?

ENDNOTES

1. Valarie A. Zeithaml, "Consumer Perceptions of Price, Quality, and Value: A Means-End Model and Synthesis of Evidence," *Journal of Marketing* 52 (July 1988): 2–21.
2. Leonard L. Berry and Manjit S. Yadav, "Capture and Communicate Value in the Pricing of Services," *Sloan Management Review* 37 (Summer 1996): 41–51.
3. Edmund Sanders, "Credit Card 'Fee Frenzy' Cost Americans $18.9B in '98," *Los Angeles Times*, syndicated article, August 1999.
4. H. T. Johnson and Robert S. Kaplan, *Relevance Lost: The Rise and Fall of Management Accounting* (Boston: Harvard Business School Press, 1987).
5. Antonella Carù and Antonella Cugini, "Profitability and Customer Satisfaction in Services: An Integrated Perspective between Marketing and Cost Management Analysis," *International Journal of Service Industry Management* 10, no. 2 (1999): 132–156.
6. Robin Cooper and Robert S. Kaplan, "Profit Priorities from Activity-Based Costing," *Harvard Business Review* (May–June 1991).
7. For a review of the literature in this area and findings from a research study, see Injazz J. Chen, Atul Gupta, and Walter Rom, "A Study of Price and Quality in Service Operations," *International Journal of Service Industry Management* 5, no. 2 (1994): 23–33.
8. Hermann Simon, "Pricing Opportunities and How to Exploit Them," *Sloan Management Review* 33 (winter 1992): 71–84.
9. Berry and Yadav, op cit.
10. Frederick F. Reichheld, *The Loyalty Effect* (Boston: Harvard Business School Press, 1996), 82–84.
11. Hermann Simon and Robert J. Dolan, "Price Customization," *Marketing Management* 7 (fall 1998): 12.
12. Sheryl E. Kimes and Richard. B. Chase, "The Strategic Levers of Yield Management," *Journal of Service Research* 1, no. 2 (November 1998): 156–166.
13. Peter Elkind, "The Hype Is Big, Really Big, at Priceline," *Fortune*, September 6, 1999, 193–202.
14. Amy E. Cortese and Marcia Stepanek, "Good-bye to Fixed Pricing?" *Business Week*, May 4, 1999, 71–84.
15. Steven M. Shugan and Jinhong Xie, "Advance Pricing of Services and Other Implications of Separating Purchase and Consumption," *Journal of Service Research*, 2, February 2000, 227–239.
16. Kalyani Vittalas, "Cashless Society Put to Test in Ontario Town," *New York Times*, September 30, 1997, p. D2.
17. See, for example, Anita Sharpe, "The Operation Was a Success; The Bill Was Quite a Mess," *Wall Street Journal*, September 17, 1997, p. 1.
18. Kathy Chen, "Miracle of the Bells: The Simplified Phone Bill," *Wall Street Journal*, April 12, 1999, pp. B1, B3.

CHAPTER 10

Customer Education and Service Promotion

Promise, large promise, is the soul of an advertisement.

SAMUEL JOHNSON

Education costs money, but then so does ignorance.

SIR CLAUS MOSER

Communication is the most visible or audible—some would say intrusive—of marketing activities, but its value is limited unless it's used intelligently in conjunction with other marketing efforts. An old marketing axiom says that the fastest way to kill a poor product is to advertise it heavily. By the same token, an otherwise well-researched and well-planned marketing strategy, designed to deliver, say, new Web-based services at a reasonable price, is likely to fail if people lack knowledge of the service and how to access it.

Through communication, marketers inform existing or prospective customers about service features and benefits, price and other costs, the channels through which service is delivered, and when and where it is available. Where appropriate, persuasive arguments can be marshaled for using a particular service, and preference can be created for selecting a specific brand. And both personal instructions and impersonal communications can be employed to help customers become effective participants in service delivery processes.

Much confusion surrounds the scope of marketing communication. Some people still define it narrowly as the use of paid media advertising, public relations, and professional salespeople, failing to recognize the many other ways that a modern organization can communicate with its customers. The location and atmosphere of a service delivery facility, corporate design features such as the consistent use of colors and graphic elements, the appearance and behavior of employees, the design of a Web site—all contribute to an impression in the customer's mind that reinforces or contradicts the specific content of formal communication messages.

In this chapter, we begin with a brief review of the tasks performed by marketing communications and related ethical issues and then proceed to explore the following questions:

1. What is distinctive about the nature of marketing communications in a service setting?
2. What are the elements of the marketing communications mix, and what are the strengths and weaknesses of each major element?
3. How does the level of customer contact affect communication strategy?
4. How should marketing communication objectives be defined?
5. What is the potential value of the Internet as a communication channel?

The Role of Marketing Communication

Marketing communications between the service firm and its customers and prospects can take many forms, some of them highly creative. In a competitive environment, effective communications play a vital role in marketing strategy, moving new customers through the purchase decision process presented in chapter 4 (refer to Figure 4.5 on p. 123) and helping to reinforce brand preference among existing customers.

Marketing Communication Tasks

Among the specific tasks performed by marketing communication are

- To inform and educate prospective customers about an organization, its brand promises, and the relevant features of the goods and services that it offers
- To persuade target customers that a specific service product offers the best solution to their needs, relative to the offerings of competing firms
- To remind customers and prospects of service availability and motivate them to act
- To maintain contact with existing customers, providing updates and further education on how to obtain the best results from the firm's products in light of each customer's documented usage behavior

As we saw in our discussion of the Flower of Service in chapter 8, information and consultation represent important ways to add value to a product. Prospective customers need information about what service options are available to them, where and when these services are available, how much they cost, specific features and functions, and the particular benefits to be gained. Prospects may also need advice on which of several alternative service packages might best meet their needs. In service businesses, many communication efforts are concerned with educating customers. This is especially true of advertising campaigns for new services or for newly introduced service features.

Persuasion involves developing arguments about why a customer should purchase and use a particular service rather than not purchase at all or buy a competing brand. Reminders may be needed to get people to act on their intentions to buy a particular service, especially when it's only offered at very specific times—like subscribing to concert programs or purchasing special holiday travel packages.

Communicating with Existing Customers

Communication efforts serve not only to attract new users but also to maintain contact with an organization's existing customers and build relationships with them. As emphasized in chapter 6, reinforcing loyalty and securing repeat sales are usually central to a firm's long-term profitability. Existing users should not be taken for granted. Techniques for keeping in touch include mailings, periodic e-mail communications, and contacts by telephone or through other forms of telecommunication, including fax and Internet. Doctors, dentists, and household maintenance services often mail annual checkup reminders to their customers. Banks and utility companies that send periodic account statements often include a brief newsletter or print customized information on each statement as a means of keeping in touch with existing customers and promoting new services; companies in both industries also make widespread use of direct mail promotions for cross-selling (persuading existing customers to use additional services) and for building customer loyalty. Some hotels, restaurants, and insurance companies remember to acknowledge special events like customers' birthdays and anniversaries. Subscription services send early renewal notices.

Nurturing customer relationships depends on a comprehensive and up-to-date customer database and the ability to make use of it in a personalized way. Although postal mailings have been the traditional channel of communication, many businesses are now turning to telecommunications to keep in touch with customers—as well as encouraging customers to visit their corporate Web sites.

Internal Communications

Several of the tools of marketing communications can be used with service employees as well as with external customers. Internal communications from senior managers to their employees play a vital role in maintaining and nurturing a corporate culture founded on specific service values. Well-planned internal marketing efforts are especially necessary in large service businesses that operate in widely dispersed sites, sometimes situated around the world. Even when employees are working far from the head office in the home country, they still need to be kept abreast of new policies, changes in service features, and new quality initiatives. Communications may also be needed to nurture a team spirit and to motivate adoption of new ways of working. Consider, for instance, the challenge of maintaining a unified sense of corporate purpose at the overseas offices of companies such as Citibank, Air Canada, Marriott, or McDonald's, where people from different cultures and speaking different languages must still pull together to create consistent levels of service.

The goals of internal communications include ensuring efficient and satisfactory service delivery; achieving productive and harmonious working relationships; and building employee trust, respect, and loyalty. Progress in reaching each goal depends, in part, on clear communication between management and employees. Commonly used media vehicles include internal newsletters and magazines; private corporate television networks; videotapes; Intranets (private networks of Web sites and e-mail, inaccessible to the general public); face-to-face briefings; and promotional campaigns using displays, prizes, and recognition programs.

Ethical Issues in Communication

The tools of communication are very powerful ones. Few aspects of marketing lend themselves so easily to misuse (and even abuse) as advertising, selling, and sales promotion. The fact that customers often find it hard to evaluate services makes them more dependent on marketing communication for information and advice. Communication messages often include promises about the benefits that customers will receive and the quality of service delivery. When promises are made and then broken, customers are disappointed because their expectations have not been met.[1] Their disappointment and even anger will be all the greater if they have wasted money, time, and effort and have either no benefits to show for it or, worse, have actually suffered a negative impact. Employees, too, may feel disappointed and frustrated as they listen to customers' complaints.

Sometimes, unrealistic service promises result from poor internal communications between operations and marketing personnel concerning the level of service performance that customers can reasonably expect. In other instances, unethical advertisers and salespeople deliberately make unrealistic statements about service features and false promises about the benefits that customers can hope to receive. Finally, there are deceptive prize promotions that lead people to think that they have a much higher chance of winning than is really the case. Fortunately, many consumer watchdogs are on the lookout for such untruthful marketing practices. They include consumer protection agencies, trade associations within specific industries, and journalists who investigate customer complaints and seek to expose fraud and misrepresentation. Once a firm gets a reputation for being untrustworthy, that can be hard to shake off.

A different type of ethical issue concerns unwanted intrusion into people's personal lives—including, perhaps, your own. You can, of course, simply turn the page if you don't want to look at an advertisement in a newspaper or magazine. Perhaps you ignore television advertising, press the mute button on your remote, and talk to friends or family members while the commercials are on. However, the increase in telemarketing is frustrating for those who receive unwanted sales calls. How do you feel if your evening meal at home is interrupted by a telephone call from a stranger trying to interest you in buying services in which you have no interest? Even if you are interested, you may feel, as many do, that your privacy has been violated and see the call as an unwanted intrusion.

Services versus Goods: Implications for Communication Strategy

Developing a communications strategy for intangible services differs in important respects from advertising and promoting physical goods. Guidelines for action need to reflect the special characteristics of services.[2] Several of the differences distinguishing services from goods have important marketing communications implications. The six most relevant differences are

- The intangible nature of service performances.
- Customer involvement in production.
- Services are harder for customers to evaluate.
- The need to balance supply and demand.
- The importance of customer-contact personnel.
- Reduced role for intermediaries.

Let's examine each of these in more detail.

Intangible Nature of Service Performances

Recognizing that service is a performance rather than an object means that ways have to be found to make the service more concrete and to clarify what the performance can achieve. George and Berry urge service providers to use tangible cues whenever possible in their advertising campaigns, especially for low-contact services that involve few tangible elements.[3] Legg and Baker argue for presenting "vivid information" that will produce a strong, clear impression on the senses.[4]

At a very basic level, some companies have succeeded in creating a tangible, recognizable symbol to associate with their corporate brand name. Many companies employ animal motifs as physical symbols for their services. Examples include the Qantas kangaroo, the eagle of the U.S. Postal Service (also employed by AeroMexico and Eagle Star Insurance), the black horse of Norfolk Southern Railroad (also shared with Britain's Lloyd's Bank), Merrill Lynch's bull, the lion of Dreyfus Funds and Royal Bank of Canada, the ram of the investment firm T. Rowe Price, and the Chinese dragon of Hong Kong's Dragonair. The use of easily recognizable symbols takes on special importance when offering services in markets where the local language is not written in Roman script or where a significant proportion of the population is functionally illiterate.

More important is making the message itself easier to grasp. Creating metaphors that are tangible in nature makes intangible claims more concrete. Faced with marketing a highly intangible product, insurance companies often use such an approach. Thus, Allstate advertises that "You're in Good Hands," Traveler's presents an umbrella motif to suggest protection, and Prudential uses the Rock of Gibraltar as a symbol of corporate solidity. But according to researcher Banwari Mittal, such an approach does not go far enough because the symbol alone doesn't explain *how* the protection is actually provided.[5]

Consider Trend Micro's problem in advertising its new antivirus monitoring service for corporate networks. Most advertisements for antivirus protection feature devils or evil-looking insects (remember the Millennium Bug used to highlight the Y2K problem?). That approach may capture the reader's interest, but it doesn't show how virus protection actually works or how devastating a virus's effects might be. In a technical context such as this, explaining the problem and its solution in ways that senior management will understand is not always possible. But using an easily grasped metaphor can get the point across. Now look at Trend Micro's clever solution, using the analogy of airport security to guard against terrorism (see Figure 10.1).

Customer Involvement in Production

Pressures to improve productivity in service organizations often involve technological innovations in service delivery. If customers will accept technology as a substitute for human effort or will agree to perform more of the work themselves in the form of self-service, then the service business may stand to cut its costs significantly. But these benefits will not be achieved if customers resist new, technologically based systems or avoid self-service alternatives. A major challenge for innovative firms is to teach their customers how to use new technologies effectively. When customers are actively involved in service production, they need training to help them perform well—just as employees do. In short, the service marketer needs to become an educator. One instructional approach recommended by advertising experts is to show service delivery in action.[6] Television is a good medium because of its ability to engage the viewer as it displays a seamless sequence of events in visual form.

Customers are often concerned about the risks associated with using a particular service (refer back to Table 4.1, p. 125). Sometimes these risks are financial or psychological in nature, but occasionally there are physical risks—as in many outdoor sports and organized adventure activities such as rock climbing, skiing, and white-water rafting. The providers of such services have both a legal and a moral responsibility to educate their clients. The better informed customers are of potential dangers and what to do in the event of, say, a raft tipping its occupants into a stretch of foaming rapids, the more likely they are to remain safe and to have an enjoyable experience. Basic information that customers may (or may not) have read earlier in instructional brochures often need to be reinforced and expanded by personal briefings from staff members. Educating customers for their own self-protection is important in indoor settings,

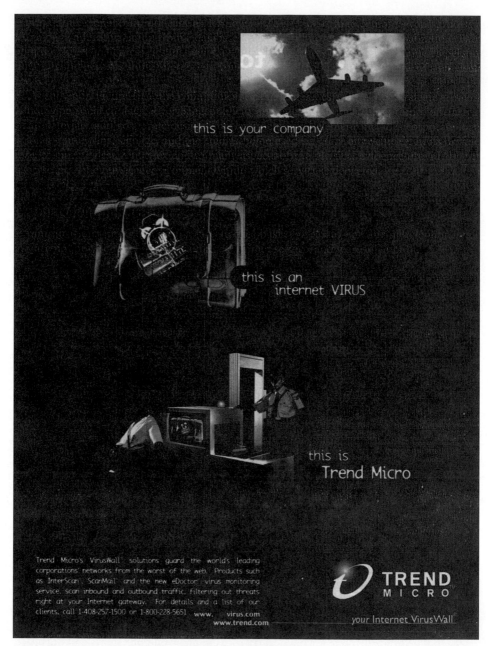

FIGURE 10.1 Providing Tangible Metaphors for Service Performance

too. For instance, Holmes Place, a chain of health and fitness centers, takes pains to ensure that clients use its facilities properly and avoid injury. All new clients are given one-to-one training on how to use different types of equipment to obtain the desired physical benefits without hurting themselves. Knowledgeable staff are on hand to offer advice and to check on clients' safety while the latter are working out.

Advertising and publicity can serve to make customers aware of changes in service features and delivery systems that require a different script. Marketers often use sales promotions to motivate customers, offering them incentives to make the necessary changes in their behavior. Publicizing price discounts is one way to encourage self-service on an ongoing basis; at self-service gas pumps, for instance, the price difference from full service is often substantial. Premiums, sampling, and prize promotions can also be used to encourage customers to adopt a new way of using an existing service. And, of course, well-trained customer-contact personnel can provide one-to-one tutoring to help customers adapt to new procedures.

Services Are Harder for Customers to Evaluate

Even if customers understand what a particular type of service is supposed to do, they may have difficulty distinguishing one firm from another and of knowing what level of performance they can expect from a particular supplier. Among the strategies that can be employed here are providing tangible clues specifically related to service performance; highlighting the quality of equipment employed; and documenting employee characteristics such as their qualifications, experience, commitment, and professionalism. For example, the advertisement shown in Figure 10.2 is one in a series featuring employees of J.P. Morgan, a major investment bank. The ads seek to build the firm's image in an industry where the caliber of a firm's professional staff is one of its principal assets. This type of advertising is often targeted at two audiences, seeking both to win new clients and to attract outstanding new recruits.

Airlines periodically address service quality issues in their advertising, sometimes to correct what research shows to be misperceptions. Reporting favorable measures calculated by a government agency is a popular device because they have more credibility than the airline's own internal measures. For instance, being rated number one in punctuality by the U.S. Department of Transportation is something to boast about in advertising, particularly if the airline in question has recently shown significant improvement. However, airlines don't like to talk overtly about safety—an ongoing customer concern—so they approach the topic obliquely, advertising the expertise of their pilots, the skills and training of their mechanics, and the newness of their aircraft.

In low-contact services, much of the firm's expertise is hidden, so it may be necessary to use communications to illustrate equipment, procedures, and employee activities that are taking place backstage. For instance, how do prospective buyers know if they are getting the best value from insurance services? Liberty Mutual has run ads using attention-getting headlines: "I love dissecting humans" is accompanied by an amusing photo of one of the company's field investigators, who then describes her work in detecting and preventing insurance fraud; "Wake up, you're dead" introduces a grim-looking auto safety expert with a Ph.D. who is researching how to prevent highway accidents caused by driver fatigue. The fraud prevention ad shows just how serious the problem of jaycustomers (introduced in chapter 3) is for the insurance industry; did you know that fraudulent claims amount to an estimated $25 billion a year? Those that go undetected simply add to the cost of insurance premiums for honest customers.

Another role for advertising that can help customers understand and evaluate a service is to encourage positive word-of-mouth comments from other customers who have already used the service and are pleased with it.[7] Word-of-mouth is a very credible medium when it comes from a trusted source. At a minimum, firms should try to determine through research what existing customers are saying about their services—negative word-of-mouth can be very damaging!

Supply and Demand Management

Because live service performances—such as a seat at the Metropolitan Opera for Friday evening's performance of *Carmen,* a room at the Marriott on Monday, or a haircut at Supercuts

FIGURE 10.2 Promoting the Caliber of a Firm's Professional Staff

on Tuesday morning—are time specific and can't be stored for resale at a later date, marketers often resort to using advertising and sales promotions to help shape demand to match the capacity available at a given time. As we discuss in chapter 13, demand management strategies include reducing usage during peak demand periods and stimulating it during off-peak periods. There are many opportunities for service providers to design, advertise, and deliver promotions that communicate an otherwise mundane price reduction in an exciting and attention-getting manner. Low demand outside peak periods poses a serious problem for service industries with high fixed costs, such as hotels. One strategy is to avoid lowering the list price too much and instead run promotions that offer extra value—such as a room upgrade and a free breakfast—in an attempt to stimulate demand without using price directly as a weapon. When demand increases, the number of promotions can be reduced or eliminated.

Importance of Contact Personnel

In high-contact services, service personnel are central to service delivery. Their presence makes the service more tangible and, in many cases, more personalized. An ad that shows employees at work helps prospective customers to understand the nature of the service encounter and implies a promise of the personalized attention that they can expect to receive (see Figure 10.3). Such advertising also reaches a second audience, the firm's employees, showing them what customers are being promised. The challenge here for advertisers is to be realistic, because these messages help to set customers' expectations. If a firm's brochures and ads show friendly, smiling workers but, in reality, most employees turn out to be glum or frazzled or just plain rude, customers will be disappointed! At a minimum, the marketer should brief staff members about the content of new advertising campaigns or brochures.

Reflecting the critical role played by service employees in enhancing customer satisfaction and building loyalty, many large service firms develop internal marketing communication campaigns directed at their own employees. These can take the form of posters, ads and stories in

FIGURE 10.3 A uniformed hotel employee leads a guest through the check-in script; her warmth humanizes the experience for him.

corporate bulletins, films, and even use of programs transmitted on private television networks (FedEx and Merrill Lynch are among the large international companies with their own networks). Employee incentive programs are often used as part of an internal marketing effort to ensure quality control in the service facility. Cash bonuses, awards, dinners, recognition programs, and eligibility for prize draws are among the many promotional incentives offered to employees for delivery of outstanding service, success in referrals to sales personnel, and achievement of quality targets.

In high-contact services, employees can help implement promotional efforts. For instance, the gift premiums offered by fast-food chains and upgrades to larger or more luxurious vehicles at car rental facilities can both be delivered personally to customers at the point of sale. When customer-contact personnel are actually responsible for sales, they can be motivated and rewarded as part of an overall sales promotion.

Reduced Role for Intermediaries

Intermediaries, such as retailers, often play a significant role in promoting products to customers and teaching them about their characteristics. But services are less likely than goods to be sold through channel intermediaries. Consumer goods marketers need to decide how to allocate funds between advertising, consumer promotion, and trade promotion (that is, promotions designed to reward retailers who agree to stock a particular brand or model). However, many service firms sell directly to customers—such as banks, restaurants, health clubs, and professional firms—and have no need for trade promotions.

Nevertheless, some service providers do rely on intermediaries for help in selling their products. Firms in the travel and insurance industries, which make extensive use of independent agents and brokers, must compete with other brands not only for physical display space but also for "top-of-mind" recall to obtain adequate push from the intermediaries in the channel of distribution. Internal communication, personal selling, motivational promotions, and effective public relations can be critical in maintaining successful working relationships and partnerships between the intermediary and the service firm.

Setting Communication Objectives

What role should communication play in helping a service firm achieve its marketing goals? A useful checklist for marketing communications planning is provided by the 5 Ws model:

Who is our target audience?
What do we need to communicate and achieve?
How should we communicate this?
Where should we communicate this?
When do the communications need to take place?

Marketers need to be clear about their objectives; otherwise, it will be difficult to formulate specific communications objectives and select the most appropriate messages and communication tools to achieve them.

For instance, a car rental agency might define as a key objective the need to increase repeat purchase rates among business travelers. To achieve this objective, the firm might decide to implement an automatic upgrade program and an express delivery and drop-off system. For this innovation to be successful, communications will be needed to inform customers of this initiative and to educate them on how to take advantage of it. A more specific set of objectives might be (1) create awareness of the new offering among all existing customers; (2) attract the

TABLE 10.1 *Common Educational and Promotional Objectives in Service Settings*

- Create memorable images of specific companies and their brands.
- Build awareness of and interest in an unfamiliar service or brand.
- Build preference by communicating the special strengths and benefits of a particular brand.
- Encourage trial by offering promotional incentives.
- Familiarize customers with service processes in advance of use.
- Teach customers how to use a service to their own best advantage.
- Stimulate demand in low-demand periods and discourage demand during peak periods (include information on the best times to use the service to avoid crowds).
- Compare a service against the competition and counter competitors' claims.
- Reduce uncertainty and the sense of risk by providing useful information and advice.
- Provide reassurance (e.g., by promoting service guarantees).
- Recognize and reward valued customers and employees.
- Reposition a service relative to the competing offerings.

attention of prospective customers in the business traveler segment, inform them of the new features, and teach them how to use the new procedures effectively; (3) stimulate inquiries and increase prebookings; and (4) generate an increase in repeat patronage of (say) 20 percent after six months.

In addition to communicating special offers, reinforcing loyalty, and encouraging repurchase, other common educational and promotional objectives for service marketers are listed in Table 10.1.

The next step is to consider which elements of the marketing communications mix will best convey the desired messages to chosen market segments. Advertising through such media as television, newspapers, magazines, and posters is usually the most visible element in a campaign, whereas radio is a commonly used audible medium. However, marketers have many other communication tools at their disposal, including personal selling, public relations, sales promotions, and corporate design. Perhaps the most exciting new medium available to marketers is the Internet, including e-mail and Web sites.

Key Planning Considerations

Planning a marketing communications campaign must be based on a good understanding of the service product and the extent to which prospective buyers are able to evaluate its characteristics in advance of purchase. Also essential is knowledge of the target market segments, their awareness of the product and attitudes toward it, and their exposure to different media. Decisions include determining the content, structure, and style of the message to be communicated; its manner of presentation; and the media most suited to reaching the intended audience. Additional considerations include the budget available for execution; time frames, as defined by such factors as seasonality, market opportunities, and anticipated competitive activities; and finally, methods of measuring and evaluating performance.

The Marketing Communications Mix

Most service marketers have access to numerous forms of communication, sometimes referred to collectively as the *marketing communications mix*. Different communication elements have distinctive capabilities relative to the types of messages that they can convey and the market segments most likely to be exposed to them.

Communication experts draw a broad division between *personal communications* (where a representative of the service firm interacts with customers on an individual basis) and *impersonal communications* (where the service firm sends messages to an audience). In the first instance, messages are personalized and move in both directions between the two parties. In the second instance, messages move in only one direction and are generally targeted at a large market segment of customers and prospects rather than at a single individual. However, as you've probably noticed in your own life as a customer, technology has created a gray area between personal and impersonal communications. It's now very easy for a firm to combine word-processing technology with information from a database to create an impression of personalization. Think about the direct-mail messages that you have received and how often they contained a personal salutation and perhaps some reference to your specific situation or your past use of a particular product.

As shown in Figure 10.4, the communications mix includes a variety of strategic elements, including personal contact, advertising, publicity and public relations, sales promotion, instructional materials, and corporate design. This last-mentioned element includes corporate logos, stationery, uniforms, signage, and the color scheme used on company vehicles. In its broadest sense, corporate design may extend to many aspects of the physical evidence provided by the servicescape—the physical environment within which service is delivered.

Personal Communications

Communications undertaken on a face-to-face basis (or ear-to-ear during telephone calls) embrace not only selling but also training, customer service, and word-of-mouth.

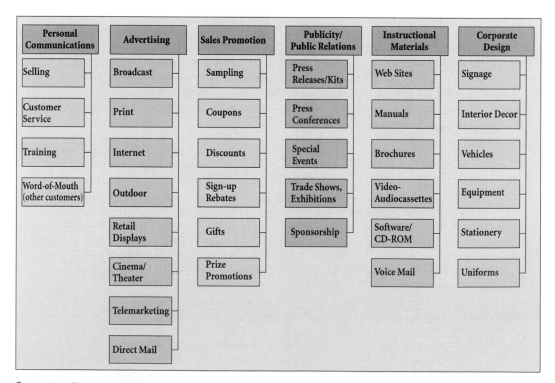

FIGURE 10.4 The Marketing Communication Mix for Services

Personal selling refers to interpersonal encounters on a face-to-face (or in telemarketing, voice-to-voice) basis in which efforts are made to educate customers and promote preference for a particular brand or product. Because face-to-face selling is usually very expensive, it is used more frequently in business-to-business markets—especially when the amounts purchased by each corporate customer are substantial. But as you know from your own experience, there is still widespread use of personal selling in consumer settings. It's often undertaken by the same customer-contact personnel responsible for service delivery. All types of service firms, from department stores to hair salons, use personal selling strategies. And for infrequently purchased services such as property, insurance, and funeral services, the firm's representative may act as a consultant to help buyers determine their needs and select from among suitable alternatives.

The direct nature of personal selling allows a sales representative or account manager to tailor the message to fit each customer's particular needs and concerns; effective teaching often benefits from one-to-one tutorial sessions. During a sales call, in person or by phone, communication flows in both directions between the marketer and the customer. The advantage for the firm is that careful listening by the sales representatives allows them to learn more about their customers. In fact, sales training often emphasizes development of good listening skills. Through one-to-one dialog, needs can be identified, questions answered, and concerns addressed.

As we saw in chapter 5, firms are increasingly aware of the importance of developing and maintaining long-term relationships with their customers and are moving away from a transaction mentality that focuses on making a quick sale. Relationship marketing strategies are often based on account management programs, where customers are assigned a designated account manager who acts as an interface between the customer and the supplier. Account management is most commonly practiced in industrial and professional firms that sell relatively complex services so that customers have an ongoing need for advice and consultation. Examples of account management for individual consumers can be found in insurance, stockbroker, and medical services. For an example of a telephone-based account management program for small business users of telecommunications services, see the case study "BT: Telephone Account Management" on pp. 615 to 624. Not all service personnel who engage in selling are, in fact, professionally trained salespeople. Professionals in businesses such as accounting, engineering, and management consulting are required to bring in new clients as well as to build lasting relationships with existing ones.

Customer Service. The primary responsibilities of employees in customer service positions usually entail creating and delivering the service in the customer's presence as well as providing information, taking reservations and receiving payment, and solving problems. New customers, in particular, often rely on customer service personnel for assistance in learning how to use a service effectively and how to resolve problems. However, it is difficult for such employees to provide good service if they themselves are insufficiently informed, trained, and supported.

When a customer has the potential to buy several different products from the same supplier, firms encourage their customer-contact staff to cross-sell additional services. However, these strategies are likely to fail if not properly planned and executed.[8] Employees who see their jobs primarily in operational terms may resent having to act as salespeople. In the banking industry, for example, the combination of a highly competitive marketplace and new technologies have forced banks to add more services in an attempt to increase their profitability. In many banks, tellers who have traditionally been evaluated against operationally oriented criteria are now expected to promote new services to their customers. Despite training, many such employees feel uncomfortable in this role and are not effective as salespeople. For an in-depth illustration of this situation, see the case study "Menton Bank" on pp. 669–677.

Training. Many companies, especially those selling complex business-to-business services, offer training courses for their customers. The purpose is to familiarize users with the product's potential and educate them on how to use the service to best advantage.

Word-of-Mouth. The comments and recommendations that customers make about their service experiences can have a powerful influence on other people's decisions. So it's realistic to classify what is often called word-of-mouth as a form of marketing communication. Strictly speaking, it's not advertising, because customers provide it voluntarily. However, some advertisers try to simulate word-of-mouth by hiring actual customers to give endorsements. The most appropriate way to think of unpaid word-of-mouth is as a form of publicity that marketers seek to cultivate and shape so that it becomes an effective supplement to other communication activities.

Research in both the United States and Sweden shows that the extent and content of word-of-mouth is related to customer satisfaction levels[9] (see Research Insights 10.1). Positive word-of-mouth can act as a powerful and highly credible selling agent. After all, whose recommendation are you most likely to accept: a trusted friend's or a professional salesperson's? At the same time, experienced customers can also be useful in helping inexperienced fellow customers and teaching them how to use a service. Conversely, negative word-of-mouth can be extremely damaging to a company's reputation and hurt its sales.

Advertising

Advertising tends to be the most dominant form of communication in consumer marketing and is often the first point of contact between service marketers and their customers. A broad array of paid advertising media are available, including broadcast (television and radio), print (magazines and newspapers), and many types of outdoor media (posters, billboards, electronic message boards, and the exteriors of vehicles such as buses). The Irish low-cost airline Ryanair has even announced its intention to transform some of its aircraft into flying billboards, featuring advertisements for products ranging from Kilkenny beer to Jaguar cars.[10]

Some media are more focused than others. Newspapers and television, for instance, tend to reach mass audiences (although research can identify who reads what sections of a newspaper or watches specific programs). Showing advertising before the main feature in movie theaters, long a popular advertising practice in many parts of the world, is now catching on in the United States and Canada, where it can reach a broad audience. Magazines and radio, by contrast, are usually more focused media because the audiences for individual titles or stations tend to be highly segmented. Advertising messages transmitted through mass media, such as billboards, television, newspapers and magazines, are sometimes reinforced by brochures or direct marketing, using mail, telephone (telemarketing), fax, or e-mail. The growth of the Internet and the World Wide Web offers interesting new opportunities for marketing communications. More

---

RESEARCH INSIGHTS 10.1

Satisfaction and Word-of-Mouth: Comparing Swedish and U.S. Customers

Do dissatisfied customers engage in more or less word-of-mouth communication than satisfied ones? People who are happy with their experience of a good or service are likely to tell others about it in positive terms, perhaps even recommending the product in question. By contrast, those who are dissatisfied may regale others with their bad experiences, make disparaging comments about the service or the supplier, and even start negative rumors.

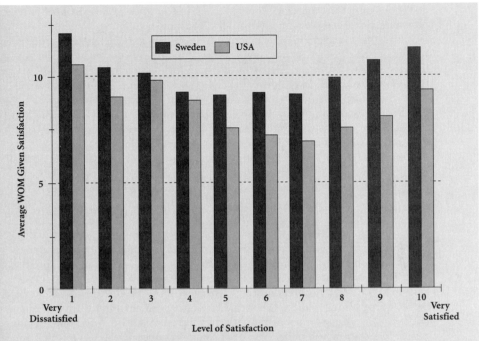

FIGURE 10.A Conditional Mean of Word-of-Mouth Comments (WOM > 0) Given Customer Satisfaction

Reviewing past research and commentary on the topic, Eugene Anderson of the University of Michigan found conflicting viewpoints and resolved to get additional insights. He analyzed data from the Swedish Customer Satisfaction Barometer (SCSB) and the American Customer Satisfaction Index (ACSI). The two projects measure individual customers' satisfaction with goods and services produced by a large sample of firms from different industries in the two countries. The 203 firms in the U.S. sample have dollar sales exceeding 40 percent of the gross national product (GNP). Each year, a national probability sample of households is screened to identify respondents with recent experience of the target firms' products. Respondents are asked multiple questions on a variety of topics, including perceived value, overall satisfaction, repurchase likelihood, word-of-mouth, and complaining behavior. The annual results show trends over the years and comparisons between industries and firms.

For customer satisfaction, respondents rate the supplier on a 10-point scale, ranging from "very dissatisfied" to "very satisfied." They report word-of-mouth activity in terms of the number of individuals they have spoken to about recent experiences with quality. Anderson analyzed these two variables, taking data from both the SCSB and the ACSI, and linked the average number of individuals spoken to with average satisfaction ratings. A simple graphic portrayal of the results is shown in Figure 10.A.

Both indexes show a U-shaped relationship between satisfaction ratings and extent of word-of-mouth; customers holding strong views are likely to tell more people about their experiences than those with milder views. In addition, extremely dissatisfied customers told more people than those who were highly satisfied. The results also showed that Swedish consumers engage in more word-of-mouth activity than Americans across all satisfaction levels.

Source: Eugene W. Anderson, "Customer Satisfaction and Word of Mouth," *Journal of Service Research* 1 (August 1998): 5–17.

and more companies are establishing Web sites as an information resource for customers and prospects. Others are using the Web as an advertising medium.

Direct marketing, which includes both direct mail and telemarketing, offers the potential to send personalized messages to highly targeted microsegments, including one-to-one communications. As noted earlier, this form of communication is most likely to be successful when marketers possess detailed information about customers and prospects. E-mail is growing as a direct advertising medium, although many e-mail address lists are still very unfocused. The problem lies with companies that sell inexpensive e-mail address lists containing millions of names. Some advertisers, often promoting dubious personal services, purchase these lists and then swamp millions of prospects with unwanted junk e-mail ("spam").

Another form of advertising, often linked to sales promotion, consists of retail displays in store windows. Some Web sites seek to replicate retail storefronts with attractive displays in cyberspace, although the time required to download the images often gets in the way of effective communication.

The Role of Advertising. In a service setting, advertising is most commonly used to create awareness and stimulate interest in the service offering, to educate customers about service features and applications, to establish or redefine a competitive position, to reduce risk, and to help "tangibilize" the intangible. Advertising plays an especially vital role in providing factual information about services and educating customers about product features and capabilities. To demonstrate this role, Grove, Pickett and Laband carried out a study comparing newspaper and television advertising for goods and services.[11] Based on a review of 11,543 television advertisements over a 10-month period and of 30,940 newspaper display adverts that appeared over a 12-month period, they found that advertisements for services were significantly more likely than those for goods to contain factual information on the following four dimensions: price, guarantees/warranties, documentation of performance, and availability (where, when, and how to acquire products). Consumers may rely more on information provided by advertising for services because they find them more difficult to evaluate than goods. For an example of a print advertisement that seeks to educate readers, see the Prudential ad reproduced in Figure 10.5 about investing for a child's college education.

Publicity and Public Relations

Public relations (PR) involves efforts to stimulate positive interest in an organization and its products and services by sending out news releases, holding press conferences, staging special events, and sponsoring newsworthy activities put on by third parties. A basic element in PR strategy is the preparation and distribution of press releases (including photos and sometimes videos) featuring stories about the company, specific services, and its employees. PR executives also arrange press conferences and distribute press kits when they feel that the story is especially newsworthy. However, unlike paid advertising, there is no guarantee that such stories will appear in the media, and if they do, they may not appear in the positive form desired by the company's PR department (or the outside PR agency retained by the firm). Good relationships with journalists and other media specialists are important in building a receptive climate for news releases. A reputation for openness and honesty is vital when something negative happens—such as an accident, injuries to customers or employees, or market rejection of a new service initiative. A key task performed by corporate PR specialists is to teach senior managers how to present themselves well at news conferences or in radio and television interviews.

Among other widely used PR techniques are recognition and reward programs, obtaining testimonials from public figures, community involvement and support, fundraising, and obtaining favorable publicity for the organization through special events and pro bono work. In

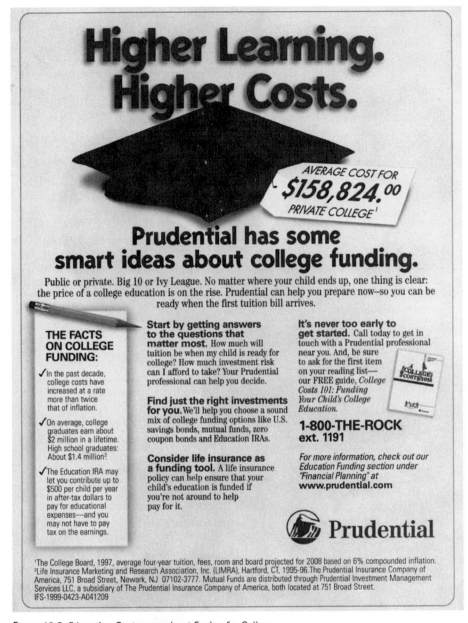

FIGURE 10.5 Educating Customers about Saving for College

this way an organization builds its reputation and credibility; forms strong relationships with its employees, customers, and the community of which it is a part; and secures an image conducive to business success. Firms can also win wide exposure through sponsorship of sporting events and other high-profile activities, where banners, decals, and other visual displays provide continuing repetition of the corporate name and symbol. For instance, by sponsoring the PGA Tour golf tournaments, Bank of America expects to get repeated exposure for its name among audiences attending these events; more importantly, it hopes to reach a much wider television audience, thus reinforcing awareness of its brand name and creating positive associations for the company. To popularize both the tour and the bank's sponsorship, Bank of America has also taken out full-page magazine advertisements (Figure 10.6).

The role of Sydney, Australia, in hosting the 2000 Summer Olympics created numerous opportunities for companies from around the world to sponsor different activities, not only during the games themselves but also during the precompetition period when interest and excitement were building for the event. The 2002 Winter Olympics in Utah will provide similar opportunities for advertisers in all countries that send teams to participate. So even though neither set of games is taking place in, for instance, Canada, many Canadian advertisers will be sponsoring teams and events because they know that the games will be closely followed back home.

Sales Promotion

A few years ago, SAS International Hotels devised an interesting promotion targeted at older customers. If a hotel had vacant rooms, guests over 65 years of age could get a discount equivalent to their years—thus, a 75-year-old could save 75 percent of the normal room price. All went well until a Swedish guest checked into one of the SAS chain's hotels in Vienna, announced his

FIGURE 10.6 Bank of American sponsors PGA Tour golf tournaments.

age as 102, and asked to be paid 2 percent of the room rate in return for staying the night. This request was duly granted, whereupon the spry centenarian challenged the general manager to a game of tennis—and obtained that, too (the results of the game, however, were not disclosed). Events such as these are the stuff of dreams for PR people. In this case, a clever promotion yields a humorous, widely reported story that places the marketing organization in a favorable light.

A useful way of looking at sales promotions is as communication attached to an incentive. Sales promotions are usually specific to a time period, price, or customer group—and sometimes all three, as in the SAS example. Typically, the objective is to accelerate the purchasing decision or to motivate customers to use a specific service sooner, in greater volume with each purchase, or more frequently. Sales promotions for service firms may take such forms as samples, coupons and other discounts, gifts, and competitions with prizes. Used in these forms, sales promotion serves to add value, provide a competitive edge, boost sales during periods when demand would otherwise be weak, speed the introduction and acceptance of new services, and generally get customers to act faster than they would in the absence of any promotional incentive.[12]

Short-term price promotions can offer marketers the following advantages that are not available through other marketing tools:

- Because promotional costs vary with volume, price promotions are a good weapon for small companies to use in challenging large competitors.
- Promotions reduce the risk of first-time purchase for customers and thus encourage trial.
- Different segments can be charged different prices for the same service when one group receives a promotional discount and the other doesn't.
- Promotions can add excitement to mundane repetitive purchases and appeal to price-conscious consumers.
- Price promotions are particularly useful for adjusting demand and supply fluctuations.[13]

Sales promotions can take many forms. At least six methods are available to service marketers, including samples, coupons, short-term discounts, enrollment rebates, gift premiums, and prize promotions.[14] Let's look briefly at each in turn.

Sampling gives customers a chance to learn more about a service by trying it free of charge. For instance, a credit card company may offer cardholders a free one-month trial of a credit card protection service, public transport services offer free rides for a day or two on a newly opened route, and hotels give guests free 15-minute previews of newly released films that are available on its internal pay-TV system. Sampling, however, is used less frequently for services than for consumer package goods. Service marketers usually prefer to offer price discounts or other promotions rather than give away the service for free.

Coupons usually take one of three forms: a straight price cut, a discount or fee waiver for one or more patrons accompanying the original purchaser, or a free or discounted enhancement of the basic service (such as free waxing with each car washing). Coupons can be printed in newspapers and magazines; sent by direct mail; printed on the backs of ATM receipts; or sold in books that allow purchasers to save on a wide array of specific services, including restaurants, dry cleaners, car servicing, and movie theaters. With the advent of electronic scanning in shops, promotional coupons can be tied to customers' purchase patterns and implemented electronically. Another approach to couponing involves issue of airline miles in return for a purchase (see Figure 10.7).

Short-term discounts are price cuts that are promoted as being available for only a limited time period, such as any form of sale designed to boost business during slow periods. Health and fitness clubs often offer charter memberships that are sold at decreasing levels of discount prior to opening the club; such strategies help to build a base of customers quickly and improve initial cash flow.

FIGURE 10.7 Promoting Purchases with Airline Miles

Sign-up rebates may be offered by membership organizations that charge a sign-up fee for applying, joining, or making connections to a network. Examples include mortgage applications, private clubs, and pay-TV systems. To attract new members or subscribers, these fees may be waived or else credited toward payment of future usage fees.

Gift premiums can add a tangible element to services and provide a distinctive image for sponsoring firms. For instance, some international airlines have used a strategy of providing passengers in first and business classes with free gifts including toiletries, pens, stationery, and playing cards. Similarly, to encourage customers (who may hold several credit cards) to either increase their credit purchases or consolidate their charges to a single account, banks and credit card companies have experimented with promotions offering prizes to customers who charged more than specified amounts over a given period. Sometimes, however, gifts are offered simply to amuse customers and create a friendly environment. The Conrad Hotel in Hong Kong places a small teddy bear on each guest's bed and a yellow rubber duck in the bathroom; it reports that many guests take these items home with them.

Prize promotions introduce an element of chance, as in a lottery or sweepstakes. They can be used effectively to add involvement and excitement to the service experience and are generally designed to encourage increased use of the service. Fast-food restaurants, video rental outlets, and gas stations sometimes offer lottery-like promotions tied to special events giving all purchasers tickets with scratch-off award categories. And radio stations may offer listeners the chance to claim instant cash and other prizes if they call within a prescribed time after the announcement is broadcast.

Instructional Materials

Promotion and education often go hand in hand. There is little point in promoting a new service—or service feature—if people are unsure of the benefits or don't know how to proceed. Although service personnel are often called on to play teaching roles, they are not always available to help in the locations where customers need them. Traditional approaches use printed materials, ranging from brochures and instruction manuals to step-by-step instructions and diagrams affixed to self-service machines (have a look at a pay phone, ATM, or ticket machine the next time you use one). But in recent years, video and audio instructions have also come to the fore. The CVS pharmacy chain offers customers the chance to telephone for recorded information about prescription medication for a variety of different diseases; the numbers to call are publicized in newspaper advertising. Supermarkets and department stores sometimes feature a touch-screen store directory. Some banks have video terminals in the lobby where customers can learn about new financial products. Airlines play videos to illustrate aircraft safety procedures and make customers aware of government regulations. The latest instructional media take the form of CD-ROMs and Web sites, which often go into considerable detail. Free telephone calls to specialized information lines are another way in which organizations can help to educate their customers.

Corporate Design

Many companies have come to appreciate the importance of creating a unified and distinctive visual appearance for all tangible elements that contribute to the corporate image. Corporate design strategies are usually created by external consulting firms and include such features as stationery and promotional literature; retail signage; uniforms; and color schemes for painting vehicles, equipment, and building interiors. These elements are created by using distinctive colors, symbols, lettering, and layout to provide a unifying and recognizable theme linking all the firm's operations in a branded service experience.

Corporate design is particularly important for companies operating in competitive markets where the challenge is to stand out from the crowd and to be instantly recognizable in different locations. The highly competitive business of gasoline retailing provides striking contrasts in corporate designs, from the bright green and yellow service stations displaying the BP shield to Texaco's red and black; Exxon's (Esso's) red, white, and blue; and Sunoco's blue and yellow.

Many companies use a trademarked symbol, rather than a name, as their primary logo. Shell, for instance, makes a pun of its English name by displaying a yellow scallop shell on a red background, which has the advantage of making its vehicles and gas stations instantly recognizable even in parts of the world that don't use the roman alphabet. McDonald's golden arches are said to be the most widely recognized corporate symbol in the world. Early restaurant designs featured an enormous arch, but today local zoning laws often restrict how this symbol may be displayed on exterior signage and limit its size. Consistent corporate design for the McDonald's chain also extends to the style of lettering used, certain aspects of the interior store appearance, and the design and colors of employee uniforms. However, international companies operating in many countries need to select their designs carefully to avoid conveying a culturally inappropriate message through unfortunate choices of names, colors, or images.

How easy to recognize are the facilities, vehicles, and personnel of your own bank, favorite fast-food restaurant, taxi service, and local public transport system? Try the quiz in the boxed insert "Can You Recognize a Service Company from These Clues?" to see how many internationally used symbols and design elements you recognize.

Companies in the highly competitive express delivery industry tend to use their names as a central element in their corporate designs. When Federal Express changed its trading name to the snappier FedEx, it also changed its logo to feature the new name in a distinctive red and purple logo, typically displayed on a white background. Consistent applications of this design were developed for use in a wide variety of contexts, ranging from business cards to boxes and from employee caps to aircraft exteriors.

Servicescape Design

As noted in chapter 8, the term *servicescape* describes the design of any physical location where customers come to place orders and obtain service delivery.[15] It consists of four dimensions: the physical facility, the location, ambient conditions (such as temperature or lighting), and personnel. Each of these elements is critical because the appearance of a firm's service facilities and personnel affect both communication and image building. Corporate design consultants are sometimes asked to advise on servicescape design, to coordinate the visual elements of both interiors and exteriors—such as signage, decor, carpeting, furnishings, and uniforms—so that they may complement and reinforce the other design elements.

Consider what conclusions you might draw about a car rental firm's service if, on arriving to rent a car, you encountered a smart-looking building with attractive signage—but on entering, you noticed in the harsh neon light that the office was small and cramped; the paintwork, peeling and clashing in color with the faded carpet; the signage, hand lettered; the desk and furnishings, in contrasting styles; and the agent, wearing a smart uniform shirt tucked into dirty jeans? We can think of the servicescape concept in terms of the design of the stage on which the service drama is enacted. A good set and costumes can't save a bad play, but they can greatly enhance the audience's enjoyment of a good one. Conversely, a bad stage set can create a poor initial impression that is hard to overcome.

Can You Recognize a Service Company from These Clues?

1. With which three rental car companies are the colors yellow, red, and green associated?
2. Which international airline has a flying kangaroo for its symbol? And which, a maple leaf?
3. Which stockbroker displays a bull as its corporate symbol?
4. How many companies can you name that use a globelike symbol?
5. Which international bank displays a four-pointed star?

The answers can be found at the end of the chapter, before the Endnotes.

Integrated Communications for Services Marketing

In a service setting, marketing communications tools are especially important because they serve to create powerful images and a sense of credibility, confidence, and reassurance. Through the use of brand names, unified and recognizable corporate design elements, and well-executed servicescapes, companies can give visibility and personality to their intangible service offerings.

Each of the different communication elements described previously is a potentially powerful tool that can be used to create and promote a distinctive corporate, brand, or product identity; communicate with current and prospective customers; and sell specific products. Marketing communications, in one form or another, are essential to a company's success. Without effective communications, prospects may never learn of a service firm's existence, what it has to offer them, or how to use its products to best advantage. Customers might be more easily lured away by competitors and competitive offerings, and there would be no proactive management and control of the firm's identity.

A key task for service marketers is to select the most appropriate mix of communication elements to convey the desired messages efficiently and effectively to the target audience. In well-planned campaigns, several different communication elements may be used in ways that mutually reinforce each other. Sequencing of different communications activities is often important because one element may pave the way for others. For example, advertising may encourage prospects to request further information by mail or draw them to a retail site where they may then be exposed to retail displays or interact directly with a salesperson.

Implications of the Internet for Marketing Communication

Changes are in store for marketing communication strategy as the Internet becomes an increasingly important channel for marketers. Users of personal computers around the world are spending more time online and less time watching television or reading printed material. Subscriptions and usage are increasing rapidly.

Marketers have grasped the importance of this development and are rushing to establish a presence on the Web, creating new and more sophisticated Web sites, advertising, and sending both customized and mass mailings via e-mail. Advertising expenditures on the Internet are expected to grow rapidly, with English-speaking countries leading the way. In many instances, one company's Web site may include advertising messages from other marketers with related but noncompeting services—take a look, for instance, at Yahoo!'s stock quotes page, which features a sequence of advertisements for a variety of financial service firms. Similarly, many Internet pages dealing with specific topics feature a small message from Amazon.com that invites consumers to see what books are available on that very topic by clicking the accompanying hyperlink button to visit the book retailer's site.

Growth Predictions for Online Advertising

Forrester Research predicts that spending for Internet advertising worldwide will reach $33 billion by 2004.[16] The firm forecasts that U.S. expenditures will account for two-thirds of this total, rising from $2.8 billion in 1999 to $22 billion in 2004, at which point it will amount to 8.1 percent of expenditures for traditional advertising—exceeding magazine, yellow pages, and radio spending. This amounts to a compound annual growth rate of 51 percent, roughly paralleling the predicted growth in online retail sales. Forrester anticipates that newspapers and direct mail may lose as much as 18 percent of their advertising revenues to the Web.

Outside the United States, Forrester projects an increase in online spending from $502 million in 1999 to $10.8 billion in 2004, with Europe accounting for about half this amount. Web advertising is also expected to accelerate in Latin America, reaching a projected $1.6 billion by 2004.

Measuring Advertising Effectiveness on the Internet. Among the factors stimulating the growth of Internet advertising is the precision with which this new technology can measure advertising effectiveness. Marketers have long worried about whether the money spent on different forms of mass communication is a good investment in terms of its impact on sales. Both P. T. Barnum, the circus entrepreneur, and Lord Cole, the founder of Unilever, have been credited with the observation, "I know that half the money I spend on advertising is wasted; unfortunately, I don't know which half!" Many traditional measures of effectiveness are based on changes in awareness, preferences, intentions, and reported media exposure and buying behavior among consumers; others compare actual sales data before, during, and after a campaign. Direct-response advertising is easier to measure; for instance, firms can look at the sales generated by responses to direct mail or telephone solicitation. But the Web-based measures are more sophisticated.

On the Internet, advertisers can not only measure the number of people who are exposed to an ad (by clicking onto the page on which it appears) but can also track how many of them click through an ad to get more information from the advertiser's own Web site. So advertising pricing can be linked directly to the number of prospective customers delivered to the Web site. The next step has involved development of techniques that measure the transition from click-throughs to purchases through the Web site in question.

New market analysis techniques—developed in Silicon Valley rather than in traditional North American advertising centers such as New York, Chicago, Los Angeles, or Toronto—can identify which customers actually made purchases, how much they bought, and what the margins were on each sale.[17] However, there is growing concern that Internet marketers may be going too far in snooping on customers.[18] More firms are using software cookies to track individual's visits to different Web sites, monitor how long they stay there, and report back the information. Because this activity usually takes place without customers' knowledge, it raises significant ethical issues.

Internet Applications. Marketers are using the Internet for a variety of communications tasks, including promoting consumer awareness and interest, providing information and consultation, facilitating two-way communications with customers through e-mail, stimulating product trial (samples of information-based services can be downloaded immediately), and enabling customers to place orders. Many companies have found that the interactive nature of the Internet increases customer involvement dramatically because it is actually a form of self-service marketing where customers are in complete control of the time and extent of contact with the Web sites they visit. This feature makes the Web particularly useful for self-paced learning in instances where a Web site features educational content. For these reasons, the Internet is fast becoming almost as common in business-to-business marketing as business cards and fax machines. Marketing through the Web allows companies to supplement conventional communications channels at a reasonable cost. But like any of the elements of the marketing communications mix, Internet advertising should be part of an integrated, well-designed communications strategy.

The ability to communicate and establish a rapport with individual customers is one of the Web's greatest strengths. These characteristics lend themselves to a new approach to marketing that Godin and Peppers have christened "permission marketing."[19] Traditional advertising, they argue, doesn't work as well as it used to. Its biggest problem is that it fights for attention by interrupting people—a 30-second spot interrupts a viewer's favorite television program, a telemarketing call interrupts a family dinner, or a print ad interrupts the flow of a magazine or newspaper article. Godin and Peppers argue that the new model is built around permission. The challenge for marketers is to persuade consumers to volunteer attention, to "raise their hands" and agree to learn more about a company and its products because they anticipate receiving or learning something useful. In other words, customers self-select into the target segment. For an illustration of how a promotional contest was employed to get customers to volunteer their attention to learn about a new tax preparation service, see Service Perspectives 10.1.

Recommendations for Web Site Design and Application

A Web site should contain information that people in a company's target market will find useful and interesting. It should also stimulate product purchase and encourage repeat visits. Early Web sites were often little more than electronic versions of corporate brochures, featuring attractive graphics that took a long time to download. Although Internet users rank content as the most important factor affecting their decision to return to a Web site (they are actually annoyed by sites—and companies—who waste their time with what they perceive to be frivolous content), they also wanted the experience to be enjoyable (either because they found the information they wanted or because the site was unique or entertaining).[20]

Transport firms, from airlines to railroads, offer interactive sites that enable travelers to evaluate alternative routes and schedules for specific dates, download printed information, and make reservations online. Some sites offer discounts on hotels and airfare if reservations are made over the Internet—a tactic designed to draw customers away from intermediaries such as

SERVICE PERSPECTIVES 10.1

Permission Marketing at H&R Block

One of the ways of attracting the attention of customers in a particular target segment is to offer people the chance to win a prize that is relevant to the service in question. When H&R Block wanted to introduce a new service called Premium Tax aimed at upper-income customers, it retained Seth Godin's firm, Yoyodyne, to create a contest. In due course, banners appeared on selected Web sites that said, "H&R Block: We'll pay your taxes sweepstakes." More than fifty thousand people clicked on those banners; they were individuals who paid taxes and probably recognized the company. In effect, they volunteered their e-mail addresses and said, "Tell me more about this promotion."

In return for the chance to have somebody else pay their taxes, these people then became players in a contest. Every week for 10 weeks, they received three e-mails, inviting them to answer trivia questions about taxes, H&R Block, and other relevant topics. They were given fun facts about the history of taxes or were sent to H&R Block's Web site to find answers to questions. Each e-mail also included a promotional message about Premium Tax. Not everybody responded to every message—on average about 40 percent did so—but over the life of the promotion, 97 percent of the people who entered the game stayed in it.

A survey was conducted at the end of the 10 weeks, focusing on three groups of respondents: those who had participated actively in the game; those who had participated, but less actively; and a control group of nonparticipants. Among nonparticipants, knowledge of Premium Tax was essentially nonexistent. Among less active participants, 34 percent had a good understanding of Premium Tax, and for active participants, the figure was 54 percent.

Source: William C. Taylor, "Permission Marketing" (interview with Seth Godin), *Fast Company,* April–May 1998, 198–212.

travel agents. Many banks now have interactive sites that allow customers to pay bills electroni-cally, apply for loans, and check their account balances. And a Web-based business called Home Debut, designed to help house buyers look for a new home online, also provides information about specific neighborhoods and links to school districts, day care, restaurants, and health care providers. Whistler/Blackholm ski resort in British Columbia uses its Web site to promote advance online purchase of lift tickets at a discount. It then provides instructions on how the online ticket window works and where to pick up the tickets, plus responses to frequently asked questions.

Perhaps the most remarkable aspect of the Internet is its ubiquity: A Web site hosted in one country can be accessed from almost anywhere in the world. Electronic marketing is the sim-plest form of international market entry available—in fact, as Christian Grönroos points out, "The firm cannot avoid creating interest in its offerings outside its local or national market."[21] However, creating international access and developing an international strategy are two very different things. We return to this issue in chapter 17.

The Need for Updating. A Web site is a very dynamic medium, and visitors expect it to be updated regularly or they soon lose interest in returning. As a communication medium the Web has become a useful additional channel for distribution of PR releases. Many corporate Web sites maintain a file of recent PR releases going back for a year or more. Unlike pamphlets and brochures, which may only be redesigned once a year, a Web presence must be constantly main-tained and upgraded, even if that just means changing the appearance of the site cosmetically by using a different layout or new illustrations. Savvy companies constantly add new content, attractive graphics and photographs, and more advanced interactive capabilities to increase the appeal of their sites to both first-time and repeat visitors. Two areas of emphasis in addition to content are ease of navigation (finding the information desired) and speed of downloading desired pages. For this reason, it's unwise to include slow-loading graphics on the most fre-quently visited pages. Many firms include an e-mail connection to the webmaster, requesting feedback from visitors and their suggestions for improvement.

Web marketers need to remember that it's very easy for customers to compare competitors' offerings on the Internet—that information is literally at their fingertips with the click of a mouse! For example, customers who are shopping for a specific product online can browse the Web sites of competing retailers in a matter of minutes before making a decision about where to shop. As Internet technology evolves, Web sites are becoming increasingly sophisticated. The combination of growing computer power and increasing bandwidth means that downloading is becoming faster and that Web designers can add more sophisticated video animation and even audio tracks to their site content.

Attracting New Visitors. Another challenge facing Internet marketers is that of attracting visitors to their sites, especially those that fit the firm's target market segments. It helps to have a memorable Web address. Perhaps the best are simple ones that relate to the firm's name or busi-ness. Unlike phone or fax numbers, it's often possible to guess a firm's Web address. Un-fortunately for firms that come late to the Internet, they often find that their preferred name has already been taken. For instance, many industries include a company called Delta, but there can only be one www.delta.com (it's Delta Financial Corporation; the airline had to use the longer address, www.deltaairlines.com).

Web addresses should be actively promoted if they are to play an integral role in the firm's overall communication and service delivery strategy. They should be displayed on all corporate communications as well as on business cards, letterhead stationery, catalogs, listings in yellow pages, and promotional items. Advertising banners and buttons on portals (such as Yahoo! or Netscape) or other organizations' Web sites are often used to draw traffic but are not necessarily the most focused or effective tool. Some firms use a direct-mail approach by sending out postcards announcing their Web addresses and offering an incentive for customers to visit the site. Alternatively, they purchase carefully targeted lists of postal or e-mail addresses to reach prospects from desired segments. Other approaches include featuring a Web site prominently in media advertising and PR releases.

An indirect method of attracting prospective customers with an interest in the firm's services is to include in the Web site useful educational information about a topic related to the firm's business. Such topic-specific pages may then get picked up by one or more of the robotic search engines that continually scan the Web for new content on almost every topic. The desired end result is that people who are using a browser to turn up information on a particular topic will find a reference to the firm's helpful information in the course of their search and promptly click to its site. For instance, a search for information on specific legal issues may lead someone to the Web site of a law firm that focuses on this area. Similarly, information on treatment for different medical conditions may be featured on Web sites of such organizations as specialist clinics, drug companies, marketers of herbal remedies, or manufacturers of other health-related products.

Conclusion

The distinctive characteristics of services suggest that the marketing communications strategy for services needs a different emphasis from that used to market goods. Emphasizing tangible clues for services that are hard to grasp, clarifying the nature and sequence of the service performance, highlighting the performance of customer-contact personnel, and educating the customer how to participate in service delivery and conduct self-service are among the tasks facing service marketers.

Many different communication elements are available to marketers as they seek to create a distinctive position in the market for both their firm and its products and to reach prospective customers. Communication tasks include dissemination of information, educating current or prospective customers, persuasion, and reminders. The options in the marketing communication mix include paid advertising, personal selling and customer service, sales promotions, public relations, corporate design, and the evidence offered by the servicescape of the service delivery site. Within advertising, a host of different media compete for promotional expenditures. Informational materials, from brochures to Web sites, often play an important role in educating customers how to make good choices and obtain the best use from the services they have purchased. Salespeople and customer service representatives may also play an educational role. Developments in information technology, especially the Internet, are changing the face of marketing communications. We return to the strategic implications of technology for service marketers in chapter 18.

Answers to Symbol Quiz on Page 306

1. Hertz (yellow), Avis (red), National (green).
2. Qantas (kangaroo), Air Canada (maple leaf). Note: some regional Canadian airlines also display a maple leaf.
3. Merrill Lynch (bull).
4. AT&T and Cable & Wireless are both quite well known; aircraft of Continental Airlines have a partial golden globe on their tailfins, whereas those of PanAm featured a complete blue and white globe. (There are others; UPS now paints a golden globe on all its trucks to emphasize its worldwide delivery capabilities.)
5. Citibank (also its parent, Citicorp).

REVIEW QUESTIONS

1. What roles do personal selling, advertising, and public relations play in (a) attracting new customers to a service business and (b) retaining existing customers?
2. Contrast the relative effectiveness of brochures and Web sites for promoting (a) a ski resort, (b) a hotel, (c) the services of a consulting firm, and (d) a full-service stockbroker.
3. In what ways do the physical aspects of a servicescape communicate?
4. Consider each of the following scenarios and then determine which elements of the marketing communications mix you would employ and for what purposes. State your reasons.
   ● A newly established hairdresser's in a suburban shopping center
   ● An established restaurant facing declining patronage due to the arrival of new competitors
   ● A large, single-office accounting firm doing business in a major city and serving primarily business clients.
5. For which categories of services are customers at greatest risk when a firm makes advertising claims that it knows to be fraudulent? And what types of customers are most likely to be hurt?
6. What are some common educational and promotional objectives in service settings? Provide a specific example for each of the objectives you list.

APPLICATION EXERCISES

1. Describe the role of personal selling in service communications. Give examples of three different situations in which you have encountered this approach.
2. Provide several current examples of public relations efforts made by local service companies.
3. Find examples of service promotional efforts in your local area and then evaluate their strengths and weaknesses as effective communication tools.
4. Locate the Web sites for three airlines, three banks, and three Internet retailers. Critique them for ease of navigation, content, and visual design. What, if anything, would you change about each site?

ENDNOTES

1. Louis Fabien, "Making Promises: The Power of Engagement," *Journal of Services Marketing* 11, no. 3 (1997): 206–214.
2. For a useful review of research on this topic, see Kathleen Mortimer and Brian P. Mathews, "The Advertising of Services: Consumer Views v. Normative Dimensions," *The Service Industries Journal* 18 (July 1998): 14–19.
3. William R. George and Leonard L. Berry, "Guidelines for the Advertising of Services," *Business Horizons*, July–August 1981, 52–56.
4. Donna Legg and Julie Baker, "Advertising Strategies for Service Firms," in *Add Value to Your Service*, ed. C. Surprenant (Chicago: American Marketing Association, 1987), 163–168.
5. Banwari Mittal, "The Advertising of Services: Meeting the Challenge of Intangibility," *Journal of Service Research* 2 (August 1999): 98–116.
6. Legg and Baker, "Advertising Strategies for Service Firms"; D. J. Hill and N. Gandhi, "Services Advertising: A Framework for Effectiveness," *Journal of Services Marketing* 3 (fall 1992): 63–76.
7. K. M. Haywood, "Managing Word of Mouth Communications," *Journal of Services Marketing* 3 (spring 1989): 55–67.
8. David H. Maister, "Why Cross Selling Hasn't Worked," in *True Professionalism* (New York: The Free Press, 1997), 178–184.

9. Eugene W. Anderson, "Customer Satisfaction and Word of Mouth," *Journal of Service Research* 1 (August 1998): 5–17; Magnus Söderlund, "Customer Satisfaction and Its Consequences on Customer Behaviour Revisited: The Impact of Different Levels of Satisfaction on Word of Mouth, Feedback to the Supplier, and Loyalty," *International Journal of Service Industry Management* 9, no. 2 (1998): 169–188.

10. Kieran Cooke, "Giant Billboards in the Skies," *Financial Times,* March 16, 1998, p. 14.

11. Stephen J. Grove, Gregory M. Pickett, and David N. Laband, "An Empirical Examination of Factual Information Content among Service Advertisements," *The Service Industries Journal* 15 (April 1995): 216–233.

12. Ken Peattie and Sue Peattie, "Sales Promotion—A Missed Opportunity for Service Marketers," *International Journal of Service Industry Management* 5, no. 1 (1995): 6–21.

13. Paul W. Farris and John A. Quelch, "In Defense of Price Promotion," *Sloan Management Review* (fall 1987): 63–69.

14. Christopher H. Lovelock and John A. Quelch, "Consumer Promotions in Services Marketing," *Business Horizons,* May–June 1983.

15. Mary Jo Bitner, "Servicescapes: The Impact of Physical Surroundings on Customers and Employees," *Journal of Marketing* 56 (April 1992): 57–71.

16. Forrester Research, *Internet Advertising Skyrockets,* press release at www.forrester.com, August 1999.

17. J. William Gurley, "How the Web Will Warp Advertising," *Fortune,* November 9, 1998, 119–120.

18. Stephen W. Wildstrom, "On the Web, It's 1984," *Business Week,* January 10, 2000, 28.

19. Seth Godin and Don Peppers, *Permission Marketing: Turning Strangers into Friends and Friends into Customers* (New York, Simon & Schuster, 1999).

20. Marshall Rice, "What Makes Users Revisit a Web Site?" *Marketing News,* March 17, 1997, 12.

21. Christian Grönroos, "Internationalization Strategies for Services," *The Journal of Services Marketing* 13, no. 4/5 (1999): 295.

Service Positioning Through Structural Change

G. Lynn Shostack

The basis of any service positioning strategy is the service itself, but marketing offers little guidance on how to craft service processes for positioning purposes. A new approach suggests that within service systems, structural process design can be used to "engineer" services on a more scientific, rational basis.

When a firm or provider establishes and maintains a distinctive place for itself and its offerings in the market, it is said to be successfully positioned. In the increasingly competitive service sector, effective positioning is one of marketing's most critical tasks.

For some marketers (e.g. Ries and Trout, 1981), positioning is strictly a communications issue. The product or service is a given and the objective is to manipulate consumer perceptions of reality. As Lovelock (1984) rightly points out, however, positioning is more than just advertising and promotion. Market position can be affected by pricing, distribution and, of course, the product itself, which is the core around which all positioning strategies revolve.

Apart from promotion, pricing, and distribution, the product is indeed a critical, manageable factor in positioning. Products often are engineered explicitly to reach certain markets, as the original Mustang was designed to reach the youth market and light beer was created to tap the calorie-conscious consumer. Sometimes products are invented first and positioned afterward. The Xerox copies and the Polaroid camera are examples of products that were first created, then positioned to various markets. Finally, an existing product may be changed in order to change its market position, as the Jeep was altered physically from a military vehicle to a vehicle for the family market.

Services are not things, however. McLuhan (1964) perhaps put it best and most succinctly more than 20 years ago when he declared that the *process* is the product. We say "airline" when we mean "air transportation." We say "movie," but mean "entertainment services." We say "hotel" when we mean "lodging rental." The use of nouns obscures the fundamental nature of services, which are processes, not objects.

As processes, services have many intriguing characteristics. Judd (1964), Rathmell (1974), Shostack (1977), Bateson (1977), and Sasser, Olsen, and Wyckoff (1978) were among the first to ponder the implications of service intangibility, service perishability, production/consumption simultaneity, and consumer participation in service processes. They found that traditional marketing, with its goods-bound approaches, was not helpful in process design, process modification, or process control.

If processes are the service equivalent of a product's "raw materials," can processes be designed, managed, and changed for positioning purposes the way physical good are? The purpose of this article is to take a closer look at processes as structural elements and suggest some ways in which they can be "engineered" for strategic service positioning purposes.

Process Characteristics

Processes have been studied for some time in disciplines other than marketing. Systematic, quantified methods for describing processes have been developed in industrial engineering (Deming, 1982), computer programming (Fox, 1982), decision theory (Holloway, 1979), and operations management (Schroeder, 1981), to name a few examples and well-known authors in each field. Though their

Reprinted with permission from *Journal of Marketing*, Vol. 51 (January 1987), 34–43, published by the American Marketing Association, Chicago, IL 60606.

techniques and nomenclatures may differ, process oriented disciplines share certain basic concepts. First, each of them provides a way of breaking any process down into logical steps and sequences to facilitate its control and analysis. Second, each includes ways to accommodate more variable processes in which outcomes may differ because of the effects of judgment, chance, or choice on a sequence. Finally, each system includes the concept of deviation or tolerance standards in recognition that processes are "real-time" phenomena that do not conform perfectly to any model or description, but rather function within a band or "norm" of some sort.

Little process description can be found in marketing literature. However, several writers on services have drawn upon manufacturing sources in using the words "standardized" and "customized" to define the poles of process continuum (see Levitt, 1976; Lovelock, 1984). "Standardized" usually implies a nonvarying sequential process, similar to the mass production of goods, in which each step is laid out in order and all outcomes are uniform. "Customized" usually refers to some level of adaptation or tailoring of the process to the individual consumer. The concept of deviation usually is treated as a quality issue, in reference to services that do not perform as they should.

Complexity and Divergence

Extracting from various approaches, we can suggest two ways to describe processes. One way is according to the steps and sequences that constitute the process; the other is according to the executional latitude or variability of those steps and sequences. Let us call the first factor the complexity of the process and the second its divergence. Deviation, a real-time operating factor, can then be thought of as an inadvertent departure from whatever process model and standards have been established for the first two factors.

We can define a service's complexity by analyzing the number and intricacy of the steps required to perform it. Accounting, for example, is more complex than bookkeeping because accounting is a more elaborated process, involving more functions and more steps. Architecture is more complex than plumbing. Plumbing is more complex than lawn mowing.

Apart from complexity, however, some processes include a high level of executional latitude and others do not. The degree of freedom allowed or inherent in a process step or sequence can be thought of as its divergence. A highly divergent service thus would be one in which virtually every performance of the process is unique. A service of low divergence would be one that is largely standardized.

Every service can be analyzed according to its overall complexity and divergence. A physician's services, for example, are highly complex. They are also highly divergent. As the service is being performed, a doctor constantly alters and shapes it by assimilating new data, weighing probabilities, reaching conclusions, and then taking action. Every case may be handled differently, yet all performances may be satisfactory from the consumer point of view. Architecture, law, consulting, and most other "professional" services have similarly high divergence (as well as high complexity), because they involve a considerable amount of judgment, discretion, and situational adaptation.

However, a process can be high in complexity and low in divergence. Hotel services, for example, are a complex aggregation of processes, but hotels standardize these processes through documentation and establishment of executional rules for every sequence from room cleaning to checkout. Telephone services are also highly complex, yet telephone companies have standardized and automated them to ensure uniformity and achieve economies of scale.

Services also can be low in complexity but high in divergence. In process terms, a singer renders the service of entertainment in one step: singing. This service is infinitely divergent, however, because each execution is unique and unlike that of any other provider. A painter "merely" paints, a teacher simply "transmits knowledge," a minister "spreads the gospel." These services do not consist of orderly, mechanical procedures, but of unique performances. Services that involve interpretational skills, artistic crafting, or highly individualized execution often appear simple in process terms, yet are highly divergent in operation. In fact, for such services, defining "what" is done in process terms is often easier than describing "how" it is done.

Blueprinting Complexity and Divergence in Service Systems

Though processes can be reduced to steps and sequences, services must be viewed as interdependent, interactive systems, not as disconnected pieces and parts. One approach for visualizing service systems is a mapping technique called "blueprinting" (Shostack, 1984a, 1984b). Blueprinting is a holistic method of seeing in snapshot form what is essentially a dynamic, living phenomenon.

For process design purposes, a blueprint should document all process steps and points of divergence in a specific service. This documentation must be carried to whatever level of detail is needed to distinguish between any two competing services. In other words, specific blueprints of real services are more productive than generic or generalized visualizations in working out position strategies based on process.

Figure 1 shows how one Park Avenue florist's service appears in blueprint form. The "fan" is borrowed from decision theory (see Holloway, 1979) in which a fan attached to a circle is used to show a range of potential events that may occur, whereas a fan attached to a square denotes a range of potential actions that may be taken. This is a useful symbol for divergence and is used throughout the following illustrations. The florist provides a service of low complexity that is highly divergent. Though the process steps are few, the fans indicate broad executional latitude stemming from the judgment and decisions of the individual performing the service.

For comparison, Figure 2 illustrates a complex but standardized service—consumer installment lending at a large commercial bank. Here, the process has many more specific steps, but the steps are executed in a strict and unvarying manner. As Levitt would say, the service has been "industrial-ized" (1976). There is one and only one permissible manner and order in which the service is provided. Parts of the process have been automated for further conformity, and the bank's design for this service does not allow employees who are part of the service system to modify or change the service in any way. Such a service may not function perfectly at all times. However, as noted before, such quality failures represent deviation from a design standard, whereas true divergence is an integral part of the process.

Figure 3 shows yet another structure—the highly complex and highly divergent service of a general medical practitioner. Here, not only is the process complex, but virtually every step involves variable execution.

Blueprints as a Tool in Consumer Research

It may be noted that this analytical approach is a useful and natural companion to market research. Lovelock (1984) noted the difficulty of researching service "attributes" for positioning purposes, which is caused at least partly by the inherent ambiguity and subjectivity of verbal descriptions. Blueprints provide visible portraits to which consumers can react, and which can facilitate exploration of more parts of the service system than just its processes. Blueprints can be used to educate consumers, focus

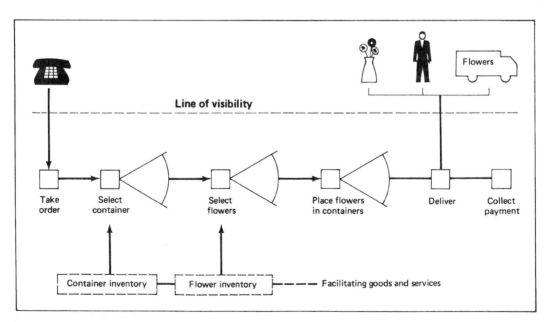

FIGURE 1 Park Avenue Florist

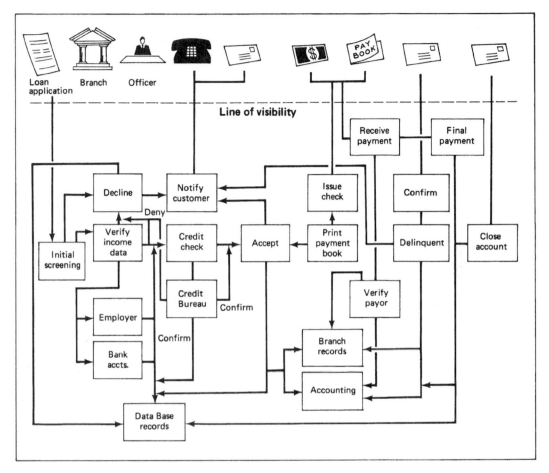

FIGURE 2 Installment Lending: Bank X

their evaluative input on various aspects of the service system, elicit comparative or competitive assessments, and generate specific responses to contemplated changes or new service concepts. As Schneider and Bowen (1984) pointed out, regardless of whether consumers are privy to or even aware of all parts of the process, their awareness of its results and evidence makes them potentially valuable participates in the design of the entire system, not just those parts they see.

Changing the Process

Complexity and divergence are not fixed and immutable. They are factors that can be changed. Once a service has been documented accurately, it can be analyzed for opportunities either to increase or decrease one or both variables.

Alternative Directions for Structural Change

A change in overall complexity or divergence generally indicates one of four overall strategic directions. Each one has management consequences as well as certain market risks.

Reduced divergence. Reducing divergence leads to uniformity which tends to reduce costs, improve productivity, and make distribution easier. It usually indicates a shift to a volume-oriented positioning strategy based on economies of scale. The positive market effects of such a move can include perceived increases in reliability—more uniform service quality and greater service availability. However, reducing divergence also can have negative market effects. It dictates conformity as well as inflexibility in operating procedures. Customers may perceive

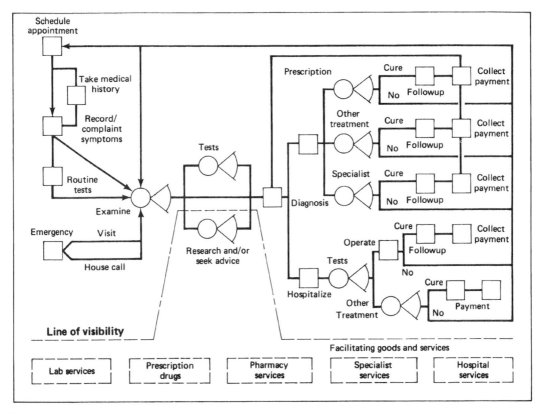

FIGURE 3 General Practitioner Services

the shift as one that lowers customization and limits their options, and may reject a highly standardized service even if it costs less.

Increased divergence. Raising divergence is the service equivalent of creating a "job shop." Greater customization and flexibility tend to command higher prices. Increased divergence usually indicates a niche positioning strategy, dependent less on volume and more on margins. The market can respond positively to such a shift if the service taps a desire for prestige, customization, or personalization. Here, too, however, care is needed in making such a shift. A divergent service is more difficult to manage, control, and distribute. Moreover, customers may not be willing to pay the price that customization demands.

Reduced complexity. Reduced complexity usually indicates a specialization strategy. As steps or functions are dropped from the system, resources can

be focused on a narrower service offering (radiology, for example, versus general medical services). Narrowing the service offering usually makes distribution and control easier. Such a service can be perceived positively by the market if the provider stands out as an expert. However, reduced complexity also can cause a service to be perceived as "stripped down" or so limited that its specialized quality is not enough to overcome the inconvenience or price of obtaining it. Reducing complexity can be competitively risky if other providers continue to offer a broader, more extensive full-service alternative.

Increased complexity. Higher complexity usually indicates a strategy to gain greater penetration in a market by adding more services or enhancing current ones. Supermarkets, banks, and retailers have expanded their service lines with this strategic goal in mind. Increasing complexity can increase efficiency by maximizing the revenue generated from each customer. In contrast, too much complexity can be confusing to customers and can cause overall service quality to fall. Thus, a highly complex service system may be vulnerable to inroads by competitors who specialize.

Marketing Strategy and Structural Change

Service industries offer numerous examples of changes in complexity and divergence and how they affect market position. Barbering, for example, is a relatively simple service, but beginning in the 1970s some providers began to reposition it. They added processes borrowed from women's beauty salons, such as tinting, body perms, and backcombing, redefined their mission, and transformed "hair cutting" into "hair styling"—a more complex, divergent service structure. Hair styling tapped or created a new market segment of men willing to pay substantially higher prices for a more elaborated process and carved a niche in the market through structural differentiation.

In retailing, there are many examples of adding to the complexity of service systems. Supermarkets began as specialty food stores and have added banking services, pharmacist services, flowers, books and magazines, and even food preparation to their basic food retailing structure. In the fast-food industry, what were once simple hamburger outlets have become providers of breakfast, dining room services, and even entertainment. Retailing also affords many examples of reducing complexity, as evidenced by the emergence of businesses specializing only in pasta, only in cookies, and only in ice cream.

For examples of lowered divergence, we need only to look at professional services. Legal services, for instance, have historically had both high complexity and high divergence. A consumer needing legal assistance first had to seek out and select an attorney, and was then dependent upon the variable performance of that individual. Over the past few years, however, this service has been repositioned through the actions of business-minded entrepreneurs who perceived a market need for less complex, less divergent alternatives. The result has been the creation of legal "clinics" and chains that offer a limited menu of services executed uniformly at published rates. This repositioning not only has opened a new market for legal services, but also has had and will continue to have a profound effect on the positioning strategies of traditional law firms.

A similar downshifting and repositioning of traditional personal accountant services was effected by the innovations of H&R Block, which tapped a vast market of consumers who did not require the variable and costly services of a personal accountant, but who were willing to pay someone else to prepare their tax returns.

Most of these examples are based on entrepreneurial response to the perception of an unmet market need. What is perhaps less clearly recognized is that such changes need not be intuitive or accidental. They can be made deliberately to support explicit positioning or competitive strategies.

Implications of Service System Changes

Let us assume that Figure 1 is an accurate representation of a specific florist's service. Assume further that in an analysis of competitors, very similar structures were found. One strategic option to reposition and differentiate the service would be to reengineer it as a less divergent system. Figure 4 illustrates a redesigned blueprint that accomplishes this objective. The number of container choices has been limited to two; there are only two groups of flowers and only two choices of arrangements for each group. Thus, only eight combinations are possible.

Obviously, the new design has implications for inventory management as well as productivity. Inventory can be ordered in larger, more economic quantities. More arrangements can be produced by the florist because the process is more standardized. These two effects will lower prices and potentially allow the service to be repositioned to a broader market. The new structure also will allow wider service distribution, because simpler blueprints are easier to replicate. FTD (Florists' Transworld Delivery) arrived at a similar conclusion and expanded florist services from a local craft into a national service industry.

However, if all the florists in a particular market had structures similar to Figure 4, a logical positioning strategy might be to move toward the design shown in Figure 1—a highly artistic, high-priced structure. Alternatively, a marketer might choose to increase complexity alone, through retailing a selection of plants and supplies, or to increase both complexity and divergence by offering flower arranging classes.

Identifying and Evaluating Strategic Choices

Services can be structurally evaluated on a stand-alone basis and also as members of service families. Within a service family, a marketer can consider positioning strategies based on structural comple-

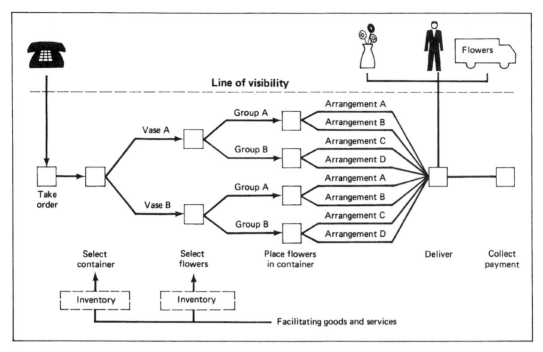

FIGURE 4 Florist Services: Alternative Design

mentarity, structural diversity, and overall developmental direction.

In Figure 2, a bank's consumer installment lending service is diagrammed. This service, of course, is only one of a constellation of services that constitute consumer banking. Though consumer banking, in its totality, is an extraordinarily complex service system, most blueprints of its component services would show low divergence stemming from 20 years of effort to standardize and automate the service system.

One strategy for a bank with this structure is to continue increasing complexity by adding more subservices while continuing to minimize divergence through standardization and automation. For a competitor, an equally valid strategy would be to adopt the counterposition, which would call for increasing the customization of services. The latter strategy is evident in banks offering "private" banking, an integrated package of services for the upscale market that includes such divergent services as customized lending, portfolio management, and financial planning.

The general practitioner previously described also has numerous strategic choices. Figure 5 illustrates the relative structural positions held by a number of medical service providers, including the general practitioner analyzed in Figure 3. From the present position, he or she can move in any direction on the scale by adding or deleting service functions to create a new family. Depending on the complexity and divergence of these functions, the overall service system's complexity and divergence will change, thus altering its relative position.

For example (Figure 6), retailing orthopedic supplies would add complexity to the doctor's overall service system, but little divergence. Adding counseling, in contrast, would add considerable divergence, but little operational complexity. Conversely, if minor surgical procedures that have been performed in the office were eliminated, the service system would be reduced in both complexity and divergence and move closer to the position held by diagnosticians, who perform no treatment themselves. At the extreme position, complexity and divergence could be lowered to the point where only the simple service, such as X-rays, is provided in a completely standardized way. Consumer research can be instrumental in facilitating this strategic process, and blueprints are a useful tool for focusing consumer input and response to new structural concepts.

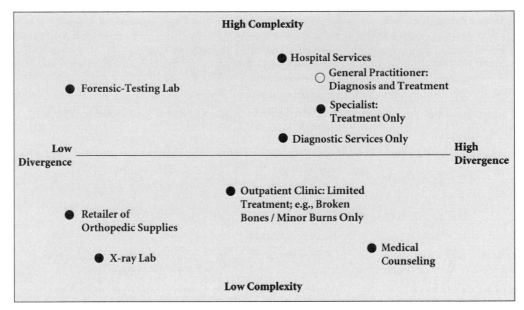

FIGURE 5 Relative Positions Based on Structural Analysis

In simplified terms, Figure 7 shows some changes that a midpriced family restaurant might consider to alter complexity and divergence for competitive purposes. Any prospective change or mix of changes can be compared with competitors' offerings to determine which mix is most likely to provide the maximum competitive differentiation.

Positioning charts are a useful tool for market analysts wishing to compare the perceived performance of competing services on two or three attributes simultaneously. Examples of such charts (also known as perceptual maps) are given by Tybout and Hauser (1981) and Lovelock (1984). Blueprinting works well in tandem with this technique by serving as a focal point for determining which parts of the service system or process components are important to the market, and in evaluating change across many elements of the system.

Implementing Change

Though processes are intangible, the means by which services are rendered are very real. There are only two, people (both providers and consumers) and facilitating goods. Any shift in overall complexity or divergence, or the introduction of any new process design, must be implemented with a clear understanding of the potential impact of these "producers" of the process.

Role of Service Employees and Customers

Considerable attention has been paid to people in the service system. Whether they are providers or consumers, the management and control of human behavior is a critical factor in process design, change, and operating quality. Mills (1985) suggests that management controls over service

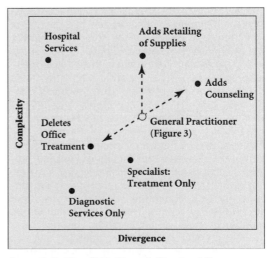

FIGURE 6 Position Shifts Through Structural Change

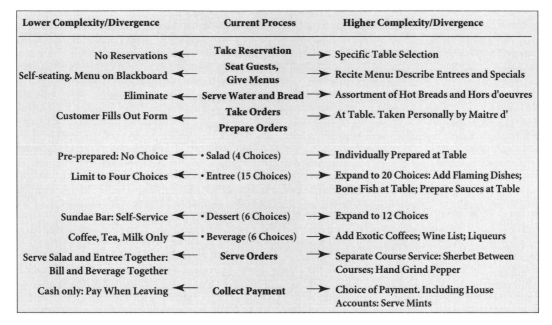

Lower Complexity/Divergence	Current Process	Higher Complexity/Divergence
No Reservations ←	**Take Reservation**	→ Specific Table Selection
Self-seating. Menu on Blackboard ←	**Seat Guests, Give Menus**	→ Recite Menu: Describe Entrees and Specials
Eliminate ←	**Serve Water and Bread**	→ Assortment of Hot Breads and Hors d'oeuvres
Customer Fills Out Form ←	**Take Orders**	→ At Table. Taken Personally by Maitre d'
	Prepare Orders	
Pre-prepared: No Choice ←	• Salad (4 Choices)	→ Individually Prepared at Table
Limit to Four Choices ←	• Entree (15 Choices)	→ Expand to 20 Choices: Add Flaming Dishes; Bone Fish at Table; Prepare Sauces at Table
Sundae Bar: Self-Service ←	• Dessert (6 Choices)	→ Expand to 12 Choices
Coffee, Tea, Milk Only ←	• Beverage (6 Choices)	→ Add Exotic Coffees; Wine List; Liqueurs
Serve Salad and Entree Together: Bill and Beverage Together ←	**Serve Orders**	→ Separate Course Service: Sherbet Between Courses; Hand Grind Pepper
Cash only: Pay When Leaving ←	**Collect Payment**	→ Choice of Payment. Including House Accounts: Serve Mints

FIGURE 7 Structural Alternatives

employees should depend on the structure of the service system. For low-contact, standardized services, behavior can be controlled through mechanistic means, such as rules and regulations. However, for high-contact, divergent services, Mills suggests that employee self-management and peer-reference techniques are more effective. Smith and Houston (1983), in contrast, propose that a script-based approach to managing customer and employee behavior can help to control expectations as well as process compliance. Bowen and Schneider (1985) speak of "boundary spanners," that is, employees with high customer interaction, as a valuable source of design information and as change agents whose acceptance and commitment are critical to success in altering any process. Schneider and Bowen (1984) as well as others (Berry, 1983; Heskett, 1986) stress that employee involvement and "internal" marketing to employees are important factors in ensuring successful service operations. Deming (1982), however, argues that both behavior and motivation are controlled by the design of the process itself and that if the process is properly designed, high motivation and effectiveness will be the natural results.

In terms of consumer participation, Lovelock and Young (1979), Chase (1978), Bateson (1985), and others have discussed whether and how to involve consumers in the service process, and the management of their involvement. Chase argues that consumer participation should be kept to a minimum in the interests of greater process efficiency. However, as we have seen, process design offers many routes to market success. A service (self-service gasoline stations, for example) can be designed for maximum consumer participation and still be profitable. In fact, Bateson's (1985) work suggests that consumers can be segmented on the basis of control needs, resulting in services that are designed to capitalize profitably on the consumer's own desire for participation.

These brief descriptions illustrate the richness and diversity of current thought about the human side of service systems. Our purpose here is not to choose one approach over another, but to underscore the fact that people are just as important as structural design. If people issues are not addressed effectively, even the best design will fail.

Role of Facilitating Goods
Facilitating goods are also important in structural planning. Educational services, for example, can be rendered by a human being who lectures in a traditional classroom setting. Education also can be rendered via videotape, television, computer, and book, to name just a few alternative facilitating goods.

For the designer of a new or different educational service, any of these choices will yield a different service structure. These structures will differ in complexity and divergence, as well as in cost dynamics, distribution constraints, and market position.

Sometimes facilitating goods are used as a replacement for human performance to reduce divergence. Computers are the prime example of a good that has been used in this way to standardize service systems. However, simplification is not the only use for technology. Technology also can be used to increase complexity and divergence. When bank automated teller machines first were introduced, for example, they could deliver only simple cash dispensing and deposit services. Now, technology has allowed the addition of funds transfer and investment services to the system, increasing its overall complexity. Tomorrow, what are called "smart" cards will make possible the delivery of a wide range of credit, payment, and information services. Ultimately, technology may even make possible a degree of customization (i.e., divergence) that only human providers can now deliver.

For all these reasons, the consideration of changes to any service structure demands an appreciation of the interrelatedness and intricacy of service systems. Unlike a product, a service cannot be engineered and then made in a factory. "Producing" a service is a dynamic, continuous event.

Conclusion

Though our discussion focuses on process design, other elements of the service system can and do affect market position. Advertising and promotion are, of course, powerful forces in the positioning process. American Express, for example, has repositioned its credit services to women solely through advertising.

Distribution channels also affect market position. Marketing stock brokerage through Sears stores is one example of positioning a service to a new, broader consumer base through a change in distribution channels. Moreover, as Shostack (1985), Blackman (1985), and others have noted, various forms of physical service evidence, from the environment in which a service is rendered to the correspondence, brochures, signage, and even people to which a customer is exposed, can affect position. Facilitating goods also can affect position, even without process change. A provider who substitutes limousines for taxicabs, for example, may succeed in charging higher prices and tapping a different market for exactly the same transportation service.

In short, the issues involved in service positioning are numerous, and this discussion by no means encompasses all of the subjects relevant to the positioning process. In a structural sense, however, processes themselves appear to have characteristics that not only affect market position, but also can be deliberately and strategically managed for positioning purposes. By manipulating complexity and divergence, a service marketer can approximate some of the product analysis and design functions that are traditional in product marketing. Moreover, the use of blueprints provides a mechanism through which services can be "engineered" at the drawing board, as well as a tool for identifying gaps, analyzing competitors, aiding in market research, and controlling implementation.

The marketplace affords evidence that both complexity and divergence are concepts that are understood an employed in service industries. Though the practice is not formalized, it works. How much more powerful the result might be if marketers brought a professional discipline, capable of crafting service systems in a rational basis, to bear on the service positioning task!

For managers in service industries, taking a structural approach can help increase their control over some of the most critical elements of service system management. For marketers, process design may be a tool that can substantially increase their impact and role in the service sector and help service marketing come of age.

REFERENCES

Bateson, John E. G. (1977). "Do We Need Service Marketing?" *Marketing Consumer Services: New Insights,* Report #77–115. Cambridge, MA: Marketing Science Institute.

———. (1985). "Perceived Control and the Service Encounter." In *The Service Encounter,* John A. Czepiel et al., eds. Lexington, MA: Lexington Books.

Berry, Leonard L. (1983). "Relationship Marketing." In *Emerging Perspectives on Services Marketing,* Leonard L. Berry et al., eds. Chicago: American Marketing Association, 25–28.

Blackman, Barry. (1985). "Making a Service More Tangible Can Make It More Manageable." In *The Service Encounter,* John A. Czepiel et al., eds. Lexington, MA: Lexington Books.

Bowen, David E., and Benjamin Schneider. (1985). "Boundary-Spanning-Role Employees and the Service Encounter." In *The Service Encounter,* John A.

Czepiel et al., eds., pp. 124–147. Lexington, MA: Lexington Books.

Chase, Richard B. (1978, November–December). "Where Does the Consumer Fit in a Service Operation?" *Harvard Business Review*, 56, 137–142.

Deming, W. Edwards. (1982). *Quality, Productivity and Competitive Position*. Cambridge, Massachusetts Institute of Technology, Center for Advanced Engineering Study.

Fox, Joseph M. (1982). *Software and Its Development*. Englewood Cliffs, NJ: Prentice Hall.

Heskett, James L. (1986). *Managing in the Service Economy*, pp. 45–74, 117–134. Boston: Harvard Business School Press.

Holloway, Charles A. (1979). *Decision Making Under Uncertainty: Models and Choices*. Englewood Cliffs, NJ: Prentice Hall.

Judd, Robert C. (1964, January). "The Case for Redefining Services." *Journal of Marketing*, 28, 58–59.

Levitt, Theodore (1976, September–October). "The Industrialization of Service." *Harvard Business Review*, 54, 63–74.

Lovelock, Christopher H. (1984). *Services Marketing, Text, Cases & Readings*, pp. 55–56, 133–139. Englewood Cliffs, NJ: Prentice Hall.

Lovelock, Christopher H., and Robert F. Young (1979, May–June). "Look to Consumers to Increase Productivity." *Harvard Business Review*, 57, 168–178.

McLuhan, Marshall (1964). *Understanding Media*. New York: McGraw-Hill.

Mills, Peter K. (1985). "The Control Mechanisms of Employees at the Encounter of Service Organizations." In *The Service Encounter*, John A. Czepiel et al., eds. Lexington, MA: Lexington Books.

Rathmell, John M. (1974). *Marketing in the Service Sector*. Cambridge, MA: Winthrop Publishers.

Ries, Al, and Jack Trout. (1981). *Positioning*. New York: McGraw-Hill.

Sasser, W. Earl, Jr., R. Paul Olsen, and D. Daryl Wyckoff. (1978). *Management of Service Operations: Text, Cases, and Readings*. Boston: Allyn & Bacon.

Schneider, Benjamin, and David E. Bowen. (1984). "New Service Design, Development and Implementation." In *Developing New Services,* William R. George and Claudia Marshall, eds., pp. 82–102. Chicago: American Marketing Association, Proceedings Series

Schroeder, Roger G. (1981). *Operations Management*. New York: McGraw-Hill.

Shostack G. Lynn. (1977, April). "Breaking Free from Product Marketing," *Journal of Marketing*, 41, 73–80.

———. (1984a). "A Framework for Service Marketing." In *Marketing Theory, Distinguished Contributions*, Stephen W. Brown and Raymond P. Fisk, eds., p. 250. New York: John Wiley.

———. (1984b, January–February). "Designing Services That Deliver." *Harvard Business Review*, 62, 133–139.

———. (1985). "Planning the Service Encounter." In *The Service Encounter*, John A. Czepiel et al., eds., pp. 243–253. Lexington, MA: Lexington Books.

Smith, Ruth A., and Michael J. Houston. (1983). "Script-Based Evaluation of Satisfaction with Services." In *Emerging Perspectives on Services Marketing*, Leonard Berry et al., eds. Chicago: American Marketing Association.

Tybout, Alice M., and John R. Hauser. (1981, Summer). "A Marketing Audit Using a Conceptual Model of Consumer Behavior: Application and Evaluation." *Journal of Marketing*, 45, 82–101.

The Strategic Levers of Yield Management

Sheryl E. Kimes
Richard B. Chase

Yield management, controlling customer demand through the use of variable pricing and capacity management to enhance profitability, has been examined extensively in the services literature. Most of this work has been tactical and mathematical rather than managerial. In this article, the authors suggest that a broader view of yield management is valuable to both traditional and nontraditional users of the approach. Central to this broader view is the recognition of how different combinations of pricing and duration can be used as strategic levers to position service firms in their markets and the identification of tactics by which management can deploy these strategic levers. The authors also propose that further development of yield management requires that when the service is delivered be treated as a design variable that should be as carefully managed as the service process itself.

Although commonly associated with marketing as a revenue management tool, yield management has significant impacts on other service business functions. It affects operations in capacity planning, human resource management in worker selection and training, and business strategy through the way the service firm positions itself in the market. Despite this widespread impact and the considerable attention it has received, formal yield management is still viewed primarily as a pricing/inventory management tool. What is lacking is a broader theory of yield management that would permit other service industries to gain the benefits of yield management-type thinking and provide insights into new areas in which experienced companies might further apply the concept. Our objective in this article is to develop the groundwork for such a theory. Our focus will be on the strategic levers available for yield management, how they have been applied in traditional yield management settings, and how they, along with some tactical tools, can be applied to other service settings.

A Modified Definition of Yield Management

A common definition of yield management is the application of information systems and pricing strategies to "sell the right capacity to the right customers at the right prices" (Smith, Leimkuhler, and Darrow 1992). Implicit in this definition is the notion of time-perishable capacity and, by extension, the notion of segmentation of capacity according to when it is booked, when and how long it is to be used, and according to the customer who uses it. In other words, "an hour is not an hour is not an hour" when it comes to customer preferences or capacity management. In light of this subtle point, we offer a slightly modified definition of the term. That is, yield management may be defined as managing the four Cs of perishable service: calendar (how far in advance reservations are made), clock (the time of day service is offered), capacity (the inventory of service resources), and cost (the price of the service) to manage a fifth C, customer demand, in such a way as to maximize profitability.

Strategic Levers

A successful yield management strategy is predicated on effective control of customer demand. Businesses have two interrelated strategic levers with which to accomplish this: pricing and duration of customer use. Prices can be fixed (one price for the same service for all customers for all times) or variable (different prices for different times or for different customer segments), and duration can be predictable or unpredictable.

Variable pricing to control demand is conceptually a straightforward process. It can take the form

Reprinted with permission from *Journal of Service Research*, Vol. 1, No. 2, November 1998, 156–166. Sponsored by Center for Service Marketing, Owen Graduate School of Management, Vanderbilt University. Copyright © 1998 by Sage Publications, Inc.

of discount prices at off-peak hours for all customers, such as low weekday rates for movies, or it can be in the form of price discounts for certain classes of customers, such as senior discounts at restaurants.

Duration control presents a more complicated decision problem but at the same time represents an area that would improve the effectiveness of yield management. By implementing duration controls, companies maximize overall revenue across all time periods rather than just during high-demand periods. If managers want to increase control over duration, they can refine their definition of duration, reduce the uncertainty of arrival, reduce the uncertainty of the duration, or reduce the amount of time between customers. We will discuss each of these tactics later.

Different industries use different combinations of variable pricing and duration control (Figure 1). Industries traditionally associated with yield management (hotel, airline, rental car, and cruise line) tend to use variable pricing and a specified or predictable duration (Quadrant 2). Movie theaters, performing arts centers, arenas, and convention centers use a fixed price for a predictable duration (Quadrant 1), whereas restaurants, golf courses, and Internet service providers use a fixed price with unpredictable customer duration (Quadrant 3). Many health care industries charge variable prices

(Medicare or private pay) but do not know the duration of patient use (Quadrant 4). There is no fixed demarcation point between quadrants, so an industry may lie partially in one quadrant and partially in another. The intent of this classification method is to help industries not currently using yield management develop a strategic framework for developing yield management. More specifically, what we are trying to show is which quadrant industries are in and what they can do to move to Quadrant 2. For example, restaurant management does not have control of duration; they need to pursue some duration management approach. Or, if hotel management does not adequately control length of stay, they may want to modify their forecasting system from room nights to arrivals to enhance their reservation system.

As indicated above, successful yield management applications are generally found in Quadrant 2 industries. The reason is that a predictable duration enables clear delineation of the service portfolio, and variable pricing enables generating maximum revenue from each service offering within the portfolio. We hasten to point out that even those industries that are listed in this quadrant have structural features that inhibit them from achieving their full profit potential. A brief review of the development of yield management in the airline and hotel industries will help illustrate these points.

		Price	
		Fixed	Variable
Duration	Predictable	**Quadrant 1:** Movies Stadiums/Arenas Convention Centers	**Quadrant 2:** Hotels Airlines Rental Cars Cruise Lines
	Unpredictable	**Quadrant 3:** Restaurants Golf Courses Internet Service Providers	**Quadrant 4:** Continuing Care Hospitals

FIGURE 1 Typical Pricing and Duration Positioning of Selected Services Industries

Airline Industry

Deregulation of the American airline industry was the major impetus for the development of yield management. Before deregulation in 1978, major carriers offered one-price service between cities. Essentially, most airlines were operating in Quadrant 1: Their flight durations were extremely predictable, and their price was fixed (Figure 2).

Immediately after deregulation, many new airlines emerged, and one airline, People's Express, developed an aggressive low-cost strategy. The People's Express story is well known: Their airfares were considerably lower than those of the major carriers, and customers were attracted to the limited service that People's Express flights offered. The major carriers such as American Airlines, United Airlines, and Delta Airlines, aided by new computerized reservation systems, employed variable pricing on a flight-by-flight basis to match or undercut fares offered by People's Express. Cost-conscious passengers then switched to the major carriers, and People's Express was eventually forced out of business. Donald Burr, the former CEO of People's Express, attributes his airline's failure to the lack of good information technology and the subsequent inability to practice yield management (Anonymous 1992; Cross 1997).

Seeing the benefits of differential pricing, most major North American carriers instituted yield management and moved into Quadrant 2. Yield management allowed airlines to determine the minimum fare (of a set mix of fares) that should be available for a specific flight. Differential pricing, in combination with the predictability of flight duration, gave them the enviable position of variable pricing with predictable duration.

Another trend that emerged after deregulation was the hub-and-spoke system. Previously, airlines operated on an origin-destination basis, and although connecting flights existed, the concept of a hub city did not. Most major airlines now operate with a hub-and-spoke system, and their forecasting and yield management systems are based around the associated flight legs (Skwarek 1996). Leg-based solutions have inherent problems and may lead to suboptimal solutions. Although the revenue on each flight leg may be optimized, revenue over the entire airline network may not. In an attempt to circumvent this problem, some airlines (notably American Airlines) developed virtual nesting systems (Smith, Leimkuhler, and Darrow 1992), in which different origin-destination pairs were classified by revenue generated. Unfortunately, current origin-destination forecasting and yield management systems have a high forecast error that results in an unreliable solution.

The lack of origin-destination forecasting may seem like a minor point, but it prevents airlines from truly managing the predictability of their duration. In a sense, the hub-and-spoke system has caused the airline industry to move into the bottom half of Quadrant 2 or the top half of Quadrant 4. The hub-and-spoke system, in combination with airline pricing systems, has created problems such as passengers attempting to obtain a lower fare by completing only one leg of their multileg flight (a

		Price	
		Fixed	Variable
Duration	Predictable	Quadrant 1: Before De-regulation	Quadrant 2: Immediately after De-regulation
	Unpredictable	Quadrant 3: None Identified	Quadrant 4: Hub-and-Spoke System

FIGURE 2 The Airline Industry

"hidden city"). The empty seat on the remaining flight leg represents lost revenue to the airlines so safeguards have been instituted to avoid this problem. Only one major carrier, Southwest Airlines, has resisted the temptation of the hub-and-spoke system. This represents a competitive advantage for their yield management system because they are better able to manage the predictability of their flight durations (Anonymous 1994b).

Hotel Industry

Unlike the airline industry, traditional hotels are usually located in Quadrant 3. Although group and tour operators have multiple negotiated rates (Hoyle, Dorf, and Jones 1991; Vallen and Vallen 1991), most traditional hotels charge essentially one room rate (or perhaps a low-season and high-season rate) for transient guests. Length of stay is not explicitly considered, and forecasts are designed to predict nightly occupancy (Figure 3). Typically, the goal of the traditional hotel is to maximize occupancy for a given night, and managers seldom look at long-term revenue generation.

After the airlines started using yield management, many hotel managers were impressed with the increased revenue claimed by the airlines and applied the concept of variable pricing to the hotel industry. When hotels started using variable pricing, they did not apply the concept of qualified rates, in which customers had to meet certain requirements to obtain a lower room rate. They instead relied on top-down pricing, in which reservation agents quoted the highest rate first and, if faced with resistance, offered the next of several lower rates until the customers acquiesced or they reached a minimum level previously established by management. Many major hotel chains still use this pricing method. Although short-term revenue gains may result from top-down pricing, customers view this practice unfavorably (Kimes 1994). Most hotels using this approach forecast room nights and use the forecasted nightly occupancy rate to develop pricing recommendations (Kimes 1989). Length-of-stay issues are not considered, and occupancy and rates are managed for one night at a time.

Some hotel chains, notably Marriott and Forte Hotels, saw the benefits associated with predictable durations (Anonymous 1994a). To reap the benefits associated with duration controls, they switched from forecasting room nights to forecasting arrivals by length of stay and/or room rate. Forte charged only one rate and concentrated solely on length of stay. Guests requesting a 2-night stay might be accepted, whereas those requesting a 1-night stay might be rejected depending on the projected demand. Marriott forecasted by arrival day, length of stay, and room rate and was able to determine the best set of reservation requests to accept. Still other hotel chains tried to implement length-of-stay controls without changing their forecasting system from room nights to arrivals. Without arrival information, they

		Price	
		Fixed	Variable
Duration	Predictable	Quadrant 1: Forte	Quadrant 2: Marriott Sheraton Holiday Inn
	Unpredictable	Quadrant 3: Traditional Hotels	Quadrant 4: Initial Yield Management Attempts

FIGURE 3 The Hotel Industry

had no way of knowing if their restrictions made sense or if they were unnecessarily turning away potential customers.

The focus on length of stay not only changed the forecasting systems in place at leading hotels but also changed the mathematical methods used to develop yield management recommendations. Many hotel chains (e.g., Holiday Inn, Hilton, Sheraton, and Hyatt) have instituted linear-programming-based systems in which length of stay and room rate are explicitly considered (Hensdill 1998; Vinod 1995).

Using the Strategic Levers

Industries in Quadrants 1, 3, and 4 can move into Quadrant 2 to achieve some of the revenue gains associated with yield management by manipulating duration and price. Although there are still problems facing the hotel and airline industries, their experience provides a rich context from which to understand the tactical tools needed to improve revenue generation. Specific tools associated with each strategic yield management lever can allow managers to move their company into a better revenue-generating position.

Duration Methods

If managers want to increase control over duration, they can refine their definition of duration, reduce the uncertainty of arrival, reduce the uncertainty of the duration, or reduce the amount of time between customers (Figure 4).

Refining the definition of duration. Duration is how long customers use a service and is measured either in terms of time (i.e., the number of nights or number of hours) or by event (i.e., a meal or a round of golf). When duration is defined as an event rather than time, forecasting the length of duration generally becomes more difficult. Thus, if duration for an industry could be defined in time rather than events, better forecasting, and hence control of duration, would likely result.

Even industries that use time-based duration definitions can refine this definition and thereby enhance their operations. Most hotels sell rooms by the day, or more specifically, they sell rooms from 3 p.m. (check-in) to noon (check-out). Sheraton Hotels and The Peninsula Hotel in Beverly Hills allow customers to check in at any time of the day and check out at any time without penalty

	Possible Approaches
Refine Definition	Time Event
Uncertainty of Arrival: **Internal Measures**	Forecasting Overbooking
Uncertainty of Arrival: **External Measures**	Penalties Deposits
Uncertainty of Duration: **Internal Measures**	Forecasting by Time of Arrival, Length of Stay, and Customer Characteristics
Uncertainty of Duration **External Measures**	Penalties Restrictions Process Analysis
Reduce Time Between **Customers**	Process Analysis

FIGURE 4 Methods of Managing Duration

(Anonymous 1997; Barker 1998). By refining their definition of duration, they have improved customer satisfaction, made better use of capacity, and increased revenue.

Uncertainty of arrival. Because many capacity-constrained firms have perishable inventory, they must protect themselves from no-shows or late arrivals. Firms can use both internal (not involving customers) and external (involving customers) approaches to decrease uncertainty of arrival.

Internal approaches. Most capacity-constrained service firms use overbooking to protect themselves against no-shows. Published overbooking models often use Markovian decision processes or simulation approaches (for example, Lieberman and Yechialli 1978; Rothstein 1971, 1985; Schlifer and Vardi 1975), but in practice many companies use service-level approaches. (Anonymous 1993; Smith, Leimkuhler, and Darrow 1992) or the critical fractile method (as suggested by Sasser, Olsen, and Wyckoff 1978). The key to a successful overbooking policy is to obtain accurate no-show and cancellation information and to develop overbooking levels that will maintain an acceptable level of customer service.

Once an overbooking policy is implemented, companies must develop good internal methods for handing displaced customers. The frontline personnel who must assist displaced customers should receive appropriate training and compensation for dealing with potentially angry consumers. Companies can choose to select which customers to displace on either a voluntary or involuntary manner. The airline industry, with its voluntary displacement system, has increased customer goodwill while increasing long-term profit (Anonymous 1993; Rothstein 1985). Other industries base their displacement decision on time of arrival (if customers are late, their reservation is no longer honored), frequency of use (regular customers are never displaced), or perceived importance (important customers are never displaced).

External approaches. External approaches to reduce arrival uncertainty shift the responsibility of arriving to the customer. The deposit policies used at many capacity-constrained service firms such as cruise lines and resorts are excellent examples of external approaches. In addition, the cancellation penalties imposed by these companies represent an attempt to make customers more responsible for arriving. Restaurants are experimenting with can-

cellation penalties and ask customers for their credit card numbers when taking reservations (Breuhaus 1998). If patrons do not arrive within 15 minutes of the reservation time, a penalty fee is charged to their credit cards. Interestingly, the car rental industry, which has considerable yield management experience, makes very limited use of external approaches. With the exception of specialty cars and vans, customers are not asked to guarantee their rental and have no responsibility for showing up. With no incentives for customers to arrive, it is not surprising that in busy tourist markets such as Florida, no-shows can account for as much as 70% of the reservations (Stern and Miller 1995). Besides these negative incentives, some companies use service guarantees to encourage people to show up on time. American Golf, for example, offers discounted or free play to golfers whose actual tee-off time is delayed by more than 10 minutes of their reservation time.

Uncertainty of duration. Reducing duration uncertainty enables management to better gauge capacity requirements and hence make better decisions as to which reservation requests to accept. As in the case of arrival uncertainty, both internal and external approaches can be used for this purpose.

Internal approaches. Internal approaches include accurate forecasting of the length of use and the number of early and late arrivals and departures and improving the consistency of service delivery. By knowing how long customers plan to use the service, managers can make better decisions as to which reservation requests to accept. If a restaurant manager knows that parties of two take approximately 45 minutes to dine and parties of four take about 75 minutes, he or she can make better allocation decisions. Likewise, knowing how many customers will change their planned duration of use enhances capacity decisions. For example, in a hotel, accurately forecasting how many customers book for 4 nights but leave after 3, or request additional nights, facilitates room and staff allocations. Similarly, if a rental car company knows that 20% of its week-long rentals are returned after 5 days, the fleet supply requirement can be adjusted accordingly.

Early research and practice in yield management focused on single flight legs or room nights and did not consider duration. Expected marginal seat revenue (EMSR) based models (Belobaba 1987; Littlewood 1972) are widely used in the airline industry (Williamson 1992) and result in allocation decisions for flight legs at various days before departure. Early hotel yield management systems based minimum rate decisions on forecasted occupancy but did not consider the impact of length of stay (Kimes 1989). Some airlines have tried to compensate for the lack of duration control by using virtual nesting (Smith, Leimkuhler, and Darrow 1992; Vinod 1995; Williamson 1992) but still have not achieved the goal of full origin-destination control (Vinod 1995).

Linear programming has been used to help make better duration and pricing allocation decisions (Kimes 1989; Weatherford 1995; Williamson 1992). The bid price, defined as the shadow price of the capacity constraint, can be used to determine the marginal value of an additional seat, room, or other inventory unit (Phillips 1994; Vinod 1995; Williamson 1992). This value can then be used to determine the minimum price available for different durations. Dynamic programming (Bitran and Mondschein 1995) has also been suggested as a possible method for considering hotel length of stay.

The accuracy of the forecast affects the effectiveness of the yield management system. Lee 1990), in his study of airline forecasting, found that a 10% improvement in forecast accuracy resulted in a 3% to 5% increase in revenue on high-demand flights.

If duration is to be explicitly addressed, forecasts of customer duration must be developed. Airlines typically forecast demand by flight leg (Lee 1990; Vinod 1995), but to truly practice duration control, airlines must forecast demand by all possible origin-destination pairs. As previously mentioned, the hub-and-spoke system has increased the number of forecasts required and the subsequent accuracy of those forecasts. Some airlines have tried to reduce the number of forecasts needed by using virtual nesting (Smith, Leimkuhler, and Darrow 1992; Vinod 1995). Preliminary research on airline-forecasting accuracy (Weatherford 1998) shows that an increase in the number of daily forecasts required increases the forecast error.

When hotels forecast customer duration, they must forecast by day of arrival, length of stay, and possible rate class (Kimes, O'Sullivan, and Scott 1998). Hotels using linear programming and bid-price approaches forecast at this level of detail, and some have developed even more detailed forecasts. The magnitude of this problem becomes apparent when you consider that for each day of arrival, a hotel might consider 10 different lengths of stay

and 10 different rate classes. If room type is included, a hotel may have 200 to 300 different forecasts per day.

Consistency of duration (i.e., most customers using the service for about the same length of time) is typically achieved through internal process changes. For example, TGI Fridays redesigned their restaurant menus and service delivery systems to make dining time more consistent as well as faster. Some restaurants in the theater district of New York City have placed an hourglass on the table of each party. When the sand in the hourglass is gone, patrons have a visual cue to finish dinner and leave so they will not be late to the theater. Or, in a much different context, if a prison warden knows that 25% of prisoners sentenced to 10 years serve only 4, additional prisoners may be incarcerated.

External approaches. External approaches for handling uncertainty of duration generally reach the customer in the form of deposits or penalties. Some hotels have instituted early and late departure fees (Miller 1995), and airlines have penalized passengers who purchase tickets through hidden cities. Although penalties may work in the short term, they risk incurring customer wrath and hurting the company in the long run. For this reason, internal approaches are generally preferable.

Reduce time between customers. Reducing the amount of time between customers (changeover time reduction), by definition, means that more customers can be served in the same or a shorter period of time. Although changeover time reduction is not normally considered a tool of yield management, it is a tactic that can be used to increase revenue per available inventory unit. Such tactics play an important role in the yield management strategy. Changeover time reduction has become a common strategy for airlines. Southwest Airlines and Shuttle by United both boast of 20-minute ground turnarounds of their aircraft (compared to the average of 45 minutes at most airlines) and have been able to increase the utilization of their planes (Kimes and Young 1997). Many restaurants have instituted computerized table management systems that track tables in use, the progress of the meal, and when the bill is paid. When customers leave, the table management system notifies bussers, and the table is cleared and reset (Liddle 1996). The result is an increase in table utilization and, hence, revenue per table.

Price

Industries actively practicing yield management use differential pricing—charging customers using the same service at the same time different prices, depending on customer and demand characteristics. Passengers in the economy section of a flight from New York City to Los Angeles may pay from nothing (for those using frequent-flyer vouchers) to more than $1,500. The fares vary according to the time of reservation, the restrictions imposed, or the group or company affiliation. In contrast to such Quadrant 2 pricing, Quadrant 1 and 3 industries use relatively fixed pricing and charge customers using the same service at the same time the same price.

Customers tend to develop reference prices for various transactions. If companies change price, they must do so carefully to avoid upsetting their customers (Kahneman, Knetsch, and Thaler 1986). Although it is possible to charge more solely based on high demand, customers may resent being charged different prices for essentially the same service. Two mechanisms—proper price mix and rate fences—provide opportunities to alter price while maintaining goodwill (Figure 5).

Proper price mix. Companies must be sure that they offer a logical mix of prices from which to choose. If customers do not see much distinction between the different prices being quoted, a differential-pricing strategy may not work. Determining the best mix of prices is difficult because management often has little information on price elasticities. This, in turn, often results in pricing decisions based solely on competitive pressures. It

should be noted, however, that airlines such as American Airlines have been working hard on the issues of elasticity and of multiple legs and have made some progress.

Optimal pricing policies, in which customers are asked to name the prices that they would consider to be cheap, expensive, too cheap to be of reasonable quality, and too expensive to be considered, have been developed by Taco Bell and have been tested for use with meeting planners (Lewis and Shoemaker 1997). Optimal pricing policies represent a relatively simple way of determining price sensitivity and acceptable price ranges.

Although not widely publicized, some restaurant companies are experimenting with menu pricing based on price elasticities. Large chain restaurant companies analyze the price elasticities of various menu items and make appropriate pricing changes (Kelly, Kiefer, and Burdett 1994).

Rate fences. The possession of a good pricing structure does not ensure the success of a variable-pricing strategy. Companies must also have a logical rationale or, in industry terms, rate fences that can be used to justify price discrimination. (Or, as one somewhat cynical hotel executive states, "We want something we can say out loud without laughing.")

Quadrant 2 industries often use rate fences, such as when the reservation is booked or when the service is consumed, to determine the price a customer will pay. Rate fences refer to qualifications that must be met to receive a discount (Hanks, Cross, and Noland 1992). Rate fences can be physi-

	Possible Approaches
Proper Price Mix	Price Elasticities Competitive Pricing Optimal Pricing Policies
Rate Fences: Physical	Type of Inventory Amenities
Rate Fences: Nonphysical	Restrictions Time of Usage Time of Reservation Group Membership

FIGURE 5 Methods of Managing Price

cal or nonphysical in nature and represent a ratio-nale for why some customers pay different prices for the same service.

Physical rate fences include tangible features such as room type or view for hotels, seat type or location for airlines, or table location for restau-rants. Other physical rate fences are the presence or absence of certain amenities (free golf cart use with a higher price, free breakfast with a higher price, or free soft drinks at a movie theater).

Nonphysical rate fences can be developed that can help shift demand to slower periods, reward regular customers, or reward reliable customers. Nonphysical rate fences include cancellation or change penalties and benefits based on when the reservation was booked, desired service duration, group membership or affiliation, and time of use.

Even today, it is common practice for companies to adopt differential pricing schemes without rate fences. Hotels use top-down pricing in which reser-vation agents quote the rack rate (generally the highest rate) and only quote lower rates if cus-tomers ask for them. Knowledgeable customers may know to ask for the lower rate, but inexperi-enced customers may not. Customers view this practice highly unfavorably (Kimes 1994).

Moving to a More Profitable Quadrant
The strategic levers described above can be used to help companies move into more profitable quad-rants by making duration more predictable and/or by varying prices. Generally, companies try to manipulate one strategic lever at a time, but it is possible, although difficult, for a company to try to simultaneously adjust price and duration. The fol-lowing examples of potential moves show the pos-sibilities for various industries.

Differential Pricing

Quadrant 1 to Quadrant 2
Movie theaters. Although reservation systems and differential pricing have been used in Europe for many years, American movie theaters usually charge the same price for all seats and offer dis-counted seats only for matinees or for senior citi-zens. However, things are changing rapidly, and some new movie houses are now offering differen-tial pricing based on seat location, time of show, and access to amenities. For example, the 70-seat Premium Cinema in Lombard, Illinois, has been booked solid since its opening April 3, 1998. Guests willing to pay $15 for access to a separate entrance with valet parking are admitted to a private lounge,

where they can purchase champagne at $12 per glass and buy prime-rib sandwiches at the same price. They offer free popcorn (all you can eat) and have a full-time concierge to get it for the cus-tomers. As of yet, they have not gone to the next step of developing an overbooking strategy.

Control Duration

Quadrant 3 to Quadrant 1
Golf courses. Golf courses seem to be in the worst possible position—they charge a fixed price for an event of unknown duration. Much of the problem stems from the definition of duration as an event, typically 18 holes of golf played during daylight hours. Alternative definitions of duration abound. The golf course could sell 9-hole rounds; it could institute shotgun golf, in which different groups start simultaneously at multiple holes; or it could use express golf, in which golfers run between holes and receive two scores, elapsed time and stroke count, at the end of each round. (The latter perhaps becoming a new Olympic event.) None of these modifications reduce variability in and of themselves; however, they do provide ways of redefining duration for more creative applications of yield management.

Arrival uncertainty could be reduced by institut-ing deposit policies or by developing good over-booking policies. Duration uncertainty could be reduced by adding marshals to help move golfers along on the course, by provision of free golf carts to speed the time between holes, and by more accurately forecasting play length based on time of day, week, and party size. More golfers could be accommodated if tee-time intervals were reduced or if party size were better regulated.

Control Duration

Quadrant 4 to Quadrant 2
Health care. Health care organizations use differ-ential pricing (often government mandated) but have difficulties managing duration. If hospital or nursing home managers do not know how long patients will be using beds or rooms, it is difficult to effectively plan and manage capacity. In a nursing home, the health of potential patients could be evaluated and actuarial tables used to estimate the duration of patient stay. In private and nonprofit facilities, attempts could be made to select the best mix of private-pay and Medicare patients with a bias toward private-pay patients with a long dura-tion.

The issue of duration control of health care has caused political controversy. During the mid-1990s, insurance companies in New York reduced the maximum length of insurable hospital stay for childbirth to 1 day. After intensive lobbying pressure from hospitals and medical associations, the state legislature outlawed this practice and guaranteed all new mothers a minimum length of stay of 48 hours.

Differential Pricing

Quadrant 3 to Quadrant 4

Internet service providers (ISPs). ISPs offer Internet bandwidth to customers. Because not all customers use their full allotment of bandwidth at the same time, the ISP overbooks the bandwidth. If too many customers try to access the Internet at once, service deteriorates.

ISPs operate at 100% capacity during certain times of the day and at other times have available bandwidth. Currently, most ISPs charge a flat monthly rate for Internet access, and there is no off-peak discount. Some customers are heavy users during the day, whereas others are heavy nighttime users. ISPs must maintain a mix of these customers to operate effectively. By identifying common demographic characteristics within each segment, ISPs could target specific types of users to add to the mix (M. Freimer, personal communication, 1998).

Conclusion

Effective use of the strategic levers of pricing and duration control can help capacity-constrained firms make more profitable use of their resources. Real potential exists for novel use of these tools in industries not typically associated with yield management. Even companies with yield management experience can improve performance by refining their deployment of these levers. The research challenge is to help managers identify yield management opportunities and to develop appropriate pricing and duration control approaches.

Beyond where to apply yield management, there are the questions of how to develop a yield management strategy, how to train people in the tools to implement it, and how to maintain and improve customer satisfaction while applying yield management practices. In the long run, achieving the full potential from yield management lies in management's ability to market and manage every available moment as a unique product. This, in turn, requires that we treat when the service is provided as a design variable that should be as carefully managed as the service process itself. Such a reformulation presents an exciting conceptual challenge to the emerging field of service research.

REFERENCES

"Adding to Forte's Fortune," (1994a), *Scorecard,* Second Quarter, 4–5.

Barker, J. (1998), "Flexible Check-in Expands," *Successful Meetings,* 47 (January), 32.

Belobaba, P. P. (1987), "Air Travel Demand and Airline Seat Inventory Management," Ph.D. thesis, Massachusetts Institute of Technology.

Bitran, G. R. and S. V. Mondschein (1995), "An Application of Yield Management to the Hotel Industry Considering Multiple Day Stays," *Operations Research,* 43, 427–43

Brehaus, B. (1998), "Handling No-Shows: Operators React to Reservation Plan," *Restaurant Business Magazine,* 1 (16), 13.

"A Conversation with Don Burr," (1992), *Scorecard,* Fourth Quarter, 6–7.

Cross, R. G. (1997), *Revenue Management: Hard-Core Tactics for Market Domination.* New York: Broadway Books.

"Flying High with Herb Kelleher," (1994b), *Scorecard,* Third Quarter, 1–3.

Freimer, M. (1998), personal communication.

Hanks, R. D., R. G. Cross, and R. P. Noland. (1992), "Discounting in the Hotel Industry: A New Approach," *Cornell Hotel and Restaurant Administration Quarterly,* 33 (3), 40–45.

Hensdill, C. (1998), "The Culture of Revenue Management," *Hotels,* March, 83–86.

"Hotel Adopts 24-Hour Check-in Policy," (1997), *Hospitality Law,* 12 (1), 7.

Hoyle, L. H., D. C. Dorf, and T. J. A. Jones (1991), *Managing Conventions and Group Business.* Washington, DC: The Educational Institute of the American Hotel and Motel Association.

Kahneman, D., J. Knetsch, and R. Thaler. (1986), "Fairness as a Constraint on Profit Seeking: Entitlements in the Market," *American Economic Review,* 76 (4), 728–41.

Kelly, T. J., N. M. Kiefer, and K. Burdett. (1994), "A Demand-Based Approach to Menu Pricing," *Cornell Hotel and Restaurant Administration Quarterly,* 34 (3), 40–45.

Kimes, S. E. (1989), "Yield Management: A Tool for Capacity-Constrained Service Firms," *Journal of Operations Management,* 8 (4), 348–63.

——— (1994), "Perceived Fairness of Yield Management," *Cornell Hotel and Restaurant Administration Quarterly*, 34 (1), 22–29.

Kimes, S. E. and Franklin Young. (1997), "Shuttle by United," *Interfaces*, 27 (3), 1–13.

Kimes, S. E., M. O'Sullivan, and D. Scott. (1998), "Hotel Forecasting Methods," working paper. Cornell University School of Hotel Administration.

Lee, A. O. (1990), "Airline Reservations Forecasting: Probabilistic and Statistical Models of the Booking Process," Ph.D. thesis, Massachusetts Institute of Technology.

Lewis, R. C. and S. Shoemaker (1997), "Price Sensitivity Measurement: A Tool for the Hospitality Industry," *Cornell Hotel and Restaurant Administration Quarterly*, 38 (2), 44–54.

Liddle, A. (1996), "New Computerized Table Management Reduces Guests' Waits, Empty Seats," *Nation's Restaurant News*, August 5, 22.

Lieberman, V. and U. Yechialli (1978), "On the Hotel Overlooking Problem: An Inventory Problem with Stochastic Cancellations," *Management Science*, 24, 1117–26.

Littlewood, K. (1972), "Forecasting and Control of Passenger Bookings," *AGIFORS Symposium Proceedings*, 12, 95–117.

Miller, L. (1995), "Check-Out Made Pricier," *Wall Street Journal*, October 20, B6.

Phillips, R. L. (1994), "A Marginal Value Approach to Airline Origin and Destination Revenue Management," in *Proceedings of the 16th Conference on System Modeling and Optimization*, J. Henry and P. Yvon, eds. New York: Springer-Verlag, 907–17.

Rothstein, M. (1971), "An Airline Overbooking Model," *Transportation Science*, 5, 180–92.

——— (1985), "OR and the Airline Overbooking Problem," *Operations Research*, 33 (2), 237–48.

Sasser, W. E., R. P. Olsen, and D. D. Wyckoff (1978), *Management of Service Operations*. Boston: Allyn and Bacon.

Schlifer E. and Y. Vardi (1975), "An Airline Overbooking Policy," *Transportation Sciences*, 9, 101–14.

"Simon Says," (1993), *Scorecard*, First Quarter, 10–12.

Skwarek, D. K. (1996), "Competitive Impacts of Yield Management System Components: Forecasting and Sell-Up Models," MIT Flight Transportation Lab Report No. R96-6. Cambridge, MA: Massachusetts Institute of Technology.

Smith, B. C., J. F. Leimkuhler, and R. M. Darrow (1992), "Yield Management at American Airlines," *Interfaces*, 22 (1), 8–31.

Stern, G. and L. Miller (1995), "Rental Car Companies Set to Impose Cancellation Penalties for No-Shows," *The Wall Street Journal*, December 26, A3.

Vallen, J. J. and G. K. Vallen (1991), *Check-In, Check-Out*. Dubuque, IA: William C. Brown.

Vinod, B. (1995), "Origin-and-Destination Yield Management," in *Handbook of Airline Economics*, D. Jenkins, ed. New York: McGraw-Hill, 459–68.

Weatherford, L. R. (1995), "Length of Stay Heuristics: Do They Really Make a Difference?" *Cornell Hotel and Restaurant Administration Quarterly*, 36 (6), 47–56.

——— (1998), "Forecasting Issues in Revenue Management," INFORMS conference presentation, Montreal, Canada, May.

Williamson, E. L. (1992), "Airline Network Seat Control," Ph.D. thesis, Massachusetts Institute of Technology.

PART IV

Planning and Managing Service Delivery

CHAPTER 11

Creating Delivery Systems in Place, Cyberspace, and Time

Companies best equipped for the twenty-first century will consider investment in real time systems as essential to maintaining their competitive edge and keeping their customers.

REGIS MCKENNA

The beginning of the twenty-first century is both an exciting and challenging time for managers responsible for service delivery. Speed has become an important factor in competitive strategy. Customers are demanding more convenience and expecting services to be delivered rapidly where and when they want them. The Internet offers an array of new possibilities to those already presented by physical sites, mail, and telephone delivery.

Delivering a service to customers involves decisions about where, when, and how. The rapid growth of the Internet means that services marketing strategy must address issues of place, cyberspace, and time, paying at least as much attention to speed, scheduling, and electronic access as to the more traditional notion of physical location. A service product and its means of distribution and delivery are often closely linked; in the case of people-processing services, the nature of the delivery system has a powerful impact on the customers' experience.

For high-contact services, the design of the physical environment and the way in which tasks are performed by customer-contact personnel jointly play a vital role in creating a particular identity for a service firm, shaping the nature of the customer's experience and enhancing both productivity and quality. Low-contact services are expanding in number, thanks to advances in electronic technology. More and more, these services, often designed specifically with improved productivity in mind, are being delivered through self-service. The challenge is for marketers to make self-service a positive experience.

In this chapter, we touch on technology issues in service delivery at several points but save detailed discussion of this topic to chapter 18. Our main focus is to review the role that delivery plays in service marketing strategy and explore the following questions:

1. How are the nature of the service product and its delivery system related to one another?
2. What are the distinctive challenges to delivery system design posed by high-contact and low-contact service processes?
3. What are the implications for a firm of delivering through both physical and electronic channels?
4. What role is played by intermediaries in service delivery?
5. Why should service managers invest money and effort in the design of the firm's servicescape?

Alternative Scenarios for Service Delivery

The nature of the service both influences and is shaped by distribution strategy. It is through delivery systems that the supplier provides service to the customer. With mature services, improvements may take the form of incremental enhancements to improve the efficiency or attractiveness of the delivery system. The thrust of the so-called experience economy, often consists of enhancing the experience associated with delivery processes as opposed to improving the core product (this is why discriminating diners find themselves disenchanted by the food served in theme restaurants). In well-designed high-contact services, customers are often so actively involved in service delivery that process and outcome become intimately entwined. In low-contact services, by contrast, customers may be far removed physically from the service provider and concerned with the delivery system simply to the extent that they can obtain service promptly whenever and wherever they want it.

But delivery processes can also drive new service innovation, as we discussed in chapter 8. Looking at the impact of the Internet, for instance, we can see numerous dot-com start-up companies optimistically seeking markets for service concepts built around the potential of this remarkable new channel that allows customers the unprecedented freedom of access in cyberspace, where and when it suits them. Meantime, many bricks-and-mortar retailers, used to operating stores in defined physical places, are trying to adapt their operations to deliver all or some of their service elements through Web sites.

Today, speed is an important factor in competitive strategy.[1] Modern business logistics have greatly speeded delivery of objects through physical channels, even to the extent of same-day delivery across significant geographic distances. Meanwhile, new telecommunications technologies, including the Internet, have given service providers the potential to deliver information-based services (and informational processes related to supplementary services) almost anywhere at the speed of light through electronic channels.

Forward-looking firms are coming up with new formats to offer face-to-face delivery in new locations, ranging from Wells Fargo's tiny bank branches occupying booths at the end of supermarket aisles to massage clinics on airport concourses. These providers recognize that customers also save time and effort when they no longer need to visit inconveniently located service factories to obtain the services they need.

Physical versus Electronic Delivery

The availability of electronic channels as well as physical ones marks a key distinction between goods and services marketing where the core product is concerned. Information-based services can be delivered through either type of channel. Equally significantly, many of the supplementary services surrounding both tangible and intangible core products can also be delivered electronically.

As we look at the eight petals of the augmented service product, we can see that no fewer than five are information based (Figure 11.1). Information, consultation, order taking, billing, and payment can all be transmitted in the digital language of computers. Although we may think of money in its metallic or paper form, more and more financial transactions today involve instructions couched in electronic form. Relatively few service businesses now require payment only in cash—most offer the option of electronic funds transfer. Even service businesses that involve physical core products, such as retailing and repair, are shifting delivery of many supplementary services to the Internet, closing physical branches, and relying on speedy business logistics to enable a new strategy of arm's-length transactions with their customers.

Considerations in the Design of Service Delivery

Decisions faced by firms in planning and configuring the service delivery process are summarized in Figure 11.2 (which picks up where the bottom of Figure 8.1 on p. 218 left off). The design of service delivery processes starts with the core product and should then be extended to include delivery of each of the different supplementary elements. Managers responsible for

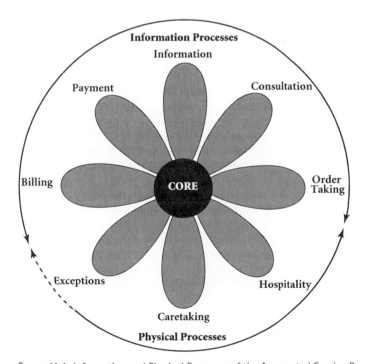

FIGURE 11.1 Information and Physical Processes of the Augmented Service Product

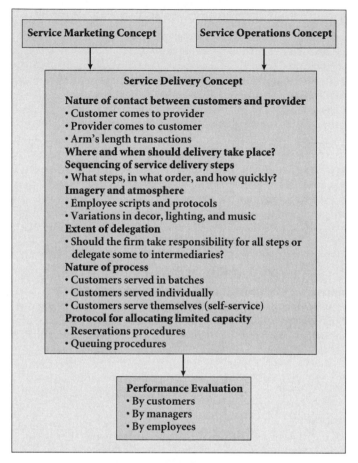

FIGURE 11.2 Service Delivery and Performance Evaluation

planning service delivery strategies find themselves addressing a series of issues, often going backward and forward between the following questions:

- *What should be the nature of contact between the service provider and its customers?* Should customers come to the provider or the other way around? Or, where feasible, should the two parties deal at arm's length, using mail and telecommunications—ranging from voice telephone to the Web? (This issue is discussed under "Selecting the Type of Contact.")
- *What should be the sequencing of the various steps in the service delivery process?* Both operational considerations and customer preferences need to be taken into account in making this decision. Blueprinting of processes, as discussed in chapter 8, helps planners to evaluate the implications of alternative sequences—for instance, paying before service is delivered versus paying afterwards.
- *Where (location) and when (scheduling) should delivery take place?* The choice today is not just between alternative geographic locations but also between physical place and cyberspace. Ideally, convenience for customers should drive such decisions, but the financial and operational implications need to be considered, too. (We examine these issues in depth later in this chapter under the heading "Place and Time Decisions.")

- *What imagery, atmosphere, and experience should the servicescape strive to create?* For a high-contact service, responding to this question will require decisions on (1) facility design and layout; (2) staff uniforms, appearance, and attitudes; (3) the type of furnishings and equipment installed; and (4) the use of music, lighting, and decor. (See "The Physical Evidence of the Servicescape" later in this chapter.)
- *Should service elements be bundled or unbundled for delivery purposes?* For instance, should a service firm take responsibility for all elements or delegate certain components to an intermediary? (See the discussion later in the chapter within the section "The Role of Intermediaries.")
- *What should be the nature of the service process at each step?* Should customers be served in batches or individually? Alternatively, should they serve themselves? The nature of the service performed often dictates whether customers can be served individually or need first to be grouped together in batches. Except for taxis, public transportation services involve batch processing of many passengers at once. Some delivery processes involve a mix of individual and batch processing—thus, admission tickets to a museum may be sold individually or to a group, with visitors being free to join a group tour or to wander around the facilities on their own. Issues relating to self-service are discussed in more depth in the sections on productivity in chapter 12.
- *What should be the serving protocol?* Should the firm operate a reservations system or work on a first-come, first-served basis, with queuing as necessary? Alternatively, should a priority system be established for certain types of customers (as many firms do for their larger industrial accounts or airlines do for their frequent flyers)? We examine these and related issues in chapter 14.

Selecting the Type of Contact: Options for Service Delivery

Decisions on where, when, and how to deliver service have an important impact on the nature of customers' service experiences by determining the types of encounters (if any) with service personnel and the price and other costs incurred to obtain service. Several factors serve to shape delivery strategy. A key question is, Does the nature of the service or the firm's positioning strategy require customers to be in direct physical contact with its personnel, equipment, and facilities? (As we saw in chapter 2, this is inevitable for people-processing services but optional for other categories.) If so, do customers have to visit the facilities of the service organization, or will the latter send personnel and equipment to customers' own sites? Alternatively, can transactions between provider and customer be completed at arm's length through use of either telecommunications or physical channels of distribution?

A second issue concerns the firm's strategy in terms of distribution sites: Should it maintain just a single outlet or offer to serve customers through multiple outlets at different locations? The possible options, combining both type of contact and number of sites, can be seen in Table 11.1, which consists of six different cells.

Customers Visit the Service Site

The convenience of service factory locations and operational schedules may assume great importance when a customer has to be physically present—either throughout service delivery or even just to initiate and terminate the transaction. Elaborate statistical analysis, in the form of retail gravity models, is sometimes used to aid decisions on where to locate supermarkets relative to prospective customers' homes and workplaces. Traffic counts and pedestrian counts help to establish how many prospective customers a day pass by certain locations. Construction of an

TABLE 11.1 *Method of Service Delivery*		
	Availability of Service Outlets	
Nature of Interaction between Customer and Service Organization	Single Site	Multiple Sites
Customer goes to service organization	Theater Barbershop	Bus service Fast-food chain
Service organization comes to customer	House painting Mobile car wash	Mail delivery Auto club road service
Customer and service organization transact at arm's length (mail or electronic communications)	Credit card company Local TV station	Broadcast network Telephone company

expressway or the introduction of a new bus or rail service may have a significant effect on travel patterns and, in turn, determine which sites are now more desirable and which are less so.

The tradition of having customers visit the service site for services other than those in the people-processing category is now being challenged by advances in telecommunications and business logistics, which are leading to a shift to services delivered from a distance.

Providers Come to the Customer

For some types of services, the supplier visits the customer. A firm like Aramark, which provides a wide variety of facilities maintenance services, must necessarily bring its tools and personnel to the customer's site because the need is location specific. This approach is essential whenever the object of the service is some immovable physical item, such as a tree that needs pruning, a large machine that needs repair, a house that requires pest-control treatment, or a building that has a temporary need for auxiliary power generation.

Because it's more expensive and time-consuming for service personnel and their equipment to travel to the customer than vice versa, the trend has been away from this approach (fewer doctors make house calls nowadays!). However, there may still be a profitable niche in serving customers who are willing to pay a premium price for the time savings and convenience of receiving personal visits from service providers. One young veterinary doctor has built her business around house calls to sick pets. She has found that customers are glad to pay extra for a service that not only saves them time but is also less stressful for the pet than waiting in a crowded veterinary clinic, full of other animals and their worried owners. Other recently established consumer services that are taken to the customer include mobile car washing, office and in-home catering, and made-to-measure tailoring services for businesspeople. In remote areas such as Alaska or Canada's Northwest Territory, service providers often fly to visit their customers. Australia is famous for its Royal Flying Doctor Service, in which physicians fly to make house calls at farms and stations in the outback.

Service firms are more likely to visit corporate customers at their premises than to visit individuals in their homes. This practice reflects the greater volume of business purchased and also the buyers' need for outsourcing services directed at their offices and factories, such as cleaning, facilities maintenance, and security. Firms may also undertake short-term rentals of both equipment and labor for special purposes or as a strategic move to increase their productive capacity during busy periods. Service Perspectives 11.1 describes the activities of an international company that rents generating and cooling equipment around the world.

SERVICE PERSPECTIVES 11.1

Power and Temperature Control for Rent

You probably think of electricity as coming from a distant power station and of air conditioning and heating in a large structure as fixed installations. So how would you deal with the following challenges? Luciano Pavarotti is giving an open-air concert in Münster, Germany, and the organizers require an uninterruptible source of electrical power for the duration of the concert, independent of the local electricity supply. A tropical cyclone has devastated the small mining town of Pannawonica in Western Australia, destroying everything in its path, including power lines, and it's urgent that electrical power be restored as soon as possible so that the town and its infrastructure can be rebuilt. In Amsterdam, organizers of the World Championship Indoor Windsurfing competition need to power 27 wind turbines that will be installed along the length of a huge indoor pool to create winds with a force of 5 to 6 on the Beaufort scale. A U.S. Navy submarine needs a shore-based source of power when it spends time in a remote Norwegian port. Sri Lanka faces an acute shortage of electricity-generating capability when water levels fall dangerously low at the country's major hydroelectric dams due to insufficient monsoon rains two years in a row. And a large power-generating plant in Oklahoma urgently seeks temporary capacity to replace one of its cooling towers, destroyed the day before in a tornado.

These are all challenges faced and met by a company called Aggreko, which describes itself as "The World Leader in Temporary Utility Rental Solutions." Aggreko operates from more than one hundred and ten depots in 20 countries around the world. It rents a "fleet" of mobile electricity generators, oil-free air compressors, and temperature-control devices ranging from water chillers and industrial air-conditioners to giant heaters and dehumidifiers.

Aggreko's customer base is dominated by large companies and government agencies. Although a lot of its business comes from needs that are foreseen far in advance, such as backup operations during planned factory maintenance or a package of services during the filming of a James Bond movie, the firm is also poised to resolve problems arising unexpectedly from emergencies.

Much of the firm's rental equipment is contained in soundproofed, boxlike structures that can be shipped anywhere in the world and coupled together to create the specific type and level of electrical power output or climate-control capability required by the client. Consultation, installation, and ongoing technical support add value to the core service. Says a company brochure, "Emphasis is placed on solving customer problems rather than just renting equipment." Some customers have a clear idea in advance of their needs; others require advice on how to develop innovative, cost-effective solutions to what may be unique problems; and still others are desperate to restore power that has been lost due to an emergency. In the last-mentioned instance, speed is of the essence because downtime can be extremely expensive, and in some cases lives may depend on the promptness of Aggreko's response.

Delivering service requires that Aggreko ship its equipment to the customer's site so that the needed power or temperature control can be available at the right place and time. Following the Pannawonica cyclone, Aggreko's West Australian team swung into action, rapidly organizing the dispatch of some thirty generators ranging in size from 60 to 750 kVA, plus cabling, refueling tankers, and other equipment. The generators were transported by means of four so-called road trains, each comprising a giant tractor unit hauling three 40-foot (13-meter) trailers. A full infrastructure team of technicians and additional equipment were flown in on two Hercules aircraft. The Aggreko technicians remained on site for six weeks, providing 24-hour service while the town was being rebuilt.

Source: Aggreko's "International Magazine," 1997; Aggreko Web site, www.aggreko.com, February 2000. Used with permission of Aggreko.

Arm's-Length Transactions

Dealing with a service firm through arm's-length transactions may mean that a customer never sees the service facilities and never meets the service personnel face-to-face. An important consequence is that the number of service encounters tends to be fewer, and those encounters that do take place with service personnel are more likely to be made by telephone or, even more remotely, by mail, fax, or e-mail. The outcome of the service activity remains very important to the customer, but much of the process of service delivery may be hidden. Credit cards and insurance are examples of services that can be requested and delivered by mail or telecommunications. Repair services for small pieces of equipment sometimes require customers to ship the product to a maintenance facility where it will be serviced and then returned again by parcel service (with the option of paying extra for express shipment).

For best results, a new business model needs to be developed when telecommunications replaces, or is added to, traditional face-to-face delivery models. First Direct's success in creating an all-telephone bank reflected the attention given to reengineering many banking processes and the careful training given to hiring and training banking representatives, whose jobs were very different from those of traditional branch-based personnel.[2]

Any information-based product can be delivered almost instantaneously through telecommunication channels to any point in the globe where a suitable reception terminal exists. As a result, physical logistics services now find themselves competing with telecommunications services. When I was writing this book, for instance, I had a choice of mail or courier services for physical shipments of the chapters in either paper or disk form. I could also fax the materials, feeding in the pages one sheet at a time. But by using e-mail, I was able to transmit chapters electronically from one computer to another, with the option of printing them out at the receiving end. In fact, I used all three methods, depending on the nature of the page (hand-drawn images were faxed) and the compatibility (or lack thereof) of the author's and publisher's software.

Place and Time Decisions

How should service managers make decisions on the places where service is delivered and the times when it is available? The answer is likely to reflect customer needs and expectations, competitive activity, and the nature of the service operation. As we noted earlier, different distribution strategies may be more appropriate for some of the supplementary service elements (the petals of the Flower of Service shown again in Figure 11.1) than for the core product itself. For instance, as a customer you are probably willing to go to a particular location at a specific time to attend a sporting or entertainment event. But you probably want greater flexibility and convenience when reserving a seat in advance, so you may expect the reservations service to be open for extended hours, to offer booking and credit card payment by phone or even the Web, and to deliver tickets by mail.

Where Should Services Be Delivered?

Deciding where to locate a service facility that will be visited by customers involves very different considerations from decisions related to locating the backstage elements, where cost savings and access to labor are often key determinants. In the former case, questions of customer convenience and preference come to the fore. Frequently purchased services that are not easily differentiated from competitors need to be easily accessible from customers' homes or workplaces. Examples include retail banks and quick-service restaurants. However, customers may be willing to travel further for specialty services that fit their needs well.

Locational Constraints. Although customer convenience is important, operational requirements set tight constraints for some services. Airports, for instance, are often inconveniently located relative to travelers' homes, offices, or destinations. Because of noise and environmental factors, finding suitable sites for construction of new airports or expansion of existing ones is a very difficult task. (A governor of Massachusetts was once asked what would be an acceptable location for a second airport to serve Boston; he thought for a moment and then responded, "Nebraska!") As a result, airport sites are often far from the city centers to which many passengers wish to travel, and the only way to make them less inconvenient is to install fast rail links, such as the recently introduced Heathrow Express in London or the rail service to Hong Kong's new airport. A different type of location constraint is imposed by other geographic factors, such as terrain and climate. By definition, ski resorts have to be in the mountains; and ocean beach resorts, on the coast.

The need for economies of scale is another operational issue that may restrict choice of locations. Major hospitals offer many different health care services—even a medical school—at a single location, requiring a very large facility. Customers requiring complex, in-patient treatment must come to this service factory, rather than being treated at home—although an ambulance (or even a helicopter) can be sent to pick them up. This is particularly necessary in cases where specialized medical and nursing care is only available in a limited number of hospitals possessing the necessary equipment and skills. Medical specialists—as opposed to general practitioners—often find it convenient to locate their offices close to a hospital because it saves them time when they need to operate on their patients.

Ministores. An interesting innovation among multisite service firms has been to create service factories on a very small scale to maximize coverage within a geographic area. Automation is one approach, as exemplified by the ATM, which offers many of the functions of a bank branch within a small, self-service machine that can be located within stores, hospitals, colleges, airports, and office buildings. Another approach to smaller facilities results from rethinking the links between the frontstage and backstage of the operation. Taco Bell is often cited for its innovative K-Minus strategy, involving restaurants without kitchens.[3] The firm now confines food preparation to a central commissary from which prepared meals are shipped to restaurants and other points of access (such as mobile food carts), where they can be reheated prior to serving.

Sometimes firms purchase space from another provider in a complementary field. Examples include minibank branches within supermarkets and donut stores like Dunkin Donuts sharing space with a quick-service restaurant like Burger King.

Locating in Multipurpose Facilities. The most obvious locations for consumer services are close to where customers live or work. Modern buildings are often designed to be multipurpose, featuring not only office or production space but also such services as a bank (or at least an ATM), a restaurant, a hair salon, several stores, and even a health club. Some companies even include an on-site children's day care facility to make life easier for busy working parents.

Interest is growing in siting retail and other services on transportation routes or even in bus, rail, and air terminals. Major oil companies are developing chains of small retail stores to complement the fuel pumps at their service stations, thus offering customers the convenience of one-stop shopping for fuel, car supplies, food, and household products. Truck stops on freeways often include laundromats, toilets, ATMs, fax machines, restaurants, and inexpensive hotels in addition to a variety of vehicle maintenance and repair services for both trucks and cars. In one of the most interesting new retailing developments, airport terminals—designed as part of the infrastructure for air transportation services—are being transformed from nondescript areas where passengers and their bags are processed into vibrant shopping malls. (See Service Perspectives 11.2.)

SERVICE PERSPECTIVES 11.2

From Airports to Air Malls

Large airports used to be places where thousands of people spent time waiting with little to keep them occupied. Airports were often bound by contract to a single food operator, which translated into expensive drinks and low-quality food at high prices. Other than visit stores selling newspapers, magazines, and paperback books, there wasn't much opportunity for travelers to shop unless they wanted to spend money on expensive (and often tawdry) souvenirs. The one exception was the tax-free shop at international airports, where opportunities to save money created a brisk trade in alcohol, perfumes, tobacco, and consumer products like cameras. But today, some airports have terminals that have been transformed into shopping malls. London's Heathrow Airport even has a branch of Harrods, the famous department store.

Three factors make investments in airport retailing very appealing. One is the upscale demographics of airline passengers, whose numbers continue to grow rapidly. A second is that many passengers have plenty of time to spare while waiting for their flights; meanwhile, passengers in transit spend time waiting for connections. Finally, many existing terminal interiors have free space that can be put to profitable use. And as terminals are expanded, new retail sites can be included as an integral part of the design.

New York's La Guardia Airport retained a Boston-based firm, MarketPlace Development, to redevelop its retailing activities in the newly renovated central terminal. At La Guardia Marketplace, national brand stores and restaurants, from Sbarro to Sunglass Hut, have replaced overpriced, cafeteria-style food vendors and generic drugstores. Tighter security requirements mean that passengers must now check in earlier for flights, so they have even more time to spend at the airport. One passenger, relaxing in La Guardia's bright, three-story atrium after making some purchases, contrasted the new facility favorably to the old, which she said, "was sort of what I had expected in a New York airport: dull, kind of dirty, and not much to do."

The first (and still the most successful) custom-built airport retail complex in the United States is the Pittsburgh Air Mall, created as part of a new airport terminal and operated under a 15-year contract by BAA International. Pittsburgh is U.S. Airways' major hub, and most of its passengers are domestic travelers. Goods and services available in the Air Mall's more than one hundred stores and restaurants range from tasty take-out sandwiches for passengers who don't expect a meal on their discount-priced flight to $15 massages for tired travelers with an aching back. Sales per passenger at shops and food stores increased from $2.40 in 1992 to $8.10 in 1999. Perhaps the most striking statistic is that sales per square foot are between four and five times those of typical U.S. regional shopping centers!

Source: MarketPlace Development Inc., 1997; Eileen Kinsella, "Noshing at New York's La Guardia Airport," *Wall Street Journal,* January 21, 1998, p. B10; BAA International, www.baa.co.uk, December 1999.

E-Commerce: The Move to Cyberspace

Selling goods and services through the Internet is a major growth trend. Personal computers and the Internet are changing the way people shop. From perusing catalogs and shopping by mail or telephone, many people are moving to shop in cyberspace for a wide array of both goods and services.

Forrester Research says that customers are lured into virtual stores by four factors, in the following order of importance: convenience, ease of research (obtaining information and searching for desired items or services), better prices, and broad selection.[4] Enjoying 24-hour service with prompt delivery is particularly appealing to customers whose busy lives leave them short of time.

Traditional retailers are having to respond to stiffer competition from Internet and telephone-based catalog retailing. One company, software and computer retailer Egghead, Inc., decided to get out of physical retailing altogether. It closed its 80 stores across the United States, dismissed 800 of its 1,000 workers, shifted its sales entirely to the Internet, and renamed itself Egghead.com.

Other retailers, such as the giant bookstore chain Barnes and Noble, have developed a strong Internet presence to complement their full-service bookstores in an effort to counter competition from cyberspace retailers such as Amazon.com, which has no stores.[5] Web sites are becoming increasingly sophisticated but also more user-friendly. They often simulate the services of a well-informed sales assistant in steering customers toward items that are likely to be of interest. Some even provide the opportunity for live e-mail dialog with helpful customer service personnel. Facilitating searches is another useful service on many sites, ranging from looking at what books by a particular author are currently available to finding schedules of flights between two cities on a specific date.

Store-based retailers are responding to this competitive challenge by trying to make the shopping experience more interesting and enjoyable. Shopping centers have become larger, more colorful, and more dramatic. Within each center, individual stores seek to create their own atmosphere, but tenancy agreements often specify certain design criteria so that each store may fit comfortably into the overall servicescape. The presence of food courts and other gathering places encourages social interaction among shoppers. Theatrical touches include live entertainment, special lighting effects, fountains, waterfalls, and eye-catching interior landscaping ranging from banks of flowers to surprisingly large trees. Individual stores try to add value by offering product demonstrations and such services as customized advice, gift wrapping, free delivery, installation, and warranty services.

When Should Service Be Delivered?

Some services have long operated 24 hours a day, every day of the year. Examples include those services that respond to emergencies, such as fire, police, and ambulance, or make repairs to vital equipment. Hospitals and first-class hotels provide 24-hour care or room service as a matter of course. Ships and long-distance trains don't stop for the night; they keep on going. Similarly, passenger aircraft operate around the clock, and telephone companies always have operators available on a 24-hour basis.

By contrast, most retail and professional services in industrialized countries used to follow a traditional and rather restricted schedule that limited service availability to about forty to fifty hours a week. In large measure, this routine reflected social norms (and even legal requirements or union agreements) as to what were appropriate hours for people to work and for enterprises to sell things. The situation caused a lot of inconvenience for working people, who either had to shop during their lunch break (if the stores themselves didn't close for lunch) or on Saturdays (if management chose to remain open a sixth day). But the idea of Sunday opening was strongly discouraged in most Christian cultures and often prohibited by law, reflecting long tradition based on religious practice. Among commercial services, only those devoted to entertainment and relaxation, such as cinemas, pubs, restaurants, and sporting facilities, geared their opening times toward weekends and evening hours when their customers were free. Even so, they often faced restrictions on hours of operation, especially on Sundays. Today, the situation is changing fast. For some highly responsive service operations, the standard has become 24/7 service—24 hours a day, seven days a week, around the world. For an overview of the factors behind the move to more extended hours, see Management Memo 11.1.

Factors That Encourage Extended Operating Hours

At least five factors are driving the move toward extended operating hours and seven-day operations. They reflect economic, legal, social, cultural, and technological developments in modern life.

- *Economic pressure from consumers.* The growing number of two-income families and single wage earners who live alone need time outside normal working hours to shop and use other services. Once one store or firm in any given area extends its hours to meet the needs of these market segments, competitors often feel obliged to follow. Retail chains have often led the way in this respect.
- *Changes in legislation.* A second factor has been the decline, lamented by some, of support for the traditional religious view that a specific day (Sunday in predominantly Christian cultures) should be legislated as a day of rest for one and all, regardless of religious affiliation. In a multicultural society, of course, it's a moot point which day should be designated as special. For observant Jews and Seventh Day Adventists, Saturday is the Sabbath; for Muslims, Friday is the holy day; and agnostics or atheists presumably don't mind. There has been a gradual erosion of such legislation in Western nations in recent years, although it's still firmly in place in some countries and locations. Switzerland, for example, still closes down most retail activities on Sundays, except for those related to bread, which people like to buy freshly baked on Sunday mornings.
- *Economic incentives to improve asset utilization.* A great deal of capital is tied up in service facilities. The incremental cost of extending hours is often relatively modest (especially when part-timers can be hired without paying them either overtime or benefits); if extending hours reduces crowding and increases revenues, then it's economically attractive. There are costs involved in shutting down and reopening a facility like a supermarket, yet climate control and some lighting must be left running all night, and security personnel must be paid to keep an eye on the place. Even if the number of extra customers served is minimal, there are both operational and marketing advantages to remaining open 24 hours.
- *Availability of employees to work during "unsocial" hours.* Changing lifestyles and a desire for part-time employment have combined to create a growing labor pool of people who are willing to work evenings and nights. Some of these workers are students looking for part-time work outside their classroom hours; some are moonlighting, holding a full-time job by day and earning additional income by night; some are parents juggling child care responsibilities; others simply prefer to work by night and relax or sleep by day; and still others are glad to obtain any paid employment, regardless of hours.
- *Automated self-service facilities.* Self-service equipment has become increasingly reliable and user friendly. Many machines now accept card-based payments in addition to coins and banknotes. Installing unattended machines may be economically feasible in places that couldn't support a staffed facility. Unless a machine requires frequent servicing or is particularly vulnerable to vandalism, the incremental cost of going from limited hours to 24-hour operation is minimal. In fact, it may be much simpler to leave machines running all the time than to turn them on and off, especially if they are placed in widely scattered locations.

Responding to Customers' Need for Convenience

U.S. and Canadian retailing have led the way toward meeting customer needs for greater convenience, but many other countries are now beginning to follow suit. A trend that began in earnest with early-morning to late-evening service in pharmacies and so-called convenience stores has now extended to 24-hour service in a variety of retail outlets, from service stations to restaurants to supermarkets.

The customer's search for convenience has not been confined to convenient times and places or to just purchase of core products. People want easy access to supplementary services, too, especially information, reservations, and problem solving.

There are now a large number of two-income families. Customers are busy with their personal lives and don't have a lot of time to handle such activities as banking, insurance, and even shopping. They expect suppliers to be available to them when it's convenient for customers, not when it's convenient for suppliers, so they want extended hours and easy access. And most of all, they expect one contact to solve their problem, rather than being asked to get in touch with a different office or dial another number.

Use of Call Centers. In many service industries, problem-solving needs were originally met by telephoning a specific store or company during its regular opening hours. But led by airlines and hotel chains, separate customer service centers have evolved, reached by calling a single number regardless of the caller's location. Some of these centers are operated by the service provider; others are subcontracted to specialist intermediaries (hotel chains, for instance, often delegate the reservations function to independent contractors). Once a firm departs from locally staffed phones and installs a centralized system, most customers will be calling from distant locations. So instead of forcing customers to pay the cost of a long-distance call, many firms have installed toll-free numbers. Once one company offers this convenience, competitors often feel obliged to follow the leader.

Providing extended-hours customer service is almost mandatory for any organization with a nationwide clientele in countries (or service regions) that cover multiple time zones. Consider a company that serves customers on both the Atlantic and Pacific coasts of North America. Between New York and Los Angeles, for instance, there is a three-hour time difference. If the switchboard closes at 5:00 P.M. Eastern time, for example, consumers on the West Coast are denied access to the number after 2:00 P.M. (the situation is even worse for those on Alaska-Hawaii time, where it's only 12:00 P.M.). The situation is reversed when the supplier is on the West Coast. Imagine a Canadian supplier in Vancouver, British Columbia, whose office opens at 8:30 A.M. Pacific time. By then it's already 12:30 P.M. Atlantic time in Halifax, Nova Scotia, and 1:00 P.M. in St. John's, Newfoundland (which has its own time zone 30 minutes ahead of Atlantic time).

Even having access between 8:30 A.M. and 5:00 P.M. local time is inconvenient for people who want to call a supplier from home before or after work. (If there's a mistake on your bank account, for instance, you're likely to discover it when you open your mail at home in the evening.)

When a North American business redefines its goal as offering continent-wide service on a daily basis, from first thing in the morning in Newfoundland to mid-evening in Alaska or Hawaii, then managers don't need a fancy calculator to figure out that customer service lines will have to be open at least 18 hours a day. At this point, why not go to 24-hour operation and cater to organizations that themselves operate on a 24-hour schedule as well as to individuals who work odd shifts and get up very early or go to bed very late? It depends on the firm's priorities, the costs involved, and the value that customers place on total accessibility. However, although operating a telephone-based customer service center may cost more for every hour added, a Web site is always open for business and can handle many transactions and queries without human backup (beyond that needed to support the computer system and servers).

Support Services. Most manufactured products create a need for accompanying services, ranging from finance and training to transportation and maintenance. Indeed, the competitiveness of a manufacturer's products in both domestic and global markets is as much a function of the availability and quality of relevant services as the quality of the core product. Increasingly, both manufacturing and service companies rely on computer-based systems to provide the supplementary services that customers need and expect. In turn, servicing these computer systems constitutes a major possession-processing industry.

Powerful computer systems—and the software to run them—have been sold to users all over the world. There are many niche players, but the market for large computer systems is supplied by a small handful of international firms. Although the applications to which they are put vary enormously, computers are only of value when they are up and running (or ready for service). System failures can have disastrous consequences for their users and also for the users' own customers. Supporting the enormous installed base of equipment and software, as well as helping users to plan for future needs, is a big business, attracting suppliers ranging from worldwide vendors to local service firms.

Historically, maintaining and repairing computers was a task that had to be performed on site. Proximity to the customer can give locally based third-party vendors a competitive edge over OEMs (original equipment manufacturers), who also tend to be more expensive. Varying educational levels among host-country nationals can also make it difficult for global OEMs such as Hewlett-Packard to ensure consistent standards of service to their customers around the world—a serious problem when dealing with complex equipment where speed and accuracy are of the essence in restoring defective hardware and software to good working order.

If a customer is dependent on a machine or a service 24 hours a day, downtime can be very disruptive. Emergencies don't just involve people. They involve vital equipment and processes, too. If a computer goes down, the consequences can range from personal inconvenience to shutdown of a major facility; if a transformer blows, electric power may be lost; if a furnace fails in below-freezing conditions, pipes may burst. Sometimes, these types of emergencies are handled by a duty person, reached by a pager or cellular phone, who drives to the site of the problem, makes a physical inspection, and undertakes whatever repairs are necessary. But by using modern telecommunications technology, engineers from companies such as IBM or Hewlett-Packard can often diagnose and fix problems involving software and hardware from a support center in another location—even in another part of the world—without ever leaving their own offices.

How Technology Is Revolutionizing Service Delivery

Technological developments during the last 20 years have had a remarkable impact on the way in which services are produced and delivered. Developments in telecommunications and computer technology in particular continue to result in many innovations in service delivery. An important result is that more than ever before, customers are now able to serve themselves, rather than requiring the assistance of an employee. This may offer opportunities for the customer to save time and for the firm to achieve higher productivity. In addition to the advantage of not requiring staffing, self-service machines can operate 24 hours a day and can be located in places where a full-service, staffed facility would not be an economic proposition. Telephone or Web-based services, of course, can be accessed from any phone or computer to which the customer has access.

Creation of freestanding, automated kiosks enables customers to conduct a variety of simple transactions. Many new applications of this technology are coming into use. One of the most frequently cited self-service innovations of the past quarter-century has been the ATM, which has revolutionized the delivery of retail banking services, making them available 24 hours a day every day of the year in a wide variety of convenient locations, often far from traditional retail branches. To expand the geographic area in which service can be delivered to their customers, banks have joined regional, national, and even global networks. This means that a bank can also offer service to customers from other banks and collect a fee for doing so. However, a bank's brand identify is weakened when the ATMs used by its customers are branded with the name of other banks or networks. Furthermore, the social bonds between customers and bank staff, which are often responsible for customers' remaining loyal to a particular bank, are severed.

Banks in many countries have embarked on programs of closing bank branches and shifting customers to cheaper, electronic banking channels in an effort to boost productivity and remain viable in an increasingly competitive marketplace. However, not all customers like to use self-service equipment, and so migration of customers to new electronic channels may require different strategies for different segments—as well as recognition that some proportion of customers will never voluntarily shift from their preferred high-contact delivery environments. An alternative that appeals to many people, perhaps because it uses a familiar technology, is banking by voice telephone.

The "*m*banx" virtual banking enterprise created by Bank of Montreal and its U.S. subsidiary, Chicago-based Harris Bank, seeks to offer customers a broad choice of 24-hour delivery channels, including telephone, fax, Internet, and ATM.

Promoting and Delivering Services in Cyberspace

Use of the telephone for selling and ordering goods and services has increased rapidly during the past few decades. More recently, entrepreneurs have taken advantage of the Internet to create new services that can be delivered through electronic channels accessed by computers in customers' homes or offices. Four innovations of particular interest are

- Development of so-called smart mobile telephones that can link users to the Internet wherever they may be.
- Voice recognition technology that allows customers to give information and request service simply by speaking into a phone or microphone.
- Creation of Web sites that can provide information, take orders, and even serve as a delivery channel for information-based services.
- Commercialization of smart cards containing a microchip that can store detailed information about the customer and act as an electronic purse containing digital money. The ultimate in self-service banking will be when you can not only use a smart card as an electronic wallet for a wide array of transactions but can also refill it from a special card reader connected to your computer modem.

Mobile telecommunications can, of course, be used by service personnel to call customers as well as the other way around. Research in France shows that when frontline personnel are equipped with mobile phones, customers obtain faster and better service; however, face-to-face contacts remain the preferred mode of exchange for complex situations.[6] The underlying theme of modern service delivery is one of offering customers more choices: Some people opt for face-to-face contact, others like telephone contact with a human being, and still others prefer the greater anonymity and control offered by more impersonal contacts. When purchasing goods, some customers like to visit the store and make a physical examination of the items that interest them. Others watch product demonstrations on television (sometimes called *infomercials*) and then call a toll-free number to place an order if they have seen something they like. Another group likes to select its purchases from a nicely printed catalog and to order by telephone or mail. Finally, a growing number of consumers are choosing to use the World Wide Web as a means of learning about and purchasing goods. In each instance, although the core product may remain the same, the wide differences in delivery systems mean that the nature of the overall service experience changes sharply as the encounter moves from high contact to low contact.

The Physical Evidence of the Servicescape

Physical evidence, one of the 8Ps of integrated service management, relates to the tangible objects encountered by customers in the service delivery environment as well as to tangible metaphors used in such communications as advertising, symbols, and trademarks. The most powerful physical evidence is experienced by customers who come to a service factory and experience employees working in a physical environment. The term *servicescape,* coined by Mary Jo Bitner, describes the style and appearance of the physical surroundings where customers and service providers interact.[7]

Servicescape Design

Servicescapes can create positive or negative impressions on each of the five senses. More and more service firms are paying careful attention to the design of the servicescapes that they offer their customers. In fact, some professional design firms have built successful practices creating and implementing carefully themed servicescapes for clients ranging across a broad cross-section of high-contact service businesses. Consider some of the evidence:

- Many traditional law firms seek to create a formal look. Their offices, which are sometimes announced on the exterior by highly polished brass plates, may feature interior walls with wood-paneling, solid furniture in an antique style, somber colors, and floor-to-ceiling bookshelves containing leather-bound law books; there is usually a conservative dress code for both professionals and other employees.
- Airlines employ corporate design consultants to help them differentiate the appearance of their aircraft and employees from those of competitors. Although the female flight attendants from many airlines look interchangeable in their black or navy blue outfits, others have distinctive uniforms that immediately identify them as employees of, say, Singapore Airlines or Southwest Airlines.
- A significant industry has grown up around theme restaurant design, with furnishings, pictures, real or fake antiques, carpeting, lighting, and choice of live or background music all trying to reinforce a desired look and style that may or may not be related to the cuisine.
- The more expensive hotels have become architectural statements. Some occupy classic buildings, lovingly restored at huge expense to a far higher level of luxury than ever known in the past and using antique furnishings and rugs to reinforce their old-world style. Modern hotels often feature dramatic atria in which wall-mounted elevators splash down in fountains. Resort hotels invest enormous sums to plant and maintain exotic gardens on their grounds.

As in a theater, scenery, lighting, music and other sounds, special effects, and the appearance of the actors (in this case the employees) and audience members (other customers) all serve to create an atmosphere in which the service performance takes place. In certain types of businesses, servicescapes are enhanced by judicious use of sounds, smells, and the textures of physical surfaces. Where food and drink are served, of course, taste is also highly relevant. For first-time customers in particular, the servicescape plays an important role in helping to frame expectations about both the style and quality of service to be provided. Because services are intangible performances and it's hard to evaluate them in advance (or even after service delivery), customers seek prepurchase clues as to service quality. Hence, first impressions are important. But as customers move beyond the entrance to a service business, continued exposure and experiences combine to create a more detailed impression. Of course, some visitors are more experienced than others. Consider the impressions recorded by a mystery shopper appraising a Toronto supermarket for a grocery trade magazine (see Service Perspectives 11.3).

SERVICE PERSPECTIVES 11.3

Let's Go Shopping (Maybe at Your Store)

5 CART [RATING]:

- Personnel
- Store Services
- Creativity
- Selection/Inventory
- Overall Store Atmosphere

"Let's Go Shopping" is a regular feature filed by "mystery shoppers" who visit grocery stores across the country to report on how stores measure up in terms of personnel, services, merchandising, selection, and overall store atmosphere.

Loblaws, #029
650 Dupont St. & Christie, Toronto
This chain-operated store's entrance was filled with tantalizing aromas from Movenpick; one of the many kiosks lining the store. The store's most unique asset is its one-stop, "under one roof" shopping experience. The Internet, in-store pharmacy, cleaners, wine store, bank machine, etc. prove to be successful additions to the store's business. Everything is done on a larger scale. This is evident in the large aisles and large signage throughout the store and increased SKUs. To enhance the mood of the environment; music, lighting and odors circulate to create customer comfort.

There were 14 cash registers in front of the store, five of which were open. The registers were completely computerized visual systems with scanning. Cashiers provide a choice between paper and plastic bags for those customers who are concerned with recycling. Shopping carts are clean and accessible at the store front with a dollar deposit. There were sufficient cart locations outside the store to attain/dispose of carts.

The pricing on the shelf after a random audit was accurate and highly visible. The overall impression of the shelves was that they were well stocked and faced with a large variety of SKUs. Presidents' Choice, the store's private label products, are aggressively promoted with signage at shelf and throughout the store.

In-Store Marketing:
The promotional weekly flyers, store signs and in-store features were promoted with large signage throughout the store. There was no loyalty card program or coupon clipping here, but there are store coupons available on the shelf. Similar to most stores they did accept manufacturers coupons. The primary displays included a variety of feature/advertised items, which are promoted on well-stocked displays throughout the store. The incremental displays were attractively done and promoted impulse purchases while the aisles are still clear and shoppable. While taking advantage of some good displays to cross promote, there were some obvious missed opportunities. The store has special racking for promoting some products, especially in the seasonal aisle. Overall the impression of in-store promotion was strong.

Staff:
Customer service is definitely not a thing of the past in this store. The staff was extremely customer-focused and seemed to enjoy the work environment. They were well groomed with clean/pressed uniforms. The knowledge of store staff when asked about an item was good. The shopper was directed to the appropriate location but was not taken directly over.

Full of color, the produce section was clean and well maintained. The deli section was also clean and the meat/salads were well stocked. The seafood section filled with the catch of the day looked fresh and inviting. The meat/butcher counter was acceptable. The staff was knowledgeable and helpful in all departments.

General Impressions:
The store's biggest strength is its one-stop shopping benefits. For a taste of international flair one must definitely shop the aisles. The one disappointment of the store was the meat department. The labels indicating specific meats were stained and the overall appearance of the department was unclean.

This store's overall ranking is outstanding. Shopping should be an excellent experience thus endorsing future loyalty to a store.

OVERALL [RATING]: 🛒 🛒 🛒 🛒

Reprinted with permission from *Canadian Grocer,* November 1997, 38.

Many servicescapes are purely functional. Firms that are trying to convey the impression of cut-rate service do so by locating in inexpensive neighborhoods; occupying buildings with a simple—even warehouse-like—appearance; minimizing wasteful use of space; and dressing their employees in practical, inexpensive uniforms, such as the bright red aprons worn at Home Depot. However, servicescapes do not always shape customer perceptions and behavior in ways intended by their creators. Veronique Aubert-Gamet notes that customers often make creative use of physical spaces and objects for different purposes.[8] For instance, businesspeople may appropriate a restaurant table for use as a temporary office desk, with papers spread around and even a laptop computer and mobile phone positioned on its surface, competing for space with the food and beverages. Smart designers keep an eye open for such trends—they may even lead to creation of a new service concept!

Customers themselves, when highly visible, also contribute to the impressions created by the overall servicescape. Consider Figure 11.3, which shows the interior of two restaurants. Imagine that you have just entered each of these two dining rooms. How is each positioning itself within the restaurant industry? What sort of meal experience can you expect? And what are the clues that you employ to make your judgments?

FIGURE 11.3 Distinctive servicescapes, from table settings to furniture and room design, create different customer expectations of these two restaurants.

Role of Physical Environments

Physical surroundings help to shape appropriate feelings and reactions among customers and employees. Consider how effectively many amusement parks use the servicescape concept to enhance their service offerings. The clean streets of Disneyland or Denmark's Legoland (both of which have established theme parks outside their respective home countries), plus employees in colorful costumes, all contribute to the sense of fun and excitement that visitors encounter on arrival and throughout their visit. Alternatively, think about the reception area of a successful professional firm—the offices of an investment bank or a consulting firm, for example—where the decor and furnishings tend to be elegant and designed to impress. Physical evidence and accompanying atmosphere impact buyer behavior in three ways:

1. As an attention-creating medium to make the servicescape stand out from those of competing establishments and to attract customers from target segments
2. As a message-creating medium, using symbolic cues to communicate with the intended audience about the distinctive nature and quality of the service experience
3. As an effect-creating medium, employing colors, textures, sounds, scents, and spatial design to create or heighten an appetite for certain goods, services or experiences

Antique stores provide a nice example of how carefully crafted design can itself become an important marketing tool. As noted by Philip Kotler:

> Many antique dealers also make use of "organizational chaos" as an atmospheric principle for selling their wares. The buyer enters the store and sees a few nice pieces and a considerable amount of junk. The nice pieces are randomly scattered in different parts of the store. The dealer gives the impression, through his prices and his talk, that he doesn't really know values. The buyer therefore browses quite systematically, hoping to spot an undiscovered Old Master hidden among the dusty canvases of third rate artists. He ends up buying something that he regards as value. Little does he know that the whole atmosphere has been arranged to create a sense of hidden treasures.[9]

Another illustration of giving more attention to the servicescape can be found in resort hotels. Club Med's villages, designed to create a totally carefree atmosphere, may have provided the original inspiration for getaway holiday environments. The new destination resorts are not only far more luxurious than Club Med but also draw for inspiration on theme park approaches to creating fantasy environments, both inside and outside. Perhaps the most extreme examples come from Las Vegas. Facing competition from numerous casinos in other locations, Las Vegas has been trying to reposition itself from an adult destination once described in a London newspaper as "the electric Sodom and Gomorrah" to a somewhat more wholesome family-fun resort. The gambling is still there, of course, but many of the huge hotels recently built (or rebuilt) have been transformed into visually striking entertainment centers that feature such attractions as erupting mechanical volcanoes, mock sea battles, and even reproductions of Venice and its canals.

The Role of Intermediaries

Many service organizations find it cost-effective to delegate certain tasks. Most frequently, this delegation concerns supplementary service elements. For instance, despite their greater use of telephone call centers and the Internet, transportation firms and hotels still rely for a significant portion of their business on travel agents who handle customer interactions such as giving out information, taking reservations, accepting payment, and ticketing. And, of course, many manufacturers rely on the services of distributors or retailers to stock and sell their physical products to end users, while also taking on responsibility for such supplementary services as information, advice, order taking, delivery, installation, billing and payment, and certain types of problem solving; in some cases, they may also handle certain types of repairs and upgrades.

Delegating Specific Service Elements

In Figure 11.4 we use the Flower of Service framework to illustrate how the original supplier may work in partnership with one or more intermediaries to deliver a complete service package to customers. In this example, the core product is still delivered by the originating supplier, together with certain supplementary elements in the informational, consultation, and exceptions categories. The remaining supplementary services packaged with this offering have been added by an intermediary to complete the offering as experienced by the customer. In other instances, several specialist outsourcers might be involved as intermediaries for specific elements. The challenge for the original supplier is to act as guardian of the overall process, ensuring that each element offered by intermediaries fits the overall service concept to create a consistent and seamless branded service experience.

Franchising

Even delivery of the core product can be outsourced to an intermediary. This is the essence of business format franchising. Franchising has become a popular way to expand delivery of an effective service concept to multiple sites without the level of investment capital that would be needed for rapid expansion of company-owned and -managed sites. A franchisor recruits entrepreneurs who are willing to invest their own time and equity in managing a previously developed service concept. In return, the franchisor provides training in how to operate and market the business, sells necessary supplies, and provides promotional support at a national or regional level to augment local marketing activities (which are paid for by the franchisee but must adhere to copy and media guidelines prescribed by the franchisor).

A disadvantage of delegating activities to franchisees is that it entails some loss of control over the delivery system and, thereby, over how customers experience the actual service. Ensuring that an intermediary adopts exactly the same priorities and procedures as prescribed by the franchisor is difficult yet vital to effective quality control. Franchisors usually seek to exercise control over all aspects of the service performance through a contract that specifies adherence to tightly defined service standards, procedures, scripts, and physical presentation. Franchisors control not only output specifications but also the appearance of the servicescape, employee performance, and such elements as service timetables. An ongoing problem is that as

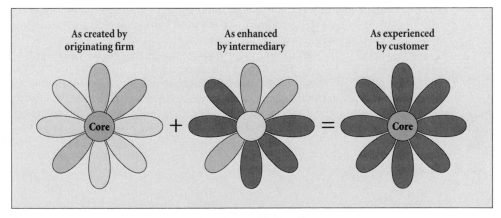

FIGURE 11.4 Splitting Responsibilities for Supplementary Service Elements

franchisees gain experience, they start to resent the various fees they pay the franchisor and believe that they can operate the business better without the constraints imposed by the agreement. The resulting disputes often lead to legal fights between the two parties.

Licensing and Distribution Agreements

An alternative to business format franchising is licensing another supplier to act on the original supplier's behalf to deliver the core product. Trucking companies regularly make use of independent agents, instead of locating company-owned branches in each of the different cities they serve; they may also choose to contract with independent owner-operators who drive their own trucks, rather than buying their own trucks and employing full-time drivers. Universities sometimes license another educational institution to deliver courses designed by the former.

Other service distribution agreements include financial services. Banks seeking to move into investment services will often act as the distributor for mutual fund products created by an investment firm that lacks extensive distribution channels of its own. Many banks also sell insurance products underwritten by an insurance company. They collect a commission on the sale but are not normally involved in handling claims.

Conclusion

"Where? When? and How?" Responses to these three questions form the foundation of service delivery strategy. The customer's service experience is a function of both service performance and delivery characteristics. "Where?" relates, of course, to the places where customers can obtain delivery of the core product, one or more supplementary services, or a complete package. In this chapter, we presented a categorization scheme for thinking about alternative place-related strategies, ranging from customers coming to the service site to service personnel visiting the customer, and finally a variety of options for arm's-length transactions, including delivery through both physical and electronic channels. The advent of the Internet and mobile telecommunications allow remote delivery of services in cyberspace, to be accessed by customers wherever is convenient for them. "When?" is involved with decisions on scheduling of service delivery. Customer demands for greater convenience are leading many firms to extend their hours and days of service, with the ultimate flexibility being offered by 24/7 service year-round. "How?" concerns channels and procedures for delivering the core and supplementary service elements to customers. Advances in technology are having a major impact on the alternatives available and on the economics of those alternatives. We return to technology issues in more depth in chapter 18.

Many service firms have a variety of options open to them, and the challenge is to select the channel that will best meet the needs of the target segment so long as price and other costs (including time and effort) remain acceptable. Responding to customer needs for flexibility, some firms offer several alternative choices of delivery channels. Although the organization that creates a service concept is much more likely than a manufacturer to control its own delivery systems, there's also a role for intermediaries, including franchisees.

REVIEW QUESTIONS

1. Compare and contrast the strategic and functional roles of servicescapes within a service organization. Give examples from retailing, airports, hotels, hospitals.

2. What are the key decisions faced by firms in designing effective service delivery systems? What are some of the key tradeoffs to be made?
3. What marketing and management challenges are raised by the use of intermediaries in a service setting?
4. In what ways do customers benefit from greater locational and time convenience in service settings? What are the implications for firms and employees?
5. What risks and opportunities are entailed for a retail service firm in adding electronic channels of delivery (a) paralleling a channel involving physical stores, (b) replacing the physical stores with an all-Internet (Web plus e-mail) channel? Give examples.

APPLICATION EXERCISES

1. Select a service organization with which you are reasonably familiar and construct a simple flowchart of service delivery. Identify the moments of truth, that is, the critical points within the service delivery process that are likely to have a significant bearing on customers' perceptions and sense of satisfaction. Clarify why these points in the process are particularly important. How would you go about managing these?
2. Using the same service organization or another of your choice, examine its use of technology in facilitating service delivery. Might there be other opportunities for technology to be employed beneficially? What are these?
3. Identify five situations in which you use self-service delivery. In each instance, what is your motivation for using this approach to delivery rather than having service personnel do it for you?
4. Using the same five situations, comment on the user-friendliness of the equipment, the mental and physical effort required (if any), the time involved, and any negative sensory experiences involved. What risks (if any) are there for you? What recommendations would you make to management to improve the experience?

ENDNOTES

1. See, for example, Regis McKenna, "Real-Time Marketing," *Harvard Business Review* 73 (July–August 1995): 87–98; Jeffrey F. Rayport and John J. Sviokla, "Exploiting the Virtual Value Chain," *Harvard Business Review* (November–December 1995): and Regis McKenna, *Real Time* (Boston: Harvard Business School Press, 1997).
2. See Christopher Lovelock, *Product Plus: How Product + Service = Competitive Advantage* (New York: McGraw-Hill, 1994), 78; and Jean-Claude Larréché, Christopher Lovelock, and Delphine Parmenter, "First Direct" (Fontainbleau: INSEAD; distributed by the European Case Clearing House, 1997).
3. James L. Heskett, W. Earl Sasser Jr., and Leonard A. Schlesinger, *The Service Profit Chain* (New York: The Free Press, 1997) 218–220.
4. Information obtained from Forrester Research's Web site: www.forrester.com, December, 1998.
5. Diane Brady, "How Barnes & Noble Misread the Web," *Business Week,* February 7, 2000, 63.
6. Marie-Christine Monnoyer-Longé, "Servuction and Mobile Telephony," *The Service Industries Journal* 19 (January 1999): 117–132.
7. Mary Jo Bitner, "Servicescapes: The Impact of Physical Surroundings on Customers and Employees," *Journal of Marketing* 56 (April 1992): 57–71.
8. Véronique Aubert-Gamet, "Twisting Servicescapes: Diversion of the Physical Environment in a Reappropriation Process," *International Journal of Service Industry Management* 8, no. 1 (1997): 26–41.
9. Philip Kotler, "Atmospherics As a Marketing Tool," *Journal of Retailing* 49, no. 4 (1973): 48–64.

Enhancing Value by Improving Quality and Productivity

Not everything that counts can be counted, and not everything that can be counted, counts.

ALBERT EINSTEIN

Productivity was one of the key managerial imperatives of the 1970s: working faster and more efficiently to reduce costs. During the 1980s and early 1990s, improving quality became a major priority. In a service context, this strategy required efforts to improve customer satisfaction by creating better service processes and outcomes. At the beginning of the twenty-first century, we're seeing growing emphasis on linking these two strategies to create better value for both customers and the firm.

Both quality and productivity were historically seen as issues for operations managers. When improvements in these areas required better employee selection, training, and supervision—or renegotiation of labor agreements relating to job assignments and work rules—then human resource managers were expected to get involved, too. But it was not until service quality was explicitly linked to customer satisfaction that marketers were also seen as having an important role to play.

Broadly defined, the task of value enhancement requires quality improvement programs to deliver and continuously enhance the benefits desired by customers; at the same time, productivity improvement efforts must seek to reduce the associated costs. Considered jointly, productivity and quality form a powerful component of the 8Ps of integrated service management. The challenge is to ensure that improvement programs in each sphere are mutually reinforcing in achieving common goals rather than operating at loggerheads with one another in pursuit of conflicting goals.

In this chapter, we review the challenges involved in improving both productivity and quality in service organizations and explore the following questions:

1. What is meant by *productivity* and *quality* in a service context, and why should they be linked when formulating marketing strategy?
2. How do we measure productivity and quality?
3. In what ways can service productivity be improved in different types of services?
4. What is the relationship between customer expectations, service quality, and customer satisfaction?
5. What are the key dimensions of service quality as described in the SERVQUAL scale?
6. What are the components of a service quality information system?

Integrating Productivity and Quality Strategies

A key theme running through this book is that where services are concerned, marketing cannot operate in isolation from other functional areas. Tasks that might be considered the sole preserve of operations in a manufacturing environment need to involve marketers because customers are often exposed to—even actively involved in—service processes. Making service processes more efficient doesn't necessarily result in a better-quality experience for customers or lead to improved benefits for them. So marketers and operations managers need to engage in dialogue. Getting service employees to work faster may sometimes be welcomed by customers, but at other times it may make them feel rushed and unwanted. So marketing, operations, and human resource managers need to work together on designing frontstage jobs. Similarly, implementing marketing strategies to improve customer satisfaction with services can prove costly and disruptive for an organization if the implications for operations and human resources have not been carefully thought through—hence, the need to consider productivity and quality improvement strategies jointly rather than in isolation from one another.

Writing in the early 1990s, Gummesson observed that although service quality must be viewed in conjunction with service productivity and profitability, quality in the service sector had been widely researched, whereas productivity had not.[1] Today, the situation is changing, and we note insights from several recent research studies on service productivity in the course of this chapter, as well as reproducing later in the book the reading by Vuorinen, Jarvinen, and Lehtinen, "Content and Measurement of Productivity in the Service Sector" (see pp. 430–443).

A Role for Marketing

What is the fundamental basis for marketing? Many theorists argue that it is to create customer value.[2] The search for value often begins with market research, which seeks to identify the benefits sought by customers or prospects for a given product category and the costs that they are willing to incur to obtain these benefits. But as Holbrook emphasizes, perceived value is highly personal and may vary widely from one customer to another.[3] In fact, variations in the benefits desired often form the basis for segmentation.

In earlier chapters, we examined some of the key tools available to service marketers for creating services that offer value to target customers. Service design—embracing the core product, supplementary services, and the delivery system—is a key element in the value equation and should be directed at enhancing desired benefits and reducing unwanted costs. Reengineering of existing production and delivery systems may be needed to improve service value, either by adding new benefits or by reducing the associated costs as a result of greater productivity.

Pricing decisions, of course, are intimately related to value for the customer: Lowering monetary prices (often a function of improved productivity) while maintaining perceived benefits will serve to increase perceived value. A marketing input is important to advise operations experts on whether or not customers may be willing to make trade-offs, such as paying a higher price to obtain more benefits or avoid unwanted time and effort. However, unless such a strategy is accompanied by either increased sales volume or lower costs from improved productivity, it may not increase profits. Finally, advertising and other communications efforts may be needed to clarify service benefits (especially when research shows that prospective users misperceive the relevant costs and benefits), to encourage trial, and to educate customers on how to obtain the best value from that service.

Marketing and Quality

Marketing's interest in service quality is obvious when one thinks about it: Poor quality places a firm at a competitive disadvantage. If customers perceive quality as unsatisfactory, they may be quick to take their business elsewhere. Recent years have witnessed a veritable explosion of discontent with service quality at a time when the quality of many manufactured goods seems to have improved significantly.

Service quality problems are not confined to traditional service industries. Many manufacturing firms are struggling to improve the quality of the supplementary services that support their products—consultation, financing, shipping and delivery, installation, training of operators, repair and maintenance, troubleshooting, and billing, for instance.

From a marketing standpoint, a key issue is whether or not customers notice differences in quality between competing suppliers. Gale puts it succinctly when he says that "value is simply quality, however the *customer* defines it, offered at the right price."[4] Improving quality in the eyes of the customer pays off for the companies that provide it: Data from the Profit Impact of Market Strategy (PIMS) show that a perceived quality advantage leads to higher profits.[5]

Marketing and Productivity

Improving productivity is important to marketers for several reasons. First, it helps to keep costs down. Lower costs either mean higher profits or the ability to hold down prices. The company with the lowest costs in an industry has the option to position itself as the low-price leader— usually a significant advantage among price-sensitive market segments. Firms with lower costs than their competitors also generate higher margins, giving them the option of spending more than the competition in such marketing activities as advertising and promotion, sales efforts, improved customer service, and supplementary service extras; they may also be able to offer higher margins to attract and reward the best distributors and intermediaries. Finally, there is the opportunity to secure the firm's long-term future through investments in new service technologies and research to create superior new services, improved features, and innovative delivery systems.

Efforts to improve productivity often have an impact on customers, and it's the marketer's responsibility to ensure that negative impacts are avoided or minimized and that new procedures are carefully presented to customers. When the impact is a positive one, then the improvements can be promoted as a new advantage. Finally, as we'll see, there are opportunities for marketers themselves to help improve productivity by involving customers actively in the service production and delivery process.

Definition and Measurement

It's commonly said that you cannot manage what you do not measure. Without measurement, managers cannot identify where their firm or products currently stand and whether desired goals are being achieved. Measurement, in turn, requires careful definition so that people agree on what they are talking about and what they are measuring. Quality and productivity are twin paths to creating value for both customers and companies. In broad terms, quality focuses on the benefits created for customers' side of the equation, and productivity ties into the financial costs incurred by the firm, which may subsequently be passed on to customers, primarily in the form of price.

Defining and Measuring Quality

The word *quality* means different things to people according to the context. Garvin identifies five perspectives.

- *The transcendent view* of quality is synonymous with innate excellence, a mark of uncompromising standards and high achievement. This viewpoint is often applied to the performing and visual arts. It argues that people learn to recognize quality only through the experience gained from repeated exposure. However, from a practical standpoint, suggesting that managers or customers will know quality when they see it is not very helpful.
- *The product-based approach* sees quality as a precise and measurable variable. Differences in quality, it argues, reflect differences in the amount of some ingredient or attribute possessed by the product. Because this view is totally objective, it fails to account for differences in the tastes, needs, and preferences of individual customers (or even entire market segments).
- *User-based definitions* start with the premise that quality lies in the eyes of the beholder; these definitions equate quality with maximum satisfaction. This subjective, demand-oriented perspective recognizes that different customers have different wants and needs.
- *The manufacturing-based approach*, in contrast, is supply based and primarily concerned with engineering and manufacturing practices. (In services, we would say that quality was operations driven.) It focuses on conformance to internally developed specifications, which are often driven by productivity and cost containment goals.
- *Value-based definitions* define quality in terms of value and price. By considering the trade-off between performance (or conformance) and price, quality comes to be defined as "affordable excellence."[6]

Garvin suggests that these alternative views of quality help to explain the conflicts that sometimes arise between managers in different functional departments. However, he goes on to argue:

> Despite the potential for conflict, companies can benefit from such multiple perspectives. Reliance on a single definition of quality is a frequent source of problems. . . . Because each approach has its predictable blind spots, companies are likely to suffer fewer problems if they employ multiple perspectives on quality, actively shifting the approach they take as products move from design to market. . . . Success normally requires close coordination of the activities of each function.[7]

Manufacturing–Based Components of Quality. To incorporate differing perspectives, Garvin developed eight components of quality that could be useful as a framework for analysis and strategic planning. These are (1) performance (primary operating characteristics), (2) features (bells and whistles), (3) reliability (probability of malfunction or failure), (4) conformance (ability to meet specifications), (5) durability (how long the product continues to provide value to the customer), (6) serviceability (speed, courtesy, competence, and ease of having problems fixed), (7) aesthetics (how the product appeals to any or all of the user's five senses), and (8) perceived quality (associations such as the reputation of the company or brand name). Note that these categories were developed from a manufacturing perspective, but they do address the notion of serviceability of a physical good.

Service-Based Components of Quality. Researchers argue that the distinctive nature of services requires an equally distinctive approach to defining and measuring service quality. Because of the intangible, multifaceted nature of many services, it may be harder to evaluate the quality of a service than a good. Because customers are often involved in service production— particularly in people-processing services—a distinction needs to be drawn between the *process* of service delivery (what Grönroos calls *functional quality*) and the actual *output* of the service (what he calls *technical quality*).[8] Grönroos and others also suggest that the perceived quality of a service will be the result of an evaluation process in which customers compare their perceptions of service delivery and its outcome against what they expected.

The most extensive research into service quality is strongly user oriented. From focus-group research, Zeithaml, Berry, and Parasuraman identified 10 criteria used by consumers in evaluating service quality (Table 12.1). In subsequent research, they found a high degree of correlation between several of these variables and so consolidated them into five broad dimensions:

- *Tangibles* (appearance of physical elements)
- *Reliability* (dependable, accurate performance)
- *Responsiveness* (promptness and helpfulness)
- *Assurance* (competence, courtesy, credibility, and security)
- *Empathy* (easy access, good communications, and customer understanding)[9]

Only one of these five dimensions, reliability, has a direct parallel in findings from Garvin's research on manufacturing quality.

Measuring Satisfaction. To measure customer satisfaction with different aspects of service quality, Parasuraman, Zeithaml, and Berry developed a survey research instrument called SERVQUAL.[10] It is based on the premise that customers can evaluate a firm's service quality by comparing their perceptions of its service with their expectations. SERVQUAL is seen as a generic measurement tool that can be applied across a broad spectrum of service industries. In its basic form, the scale contains 21 perception items and a series of expectation items, reflecting the five dimensions of service quality just described (Table 12.2). Respondents complete a series of scales that measure their expectations of companies in a particular industry on a wide array of specific service characteristics; subsequently, they are asked to record their perceptions of a specific company whose services they have used on those same characteristics. When perceived performance ratings are lower than expectations, this is a sign of poor quality; the reverse indicates good quality.

Although SERVQUAL has been widely used by service companies, doubts have been expressed with regard to both its conceptual foundation and methodological limitations.[11] To evaluate the stability of the five underlying dimensions when applied to a variety of different service industries, Mels, Boshoff, and Nel analyzed data sets from banks, insurance brokers, vehicle repair shops, electrical repair shops, and life insurance firms.[12] Their findings suggest that in reality, SERVQUAL difference scores measure only two factors: intrinsic service quality (resembling what Grönroos termed *functional quality*) and extrinsic service quality (which

TABLE 12.1. *Generic Dimensions Used by Customers to Evaluate Service Quality*

Dimension	Definition	Examples of Questions That Customers Might Raise
Credibility	Trustworthiness, believability, honesty of the service provider	Does the hospital have a good reputation? Does my stockbroker refrain from pressuring me to buy? Does the repair firm guarantee its work?
Security	Freedom from danger, risk, or doubt	Is it safe for me to use the bank's ATMs at night? Is my credit card protected against unauthorized use? Can I be sure that my insurance policy provides complete coverage?
Access	Approachability and ease of contact	How easy is it for me to talk to a supervisor when I have a problem? Does the airline have a 24-hour toll-free phone number? Is the hotel conveniently located?
Communication	Listening to customers and keeping them informed in language they can understand	When I have a complaint, is the manager willing to listen to me? Does my doctor avoid using technical jargon? Does the electrician call when unable to keep a scheduled appointment?
Understanding the customer	Making the effort to know customers and their needs	Does someone in the hotel recognize me as a regular customer? Does my stockbroker try to determine my specific financial objectives? Is the moving company willing to accommodate my schedule?
Tangibles	Appearance of physical facilities, equipment, personnel, and communication materials	Are the hotel's facilities attractive? Is my accountant dressed appropriately? Is my bank statement easy to understand?
Reliability	Ability to perform the promised service dependably and accurately	When a lawyer says she will call me back in 15 minutes, does she do so? Is my telephone bill free of errors? Is my television repaired right the first time?
Responsiveness	Willingness to help customers and provide prompt service	When there's a problem, does the firm resolve it quickly? Is my stockbroker willing to answer my questions? Is the cable TV company willing to give me a specific time when the installer will show up?
Competence	Possession of the skills and knowledge required to perform the service	Can the bank teller process my transaction without fumbling around? When I call my travel agent, is she able to obtain the information I need? Does the dentist appear to know what he is doing?
Courtesy	Politeness, respect, consideration, and friendliness of contact personnel	Does the flight attendant have a pleasant demeanor? Are the telephone operators consistently polite when answering my calls? Does the plumber take off his muddy shoes before stepping on my carpet?

Source: Adapted from Valarie A. Zeithaml, A. Parasuraman, and Leonard L. Berry, *Delivering Quality Service: Balancing Customer Perceptions and Expectations* (New York: The Free Press, 1990).

TABLE 12.2 *The SERVQUAL Scale*

The SERVQUAL scale includes five dimensions: tangibles, reliability, responsiveness, assurance, and empathy. Within each dimension are several items measured on a seven-point scale from *strongly agree* to *strongly disagree*, for a total of 21 items.

SERVQUAL Questions

Note: For actual survey respondents, instructions are also included, and each statement is accompanied by a seven-point scale ranging from "strongly agree = 7" to "strongly disagree = 1." Only the end points of the scale are labeled—there are no words above the numbers 2 through 6.

Tangibles

- Excellent banks [refer to cable TV companies, hospitals, or the appropriate service business throughout the questionnaire] will have modern-looking equipment.
- The physical facilities at excellent banks will be visually appealing.
- Employees at excellent banks will be neat in appearance.
- Materials associated with the service (like brochures or statements) will be visually appealing in an excellent bank.

Reliability

- When excellent banks promise to do something by a certain time, they will do so.
- When customers have a problem, excellent banks will show a sincere interest in solving it.
- Excellent banks will perform the service right the first time.
- Excellent banks will provide their services at the time they promise to do so.
- Excellent banks will insist on error-free records.

Responsiveness

- Employees of excellent banks will tell customers exactly when service will be performed.
- Employees of excellent banks will give prompt service to customers.
- Employees of excellent banks will always be willing to help customers.
- Employees of excellent banks will never be too busy to respond to customer requests.

Assurance

- The behavior of employees of excellent banks will instill confidence in customers.
- Customers of excellent banks will feel safe in their transactions.
- Employees of excellent banks will be consistently courteous with customers.
- Employees of excellent banks will have the knowledge to answer customer questions.

Empathy

- Excellent banks will give customers individual attention.
- Excellent banks will have operating hours convenient to all their customers.
- Excellent banks will have employees who give customers personal attention.
- The employees of excellent banks will understand the specific needs of their customers.

Adapted from A. Parasuraman, Valarie A. Zeithaml, and Leonard Berry, "SERVQUAL: A Multiple Item Scale for Measuring Consumer Perceptions of Service Quality," *Journal of Retailing* 64 (1988): 12–40.

refers to the tangible aspects of service delivery and "*resembles to some extent* what Grönroos refers to as technical quality"). In another study, Lam and Woo found that the SERVQUAL scale was not stable over time, as revealed by insignificant correlations between test scores and retest scores.[13] Although scores on items in the expectation battery remained fairly stable over time, the performance items were subject to instability even in a one-week test-retest interval.

These findings do not undermine the value of Zeithaml, Berry, and Parasuraman's achievement in identifying some of the key underlying constructs in service quality, but they do highlight the difficulty of measuring customer perceptions of quality. Smith notes that the majority of researchers using SERVQUAL have omitted from, added to, or altered the list of statements purporting to measure service quality.[14]

There are some risks, however, to defining service quality primarily in terms of customers' satisfaction with outcomes relative to their prior expectations. If customers' expectations are low and actual service delivery proves to be marginally better than the dismal level that had been expected, we can hardly claim that customers are receiving good-quality service!

Satisfaction-based research into quality assumes that customers are dealing with services that are high in search or experience characteristics (see chapter 4). A problem arises when they are asked to evaluate the quality of those services that are high in *credence* characteristics, such as complex legal cases or medical treatments, which they find hard to evaluate even after delivery is completed. In short, the customers may not be sure what to expect in advance, and they may not know for years—if ever—how good a job the professional actually did. A natural tendency in such situations is for clients or patients to evaluate quality in terms of process factors, such as whether or not they liked the providers' personal style and how satisfied they were with the perceived quality of those supplementary elements that they are competent to evaluate (for example, the tastiness of hospital meals or the clarity of bills for legal services). Consequently, measuring the quality of professional performance may require adding peer reviews of both process and outcomes as these relate to service execution on the core product.

Devlin and Dong offer guidelines on how to measure service quality across every aspect of the business in a real-world setting.[15] To help customers recall and evaluate their service experiences, these authors suggest taking them through each step of their service encounters (this approach is sometimes referred to as a *walk-through audit*). Stuart and Tax demonstrate the value of the quality function deployment (QFD) process for both strategic service positioning and quality of service delivery; in particular, they illustrate how the "voice of the customer" can be related to each individual service encounter.[16]

Defining and Measuring Productivity

Simply defined, *productivity* measures the amount of output produced by an organization relative to the amount of inputs required. Hence, improvements in productivity require an increase in the ratio of outputs to inputs. An improvement in this ratio might be achieved by cutting the resources required to create a given volume of output or by increasing the output obtained from a given level of inputs.

Input. What do we mean by *input* in a service context? Input varies according to the nature of the business but may include labor (both physical and intellectual), materials, energy, and capital (consisting of land, buildings, equipment, information systems, and financial assets). The intangible nature of service performances makes it more difficult to measure the productivity of service industries than that of manufacturing. The problem is especially acute for information-based services. A manufacturer's output consists of products like cars, packages of soap powder, transformers, or drill bits that can all be counted and readily sorted into different models or categories. Because production and consumption are separated in time, defective items that are caught by quality control inspectors will either be recycled or reworked, thus adding to their respective input costs.

Output. Measuring productivity is difficult in services when the output is hard to define. In a people-processing service, such as a hospital, we can look at the number of patients treated in the course of a year and at the hospital's census, or average bed occupancy. But how do we account for the different types of interventions performed—removal of cancerous tumors, treatment of diabetes, or setting of broken bones—and the almost inevitable variability between one patient and another? And how do we evaluate the inevitable difference in outcomes? Some patients get better, some develop complications, and sadly, some even die. There are relatively few standardized procedures in medicine that offer highly predictable outcomes.

The measurement task is perhaps simpler in possession-processing services, because many are quasi-manufacturing organizations, performing routine tasks with easily measurable input and output. Examples include garages that change a car's oil and rotate its tires or fast-food restaurants that offer limited and simple menus. But the task gets more complicated when the garage mechanic has to find and repair a water leak or when we are dealing with a French restaurant known for its varied and exceptional cuisine. And what about information-based services? How should we define the output of a bank or a consulting firm? And how does the latter's output compare to a law firm's? Lawyers like to boast (or keep quiet) about their billable hours—but what were they actually doing during those hours, and how do we measure their output as opposed to their fees?

Efficiency, Effectiveness, and Productivity. Klassen, Russell, and Chrisman distinguish between efficiency, productivity, and effectiveness.[17] *Efficiency* involves comparison to a standard that is usually time based—such as how long it takes for an employee to perform a particular task relative to a predefined standard. *Productivity,* however, involves financial valuation of outputs to inputs. *Effectiveness,* by contrast, can be defined as the degree to which an organization is meeting its goals.

A major problem in measuring service productivity concerns variability. As Heskett points out, traditional measures of service output tend to ignore variations in the quality or value of service. In freight transport, for instance, a ton-mile of output for freight that is delivered late is treated the same for productivity purposes as a similar shipment delivered on time.[18]

Another approach, counting the number of customers served per unit of time, suffers from the same shortcoming: What happens when an increase in customer throughput is achieved at the expense of perceived service quality? Suppose a hairdresser serves three customers per hour and finds she can increase her output to one every 15 minutes—giving what is technically just as good a haircut—by using a faster but noisier hairdryer, eliminating all conversation, and generally rushing her customers. Even if the haircut itself is just as good, the delivery process may be perceived as functionally inferior, leading customers to rate the overall service experience less positively.

The problem is that classical techniques of productivity measurement focus on outputs rather than outcomes; they stress efficiency but neglect effectiveness. In the long run, organizations that are more effective in consistently delivering outcomes desired by customers should be able to command higher prices for their output. The need to emphasize effectiveness and outcomes suggests that issues of productivity cannot be divorced from those of quality and value. As noted in chapter 5, loyal customers who remain with a firm tend to become more profitable over time, an indication of the payback to be obtained from providing quality service. In this vein, Shaw suggests that measures of productivity growth in services should focus on customers as the denominator.[19] He proposes the following units of analysis and comparison:

- Profitability by customer
- Capital employed per customer
- Shareholder equity employed per customer

These measures tell the firm how it is doing. But what managers and employees also need are insights as to how better results may be achieved. One insight in this respect comes from Frei and Harker, who focus on the underlying processes in retail banking and have developed a methodology to help managers understand how much inefficiency in a business process is due to the process design employed and how much is due to process execution.[20]

Identifying and Correcting Service Quality Shortfalls

If one accepts the view that quality entails consistently meeting customers' expectations, then the manager's task is to balance customer expectations and perceptions and to close any gaps between the two.

Before customers purchase a service, they have expectations about service quality that are based on individual needs, past experiences, word-of-mouth recommendations, and a service provider's marketing communications (refer to chapter 4 for a detailed discussion of how expectations are formed and the zone of tolerance between desired and adequate service). After buying and consuming the service, customers compare the expected quality of the service with what they actually received. Service performances that surprise and delight customers by falling above their desired service levels will be seen as superior in quality. If service delivery falls within their zone of tolerance, customers will feel that service quality is adequate.

Gaps in Service Design and Delivery

Zeithaml, Berry, and Parasuraman identify four potential shortfalls—or gaps—within the service organization that may lead to the fifth and most serious gap, the difference between what customers expected and what they perceived was delivered.[21] The other shortfalls are

- Not knowing what customers expect
- Specifying service quality standards that do not reflect what management believes to be customers' expectations
- Failing to ensure that service performance matches specifications
- Not living up to the levels of service performance that are promised or implied by marketing communications

Improving quality requires identifying the specific causes of each gap and then developing strategies to close them.

We have adapted and extended their framework to identify a total of seven types of gaps that can occur at different points during the design and delivery of a service performance (Figure 12.1).

1. *The knowledge gap*—the difference between what service providers believe customers expect and customers' actual needs and expectations
2. *The standards gap*—the difference between management's perceptions of customer expectations and the quality standards established for service delivery
3. *The delivery gap*—the difference between specified delivery standards and the service provider's actual performance on these standards

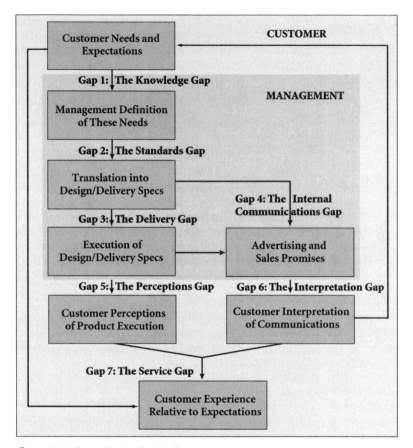

FIGURE 12.1 Seven Service Quality Gaps
Source: Adapted from an earlier model by V. A. Zeithaml, A. Parasuraman, and L. L. Berry.

4. *The internal communications gap*—the difference between what the company's advertising and sales personnel think are the product's features, performance, and service quality level and what the company is actually able to deliver
5. *The perceptions gap*—the difference between what is actually delivered and what customers perceive they have received (because they are unable to accurately evaluate service quality)
6. *The interpretation gap*—the difference between what a service provider's communication efforts (in advance of service delivery) actually promise and what a customer thinks was promised by these communications
7. *The service gap*—the difference between what customers expect to receive and their perceptions of the service that is actually delivered

As clarified by the diagram, Gaps 1, 6, and 7 represent external gaps between the customer and the organization. Gaps 2 through 5 are internal gaps occurring between different functions and departments within the organization.

Any of the seven quality gaps can damage relationships with customers. The service gap (number 7) is the most critical, because it represents the difference between the customer's overall assessment of what was expected as compared to his or her perceptions of what was delivered. The ultimate goal in improving service quality is to narrow this gap as much as possible. But to achieve this, service providers may have to reduce or close the six other gaps shown in Figure 12.1. Improving service quality requires identifying the specific causes of each gap and then developing strategies to close them.

Zeithaml, Parasuraman, and Berry propose a series of generic steps for closing gaps 1 through 4. Their prescriptions (relabeled to conform to the terminology of Figure 12.1), are summarized in Table 12.3.[22] What of gaps 5 and 6? As shown in Figure 12.1, these two gaps may interact with each other.

Gap 5—the perceptions gap—reflects the fact that customers do not always correctly understand what the service has done for them. This situation is particularly likely to occur with credence services where it is hard to judge performance even after delivery. Some service personnel make a point not only of keeping customers informed during service delivery but also of debriefing them at the end and, sometimes, of offering tangible evidence. For instance, a doctor may explain to a patient what took place during a medical procedures such as surgery, what was found—if anything—that differed from what was expected, and what the patient can expect for the future. To explain the nature of a complex repair, a technician may give a similar debriefing to the customer personnel who commissioned it and provide physical evidence in the form of showing the damaged components that had to be replaced. To reduce Gap 6—the interpretation gap—communication specialists in the firm need to pretest all advertising, brochures, telephone scripts, and Web site content *before* they are published. Pretesting, widely used by advertising agencies, involves presenting communication materials to a sample of customers in advance of publication. Those participating in the pretest can be asked their opinion of the communications in question and what they interpret the specific or implied promises to mean. If their interpretation is not what the firm intended, then changes to text copy or images will be needed. Service personnel who communicate with customers directly—including, but not limited to, sales and customer service—should ensure through questioning that customers understand their presentations correctly.

The strength of the gap methodology is that it offers generic insights and solutions that can be applied across different industries. What it doesn't attempt, of course, is to identify specific quality failures that may occur in particular service businesses. Each firm must develop its own customized approach to ensure that service quality becomes and remains a key objective.

Identifying Failure Points

A powerful tool for understanding the activities and processes involved in delivering a particular type of service is blueprinting (discussed in chapter 8). A well-constructed blueprint (or flowchart) enables us to visualize the process of service delivery by depicting the sequence of frontstage interactions that customers experience as they encounter service providers, facilities, and equipment, together with supporting backstage activities, which are hidden from the customers and not part of the actual service experience.

But it's important to recognize that backstage problems may well have undesirable frontstage outcomes. As noted earlier, blueprinting can be undertaken at different levels of detail. A basic blueprint provides a bird's-eye view of the overall service delivery process (take another look at the restaurant blueprint in Figure 8.4 on p. 226–229). Such a diagram displays the major elements of service (both core product and supplementary services), showing the principal interactions with customers and a plausible sequence in which they might take place. This is very helpful for clarifying the elements of the service (is anything missing?), showing the sequence in which these elements are delivered (is this the most appealing sequence for the customer?), and identifying the standards applying to each activity (are these being met?).

TABLE 12.3 *Prescriptions for Closing Service Gaps*

Gap 1 Prescription: Learn What Customers Expect

Understand customer expectations through research, complaint analysis, customer panels, etc.

Increase direct interactions between managers and customers to improve understanding.

Improve upward communication from contact personnel to management.

Turn information and insights into action.

Gap 2 Prescription: Establish the Right Service Quality Standards

Ensure that top management displays ongoing commitment to quality as defined by customers.

Set, communicate, and reinforce customer-oriented service standards for all work units.

Train managers in the skills needed to lead employees to deliver quality service.

Become receptive to new ways of doing business that overcome barriers to delivering quality service.

Standardize repetitive work tasks to ensure consistency and reliability by substituting hard technology for human contact and improving work methods (soft technology).

Establish clear service quality goals that are challenging, realistic, and explicitly designed to meet customer expectations.

Clarify which job tasks have the biggest impact on quality and should receive the highest priority.

Ensure that employees understand and accept goals and priorities.

Measure performance and provide regular feedback.

Reward managers and employees for attaining quality goals.

Gap 3 Prescription: Ensure That Service Performance Meets Standards

Clarify employee roles.

Ensure that all employees understand how their jobs contribute to customer satisfaction.

Match employees to jobs by selecting for the abilities and skills needed to perform each job well.

Provide employees with the technical training needed to perform their assigned tasks effectively.

Develop innovative recruitment and retention methods to attract the best people and build loyalty.

Enhance performance by selecting the most appropriate and reliable technology and equipment.

Teach employees about customer expectations, perceptions, and problems.

Train employees in interpersonal skills, especially for dealing with customers under stressful conditions.

Eliminate role conflict among employees by involving them in the process of setting standards.

Train employees in priority setting and time management.

Measure employee performance and tie compensation and recognition to delivery of quality service.

Develop reward systems that are meaningful, timely, simple, accurate, and fair.

Empower managers and employees in the field by pushing decision-making power down the organization; allow them greater discretion in the methods they use to reach goals.

Ensure that employees working at internal support jobs provide good service to customer-contact personnel.

Build teamwork so that employees work well together, and use team rewards as incentives.

Treat customers as partial employees; clarify their roles in service delivery, train and motivate them to perform well in their roles as coproducers.

Gap 4 Prescription: Ensure That Communication Promises Are Realistic

Seek inputs from operations personnel when new advertising programs are being created.

Develop advertising that features real employees performing their jobs.

Allow service providers to preview advertisements before customers are exposed to them.

Get sales staff to involve operations staff in face-to-face meetings with customers.

Develop internal educational, motivational, and advertising campaigns to strengthen links among marketing, operations, and human resource departments.

Ensure that consistent standards of service are delivered across multiple locations.

Ensure that advertising content accurately reflects those service characteristics that are most important to customers in their encounters with the organization.

Manage customers' expectations by letting them know what is and is not possible—and the reasons why.

Identify and explain uncontrollable reasons for shortcomings in service performance.

Offer customers different levels of service at different prices, explaining the distinctions.

Source: Distilled from chapters 4, 5, 6, and 7 of Valarie A. Zeithaml, A. Parasuraman, and Leonard L. Berry, *Delivering Quality Service: Balancing Customer Perceptions and Expectations* (New York: The Free Press, 1990).

Blueprints can also highlight the points where failures are most likely to occur, helping planners to identify how failures at one point (such as in overbooking reservations) may have a ripple effect later on in the process (the customer arrives at the restaurant and is told that no tables are available for the chosen time).

A more detailed blueprint might focus on a specific activity—such as making a reservation—that can be exploded into a series of subactivities. For a customer, these actions may include seeking the restaurant's phone number, telephoning and waiting for an answer, getting a response, asking for information about the restaurant and its menus, requesting a table for a specific time and date, receiving confirmation for the chosen time (or being offered an alternative if no tables are free), being asked for his or her name and phone number, receiving a final confirmation of all the details, and putting down the phone. Paralleling the customer's actions are those of the employee, who should be following a well-defined script for this important task.

Time lines can be attached to each activity to help set standards for speed of service and thus avoid unwanted waits. Managers can then identify the specific types of failures that might occur, take preventive actions to stop such failures from happening, and develop contingency plans for handling failures due to external causes (e.g., a power failure) that they cannot easily prevent.

Building a Service Quality Information System

Customer-defined standards and measures of service quality can be grouped into two broad categories: soft and hard. Soft measures are those that cannot easily be observed and must be collected by talking to customers, employees, or others. As noted by Zeithaml and Bitner, "Soft standards provide direction, guidance and feedback to employees in ways to achieve customer satisfaction and can be quantified by measuring customer perceptions and beliefs."[23] SERVQUAL is an example of a sophisticated soft measurement system.

By contrast, hard standards and measures relate to those characteristics and activities that can be counted, timed, or measured through audits. Measures may include such things as how many telephone calls were abandoned while the customer was on hold, how many minutes customers had to wait in line at a particular stage in service delivery, the time required to complete a specific task, the temperature of a particular food item, how many trains arrived late, how many bags were lost, how many patients made a complete recovery following a specific type of operation, and how many orders were filled correctly. Standards are often set with reference to the percentage of occasions on which a particular measure is achieved. The challenge for service marketers is to ensure that operational measures of service quality reflect customer input.

Organizations that are known for excellent service make use of both soft and hard measures. Among other things, they are good at listening to both their customers and their customer-contact employees. The fact that everyone was satisfied with this month's performance does not mean that the situation may not change for the worse in the months to come. The larger the organization, the more important it is to create formalized feedback programs using a variety of professionally designed and implemented research procedures. Here we will look at some procedures for measuring performance against soft standards of service quality. Later in the chapter, we will examine measurement against hard standards.

Berry and Parasuraman state that companies need to establish ongoing service research processes, using multiple methods among different customer groups, that provide timely, relevant trend data that managers can use in their decision making. An individual service quality study is a snapshot taken at a point in time and from a particular angle. Deeper insight and more informed decision making come from a continuing series of snapshots, taken from various angles and through different lenses, that form the essence of systematic listening.[24]

Among the possible techniques in their recommended portfolio of approaches are the following:

- Analysis of customers' complaints
- Posttransaction surveys (similar to the guest surveys used by hotels)
- Ongoing surveys of account holders by telephone or post, using scientific sampling procedures to determine customers' satisfaction in terms of broader relationship issues
- Customer advisory panels to offer feedback and advice on service performance
- Employee surveys and panels to determine perceptions of the quality of service delivered to customers on specific dimensions, barriers to better service, and suggestions for improvement
- Focus-group interviews, conducted separately with both customers and customer-contact employees to study qualitative issues in depth
- "Mystery shopping" of service providers to measure the service behavior of individual employees (this research is often used by human resource managers as well as marketers)
- Total market surveys to compare a firm's performance relative to its competitors, benchmark the leaders, and identify relevant trends.
- Capture of service operating data, including service response times, failure rates, and delivery costs

(For more details, see the reading by Leonard Berry and A. Parasuraman, "Listening to the Customer—The Concept of a Service Quality Information System," on pp. 182.)

Designing and implementing a large-scale customer survey to measure service across a wide array of attributes is no simple task. Line managers may view the findings as threatening when they involve direct comparisons of the performance of different departments or branches.

Return on Quality

Despite the attention paid to improving service quality, many companies have been disappointed by the results of their efforts to do so. Firms that have been praised for their quality efforts have sometimes run into financial difficulties, in part because they spent too lavishly on quality improvements. For instance, Florida Power & Light spent millions of dollars to compete for Japan's prestigious Deming Prize. Unfortunately, management's lack of attention to rising costs caused a backlash by ratepayers, resulting in the program's being discontinued. As Rust, Zahonik, and Keiningham wryly observe, "The quality revolution is not without its casualties."[25]

In some instances, such outcomes can be blamed on poor or incomplete execution of the quality program itself. In other instances, improved measures of service quality do not seem to translate into bigger profits, increased market share, or higher sales. Consequently, Rust and his colleagues argue for a Return on Quality (ROQ) approach, based on the assumptions that (1) quality is an investment, (2) quality efforts must be financially accountable, (3) it's possible to spend too much on quality, and (4) not all quality expenditures are equally valid. An important implication of the ROQ perspective is that quality improvement efforts may benefit from being related to productivity improvement programs.

To determine the feasibility of new quality improvement efforts, they must be carefully costed in advance and then related to anticipated customer response. Will the program enable the firm to attract more customers and, if so, how much additional net income will they generate? Alternatively, will existing customers be willing to spend more? Yet another financial consideration is whether a documented trend of losing existing customers due to quality problems can be arrested.

With the aid of good documentation, it is sometimes possible for a firm that provides similar services in multiple locations to look back and determine whether there has been a past relationship between service quality and revenues. (See Research Insights 12.1.)

RESEARCH INSIGHTS 12.1

Quality of Facilities and Room Revenues at Holiday Inn

Do better-maintained facilities enable a service firm to command higher prices? To determine the relationship between product quality and financial performance in a hotel context, Sheryl Kimes of Cornell University analyzed three years of quality and operational performance data from 1,135 franchised Holiday Inn hotels in the United States and Canada.

Indicators of product quality came from the franchisor's quality assurance reports. These reports were based on unannounced, semiannual inspections by trained quality auditors who were rotated among different regions and who spent most of a day inspecting and rating 19 different areas of each hotel. Twelve of these areas were included in the study, 2 relating to the guest rooms (bedroom and bathroom) and 10 relating to so-called commercial areas (e.g., exterior, lobby, public restrooms, dining facilities, lounge facilities, corridors, meeting area, recreation area, kitchen, and back of house). Each area typically included 10 to 12 individual items that could be passed or failed. The inspector noted the number of defects for each area and the total number for the entire hotel.

Holiday Inn Worldwide also provided data on revenue per available room (RevPAR) at each hotel. To adjust for differences in local conditions that affected pricing levels, Kimes analyzed sales and revenue statistics obtained from thousands of U.S. and Canadian hotels and reported in the monthly Smith Travel Accommodation Reports (a widely used service in the travel industry). This data enabled Kimes to calculate the RevPAR for the immediate midscale competitors of each Holiday Inn hotel; the resulting information was then used to normalize the RevPARs for all Holiday Inns in the sample so that they were now truly comparable. The average daily room rate at the time was about $50.

The analysis was conducted using six-month intervals over the three-year period from 1990 through 1992. For the purposes of the research, if a hotel had failed at least one item in an area, it was considered defective in that area. A comparison was then made, on an area-by-area basis, of the average normalized RevPAR for hotels that were defective in an area against those that were nondefective.

The findings showed that as the number of defects in a hotel increased, the RevPAR decreased. Hotel areas that showed a particularly strong impact on RevPAR were the exterior, the guest room, and the guest bathroom. Even one deficiency had a statistically significant effect on RevPAR, but the combination of deficiencies in all three areas showed an even larger effect on RevPAR over time.

The next step in the study involved categorizing the hotels based on the quality assurance results in the first six-month period. The 607 hotels that had deficiencies in all three areas in the first half-year were defined as defective hotels; the 528 others were defined as nondefective hotels. Comparative analysis of the RevPAR obtained within each of these two categories over each of the six-month periods showed that defective hotels had a RevPAR of nearly $3 less than those in the nondefective group; these results were significant at the $p < .0001$ level. Kimes calculated that the average annual revenue impact on a defective hotel was $204,400.

Using an ROQ perspective, the implication is that the primary focus of increased expenditures on housekeeping and preventive maintenance should be the hotel exterior, guest rooms, and bathrooms. (This does not mean, of course, that deficiencies in other areas can be ignored.)

Source: Sheryl E. Kimes, "The Relationship between Product Quality and Revenue per Available Room at Holiday Inn," *Journal of Service Research* 2 (November 1999): 138–144.

Problem Solving and Prevention

We've already discussed blueprints (and their simpler form, flowcharts) in some depth. Their role is to help managers understand the underlying processes behind service delivery and to set realistic hard standards that reflect both customer expectations and operational realities. Analysis of blueprints also results in identification of potential failure points, which represent weak links in the chain. Knowing what can go wrong (and where) is an important first step in preventing service quality problems.

Even businesses that generally perform well on providing quality service still have to deal from time to time with dissatisfied customers. Although the first law of quality might be "do it right the first time," no quality-minded business can afford to be without contingency plans for how to act when things go wrong. Many problems result from internal failures—faulty merchandise, rude personnel, lengthy delays, defective execution, or billing errors. Others are caused by factors outside the firm's immediate control, such as failures in the public infrastructure (phone lines are cut), weather (service facilities are flooded), criminal activities (arson, break-ins, vandalism), or personal troubles for customers (a missing child, a medical emergency, or a lost wallet).

How well a firm handles complaints and problem resolution—a key petal on the Flower of Service presented in chapter 8—will be a major determinant of whether it retains or loses the customers in question. If a company has thought through all such possibilities, developed contingency plans, and then trained its employees accordingly, its people will know what to do and will have the authority to work toward solving the problem.

Hard Measures of Service Quality

When a problem is caused by controllable, internal forces, there's no excuse for allowing it to recur. In fact, maintaining customers' goodwill after a service failure depends on keeping promises made to the effect that "we're taking steps to ensure it doesn't happen again!" With prevention in mind, let's look briefly at some tools for monitoring service quality and determining the root cause of specific problems that upset customers.

Control Charts to Monitor a Single Variable. These charts offer a simple method of displaying performance over time against specific quality standards. Because they are visual, trends are easily identified. Figure 12.2 shows an airline's performance on the important hard standard of on-time departures; the trends displayed suggest that this issue needs to be addressed by management because performance is erratic and not very satisfactory. Of course, control charts are only as good as the data on which they are based.

Service Quality Indexes. In a complex service operation, there will be multiple measures of service quality recorded at many different points in the various processes that create the outcome desired by customers. In low-contact services where the customer is not deeply involved in the service delivery process, there's a natural tendency to create many operational measures that apply only to backstage activities, which may have only a second-order effect on activities experienced by customers.

Federal Express was one of the first companies to understand the need for a companywide index of service quality that embraced all the key activities that had an impact on customers. By publishing a single, composite index on a frequent basis, senior managers hoped to motivate all FedEx employees to work toward improving quality. The firm recognized the danger of using

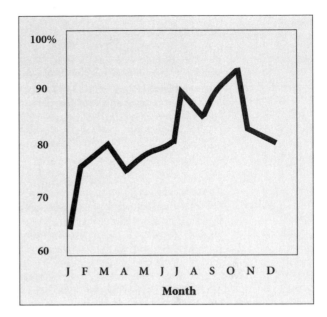

FIGURE 12.2 Control Chart of Departure Delays Showing Percentage of Flights Departing within 15 Minutes of Schedule

percentages as targets because they might lead to complacency. In an organization as large as FedEx, which ships millions of packages a day, even delivering 99 percent of packages on time or having 99.9 percent of flights arrive safely would lead to horrendous problems. Instead, it was decided to approach quality measurement from the baseline of zero failures. As noted by one senior executive:

> It's only when you examine the types of failures, the number that occur of each type, and the reasons why, that you begin to improve the quality of your service. For us the trick was to express quality failures in absolute numbers. That led us to develop the Service Quality Index or SQI [pronounced *sky*], which takes each of 12 different events that occur every day, takes the numbers of those events and multiplies them by a weight . . . based on the amount of aggravation caused to customers—as evidenced by their tendency to write to Federal Express and complain about them.[26]

This design of this hard index reflected the findings of extensive soft customer research (and has been periodically modified in the light of new research insights). Looking at service failures from the customer's perspective, the SQI measures daily the occurrence of 12 different activities that are likely to lead to customer dissatisfaction. The index is comprised by taking the raw number of each event and multiplying it by a weighting—which highlights the seriousness of that event for customers—to give a point score for each item. The points are then totaled to provide an overall index (Table 12.4). Like a golf score, the lower the index, the better the performance. However, unlike golf, the SQI involves substantial numbers—typically on the order of six figures—reflecting the huge number of packages shipped daily. An annual goal is set for the average daily SQI, based on reducing the occurrence of failures over the previous year's total.

To ensure a continuing focus on each separate component of the SQI, FedEx established 12 Quality Action Teams, one for each component, and charged them with understanding and correcting the root causes underlying the observed problems.

TABLE 12.4 *Composition of Federal Express's Service Quality Index (SQI)*		
Failure type	Weighting Factor × No. of incidents	= Daily points
Late delivery—right day	1	
Late delivery—wrong day	5	
Tracing requests unanswered	1	
Complaints reopened	5	
Missing proofs of delivery	1	
Invoice adjustments	1	
Missed pickups	10	
Lost packages	10	
Damaged packages	10	
Aircraft delays (minutes)	5	
Overgoods (packages missing labels)	5	
Abandoned calls	1	
Total Failure points (SQI)		XXX,XXX

Source: Christopher Lovelock, *Product Plus.* New York: McGraw-Hill, 1994, 131.

Root–Cause Analysis: The Fishbone Chart. Cause-and-effect analysis employs a technique first developed by the Japanese quality expert Kaoru Ishikawa. Groups of managers and staff brainstorm all the possible reasons that might cause a specific problem. The resulting factors are then categorized into one of five groupings—Equipment, Manpower (or People), Material, Procedures, and Other—on a cause-and-effect chart, popularly known as a fishbone chart because of its shape. This technique has been used for many years in manufacturing and, more recently, in services.

To sharpen the value of the analysis for use in service organizations, we show an extended framework that comprises eight rather than five groupings.[27] The People category has been broken into Frontstage Personnel and Backstage Personnel to highlight the fact that frontstage service problems are often experienced directly by customers whereas backstage failures tend to show up more obliquely through a ripple effect. The Information category has taken from Procedures in recognition that many service problems result from information failures, especially failures by frontstage personnel to tell customers what to do and when. In an airline context, for instance, poor announcement of departures may lead passengers to arrive late at the gate. Finally, there is a new category: Customers.

In manufacturing, customers have little impact on day-to-day operational processes, but in high-contact services, they are involved in frontstage operations. If they don't play their own roles correctly (assuming that they have even been informed of what is expected of them), they may reduce service productivity, causing quality problems for themselves and other customers. For instance, an aircraft can be delayed if a passenger tries to board at the last minute with an oversized suitcase that then has to be loaded into the cargo hold. An example of the extended fishbone is shown in Figure 12.3, displaying 27 possible reasons for late departures of passenger aircraft.[28] We should recognize, of course, that failures are often sequential, with one problem leading to another.

Pareto analysis (named after the Italian economist who first developed it) seeks to identify the principal causes of observed outcomes. This type of analysis underlies the so-called 80/20 rule, because it often reveals that around 80 percent of the value of one variable (in this instance,

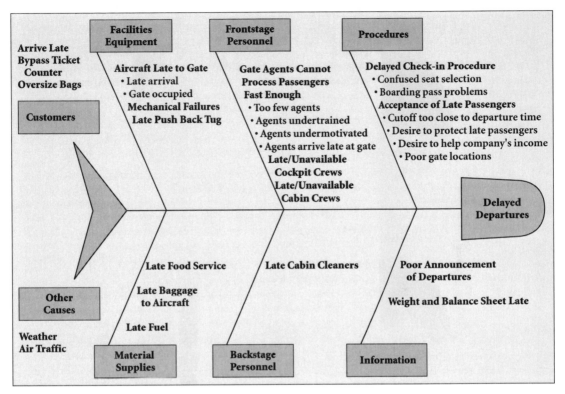

FIGURE 12.3 Cause-and-Effect Chart for Airline Departure Delays

number of service failures) is accounted for by only 20 percent of the causal variable (i.e., number of possible causes).

In the airline example given previously, findings showed that 88 percent of the company's late-departing flights from the airports that it served were caused by only four (15 percent) of all the possible factors. In fact, more than half the delays were caused by a single factor: acceptance of late passengers (situations when the staff held a flight for one more passenger who was checking in after the official cutoff time). On such occasions, the airline made a friend of that late passenger—possibly encouraging repetition of this undesirable behavior on a future occasion—but risked alienating all the other passengers who were already on board, waiting for the aircraft to depart. Other major delays included waiting for pushback (a vehicle must arrive to pull the aircraft away from the gate), waiting for fueling, and delays in signing the weight and balance sheet (a safety requirement relating to the distribution of the aircraft's load that the captain must observe on each flight). Further analysis showed some significant variations from one airport to another (see Figure 12.4). Note the problem of late cabin cleaners at Newark.

A New Quality Goal: Zero Defections

Quality failures weaken customers' loyalty to companies and brands. When disappointed customers have a choice of service suppliers, they may decide to abandon the one that has let them down in favor of a competitor. Reichheld and Sasser popularized the term *zero defections*, which they define as keeping every customer the company can profitably serve. When customers have

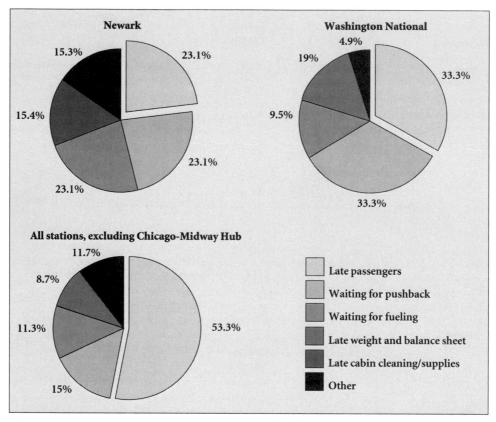

FIGURE 12.4 Analysis of Causes of Flight Departure Delays
Source: Based on D. Daryl Wyckoff, "New Tools for Achieving Service Quality," *Cornell Hotel and Restaurant Administration Quarterly*, November 1984.

a membership relationship with an organization, their use of the service can be tracked on an individual-account basis. Declining usage—say, less frequent visits to a hotel chain for a business traveler, reduced purchases from a retail store, fewer transactions at a bank—are often a good predictor of potential defection. Intervention at this point (with a view to restoring loyalty) is preferable to waiting until the customer ceases all activity or formally closes an account. Not only does a rising defection rate indicate that something is already wrong with quality (or that competitors offer better value), but it also signals a probable profit slump ahead.

Reichheld has studied both customer and employee retention in several dozen industries and has worked on retention issues with clients around the world. He says that it's much harder to engineer higher loyalty into a business system than most managers suspect. At the root of the problem, he notes, is that most business people don't recognize the full economic implications of loyalty; they agree intuitively with the concept but haven't made the required investments. The trouble is that they underestimate the value of loyalty but overestimate the ease of creating it. He adds: "Managers tend to look for ad hoc solutions, such as better recovery efforts, pricing and promotional incentives, and reward programs for regular customers of the 'frequent fliers' variety. But the impact of such efforts is often quite modest, particularly if they're easily copied by competitors."[29] Top managers must recognize that building and maintaining loyalty is a systemwide challenge, not just a tactical embellishment. Customer loyalty should be seen as standing at the core of sustained competitive success (refer to chapter 5).

Clearly, to the extent that service marketers can uncover customer dissatisfaction and resolve it promptly, the chances of retaining desirable customers are improved. But good complaints-handling procedures (see chapter 6), although highly desirable, can do little more than treat symptoms that in many cases have avoidable causes. So it's imperative to work continuously to improve the overall service delivery system and its constituent processes as well. That means getting to the bottom of service problems and making sure they don't recur.

How Productivity Improvement Impacts Quality and Value

The task of improving service productivity has traditionally been assigned to operations managers, whose approach has typically centered on such actions as the following:

- Careful control of costs at every step in the process
- Efforts to reduce wasteful use of materials or labor
- Matching productive capacity to average levels of demand rather than peak levels, so that workers and equipment are not underemployed for extended periods
- Replacement of workers by automated machines
- Providing employees with equipment and data bases that enable them to work faster or to a higher level of quality
- Teaching employees how to work more productively (faster is not necessarily better if it leads to mistakes or unsatisfactory work that has to be redone)
- Installing expert systems that allow paraprofessionals to take on work previously performed by more experienced individuals earning higher salaries

Restructuring or reengineering the ways in which tasks are performed has significant potential to increase output, especially in many backstage jobs.[30] Also, broadening the array of tasks that a service worker can perform (which may require revised labor agreements) can eliminate bottlenecks and wasteful downtime by allowing managers to deploy workers wherever they are most needed at any given time.

In general, however, managers would do well to examine productivity from the broader perspective of the business processes used to transform resource inputs into the outcomes desired by customers—processes that not only cross departmental and sometimes geographic boundaries but also link the backstage and frontstage areas of the service operation. Armistead and Machin adopted this approach in a study of a national postal service, in the course of which they mapped (blueprinted) the processes through which mail products were delivered through the "integrated product pipeline" to customers in accordance with quality standards.[31] They concluded that business process management helps a large organization to position service productivity against quality and to better understand the complex links between customer satisfaction (via the overall performance of processes) and productivity.

How Backstage Changes May Impact Customers

The marketing implications of backstage changes depend on whether or not they affect or are noticed by customers. If airline mechanics develop a procedure for servicing jet engines more quickly without incurring increased wage rates or material costs, then the airline has obtained a productivity improvement that has no impact on the customer's service experience.

Other backstage changes, however, may have a ripple effect that extends frontstage and affects customers. Marketers should keep abreast of proposed backstage changes, not only to identify such ripples but also to prepare customers for them. At a bank, for instance, the decision to install new computers and printer peripherals may be driven by plans to improve internal quality controls and reduce the cost of preparing monthly statements. However, this new equipment may change the appearance of bank statements and the time of the month when they are posted. If customers are likely to notice such changes, an explanation may be warranted. If the new statements are easier to read and understand, then the change may be worth promoting as a service enhancement.

Unfortunately, technological changes are often implemented by specialists, such as accountants and systems engineers, who have never been briefed on customer concerns. Instead of a better statement, the net result may be a format that makes the statement difficult to interpret and truncation of the customer's name (CHRISTOPHER H. LOVEL or CHRISTO LOVELOCK, for example) as the data-processing department tries to reduce the amount of storage space required or ensure that all names fit on a single printed line. In this example, a backstage productivity gain may appear to customers as a decline in the quality of frontstage output.

Frontstage Efforts to Improve Productivity

In high-contact services, many productivity enhancements are quite visible. Some changes simply require passive acceptance by customers; others require customers to adopt new patterns of behavior in their dealings with the organization. If substantial changes are proposed, then it makes sense to conduct market research first to determine how customers may respond. Failure to think through impacts on customers may result in loss of business and cancel out anticipated productivity gains. Once the nature of the changes has been decided, marketing communication can help prepare customers for the change, explaining the rationale, the benefits, and what customers will need to do differently in the future.

From time to time, a major innovation results in a radical change to some aspect of service delivery. Sometimes, such a change offers significant marketing advantages as well as operational improvements. Consider a couple of important historical examples. When jet-powered de Havilland Comet 4s and Boeing 707s replaced propeller-driven aircraft on transatlantic routes in 1957, both passengers and airlines benefited. The former enjoyed the comfort of smoother, quieter, and much faster flights (for which many were prepared to pay a premium price). The airlines, in turn, found their productivity much increased because the 707s could carry almost five times as many passengers in a year as the Boeing Stratocruisers or Douglas DC-7s that they replaced—a function of the new airliners' greater speed and capacity as well as the higher daily utilization that was possible with the more reliable jet engines. Crew members, too, became more productive in terms of the passenger-miles of service provided each month.

But radical change is not always understood and appreciated. Consider the case of the universal product code (UPC), designed to simplify both backstage and frontstage activities in supermarkets. By marking packaged goods with UPC bar codes unique to each stock-keeping unit (SKU) and then scanning each item electronically at the checkout, supermarket executives expected to achieve major advantages and efficiencies.[32] They would save the cost of price marking each individual package (and changing those prices whenever the price of an SKU changed); all that would be necessary was to program (or reprogram) the price data for that SKU in the computer. They also expected to reduce clerical time and errors at checkouts (a benefit to customers, too), provide more detailed receipts (also a customer benefit), and generate valuable data from the scanners on product sales.

Unfortunately, things didn't quite work out as planned. UPC symbols began appearing on thousands of consumer products in 1973, but installation of scanners at checkouts took place far more slowly than anticipated. In fact, some large supermarket chains did not make the changeover until the late 1980s. Union resistance and the high cost of the equipment were two factors, but consumer concerns also proved to be a major problem. Consumer groups opposed the new technology on the grounds that removal of individual price marking would allow stores to put through surreptitious price increases. Laws were passed in many U.S. states mandating that packages still had to be individually marked. Supermarket executives later conceded that they had done a poor job of preparing customers for the change, highlighting the benefits, and allaying customer concerns. One firm admitted that it would have been wiser to bring customers into the decision-making process when installation was first planned. Today's managers, looking to improve productivity through access to the Internet and other technological innovations, would do well to consider the insights to be obtained from past failures and successful solutions. History often has a tendency to repeat itself!

A Caution on Cost-Reduction Strategies

In the absence of new technology, most attempts to improve service productivity tend to center on efforts to eliminate waste and reduce labor costs. Skinner sounds a note of caution: "Resolutely chipping away at waste and inefficiency—the heart of most productivity programs—is not enough to restore competitive health. Indeed, a focus on cost reductions (that is, on raising labor output while holding the amount of labor constant or, better, reducing it) is proving harmful."[33]

Skinner was writing about manufacturing, but he might just as well have been writing about services. Cutbacks in frontstage staffing either mean that the remaining employees have to work harder and faster or that there are insufficient personnel to serve customers promptly at busy times. Although employees may be able to work faster for a brief period of time, few can maintain a rapid pace for extended periods; they become exhausted, make mistakes, and treat customers in a cursory manner. Workers who are trying to do two or three things at once—serving a customer face-to-face while simultaneously answering the telephone and sorting papers, for example—may do a poor job of each task. Excessive pressure breeds discontent and frustration among all employees but especially among customer-contact personnel who are caught between trying to meet customer needs and attempting to achieve management's productivity goals.

Attempts to economize on materials and equipment in the name of avoiding wasteful duplication may similarly backfire. I once asked a hotel receptionist why it had taken so long to check me out. The employee replied with a tired smile that the four receptionists on the front desk had to share a single stapler for clipping credit card receipts to the customers' bills, so she had to wait her turn in line to use it—a perfect example of the old nautical metaphor of "spoiling the ship for want of a ha'p'orth [half-penny's worth] of tar."

Customer-Driven Approaches to Improving Productivity

In situations where customers are deeply involved in the service production process (typically, people-processing services), operations managers should be examining how customers' inputs can be made more productive.[34] And marketing managers should be thinking about what marketing strategies should be employed to influence customers to behave in more productive ways. We review three strategies: changing the timing of customer demand, involving customers more actively in the production process, and asking customers to use third parties.

Changing the Timing of Customer Demand

Managing demand in capacity-constrained service businesses has been a recurring theme in this book. We introduced it briefly in chapter 2 and discuss it at greater length in chapter 13. Customers often complain that the services they use are crowded and congested, reflecting time-of-day, seasonal, or other cyclical peaks in demand. During the off-peak periods in those same cycles, managers often worry that there are too few customers and that their facilities and staff are not fully productive. By shifting demand away from peaks, managers can make better use of their productive assets and provide better service. Post office advertising campaigns encouraging people to post early for Christmas have had some success in getting people to plan ahead, rather than leaving it until a few days before Christmas to post their cards and packages.

However, some demand cannot easily be shifted without the cooperation of third parties such as employers and schools, who control working hours and holiday schedules. To fill idle capacity during off-peak hours, marketers may need to target new market segments with different needs and schedules, rather than focusing exclusively on current segments. If the peaks and valleys of demand can be smoothed, using the tools and strategies we've discussed in earlier chapters, productivity will improve.

Involve Customers More in Production

Customers who assume a more active role in the service production and delivery process can take over some labor tasks from the service organization. Benefits for both parties may result when customers perform self-service.

Many technological innovations are designed to get customers to perform tasks previously undertaken by service employees. A classic example of such a change, with nationwide implications, was AT&T's automation of the long-distance telephone network. Originally, customers had to ask an operator to connect them to numbers outside their local areas. In the early 1960s, it was said that if the number of long-distance telephone calls continued to grow at the same exponential rate, by the year 2000 every second employee in the United States would be working as a telephone operator! By 1970, AT&T had installed the direct-dialing technology that would allow it to achieve major increases in internal productivity by reducing the number of long-distance operators it employed. Yet almost half of all long-distance calls were still being placed with the operator.

So the company launched a major marketing effort to encourage subscribers to dial their own long-distance calls. Substantial price discounts were offered for direct-dial calls, and a national advertising campaign encouraged callers to dial direct rather than getting an operator to place the call for them. The adverts said, "We have two reasons for urging you to dial long-distance calls direct. You save and we save too." After three years, directly dialed calls accounted for almost 75 percent of long-distance calls.

Today, many companies are trying to encourage customers who have access to the Internet to obtain information from the firm's corporate Web sites and even to place orders through the Web, rather than telephoning employees at the company's offices. For such changes to succeed, Web sites must be made user-friendly and easy to navigate, and customers must be convinced that it is safe to provide credit card information over the Web. Some companies have been offering promotional incentives (such as a credit of air-miles to a frequent-flyer program) to encourage customers to make an initial order on the Web.

Restaurants, which have traditionally had a high labor component and relatively low productivity, represent another service in which customers have been asked to do more of the work. We've become accustomed to self-service salad bars and buffets. But despite the reduction in personal service, this innovation has been positioned as a benefit that lets customers select the foods they want, without delay, in the quantities they desire.

Some customers may be more willing than others to serve themselves. In fact, research suggests that this may be a useful segmentation variable. A large-scale study presented respondents with the choice of a do-it-yourself option versus traditional delivery systems at gas stations, banks, restaurants, hotels, airports, and travel services.[35] For each service, a particular scenario was outlined, because earlier interviews had determined that decisions to choose self-service options were very situation specific, depending on such factors as time of day, weather conditions, presence or absence of others in the party, and the perceived time and cost involved.

The results showed that in each instance a sizable proportion of respondents would select the self-service option—even in the absence of time or monetary savings. When these inducements were added, the proportions choosing self-service increased. Further analysis showed some overlap between different services; if respondents didn't serve their own fuel, for instance, they were less likely to use an ATM and more likely to prefer being served by a bank clerk.

Quality and productivity improvements often depend on customers' willingness to learn new procedures, follow instructions, and interact cooperatively with employees and other people. Customers who arrive at the service encounter with a set of preexisting norms, values, and role definitions may resist change. Goodwin suggests that insights from research on socialization can help service marketers redesign the nature of the service encounter in ways that increase the chances of gaining customer cooperation.[36] In particular, she argues that customers will need help to learn new skills, form a new self-image ("I can do it myself"), develop new relationships with providers and fellow customers, and acquire new values.

Ask Customers to Use Third Parties

In some instances, managers may be able to improve service productivity by delegating one or more marketing support functions to third parties. The purchase process often breaks down into four components: information, reservation, payment, and consumption. When consumption of the core product takes place at a location not easily accessible from customers' homes or workplaces (for instance, an airport, theater, stadium, or a hotel in a distant city), it makes sense to delegate delivery of supplementary service elements to intermediary organizations.

Specialist intermediaries may enjoy economies of scale, enabling them to perform the task more cheaply than the core service provider, allowing the latter to focus on quality and productivity in its own area of expertise. Some intermediaries are identifiable local organizations, such as travel agencies, which customers can visit in person. Others, such as hotel reservations centers, often subjugate their own identity to that of the client service company. When intermediaries offer service 24 hours a day nationwide, customer calls can be spread over a broader time base. The peaks and valleys of call demand are further smoothed when the call center serves an entire continent such as North America, which has multiple time zones, because busy times in (say) Montreal or New York may be quiet periods on the Pacific Coast (and vice versa). The call-center industry is booming in Europe, with Britain, Ireland, and the Netherlands hosting the largest number of centers. International call centers, with provision for different languages, are increasing rapidly in number. Countries such as the United States, Canada, and Australia, which have large immigrant populations, may have an advantage here because they often have a ready supply of native speakers. As with any change in procedures, a move to employ intermediaries to provide supplementary services will succeed only if customers know how to use them and are willing to do so. At a minimum, a promotional and educational campaign may be needed to launch such a change.

Sensitivity to Customers' Reluctance to Change

Customer resistance to changes in familiar environments and long-established behavior patterns can thwart attempts to improve productivity and even quality. All too often, management's failure to look at such changes from the customer's standpoint actually causes resistance. Managers of service operations can, and should, avoid such insensitivity toward their customers. Six possible steps suggest themselves:

1. *Develop customer trust.* It's harder to introduce productivity-related changes when people are basically distrustful of the initiator, as they often are in the case of large, seemingly impersonal institutions. Customers' willingness to accept change may be closely related to the degree of goodwill they bear toward the organization. If a firm does not have a strong positive relationship with its customers, the latter may be able to block productivity improvements.

2. *Understand customers' habits and expectations.* People often get into a routine around the use of a particular service, with certain steps being taken in a specific sequence. In effect, they have their own individual flowchart in mind. Innovations that disrupt ingrained routines are likely to face resistance unless consumers are carefully briefed as to what changes to expect. For instance, in introducing the UPC, many retailers seem to have ignored the typical shopper's habit of examining price markings on packages and then watching the cashier punch in the prices on the cash register. Retailers made little effort to prepare consumers for the change and how it would affect them, let alone explain the rationale for this innovation or promote its benefits.

3. *Pretest new procedures and equipment.* Before introducing new procedures and equipment, or Internet-based services, marketers need to determine probable customer response. These efforts may include concept and laboratory testing and/or field testing at one or more sites. When replacing service personnel by automatic equipment, it's particularly important for an organization to develop machines that customers of almost all types and backgrounds will find easy to use. Some self-service equipment looks as if it has been designed by engineers for engineers. Even the phrasing of instructions needs careful thought. Ambiguous, complex, or authoritarian instructions may discourage customers with limited command of the language or poor reading skills as well as people used to personal courtesies from the service personnel whom the machine replaces.

4. *Publicize the benefits.* Introduction of self-service equipment or procedures requires consumers to perform part of the task themselves. Although this additional work may be associated with such benefits as extended service hours, time savings, and (in some instances) monetary savings, these benefits are not necessarily obvious—they have to be promoted. Useful strategies may include use of mass-media advertising; on-site posters and signage; and personal communications to inform people of the innovation, arouse their interest in it, and clarify the specific benefits to customers of changing behavior and using new delivery systems.

5. *Teach customers to use innovations and promote trial.* Simply installing self-service machines and supplying printed instructions may not win over many customers, especially those resistant to technology or to change in general. Experience with ATMs shows that assigning service personnel to demonstrate new equipment and answer questions—providing reassurance as well as educational assistance—is a key element in gaining acceptance of new procedures and technology. The costs of such demonstration programs can be spread more widely in multiple-outlet operations by moving staff members from one site to another as the innovation spreads to new locations. Promotional incentives and price discounts may also serve to stimulate initial trial. Once customers have actually tried a self-service option

(particularly an electronically based one) and found that it works well, they will be more likely to use it regularly in the future.

6. *Monitor performance and continue to seek improvements.* Introducing quality and productivity improvements is an ongoing process. Today's quality advantage may be trumped tomorrow by a competitor's response. And the competitive edge provided by productivity improvements may quickly be erased as other firms adopt similar or better procedures. Service managers have to work hard to keep up the momentum so that programs achieve their full potential and are not allowed to flag. For instance, managers of firms that have installed pages on the World Wide Web containing information about the company and its services should be checking on whether the number of visits to their Web pages are increasing over time and whether customers who seek information are switching back from the Web to use of the firm's toll-free telephone number.

The important thing is for managers to learn from experience (both good and bad), to take corrective action where needed (whether it involves redesign of facilities and procedures, better communications and educational activities, more dramatic promotional efforts, or more compelling incentives), and to continue searching for new ways to boost quality and productivity.

Conclusion

Enhancing service quality and improving service productivity are often two sides of the same coin, which is why we treat them jointly as a component of the 8 Ps of integrated service management. Together, they offer powerful potential to improve value for both customers and the firm. A key challenge for any service business is to deliver satisfactory outcomes to its customers in ways that are cost-effective for the company. If customers are dissatisfied with the quality of a service, they won't be willing to pay very much for it—or even to buy it at all if competitors offer better quality. Low sales volumes mean unproductive assets. Needlessly low prices may result in low returns on investment, which also means less productive assets.

The notion that customers are the best judges of the quality of a service process and its outcome is relatively new and replaces (or supplements) other concepts of quality. When the customer is seen as the final arbiter of quality, marketing managers come to play a key role in defining expectations and in measuring customer satisfaction. However, service marketers need to work closely with other management functions in service design and implementation.

This chapter presented a number of frameworks and tools for defining, measuring, and managing quality, including research programs to identify quality gaps and cause-and-effect charts to identify the root causes of failure in service delivery. Peer review may also be an important alternative approach when measuring the core product quality on services that are high in credence characteristics.

Marketing managers should be included in productivity improvement programs whenever these efforts are likely to have an impact on customers. And because customers are often involved in the service production process, marketers should keep their eyes open for opportunities to reshape customer behavior in ways that may help the service firm to become more productive. Possibilities for cooperative behavior include adopting self-service options, changing the timing of customer demand to less busy periods, and making use of third-party suppliers of supplementary services.

In summary, value, quality, and productivity are all of great concern to senior management because they relate directly to an organization's survival in the competitive marketplace. Strategies designed to enhance value are dependent in large measure on continuous improvement in service quality (as defined by customers) and productivity improvements that reinforce rather than counteract customer satisfaction. The marketing function has much to offer in reshaping our thinking about these three issues as well as in helping to achieve significant improvements in all of them.

REVIEW QUESTIONS

1. How do definitions of service quality differ from those relating to the quality of manufactured products?
2. Explain the relationship between service productivity and service quality.
3. Under what circumstances will improvements in service quality and productivity lead to both increased value for customers and higher profits for the firm?
4. Review the five dimensions of service quality. What do *tangibles* mean in the context of (a) an industrial repair shop, (b) a retail bank, (c) a hotel, (d) a telephone company, and (e) a Big 5 accounting firm?
5. Identify the gaps that can occur in service quality and how service marketers can prevent them.
6. Why is productivity a more difficult issue for service firms than for manufacturers?
7. What relationship do you see between service productivity and return on quality?

APPLICATION EXERCISES

1. Consider your own recent experiences as a service consumer. On which dimensions of service quality have you most often experienced a large gap between your expectations and your perceptions of the actual service performance? What do you think the underlying causes might be? What steps should management take to improve quality?
2. Specify the different ways that you, as a consumer, can help to improve productivity for at least five service organizations that you patronize. What distinctive characteristics of each service make some of these actions possible?

ENDNOTES

1. Evert Gummesson, "Service Management: An Evaluation and the Future," *International Journal of Service Industry Management* 5, no. 1 (1994): 77–96.
2. See, for example, the classic article by Philip Kotler, "A Generic Concept of Marketing, *Journal of Marketing* 36, (April 1972): 46–54.
3. Morris Holbrook, "The Nature of Customer Value: An Anthology of Services in the Consumption Experience," in *Service Quality: New Directions in Theory and Practice,* ed. R. T. Rust and R. L. Oliver (Thousand Oaks, CA: SAGE Publications, 1994), 21–71.
4. Bradley T. Gale, *Managing Customer Value* (New York: The Free Press, 1994), 26.
5. Robert D. Buzzell and Bradley T. Gale, *The PIMS Principles—Linking Strategy to Performance* (New York: The Free Press, 1987).
6. David A. Garvin, *Managing Quality* (New York: The Free Press, 1988), especially chap. 3.
7. Ibid., 48–49.
8. Christian Grönroos, *Service Management and Marketing* (Lexington, MA: Lexington Books, 1990), chap. 2.
9. Valarie A. Zeithaml, A. Parasuraman, and Leonard L. Berry, *Delivering Quality Service* (New York: The Free Press, 1990).
10. A. Parasuraman, Valarie A. Zeithaml, and Leonard Berry, "SERVQUAL: A Multiple Item Scale for Measuring Consumer Perceptions of Service Quality," *Journal of Retailing* 64 (1988): 12–40.

11. See, for instance, Francis Buttle, "SERVQUAL: Review, Critique, Research Agenda," *European Journal of Marketing* 30, no. 1 (1996): 8–32; and Simon S. K. Lam and Ka Shing Woo, "Measuring Service Quality: A Test-Retest Reliability Investigation of SERVQUAL," *Journal of the Market Research Society* 39 (April 1997): 381–393.

12. Gerhard Mels, Christo Boshoff, and Denon Nel, "The Dimensions of Service Quality: The Original European Perspective Revisited," *The Service Industries Journal* 17 (January 1997): 173–189.

13. Lam and Woo, "Measuring Service Quality."

14. Anne M. Smith, "Measuring Service Quality: Is SERVQUAL Now Redundant?" *Journal of Marketing Management* 11 (January/February/April 1995): 257–276.

15. Susan J. Devlin and H. K. Dong, "Service Quality from the Customers' Perspective," *Marketing Research* 6, no. 1 (1994): 5–13.

16. F. Ian Stuart and Stephen S. Tax, "Planning for Service Quality: An Integrative Approach," *International Journal of Service Industry Management* 7, no. 4 (1996): 58–77.

17. Kenneth J. Klassen, Randolph M. Russell, and James J. Chrisman, "Efficiency and Productivity Measures for High Contact Services," *The Service Industries Journal* 18 (October 1998): 1–18.

18. James L. Heskett, *Managing in the Service Economy* (New York: The Free Press, 1986).

19. John C. Shaw, *The Service Focus* (Homewood, IL: Dow Jones-Irwin, 1990), 152–153.

20. Frances X. Frei and Patrick T. Harker, "Measuring the Efficiency of Service Delivery Processes: An Application to Retail Banking," *Journal of Service Research* 1 (May 1999): 300–312.

21. Valarie A. Zeithaml, Leonard L. Berry, and A. Parasuraman, "Communication and Control Processes in the Delivery of Service Processes," *Journal of Marketing*, 52 (April 1988): 36–58.

22. Zeithaml, Parasuraman, and Berry, *Delivering Quality Service*.

23. Valarie A. Zeithaml and Mary Jo Bitner, *Services Marketing*, 2d ed. (New York: McGraw-Hill, 2000), 228–229.

24. Leonard L. Berry and A. Parasuraman, "Listening to the Customer—The Concept of a Service Quality Information System," *Sloan Management Review*, spring 1997, 65–76.

25. Roland T. Rust, Anthony J. Zahonik, and Timothy L. Keiningham, "Return on Quality (ROQ): Making Service Quality Financially Accountable," *Journal of Marketing* 59 (April 1995): 58.

26. Comments by Thomas R. Oliver, then senior vice president, sales and customer service, Federal Express, reported in Christopher H. Lovelock, "Federal Express: Quality Improvement Program," IMD case study (Cranfield, UK: European Case Clearing House, 1990).

27. Christopher Lovelock, *Product Plus: How Product + Service = Competitive Advantage* (New York: McGraw-Hill, 1994), 218.

28. These categories and the research data that follow have been adapted from information in D. Daryl Wyckoff, "New Tools for Achieving Service Quality," *Cornell Hotel and Restaurant Administration Quarterly*, November 1984.

29. Quoted in Lovelock, *Product Plus*, 221.

30. See, for example, Michael Hammer and James Champy, *Reengineering the Corporation* (New York: Harper Business, 1993).

31. Colin Armistead and Simon Machin, "Business Process Management: Implications for Productivity in Multi-stage Service Networks," *International Journal of Service Industry Management* 9, no. 4 (1998): 323–336.

32. A stock-keeping unit (SKU) represents a specific brand of a product category in a given package size or format. Thus, 4-oz., 8-oz., and 1-lb. jars of Maxwell House instant coffee represent three different SKUs; the same three package sizes of Maxwell House decaffeinated instant coffee represent another three SKUs; and other brands, in turn, would represent other SKUs.

33. Wickham Skinner, "The Productivity Paradox," *McKinsey Quarterly* (winter 1987), 36–45.

34. This discussion has its origins in ideas first presented in Christopher H. Lovelock and Robert F. Young, "Look to Consumers to Increase Productivity," *Harvard Business Review* (May–June 1979): 168–178.

35. Eric Langeard, John E. G. Bateson, Christopher H. Lovelock, and Pierre Eiglier, *Services Marketing: New Insights from Consumers and Managers* (Cambridge, MA: Marketing Science Institute, 1981), especially chap. 2. A good summary of this research is provided in J. E. G. Bateson, "Self-Service Consumer: An Exploratory Study," *Journal of Retailing* 51 (fall 1985): 49–76.

36. Cathy Goodwin, "I Can Do It Myself: Training the Service Consumer to Contribute to Service Productivity," *Journal of Services Marketing* 2 (fall 1988): 71–78.

CHAPTER **1 3**

Balancing Demand and Capacity

Balancing the supply and demand sides of a service industry is not easy, and whether a manager does it well or not makes all the difference.

W. EARL SASSER JR.

Unlike manufacturing, service operations create a perishable inventory that cannot be stockpiled for sale at a later date. That's a problem for any capacity-constrained service that faces wide swings in demand.

Fluctuating demand for service occurs among a huge cross-section of businesses serving both individual and corporate customers. The problem is most commonly found in service organizations that process people or physical possessions—such as those providing transportation, lodging, food service, repair and maintenance, entertainment, and health care. It also affects labor-intensive, information-processing services such as accounting and tax preparation.

These demand fluctuations, which may range in frequency from as long as a season of the year to as short as hourly, play havoc with efficient use of productive assets. Solving—or at least minimizing—this problem is an important goal for many service organizations because it can make the difference between financial success and failure. Creating effective strategies for balancing demand and capacity is also essential for improving productivity and preventing degradation of service quality. Such strategies typically require close cooperation between marketing, operations, and human resource managers. Teamwork is vital because there are real limits as to what managers from any one of these functions can achieve alone.

In this chapter, we consider the nature of both demand and capacity in a service context and explore such questions as:

1. What factors cause demand to follow predictable cycles?
2. How can the tools of marketing be used to smooth these cycles?

390

3. What are the elements that compose productive capacity for a service organization?
4. How can capacity management techniques be employed to meet variations in demand?
5. How can well-designed waiting environments reduce the perceived burden for customers of having to wait for service?

The Ups and Downs of Demand

The situation is a familiar one around the world. "It's either feast or famine for us!" sighs the manager. "In peak periods, we're turning customers away. In low periods, our facilities are idle, and our employees are standing around looking bored."

The Problem of Perishable Output

Most services are unable to store their finished output. This lack of inventory doesn't matter when demand levels are relatively stable and predictable. However, it raises problems for organizations that face wide swings in demand, especially when their capacity is relatively fixed. The factors of production may be in place and ready to serve, but an empty seat loses its chance to earn money for the airline on a specific flight once the aircraft takes off. The same is true of hotels that sell room nights, professionals who sell their time, industrial repair shops that sell a combination of labor and use of expensive maintenance equipment, theaters that sell seats, and warehouses that rent storage space. Readiness to serve is wasted if there are no customers to purchase the service at that time.

Services involving tangible actions to customers or their possessions are more likely to be subject to capacity constraints than are information-based services. In the latter instance, however, similar capacity problems may occur when customers are obliged to come to a service site for delivery, as in live entertainment or traditional retail banking. Cyclical shifts in demand are often a problem for labor-intensive, information-processing services—accounting and tax preparation are cases in point.

Financial success in these capacity-constrained industries is, in large measure, a function of management's ability to use productive capacity—staff, labor, equipment, and facilities—effectively. However, the goal shouldn't be to utilize staff, labor, equipment, and facilities as *much* as possible but rather to use them as *productively* as possible. As you will see, this chapter is relevant to issues of productivity and quality, which we introduced in chapter 1 and discussed in more depth in chapter 12. Successful service managers recognize that managing demand and capacity are essential not only to productive use of the firm's assets but also for giving customers the quality service experiences that they are looking for.

From Excess Demand to Excess Capacity

At any given moment, a fixed-capacity service may face one of four conditions (Figure 13.1):

● *Excess demand*—The level of demand exceeds maximum available capacity, with the result that some customers are denied service and business is lost.
● *Demand exceeds optimum capacity*—No one is actually turned away, but conditions are crowded, and all customers are likely to perceive a deterioration in the quality of service delivered.
● *Demand and supply are well balanced* at the level of optimum capacity. Staff and facilities are busy without being overworked, and customers receive good service without delays.

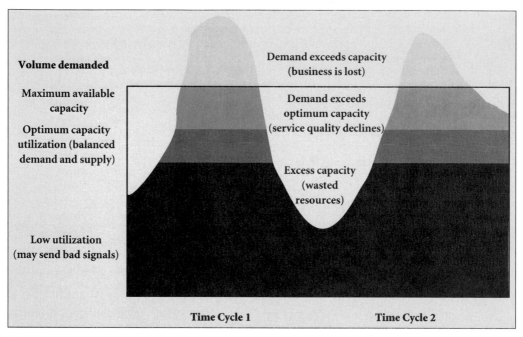

Volume demanded

Maximum available capacity

Optimum capacity utilization (balanced demand and supply)

Low utilization (may send bad signals)

Demand exceeds capacity (business is lost)

Demand exceeds optimum capacity (service quality declines)

Excess capacity (wasted resources)

Time Cycle 1   **Time Cycle 2**

FIGURE 13.1 Implications of Variations in Demand Relative to Capacity

- *Excess capacity*—Demand is below optimum capacity and productive resources are under-utilized, resulting in low productivity. Those customers who do come may find the experience disappointing or have doubts about the viability of the service.

You'll notice that we've drawn a distinction between *maximum capacity* and *optimum capacity*. When demand exceeds maximum available capacity, some potential customers may be turned away, and their business may be lost forever. But when demand is operating between optimum and maximum capacity, there's a risk that all customers being served at that time may start to receive inferior service. In such conditions, Armistead and Clark argue that service managers need to employ what they call a *coping strategy* to control the fall in service standards and thus prevent customer dissatisfaction.[1]

Sometimes optimum and maximum capacities are one and the same. At a live theater or sports performance, a full house is grand because it stimulates the players and creates a sense of excitement and audience participation. The net result? A more satisfying experience for all. But with most other services, you probably feel that you get better service if the facility is not operating at full capacity. The quality of restaurant service, for instance, often deteriorates when every table is occupied, because the staff are rushed and there's a greater likelihood of errors or delays. And if you're traveling alone in an aircraft with high-density seating, you tend to feel more comfortable if the seat next to you is empty. When repair and maintenance operations are fully scheduled, delays may result if there is no slack in the system to allow for unexpected problems in completing particular jobs.

There are two basic solutions to the problem of fluctuating demand. One is to adjust the level of capacity to meet variations in demand. This approach, which entails cooperation between operations and human resource management, requires an understanding of what constitutes productive capacity and how it may be increased or decreased on an incremental basis.

Cape Cod: A Seasonal Tourist Destination

Cape Cod is a remarkable peninsula of narrow land, about fifty miles (80 km) south of Boston. Jutting out into the Atlantic off the Massachusetts coast, its shape resembles a long arm bent at the elbow. Native Americans have lived there for thousands of years. The Pilgrims landed there in 1619 but continued across Cape Cod Bay to found Plymouth; however, not long afterwards, more immigrants from England settled on the cape itself. Fishing, whaling, agriculture, and salt works were among the principal industries in the nineteenth century. By the mid-twentieth century, all but fishing—itself in decline—had virtually disappeared, and tourism was beginning to assume some significance.

Events in the early 1960s put the cape firmly in the public eye. John F. Kennedy became president of the United States and was regularly photographed at his family's vacation home in Hyannisport; while in office he signed legislation creating the Cape Cod National Seashore, pre-serving large areas of the Outer Cape as a national park. And the song "Old Cape Cod," commis-sioned by tourism promoters and sung by the popular Patti Page, unexpectedly climbed to the top of the charts and was heard around the world. With its beaches and salt marshes, sand dunes and fishing harbors, picturesque towns and lobster dinners, the cape rapidly became a destina-tion resort. Today, it draws millions of visitors each year from the eastern United States and Canada and is increasingly attracting European tourists.

In summer, the cape is a busy place. Colorful umbrellas sprout like giant flowers along the miles of sandy beaches. The parking lots are full. There are lines outside most restaurants, and managers complain about the difficulty of hiring and retaining sufficient serving staff. (In fact, hundreds of young people are recruited from Europe each summer to work on the cape, many of whom are students looking for an enjoyable working vacation; they are joined by workers from Caribbean countries such as Jamaica.) Shops and cinemas are busy, especially when it rains. The Mid-Cape Highway is clogged. Hotels sport "no vacancy" signs. Fishing trips have to be booked well in advance. Holiday cottages are fully rented, it's hard to get a car reservation on the ferries to the islands of Nantucket or Martha's Vineyard, and the visitor centers at the Cape Cod National Seashore are crowded with tourists.

Return for a weekend in midwinter, and what do you find? A few walkers brave the chill winds on the otherwise empty beaches. You can park in almost any legal space you wish. Many restaurants have closed (their owners are wintering in Florida), and only the most popular of the remaining establishments even bother to suggest reservations. Student workers have gone back to college, and the shops have laid off seasonal workers and, in some cases, cut the hours of remaining employees. As a result, there is seasonal unemployment among some of the full-time residents.

It's rare in February to be unable to see the film of your choice at your preferred time. The main problem on the Mid-Cape Highway is being stopped for speeding. If a motel sports a "no vacancy" sign, that means it's closed for the season; others offer bargain rates. Recreational fish-ing? You must be crazy—there may even be ice on Cape Cod Bay! Owners of holiday cottages have drained their water systems and boarded up the windows. You can probably drive your vehi-cle straight onto one of the car ferries to the islands (although the sailing schedules are more limited), and the rangers at the visitor centers are happy to talk with the few visitors who drop by during the limited operating hours.

Faced with such a sharply peaked season, economic development agencies have stopped promoting the cape in summer and are working to extend its tourism season beyond the peak months of July and August, seeking to build demand in spring and autumn. Their efforts—and those of individual hotels and resorts—are proving quite successful. Among their targets are tourists from Europe, who appreciate the old-world charm of the cape and tend to spend more money than visitors from Boston or New York.

The second approach is to manage the level of demand, using marketing strategies to smooth out the peaks and fill in the valleys so as to generate a more consistent flow of requests for service. Many firms use both approaches. But in some instances, such as seasonal vacation destinations, there are real limits to the possibilities. Consider the situation on Cape Cod, where the year-round population of about two hundred and fifteen thousand jumps to over five hundred thousand in the summer (see Service Perspectives 13.1).

Measuring and Managing Capacity

What do we mean by *productive capacity?* The term refers to the resources or assets that a firm can employ to create goods and services. In a service context, productive capacity can take at least five potential forms.

1. *Physical facilities designed to contain customers* and used for delivering people-processing services or mental stimulus–processing services. Examples include medical clinics, hotels, passenger aircraft, buses, restaurants, swimming pools, theaters, concert halls, and college classrooms. In these situations, the primary capacity constraint is likely to be defined in terms of such furnishings as beds, rooms, seats, tables, or desks. In some cases, local regulations may set an upper limit to the number of people allowed in the interest of health or fire safety.
2. *Physical facilities designed for storing or processing goods* that either belong to customers or are being offered to them for sale. Examples include supermarket shelves, pipelines, warehouses, parking lots, freight containers, or railroad cars.
3. *Physical equipment used to process people, possessions, or information* may embrace a huge range of items and be very situation specific(machinery, telephones, hair dryers, computers, diagnostic equipment, airport security detectors, toll gates on roads and bridges, cooking ovens, bank ATMs, repair tools, and cash registers are among the many items whose absence in sufficient numbers for a given level of demand can bring service to a crawl (or a complete stop).
4. *Labor,* a key element of productive capacity in all high-contact services and many low-contact ones, may be used for both physical and mental work. Abraham Lincoln captured it well when he remarked that "a lawyer's time and expertise are his stock in trade." Staffing levels for personnel, from restaurant servers and nurses to telephone operators, must be sufficient to meet anticipated demand—otherwise, customers will be kept waiting or service will be rushed. Professional services are especially dependent on highly skilled staff to create high value-added, information-based output.
5. *Infrastructure.* Many organizations are dependent on access to sufficient capacity in the public or private infrastructure to be able to deliver quality service to their own customers. Capacity problems of this nature may include busy telephone circuits, electrical power failures (or so-called brownouts caused by reduced voltage), congested airways that lead to air-traffic restrictions, and traffic jams on major roads.

Measuring Capacity

Measures of capacity utilization include the number of hours (or percentage of total available time) that facilities, labor, and equipment are productively employed in revenue operation and the percentage of available space (e.g., seats, cubic freight capacity, or telecommunications bandwidth) that is actually utilized in revenue operations. Human beings tend to be far more variable than equipment in their ability to sustain consistent levels of output over time. One tired or poorly trained employee staffing a single station in an assembly-line operation such as a cafeteria restaurant can slow the entire service to a crawl. In a well-planned, well-managed service operation, the capacity of the facility, supporting equipment, and service personnel will be in balance. Similarly, sequential operations will be designed to minimize the likelihood of bottlenecks at any point in the process. In practice, however, it's difficult to achieve this ideal all the time.

Stretching and Shrinking the Level of Capacity

Some capacity is elastic in its ability to absorb extra demand. A subway car, for instance, may offer 40 seats and allow standing room for another 60 passengers with adequate handrails and floor space for all. Yet at rush hours, when there have been delays on the line, perhaps 200 standees can be accommodated under sardine-like conditions. Service personnel may be able to work at high levels of efficiency for short periods of time but would quickly tire and begin providing inferior service if they had to work that fast all day long.

Even where capacity appears fixed, as when it's based on the number of seats, there may still opportunities to accept extra business at busy times. Some airlines, for instance, increase the capacity of their aircraft by slightly reducing legroom throughout the cabin and cramming in another couple of rows. Similarly, a restaurant may add extra tables and chairs. Upper limits to such practices are often set by safety standards or by the capacity of supporting services, such as the kitchen.

Another strategy for stretching capacity is to use the facilities for longer periods. Examples of this include restaurants that open for early dinners and late suppers, universities that offer evening classes and summer programs, and airlines that extend their schedules from, say, 14 to 18 hours a day. Alternatively, the average amount of time that customers (or their possessions) spend in process may be reduced. Sometimes this is achieved by minimizing slack time, as when the bill is presented promptly to a group of diners relaxing at the table after a meal. In other instances, it may be achieved by cutting back the level of service–say, offering a simpler menu at busy times of day.

Chasing Demand

Another strategy, known as *chasing demand,* involves tailoring capacity to match variations in demand. Possible ways to adjust capacity as needed include:

- *Schedule downtime during periods of low demand.* To ensure that 100 percent of capacity is available during peak periods, repairs and renovations should be conducted when demand is expected to be low, and employee holidays should be taken then.
- *Use part-time employees.* Many organizations hire extra workers during their busiest periods. Examples include postal workers and retail shop assistants at Christmastime, extra staff within tax preparation service firms at the end of the financial year, and additional hotel employees during holiday periods and major conferences.
- *Rent or share extra facilities and equipment.* To limit investment in fixed assets, a service business may be able to rent extra space or machines at peak times. Firms with complementary demand patterns may enter into formal sharing agreements.
- *Cross-train employees.* Even when the service delivery system appears to be operating at full capacity, certain physical elements—and their attendant employees—may be underutilized. If employees can be cross-trained to perform a variety of tasks, they can be shifted to bottle-

neck points as needed, thereby increasing total system capacity. In supermarkets, for instance, the manager may call on stockers to operate cash registers when checkout lines start to get too long. Likewise, during slow periods, the cashiers may be asked to help stock shelves.[2]

Creating Flexible Capacity

Sometimes, the problem lies not in the overall capacity but in the mix that's available to serve the needs of different market segments. For instance, on a given flight, an airline may have too few seats in economy class even though there are empty places in the business-class cabin, or a hotel may find itself short of suites one day when there are standard rooms still available. One solution lies in designing physical facilities to be flexible. For example, some hotels build rooms with connecting doors. With the door between two rooms locked, the hotel can sell two bedrooms; with the door unlocked and one of the bedrooms converted into a sitting room, the hotel can now offer a suite.

Facing stiff competition from Airbus Industrie, Boeing received what were described, tongue in cheek, as "outrageous demands" from prospective customers when it was designing its new 777 airliner. The airlines wanted an aircraft in which galleys and lavatories could be relocated, plumbing and all, almost anywhere in the cabin within a matter of hours. Boeing gulped but solved this challenging problem. Airlines can rearrange the passenger cabin of the "Triple Seven" within hours, reconfiguring it with varying numbers of seats allocated among one, two, or three classes.

One nice example of highly flexible capacity comes from an ecotourism operator in the South Island of New Zealand. During the spring, summer, and early autumn months the firm provides guided walks and treks, and during the snow season it offers cross-country skiing lessons and trips. Bookings all year round are processed through a contracted telephone-answering service, guides and instructors are employed on a part-time basis as required, the firm has negotiated agreements to use national park huts and cabins, and it has an exclusive arrangement with a local sporting goods store whereby equipment can be hired or purchased by clients at preferential rates. As needed, they can arrange charter bus service for groups. Yet despite this capacity to provide a range of services, the owners' capital investment in the business is remarkably low.

Strategic Application of Unsold Service Capacity

Not all productive capacity is sold. Ng, Wirtz, and Lee note that unsold capacity can be put to a variety of strategic uses that help the firm build relationships with customers, suppliers, employees, and intermediaries.[3] Possible applications include customer development through free trials, employee rewards, pledging to intermediaries, and bartering. A very different application is to expand capacity to discourage competitors from entering a market—often encountered in the airline and lodging industries.

Pledging. To demonstrate commitment to their intermediaries, firms in the travel industry often pledge a defined amount of capacity to the intermediaries before the season begins. One of the goals is to enable employees to become familiar with the offering (such as the "fam" trips widely employed by hotels, resorts, and airlines to build relationships with travel agents). Couriers accompanying tour groups are usually provided with free travel and accommodation.

Bartering. Some service capacity is bartered with other suppliers. This practice has long been common in informal economies, where people will trade work in their area of expertise against services created by someone else. At a corporate level, we need to distinguish between planning a strategy to barter capacity in advance with another supplier and simply doing so as a last resort when all other attempts to sell surplus capacity have been exhausted. Bartering allows for much more creativity than cash deals because it can be used to obtain other services of value to the firm, thus helping reduce costs. For instance, radio stations may offer an advertiser free (or discounted) air time in return for free use of a specified amount of that advertiser's own services—as long ago as 1992, bartering for advertising had an estimated value of $3 billion.[4] Among the most widely bartered services are airline seats and hotel rooms.

Understanding the Patterns and Determinants of Demand

Now let's look at the demand side of the equation. To control variations in demand for a particular service, managers need to determine what factors govern that demand. Research should begin by getting some answers to a series of important questions.[5]

What Determines Demand?

1. Do demand levels follow a predictable cycle? If so, is the duration of the cycle:
   - One day (varies by hour)
   - One week (varies by day)
   - One month (varies by day or by week)
   - One year (varies by month or by season or reflects annually occurring public holidays)
   - Some other period
   Often, multiple cycles operate simultaneously. Thus, demand for passenger transport may vary by time of day, day of the week, and season all at once.

2. What are the underlying causes of these cyclical variations?
   - Employment timetables
   - Billing and tax payment/refund cycles
   - Wage and salary payment dates
   - School hours and holidays
   - Seasonal changes in climate
   - Occurrence of public or religious holidays
   - Natural cycles, such as coastal tides

3. Do demand levels seem to change randomly? If so, could the underlying causes be
   - Day-to-day changes in the weather (Consider how rain and cold affect the use of indoor and outdoor recreational or entertainment services.)
   - Health events whose occurrence cannot be pinpointed exactly (Heart attacks and births affect the demand for hospital services.)
   - Accidents, natural disasters (such as earthquakes), and certain criminal activities (These require fast response from firefighters, police, and ambulance and also from disaster recovery specialists and insurance firms.)

4. Can demand for a particular service over time be disaggregated by market segment to reflect such components as
   - Use patterns by a particular type of customer or for a particular purpose?
   - Variations in the net profitability of each completed transaction?

Multiple Influences on Demand

Most periodic cycles influencing demand for a particular service vary in length from one day to 12 months. In many instances, multiple cycles may operate simultaneously. For example, demand levels for public transport may vary by time of day (highest during commuter hours), day of week (less travel to work on weekends but more leisure travel), and season of year (more travel by tourists in summer). The demand for service during the peak period on a Monday in summer may be different from the level during the peak period on a Saturday in winter, reflecting day-of-week and seasonal variations jointly.

Figure 13.2 shows how the combination of 4 time-of-day periods (morning peak, midday, afternoon peak, evening/night), 2 day-of-week periods (weekday, weekend), and 3 seasonal periods (peak, shoulder, off-peak) can be combined to create 24 different demand periods. In theory, each of these might have its own distinct demand level (at a given price) and customer profiles (with resulting differences in needs and expectations). But in practice, analysis might show close similarities between many of the periods. Such a finding would make it possible to collapse the framework into a total of perhaps three to six cells, each requiring a distinct mar-

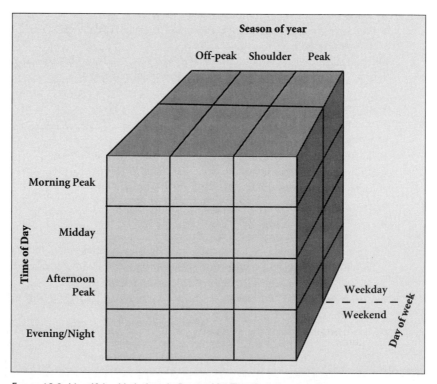

FIGURE 13.2 Identifying Variations in Demand by Time Period

keting treatment to optimize the use of available capacity and obtain the most desirable customer mix.

Analyzing and Forecasting Demand

Keeping good records of each transaction helps enormously when it comes to analyzing demand patterns based on past experience. Computer-based services, such as telecommunications, can track customer consumption patterns by date and time of day automatically. Where relevant, it's also useful to record weather conditions and other special factors (a strike, an accident, a big convention in town, a price change, launch of a competing service, etc.) that might have influenced demand.

Random fluctuations are usually caused by factors beyond management's control. But analysis will sometimes reveal that a predictable demand cycle for one segment is concealed within a broader, seemingly random pattern. This fact illustrates the importance of breaking down demand on a segment-by-segment basis. For instance, a repair and maintenance shop that services industrial electrical equipment may already know that a certain proportion of its work consists of regularly scheduled contracts to perform preventive maintenance. The balance may come from walk-in business and emergency repairs. Although it might seem hard to predict or control the timing and volume of such work, further analysis could show that walk-in business was more prevalent on some days of the week than others and that emergency repairs were frequently requested following damage sustained during thunderstorms (which tend to be seasonal in nature and can often be forecast a day or two in advance).

Telephone call centers are acutely affected by demand variations. Because experience shows that call volumes vary widely, it makes sense for such businesses to forecast demand and then set staffing levels by time of day, week, or season with reference to those forecasts. Research Insights 13.1 describes how researchers created a forecasting model for L.L. Bean, the well-known retailer of outdoor goods and apparel.

Organizations serving several different types of customers have to forecast the level of demand from each segment. For instance, a quick-service restaurant may serve customers who come in for a meal; customers who come to the counter for take out; and customers who arrive at the drive-up window, also seeking take out.[6] Depending on the demand levels forecast from each group, the manager has to decide how many staff will be needed at certain times of day or week and which tasks to assign them to. Busy times at the drive-up window may require two staff members; at other times one may suffice. If there are, say, four counter stations for walk-in customers, decisions must be made on how many to open at specific times. Finally, the restaurant will get dirtier when more people are eating in, so someone needs to be assigned to clean periodically.

Not all demand is desirable. In fact, some requests for service are inappropriate and make it difficult for the organization to respond to the legitimate needs of its target customers. Have you ever wondered what it's like to be a dispatcher for an emergency service such as 911? People differ widely in what they consider to be an emergency. Imagine yourself in the huge communications room at police headquarters in New York City. A gray-haired sergeant is talking patiently by phone to a woman who has dialed 911 because her cat has run up a tree and she's afraid it's stuck there. "Ma'am, have you ever seen a cat skeleton in a tree?" the sergeant asks her. "All those cats get down somehow, don't they?" After the woman has hung up, the sergeant turns to a visitor and shrugs. "These kinds of calls keep pouring in," he says. "What can you do?" The trouble is, when people call the emergency number with complaints about noisy parties next door or pleas to rescue cats, they may be slowing response times to fires, heart attacks, or violent crimes. Discouraging undesirable demand through marketing campaigns or screening procedures will not, of course, eliminate random fluctuations in the remaining demand. But it may help to keep peak demand levels within the organization's capacity to serve.

Forecasting Telephone Call–Center Volume at L.L. Bean

The majority of L.L. Bean's sales volume is generated by telephone orders to the firm's 24/7 customer service center, stimulated by catalogue mailings. In 1998, the firm mailed more than one hundred fifty million catalogues in 50 different versions and received 15 million toll-free calls. During peak periods that year, the company employed 3,300 telephone representatives (some of them multilingual). The busiest single day of 1998 was December 7, when 148,506 calls were received. Other methods of purchase include mail and fax orders, Internet orders (increasing steadily), and visits to the company's store in Freeport, Maine, or to its several factory outlets.

Telephone calls to L.L. Bean fit into two major classifications: telemarketing (TM), which is primarily concerned with receiving orders, and telephone inquiry (TI), which involves customers who call about the status of their orders, report order problems, or discuss other matters. The volume and average duration of these two types of calls are quite different; annual volumes for TM calls vastly outnumber TI calls, but the latter are longer and more complex and thus require agents with more skill and training.

Several years ago, the company retained consultants to create models that could forecast TM and TI call volumes three weeks ahead so that managers could create weeklong staffing schedules and post agent work schedules in advance. Inaccurate forecasts are costly to the company, because inadequate staffing of TM agents leads to lost orders; meanwhile, understaffing of TI agents decreases customer satisfaction and threatens loyalty and future orders. Excessive waiting for an agent to respond not only irritates customers by costing them time but also drives up telephone connect charges, which are paid by L.L. Bean. Overstaffing, by contrast, is expensive in that it drives up direct-labor costs unnecessarily. Staffing decisions are complicated by the erratic nature and extreme seasonality of L.L. Bean's business. Nearly 20 percent of the company's annual sales volume comes from a three-week period prior to Christmas. During that peak season, the company more than doubles the number of agents and quadruples the quantity of telephone lines.

The consultants (Bruce Andrews and Shawn Cunningham of the University of Southern Maine) built forecasting models for both types of calls using the autoregressive/integrated/moving average (ARIMA) methodology, which has been widely used for modeling time-series data with strongly seasonal patterns.

Plots of daily call data for TM and TI showed strong day-of-week patterns, with Monday typically generating the highest volume and each successive day decreasing monotonically to the weekly low on Sunday. Full-year time-series plots showed strong seasonal patterns. Although call volumes are reasonably stable during the second and third quarters of the year, both TM and TI volumes begin to increase during the fourth quarter and explode during December (although TM volumes ramp up more steeply than TI). Both then fall back again during the first quarter. TI volumes consistently peak two to three weeks later than TM, reflecting the lagged effect of placing an order and later calling to inquire about its status or report a problem. Other factors that disrupt the underlying daily and seasonal patterns are holidays (during which call volumes are much lower) and catalogue mailings (which are usually timed to arrive in customers' homes on a Tuesday).

The complex models developed by the consultants treated each holiday and each catalogue as an independent variable and even allowed the model to accommodate a change in the size or circulation of a particular catalogue. The final models were identified and calibrated with a data set that spanned five years. Following implementation, the firm calculated that the increased precision of the forecasts translated into annual savings of approximately $300,000 for L.L. Bean.

Source: Bruce H. Andrews and Shawn M. Cunningham, "L.L. Bean Improves Call-Center Forecasting," *Interfaces* 25 (November–December 1995): 1–13; and www.llbean.com/customerservice/aboutLLBean, March 2000.

Strategies for Managing Demand

In a well-designed, well-managed service operation, the capacity of the facility, supporting equipment, and service personnel will be in balance with each other and with demand. Similarly, sequential operations will be designed to minimize the risk of bottlenecks at any point in the process. This ideal, however, may prove difficult to achieve. Not only does the level of demand vary over time, often randomly, but the time and effort required to process each person or thing may vary widely at any point in the process. In general, processing times for people are more variable than for objects or things, reflecting varying levels of preparedness ("I've lost my credit card"), argumentative versus cooperative personalities ("If you won't give me a table with a view, I'll have to ask for your supervisor"), and so forth. In both professional services and repair jobs, diagnosis and treatment times vary according to the nature of the customers' problems.

Disaggregating Demand by Market Segment

Can marketing efforts smooth out random fluctuations in demand? The answer is generally no, because these fluctuations are usually caused by factors beyond the management's control. But detailed market analysis may sometimes reveal that a predictable demand cycle for one segment is concealed within a broader, seemingly random pattern. For example, a retail store might experience wide swings in daily patronage but note that a core group of customers visited every weekday to buy staple items such as newspapers and lottery tickets.

The ease with which total demand can be broken down into smaller components depends on the nature of the records kept by management. If each customer transaction is recorded separately and backed up by detailed notes (as in a medical or dental visit or an accountant's audit), then the task of understanding demand is greatly simplified. In subscription and charge account services, when each customer's identity is known and itemized monthly bills are sent, managers can gain some helpful insights into usage patterns. As noted earlier, some services, such as telephone and electricity, even have the ability to track subscriber consumption patterns by time of day. Although these data may not always yield specific information on the purpose for which the service is being used, it is often possible to make informed judgments about the volume of sales generated by different user groups.

No strategy for smoothing demand is likely to succeed unless it is based on an understanding of why customers from a specific market segment choose to use the service when they do. For example, most hotels find it difficult to convince business travelers to remain on Saturday nights because few executives do business over the weekend. Instead, hotel managers should consider promoting use of their facilities for other purposes at weekends, such as conferences or pleasure travel. Similarly, attempts to get people traveling to work on public transport to shift their travel to off-peak periods will probably fail, because the timing of such travel is determined by people's employment hours. Instead, marketing efforts should be directed at employers to persuade them to adopt flextime or staggered working hours.

There are no real limits to the ability of price discounting to develop business out of season. However, resort areas, such as Cape Cod or Canada's Prince Edward Island, may have good opportunities to build business during the so-called shoulder seasons of spring and autumn by promoting different attractions—such as hiking, bird watching, bicycling, visiting museums and historic sites, and looking for bargains in antique stores—and then altering the mix and focus of services to target a different type of clientele than those who visit in the summer.

Managing Demand under Different Conditions

There are five basic approaches to managing demand. The first, which has the virtue of simplicity but little else, involves *taking no action and leaving demand to find its own levels.* Eventually customers learn from experience or word-of-mouth when they can expect to stand in line to use the service and when it will be available without delay. The trouble is that they may also learn to find a competitor who is more responsive! More interventionist approaches involve influencing the level of demand at any given time, by taking active steps to *reduce demand in peak periods* and to *increase demand when there is excess capacity.*

Two more approaches both involve *storing demand until capacity becomes available.* A firm can accomplish this either by introducing a booking or reservations system that promises customers access to capacity at specified times, or by *creating formalized queuing systems* (or by a combination of the two).

Table 13.1 links these five approaches to the three basic situations of excess demand, sufficient capacity, and excess capacity and provides a brief strategic commentary on each. Many service businesses face all three situations at different points in the cycle of demand and so should consider use of the interventionist strategies described.

Using Marketing Strategies to Shape Demand Patterns

Four of the elements of integrated service management introduced in chapter 1 have a role to play in stimulating demand during periods of excess capacity and in decreasing it *(demarketing)* during periods of insufficient capacity. Manipulating price and other user costs is often the first strategy adopted for bringing demand and supply into balance, but changes in product elements, variations in the place and time of service delivery, and the use of promotional and educational efforts can also play important roles. Although each element is discussed separately, effective demand management efforts often require changes in two or more elements jointly.

Price and Other User Costs. One of the most direct ways of reducing excess demand at peak periods is to charge customers more money to use the service during those periods. Increasing other outlays may have a similar effect. For instance, if customers learn that they are likely to face increased time and effort during peak periods, this information may lead those who dislike spending time waiting in crowded and unpleasant conditions to try later. Similarly, the lure of cheaper prices and an expectation of no waiting may encourage some people to change the timing of their behavior, whether it be shopping, travel, or visiting a museum

Some firms use pricing strategy in sophisticated ways to balance supply and demand. For the monetary price of a service to be effective as a demand management tool, managers must have some sense of the shape and slope of a product's demand curve—that is, how the quantity of service demanded responds to increases or decreases in the price per unit at a particular point in time (see Figure 13.3). It's important to determine whether the demand curve for a specific service varies sharply from one time period to another (will the same person be willing to pay more for a weekend stay in a hotel on Cape Cod or Prince Edward Island in summer than in other seasons? The answer is probably yes.). If so, significantly different pricing schemes may be needed to fill capacity in each time period. To complicate matters further, there may be separate demand curves for different segments within each time period; for instance, business travelers are usually less price sensitive than tourists (see Figure 13.4)

One of the most difficult tasks facing service marketers is to determine the nature of all these different demand curves. Research, trial and error, and analysis of parallel situations in other locations or in comparable services are all ways of obtaining an understanding of the situation. Many service businesses explicitly recognize the existence of different demand curves by

TABLE 13.1 *Alternative Demand Management Strategies for Different Capacity Situations*

Approach Used to Manage Demand	Capacity Situation Relative to Demand		
	Insufficient Capacity (Excess Demand)	Sufficient Capacity* (Satisfactory Demand)	Excess Capacity (Insufficient Demand)
Take no action	Unorganized queuing results. (May irritate customers and discourage future use)	Capacity is fully utilized. (But is this the most profitable mix of business?)	Capacity is wasted. (Customers may have a disappointing experience for services like theater.)
Reduce demand	Pricing higher will increase profits. Communication can be employed to encourage usage in other time slots. (Can this effort be focused on less profitable/desirable segments?)	Take no action (but see above).	Take no action (but see above).
Increase demand	Take no action unless opportunities exist to stimulate (and give priority to) more profitable segments.	Take no action unless opportunities exist to stimulate (and give priority to) more profitable segments.	Price lower selectively (try to avoid cannibalizing existing business; ensure all relevant costs are covered). Use communications and variation in products/distribution (but recognize extra costs, if any, and make sure appropriate trade-offs are made between profitability and usage levels).
Inventory demand by reservation system	Consider priority system for most desirable segments. Make other customers shift (a) to outside peak period or (b) to future peak.	Try to ensure most profitable mix of business.	Clarify that space is available and that no reservations are needed.
Inventory demand by formalized queuing	Consider override for most desirable segments. Seek to keep waiting customers occupied and comfortable. Try to predict wait period accurately.	Try to avoid bottleneck delays.	Not applicable.

Sufficient capacity may be defined as maximum available capacity or optimum capacity, depending on the situation.

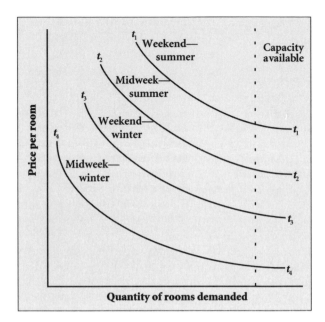

FIGURE 13.3 Variations in Demand Curves by Time Period (Hypothetical Example for Vacation Hotel Stays)

establishing distinct classes of service, each priced at levels appropriate to the demand curve of a particular segment. In essence, each segment receives a variation of the basic product, with value being added to the core service through supplementary services to appeal to higher-paying segments. For instance, first-class service on airlines offers travelers larger seats, free drinks, and better food; in computer services and printing services, product enhancement takes the form of consultation, faster turnaround, and more specialized options; and in hotels, a distinction is made between rooms of different size and amenities and with different views.

In each case, the objective is to maximize the revenues received from each segment. When capacity is constrained, however, the goal in a profit-seeking business should be to ensure that as much capacity as possible is assigned to the most profitable segments available at any given time. For instance, airlines will hold a certain number of seats for business passengers paying full fare and place restrictive conditions on excursion fares for tourists (such as requiring advance purchase and a Saturday night stay) to prevent business travelers from taking advantage of cheap fares designed to attract tourists who can help fill the aircraft. Pricing strategies of this nature are known as *yield management* and were discussed in chapter 9.

Changing Product Elements. Although pricing is often a commonly advocated method of balancing supply and demand, it is not quite as universally feasible for services as for goods. A rather obvious example is provided by the respective problems of a ski manufacturer and a ski-slope operator during the summer. The former can either produce for stock or try to sell skis in the summer at a bargain price. If the skis are sufficiently discounted, some customers will buy before the ski season to save money. However, in the absence of skiing opportunities, no skiers would buy lift tickets for use on a midsummer day at any price. So to encourage summer use of the lifts, the operator has to change the service product offering. For instance, resorts such as Vail, Colorado, or Mont Tremblant, Quebec, encourage summer visitors to ride lifts high up the mountain, see the view, go hiking, and eat at the restaurant on the summit. Ski resorts have

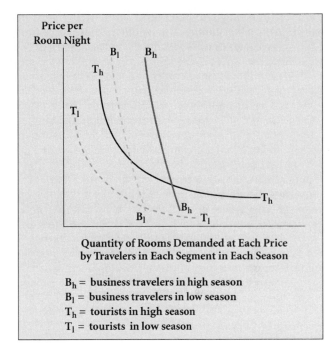

Price per Room Night

Quantity of Rooms Demanded at Each Price by Travelers in Each Segment in Each Season

B_h = business travelers in high season
B_l = business travelers in low season
T_h = tourists in high season
T_l = tourists in low season

FIGURE 13.4 Differing Demand Curves for Different Segments in Two Time Periods (Hypothetical Transportation Example)

always tried to attract summer hikers. Now some are taking advantage of the mountain-biking craze. At a growing number of resorts, mountain bikers can rent bikes from the lodge at the base, take them up to the summit on specially equipped lift chairs, and ride them down the trails (a few hardy souls have even been observed riding their bikes up the mountains, too!). Ski resorts also look for a variety of additional ways to attract guests to their hotels and rental homes in the summer. Possibilities include offering such activities and facilities as a championship golf course, tennis, water sports, rollerblading, and a children's day camp.

Similar thinking prevails at a variety of other seasonal businesses. Thus, tax preparation firms offer bookkeeping and consulting services to small businesses in slack months, educational institutions offer weekend and summer programs for adults and senior citizens, and sightseeing boats offer cruises in the summer and a dockside venue for private functions in winter months. These firms recognize that no amount of price discounting is likely to develop business out of season.

Many service offerings remain unchanged throughout the year, but others undergo significant modifications according to the season. Hospitals, for example, usually offer the same array of services throughout the year. By contrast, resort hotels sharply alter the mix and focus of their peripheral services such as dining, entertainment, and sports to reflect customer preferences in different seasons.

There can be variations in the product offering even during the course of a 24-hour period. Some restaurants provide a good example of this, marking the passage of the hours with changing menus and levels of service, variations in lighting and decor, opening and closing of the bar, and the presence or absence of entertainment. The goal is to appeal to different needs within the same group of customers, to reach out to different customer segments, or to do both according to the time of day.

Modifying the Place and Time of Delivery. Rather than seeking to modify demand for a service that continues to be offered at the same time in the same place, some firms respond to market needs by modifying the time and place of delivery. Three basic options are available.

The first represents a strategy of *no change*: regardless of the level of demand, the service continues to be offered in the same location at the same times. By contrast, a second strategy involves *varying the times when the service is available* to reflect changes in customer preference by day of week, by season, and so forth. Theaters often offer matinees on weekends when people have more leisure time throughout the day. During the summer, cafés and restaurants may stay open later because of extended daylight hours and the general inclination of people to enjoy the longer, balmier evenings outdoors. In the lead-up to Christmas, many shops extend their opening hours.

A third strategy involves *offering the service to customers at a new location.* One approach is to operate mobile units that take the service to customers, rather than requiring them to visit fixed-site service locations. Traveling libraries, mobile car wash services, in-office tailoring services, home-delivered meal and catering services, and vans equipped with primary-care medical facilities are examples of this. A cleaning and repair firm that wishes to generate business during low-demand periods might offer free pickup and delivery of portable items that need servicing. Alternatively, service firms whose productive assets are mobile may choose to follow the market when that, too, is mobile. For instance, some car rental firms establish seasonal branch offices in popular holiday locations. They transport large numbers of cars to these towns so that vacationers arriving by air, train, or cruise ship will be able to have a car available.

Promotion and Education. Even if the other marketing variables remain unchanged, communication efforts alone may be able to help smooth demand. Signage, advertising, publicity, and sales messages can be used to educate customers about the timing of peak periods and encourage them to avail themselves of the service at off-peak times when there will be fewer delays. Examples include post office requests to mail early for Christmas, public transport messages urging noncommuters—such as shoppers or tourists—to avoid the crush conditions of the rush hours, and communications from sales representatives for industrial maintenance firms advising customers of periods when preventive maintenance work can be done quickly. In addition, management can ask service personnel (or intermediaries such as travel agents) to encourage customers with discretionary time to favor off-peak periods.

Changes in pricing, product characteristics, and distribution must be communicated clearly. If a firm wants to obtain a specific response to variations in marketing mix elements it must, of course, inform customers fully about their options. As discussed in chapter 11, short-term promotions, combining both pricing and communication elements as well as other incentives, may provide customers with attractive incentives to shift the timing of service usage.

Storing Demand through Queuing and Reservations. What can a manager do when the possibilities for shaping demand and adjusting capacity have been exhausted and yet supply and demand are still out of balance? Not taking any action and leaving customers to sort things out is no recipe for service quality or customer satisfaction. Rather than allowing matters to degenerate into a random free-for-all, customer-oriented firms try to develop strategies for ensuring order, predictability, and fairness. In businesses where demand regularly exceeds supply, managers can often take steps to inventory demand. This task can be achieved in one of two ways: (1) by asking customers to wait in line (queuing), usually on a first-come, first-served basis, or (2) by offering them the opportunity of reserving space in advance. In chapter 14, we examine these two options in depth.

Information Needs

Managers require substantial information to help them develop effective demand management strategies and then monitor marketplace performance. Needs include

- *Historical data* on the level and composition of demand over time, including responses to changes in price or other marketing variables
- *Forecasts* of the level of demand for each major segment under specified conditions
- *Segment-by-segment data* to help management evaluate the impact of periodic cycles and random demand fluctuations
- *Sound cost data* to enable the organization to distinguish between fixed and variable costs and to determine the relative profitability of incremental unit sales to different segments and at different prices
- In multisite organizations, identification of meaningful variations in the levels and composition of demand on a site-by-site basis
- *Customer attitudes* toward queuing under varying conditions
- *Customer opinions* on whether the quality of service delivered varies with different levels of capacity utilization

Where might all this information come from? Although some new studies may be required, much of the needed data are probably already being collected within the organization—although not necessarily by marketers. A stream of information comes into most service businesses, especially from transaction data. Sales receipts alone often contain vast detail. Most service businesses collect detailed information for operational and accounting purposes. Although some do not record details of individual transactions, a majority have the potential to associate specific customers with specific transactions. Unfortunately, the marketing value of these data is often overlooked, and they are not always stored in ways that permit easy retrieval and analysis for marketing purposes. Nevertheless, collection and storage of customer transaction data can often be reformatted to provide marketers with some of the information they require, including how existing segments have responded to past changes in marketing variables.

Other information may have to be collected through special studies, such as customer surveys or reviews of analogous situations. It may also be necessary to collect information on competitive performance because changes in the capacity or strategy of competitors may require the firm to respond with a change in its own strategy.

Conclusion

Fluctuating demand for service is a problem for numerous service businesses, especially those with expensive fixed capacity. Because service output can rarely be produced and then stocked for future sale, strategies must be developed to balance demand against available capacity. Designing and implementing such strategies typically require close cooperation between marketing, operations, and human resource managers.

Options range from using marketing efforts to smooth the peaks and valleys of demand to managing the level of available capacity to match the level of demand. When demand exceeds supply, lines may develop and lead to customer frustration unless carefully organized. As shown in the next chapter, reservations systems can be used to guarantee customers access to the desired service at a specified time and thus save them from having to wait in line. But if they do have to wait, then there are a variety of ways to organize the queuing process.

Several of the 8 Ps of integrated service management underlie the discussion in this chapter. The first is productivity. Because many capacity-constrained service organizations have heavy fixed costs, even modest improvements in capacity utilization can have a significant effect on the bottom line. In this chapter we have also shown how managers can transform fixed costs into variable costs through such strategies as using rented facilities or part-time labor. Creating a more flexible approach to productive capacity allows a firm to adopt the strategy of chasing demand, thereby improving productivity.

Decisions on place and time are closely associated with balancing demand and capacity. Demand is often a function of where the service is located and when it is offered. As we saw with the discussion of mountain resorts, the appeal of many destinations varies with the seasons. Marketing strategies involving use of product elements, price and other costs, and promotion and education are often useful in managing the level of demand for a service at a particular place and time.

REVIEW QUESTIONS

1. Why is capacity management particularly significant in a service setting?
2. What is meant by *chasing demand?* Give examples of how you would apply such a strategy in freight shipment.
3. What does *inventory* mean for service firms, and why is it perishable?
4. Distinguish between optimum and maximum capacity. What are their respective implications for customers, employees, and managers?
5. Define *capacity* in relation to all the service elements offered to customers by (a) an airline, (b) a hotel, (c) a management consulting firm, and (d) a full-service restaurant.
6. List at least two implications of each of the cyclical events outlined on page 397 for different types of services available on Cape Cod.
7. Review the five approaches to managing demand. Give examples of their applicability to different types of business-to-business services.

APPLICATION EXERCISES

1. Identify five services that you use at school, at work, or during your leisure time. In each case, how would you define their capacity to serve? How would you measure this capacity? Is any attempt made to vary the amount of capacity to correspond to variations in demand?
2. Select a service organization with which you are familiar and identify its particular patterns of demand with reference to Figure 13.1:
   (a) What is the nature of this service organization's approach to capacity and demand management?
   (b) What changes would you recommend in relation to its management demand and why?
3. Interview a manager from a local firm that undertakes repair and maintenance services (e.g., plumber, garage, electrician, facilities maintenance, computer services). Determine how they schedule time for emergency repairs relative to routine work—is slack built into the schedule, or do other customers get bumped?
4. Compare and contrast the impact of peak demand on capacity to serve in (a) a telephone call center, (b) a web site that accepts orders, and (c) a retail store.

ENDNOTES

1. Colin G. Armistead and Graham Clark, "The 'Coping' Capacity Management Strategy in Services and the Influence on Quality Performance," *International Journal of Service Industry Management* 5, no. 2 (1994): 5–22.
2. Based on material in James A. Fitzsimmons and Mona J. Fitzsimmons, *Service Management: Operations, Strategy, and Information Technology,* 2d ed. (New York: Irwin McGraw-Hill, 1998); and W. Earl Sasser Jr., "Match Supply and Demand in Service Industries," *Harvard Business Review* 54 (November–December 1976): 133–140.
3. Irene C. L. Ng, Jochen Wirtz, and Khai Sheang Lee, "The Strategic Role of Unused Service Capacity," *International Journal of Service Industry Management* 10, no. 2 (1999): 211–238.
4. J. P. Vaccaro and W. W. Kassaye, "Taking Advantage of Barter in Radio," *Journal of Services Marketing* 11, no. 2 (1997): 118–127.
5. Christopher H. Lovelock, "Strategies for Managing Demand in Capacity-Constrained Service Organizations," *Service Industries Journal* 4 (November 1984): 12–30.
6. James L. Heskett, W. Earl Sasser Jr., and Christopher W. L. Hart, *Service Breakthroughs* (New York: The Free Press, 1990), 135–158.

CHAPTER 14

Managing Customer Waiting Lines and Reservations

They also serve who only stand and wait.

JOHN MILTON

In an ideal world, nobody would ever have to wait to conduct a transaction at any service organization. But firms cannot afford to provide extensive extra capacity that would go unutilized most of the time. As shown in the previous chapter, there are a variety of procedures for bringing demand and supply into balance. But what's a manager to do when the possibilities for shaping demand and adjusting capacity have been exhausted and yet supply and demand are still out of balance? Not taking any action and leaving customers to sort things out is no recipe for service quality or customer satisfaction. Rather than allowing matters to degenerate into a random free-for-all, customer-oriented firms try to develop strategies for ensuring order, predictability, and fairness.

In businesses where demand regularly exceeds supply, managers can often take steps to inventory demand. This task can be achieved in one of two ways: (1) by asking customers to wait in line (queuing), usually on a first-come, first-served basis, or (2) by offering them the opportunity of reserving or booking space in advance.

In this chapter, we consider the role that marketing can play in a field that has often been regarded simply as the province of operations and explore such questions as

1. How can well-designed waiting environments reduce the perceived burden for customers of waiting for service?
2. In what different ways can waiting lines be designed, and what are their implications for customers?
3. What data do we need to be able to predict how long a customer will have to wait in line under defined conditions?

4. What are the basics of designing an effective reservation system?
5. How do advance reservations relate to yield management strategy?

Waiting to Get Processed

You asked for a table for two last Saturday at a restaurant but were told that there would be a 40-minute wait, there were no washing machines free when you went to the laundromat last night, your travel agent told you the flight you wanted to take on vacation is fully booked, and the line to get into the latest blockbuster movie stretches around the block. Groan! A friend's car is having problems, but the local garage told her that they can't deal with it until next Tuesday. At least that is better than the plumber, who cannot get to your apartment to fix that annoying dripping tap for another 10 days. Calling another airline to check on schedules, you were put on hold and had to listen to a combination of canned music and ads for Florida vacations for 9 minutes. That delay came on top of the 6 minutes you waited in line in the bookstore at lunchtime to pay for books and the extra 25 minutes you waited this afternoon at your doctor's office beyond the appointment time you set up three weeks ago. Life is such a hassle! You begin to understand road rage.

All these disappointments result from too many people wanting the same service at the same time. One of the challenges of services is that because they are performances, they cannot normally be stored for later use: They must be delivered in real time.

The Universality of Waiting

It's estimated that Americans spend thirty-seven billion hours a year (an average of almost one hundred fifty hours per person) waiting in lines, "during which time they fret, fidget, and scowl," according to the *Washington Post*.[1] Similar (or worse) situations seem to prevail around the world. Richard Larson suggests that when everything is added up, the average person may spend as much as half an hour per day waiting in line, which would translate to 20 months of waiting in an 80-year lifetime![2]

Nobody likes to be kept waiting. It's boring, time wasting, and sometimes physically uncomfortable, especially if there is nowhere to sit or you are out-of-doors. And yet waiting for a service process is an almost universal phenomenon: Virtually every organization faces the problem of waiting lines somewhere in its operation. People are kept waiting on the phone, they line up with their supermarket carts to check out their grocery purchases, and they wait for their bills after a restaurant meal. They sit in their cars waiting for traffic lights to change, to enter drive-in car washes, and to pay at tollbooths.

Physical and inanimate objects wait for processing, too. Letters pile up on an executive's desk, shoes await repair, checks wait to be cleared at a bank, and an incoming phone call waits to be switched to a customer service rep. In each instance, a customer may be waiting for the outcome of that work—an answer to a letter, a pair of shoes ready to be picked up, a check credited to the customer's balance, or useful contact with the service rep—instead of being kept on hold listening to a recorded message that keeps repeating, "Your call is important to us (Figure 14.1)."

The Nature of Queues

Waiting lines—known to operations researchers (and also the British) as *queues*—occur whenever the number of arrivals at a facility exceeds the capacity of the system to process them. In a very real sense, queues are basically a symptom of unresolved capacity management problems. Analysis and modeling of queues is a well-established branch of operations management.

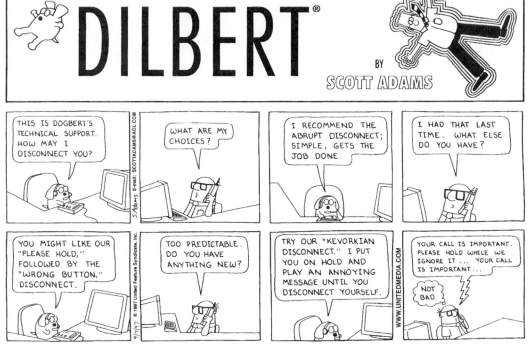

FIGURE 14.1 The Customer Comes Last
Source: Dilbert © UFS. Reprinted by permission.

Queuing theory has been traced back to 1917, when a Danish telephone engineer was charged with determining how large the switching unit in a telephone system had to be to keep the number of busy signals within reason.[3]

As the telephone example suggests, not all queues take the form of a physical waiting line in a single location. When customers deal with a service supplier at arm's length, as in information-processing services, they call from their home, office, or college using telecommunication channels such as voice telephone or the Internet. Typically, calls are answered in the order received, often requiring customers to wait their turn in a virtual line. Some physical queues are geographically dispersed. Travelers wait at many different locations for the taxis they have ordered by phone to arrive and pick them up.

The advent of sophisticated Web sites now makes it possible for people to do things for themselves, such as obtaining information or making reservations, that formerly required making telephone calls or visiting a service facility in person. Companies often promote the time savings that can be obtained (Figure 14.2). Although accessing the Web can be slow sometimes, at least the wait is conducted while the customer is comfortably seated and able to attend to other matters while waiting.

Adding extra capacity is not always the optimal solution in situations where customer satisfaction must be balanced against cost considerations. Managers should consider a variety of alternatives, such as

- Rethinking the design of the queuing system
- Redesigning processes to shorten the time of each transaction

FIGURE 14.2 United Airlines advises customers to make reservations and select seats on their own computers to avoid waiting in line at the airport.

Source: Used with the permission of United Airlines

- Managing customers' behavior and their perceptions of the wait
- Installing a reservations system

Elements of a Queuing System

We can divide queuing systems into seven elements, as shown in Table 14.1.[4] Let's take a look at each of them, recognizing that strategies for managing waiting lines can exercise more control over some elements than others.

Customer Population. When planning queuing systems, operations managers need to know who their customers are and something about their needs and expectations. There is, obviously,

TABLE 14.1 *Elements of a Queuing System*
1. The *customer population* from which demands for service originate (sometimes known to operations researchers as the *calling population*)
2. The *arrival process*—times and volumes of customer requests for service
3. *Balking*—decision by an arriving customer not to join the queue
4. *Queue configuration*—design of the system in terms of the number, location, and arrangement of wait lines
5. *Reneging*—decision by a customer already in the queue who has not yet been served to leave the line rather than wait any longer
6. *Customer selection policies*—formal or ad hoc policies on whom to serve next (also known as *queue discipline*)
7. The *service process*—physical design of the service delivery system, roles assigned to customers and service personnel, and flexibility to vary system capacity

a big difference between a badly injured patient arriving at a hospital emergency unit and a sports fan arriving at a stadium ticket office. Although neither are inanimate physical objects at a repair shop that could, in theory, be left to wait for several weeks, the hospital needs to be more geared for speed than the stadium. Based on customer research, the population can often be divided into several distinct market segments, each with differing needs and priorities.

Arrival Process. The rate at which customers arrive over time—relative to the capacity of the serving process—and the extent to which they arrive individually or in clusters will determine whether or not a queue starts to form. We need to draw a distinction between the *average* arrival rate (e.g., 60 customers per hour = 1 customer every minute) and the *distribution* of those arrivals during any given minute of that hour. In some instances, arrival times are largely random (for instance, individuals entering a store in a shopping mall). In other instances, some degree of clustering can be predicted, such as arrivals of students in a cafeteria within a few minutes of classes ending. Managers who anticipate surges of activity at specific times can plan their staff allocations around such events (for instance, opening an additional checkout line).

Balking. If you're like most people, you tend to be put off by a long line at a service facility and may often decide to come back later (or go somewhere else) rather than waiting. Sometimes this is a mistake, as the line may actually be moving faster than you think. Managers can disguise the length of lines by having them wind around corners, as often happens at theme parks. Alternatively, they may indicate the expected wait time from specific locations in the queuing area by installing information signs.

Queue Configuration. There are a variety of different types of queues. Here are some common ones that you may have experienced yourself in people-processing services (see also Figure 14.3 for diagrams of each type).

- *Single line, single stage.* Customers wait to conduct a single service transaction. Waiting for an elevator or a bus is an example.
- *Single line, sequential stages.* Customers proceed through several serving operations, as in a cafeteria line. In such systems, bottlenecks will occur at any stage where the process takes longer to execute than at previous stages. Many cafeterias often have lines at the cash register because the cashier takes longer to calculate how much you owe and to make change than the servers take to slap food on your plate.

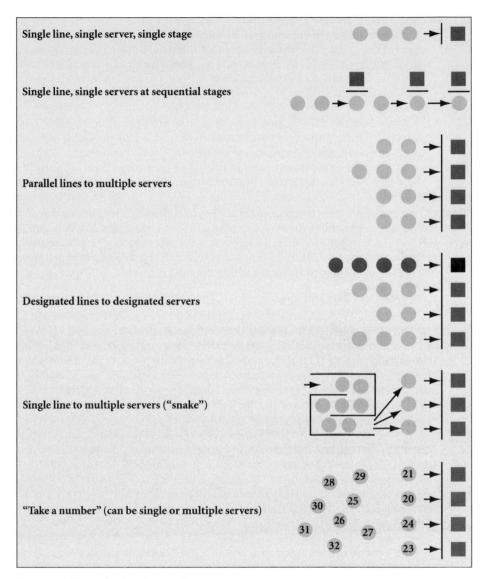

FIGURE 14.3 Alternative Queuing Configurations

- *Parallel lines to multiple servers (single or sequential stages).* This system offers more than one serving station, allowing customers to select one of several lines in which to wait. Fast-food restaurants usually have several serving lines in operation at busy times of day, with each offering the full menu. A parallel system can have either a single stage or multiple stages. The disadvantage of this design is that lines may not move at equal speed. How many times have you chosen what looked like the shortest line only to watch in frustration as the lines either side of you move at twice the speed because someone in your line has a complicated transaction?
- *Designated lines.* Different lines can be assigned to specific categories of customer. Examples include express lines (for instance, six items or less) and regular lines at supermarket checkouts and different check-in lines for first-class, business-class, and economy-class airline passengers.

- *Single line to multiple servers ("snake").* Customers wait in a single line, often winding sinuously back and forth between rope barriers (hence the name). As each person reaches the head of the queue, he or she is directed to the next available serving position. This approach is encountered frequently in bank lobbies, post offices, and at airport check-ins. Its big advantages are fairness and reduced anxiety. The presence of ropes or other barriers makes it difficult for inconsiderate people to break into line. At the margin, it may also discourage reneging.
- *Take a number.* In this variation of the single line, arriving customers take a number and are then called in sequence, thus saving the need to stand in a queue. This procedure allows them to sit down and relax (if seating is available) or to guess how long the wait will be and do something else in the meantime—but risk losing their place. Users of this approach include large travel agents or specialized departments in supermarkets, such as the butcher or baker.

Hybrid approaches to queue configuration also exist. For instance, a cafeteria with a single serving line might offer two cash register stations at the final stage. Similarly, patients at a small medical clinic might visit a single receptionist for registration; proceed sequentially through multiple channels for testing, diagnosis, and treatment; and conclude by returning to a single line for payment at the receptionist's desk.

Reneging. You know the situation (perhaps all too well!). The line is not that long, but it's moving at a snail's pace. The person at the front of the queue has been there for at least five minutes and his problem seems nowhere near solution. There are two other people ahead of you, and you have an uneasy feeling that their transactions are not going to be brief either. You look at your watch for the third time and realize that you have only a few minutes left before your next appointment. Frustrated, you turn on your heel and leave the line. In the language of queue management, you have *reneged.* One of the things planners need to determine is how long a wait has to be before customers are likely to start reneging. The consequences may include irritated customers who will return later as well as lost business.

Customer Selection Policies. Most waiting lines work on the principle of first come, first served. Customers tend to expect this—it's only fair, after all. In many cultures (but not all), people get very resentful if they see later arrivals being served ahead of them for no good reason. There are, however, some valid exceptions. Medical services will give priority to emergency cases, and airline personnel will allow passengers whose flights are soon due to leave to check in ahead of passengers taking later flights.

Service Process. Poorly designed service processes can lead to waits that are longer and more burdensome than necessary. All of the elements of the service system that we discussed in chapter 3 come into play here. The root cause for waits is sometimes to be found in one or more delays behind the scenes, resulting in customer-contact employees themselves being kept waiting for a necessary action to occur somewhere else in the system. Flowcharts, employee interviews, and analysis of past service failures can help to pinpoint where such problems might occur. The physical design of the frontstage service delivery system (refer back to chapters 3 and 11) plays a key role in effective queue management. Important design issues include

1. How customers are served: Batch processes serve customers in groups, whereas flow processes serve them individually.
2. Whether customers will be served by personnel, by equipment (self-service), or a combination of the two.
3. How quickly service transactions can be executed (thus determining capacity).

4. Whether service comes to the customers or whether they must come to the service site and move from one step to another.
5. The quality of the serving and waiting experiences, including personal comfort and design issues such as the impression created by the servicescape (see chapter 9).

Matching Queuing Systems to Market Segments

Although the basic rule in most queuing systems is first come, first served, not all queuing systems are organized on this basis. Market segmentation is sometimes used to design queuing strategies that set different priorities for different types of customers. Allocation to separate queuing areas may be based on

- *Urgency of the job*—At many hospital emergency units, a triage nurse is assigned to greet incoming patients and decide which ones require priority medical treatment and which can safely be asked to register and then sit down while they wait their turn.
- *Duration of service transaction*—Banks, supermarkets, and other retail services often institute express lanes for shorter, less complicated tasks
- *Payment of a premium price*—Airlines usually offer separate check-in lines for first-class and economy-class passengers, with a higher ratio of personnel to passengers in the first-class line, resulting in reduced waits for those who have paid more for their tickets.
- *Importance of the customer*—A special area may be reserved for members of frequent-user clubs. Airlines often provide lounges, offering newspapers and free refreshments, where frequent flyers can wait for their flights in greater comfort.

Minimizing the Perceived Length of the Wait

Operations managers should know better than to treat people who are waiting for service like inanimate objects (although that doesn't stop many some organizations from doing so!). As we saw in chapter 11, customers may view the time and effort spent on consuming services as a cost. People don't like wasting their time on unproductive activities any more than they like wasting money. They also prefer to avoid unwanted mental or physical effort, including anxiety or discomfort.

Research shows that people often think they have waited longer for a service than they actually did. Studies of public transportation use, for instance, have shown that travelers perceive time spent waiting for a bus or train as passing one and a half to seven times more slowly than the time actually spent traveling in the vehicle.[5] Tolerance for waiting may also be related to the nature of the institution providing service. A study conducted in Switzerland among customers of the Swiss postal service and those of the country's leading retailer, Migros, found that what customers defined as a tolerable waiting time for service was 30 percent higher for the retailer than for the post office. Kostecki hypothesized that this was because shopping at Migros was seen as a more pleasant experience than going to the post office.[6]

The Psychology of Waiting Time

The noted philosopher William James observed, "Boredom results from being attentive to the passage of time itself." Based on this observation, David Maister formulated 8 principles about waiting time.[7] Adding two additional principles gives us a total of 10, summarized in Table 14.2. Let's examine each proposition in turn and review some appropriate actions.

TABLE 14.2 *Ten Propositions on the Psychology of Waiting Lines*
1. Unoccupied time feels longer than occupied time.
2. Pre- and postprocess waits feel longer that in-process waits.
3. Anxiety makes waits seem longer.
4. Uncertain waits are longer than known, finite waits.
5. Unexplained waits are longer than explained waits.
6. Unfair waits are longer than equitable waits.
7. The more valuable the service, the longer people will wait.
8. Solo waits feel longer than group waits.
9. Physically uncomfortable waits feel longer than comfortable waits.
10. Unfamiliar waits seem longer than familiar ones.

Unoccupied Time Feels Longer than Occupied Time. When you're sitting around with nothing to do, time seems to crawl. The challenge for service organizations is to give customers something to do or to distract them while waiting. A supermarket chain found from research that customers do not see themselves as waiting in line if there is only one person ahead of them at the checkout so long as there is space for them to begin unloading their trolleys, which keeps them busy.[8] Doctors and dentists stock their waiting rooms with piles of magazines (all too often, many months old and irrelevant to patients' interests) for people to read while waiting. Car repair facilities may have a television for customers to watch. One tire dealer goes further, providing customers with free popcorn, soft drinks, coffee, and ice cream while they wait for their cars to be returned. Theme parks supply roving bands of entertainers to amuse customers waiting in line for the most popular attractions.

Pre- and Postprocess Waits Feel Longer than In-Process Waits. There's a difference between waiting to buy a ticket to enter a theme park and waiting to ride on a roller coaster once you're in the park. There's also a difference between waiting for coffee to arrive near the end of a restaurant meal and waiting for the server to bring you the check once you're ready to leave. Rental car firms sometimes get the process started early by assigning an agent to obtain information on customers' needs while they wait in line; in that way, service delivery—namely, assigning a specific car—can begin as soon as each person reaches the head of the line. These firms also try to minimize customer waiting when the car is returned, employing agents with wireless, handheld terminals to meet customers in the parking area, enter fuel and mileage, and then compute and print bills on the spot.

Anxiety Makes Waits Seem Longer. Can you remember waiting for someone to show at a rendezvous and worrying about whether you had got the time or the location correct? While waiting in unfamiliar locations, especially out-of-doors and after dark, people often worry about their personal safety.

Uncertain Waits Are Longer than Known, Finite Waits. Although any wait may be frustrating, we can usually adjust mentally to a wait of known length. It's the unknown that keeps us on edge. Imagine waiting for a delayed flight and not being told how long the delay is going to be. You don't know whether you have the time to get up and walk around the terminal or whether to stay at the gate in case the flight is called any minute.

Unexplained Waits Are Longer than Explained Waits. Have you ever been in a subway or elevator that has stopped for no apparent reason without anyone telling you what is going on? Not only is there uncertainty about the length of the wait, but there's also added worry about what is going to happen. Has there been an accident on the line? Will you have to leave the train in the tunnel? Is the elevator broken? Will you be stuck for hours in close proximity with dubious-looking strangers?

Unfair Waits Are Longer than Equitable Waits. Expectations about what is fair or unfair sometimes vary from one culture or country to another. In countries like the United States, Canada, or Britain, for example, people expect everybody to wait their turn in line and are likely to get irritated if they see others jumping ahead or being given priority for no apparent good reason.

The More Valuable the Service, the Longer People Will Wait. People will queue overnight under uncomfortable conditions to get good seats at a major concert or sports event that is expected to sell out.

Solo Waits Feel Longer than Group Waits. Waiting with one or more people you know is reassuring. Conversation with friends can help to pass the time, but not everyone is comfortable talking to a stranger.

Physically Uncomfortable Waits Feel Longer than Comfortable Waits.[9] "My feet are killing me!" is one of the most frequently heard comments when people are forced to stand in line for a long time. And whether seated or unseated, a wait seems more burdensome if the temperature is too hot or too cold, if it's drafty or windy, and if there is no protection from rain or snow.

Unfamiliar Waits Seem Longer than Familiar Ones.[10] Frequent users of a service know what to expect and are less likely to worry while waiting. New or occasional users of a service, by contrast, are often nervous, wondering not only about the probable length of the wait but also about what happens next. They may also be concerned about such issues as personal safety.

The implications? When increasing capacity is simply not feasible, you should try to be creative and look for ways to make waiting more palatable for customers. An experiment at a large bank in Boston found that installing an electronic news display in the lobby didn't reduce the perceived time spent waiting for teller service, but it did lead to greater customer satisfaction.[11] Heated shelters equipped with seats make it more pleasant to wait for a bus or train in cold weather. Restaurants solve the waiting problem by inviting dinner guests to have a drink in the bar until their table is ready (that approach makes money for the house as well as keeping the customer occupied). In similar fashion, guests waiting in line for a show at a casino may find themselves queuing in a corridor lined with slot machines. And the doorman at a Marriott Hotel has taken it upon himself to bring a combination barometer/thermometer to work each day, hanging it on a pillar at the hotel entrance where guests waiting can spend a moment or two examining it while they wait for a taxi or for their car to be delivered from the valet parking.[12] Theme park operators cleverly design their waiting areas to make the wait look shorter than it really is, find ways to give customers in line the impression of constant progress, and make time seem to pass more quickly by keeping customers amused or diverted while they wait.

Giving Customers Information on Waits

Does it help to tell people how long they are likely to have to wait for service? Common sense would suggest that this is useful information for customers because it allows them to make decisions as to whether they can afford to take the time to wait now or should come back later. It also enables them to plan the use of their time while waiting. An experimental study in Canada looked at how students responded to waits while conducting transactions by computer—a situation similar to waiting on the telephone in that there are no visual clues as to the probable wait time.[13] The study examined dissatisfaction with waits of 5, 10, or 15 minutes under three conditions: (1) the student subjects were told nothing, (2) they were told how long the wait was likely to be, or (3) they were told what their place in line was. The results suggested that for 5-minute waits, it was not necessary to provide information to improve satisfaction. For waits of 10 or 15 minutes, offering information appeared to improve customers' evaluations of service. However, for longer waits, the researchers suggest that it may be more positive to let people know how their place in line is changing than to let them know how much time remains before they will be served. One conclusion we might draw is that people prefer to see (or sense) that the line is moving rather than to watch the clock.

SERVICE PERSPECTIVES 14.1

Cutting the Wait at First National Bank of Chicago

How should a big retail bank respond to increased competition from new financial service providers? The First National Bank of Chicago decided that enhancing service to its customers would be an important element in its strategy. One opportunity for improvement was to reduce the amount of time that customers spent waiting in line for service in the bank's retail branches—a frequent source of complaints. Recognizing that no single action could resolve the problem satisfactorily, the bank adopted a three-pronged approach.

First, technological improvements were made to the service operation, starting with introduction of an electronic queuing system that not only routed customers to the next available teller station but also provided supervisors with online information to help match staffing to customer demand. Meantime, computer enhancements provided tellers with more information about their customers, enabling them to handle more requests without leaving their stations. And new cash machines for tellers saved them from selecting bills and counting them twice (yielding a time savings of 30 seconds for each cash withdrawal transaction).

Second, changes were made to human resource strategies. The bank adopted a new job description for teller managers that made them responsible for customer queuing times and for expediting transactions. It created an officer-of-the-day program, under which a designated officer was equipped with a beeper and assigned to help staff with complicated transactions that might otherwise slow them down. A new job category of peak-time teller was introduced, paying premium wages for 12 to 18 hours of work a week. Existing full-time tellers were given cash incentives and recognition to reward improved productivity on predicted high-volume days. Lastly, management reorganized meal arrangements. On busy days, lunch breaks were reduced to half-hour periods, and staff received catered meals; meanwhile, the bank cafeteria was opened earlier to serve peak-time tellers.

A third set of changes centered on customer-oriented improvements to the delivery system. Quick-drop desks were established on busy days to handle deposits and simple requests, whereas newly created express teller stations were reserved for deposits and check cashing. Lobby hours were expanded from 38 to 56 hours a week, including Sundays. A customer brochure, *How to Lose Wait*, alerted customers to busy periods and suggested ways of avoiding delays.

Subsequently, internal measures and customer surveys showed that the improvements had not only reduced customer wait times but also increased customer perceptions that First Chicago was the best bank in the region for minimal waits in teller lines. The bank also found that adoption of extended hours had deflected some of the noon rush to before-work and after-work periods.

Source: Based on an example in Leonard L. Berry and Linda R. Cooper, "Competing with Time-Saving Service," *Business* 40, no. 2 (1990): 3–7.

Clearly there are a variety of solutions to dealing with the problem of long waits, ranging from addressing the capacity side—by adding more staff at peak hours or extending service hours—to establishing segmented queuing systems, giving customers more information and encouraging them to use the service outside peak times. For an example of a mixed strategy, see Service Perspectives 14.1.

Calculating Wait Times

Queue management involves extensive data gathering. Questions of interest include the rate at which customers (or things requiring service) arrive per unit of time and how long it takes to serve each one.

A typical operations strategy is to plan on the basis of average throughput to optimize use of employees and equipment. So long as customers (or things) continue to arrive at this same average rate, there will be no delays. However, fluctuations in arrivals (sometimes random, sometimes predictable) will lead to delays at times as the line backs up following a clump of arrivals. Planners also need to know how easily customers will just walk away when they spot a lengthy line *(balking)* and how long customers will wait for service before giving up and leaving *(reneging)*.

To streamline its check-in service at a major airport, an airline commissioned a consulting firm to study the existing queuing system and determine how much time passengers were spending waiting in line. Technicians from the firm installed pressure-sensitive rubber mats on the floor in front of the ticket counters. Pressure from each customer's foot on approaching or leaving the counter recorded the exact time on an electronic device embedded in the mats. From these data, the consultant was able to profile the waiting situation at the airline's counters, including average waiting times, how long each transaction took, how many customers waited longer than a given length of time (and at what hours on what days), and even how many bailed out of a long line. Analysis of these data, collected over an extended period, yielded information that helped the airline to match its staffing more closely to the demand levels projected at different times.

Predicting the Behavior of Simple Queuing Systems

Underlying the practice of queue management are mathematical models that enable planners or consultants to calculate a variety of statistics about queue behavior and thus make informed decisions about changes or improvements to existing queuing systems. For basic queuing situations, the formulas are quite simple and yield interesting insights (see Management Memo 14.1). More complex environments may require powerful simulation models that are beyond the scope of this book.

Reservations

Ask someone what services come to mind when you talk about *reservations* and most likely they will cite airlines, hotels, restaurants, car rentals, and theater seats. Suggest synonyms such as *bookings* or *appointments* and they may add haircuts, visits to professionals such as doctors and consultants, vacation rentals, and service calls to fix anything from a broken refrigerator to a neurotic computer.

MANAGEMENT MEMO 14.1

Calculating Statistics for Simple Queues

Managers periodically have to make decisions concerning the trade-off between the expense of adding extra capacity to serve waiting customers (or objects) and the risk of customer dissatisfaction due to wasted time and delayed outcomes.

Given certain information about a particular queuing situation, formulas can be used to calculate such statistics as (1) average queue length, (2) average wait times for customers, (3) average total time for customers in the service system, (4) the impact of increasing the number of service channels, and (5) the impact of reducing average serving time. The math is easy but requires reference to a one-page statistical table (reproduced as an appendix at the end of this chapter). By using the following information in conjunction with the table, you will be able to make simple calculations about queue waiting times and how many people are likely to be waiting in a given queue under specified conditions.

Terminology
Certain terms and notation are used in queue analysis:

M = number of serving channels
λ (lambda) = average number of customers actually arriving per unit of time (60 minutes)
μ (mu) = average number of customers per channel served per unit of time (60 minutes)
ρ (rho) = λ/μ = flow intensity through serving channel (percent utilization)
$U = \lambda/M\mu$ = capacity utilization of the overall facility
L_q = expected length of line (number of people or objects waiting)
$W_q = L_q/\lambda$ = expected waiting time before being served

Note that unless the average number of customers served (μ) exceeds the average number of arrivals (λ), it will never be possible to serve all the customers desiring service.

Let's take a simple example. Consider the case of a theater ticket office which has one agent *(M)* who, on average, can serve 25 customers per hour (μ). This implies an average serving time of $60/25 = 2.4$ minutes per customer. Let's assume that customers arrive at an average rate of 20 per hour (λ) in the busy period, which means that $\rho = 20/25 = 0.80$. We can now use the table in the appendix on page 428 to calculate

● *Expected length of the line* (L_q): Looking down the column for one serving line (M) to $\rho = 0.80$, we can see that the line length will average 3.2 persons.
● *Expected waiting time* (W_q): $3.2 \times 60/20 = 9.6$ minutes.
● *Expected total time in system* $(W_q + 60/\mu)$: 9.6 minutes + 2.4 minutes = 12.0 minutes.
● *The average percentage utilization (U)*: $\lambda/M\mu = 20/1 \times 25 = 80$ percent (in other words, 20 percent of the time, the agent will be idle).

Let's suppose that customers are complaining about this wait and management wants to speed up service. The choices are to add a second agent (maintaining a single line) or to purchase new equipment that halves the time required to issue a ticket and receive payment. Here are the comparative results:

1. Using the table in the appendix, when $M = 2$ and $\rho = 0.80$:

The expected line length (L_q) will be only 0.15 persons.

The expected wait $(W_q) = L_q/\lambda = 0.15 \times 60/20 = 0.45$ minutes, plus 2.40 minutes for service = 2.85 minutes (down from 12.0 minutes).

2. However, if instead we halve the service process time, from 2.4 to 1.2 minutes, we can now serve a maximum of 50 customers per hour per channel and the following results occur:

The expected line length, when $M = 1$ and $\rho = 20/50 = 0.4$, is 0.27 persons.

The expected wait is $0.27 \times 60/20 = 0.81$ minutes $+ 1.2 = 2.01$ minutes total.

Both approaches cut the time sharply, but halving the service process time yields slightly better time savings than doubling the number of channels. In this instance, the decision on which approach to adopt would probably depend on the relevant costs involved—the capital cost of adding a second channel plus the wages and benefits paid to a second employee versus the capital costs of investing in new technology and training (assuming no increase in wages).

Reservations go beyond the simple placing of an order because they are supposed to guarantee that the service will be available at a specified time that is agreed with the customer. Systems vary from a simple appointments book for a doctor's office, using handwritten entries, to a central, computerized data bank for an airline's worldwide operations. When goods require servicing, their owners may not wish to be parted from them for long. Households with only one car, for example, or factories with a vital piece of equipment often cannot afford to be without such items for more than a day or two. So a reservations system may be necessary for service businesses in fields such as repair and maintenance. By requiring reservations for routine maintenance, management can ensure that some time will be kept free for handling emergency jobs that, because they carry a premium price, generate a much higher margin.

Designing a Reservations System

Reservation systems are commonly used by many people-processing services including restaurants, hotels, airlines, hairdressing salons, doctors, and dentists. The presence of such systems enables demand to be controlled and smoothed out in a more manageable way. By capturing data, reservation systems also help organizations to prepare financial projections.

Taking bookings also serves to presell a service, to inform customers and to educate them about what to expect. Customers who hold reservations should be able to count on avoiding a queue because they have been guaranteed service at a specific time. A well-organized reservations system allows the organization to deflect demand for service from a first-choice time to earlier or later times, from one class of service to another *(upgrades* and *downgrades),* and even from first-choice locations to alternative ones.

However, problems arise when customers fail to show or when service firms overbook. Marketing strategies for dealing with these operational problems include

- Requiring a deposit
- Canceling nonpaid bookings after a certain time
- Providing compensation to victims of overbooking

The challenge in designing reservation systems is to make them fast and user-friendly for both staff and customers. Many firms now allow customers to make their own reservations on a Web site—a trend that seems certain to grow. Whether customers talk with a reservations agent or make their own bookings, they want quick answers to queries about service availability at a preferred time. They also appreciate it if the system can provide further information about the type of service they are reserving. For instance, can a hotel assign a specific room on request? Or at least, can it assign a room with a view of the lake rather than one with a view of the parking lot and the nearby power station?

Segmentation Issues in Reservations Strategy

Yield analysis (introduced in chapter 9) forces managers to recognize the opportunity cost of accepting business from one customer or market segment when another might subsequently yield a higher rate. Consider the following problems facing sales managers for different types of capacity-constrained service organizations:

- Should a hotel accept an advance booking from a tour group of 200 room-nights at $80 each when these same room-nights might possibly be sold later at short notice to business travelers at the full posted rate of $140?
- Should a railroad with 30 empty freight cars at its disposal accept an immediate request for a shipment worth $900 per car or hold the cars idle for a few more days in the hope of getting a priority shipment that would be twice as valuable?
- How many seats on a particular flight should an airline sell in advance to tour groups and passengers traveling at special excursion rates?
- Should an industrial repair and maintenance shop reserve a certain proportion of productive capacity each day for emergency repair jobs that offer a high contribution margin and the potential to build long-term customer loyalty, or should it simply follow a strategy of making sure that there are sufficient jobs, mostly involving routine maintenance, to keep its employees fully occupied?
- Should a print-shop process all jobs on a first-come, first-served basis, with a guaranteed delivery time for each job, or should it charge a premium rate for rush work and tell customers with standard jobs to expect some variability in completion dates?

Decisions on such problems deserve to be handled with a little more sophistication than just resorting to the "bird in the hand is worth two in the bush" formula. So managers need a way of figuring out the chances of getting more profitable business if they wait. Good information, based on detailed record keeping of past usage and supported by current market intelligence and good marketing sense, is the key. The decision to accept or reject business should represent a realistic estimate of the probabilities of obtaining higher-rated business, together with a recognition of the importance of maintaining established (and desirable) customer relationships. Managers who make reservations decisions on the basis of guesswork and gut feelings are little better than gamblers who bet on rolls of the dice.

Focusing on Yield Rather Than Capacity Utilization

Service organizations often use percentage of capacity sold as a measure of operational efficiency. Transport services talk of the *load factor* achieved, hotels of their *occupancy rate*, and hospitals of their *census*. Similarly, professional firms can calculate what proportion of a partner's or an employee's time is classified as billable hours, and repair shops can look at utilization of both equipment and labor. By themselves, however, these percentage figures tell us little of the relative profitability of the business attracted, because high utilization rates may be obtained at the expense of heavy discounting—or even outright giveaways. As emphasized in chapter 9, pricing strategies should be designed in ways that avoid giving discounts to those who are prepared to pay more. In turn, this requires establishing what are known as *fences*, between different rate classes. These fences act as a barrier to prevent—or at least discourage—customers willing to pay a higher price from taking advantage of lower prices designed to attract more price-sensitive buyers (for a diagrammatic example, refer back to Figure 9.5 on p. 275).

More and more, service firms are looking at their *yield*—that is, the average revenue received per unit of capacity. The aim of an effective reservations strategy is to maximize this yield to improve profitability. Strategies designed to achieve this goal are collectively known as *yield management* and are widely used in such capacity-constrained industries as passenger airlines, hotels, and car rentals (for an in-depth treatment of this topic, see the reading by Sheryl Kimes and Richard Chase, "The Strategic Levers of Yield Management," on pp. 325 to 335). Formalized yield management programs, based on mathematical modeling, are of greatest value for service firms that find it expensive to modify their capacity but incur relatively low costs when they sell another unit of available capacity.[14] Other characteristics encouraging use of such programs include fluctuating demand levels, ability to segment markets by extent of price sensitivity, and sale of services well in advance of usage.

Planning Capacity Allocation

Based on analysis of past performance and current market data, reservations planning should indicate how much capacity to allocate on specific dates to different types of customers at certain prices. Based on this plan, selective-sell targets can be assigned to advertising and sales personnel, reflecting allocation of available capacity among different market segments on future dates. The last thing a firm wants its sales force to do is to encourage price-sensitive market segments to buy capacity on dates when sales projections predict that there will be strong demand from customers willing to pay full price. Unfortunately, in some industries, the lowest-rated business often books the furthest ahead: Tour groups, which pay much lower rates than individual travelers, may ask airlines and hotels to block space more than a year in advance.

Figure 14.4 illustrates capacity allocation in a hotel setting, where demand from different types of customers varies not only by day of the week but also by season. These allocation decisions by segment, captured in reservation databases that are accessible worldwide, tell reservations personnel when to stop accepting reservations at certain prices, even though many rooms may still remain unbooked.

Charts similar to those presented in Figure 14.4 can be constructed for most capacity-constrained businesses. In some instances, capacity is measured in terms of seats for a given performance, seat-miles, or room-nights; in others it may be in terms of machine time, labor time, billable professional hours, vehicle miles, or storage volume—whichever is the scarce resource. Unless it's easy to divert business from one facility to a similar alternative, allocation-planning decisions will have to be made at the level of geographic operating units. So each hotel, repair and maintenance center, or computer service bureau may need its own plan. On the other hand, transport vehicles represent a mobile capacity that can be allocated across any geographic area that the vehicles are able to serve.

In large organizations, such as major airlines or hotel chains, the market is very dynamic because the situation is changing all the time. For instance, the demand for both business and pleasure travel reflects current or anticipated economic conditions. Although many business travelers are not price sensitive, some companies insist that employees shop for the best travel bargains they can find within the constraints of their business travel needs. The Internet has added a new dynamic to this task. Pleasure travelers are often very price sensitive; a special promotion, involving discounted fares and room rates, may encourage people to undertake a trip that they would not otherwise have made. Alternatively, consumers may offer a low bid through a reverse-auction service such as Priceline.com.

Viewed from the perspective of the individual hotel or airline, competitive activity has the potential to play havoc with patronage forecasts. Imagine that you are a hotel owner and a new hotel opens across the street with a special discount offer. How will it affect you? Alternatively, consider the impact if an existing competitor burns down! The airline business is notoriously changeable. Fares can be slashed overnight. A competitor may introduce a new nonstop service between two cities or cut back its existing schedule on another route. Travel agents and savvy

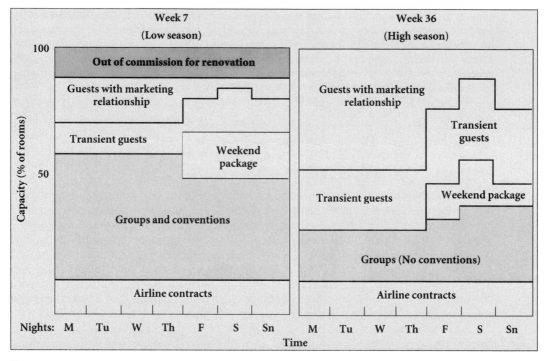

FIGURE 14.4 Setting Capacity Allocation Sales Targets over Time

customers watch these movements like hawks and may be quick to cancel one reservation (even if it involves paying a penalty) to take advantage of a better price or a more convenient schedule that can be obtained elsewhere.

There's evidence that yield management programs can improve revenues significantly—many airlines report increases of 5 percent or more after starting such programs. But a word of warning is in order at this point. Yield management shouldn't necessarily mean short-term yield maximization at all cost. Strategies can easily become rigid, full of rules and regulations designed to prevent less price-sensitive segments from trading down to take advantage of lower-priced offers, penalties for canceled reservations, and cynical overbooking without thought for the consequences to disappointed customers, who thought they had a firm reservation. To maintain goodwill and build relationships, managers have to take the long-term perspective. So yield management programs should build in strategies for retaining valued customer relationships, even to the extent of not charging the maximum feasible amount on a given transaction (perceptions of price gouging do not build trust). There should also be thoughtfully planned contingencies for victims of overbooking, with recovery programs designed to maintain goodwill even under conditions of inherent disappointment.

Marketing's Role in Yield Management

Clearly, the adoption of customer-mix sales targets that may vary from day to day—or even from hour to hour—puts a premium on accurate market analysis and forecasting. But the economic and strategic benefits are likely to outweigh the planning and research costs involved. Setting specific sales targets by segments, with recommended prices for each segment, reduces the risk that business will be booked in advance at a discount when there is a high probability of later obtaining business for the rate in question from a higher-paying segment. Sales targets also reduce the risk that potential business from lower-rated segments will be turned away in the hope of obtaining a higher-priced sale when the chances of obtaining the latter are actually very small. Similarly, operations personnel will be better able to plan service levels, staffing, and availability of special features if they have a good idea of the business mix that is likely to be obtained on specific dates.

One possible constraint on management's desire to maximize yield in the short term is the need to maintain good customer relations, especially with customers who provide extensive repeat business or use substantial capacity during periods of low demand. In the former instance, perceived price gouging during peak periods may alienate customers and result in bad word-of-mouth publicity. In the second instance, it may sometimes be necessary to take low-rated business in the peak period to ensure continued patronage during off-peak periods. Each case should be taken on its own merits, with careful assessment being made of who needs whom the most—the buyer or the seller.

Conclusion

The time-bound nature of services is a critical management issue today, especially with customers becoming more time sensitive and more conscious of their personal time constraints and availability. People-processing services are particularly likely to impose the burden of unwanted waiting on their customers because the latter cannot avoid coming to the "factory" for service.

Reservations can shape the timing of arrivals, but sometimes queuing is inevitable. Managers who can act to save customers time (or at least make time pass more pleasantly) may be able to create a competitive advantage for their organizations. Use of yield management techniques, meanwhile, can help firms in certain capacity-constrained industries to develop sophisticated reservations strategies designed to improve profitability by selling to different segments at different prices.

REVIEW QUESTIONS

1. Why should service marketers be concerned about the amount of time that customers spend in (a) preprocess waits and (b) in-process waits?

2. How might the principles of yield management be applied to rental car companies?

3. Review the 10 propositions on the psychology of waiting lines. Which are the most relevant in (a) a supermarket; (b) a city bus stop on a cold, dark evening; (c) check-in for a flight at the airport; (d) a doctor's office where patients are seated; (e) a ticket line for a football game that is expected to be a sellout?

4. What are the seven elements of a queuing system? Which are under the control of the customer and which of the service provider?

5. For an organization serving a large number of customers, what do you see as the advantages and disadvantages of the different types of queues?

6. Using the formulas on p. 422, please calculate answers to the following problems:
   a. At Jack's office cafeteria, customers select their meals from different food stations and then go to the checkout to pay. He knows that Betty, the speedy cashier, can check out a customer every 20 seconds on average. With an arrival rate of 90 customers an hour during the 11 A.M.–2 P.M. lunch period, what is the average length of the line that Jack can expect at the checkout? How many minutes will he have to wait ?

   b. Betty goes on maternity leave and is replaced by Judd, whom Jack times at 1 customer every 36 seconds. On average, how much longer will the line now be, and how long can Jack expect to wait?

   c. In response to complaints about delays at the checkout line, management assigns Kathi to operate a second cash register during Betty's absence. Kathi, like Judd, can process the average customer in 36 seconds. How long on average will each line now be, and how many minutes can Jack expect to wait (in either line)?

   d. Judd is off sick one day, so Kathi must work alone. But she managed to improve her performance and to process 1 customer every 30 seconds. Now how long on average is the line? And the wait?

APPLICATION EXERCISES

1. Give examples, based on your own experience, of reservations systems that worked really well or really badly.

2. Identify five situations in which you have had to wait in line during the past week. In each instance identify the nature of the queuing configuration and any activities or features that served to (a) advise you of the probable waiting time and (b) make the wait less burdensome. What improvements or changes would you recommend?

APPENDIX: POISSON DISTRIBUTION TABLE

Calculating the Expected Number of People Waiting in Line for Various Values of M and ρ

	Number of Service Channels (M)			
Flow Intensity (ρ)	1	2	3	4
0.10	0.0111			
0.15	0.0264	0.0008		
0.20	0.0500	0.0020		
0.25	0.0833	0.0039		
0.30	0.1285	0.0069		
0.35	0.1884	0.0110		
0.40	0.2666	0.0166		
0.45	0.3681	0.0239	0.0019	
0.50	0.5000	0.0333	0.0030	
0.55	0.6722	0.0149	0.0043	
0.60	0.9000	0.0593	0.0061	
0.65	1.2071	0.0767	0.0084	
0.70	1.6333	0.0976	0.0112	
0.75	2.2500	0.1227	0.0147	
0.80	3.2000	0.1523	0.0189	
0.85	4.8166	0.1873	0.0239	0.0031
0.90	8.1000	0.2285	0.0300	0.0041
0.95	18.0500	0.2767	0.0371	0.0053
1.0		0.3333	0.0454	0.0067

ENDNOTES

1. Malcolm Galdwell, "The Bottom Line for Lots of Time Spent in America," *Washington Post* (syndicated article, February, 1993).
2. Dave Wielenga, "Not So Fine Lines," *Los Angeles Times,* November 28, 1997, p. E1.
3. Richard Saltus, "Lines, Lines, Lines, Lines . . . The Experts Are Trying to Ease the Wait," *Boston Globe,* October 5, 1992, pp. 39, 42.
4. This section is based in part on James A. Fitzsimmons and Mona J. Fitzsimmons, *Service Management for Competitive Advantage* (New York: McGraw-Hill, 1994), 264–290; and David H. Maister, "Note on the Management of Queues," 9–680–053, Harvard Business School Case Services 1979, rev. 2/84.
5. Jay R. Chernow, "Measuring the Values of Travel Time Savings," *Journal of Consumer Research* 7 (March 1981): 360–371. [Note: this entire issue was devoted to the consumption of time.]
6. Michel Kostecki, "Waiting Lines as a Marketing Issue," *European Management Journal* 14, no. 3 (1996): 295–303.
7. David H. Maister, "The Psychology of Waiting Lines," in *The Service Encounter,* ed. J. A. Czepiel, M. R. Solomon, and C. F. Surprenant (Lexington, MA: Lexington Books/D.C. Heath, 1986), 113–123.
8. Tim Mason, "The Best Shopping Trip? How Tesco Keeps the Customer Satisfied," *Journal of the Market Research Society* 40, no. 1 (January 1998): 5–12.
9. M. M. Davis and J. Heineke, "Understanding the Roles of the Customer and the Operation for Better Queue Management," *International Journal of Operations and Production Management* 14, no. 5 (1994): 21–34.
10. Peter Jones and Emma Peppiatt, "Managing Perceptions of Waiting Times in Service Queues," *International Journal of Service Industry Management* 7, no. 5 (1996): 47–61.
11. Karen L. Katz, Blaire M. Larson, and Richard C. Larson, "Prescription for the Waiting-in-Line Blues: Entertain, Enlighten, and Engage," *Sloan Management Review* 31 (winter 1991): 44–53.
12. Bill Fromm and Len Schlesinger, *The Real Heroes of Business and Not a CEO Among Them* (New York: Currency Doubleday, 1994), 7.
13. Michael K. Hui and David K. Tse, "What to Tell Customers in Waits of Different Lengths: An Integrative Model of Service Evaluation," *Journal of Marketing* 80, no. 2 (April 1996): 81–90.
14. Sheryl E. Kimes, "Yield Management: A Tool for Capacity-Constrained Service Firms," *Journal of Operations Management* 8, no. 4 (October 1989): 348–363; Shcryl E. Kimcs and Richard B. Chase, "The Strategic Levers of Yield Management," *Journal of Service Research* 1 (November 1998): 156–166.

Content and Measurement of Productivity in the Service Sector: A Conceptual Analysis with an Illustrative Case from the Insurance Business

Ismo Vuorinen, Raija Järvinen, and Uolevi Lehtinen

The concept of productivity has historically emphasized manufacturing rather than service operations. Measuring service productivity requires examining both the quantity and quality dimensions of service output. The article considers the approaches employed by a major insurance company.

Introduction

During the last decade, the significance of service industries to the prosperity of modern economies has been widely recognised (Allen, 1988; Charles, 1993; Grönroos, 1990; Johnston, 1988). In the business disciplines, the issue of service management has attracted increasing interest amongst scholars (especially among the Nordic School of Services, see Gummesson *et al.*, 1997). According to these authors, the line of reasoning has for too long been dominated by the logic of manufacturing operations. Owing to the specific nature of services, a different strategic approach is called for in the case of service management (e.g. Wilson, 1988).

The concept of productivity is deeply rooted in the context of mass manufacturing, and this may be the main reason for the prolonged neglect of the productivity issue by writers on service management (Adam and Gravesen, 1996; Adam *et al.*, 1995; Holmlund and Ravald, 1992). However, the importance of productivity management in the service industries is widely accepted in the literature (e.g. Gummesson, 1993; van Biema and Greenwald, 1997; Wilson, 1988). While comparing productivity between service and manufacturing operations, one of the basic claims has been that the special characteristics of services demand a more holistic approach including a customer-orientation to pro-

ductivity (Blois, 1985, Grönroos, 1990). More specifically, several researchers (e.g. Giarini, 1991; Grönroos, 1990) have argued that quality and productivity cannot be dealt with separately in the case of services. However, many authors still apparently regard them as separate concepts (e.g. Brignall and Ballantine, 1996; cf. Heskett *et al.*, 1994). Consequently, there seems to be a growing need for a thorough analysis of the productivity concept in the context of services.

The current debate on service productivity is in its infancy, and it is for this reason that we must begin from the basics. We believe that the introductory step is to elaborate the conceptual underpinnings of service productivity. We have to decide first what we are trying to capture before making any attempt to measure (cf. Gummesson, 1992), and a meaningful definition of service productivity has to keep the concept analytically distinct from related concepts like efficiency and effectiveness. After the elucidation of the productivity concept itself, it is reasonable to take a second step by discussing the opportunity for operationalisation in the form of measurement. Initial operationalisation efforts are usually bound to the measurement of the phenomenon at a certain moment in time (i.e. static measures). The third step in the elaboration process might be to make the formulation a dynamic one; this would be achieved by contemplating the possibility of cause-effect relationships (e.g. Collier, 1995; Heskett *et al.*, 1994) and by pondering over the possibility of enhancing service productivity over time (e.g. van Biema and Greenwald, 1997). The last-mentioned aspects are of particular interest in the management of productivity within the service sector.

Reprinted with permission from *International Journal of Service Industry Management*. Vol. 9, No. 4, 1998, pp. 377–396.

The purpose of this article is to elucidate the concept and measurement of productivity in the service sector. We will focus on the first two steps in the above elaboration process, that is, the productivity concept itself and its operationalisation at a certain moment in time. Hence, we will not extend our analysis to the measurement of the dynamics of service productivity. Consequently, it is not our aim to cover the issue of productivity management in the following analysis, although some topics related to it will inevitably come up in our discussion.

The productivity concept deals with the economic performance of a firm. We may differentiate between the operational and financial performance of a service firm—the former being based on the real process (from inflows of factors of production to outflows of services) and the latter on the monetary process (inflows and outflows of money). In this respect, the service productivity concept adopted in this article focuses on the dimension of operational (real) performance. However, we will briefly deal with the relationship between operational and financial performance while discussing the measurement issue.

We will demonstrate our approach, and especially the dimensions of productivity, through a case study of the second largest insurance company in Finland, The Pohjola Insurance Group, offering the entire spectrum of insurance services. Because our empirical data cover only a single case, it will be used for illustrative purposes. Our reasons for selecting the case from the insurance sector are as follows. First, the insurance industry has often been considered quite complicated, because it is the one that markets the most intangible of intangibles of all service industries (see Majaro, 1982; 1985), i.e. a piece of paper called an insurance policy to protect a policy holder. This makes a sharp contrast to the conventional manufacturing business and its approach to productivity. Second, mergers around the world within the insurance sector and between insurance and banking companies are questions of the day to achieve economies of scale. As a consequence, the whole industry is now changing its operations towards more efficient action, which we find extremely interesting from the viewpoint of productivity. Third, in Finland, this sector has been able to act in the protected domestic markets and to avoid stiff competition until Finland's EU membership in 1995. The years of recession at the beginning of the 1990s were a pilot lesson about the non-existence of everlasting growth in the entire sector. These lines of develop-

ment make the insurance sector a current topic from the viewpoint of service management in Finland. And, finally, there emerges the issue of access: one of the co-authors has been employed by the insurance company in question. This allowed us to use both various kinds of data collection methods (including direct observation) and an insider view in the interpretation of the material gathered.

The Content of Service Productivity

Regarding the economic evaluation of the performance level achieved in the production process, productivity, efficiency and effectiveness are three of the most frequently mentioned criteria. The concept of productivity has been rooted in the production function approach describing the relationship between factor inputs and product outputs (Vehmanen, 1994). Productivity has come to be interpreted as the ratio between output and input. In this way, productivity is conceptually defined as distinct from the value measurement of the monetary process.

Efficiency and effectiveness are usually treated as related but separate concepts. Efficiency describes the degree to which an activity generates a given quantity of outputs with a minimum consumption of inputs, or generates the largest possible outputs from a given quantity of inputs (e.g. Anthony, 1965). Effectiveness, in turn, indicates the ability to attain a goal or a purpose. Effectiveness relates the output to the goal(s) set for the operation, whereas efficiency relates the output to the resources used (input). Efficiency is about doing things right and effectiveness is about doing the right things (e.g. Adam et al., 1995).

There exists a clear distinction between effectiveness and productivity: effectiveness is tied to the ability of the organization to attain its specified objectives, whereas productivity concerns the relationship between outputs and inputs. Hence, increasing productivity is not a sufficient condition for enhancing an organization's effectiveness. In fact, productivity may be increased at the cost of effectiveness in meeting the goals set for the organization (Blois, 1985).

Efficiency is a common but loosely defined concept in the business disciplines. It may be seen as a quantitative (technical efficiency) or a value (economic efficiency) concept (e.g. Vehmanen, 1994). Technical efficiency may be considered synonymous with productivity as a ratio between output and input, although efficiency has sometimes been defined as the inverse to productivity (i.e. the amount of resources used to produce one unit of output, see e.g. Etzioni, 1964). When efficiency is defined in value terms, one tries to make compatible the effects of various input and output factors in the production process (cf. Amey, 1969). This interpretation has led to formulations in which efficiency is seen as costs per product.

Technical efficiency and productivity may be defined as distinct concepts by taking the standard of comparison as a frame of reference (Uusi-Rauva, 1987): in the case of a productivity ratio, the aim is to compare the output-input ratios across units and time, whereas in the case of an efficiency ratio, the comparison is made against a predetermined standard or ideal. If a meaningful interpretation can be given to ideal performance, it is reasonable to perceive an efficiency ratio as an indicator of the extent to which actual performance has achieved the ideal level (overall efficiency) or the best observed performance (observable efficiency, cf. Frei and Harker, 1995).

According to the basic principle of economic rationality, the purpose is to achieve a given result with the minimal resources, or to get the maximum result with a given set of resources. However, it is very difficult to talk about the maximum level of performance in the production of services. Hence, we will elaborate the economic evaluation of service operations on the basis of the concept of productivity.

Because of its origin in manufacturing, the conventional definition of productivity may be regarded as narrow and value-laden (cf. Adam *et al.*, 1995). It is our conviction that productivity in the context of services has to be interpreted more broadly than in the traditional sense. More specifically, we include quality in the analysis of the productivity of service operations (cf. Grönroos, 1990; Shaw and Capoor, 1979). At the outset, we define service productivity as the ability of a service organization to use its inputs for providing services with quality matching the expectations of customers (cf. Järvinen *et al.*, 1996).

The quantity and quality dimensions of service offering cannot be treated in isolation. Due to their interrelationship, it may be impossible to separate the impact of a service process on conventional productivity from its impact on service quality. Hence, both the quantity and quality aspects must be considered together to provide a joint impact on the total productivity of the service firm. We simply call it service productivity and it may be presented as a general formula:

$$\text{Service productivity} = \frac{\text{Quantity of output and Quality of output}}{\text{Quantity of input and Quality of input}}$$

The holistic view underlining the interaction between factors has its advantages and disadvantages. In the light of the views expressed in the service literature, this formula seems to cover the key success factors of a service firm (e.g. Grönroos, 1990; Gummesson, 1993; McLaughlin and Coffey, 1990). Without taking an explicit stand on the mathematical form (additive, multiplicative, exponential, etc.) of the above formula, we will elucidate our concept by a more detailed analysis of the factors inside the formula.

The Quantity Aspect

Regarding the quantity aspect of service productivity, the input factors of services are the same means of production as in manufacturing: raw materials, labour and capital. Owing to the labour-intensiveness of service production, the productivity of many service sectors has been labelled as very low compared to manufacturing operations (Charles, 1993; Wilson, 1988). As a consequence, many service providers have invested heavily in technology as a substitute for labour; e.g. automated teller machines to replace bank tellers, self-service insurance policy machines to replace clerks (Levitt, 1972). The service industries have also been identified as the biggest buyers of the new information technology (Charles, 1993). This raises a crucial issue in the light of the service productivity concept: has the enhancement in labour productivity, as a result of heavy investments in technology, been achieved at the cost of capital productivity? We underline in our formula the need to gauge the formation of productivity from a holistic point of view. Decisions made to enhance service productivity should not be based on partial productivity measures.

The output, volume or amount of service offered, may first seem to be a straightforward issue. When the service offered consists of a single component or of a number of standardised components which allow cloning and mixing across a wide range of applications, the volume of service may be easily determined (cf. Quinn and Paquette, 1990). In contrast, the output may consist of highly customised services (as in the case of a unique service package), and the definition of the service output becomes a more laborious task. This task is often complicated by the intangible nature of services.

The relationship between inputs and outputs in terms of service volume is often seen to be problematic due to the lack of storability of services (Blois, 1985). A strategic decision for the service provider is the acquisition of resources in order to generate enough capacity to match the demand for the service. As such, this strategic choice is volume-oriented. However, from the customer's view, the volume of the service output is hardly a significant issue because the customer usually buys only one unit of output (e.g. a haircut) or one package of services (e.g. a holiday tour). The customer is therefore inclined to give priority to service quality instead of quantity. Yet, the actual volume of operations is determined by the variation of demand over time (McLaughlin, 1996). As a consequence, the productivity ratio of service operations may vary greatly from one time period to another, provided it is measured as a quantity ratio. Hence, due to the variation in the amount of the total demand across time, the service provider has to solve two basic problems related to the quantity aspect: capacity size and capacity scheduling (McLaughlin et al., 1991).

The Quality Aspect

The quality aspect is a dimension that is difficult to define objectively. In the case of manufacturing products, the quality dimension has usually been operationalised as conformance to specifications and as actual product performance (McLaughlin et al., 1991). However, this notion of quality has been regarded as inadequate in the case of services. According to Gummesson (1992), there is a humanistic quality approach, at the one extreme stressing customers, personnel, leadership and culture, whereas at the other end lies a technical approach concerning operations management, statistics and methods of measurement. Gummesson divides quality into services, tangibles and software, but he stresses the importance of a total service offering. Lehtinen and Lehtinen (1991) talk about physical quality, interactive quality and corporate quality and, on the other hand, about process and output quality. As our formula suggests, we divide quality into input and output dimensions, which are parallel to Lehtinen and Lehtinen's latter division of dimensions. Drawing on the above notions, the output consists of a total service offering in terms of quality, and the input includes both tangible and intangible elements.

The output in the form of quality is what the customer in fact pays for, which is to a large extent intangible and may be difficult to quantify (Adam et al., 1995). Service quality is generally defined as customer perceived quality which stresses the individuals' assessment of the value of the total service offering (e.g. Gummesson, 1994). Grönroos (1982; 1983) describes perceived service quality as the difference between expected service quality and experienced service quality. This has a link to the gap model (Parasuraman et al., 1985; 1994) and other service quality models (e.g. Bitner, 1990; Bolton and Drew, 1991; Oliver, 1993). On the other hand, Berry et al., (1985) divides service quality into two types: regular services, and handling of exceptions/problems to ensure that appropriate procedures are taken to deal with inevitable failures (see also Johnston, 1995). We accept customer perceived quality as the basis of our notion of service quality.

When purchasing services, customers' attention is often limited to a small number of tangible inputs (Zeithaml, 1984). Physical environment—buildings, offices and interior design—affects customer beliefs, attitudes and satisfaction (Bitner, 1986; Zeithaml and Bitner, 1996), and provides an opportunity to tell the "right" story about a given service (Berry, 1984). Matters such as how contact personnel dresses, articulates, writes designs and presents proposals are likewise not without meaning (Levitt, 1981, 1983). Tangibilising the intangible is important, because customers do not usually know what they are getting until they do not get it (Levitt, 1981; 1983).

As intangible input, the service personnel represents the service, the organization and the marketers in the customers' eyes (Zeithaml and Bitner, 1996). The quality management of personnel includes such things as motivating, managing information, training, career planning, and recruiting and retaining of right people (Normann, 1991; Zeithaml and Bitner, 1996). It is true that service business is personnel-intensive, meaning that quality supplied to the customer is essentially a result of the way personnel perform (cf. Normann, 1991). Schneider (1980) shows that both employees and customers will experience more positive outcomes when the organization operates with a customer service orientation and management supports it (see also Blois, 1989). This may be linked to the external service value within the service-profit chain by Heskett et al., (1994), which describes employee satisfaction as the underlying factor in the formation of customer perceived quality.

In addition, there are attempts to include customers in the service providing organization, at least on a temporary basis (Gummesson, 1994; see also Handy, 1990; Lovelock and Young, 1979; Quinn and Paquette, 1990), which provides an opportunity to utilise customers as free inputs to increase productivity from the viewpoint of service provider (Ojasalo, 1997). Furthermore, functional organizational plans have tended not to work as well in service organizations, partly because of difficulties in predefining end product variables and standards for services (Shaw and Capoor, 1979). Therefore, it can be concluded that the way customers perceive service and how service production and delivery are organized cannot be considered in isolation from each other.

The other important intangible element is service culture, and, by participating in the production process, customers influence and even create perceived service culture (Lehtinen, 1986). High levels of intangibility call for image building and maintenance to attain reliance based on reputation and subjective impressions of the service (Cowell, 1988). In the long run, image depends mainly on what the company actually provides, but in the short run, image can be used as a tool for the creation of new reality (Normann, 1991).

Today, many service operations are heavily dependent on information technology (IT). Customers, while interacting either with a contact person or a machine, have an interface to computers: a bank teller processes the transactions through a computer while a customer watches, or customers themselves use automated teller machines (cf. Gummesson, 1992). Normann (1991) sees five reasons for utilising IT:

(1) reducing costs by substituting service officers for IT (see also Levitt, 1983);
(2) standardising services;
(3) increasing availability, e.g. through automated 24-hour branch offices or machines;
(4) linking customers tightly into the service system; and
(5) affecting customer and personnel relationships and behaviour (see also Zeithaml and Bitner, 1996).

Figure 1 summarises our view of the content of service productivity concept.

The Measurement of Service Productivity

From the viewpoint of measurement theory, the representativeness of a chosen measure becomes a crucial issue. In the social sciences, this is usually evaluated through two basic criteria: validity and reliability. According to Kerlinger (1973), validity and reliability are the operationalised counterparts of the criteria developed in mathematical measure-

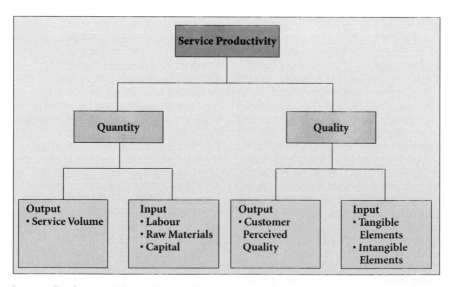

FIGURE 1. The Content of Service Productivity

ment theory (see also Mock, 1976). Validity is usually seen to encompass both the reliability criterion and freedom from systematic bias.

Our concept of productivity covers the basic criteria of evaluation within service operations: both quantity and quality are deemed significant among the writers on service management. As such, it seems to offer a valid representation of the economic dimension of service operations. From the viewpoint of reliability, the problems of measurement may be stated as follows:

- How can the quantity of inputs and outputs be measured?
- How can the quality of inputs and outputs be measured?
- How can the interrelationship of different output and input factors be operationalized?

These problems come close to the dimension of complexity of inputs and outputs in service productivity measures, which is part of the classification scheme outlined by McLaughlin and Coffey (1990).

Considering the volume of inputs and outputs, rather direct measurement seems to be possible in many services. The quantity of inputs, for example, may be operationalised as the number of employees or labour hours, or as the number of hours the service is available to customers. Likewise, the output measure may comprise the number of customers or customer contacts, or the number of transactions or actual service hours. However, due to the heterogeneity of inputs and outputs, a transfer to value measurement with the help of unit prices has been offered as a common solution to generate an economically meaningful ratio (cf. Amey, 1969). Consequently, we may have to content ourselves with a surrogate measure based on monetary measurement (e.g. turnover per the total monetary value of inputs) to combine the volumes of inputs and outputs in a meaningful way (cf. Ojasalo, 1997).

The subjective nature of the quality of inputs and outputs presents a tough challenge to reliable measurement, and this is exacerbated by the interpretation of quality from the customers' point of view. The gap-model operationalisation is based on the idea of comparing customer experience with customer expectations (e.g. Parasuraman et al., 1988; the SERVQUAL). In general, the systematic use of customer feedback is a vehicle to operationalise the measurement of service quality. Even though customer satisfaction may be difficult to measure directly, more indirect ways are available as surrogate measures. Empirical studies usually support the hypothesis that satisfied customers do not usually give any direct feedback to the service producer, whereas dissatisfied customers are tempted to give voice (see e.g. Järvinen et al., 1996). Consequently, it may be possible to quantify customer dissatisfaction (e.g. as a ratio between the number of customer complaints vs. the total number of customer handlings). Other ways to circumvent the problem of service quality measurement include direct observation of the service process and comprehensive process documentation (McLaughlin and Coffey, 1990; McLaughlin et al., 1991).

One of our claims regarding service productivity has been that the impact of the components is not an additive function which would allow the measurement of impacts separately at first and then summing these sub-measures up in order to get an all-encompassing measure. As a consequence, the joint effects of various input and output factors may be approached only by using indirect methods of measurement (e.g. associative measurement based on the presumed relationships between factors). The cumulative effect of the various components manifests itself at the level of overall performance, which is usually judged against the goals set for the business. This leads to the measurement of service productivity at the aggregate level (e.g. firm, unit) only, but the question of measurement at the disaggregate level (e.g. service, process) remains unsettled (cf. McLaughlin and Coffey, 1990).

This brings us to the criterion of relevance of the chosen approach to productivity. A service firm strives for productivity to achieve the goals set for the business, and the fundamental goal is to make a profit in the markets. The relationship between the productivity concept outlined above and the financial success of the service firm may be called into question. This relationship has been one of the cornerstones of an ongoing Swedish research effort (the QP&P Program) focusing on the interaction between service quality, productivity and profitability (Gummesson, 1994). The tentative conclusions of the QP&P Program underline, amongst other things, the interaction between service provider and customer, and between customers themselves, as two main sources of service quality and productivity, leading consequently to profitability.

Storbacka (1994) emphasizes the importance of linking the consideration of productivity with profitability. It is possible to create a link from our concept of productivity to profitability. The first step is a transfer to value measurements in input factors with the help of unit prices (cf. Gummesson, 1993). The second step is to determine the value of output less the value of input, to get a measure of a surplus/deficit which may further be related to the money capital invested in the firm to attain a measure of profit/loss. Even though many problems regarding measurement must be solved, it is, in principle, possible to link our concept of service productivity to overall profitability.

According to Bååthe and Mattsson (1993), knowledge of the measurement of quality and productivity is relatively little developed in service companies. However, there have been attempts to develop appropriate methods of measurement in the service literature (see e.g. a review by McLaughlin and Coffey, 1990).

To summarise this section, we consider that the following requirements must be met to obtain a comprehensive measure of service productivity:

(1) both the quantity and quality aspects of service productivity must be operationalised;
(2) the operationalisation must be implemented through a commensurable unit of measurement; and
(3) the possibility of cumulative effects has to be accounted for in the measurement effort.

In practice, the development of a single measure of service productivity fulfilling the requirements outlined above is likely to prove a tough challenge. On the other hand, this does not undermine our approach to conceptualise service productivity, because there seem to be opportunities to resort to proxy measures in the operationalisation efforts.

An Illustration: Service Productivity in an Insurance Firm

Following the conceptual logic outlined in Figure 1, our illustration introduces the basic elements of service productivity, namely the concept divided into quantity and quality dimensions, and further into output and input elements. Moreover, we will describe the current measurement practice within the target firm. Consequently, we want to emphasise that the elements of output and input in our case firm provide the level of analysis in this section, i.e. the aim is to show that the dimensions and elements discussed earlier in this article can be identified in our target firm. However, this does not mean that our target firm would currently evaluate its operations according to our notion of service productivity. We conclude with a brief summary of the empirical analysis as compared to the conceptual foundations adopted in this article.

The Target Firm

Our case company is the Pohjola Insurance Group, an insurance company grouping covering the entire spectrum of insurance services: non-life, travel, life and pension insurance. The parent companies of The Pohjola Group were established in 1890 and 1891. The Group's co-operation is based on mutual shareholdings and agreements, and it has a joint organization. The Pohjola Group earned 2.7 billion USD in insurance premium in 1996. With the number of employees reaching 3,341 on average, the group is the second largest in its branch in Finland (Pohjola, 1996). Like other insurance companies, Pohjola recently invested in information technology, although it has been dependent on computerised insurance registers over two decades. To foster its position in the market, Pohjola started large development projects in 1994, the objectives of which are not only better utilisation of technology, service value chains and multi-skilled personnel, but also productivity. The quality policy was determined simultaneously, and, as a consequence, the importance of quality and productivity has now been acknowledged. However, at this stage, the development processes ongoing in the target firm and their possible implications in the future are not included in our illustration.

Methodology

In the case of The Pohjola Group, we studied three different entities responsible for three different insurance types:

(1) the motor and comprehensive insurance sale and claims organizations responsible for car dealers as intermediaries;
(2) the travel insurance sale and claims organizations responsible for travel agencies as intermediaries; and
(3) the statutory workers' compensation insurance organization.

All the entities studied have recently electronicised their channels either towards intermediaries or customers, and the company-based development projects mentioned earlier concern each of them. The study was carried out by interviewing the key actors (11 persons), among them regional managers, claims managers, a manager of training and quality, and insurance contact persons responsible for each insurance type. Patton (1990) confirms that a qualitative inquiry typically focuses on relatively small samples, even single cases, selected deliberately. The underlying logic is in selecting information-rich cases and respondents for study in depth.

Each actor was interviewed separately, and at first the interviews were standardised by the equal written open-ended forms, but later we used more specialised lists of questions, adapted to gather more detailed information on specific areas. The standardised interview is used when it is important to minimise variation in the questions posed to interviewees. This reduces the risk of bias that comes from having different interviews for different people including the problem of obtaining more comprehensive data from certain persons while getting less systematic information from others (see Patton, 1990). For this reason, we started by standardised interviews, but ended up with specialised non-standardised forms in order to get in-depth data. The interviews were held in June–July 1994, April 1995 and February 1996, and some follow-up questions were asked in May–August 1996. The secondary data consists of the material provided by Pohjola, including statistics and reports, in-house newsletters, information letters and customer journals.

Quantitiy Dimension of Service Productivity
At Pohjola, the traditional approach to analysing productivity is quantitative, and only recently have the qualitative elements received explicit attention. The output of the quantity dimension is based on the volume of insurance services; the amount of insurance services sold, or the amount of different insurance types (i.e. assortment) in the whole portfolio. Increasing the insurance volume usually means selling a larger variety of insurance services to the existing customers or attracting new customer segments. In addition, the market share (total and per insurance type) is monitored at Pohjola, as in other insurance companies.

Within Pohjola, labour is the key input to productivity as salaries, commissions and social expenses account for 70 per cent of operating costs. The personnel policy prefers job rotations, amendments in job descriptions and job retraining instead of redundancies, which so far have been exceptional cases. Work process re-engineering, and analysing overtime and bottlenecks are valuable means of controlling the amount of labour input at Pohjola. Extra working hours and waste of time are eliminated by minimising errors, which is emphasised by the campaign "first pass quality policy."

The capital invested has mainly been in IT, electronic channels and physical environment. Technology offers an opportunity for automated service environment, although it is important to utilise the technology on the company's own terms and to its own benefit. Service processes are dependent on technological development, as all insurance registers are computer-based, that is, every clerk is skilled in data processing through data terminals or personal computers. IT assists in decreasing the amount of the paper handling a clerical work, and thus saves time, human resources, and helps to avoid errors by eliminating manual data entries at each handling stage.

Pohjola has built electronic channels step-by-step towards their intermediaries and customers. Travel agencies and car dealers were the first to connect their links in 1993, and interorganizational data transfer (IDT) towards customers concerning statutory workers' compensation insurance was introduced in 1995, even though the technology at the customers' end proved to be a bottleneck in many cases (see also Järvinen *et al.,* 1996). In addition, Pohjola has self-service insurance policy machines and its insurance services are available at the automated teller machines in the largest bank group in Finland, but this "service" has so far not attracted customers.

The physical environment covers both headquarters and the extensive branch office network (around 95 outlets) ensuring availability of insurance services. Insurance applications are still handled in back-offices which are often located elsewhere, and consequently, customers do not take part into the production process. So far, Pohjola has only a few years' experience of telework that offers an opportunity to adjust the amount of back-office facilities, as it enables clerks to be located practically anywhere the technology is available. Because of the high intangibility of insurance services, raw material is an unimportant element is in this case.

Quality Dimension of Service Productivity
Lack of homogeneity and consequent difficulties in controlling quality are often used to distinguish services (Foxall, 1985). However, the insurance services in question are standardised, and the only situation lacking homogeneity is the service encounter, i.e. interaction between a customer and a clerk. At Pohjola, quality is interpreted as customer satisfaction. The customer satisfaction studies have revealed that the most important factor at Pohjola is claims handling, and the major strength was considered to be customer service in selling situations, but a serious weakness seems to be the lack of information concerning insurance terms and conditions.

As more and more customer contacts are conducted at arm's length, access time becomes a tool for better service quality. Pohjola's own Internet connections offer full-time access and telephone response services 12 hours a day. Customer co-production is a path Pohjola has chosen to proceed. More and more insurance data entries are made at the customers' end, and thus they carry out the job for Pohjola. Customers feel satisfied because this does not increase their duties either, but they are able to enjoy correct and up-dated insurance registers. Moreover, additional information requests are avoided when customers themselves take the responsibility for providing accurate and adequate data.

Providing excellent service is a demanding job and this has been recognised at Pohjola, which tries to attain and retain highly talented personnel capable of using the most advanced technology in solving customer' problems. The change from routine work to more creative and demanding tasks, as in expert activities or in customer service, presents a formidable challenge to the skills of the personnel. Therefore, individual development programmes are offered for the personnel in these instances, although systematic career planning is not included in the personnel policy. In addition to the organization redesign, teamwork has been introduced as a solution, offering a way to decrease the number of organization levels, although the organization structure has remained functional. The personnel's performance criteria are operationalised by using special themes, e.g. optimal time for telephone, letter and e-mail responses. Special attention has been given to the response to customer complaints.

The insurance business is nowadays a combination of information and technology, both of which are critical cornerstones for successful operation. IT requires its own quality indicators, e.g. security of insurance registers (backups) and ensuring the functioning of computer systems in all situations, as well as management of high quality information. This is evaluated by the amount of unavoidable computer breakdowns and system errors.

Physical environment in a quality sense is mainly a concern of the locations and interiors where customers visit, and this has always been a matter of great importance within Pohjola. The branch office network covers the whole of Finland and the interiors are carefully designed. As Pohjola has already operated 105 years, the organization culture can be characterised as traditional. One important aim of the development projects is to modernise this self-image in which in-house news-letters and information sharing provide the most important means. Moreover, the stakeholder information bears the same message, but aims at improved corporate image.

Measurement of Service Productivity

Pohjola uses conventional ways to measure the quantity dimension of service productivity, such as the amount of insurance handled per clerk in a certain time period (usually one month) and the turn-around time of one application through various work stages. The workload of the teleworkers is compared with that of the main office clerks and the workers before their shift to telework. In addition, the amount of various insurance types in the total insurance portfolio is followed, and the investments are evaluated by the aid of pay-back periods. The quantity elements can be made commensurable by the aid of monetary values, e.g. by using premium as a quantity of insurance services and the salaries of labour accordingly, not forgetting that the total amount of premiums may be affected either through pricing or sales policy.

Pohjola's quality policy is operationalised in four measurable dimensions:

(1) customer satisfaction;
(2) employee satisfaction, covering aspects from routine tasks to working environment;
(3) high quality work performance; and
(4) profitability, of which the first refers to service quality output and the next two to intangible input elements.

The first three items are expected to have a positive impact on profitability in due course, and this is the reason for including profitability in the quality policy. The quality dimension of service productivity is measured by customer satisfaction studies, customer complaints, and employee satisfaction studies. The evaluation criteria of The Finnish Quality Award System for self-evaluation purposes are utilised in this context.

Summary of the Analysis of the Target Firm

Most of the elements of quantity and quality dimensions of service productivity are interrelated. It is difficult to analyse each element one by one in logical order. Although we have tried to do this, we believe that it is most important to understand the elements constituting a whole. However, both the quantity and quality dimensions of the target firm are summarised in Table I and Table II.

TABLE I *The Quantity Dimension of the Service Productivity in the Insurance Firm*

Quantity dimension of service productivity		
Service quantity output	**Labour input**	**Capital input**
Service volume	Amount of labour	Information technology
Assortment	Recruitment	Electronic channels
Market share	Job rotations	Self-service policy machines
Customer segments	Job descriptions	Headquarter and office network
	Service process re-engineering	Telework facilities
	Error avoidance	
	Overtime	

Tables I and II show that the various elements of quantity and quality can be distinguished in our target firm. However, Pohjola itself does not include all the elements we present in Tables I and II in its productivity concept. The elements of the quantity dimension seem to be covered by the current measurement practice within Pohjola. Regarding the quality dimension, the intangible elements have not been systematically developed at Pohjola, because it has not tangibilised its offerings in the way suggested by the service marketing literature. Hence, a critique against the lack of integrity of various elements of the quality dimension seems justified, although the quality policy can be considered as an attempt in that direction.

The management of Pohjola has already acknowledged that the current way of measuring is not sufficient, and new tools are to be developed.

The concept introduced in this paper would widen the perspective and provide a comprehensive formula to evaluate total service productivity. Moreover, new measurements, such as our suggestions concerning quality aspects would bring the customer perceptions closer to the traditional quantity aspects. Even in the case of the quantitative dimension of service productivity, there are several alternatives to develop new measurement techniques, and to start with, attention has to be paid to the commensurability between the various elements of quantity output, labour input and capital input.

Summary and Conclusions

This article has outlined an approach to the evaluation of productivity in service operations. By taking the quantity and quality aspects of service offerings

TABLE 2 *The Quality Dimension of Service Productivity in the Insurance Firm*

Quality dimension of service productivity		
Service quality output	**Intangible input**	**Tangible input**
Customer satisfaction	Employee satisfaction	Branch office locations
Customer encounter and service	Expertise and skills	Branch office interiors
Standardised services	Performance criteria	
Access time	Recruitment and retaining personnel	
Customer co-production	Personnel development programmes	
Correct insurance registers	Teamwork	
Corporate image	Organisation structure	
	Corporate culture	
	IT backups, breakdowns and system errors	

as our point of departure, we analysed the conceptual underpinnings of the productivity concept in services. In addition, we summarised our approach in a general formula and discussed operationalisation in terms of measurement. It must be stressed again that our intention was not to take a definitive stand on the issue of how to model the relationships between the components included in our formula. In fact, we want to provide an opportunity to develop various models to operationalise the relationships between quantity and quality dimensions, and further, between output and input factors. As a result, these operationalisation efforts may lead to additive, multiplicative, exponential or other functions. After the conceptual analysis, an attempt was made to illustrate our way of thinking in an empirical setting in order to show the relevance of our concept to the management of services.

Generally, this type of service productivity concept offers a step forward from the conventional line of reasoning centred around the concept of productivity. The conventional way has reflected its manufacturing origins by focusing on the use of industrial methods (industrialization) even in the case of services (Levitt, 1983). This has resulted in quantitative measurement, volume orientation, heavy investments, specialisation and automation as means to increase productivity even in service operations. In standardised services like travel insurance, this may be a valid approach to the enhancement of productivity. However, by ignoring the impacts on perceived quality, the traditional approach may develop into a vicious circle (Grönroos, 1990) leading to inferior financial performance in the long run. This may be true especially in the case of customised services like personal life insurance. Different types of services call for different approaches in the formulation of service productivity. As a consequence, the quantity and quality dimensions may receive different weightings in our formula depending on the nature of the service in the eyes of the customer.

Owing to the shortcomings of the conventional way of thinking, several writers have approached the problem of service productivity or efficiency (e.g. Blois, 1985; Grönroos, 1990; Gummesson, 1993; McLaughlin and Coffey, 1990). Based on the case studies carried out in the QP&P Program and on the papers presented at the First International Research Workshop on Service Productivity held in Brusssels 1994, Adam *et al.* (1995) put forward six general requirements to guide the formulation of a service productivity concept in the future:

(1) Service output has to be seen as the value for the customer and from the perspective of the customer.
(2) Service output must be defined by its quality level.
(3) The customer must become a part of the productivity concept.
(4) Measures of productivity must be more customer-related.
(5) Dynamic indicators of productivity must be used instead of static output/input measures.
(6) Situation specific measures have to be available to allow for the complexity and diversity of service operations.

The first four criteria are among the basic underpinnings of our conceptual analysis of the content and measurement of service productivity. More specifically, the value for the customer is the vital point in the quality dimension of our concept, and with this dimension the traditional productivity concept is broadened to include the customer. Through the quality-of-output component in our formula, the second criterion of including the quality level is met. Our illustration also shows that customer and quality orientation are evolving trends within the target firm.

Regarding the fact that little knowledge has accumulated so far in the field of service productivity, a satisfactory solution fulfilling the fifth criterion presented above seems at present to be beyond our reach. If a meaningful operationalisation of the formula outlined in this article is available, cross-sectional data measured at discrete points of time may reveal changes in the quantity and/or quality components. A more advanced alternative would be to include lag and lead elements, i.e. time-dependent effects, explicitly in our formula. However, our formula does not even try to uncover the process of changing service productivity as cause-effect relationships between different factors (cf. Collier, 1995; Heskett *et al.*, 1994).

In principle, our approach to service productivity is not dependent on the aggregation level under consideration in the measurement effort. The need for situation specific productivity measures within service firms is closely related to the issue of the appropriate aggregation level. On the basis of our empirical illustration, the suggested approach to service productivity is a fruitful one at the level of a firm and from the perspective of service management. Firm-specific operationalisation efforts are a logical first step in the measurement of service productivity, and in many service industries like insurance the large number of delivery units allows for measurement in comparative terms (cf. McLaughlin and Coffey, 1990).

When analysing the content of productivity in services, the authors soon encountered a dilemma: the deeper we wanted to go in our line of reasoning, the less we seemed to know to form an informed opinion on the issue. The same argument holds in the case of developing measurement methods based on the service productivity concept. In conclusion, these arguments call for genuine cooperative research efforts between the scholars representing different business disciplines.

REFERENCES

Adam, K, and Gravesen, I. (1996), "Is service productivity a viable concept?" paper presented in *The Second International Research Workshop on Service Productivity,* April 18–19, Madrid.

Adam, K., Johanson, M. and Gravesen, I. (1995), "Service productivity: a vision or a search for a new outlook," paper presented at *The Ninth World Productivity Congress,* Istanbul, June 4–7.

Allen, M. (1988), "Strategic management of consumer services," *Long Range Planning,* Vol., 6, pp. 20–26.

Amey, L. (1969), *The Efficiency of Business Enterprises,* New York, NY.

Anthony, R. (1965), *Planning and Control Systems: A Framework for Analysis,* Boston, MA.

Blååthe, J. and Mattsson, J. (1993), *Produktivitets- och Kvalitetsmätning i Några Svenska Tjänsteföretag,* (Productivity and quality measurement in some Swedish service firms), CTF, Research Report 93:3, Karlstad.

Berry, L. (1984), "Services marketing is different," in Lovelock, C. (Ed.), *Service Marketing,* Englewood Cliffs, pp. 29–37.

Berry, L.L., Zeithaml, V.A. and Parasuraman, A. (1985), "Quality counts in services, too," *Business Horizons,* May–June pp. 44–52.

Bitner, M.J. (1986), "Consumer responses to the physical environments in service settings," in Venkatesan M., Schmalensee, D.M. and Marshall, G. (Eds), *Creativity in Services Marketing: What's New, What Works, What's Developing,* AMA ,Chicago, pp. 89–92.

Bitner, M.J. (1990), "Evaluating service encounters: the effect of physical surroundings and employee responses," *Journal of Marketing,* Vol. 54, April, pp. 69–82.

Blois, K.J. (1985), "Productivity and effectiveness in service firms," in Foxall, G. (Ed.), *Marketing in the Service Industries,"* pp. 45–60.

Blois, K.J. (1989), "The structure of service firms and their marketing policies," in Bateson, J.E.G. (Ed.), *Managing Services Marketing,* Chicago, pp. 522–31.

Bolton, R.N. and Drew, J.H. (1991), "A multistage model of customers' assessments of service quality and value," *Journal of Consumer Research,* Vol. 17, March, pp. 375–84.

Brignall, S. and Ballantine, J. (1996), "Performance measurement in service businesses revisited," *International Journal of Service Industry Management,* Vol. 7 No. 1, pp. 6–31.

Charles, S. (1993), "Conceptualizing services sector productivity," *Social and Economic Studies,* Vol. 42 No. 4, pp. 95–113.

Collier, D.A. (1995), "Modelling the relationships between process quality errors and overall service process performance," *International Journal of Service Industry Management,* Vol. 6 No. 1, pp. 4–19.

Cowell, D. (1988), *The Marketing of Services,* London.

Etzioni, A. (1964), *Modern Organizations,* Englewood Cliffs, NJ.

Foxall, G. (1985), "Marketing is service marketing," in Foxall, G. (Ed.), *Marketing in the Service Industries,* London, pp. 1–6.

Frei, F.X. and Harker, P.T. (1985), "Process efficiency in retail banking: methods and empirical results," *Workshop on Quality Management in Services V,* May 11–12, Tilburg, The Netherlands, pp. 127–46.

Giarini, O. (1991), "Notes on the concept of service quality and economic value," in Brown, S.W. *et al.* (Eds), *Quality in Service: Multidisciplinary and Multinational Perspectives,* Lexington, MA, pp. 57–70.

Grönroos, C. (1982), *Strategic Management and Marketing in the Service Sector,* Research Reports No. 8, Swedish School of Economics and Business Administration, Helsinki.

Grönroos, C. (1983), Marknadsföring Tjänsteföretag, (Marketing in Service Firms), Malmö.

Grönroos, C. (1990), *Service Management and Marketing,* Lexington, MA.

Gummesson, E. (1992), "Quality dimensions: what to measure in service organizations," in Swartz, T.A., Bowen, D.E. and Brown, S.W. (Eds), *Advances in Services Marketing and Management,* Greenwich, CT, pp. 177–205.

Gummesson, E. (1993), "Service productivity, service quality and profitability," paper presented at the *Eighth International Conference of the Operations Management Association,* May 25–26,Warwick.

Gummesson, E. (1994), "Service quality and productivity in the imaginary organization," paper presented at the *3rd International Research Seminar in Service Management,* May 24–27, France.

Gummesson, E., Lehtinen, U. and Grönroos, C. (1997), "Comment on 'Nordic perspectives on relationship marketing,' " *European Journal of Marketing,* Vol. 31 No. 1, pp. 10–16.

Handy, C. (1990), *The Age of Unreason,* Boston, MA.

Heskett, J.L., Jones, T.O. and Loveman, G.W. (1994), "Putting the service-profit chain to work," *Harvard Business Review,* March–April, pp. 164–74.

Holmlund, M. and Ravald, A. (1992), *Produktivite-tsstyrning i Tjänsteföretag,* (Management of Productivity in Service Firms), publications of Swedish School of Economics and Business Administration, Helsinki.

Johnston, R. (1988), "Service industries—improving competitive performance," *The Service Industries Journal,* Vol. 8 No. 2, April, pp. 202–11.

Johnston, R. (1995), "Service failure and recovery: impact, attributes and process," in Swartz, T.A., Bowen, D.E. and Brown, S.W. (Eds), *Advances in Services Marketing and Management,* Greenwich, CT, pp. 211–28.

Järvinen, R., Lehtinen, U. and Vuorinen, I. (1996), "The change process of industrialisation, electronising service channels and redesigning organization in the financial sector from the productivity viewpoint," paper presented at the *Second International Research Workshop on Service Productivity,* April 18–19, Madrid.

Kerlinger, F. (1973), *Foundations of Behavioral Research,* New York, NY.

Lehtinen, J.R. (1986), *Quality Oriented Services Marketing,* publications of the University of Tampere, Tampere.

Lehtinen, U. and Lehtinen, J.R. (1991), "Two approaches to service quality dimensions," *The Service Industries Journal,* Vol. 11 no. 3, July, pp. 287–303.

Levitt, T. (1972), "Production-line approach to service," *Harvard Business Review,* September–October, pp. 63–76.

Levitt, T. (1981), "Marketing intangible products and product intangibles," *Harvard Business Review,* September–October, pp. 41–52.

Levitt, T. (1983), *The Marketing Imagination,* New York NY.

Lovelock, C.H. and Young, R.F. (1979), "Look to consumers to increase productivity," *Harvard Business Review,* Vol. 57 No. 3, May–June, pp. 168–78.

Majaro, S. (1982), "Insurance, too, needs marketing," in Majaro, S. (Ed.), *Marketing in Perspective,* London, pp. 193–207.

Majaro, S. (1985), "Marketing insurance services: the main challenges," in Foxall, G. (Ed.), *Marketing in the Service Industries,* pp. 77–91.

McLaughlin, C. (1996), "Why variation reduction is not everything: a new paradigm for service operations," *International Journal of Service Industry Management,* Vol. 7 No. 3, pp. 17–30.

McLaughlin, C. and Coffey, S. (1990), "Measuring productivity in services," *International Journal of Service Industry Management,* Vol. 1 No. 1, pp. 46–63.

McLaughlin, C., Pannesi, R. and Kathuria, N. (1991), "The different operations strategy planning process for service operations," *International Journal of Operations & Production Management,* Vol. 11 No. 3, pp. 63–76.

Mock, T. (1976), *Measurement and Accounting Information Criteria,* AAA, Sarasota, FL.

Normann, R. (1991), *Service Management,* 2/E. Chichester: John Wiley & Sons.

Ojasalo, K. (1997), *Measuring Service Productivity,* Working Paper No. 345, Swedish School of Economics and Business Administration, Helsinki.

Oliver, R.L. (1993), "A conceptual model of service quality and service satisfaction: compatible goals, different concepts," in Swarz, T.A., Bowen, D.E. and Brown, S.W. (Eds), *Advances in Services Marketing Management,* Vol. 2, Greenwich, CT, pp. 65–85.

Parasuraman, A., Zeithaml, V.A. and Berry, L.L. (1985), "A conceptual model of service quality," *Journal of Retailing,* Vol. 64 No. 1, Spring, pp. 12–40.

Parasuraman, A., Zeithaml, V.A. and Berry, L.L. (1988), "SERVQUAL: a multiple-item scale for measuring consumer perceptions of service quality," *Journal of Retailing,* Vol. 64 No. 1, Spring, pp. 12–40.

Parasuraman, A., Zeithaml, V.A. and Berry, L.L. (1994), "Reassessment of expectations as a comparison standard in measuring service quality: implications for future research," *Journal of Marketing,* Vol. 58, January, pp. 111–24.

Patton, M.Q. (1990), *Qualitative Evaluation and Research Methods,* Newberry Park, CA.

Pohjola 1996, *Annual Report,* Helsinki.

Quinn, J.B. and Paquette, P.C. (1990), "Technology in services: creating organizational revolutions," *Sloan Management Review,* Winter, pp. 67–78.

Schneider, B. (1980), "The service organization: climate is crucial," *Organizational Dynamics,* Autumn, pp. 52–65.

Shaw, J.C. and Capoor, R. (1979), "Quality and productivity: mutually exclusive or interdependent in service organizations?" *Management Review,* March, pp. 25–39.

Storbacka, K. (1994), *The Nature of Customer Relationship Profitability. Analysis of Relationships and Customer Bases in Retail Banking,* publications of the Swedish School of Economics and Business Administration, No. 55, Helsinki.

Uusi-Rauva, E. (1987), *Palveluyrityksen Tunnusluvut,* (Key Figures of a Service Firm), Helsinki.

van Biema, M. and Greenwald, B. (1997), "Managing our way to higher service-sector productivity," *Harvard Business Review,* July–August, pp. 87–95.

Vehmanen, P. (1994), "Efficiency—the cornerstone of conceptual frameworks for management accounting," paper presented at the *17th Annual Congress of the European Accounting Association,* April 6–8, Venice.

Wilson, I. (1988), "Competitive strategies for service businesses," *Long Range Planning,* Vol. 6, pp. 10-12.

Zeithaml, V. (1984), "How consumer evaluation process differ between goods and services," in Lovelock, C. (Ed.), *Service Marketing,* Prentice-Hall, Englewood Cliffs, NJ, pp. 191–99.

Service Markets and the Internet

John Deighton

How will Web-based technologies impact the practice of services marketing? This article considers the implications for pricing strategy, the way firms align themselves with distributors and collaborators, and the nature of marketing communications. It also examines possible limits to the transformative power of the Internet.

How will the Internet change the way services are marketed? To attempt to answer that question is to try to predict the full flowering of an age from its infancy. We are barely into the transformation that began when, in 1993, Web browsers first gave the general public the power to play on the World Wide Web. Only the most reckless of prognosticators would claim a confident vision of the future to which the browser gave birth. Nevertheless, someone at Microsoft is alleged to have said that in times of change perspective is worth 30 IQ points, and this article offers a perspective.

The article selects three questions, arguably three of the most important questions, about the impact of the Internet on services markets. First, what is happening to the pricing of services? We know that service pricing is of the greatest importance because services are perishable. If supply can be rationed and demand shifted, the consequences for profitability can be very substantial. How will information-age technologies be used to transform the pricing process?

Second, what will be the effect of the Internet on the way firms align themselves with distributors and collaborators? By reducing many transaction costs for consumers and service providers, the Internet changes the sizes and kinds of firms needed to make service markets work. We contend that whole supply chains are moving onto the Web, transforming themselves from straight-line chan-nels to networks. We examine infomediaries and service hubs in particular, because they are the new organizational forms that threaten (or promise) to disrupt today's service marketing institutions.

Third, how will service marketers communicate with their consumers? Service marketers used to have to choose between broadcasting and personal contact. In the future they will be able to use something more like automated conversation. We view the Web as the latest step in a transformation from broadcast, to direct mail, to database marketing, to truly interactive one-to-one marketing.[1] We ask how this new frontier of communication possibilities is changing the work of marketing managers in service industries from hotels to airlines and banks.

Before we pose these questions, we shall review some features of nascent information age technologies that seem particularly salient.[2]

What Is the Web and What Is It Good For?

A person who uses the Web today is drawing on a chain of technology advances that began in the 1970s and shows no sign of slowing down. The volatility of technological innovation is what makes the task of the forecaster intrinsically difficult. Yet, paradoxically, the same fecundity of possibility simplifies the task, because with surprising regularity the need for a tool is all that is required for the tool to be discovered.

First came the *Internet,* a network of computers that spans the globe. It grew out of experiments to link together the main computers of the U.S. Department of Defense in the early 1970s, but many date its birth from 1983 when the Department of Defense imposed rules for information exchange on all users. In 1985 the Internet began to grow explosively after the National Science

Foundation connected six supercomputer centers with a high-speed "backbone" that gave scientists the ability to move files across the system. The number of host computers that make up the Internet has doubled every year since 1985 and may well continue to double annually for some time. A simple system that uses only the first stage of the Internet is e-mail. Today more individuals use this Internet application than any other.

Second came the *World Wide Web* in 1989. The Web is no more than a set of rules governing a library of files (text, pictures, sound, or video) stored on the computers that make up the Internet. It is termed a web because any one file can contain pathways to many other files. In this sense, any file on the Internet that conforms to the Web's rules can be said to include the content of every other file to which it is linked, wherever in the world it is physically stored.

Third came the *browsers,* the first being Mosaic in 1993, which a year later became Netscape. These software products are called browsers because they let personal computer users browse easily from one file on the Web to another. Only after browsers became widely available in 1994 did the Web begin to be noticed for its commercial potential. Quite suddenly the Internet was seen not as a way to run computers from a distance but rather as a two-way highway that could carry things as disparate as telephony, television, radio, and mail, and combine their functions into a whole more effective than any of the parts. The term browser has largely vanished from Web discourse recently, as browsers like Yahoo! and Excite added content and became known as portals, or points of entry to the riches of the Internet with the power to sell traffic to one destination or another. *Internet Service Providers* (ISPs), the companies that linked individual personal computers to the computers of the Internet for a fee, had existed since before the Web was born in 1989, because they were needed to send and receive e-mail. But demand for browsers created demand for ISP services. One ISP in particular, AOL, had the good sense to combine the ISP service with the portal function and, as a result, became the first child of the e-commerce industry to cross into the mainstream communication economy.

Fourth came *broadband access.* Early traffic on the Internet tended to travel on telephone wires. Consequently, the early Web experience was frustratingly slow, leading some to call it the "World Wide Wait." In the late 1990s, telephone and cable television companies began to build new transmission capacity, designed expressly to transmit data

in large quantities. Its rollout was slow, and by the end of the twentieth century, fewer than 2 percent of U.S. homes could participate in the Web on these transmission lines. For these consumers, however, the experience was transformed. The full flowering of the Web as a commercial medium with mass-market reach could now be seen to depend on the rate at which broadband access would roll out.

An industry is taking shape to support commerce on the Internet that is a relatively complex structure of collaborators and competitors. Figure 1 indicates the main functions that the industry performs and identifies some of the firms that compete to do the work. The shaded boxes indicate the "consumables" or finished products of the industry, classified as transactions, content (information and entertainment), and consumer services such as e-mail. The unshaded boxes indicate the suppliers who help to create the finished products. The allocation of firms to functions is fluid at this stage in the evolution of the industry, and there is a vigorous rate of vertical integration by firms who attempt to anticipate the future structure of the industry. Thus AOL has acquired Netscape and Time Warner, and Microsoft and Yahoo! have acquired a number of small suppliers of electronic commerce services.

What does this loosely linked confederacy of firms amount to? What is it that the Web brings to the toolkit of services industry market-making that was not there before? Distinctive features of digital interactive media include the following[2]:

Any-to-any, not one-to-many communication. Like the telephone, the Internet allows any participant to interact with any other. This democratic (and at times, anarchic) structure empowers the individual over the corporation in a way that traditional media do not. Consumers can collaborate to build a community with buying power or to caution other consumers against a brand. The same Web search that leads a consumer to a manufacturer's advertisement may well discover a page erected by disgruntled purchasers.

Content can be perpetually fresh. Unlike catalogs, brochures, and CD-Roms, whose content is fixed at the time of manufacture, digital interactive media can be refreshed continuously. The *USA TODAY Online* newspaper, for example, updates its front page every 10 minutes, 7 days a week. For Web catalogs, out-of-stock items can be deleted and prices can be revised in line with demand and supply.

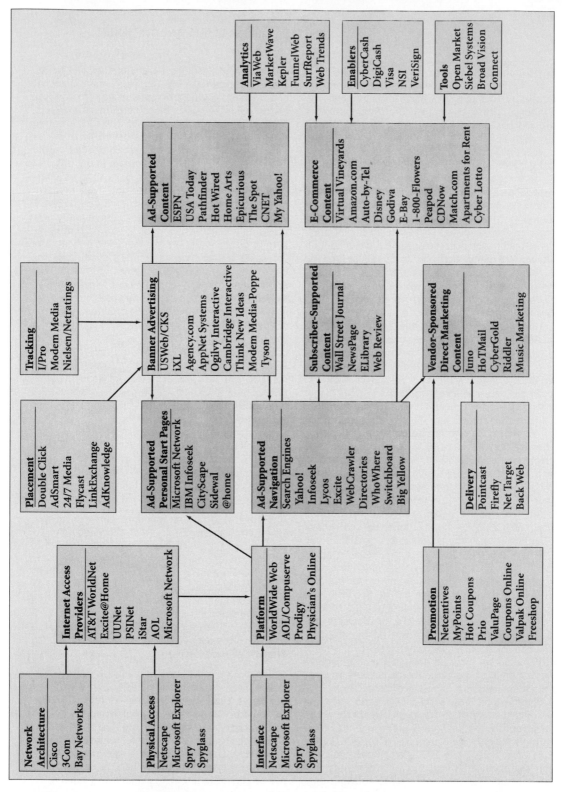

FIGURE 1. Structure of the Internet Marketing Communication Industry

Consumers can select information. Vast databases and increasingly sophisticated search and indexing engines make unimagined resources available to Internet users. Pirolli and Carol estimate that a person sitting at a desk today can reach out to the information in 275 million public Web pages via the Web, compared to perhaps 1,000 paper pages 5 years ago.[3]

Communities can form across space or time. Individuals can link themselves to others with related interests and in doing so gain access to the links that those individuals have created. Although communities of interest are a common feature of many markets in the broadcast world, digital interactive media allow them to form faster and over wider areas than has been possible before.

Digital interactivity redefines privacy and identity. In the physical world, privacy is the reciprocal of identity. The more privacy is assured, the narrower is the circle within which one has identity. On the Web, however, it is possible to decouple privacy and identity. A Web user may preserve anonymity yet benefit from a constructed Web persona that receives individually tailored communications from marketers who, through services provided by auditing firms and through direct questioning, know the user's previous destinations, psychographics, and preferences.

Interactivity enables hyperimpulsivity. The Web permits a closer conjunction of desire, transaction, and payment than any other environment yet created apart from personal selling.

In summary, although it is easy to overclaim for information-age technologies, we believe that they have a central role in the increasingly interactive future of service marketing practice. These technologies are raising the scope and power of interactive marketing to a new level, combining individual addressability, instant response, round-the-clock availability, and global reach. In the following three sections we support this assertion in three specific areas: pricing, distribution, and communication.

Pricing in the Information Age: From Posted Prices to Dynamic Prices

Price, the information signal by which supply and demand are brought as near as possible to alignment, is disproportionately important to service marketers because services are perishable. An unsold airline seat on a particular flight, or a hotel bed on a particular night, or a consultant's services on a particular day, have no salvage value the following day. For as long as there have been service marketers, therefore, there have been price tools to shift demand from times of excess demand to times of insufficient demand. The Internet and related information-age technologies have made it easier to use price creatively, because they reduce transaction costs. The most obvious transaction cost to be reduced by the information age is search cost (what must be expended to find the right price to pay or to charge); but menu costs (the costs associated with changing price) have also declined.

We shall identify several specific consequences of reduced transaction costs for pricing in service markets. The general idea underlying these specific instances is that the need to declare a price and stick to it for all comers (what economists call posting a price) is disappearing in favor of dynamic price generation, whether at the vendor's instigation (discounting, customization), or the consumer's (auctions, reverse auctions), or an intermediate form (negotiation). The one-price-for-all character of a posted price leaves uncaptured much of the value created in a market. Prices that vary dynamically, over time and across customers, do a better job of equating value created to value captured. Consequently they improve the welfare of both producers and consumers.

Discounting
The very name of the British Internet startup, www.Lastminute.com, makes explicit that it traffics in discounted perishable services. It offers last-minute deals on many services, including vacations, air travel, car rental, and hotel accommodation. Its competitors are legion, both agents and principals. The largest service providers go directly to the consumer to offer discounted services. Airlines, for example, discount prices with the help of e-mail. Subscribers to American Airlines' NetSAAver service (www.AA.com) receive e-mail notification each week of the week's flights that, because of lack of demand, can be bought at substantially reduced prices on the condition that travel commences after 7:00 P.M. on that Friday and the return leg starts by the following Tuesday. Ticketmaster Online (www.Ticketmaster.com) offers an assortment of discounted entertainment alternatives customized to a site visitor's home state.

Price Customization
Profitability in service industries is acutely sensitive to utilization. Hotels, for example, break even

at occupancies of about 65 percent. At higher occupancies, most of the revenue flows to the bottom line. It is common in the industry to appoint a revenue manager to each hotel property, who oversees the many day-to-day decisions that affect hotel revenue of which the most powerful is the customization of prices to particular customers. One tool widely used to implement price customization in this industry, and in others such as airlines and car rental, is yield management. Yield management models are probabilistic algorithms that help the revenue manager set reservations policy. They use past history and other statistical data to make continuously updated recommendations in three areas: when to overbook a hotel, when to let it stay underbooked, and what price to offer a particular guest. Simulation studies have shown that when the reservations function is guided by a good yield management model, a company's revenue can increase by 20 percent over a simple "first come, first served, fixed price" reservation policy.[4] In the hotel industry overbooking means that a prospective guest may be accepted even when no rooms are available, if the model predicts that a room is highly likely to come available due to cancellation or no-show. Underbooking means rejecting a prospective guest even when rooms are available, if the model predicts that a higher-paying or longer-staying guest is likely to come along. Variable pricing means that the rate charged for a room depends not only on its size and fittings but also on the day of booking, the day of occupation, length of stay, and customer characteristics. Of these factors, customer characteristics are the most problematic.

Customer characteristics are needed by yield management models to estimate *walking cost,* the cost of turning a customer away. That cost in turn depends on the customer's future lifetime value to the chain, their willingness to pay, and past loyalty to the chain. These are considered soft variables but are notoriously hard to estimate. The better the historical information on a customer, however, the better the estimate. Tools of the information age, such as transaction databases and rapid data transmission over corporate Intranets, are allowing the hotel industry to make real-time pricing decisions informed by full information on customer characteristics.

Yield management and selective discounting are attractive price-setting tools for large service providers with rich information at their disposal. For the smaller service provider, the Internet can offer automated negotiation.

Price Negotiation

The technology for online negotiation is in its infancy, but its potential is apparent. The Internet start-up Make Us an Offer (www.makeusanoffer.com) is an intriguing case. An animated cartoon character, Chester, engages in real time, online haggling controlled by artificial intelligence algorithms to entice customers who are willing to play along with him. Chester adopts colorful haggling language to bait the other party to the transaction into closing on the deal. He welcomes customers with, "I'm Chester, and my job is to sell you quality merchandise at any price we can agree upon. Just find what you like, tell me what you're willing to pay, and I'll see what I can do!" Although most of what is sold on this site today is products, the format lends itself well to services.

There are two Internet start-up firms, Mercata (www.Mercata.com) and Accompany (www.Accompany.com), pioneering the principle of buying power aggregation. Their sites invite buyers to pool their demand to negotiate lower prices. By buying in quantity, each consumer in the pool plays a lower price for products and services offered by supplier partners than they would pay if buying alone.

Auctions

Auctions have one characteristic of particular appeal to perishable service vendors—subject only to the constraint of a reserve price, an auction ensures that the offered service will be sold. Despite this feature, while auctioning of services was possible in the pre-information-age world, it was seldom done because auction markets were limited in size and costly to administer. The success of the online auctioneer eBay has spurred a reassessment of the auction method by service vendors. Although none of the standard categories on the eBay site or its competitor Yahoo! is a service category, both sites offer a growing number of service offerings such as travel, entertainment tickets, phonecards, and educational courses. Last_minute.com has added an auction element to its site.

Reverse Auctions

The most radical of the innovations that the Internet has introduced into the service pricing process is the principle of reverse auctions, most familiarly associated with the name of Priceline.com. It is significant that Priceline began as a vendor of perishable services, in particular airline seats, because the price-setting process is particularly appropriate for items that cannot be inventoried and resold and where the supplier has an incentive to give the vendor a guaranteed supply of items to sell.

In the Priceline model, the buyer offers a price and commits *irrevocably* to buy the service if a supplier can be found to meet it within a reasonable zone of latitude. For example, an airline passenger is obliged to accept a change of planes en route, any departure or arrival time on the requested days, and any airline. Armed with a guaranteed sale, Priceline can then auction the customer across suppliers of the service. Priceline is extending its assortment to include rental cars, home financing services, and long distance phone service.

The particular appeal of auctions and reverse auctions on the Web is the evidence they generate of buyer reservation prices. Even an unsuccessful auction bid is informative in this respect. It reveals that the bidder is potentially a consumer of the category of services and indicates a willingness to pay at the bid price. Onsale, a predecessor company of Egghead.com, obtained a 30 percent response rate to e-mails sent after auctions to unsuccessful bidders offering alternatives for sale at close to the bidder's last bid.[5]

In sum, the efficiency with which the Internet can allow vendors to post prices, revise prices, invite consumers to offer prices, and match prices to demand fluctuations, is a benefit to all producers. To service industries, where the optimization of revenues from a fixed and perishable service production capacity is often the difference between profit and loss, mastery of this benefit is a competitive priority.

Distribution Channels and Alliances: From Supply Chains to Service Hubs

The argument to be made here is that the effect of the Internet on service markets is not simply to favor one firm over another but to change the kinds of firms that make up the industry. It is not simply that the first firm to master the technology will gain some simple advantage and therefore thrive but rather that the work of the industry will change, new institutional forms will emerge, and others will become obsolete. As a general rule, many individual firms will become smaller as firms outsource nonessential functions and reorganize themselves into networks and alliances, and direct-to-consumer channels will displace multilayered channels.

Retailing Personal Computers

The rise of Dell Computer Corporation to dominance in the retailing of personal computers illustrates this contention. In the market that operated before Dell entered, the largest firms were Compaq and IBM. The stylized diagram in Figure 2 depicts their role in the market as captains of the supply chain. The role of original equipment manufacturers (OEMs) as supply chain captain was in essence to coordinate the activities of the other firms that made up the chain, some working as suppliers and some as distributors, to anticipate and fill the needs of consumers. The inevitable uncertainties about end-consumer demand showed up in the form of inventories at each link in the chain. In that sense, inventories were the concrete manifestation of uncertainty.

The next stage in the transformation of the supply chain by information technology came when adjacent elements of the supply chain agreed to share information using electronic data interchange (EDI) protocols. The result was better coordination of each firm with its neighbors and therefore a reduction in the inventories that each firm needed to carry, as shown in Figure 3. This change did not change the organization of the market, however. On the contrary, it strengthened the

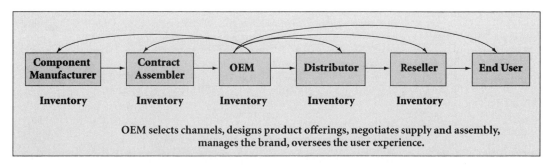

FIGURE 2. Role of the OEM in the Traditional Supply Chain

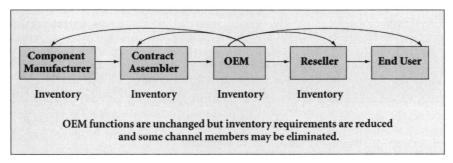

FIGURE 3. Role of the OEM in the Supply Chain with EDI

incumbent firms, binding them together in mutually nourishing partnerships, which went under the name of customer relationship management (CRM). In fact, EDI was the technological face of CRM.

Dell entered the market in the early 1980s with what it called the Dell Direct model (private label products sold by mail order and made-to-order), serving the segment of end users who were willing to buy from an OEM.[6] Initially, Dell's model amounted to little more than a tweak on the integrated supply chain used by every other OEM, as illustrated in Figure 4. The tweak had a cost advantage for those customers willing to do without the services of a value-added reseller or a systems integrator or a retailer, the three service providers who lived downstream from Compaq and IBM, because the costs of these service providers was eliminated. It also eliminated the inventories carried by these distributors and in an industry where product life cycles were of the order of six months, that meant that Dell could get upstream innovations like faster chips or larger hard drives into the hands of customers faster. But essentially it was no reorganization of the market.

The radical change came with the introduction of Dell Online (www.Dell.com) in 1996. Not only the customer-facing activities but also the supplier-facing activities began to occur on the Internet. The market began to evolve toward the structure shown in Figure 5. Dell began to function as a service hub, receiving orders on the Web and sourcing the components and assembly services needed to fulfill these orders on the Web, too. A hub on the Internet is quite different from a supply chain linked by an EDI system. First, it is not a slave to legacy systems. It uses protocols such as XML to create, share, and process information in a fashion that is consistent across members of the network. Second, it is flexible, allowing the network's active members to change as easily as new market circumstances require.

Service Hubs

The term *service hub* applies because in its pure form the trader carries no inventory, operating instead as a market-making service for upstream and downstream customers. Dell's hub has begun to make markets for manufacturers who were once viewed as serving different markets, or as competitors. It sells printers, modems, and software, and sources its notebook computers from other OEMs under the Dell brand.

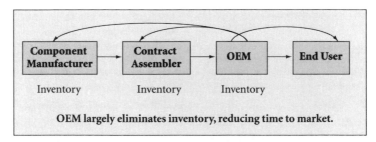

FIGURE 4. Role of the OEM in the Supply Chain with Direct-to-Consumer Selling

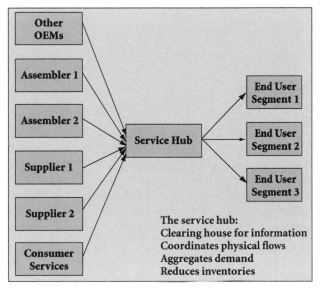

FIGURE 5. OEM Becomes Service Hub

Of course a pure service hub is a romantic notion, a business model with no risk, no investment, and no responsibility. What are the essential business functions that must be performed to earn the right to be a broker between demand and supply? Peter Drucker identified them as long ago as 1954 when he declared that the crucial tasks of any firm were innovation and marketing.[7] All else, he implied, was peripheral to the mission of the firm. If we label these functions with the analogous terms of branding and design, we have the core competencies of a service hub. To be assured of a place in the internetworked economy, a firm must own a brand that establishes an expectation and inspires trust for its offering. The firm must possess the design skills to orchestrate the production of products and services that live up to that trust. The rest, arguably, is detail.

The U.S. automotive industry shows signs of reorganizing from three large vertically integrated and self-contained industrial fortresses into a system of service hubs. Ford and General Motors both announced in 1999 that they would create procurement hums capable of supporting transactions (in Ford's case) worth $80 billion a year.[8] Ford's is known as AutoXchange, and General Motors' is MarketSite. Competitors are invited to join these procurement hubs, and already Toyota has accepted. Each is engaged in experiments with direct-to-consumer retailing, General Motors under the name of GM BuyPower and Ford as Auto Vantage. They face independent Web competitors such as Autobytel (www.Autobytel.com) and CarsDirect (www.CarsDirect.com). The *Economist* offered the opinion,

> Before too long, both Ford and GM should be able to make cars in the same way as Dell makes computers—each built to order and delivered within a few days. They may even realize that they no longer need to make cars at all, deciding to follow the example of Cisco Systems, a data-networking firm, by becoming virtual companies whose expertise lies in design and brand marketing.[9]

If such an eventuality were to come into being, the product-manufacturing function of these companies would have been transformed into a market-making service.

In the examples discussed so far, OEMs compete to become the service hub for the industry. If the returns to scale of the service providers in the industry are not great, a newcomer may enter to play the hub role, capturing information flows in the industry and selling coordination services to upstream and downstream firms. These intruders are called *infomediaries* in the parlance of the Web. They are intermediaries in the channel only with respect to information.

Declining	Emerging	Declining
The Old Branded Goods View of the Customer	**The View of the Customer on the Web**	**The Old Services View of the Customer**
A needy but inert media audience.	One-to-one interaction.	The customer meets the service provider face-to-face in the service encounter.
Low involvement, fickle attention.	Focused attention.	High involvement.
Broadcast communication, hard to customize.	Optimum combination of customized and standardized communication.	Communication occurs in the field, hard to standardize.

FIGURE 6. Convergence in the Vocabulary of Marketing: On the Web, Goods and Services Paradigms are Coming Together.

Communication:
From Broadcasting to Interaction

The difference between the toolkits of goods marketers and service marketers can be summed up, at the risk of a little oversimplifying, as follows. Goods marketers use broadcast tools. The broadcast image, with its all-powerful transmitting center and a passive receiving periphery, has given packaged goods marketing practice its basic architecture and product marketing scholarship its problems to solve. The broadcast paradigm envisaged a needy but inert audience for manufacturers to deal with, a "target" whose most irksome property was its fickle attention. Know the customer, then build a brand that gets noticed, is relevant, is likable, is clearly positioned relative to competitors' brands, and then is available at the point of purchase: these were the core prescriptions of the broadcast paradigm applied to product markets, and marketing scholarship was largely concerned with refining the concepts and measures of these practices.

Service marketers, by contrast, tended to use interactive tools. Their skill was in making things happen in front of consumers, frequently with the help of the customers. Their main tool was face-to-face interchange executed by the service provider in the course of a service encounter. Service marketing's architecture was the reverse of goods marketing's. The critical activities took place at the periphery where commercial intercourse occurred beyond the sight and control of a usually weak and ill-informed center. Tools to improve standardization of the service experience, such as automation, blueprinting of the service encounter, and alignment of compensation systems with service delivery objectives, were the key to success. What broadcasting was to product marketing, the skills of managing interaction were to service marketing.

The problem that broadcast communication faced was that it was not very intimate. Its messages were heard by the whole market and so marketers were obliged to frame their arguments in the most general terms. Because they were often not personally relevant, consumers paid them little attention and so a lot of effort was needed to have quite small effects. That was a problem that service marketers seldom faced. Their problem was controlling communication in the service encounter. All the advertising in the world could be rendered irrelevant by a bad experience at the hands of a service provider. The challenge of service communication was usually to deliver consistent content across many field service settings.

The information age has produced something that solves the problem of goods marketing's lack of customer intimacy as surely as it solves the service marketer's problem of field coordination. This tool is the Internet. It offers us a new marketing vocabulary in which the distinctions between services and goods are not as divisive as they once were (see Figure 6).

Two critical features of a digital networked communication such as the Internet exist. First, addressability: the communication is not broadcast to all who can receive it but is directly addressable to individuals. Second, responsiveness: the communication is no longer broadcast in the sense that it is no longer indifferent to its effect on the receiver. Instead, it is alert to the receiver's response.

Conversational Marketing

When addressability and responsiveness coexist, a medium has the potential to carry conversation. The mark of whether a marketing communication is conversational or not lies in the third round of the exchange. The first round is the marketer's overture. The second round is the consumer's response. The third round indicates whether the exchange is a conversation or merely two parties talking at one another. The test is whether the response of the marketer takes into account what the consumer said in the second round.

Conversation makes intimacy all but inevitable. Where a broadcast communicator can keep going despite the audience's lack of interest, a conversation as defined in the previous paragraph fails as soon as one party becomes disengaged. Thus conversation has the capability of being self-correcting, of converging toward intimacy, as long as both parties are intelligent. And in digital conversation, where the messages of both parties are machine-readable, and the machines are intelligent, this convergence toward intimacy can occur almost costlessly. That is, each machine learns and remembers costlessly the preferences and capabilities of the other. When the machines function as agents of buyers and sellers, the result is a high order of matching of tasks and offerings, and a tightly coordinated marketing system. To the extent that a service marketer can move the service encounter onto the Web, whether at a Web-linked automatic teller machine, a hotel cable television interface, a retail store kiosk, or a conventional Web site, the problem of delivering consistent service quality in the field is reduced considerably.

Impediments to Conversation Marketing

Service industries in which the customer interface demands consistent and accurate service and deep access to information, like stockbroking, bill payment, and retailing in categories where the inventory is rich, like books and CDs, have been the first to migrate to the Web. It is easy, however, to overestimate the power of the Web to "Amazon" every service industry. There are definite limitations to the tailoring of Web communication to the needs of service industries. Consider the following three limitations in particular.

First, audience attention on the Web is much more fragmented than on broadcast media. Because even a child can launch a Web site, and any twenty-something with a clever Web publishing idea can mobilize capital to test it, content creation on the Web is a fecund, turbulent process that segments, rather than aggregates, audiences. It is far easier to imagine a service business on the Web than it is to solve the communication problem of getting noticed by enough people to achieve economies of scale and become a going concern.

Second, if customers come to expect interactivity, the burden on the organization to deliver it can be overwhelming. E-mail is easier to use than the telephone. But as a result, consumers expect to speak and to be heard and responded to. Few firms that use digital media have yet solved the problems of scalability in managing conversation to build intimacy, to foster customer relationships, and, most radically, to cultivate consumer communities. Customer service expectations rise with interactivity and disappointing them is easy.

Third, the Web is really quite boring when compared to television. Although the Web enables ever more intimate conversation with and among consumers, it is a medium with little power to command emotional involvement or indulge fantasy. It is an instrumental medium, a tool for action, but not an inspirer of action.

This litany of limitations goes some way to explaining why the Web has not wrought more material damage to consumer service industries yet. It is beginning to be used by airlines to wrest some of the control of their customer relationships back from travel agents, by start-ups to disrupt the control of banks over mortgage loan origination, by banks to reduce branch costs with online banking, and by pharmacies to reduce chronic drug prescribing costs, but in each of these instances the disruption is far from material yet. In none of these service industries does the volume of online business amount to more than the rounding error on traditional business despite the volumes of publicity given to Internet firms.

Arguably the most important communications applications of the Internet will go unpublicized. Some of the most consequential conversations on the Web may occur in the background of the consumer's life. Some indeed may disregard human audiences and take place directly between consumers' computers and the systems of service providers, as remote from human consciousness as plumbing. Examples are repetitive bill payment services, automatic replenishment of household goods, shopping by bot (a bot is a device that scours the Web for the best deal on an item of merchandise), time management and appointment scheduling services, and custom publishing of news and information.

Conclusion

The Internet is, as Jim Barksdale, the former chief executive of Netscape, observed, "a huge, transforming event."[10] This article has shown that services industries, in common with every other sector of the economy, can expect to be buffeted and disrupted by innovations that marshal the power of the Web.

We have explored what the Web can do for and to the service economy in three respects. We have seen how service pricing will change as the notion of posting fixed prices for all comers gives way to differentiated pricing and consumer-initiated pricing. We have seen that the structure of distribution will be reorganized in many industries and that indeed the very boundaries of service firms will in many cases be redrawn, with more outsourcing and more alliances. We have seen that the communication that binds consumers and service firms together will be able to be more intimate and, therefore, that customer relationships will likely be direct and stronger in the future enabled by information technology.

However, there are limits to the transformative power of the Internet and this article will end on a note of moderation. Bill Gates popularized the idea that the Web would presage "friction-free capitalism." If he were right, it would be a disturbing idea for marketers. Markets without friction are, usually, markets without marketing. The most frictionless markets, large stock markets and exchanges trading contracts in commodities, require very little of the work of marketing in order to operate. It is inefficient markets, such as the market in political ideas

and the market for entertainment and pleasure, which attract advertisers, publicists, promoters, distributors, market researchers, and the rest of the armamentarium of the profession. The tools of the information age seem designed to make markets more efficient and marketing less important. But, fortunately perhaps for the profession, they must still contend with the imperfections of human nature and the frailties of technology. The Internet may help markets to work better, but it will not make them work perfectly.

ENDNOTES

1. John Deighton and Patrick Barwise, "Digital Marketing Communications," in *Digital Marketing,* ed. Jerry Wind and Vijay Mahajan (New York: John Wiley and Sons, forthcoming).
2. John Deighton, "Note on Marketing and the World Wide Web, " Case number 9-597-037 (Boston: Harvard Business School Publishing, 1999).
3. Peter Pirolli and Stuart Carol, "Information Foraging," *Psychological Review* 106 (October 1999).
4. Timothy K. Baker, "A Comparative Revenue Analysis of Hotel Yield Management Heuristics," *Decision Sciences* 30 (1999): 1239–1264.
5. Youngme Moon, "Onsale, Inc." Case Number 9-599-091 (Boston: Harvard Business School Publishing, 1999).
6. Facts in this section are drawn from Das Narayandas and V. Kasturi Rangan, "Dell Computer Corporation," Case number 9-596-058 (1995) and V. Kasturi Rangan, "Dell Online," Case number 9-598-116 (1998) (Boston: Harvard Business School Publishing).
7. Peter Drucker, *The Practice of Management,* (New York: Harper and Row, 1954).
8. "Riding the Storm," *Economist,* November 6, 1999, 63–64.
9. Ibid.
10. Steve Hamm, "Jim Barksdale, Internet Angel," *Business Week,* May 10, 1999, 60–62.

PART V

Issues for Senior Management

CHAPTER 15

Managing People in Service Organizations

The old adage "People are your most important asset" is wrong. The right people are your most important asset.

JIM COLLINS

Companies that do right by employees seem to do right by stockholders.

ROBERT LEVERING AND MILTON MOSKOWITZ

Among the most demanding jobs in service businesses are so-called *boundary-spanning positions,* where employees are expected to be fast and efficient at executing operational tasks as well as courteous and helpful in dealing with customers. As a result, many service encounters have the potential to be a three-cornered fight among the needs of partially conflicting parties: the customer, the server, and the service firm. If the job is not designed carefully or the wrong people are picked to fill it, there's a real risk that employees may become stressed and unproductive.

Most of the published research in service management—and most of the service employment coverage in business magazines—tends to focus on employees in high-contact environments. This is not entirely surprising because the people in these jobs are so visible. After all, they are the actors who appear frontstage in the service drama when they serve customers. But a growing number of service jobs are being created in telephone-based call centers. In these instances, customer contact is ear-to-ear rather than face-to-face, and we hear only the voices of these employees; from a dramatic standpoint, their role is akin to that of actors in a radio drama. Yet effective service performance in such jobs remains vital, and the human resources (HR) task requires a distinctive approach.

And what of the numerous employees who appear to have no customer contact at all? In some respects, their jobs may seem closer to those of workers in a manufacturing environment. However, like backstage workers in a theater, many of them provide real-time support to the actors appearing frontstage, and any shortcomings in executing their designated tasks may quickly—perhaps even instantaneously—become apparent to customers. It can be useful to view these jobs from the standpoint of providing services to internal customers who are themselves serving external customers.

Findings from research on service quality have contributed to greater awareness among top management of the key role that service employees play in both creating customer satisfaction and working toward service recovery when things go wrong. There is also greater appreciation in management circles of the competitive advantage inherent in a dedicated, motivated set of employees who support the corporate mission, understand how their individual work activities contribute—directly or indirectly—to customer satisfaction, and have the skills and tools needed to be both productive and quality oriented.

In this chapter, we focus on the *people* element of integrated service management, demonstrating the distinctive role played by human resources and exploring such questions as

1. Why is it important that top managers should see expenditures on human resources as an investment that will pay dividends rather than a cost to be minimized?
2. What is the strategic importance of recruitment, selection, training, motivation, and retention of employees?
3. What is meant by the control and involvement models of management?
4. When is a strategy of empowering employees appropriate, and what are its benefits and implications?
5. How do different approaches to HR management affect customer satisfaction and retention?

Human Resources: An Asset Worthy of Investment

Almost everybody can recount some horror story of a dreadful experience they have had with a service business—and usually, they love to talk about it! If pressed, many of these same people can also recount a really good service experience. Service personnel usually feature prominently in such dramas—either in roles as uncaring, incompetent, mean-spirited villains or as heroes who went out of their way to help, anticipating customer needs for resolving problems in a supportive and empathetic manner. Consider your own recent service experiences: In what ways have you been treated particularly well or badly lately by service personnel, either in face-to-face contacts or over the telephone?

As customers, most of our involvement with service employees is with low-level contact personnel, not managers. At the department store, you're served by sales clerks, not the chairperson. Whom do you encounter at a fast-food restaurant? Not a vice president, that's for sure—more likely a teenage cashier. Call a professional firm, and you may have to go through a switchboard operator before you reach the busy man or woman you want to talk to (chances are, they're so busy that you'll have to leave a message with a secretary, anyway). When you visit your bank (if you still do), you probably deal with tellers, customer service reps, or loan officers most of the time. And you often have to be a VIP to get even a greeting from the general manager of a big hotel.

Many organizations have used the slogan "People are our most important asset," but all too few act as though top management really believes it. However, behind most of today's successful service organizations stands a commitment to effective management of human resources, including recruitment, selection, training, and retention of employees. Management styles and corporate cultures may differ widely, but in high-contact service organizations especially there is a recognition that the quality of personal service encounters plays an important role in creating customer satisfaction and, in the private sector, competitive advantage. In the public sector and many nonprofits, too, creative new approaches to service delivery and nontraditional ways of managing employees go hand in hand when the goal is to provide better service to customers.

Successful service firms are characterized by a distinctive culture of service, leadership, and role-modeling by members of top management and active involvement of HR managers in strategic decisions. Employees are seen as a resource to be nurtured, rather than a cost to be minimized, and are empowered to make decisions on their own, rather than having to go continually to their supervisors to ask for permission. Hal Rosenbluth, owner of a chain of successful travel agencies, argues in his book, *The Customer Comes Second,* that a company's first focus should be on its employees: "Only when people know what it feels like to be first in someone else's eyes," he writes, "can they sincerely share that feeling with others."[1] Within a service organization, other employees may serve internal suppliers and internal customers as they work backstage to support the efforts of frontstage colleagues who are serving end-customers directly.

In high-contact service encounters, we tend to remember the role played by frontstage personnel better than any other aspect of the operation. In many respects, these employees *are* the service. A single employee may play many roles: part of the product and part of the delivery system, adviser and teacher, marketer, and even—if the customers get unruly—police officer (like a bouncer in a bar). Yet service people may also play a vital role in lower-contact jobs where customers interact with the firm by telephone and an agent's voice is the only form of human contact.

Boundary Spanning

Customer-contact personnel must attend to both operational and marketing goals. On the one hand, they help to "manufacture" the service output. At the same time, they may also be responsible for marketing it (for instance, "We've got some nice desserts to follow your main course" or "We could clean your machine at the same time that we repair the electric motor" or "Now would be a good time to open a separate account to save for your children's education"). In the eyes of their customers, service personnel may also be seen as an integral part of the service experience. In short, the service person may perform a triple role as operations specialist, marketer, and part of the service product itself.

This multiplicity of roles—known as *boundary spanning*—may lead to role conflict among employees, especially when they feel as physically and psychologically close to customers as they do to managers and other employees.[2] In general, organizations whose services involve extensive service encounters tend to be harder to manage than those without such encounters. Because of the human element, consistent service delivery becomes that much harder to achieve, thereby complicating the task of those responsible for productivity and quality improvement efforts. Research Insights 15.1 offers insights into how telephone-based service employees cope with the inevitable tension between productivity and quality achievement in frontline jobs.

Reflecting such challenges, several special characteristics may be important in recruiting and training boundary-spanning employees. These include interpersonal skills, personal appearance and grooming (where face-to-face contact with customers is required), voice, knowledge of the product and the operation, selling capabilities, and skills in coproduction (that is, working jointly with customers to create the desired service). Additional characteristics, particularly valuable in selling situations, include monitoring nonverbal clues (such as the customer's body language) and adjusting one's behavior in the context of social situations. Both technical and interpersonal skills are *necessary,* but neither alone is *sufficient* for optimal job performance.[3]

Performance Productivity and Quality of Frontline Service Employees

What mechanisms govern productivity and quality for frontline service employees? Does the tension of competing demands from customers and management have dysfunctional consequences? And what resources help to counter these dysfunctional effects? Seeking answers, Professor Jaydip Singh of Case Western Reserve University conducted a survey of full-time employees working in customer contact jobs at a financial service company's telephone call center.

The nature of the job required these frontline employees (FLEs) to coordinate tasks with their co-workers and to receive regular directions and guidelines from supervisors. They were expected to meet daily quotas for call volumes and were randomly monitored against service quality standards. Their work setting contained many characteristics of a burnout environment, including long hours, lack of autonomy, insufficient resources, and ongoing demands to meet quotas and goals.

All employees received a survey packet at their homes, containing a questionnaire, a cover letter from the researchers, a letter of endorsement from the company president, and a postage-paid return envelope addressed to the researchers. Participants were assured of anonymity and asked to complete the survey at home. Usable responses were received from 306 FTEs, representing a response rate of 30%.

The questionnaire included scales designed to measure a variety of constructs:

- Role stressors measured the ambiguity perceived by FTEs concerning both the company (in terms of such dimensions as task flexibility, priorities, workload, and getting promoted) and customers (nature of interactions, amount of service offered, handling objections and criticism, and presenting company strengths). Stressors also measured the role conflict inherent for FTEs in trying to meet conflicting demands from different departments while lacking the training and resources needed to get the required volume of work done well.
- Burnout tendencies measured emotional feelings about top management (dismay, alienation, and emotional exhaustion from trying to meet expectations), and about customers (strain, indifference towards and depersonalization of customers, and overwork).
- Task Control and Boss Support measured FTEs' perceived ability to influence the tasks and decisions affecting their jobs, as well as their perceptions of the boss's fairness, supportiveness, and competence.
- Job Outcomes measured employees' level of commitment and likelihood of quitting.
- Performance Productivity and Quality. Productivity addressed both contact output (customer contact time—measured automatically—meeting quotas and targets, following procedures) and backroom work (accurate completion of paperwork and adherence to company policies and procedures). Quality included building customer trust and confidence, giving prompt and individualized attention, going beyond defined responsibilities to help customers even at the expense of not meeting productivity goals, consistently resolving customer concerns the first time, and providing accurate information.

The findings showed FLE productivity to be unaffected by burnout tendencies but negatively impacted by conflict between resources and demands and by role ambiguity relative to customers. Singh believes that employees seek to maintain their productivity, even in the face of burnout, because the relevant indicators are visible and relate to pay and job retention. By contrast, FLE quality—which is less quantifiable and less visible—is likely to be damaged directly as employees burnout on customers. An unexpected finding was the negative correlation between organizational commitment and service quality, indicating that FLEs who are more committed to the organization may be less committed to customers, and vice versa. Providing greater task control and boss support helps to shield employees from role stress, burnout, and thoughts of quitting, while also enhancing positive attitudes.

Source: Jagdip Singh, "Performance Productivity and Quality of Frontline Employees in Service Organizations," Journal of Marketing, 64, April 2000, 15-34.

Emotional Labor

Service encounters entail more than just correct technical execution of a task. They also involve such human elements as personal demeanor, courtesy, and empathy. This brings us to the notion of *emotional labor,* defined by Arlie Hochschild in her book, *The Managed Heart,* as the act of expressing socially desired emotions during service transactions.[4] For instance, some jobs require service workers to act in a friendly fashion toward customers, whereas others require them to appear compassionate, sincere, or even self-effacing—emotions that can be conveyed through both facial expressions and gestures. The problem is that the employee may not feel such emotions. Trying to conform to customer expectations on these dimensions can prove to be a psychological burden for some service workers when they perceive themselves as having to act out emotions they do not feel. At worst, policies that impose such requirements raise troubling ethical questions about how far it is appropriate for organizations to control and shape the social aspects of work.[5]

Customer-contact employees comply with so-called display rules through both acting and the expression of spontaneous and genuine emotion.[6] Display rules generally reflect the norms imposed both by society—which may vary from one culture to another—and by specific occupations and organizations. For instance, our expectations for nurses are usually different from what we expect of bill collectors. Expectations may also reflect the nature of a particular encounter (what emotions would you expect a waiter to display if you discovered a cockroach in your water glass?). Surface acting requires employees to simulate emotions that they do not actually feel, accomplished by careful presentation of verbal and nonverbal cues, such as facial expression, gestures, and vocal tone. Within limits, such acting skills can be taught; some people are natural actors. Deep acting goes further; it involves trying to psych oneself into actually experiencing the desired emotion. One way to do this in a service context is to try to imagine how the customer is currently feeling. Under certain conditions, service providers may spontaneously experience the expected emotion without any need for acting, as when a firefighter feels sympathy for an injured child taken from a burning building.

HR managers need to be aware that performing emotional labor, day after day, can be stressful for employees as they strive to display toward customers feelings that may be false. From a marketing standpoint, however, failure to display the emotions that customers expect can be damaging and may lead to complaints that employees don't seem to care. The challenge for HR managers is to determine what customers expect, recruit the most suitable employees, and train them well. Grayson concludes that investment in such HR strategies—which can be quite expensive—is most worthwhile for service situations in which exchanges between employees and customers take place in the context of long-term relationships but less important when exchanges are simply discrete transactions in which the two parties are unlikely to encounter each other again.[7]

When service personnel have been exposed to traumatic events, such as injuries or death involving customers or coworkers, professional counseling may be needed to allow the workers to express their feelings and share them with others. Special training on how to handle such emotions is often offered to workers in such fields as policing, firefighting, and emergency medical care because of the frequency with which they are likely to be exposed to traumatic situations in the normal course of their jobs. Managers need to be aware of ongoing emotional stress and to devise ways of alleviating it (see Service Perspectives 15.1).

Job Design and Recruitment

The goal of job design is to study the requirements of the operation, the nature of customer desires, the needs and capabilities of employees, and the characteristics of operational equip-

SERVICE PERSPECTIVES 15.1

Reducing the Risks of Emotional Stress in a Hospital Emergency Unit

Consider for a moment what it must be like to work in a hospital emergency unit (EU) as you reflect on the comments of this young nurse, talking to a television reporter about a critically injured victim of a motor vehicle accident who has been treated in the EU at Boston's Beth Israel Hospital before being transferred to the intensive care unit—where he may or may not survive:

> There are some [patients] that affect you more than others . . . like this person. You don't know his name, you don't know his family . . . but you just wonder if there is someone out there waiting for him to come home. . . . As much as [the work] is task oriented, you can't take the human side out. . . . You never get used to that part!

Managers at Beth Israel recognize that such events are potentially damaging emotionally, so they have taken steps to minimize the risks for nurses working in the EU. Although the EU is among the most stressful areas for a nurse to work in, there is one advantage: Things change every minute. As the unit's nurse manager reported, "My staff leave here at the end of the worst day they could ever have and the next day it's totally different."

To give nurses some degree of control over their activities, each day they are offered the opportunity to choose in which of three different areas of the EU they would like to work—an acute treatment area, an intermediate area, and a triage position, which involves deciding whether an incoming patient needs immediate treatment (and if so, where) or can be asked to be seated and wait until medical staff are available to see them.

Another strategy to reduce stress involves encouraging the nursing staff to get involved in activities beyond direct patient care. "What made for burnout was no break from direct patient care, 40 hours a week, week in, week out," commented the nurse manager, who herself worked regularly in the EU when not involved in managerial activities and had noticed that staff who were involved in other unit projects complained less and were more satisfied with their work. "It's very important to channel some of your hours at work into other professional activities." As a result, almost every nurse in the unit is involved in some work-related area of interest in the course of the week, including a victims of violence committee, a patient education group, and quality assurance activities.

Source: Christopher Lovelock, *Product Plus: How Product + Service = Competitive Advantage* (New York: McGraw-Hill, 1994), 336–337.

ment to develop job descriptions that strike the best balance between these sometimes conflicting demands.

Recruiting the Right People for the Job

There's no such thing as the perfect, universal employee. First, some service jobs require prior qualifications, as opposed to giving employees the necessary training after they are hired. A school teacher can apply for a job as a hotel receptionist, but the reverse is not true unless the applicant has the necessary teaching credentials. Second, different positions—even within the same firm—are best filled by people with different styles and personalities. It helps to have an outgoing personality in many frontstage jobs that involve constantly meeting new customers; a shy, retiring person, by contrast, might be more comfortable working backstage and always dealing with the same people. Someone who loves to be physically on the go might do better as a restaurant server or courier than in a more sedentary job as a reservation agent or bank teller. Finally, as Levering and Moskowitz stress: "No company is perfect for everyone. This may be especially true in good places to work since these firms tend to have real character . . . their own culture. Companies with distinctive personalities tend to attract—and repel—certain types of individuals."[8]

Recruiting criteria should reflect the human dimensions of the job as well as the technical requirements. This brings us back to the notions of emotional labor and service as theater. The Walt Disney Company, which is in the entertainment business, actually uses the term *casting* and assesses prospective employees in terms of their potential for on-stage or backstage work. On-stage workers, known as *cast members,* are assigned to those roles for which their appearance, personalities, and skills provide the best match.

In trying to become more customer oriented, a number of service firms have put their frontstage employees through so-called charm schools, trying to create warmer, friendlier staff members who can relate better to customers. A related approach is to use a combination of control and incentives to obtain the desired behaviors. But HR managers have discovered that although good manners and the need to smile and make eye contact can be taught, warmth itself cannot. In fact, a cool and insincere smile may be worse than no smile at all. The only realistic solution is to change the organization's recruitment criteria to favor candidates with naturally warm personalities. As Jim Collins observes (in a follow-on from the chapter's opening quote), "The right people are those who would exhibit the desired behaviors anyway, as a natural extension of their character and attitude, regardless of any control and incentive system."[9]

What makes outstanding service performers so special? Often it's things that *cannot* be taught, qualities that are intrinsic to the people, qualities they would bring with them to any employer. As one study of high performers observed: "Energy . . . cannot be taught, it has to be hired. The same is true for charm, for detail orientation, for work ethic, for neatness. Some of these things can be enhanced with on-the-job training . . . or incentives. . . . But by and large, such qualities are instilled early on."[10]

The logical conclusion is that service businesses that are dependent on the human qualities of their frontstage service personnel should devote great care to attracting and hiring the right candidates. As part of this strategy, service firms should also review their recruitment advertising to capture the human challenges of the work instead of just emphasizing the technical aspects and the glamour (if any).

Recruitment Procedures and Criteria

A number of progressive companies have come to the conclusion that the selection process should start not with the candidate but with the individuals responsible for recruiting. In a sense, it is the recruiters who must ensure that new hiring decisions reflect and reinforce the company's distinctive culture. Consider the approach at Southwest Airlines, regularly rated as one of the best companies to work for in the United States.[11] Everyone hired to work in the airline's People Department—Southwest doesn't use the terms *human resources* or *personnel*—comes from a marketing or customer-contact background. This marketing orientation is displayed in internal research on job descriptions and selection criteria, whereby each department is asked, "What are you looking for?" rather than told, "This is what we think you need!" Southwest invites supervisors and peers (with whom future candidates will be working) to participate in the in-depth interviewing and selection process. More unusually, it invites its own frequent flyers to participate in the initial interviews for flight attendants and to tell candidates what they, the passengers, value. The People Department admits to being amazed at the enthusiasm with which these busy customers have greeted this invitation and at their willingness to devote time to this task.

Southwest's painstaking approach to interviewing continues to evolve in the light of experience; it's perhaps at its most innovative in the selection of flight attendants. A daylong visit to the company usually begins with applicants gathered in a group; recruiters watch how well they interact with each other (another chance for such observation will come at lunchtime). Because there are usually several job openings to be filled at once, it's possible that all (or none) of the applicants from any one group might be selected.

Then come a series of personal interviews. Each candidate has three one-on-one "behavioral-type" interviews during the course of the day. Based on input from current employees and supervisors in a given job category, interviewers target 8 to 10 dimensions for each position. For a flight attendant, these might include a willingness to take initiative, compassion, flexibility, sensitivity to people, sincerity, a customer service orientation, and a predisposition to be a team player. The interviewers then create questions of a situational nature to examine these characteristics in each applicant. The goal, as one interviewer explains, is to look at the applicant's past behaviors:

> A 20-year old applicant for flight attendant won't have any previous experience in that job. So instead of asking: "What would you do if . . . ?" which wouldn't be fair, we ask, "What did you do when . . . ?" The behavior is the issue, not the technical skills. So we ask about relevant experience at school, in part-time jobs, and with their families. Much the same is true for a mature woman returning to the workplace after bringing up a family. Being a mother and housewife can often provide great experience for working in a customer service position. By having them relive past experiences—say, how they reacted to an emergency or a threatening situation—we hear exactly what they did, we see the emotions, and so it's not a textbook answer. More than just "what did you do?" we also ask, "Why? What motivated you to do that?"[12]

Southwest describes the ideal interview as "a conversation" in which the goal is to make candidates comfortable. "The first interview of the day tends to be a bit stiff, the second is more comfortable, and by the third they tell us a whole lot more. It's really hard to fake it under those circumstances."[13] The three interviewers don't discuss candidates during the day but compare notes afterwards, which reduces the risk of bias. The People Department also invites participation in interviewing and selection from supervisors and from the peers with whom successful candidates will be working. In this way, existing employees buy into the recruitment process and feel a sense of responsibility for mentoring new recruits and helping them to become successful in the job (rather than wondering, as an interviewer put it, "who hired this turkey?").

If a good personality match is important, even more so is a good fit between personal and corporate values, especially at high levels in the organization. Consider this observation from Mitchell T. Rabkin, M.D., formerly president of Boston's Beth Israel Hospital (now Beth Israel Deaconess Medical Center):

> One of the things that I look for when we're recruiting is whether people are willing to "join the village." We tend to get two kinds of response when recruiting physician-scientists at a fairly high level: those who show they appreciate the characteristics of our "village" and are willing to join it, and those who only talk about the resources he or she will require to do the job.
>
> Medicine is a very giving kind of profession. We want people who are going to be nurturing it's tough to be sick, and when you are, you need some caring. There's a huge difference between looming large over the bed, looking at your watch, and saying "How ya doing today?" and sitting down nose to nose and asking how things have gone today. You may spend the same amount of time, but it's the difference between night and day.[14]

Challenges and Opportunities in Recruiting Workers for Technology-Based Jobs

Rapid developments in information technology are permitting service businesses to make radical improvements in business processes and even completely reengineer their operations.[15] These developments sometimes result in wrenching changes in the nature of work for existing employees. In instances where face-to-face contact has been replaced by use of the Internet or telephone-based services, firms have redefined and relocated jobs, created new employee profiles for recruiting purposes, and sought to hire employees with a different set of qualifications.

As a result of the growing shift from high-contact to low-contact services (for both the core product and for information-based supplementary services), a large and increasing number of customer contact employees work by telephone, never meeting customers face-to-face. At best, when well designed, such jobs can be very rewarding. At worst, they can place employees in an electronic equivalent of the old-fashioned sweatshop. Telemarketers are infamous for recruiting part-timers, giving them set scripts to read verbatim, and locating them in windowless warehouse or basement offices—often described as "boiler room" environments. As described in Service Perspectives 15.2, some of the keys to success in this area involve screening applicants to make sure they already know how to present themselves well on the telephone and have the potential to learn additional skills, training them carefully, and giving them a well-designed working environment.

SERVICE PERSPECTIVES 15.2

Recruiting Employees Who Work by Phone

BT is not only a major supplier of telecommunication services but also an active user of its own medium, the telephone, for managing relationships with its business accounts. Like a growing number of firms that do business by phone, it is very dependent for its success on being able to recruit and retain employees who are good at telephone-based transactions with customers whom they never see. Managers responsible for BT's telephone account management (TAM) operation, serving small-business customers, are highly selective in their recruitment efforts. They look for bright, self-confident people who can be trained to listen to customers' needs and use structured, probing questions to build a database of information on each of the 1,000 accounts for which an account manager is responsible.

BT begins its recruitment process with a telephone interview to see if candidates have the poise, maturity, and good speaking voice to project themselves well and inspire trust in a telephone-based job. (Curiously, most recruiters of telephone-based employees leave this all-important telephone test until much later in the process.) Those who pass this screen proceed to written tests and personal interviews.

Successful candidates receive intensive training. BT has built special training schools to create a consistent approach to customer care. Would-be account managers receive 13 weeks of training over a 12-month period, interspersed with live frontline experience at their home bases. They must develop in-depth knowledge of all the services and customer-premises equipment that BT sells as well as the skills needed to build relationships with customers and understand their business needs. Modern telecommunications technology is bewildering, for so much is changing so rapidly. Customers need a trusted adviser to act as consultant and problem solver. And it is this role that BT's TAM program has succeeded in filling. For all the impressive supporting technology, the program would fail without good people at the other end of the phone.

Source: Based on information in the case, "BT: Telephone Account Management," reproduced on pp. 615–624.

Another implication of technology is that it can help employees to work at a higher level. Expert systems can be used to leverage employees' skills to perform work that previously required higher qualifications, more extensive training, or simply years of experience. An expert system contains three elements: a knowledge base about a particular subject; an inference engine that mimics a human expert's reasoning to draw conclusions from facts and figures, solve problems, and answer questions; and a user interface that gathers information from—and gives it to—the person using the system.

Like human experts, such systems can give customized advice and may accept and handle incomplete and uncertain data. Some systems are designed to train novices by gradually enabling them to perform at higher levels. Many expert systems capture and make available to all the scarce expertise of outstanding performers. American Express uses a well-known expert system called Authorizer's Assistant (originally called Laura's Brain, after a star authorizer), which contains the expertise of its best credit authorizers. It has improved the quality and speed of credit decisions dramatically and contributed enormously to corporate profitability.[16]

Dealing with Tight Labor Markets. When employment is booming, service businesses find their recruitment options more restricted. The problem is often most severe for low-paid, low-skilled jobs in fields such as cleaning, food preparation, housekeeping in hotels and hospitals, and retailing. Although few of these jobs entail more than limited customer contact and many are backstage, failure to fill them with effective workers can lead to deterioration in overall service quality. Some firms have experience in hiring immigrants and individuals previously on welfare support, reflecting a management commitment to playing a broader social role. The Marriott hotel chain has been one of the leaders in this endeavor. For many service businesses, good economic times create tough recruitment, training, and retention problems as they try to transform mostly young, less educated people from diverse cultural backgrounds into effective performers who will remain with the organization and even grow with it.[17]

What are some of the actions taken by experienced employers to make lower-rung workers more productive and more likely to remain with the firm? Aramark, a major supplier of support services in areas such as food, facilities maintenance, and laundry, trains employees about not only specific job skills but also customer service and conflict resolution. Like many firms, it emphasizes English classes for immigrants to build their self-confidence and help them interact better with coworkers and customers. A number of employers assist immigrant employees to adjust to the unfamiliar U.S. or Canadian culture, including such issues as punctuality and personal hygiene. Some also get involved in helping those who are new to the job market to organize their personal lives better so that crises at home won't result in absenteeism. One hotel offers free bus service, one free meal a day, and subsidized on-site child care and helps new recruits search for subsidized housing.

Employee Retention. Marketing theory argues that successful relationships are built on mutually satisfying exchanges from which both customers and suppliers gain value. This same notion of value can be applied to any employee who has a choice of whether or not to work for a particular organization; the best employees usually do have opportunities to move on if dissatisfied.

The Concept of Exchange Applied to Employment

The net value of a job is the extent to which its benefits exceed its associated costs. The most obvious benefits are pay, health insurance, and pension funding. However, most jobs also generate other benefits. Some offer learning or experience-building opportunities; some positions provide deep satisfaction because they are inherently interesting or provide a sense of accomplishment; and still others provide companionship, a valued chance to meet other people, feelings of dignity and self-worth, opportunities to travel, and the chance to make a social contribution.

But working in any job has its costs, too, beginning with the time spent on the job and traveling to and from work. Most jobs also entail some monetary costs, ranging from special clothes to commuting and child care. Stress can be a psychological and physical cost in a demanding job. Unpleasant working conditions may involve exposure to noise, smells, and temperature extremes. And, of course, some jobs require intense physical or mental effort. It can be helpful for HR managers to view employees as customers who may leave if dissatisfied. Measuring employee satisfaction can help to identify what workers see as the benefits of their job and what they see as drawbacks.[18] Decisions to change the nature of the service operation frequently affect employees, too. The perceived value of their jobs may go up or down as a result. But not everybody has the same priorities and concerns—there is segmentation among employees as well as among customers. Part of the HR challenge is to match round pegs to round holes of the right diameter.

Frontstage service jobs add another dimension: frequent customer contact—sometimes but not always involving extended relationships with the same customers. Depending on the employee's personality, such encounters may be seen in the abstract as a benefit to enjoy or a cost to be borne. In reality, good training, good support, and satisfied customers should increase the pleasure (or diminish the pain), although the reverse will also be true.

Job design cannot be restricted just to ensuring that the firm gets its money's worth out of employees. It must also consider the design of the working environment and whether employees have the tools and facilities they need to deliver excellent service. Savvy HR managers know that if a job is changed through redesign, it will become more or less attractive to certain types of employees—and they can usually predict which ones. To an increasing degree, health and safety legislation is requiring changes in the workplace to eliminate physical and even psychological hazards, but only management can create a positive working climate—and that takes a long time. Reducing the negative aspects of the job and improving its positive ones may make it easier for firms to hire and retain the best available employees without having to pay premium salaries and load up on conventional benefits. Employees who enjoy their work are more likely than unhappy ones to give good service to customers.

In industrialized countries around the world, significant changes are taking place in the context of employment, relationships between employers and employees, and in the nature of jobs themselves.[19] Technology is radically changing the nature of some jobs, eliminating others, and creating new ones. Backstage service jobs and those based on telecommunication links, such as customer service centers, are being shifted to new geographic locations—sometimes even to a different country or a different continent. In the absence of legal protection afforded by an employee organization such as a union, the balance of power has shifted between employers and labor, with the former the beneficiaries. Under such circumstances, it is relatively easier for senior managers to take decisions that favor shareholders rather than employees, often in ways that should raise ethical concerns.

For many workers and managers, these broad environmental changes can lead to feelings of insecurity. Others, by contrast, may come to the conclusion that they are responsible for their own career paths and owe no loyalty to their present employers. The latter, it should be noted, are often the very employees whom firms should be trying to retain, either because they are ambitious and high-performing or because their skills are in short supply.

Employee Retention and Customer Retention

Researchers have found strong correlations between employees' attitudes and perceptions of service quality among customers of the same organization.[20] One retail banking study showed that when employees reported a strong service orientation imperative in the branch where they worked, customers reported that they received higher-quality service. A follow-up study determined that customer intentions to switch to a competitor could be predicted, based on employee perceptions of the quality of service delivered. It also found that employee turnover probabilities were predictable, based on customer perceptions of service quality. Simply put, where customers reported high service quality, employees were less likely to leave. A reasonable inference is that it is not very rewarding to work in an environment where service is poor and customers are dissatisfied. A study of a truck rental business found that higher levels of employee satisfaction were related to both lower turnover and lower worker's compensation claims.[21]

When jobs are low paid, boring, and repetitive, with minimal training, service is poor and turnover is high. Poor service generates high customer turnover, too, making the working environment even less rewarding. As a result, the firm spends all its resources trying to recruit both new customers and new employees. Loyal employees, by contrast, know the job and, in many cases, the customers, too. To the extent that long-term employees are customer oriented and knowledgeable and remain motivated, better service and higher customer retention should result.

Researchers have been able to document the economic value of both customer retention (see chapter 7) and employee retention.[22] Yet, many companies diminish their economic potential through HR strategies that are practically guaranteed to ensure high employee turnover.

Cycles of Failure, Mediocrity, and Success

All too often, bad working environments translate into dreadful service, with employees treating customers the way their managers treat them. Businesses with high employee turnover are frequently stuck in what has been termed the *cycle of failure*. Other organizations, which offer job security but little scope for personal initiative, may suffer from an equally undesirable *cycle of mediocrity*. However, there is potential for both vicious and virtuous cycles in service employment, with the latter being termed the *cycle of success*.[23]

The Cycle of Failure. In many service industries the search for productivity is on with a vengeance. One solution takes the form of simplifying work routines and hiring workers as cheaply as possible to perform repetitive tasks that require little or no training. Among consumer services, fast-food restaurants are often cited as examples of this problem (although it is not true for every chain). The cycle of failure captures the implications of such a strategy, with its two concentric but interactive cycles: one involving failures with employees and another, with customers (Figure 15.1).

The employee cycle of failure begins with a narrow design of jobs to accommodate low skill levels, emphasis on rules rather than service, and use of technology to control quality. A strategy of low wages is accompanied by minimal effort on selection or training. Consequences include bored employees who lack the ability to respond to customer problems, become dissatisfied, and develop a poor service attitude. Outcomes for the firm are low service quality and high employee turnover. Because of weak profit margins, the cycle repeats itself with hiring of more low-paid employees to work in this unrewarding atmosphere.

The customer cycle of failure begins with repeated emphasis on attracting new customers who become dissatisfied with employee performance and the lack of continuity implicit in continually changing faces. These customers fail to develop any loyalty to the supplier and turn over as rapidly as the staff, thus requiring an ongoing search for new customers to maintain sales volume. The departure of discontented customers is especially worrying in light of the potential greater profitability of a loyal customer base (see Chapter 5). For conscientious managers, it should be deeply disturbing to contemplate the social implications of an enormous pool of

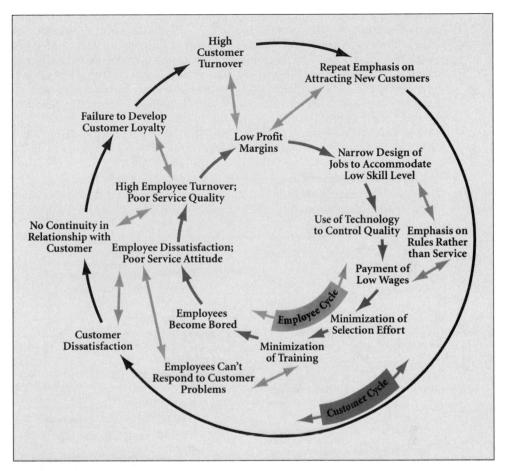

FIGURE 15.1 The Cycle of Failure
Source: Leonard L. Schlesinger and James L. Heskett, "Breaking the Cycle of Failure in Services," *Sloan Management Review* 31 (spring 1991): 17–28. Copyright © 1991 by Sloan Management Review Association. All rights reserved.

nomadic service employees moving from one low-paying employer to the next and experiencing a stream of personal failures in part because of the unwillingness of these employers to invest in efforts to break the cycle.

Managers have offered a veritable litany of excuses and justifications for perpetuating this cycle:

- "You just can't get good people nowadays."
- "People just don't want to work today."
- "To get good people would cost too much, and you can't pass on these cost increases to customers."
- "It's not worth training our frontline people when they leave you so quickly."
- "High turnover is simply an inevitable part of our business. You've got to learn to live with it."[24]

Too many managers make short-sighted assumptions about the financial implications of low-pay/high-turnover HR strategies. Part of the problem is failure to measure all relevant costs. Often omitted are three key cost variables: the cost of constant recruiting, hiring, and training (which is as much a time cost for managers as a financial cost); the lower productivity of inexperienced new workers; and the costs of attracting new customers (requiring extensive advertising and promotional discounts). Also ignored are two revenue variables: future revenue streams that might have continued for years but are lost when unhappy customers take their business elsewhere and potential income from prospective customers who are turned off by negative word-of-mouth. Finally, there are less easily quantifiable costs such as disruptions to service while a job remains unfilled and loss of the departing employee's knowledge of the business.

The Cycle of Mediocrity. Another vicious employment cycle is the cycle of mediocrity (Figure 15.2). It's most likely to be found in large, bureaucratic organizations—often typified by state monopolies, industrial cartels, or regulated oligopolies—where there is little incentive to

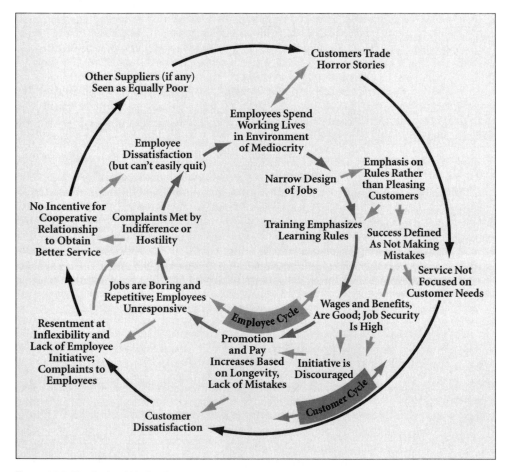

FIGURE 15.2 The Cycle of Mediocrity
Source: Christopher Lovelock, "Managing Services: The Human Factor" in *Understanding Service Management,* ed. W.J. Glynn and J.G. Barnes (Chichester: Wiley, 1995), 228.

improve performance and where fear of entrenched unions may discourage management from adopting more innovative labor practices.

In such environments (which today are in decline), service delivery standards tend to be prescribed by rigid rule books, oriented toward standardized service, operational efficiencies, and prevention of both employee fraud and favoritism toward specific customers. Employees often expect to spend their entire working lives with the organization. Job responsibilities tend to be narrowly and unimaginatively defined, tightly categorized by grade and scope of responsibilities, and further rigidified by union work rules. Salary increases and promotions are based on longevity, with successful performance in a job being measured by absence of mistakes rather than by high productivity or outstanding customer service. Training, such as it is, focuses on learning the rules and the technical aspects of the job, not on improving human interactions with customers and coworkers. Because there are minimal allowances for flexibility or employee initiative, jobs tend to be boring and repetitive. However, in contrast to cycle-of-failure jobs, most positions provide adequate pay and often good benefits, combined with high security— thus making employees reluctant to leave. This lack of mobility is compounded by an absence of marketable skills that would be valued by organizations in other fields of endeavor.

Customers find such organizations frustrating to deal with. Faced with bureaucratic hassles, lack of service flexibility, and unwillingness of employees to make an effort to serve them better on grounds such as "That's not my job," users of the service may become resentful. What happens when there is nowhere else for customers to go—either because the service provider holds a monopoly or because all other available players are perceived as being as bad or worse? We shouldn't be surprised if dissatisfied customers display hostility toward service employees who, feeling trapped in their jobs and powerless to improve the situation, protect themselves through such mechanisms as withdrawing into indifference, playing overtly by the rule book, or countering rudeness with rudeness. The net result? A vicious cycle of mediocrity in which unhappy customers continually complain to sullen employees (and also to other customers) about poor service and bad attitudes, generating ever greater defensiveness and lack of caring on the part of the staff. Under such circumstances, there is little incentive for customers to cooperate with the organization to achieve better service.

The Cycle of Success. Some firms reject the assumptions underlying the cycles of failure or mediocrity. Instead, they take a long-term view of financial performance, seeking to prosper by investing in their people in order to create a cycle of success (Figure 15.3). As with failure or mediocrity, success applies to both employees and customers. Broadened job designs are accompanied by training and empowerment practices that allow frontstage personnel to control quality. With more focused recruitment, more intensive training, and better wages, employees are likely to be happier in their work and to provide higher-quality, customer-pleasing service. Regular customers also appreciate the continuity in service relationships resulting from lower turnover and so are more likely to remain loyal. Profit margins tend to be higher, and the organization is free to focus its marketing efforts on reinforcing customer loyalty through customer retention strategies, which are usually much less costly to implement than strategies for attracting new customers.

Deregulation of many service industries and privatization of government corporations have often been instrumental in rescuing organizations from the cycle of mediocrity. In both the United States and Canada, formerly monopolistic regional telephone companies have been forced to adopt a more competitive stance. In many countries, once mediocre public corporations have undergone radical culture changes in the wake of privatization and exposure to a more competitive environment. A slimming down of the ranks (usually resulting in retention of the more dynamic and service-oriented employees), redefinition of performance criteria, intensive training,

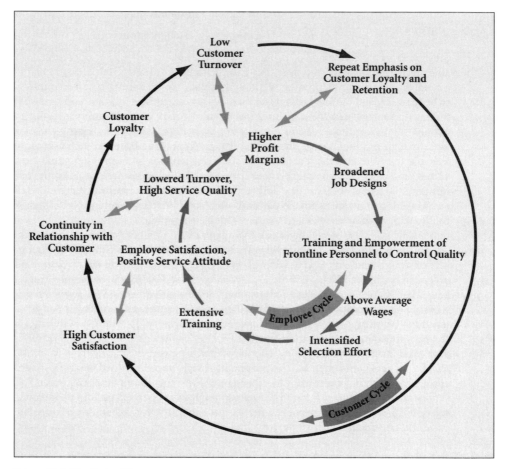

FIGURE 15.3 The Cycle of Success
Source: Leonard L. Schlesinger and James L. Heskett, "Breaking the Cycle of Failure in Services," *Sloan Management Review* 31 (spring 1991): 17–28. Copyright © 1991 by Sloan Management Review Association. All rights reserved.

and major reorganizations have created service firms that are much better placed to offer customers good service. In many parts of the world, such changes are currently in full swing.

Keeping People Challenged and Energized

Stressed and burned-out employees pose risks for any organization but especially when they are in frontstage service positions, where customers may be quick to sense dispirited feelings or a lack of energy, focus, and caring. What can an organization do to prevent burnout,—or cure it once it takes hold?

The insights of a physician–turned–chief executive of a major teaching hospital are perhaps a good place to start. Beth Israel's Dr. Rabkin has argued that burnout has less to do with hard work and more to do with powerlessness. It can come from working hard and seeing things that are incongruous and inappropriate and being unable to do anything about it. The first task in addressing and preventing burnout, he says, is to identify situations in which employees feel that way and to deal with those situations: "You need to encourage people to voice their concerns and questions, their suggestions for change, and to give good answers."[25]

Rabkin's views highlight the need for an organization-wide dialogue between management and employees, which may range from one-on-one discussions between employees and supervisors to a formalized feedback mechanism such as the Survey-Feedback-Action (SFA) program at Federal Express. Like many companies, FedEx has conducted a confidential, annual employee survey for many years that serves as a basis for airing concerns and resolving work-group problems. The survey consists of questions about pay, working conditions, views on senior management, feelings about the company, and the importance of quality in the work group. Employees are asked to agree or disagree with a series of statements, using a five-point scale ranging from "strongly agree" to "strongly disagree." Participation exceeds 99 percent. Scores are only reported for work groups, so no one knows the responses made by an individual employee. The first 10 questions on this survey (see Table 15.1) concern an employee's view of his or her manager. In turn, managers evaluate their own superiors. The percentage of favorable responses throughout the firm on these 10 items constitute what is known as the SFA Leadership Index.

Take a look at the statements in the SFA Leadership Index for a moment and consider how they relate to helping employees improve quality. At least 6 items concern the ease and content of communications between manager and employees (who might themselves be managers of other employees). The other items deal with behavior—both positive (helpfulness, respect) and negative (favoritism, interference). Although the concept may seem threatening at first, managers at FedEx and other companies using similar approaches state that they soon come to welcome the insights that these ratings, and follow-up discussions, provide.

Sometimes the problem of burnout is ascribed to people's staying too long in the same job. Providing ample opportunities to move internally within the company (subject to a certain minimum period in any position) is a way to keep people challenged and energized. Having hands-on managers and supervisors who believe in MBWA (management by wandering around) plays an important role in spotting employees who are unfulfilled in their present positions. Being short-tempered with customers (or other employees) is a common symptom, so supervisors need to be on the lookout for such employees and to encourage them to share their concerns and feelings about their jobs.

TABLE 15.1 *Survey Feedback Action Program: Components of Leadership Index*

1. I can tell my manager what I think.
2. My manager tells me what is expected.
3. Favoritism is not a problem in my work group.
4. My manager helps us to do our job better.
5. My manager listens to concerns.
6. My manager asks for my ideas about work.
7. My manager tells me when I do a good job.
8. My manager treats me with respect.
9. My manager keeps me informed.
10. My manager does not interfere.

Note: The above sentences paraphrase the actual wording used in compiling the Leadership Index. Employees were asked to review each statement carefully and then to express their agreement or disagreement with that statement on a 5-point scale.

Source: Christopher H. Lovelock, "Federal Express: Quality Improvement Program," exhibit 3 from case published by IMD, Lausanne, Switzerland, 1990. Courtesy of International Institute for Management Development.

Like many strong service performers, Southwest Airlines has a commitment to promotion from within; 80 percent of movement within the company is internal. The airline offers a one-day course entitled "Is Management for Me?" (which gives participants a good idea of what is entailed and helps reduce the risk of the Peter Principle: promoting people to their level of incompetence). Another course, "Career Directions," asks people to look into themselves and figure out what their strengths and weaknesses are. Helping people to recognize what they like and dislike about a job and how these factors relate to their own situations may lead to a career change or development of more positive feelings about an existing job.

Commenting on the positive changes they have seen in their years of studying employees and the workplace, Levering and Moskowitz include the rather surprising one of "more fun." They observe wisely that "having more fun is not inconsistent with operating a serious, profit-making business" and warn: "Watch out for companies where there is no sense of humor."[26] After all, humor often provides a way of alleviating boredom and defusing—or even preempting—stress. Humor may also help to build commitment, stimulate creativity, and enhance rapport with colleagues and customers.

Empowerment of Employees

How important is the much-advocated practice of empowering employees to use their own discretion to serve customers better?[27] Job designs should reflect the fact that service personnel may encounter customer requests for assistance at distant sites, often at short notice and even outside normal working hours. For instance, police officers, cable television installers, electricians, plumbers, and cleaners spend most of their time out in the community, often entering people's homes or workplaces. Under the right conditions, providing employees with greater discretion (and training in how to use their judgment) may enable them to provide superior service on the spot without referring to rule books or taking time to seek permission from higher authority. From a humanistic standpoint, the notion of encouraging employees to exercise initiative and discretion is an appealing one. Empowerment looks to the performer of the task to find solutions to service problems and to make appropriate decisions about customizing service delivery. It depends for its success on what is sometimes called *enablement*—giving workers the tools and resources they need to take on these new responsibilities.

Is Empowerment Always Appropriate?

Advocates claim that the empowerment approach is more likely to yield motivated employees and satisfied customers than the production-line alternative, in which management designs a relatively standardized system and expects workers to execute tasks within narrow guidelines. But is the choice between these two approaches really so obvious? The truth is that different situations may require different solutions.

As shown in Management Memo 15.1, a strategy of empowerment is most likely to be appropriate when certain factors are present within the organization and its environment. It's important to emphasize that not all employees are necessarily eager to be empowered. Many employees do not seek personal growth within their jobs and would prefer to work to specific directions rather than having to use their own initiative. Moreover, Chris Argyris warns that many employees have become cynical about the gap between the myth and the reality of empowerment. Most corporate talk of empowerment is lip service, he says. Many executives claim to be empowering their employees, but the latter find that they are either second-guessed or left out in the cold on big decisions.[28]

David Bowen and Edward Lawler suggest that different situations may require different solutions, declaring that "both the empowerment and production-line approaches have their

> ### MANAGEMENT MEMO 15.1
>
> ## Should You Empower Your Service Employees?
>
> Not every service business is an obvious candidate for employee empowerment. A strategy of empowerment tends to work best in service organizations that meet the following criteria:
>
> - The firm's business strategy is based on competitive differentiation and on offering personalized, customized service.
> - The approach to customers is based on extended relationships rather than on short-term transactions.
> - The organization uses technologies that are complex and nonroutine in nature.
> - The business environment is unpredictable, and surprises are to be expected.
> - Existing managers are comfortable with letting employees work independently for the benefit of both the organization and its customers.
> - Employees have a strong need to grow and deepen their skills in the work environment, are interested in working with others, and have good interpersonal and group process skills.
>
> *Source:* David E. Bowen and Edward E. Lawler III, "The Empowerment of Service Workers: What, Why, How and When," *Sloan Management Review* 32 (spring 1992): 32–39.

advantages . . . and . . . each fits certain situations. The key is to choose the management approach that best meets the needs of both employees and customers." The payoffs from greater empowerment, they argue, must be set against increased costs for selection and training, higher labor costs, slower service as customer-contact personnel devote more time to individual customers, and less consistency in service delivery. Bowen and Lawler also warn against being seduced into too great a focus on recovery at the expense of service delivery reliability, noting that "it is possible to confuse good service with inspiring stories about empowered employees excelling at the art of recovery."

Control versus Involvement. The production-line approach to managing people is based upon the well-established control model of organization design and management, with its clearly defined roles, top-down control systems, hierarchical pyramid structure, and assumption that management knows best. Empowerment, by contrast, is based upon the involvement (or commitment) model, which assumes that most employees can make good decisions—and produce good ideas for operating the business—if they are properly socialized, trained, and informed. It also assumes that employees can be internally motivated to perform effectively and that they are capable of self-control and self-direction. Although broad use of the term *empowerment* is relatively new, the underlying philosophy of employee involvement is not.

In the control model, four key features are concentrated at the top of the organization, although in the involvement model, by contrast, these features are pushed down through the organization:

1. Information about organizational performance (e.g., operating results and measures of competitive performance)
2. Rewards based on organizational performance (e.g., profit sharing and stock ownership)
3. Knowledge that enables employees to understand and contribute to organizational performance (e.g., problem-solving skills)
4. Power to make decisions that influence work procedures and organizational direction (e.g., through self-managing teams)

Levels of Employee Involvement. The empowerment and production-line approaches are at opposite ends of a spectrum that reflects increasing levels of employee involvement as additional knowledge, information, power, and rewards are pushed down to the frontline. Empowerment can take place at several levels:

- *Suggestion involvement* empowers employees to make recommendations through formalized programs, but their day-to-day work activities do not really change. McDonald's, often portrayed as an archetype of the production-line approach, listens closely to its frontline; innovations ranging from the Egg McMuffin to methods of wrapping burgers without leaving a thumbprint on the bun were invented by employees.
- *Job involvement* represents a dramatic opening up of job content. Jobs are redesigned to allow employees to use a wider array of skills. In complex service organizations such as airlines and hospitals, where individual employees cannot offer all facets of a service, job involvement is often accomplished through use of teams. To cope with the added demands accompanying this form of empowerment, employees require training, and supervisors need to be reoriented from directing the group to facilitating its performance in supportive ways.
- *High involvement* gives even the lowest-level employees a sense of involvement in the company's overall performance. Information is shared. Employees develop skills in teamwork, problem solving, and business operations, and they participate in work-unit management decisions. There is profit sharing and employee ownership of stock in the business.

For an illustration of a high-involvement company, see the Service Perspectives 15.3. Another example, this time in a professional services setting, is provided in the case study "R Cubed" (reproduced on pp. 678 to 687).

The Role of Unions

If innovations in the way that a firm's employees are organized and managed are to achieve their full potential, employee cooperation is often essential. The power of organized labor is widely cited as an excuse for not adopting new approaches in both service and manufacturing businesses. "We'd never get it past the unions," managers say, wringing their hands and muttering darkly about restrictive work practices. Unions are often portrayed as villains in the press, especially when high-profile strikes inconvenience millions.

Many managers seem to be rather antagonistic toward unions. Jeffrey Pfeffer has observed wryly that "the subject of unions and collective bargaining is . . . one that causes otherwise sensible people to lose their objectivity."[29] He urges a pragmatic approach to this issue, emphasizing that "the effects of unions depend very much on what *management* does." The higher wages, lower turnover, clearly established grievance procedures, and improved working conditions often found in highly unionized organizations may yield positive benefits in a well-managed service organization where there is mutual respect between management and other employees. From a marketing perspective, greater experience on the job and long-term familiarity with customers may help to boost productivity and quality, as well as cementing customer loyalty. We need to be careful to avoid stereotyping unions in the mold of militantly antagonistic environments where extreme demarcation of job responsibilities leads to slow, surly, and unresponsive service for customers, punctuated by frequent work stoppages. That's an outdated and unhelpful perspective in most countries today.

Many of the world's most successful service businesses are, in fact, highly unionized. The inescapable conclusion is that the presence of unions in a service company is not an automatic barrier to high performance and innovation unless there is a long history of mistrust, acrimo-

Empowerment Based on Values

AES Corporation operates electricity-generating plants around the world. It was founded in 1981 by its current chairman and CEO, respectively Roger Sant and Dennis Bakke, who firmly believe that empowerment must go beyond technique and strategy to include values. They sought to build a company that "embodied the four principles that we felt mattered in any kind of community, be it a business, church, village, or whatever: fairness, integrity, social responsibility, and fun." Sant and Bakke want AES to be a fun place to work, but not just in terms of parties: "It's fun because the people who work here are fully engaged. They have total responsibility for decisions. They are accountable for results."

AES has grown fast and is now a large company. Much of the growth has been through acquisition. Marketing often takes the form of bidding for large-scale, long-term electricity supply contracts. By 1999, AES had some ninety electricity plants in 33 countries and employed 40,000 people. But the founders have avoided the temptation to add hierarchical layers of management ("The more authority figures you have above you, the more likely it is that you won't make decisions yourself."). Instead, the company is organized around a series of small teams. Bakke describes the firm's structure and practices as being like an ecosystem: "Everything about how we organize gives people the power and the responsibility to make important decisions, to engage with their work as businesspeople, not as cogs in a machine." There is no corporate HR department—plants do their own hiring, and there is upward mobility into senior positions. Within each plant, the manager oversees a number of teams containing a team leader and between 5 to 20 team members, responsible for a particular area of activity such as the control room, water treatment, or fuel. Unlike most of the industrial world, where responsibility for operations is separated from maintenance, AES is moving toward having each team responsible for both activities within its area of responsibility. Bakke says, "We want people to take ownership of the whole—the way you care about your house. You run it, you keep it up, you fix it. When something goes wrong, you own the problem from start to finish. And nobody has to tell you to do it, because the responsibility is all yours—operating and maintaining."

To make empowerment work, AES believes in information sharing, accountability, and a willingness to be supportive and forgiving about initial mistakes. Compensation includes the potential for significant bonuses. The founders see sharing of information as essential for success. All financial and market information is widely circulated (in fact, for Securities and Exchange Commission [SEC] purposes, every employee is considered an insider from the standpoint of stock trading). Although serious mistakes are penalized financially, there are none for first-time mistakes that do not have serious consequences and that are made as people learn. It's part of AES values to accept mistakes as long as people own up to them. Safety failures, however, are treated as more than just an individual responsibility. At some plants, one accident means a 25 percent reduction in everybody's bonus; two accidents means a 50 percent cut, and by the third, there's no bonus for anyone.

Despite predictions that the AES way of doing things wouldn't work outside the United States, the firm has successfully exported its emphasis on empowerment to numerous other countries. However, Sant concedes that people from some cultures may take longer to trust AES leaders and the AES approach, as well as to trust themselves to take responsibility.

Source: Suzy Wetlaufer, "Organizing for Empowerment: An Interview with AES' Roger Sant and Dennis Bakke," *Harvard Business Review* 77 (January–February 1999).

nious relationships, and confrontation. However, management cannot rule by fiat: Consultation and negotiation with union representatives are essential if employees are to accept new ideas (conditions that are equally valid in nonunionized firms, too).

HR Management in a Multicultural Context

The trend toward a global economy means that more and more service firms are operating across national frontiers (see Chapter 17). Other important trends are increased tourism and business travel plus substantial immigration of people from different cultural backgrounds into developed economies. The net result is pressure on service organizations to serve a more diverse array of customers—with different cultural expectations and speaking a variety of languages— and to recruit a more diverse workforce.

Striking a balance between diversity and conformity to common standards is not a simple task because societal norms vary across cultures. When McDonald's opened a fast-food restaurant in Moscow, management trained staff members to smile at customers. However, this particular norm did not exist in Russia, and some patrons concluded that staff members were making fun of them! Another example of how transferring U.S. standards to European operations may run into cultural conflicts comes from the troubled early history of Euro Disney (see the case, "Euro Disney: An American in Paris," pp. 602 to 614.)

Part of the HR management challenge as it relates to culture is to determine which performance standards are central and which should be treated more flexibly. For instance, some public service agencies that require employees to wear uniforms have been willing to allow Sikh employees to wear a matching-color turban with badge. But others have generated conflict by insisting on use of traditional uniform caps. Multiculturalism may also require new HR management procedures. Thus, the decision to be more responsive to customers (and even employees) whose first language is not English may require changes in recruiting criteria, use of role-playing exercises, and language training.

Conclusion

Successful service organizations are committed to effective management of human resources, including recruitment, selection, training, and retention of employees. They recognize that the quality of personal service encounters plays an important role in creating customer satisfaction and competitive advantage.

It's probably harder to duplicate high-performance human assets than any other corporate resource. To the extent that employees understand and support the goals of an organization, have the skills needed to succeed in performing their jobs, work well together in teams, recognize the importance of ensuring customer satisfaction, and have the authority and self-confidence to use their own initiative in problem solving, the marketing and operational functions should actually be easier to manage. In the following chapter, we examine the leadership task of integrating marketing, operations, and human resources in a strategic partnership.

STUDY QUESTIONS

1. List five ways in which investment in hiring and selection, training, and ongoing motivation of employees will pay dividends in customer satisfaction for such organizations as (a) an airline, (b) a hospital, and (c) a restaurant.

2. Define what is meant by the *control and involvement models* of management.
3. What is emotional labor? Explain the ways in which it may cause stress for employees in specific jobs. Illustrate with suitable examples.
4. Identify the factors favoring a strategy of employee empowerment.
5. What is the distinction between empowerment and enablement? Can you have one without the other?
6. Highlight specific ways in which technology—particularly information technology (IT)—is changing the nature of service jobs. Provide examples of situations in which use of IT is likely to (a) enhance and (b) detract from employee job satisfaction.
7. What can a marketing perspective bring to the practice of HR management?
8. What important ethical issues do you see facing HR managers in high-contact service organizations?

APPLICATION EXERCISES

1. An airline runs a recruiting advertisement for cabin crew that shows a picture of a small boy sitting in an airline seat and clutching a teddy bear. The headline reads: "His mom told him not to talk to strangers. So what's he having for lunch?" Describe the types of personalities that you think would be (a) attracted to apply for the job by that ad and (b) discouraged from applying.
2. Consider the following jobs: emergency ward nurse, bill collector, computer repair technician, supermarket cashier, dentist, flight attendant, kindergarten teacher, prosecuting attorney, minister officiating at a baptism, police officer on highway patrol, server in a family restaurant, server in an expensive French restaurant, stockbroker, undertaker. What type of emotions would you expect each of them to display to customers in the course of doing their job? What drives your expectations?

ENDNOTES

1. Hal E. Rosenbluth, *The Customer Comes Second* (New York: William Morrow, 1992), 25.
2. David E. Bowen, and Benjamin Schneider, "Boundary-Spanning Role Employees and the Service Encounter: Some Guidelines for Management and Research," in *The Service Encounter,* ed. J. A. Czepiel, M. R. Solomon, and C. F. Surprenant (Lexington, MA: Lexington Books, 1985), 127–148.
3. David A. Tansik, "Managing Human Resource Issues for High Contact Service Personnel," in *Service Management Effectiveness,* ed. D. E. Bowen, R. B. Chase, T. G. Cummings, and associates (San Francisco: Jossey-Bass, 1990), 152–176.
4. Arlie R. Hochschild, *The Managed Heart: Commercialization of Human Feeling* (Berkeley: University of California Press, 1983).
5. Robin Leidner, "Emotional Labor in Service Work," in R. J. Steinerg and D. M. Figart. *Emotional Labor in the Service Economy. The Annals of the American Academy of Political and Social Science,* January 1999, 81–95.
6. Blake E. Ashforth and Ronald W. Humphrey, "Emotional Labor in Service Roles: The Influence of Identity," *Academy of Management Review* 18, no. 1 (1993): 88–115.
7. Kent Grayson, "Customer Responses to Emotional Labour in Discrete and Relational Service Exchange," *International Journal of Service Industry Management* 9, no. 2 (1998): 126–154.
8. Robert Levering and Milton Moskowitz, *The 100 Best Companies to Work for in America* (New York: Currency/Doubleday, 1993), xvii.
9. Jim Collins, "Turning Goals into Results,: The Power of Catalytic Mechanisms," *Harvard Business Review* 77 (July–August 1999): 77.
10. Bill Fromm and Len Schlesinger, *The Real Heroes of Business* (New York: Currency Doubleday, 1994), 315–316.

11. Robert Levering and Milton Moskowitz, "The 100 Best Companies to Work for in America," *Fortune,* January 10, 2000, 82–110.

12. Christopher Lovelock, *Product Plus: How Product + Service = Competitive Advantage* (New York: McGraw-Hill, 1994), 325–326.

13. Ibid., 326.

14. Ibid., 323.

15. Thomas H. Davenport, *Process Innovation: Reengineering Work through Information Technology* (Boston: Harvard Business School Press, 1993).

16. Rajendra Sisodia, "Expert Marketing with Expert Systems," *Marketing Management,* spring 1992, 32–47.

17. Catherine Yang et al., "Low-Wage Lessons," *Business Week,* November 11, 1996, 108–116.

18. Roland T. Rust, Greg L. Stewart, Heather Miller, and Debbie Pielack, "The Satisfaction and Retention of Frontline Employees: A Customer Satisfaction Measurement Approach," *International Journal of Service Industry Management* 7, no. 5 (1996): 62–80.

19. Joel Bonamy and Nicole May, "Service and Employment Relations," *The Service Industries Journal* 17, no. 4 (1997): 544–563.

20. This research is summarized in Benjamin Schneider and David E. Bowen, *Winning the Service Game* (Boston, Harvard Business School Press, 1995); and Benjamin Schneider, Susan S. White, and Michelle C. Paul, "Linking Service Climate and Customer Perceptions of Service Quality: Test of a Causal Model," *Journal of Applied Psychology* 83, no. 2 (1998): 150–163.

21. Schneider, Benjamin, "HRM—A Service Perspective: Towards a Customer-Focused HRM?" *International Journal of Service Industry Management* 5 , no. 1 (1994): 64–76.

22. James L. Heskett, W. Earl Sasser Jr., and Leonard A. Schlesinger, *The Service Profit Chain* (New York: The Free Press, 1997).

23. The terms *cycle of failure* and *cycle of success* were coined by Leonard L. Schlesinger and James L. Heskett, "Breaking the Cycle of Failure in Services," *Sloan Management Review* (spring 1991): 17–28. The term *cycle of mediocrity* comes from Christopher H. Lovelock, "Managing Services: The Human Factor," in *Understanding Services Management,* ed. W. J. Glynn and J. G. Barnes (Chichester, UK: John Wiley & Sons, 1995), 228.

24. Schlesinger and Heskett, "Breaking the Cycle."

25. Lovelock, *Product Plus,* 335.

26. Levering and Moskowitz, "The 100 Best Companies," 1993, xiii.

27. Parts of this section are closely based on David E. Bowen and Edward E. Lawler III, "The Empowerment of Service Workers: What, Why, How and When," *Sloan Management Review* 32 (spring 1992): 32–39.

28. Chris Argyris, "Empowerment: The Emperor's New Clothes," *Harvard Business Review* 76 (May–June 1998).

29. Jeffrey Pfeffer, *Competitive Advantage through People* (Boston: Harvard Business School Press, 1994), 160.

30. Lovelock, *Product Plus,* chap. 19.

CHAPTER 16

Organizing for Service Leadership

Marketing is so basic that it cannot be considered a separate function. . . . It is the whole business seen from the point of view of its final result, that is, from the customer's point of view. Concern and responsibility for marketing must, therefore, permeate all areas of the enterprise.

PETER DRUCKER

The increasingly fast-moving and competitive environment we will face in the twenty-first century demands more leadership from more people to make enterprises prosper.

JOHN P. KOTTER

What comes to mind when you hear the term *service leadership?* Do you think of market leadership, focusing on those companies that are viewed as front-runners in a particular service industry? Alternatively, do you associate leadership with individuals, thinking of the role of the chief executive in guiding the organization or of leadership positions at different levels in a service business, right down to that of someone leading a team and motivating its members to provide good service to customers?

In practice, service leadership embraces both perspectives. Realistically, it's very difficult for a firm to achieve and maintain leadership in an industry if it lacks human leaders who can articulate a vision and help to bring it about—whether it emphasizes setting the standards for service quality, initiating important innovations, using new technologies for competitive advantage, defining the terms on which other companies seek to compete, or creating an outstanding place to work.

This chapter recognizes that marketing activities in service organizations extend beyond the responsibilities assigned to a traditional marketing department. We examine the challenging task of leading a market-oriented service business and raise such questions as

1. What is the distinction between being market oriented and customer led?
2. What actions are required to move a service firm from a reactive position of merely being available for service toward the status of world-class service delivery?
3. To what extent are the marketing, operations, and human resource management functions interdependent in service organizations?
4. What are the causes of interfunctional tensions, and how can they be avoided?
5. How does leading differ from managing?

Marketing's Role in the Service Firm

Many Canadian engineers wear an iron ring on the little finger of their working hand. This ring is presented to engineering graduates when they participate in what is known as the Ceremony of the Calling of an Engineer, during which they commit themselves to high standards of integrity in their professional careers. Legend has it that the metal for these rings originally came from the wreckage of the Quebec Bridge, which collapsed into the St. Lawrence River in 1909 with the loss of 75 lives. It remains the worst bridge construction disaster in history. A subsequent inquiry blamed the collapse on structural design flaws and shortcomings in construction. By wearing a memento of that calamitous event—or so the legend goes—engineers would add humility to the pride they felt in their profession.

Marketing as a Bridging Function

Marketers like to be thought of as professionals, too. Part of their role is to serve as social engineers, shaping behavior and building relationships. In a company with a strong customer focus, marketers build numerous relationship bridges to link the businesses for which they work to the customers who use the firm's services. How many customer relationships, one wonders, collapse because marketers fail to do a good job of designing, constructing, and maintaining them? But we need to take our bridge analogy one step further, seeing the marketing function itself as a bridge that links the entire organization to the markets in which it competes. Unless this link is well designed, maintained in good working order, and open to free-flowing traffic in both directions, the firm will lose touch with the marketplace.

In earlier chapters, we have seen that customers are closely involved in the creation and delivery of many services, sometimes to the extent of actually participating in production. Customers' satisfaction with a service may be conditioned as much by the processes in which they are involved—including interactions with operating systems, service employees, and even other customers—as by the outcome of those processes. So, unlike the situation that often prevails in manufacturing (especially production of consumer packaged goods), the marketing function in services cannot easily be separated from other management activities without damage to the latter's effectiveness. After all, any action involving or affecting customers has marketing implications.

Evert Gummesson has long emphasized that the work of the traditional marketing department embraces only a small portion of the overall marketing function in a service business—a point also stressed by Christian Grönroos.[1] More recently, Gummesson notes the move to *network organizations* and what is sometimes called the *virtual corporation*, in which functional boundaries are fuzzy around a core competence and relationships are highly flexible.[2] These networks, of course, extend to more than just customers; they also include suppliers, intermediaries, and other partners with whom the service firm needs to work. Organizational structures are starting to move away from the traditional hierarchical model, requiring leadership to be exercised in new ways. In fact, the traditional organization chart really tells us very little about the nature of a service business and the role that different management functions should play. For a creative look at visual ways of capturing what an organization does, how it works, and the manner in which it relates to customers, see the reading by Henry Mintzberg and Ludo Van der Heyden, "Organigraphs: Drawing How Companies Really Work," on pp. 564 to 573.

Customer-Led versus Market-Oriented Philosophies of Management

Is it possible for a firm to be too focused on its current customers? Although the pursuit of customer satisfaction is very important, there may be limits as to how far a firm should allow itself to be led by its customers, especially during times of rapid change. In their analysis of the impact of disruptive technologies on industry evolution, Christensen and Bower conclude that "firms lose their position of industry leadership . . . because they listen too carefully to their customers."[3]

According to Slater and Narver, there is a fundamental distinction between a firm that is customer led and one that is market oriented.[4] Customer-led businesses, these researchers argue, focus on understanding the expressed desires of customers in their currently served markets. They use focus groups and customer surveys to enhance the firm's understanding of customer wants and their perceptions of current services as well as techniques such as conjoint analysis and concept testing to guide the development of new services (examples of which were discussed in chapter 8). This approach may work well in a relatively stable environment, but is risky in a more turbulent one because it leads managers to see the world only through their current customers' eyes. Another problem is that efforts to measure customer satisfaction can easily overwhelm other strategic performance indicators. If that happens and improving customer satisfaction is allowed to become the over-riding goal, then management is likely to focus only on short-term incremental improvements to current products and processes.

Market-oriented businesses go further, being committed to understanding both the expressed and latent needs of their customers as well as the capabilities and plans of their competitors. Compared to customer-led businesses, market-oriented firms scan the market more broadly and have a longer-term focus. They combine traditional research methods with other techniques, notably continuous experimentation and observation of customers' behavior before, during, and after service delivery. They also work closely with lead users, not just with large customers whose purchases are important to the existing business. Lead users—who may even be prospects rather than current customers—have more advanced needs than most existing customers and expect to benefit significantly from a solution to those needs. As Slater and Narver observe, "A true lead user should be a window into the future and not an anchor in the past."

To be a service leader, therefore, it's not enough for a firm to have good relations with its existing customers. Top management must charge marketers with maintaining a bridge to the broader marketplace and enabling a free flow of information and insights about customer behavior, competitive activity, new technologies, and market evolution. Service leadership involves creating a climate in which curiosity, experimentation, and risk taking are supported rather than frowned upon. It also requires provision of the financial support needed for ongoing experimentation.

Consider the evolution of ski resorts. The original ski slopes consisted of a base lodge plus machinery that operated simple tows or chairlifts to transport skiers up the mountain. Later, accommodations were added, and some people built cabins nearby, and thus the ski slope became a place to stay for several days (or more) rather just than a day excursion for those

Creating a Formula for Success in Ski Resorts

Soaring high in the Coast Mountain range of British Columbia, Whistler/Blackcomb ski resort receives an average of some thirty feet (9 meters) of snow each year and claims to offer the longest ski season and largest skiable terrain in North America. The twin mountains are owned by Vancouver-based Intrawest Corporation, whose other ski properties include Mammoth in California, Copper Mountain in Colorado, Stratton in Vermont, and Tremblant in Quebec, to name a few.

Whistler/Blackcomb, located 75 miles (120 km) northeast of Vancouver, offers the greatest vertical drop of any ski mountain in North America—no less than one mile (1,600 meters). Day trippers from Vancouver and its suburbs have long ceased to be Whistler/Blackcomb's only source of business—although the resort still courts their loyalty with big savings on season passes. By creating a major destination resort, Intrawest has been able to appeal to vacationers from across the continent and even overseas. Whistler's appeal is evident from the fact that it has been named the number one ski resort on the North American continent by three different ski magazines. Intrawest's management believes that it has created a formula for success that can be transferred to other ski resorts.

Their multistep process begins with enhancing the skiing experience on each mountain. To keep skiers loyal, the experience on the slopes must be a good one, requiring a choice of well-maintained terrain that will satisfy skiers from beginners to experts plus sufficient lift capacity to avoid lengthy delays. The second step is to build an attractive and animated resort community so that people will want to stay longer. After all, for many people, après-ski activities are part of the appeal of a skiing vacation! Satisfied skiers not only start coming back more often but also tell their friends and spend more money. In turn, higher patronage justifies the third step, which is construction of more lodging and additional attractions, drawing yet more people to the resort which now, in the fourth stage, sees expansion of year-round facilities, thus maximizing the use of shops, hotels, convention facilities, and restaurants. By this point, the resort is appealing to nonskiers as well.

The purchase of a condominium or chalet at a resort tends to bring owners back more often throughout the year—even when there is no snow. After all, the mountains are lovely in summer and fall as well as in winter and early spring when there is snow on the slopes. And the resort operators can also manage properties on behalf of their owners, who derive income from renting to other visitors.

Maintaining the quality of a ski resort requires ongoing investment. Thanks to inexpensive airfares, skiers can choose between many different resorts for their vacations, and their expectations—which have been rising in recent years—tend to be shaped by the best facilities they have experienced, heard about from their friends, seen on television, or read about in magazines. In 1997, Intrawest spent $16 million to improve facilities at Whistler/Blackcomb. Investments included replacing old chairlifts by new express "quads." This action was intended to improve reliability, reduce waiting times, and increase lift capacity. A wide range of new trails was opened at Blackcomb. Recognizing the growing popularity of snowboarding, the company also purchased a new Pipe Dragon, a unique machine used to shape and groom snowboard half-pipes. Other investments included the purchase of new snow cats for trail grooming and upgrades to snow-making equipment to ensure good skiing conditions, even on days when Mother Nature is not cooperative. To appeal to summer visitors, investments were also being made in an expanded trail system for the Whistler Mountain Bike Park.

Finally, recognizing the importance of attracting and retaining loyal employees—who form an important element in creating visitor satisfaction—the company made plans for constructing numerous units of employee housing at the resort.

Source: Based on information in *Intrawest Annual Report 1997* and *Whistler Resort: 1997–98 Winter Ski Season* (Vancouver, BC: Intrawest Corporation, 1998), plus additional information from www.intrawest.com, January 2000.

within driving distance. However, the snow doesn't last all year and is not always guaranteed, so the facilities remained idle for perhaps 70 percent of the year. Nevertheless, some people returned in the summer or fall to enjoy the mountains under very different conditions. Noticing this, some ski operators started developing summer activities on and around the mountain as well as developing real estate in the vicinity. Today the best-known ski slopes have been transformed into year-round resorts, offering a wide array of activities that even draw nonskiers in midwinter.

Take a moment to review the information in Service Perspectives 16.1 about Intrawest Corporation, one of the North American leaders in the skiing industry, and ask yourself how much of its strategy is likely to have been based on satisfaction surveys of existing skiers and how much may have resulted from observation of lead users and evaluation of mountain resort communities in Europe, where skiing centers often grew up around existing villages.

Changing Relationships between Marketing, Operations, and Human Resources

One of the challenges facing senior managers in any type of organization is to avoid what are sometimes referred to as "functional silos" in which each function exists in isolation from the others, jealously guarding its independence. Functionalism based on specialization in specific task areas represents a long tradition in business. But as the list of service management challenges presented earlier suggests, the three functions of marketing, operations, and human resources need to work closely together if a service organization is to be responsive to its different stakeholders. In short, compartmentalizing management functions or subjugating one function to another is not an appropriate way to organize a modern service firm.

Using the concept of what they call the Service Profit Chain, Heskett et al. lay out a series of causal links in achieving success in service businesses.[5] These links are summarized in Table 16.1. (For more detail, see the reading, "Putting the Service Profit Chain to Work," on pp. 574 to 584.)

In a subsequent book, Heskett, Sasser, and Schlesinger cite several leadership behaviors that are critical to managing the different links in the service profit chain.[6] Some behaviors relate to employees (links 4–7) and include spending time on the frontline, investing in the development of promising managers, and supporting the design of jobs that offer greater latitude for employees; also included in this category is promoting the notion that paying higher wages actually reduces labor costs after reduced turnover, higher productivity, and higher quality are taken into account. Another set of service leadership behaviors focus on customers (links 1–3) and include

TABLE 16.1 *Causal Links in the Service Profit Chain*

1. Customer loyalty drives profitability and growth
2. Customer satisfaction drives customer loyalty
3. Value drives customer satisfaction
4. Employee productivity drives value
5. Employee loyalty drives productivity
6. Employee satisfaction drives loyalty
7. Internal quality drives employee satisfaction
8. Top management leadership underlies the chain's success

Source: James L. Heskett, Thomas O. Jones, Gary W. Loveman, W. Earl Sasser Jr., and Leonard A. Schlesinger "Putting the Service-Profit Chain to Work." *Harvard Business Review,* 7, March–April, 1994, 164–174.

an emphasis on identifying and understanding customer needs, investments to ensure customer retention, and a commitment to adopting new performance measures that track such variables as satisfaction and loyalty among both customers and employees.

These themes and relationships illustrate the mutual dependency that exists among marketing, operations, and human resources. Although managers within each function may have specific responsibilities, strategic planning and the execution of specific tasks must be well coordinated. Responsibility for the tasks assigned to each function may be present entirely within one firm or distributed between the originating service organization and its subcontractors, who must work in close partnership if the desired results are to be achieved. Although other functions, such as accounting or finance, are central to the effective functioning of a service business, they present less need for close integration because of their lesser involvement in the ongoing processes of service creation and delivery.

The Marketing Function

Production and consumption are usually clearly separated in manufacturing firms. In most instances, a physical good is produced in a factory in one geographic location, shipped to a retailer or other intermediary for sale in a different location, and consumed or used by the customer in a third location. As a result, it's not normally necessary for production personnel to have direct involvement with customers, especially for consumer goods. In such firms, marketing acts to link producers and consumers, providing the manufacturing division with guidelines for product specifications that reflect consumer needs as well as projections of market demand, information on competitive activity, and feedback on performance in the marketplace. In this linking role, marketing also works with logistics and transportation specialists to develop strategies for distributing the product to prospective purchasers.

In service firms, things are different. Many service operations—especially those involved in delivering services that require the customer's presence throughout service delivery—are literally "factories in the field" that customers enter at the specific time that they need the service. In a large chain (such as hotels, fast-food restaurants, or car rental agencies), the company's service delivery sites may be located across a country, a continent, or even the entire world. When customers are actively involved in production and the service output is consumed as it is produced, there has to be direct contact between production (operations) and consumers. Even when customers are not involved in production—as in the case of cleaning or repair and maintenance—they may still have close relationships with those who do the work. Dropping off your car for repair, for instance, often involves a discussion about what seems to be wrong and what the symptoms are. On returning to collect the car, you may want to talk with a mechanic to learn what caused the problem, how it has been fixed, and how to avoid the risk that it could happen again. In some instances, of course, there's no contact with personnel because customers are expected to serve themselves independently or communicate through more impersonal media such as mail, fax, or Web sites.

How should marketing relate to operations and human resources in frontstage service delivery environments? In manufacturing firms, marketers assume full responsibility for the product once it leaves the production line, often working closely with channel intermediaries such as retailers. In many services, by contrast, operations management is responsible for running service distribution systems, including retail outlets. Moreover, contact between operations personnel and customers is the rule rather than the exception—although the extent of this contact varies according to the nature of the service, with many employees working backstage and never encountering end users. Yet there remains a need in service businesses for a strong, efficient marketing organization to perform the following tasks:

- Evaluate and select the market segments to serve.
- Research customer needs and preferences within each segment.
- Monitor competitive offerings, identifying their principal characteristics, quality levels, and the strategies used to bring them to market.
- Design the core product, tailor its characteristics to the needs of chosen market segments, and ensure that they match or exceed those of competitive offerings.
- Select and establish service levels for supplementary elements needed to enhance the value and appeal of the core product or to facilitate its purchase and use.
- Participate with operations in designing the entire service process to ensure that it is user-friendly and reflects customer needs and preferences.
- Set prices that reflect costs, competitive strategies, and consumer sensitivity to different price levels.
- Tailor location and scheduling of service availability to customers' needs and preferences.
- Develop communications strategies, using appropriate media to transmit messages informing prospective customers about the service and promoting its advantages.
- Develop performance standards for establishing and measuring service quality levels.
- Ensure that all customer-contact personnel—whether they work for operations, marketing, or an intermediary—understand the firm's desired market position and customer expectations of their own performance.
- Create programs for rewarding and reinforcing customer loyalty.
- Conduct research to evaluate customer satisfaction following service delivery and identify any aspects requiring changes or improvements.

The net result of these requirements is that the marketing function in service businesses is closely interrelated with—and dependent on—the procedures, personnel, and facilities managed by the operations function as well as on the quality of the service personnel recruited and trained by the HR function. To a greater degree than in manufacturing, the marketing, operations, and HR functions must work together day-to-day. Although initially seen as a poor sister by many operations managers, marketing has now acquired significant management clout in many service businesses, with important implications for strategy, organizational design, and assignment of responsibilities. Human resources, too, is taking on a more strategic role.

The Operations Function

Although marketing's profile has risen, the operations function still dominates line management in most service businesses. This is hardly surprising because operations—typically the largest area of activity within the firm—remains responsible for most of the processes involved in creating and delivering the service product. Operations managers are responsible not only for equipment, technology, and backstage procedures but also for company-owned retail outlets and other customer facilities. In high-contact services, operations managers may direct the work of large numbers of employees, including many who serve customers directly. In technology-driven firms, operations managers take primary responsibility for the technological infrastructure and interface with research and development specialists to design and introduce innovative delivery systems. They also take responsibility for reengineering existing operations to make them more efficient.

In tradition-oriented service firms, most operations managers have been with the organization longer than their marketing colleagues and believe that they understand it better. Yet even here, there's growing recognition of the contributions that marketers can make, not least in understanding customer motivations and habits, identifying opportunities for new product development and entry into new markets, telling customers and prospects about the product, and creating strategies to build customer loyalty in highly competitive environments. Although, in some traditional firms, operations managers may continue to believe that marketing should not become directly involved in line management, they are more willing today to recognize that marketing specialists can provide useful inputs to service design.

Service firms that are acknowledged for leadership in operations have moved beyond the mass production of standardized services to a mass-customization approach that enables the firm to be more responsive to variations in customer needs without losing sight of the need to improve productivity. Bowen and Youngdahl argue for a lean approach to service operations that focuses on what customers are looking for and then minimizes the costs of delivering the desired service.[7] Essential to such a strategy, they argue, are state-of-the art operations practices (sometimes based on studies of manufacturing operations) allied to use of blueprinting to eliminate non-value-added activities. Rounding out the picture are increased customer involvement in service design, employee training, and investment in practices that permit employee empowerment (discussed in chapter 15).

The Human Resources Function

Few service organizations are so technologically advanced that they can be operated without employees. Indeed, many service industries remain highly labor intensive. People are needed for operational tasks (either frontstage or backstage), to perform a wide array of marketing and customer service activities, and for administrative support.

Human resources emerged as a coherent management function during the 1980s. Historically, responsibility for matters relating to employees was often divided among a number of different departments, such as personnel, compensation, industrial relations, and organization development (or training). In their daily work, many employees report to operations departments. As defined by academic specialists, "Human resource management . . . involves all managerial decisions and actions that affect the nature of the relationship between the organization and its employees—its human resources."[8]

Just as some forward-looking service businesses have developed an expanded vision of marketing, viewing it from a strategic perspective rather than a narrow functional and tactical one, so is HR management coming to be seen as a key element in business strategy. People-related activities in a modern service corporation can be subsumed under four broad policy areas:[9]

1. *Human resource flow* is concerned with ensuring that the right number of people and the right mix of competencies are available to meet the firm's long-term strategic requirements. Issues include recruitment, training, career development, and promotions.
2. *Work systems* involve all tasks associated with arranging people, information, facilities, and technology to create (or support) the services produced by the organization.
3. *Reward systems* send powerful messages to all employees as to what kind of organization management seeks to create and maintain, especially in terms of desired attitudes and behavior. Not all rewards are financial in nature; recognition may be a powerful motivator.
4. *Employee influence* relates to employee inputs concerning business goals, pay, working conditions, career progression, employment security, and the design and implementation of work tasks. The movement toward greater empowerment of employees represents a shift in the nature and extent of employee influence.[10]

In many service businesses, the caliber and commitment of the labor force have become a major source of competitive advantage, especially in high-contact services where customers can discern differences among the employees of competing firms.[11] A strong commitment by top management to human resources is a feature of many successful service firms.[12] To the extent that employees understand and support the goals of their organization, have the skills and training needed to succeed in their jobs, and recognize the importance of creating and maintaining customer satisfaction, both marketing and operations activities should be easier to manage. Service Perspectives 16.2 illustrates the key role of people at Southwest Airlines, which has been rated on numerous occasions as one of the best companies to work for.[13]

To adopt a strategic role, human resources needs to shift its emphasis away from many of the routine, bureaucratic tasks such as payroll and benefits administration that previously con-

---

SERVICE PERSPECTIVES 16.2

Leadership through People at Southwest Airlines

What makes Southwest so successful? This extract from one of the company's recent annual reports provides some insights. Note the words that the company chooses to highlight by capitalizing their first letter.

Southwest Airlines believes our number one asset is our People; therefore, we devote a significant amount of time and effort hiring, training, and retaining our Employees. At Southwest, we are not interested in hiring clones. We target individuals from diverse backgrounds who will support and enhance our Culture. Regardless of the job, we hire People with attitudes that are outrageously positive. Our Employees enjoy working together as a team and take pleasure in team results, rather than emphasizing individual accomplishments.

Southwest Employees are not afraid to "color outside the lines." We encourage our Employees to be creative and have fun on the job. As a result, our Employees tend to go out of their way to ensure our Customers have an enjoyable and memorable flight. Although our Employees take our Customers very seriously, they do not take themselves seriously. They are warm, caring, compassionate, and always willing to go the extra mile to deliver Positively Outrageous Service to our Customers as well as the communities we serve.

Finding a person who fits that bill is not an easy task! In fact, we accepted approximately 124,000 external job applications in 1995 and interviewed 38,000 individuals for 5,473 positions.

Once Southwest hires someone to join our Family, we focus on nurturing and developing that Employee. We provide exceptional training programs which are specifically designed to help our Employees excel and succeed in an extremely competitive and dynamic environment.

Without sufficient retention of our incredibly talented Employees, our recruiting, hiring, and training efforts would be in vain. What is our secret? Although we offer competitive compensation packages, including, among other things, competitive wages and generous profitsharing, it is the psychic satisfaction of pride, excitement, fun, and collective fulfillment that is the key to our Culture and retaining the best Employees in America.

It is Southwest's philosophy that Employees with a sense of ownership in the Company will focus more on longterm versus shortterm goals. Empowerment to each and every Employee not only provides high spirit but avoids complacency and prevents a hierarchy or bureaucracy from slowing down creativity and innovation. In other words, the Southwest Spirit and Culture enhance job satisfaction which translates into thousands and thousands of dedicated Employees.

In every respect, our Employees are the best. And even though our competition may try to imitate Southwest, they cannot duplicate the most important element of our success—the Southwest Spirit inherent in each and every one of our 20,000 Employees.

Source: Southwest Airlines Co., *1995 Annual Report* (Dallas, TX, 1996), 14.

sumed much of management's time. Investments in technology can reduce some of the burden, but progressive firms are going even further, outsourcing many noncore administrative tasks. Recently, the giant oil company BP Amoco, whose businesses include many service elements, announced a $750 million, five-year contract to outsource the transactional elements of its worldwide HR activities.[14] However, work related to the company's strategy and hiring will continue to be performed in-house.

For human resource management to succeed, argues consultant Terri Kabachnick, "it must be a business-driven function with a thorough understanding of the organization's big picture. It must be viewed as a strategic consulting partner, providing innovative solutions and influencing key decisions and policies."[15] Among the tasks that she believes that human resources should perform are

- Installing systems that measure an applicant's beliefs and values for comparison to the company's beliefs and values to replace gut-instinct hiring decisions that often result in rapid turnover
- Studying similar industries and identifying what lessons can be learned from their HR policies
- Challenging corporate personnel policies if they no longer make sense in today's environment, demonstrating how proposed changes (e.g., job sharing) will affect the bottom line
- Demonstrating that human resources is in the business of developing and retaining productive workers rather than just being a training department

Rethinking training and education programs is central to progressive service businesses. It's important not to assume that all workers require the same training. After first assessing what individuals already know and do well, human resources should provide the tools that allow employees to pace and control their own learning. This task includes providing opportunities for managers to learn leadership skills, based on a knowledge of how individual managers currently perform on leading their existing employees.

The Search for Synergy in Service Management

Managing any type of organization entails conflict between differing goals and agendas. To achieve strategic synergy, service managers need to search for compatibility between four basic forces in a service business: What top management wants for the organization; what its employees, intermediaries, and other partners want; what its customers want; and what the organization is actually capable of doing. These four forces are represented as four intersecting circles in Figure 16.1. Senior managers need to consider each of the six intersections between these circles.

- *Is what we (management) want something that we (the firm) can do?* If not, we should either change our goals or place priority on making the necessary improvements to the organization's capabilities.
- *Is what we want what our customers want?* If not, we may gain a reputation as being a tight-fisted, uncaring, even unethical organization, unwilling to emphasize responsiveness to customers and interested only in its own goals and agendas.
- *Is what we want what our employees, suppliers, and other partners want?* If not, we may not be able to win their enthusiastic participation; at worst, we may not be able to attract and retain them.
- *Is what employees, suppliers, and other partners want what customers want?* If not, customers will quickly detect a failure to understanding of their priorities, disinterest in meeting their needs, and a lack of enthusiasm for providing them with a quality experience.

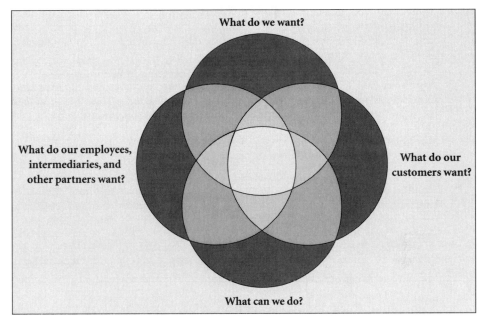

FIGURE 16.1 The Search for Synergy: A Top Management Perspective

- *Is what we can do what our customers want?* If not, both parties are barking up the wrong tree. Either we must look for different market segments—ones that value what our firm has to offer—or we must change what we do to bring it into line with what customers want.
- *Is what employees, intermediaries, and other partners want what we can do?* If not, the firm may not be offering the training and technological leverage that many service providers require to operate productively and create high-quality performances; similarly, the firm may not be providing satisfactory working conditions or paying competitive wages and fees.

Service leaders try to bring these four circles into the closest possible convergence so as to maximize the shaded area in the middle—the win-win-win-win zone where all parties enjoy a mutually rewarding relationship. To achieve this success, top management needs to ensure that marketing, operations, and human resources pull together in pursuit of common goals, rather than each pursuing independent and potentially conflicting agendas. However, alignment around an overly narrowly set of goals can put an organization at risk in the long run.[16]

Interfunctional Conflict

As service firms place more emphasis on developing a strong market orientation and serving customers well, there's increased potential for conflict among the three functions, especially between marketing and operations. Marketing managers are likely to see the operations perspective as narrow and one sided. Similarly, they get frustrated by employee resistance to change or by labor agreements that constrain the firm's ability to introduce new services and innovative delivery systems.

How comfortably can the three functions coexist in a service business, and how are their relative roles perceived? Sandra Vandermerwe makes the point that high-value-creating enterprises should be thinking in term of activities, not functions.[17] Yet in many firms, we still find individuals from marketing and operations backgrounds at loggerheads with one another. For instance, marketers may see their role as one of constantly adding superiority to the product offering to enhance its appeal to customers and thereby increase sales. Operations managers, by contrast, often take the view that their role is to pare back these elements to reflect the reality of service constraints—staff, equipment, and so forth—and the accompanying need for cost containment. Conflicts may also occur between human resources and the other two functions, especially where employees are in so-called boundary-spanning roles that require them to serve the seemingly conflicting goals imposed by marketing and operations.

Marketing Concerns with Operational Goals. Marketers who want to avoid conflicts with operations would do well to familiarize themselves with the issues that often underlie operations strategy (some of which relate to deployment of customer-contact staff). The left-hand column of Table 16.2 lays out 10 common operational issues that are particularly relevant to operations management of high-contact services. The center column identifies some typical operations goals associated with that issue. And the right-hand column identifies common marketing concerns that arise as a result.

To the extent that marketers and operations managers can engage in open dialogue about each other's goals and can explain their underlying rationale, there is a better chance that strategies and goals can be adapted so as to minimize the risk of potential negative impacts.

Conflicting Goals for Workers in Boundary-Spanning Jobs. The problem with high-contact, boundary-spanning jobs—positions that involve serving customers while working in an operational department—is that employees may find themselves caught in the middle of a fight between marketing and operations for turf and influence. For instance, operations may demand that customer-contact personnel focus on speed and efficiency, dealing with each customer as quickly as possible to improve productivity and reduce costs. Marketing, by contrast, may insist that employees should spend more time with customers, treat each one as an individual, display appropriate emotions, and try to sell additional services. Conflicting demands such as these are a recipe for stress and burnout. Instead, both functions need to work with human resources to come up with compatible goals for employee performance, clarify the skills and personal traits needed among employees in particular positions, and provide the necessary support and motivational structure.

Cost versus Revenue Orientation. Operations managers tend to focus on standardization, improving productivity, and other approaches to keeping down costs, whereas marketers look for opportunities to increase sales, improve service quality, and build customer loyalty. Although a proposed marketing innovation may have the potential to attract customers and offer the likelihood of increased sales, the financial and opportunity costs may sometimes be too high to permit its profitable introduction. Marketers who take the trouble to understand the nature and limitations of the existing operation are less likely to fall into the trap of pushing a new service that represents a poor fit with existing facilities, skills, and procedures. Moreover, marketers who have earned credibility with their colleagues in operations and human resources may be able to make the case for investment in new facilities and equipment, changes in labor agreements, and retraining of current personnel in new procedures (or even new hires).

Different Time Horizons. Marketing and operations often have different priorities in terms of how quickly specific strategies need to be implemented. Marketers may be oriented to current customer concerns and eager to achieve an early competitive advantage (or to regain competi-

TABLE 16.2 Differing Perspectives on Operational Issues among Operations and Marketing

Operational Issues	Typical Operations Goals	Common Marketing Concerns
Productivity improvement	Reduce unit cost of production	Strategies may cause decline in service quality
Make-versus-buy decisions	Trade off control of service delivery against comparative advantage and cost savings from outsourcing	"Make" decisions may result in lower quality and lack of market coverage; "buy" decisions may transfer control to unresponsive suppliers, divorce the firm from customer contact, and hurt its image
Facilities location	Reduce costs; provide convenient access for suppliers and employees	Customers may find location unattractive and inaccessible
Layout and design of service facilities	Control costs; improve efficiency by ensuring proximity of operationally related tasks; enhance safety and security	Customers may be confused by layout, find facility unattractive and inconvenient, and resent being shunted around needlessly from their perspective
Standardization	Keep costs low and quality consistent; simplify operational tasks; reduce errors; permit hiring of low-skilled, low-cost employees	Customers may prefer choice and variety and desire customization; difficult for marketers to target several segments
Job design	Minimize error, waste, and fraud; simplify tasks for standardization; facilitate rapid hiring; limit discretion; make efficient use of technology	Operationally oriented employees with narrowly defined roles may be unresponsive to consumer needs
Batch versus unit processing	Seek economies of scale, consistency, and efficient use of capacity by serving customers in groups	Customers may be forced to wait for a group to form, feel just "one of a crowd," and be turned off by other customers
Management of capacity	Keep costs down by not expanding capacity to meet peak demand, thus avoiding wasteful underutilization of resources at other times	Service may be unavailable to many customers at their preferred times; quality may be compromised during high-demand periods
Management of queues	Optimize use of available capacity by planning for average throughput; maintain customer order and discipline during wait	Customers may become bored and frustrated during wait and see firm as unresponsive
Quality control	Ensure that service execution conforms to predefined standards based on operational perspectives	Operational definitions of quality may not reflect customer needs and expectations

Source: Adapted from Christopher Lovelock, "Managing Interactions Between Operations and Marketing and Their Impact on Customers," in *Service Management Effectiveness*, ed. D. E. Bowen, R. B. Chase, and T. G. Cummings (San Francisco: Jossey Bass, 1990), 362.

tive parity) by introducing a new product. Operations managers, by contrast, may prefer to adopt a longer time horizon to depreciate existing assets, develop a new technology, or refine new operating procedures. Similarly, HR managers may caution against rushing to change the nature of employees' jobs, especially in situations where it may take time to obtain acceptance and commitment from employee associations or union leaders.

Perceived Fit of New Products with Existing Operations. Another problem relates to compatibility. How well does a new product, which may be very appealing to existing and prospective customers, fit into the operation? A classic example of incompatibility comes from an executive in a fast-food restaurant chain who related the operational problems attending the introduction of a new menu item:

> It was a big mistake. Our stores are small. They didn't have space for the new equipment that was needed. It really didn't fit with our existing business and was just a square peg in a round hole. Of course, just because it wasn't right for us doesn't mean it wouldn't have been a great success in another quick service restaurant company. It was really popular with our customers, but it started to mess up the rest of our operation.[18]

If a new product is incompatible with existing production facilities, expertise, and employee skills, it follows that good-quality execution may be infeasible. There is, of course, a difference between a permanently bad fit and short-term start-up problems. Resistance by operating personnel is one such start-up problem. There's often a natural tendency to want to make the job as easy as possible, and supervisors may be reluctant to disturb existing patterns by imposing new procedures on employees.

Improving Intraorganizational Coordination

Top management's responsibility is to develop structures and procedures that harness the energy of managers across different functions, rather than allowing it to be dissipated in internal disputes or permitting managers from one group to dominate (and thereby frustrate) the others. There are a number of ways in which service firms seek to improve intraorganizational coordination and reduce tension.

Transfers and Cross-Training. One approach is to transfer managers from one functional department to another to ensure better understanding of differing perspectives. By working in another department, the transferred manager learns the language and concepts of the other function, understands its opportunities and constraints, and recognizes how its priorities are established. A related approach is to cross-train managers and employers to perform a broader variety of tasks, rather than remaining narrow specialists.

Creating Cross-Functional Task Forces. Another approach is to create a task force for a specific project—such as planning the introduction of a new service, improving quality, or enhancing productivity. Such groups are normally formed on a temporary basis with a defined time deadline for completing a specific task. Ideally, groups should be composed of individuals from each functional area who are well attuned to the others' viewpoints. In operations, this means looking for what one manager has termed "field hands"—personnel who are practical and understand how to deal with people, rather than being totally systems and technology oriented. For marketers, task-force membership requires an orientation toward operating systems and what is involved in making them work from both a staffing and technical perspective; it doesn't necessarily require detailed technical training or an understanding of the inner workings of technology. Properly planned and managed, the team environment provides a forum for discussion and resolution of many of the problems likely to occur during, say, the development and commercialization of an innovative service.

New Tasks and New People. Organizational change requires that new relationships be developed, jobs redefined, priorities restructured, and existing patterns of thought and behavior modified—often sharply. There are two schools of thought here. One involves taking the existing players and redirecting them. The other calls for replacing these people with new ones. Larger firms obviously have a bigger pool of people from which to draw; they have managers and specialists in other divisions or regions who have not been "contaminated" by close exposure to the activity in question yet are sufficiently knowledgeable about the organization that they can quickly be productive in a new project.

Process Management Teams. A more permanent form of team is one that is organized around a specific process. In a marketing context, this approach may include brand management organizations created to plan and coordinate the design and delivery of all frontstage elements for a particular product. One example is found in the brand management teams that are responsible for planning and managing each of British Airways's different classes of service; they are composed of employees from a broad cross section of jobs, including cabin crew.[19] Another example is found in the executive operating committees that manage individual hotels within a chain.

Integrating the Firm's Personnel with the Customer's Organization. Some business-to-business service firms maintain ongoing relationships with customers by locating their own personnel at the customer's site or by bringing customers into their own organization. Taking operations and HR managers on sales calls or service follow-ups is a related approach. Such activities serve to highlight customer needs and concerns, thus driving home the notion that marketing is everybody's business.

Instituting Gain-Sharing Programs. These programs allow employees to share in improved profits (or in the cost savings achieved at a nonprofit organization). The most significant form of sharing in the fortunes of a business comes through employee stock-ownership programs (ESOPs), especially when participation is broadly based and employees own a substantial share of the equity. Another option is year-end bonuses. Nonprofit organizations can develop programs for sharing a proportion of the value of cost savings with their employees. One large hospital, for instance, issues specially colored checks to all employees at the end of each quarter during which cost savings have been achieved. Although the amounts are modest relative to wages and salaries, the motivational impact is high.

Installing Corporate Intranets. Few things break down departmental silos better than sharing information. Many firms have developed corporate Intranets (a secure, private, Internet-like network, complete with a wide variety of internal Web sites) to make it easy for managers and employees to obtain and exchange information across a wide array of topics. These networks can be extended to include suppliers, intermediaries, and even key customers (in which instance they are sometimes termed *Extranets*). Web sites can feature the activities of innovative projects, process teams, individual service delivery sites, staff departments, countrywide activities around the world, performance against standards, customer satisfaction ratings, complaint trends, competitive intelligence, financial performance, and so forth.

Three Imperatives

Changing traditional organizational perspectives doesn't come readily to managers who have been comfortable with established approaches. It's easy for them to become obsessed with their own functional tasks, forgetting that all areas of the company must pull together to create a customer-driven organization. As long as a service business continues to be organized along functional lines (and many are), achieving the necessary coordination and strategic synergy requires that top management establish clear imperatives for each function

Each imperative should relate to customers and define how the function in question contributes to the overall mission. Although a firm will need to phrase each imperative in ways that are specific to its own business, we can express them generically as follows:

- *The Marketing Imperative.* The firm will target specific types of customers whom it is well equipped to serve and then create profitable relationships with them by delivering a carefully defined augmented service package that they desire to purchase. Customers will recognize this package as being one of consistent quality that delivers solutions to their needs and offers superior value to competing alternatives.
- *The Operations Imperative.* To create and deliver the specified service package to targeted customers, the firm will select those operational techniques that allow it to consistently meet customer-driven cost, schedule, and quality goals and also enable the business to reduce its costs through continuing improvements in productivity. The chosen processes will match skills that employees or contractors currently possess or can be trained to develop. The firm will have the resources not only to support these operations with the necessary facilities, equipment, and technology but also to avoid negative impacts on employees and the broader community.
- *The Human Resources Imperative.* The firm will recruit, train, and motivate managers, supervisors, and employees who can work well together for a realistic compensation package to balance the twin goals of customer satisfaction and operational effectiveness. People will want to stay with the firm and to enhance their own skills because they value the working environment, appreciate the opportunities that it presents, and take pride in the services they help to create and deliver.

Part of the challenge of service management is to ensure that each of these three functional imperatives is compatible with the others and that all are mutually reinforcing.

Creating a Leading Service Organization

In your own life as a consumer, you have probably encountered an array of service performances ranging from highly competent and very satisfying to infuriatingly bad. There may be some organizations that you know you can always trust to deliver good service as well as to be among the first to innovate, whereas others are rather unpredictable, offering good service one day and indifference the next. Perhaps there are even a few organizations you know that consistently deliver bad service and demean their customers.

From Losers to Leaders: Four Levels of Service Performance

Service leadership is not based on outstanding performance within a single dimension. Rather, it reflects excellence across multiple dimensions. In an effort to capture this performance spectrum, we need to evaluate the organization within each of the three functional areas described earlier—marketing, operations, and human resources. Table 16.3 modifies and extends an earlier, operations-oriented framework proposed by Chase and Hayes.[20] It categorizes service performers into four levels: loser, nonentity, professional, and leader. At each level, there is a brief description of a typical organization across 12 dimensions. Under the marketing function, we look at the role of marketing in the organization, competitive appeal, customer profile, and service quality. Under the operations function, we consider the role of operations, service delivery (frontstage), backstage operations, productivity, and introduction of new technology. Finally, under the HR function, we consider the role of human resources, the workforce, and first-line management. Obviously, there are overlaps between these dimensions and across functions. There may also be variations in the relative importance of some dimensions between industries. However, the goal is to obtain some insights into what needs to be changed in organizations that are not performing as well as they might.

Service Losers. These are organizations at the bottom of the barrel from both customer and managerial perspectives. They get failing grades in marketing, operations, and HR management alike. Customers patronize them for reasons other than performance; typically, because there is no viable alternative—which is one reason why service losers continue to survive. Service delivery is seen as a necessary evil, new technology is only introduced under duress, and the uncaring workforce is a negative constraint. You will recognize how such organizations behave from the cycles of failure and mediocrity presented in chapter 15 (see Figures 15.1 and 15.2).

Service Nonentities. Although their performance still leaves much to be desired, nonentities have eliminated the worst features of losers. As shown in Table 16.3, they are dominated by a traditional operations mind-set, typically based on achieving cost savings through standardization. They employ rudimentary marketing strategies and the role of human resources and operations might be summed up, respectively, by the philosophies "adequate is good enough" and "if it ain't broke, don't fix it." Consumers neither seek out nor avoid such organizations; often, there are several such firms competing in desultory fashion within a given marketplace, and each one may be almost indistinguishable from the others. Periodic price discounts tend to be the primary means of trying to attract new customers.

Service Professionals. These organizations are in a different league than nonentities and have a clear positioning strategy. Customers within the target segments seek out these firms based on their sustained reputation for meeting expectations. Marketing is more sophisticated, using targeted communications and pricing based on value. Research is used to measure customer satisfaction and obtain ideas for service enhancement. Operations and marketing work together to introduce new delivery systems and recognize the trade-off between productivity and customer-defined quality. There are explicit links between backstage and frontstage activities and a much more proactive, investment-oriented approach to HR management than is found among nonentities.

Service Leaders. These organizations are the crème de la crème of their respective industries. Although service professionals are good, service leaders are outstanding. Their company names are synonymous with service excellence and an ability to delight customers. They are recognized for their innovation in each functional area of management as well as for their excellent internal communications and coordination among these three functions—often the result of a relatively flat organizational structure and extensive use of teams. As a result, service delivery is a seamless process organized around the customer. Marketing efforts make extensive use of relational databases that offer profound insights into customers, who are often addressed on a one-to-one basis. Concept testing, observation, and contacts with lead customers are employed in develop-

TABLE 16.3 *Four Levels of Service Performance*		
Level	1. Loser	2. Nonentity
Marketing Function		
Role of marketing	Tactical role only; advertising and promotions lack focus; no involvement in product or pricing decisions	Employs mix of selling and mass communication using simple segmentation strategy; makes selective use of price discounts and promotions; conducts and tabulates basic satisfaction surveys
Competitive appeal	Customers patronize firm for reasons other than performance	Customers neither seek out nor avoid the firm
Customer profile	Unspecified; a mass market to be served at a minimum cost	One or more segments whose basic needs are understood
Service quality	Highly variable, usually unsatisfactory Subservient to operations priorities	Meets some customer expectations; consistent on one or two key dimensions
Operations Function		
Role of operations	Reactive, cost oriented	The principal line management function: Creates and delivers product, focuses on standardization as key to productivity, defines quality from internal perspective
Service delivery (frontstage)	A necessary evil. Locations and schedules are unrelated to preferences of customers, who are routinely ignored	Sticklers for tradition; "if it ain't broke, don't fix it;" tight rules for customers; each step in delivery run independently
Backstage operations	Divorced from frontstage; cogs in a machine	Contributes to individual frontstage delivery steps but organized separately; unfamiliar with customers
Productivity	Undefined; managers are punished for failing to stick within budget	Based on standardization; rewarded for keeping costs below budget
Introduction of new technology	Late adopter, under duress, when necessary for survival	Follows the crowd when justified by cost savings
Human Resources Function		
Role of human resources	Supplies low-cost employees that meet minimum skill requirements for the job	Recruits and trains employees who can perform competently
Workforce	Negative constraint: poor performers, don't care, disloyal	Adequate resource, follows procedures but uninspired; turnover often high
Frontline management	Controls workers	Controls the process

Note: This framework was inspired by—and expands upon—work in service operations management by Richard Chase and Robert Hayes.

3. Professional	4. Leader
Marketing Function	
Has clear positioning strategy against competition; employs focused communications with distinctive appeals to clarify promises and educate customers; pricing is based on value; monitors customer usage and operates loyalty programs; uses a variety of research techniques to measure customer satisfaction and obtain ideas for service enhancements; works with operations to introduce new delivery systems	Innovative leader in chosen segments, known for marketing skills; brands at product/process level; conducts sophisticated analysis of relational databases as inputs to one-to-one marketing and proactive account management; employs state-of-the-art research techniques; uses concept testing, observation, and use of lead customers as inputs to new product development; close to operations/HR
Customers seek out the firm based on its sustained reputation for meeting customer expectations	Company name is synonymous with service excellence; its ability to delight customers raises expectations to levels that competitors can't meet
Groups of individuals whose variation in needs and value to the firm are clearly understood	Individuals who are selected and retained based on their future value to the firm, including their potential for new service opportunities and their ability to stimulate innovation
Consistently meets or exceeds customer expectations across multiple dimensions	Raises customer expectations to new levels; improves continuously
Operations Function	
Plays a strategic role in competitive strategy; recognizes trade-off between productivity and customer-defined quality; willing to outsource; monitors competing operations for ideas, threats	Recognized for innovation, focus, and excellence; an equal partner with marketing and HR management; has in-house research capability and academic contacts; continually experimenting
Driven by customer satisfaction, not tradition; willing to customize, embrace new approaches; emphasis on speed, convenience, and comfort	Delivery is a seamless process organized around the customer; employees know who they are serving; focuses on continuous improvement
Processes explicitly linked to frontstage activities; sees role as serving "internal customers" who in turn serve external customers	Closely integrated with frontstage delivery, even when geographically far apart; understands how own role relates to overall process of serving external customers; continuing dialogue
Focuses on reengineering backstage processes; avoids productivity improvements that will degrade customers' service experience; continually refining processes for efficiency	Understands concept of return on quality; actively seeks customer involvement in productivity improvement; ongoing testing of new processes and technologies
An early adopter when it promises to enhance service for customers and provide a competitive edge	Works with technology leaders to develop new applications that create first-mover advantage; seeks to perform at levels competitors can't match
Human Resources Function	
Invests in selective recruiting, ongoing training; keeps close to employees, promotes upward mobility; strives to enhance quality of working life	Sees quality of employees as strategic advantage; firm is recognized as outstanding place to work; HR helps top management to nurture culture
Motivated, hard-working, allowed some discretion in choice of procedures, offers suggestions	Innovative and empowered; very loyal, committed to firm's values and goals; creates procedures
Listens to customers; coaches and facilitates workers	Source of new ideas for top management; mentors workers to enhance career growth, value to firm

ment of new, breakthrough services that respond to latent needs. Operations specialists work with technology leaders around the world to develop new applications that will create first-mover advantage and enable the firm to perform at levels that competitors cannot hope to reach for some considerable time. Senior executives see quality of employees as a strategic advantage. Human resources works with them to develop and maintain a service-oriented culture and to create an outstanding working environment that simplifies the task of attracting and retaining the best people. The employees themselves are committed to the firm's values and goals; empowered and quick to embrace change, they are an ongoing source of new ideas.

Moving Up the Performance Ladder to a Higher Level

Firms can move either up or down the performance ladder. Once-stellar performers can become complacent and sluggish. Organizations that are devoted to satisfying their current customers may miss important shifts in the marketplace and find themselves turning into has-beens that continue to serve a loyal but dwindling band of conservative customers but are unable to attract demanding new consumers with different expectations. Companies whose original success was based on mastery of a specific technological process may find that in defending their control of that process, they have encouraged competitors to find higher-performing alternatives. And organizations whose management has worked for years to build up a loyal workforce with a strong service ethic may find that such a culture can be quickly

---

MANAGEMENT MEMO 16.1

Are You Suffering from Active Inertia?

Active inertia is insidious by nature. Because it grows out of success, it often spreads unnoticed in corporations. Sometimes, in fact, what managers consider to be their company's strengths are actually signs of weakness. If many of the following signs of weakness ring true for your company, you may want to take a look at your strategic frames, processes, relationships, and values.

"We know our competitors inside out."
"Our top priority is keeping our existing customers happy."
"We're not the world's greatest innovators, but we run a tight ship."
"Our processes are so well-tuned that the company could practically run itself."
"We focus R&D on product refinements and extensions, not on product breakthroughs."
"We're skeptics. In our view, the leading edge is the bleeding edge."
"We can't allow ourselves to get distracted by all the new fads in the marketplace."
"We have a very stable top management team."
"We have a well-entrenched corporate culture."
"We will never relinquish our core competency."
"Our processes are world class and we follow them religiously."
"If it ain't broke, we don't fix it."
"We have very high levels of employee loyalty, but when we bring in talented new people, they often get frustrated and leave."
"We've carved out an enduring leadership position in our industry."
"We view our current distributors as key strategic partners. We don't want to alienate them by rushing into new channels."
"Our corporate values are sacred; we will never change them."

Source: Donald N. Sull, "When Good Companies Go Bad," *Harvard Business Review* 77 (July–August 1999): 42–56. Copyright © 1999 by the President and Fellows of Harvard College. All rights reserved.

destroyed as a result of a merger or acquisition that brings in new leaders who emphasize short-term profits. Senior managers sometimes delude themselves into thinking that their company has achieved a superior level of performance when, in fact, the foundations of that success are actually crumbling. Management Memo 16.1 provides a sobering checklist of delusional statements that may signal danger ahead.

Moving up the service leadership ladder does not necessarily require simultaneous shifts across each of the 12 components featured in Table 16.3. Businesses don't necessarily rank in the same level across all components. But turnaround strategies require a thoughtful evaluation of where change is needed and determination of the logical sequence in which improvements need to be made.

In Search of Service Leadership

Service leaders are those firms that stand out in their respective markets and industries. But human leaders must take them in the right direction, set the right strategic priorities, and ensure that the relevant strategies are implemented throughout the organization. Much of the literature on leadership is concerned with turnarounds and transformation. It is easy to see why poorly performing organizations may require a major transformation of their culture and operating procedures to make them more competitive. But in times of rapid change, even high-performing firms need to evolve on a continuing basis, transforming themselves in evolutionary fashion.

Leading a Service Organization

John Kotter, perhaps the best-known writer on leadership, argues that in most successful change management processes, people need to move through eight complicated and often time-consuming stages:

- Creating a sense of urgency to develop the impetus for change
- Putting together a strong enough team to direct the process
- Creating an appropriate vision of where the organization needs to go
- Communicating that new vision broadly
- Empowering employees to act on that vision
- Producing sufficient short-term results to create credibility and counter cynicism
- Building momentum and using that to tackle the tougher change problems
- Anchoring the new behaviors in the organizational culture[21]

Leadership versus Management. The primary force behind successful change is leadership, which is concerned with the development of vision and strategies and the empowerment of people to overcome obstacles and make the vision happen. Management, by contrast, involves keeping the current situation operating through planning, budgeting, organizing, staffing, controlling, and problem solving. Bennis and Nanus distinguish between leaders who emphasize the emotional and even spiritual resources of an organization and managers who stress its physical resources, such as raw materials, technology and capital.[22] Says Kotter:

> Leadership works through people and culture. It's soft and hot. Management works through hierarchy and systems. Its harder and cooler. . . . The fundamental purpose of management is to keep the current system functioning. The fundamental purpose of leadership is to produce useful change, especially nonincremental change. It's possible to have too much or too

little of either. Strong leadership with no management risks chaos; the organization might walk right off a cliff. Strong management with no leadership tends to entrench an organization in deadly bureaucracy.[23]

However, leadership is an essential and growing aspect of managerial work because the rate of change has been increasing. Reflecting both competition and technological advances, new services or service features are being introduced at a faster rate and tend to have shorter life cycles (if, indeed, they even survive the introductory phase). Meantime, the competitive environment shifts constantly as a result of international firms entering new geographic markets, mergers and acquisitions, and the exit of former competitors from a given market due to takeover, bankruptcy, or a decision to refocus efforts on other business activities. And the process of service delivery itself has speeded up, with customers demanding faster service and faster responses when things go wrong. As a result, declares Kotter, effective top executives may now spend up to 80 percent of their time leading, double the figure required not that long ago. Even those at the bottom of the management hierarchy may spend at least 20 percent of their time on leadership.

Setting Direction versus Planning. People often confuse these two activities. Planning, according to Kotter, is a management process, designed to produce orderly results, not change. Setting a direction, by contrast, is more inductive than deductive. Leaders look for patterns, relationships, and linkages that help to explain things and suggest future trends. Direction setting creates visions and strategies that describe a business, technology, or corporate culture in terms of what it should become over the long term and articulate a feasible way of achieving this goal. Many of the best visions and strategies are not brilliantly innovative; rather, they combine some basic insights and translate them into a realistic competitive strategy that serves the interests of customers, stockholders, and employees. Some visions, however, fall into the category that Hamel and Pralahad describe as "stretch," striving to attain new levels of performance and competitive advantage that might, at first sight, seem to be beyond the organization's reach.[24] Stretching to achieve such bold goals may require creative reappraisal of traditional ways of doing business, seeking to leverage existing resources through partnerships, and creating the energy and the will among managers and employees alike to perform at higher levels than they believed themselves able to do.

Planning follows and complements direction setting, serving as a useful reality check and a road map for strategic execution. A good plan provides an action agenda for accomplishing the mission, using existing resources or identifying potential new sources.

Leadership Qualities

Many commentators have written on the topic of leadership. It has even been described as a service in its own right.[25] The qualities that are often ascribed to leaders in general include vision, charisma, persistence, high expectations, expertise, empathy, persuasiveness, and integrity. Typical prescriptions for leader behavior stress the importance of such activities as establishing (or preserving) a culture that is relevant to corporate success, putting in place an effective strategic planning process, instilling a sense of cohesion in the organization, and providing continuing examples of desired behaviors. For instance, the late Sam Walton, the legendary founder of the Wal-Mart retail chain, proclaimed the importance of managers as "servant leaders."[26]

Leonard Berry argues that service leadership requires a special perspective: "Regardless of the target markets, the specific services, or the pricing strategy, service leaders visualize quality of service as the foundation for competing."[27] Recognizing the key role of employees in delivering service, he emphasizes that service leaders need to believe in the people who work for them and to make communicating with employees a priority. Love of the business is another service leadership characteristic he highlights, to the extent that it combines natural enthusiasm with the right setting in which to express it. Such enthusiasm motivates individuals to teach the business to others and to pass on to them the nuances, secrets, and craft of operating it. Berry also stresses the importance for leaders of being driven by a set of core values that they infuse into the organization, arguing that "a critical role of values-driven leaders is cultivating the leadership qualities of others in the organization." And he notes that "values-driven leaders rely on their values to navigate their companies through difficult periods."[28]

In hierarchical organizations, structured on a military model, it's often assumed that leadership at the top is sufficient. However, as Sandra Vandermerwe points out, forward-looking service businesses need to be more flexible. Today's greater emphasis on using teams within service businesses means that

> leaders are everywhere, disseminated throughout the teams. They are found especially in the customer facing and interfacing jobs in order that decision-making will lead to long-lasting relationships with customers. . . . Leaders are customer and project champions who energize the group by virtue of their enthusiasm, interest, and know-how.[29]

Internal and External Leadership

There are important distinctions between leading a successful organization that is functioning well or redirecting a successful firm into new areas of activity and trying to turn around a dysfunctional one. In the case of Wal-Mart, Sam Walton created both the company and the culture, so his task was to preserve that culture as the company grew and to select a successor who would maintain an appropriate culture as the company continued to grow. J. W. (Bill) Marriott Jr. inherited from his father the position of chief executive of the company that bears the family name. Although it was the son who transformed the company from an emphasis on restaurant and food service into a global hotel corporation, he strove to maintain the corporate culture that flowed from the founder's philosophy and values: "'Take care of the employees and customers,' my father emphasized. . . . My father knew that if he had happy employees, he would have happy customers, and then that would result in a good bottom line."[30]

Transformation can take place in two different ways. One involves Darwinian-style evolution—constant mutations designed to ensure the survival of the fittest. Charles Schwab has been very successful in building the innovative brokerage house that bears his name. Over the years, he and his top executives have evolved the focus and strategy of the firm to take advantage of changing conditions. Without a continuing series of mutations, however, it is unlikely that Schwab would have maintained its success in the dynamic marketplace of financial services. A different type of transformation occurs in turnaround situations. For instance, Jan Carlzon, the former chief executive of SAS (Scandinavian Airlines System), sought to transform the inappropriate strategy and culture he found at the airline, moving it from an operations focus to a customer focus (highlighting moments of truth), with a particular emphasis on serving the needs of the business traveler.[31] Central to achieving these goals were his efforts to "flatten the pyramid" by delegating authority downwards toward those employees who dealt directly with customers. During the 1980s, his strategy proved highly successful. Unfortunately, he failed to continue adapting the airline in a changing environment. Transformational roles have been adopted not only by CEOs of failing companies but also by many of the chief executives who have worked to wake up sluggish organizations that were previously sheltered and constrained by government ownership, regulation, or protection against foreign competition.

One of the traits of successful leaders is their ability to role-model the behavior they expect of managers and other employees. Often, this requires the approach known as "management by wandering around," popularized by Peters and Waterman in their book *In Search of Excellence.*[32] Wandering around involves regular visits, preferably unannounced, to different areas of the company's operation. It provides insights into both backstage and frontstage operations as well as the ability to observe and meet both employees and customers and to see how corporate strategy is implemented on the frontline. Periodically, it may lead to a recognition that changes are needed in that strategy.

In addition to internal leadership, chief executives such as Walton, Marriott, Carlzon, and Schwab have also assumed external leadership roles, serving as ambassadors for their companies in the public arena and promoting the quality and value of their firms' services. Carlzon, in particular, became a high-profile figure in international business, gaining valuable publicity for his company. Marriott and Schwab have often appeared in their company's advertising.

There is a risk, of course, that prominent leaders may become too externally focused at the risk of their internal effectiveness. CEOs who enjoy enormous incomes (often through exercise of stock options), maintain princely lifestyles, and bask in widespread publicity may even turn off low-paid service workers at the bottom of the organization. Another risk is that a leadership style and focus that has served the company well in the past may become inappropriate for a changing environment. Jan Carlzon—whom management guru Tom Peters once described as a model leader—ignored the need in a changing economic environment to improve productivity and reduce SAS's high costs. Instead, he spent money to expand the company and invest in new acquisitions. As losses mounted during an economic downturn, he was eventually forced out.[33] And family dynasties may come to an end, too, if the successors to the founder prove ineffectual. As noted in the discussion of Club Med in chapter 4, although Gilbert Trigano and, later, his son Serge were effective leaders for many years, the family was ousted after it proved unable to lead the company in the new directions required by the changing social and economic environment of the 1990s.

Evaluating Leadership Potential

The need for leadership is not confined to chief executives or other top managers. Leadership traits are needed of everyone in a supervisory or managerial position, including those heading teams. Federal Express believes this so strongly that it requires all employees interested in entering the ranks of frontline management to participate in its Leadership Evaluation and Awareness Process (LEAP).

LEAP's first step involves participation in an introductory, one-day class that familiarizes candidates with managerial responsibilities. About one candidate in five concludes at this point that management is not for him or her. The next step is a three- to six-month period during which the candidate's manager coaches him or her based on a series of leadership attributes identified by the company. A third step involves peer assessment by a number of the candidate's coworkers (selected by the manager). Finally, the candidate must present written and oral arguments regarding specific leadership scenarios to a group of managers trained in LEAP assessment; this panel compares its findings with those from the other sources above.

Federal Express continues its emphasis on leadership at every level through its Survey-Feedback-Action surveys, including the Leadership Index in which subordinates rate their managers along 10 dimensions (refer to chapter 15, especially Table 15.2). Unfortunately, not every company is equally thorough in addressing the role of leadership among managers at all levels in the organization. In many firms, promotional decisions often appear totally haphazard or based on such criteria as duration of tenure in a previous position.

Leadership, Culture, and Climate

To close this chapter, we take a brief look at a theme that runs throughout this chapter and, indeed, the book: the leader's role in nurturing an effective culture within the firm.[34] In an organizational context, the word *culture* can be defined as including

- Shared perceptions or themes regarding what is important in the organization
- Shared values about what is right and wrong
- Shared understanding about what works and what doesn't work
- Shared beliefs and assumptions about *why* these things are important
- Shared styles of working and relating to others

Climate can be thought of as the more immediately tangible surface layer on top of the organization's underlying culture, its working environment. Among six key factors that influence an organization's working environment are its *flexibility*—how free employees feel to innovate; their sense of *responsibility* to the organization; the level of *standards* that people set; the perceived aptness of *rewards;* the *clarity* that people have about mission and values; and the level of *commitment* to a common purpose.[35] From an employee perspective, climate represents shared perceptions concerning the practices, procedures, and types of behaviors that get rewarded and supported in a particular setting. Multiple climates often exist simultaneously within a single organization, with each one referring to something specific—for instance, service, support, innovation, or safety.

A *climate for service* refers to employee perceptions of those practices, procedures, and behaviors that are expected with regard to customer service and service quality and that bring rewards for those who perform them well. Why are some leaders more effective than others in bringing about a desired change in climate or working atmosphere? Research Insights 16.1 suggests that it may be a matter of style.

RESEARCH INSIGHTS 16.1

The Impact of Leadership Styles on Climate

Daniel Goleman, an applied psychologist at Rutgers University, is known for his work on emotional intelligence—the ability to manage ourselves and our relationships effectively. Having earlier identified six different styles of leadership, he investigated how successful each style has proved to be in affecting climate or working atmosphere, based on a major study of the behavior and impact on their organizations of thousands of executives.

Coercive leaders demand immediate compliance ("Do what I tell you") and were found to have a negative impact on climate. Goleman comments that this controlling style, often highly confrontational, has value only in a crisis or in dealing with problem employees. *Pacesetting leaders* set high standards for performance and exemplify these through their own energetic behavior; this style can be summarized as "Do as I do, now." Somewhat surprisingly, they, too, were found to have a negative impact on climate. In practice, the pacesetting leader may destroy morale by assuming too much, too soon, of subordinates—expecting them to know already what to do and how to do it. Finding others to be less capable than expected, the leader may lapse into obsessing over details and micromanaging. This style is only likely to work when seeking to get quick results from a highly motivated and competent team.

The research found that the most effective style for achieving a positive change in climate came from *authoritative leaders,* who have the skills and personality to mobilize people toward a vision, building confidence and using a "Come with me" approach. The research also identified three other styles that had quite positive impacts on climate: *affiliative leaders,* whose motto is "People come first" and who seek to create harmony and build emotional bonds; *democratic leaders,* who forge consensus through participation ("What do you think?"); and *coaching leaders,* who work to develop people for the future and whose style might be summarized as "Try this."

Source: Daniel Goleman, "Leadership that Gets Results," *Harvard Business Review* 78 (March-April 2000): 78–93.

Leaders are responsible for creating cultures and the service climates that go along with them. Transformational leadership may require changing a culture that has become dysfunctional in the context of what it takes to be successful.

Creating a new climate for service, based on an understanding of what is needed for market success, may require a radical rethinking of HR management activities, operational procedures,

---

SERVICE PERSPECTIVES 16.3

How a Hospital President Sees the CEO's Role

Although recognizing that leadership is needed at every level, the ultimate responsibility for shaping and maintaining the culture of the organization lies with its CEO. Let's look at how one very experienced CEO, Mitchell T. Rabkin, M.D., recently retired as president of Boston's Beth Israel Hospital (now Beth Israel Deaconess Medical Center), sees some of the key aspects of the CEO's job: "My feeling about the role of chief executive officer is that of a role model and a source of information," he says. "I don't think that one can be so separate from a service organization that one's impact is made only in an intellectual way—or at a distance—and be effective."

What advice would Rabkin give to a newly appointed CEO who was moving to an organization from another company?

Do a lot of listening without making any commitments. Listen to everybody, recognizing that you don't know the quality of the "facts" and "advice" that people are giving you. Try to examine as closely as you can—and as critically and as quickly as you can—the information system that will be telling you what is going on, so that you know what it is that you are measuring. Work hard to create an atmosphere where people are not afraid to speak their minds. You learn a lot from "management by wandering around." And you're also seen. When I visit another hospital and am given a tour by its CEO, I watch how that CEO interacts with other people, and what the body language is in each instance. It's very revealing. Even more, it's very important for role modeling. People learn to *do* as a result of the way they see you and others *behave*.

One classic example of role modeling at Beth Israel (BI) that has now reached almost legendary status occurred not long after Dr. Rabkin, then in his late thirties, had assumed the top administrative position at the hospital. As a not-for-profit institution, BI was governed by a board of trustees, many of whom were generous donors and took a keen interest in the hospital's operations. Dr. Rabkin tells the story of a visit from a trustee:

One of our trustees, the late Max Feldberg, head of the Zayre Corporation, asked me one time to take a walk around the hospital with him and inquired, "Why do you think there are so many pieces of paper scattered on the floor of this patient care unit?"

"Well, it's because people don't pick them up," I replied.

He said, "Look, you're a scientist. We'll do an experiment. We'll walk down this floor and we'll pick up every other piece of paper. And then we'll go upstairs, there's another unit, same geography, statistically the same amount of paper, but we won't pick up anything."

So this 72-year old man and I went picking up alternate bits of the litter on one floor and nothing on the other. When we came back 10 minutes later, virtually all the rest of the litter on the first floor had been removed and nothing, of course, had changed on the second.

And "Mr. Max" said to me, "You see, it's not because *people* don't pick them up, it's because *you* don't pick them up. If you're so fancy that you can't bend down and pick up a piece of paper, why should anybody else?"

Source: Christopher Lovelock, *Product Plus* (New York: McGraw-Hill, 1994), 338–339.

and the firm's reward and recognition policies. Newcomers to an organization must quickly familiarize themselves with the existing culture; otherwise they will find themselves being led by it, rather than leading through it and, if necessary, changing it. In Service Perspectives 16.3, a former hospital CEO discusses his thoughts on the importance for chief executives of observing, listening, and role modeling.

Dr. Rabkin's story of picking up the bits of litter is a wonderful illustration of the power of role modeling. But role modeling is not just confined to chief executives. Every manager should be a role model to his or her peers and subordinates. All supervisors should be role models to those whose work they supervise. And experienced employees should be mentors and role models for new employees. But we need to recognize that the impact of role modeling is often slow and cumulative. The skills and behaviors that are taught in training sessions must be exemplified day in and day out on the job. Otherwise much of the effort put into careful recruitment will be wasted, and leadership will degenerate into "Do as I say, not as I do."

Conclusion

No organization can hope to achieve and maintain leadership in an industry without human leaders who can articulate a vision and help to bring it about. Service leadership encompasses high performance across a variety of dimensions that fall within the scope of the marketing, operations, and HR functions. However, because these functions often overlap and are interdependent, it is difficult to perform really well without internal collaboration and cooperation.

Within any given service organization, marketing has to coexist with operations—traditionally the dominant function—whose concerns are cost and efficiency centered rather than customer centered. Marketing must also coexist with HR management, which usually recruits and trains service personnel, including those who have direct contact with the customers. An ongoing challenge is to balance the concerns of each function, not only at head office but also in the field.

REVIEW QUESTIONS

1. Explain the significance of Gummesson's statement that the work of the traditional marketing department embraces only a small portion of the overall marketing function in a service business.
2. Identify the nature of the tasks that are traditionally assigned to the marketing, operations and HR functions. Identify which of the tasks in one function have an impact on one or both of the others.
3. What do you see as the causes of tension between the marketing, operations, and HR functions? How might they vary from one industry to another?
4. What are the four levels of service performance in firms? And what are the key dimensions that can be used to measure how far a firm has progressed toward reaching the status of service leader?
5. How does leading differ from managing and planning?

APPLICATION EXERCISES

1. Contrast the roles of marketing, operations and human resources in (1) an airline, (2) a hotel, (3) a progressive brokerage firm, and (4) an insurance company.

2. Select a company that you know well and obtain additional information from a literature review, Web site, company publications, and so on. Evaluate it on as many dimensions of service performance as you can, identifying where you believe it fits on the service performance spectrum shown in Table 16.3.

3. Research a service organization (it could be a company, nonprofit, or government agency) that has either greatly improved or significantly declined in recent years. Identify and evaluate the reasons, relating them to strong (or weak) leadership within the organization.

ENDNOTES

1. Evert Gummesson, "The Marketing of Professional Services: An Organizational Dilemma," *European Journal of Marketing* 13, no. 5 (1979): 308–318; Christian Grönroos, *Service Management and Marketing* (Lexington, MA: Lexington Books, 1990), 175–178.

2. Evert Gummesson, "Service Management: An Evaluation and the Future," *International Journal of Service Industry Management* 5, no. 1 (1994): 77–96.

3. Charles Christensen and Joseph Bower, "Customer Power, Strategic Investment, and the Failure of Leading Firms," *Strategic Management Journal* 17, no. 3 (1996): 198.

4. Stanley F. Slater and John C. Narver, "Customer-Led and Market-Oriented: Let's Not Confuse the Two," *Strategic Management Journal* 19 (1998): 1001–1006.

5. James L. Heskett, Thomas O. Jones, Gary W. Loveman, W. Earl Sasser Jr., and Leonard A. Schlesinger, "Putting the Service Profit Chain to Work," *Harvard Business Review* 72 (March–April 1994): 164–174; Roger Hallowell and Leonard A. Schlesinger, "The Service Profit Chain: Intellectual Roots, Current Realities, and Future Prospects," in *Handbook of Services Marketing and Management,* ed. T. Schwartz and D. Iacobucci (Thousand Oaks, CA: Sage Publications, 2000), 203–222.

6. James L. Heskett, W. Earl Sasser Jr., and Leonard A. Schlesinger, *The Service Profit Chain* (New York: The Free Press, 1997), 236–251.

7. David E. Bowen and William E. Youngdahl, "'Lean' Service: In Defense of a Production-Line Approach," *International Journal of Service Industry Management* 9, no. 3 (1998): 207–225.

8. M. Beer, B. Spector, P. R. Lawrence, D. Q. Mills, and R. E. Walton, *Human Resource Management: A General Manager's Perspective* (New York: The Free Press, 1985).

9. Ibid.

10. David E. Bowen and Edward T. Lawler III, "The Empowerment of Service Workers: What, Why, How and When," *Sloan Management Review* 32 (Spring 1992): 31–39.

11. See, for example, Jeffrey Pfeffer, *Competitive Advantage through People* (Boston: Harvard Business School Press, 1994).

12. See, for example, Benjamin Schneider and David E. Bowen, *Winning the Service Game* (Boston: Harvard Business School Press, 1995); and Leonard L. Berry, *On Great Service: A Framework for Action* (New York: The Free Press, 1995), chaps. 8–10.

13. Robert Levering and Milton Moskowitz, "The 100 Best Companies to Work For," *Fortune,* January 10, 2000, 82–110.

14. Julia Flynn and Bhushan Bahree, "BP Amoco Set to Outsource Human Resources," *Wall Street Journal Europe,* November 24, 1999, p. 4.

15. Terri Kabachnick, "The Strategic Role of Human Resources," *Arthur Andersen Retailing Issues Letter* 11, no. 1 (January 1999): 3.

16. Danny Miller, *The Icarus Paradox* (New York: HarperBusiness, 1990).

17. Sandra Vandermerwe, *From Tin Soldiers to Russian Dolls* (Oxford: Butterworth-Heinemann, 1993), 82.

18. Eric Langeard, John E. G. Bateson, Christopher H. Lovelock, and Pierre Eiglier, *Services Marketing: New Insights from Consumers and Managers* (Cambridge, MA: Marketing Science Institute, 1981), 89.

19. Torin Douglas, "The Power of Branding," *Business Life,* April–May 1988.

20. Richard B. Chase and Robert H. Hayes, "Beefing Up Operations in Service Firms," *Sloan Management Review* 31 (fall 1991): 15–26.

21. John P. Kotter, *What Leaders Really Do* (Boston: Harvard Business School Press, 1999), 10–11.

22. Warren Bennis and Burt Nanus, *Leaders: The Strategies for Taking Charge* (New York: Harper and Row, 1985), 92.
23. Kotter, *What Leaders Really Do,* 10–11.
24. Gary Hamel and C. K. Pralahad, *Competing for the Future* (Boston: Harvard Business School Press, 1994).
25. See, for instance, the special issue, "Leadership as a Service" (Celeste Wilderom, guest editor), *International Journal of Service Industry Management* 3, no. 2 (1992).
26. James L. Heskett, W. Earl Sasser Jr., and Leonard A. Schlesinger, *The Service Profit Chain* (New York: The Free Press, 1997), 236.
27. Leonard L. Berry, *On Great Service* (New York: The Free Press, 1995), 9
28. Leonard L. Berry, *Discovering the Soul of Service* (New York: The Free Press, 1999), 44, 47.
29. Sandra Vandermerwe, *From Tin Soldiers to Russian Dolls* (Oxford: Butterworth-Heinemann, 1993), 129.
30. M. Sheridan, "J. W. Marriott, Jr., Chairman and President, Marriott Corporation," *Sky Magazine,* March 1987, 46–53.
31. For an interesting discussion of Carlzon's philosophy of leadership, see K. J. Blois, "Carlzon's Moments of Truth—A Critical Appraisal," *International Journal of Service Industry Management* 3, no. 3 (1992): 5–17.
32. Thomas J. Peters and Robert H. Waterman, *In Search of Excellence* (New York: Harper & Row, 1982), 122.
33. Michael Maccoby, "Narcissistic Leaders: The Incredible Pros, the Inevitable Cons," *Harvard Business Review* 78 (January–February 2000): 68–78.
34. This section is based in part on Benjamin Schneider and David E. Bowen, *Winning the Service Game* (Boston: Harvard Business School Press, 1995); and David E. Bowen, Benjamin Schneider and Sandra S. Kim, "Shaping Service Cultures through Strategic Human Resource Management," in *Handbook of Services Marketing and Management,* ed. Schwartz and Iacobucci, 439–454.
35. Daniel Goleman, "Leadership That Gets Results," *Harvard Business Review* 78 (March–April 2000): 78–93.

CHAPTER 17

International and Global Strategies in Service Management

Think globally, act locally.

JOHN NAISBITT

Throughout this book, we've sought to provide an international perspective on services market-ing, presenting examples, cases, and research findings not only from within North America but also from countries on other continents. With only a few exceptions, however, most of our discus-sion of strategy and execution has emphasized activities taking place within a specific national market—what can be termed *local* or *domestic marketing*. In this chapter, we will consider the 8 Ps of integrated service management in the broader context of developing an international strategy for service businesses and examine the forces that drive globalization. These are issues for government policy makers as well as corporate managers.

When discussing international services marketing, it's easy to forget that some services were international in scope long before the term *scientific management* was ever invented or the first marketing course was taught. Shipping was an essential ingredient in opening up early trade routes, with banking and insurance facilitating and then following them. In time, large shipping companies emerged to operate international freight, mail, and passenger services, developing a network of agents in different ports to represent them. With the enhancement of technologies relating to radio, telegraph, and telephone in the early twentieth century came international telecommunication companies. Perhaps the most famous of these—still in existence today—was Cable & Wireless, which was created to link London to Britain's imperial territories around the world. Both the opportunity and the need for international delivery of a wide array of services have grown dramatically in recent years, either displacing or complementing parallel delivery of similar services by purely domestic operations.

As more and more organizations offer services in foreign markets—often around the world—and as international trade in services increases, important questions are being raised concerning the design and implementation of international service marketing strategies.

In this chapter, we analyze the nature of international services and consider such questions as

1. What factors are stimulating internationalization of service businesses?
2. Does a service firm have to go abroad to have an impact on international trade?
3. How does marketing services internationally differ from marketing inside a federal nation covering a large geographic area?
4. What is the distinction between a transnational strategy and a multilocal one?
5. What role does IT play in international trade in services?

Services in the Global Economy

Although the service sector dominates manufacturing in most domestic economies, that's not true of international trade. The WTO estimates that exports of merchandise from all countries worldwide totaled $5.2 trillion in 1998, but those of commercial services were $1.3 trillion (by way of comparison, the GDP of the United States that year amounted to some $8.8 trillion).[1]

Factors stimulating international trade in services include economic growth, which leads companies to seek new market opportunities and individuals to travel more often for both business and pleasure; improved transportation (itself a service), which makes travel and freight shipments faster and easier; advances in IT that improve communication and data flows between countries; a search for efficiency and expertise that leads companies and consumers to seek out the best locations for performing certain tasks; and the growth in trade of manufactured products, which themselves will require a variety of services (including finance, transportation, installation, maintenance, repair, and so forth) far from the place where they were first manufactured.

By any standards, the figure for trade in services is a huge amount. But until recently, national and international debates always focused on a country's performance in physical goods, with services being lumped under the rather disparaging term *invisibles*. The very use of the term *export* (which means literally "to carry away") is somewhat questionable when discussing intangible performances. As we'll see, service delivery can take place domestically and still have an impact on international trade flows. Service Perspectives 17.1 illustrates some of the complexity surrounding both definition and measurement.

What Is a Service Export?

The traditional notion of trade is of physical goods (including agricultural products and raw materials) leaving country A, where they are defined as exports, and being transported to country B, where they are defined as imports. But services, being intangible performances, don't necessarily fit into that mold. Consider the case of the Qantas airliner arriving in Hong Kong described in Service Perspectives 17.1. Much of the freight in the hold can certainly be classified as exports, including the wine. Even the souvenirs of Australia, which many of the passengers have packed in their bags, represent exports if they were manufactured in that country and purchased before departure by foreign visitors.

But the passengers themselves aren't exports, so how is Qantas contributing to Australia's balance of trade? Basically, by selling tickets to foreigners—such as the passengers from China, Belgium, the United States, and so forth, who pay in foreign currencies. Australian passengers

SERVICE PERSPECTIVES 17.1

Flight to Hong Kong: A Snapshot of Globalization

A white and red Boeing 747, sporting the flying kangaroo of Qantas, banks low over Hong Kong's dramatic harbor, crowded with merchant vessels, as it nears the end of its 10-hour flight from Australia. Once landed, the aircraft taxis past a kaleidoscope of tail fins, representing airlines from more than a dozen different countries on several continents—just a sample of all the carriers that offer service to this remarkable city.

The passengers include business travelers and tourists as well as returning residents. After passing through immigration and customs, most visitors will be heading first for their hotels, many of which belong to global chains (some of them, Hong Kong based). Some travelers will be picking up cars, reserved earlier from Hertz or one of the other well-known rental car companies with facilities at the airport. Others will take the fast train into the city. Tourists on packaged vacations are actively looking forward to enjoying Hong Kong's renowned Cantonese cuisine. Parents, however, are resigned to having their children demand to eat at the same fast-food chains that can be found back home. Many of the more affluent tourists are planning to go shopping, not only in distinctive Chinese jewelry and antiques stores but also in the internationally branded luxury stores that can be found in most world-class cities.

What brings the business travelers to this special administrative region (SAR) of China? Many are negotiating supply contracts for manufactured goods ranging from clothing to toys to computer components, whereas others have come to market their own goods and services. Some are in the shipping or construction businesses; others represent an array of service industries ranging from telecommunications to entertainment and international law. The owner of a large Australian tourism operation has come to negotiate a deal for package vacations on Queensland's famous Gold Coast. The Brussels-based, Canadian senior partner of a Big 5 accounting firm is halfway through a grueling round-the-world trip to persuade the offices of an international conglomerate to consolidate all its auditing business on a global basis with his firm alone. A U.S. executive and her British colleague, both working for a large Euro-American telecom partnership, are hoping to achieve similar goals by selling a multinational corporation on the concept of employing their firm to manage all its telecommunications activities worldwide. And more than a few of the passengers either work for international banking and financial service firms or have come to Hong Kong, one of the world's most dynamic financial centers, to seek financing for their own ventures.

In the Boeing's freight hold can be found not only passengers' bags but also cargo for delivery to Hong Kong and other Chinese destinations. The freight includes mail, Australian wine, some vital spare parts for an Australian-built high-speed ferry operating out of Hong Kong, a container full of brochures and display materials about the Australian tourism industry for an upcoming trade promotion, and a variety of other high-value merchandise. Waiting at the airport for the aircraft's arrival are local Qantas personnel, baggage handlers, cleaners, mechanics and other technical staff, customs and immigration officials, and, of course, people who have come to greet individual passengers. A few are Australians, but the great majority are local Hong Kong Chinese, many of whom have never traveled very far afield. Yet in their daily lives, they patronize banks, fast-food outlets, retail stores, and insurance companies whose brand names—promoted by global advertising campaigns—may be equally familiar to their expatriate relatives living in countries such as Australia, Britain, Canada, Singapore, and the United States. They can watch CNN on cable television, listen to the BBC World Service on the radio, make phone calls through Hong Kong Telecom (itself part of a worldwide operation), and watch movies from Hollywood either in English or dubbed into the Cantonese dialect of Chinese. Welcome to the world of global services marketing!

paying in Australian dollars contribute to Qantas' bottom line but do not individually impact Australian trade figures until they start spending following their arrival at their overseas destination (at which point their impact is negative). To assess the airline's net impact, it must deduct from its earnings in foreign currencies the costs in Hong Kong dollars (and other currencies) associated with its overseas airport operations, city offices, and promotional expenditures. But the situation will be reversed for Australian or Hong Kong travelers who have selected the Cathay Pacific flight from Sydney, which will arrive one hour behind the Qantas flight. Because Cathay is a Hong Kong airline, Australian passengers purchasing tickets on that flight will create debits for the Australian trade figures and credits for those of the SAR (Hong Kong).

What about purchases of services on the ground after arrival? Visitors who pay for hotels, rental cars, entertainment, meals, and taxis with foreign credit cards, travelers' checks, or local money that has been exchanged against foreign currencies will boost Hong Kong's service exports—even though the performance itself takes place locally. Tourism purchases are a vital source of foreign earnings for many countries, but these earnings will be offset when a country's own citizens go abroad on vacation. If the Queensland tour operator can sell her company's packaged tours to Hong Kong travel agencies (for resale, with markup, to Chinese tourists), there will be foreign earnings down under for airlines, hotels, car rentals, restaurants, bus companies, theaters, and many other businesses selling to these visitors.

What about telecommunications service? How does that contribute to international trade? The charge to the customer for an international phone call includes not only local taxes and payments to both the originating and receiving phone companies—say, AT&T and Hong Kong Telecom—for switching the calls and use of their domestic lines but also a fee for use of the international cables or satellite connections. Today, there is often a choice of different ways to route the call, selecting among several international long-distance carriers who, in turn, contract with different cable and satellite operators if they don't already have an ownership position themselves.

If a Hong Kong resident buys a Big Mac from a local branch of McDonald's and then goes to see a Hollywood movie in a nearby Canadian-owned movie theater, what impact does that have on international trade? Here, the trade flows involve royalty payments by the regional franchisee to McDonald's Chicago headquarters; payments to the film distributor in, say, Los Angeles; and any transfer of theater profits (net of Hong Kong tax) to the theater owner, who might be a Chinese-born Canadian citizen currently living in Vancouver.

In summary, the nature of international trade in services and how to measure it are not as easy to grasp as they are for physical merchandise. This fact may help explain (but certainly not justify) the relative paucity of academic research on the topic.[2]

The Attraction of International Markets

What drives service businesses to seek their fortunes in international markets? There are a variety of motivations, operating either singly or in conjunction.

Expanding Sales. Some firms are driven by a growth imperative. They may feel that they have exhausted growth opportunities in their domestic markets, either because of market size or because of the extent of competition. International expansion may be particularly appealing to firms operating in small countries or in narrow niche markets. Foreign markets are sometimes at an earlier stage in their development than the home market, with local firms lacking the same level of skills and technology. Alternatively, managers may believe that the opportunities to improve profitability are greater abroad, offering a potential for lower costs, higher prices, or both. Another approach to expanding sales involves attracting foreign customers to patronize an existing domestic location, as when hotels on Cape Cod in the northeastern United States try to attract European visitors to fill empty rooms during the spring and fall shoulder seasons.

Following Customers. Some firms—such as American Express—have grown by following their customers into new markets. Sometimes, in business-to-business services, a customer may request that a supplier provide services in a new location. This situation is increasingly common in fields such as management consulting, legal and accounting services, banking, and many types of outsourcing.

Following Competitors. Not every service firm operating abroad was the first foreign entrant into each of its markets. Some saw their competitors moving there and felt obliged to follow suit to stake out a position before it was too late.

Building Expertise. Some markets are seen as lead countries where innovation in both technology and strategy takes place earlier than in others. It's not always the same country for every service. The United States leads in many areas, but not in all. For instance, Finland leads in mobile phones. Firms may wish to operate in a lead country, even to the extent of buying an existing supplier, to gain experience and expertise that can then be fed back to their home markets.

Making Preemptive Strikes. Being the first firm to enter a new country market usually conveys first-mover advantages if the entry is handled well. When one company sees its competitors starting to move into other countries, it may seek to enter a different but promising foreign market with the goal of building a strong position there before the competitors arrive (this may be a more appealing alternative than always following the leader, particularly when acquisition of local firms is the primary mode of expansion). Fujitsu, the Japanese computer and IT services company, has grown to worldwide status through a combination of both internal growth and strategic acquisitions (see Figure 17.1).

How Service Processes Affect Market Entry

What are the alternative ways for a service company to tap the potential of international markets? It depends in part on the nature of the underlying process (see chapter 2) and the delivery system (see chapter 11).

People-Processing Services. We defined these earlier as involving services to the customer's body such that direct contact must be established with the customer for the service to be delivered. They include lodging, food service, health care, and passenger transportation. Three options present themselves:

- *Exporting the service concept.* Acting alone or in partnership with local suppliers, the firm establishes a service factory in another country. The objective may be to reach out to new customers or to follow existing corporate or individual customers to new locations (or both). This approach is commonly used by chain restaurants, hotels, car rental firms, and weight-reduction clinics where a local presence is essential to be able to compete. For corporate customers, the industries are likely to be in fields such as banking, professional services, and business logistics (among others). An entry strategy of this nature often directly threatens local firms, yet it can also present opportunities (see Service Perspectives 17.2).
- *Importing customers.*[3] Customers from other countries are invited to come to a service factory with distinctive appeal or competences in the firm's home country. People will travel

FIGURE 17.1 BOTH GLOBAL AND LOCAL: FUJITSU PROMOTES ITS WORLDWIDE IT SERVICES

from abroad to ski at outstanding resorts, such as Whistler/Blackcomb in British Columbia or Vail in Colorado. If they can afford it, they may also travel for specialist medical treatment at famous hospitals and clinics.

- *Transporting customers to new locations.* In the case of passenger transportation, entering international service takes the form of opening new routes to desired destinations. This strategy is generally used to attract new customers in addition to expanding the choices for existing customers.

Possession-Processing Services. This category involves services to the customer's physical possessions and includes repair and maintenance, freight transport, cleaning, and warehousing. Most services in this category require an ongoing local presence, regardless of whether customers drop off items at a service facility or personnel visit the customer's site. Sometimes, however, expert personnel may be flown in from a base in another country. In a few instances, a transportable item of equipment may be shipped to a foreign service center for repair, maintenance, or upgrade. Like passenger carriers, operators of freight transport services enter new markets by opening new routes.

Information-Based Services. This group includes two categories, *mental-processing services* (services to the customer's mind, such as news and entertainment) and *information-processing services* (services to customers' intangible assets, such as banking and insurance). Information-based services can be distributed internationally in one of four ways:

SERVICE PERSPECTIVES 17.2

How Jollibee Learned from McDonald's in the Philippines

The arrival in a country of an experienced global company may threaten existing local service providers, who are often fearful of going head-to-head against a daunting new competitor. Yet such events can offer important learning experiences for the home players. Consider the case of Jollibee, the Philippines-based fast-food chain.

When McDonald's began opening stores in Manila in 1981, few believed that the tiny, 11-store local chain could survive. But Jollibee's management team decided to benchmark the U.S. giant as an opportunity to bring their own chain up to world-class standards. First, they learned about the sophisticated operating systems that enabled McDonald's to control its quality, costs, and service at the store level—an area of weakness in the local firm that had constrained further expansion. Making the necessary improvements enabled Jollibee to increase its network to 65 stores over the next nine years, far outpacing McDonald's own Philippines expansion.

Jollibee also looked for ways to innovate. As its CEO gained a better understanding of McDonald's business model, he recognized the gaps in the latter's strategy. Simply put, its standard product line and U.S.-dominated decision processes were not very responsive to local taste preferences. Jollibee developed a more consumer-sensitive menu, including an innovative chicken product, that earned the loyalty of existing consumers and attracted new ones as the firm opened more of its efficient new stores.

The insights gained from competing against McDonald's taught Jollibee how to move abroad itself. It developed the Jollimeal, a rice-based dish that could be adapted to the local cuisine of nearby Asian markets, beginning with smaller countries such as Brunei, Guam, and Vietnam, where fast food was not yet well established at the time. These new ventures helped Jollibee refine its strategy, learn about the problems of managing offshore franchises, and prepare for entry into much larger and more competitive markets, such as Hong Kong and Indonesia, where niche products were added to the basic product line. By the early 1990s, Jollibee was operating in 10 countries in southeast Asia and the Middle East. In 1998, the firm successfully entered the most demanding fast food market in the world—California.

Source: Christopher A. Bartlett and Sumantra Ghoshal, "Going Global: Lessons from Late Movers," *Harvard Business Review* 78 (March–April 2000): 132–145.

- *Export the service to a local service factory.* The service can be made available in a local facility that customers visit. For instance, a film made in Hollywood can be shown in movie theaters around the world, and a college course can be designed in one country and then offered by approved teachers elsewhere.
- *Import customers.* Customers may travel abroad to visit a specialist facility, in which case the service takes on the characteristics of a people-processing service. For instance, large numbers of foreign students study in U.S. and Canadian universities, and foreigners travel to Stratford-upon-Avon to see Shakespeare's plays performed in the English town where he was born.
- *Transform the service into a physical good and export it.* Information-based services can be recorded and transformed into what are sometimes called *object-based services* (physical goods such as CDs, cassettes, or printed materials) and then shipped directly to customers or sold through local distribution channels.[4]
- *Export the information via telecommunications and transform it locally.* Rather than ship object-based services from their country of origin, the data can be downloaded from that country for physical production in local markets (even by customers themselves).

In theory, none of these information-based services requires face-to-face contact with customers, because all can potentially be delivered at arm's length through telecommunications or mail. Banking and insurance are good examples of services that can be delivered from other countries, with cash delivery available through global ATM networks. In practice, however, a local presence may be necessary to build personal relationships, conduct on-site research (as in consulting or auditing), or even to fulfil legal requirements.

Entry Channel Strategies

Few firms are in a position to move swiftly from a purely domestic posture to a broad international presence. Typically, the move takes place over many years, often proceeding one country at a time. As with domestic expansion, several options are available. Service firms wishing to deliver their services in another country may be able to choose among several options: start-up, franchising, purchase of existing firms, use of intermediaries, and the Internet.

Start-ups. When services are delivered through a physical "factory," firms are often concerned to replicate the technology and HR practices that contributed to their success at home. Start-ups offer the highest degree of control in this respect. One option is to invest the firm's own funds in the necessary facilities and operate them directly under the company's own brand name. However, that requires a lot of capital, so alternative financial arrangements include leasing or partnerships with local investors who own the buildings while guaranteeing the service provider a management contract that gives it responsibility for hiring and actual operations. This strategy is often used for hotels.

Franchising. Business format franchising involves licensing a local entrepreneur to market and deliver the franchisor's services according to tightly defined specifications. Franchisees invest their own funds and pay royalties and other fees to the franchisor in return for a tested concept, training, a brand name that is promoted by national and international advertising, and (sometimes) provision of certain supplies. A common practice for international franchisors in such fields as car rentals, copy shops, and fast-food restaurants is to sign national (or regional) agreements with one or more master franchisees who are nationals of the country in question and who take responsibility for recruiting and signing up local franchisees for individual locations. Franchises can often expand faster than company-operated outlets, not only for financial reasons but also because locally based franchisees usually have established business networks and experience in dealing with government officials.

Purchase of Existing Firms. Start-ups and franchises require time to build market share. An alternative is to *buy* market share by purchasing existing service suppliers outright (or forming a partnership with local owners or investors). Acquisition is often the preferred route for a service firm that wants to acquire an existing domestic customer base. It may also be the simplest way to obtain a higher share of a client's global business. For instance, if an accounting firm already serves the same client in several countries, it may add to the network simply by buying that client's existing service provider in another country (for an illustration of this practice in the auditing field, see the case "Peters & Champlain" on pp. 688 to 693). The growth of global express shipment networks, such as those operated by UPS and FedEx, was accomplished in part through purchase of successful local operations.

The acquisition route is, of course, faster than internal expansion and allows immediate access to operating systems and personnel. The downside is that substantial reorganization and reeducation of employees may be needed to bring the new acquisition into alignment with the purchaser's existing operation and culture. This task may result in a disruptive period during which quality declines, valued personnel leave, and others have to be let go, leading to customer confusion and even defection to competitors. For this reason, immediate brand-name changes may be unwise.

Use of Agents and Intermediaries. Rather than establishing a local presence of its own in another country, a service firm may choose to employ agents or intermediaries to represent its interests and provide local delivery. Banks, for instance, often establish corresponding relationships with foreign banks in other countries for the benefit of their own customers who may need financial services abroad. Some logistics firms employ local suppliers to extend their networks, delivering and picking up packages in locations where it would not be economic to maintain a dedicated office and workforce. Insurance brokers may represent overseas underwriters and obtain business for them. The downside is that this type of approach provides little leverage for control and minimizes opportunities for learning about local customers and local markets. Sometimes, however, agency relationships may subsequently be transformed into partnerships through direct investment or even outright purchase.

Internet. The remarkable thing about the World Wide Web is that a site designed for use in one country automatically becomes accessible in all other countries with unfettered links to the Internet.[5] In this instance, the service provider may receive orders for information-based services or merchandise without ever having made a conscious effort to evaluate international markets, let alone invest in reaching them. The customer can easily make payment by credit card through the Web site so long as the currencies involved are freely convertible. Information-based services, such as software, music, or research data, can then be delivered immediately through the Net. Merchandise, however, will have to be shipped through the mails or other physical channels, posing requirements back home for knowledge of international shipping and customs regulations. Web-based service providers need to recognize the global reach of their sites and may wish to review their Web site's content for ease of comprehension and potential cultural bias; they should also be prepared to respond to queries from prospective customers in other countries. One approach to tailoring site content (including language) to specific international markets is to have a different site address in each country (for instance, Amazon.com's British site is amazon.co.uk). Another approach is to display separate buttons on the home page for visitors from designated countries or language backgrounds.

Barriers to International Trade in Services

Operating successfully in international markets is more difficult for some services than for others. Despite the efforts of the WTO and its predecessor, the General Agreement on Trade and Tariffs (GATT), to encourage different governments to negotiate easier access to service markets, there are many hurdles to overcome. Airline access is a sore point. Many countries require bilateral (two-country) agreements on establishing new routes. If one country is willing to allow entry by a new carrier but the other is not, then access will be blocked. Compounding government restrictions of this nature are capacity limits at certain major airports that lead to denial of new or additional landing rights for foreign airlines. Both passenger and freight transport are affected by such restrictions.

Other constraints may include administrative delays, refusals by immigration offices to provide work permit applications for foreign managers and workers, heavy taxes on foreign firms, domestic preference policies designed to protect local suppliers, legal restrictions on operational and marketing procedures (including international data flows), and the lack of broadly accepted accounting standards for services. Different languages and cultural norms may require expensive changes in the nature of a service and how it is delivered and promoted. The cultural issue has been particularly significant for the entertainment industry. Many nations are wary of seeing their own culture swamped by U.S. imports. France and Canada are among the countries that seek to protect their own artists and entertainment industries, using a variety of measures to restrict the amount of U.S. content in local media.

Moving from Domestic to Transnational Marketing

Numerous firms whose national origins are rooted in individual countries around the world are now operating across national frontiers, but relatively few have developed a coherent international strategy. In many cases, each country market is treated as a separate entity with little or no strategic connection to the home (domestic) market or to other country markets.

Distinguishing Between Transnational and Multilocal Strategies

From a strategic perspective, there are often advantages to be gained if planning and execution of the different management functions can be integrated across national frontiers, rather than being compartmentalized on a domestic basis within each individual national market. *Transnational* strategy involves the integration of strategy formulation and its implementation across all the countries in which the company elects to do business. Such a strategy contrasts to a *multilocal* (or *multidomestic*) approach that provides for the independent development and implementation of strategy by management units within each country.[6] In its broadest geographic application, transnational strategy becomes global in form, and we then speak of globalization.

Historically, companies were often defined as multinational if they operated in the so-called triad of the United States, Europe, and Japan. But such coverage is not sufficient to be regarded as global because it completely excludes countries in the Southern Hemisphere. There is no universally accepted definition of *globalization,* but it can argued that to be truly global, a company should be operating on at least four continents, located in each of the four quadrants of the globe (that is, in both the eastern and western halves of the Northern and Southern Hemispheres).[7] Under such conditions, firms need to be sufficiently resourceful to adapt to wide differences in time zones, physical distances, climate, terrain, languages, culture, governmental structures, regulations, and currencies.

Although we can see a growing number of well-known service brand names popping up around the world, this does not mean that the companies behind the brands have a truly global strategy. The same concern holds true at a regional level when firms operate within a more narrowly defined geographic area, such as the 15-country EU. Many allegedly European strategies today are basically multidomestic in nature rather than truly pan-European. For instance, even though a number of European retail banks now have offices and even networks outside their countries of origin, in most instances there is little transnational integration. One reason for this situation is that few retail customers need to conduct business in several different countries; when people travel within Europe, their main financial need is usually to have a debit or credit card that can be used to make retail purchases and ATM withdrawals across the continent. To achieve this, all that is needed is for the bank that issues the card to be affiliated with a global network such as Visa or MasterCard. However, the situation is predictably different in corporate and investment banking because pan-European corporations increasingly demand pan-European financial services.

Research into global strategy for service businesses is still in an evolutionary stage. One key research theme is that globalization potential depends on industry characteristics[8]—and particularly on specific industry drivers.[9] A second key theme is that the use of global strategy should differ by dimension of strategy and for different elements of the value-adding chain.

How should different types of service firms move from multilocal strategies to creation of truly transnational ones? Later in this chapter, we discuss the elements of transnational strategy and examine five drivers that stimulate the internationalization of an industry: market factors, costs, technology, favorable government policies, and competition.[10] We then link the five industry globalization drivers to the different types of service processes introduced earlier in the book. Further insights come from examining how the concept of core and supplementary services can be applied to both standardization and customization of services in a global setting. But first, let's consider how the challenges of creating a global strategy compare to those of operating within a single country.

Insights for Globalization from Studying Service Strategies in the United States

It's useful to recognize that some of the challenges facing managers involved in transnational marketing are an extension of those already found in large, domestic economies—but taking place on a much larger stage that presents sharper economic, cultural, and political distinctions.

A significant dimension of international services marketing concerns questions of scale and diversity. There are already, of course, important differences between marketing services within a compact domestic economy—such as (say) Ireland, Taiwan, Venezuela, or New Zealand—and marketing in a federal nation covering a large geographic area, such as Canada or Australia. In the latter two countries, physical logistics immediately become more challenging for many types of service because of the distances involved and the existence of multiple time zones. Multiculturalism is also an issue in both countries because of the growing proportion of immigrants and the presence of indigenous peoples. And firms marketing across Canada have to work in two official languages, English and French (the latter is spoken in parts of New Brunswick—which is officially bilingual—and northeastern Ontario as well as throughout Quebec). Finally, there are differences within each country between the laws and tax rates of the various Canadian provinces (or Australian states) and their respective federal governments. But even these challenges pale in comparison to those facing service marketers in the mega-economy of the United States.

Visitors from overseas who tour the United States are often overwhelmed by the immense size of the country, surprised by the diversity of its people, astonished by the climatic and topographic variety of the landscape, and impressed by the scale and scope of some of its business undertakings. Consider some of the statistics. Marketing at a national level in the lower 48 states of the United States involves dealing with a population of over 275 million people and transcontinental distances that exceed 2,500 miles (4,000 km). If Hawaii and Alaska are included, the market embraces even greater distances, covering six time zones, incredible topographic variety, and all climatic zones from arctic to tropical. From a logistical standpoint, serving customers in all 50 states might seem at least as complex as serving customers throughout, say, Europe, North Africa, and the Middle East—were it not for the fact that the United States has an exceptionally well developed communications, transportation, and distribution infrastructure.

The United States is less homogeneous than national stereotypes might suggest. As a federal nation, it has a diverse patchwork of government practices. In addition to observing federal laws and paying federal taxes, service businesses operating nationwide may also need to conform to relevant state and municipal laws and plan for variations in tax policies from one state to another. Because cities, counties, and special districts (such as regional transit authorities) have taxing authority in many states, there are thousands of variations in sales tax across the United States! Some states deliberately seek out new business investments by promoting their lower tax rates or offering tax incentives to encourage firms to establish or relocate factories, call centers, or back-office operations.

Meanwhile, changes in both state and federal regulations are opening up new opportunities for many service businesses and encouraging regional and national consolidation. A case in point is retail banking, once legally constrained to operate in limited geographic areas such as statewide or even, within a state, just countywide. Today, the move is toward national banking, and many banks are expanding rapidly to take advantage of economies of scale. Other areas of consolidation include railroads, retailing, telecommunications, health care, cable television (now converging and merging with entertainment, news, telephone service, and distribution of Internet services), electric power generation, and electricity distribution. In each instance, the primary method of expansion appears to be merger or acquisition, rather than just relying on organic growth.

As the U.S. population becomes increasingly mobile and multicultural, market segmentation issues have become more complex for U.S. service marketers operating on a national scale. In addition to the varied accents and even dialects of U.S. English, marketers encounter growing populations of immigrants (as well as visiting tourists) who speak many other languages, headed by Spanish. A profile of students attending schools in Cambridge, Massachusetts, a city of some ninety thousand inhabitants within the greater Boston conurbation, revealed that between them they spoke no fewer than 56 languages at home! Many U.S. service marketers are now developing communication strategies targeted at different minority-language segments.[11] U.S. economic statistics show a wider range of household incomes and personal wealth (or lack thereof) than is found almost anywhere else on earth. Corporate customers, too, often present considerable diversity, although the relevant variables may be different.

Faced with an enormous and diverse domestic marketplace, most large U.S. service companies simplify their marketing and management tasks by targeting specific market segments (refer to chapter 7). Some firms segment on a geographic basis. Others target certain groups based on demographics, lifestyle, needs, or—in a corporate context—on industry type and company size. Smaller firms wishing to operate nationally usually choose to seek out narrow market niches, a task made easier today by the growing use of Web sites and e-mail. Yet the largest national service operations face tremendous challenges as they seek to serve multiple segments across the huge geographic area encompassed by the United States. They must strike a balance between standardization of strategies across all the elements embraced by the 8 Ps (see chapter 1) and adaptation to local market conditions—decisions that are especially challenging when they concern high-contact services where customers visit the delivery site in person.

To obtain the cost efficiencies needed for competitive pricing, a growing number of service firms have elected to relocate their backstage operations to areas of the United States that offer either low-cost operations or geographical advantages. (Today, some are even moving certain operations outside the United States.) When, in the 1970s, Citicorp relocated its back-office credit card–processing operations from New York to South Dakota—far from its retail market area at the time—the move caused a sensation. Today, it would be much less noteworthy.

Moving to an Even Larger International Arena

Transnational strategy must address similar problems to those facing service firms doing business solely within the United States. The arena is larger and the context sometimes more vexing, yet the managerial problems have many parallels. Barriers to entry—historically a serious problem for foreign firms wishing to do business abroad—are slowly diminishing. The passage of free trade legislation in recent years has been an important facilitator of transnational operations. Notable developments include NAFTA (linking Canada, Mexico, and the United States), such Latin American economic blocs as Mercosur and Pacto Andino, and the EU, which is expected to expand its membership in coming years (see Service Perspectives 17.3, "The European Union: Moving to Borderless Trade").

As with the countries of the EU, NAFTA is drawing the markets of Canada, Mexico, and the United States closer together. But here, too, political and cultural factors pose barriers to closer integration in service industries ranging from airlines and banking to broadcasting and telecommunications. By 2005, some major shifts will probably have taken place, similar to recent and proposed transborder mergers between the U.S. and Canadian railroad industries and such banking initiatives as Bank of Montreal's purchase of Harris Bank in Chicago and an equity share in Mexico's Grupo Financiero Bancomer.

Operating in multiple countries will always be more complex than operating within just one, however large. But with reduced barriers to entry, management decisions to expand service operations to other countries will certainly take on more of the characteristics of a firm seeking

SERVICE PERSPECTIVES 17.3

The European Union: Moving to Borderless Trade

Many of the challenging strategic decisions facing service marketers in pan-European markets are extensions of decisions already faced by firms operating at a national basis in the United States. Although geographically more compact than the United States, the 15-country EU has an even larger population (375 million versus 275 million) and is culturally and politically more diverse, with more distinct variations in tastes and lifestyles plus the added complication of 11 official national languages and a variety of regional tongues, from Catalan to Welsh. As new countries join the EU, the "single market" will become even larger. The anticipated admission of several countries in Eastern Europe early in the twenty-first century and the possibility of a formal link to Turkey (whose land area straddles Europe and Asia) will add further cultural diversity and bring the EU market closer to Russia and the countries of central Asia.

Within the EU, the European Commission has made huge progress in harmonizing standards and regulations to level the competitive playing field and discourage efforts by individual member countries to protect their own service and manufacturing industries. The results are already evident, with German companies operating mobile phone services in Britain, the British operating French airlines, and the French operating water-related services in several European countries (as well as overseas). But the task remains incomplete, and there are various subtle ways in which governments (notably the French) can drag their feet on compliance. Another important economic step facilitating transnational marketing on a pan-European basis is monetary union. In January 1999, the exchange values of 11 national European currencies were linked to a new currency, the euro (worth about $1), which will completely replace these currencies in 2002. Soon, services will be priced in euros from Finland to Portugal. Other European countries, including Britain and Sweden, are predicted to switch to euros in due course.

However, although the potential for freer trade in services within the EU is increasing at a rapid rate, we need to recognize that greater Europe, ranging from Iceland to Russia west of the Ural Mountains, includes many countries that are likely to remain outside the union for some years to come. Some of these countries, such as Switzerland and Norway (which both rejected membership), tend to enjoy much closer trading relations with the EU than others. Whether there will ever be full political union—a United States of Europe—remains a hotly debated and contested issue. But from a services marketing standpoint, the EU is certainly moving toward the U.S. model in terms of both scale and freedom of movement.

to expand across the United States. For instance, is there a tax advantage to using one country as a major base of operations rather than another? Is it necessary to have a service facility in a particular city to complete a network designed to serve global customers? To what extent will modifications to service features and marketing strategy have to be made to accommodate climatic differences or cultural preferences? Are there cost advantages to locating certain service operations in a country other than the firm's traditional home base?

Factors Favoring Adoption of Transnational Strategies

Several forces, more precisely termed *industry drivers,* influence the trend toward globalization and the creation of transnationally integrated strategy.[12] As applied to services, these forces are *market drivers, competition drivers, technology drivers, cost drivers,* and *government drivers.* Their relative significance may vary by type of service.

Market Drivers. Market factors that stimulate the move toward transnational strategies include common customer needs across many countries, global customers who demand consistent service from suppliers around the world, and the availability of international channels in the form of efficient physical supply chains or electronic networks. As large corporate customers become global, they often seek to standardize and simplify the suppliers they use in different countries for a wide array of business-to-business services. For instance, companies that operate globally often seek to minimize the number of auditors they use around the world, expressing a preference for using Big 5 accounting firms that can apply a consistent approach (within the context of the national rules prevailing within each country of operation). A second example comes from the move to global management of telecommunications, such as the Concert service jointly offered by AT&T and BT, which enables multinational corporations to outsource management of their international telecommunications needs. Corporate banking, insurance, and management consulting are further examples. In each instance, there are real advantages to the customer in consistency, ease of access, consolidation of information, and accountability. Similarly, international business travelers and tourists often feel more comfortable with predictable international standards of performance for such travel-related services as airlines and hotels. And the development of international logistics capabilities among such firms as FedEx and UPS has encouraged many manufacturers to outsource responsibility for their logistics function to a single firm, which then coordinates transportation and warehousing operations.

Competition Drivers. The interdependence of countries, the presence of competitors from different countries, and the transnational policies of competitors themselves are among the key drivers that exercise a powerful force in many service industries. Firms may be obliged to follow their competitors into new markets to protect their positions elsewhere. Similarly, once a major player moves into a new foreign market, a scramble for territory among competing firms may ensue, particularly if the preferred mode of expansion involves purchasing or licensing the most successful local firms in each market.

Technology Drivers. These factors tend to center around advances in IT such as enhanced performance and capabilities in telecommunications, computerization, and software, all of which serve to tie markets together more closely. For information-based services, the growing availability of broadband telecommunication channels, capable of moving vast amounts of data at great speed, is playing a major role in opening up new markets. Access to the Internet or World Wide Web is accelerating around the world. But there may be no need to duplicate all informational elements in each new location. Significant economies may be gained by centralizing information hubs on a continent-wide or even global basis. Firms can take advantage of favorable labor costs and exchange rates by consolidating operations of supplementary services (such as reservations) or back-office functions (such as accounting) in just one or a few selected countries. Moreover, advances in those technologies that lead to faster and cheaper transportation—including materials, power, and physical design—also help to shrink distance and bring countries closer together.[13]

Cost Drivers. Big is sometimes beautiful from a cost standpoint. There may be economies of scale to be gained from operating on an international or even global basis plus sourcing efficiencies as a result of favorable logistics and lower costs in certain countries. Lower operating costs for telecommunications and transportation, accompanied by improved performance, facilitate entry into international markets. The effect of these drivers varies according to the level of fixed costs required to enter an industry and the potential for cost savings. Barriers to entry caused by the up-front cost of equipment and facilities may be reduced by such strategies as equipment leasing (as in airlines), seeking investor-owned facilities such as hotels and then obtaining management contracts, or awarding franchises to local entrepreneurs. However, cost drivers may be less applicable for services that are primarily people based. When most elements of the service factory have to be replicated in multiple locations, scale economies tend to be lower and experience curves flatter.

Government Drivers. Government policies can serve to encourage or discourage development of a transnationally integrated strategy. Among these drivers are favorable trade policies, compatible technical standards, and common marketing regulations. For instance, the actions taken by the European Commission to create a single market throughout the EU are a stimulus to the creation of pan-European service strategies in numerous industries. Looking at a broader global picture, we can expect government drivers to be more favorable for people-processing and possession-processing services that require a significant local presence because these services can create local employment opportunities. In contrast, governments often impose regulations to protect home-based services, such as passenger and freight transportation, from the threat of competition by foreign carriers operating on the same routes (although such restrictive practices are increasingly under attack). A typical action involves restricting foreign airlines' landing rights or their ability to pick up passengers at an intermediate stop on a scheduled flight between two other countries.

Governments can play an important role in requiring adoption of internationally compatible technical standards. However, unrestricted imports of services in categories ranging from entertainment to finance are often seen as both an economic and cultural threat—hence, such government actions as regulating international banking (widely practiced), banning private ownership of satellite dishes (implemented in past years in China, Iran, Singapore, and Saudi Arabia), or seeking to limit access to services on the Internet.[14]

With government assistance, old manufacturing centers have sometimes succeeded in recasting themselves as centers of service activity. But manufacturing and services are not necessarily mutually exclusive. In his article, "The Evolution of Services Management in Developing Countries: Insights from Latin America," Javier Reynoso describes the renaissance of the old industrial city of Monterrey, Mexico (see pp. 585 to 592). Meanwhile, the government of Panama is seeking to capitalize on the strategic advantage of the Panama Canal—the country's principal service business—by developing new activities in what used to be the U.S.-controlled Panama Canal Zone. In southeast Asia, Singapore's government has invested heavily and continually in airport and seaport facilities to exploit this island nation's location as a natural hub for both air routes and marine shipping, reinforcing these advantages with a policy of investment in a telecommunications infrastructure designed to create a wired nation.

How the Nature of Service Processes Affects Opportunities for Globalization

Are some types of services easier to internationalize than others? Our analysis suggests that this is, indeed, the case. As emphasized throughout this book, not all services are the same. Table 17.1 summarizes important variations in the impact of each of the five groups of drivers on three broad categories of services: people-processing services, possession-processing services, and information-based services (see the discussion earlier in this chapter on pp. 512 to 515).

People-processing services involve physical interactions with customers and necessarily require either that these people travel to the service factory or that service providers and equip-

TABLE 17.1 *Impact of Globalization Drivers on Different Service Categories*

Globalization Drivers	People Processing	Possession Processing	Information–Based
Competition	Simultaneity of production and consumption limits leverage of foreign-based competitive advantage in frontstage of service factory, but advantage in management systems can be basis for globalization.	Lead role of technology creates driver for globalization of competitors with technical edge (e.g., Singapore Airlines' technical servicing for other carriers' aircraft).	Highly vulnerable to global dominance by competitors with monopoly or competitive advantage in information (e.g., BBC, Hollywood, CNN), unless restricted by governments.
Market	People differ economically and culturally, so needs for service and ability to pay may vary. Culture and education may affect willingness to do self-service.	Less variation for service to corporate possessions, but level of economic development impacts demand for services to individually owned goods.	Demand for many services is derived to a significant degree from economic and educational levels. Cultural issues may affect demand for entertainment.
Technology	Use of IT for delivery of supplementary services may be a function of ownership and familiarity with technology, including telecommunications, and intelligent terminals.	Need for technology-based service delivery systems is a function of the types of possessions requiring service and the cost trade-offs in labor substitution.	Ability to deliver core services through remote terminals may be a function of investments in computerization, quality of telecommunications infrastructure, and education levels.
Cost	Variable labor rates may impact on pricing in labor-intensive services (consider self-service in high-cost locations).	Variable labor rates may favor low-cost locations if not offset by shipment costs. Consider substituting equipment for labor.	Major cost elements can be centralized and minor cost elements localized.
Government	Social policies (e.g., health) vary widely and may affect labor costs, role of women in frontstage jobs, and hours/days on which work can be performed.	Tax laws, environmental regulations, and technical standards may decrease/increase costs and encourage/discourage certain types of activity.	Policies on education, censorship, public ownership of communications, and infrastructure standards may impact demand and supply and distort pricing.

ment come to the customer. In both instances, the service provider needs to maintain a local geographic presence, stationing the necessary personnel, buildings, equipment, vehicles, and supplies within reasonably easy reach of target customers. If the customers are themselves mobile—as in the case of business travelers and tourists—then the same customers may patronize a company's offerings in many different locations and make comparisons among them.

Possession-processing services may also be geographically constrained in many instances. A local presence is still required when the supplier must come to repair or maintain objects in a fixed location, but smaller, transportable items can be shipped to distant service centers—although transportation costs, customs duties, and government regulations may constrain shipment across large distances or national frontiers. On the other hand, modern technology now allows certain types of service processes to be administered from a distance through electronic diagnostics and transmission of so-called remote fixes.

Information-based services are perhaps the most interesting category of services from the standpoint of global strategy development because they depend on the transmission or manipulation of data to create value. The advent of modern global telecommunications, linking intelligent machines to powerful databases, makes it increasingly easy to deliver information-based services around the world. Local presence requirements may be limited to a terminal—ranging from a simple telephone or fax machine to a computer or more specialized equipment such as a bank ATM—connected to a reliable telecommunications infrastructure. If the local infrastructure is not of sufficiently high quality, then use of mobile or satellite communications may solve the problem in some instances.

Many of the factors driving internationalization and adoption of transnational strategies also promote the trend to nationwide operations among service industries that previously operated only at a local level. The market, cost, technological, and competitive forces that encourage creation of nationwide service businesses or franchise chains are often the same as those that subsequently drive some of the same firms to operate transnationally. Yet many types of services, from plumbers to landscaping, still remain purely local in scope, as a review of business categories in any city's Yellow Pages reveals.

Transnational Strategy for Supplementary Services

So far, we've focused on describing global strategy as it relates to different categories of core services. However, as we saw in chapter 8, the core product—a bed for the night, restoring a defective computer to good working order, or a bank account—is typically accompanied by a variety of supplementary elements. Many manufacturing businesses offer a variety of services related to their products. These supplementary elements not only add value and provide the differentiation that separates successful firms from the also-rans but also offer opportunities for firms to develop effective transnational strategies.

Standardization versus Customization for Supplementary Services

The Flower of Service model (see Figure 8.5 on p. 233 and Tables 8.1–8.8) groups supplementary services into eight categories (information, consultation, order taking, hospitality, safekeeping, exceptions, billing, and payment). Not every core product—whether a good or a service—is surrounded by supplementary elements from all eight clusters, of course. In practice, the nature of the product, customer requirements, and competitive practices help managers to determine which supplementary services should be offered in a particular market and the extent to which they should be standardized across markets. Let's look at the implications of creating a transnational strategy for each of the eight groups of supplementary services.

Information. To obtain full value from any good or service, customers need relevant information about it. New customers and prospects are especially information hungry. Transnationalization affects both the location of information access and the nature of that information (including the languages and format in which it is provided).

Consultation and Advice. In contrast to information, consultation and advice involve a dialogue to probe customer requirements and then develop a tailored solution. Customers' need for advice may vary widely around the world, reflecting such factors as level of economic development, nature of the local infrastructure, topography and climate, technical standards, and educational levels.

Order Taking (including reservations). Once customers are ready to buy, a key supplementary element should come into play: accepting applications, orders, and reservations. Transnationalization affects both the nature and location of order-taking access, such as the potential for instituting multilingual global reservation systems, accessible through a local telephone number or the Internet.

Hospitality: Taking Care of the Customer. A well-managed business should try, at least in small ways, to treat customers as guests when they visit the supplier's facilities. Cultural definitions of appropriate hospitality may differ widely from one country to another, such as the tolerable length of waiting time (much longer in Russia than in North America) and the degree of personal service expected (higher in France, for instance, than in the Scandinavian countries).

Safekeeping: Looking After the Customer's Possessions. When visiting a service site, customers often want assistance with their personal possessions. Expectations often vary by country, reflecting culture and levels of affluence. For example, most restaurants in the United States bar dogs, but in France most will tolerate them, and in China some restaurants may even cook them for you!

Exceptions. Exceptions fall outside the routine of normal service delivery. They include special requests, problem solving, handling of complaints/suggestions/compliments, and restitution (compensating customers for performance failures). Special requests are particularly common in people-processing services, as in the travel and hotel industries. International airlines, for example, find it necessary to respond to an array of dietary needs, sometimes reflecting religious and cultural values. They must also be prepared for medical emergencies. Dealing with problems is often more difficult for people who are traveling abroad than it would be in the familiar environment of their native country. Travel service firms such as American Express and Diners Club often capitalize on their ability to help cardholders facing medical or other emergencies far from home.

Billing. Customers need clear, timely bills that explain how charges are computed. With abolition of currency exchange restrictions in many countries, travelers now expect to be able to make purchases on their charge cards almost anywhere and to have bills converted to their home currencies. In a global setting, therefore, currencies and conversion rates need to be clarified on billing statements.

Payment. Ease and convenience of payment (including credit) are important to customers when purchasing a broad array of goods and services. Acceptance of major charge cards and travelers' checks solves the problem of paying in foreign funds for many retail purchases, but some tourist-oriented stores go even further to accommodate customers by accepting foreign currencies.

Factors Favoring Transnational Strategies for Information-Based Supplementary Services

A majority of supplementary services are information-based and can potentially be delivered from remote locations. In theory, a global company could centralize its billing on a global basis, using postal or telecommunication distribution channels to deliver the bills to customers, suitably converted to the relevant currency. Similarly, information, consultation, order taking/reservations, problem solving, and payment can all be handled through telecommunications. So long as the appropriate languages are available, many such service elements could be delivered from almost anywhere. By contrast, hospitality and safekeeping will always have to be provided locally because they are responsive to the physical presence of customers and their possessions.

Elements of Transnational Strategy

How do we determine whether a firm's international strategy can realistically be described as transnational rather than multilocal? And how might the distinctive characteristics of service businesses affect the ability or necessity to adopt and implement specific aspects of a transnational approach? Is the axiom "think globally but act locally" consistent with transnational strategy?

Transnational Strategy Levers

Five transnational strategy levers serve to determine whether international strategy is primarily multilocal (recreated independently in each location) or primarily transnational.[15] They are *market participation, product features, location of value-adding supplementary services, marketing activities,* and *competitive moves.* Within each dimension, strategic options cover a spectrum that ranges from a strictly multilocal orientation to a completely global one. Let's look at the latter end of the spectrum for each of these five dimensions. Judicious use of these strategy levers can enable a firm to obtain important benefits including cost reductions, improved quality of products and processes, greater customer preference, and increased competitive leverage.

Global Market Participation. Management selects countries in which to market its services not just on the basis of stand-alone attractiveness; it also considers the potential of each market to contribute to broader globalization benefits such as completing a global network, competing in a state-of-the art market where the firm hopes to gain insights for transfer to other regions, or providing convenience for important clients when traveling.

Delivering Global Products. The firm offers one or more standardized core products (either a good or a service) that require a minimum of local adaptation. In some instances, the firm may offer a broader product line in some markets than others, but each core product conforms to standard specifications wherever it is marketed.

Global Location of Value-Adding Supplementary Services. The value chain is broken up across different countries, with management adopting a strategy of creating supplementary services in one country (or a limited number of countries) for worldwide delivery rather than duplicating each activity in each country. Looking at this another way, we could say that in a given location, the Flower of Service is pieced together with individual petals imported electronically from around the world. Technology allows information-based petals to be delivered in real time to the service site from anywhere with good telecommunication links.

Global Marketing Activities. Management employs a consistent marketing approach around the world, although not all elements of the marketing mix need be identical. Typically, corporate design is identical (except for language variations), and advertising themes and execution are recognizably similar. Market positioning, however, may vary somewhat in the light of local competitive offerings. Similarly, pricing may reflect positioning strategy, competitive activities, and local costs and taxes.

Global Competitive Moves. These actions are integrated across countries. The same type of move may be made in different countries at exactly the same time or in some systematic sequence. In highly competitive industries, a competitor may be attacked in one country to drain the resources that it was planning to apply in another country, or an assault by a competitor on the firm's own position in one country may be countered by a vigorous marketing campaign against that same competitor in a different country.

Some Industry-Specific Issues in Transnational Strategy

Certain types of services seem very easy to spread across the NAFTA countries, across Europe, or even around the world, whereas others seem very difficult. In the easy category fall simple service concepts that are replicable without difficulty and therefore franchisable. Some essential services, such as postal service and health care, are either government-owned or operate in heavily regulated environments, making it a challenge to penetrate foreign markets.

Historically, businesses that rely on trust and the reputation of their personnel—such as law firms and other professional service providers—have found it difficult to demonstrate service quality to potential foreign customers and to adopt a professional style that fits the local culture. Ways to overcome such hurdles include not only extensive advertising and public relations but also hiring host-country nationals who have obtained education and work experience in other countries. Another approach is through mergers and alliances.

For network firms, highly specific geographic locations may be seen as essential. No financial service firm with global ambitions, for instance, can afford not to have a presence in New York, London, or Tokyo. Even in this electronic age, birds of a feather still find value in flocking together! Similarly, there is intense competition among airlines for landing rights and gates at key global hub airports such as London-Heathrow, New York-JFK, and Los Angeles International.

In the case of travel-related services, wider global market participation makes a brand more valuable to customers. Thus, American Express traveler's checks and credit cards are useful precisely because they are widely accepted in most countries. Similarly, international airlines enhance their appeal as they fly to more destinations and provide more connections at their hubs. There is a growing trend for airlines to form global partnerships with carriers that have complementary routes and then to coordinate their schedules so as to feed passengers to each other's services. One example is the Star Alliance, whose members in early 2000 included Air Canada, Air New Zealand, Ansett Australia, Lufthansa, SAS, Thai, Varig, and United Airlines (see the advertisement in Figure 17.2); a second is oneworld, whose membership at that time comprised American Airlines, British Airways, Cathay Pacific, Finnair, Iberia, LAN Chile, and Qantas.

Not all service businesses that are successful in their home markets have achieved the same level of success abroad. One reason for failure may lie in not being able to transfer home-based sources of advantage. Euro Disney cannot duplicate at Paris Disneyland in northern France the sunny weather of Florida and southern California, and neither (so far) has it been able to recreate within the ranks of its French "cast" the friendliness of its American staffers (see the "Euro Disney" case on pp. 602). By contrast, Club Med has succeeded in duplicating almost all of its

Figure 17.2 Star Alliance: A Global Network of International Airlines

value chain in each of its warm-weather locations, meticulously reproducing its successful core formula, which includes a unique staff (the famous Club Med G.O.'s—*Gentils Organisateurs*—who enjoy a lot more flexibility than do Disney staffers), a village near the water, fun and games, and a high probability of pleasant weather. However, as noted in chapter 5, the company has had more difficulty in adjusting to changing market trends in what vacationers desire. Except for advance information and reservations—usually delivered by travel agents—most supplementary services are duplicated at each site. Similarly, there is a different core product but a high degree of consistency at Club Med ski locations, where the company also duplicates most supplementary services from food and après-ski entertainment to ski rentals and instruction. Service Perspectives 17.4 describes some of the ways in which a major international hotel chain has grown around the world without losing sight of its core competences.

Service firms can exploit differences in national comparative advantages as they seek to build more efficient value chains. A growing number of service-based businesses have identified key backstage activities that can be conducted more cheaply but without loss of quality in a different country than where most of their customers are located. For example, some U.S. banks and insurance companies now send checks and claims to be processed in East Asia or Ireland.

SERVICE PERSPECTIVES 17.4

Groupe Accor: Hotel Innovation in a Global Setting

Paris-based Groupe Accor is one of the world's leaders in several complementary and integrated services: hotels, travel agencies, and car rentals. According to industry experts, Accor is one of only three truly global hotel companies, each represented in more than sixty countries (the other two are Sheraton and Holiday Inn). Over the years, the group has proved itself to be a highly innovative service provider, as reflected by its in-depth market opportunity analysis, integrated offerings, and international growth strategies.

Accor has gone from being the first truly European hotel chain to the largest hotel chain in the world. It operates several distinct categories of hotel, such as the four/five-star Sofitel brand, three/four-star Novotel, three/four star Mercure, and two/three-star Ibis. Accor has also pioneered an easily prefabricated replicable budget hotel concept known as the Formula 1 chain. In the United States, Accor operates the Motel 6 chain of budget motels and Red Roof Inns and has plans for other acquisitions. Care is given to maintaining the distinctive identities of each of its hotel brands.

Accor's CEO, Jean-Marc Espalioux, seeks to give the company the integrated structure it needs to operate and compete on a global basis. Hotel activities have been restructured into three strategic segments, reflecting their market positioning. There are also two functional divisions. The first, a global services division, is being created to spearhead the major functions common to all hotel activities: information systems, reservation systems, maintenance and technical assistance, purchasing, key accounts, and partnerships and synergy between hotel and other activities. The second, the hotel development division, is structured by brand and by region and is responsible for working with the management of each hotel to prepare marketing, service development, and growth strategies. Says Espalioux: "In view of the revolution in the service sector which is now taking place, I do not see any future for purely national hotel chains—except for very specific niche markets with special architecture and locations, such as Raffles in Singapore or the Ritz in Paris. National chains can't invest enough money."

All told, Accor hotels are present in 140 countries, with more than 60 percent of hotel sales, and 75 percent of income, coming from outside France. The group is continuing its internationalization drive, focusing on further consolidating and integrating its network, as well as building a presence in such emerging markets as Poland, Hungary, and other ex–Soviet bloc countries. Espalioux is also very aware that the underlying obstacle to successful globalization in services is people: "Globalization brings considerable challenges which are often underestimated. The principal difficulty is getting our local management to adhere to the values of the group. [They] must understand our market and culture, for example, and we have to learn about theirs."

Because international cooperation, communication, and teamwork are integral to achieving global consistency, Accor has done what it can to eliminate hierarchy, rigid job descriptions and titles, and even organizational charts. Employees are encouraged to interact as much as possible both with their colleagues and with guests. They define the limits of their jobs within the context of the overall customer experience and are recognized and rewarded on how well they meet these definitions. In addition to these structural and organizational initiatives, video conferencing and other technologies are used extensively to create and reinforce a common, global culture among Accor employees around the world. All of the group's European hotels are being linked together through a sophisticated IT network, which may eventually be expanded worldwide.

Source: Andrew Jack, "The Global Company: Why There Is No Future for National Hotel Chains," *Financial Times,* October 10, 1997; W. Chan Kim and Renee Mauborgne, "Value Innovation: The Strategic Logic of High Growth," *Harvard Business Review* 75 (January–February 1997); and Ken Irons, *The World of Superservice: Creating Profit through a Passion for Customer Service* (London: Addison-Wesley, 1997), 121–123; and the firm's Web site, www.accor.fr, January 2000.

Meanwhile, Swissair has transferred part of its accounting operations to India; and American Express Europe processes all its continent-wide billing activities in Brighton, on the south coast of England. This strategy is being adopted for frontstage service elements, too, as companies build global reservation and customer service systems that are networked around the world.

Transnational Service Management: How Far Should Standardization Go?

To close this chapter, we look briefly at the implications of globalization for each of the 8 Ps of integrated service strategy.

Product Elements. Our prior discussion in this chapter suggests that there is a growing trend to standardization of core service products around the world but that supplementary services—particularly hospitality—are often adapted to meet local needs to facilitate an appropriate positioning strategy against local competition. In certain instances, cultural values or political factors are so significant that the core itself must be adapted. One example is McDonald's development of Veggie Burgers for the Indian market, where beef is not eaten because Hindus regard the cow as a sacred animal.

Price and Other User Costs. The financial price of a service may vary between countries, reflecting both local costs and local taxes. But even if the product costs approximately the same around the world (in terms of currency conversions), marketing managers should recognize that there may still be a wide divergence in its relative affordability. Buying a Big Mac in the United States or Canada does not burn a hole in most people's pockets, but in Russia or China, say, a visit to McDonald's may be considered a bit of a luxury that consumes a high percentage of the buyer's discretionary spending budget. For the other customer outlays, such as time and effort, consistency is more important. Services that are designed to save customers time and hassle should normally retain those characteristics in an international setting because they may create valuable differentiation over traditional offerings.

When corporate customers have operations in different countries, many service businesses try to avoid charging the same customer different prices for the same service without good justification. Increasingly, the purchasing departments of multinational companies are beginning to behave as transnational rather than multilocal customers. Recognizing this development, Hewlett-Packard offers worldwide contracts to its major global accounts for both manufactured products and services.

Promotion and Education. In general, services seem to make more use of consistent international branding than do manufacturing firms, especially in consumer markets. When companies grow through international acquisitions, there is often a phased replacement of the acquired company's name. The uncertainty created by intangibility can be offset by strong branding, so the primary task of the brand name or trademark for a service is to offer recognition and reassurance, rather than performing other functions such as positioning or local adaptation. McDonald's operates under the same name and golden arches trademark around the world so that both locals and travelers know that they will get the genuine McDonald's experience. Travel-related services virtually require the same brand name globally. How much value would an American Express card lose in terms of customer confidence if the local brand in Moscow were named Russian Express? International branding is supported by transnational advertising and consistent corporate design, featuring recognizable color schemes (yellow for Hertz, bright green for BP service stations) and an easily identified logo and trademark. The challenge is to avoid a using a corporate motif, name, or color that has unintended meanings or undesirable connotations in another language or culture.

Transnational or global advertising campaigns designed to build brand recognition and preference—sometimes termed *strategic advertising* as distinct from local, or *tactical,* promotions—often employ the same print artwork or video sequences around the world with text or voice-over in the local language. When developing global campaigns, it's essential to create visual themes that will travel well across different cultures. The need to be able to create and implement such campaigns for global clients has been an important factor in globalization of the advertising industry.[16] There is usually still a need for local, tactical advertising. Among the roles that this may serve are educating prospects in local markets about service features and capabilities, positioning the service against local competitors, and engaging in promotions designed to encourage trial and boost sales in periods of low demand. Educating customers and prospects may be especially important when moving to a new market where prospective customers are relatively less familiar with the service. Ways to build such expertise include well-trained salespeople and contact personnel, brochures, Web sites, and presentations at trade shows.

Place, Cyberspace, and Time. As discussed earlier in the chapter, delivery strategies vary according to the type of process involved. Information-based services lend themselves most readily to electronic delivery in cyberspace, even making possible delivery though a global network from a single, centralized source (although languages and preferred delivery schedules must still be taken into account). Delivery of high-contact services requires physical facilities, where the choice of delivery locations, building design, and operating schedules (time) may need to conform to local lifestyles, regulations, and climate.

Productivity and Quality. One of the challenges for international firms is achieving the same levels of productivity and quality that are the norm at home. The more that strategic success is dependent on consistent performance across countries in these two areas, the greater the effort that should be made to set global goals and standards. In network services, such as telecommunications, transportation, or business logistics, weaker quality standards in one location may prove to be the weak link in a global chain. Poor local infrastructures and difficulty in recruiting local personnel with the required skills and attitudes can make early parity in quality an unrealistic goal. On the other hand, lower productivity may be less of a problem if local labor costs are much lower than in the home country.

People. Can a global company develop a consistent, recognizable global culture? The answer is generally yes, given careful hiring and training, motivation, and role modeling. The task is greatly facilitated if the firm recruits against similar personality and value traits as are found among successful employees in other countries. However, success takes time. Some firms make a point of sending local managers to the company's home country for a period of training and familiarization with corporate routines. One of the challenges is to ensure that the global corporate culture can coexist with the local national culture without causing ethical conflicts or discomfort among employees and customers. To the extent that a North American company is comfortable with multicultural diversity among its employees at home, it will probably find it easier to manage its human resources abroad.

Processes. If a particular process offers a distinctive competitive advantage, a firm may want to ensure use of that process worldwide. As we've noted at several points in the book, some service industries are in transition from high-contact, people-based processes to low-contact, technology-based processes. But this transition cannot be expected to take place simultaneously around the world, especially when there is wide variation across countries in the level of infrastructure or customer sophistication. Moreover, some cultures may be more conservative and resistant to change than others. Hence, firms may have to base their international strategies on rolling out new technologies in sequence across different countries as customers become ready for change and the necessary infrastructure becomes available. Operating across many different countries has the advantage of allowing firms to create test markets in one or more of these countries to evaluate new processes that may eventually be adopted worldwide.

Physical Evidence. In terms of appearance and architectural design, service factories have started to look the same around the world, but this type of standardization is not necessarily required or even appropriate for effective execution of transnational strategy. In the hotel business, for instance, monotonously similar building exteriors and interiors are not always appreciated, even within the confines of a single country. Nevertheless, in consumer services, international travelers may seek some identifiable cues that speak to quality and positioning issues as well as confirmation that they are dealing with the same global supplier with which they are familiar from another country. Recognizable consistency in uniform design is one way to provide reassurance, although firms must be careful to create suitable variations for different climates and be aware of different cultural norms for appropriate dress, especially among women.

Conclusion

More and more service businesses are now marketing across national borders. However, an international strategy needs to be more than just a collection of domestic (or multilocal) strategies. A truly transnational strategy—whether it be pancontinental in scope or even global—requires selecting countries on more than just stand-alone attractiveness; it must also consider the potential of each market to contribute to the broader benefits associated with a large international business. Delivering global products requires that the firm offer a standardized core product (either a good or a service) that requires a minimum of local adaptation. Supplementary services, however, offer flexibility in that many can be either standardized or tailored to meet the needs of customers in local markets. Transnational marketing requires that management should use a consistent marketing approach in every country where it does business, although not all elements of the marketing mix need be identical. Market positioning, however, may vary somewhat in the light of local competitive offerings. Finally, competitive moves should be integrated across countries, with the same type of move being made in different countries at the same time or in some systematic sequence.

Stimulating (or constraining) the move to transnational strategies are such industry drivers as market factors, costs, technology, government policies, and competitive forces. However, significant differences exist in the extent to which the various drivers apply to people-processing, possession-processing, and information-based services. Within each broad service category, it's important to analyze each industry systematically to determine not only how specific drivers currently affect that particular industry but also to project how they might change over time. Similarly, managers need to evaluate alternative strategies for their own company, in the light of its size and market position, as well as corporate objectives, values, and investment criteria.

Managers should also consider the opportunities that exist to standardize each supplementary service element as well as the core product. Continuing advances in IT make even global strategies feasible for many information-based elements. As a result, certain supplementary services can be delivered from a central location, using conventional telecommunications or the

Internet. Others, however, require localized delivery systems, including local personnel and facilities. The combination of a globally standardized core product and customized supplementary services may offer service firms the opportunity to achieve the benefits of both system-wide efficiency and local market appeal.

REVIEW QUESTIONS

1. What are the key motivations for service firms to enter international markets?
2. Explain the distinction between multilocal and transnational marketing strategies as they relate to (a) the United States or Canada and (b) the world.
3. What can service marketers who are planning transnational strategies learn from studying national marketing strategies in the United States?
4. Review the five transnational strategy levers. Define the local (that is, country-specific) end of the spectrum for each of these five dimensions. What actions might be required to move a service firm toward the global end of the spectrum on each dimension?
5. To what extent should service businesses attempt to standardize both core and supplementary service elements when marketing in a large number of countries? Suggest specific instances where you believe that a strategy of mass customization would be more appropriate for some of the supplementary services.
6. How does the nature of the service process affect (a) the opportunities for globalization and (b) market entry strategies?

APPLICATION EXERCISES

1. Select three different service industries. In each instance, which do you see as the most significant of the five industry drivers as forces for globalization and why?
2. Choose an international service company from each of two different industries, one focusing on individual customers and the other on corporate customers. Using each firm's annual report, Web site, and published reports and stories in the mass media, profile its international activities and obtain evidence to show where the firm's strategy falls on the spectrum from transnational to multilocal.
3. Obtain recent statistics for international trade in services for the U.S. and another country of your choice. What are the dominant categories of service exports and imports? What factors do you think are driving trade in specific service industries? What differences do you see between the countries?

ENDNOTES

1. World Trade Organization, "World Trade Growth Slower in 1998 after Unusually Strong Growth in 1997," WTO press release, April 16, 1999, www.wto.org.
2. Gary Knight, "International Services Marketing: Review of Research, 1980–98," *Journal of Services Marketing* 13, no. 4/5 (1999): 347–360.
3. This term was coined by Curtis P. McLaughlin and James A. Fitzsimmons, "Strategies for Globalizing Service Operations," *International Journal of Service Industry Management* 7, no. 4 (1996): 43–57.

4. Sandra Vandermerwe and Michael Chadwick, "The Internationalization of Services," *The Service Industries Journal* 9 (January 1989): 79–93; Terry Clark and Daniel Rajaratnam, "International Services: Perspectives at Century's End," *Journal of Services Marketing* 13, no. 4/5 (1999): 298–310.

5. Christian Grönroos, "Internationalization Strategies for Services," *Journal of Services Marketing* 13, no. 4/5 (1999): 290–297.

6. See Thomas Hout, Michael E. Porter, and Eileen Rudden, "How Global Companies Win Out," *Harvard Business Review* 60 (September–October 1982): 98–108; C. K. Pralahad and Yves L. Doz, *The Multinational Mission: Balancing Local Demands and Global Vision* (New York: The Free Press, 1987); and George S. Yip, "Global Strategy . . . in a World of Nations?" *Sloan Management Review* 31 (fall 1989): 29–41.

7. Christopher H. Lovelock and George S. Yip, "Developing Global Strategies for Service Businesses," *California Management Review* 38 (winter 1996): 64–86.

8. Michael E. Porter. "Changing Patterns of International Competition," *California Management Review* 28 (winter 1986): 9–40.

9. George S. Yip, *Total Global Strategy: Managing for Worldwide Competitive Advantage* (Englewood Cliffs, NJ: Prentice Hall, 1992).

10. Lovelock and Yip, "Developing Global Strategies."

11. Christopher Lovelock, "What Language Shall We Put It In?" *Marketing Management* 3 (winter 1994): 36–48.

12. Johny K. Johansson and George S. Yip, "Exploiting Globalization Potential: US and Japanese Strategies," *Strategic Management Journal*, October 1994, 579–601. Note: The original framework embraced four drivers; we have broken out technology as a fifth and separate driver.

13. Frances Cairncross, *The Death of Distance* (Boston: Harvard Business School Press, 1997).

14. See, for example, "An Intruder in the Kingdom: Saudi Officials Try to Police Taboo Subjects on the Internet," *Business Week,* August 21, 1995, 40; "Chat Rooms and Chadors. Iran: Will the Internet Open a Closed Society?" *Newsweek,* August 21, 1995, 36.

15. See Yip, *Total Global Strategy,* especially 15–23.

16. P. W. Daniels, "The Internationalization of Advertising Services in a Changing Regulatory Environment," *Service Industries Journal* 15, no. 3 (July 1995): 276–294.

CHAPTER 18

Technology and Service Strategy

I believe that technology is creating a marketplace where everything is going to become more service-like.

REGIS McKENNA

Somebody once characterized *technology* as meaning anything that was invented during one's own lifetime. It's true that recency of invention tends to add interest, but sometimes it helps to take a historical perspective and understand the impact that now mature or even obsolete technologies had when they were first introduced. Although some inventions are highly specialized and don't change the lives of ordinary people, others have a significant impact on the way we live and the way business is organized. In short, they transform society and the economy.

For people living in the nineteenth century, the key transforming technologies of the Industrial Revolution included water power, steam power, railroads, and later, electricity. During the twentieth century, key transforming technologies included the telephone and internal combustion engine, air travel, jet engines, radio, television, computers, and space satellites.

New and evolving technologies continue to transform our lives. Our interest in this chapter lies in those technologies that impact the way in which services are produced, delivered, and marketed. In particular, advances in telecommunications and computers continue to generate innovations in service delivery, most notably through the medium of the Internet. Collectively, these are usually referred to as *information technology* (IT). However, technological advances in fields such as biology, physical design, power and energy, methods of working, and materials also have significant implications for services.

We've already made extensive reference to IT in earlier chapters. For instance, chapter 3 explored the shift from high-contact to low-contact services made possible by IT in information-based services such as banking. Subsequently, we demonstrated its applications to pricing in Chapter 9, communications in Chapter 10, and service delivery in Chapter 11.

This chapter begins with a broad review of technology applications in services before moving to focus on strategic issues in IT, with particular emphasis on the Internet and World Wide Web. It can usefully be read in conjunction with John Deighton's article, "Service Markets and the Internet," on pp 444 to 454. We raise such questions as:

1. What types of technology are relevant to different service processes?
2. How do the various types of technology relate to each other?
3. What factors underlie the rapid growth of IT?
4. How does IT affect the augmented service product?
5. In what ways is the Internet transforming service strategy?
6. What alternatives are available to traditional retailers faced by Internet competition?

The Meaning of Technology

Every generation tends to use the word *technology* to describe, rather loosely, the practical application of cutting-edge tools and procedures. Today, when people say, "Isn't technology wonderful?" they are probably referring to advances (or failures, depending on the tone of voice) in IT. Yet for all the modern marvels, many inventions remain very durable. We still benefit on a daily basis from technologies that have evolved only modestly from their nineteenth-century predecessors, from flush toilets to asphalt-surfaced highways and from electric railroads to the coal-fired generating stations that still power many of them—and some of our computers, too.

Examples of Different Technologies

It's important not to define technology too narrowly because there's much more to the technological transformation of services than just IT. In fact, at least six types of technology have implications for the service sector. These are the technologies of power and energy, physical design, materials, methods, genetic biology, and information. As we look at each, you should be considering the extent to which the application of one technology in a given service industry may be dependent for its success on leverage from one of more others.

1. *Power and energy technology.* Recent developments center around two areas. The first concerns more sophisticated approaches to renewable energy, such as solar and wind power. The equipment is often owned by entrepreneurs who act as small generating services, selling power to utility companies. More significantly for the service sector, there has been huge progress in miniaturization of batteries; their bulk and weight have been reduced even as battery life and strength has increased. Such batteries power small, portable IT equipment such as laptop computers, pagers, and cellular phones that are widely used by many service businesses. By facilitating mobile communications and service delivery in cyberspace, they enhance employee responsiveness and give customers greater flexibility.
2. *Physical design technology.* Creating smaller, lighter, faster, or more efficient equipment often requires new approaches to design. Laptops and cellular phones are very different from desktop computers and conventional telephones. High-speed catamaran ferries, featuring new hull designs and water jet-propulsion systems, are starting to revolutionize marine transportation.
3. *Materials technology.* New manufacturing techniques and materials have produced advanced plastics and metal alloys that make possible not only high-speed airfoils or miniaturized high-tech hardware but also such mundane objects as energy-saving lighting to pro-

vide better security in shopping-mall parking lots and lightweight, corrosion-resistant plastic piping to transport natural gas to distant customers. A modern train car makes widespread use of materials technology, including metal composites for lightweight bodies, vandal-resistant plastics and artificial fibers for easy cleaning, and shatterproof insulating glass for good views without compromising climate control and safety.

4. *Methods technology* relates to the development of new ways of working. It includes the design of the workplace and the service delivery environment as well as the activities that take place within them. Methods technology can be as simple as furnishing hotel bedrooms with box beds to simplify the cleaning task for housekeepers or installing beverage dispensers with automatic metering in a restaurant so that workers can perform other tasks while cups are filling.[1] And it can be as complex as designing the working environment for a hospital emergency room, an all-telephone bank, or an automated warehouse. To be successful, methods technology must take account of human involvement because employees and customers may be asked to perform unfamiliar new tasks. *User-friendly* must be the watchword, requiring operations managers to seek early and full participation of HR and marketing specialists.

5. *Biotechnology* includes research into the development and application of such procedures as gene splicing and gene therapy. Relevant service applications center around advances in medical treatments or development of genetically altered foods that might be served in restaurants. However, the long-term impact of these practices remains uncertain and their use—especially for broader public consumption—requires rigorous advance testing and thoughtful appraisal against ethical criteria.

6. *IT* encompasses several key elements, beginning with the capture of data and its storage in memory systems that may range in scope from the 200 bytes (equivalent to roughly three lines of typescript) in a credit card's magnetic strip to the terabytes of a super computer or data warehouse. IT is often identified with sophisticated hardware, but in fact software is the key to turning data into useful information (such as customer account profiles) or into the intelligence found in expert systems that tell users—or even machines—what decisions to make. Unfortunately, user-hostile equipment and software design, combined with lack of user training and complicated instructional manuals written in techspeak, may turn users into hostages and servants of IT systems rather than their masters. As we shall see in this chapter, almost every aspect of service can potentially be impacted by IT.

Technology and Innovation

New technologies permit service businesses to do things that weren't previously possible as well as to do existing things better or more productively. Despite all the excitement surrounding the growth of the Internet and the resulting scramble to profit from its transformational impact on business and society, economic historians point out that several past innovations have created similar levels of entrepreneurial frenzy. As Justin Fox observes:

> Once you look back at the early days of the factory, the railroad, the automobile, and especially the harnessing of electricity, a lot of what seems new about the Internet starts looking familiar. . . . In truth, the advent of almost every new product or technology during the past century and a half has spawned a free-for-all of entrepreneurs speeding to market with new designs. . . . The truly crucial technological innovations from an electronic standpoint are those that make us more productive. . . . If computers and the Internet do lead to sustained productivity gains, it will be . . . one of those great leaps into the future that make the world a vastly more prosperous place. It just won't be unprecedented. So what about the Digital

Age really is really new? Mainly, the rise of information—easily digitized, easily copied information—as a major economic product.[2]

Technological innovations may present opportunities for—or even require—a change of strategy for existing firms. Innovators, by contrast, can start with a clean state. For instance, many firms are moving to the Internet in search of greater productivity. Some bricks-and-mortar stores such as Kinko's have integrated the Internet into their business model and are

---

SERVICE PERSPECTIVES 18.1

Kinko's: From Local Copy Shop to Global Business Service Provider

In 1970, 22-year-old Paul Orfalea, just out of college, borrowed enough money to open a photocopy shop in Isla Vista, near the campus of the University of California at Santa Barbara. Covering just 100 square feet (less than 10 square meters), the tiny store contained one copy machine and also sold film processing and felt-tip highlighter pens. Orfalea, the son of Lebanese immigrants, called the store Kinko's after the nickname given to him by his college buddies because of his curly reddish hair. Thirty years later, Kinko's boasted a chain of almost one thousand printing and copying stores, operating 24 hours a day from coast to coast in the United States as well as in Canada, Britain, the Netherlands, Australia, United Arab Emirates, and three Asian countries.

Technological innovations in IT and printing have revolutionized Kinko's business model and created new methods of working for customers and the firm alike. At its stores, Kinko's customers can print in color in almost any size, bind their documents as they like, send faxes, and work on in-house computers. Many locations offer videoconferencing technology, and the company provides an array of other services and products, including rentals of conference rooms, notary public service, and sale of office supplies.

The firm's objective is to create a global online network to take advantage of digital technologies. Using Kinkonet, the firm's online service, customers can order supplies or submit files for printing. Thanks to digital file transmission, customers can compose reports in, say, Minneapolis and transmit them electronically to, say, Montreal where they can be printed and bound for a meeting. This procedure may eventually replace the traditional approach of first, creating documents and graphics; next, printing and binding them; and finally, distributing them physically to another location.

Kinko's seeks to change companies' existing working procedures through services that include productivity consultation and outsourcing of document management. In particular, it appeals to business travelers who may need to develop and deliver presentations, reports, and proposals far from their home offices (a few years ago, Kinko's even ran a national advertising campaign, positioning the firm as "Your Branch Office").

Recognizing that not all customers are in a position to transfer document files by modem and that printed materials may need to be delivered physically to their final destination, the firm has formed a partnership with FedEx, which is installing what it calls World Service Centers at selected Kinko's branches. These centers offer a full complement of express shipping solutions and provide access to late pickups.

In March 2000, the firm announced the creation of a separate company, Kinkos.com, combining Kinko's existing Internet-based activities with the e-business expertise, online design tools, and proprietary technology of a company called liveprint.com. The stated objective for Kinkos.com is to become a leading online resource for the small office/home office (SOHO) market, aided by a joint marketing relationship with AOL. The new Kinkos.com will have a clicks-and-mortar relationship with the store-based company, using the latter's physical locations for in-store marketing, customer acquisition, and physical distribution.

Source: Ann Marsh, "Kinko's Grows Up—Almost," *Forbes,* December 1, 1997, 270–272; and www.kinkos.com, April 2000.

adding the Internet as an additional channel; the new strategy is sometimes known as *clicks and mortar* (see Service Perspectives 18.1). Others such as the software retailer Egghead (now Egghead.com) are abandoning physical space entirely in favor of the cyberspace alternative. By contrast, Amazon.com and other pure Internet firms are spared the challenges of either changing horses in midstream or trying to ride two horses at once.

One important consideration is that different types of customers may prefer different channels. In chapter 5, we introduced the concept of technographic segmentation, a way of categorizing customers according to their propensity to use new technologies such as the Internet.[3] Not everyone is eager to use the Web, and there may be situations under which even an experienced user may prefer to obtain personal advice by telephone or visit a retail store to compare and contrast competing merchandise. Personal characteristics and beliefs also play a role. Among the dimensions that Parasuraman found to be associated with readiness to embrace new technologies were innovativeness, a positive view of technology, and belief that it offers people increased control, flexibility, and efficiency in their lives. Negative correlates included distrust, a perceived lack of control, feelings of being overwhelmed by technology, and skepticism about its ability to work properly.[4]

Creating New Ways of Working

Before implementing new strategies to take advantage of new or improved technologies, managers have to ask how existing work patterns will need to change if the innovation is to fulfill its promise. Much is currently being made of the Internet's potential for improving business productivity, not least through savings in activities such as purchasing and delivery costs.[5] But technology is not just about saving money. Hammer and Champy make the point that companies often use technology simply to speed up existing processes. They claim that "the real power of technology is not that it can make the old processes work better, but that *it enables organizations to break old rules and create new ways of working*"[6] (emphasis added). In the case of IT, they argue that instead of "embedding outdated processes in silicon and software, we should be using the power of technology to radically redesign business procedures and dramatically improve their performance."[7] This point assumes that firms are fully aware of what their existing processes are and underlines the value of blueprinting (see chapter 8) as a visual tool for process design or redesign.

Service leaders employ technology as an active component of strategy. Many firms have their own technology units whose work is devoted to exploring how innovations might best be employed to create value for customers and stockholders, higher quality, greater productivity, and a competitive advantage for the firm. The most desirable innovations are those that fulfill several—or even all—of these objectives simultaneously. An innovation that is designed with only a single purpose in mind may have unanticipated negative impacts on other activities.

Companies that seek to be on the cutting edge of new technology applications often work closely with university researchers and innovative manufacturers to shape the development of emerging technologies. This approach helps to create and reinforce a corporate culture that welcomes change and new methods of working.

A former chief information officer at Federal Express (now FedEx) highlighted his own company's eagerness to gain early experience with new technologies and used an interesting metaphor to describe alternate ways of applying new developments:

> One of the keys to our success is that we constantly embrace new technology. For most companies, that's very painful and they don't like it. It's painful to leave what works and is cheap for new, expensive unknown approaches. . . . [W]e would rather get an innovation a year earlier and develop back-up systems to counter a relatively high failure rate than to wait

until the failure rate—and the price—has been reduced to more acceptable levels. Most folks prefer to wait until a technology matures.

You can view technology as a wave in the ocean, washing in debris. Most people concentrate on the debris that floats in. "Oh, isn't this neat?" they'll say of some device. "Where can I use it?" And that's where I think they mess up. I view technology as the wave itself, not the individual things that are brought to shore. We knew what we wanted to do ten years ago, but the technology wasn't there. So we were waiting for the wave and constantly prodding manufacturers to create what we needed as that wave rolled in.[8]

FedEx continues to be known for its strategic emphasis on technology. In addition to its research into IT applications, the firm is also a leader in the materials-handling technologies needed for physical logistics. Its Superhub in Memphis features a remarkable matrix like system for processing and sorting millions of packages daily. In recent years, the company has also invested heavily in use of the Internet. However, in early 2000, some industry observers wondered if FedEx was getting sufficient returns on these investments relative to its less glamorous competitor, UPS.[9] If a firm becomes too enamored of one technology, there's a risk that it may overengineer its systems without reflecting sufficiently on how they add value for both customers and the business.

Managers also need to remember that the value of IT is a function of the quality of the data that it collects, stores, and distributes. In short, they should be aware of the risk of the phenomenon known as *GIGO* (garbage in, garbage out).

The Historical Evolution of IT

The technology of information has gone through a series of major transformations over several millennia. The first major advance, more than three thousand years ago, was the invention of the alphabet and other scripts, which allowed the spoken word to be recorded by scribes on stone, clay tablets, paper, or other media. Written messages—as opposed to verbal ones—could then be transferred from one location to another, and information could be recorded for posterity. Replacement of the cumbersome Roman numbering system by the Hindu-Arabic one, which took place in Europe from the twelfth century onwards, introduced true decimalization and the concept of zero and enabled the rise of modern mathematics and its application to accounting and insurance.[10] The invention of the printing press by Johannes Gutenberg in the fifteenth century marked a watershed in communications, making possible the mechanical reproduction of multiple copies of even lengthy texts instead of having to laboriously copy each one by hand.

As long as information was available only in printed form, it required physical transportation. Hence, improvements in transportation were highly relevant for communication. The creation of reliable national mail services during the nineteenth century greatly reduced the elapsed time between sending a letter, document, or package and its delivery to the recipient. As trains replaced stagecoaches, the mails became faster and more predictable. The big leap forward in international communications came with the introduction of steamship services that were not only much faster than the sailing ships they replaced but also operated fairly punctually against published schedules.

Regular transportation and mail services marked the beginning of modern marketing, creating a much broader marketplace than was feasible under face-to-face conditions. Retailers could now place orders from suppliers in distant locations and expect to receive shipments reasonably promptly. Similarly, customers in isolated farming, mining, and fishing communities could order goods by mail. In 1893, a new retailing company called Sears Roebuck conceived the idea of creating a catalogue featuring an array of goods that could be ordered and delivered by mail. Customers could request a copy of the catalogue, look through it at home, and place orders for the goods they desired to purchase (see Service Perspectives 18.2).

With the development of the telegraph and the telephone in the late nineteenth century, it became possible to transmit short printed messages or voice conversations by wire, and for the first time the link between communication and transportation was broken. Once refined and more broadly available, these media offered the potential for interactive commercial and personal communications, including the placement of orders and reservations. By contrast, the

---

SERVICE PERSPECTIVES 18.2

The Evolution of Sears: From Mail Order Catalogues to Bricks and Clicks

Richard Sears began his career as a station agent on the railroad. To supplement his income, he sold watches. In 1887, he decided to make selling his career and moved to Chicago where he hired Alvah Roebuck, a watchmaker. The first Sears catalogue was published in 1888 and featured only jewelry and watches. When this venture proved successful, the company, now known as Sears, Roebuck, expanded its array of merchandise. By 1895, the catalogue had been expanded to no less than 532 pages.

The company's catalogue retailing service grew rapidly, and in 1906 Sears, Roebuck opened a $5 million mail-order plant and office building on Chicago's South Side. With more than three million square feet (280,000 m^2) of floor space, it was then the largest business building in the world. Merchandise was ordered from an array of manufacturers, and orders were filled using a sophisticated assembly-line operation that provided inspiration to Henry Ford. Later, the company opened an additional distribution center in Texas.

With city populations growing and transportation improving, Sears, Roebuck was obliged to join the trend of operating retail stores, where city dwellers preferred to shop. The first Sears retail store opened in the firm's catalogue center in 1925 and was an immediate success. Over time, more and more stores were opened in cities across the United States, and a subsidiary operation was later opened in Canada. By 1931, sales through retail stores exceeded mail-order sales. In smaller towns, catalogue stores were established. They contained some display items, and catalogues were available for perusal by customers. An agent in the store took orders for mail delivery.

By the 1980s, the catalogue merchandise distribution operations were becoming unprofitable and were finally discontinued in 1993—an event that many economic commentators saw as marking the end of an era. However, these operations were succeeded by a smaller, successful, direct-response business, using a variety of specialized catalogues rather than one giant one.

After a period of decline during the 1990s in the face of competition from discount retailers and so-called category-killer stores (for instance, Circuit City and Home Depot), Sears revamped its remaining 2,950 stores and created Sears Shop at Home Service, which publishes specialty catalogues through licenses with third-party distributors. Another service, Sears HomeCentral, offers franchised repair services on many appliance brands, installation of home improvements, homeowner services such as carpet cleaning, pest control, heating and cooling, and maintenance contracts. Its slogan takes advantage of the power of the Sears brand: "One central source for a houseful of services: Sears Home Central. Call Someone You Know. 1-800-4-MY-HOME."

In 1999, Sears entered the Internet retailing business through its Web site, Sears.com—a significant cultural change for a traditional organization. Initially, sales were confined to appliances, parts, and tools. But the company plans to add additional merchandise categories and to let customers order repair services online.

Source: Eryn Brown, "Big Business Meets the e-World," *Fortune,* November 8, 1999, 88–98; "About the Company," www.sears.com, February 2000. Used with permission of Sears, Roebuck & Co.

invention of radio and television resulted primarily in one-way communications to a mass audience from a broadcaster, sponsor, or advertiser.

When computers were developed for commercial purposes, they were used primarily for backstage operations and recordkeeping in large companies. Individual customers first noticed their application in fields such as banking in the late 1950s and airline reservations in the 1960s. By the 1970s, the technology of transmitting data by telecommunications was sufficiently robust to permit creation of ATM networks in retail banking. The 1980s saw the advent of personal computers, modems, and fax machines, enabling customers and businesses to contact each other in new ways (although computer applications through modems required specialized software).

Today, everybody's eyes are on the Internet, whose early marketing applications first started attracting attention in the mid-1990s. Some of the service marketing activities that the Internet permits are simply enhancements of what was previously done by mail, printed brochures, or telephone calls. Others, based on digital technology, represent a radically new approach to doing business.

The Digital Revolution

Driving modern IT applications is the merger of two separate technologies—that of computers and that of telecommunications. George Gilder described this phenomenon back in 1991 as "one of the greatest transformations—perhaps *the* greatest transformation—in the history of technology. It's a technology of sand, and glass, and air."[11] The sand, he explained poetically, represented the microchip, which came in the form of "a silicon sliver the size of your thumbnail and containing a logical pattern as complex as a street map of America, switching its traffic in trillionths of seconds." The technology of glass was that of fiber optics: "threads of glass as thin as a human hair, as long as Long Island, fed by lasers as small as a grain of salt and as bright as the sun." The contribution of the air came in the form of a major enlargement in the use of the electromagnetic spectrum.

Underlying this global revolution, which Gilder describes as a change that "leaves all previous technological history in its wake," are five key drivers:

1. An enormous and sustained increase in computing power, paralleled by a rapid fall in the cost of this power (Moore's Law predicts a doubling of computing power for the same price every 18 months).[12]
2. Digitization of all types of information—from the analog waves of radio, television, and telephone calls to the images of movies and graphics—so that they can be stored and manipulated in the binary language of computers.
3. A huge increase in the capacity of telecommunication links as new satellite and microwave linkages are installed and as fiber-optic cable replaces conventional twisted-pair and coaxial cables.
4. A miniaturization of hardware and batteries that makes it possible to create a wide array of portable telecomputing devices.
5. Advances in software, digital switching technology, and network architecture that enable high-quality voice, picture, and data transmissions to move seamlessly between different types of terminals located all over the world.

Collectively, these developments are driving the rapid evolution of the Internet and its best-known component, the World Wide Web. As a global network of networks, the Internet is constructed of huge numbers of servers (large computers that control customers' e-mail and Web pages) around the world. The challenge for service managers is to decide how best to use this enormous potential.

Applying Technology to Services

In earlier chapters we saw some dramatic instances of how technology has stimulated and facilitated innovation in the service sector. Examples included Firstdirect, the all-telephone bank; Priceline.com, the Web-based reverse auction for purchasing hotel rooms, airline seats, and other services; and Hewlett-Packard's remote diagnostics and fixes of computer problems across vast distances.

Because of its remarkable capabilities, IT is, predictably, subject to hype. In his book *Megamistakes: Forecasting and the Myth of Technological Change*, Steven Schnaars writes of what he calls a bias toward optimism. "Optimism," he says, "results from being enamored of technological wonder. It follows from focusing too intently on the underlying technology."[13] The innovations most likely to succeed are those offering clearly perceived value not only to the adopting organization but also to those employees and customers who are expected to interact with them.

Managers need to create a business model for their organizations that uses technology for strategic purposes—adding value for customers, tying the organization more closely to both customers and suppliers, leveraging employees' work and liberating them from mundane tasks, increasing productivity, and having a positive financial impact on the bottom line. But they should beware of viewing technology as a magic elixir that guarantees successful results. Rushing to adopt new Web-based strategies without thinking through the implications for employees, customers, and the overall operating system can be a recipe for pain. Gregory Hackett has described past investments in computers and communication technology as a potential "service sector sinkhole," citing hundreds of billions of dollars spent on hardware and software with disappointing results.[14] Many of the once high-flying dot-com companies that bet heavily on the Web have already failed for lack of an effective business model.

Technology and Service Processes

The nature of the process underlying creation and delivery of the core product necessarily affects the type of technology needed to create and deliver it. As we saw in chapter 2, there are four underlying types of service processes: (1) *people processing*, which involves tangible actions to the physical person of the customer (e.g., hotels, health clubs); (2) *possession processing*, involving tangible actions to physical objects that customers desire to have serviced in some fashion (e.g., freight transport, repairs); (3) *mental stimulus processing*, which describes intangible services to the customer's mind (e.g., news, education); and (4) *information processing*, which is concerned with intangible actions relating to intangible assets (e.g., insurance, stockbroking). In our analysis below, we have combined the third and fourth categories into what we refer to as *information-based processes*.

People-Processing Services. Because customers interact directly with the physical organization, this category of service places a heavy emphasis on the physical design and materials technology of frontstage facilities and supporting equipment as well as the power sources needed to drive them. Methods technologies are concerned with how employees, customers, and physical elements interact on site to create the desired service.

Many technologies have been refined to serve the needs of specific industries. All transportation industries are shaped by new developments in power technologies because these affect speed, fuel consumption, and both noise and air pollution. Hospitals are the beneficiaries of advances in the physical design of new equipment needed to diagnose and treat patients as well as those in biotechnology. Methods of treatment in health care are constantly evolving, too, requiring both human and technical skills that are often exercised in a team setting. Restaurants have improved their productivity by investing in new food-related technologies (such as prepre-pared meals and improved strains of vegetables) as well as in devices to simplify food prepara-tion and cooking; however, methods of food preparation and service vary widely from those at a fast-food restaurant, where customers serve themselves in a highly industrialized setting, to those of a full-service restaurant, where the customer plays a much more passive role.

Possession–Processing Services. These services also emphasize power, design, materials, and methods technologies because the core products tend to involve physical activities, ranging from transport to storage, from installation to cleaning, and from fueling to repair. But there's a key difference between people and things. Unlike people, whose size and shape are more or less a given, physical possessions can be redesigned to make them easier to service: In fact, the first and best service that manufacturers and architects can give their customers is to design *service-ability* into physical goods and facilities. Unfortunately, this goal is often ignored; we still find equipment that is difficult to package and transport, machines that have to be totally disassem-bled by an expert to replace a simple part, electronic controls that only an 11-year-old video-game specialist understands how to operate, and buildings that are hard to clean and maintain.

Information–Based Services. This group includes both mental stimulus–processing services and information-processing services. Predictably, strategic developments in this category are driven primarily by IT. Advances in telecommunications, from cellular phones to satellite links and addressable cable TV, have opened up significant new possibilities for the information, news, entertainment, and education industries. IT-based telemedicine allows health care providers to transmit real-time patient information—including scans, X rays, and data from monitoring equipment—to a distant expert who can provide immediate consultation and advice.

Miniaturization of power sources (such as tiny batteries) also facilitates creation of smaller and lighter devices, such as flat screens, lightweight modems, portable faxes, cellular telephones, and pocketable hard disks capable of holding gigabytes of data. Combining portability with wireless networks frees users from the constraints of fixed-site installations and dramatically extends the usefulness of the Internet and World Wide Web.

Modern information-based services enable firms to dispense with the physical frontstage almost completely. To an increasing degree, all that customers need is access to some form of input-output device—a telephone, a keypad, a display screen, a card reader—connected elec-tronically to a remote backstage, which nowadays could be anywhere in the world. Many busy locations feature electronic kiosks where customers can conduct business with distant service providers (see Service Perspectives 18.3).

IT and the Augmented Service Product

What do advances in IT mean for the augmented service product? As shown in chapter 8, the supplementary services that surround the core, facilitating its use and enhancing its value, can be divided into eight categories: information, consultation, order taking, hospitality, safekeep-ing, exceptions, billing, and payment. We used the metaphor of a flower to depict the aug-mented service product as a core encircled by eight petals. In chapter 11, we noted that a major-ity of these petals are information dependent and can therefore be delivered electronically

SERVICE PERSPECTIVES 18.3

Selling Commercial and Government Services through Electronic Kiosks

Machines similar to bank ATMs are now being used to deliver a broadening array of services. In an effort to make profitable use of hallway space in shopping malls, airports, and other locations, building owners have encouraged installation of a variety of electronic kiosks. Public Internet connections are also being made available in an array of locations—you don't necessarily have to search for a cybercafé!

ATM manufacturers point out that any relatively small item that can be printed on paper or card stock or dispensed from a machine is a possible candidate for their products. So-called Super ATMs can be programmed to dispense coupons or job leads or to sell bus passes, ski-lift tickets, gift certificates, airline tickets, theater tickets, postage stamps, and long-distance telephone cards. In some locations, such as airports, they even dispense foreign currencies. The cost, plus a handling fee, is automatically deducted from the customer's bank account. The latest ATMs often include voice commands and animated color graphics; some even show movie clips and commercials while you wait for your transaction to be completed.

Government agencies have been using electronic kiosks for several years to dispense information about public services, tourist attractions, and bus routes. Now, in an effort to cut administrative budgets and provide 24-hour service in convenient locations, a number of agencies are using kiosks to automate a variety of transactions. Consumers touch the screen to choose from a menu of services, which can be programmed in multiple languages. They can pay parking tickets, speeding fines, and property taxes; obtain dog licenses and copies of birth certificates; and order license plates for their cars.

In Utah, Quickcourt kiosks assist people in filling out paperwork for no-fault divorces—a process that takes about 45 minutes, requires no lawyer, and costs only $10. Quickcourt also computes child-support payments. In San Antonio, Texas, kiosks sell permits to hold garage sales and print out information on property taxes and city job openings. Users can also view pictures of animals available for adoption at the city pound. In New York, users can look up certain kinds of records, such as landlords' histories of building code violations, and swipe their credit cards to pay municipal taxes, license fees, or speeding fines; a fee of $3.50 is added to card transactions.

Source: De'Ann Weimer, "Can You Keep 'Em Down on the Mall?" *Business Week,* December 15, 1997, 66, 70; Carol Jouzaitis, "Step Right Up and Pay Your Taxes and Tickets," *USA Today,* October 2, 1997, p. 4A; and Kara K. Choquette, "Super ATMs Sell Lift Tickets, Exchange Currencies," *USA Today,* January 19, 1998, B1.

through such media as telephone, fax, electronic kiosks, or the Internet, rather than physically. When the core product itself is information based, then it, too, can be delivered through electronic channels.

As a result, there are numerous opportunities to employ IT when designing service strategy. And even though hospitality and safekeeping involve physical processes, there is still a need to record information about customer preferences and behavior relating to these supplementary elements. Figure 18.1 illustrates ways in which a Web site can be used to deliver or enhance service for each of the petals of the Flower of Service. Let's now examine in more detail some of the ways in which IT can be used to deliver different types of supplementary services.

Information and Consultation. Customers need information about the goods and services that they buy, including confirmation of orders and documentation of account activity. Today, the emphasis is on using the Web. Well-designed sites provide the information that customers need about the firm and its services. Many sites include a section labeled FAQ (for "frequently asked questions") and an e-mail connection for additional follow-up to a customer service rep

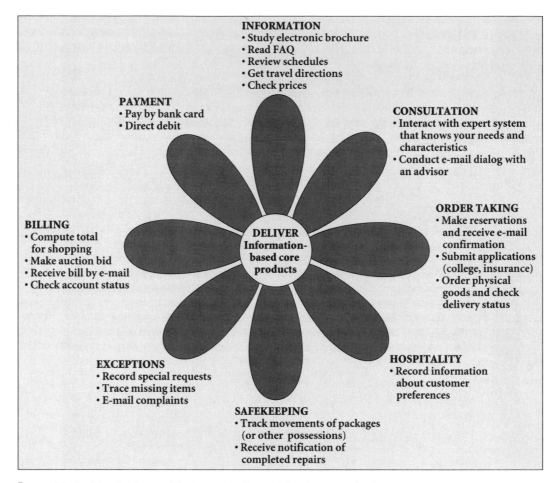

FIGURE 18.1 Applying the Power of the Internet to Core and Supplementary Services

or specialist. Some even offer company-sponsored chat rooms where customers can talk with each other.

Employees can be transformed into instant experts by giving them easy access to relevant information. When a customer in Boston telephoned FedEx late one afternoon to request a pickup, the agent told him it was too late. However, there was still time, she added, to deposit his package in a FedEx drop box—would he like street directions to the nearest one? When he said yes, she gave him easily understood instructions on how to find the box, including references to local landmarks. The customer was impressed, complimented her on the clear directions, and said, "You really know Boston well; you must come from around here!" "No," she replied, "I work in the Chicago area, and I've never even been to Massachusetts. I'm just reading this information off my computer screen!" FedEx had used the knowledge of local employees in Boston to create and record directions that any employee could subsequently access and provide with confidence. However, because even landmarks can change, such information needs to be periodically reviewed for accuracy.

Order Taking. How can technology make it easier for customers to place orders and for suppliers to take them? Placing orders in person, by voice telephone, or by mail and fax are still widespread practices. The key to improving productivity and quality in order-entry processes lies in minimizing the time and effort required of both parties while also ensuring completeness and accuracy.

Automated telephone ordering is one option, with a computer-generated voice probing for item codes and number of units required and the customer responding via the telephone keypad. Web sites are now widely used for order taking. Airlines, for example, encourage customers to check flight schedules and make their own reservations; hotel chains enable customers to research different offerings in each city served, review maps of hotel locations, and then make room bookings. And, of course, there has been a tremendous growth in online retailing, with participation by traditional retailers such as Sears and Wal-Mart; catalogue merchants such as Lands' End; and new, Internet-only providers such as Amazon.com. Online ordering has also surged in business-to-business marketing, and its sales volume greatly exceeds that of online consumer sales.

Large customers may be given access to customized and password-protected Web pages on restricted sites. There, corporate purchasers will find all the items that their firm normally orders at the prices previously negotiated plus such useful information as ordering history and typical order quantities. The Web site may also prompt the buyer to consider additional products that might be useful in the light of those that are being ordered. Another customer's pages will probably contain a different mix of merchandise at somewhat different prices.

Whether customers order physical goods by mail, telephone, Internet, or another medium, a vital challenge is to manage an effective order-fulfilment process. Prompt execution of each order involves tasks such as order picking in the warehouse, packaging, and shipment. More and more firms are contracting out the shipping task to specialized intermediaries such as UPS, FedEx, and national postal services.

McKesson, a San Francisco–based distributor of drugs, pioneered new methods of filling orders from retail druggists. Electronic orders are entered into the central computer at McKesson's warehouse. From there, each order is transmitted wirelessly to an order filler in the warehouse who wears a two-way radio and computer on the forearm and a laser scanner strapped to the back of the hand. The order is displayed on the three-square-inch computer screen, telling the worker where the items are and laying out the most efficient route through the 22,000-item warehouse to get them. As *Fortune* described this innovation when it first appeared:

> Dick Tracy would gasp with astonishment. . . . As the employee chooses each item, he points a finger, like some lethal space invader, at the bar-coded shelf label beneath it, shooting a laser beam that scans the label and confirms that he has picked the right product. When the order is complete, his arm-borne computer radios the warehouse's main computer, updating inventory numbers and the bill. The result: a 70% reduction in order errors and a hefty rise in the productivity of order takers.

The McKesson example illustrates the need to change work methods to take advantage of new IT developments. In this instance, employees were actively involved in a pretest of the new technology, offering suggestions for design refinements. Now, they way they work has changed, and the machine prompts them on how best to proceed.

Hospitality, Safekeeping, and Exceptions. Hospitality and safekeeping elements, which usually involve tangible actions in physical settings, help to make customers' visits more pleasant by treating them as welcome guests and taking care of a variety of needs. The category known as exceptions includes both special requests (often presented at the time of reservation) and problem solving when things go wrong.

Special requests, especially those involving medical and dietary needs, are common in the travel and lodging industries. The basic challenge is to ensure that each request is passed on to those employees who will be responsible for fulfilling it. The role of IT consists of storing such requests, passing them on to the relevant department or person, and documenting execution.

Technology speeds problem solving, too. USAA, a Texas-based firm specializing in insurance for military families and their dependents around the world, scans all documents electronically and stores them on optical disks. It also digitizes recordings of telephone calls reporting accidents and stores them with scans of photos and reports from lawyers, doctors, and appraisers concerning the same claim. The space required to store claim dossiers has already been enormously reduced (the company used to have a large warehouse), and the time wasted searching for missing dossiers—which were often on somebody's desk—has been eliminated.

Billing and Payment. Bills and account statements are important documents, whether displayed in paper or electronic form. Customers like them to be clear, informative, and itemized in ways that make plain how the total was computed. Forward-looking companies use market research to determine what customers expect from financial statements in terms of structure and detail and then employ IT to organize and highlight the information in useful ways.

When a Boston-based bank surveyed customers' preferences for bank statement formats, it found that people's opinions varied. Rather than trying to design a new statement that incorporated something for everybody but would have delighted nobody, the bank created three different formats offering varying degrees of detail and emphasis and let customers select the one they preferred. The computer then organizes account data in the preferred format.

Merrill Lynch continues to enhance the way it documents information on its award-winning monthly cash management account (CMA) statements, which have to integrate data on investment activity—including purchases, sales, dividend and interest receipts, and investment value—with details of checking and Visa platinum card transactions. The first page provides boxed summaries, with comparative data for the previous month and year to date, plus charts showing asset distribution and trends in total account value during recent months. Clients can also review their account data on password-protected Web sites. At year end, clients also receive an annual summary of checking and platinum card activity, organized by expense category, both monthly and for the year. Many clients find this information useful when preparing their taxes.

Wireless networks allow firms to take the checkout to the customer rather than vice versa. At many rental car–return lots, attendants take details of your contract, fuel reading, and mileage and then use a handheld device to print out your bill on the spot. In France, restaurant servers bring a wireless card reader to the table when it's time to pay the bill. The amount is entered, the user's card is verified, and then the machine (about the size of a handheld video game) prints out the bill for the customer to sign. Machines such as these save time for customer and supplier alike, as well as reducing paperwork and minimizing the potential for errors that comes from manual transfer of data.

Recreating Customer Intimacy through IT

Regis McKenna, a consultant to high-technology companies, argues that marketing's traditional, research-based connections to customers are no longer sufficient in a real-time world:

> [M]ore continuous connections with customers can provide information that focus groups and surveys cannot. . . . The knowledge of individual customer needs that that companies

can capture through technology harkens back to the days when the butcher, baker, and candlestick maker knew their clientele personally. . . . In that setting, customer service relationships were built in face-to-face transactions. . . . Today's technology can recreate the conversation between the shopkeeper and the customer.[15]

As service firms grow larger and extend their operations across broader geographic areas, corporate managers may become far removed from the day-to-day operations of the business—and thus from intimate dialogue with their customers. This development requires new efforts to understand and record customer needs so that representatives of the firm can reach out to each customer across time and geography. IT can often help provide the solution. Computer technology and telecommunications make it possible to provide national (or even global) online or telephone service out of a central location to serve customers who require information, wish to place orders, or seek to resolve problems. At the same time, technology is creating opportunities to capture real-time feedback from the marketplace.

An effective IT system has the potential to link specialized databases, thereby integrating key activities relating to customer service. The simplified airline blueprint shown in Figure 18.2 summarizes the links among databases on passengers, reservations, meals, and baggage. It also shows how information is used to track the movement of physical objects (such as bags or special meals). For instance, if a bag fails to show up at the destination airport, the IT system should be able to find out where it is so that it may be retrieved. Note, from the figure, how backstage information flows run parallel to the frontstage movements of the passenger.

Marketing Implications of the Internet

Recent years have witnessed an explosive rate of growth in Internet commerce for both goods and services. The potential of the Internet (which includes both e-mail and the Web) extends to every element of the 8Ps of integrated service management. It offers marketers exciting opportunities for service innovation, allowing them to create new offerings as well as adding new product elements and introducing new dynamics to communication, pricing, and distribution strategies (see the reading by John Deighton, "Service Markets and the Internet," on pp. 444 to 454). Although an intangible medium in itself, the Web's ability to integrate text, sound, and video creates interesting opportunities to simulate physical evidence of services.

Many companies are attracted to the Internet by its potential for improving the productivity of service processes. At the same time, the Net's ability to combine the control of centralization with the responsiveness of speed and customization can, if properly implemented, lead to improvements in service quality, too. One way in which the Web improves productivity is by enabling customers to perform more self-service; as a result, the human factor plays a lesser role on the Web than in face-to-face or even telephone-based contact. However, thoughtful Internet strategists recognize that the people dimension still has a vital role to play in problem solving and service recovery.

Marketing researchers accept that the advent of the Internet is fueling a radical change in the marketing of both goods and services, but they do not always agree on the ways in which the Internet will evolve as a commercial medium and its consequent managerial implications.[16] Some have suggested that it will blur the preexisting differences between consumer and business-to-business marketing.[17] Our focus in this final section of the chapter is on understanding the power of networks; the distinctions between the Internet, intranets, and extranets; some service-relevant applications of the Web; the importance of creating a viable business model; and how competitive Internet service strategies can be successfully integrated with more traditional approaches. The "VerticalNet" case (p. 653) provides further insights.

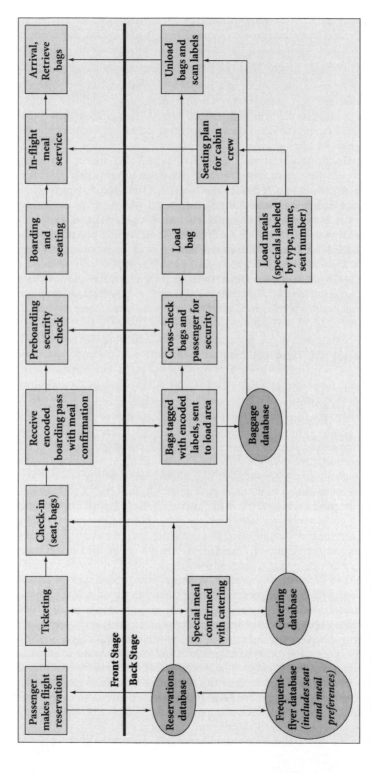

FIGURE 18.2 Using IT to Customize Service to Airline Passengers

The Power of Networks

As a network of networks connecting both individuals and businesses around the world, the Internet is open to all who can link to it. Commercial use of the Web emphasizes use of that network to exchange information, place and pay for orders, deliver *digital* products directly, arrange for later delivery of physical products, and resolve any problems that may arise.

Metcalfe's Law of Networks. A fundamental characteristic of networks, known as Metcalfe's Law (named for Robert Metcalfe, founder of 3Com Corporation) is that they increase in value dramatically with each additional node or user.[18] This law specifies that the utility of a network—whether of telephones, computers, or people—is the square of its number of users. Consider your telephone. It is useless if disconnected. It would be of only limited value if few of your friends, family members, or organizations that you needed to contact had telephones. The more people you can reach—and the more who can reach you—the more valuable the network. This fact helps to explain the early emphasis placed by Web start-ups such as eBay and Amazon.com on growing their customer bases instead of seeking immediate profits. Stimulating rapid growth requires not only an attractive, well-executed service but also heavy expenditures on marketing communication, thus necessitating substantial working capital.

The larger the number of households and businesses gaining access to the Internet (preferably through fast, broadband connections), the greater its potential as a commercial medium. With no cost penalties to either suppliers or customers for accessing geographically distant sites, the size of the potential market for many products is greatly expanded. In turn, customers may be exposed to more choices and can more easily compare prices. However, when physical goods arc ordered through the Web, there is still the cost of shipping to be considered and the possibility of having to pay higher rates for greater distances, especially for international shipments.

E-commerce: New Paradigms in Communication and Distribution. The Internet offers marketers a fast, versatile, and inexpensive communication medium. Unlike traditional broadcast networks, it is interactive. Through use of e-mail, firms can contact customers and prospects (and vice versa) faster and more cheaply than through such alternatives as postal mail, telephone, or fax. The Web can be used as a communication channel to supplement or replace traditional brochures, instruction manuals, press releases, sales promotion, and advertising. However, managers need to recognize that creating and maintaining Web sites and their content is not free and that companies incur costs in composing and responding to e-mail messages. If a firm fails to respond promptly and effectively to customer e-mails, it will lose those customers and generate negative word-of-mouth.

Key characteristics of Web sites include their ease of access, the speed with which information can be updated, and their economies of scale. The interactive nature of the Web facilitates dialogue among customers and suppliers concerning customized information, advice, order entry, order status, and complaints. It shifts power from sellers to buyers by facilitating dialogue between customers themselves through such mechanisms as chat rooms and user groups. Independent communities of interest may grow up around specific topics, ranging from hobbies to health care. In a few instances, groups of discontented customers have even created negative Web sites (some bearing a variant of the corporate name plus the suffix *sucks*) to air their complaints.[19]

For many people, the term *e-commerce* conjures up images of purchasing from high-profile retail sites, making airline reservations, or conducting banking transactions on-line. In practice, however, the use of the Net is far more pervasive in business and industrial settings, where speed, choice, and cost savings have become key forces in business procurement. Research suggests that business-to-business e-commerce has the potential to cut the cost of doing business from 2 percent in the case of the coal industry to as much as 29 to 39 percent for electronic components. Most industries can expect savings in the range of 10 to 20 percent.[20] These savings are being achieved by reorganizing the procurement function and reengineering traditional value chains. In their book *Blown to Bits,* Evans and Wurster describe how existing supply chains are being completely dismantled and reformulated in a process they call *deconstruction.*[21]

Forrester Research forecasts that business-to-business e-commerce (defined as inter-company trade in which the final order is placed over the Internet) will amount to $2.7 *trillion* by 2004.[22] It predicts that more than half of all sales will be accounted for by what it calls eMarketplaces, which bring buyers and sellers together in auctions, exchanges, and consolidated purchasing arrangements, in contrast to Internet sales involving the traditional model of one-to-one business connections.

Although much e-commerce consists of companies marketing their products directly to end users, some entrepreneurs have created Web-based brokerages, using the power of the network to bring buyers and sellers together in innovative ways. For an example of a successful business-to-business Internet start-up of this nature, BizBuyer.com, see Service Perspectives 18.4.

Although both conventional and Internet wholesale and retail organizations operate service businesses, much of what they sell are physical products. Manufacturers who engage in selling directly through Web sites are marketing goods *through service.* The strategic issue for them is how to add more value through Internet-based relationships than they might through conventional distribution in the form of face-to-face contacts, telephone contacts, or mail order. The actual delivery of their products usually requires the services of a specialized logistics supplier.

The Internet, Intranet, and Extranet

To make the best use of Internet technology, marketers need to understand the difference between the Internet and the more restricted networks known as intranets and extranets. Figure 18.3 clarifies their different characteristics and how they relate to each other.

The Internet is a public network, accessible to all. It's an open, free-ranging array of millions of computer hosts, providing information on companies (including a firm's competitors), government agencies, economic activities, vital statistics, the media, and academia. It includes all Web and other activity that is open and available to any user—including current and potential customers—around the world. As experience has shown, it is vulnerable to attack from hackers.

Intranets are composed of e-mail and Web site networks that are internal to specific organizations, available only to authorized employees and other personnel, and (ideally) protected by an effective firewall from outside access. In some cases, they represent an upgrading to Internet standards and protocols of preexisting private communication networks based on sharing electronic files through software such as Lotus Notes. For security reasons, some companies deliberately keep their intranets disconnected from the outside world. Corporate intranets serve to link the vital activities of the company, facilitate access to important information—including that needed to serve customers better—and speed communication among different departments and geographically separated offices. In a sense, intranets help a widely dispersed organization to create a virtual corporation in cyberspace.

Extranets link an enterprise's extended family. They form the core of most Internet business-to-business commerce and are generally open to suppliers, distributors, retailers, and other alliance partners as well as to large corporate customers. However, they can also be found in consumer settings, especially among those businesses promoting sales to a group of known customers. Extranets are often reached through a published Web site address that contains a secured link to a restricted site, whose access is limited to authorized users. Access may require advance registration and use of a password. Extranets enable firms to engage in active conversations with a known user and thus offer a high degree of personalization. They have become

BizBuyer.com: Brokering the Buying and Selling of Business Services

On a visit to Paris in 1995, Home Depot executive Bernard Louvat saw a presentation about the potential for retailing on the Internet, then a novel concept. "That evening," he recalled, "I had an epiphany. I saw something that would revolutionize the way we live and do business." Six months later, he moved to Los Angeles and, seeking to gain experience of this new technology, joined an online firm that delivered city guides through the Web.

Determined to found his own Internet company, Louvat was struck by the lack of applications for small businesses. Noting the success of eBay's auction site, Louvat decided to develop a reverse-auction model for businesses in need of specific goods or services. Buyers would file a request for quotes (RFQ) on his site, and suppliers would then bid to fill the order, using a procedure of progressively lower quotes. Traditional methods of seeking RFQs involved advertising, direct mailings to purchased lists of suppliers, telephone calls, and use of brokers. They were often slow and ineffective.

Investors funded the new start-up, and BizBuyer.com was launched after months of planning. By early 2000, after a year of operation, the firm offered 18 categories of business activity. A few were dedicated to physical goods, but most featured services. Categories included telecommunications; consulting; insurance; Internet services; employee benefits; sales, marketing, and creative services; financial services; accounting; legal; real estate; and translation.

BizBuyer requires potential buyers to define their needs on its highly specific request form. It offers guides for each category, explaining the features and issues to consider before purchasing. Once an RFQ has been submitted, e-mails are sent to vendors registered in that category, inviting them to view the details on the Web site and then respond. Buyers see a side-by-side comparison of the vendors' resulting bids, which usually start arriving within 24 hours, much faster than under traditional RFQ procedures.

Firms seeking an RFQ pay nothing. The firm's revenue model is based on a fee of $4 to $10 per bid from sellers plus a commission ranging by category from 0.5 percent to 20 percent of the agreed selling price. Sellers don't learn the identity of the buyer until the latter is ready to make a decision. To protect its buyers, BizBuyer.com checks the credit rating and business standing of every vendor, as well as sharing buyers' ratings of their experiences with specific vendors.

Many small to medium-sized firms rely on receiving RFQs as a basis for seeking business from new clients. Internet-based services like those of BizBuyer.com (there are now several competing firms) offer sellers lower customer acquisition costs, a broader geographic market, and higher closure rates. Because the buyer's needs are more clearly expressed than in many traditional RFQs, the leads are more easily evaluated for fit with the seller's capabilities. For buyers, the advantages include much less effort in identifying and reaching prospective suppliers, faster responses, and a more rapid closure.

Says BizBuyer's general manager, Paolo Consiglio, "Entrepreneurs who register [with us] as vendors have immediate access to a market consisting of thousands of businesses. Compared to other lead generation engines, such as the Yellow Pages, a potential buyer using RFQs is much more qualified and is already in purchase mode."

Source: Leigh Gallagher, "Best of the Web: Booting Up Your Own Business," *Forbes.com*, February 2000; Dana James, "Request for Cash: Online RFQ Services Provide Small Biz with Needed Tools," *Marketing News*, March 27, 2000, p. 11; www.bizbuyer.com, April 2000.

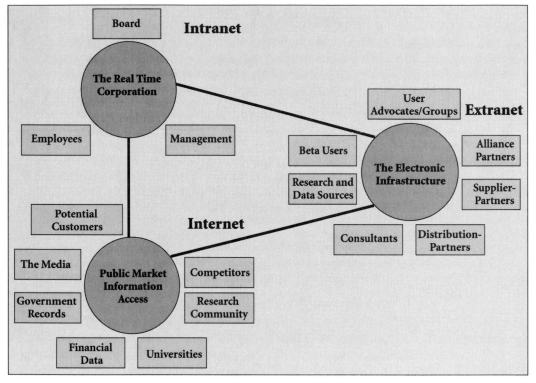

FIGURE 18.3 The Intranet, Extranet, and Internet

Source: Regis McKenna, *Real Time.* Boston: Harvard Business School Press, 1997, p. 112. Copyright © 1997 by the President and Fellows of Harvard College. All rights reserved.

common in supply chains and are leading to a restructuring of these chains, with particular emphasis on creation of electronic hubs.[23]

Business Models for the Web

As any Web surfer knows, not all Web sites are created equal.[24] Apart from ease of use, quality of presentation, and volume of information, they also differ at a strategic level in terms of what they can do for customers and how they generate revenues for the firm. Many early Web sites were little more than electronic brochures, designed to supplement other elements in the marketing communication mix, without attempting to link exposure directly to sales. Today, Internet strategists focus on employing the characteristics of the Web to generate revenues from advertisers or direct-sales responses, thus shifting Web sites from a promotional tool to a revenue-generating model. A variety of different business models now exist.

Types of Web Site. Ward Hanson identifies three different levels of Web site, each offering different capabilities.

1. *Publishing sites* are basically electronic brochures, catalogues, newspapers, magazines, or even encyclopedias that can be updated as frequently as the sponsor wishes. They offer the

same information to all visitors and are best thought of as a broadcasting medium. However, they aren't necessarily dull because they can contain numerous pages organized around many different topics, which users can search and retrieve as they wish. They can also contain animated graphics and sound. What is limited is the dialogue between Web site and user. In a simple publishing site, the only data returning to the publisher are from the clicks by visitors.

2. *Databases and forms.* These second-level Web sites combine publishing power with search engines that enable visitors to retrieve information in response to requests. Hence, they offer interactivity and dialogue. Much basic e-commerce is accomplished with capabilities that include the ability to get customized information, select products, and submit purchase orders. A user's interrogation of the site might include such questions as: Where is the nearest store to my home postal code, and how do I get there? Or, What flights are available tomorrow between Houston and Mexico City?

3. *Personalization* is the most sophisticated approach. It requires development of a site capable of dynamically creating a page catering to a specific individual. Moving beyond an ask-respond interaction into a dialogue, it may anticipate user choices and suggest possible alternatives. Users must be prepared to reveal at least part of their identities, wants, and preferences to benefit from such customization; similarly, the site must be programmed to respond appropriately.

Creation of interactive Web sites has become a demanding activity that requires frequent updates. Customers are intolerant of failures on the Internet and are only a click away from the competition. Constructing, maintaining, and upgrading sophisticated sites is an expensive proposition, and the task is often outsourced. In fact, a service industry has grown up around the business of Web site design and maintenance, with many firms offering to perform this task for client organizations.

Provider–Based Revenue Models. This approach to doing business on the Web is based on obtaining fees from other companies that seek to reach visitors to that site. There are four types of provider-based model:

1. *Content sponsorship* requires one or more sponsors to pay a fixed price for a defined period, based on the projected number of visitors, in return for having their names prominently displayed on the site, typically in some form of banner advertising. If the number of visitors changes in the future, then so will the price—much as happens with newspaper circulation or TV viewership—because the goal is exposure to the advertiser's name. This approach can work well for publishing sites, especially when the site owner does not expect to charge customers for access or downloading.

2. *Retail alliances* involve exclusive or near-exclusive deals for a firm to be the referred vendor in a specific product category (e.g., books, music, or cars). Vendors pay substantial fees—often millions of dollars a year on popular sites—for the right to have a clickable button in a prominent spot on the site. Deals are shaped by the anticipated volume of traffic and the extent of competitive exclusion.

3. *Prospect fees (also known as click-through fees)* tie the payments for clickable buttons to the number of visitors who complete some action. At the simplest level, it's based on the number of site visits. More sophisticated measures of performance include marketing-relevant behavior such as filling out a form or downloading of software.

4. *Syndicated selling* involves payment of sales commissions to affiliated sites when a customer clicks through from one site (an affiliate) to make a purchase on another, linked site. Online booksellers such as Barnes and Noble often enter into affiliate relationships with sites that can promote sales of books on particular topics.

From the standpoint of the site owner, fixed sponsorship fees, once received, offer the advantage of up-front payments that can help finance future improvements. Moving from fixed fees to prospect fees or sales commissions is more risky because the site's revenue is dependent on the advertiser's performance as well as that of the original site. If a Web site fails to attract many visitors and only a small percentage of them click through to the advertiser and buy something, then the revenue stream will be minimal.

User–Based Revenue Models. The most widespread form of e-commerce involves receipt of revenues directly from customers. Such an approach makes the entire process accountable and easy to evaluate for effectiveness and profitability. Revenues from customer transactions may include direct sales of merchandise or services, subscription fees for a period of access to a restricted Web site with valued content, or pay-per-use transaction fees, such as accessing and downloading copies of articles from a publishing site. In the case of auction sites, revenues usually take the form of commissions paid by the seller based upon the selling price.

Strategy and the Internet

A key question for service marketers is the extent to which the Internet should become the driving force behind a firm's business strategy as opposed to an enhancement of the existing, more traditional strategy. Motivations for existing firms to adopt use of the Internet include fear of losing customers to new Internet start-ups, seeking new customers in an expanded marketplace, and a search for cost savings. The self-service nature of the Internet offers the potential for sharply lower transaction costs. Consider the transaction costs for retail banking: Customers transacting at a branch cost the average bank $1.07, as compared with $0.27 at an ATM and only $0.10 by the Internet.[25]

Many companies have chosen to hedge their bets, viewing the Web as an additional medium for marketing communications, a supplement to telephone ordering procedures, or another way to deliver information-based services. However, unless well executed, a strategy of adding new delivery channels may result in sharply different service experiences for customers and lead to cultural and organizational conflicts within established service providers. Managers should recognize that Web sites can play a variety of tactical and strategic roles and should choose the approach that best leverages their strategy at a particular point in time.

Adaptive versus Transformative Applications. Faced with the opportunities presented by the Internet (and the threat posed by new, Internet-based competitors), how should existing firms respond? Alternative strategies can be divided into two broad groups—*adaptive applications,* in which the Web supplements existing marketing arrangements, and *transformative applications,* in which use of the Internet becomes the major driver of the firm's strategy. The example of Sears (in Service Perspectives 18.2, p. 541) showed a large, traditional firm in the early stages of an adaptive mode in 2000. At that time, by contrast, Kinko's (see Service Perspectives 18.1, p. 538) was already moving to an advanced adaptive mode with the formation of Kinkos.com as a separate but complementary company. For an example of shifting from an adaptive to a transformative strategy, consider the evolution of Charles Schwab, the brokerage firm, as described in Service Perspectives 18.5.

Competing on the Internet. The last years of the twentieth century were marked by explosive growth in both Internet sales and in the number of Internet start-up companies. Many established firms found themselves left behind in the rush to add a Web presence and were struggling to catch up. By contrast, if the history of past business innovations is any guide, the early years of the twenty-first century will see the disappearance of a majority of these start-ups through bankruptcy, merger, or takeover. A number of traditional firms, especially channel

SERVICE PERSPECTIVES 18.5

Technology and the Evolution of Charles Schwab

Charles Schwab & Co., the largest discount securities broker in the United States, was founded in 1975 when fixed commission rates were abolished. The company's initial service was very basic—accurate and timely execution of investment transactions for clients who conducted their own research and made their own investment decisions. By 1980, Schwab's expanding customer base and transaction volumes enabled the firm to make significant investments in back-office technology and to offer new services such as money-market mutual funds and asset management accounts. By adding value through automation, Schwab altered its market position from one based on low-price transactions to one that promoted value-added service at a low price.

In 1995 Schwab introduced its StreetSmart software package, which allowed account holders to trade through their computers and to obtain online access to current investment information. But in 1996, a new and well-funded competitor, E*TRADE, offered online trading at a flat rate of $29.99 a trade. Schwab promptly launched Web-based online trading through a separate business unit called e-Schwab. Pricing soon became a sore point: Customers who telephoned their orders to a Charles Schwab call center still paid a commission, averaging $80 a trade, whereas the price at e-Schwab (originally $39) had been reduced to $29.95 in response to E*TRADE's cut to $19.95.

In 1998, the firm made a strategic shift, merging e-Schwab with Charles Schwab, adopting a single low rate scale for all customers, and rebuilding its business model around the Internet. Thanks to rapid growth, the firm recovered from the revenue impact of this move in only 14 months. Its goal was to create a new segment in the brokerage business—the mid-tier broker—offering most of the service and advice provided by a full-service broker at a fraction of the cost.

To attract new customers, the firm changed its message from one emphasizing technology to one that demystified online investing and focused on the customer's whole experience with Schwab. It emphasized value, based on such innovations as online access to expert systems that help customers match their investment goals to, say, specific mutual funds. Unlike E*TRADE's customers, Schwab's customers could choose between doing business online, by telephone, or in one of the firm's bricks-and-mortar stores. They could get advice by downloading articles, participating in online investment forums with experts and business leaders, sharing ideas with other Schwab investors, or—for a fee of several hundred dollars—meeting with a specialist for an in-depth portfolio analysis and consultation.

Schwab's success is forcing traditional full-service brokers to reexamine their pricing policies and to offer online service, too. Meanwhile, however, Schwab has taken steps to strengthen its appeal to those long-time customers—around 175,000 out of a total of 6.6 million—who now have investable assets of more then $1 million and are at risk of defecting to high-service private banks. In January 2000, Charles Schwab announced the purchase of U.S. Trust Co., an asset management firm catering to the very wealthy.

Source: Kent Dorwin, "Repositioning a Leading Stockbroker," *Long Range Planning,* November–December 1988, 13–19; Jeffrey M. Laderman, "Remaking Charles Schwab," *Business Week,* May 25, 1998, 122–129; Mary Modahl, *Now or Never* (New York: Harper Business, 2000), 119–125; and Louise Lee and Mike McNamee, "Can Schwab Hang On to Its Heavy Hitters?" *Business Week,* January 31, 2000, 46.

intermediaries in business-to-business supply chains that no longer add value, will also disappear. Management Memo 18.1 suggests possible strategic responses to technology for existing bricks-and-mortar retailers.

Established companies with deep pockets and a willingness to change their organizational cultures may be able to profit from the shakeout. Although some of the failing start-ups lack an effective business model, don't have a well-differentiated product, or are competing with too many other firms for too small a market, others have potential. The problem facing this last

MANAGEMENT MEMO 18.1

How Should Bricks–and–Mortar Retailers Respond to Technology?

In the past, life was simpler for retailers. They connected to customers through their stores and salespeople; through the brands and packages they sold; and through in-store displays, advertising, and direct mail. Today, suggests Professor Raymond Burke of Indiana University, "[t]here are dozens of new ways to attract and engage customers—and none are more tempting than those fueled by new technologies." Although technology will change the way retailers interface with customers in the future, he cautions that not all of the new technical innovations now on offer will be successful.

In deciding which technologies to embrace and which to reject, it helps to consider past successes and failures. One major success story has been the shopping cart, introduced in 1936, which changed the method by which customers shopped and greatly increased how much they could purchase at once. Another success is the universal product code, introduced in the 1970s (although it was initially slow to gain acceptance). Scanning has made checkouts faster and more accurate, as well as providing retailers with a rich source of market research data.

But failures abound, too. They include the Checkout Channel, a network of five-inch color monitors located by grocery store checkout counters. It ran a continuous loop of CNN programming and advertisements. Customers didn't like it, and neither did the checkers. After one year, it was only available in 840 stores. In 1993, Turner Broadcasting pulled the plug. VideOcart looked promising, too, when first launched in 1989. It offered a wireless system of LCD screens and computers mounted on the pushbars of shopping carts. The screens could show maps of the aisles, highlight specials, and track how customers moved through the stores. But it cost from $100,000 to $150,000 per store and took up valuable display space. After four years, the manufacturer filed for bankruptcy in 1993, having installed systems in a mere 220 stores.

Technology firms need to understand that retailers expect a return on their investments and that hardware and software systems require new expertise to implement and maintain. From the consumers' viewpoint, many technologies actually make shopping harder rather than easier. People also worry that data-gathering technology is becoming too intrusive.

Professor Burke offers retailers 10 guidelines based on recent research conducted at Indiana University's Customer Interface laboratory and at other academic and commercial institutions.

1. *Use technology to create an immediate, tangible benefit for consumers.* If they don't see how it is going to help them, consumers often assume it's going to be used against them.
2. *Make the technology easy to use.* On average, it takes customers 20 to 30 minutes to learn how to shop in most text-based Internet grocery shopping programs. By contrast, it takes them only 2 to 3 minutes to learn in a three-dimensional virtual store modeled after a bricks-and-mortar store, because the latter is more intuitive.

group of start-ups is that although their service concepts may be promising, more time and money is needed to develop the market and refine the offerings than the firm in question can afford from its dwindling supply of working capital—hence the opportunity for takeovers by well-established firms eager to create or expand an Internet presence.

Christiansen and Tedlow point out that retailing has gone through four stages of disruptive change: the creation of department stores, mail-order catalogue retailing, the rise of discount department stores, and now the Internet.[26] The advantages of Internet retailing—its ease of access from anywhere at any time, its ability to feature a broader inventory than any physical store, and its potential for lower costs and higher margins—are too attractive to be ignored by most traditional retailers.

3. *Execution matters: prototype, test, and refine.* Many potentially viable concepts fail from poor execution. For instance, when customers used a so-called meal-solution video kiosk at one supermarket, they became frustrated by their inability to print out a menu. The source of the problem? When the printer ran out of paper, there was no screen message to communicate this fact.

4. *Recognize that customers' responses to technology vary.* Research shows that customers can be segmented according to their attitudes toward, and use of, different types of technology.

5. *Build systems that are compatible with the way customers make decisions.* Designers need to learn more about consumers' behavior and observe them in action. One Internet start-up launched a grocery shopping system that grouped cold cereals by their main ingredients—rice, corn, wheat, and so on. Unfortunately, many shoppers had trouble finding their favorite brands because they didn't know the ingredients!

6. *Study the effects of technology on what people buy and on how they shop.* Research in the United States shows that text-based home-shopping systems make consumers more price sensitive than those that display realistic images of the merchandise. In Sweden, a grocery store experimented with electronically adjusting prices according to the time of day; it found that a strategy of reducing prices in the evening increased evening sales by 40 percent and doubled store traffic.

7. *Coordinate all technologies that touch the customer.* Whether a customer encounters a retailer via the Internet, a catalogue, by telephone, or in the physical store, there should be some commonalities to the experience. Customers expect a specific firm to offer the same merchandise at the same prices accompanied by the same knowledgeable and courteous service.

8. *Revisit technologies that have failed in the past.* Just because a technology failed to meet its promise in years past doesn't necessarily mean that it will never work. Improved performance and lower prices may offer new opportunities to create value for today's customers.

9. *Use technology to tailor marketing programs to individual customers' requirements.* Treating all customers alike puts traditional retailers at a disadvantage to those electronic retailers who customize their marketing programs instantly to match the needs of individual shoppers, based on records of past purchases or other data.

10. *Build systems that leverage existing competitive advantages.* Despite the role of cyberspace in electronic retailing, the constraints of time and space still exist. Consumers may not want to wait for a physical product to be shipped to them (even assuming it can be shipped at all). They may feel that a picture and specifications on a computer screen cannot fully compensate for not being able to see and touch the real thing. Bricks-and-mortar retailers should use technology to magnify the positive differences that separate them from purely electronic competitors.

Source: Based on information in "Retailing: Confronting the Challenges That Face Bricks and Mortar Stores" (introduced by Regina Fazio Maruca), *Harvard Business Review* 77 (July–August 1999): 159–170.

Part of the competitive challenge when a firm markets through multiple channels under the same identify is to create a consistent brand experience across those channels and to use each one to leverage the others.[27] For example, if a service firm is known and liked for its friendly, informal approach in physical settings, then telephone agents and Web sites should try to express that same spirit in their respective environments.

Doing business on the Web is itself evolving. As the novelty of visiting Web sites and making electronic purchases wears off, customers are starting to become more demanding. As in conventional retailing, some firms seek to add value through service innovations, whereas others just compete on price. One of the Web's appeals for sellers is that transactions are cheaper to execute when customers must perform self-service than when sales are made by telephone or face-to-face. However, retail firms that seek to provide high levels of Internet service recognize that purchasers need to feel as comfortable making decisions online as they would in a store, where they can examine the merchandise and speak with a sales rep.

Lands' End, the direct-sales clothing marketer, is seeking to revolutionize the way clothes are sold on the Web. The firm has a strong motivation to move its customers from telephone use to Web use because printing and mailing 250 million catalogues a year accounts for no less than 43 percent of its total operating costs.[28] Operating a 3,000-person call center is also expensive. One of its innovations has been to allow female customers to evaluate clothes on its Web site by creating and saving online what it calls Your Personal Model. By entering the relevant information, customers can build a three-dimensional model that matches their body shape, hair style and color, skin tone, and face shape. With a single click, they can dress this customized model in selected clothing items and view it from different perspectives.

Lands' End is also moving to integrate its Web site and telephone call center, just as it earlier integrated toll-free telephone calling with its mail-order catalogue. While online, customers can contact a call-center agent by clicking on a callback button and entering the number of an available telephone for the agent to call. Alternatively, they can click on an instant text-message button and chat online in a text dialogue. In both instances, the customer's and agent's browsers are linked so that both can view the same Web page as they converse. As one researcher at the firm commented:

> We wanted a way to increase customer service. While some sites have taken the notion that the more they can reduce human interaction, the more cost effective their site would be, we've taken the exact opposite view. In the past few years, e-commerce was a novelty. But . . . now that people are used to the concept of shopping on line, they are starting to expect more. They want the same level of service they find when walking into a store or contacting a traditional call center. They want answers and access to knowledgeable agents.[29]

Not every service business can be an all-Internet operation.[30] That option is available only to companies marketing information-based services that can be delivered directly through the Web. People-processing services, such as airlines and hotels, will still require their customers to visit the physical locations where service is delivered. For them, the Web is a way to build closer relationships with customers at the same time that they minimize the cost of taking reservations through intermediaries such as travel agents or outsourced telephone call centers. Traditional retailers of physical goods will always need physical channels of distribution to get their merchandise to customers. Their choice is one of whether to continue operating retail stores or whether to focus (like Lands' End) on merchandise selection, marketing, and order taking while contracting out the physical distribution aspects to a specialist logistics firm.

It's appropriate to conclude this chapter as we began it, with a reminder that technology in services means much more than just use of the Internet, as important and exciting as that may be. Management Memo 18.1 focuses on bricks-and-mortar retailers, but it holds lessons for all types of established service businesses faced with adapting to new technologies.

Conclusion

Technology in services goes beyond just IT, central though that may be to modern life. Service managers also need to keep their eyes on developments in power and energy, biotechnology, physical design, methods of working, and materials. Changes in one technology often have a ripple effect, requiring leverage from other technologies to achieve their full potential. Every time technology changes, it creates threats to established ways of doing business and opportunities for new ways to offer service. Managers need to be watching developments proactively to determine their potential impact. Leading firms often seek to shape the evolution of technological applications to their own advantage.

Although there has been a rapid increase in the volume of electronic commerce, we are still in the early stages of the so-called Internet Revolution. Experts continue to disagree on what its ultimate impact will be. What is clear is that many customers are choosing to move away from face-to-face contacts with suppliers in fixed locations that only operate during fixed hours to remote contacts anywhere, anytime. As more and more households acquire computers with Internet capability, electronic commerce is likely to continue expanding. However, this doesn't necessarily mean an early end to physical retailing activities as we know them—shopping for many types of goods and services will retain its appeal as a social experience.

People-processing services will continue to require customers to visit in person; what will matter most is the nature and quality of the experience. Possession-processing services (which include the retailing of goods) may need different physical distribution channels as more and more customers choose to shop by click rather than make purchases at bricks-and-mortar stores. What seems most likely is that they will contract out their distribution and delivery requirements to specialist outsourcers who have mastered the techniques of effective business logistics, in which key requirements for success include expertise in transportation, materials handling, and IT.

Information-based services, by contrast, are likely to be transformed by the advent of the Internet. The big question here is how long it will take to attract customers who prefer the present high-contact systems (as in retail banking) and see no reason to change. In this instance, ongoing monitoring of technographic segments will help firms plan effective strategies for smooth, but possibly extended, transitions.

The underlying goal of modern service delivery systems should be to offer customers more choices, recognizing that some people opt for face-to-face contact, others like telephone contact with a human being, and still others prefer the greater anonymity and control offered by more impersonal contacts such as mail order or a Web site. When purchasing goods and services, some customers prefer to visit the store to make a physical examination of the items that interest them or discuss the performance characteristics of a service with a knowledgeable seller face-to-face, others are content to call a toll-free number to place an order when they see an advertisement for something they like, and yet another group likes to select its purchases from a nicely printed catalogue and to order by telephone or mail. Finally, a fast-growing number of consumers are comfortable examining and purchasing via the World Wide Web. In each instance, although the core product may remain the same, the wide differences in delivery systems mean that the nature of the overall service experience changes sharply as the encounter moves from high contact to low contact.

REVIEW QUESTIONS

1. Why should service marketers concern themselves with new developments in technology?
2. How have changes in both technology and society shaped the evolution of Sears?
3. What insights does blueprinting provide for effective use of methods technology and IT?
4. How do Internet applications for people-processing and possession-processing services differ from mental stimulus–processing and information-processing services? Give examples.
5. What ethical issues do you see arising as a result of the boom in electronic commerce?
6. What is the distinction between an adaptive strategy and a transformative strategy when an established firm seeks to incorporate the Internet into its business activities?

APPLICATION EXERCISES

1. Review the six different technologies described earlier in the chapter and identify specific instances in which the application of one technology may be dependent for its success on one of more other of the technologies described.

2. Prepare illustrations of the electronic Flower of Service as applied to (a) retail banking, (b) hotels, (c) freight transport, and (d) car insurance. In each instance, prepare a flower diagram that shows relevant activities for each of the different petals comprising the augmented service product

3. Select a specific industry with multiple competitors and visit the Web sites of four different firms in that industry. Compare and contrast both their capabilities and the quality of execution, including ease of navigation. What conclusions do you draw concerning the strategic role that each plays for the company in question?

4. You are consulting for a long-established retailing firm that is eager to encourage customers to switch from using stores and call centers to going to its Web site to make purchases. Explain how the insights from technographic segmentation studies would help the firm plan an appropriate strategy and set reasonable goals.

ENDNOTES

1. James L. Heskett, W. Earl Sasser Jr., and Christopher W. L. Hart, *Service Breakthroughs* (New York: The Free Press, 1990), 181.

2. Justin Fox, "How New Is the Internet, Really?" *Fortune*, November 22, 1999, 176, 180.

3. For a detailed discussion of technographics, see Mary Modahl, *Now or Never: How Companies Must Change Today to Win the Battle for Internet Consumers* (New York: HarperBusiness, 2000).

4. A. Parasuraman, "Technology Readiness Index [TRI]: A Multiple-Item Scale to Measure Readiness to Embrace New Technologies," *Journal of Service Research* 2 (May 2000), 307–320.

5. Jennifer Reingold, Marcia Stepanik, and Diane Brady, "Why the Productivity Revolution Will Spread," *Business Week*, February 14, 2000, 112–118.

6. Michael Hammer and James Champy, *Reengineering the Corporation* (New York: Harper Business, 1993), 90.

7. Ibid.

8. Ron J. Ponder, quoted in "Federal Express: Quality Improvement Program," in Christopher H. Lovelock, *Managing Services: Marketing, Operations, and Human Resources* (Englewood Cliffs, NJ: Prentice Hall, 1992), 274.

9. Brian O'Reilly, "They've Got Mail," *Fortune*, February 7, 2000, 100–112.

10. Peter L. Bernstein, *Against the Gods: The Remarkable Story of Risk* (New York: Wiley, 1996).

11. George Gilder, "Into the Telecosm," *Harvard Business Review* (March–April 1991): 150.

12. Larry Downes and Chunka Mui, *Unleashing the Killer App* (Boston: Harvard Business School Press, 1997).

13. Stephen Schnaars, *Megamistakes: Forecasting and the Myth of Rapid Technological Change* (New York: The Free Press, 1989).

14. Gregory Hackett, "Investment in Technology: The Service Sector Sinkhole?" *Sloan Management Review* (winter 1990): 97–103.

15. Regis McKenna, "Real-Time Marketing," *Harvard Business Review* (July-August 1995): 87–98.

16. For an example of some early predictions, see Robert A. Petersen, Sridhar Balasubramanian, and Bart J. Bronnenberg, "Exploring the Implications of the Internet for Consumer Marketing," *Journal of the Academy of Marketing Science* 25, no. 4 (1997): 329–346; and Raymond R. Burke, "Do You See What I See? The Future of Virtual Shopping," *Journal of the Academy of Marketing Science* 25, no. 4 (1997): 352–362.

17. John Deighton, "Commentary on 'Exploring the Implications of the Internet for Consumer Marketing,'" *Journal of the Academy of Marketing Science* 25, no. 4 (1997): 347–351.

18. Downes and Mui, *Unleashing the Killer App,* 5.
19. Wendy Zellner, "A Site for Soreheads," *Business Week,* April 12, 1999, 86.
20. Laura Cohn, Diane Brady, and David Welch, "B2B: The Hottest Net Bet Yet?" *Business Week,* January 17, 2000, 36–37.
21. Philip Evans and Thomas S. Wurster, *Blown to Bits: How the New Economics of Information Transforms Strategy* (Boston: Harvard Business School Press, 2000).
22. "e-Marketplaces Will Lead U.S. Business eCommerce to $2.7 trillion in 2004, According to Forrester," Forrester Research press release, February 7, 2000.
23. Steven Kaplan and Mohanbir Sawhney, "Ethics: The New B^{2}B Marketplaces," *Harvard Business Review,* 78 (May–June 2000): 97–103.
24. This section is based on Ward Hanson, *Principles of Internet Marketing* (Cincinnati: South-Western College Publishing, 2000); see especially 131–141.
25. Downes and Mui, *Unleashing the Killer App,* 45. (Note: the same data included an average cost of $0.68 for a telephone transaction, but much depends on the type of telephone technology employed. Transactions conducted at a custom-designed, telephone-only bank such as FirstDirect cost much less.)
26. Clayton M. Christensen and Richard S. Tedlow, "Patterns of Disruption in Retailing," *Harvard Business Review* 78 (January–February 2000): 42–45.
27. Ranjay Gulati and Jason Garino, "Get the Right Mix of Bricks and Clicks," *Harvard Business Review,* 78, (May–June 2000): 107–114.
28. Modahl, *Now or Never,* 201.
29. George V. Hulme, "Help! Companies Are Turning to Their Call Centers to Improve Customer Service on the Web," *Sales and Marketing Management* (February 2000): 78–82.
30. Jon Anton, "The Past, Present and Future of Customer Access Centers," *International Journal of Service Industry Management* 11, No. 2 (2000): 120–130.

Organigraphs: Drawing How Companies Really Work

Henry Mintzberg and Ludo Van der Heyden

A creative new approach to org charts helps managers see critical relationships—and competitive opportunities, too.

Walk into any organization—not the nice, neat managerial offices but the factory, design studio, or sales department—and take a good look. In one corner, a group of people are huddled in debate over a vexing logistics problem. In another, someone is negotiating with a customer halfway around the world on the Internet. Everywhere you look, people and products are moving, crisscrossing this way and that. You get a snapshot of the company in action.

Ask for a picture of the place, however, and chances are you'll be handed the company's org chart, with its orderly little boxes stacked atop one another. The org chart would show you the names and titles of managers, but little else about the company—not its products, processes or customer—perhaps not even its line of business. Indeed, using an org chart to "view" a company is like using a list of municipal managers to find your way around a city.

The fact is, organizational charts are the picture albums of our companies, but they tell us only that we are mesmerized with management. No wonder they have become so irrelevant in today's world. With traditional hierarchies vanishing, and new-fangled—and often quite complex—organizational forms taking their place, people are struggling to understand how their companies work. What parts connect to one another? How should processes and people come together? Whose ideas have to flow where? The answers to those questions not only help individuals understand how they fit into the grand scheme of things but also reveal all sorts of opportunities for competitive advantage.

For the past several years, we have been experimenting with a new way to draw—and thus, see—organizations. We call our approach an *organigraph*, a tip of the hat to the word *organigramme*, the French term for organizational charts. Organigraphs don't eliminate the little boxes altogether. But they do introduce new components called hubs and webs—forms that we believe reflect the varied ways people organize themselves at work today. Organigraphs are more than just pictures; they are also maps. They do not show individuals or positions so much as they provide an overview of a company's territory—its mountains, rivers, and towns, and the roads that connect them.

We have created organigraphs for about a dozen companies and have found that they are much more useful than traditional charts in showing *what* an organization is—why it exists, what it does. Organigraphs have been able to demonstrate *how* a place works, depicting critical interactions among people, products, and information. Moreover, executives have used their organigraphs to stimulate conversations about how best to manage their operations and which strategic options make the most sense, much as hikers use maps to investigate possible routes.

Take a look at the exhibit "Organigraph of a Petrochemical Company." It shows how the company operates like a traditional chain: raw materials are found or purchased, perhaps traded, and then refined and sold. Those activities constitute the main petroleum business. The organigraph also shows how the company's chemicals division connects with this chain in a more iterative, weblike way, drawing out materials from the refinery and feeding them in at another stage, at the retail gas pumps. While the sequential business relationships could very naturally be managed by a centralized planning office, the more weblike ones—with their need for negotiation of transfer prices and the like—may call for a more decentralized approach. Seeing such relationships illustrated can help a company understand the need for different managerial mind-sets throughout the organization.

That businesses need a new way to depict their organizations is hardly a novel contention. In 1993, an article in *Business Week* suggested that companies begin to replace their org charts with figures that look like starbursts, shamrocks, and pizzas. Some commentators have even suggested that the org charts be stood on their heads, putting operating employees on the top and bosses on the bottom. But all turning them upside down would do is provide a better depiction of the senior manager's headache. Organigraphs, instead, offer a new way to look at our companies. They are pictures that show not headaches but real businesses and their opportunities.

The Basic Forms of Organizing

Organigraphs contain two rather conventional components. The first is a *set*. Every organization is a set of items, such as machines or people. Sometimes these items barely connect with one another, and so they remain just that—sets. Parts in a warehouse, for example, wait there as independent items, as do the finished products of a factory before they are shipped off. Many professional service firms, such as law offices, operate as sets, with professionals working almost exclusively with their own clients. The same can be said about the divisions of a conglomerate company or the professors teaching and doing research at a university: all of these function rather independently. They are loosely coupled as a collection, a group, or a portfolio. These sets usually share common resources—facilities, funds, overall management—or else they would not be found in the same organization. But otherwise, they are on their own.

More commonly, though, organizations don't exist to house sets. They exist for purposes of connection. And connection is usually shown by the second conventional form, the *chain*. Materials enter a factory to be transformed into parts, which are combined into subassemblies, which are combined into final assemblies and then shipped to customers. The assembly line in an automobile factory is the prototypical example of this linear connecting process—here, chains prevail. Indeed, chains are so embedded in business imagery that many managers describe their strategies in terms of value chains and their logistics in terms of supply chains.

The preponderance of chains in business thinking is certainly understandable. Because chains are linear, the promote standardization and therefore enhance reliability. They can clarify and systemize the many complex processes that constitute business today. Imagine an automobile factory without chains! But do chains really describe all the activities and relationships within a company? Obviously not. Think of the buzzing confusion of a customer service office or the zigs and zags of new product development. And what of airports and trading floors? These, we would suggest, are better depicted in different ways—as hubs and webs.

Hubs first. A *hub* serves as a coordinating center. It is any physical or conceptual point at which people, things, or information move. A building can be a hub—think of a school or an airport. So can a

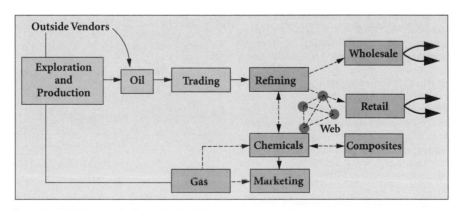

FIGURE 1 Organigraph of a Petrochemical Company

machine—a computer, for example. A manager can be a hub. Just think of a football coach. And so can a core competence, such as optics at Canon or bonding and coating at 3M. In fact, places that we usually consider chains may also be considered hubs. Draw a big circle around a factory, including its assembly line (a chain), and the whole place looks like a hub, to which parts and people flow and from which products emerge.

Hubs depict movement to and from one focal point. But oftentimes connections are more complicated than that. That's where *webs* come in. We are constantly being reminded that we live in the age of the network, where different "nodes"—be they people, teams, computers, or whatever else—connect in all kinds of ways. Webs, as we have come to see, are grids with no center; they allow open-ended communication and continuous movement of people and ideas.

Take new product development, for example. In the midst of a launch, the cast of characters talking to one another—often in very circuitous ways—will include managers, engineers, salespeople, and customers. Any complex project these days can be seen as a web. Think of how the Olympic Games are organized or how a movie is made. Everyone talks to everyone else, often with creative and unexpected outcomes.

The new vocabulary of organigraphs can expand how we view our organizations; it can even expand our thinking about strategic direction. Consider the exhibit "Organigraphs of a Canadian Bank." For years, the company had been a classic "silo" organization, with its businesses, such as insurance and brokerage, approaching customers independently. Then, as information sharing and cross-selling became competitive necessities, the bank began exploring other ways of organizing. One was to assign company representatives—personal finance advisers—to deal with customers for all the businesses, so as to present an integrated front. These advisers become, in effect, a hub for the customer. Another option was to place representatives from the different businesses in adjacent offices so that they could work cooperatively in dealing with customers—passing on leads and so forth. That way, the business representatives could work as a team—a web—while doing business with customers. Such options would have been available to the bank without organigraphs, of course, but the new vocabulary, and associated pictures, brought the choices into high relief.

Given the propensity of hubs and webs in organizations today, where does that leave the tradi-

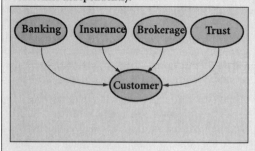

This organigraph depects the bank's original structure. Each division operates as a silo—a member of a set—and approaches the customer independently.

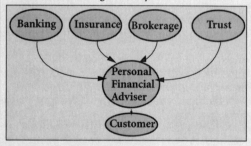

A second organigraph depicts one strategic option. All divisions converge on financial advisers—acting as a hub—who can approach each customer in an integrated way.

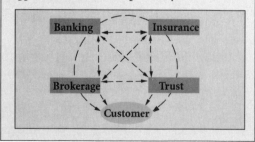

A third organigraph illuminates another strategic option. Representatives from each business work cooperatively —as a web—at each branch, but approach customers independently.

FIGURE 2 Organigraphs of a Canadian Bank

tional organizational chart? The organizational chart treats everyone and everything as an independent box. And every one of those boxes is connected by a vertical chain—that is, a chain of authority. If that is how we see organizations, is it any wonder there has been so much restructuring and delayering, so much merging and outsourcing? These changes are initially driven by a reshuffling of boxes on paper—too often without careful consideration of an organization's real ways of doing business and of creating value.

Organigraphs in Action

When you try to draw an organigraph using sets, chains, hubs, and webs, what happens? Almost anything. There is no right organigraph. Unlike the org chart with its strict rules of arrangement, an organigraph requires managers to create a customized picture of their company, something that involves imagination and an open mind. (Organigraphs can, in fact, include shapes besides sets, chains, hubs, and webs—as long as the shapes convey meaning. For instance, some organigraphs include funnels, suggesting a chain in which a transformation takes place.) Organigraphs can be disconcerting to those accustomed to doing things the traditional way. One manager we worked with resisted them initially, saying, "But I like org charts. When something goes wrong in my company, I know exactly whom to call to fix it." Always formal authority! To draw an organigraph, you must accept

the fact that it has less to do with names and titles than with relationships and processes.

To see how an organigraph works, let's look at the exhibit "Organigraph of a Newspaper." A newspaper brings in a variety of materials from society—news, photographs, and the like. Employees at the newspaper screen the material, transform it, and assemble it into a single document. The document then goes to a plant for reproduction, and the copies are distributed back to society, indeed to many of the same people responsible for the inputs, such as letters to the editor and classified ads.

The newspaper organigraph shows that while the organization's overall flow is a chain, other forms coexist within it. The reporters' relationship with the community, for example, can be seen as a web: the stock-in-trade of many reporters is to build networks of sources. And the whole newspaper might be considered a hub, upon which all sorts of inputs converge—classified and other advertisements, letters to the editor, article ideas, and so on—to be dispersed back into society. Because they are not integral to the main linear flow of the organization, various support and administrative functions, such as purchasing and finance, are shown around the hub, not within it.

What a different picture than the traditional org chart! (For a comparison, see the exhibit "Newspaper Org Chart.") Those little stacked boxes imply an organization consisting of independent agents. The picture doesn't even show advertisers, and it

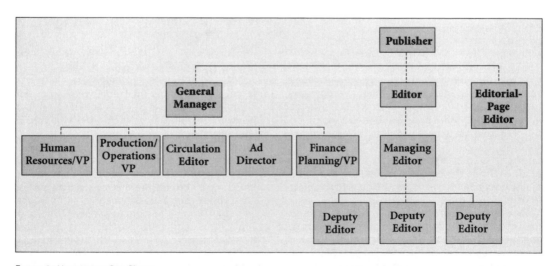

FIGURE 3 Newspaper Org Chart

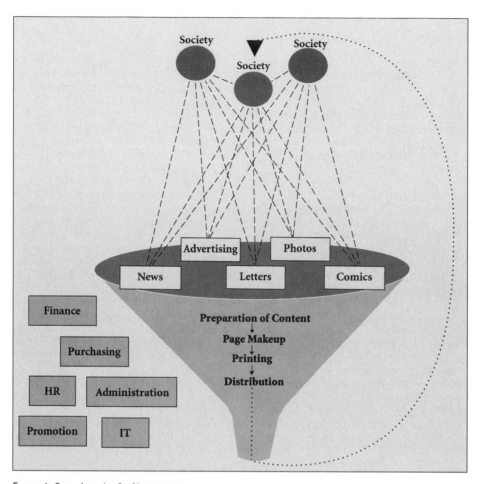

FIGURE 4 Organigraph of a Newspaper

suggests that the human resources department is somehow in the thick of the company's operating processes. The organigraph, in contrast, shows that advertisers are both sources of content (as part of the web) and customers and puts HR's role in perspective. It also draws attention to the scope of the business, suggesting which activities ought to be retained inside the core of the company and which might be candidates for outsourcing, such as printing and distribution.

The exhibit "Organigraph of Electrocomponents," showing a British distributor of electrical and mechanical items, depicts an entirely different business than that of the newspaper. When you actually visit the company, it *appears* to function

like a web: an automatic machine picks a variety of different items from all over large warehouses and moves them to packing. But this activity is, in fact, more like a set of chains: each order is picked in careful sequence.

Overall, the company's work is a chain. Electrocomponents procures thousands of items, which are held in inventory. When customers place orders, products are picked off the shelves and delivered on a day's notice. But as is often the case, the company actually combines organizational forms. For example, the company's relationships with customers can also be seen as a web. Several times a year, Electrocomponents sends out catalogs to its customers, most of whom are engineers. They

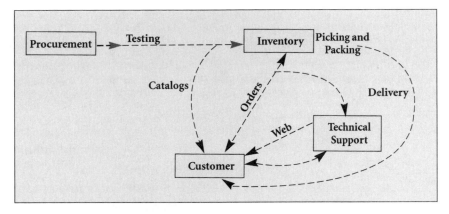

FIGURE 5 Organigraph of Electrocomponents

phone in their orders and can use the same call to ask for advice from the technical support staff, who are also engineers.

The organigraph we developed with Electrocomponents allowed managers to see nearly a dozen new opportunities to expand the business. "The picture forced us to think about what our real expertise was," recalls CEO Bob Lawson. "And we decided that it was in business-to-business relationships, not with consumers." As a result of that insight, Electrocomponents decided to expand significantly in Asia and to increase its Internet business. Further, the organigraph helped the company's managers see the strategic logic of segmenting its catalog. Having sent out only one version before, it now issues six specialized versions. The organigraph also showed managers opportunities to expand and sell the company's testing services. "At a glance, that diagram allowed us to see all sorts of new possibilities," Lawson says.

A Nest of Organizational Forms

Chains, hubs, webs, and sets can be found throughout most organizations. In the exhibit "Organigraph of Médecins Sans Frontières" (Doctors Without Borders), we take that concept one step further, depicting the nesting of such relationships—hubs within hubs within sets.

The organigraph shows a nonprofit that establishes emergency hospitals in disaster areas. Médecins Sans Frontières is made up of a set of national offices. There is no world headquarters—no hub. Rather, CEOs from the national offices meet periodically, and when a crisis arises, people from the offices communicate informally with one another. They form a loose web.

Each national office is, however, a hub unto itself. (See the largest circle in the exhibit.) The office is the focal point for the collection of professionals, supplies, funds, and procedures. Each office, for instance, holds its own donations in the bank and has a list of physicians prepared to go on assignment. When a crisis occurs, a national office assembles resources—people, supplies, and money. It then ships them to the troubled area. There, a hospital is created— a temporary organization— itself a hub to which the ill are brought. Each patient also becomes a hub in his or her own right, on the receiving end of various health care professionals, medicines, and food.

The organigraph shows that there are four distinct areas of operation within this nonprofit:

- a national office coordinates resources available for relief operations;
- that office also assembles those resources at the time of a particular relief operation;
- a chain transfers the relief resources from the national office to the hospital site;
- that hospital then delivers health care.

The organigraph makes clear the managerial realities the nonprofit faces. For example, one can see from the illustration that the burden of promoting the organization and raising money for it lies on the national offices themselves. The loose web that serves as an umbrella for the set of national offices is not organized to do so. Further, the organigraph shows operating autonomy on

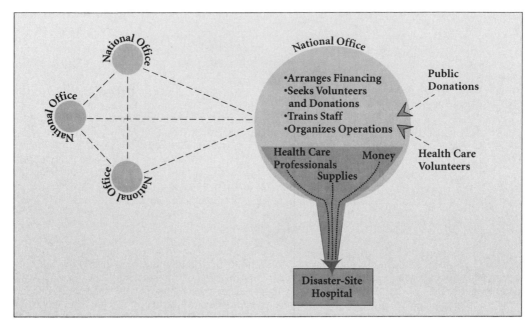

FIGURE 6 Organigraph of Médecins Sans Frontières

site—yet simultaneously illuminates the need to facilitate information flow between the national office and the disaster area.

Competencies as Hubs

Earlier we described a conglomerate as a set of loosely coupled businesses. That certainly makes sense for highly diversified operations, especially ones that have grown through the acquisition of businesses in unrelated industries. The divisions constitute a portfolio, held together by a headquarters that manages the flow of capital and imposes financial standards of performance.

But these days, the notion of conglomeration has given way to the concept of core competence: that the many products of companies such as Canon or 3M—which have grown more by the internal development of new products than by the acquisition of external businesses—are held together by some core of knowledge, skills, or resources. These competencies, then, can be seen as the *hub* of the organization, to which all activities relate.

Consider the exhibit "Organigraph of Frontec," which shows a Canadian company with about $130

million (Canadian) in annual sales. Founded in 1986, Frontec's first business was providing staff and supplies to the military's early warning stations in the far north. From there, it branched into other activities, such as construction, the running of hotels and airports, and a contract for the installation of communications equipment on military vehicles—mostly in remote, dangerous locations, often with challenging logistics. Frontec employees have worked with polar bears nearby—one operation is 400 miles from the North Pole—and sometimes have to fly helicopters in whiteouts. Such conditions explain why a primary core competence of the company is people development. The most important job for senior managers is to ensure that the right people are in charge of field operations. They do so by carefully selecting and developing key personnel.

A second core competence is business development, shown in the organigraph as closer to the field operations. The various ventures are listed all around the business development competence, as satellites, or quasi-independent business activities, which are shown to be associated with various categories such as Airport Services and Northern Enterprises.

The organigraph helped Frontec's senior managers communicate their self-image of a "frontier venturer" to a board of directors that was accustomed to more conventional organizations. It allowed managers to illustrate the company's character—that it is a company organized around competencies that allow it to venture into new and daring businesses in uncharted locations.

Putting Management in Its Place

One of the greatest benefits of seeing organizations differently is that we begin to see management differently. Isn't it about time? In the traditional organizational chart, senior managers always appear on top. But is that always the best place for them?

We think not. The very notion of "top management" may long have had a debilitating effect on organizations and on the behaviors of managers themselves. Bear in mind that "top management" is just a metaphor. In reality, the top manager is on top of nothing but a chart. Managers who see

themselves on top of their organizations may not really be on top of what takes place there. They may simply be too distant from the actual work being done.

Each organizational form suggests a different philosophy of managing. Sets suggest that managers stay away from the action, watching and comparing. In a conglomerate, for example, executives at headquarters oversee the divisions for the purposes of allocation. Their job, basically, is to decide who gets what resources.

The chain puts a boss above as well, but in this case above each link—a manager for each and a manager for all. In other words, the chain of command is laid over the chain of operations. The chain of operations is clear and orderly, and the chain of management exists primarily to keep it that way—for control.

It is when we move on to hubs and webs that management moves off its pedestal. In the hub, management appears in the center, around which

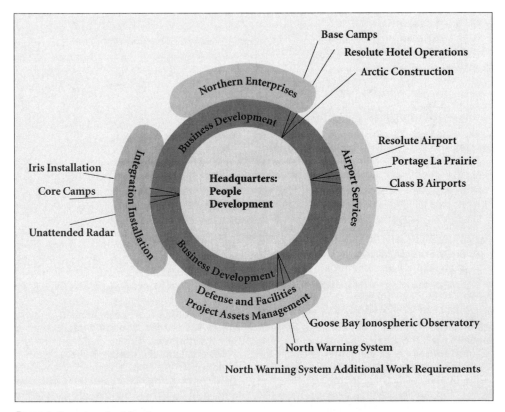

FIGURE 7 Organigraph of Frontec

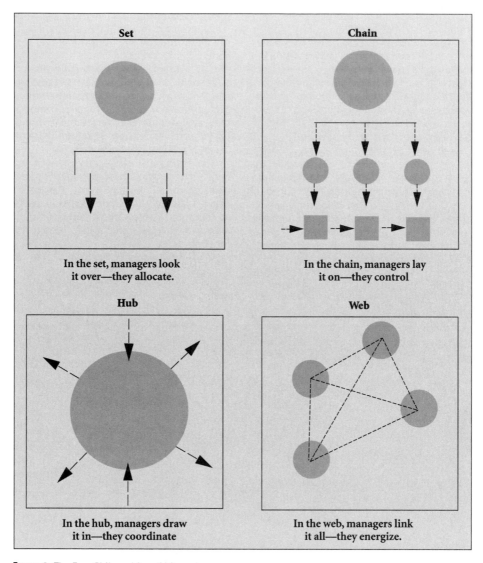

FIGURE 8 The Four Philosophies of Managing

activities revolve, as can be seen in the organigraphs of Médecins Sans Frontières and Frontec. Management at the center has an interesting implication: whoever is at the center *becomes* the manager. For example, if the hospital patient is a hub, then the nurse—not the doctor, not the chief of staff—is the manager. Why? Because the nurse coordinates the array of services that converge on the patient. In a real sense, nursing is managing—which means that managing can extend beyond formal authority.

Managing at the center implies something profoundly different from managing on top. While the chain controls, the hub coordinates. The chain may pretend to empower; the hub brings together people who are intrinsically empowered. As suggested in Frontec's organigraph, the center holds the whole together by working to reinforce the organization's competencies at its core.

And where can we find management in the web? At first glance, the answer is not clear. A more careful look, however, suggests that good management acts throughout the web. In a network—a project or an alliance, for example—managers have to be *everywhere*. In practical terms, that means out from behind their desks—in design studios, in airplanes on the way to offices and clients, and in other places where real work happens. Management that is not everywhere in the web is nowhere. The web is so fluid that managers cannot afford to remain in the center. In the web, managers have to move around, literally as well as figuratively, in order to facilitate collaboration and energize the whole network. They need to encourage people who already know how to do their work and do it well.

In a web, management can also be *everyone*. Whoever draws things together becomes a de facto manager. All kinds of people are managers who do not carry that official title, be it scientists in a research lab or salespeople in the field. (For an illustration of this point, see the exhibit "The Four Philosophies of Managing.")

In one sense, these philosophies of managing—allocating in the set, controlling in the chain, coordinating in the hub, and energizing in the web—are apt metaphors. Chains are heavy, webs are light. Hubs, in between, can explode or implode if not managed correctly. Follow a chain and you know where you will end up. Just don't try to go anywhere else! Find a hub and you know where to begin or end. Not so for the set, which can start and end in different places. The web, by contrast, can take you every which way. That can leave you flexible or flustered—and often both.

For companies to thrive in today's economy, management has to be put in its place—in another place, that is. Not atop the chart—at least not in all but the most tightly controlled, highly programmed bureaucracies—but down into its essence, whether at a center, as a hub, or throughout, as a web. That way those old charts can be put in their place, too (in something round that sits on the floor but is not a hub). By viewing management in this way, we can recognize it for what it has to be: the servant of the organization, not its purpose.

Do you see?

Putting the Service-Profit Chain to Work

James L. Heskett, Thomas O. Jones, Gary W. Loveman,
W. Earl Sasser, Jr., and Leonard A. Schlesinger

When service companies put employees and customers first, a radical shift occurs in the way they manage and measure success. The service profit chain puts "hard" values on "soft" measures, relating profitability, customer loyalty, and customer satisfaction to the value of services created by satisfied, loyal and productive employees.

Top-level executives of outstanding service organizations spend little time setting profit goals or focusing on market share, the management mantra of the 1970s and 1980s. Instead, they understand that in the new economics of service, frontline workers and customers need to be the center of management concern. Successful service managers pay attention to the factors that drive profitability in this new service paradigm: investment in people, technology that supports frontline workers, revamped recruiting and training practices, and compensation linked to performance for employees at every level. And they express a vision of leadership in terms rarely heard in corporate America: an organization's "patina of spirituality," the "importance of the mundane."

A growing number of companies that includes Banc One, Intuit Corporation, Southwest Airlines, ServiceMaster, USAA, Taco Bell, and MCI know that when they make employees and customers paramount, a radical shift occurs in the way they manage and measure success. The new economics of service requires innovative measurement techniques. These techniques calibrate the impact of employee satisfaction, loyalty, and productivity on the value of products and services delivered so that managers can build customer satisfaction and loyalty and assess the corresponding impact on profitability and growth. In fact, the lifetime value of a loyal customer can be astronomical, especially when referrals are added to the economics of customer retention and repeat purchases of related products. For example, the lifetime revenue stream from a loyal pizza eater can be $8,000, a Cadillac owner $332,000, and a corporate purchaser of commercial aircraft literally billions of dollars.

The service-profit chain, developed from analyses of successful service organizations, puts "hard" values on "soft" measures. It helps managers target new investments to develop service and satisfaction levels for maximum competitive impact, widening the gap between service leaders and their merely good competitors.

The Service-Profit Chain

The service-profit chain establishes relationships between profitability, customer loyalty, and employee satisfaction, loyalty, and productivity. The links in the chain (which should be regarded as propositions) are as follows: Profit and growth are stimulated primarily by customer loyalty. Loyalty is a direct result of customer satisfaction. Satisfaction is largely influenced by the value of services provided to customers. Value is created by satisfied, loyal, and productive employees. Employee satisfaction, in turn, results primarily from high-quality support services and policies that enable employees to deliver results to customers. (See the chart, "The Links in the Service-Profit Chain.")

The service-profit chain is also defined by a special kind of leadership. CEOs of exemplary service companies emphasize the importance of each employee and customer. For these CEOs, the focus on customers and employees is no empty slogan tailored to an annual management meeting. For example, Herbert Kelleher, CEO of Southwest Airlines, can be found aboard airplanes, on tarmacs, and in terminals, interacting with employees and customers. Kelleher believes that hiring employees that have the right attitude is so important that the hiring process takes on a "patina of spirituality." In addition, he believes that "anyone who looks at things solely in terms of factors that can easily be quantified is missing the heart of business, which is people." William Pollard, the chairman of Service-Master, continually underscores the importance of "teacher-learner" managers, who have what he calls "a servant's heart." And John McCoy, CEO of Banc One, stresses the "uncommon partnership," a system of support that provides maximum latitude to individual bank presidents while supplying information systems and common measurements of customer satisfaction and financial measures.

A closer look at each link reveals how the service-profit chain functions as a whole.

Customer Loyalty Drives Profitability and Growth

To maximize profit, managers have pursued the Holy Grail of becoming number-one or two in their industries for nearly two decades. Recently, however, new measures of service industries like software and banking suggest that customer loyalty is a more important determinant of profit. (See Frederick F. Reichheld and W. Earl Sasser, Jr., "Zero Defections: Quality Comes to Services," HBR September–October 1990). Reichheld and Sasser estimate that a 5% increase in customer loyalty can produce profit increases from 25% to 85%. They conclude that *quality* of market share, measured in terms of customer loyalty, deserves as much attention as *quantity* of share.

Banc One, bases in Columbus, Ohio, has developed a sophisticated system to track several factors involved in customer loyalty and satisfaction. Once driven strictly by financial measures, Banc One now conducts quarterly measures of customer retention; the number of services used by each customer, or *depth of relationship;* and the level of customer satisfaction. The strategies derived from this information help explain why Banc One has achieved a return on assets more than double that of its competitors in recent years.

Customer Satisfaction Drives Customer Loyalty

Leading service companies are currently trying to quantify customer satisfaction. For example, for several years, Xerox has polled 480,000 customers per year regarding product and service satisfaction using a five-point scale from 5 (high) to 1 (low). Until two years ago, Xerox's goal was to achieve 100% 4s (satisfied) and 5s (very satisfied) by the end of 1993. But in 1991, an analysis of customers who gave Xerox 4s and 5s on satisfaction found that the relationships between the scores and actual loyalty differed greatly depending on whether the customers were very satisfied or satisfied. Customers giving Xerox 5s were six times more likely to repurchase Xerox equipment than those giving 4s.

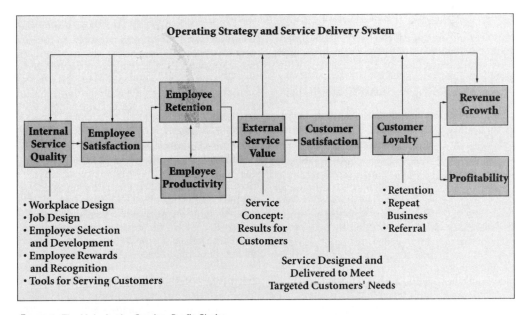

FIGURE 1 The Links in the Service-Profit Chain

This analysis led Xerox to extend its efforts to create *apostles*—a term coined by Scott D. Cook, CEO of software producer and distributor, Intuit Corporation, describing customers so satisfied that they convert the uninitiated to a product or service. Xerox's management currently wants to achieve 100% apostles, or 5s, by the end of 1996 by upgrading service levels and guaranteeing customer satisfaction. But just as important for Xerox's profitability is to avoid creating *terrorists:* customers so unhappy that they speak out against a poorly delivered service at every opportunity. Terrorists can reach hundreds of potential customers. In some instances, they can even discourage acquaintances from trying a service or product. (See the graph "A Satisfied Customer Is Loyal.")

Value Drives Customer Satisfaction

Customers today are strongly value oriented. But just what does that mean? Customers tell us that value means the results they receive in relation to the total costs (both the price and other costs to customers incurred in acquiring the service). The insurance company, Progressive Corporation, is creating just this kind of value for its customers by processing and paying claims quickly and with little policyholder effort. Members of the company's CAT (catastrophe) team fly to the scene of major accidents, providing support services like transportation and housing and handling claims rapidly. By reducing legal costs and actually placing more money in the hands of the injured parties, the CAT team more than makes up for the added expenses the organization incurs by maintaining the team. In addition, the CAT team delivers value to customers, which helps explain why Progressive has one of the highest margins in the property-and-casualty insurance industry.

Employee Productivity Drives Value

At Southwest Airlines, the seventh-largest U.S. domestic carrier, an astonishing story of employee productivity occurs daily. Eighty-six percent of the company's 14,000 employees are unionized. Positions are designed so that employees can perform several jobs if necessary. Schedules, routes, and company practices—such as open seating and the use of simple, color-coded, reusable boarding passes—enable the boarding of three and four times more passengers per day than competing airlines. In fact, Southwest deplanes and reloads two-thirds of its flights in 15 minutes or less. Because of aircraft availability and short-haul routes that don't require long layovers for flight crews, Southwest has roughly 40% more pilot and aircraft utilization than its major competitors: its pilots fly on average 70 hours per month versus 50 hours at other airlines. These factors explain how the company can charge fares from 60% to 70% lower than existing fares in markets it enters.

At Southwest, customer perceptions of value are very high, even though the airline does not assign seats, offer meals, or integrate its reservation system with other airlines. Customers place high value on Southwest's frequent departures, on-time service, friendly employees, and very low fares. Southwest's management knows this because its major marketing research unit—its 14,000 employees—is in daily contact with customers and reports its findings back to management. In addition, the Federal Aviation Administration's performance measures show that Southwest, of all the major airlines, regularly achieves the highest level of on-time arrivals, the lowest number of complaints, and the fewest lost-baggage claims per 1,000 passengers. When combined with Southwest's low fares per seat-mile, these indicators show the higher value delivered by Southwest's employees compared with most domestic competitors. Southwest has been profitable for 21 consecutive years and was the only major airline to realize a profit in 1992. (See the graph "How Southwest Compares with Its Competitors.")

Employee Loyalty Drives Productivity

Traditional measures of the losses incurred by employee turnover concentrate only on the cost of recruiting, hiring, and training replacements. In most service jobs, the real cost of turnover is the loss of productivity and decreased customer satisfaction. One recent study of an automobile dealer's sales personnel by Abt Associates concluded that the average monthly cost of replacing a sales representative who had five to eight years experience with an employee who had less than one year of experience was as much as $36,000 in sales. And the costs of losing a valued broker at a securities firm can be still more dire. Conservatively estimated, it takes nearly five years for a broker to rebuild relationships with customers that can return $1 million per year in commissions to the brokerage house—a cumulative loss of at least $2.5 million in commissions.

Employee Satisfaction Drives Loyalty

In one 1991 proprietary study of a property-and-casualty insurance company's employees, 30% of

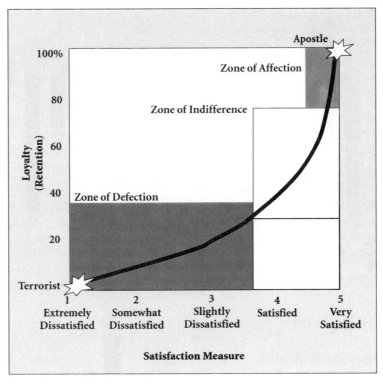

FIGURE 2 A Satisfied Customer Is Loyal

all dissatisfied employees registered an intention to leave the company, a potential turnover rate three times higher than that for satisfied employees. In this same case, low employee turnover was found to be linked closely to high customer satisfaction. In contrast, Southwest Airlines, recently named one of the country's ten best places to work, experiences the highest rate of employee retention in the airline industry. Satisfaction levels are so high that at some of its operating locations, employee turnover rates are less than 5% per year. USAA, a major provider of insurance and other financial services by direct mail and phone, also achieves low levels of employee turnover by ensuring that its employees are highly satisfied. But what drives employee satisfaction? Is it compensation, perks, or plush workplaces?

Internal Quality Drives Employee Satisfaction

What we call the *internal quality* of a working environment contributes most to employee satisfaction.

Internal quality is measured by the feelings that employees have toward their jobs, colleagues, and companies. What do service employees value most on the job? Although our data are preliminary at best, they point increasingly to the ability and authority of service workers to achieve results for customers. At USAA, for example, telephone sales and service representatives are backed by a sophisticated information system that puts complete customer information files at their fingertips the instant they receive a customer's call. In addition, state-of-the-art, job-related training is made available to USAA employees. And the curriculum goes still further, with 200 courses in 75 classrooms in a wide range of subjects.

Internal quality is also characterized by the attitudes that people have toward one another and the way people serve each other inside the organization. For example, ServiceMaster, a provider of a range of cleaning and maintenance services, aims to maximize the dignity of the individual service worker. Each year, it analyzes in depth a part of the

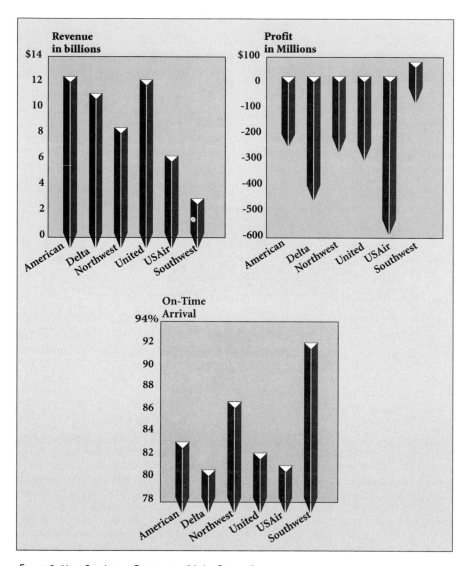

FIGURE 3 How Southwest Compares with Its Competitors

maintenance process, such as cleaning a floor, in order to reduce the time and effort needed to complete the task. The "importance of the mundane" is stressed repeatedly in ServiceMaster's management training—for example, in the seven-step process devised for cleaning a hospital room: from the first step, greeting the patient, to the last step, asking patients whether or not they need anything else done. Using this process, service workers develop communication skills and learn to interact with patients in ways that add depth and dimension to their jobs.

Leadership Underlies the Chain's Success

Leaders who understand the service-profit chain develop and maintain a corporate culture centered around service to customers and fellow employees. They display a willingness and ability to listen. Successful CEOs like John Martin of Taco Bell, John

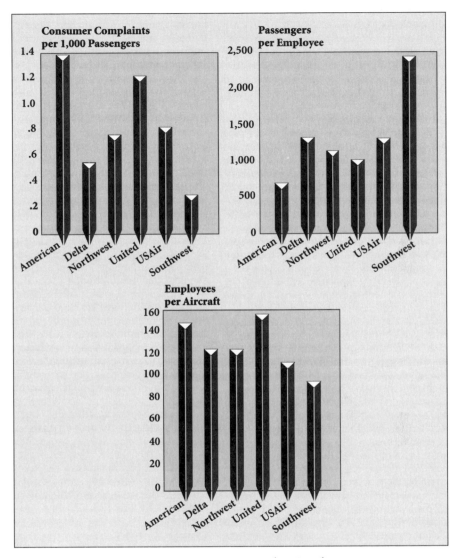

FIGURE 3 How Southwest Compares with Its Competitors (*continued*)

McCoy of Banc One, Herb Kelleher of Southwest, and Bill Pollard of ServiceMaster spend a great deal of time with customers and employees, experiencing their companies' service processes while listening to employees for suggestions for improvement. They care about their employees and spend a great deal of time selecting, tracking, and recognizing them.

For example, Brigadier General Robert McDermott, until recently chairman and CEO of USAA, reflected, "Public recognition of outstanding employees flows naturally from our corporate culture. That culture is talked about all the time, and we live it." According to Scott Cook at Intuit, "Most people take culture as a given. It is around you, the thinking goes, and you can't do anything about it. However, when you run a company, you have the opportunity to determine the culture. I find that when you champion the most noble values—including service, analysis, and database decision making—employees rise to the challenge, and you forever change their lives."

Relating Links in the Chair for Management Action

While many organizations are beginning to measure relationships between individual links in the service-profit chain, only a few have related the links in meaningful ways—ways that can lead to comprehensive strategies for achieving lasting competitive advantage.

The 1991 proprietary study of a property-and-casualty insurance company, cited earlier, not only identified the links between employee satisfaction and loyalty but also established that a primary source of job satisfaction was the service workers' perceptions of their ability to meet customer needs. Those who felt they did meet customer needs registered job satisfaction levels more than twice as high as those who felt they didn't. But even more important, the same study found that when a service worker left the company, customer satisfaction levels dropped sharply from 75% to 55%. As a result of this analysis, management is trying to reduce turnover among customer-contact employees and to enhance their job skills.

Similarly, in a study of its seven telephone service centers, MCI found clear relationships between employees' perceptions of the quality of MCI service and employee satisfaction. The study also linked employee satisfaction directly to customer satisfaction and intentions to continue to use MCI services. Identifying these relationships motivated MCI's management to probe deeper and determine what affected job satisfaction at the service centers. The factors they uncovered, in order of importance, were satisfaction with the job itself, training, pay, advancement fairness, treatment with respect and dignity, teamwork, and the company's interest in employees' well-being. Armed with this information, MCI's management began examining its policies concerning those items valued most by employees at its service centers. MCI has incorporated information about its service capabilities into training and communications efforts and television advertising.

No organization has made a more comprehensive effort to measure relationships in the service-profit chain and fashion a strategy around those relationships than the fast-food company Taco Bell, a subsidiary of PepsiCo. Taco Bell's management tracks profits daily by unit, market manager, zone, and country. By integrating this information with the results of exit interviews that Taco Bell conducts with 800,000 customers annually, management has found that stores in the top quadrant of customer satisfaction ratings outperform the other stores by all measures. As a result, Taco Bell has linked operations managers' compensation in company-owned stores to customer satisfaction, realizing a subsequent increase in both customer satisfaction ratings and profits.

However, Taco Bell's efforts don't stop there. By examining employee turnover records for individual stores, Taco Bell has discovered that the 20% of the stores with the lowest turnover rates enjoy double the sales and 55% higher profits than the 20% of stores with the highest employee turnover rates. As a result of this self-examination, Taco Bell has instituted financial and other incentives in order to reverse the cycle of failure that is associated with poor employee selection, subpar training, low pay, and high turnover.

In addition, Taco Bell monitors internal quality through a network of 800 numbers created to answer employees' questions, field their complaints, remedy situations, and alert top-level management to potential trouble spots. It also conducts periodic employee roundtable meetings, interviews, as well as a comprehensive companywide survey every two or three years in order to measure satisfaction. As a result of all this work, Taco Bell's focus on employee satisfaction involves a new selection process, improved skill building, increased latitude for decision making on the job, and further automation of unpleasant "back room" labor.

Relating all the links in the service-profit chain may seem to be a tall order. But profitability depends not only on placing hard values on soft measures but also linking those individual measures together into a comprehensive service picture. Service organizations need to quantify their investments in people—both customers and employees. The service-profit chain provides the framework for this critical task.

Service-Profit Chain Audit

A service-profit chain audit helps companies determine what drives their profit and suggests actions that can lead to long-term profitability. As they review the audit, managers should ask themselves what efforts are underway to obtain answers to the following questions and what those answers reveal about their companies.

Profit and Growth

1. How do we define loyal customers?

Customers often become more profitable over time. And loyal customers account for an unusually high proportion of the sales and profit growth of successful service providers. In some organizations, loyalty is measured in terms of whether or not a customer is on the company rolls. But several companies have found that their most loyal customers—the top 20% of total customers—not only provide all the profit but also cover losses incurred in dealing with less loyal customers.

Because of the link between loyal customers and profit, Banc One measures *depth of relationship*—the number of available related financial services, such as checking, lending, and safe deposit, actually used by customers. Recognizing the same relationship, Taco Bell drives its desire to increase "share of stomach" by broadening the selection of food purchases a customer can potentially make. As a result, the fast-food chain is trying to reach consumers through kiosks, carts, trucks and the shelves of supermarkets.

2. Do measurements of customer profitability include profits from referrals?

Companies that measure the stream of revenue and profits from loyal customers (retention) and repeat sales often overlook what can be the most important of the three Rs of loyalty: referrals. For example, Intuit provides high-quality, free lifetime service for a personal finance software package that sells for as little as $30. The strategy makes sense when the value of a loyal customer is considered—a revenue stream of several thousands of dollars from software updates, supplies, and new customer referrals. With this strategy in place, Intuit increased its sales to more than $30 million with just two U.S. field sales representatives.

3. What proportion of business development expenditures and incentives are directed to the retention of existing customers?

Too many companies concentrate nearly all their efforts on attracting new customers. But in businesses like life insurance, a new policyholder doesn't become profitable for at least three years. In the credit-card finance business, the break-even point for a new customer is often six or more years because of high-marketing and bad-debt costs in the first year of a relationship with cardholders. These costs must be defrayed by profits from loyal customers, suggesting the need for a careful division of organizational effort between customer retention and development.

1. Why do our customers defect?

It's important to find out not only where defectors go but also why they defect. Was it because of poor service, price or value? Answers to these questions provide information about whether or not existing strategies are working. In addition, exit interviews of customers can have real sales impact. For example, at one credit-card service organization, a phone call to question cardholders who had stopped using their cards led to immediate reinstatement of one-third of the defectors.

Customer Satisfaction

5. Are customer satisfaction data gathered in an objective, consistent, and periodic fashion?

Currently, the weakest measurements being used by companies we have studied concern customer satisfaction. At some companies, high levels of reported customer satisfaction are contradicted by continuing declines in sales and profits. Upon closer observation, we discovered that the service providers were "gaming" the data, using manipulative methods for collecting customer satisfaction data. In one extreme case, an automobile dealer sent a questionnaire to recent buyers with the highest marks already filled in, requiring owners to alter the marks only if they disagreed. Companies can, however, obtain more objective results using "third party" interviews; "mystery shopping" by unidentified, paid observers; or technologies like touch-screen television.

Consistency is at least as important as the actual questions asked of customers. Some of Banc One's operating units formerly conducted their own customer satisfaction surveys. Today the surveys have been centralized, made mandatory, and are administered by mail on a quarterly basis to around 125,000 customers. When combined with periodic measurement, the surveys produce highly relevant trend information that informs the managerial decision-making process. Similarly, Xerox's measures of satisfaction obtained from 10,000 customers per month—a product of an unchanging set of survey questions and very large samples—make possible period-to-period comparisons that are important in measuring and rewarding performance.

6. What are the listening posts for obtaining customer feedback in your organization?

Listening posts are tools for collecting data from customers and systematically translating those data into information in order to improve service and products. Common examples are letters of complaint. Still more important listening posts are reports from field sales and service personnel or the logs of telephone service representatives. Intuit's content analysis of customer service inquiries fielded by service representatives produced over 50 software improvements and 100 software documentation improvements in a single year. USAA has gone one step further by automating the feedback process to enter data online, enabling its analysis and plans departments to develop corrective actions.

7. How is information concerning customer satisfaction used to solve customer problems?

In order to handle customer problems, service providers must have the latitude to resolve any situation promptly. In addition, information regarding a customer concern must be transmitted to the service provider quickly. Customers and employees must be encouraged to report rather than suppress concerns. For example, one Boston-area Lexus dealer notified its customers, "If you are experiencing a problem with your car or our service department and you can't answer '100% satisfied' when you receive your survey directly from Lexus, please give us the opportunity to correct the problem before you fill out the survey. Lexus takes its customer surveys very seriously."

External Service Value

8. How do you measure service value?

Value is a function not only of costs to the customer but also of the results achieved for the customer. Value is always relative because it is based both on perceptions of the way a service is delivered and on initial customer expectations. Typically, a company measures value using the reasons expressed by customers for high or low satisfaction. Because value varies with individual expectations, efforts to improve value inevitably require service organizations to move all levels of management closer to the customer and give frontline service employees the latitude to customize a standard service to individual needs.

9. How is information concerning customers' perceptions of value shared with those responsible for designing a product or service?

Relaying information concerning customer expectations to those responsible for design often requires the formation of teams of people responsible for sales, operations, and service or product design, as well as the frequent assignment of service designers to tasks requiring field contact with customers. Intuit has created this kind of capability in product development teams. And all Intuit employees, including the CEO, must periodically work on the customer service phones. Similarly, at Southwest, those responsible for flight scheduling periodically work shifts in the company's terminals to get a feel for the impact of schedules on customer and employee satisfaction.

10. To what extent are measures taken of differences between customers' perceptions of quality delivered and their expectations before delivery?

Ultimately, service quality is a function of the gap between perceptions of the actual service experienced and what a customer expected before receiving that service. Actual service includes both final results and the process through which those results were obtained. Differences between experiences and expectations can be measured in generic dimensions such as the reliability and timeliness of service, the empathy and authority with which the service was delivered, and the extent to which the customer is left with tangible evidence (like a calling card) that the service has been performed.

11. Do our organization's efforts to improve external service quality emphasize effective recovery from service errors in addition to providing a service right the first time?

A popular concept of quality in manufacturing is the importance of "doing things right the first time." But customers of service organizations often allow one mistake. Some organizations are very good at delivering service as long as nothing goes wrong. Others organize for and thrive on service emergencies. Outstanding service organizations do both by giving frontline employees the latitude to effect recovery. Southwest Airlines maintains a policy of allowing frontline employees to do whatever they feel comfortable doing in order to satisfy customers. Xerox authorizes frontline service employees to replace up to $250,000 worth of equipment if customers are not getting results.

Employee Productivity

12. How do you measure employee productivity?

13. To what extent do measures of productivity identify changes in the quality as well as the quantity of service produced per unit of input?

In many services, the ultimate measure of quality may be customer satisfaction. That measure should be combined with measures of quantity to determine the total output of the service organization. At ServiceMaster, for example, measures of output in the schools and hospitals cleaned under the company's supervision include both numbers of work orders performed per employee hour and quality of the work done, as determined by periodic inspections performed by ServiceMaster and client personnel. Similarly, Southwest Airlines delivers relatively high levels of productivity in terms of both quality and quantity. In fact, outstanding service competitors are replacing the typical "either/or" trade-off between quality and quantity with an "and/also" imperative.

Employee Loyalty

14. How do you create employee loyalty?

Employee loyalty goes hand in hand with productivity, contradicting the assumption that successful service providers should be promoted to larger supervisory responsibilities or moved to a similar job in a larger business unit. ServiceMaster and Taco Bell have expanded jobs without promoting good service workers. At ServiceMaster, effective single-unit managers are given supervisory responsibilities for custodial, maintenance, or other workers at more than one hospital or school. Taco Bell gives restaurant general managers a "hunting license" to help identify and operate new satellite feeding locations in the neighborhoods served by their restaurants and rewards them for doing it.

15. Have we made an effort to determine the right level of employee retention?

Rarely is the right level of retention 100%. Dynamic service organizations require a certain level of turnover. However, in calibrating desired turnover levels, it is important to take into account the full cost of the loss of key service providers, including those of lost sales and productivity and added recruiting, selection, and training.

Employee Satisfaction

16. Is employee satisfaction measured in ways that can be linked to similar measures of customer satisfaction with sufficient frequency and consistency to establish trends for management use?

Taco Bell studies employee satisfaction through surveys, frequent interviews, and roundtable meetings. Customer satisfaction is measured by interviews with customers conducted biannually and includes questions about satisfaction with employee friendliness and hustle. Both the employee

and customer satisfaction rankings are comprehensive and conducted on a regular basis. With these data, the company can better understand overall trends and the links between employee and customer satisfaction.

17. Are employee selection criteria and methods geared to what customers, as well as managers, believe are important?

At Southwest Airlines, for example, frequent fliers are regularly invited to participate in the auditioning and selection of cabin attendants. And many take time off from work to join Southwest's employee selection team as it carries out its work. As one customer commented, "Why not do it? It's my airline."

18. To what extent are measures of customer satisfaction, customer loyalty, or the quality and quantity of service output used in recognizing and rewarding employees?

Employee recognition may often involve little more than informing individual employees or employees as a group about service improvements and individual successes. Banc One goes one step further, including customer satisfaction measures for each banking unit in its periodic report of other performance measures, mostly financial, to all units.

Internal Service Quality

19. Do employees know who their customers are?

It is particularly difficult for employees to identify their customers when those customers are internal to the company. These employees often do not know what impact their work has on other departments. Identifying internal customers requires mapping and communicating characteristics of work flow, organizing periodic cross-departmental meetings between "customers" and "servers," and recognizing good internal service performance.

In 1990, USAA organized a PRIDE (Professionalism Results in Dedication to Excellence) team of 100 employees and managers to examine and improve on a function-by-function basis all processes associated with property-and-casualty insurance administration, which included analyzing customer needs and expectations. The PRIDE effort was so successful that it led to a cross-functional review of USAA's service processing. Service processing times has been reduced, as have handoffs of customers from one server to another.

20. *Are employees satisfied with the technological and personal support they receive on the job?*

The cornerstone of success at Taco Bell is the provision of the latest in information technology, food service equipment, simple work-scheduling techniques, and effective team training. This practice led to the establishment of self-managing teams of service providers. Also, the quality of work life involves selecting the right workers. Better employees tend to refer people who, like themselves, are motivated by ownership and responsibility to create customer satisfaction. Internal service quality can also be thought of as the quality of work life. It is a visible expression of an organization's culture, one influenced in important ways by leadership.

Leadership

21. *To what extent is the company's leadership:*

  a. *energetic, creative vs. stately, conservative?*
  b. *participatory, caring vs. removed, elitist?*
  c. *listening, coaching, and teaching vs. supervising and managing?*
  d. *motivating by mission vs. motivating by fear?*
  e. *leading by means of personally demonstrated values vs. institutionalized policies?*

22. *How much time is spent by the organization's leadership personally developing and maintaining a corporate culture centered around service to customers and fellow employees?*

Leaders naturally have individual traits and styles. But the CEOs of companies that are successfully using the service-profit chain possess all or most of a set of traits that separate them from their merely good competitors. Of course, different styles of leadership are appropriate for various stages in an organization's development. But the messages sent by the successful leaders we have observed stress the importance of careful attention to the needs of customers and employees. These leaders create a culture capable of adapting to the needs of both.

Relating the Measures

23. *What are the most important relationships in your company's service-profit chain?*

24. *To what extent does each measure correlate with profit and growth at the frontline level?*

25. *Is the importance of these relationships reflected in rewards and incentives offered to employees?*

Measures drive action when they are related in ways that provide managers with direction. To enjoy the kind of success that service organizations like Southwest Airlines, ServiceMaster, and Taco Bell have enjoyed, looking at individual measures is not enough. Only if the individual measures are tied together into a comprehensive picture will the service-profit chain provide a foundation for unprecedented profit and growth.

The Evolution of Services Management in Developing Countries: Insights from Latin America

Javier Reynoso

Structural, social, and political differences make the evolution of service management a complex process in regions like Latin America. Deregulation and privatization programs are stimulating competitive activity and innovation. However, there are radical differences between the needs and behavior of middle-class customers and the large numbers of people living in poverty.

Introduction

The most important, state of the art contributions in the area of services management have been developed in Europe and the United States over the last two decades. However, the service sector is becoming increasingly important in the economic growth of Latin America. In Mexico, for example, the contribution of this sector to the GNP during 1997 was 66 percent (INEGI 1998), while employment level exceeded 50 percent. Many other Latin American countries show similar trends. Furthermore, the abolition of trade frontiers among our countries due to NAFTA, Mercosur, and Pacto Andino has increased even more the strategic importance of the service sector in our continent.

The Service Sector in Latin America
Stages of Economic Development

In discussing the role of services in an economy, different stages of economic development can be identified. Based on the work of sociologist Daniel Bell, Fitzsimmons and Fitzsimmons (1994) highlight three main stages in society: preindustrial, industrial, and postindustrial. Characterized as a game against nature, a preindustrial society is mainly about subsistence. At this stage, the labor force is engaged in agriculture, mining, and fishing. While

an industrial society defines the standard of living by the quantity of goods, the postindustrial society is concerned with the quality of life, as measured by services such as health, education, and recreation. In this framework, the key element in the transformation from industrial to postindustrial society is the natural development of services.

It could be argued that most developed countries present a more homogeneous society where health and education are standard requirements for entry into a postindustrial society. In contrast, developing countries in Latin America present a more complex situation. Most countries could coexist among the three different stages of economic development. The movement from rural to urban societies is certainly an illustration of this situation (World Bank 1995a). In Mexico, for example, there are regions where economy is based on agriculture, mining, and fishing. There are other areas of the country supported by industrial activities, and indeed some of these areas are now moving into postindustrial activities. The case of the Mexican city of Monterrey is a good example of this transformation.

Monterrey is internationally known for being the place where some of the most important Mexican manufacturing industries were born. Companies producing glass, steel, cement, beer, chemicals, and so on, gave Monterrey its international reputation as an industrial city. Today, such industries remain important, but service companies have also appeared. A number of service industries, including insurance, financial services, retailing, and banking and telephony, among others, are also becoming symbols of the economic power of this city.

Chile is another interesting case. During interviews with the author, Chilean executives have claimed that their country presents the peculiar case of having moved from a preindustrial to a postindustrial society. With a unique geography concentrating a high percentage of its population in Santiago—the capital—and the surrounding areas, the country that once based its economic growth in the primary sector is now moving very quickly towards the development of new economic activities, including telecommunications, financial services, and other services.

Bolivia provides a contrasting illustration. As a less developed country, following a number of years of political conflicts, and with a high percentage of indigenous population, Bolivia is now facing the beginning of a new economy. The coexistence of the three aforementioned societies becomes clear when we realize the importance of agriculture for the subsistence of its rural population, combined with the incipient industrial base and the arrival of the foreign capital that is currently being invested in the service sector. Airlines, trains, telephones, and banking are some examples of this effort to participate more actively in the service economy.

The three cases illustrated here are indeed representative of what is happening in the service sector in Latin America. Similar situations are to be found in Brazil, Argentina, Venezuela, Colombia, and other countries in the region. The examples of Mexico, Chile, and Bolivia lead us to understand why services management in developing countries could not necessarily evolve in the same way as it has in developed countries. Structural, social, and political differences make the evolution of services management a complex process in regions like Latin America.

Importance of the Service Economy in Latin America

Without pretending to make this contribution an economic debate, some data are presented here. These data should be evaluated with the appropriate caution, as there are always some statistical problems with international comparisons. According to the World Bank, countries can be grouped by income level into low, low-medium/medium, medium-high, and high. As *Table 1* shows, the contribution to GNP by the service sector seems to be associated with the income level of the countries. While the average contribution of those nations included within the low-level segment remained stable at 40 percent during the 1970–1993 period, those countries representing the high-income group increased their GNP contribution on services activities from 54 to 64 percent in the same period.

TABLE 1 Service Sector Contribution to GNP by Income Level

Countries by Income Level	Services as a Percent of GNP	
	1970	1993
Low	40	40
Low-Medium/Medium	49	48
Medium-High	46	54
High	54	64

Source: World Bank 1995b

TABLE 2 Service Sector Contribution to GNP in Latin America and The Caribbean

Country	Services as a Percent of GNP	
	1980	1996
Argentina	52	63
Bolivia	47	n.a.
Brazil	45	50
Chile	55	n.a.
Colombia	49	64
Costa Rica	55	60
Ecuador	50	51
El Salvador	40	60
Guatemala	n.a.	56
Haiti	n.a.	45
Honduras	52	47
Jamaica	54	55
Mexico	59	68
Nicaragua	45	44
Panama	69	73
Paraguay	44	54
Peru	48	56
Puerto Rico	58	n.a.
Dominican Republic	52	55
Trinidad and Tobago	38	53
Uruguay	53	65
Venezuela	49	49

n.a. = not available

Source: World Bank 1998

In this vein, the average contribution to GNP from the service sector in Latin American and Caribbean countries has increased from 50.7 percent in 1980 to 56.2 percent in 1996 (World Bank 1998). More than half the economy of these countries is already based in service activities. *Table 2* shows data for individual countries in the region.

What is striking is that, although Latin America and the Caribbean are not considered affluent regions, by as early as 1980 most, if not all countries were already producing about 50 percent of GNP through service activities. This situation illustrates the increasing importance of the service economy in Latin America. Service contribution to GNP in Mexico, for example, has moved from 52.7 percent in 1895 to about 66 percent in 1997 (INEGI 1998). De Mateo (1991) illustrates this point:

> The Mexican economy is a service economy. This characteristic is not new, it has been like this for almost a century. Since 1895 services contribution was more than half of the production of the country. From then, that contribution has been incremented by about ten points.

Another indicator of the service economy presented here is labor force. Again, as it can be seen from *Table 3*, in most Latin American and Caribbean countries, more than half of their registered working population participate in service activities. Ranging from 25.6 to 79.1 percent, the average labor force in service is 55.5 percent. Noticeable exceptions are Haiti, Guatemala, and Cuba. Cuba, in particular, presents a peculiar case, where a rather balanced distribution of the working force can be noticed.

Informal ("underground") employment is a critical issue. Developing countries present the problem, or opportunity, of having an increasingly important informal economy, most of which comes from the service sector. A large number of people are working in undocumented jobs.

Entering into the Service Revolution

Despite the evidence presented above of the increasing importance of the service economy in Latin America, in most countries this sector, with the exception of specific activities, has not been

TABLE 3 *Labor Force Distribution in Latin America and The Caribbean*			
Country	Agriculture	Industry	Services
Argentina	12.1	31.5	56.5
Bahamas	5.7	16.5	77.9
Barbados	10.1	10.9	79.1
Bolivia	1.2	24.8	74.0
Brazil	22.2	23.4	52.4
Chile	19.1	26.3	56.4
Costa Rica	25.0	26.9	48.0
Cuba	32.2	40.0	27.9
Ecuador	31.2	18.1	50.8
El Salvador	10.7	29.2	60.2
Guatemala	49.9	18.3	31.8
Haiti	65.7	8.8	25.6
Honduras	36.9	20.9	42.3
Mexico	22.6	27.8	49.6
Panama	27.0	16.0	57.1
Puerto Rico	3.6	26.3	70.2
Dominican Republic	23.6	18.1	58.3
Surinam	9.3	21.8	69.0
Trinidad and Tobago	10.4	32.5	57.1
Uruguay	14.6	25.8	59.6
Venezuela	11.4	27.7	61.0

Source: World Bank 1995b

inserted completely into the so-called service revolution. Somewhat understandably, industrial development of countries has had an important influence on this situation. In most of the cases, the importance of the service economy is not yet fully realized or is just beginning to be noticed. In many cases, the way service organizations are managed does not reflect an adequate awareness of the economy of the continent. For many years industrialization was the key to development. The importance of the service sector in this process, however, was overlooked. In this respect De Mateo (1991) claims:

Mexico is not completely into the service revolution yet. To a great extent, the reason for this is that while the industrial sector has changed its model for a more appropriate one to participate in the international economy, many of the existing regulations for service industries come from the days when the country's growth was focused on industrial activity through imports substitution. Services were oriented to support that model and therefore, neither quality nor price were important factors.

The abolition of trade frontiers among our countries due to NAFTA, Mercosur, and Pacto Andino, has started to change this situation in recent years. Open competition in the service sector is twisting the picture dramatically. It has increased even more the strategic importance of the service sector in our continent. Mexican economy, for example, is currently entering into the battles of telephony, telecommunications, software, airlines, banking, saving funds, retailing, entertainment, tourism, industrial transportation, and many other sectors.

The case of many other countries is similar. Privatization programs in Argentina, Venezuela, Brazil, Peru, and Bolivia, for instance, are forcing governments and organizations to enter into the new era of competition in the service arena. This situation, which is attracting a great deal of foreign investment in different sectors, is making traditionally protected service companies experience and adapt to these changes in order to survive. As can be seen from *Table 4,* privatization programs in Latin American countries produced more than $63 billion from almost 700 transactions during the 1990–1995 period. Mexico, Argentina, and Brazil produced about 50 percent of all transactions, representing 82 percent of the generated income. In terms of the sectors involved, it can be noticed that privatization of services accounted for 44 percent

of all transactions and produced 68 percent of the generated income during the 1990–1995 period.

As part of this privatization process in Latin America, information technology has been identified as a critical factor in the internationalization of services in developing countries. Primo (1996), claims that:

The most dynamic trade routes of the twenty-first century will be dominated by transactions in intangibles rather than goods. Service industries will be responsible for the "roads" of the global "infostructure" and they will be the main providers of the content to be traded via electronic means. The adoption of a liberal trade and investment regime is essential for countries to maximize the benefits to be derived from the internationalization of services and to move toward the information age. This is particularly true for developing countries.

These macroeconomic and technological trends are inevitably leading to rapid and unprecedented changes. They are transforming Latin American societies into service societies and redefining the ways service organizations are competing to be profitable in the long term. Such a situation would seem to suggest that Latin America is moving smoothly towards a new stage of economic development, as countries in the so-called Western world have done. However, it is important to realize the existence of characteristics in developing countries such as the distribution of income and poverty, for a better understanding of that journey. Factors like these make the service revolution a complex, peculiar phenomenon in Latin America, and they cannot be ignored. *Table 5* shows that poverty (defined as income of less than $60 a month) has increased from 26.5 percent of total population in 1980 to 31 percent in 1989. Whereas there is a higher proportion of poor people living in rural than in urban areas, it can also be noticed that more than 50 percent of the population in poverty was already living in urban areas by 1989. Despite the great variety of forms used by economists to measure it and its subjective nature, poverty levels and distribution are certainly important factors to better understand the service revolution in Latin America and indeed in other developing regions like Asia or Africa. The design, marketing, and delivery of services to segments of society with significantly different income distribution require complex strategic arrangements for organizations. First, there are strategies directed to a small group of

TABLE 4 *Privatization in Latin America 1990–1995*

Country	Infrastructure	Financial Services	Primary Sector	Industry	Other Services	Total	Number of Transactions
	(Millions of Dollars)						
Argentina	12,498	263	4,976	618	91	18,446	123
Barbados	24	0	0	10	17	51	6
Belize	59	0	0	0	0	59	4
Bolivia	615	0	11	10	1	637	28
Brazil	583	0	1,862	6,600	91	9,136	45
Chile	512	0	672	11	64	1,259	14
Colombia	0	645	6	56	27	734	16
Costa Rica	0	0	0	42	3	45	4
Ecuador	0	1	0	95	0	96	9
Honduras	12	0	25	33	4	74	32
Jamaica	111	23	88	51	43	316	26
Mexico	8,052	12,989	1,491	1,517	222	24,271	174
Nicaragua	0	0	83	24	19	126	75
Panama	18	0	19	61	3	100	9
Paraguay	22	0	0	0	0	22	1
Peru	2,437	583	989	282	64	4,356	72
Trinidad and Tobago	138	0	8	302	1	448	17
Uruguay	2	15	0	0	0	17	7
Venezuela	2,128	163	53	147	18	2,510	29
Latin America	27,211	14,682	10,283	9,858	669	62,703	
%	43	23	16	16	1	100	
Number of Transactions	167	53	210	180	81		691
%	24	8	30	26	12		100

Infrastructure includes: airlines and airports, railways, transportation, telecommunications, ports and shipment, energy (electricity and gas), water and sanity; **Financial Services** include: banks, insurance, real estate; **Primary Sector** includes: agriculture and farming, cattle raising and fishing, mining, oil; **Industry** includes: manufacturing, steel, chemicals, construction materials; **Other Services** include: tourism, international commerce, retailing, other services, not classified.

Source: adapted from IMF (1995), *Informe del Desarrollo Económico y Social de América Latina*, Chap. 5.

wealthy people who operate internationally and have sophisticated expectations. Second, strategies can focus on a middle-class group, increasingly aspiring to many goods and services available in developed countries. And third, strategies may be oriented to a large segment of poor people in both urban and rural areas who, even with very low incomes, have the need for basic services.

Increasing levels of population moving to urban areas in Latin American countries and the increasing levels of poverty and extreme poverty in a number of the countries over the past decade—although this trend appears to have slowed in the early 1990s (Rosenthal 1996)—are valuable points for reflection for those interested in the evolution of services in this region. Most of the research on services has been conducted in developed societies where income distribution, poverty levels, and social welfare conditions are, in most cases, different from Latin American countries. In this respect, it is important to realize the existence of the so-called informal economy as an increasingly important phenomenon that has emerged in most of these countries as a result of the erosion of real incomes, increasing unemployment levels, and the contrast between income extremes, among other

TABLE 5	Poverty in Latin America, 1980 and 1989		
Country	Total Population (millions)	Population in Poverty (millions)	%
1980			
Total	345.5	91.4	26.5
Urban	227.4	38.2	16.8
Rural	118.1	53.2	45.1
1989			
Total	421.4	130.8	31.0
Urban	300.1	66.0	22.0
Rural	121.3	64.8	53.4
Increase, 1980–89			
Total	76.0	39.4	
Urban	72.7	27.8	
Rural	3.3	11.6	

Source: Samuel A. Morley (1995), *Poverty and Inequality in Latin America,* The Johns Hopkins University Press, London, p. 44.

factors. In fact, according to Rosenthal (1996), the informal sector had the highest annual rate of growth (more than 6 percent) during the 1980–1989 period in Latin America.

People have had to be very creative in order to survive. Thus, a number of informal service jobs have surged in most countries. Many ancient activities have been transformed into traditional and local activities to produce a growing informal, underground service economy in the region. Although many of these service activities have been originally oriented for serving the poor, today middle and even wealthy classes are participating in the benefits of such services. A great variety of services are offered and sold everyday and everywhere. Perhaps one of the most important characteristics of such services is that, whereas businesses such as airlines, hotels, and telecommunications rely more and more on technology, informal activities rely on cheap and creative labor, creating a demand for affordable services like urban transportation, technical and domestic services, and local trade, for example.

For many people this informal economy is a growing problem, for others it is an opportunity in many respects. In his book, *The Other Path,* De Soto (1987) presents one of the most interesting analyses and critiques of this phenomenon focusing on the case of Peru. His analysis and insights certainly helps in clarifying that economic, social, political, and legal conditions play crucial roles in the difficult coexistence of wealth creation and development in Latin America.

The framework discussed here presents a promising but challenging horizon for Latin America. Governments, organizations, and society still have to insert themselves completely into the so-called service revolution before we will start to see profound changes in how services are going to be managed in the twenty-first century. Latin America faces the challenge of increasing service competition within a complex, diverse environment.

The Need to Break Service Myths

After five years of conducting a number of research projects and other academic activities in various Latin American countries, the author of this article has found that in many cases, the service concept is associated with two main issues: *customer care* and *service quality.* It is very common today to find executives, managers, and staff in organizations *talking* about "customer service," "customer care," "customer satisfaction," "service quality," and so on. Unfortunately, in most cases these terms are being handled merely as motivational and promotional tools. Everybody can *talk* about customer satisfaction, but it is rare to find companies engaged in developing a systematic and reliable approach to measure it. Radio, television, and press are plagued with advertisements in which the central element of publicity is service. Sadly, in many cases service still is a variable of one dimension, this being "attention to the customer." This particular situation might also be influenced by cultural factors. The sense of obedience and even submission developed over the centuries in conquered countries that are now independent in Latin America, could probably influence the willingness to provide excellent *attention.* In most Latin American countries, people are recognized for their attitude in providing warm, friendly, and courteous service.

Academic and Research Development in Services

Not surprisingly, services have received very little attention from the academic perspective. Apart from the economic field, which has produced profiles illustrating and explaining the evolution of service economies in different countries of the continent (e.g., Chavez 1995; Ibarra 1995), not much effort has been made so far in understanding and developing knowledge on service. It has to be said, though, that researchers from traditional disciplines in management have always included in their studies information about service industries. An important difference, however, is that the focus, in most cases, is not to explain a phenomenon from the service perspective but rather to understand and explain issues related to the traditional discipline involved (e.g., organization, human resources, operations, or marketing). In this respect, a limited number of business schools have introduced services-marketing courses within their MBA programs. In some countries (e.g., Brazil, Mexico, and Argentina), postgraduate students are already conducting research projects in the service field for their master's and Ph.D. theses. This evidence seems to suggest that what is needed is the integration of work that has been done across different disciplines into a more structured service management framework.

The Graduate School of Management and Leadership (EGADE) at Monterrey Institute of Science and Technology (ITESM) in Monterrey, Mexico, has taken the initiative to actively participate in the development of services management in the region. During 1996, the initiative to create the Latin American Academy of Services Management was launched. The main objective of this initiative is to integrate a community which, sharing the common intellectual passion for service, would work towards the development of science, art, and practice in services management, in order to contribute to the progress of this important field in Latin America. By the end of 1999, the Academy had integrated 26 business schools and universities from 14 countries. Three years after its founding, members of the Academy made possible the first special issue ever dedicated to service research in Latin America and published by the *International Journal of Services Industry Management* (IJSIM).

Conclusion

Services management has evolved rapidly in most developed countries over the last 20 years, as a consequence of the transformation into a post-industrial society. Most developing countries in Latin America already participate in a service economy or are about to do so. However, the complexities imposed by the presence of different levels of economic development co-existing together makes

the evolution of services management in Latin America both distinctive and challenging. Open competition in the service sector is changing the name of the game. Deregulation and privatization programs are leading governments and organizations to face the challenge of becoming more competitive and profitable. On the other hand, growth of poverty in urban cities and the important role of the informal economy in the region are factors that cannot be ignored when seeking a better understanding of the evolution of services in this part of the world.

This situation calls for an urgent need to broaden the perspective of policy makers and public administrators, as well as executives and managers, in order for them to be capable of facing the unique challenges this sector is presenting today. It is crucial for our leaders to listen, to understand, and to interpret the contrasting needs of an increasingly demanding and dynamic environment in the so-called service economy. It is also very important to break with those service myths that still prevail in people's minds, making service more an attitude than an economic and entrepreneurial activity. The above challenges require also a great deal of passion, commitment, and human talent to create and disseminate knowledge on the management of service activities in the region. Only then will Latin America communities and organizations be able to establish competitive strategies searching for the coexistence of wealth creation and social development, making sense of the reality not only of their own businesses but also of the culture of their own countries.

REFERENCES

Chavez, F. J., *Los Servicios en Mexico: Crecimiento, Empleo y Rentabilidad* (Mexico City: Universidad Autonoma Metropolitana, 1995).

De Mateo, F., "El Sector Servicios en Mexico y su Contribucion al Desarrollo," in *Mexico Una Economia de Servicios* (New York: United Nations, 1991).

De Soto, H., *The Other Path: The Invisible Revolution in the Third World* (New York: Harper and Row, 1989).

Fitzsimmons, J. A., and M. J. Fitzsimmons, *Service Management for Competitive Advantage* (New York: McGraw-Hill, 1994).

Ibarra, G., *Economía Terciaria y Desarrollo Regional en México* (México: UAS, INSEUR-NL, 1995).

INEGI, *Cuaderno de Información Oportuna* (Mexico, 1998).

Morley, S. A., *Poverty and Inequality in Latin America* (London: Johns Hopkins University Press, 1995).

Primo, C. A., "The Impact of the Internalization of Services on Developing Countries," *Finance & Development,* March 1996, 34–37.

Rosenthal, G., "On Poverty and Inequality in Latin America," *Journal of Interamerican Studies and World Affairs* 38 (Summer/Fall 1996): 15–37.

World Bank, *Better Urban Services* (Washington, D.C.: The Internationas Bank of Reconstruction and Development, 1995a).

World Bank, *El Mundo del Trabajo en una Economia Integrada* (Washington, D.C.: 1995b).

World Bank, *World Development Indicators* (Washington, D.C.: 1998).

Note on Studying and Learning from Cases

Introduction to Cases

The cases featured in this book are representative of real-world problems that managers in different service organizations have to face and resolve. They describe problems from a wide variety of industries in several different countries. Some of the events depicted took place quite recently, others occurred a number of years ago but still contain important lessons and insights for the managers of tomorrow.

Unlike methods of instruction that use lectures and textbooks, the case method of instruction does not present students with a body of tried and true knowledge about how to be a successful manager. Instead, it provides an opportunity for you to learn by doing.

Dealing with cases is somewhat like working with the actual problems that people encounter in their jobs as managers. In most instances, you'll be identifying and clarifying problems facing the management of a company or nonprofit organization, analyzing qualitative information and quantitative data, evaluating alternative courses of action, and then making decisions about what strategy to pursue for the future. You may enjoy the process more—and will probably learn more—if you accept the role of an involved participant rather than that of a disinterested observer who has no stake, or interest, in resolving the problems in question.

The goal of case analysis is not to develop a set of "correct" facts but to learn to reason well with available data. Cases mirror the uncertainty of the real-world environment in that the information they present is often imprecise and ambiguous. You may be frustrated to find that there is no one right answer or correct solution to any given case. Instead, there are often a number of feasible strategies management might adopt, each with somewhat different implications for the future of the organization and each involving different trade-offs.

Cases and the Real World

Cases differ from real-world management situations in several important respects. First, the information is prepackaged in written form. By contrast, managers accumulate their information through memoranda, meetings, chance conversations, research studies, observations, news reports, and other externally published materials.

Second, cases tend to be selective in their reporting because they are designed with specific teaching objectives in mind. Each must fit a relatively short class period and focus attention on certain types of issues within a given subject area. In the real world, management problems are usually dynamic in nature. They call for some immediate action, with further analysis and major decisions being delayed until some later time. Managers are rarely able to wrap up their problems, put them away, and go on to the next "case." In contrast, discussing a case in class or writing an analysis of a case is more like examining a snapshot taken at a particular point in time—although sometimes a sequel case provides a sense of continuity and poses the need for future decisions within the same organization.

A third, and final, contrast between case analyses and real-world management is that participants in case discussions and authors of written case reports aren't responsible for implementing their decisions, nor do they have to live with the consequences. However, this doesn't mean that you can be frivolous when making recommendations. Instructors and classmates are likely to be critical of contributions

The contributions of Charles B. Weinberg are gratefully acknowledged.

that aren't based on careful analysis and interpretation of the facts.

Preparing a Case

Just as there is often no one right solution to a case, there is also no single correct way of preparing a case for class discussion or for a written assignment. With practice, you should be able to establish a working style with which you feel comfortable.

Initial Analysis

First, it's important to gain a feel for the overall situation by skimming quickly through the case. Ask yourself:

- What sort of organization does the case concern?
- What is the nature of the industry (broadly defined)?
- What is going on in the external environment?
- What problems does management appear to be facing?

After an initial fast reading, without making notes or underlining, you'll be ready to make a very careful second reading of the case. This time, seek to identify key facts so that you can develop a situation analysis and clarify the nature of the problems facing management. As you go along, try to make notes in response to such questions as:

- What decisions need to be made, and who will be responsible for making them?
- What are the objectives of the organization itself and of each of the key players in the case? Are these objectives compatible?
- What resources and constraints are present that may help or hinder attempts by the organization to meet its objectives?

Try to establish the significance of any quantitative data presented in the text of the case or, more often, in the exhibits. See if new insights may be gained by combining and manipulating data presented in different parts of the case. But don't accept the data blindly. In the cases, as in real life, not all information is equally reliable or equally relevant. On the other hand, case writers won't deliberately misrepresent data or facts to try to trick you.

Developing Recommendations

Now you should be in a position to summarize your evaluation of the situation and to develop some recommendations for management. First, identify the alternative courses of action open to the organization.

Next, consider the implications of each alternative, including possible undesirable outcomes, such as provoking responses from stronger competitors. Ask yourself how short-term tactics fit with longer-term strategies. Relate each alternative to the objectives of the organization (as defined or implied in the case, or as redefined by you). Then, develop a set of recommendations for future action, making sure that these recommendations are supported by your analysis of the case data.

Your recommendations won't be complete unless you give some thought to how the proposed strategy should be implemented:

- What resources—human, financial, or other—will be required?
- Who should be responsible for implementation?
- What time frame should be established for the various actions proposed?
- How should subsequent performance be measured?

Small-Group Discussions

The best results in the early stages of case preparation generally are achieved by working alone. But a useful step, prior to class discussion, is to discuss the case with a small group of classmates. (In some instances, you may find yourself assigned to a small discussion group or you may be required to work with others to develop a written report for possible group presentation.) These small groups facilitate initial testing of ideas and help to focus discussion on the main considerations. Present your arguments and listen to those of other participants. The focus of small-group discussions should be on analysis and decision making: What are the facts? What do they mean? What alternatives are available? What specifically should management do? How and when?

Class Discussion

In class, you may find that the role played by an instructor when teaching cases differs from that when lecturing. The instructor's role in case discussions is often similar to that of a moderator—calling on students, guiding the discussion, asking questions, and periodically synthesizing previous comments. Teaching styles vary, of course, from one instructor to another. Some professors like to begin the class by asking a student to "lay out" the case, which may involve your being asked to identify key problems and opportunities, to present some preliminary analysis, and perhaps to outline a possible course of action. Others prefer to work through each of the discussion questions in turn.

Instead of being a passive note-taker, as in lecture classes, you'll be expected to become an active participant in case discussions. Indeed, it's essential that you participate, for if nobody participates there can be no discussion! If you never join in the debate, you'll be denying other participants the insights that you may have to offer. Moreover, there's significant learning involved in presenting your own analysis and recommendations and debating them with your classmates—who may hold differing views or else seek to build on your presentation. But don't be so eager to participate that you ignore what others have to say. Learning to be a good listener is also an important element in developing managerial skills.

Occasionally, it may happen that you are personally familiar with the organization depicted in a case. Perhaps you have access to additional information not contained in the case, or perhaps you know what has happened since the time of the case decision point. If so, keep this information to yourself unless, and until, the instructor requests it. (This advice also holds true for written reports and case exams.) There are no prizes for 20/20 hindsight and injecting extra information that nobody else has is more likely to spoil a class discussion than to enhance it.

Four Customers in Search of Solutions

Christopher Lovelock

Four suburban subscribers call their telephone company to complain about a variety of different problems. How should the phone company respond to each?

Among the many customers of Bell Canada in Toronto, Ontario, are four individuals living on Willow Street in a middle-class suburb of the city. Each of them has a telephone-related problem and decides to call the company about it.

Winston Chen

Winston Chen grumbles constantly about the amount of his home telephone bill (which is, in fact, in the top 2 percent of all household phone bills in Ontario). There are many calls to countries in Southeast Asia on weekday evenings, almost daily calls to Kingston (a smaller city not far from Toronto) around mid-day, and calls to Vancouver, British Columbia, most weekends. One day, Mr. Chen receives a telephone bill which is even larger than usual. On reviewing the bill, he is convinced that he has been overcharged, so he calls Bell's customer service department to complain and request an adjustment.

Marie Portillo

Marie Portillo has missed several important calls recently because the caller received a busy signal. She phones the telephone company to determine possible solutions to this problem. Ms. Portillo's telephone bill is at the median level for a household subscriber. Most of the calls from her house are local, but there are occasional international calls to Mexico or to countries in South America. She does not subscribe to any value-added services.

Eleanor Vanderbilt

During the past several weeks, Mrs. Vanderbilt has been distressed to receive a series of obscene telephone calls. It sounds like the same person each time. She calls the telephone company to see if they can put a stop to this harassment. Her phone bill is in the bottom 10 percent of all household subscriber bills and almost all calls are local.

Richard Robbins

For more than a week, the phone line at Rich Robbins's house has been making strange humming and crackling noises, making it difficult to hear what the other person is saying. After two of his friends comment on these distracting noises, Mr. Robbins calls Bell and reports the problem. His guess is that it is being caused by the answering machine, which is getting old and sometimes loses messages. Mr. Robbins's phone bill is at the 75th percentile for a household subscriber. Most of the calls are made to locations within Canada, usually on evenings and weekends, although there are a few calls to the United States, too.

Study Questions

1. Based strictly on the information in the case, how many possibilities do you see to segment the telecommunications market?
2. As a customer service rep at the telephone company, how would you address each of the problems and complaints reported?
3. Do you see any marketing opportunities for Bell in any of these complaints?

Sullivan's Auto World Ford

Christopher Lovelock

A young health care manager unexpectedly finds herself responsible for running a family-owned car dealership that is in trouble. She is very concerned about the poor performance of the service department and wonders if a turnaround is possible.

Viewed from Wilson Avenue, the dealership presented a festive sight. Strings of triangular pennants in red, white, and blue fluttered gaily in the late afternoon breeze. Rows of new model cars gleamed and winked in the sunlight. Geraniums graced the flowerbeds outside the showroom entrance. A huge rotating sign at the corner of Wilson Avenue and Lincoln Street sported the Ford logo and identified the business as Sullivan's Auto World Ford. Banners below urged "Let's Make a Deal!"

Inside the handsome, high-ceilinged showroom, three of the new model Fords were on display—a dark-green 4×4 sports utility vehicle, a red convertible, and a white Taurus. Each vehicle was polished to a high sheen. Two groups of customers were chatting with salespeople, and a middle-aged man sat in the driver's seat of the convertible, studying the controls.

Upstairs in the comfortably furnished general manager's office, Carol Sullivan-Diaz finished running another spreadsheet analysis on her laptop. She felt tired and depressed. Her father, Walter Sullivan, had died four weeks earlier at the age of 56 of a sudden heart attack. As executor of his estate, the bank had asked her to temporarily assume the position of general manager of the dealership. The only visible changes that she had made to her father's office were installing a fax machine and laser printer, but she had been very busy analyzing the current position of the business.

Sullivan-Diaz did not like the look of the numbers on the printout. Auto World's financial situation had been deteriorating for 18 months, and it had been running in the red for the first half of the current year. New car sales had declined, reflecting a downturn in the regional economy. Margins had been squeezed by promotions and other efforts to move new cars off the lot. Industry forecasts of future sales were discouraging and so were her own financial projections for Auto World's sales department. Service revenues, which were below average for a dealership of this size, had also declined, although the service department still made a small surplus.

Had she had made a mistake last week, Carol wondered, in turning down Bill Froelich's offer to buy the business? It was true that the price offered had been substantially below the offer from Froelich that her father had rejected two years earlier, but the business had been more profitable then.

The Sullivan Family

Walter Sullivan had purchased a small Ford dealership in 1981 and had built it up to become one of the best known in the metropolitan area. Six years back, he had borrowed heavily to purchase the current site at a major suburban highway intersection, in an area of town with many new housing developments.

There had been a dealership on the site, but the buildings were 30 years old. Sullivan had retained the service and repair bays, but torn down the showroom in front of them and replaced it by an attractive modern facility. On moving to the new location, which was substantially larger than the old one, he had renamed his business Sullivan's Auto World Ford.

Everybody had seemed to know Walt Sullivan. He had been a consummate showman and entrepreneur, appearing in his own radio and television commercials and active in community affairs. His approach to car sales had emphasized promotions, discounts, and deals in order to maintain volume. He was never happier than when making a sale.

Carol Sullivan-Diaz, aged 28, was the eldest of Walter and Carmen Sullivan's three daughters. After obtaining a bachelor's degree in economics, she had gone on to take an MBA degree and had then embarked on a career in health care management. She was married to Dr. Roberto Diaz, a surgeon at St. Luke's Hospital. Her 20-year-old twin sisters, Gail and Joanne, who were students at the local university, lived with their mother.

In her own student days, Sullivan-Diaz had worked part-time in her father's business on secretarial and bookkeeping tasks and also as a service writer in the service department, so she was quite familiar with the operations of the dealership. At business school, she had decided on a career in health care management. After graduation, she had worked as an executive assistant to the president of St. Luke's, a large teaching hospital. Two years later, she joined Metropolitan Health Plan as assistant director of marketing, a position she had now held for almost three years. Her responsibilities included attracting new members, complaint handling, market research, and member retention programs.

Carol's employer had given her a six-week leave of absence to put her father's affairs in order. She doubted that she could extend that leave much beyond the two weeks still remaining. Neither she nor other family members were interested in making a career of running the dealership. However, she was prepared to take time out from her health care career to work on a turnaround if that seemed a viable proposition. She had been successful in her present job and believed it would not be difficult to find another health management position in the future.

The Dealership

Like other car dealerships, Sullivan's Auto World operated both sales and service departments, often referred to in the trade as "front end" and "back end," respectively. Both new and used vehicles were sold, since a high proportion of new car and van purchases involved trading in the purchaser's existing vehicle. Auto World would also buy well-maintained used cars at auction for resale. Purchasers who decided that they could not afford a new car would often buy a "preowned" vehicle instead, while shoppers who came in looking for a used car could sometimes be persuaded to buy a new one. Before being put on sale, each used vehicle was carefully serviced, with parts being replaced as needed. Dents and other blemishes were removed at a nearby body shop and occasionally

the vehicle's paintwork was resprayed, too. Finally, it was thoroughly cleaned and polished, inside and out, by a detailer whose services were hired as needed.

The front end of the dealership employed a sales manager, seven salespeople, an office manager, and a secretary. One of the salespeople had given notice and would be leaving at the end of the following week. The service department, when fully staffed, consisted of a service manager, a parts supervisor, nine mechanics, and two service writers. The Sullivan twins often worked part-time as service writers, filling in at busy periods, when one of the other writers was sick or on vacation, or when—as currently—there was an unfilled vacancy. The job entailed scheduling appointments for repairs and maintenance, writing up each work order, calling customers with repair estimates, and assisting customers when they returned to pick up the cars and pay for the work that had been done.

Sullivan-Diaz knew from her own experience as a service writer that it could be a stressful job. Few people liked to be without their car, even for a day. When a car broke down or was having problems, the owner was often nervous about how long it would take to get it fixed and, if the warranty had expired, how much the labor and parts would cost. Customers were quite unforgiving when a problem was not fixed completely on the first attempt and they had to return their vehicle for further work.

Major mechanical failures were not usually difficult to repair, although the parts replacement costs might be expensive. It was often the "little" things like water leaks and wiring problems that were the hardest to diagnose and correct, and it might be necessary for the customer to return two or three times before such a problem was resolved. In these situations, parts and materials costs were relatively low, but labor costs mounted up quickly, being charged out at $45 an hour. Customers could sometimes become abusive, yelling at service writers over the phone or arguing with service writers, mechanics, and the service manager in person.

Turnover in the service writer job was high, which was one reason why Carol—and more recently her sisters—had often been pressed into service by their father to "hold the fort" as he described it. More than once, she had seen an exasperated service writer respond sharply to a complaining customer or hang up on one who was being abusive over the telephone. Gail and Joanne were currently taking turns to cover the vacant position, but there were times when both of them had classes and the dealership had only one service writer on duty.

By national standards, Sullivan's Auto World was a medium-sized dealership, selling around 1,100 cars a year, equally divided between new and used vehicles.

In the most recent year, its revenues totaled $26.6 million from new and used car sales and $2.9 million from service and parts—down from $30.5 million and $3.6 million, respectively, in the previous year. Although the unit value of car sales was high, the margins were quite low, with margins for new cars being substantially lower than for used ones. The reverse was true for service. Industry guidelines suggested that the contribution margin (known as the departmental selling gross) from car sales should be about 5.5 percent of sales revenues, and from service, around 25 percent of revenues. In a typical dealership, 60 percent of the selling gross had traditionally come from sales and 40 percent from service, but the balance was shifting from sales to service. The selling gross was then applied to fixed expenses, such as administrative salaries, rent or mortgage payments, and utilities.

For the most recent 12 months at Auto World, Sullivan-Diaz had determined that the selling gross figures were 4.6 percent and 24 percent, respectively, both of them lower than in the previous year and collectively insufficient to cover the dealership's fixed expenses. Her father had made no mention of financial difficulties, and she had been shocked to learn from the bank after his death that Auto World had been two months behind in mortgage payments on the property. Further analysis also showed that accounts payable had also risen sharply in the previous six months. Fortunately, the dealership held a large insurance policy on Sullivan's life, and the proceeds from this had been more than sufficient to bring mortgage payments up to date, pay down all overdue accounts, and leave some funds for future contingencies.

The opportunities for expanding new car sales did not appear promising, given rising interest rates and recent layoffs at a local factory that was expected to hurt the local economy. However, recent promotional incentives had reduced the inventory to manageable levels. From discussions with Larry Winters, Auto World's sales manager, Sullivan-Diaz had concluded that costs could be reduced by not replacing the departing sales rep, maintaining inventory at somewhat lower levels, and trying to make more efficient use of advertising and promotion. Although Winters did not have Walter's exuberant personality, he had been Auto World's leading sales rep before being promoted and had shown strong managerial capabilities in his current position.

As she reviewed the figures for the service department, Sullivan-Diaz wondered what potential might exist for improving its sales volume and selling gross. Her father had never been very interested in the parts and service business, seeing it simply as a necessary adjunct of the dealership. "Customers always seem to be miserable back there," he had once remarked to her. "But here in the front end, everybody's happy when someone buys a new car." The service facility was not easily visible from the main highway, being hidden behind the showroom. Although the building looked old and greasy, the equipment itself was modern and well maintained. There was sufficient capacity to handle more repair work, but a higher volume would require hiring one or more new mechanics.

Customers were required to bring cars in for servicing before 8:30 A.M. After parking their cars, customers entered the service building by a side door and waited their turn to see the service writers, who occupied a cramped room with peeling paint and an interior window overlooking the service bays. Customers stood while work orders for their cars were prepared. Ringing telephones frequently interrupted the process. Filing cabinets containing customer records and other documents lined the far wall of the room.

If the work were of a routine nature, such as an oil change or tune-up, the customer was given an estimate immediately. For more complex jobs, they would be called with an estimate later in the morning once the car had been examined. Customers were required to pick up their cars by 6:00 P.M. on the day the work was completed. On several occasions, Carol had urged her father to computerize the service work-order process, but he had never acted on her suggestions, so all orders continued to be handwritten on large yellow sheets, with three carbon copies below. The top sheet became the work order, the second was the customer receipt, the third was filed alphabetically by customer name and the fourth was filed in chronological sequence.

The service manager, Rick Obert, who was in his late forties, had held the position since Auto World opened at its current location. The Sullivan family considered him to be technically skilled, and he managed the mechanics effectively, with low turnover. However, his manner with customers could be gruff and argumentative.

Customer Survey Results

Another set of data that Sullivan-Diaz had studied carefully were the results of the customer satisfaction surveys that were mailed to the dealership monthly by a research firm retained by the Ford Motor Company.

Purchasers of all new Ford cars were sent a questionnaire by mail within 30 days of making the purchase and asked to use a five-point scale to rate their satisfaction with the dealership sales department, vehicle preparation, and the characteristics of the vehicle itself. The questionnaire asked how likely the purchaser would be to recommend the dealership, the salesperson, and the manufacturer to someone else. Other questions asked if the customers had been introduced to the dealer's service department and been given explanations on what to do if their cars needed service. Finally, there were some classification questions relating to customer demographics.

A second survey was sent to new car purchasers nine months after they had bought their cars. This questionnaire began by asking about satisfaction with the vehicle and then asked customers if they had taken their vehicles to the selling dealer for service of any kind. If so, respondents were then asked to rate the service department on 14 different attributes—ranging from the attitudes of service personnel to the quality of the work performed—and then to rate their overall satisfaction with service from the dealer.

Customers were also asked about where they would go in the future for maintenance service, minor mechanical and electrical repairs, major repairs in those same categories, and bodywork. The options listed for service were selling dealer, another Ford dealer, "some other place," or "do-it-yourself." Finally, there were questions about overall satisfaction with the dealer sales department and the dealership in general, as well as the likelihood of their purchasing another Ford Motor Company product and buying it from the same dealership.

Dealers received monthly reports summarizing customer ratings of their dealership for the most recent month and for several previous months. To provide a comparison with how other Ford dealerships performed, the reports also included regional and national rating averages. After analysis, completed questionnaires were returned to the dealership; since these included each customer's name, a dealer could see which customers were satisfied and which were not.

In the 30-day survey of new purchasers, Auto World achieved better than average ratings on most dimensions. One finding that puzzled Carol was that almost 90 percent of respondents answered "yes" when asked if someone from Auto World had explained what to do if they needed service, but less than a third said that they had been introduced to someone in the service department. She resolved to ask Larry Winters about this discrepancy.

The nine-month survey findings disturbed her. Although vehicle ratings were in line with national averages, the overall level of satisfaction with service at Auto World was consistently low, placing it in the bottom 25 percent of all Ford dealerships.

The worst ratings for service concerned promptness of writing up orders, convenience of scheduling the work, convenience of service hours, and appearance of the service department. On length of time to complete the work, availability of needed parts, and quality of work done ("was it fixed right?"), Auto World's rating was close to the average. For interpersonal variables such as attitude of service department personnel, politeness, understanding of customer problems, and explanation of work performed, its ratings were relatively poor.

When Sullivan-Diaz reviewed the individual questionnaires, she found that there was a wide degree of variation between customers' responses on these interpersonal variables, ranging all the way across a 5-point scale from "completely satisfied" to "very dissatisfied." Curious, she had gone to the service files and examined the records for several dozen customers who had recently completed the nine-month surveys. At least part of the ratings could be explained by which service writers the customer had dealt with. Those who had been served two or more times by her sisters, for instance, gave much better ratings than those who had dealt primarily with Jim Fiskell, the service writer who had recently quit.

Perhaps the most worrying responses were those relating to customers' likely use of Auto World's service department in the future. More than half indicated that they would use another Ford dealer or "some other place" for maintenance service (such as oil change, lubrication, or tune-up) or for minor mechanical and electrical repairs. About 30 percent would use another source for major repairs. The rating for overall satisfaction with the selling dealer after nine months was below average, and the customer's likelihood of purchasing from the same dealership again was a full point below that of buying another Ford product.

Sullivan-Diaz pushed aside the spreadsheets she had printed out and shut down her laptop. It was time to go home for dinner. She saw the options for the dealership as basically twofold: either prepare the business for an early sale at what would amount to a distress price, or take a year or two to try to turn it around financially. In the latter instance, if the turnaround succeeded, the business could subsequently be sold at a higher price than it presently commanded, or the family could install a general manager to run the dealership for them.

Bill Froelich, owner of another nearby dealership plus three others in different suburbs, had offered to buy Auto World for a price that represented a fair valuation of the net assets, according to Auto World's accountants, plus $150,000 in goodwill. However, the rule of thumb when the auto industry was enjoying good times was that goodwill should be valued at $1,000 per vehicle sold each year. Carol knew that Froelich was eager to develop a network of dealerships in order to achieve economies of scale. His prices on new cars were very competitive and his nearest dealership clustered several franchises—Ford, Lincoln-Mercury, and Jaguar—on a single large property.

Carol knew that Froelich subscribed to an Internet-based car-buying service that allowed consumers to specify their exact requirements for a particular model of car and then submit a purchase request for their choice. In return for a sign-up fee of about $5,000 for each of his franchises and a monthly subscription of about $1,000 each, Froelich's dealerships had been given exclusive rights to the metropolitan area. When a consumer from this area submitted a purchase request, the dealer was obligated to call the individual within 24 hours and offer a low, competitive, no-haggle, no-hassle price. The customer (who paid no fee for the service) was under no obligation to buy. If the quote led to a purchase, the dealer would coordinate financing, if needed, and arrange delivery. In many cases, the customer never even set foot in the dealership.

Carol recognized that the procedure represented a radical change in car selling. Although it led to lower prices, it also reduced selling time and expenses. She had received a call only that morning from a competing Internet company that offered separate services for new and used cars. To become a franchisee of the latter service, dealers had to agree to submit each car to a 135-point certification program and to institute a 72-hour, 100 percent money-back return policy, as well as a 3-month limited warranty. This firm's services were cheaper than the one Froelich subscribed to; there was no sign-up charge and annual fees for each of the two services averaged about $800. However, there was no geographic exclusivity and, for each completed sale, the dealer paid a commission of $29.

An Unwelcome Disturbance

As Carol left her office, she spotted the sales manager coming up the stairs leading from the showroom floor. "Larry," she said, "I've got a question for you."

"Fire away!" replied the sales manager.

"I've been looking at the customer satisfaction surveys. Why aren't our sales reps introducing new customers to the folks in the Service Department? It's supposedly part of our sales protocol, but it only seems to be happening about one-third of the time!"

Larry Winters shuffled his feet. "Well, Carol, basically I leave it to their discretion. We tell them about service, of course, but some of the guys on the floor feel a bit uncomfortable taking folks over to the service bays after they've been in here. It's quite a contrast, if you know what I mean."

Suddenly, the sound of shouting arose from the floor below. A man of about 40, wearing a windbreaker and jeans, was standing in the doorway yelling at one of the salespeople. The two managers could catch snatches of what he was saying in between various obscenities: ". . . three visits . . . still not fixed right . . . service stinks . . . who's in charge here?" Everybody else in the showroom had stopped what they were doing and had turned to look at the newcomer.

Winters looked at his young employer and rolled his eyes. "If there was something your dad couldn't stand, it was guys like that, yelling and screaming in the showroom and asking for the boss. Walt would go hide out in his office! Don't worry, Tom'll take care of that fellow and get him out of here. What a jerk!"

"No," said Sullivan-Diaz, "I'll deal with him! One thing I learned when I worked at St. Luke's was that you don't let people yell about their problems in front of everybody else. You take them off somewhere, calm them down, and find out what's bugging them."

She stepped quickly down the stairs, wondering to herself, "What else have I learned in health care that I can apply to this business?"

Study Questions

1. How does marketing cars differ from marketing service for those same vehicles?
2. Compare and contrast the sales and service departments at Auto World.
3. Prepare a flowchart of the servicing of a car that comes in for repair or maintenance.
4. What useful parallels do you see between running an automobile sales and service dealership and running health care services?
5. What advice would you give to Carol?

Euro Disney: An American in Paris

Christopher Lovelock
Ivor P. Morgan

The new Disney theme park and resort near Paris has not met its attendance and revenue projections. Management is evaluating the situation and seeking a turnaround strategy.

"Last call for the Euro-Disneyland Express. . . ." The recorded American voice boomed out loud and clear even as the express disappeared from view down the tracks. The crowds still waiting behind the station barriers muttered to themselves in a variety of languages, complaining that station employees had failed yet again to fill all the empty seats on the train. One visitor remarked to a companion that, although they had passed the "Maximum 30 Minutes Wait" sign at the station entrance over 45 minutes earlier, they had at their present rate of progress at least that long to wait again. "Let's try something else!" he said to his friend.

It was a cool autumn Saturday at Euro Disneyland, near Paris, and raining hard. Main Street, USA, flanked principally by stores selling Disney paraphernalia, was almost deserted. Only a few individuals wearing bright yellow rain capes with a Mickey Mouse insignia lit up the street. The absence of people outside the station suggested, at least, quick access to the rest of the park's attractions and restaurants.

This was not a promising start to a day at the Walt Disney Co.'s newest theme park, the fourth in a series, each of which had previously seemed a guaranteed success no matter where located. The company's ventures in California and Florida had become a staple "must visit" for many American families and also a draw for visitors from other parts of the world,

including Europe and Asia. Tokyo Disneyland, opened in 1983, had been successful, too, even though Japanese culture was widely accepted as being very different from that of the United States. But more than two years after its April 1992 opening, managers of the Euro Disney resort (which comprised both the Euro Disneyland theme park and an adjoining cluster of six hotels) were struggling to boost park attendance and hotel occupancy to help it turn around its continuing financial problems.

Background

Walt Disney dreamed in the 1950s of a new type of entertainment, which came to be known as the theme park. Seeing the amusement parks of that time as dirty, phony places run by tough-looking people, he envisioned something better. Disneyland opened in 1955 on an 80-acre (32 hectare) site in the suburban town of Anaheim, easily accessible from both Los Angeles and San Diego. The park featured many of Walt's famous cartoon figures, including Mickey Mouse, Goofy, and other characters from Disney movies.

Walt Disney died in 1966 but his company continued to prosper. In 1971, it opened a second theme park in central Florida, named Walt Disney World. The new park, which most people called simply "Disney World," was located within the company's huge landholdings outside Orlando. The development included on-site hotels and, subsequently, the futuristic Epcot Center. Stimulated by the success of Disney World, Orlando became a boom area boasting numerous other attractions and hotels. The third

This case was developed from published sources and the personal experiences of individual Euro Disney visitors.

Exchange rates for the French franc (FFr) against other currencies varied widely during the early 1990s. Representative rates for this period: FFr 1.00 = US $0.19 or C$0.26

Exhibit 1 Comparative Rainfall and Temperature Statistics
Monthly Rainfall by Frequency and Volume

	Los Angeles California		Orlando Florida		Tokyo Japan		Paris France		Barcelona Spain	
	days	inches	days	inches	days	inches	days	inches	days	inches
Jan.	6	2.7	6	2.1	5	2.2	17	1.5	5	1.4
Feb.	6	3.0	7	2.8	6	2.8	14	1.2	5	1.3
Mar.	6	2.2	8	3.2	10	4.4	12	1.6	8	2.7
Apr.	4	0.5	5	2.2	10	4.9	13	1.7	9	2.0
May	2	0.2	9	4.0	10	5.7	12	2.1	8	1.4
Jun.	1	0.1	14	7.4	12	6.5	12	2.3	6	1.3
Jul.	—	—	17	7.8	10	5.3	12	2.2	4	1.1
Aug.	—	—	16	6.3	9	5.7	13	2.2	6	1.4
Sep.	1	0.3	14	5.6	12	8.7	13	2.0	7	3.0
Oct.	2	0.7	8	2.8	11	7.4	13	2.3	9	3.0
Nov.	3	1.0	6	1.8	7	4.2	15	1.8	6	1.8
Dec.	6	2.3	6	1.8	5	2.1	16	1.7	6	1.7

Note: "days" refers to average number of days per month during which rain falls; "inches" refers to average rainfall volume during that month (1 inch = 25mm). Florida's rainfall is usually concentrated in short but extremely heavy showers, whereas in Paris rain may fall steadily for many hours.

Average Daily Temperatures: High and Low for Each Month (in degrees Celsius)

	Los Angeles California		Orlando Florida		Tokyo Japan		Paris France		Barcelona Spain	
	high	low	high	low	high	low	high	low	high	low
Jan.	18°	8°	22°	10°	8°	−2°	6°	1°	13°	6°
Feb.	19	8	23	10	9	−1	7	1	14	7
Mar.	19	9	26	13	12	2	12	4	16	9
Apr.	21	10	29	16	17	8	16	6	18	11
May	22	12	31	19	22	12	20	10	21	14
Jun.	24	13	33	22	24	17	23	13	25	18
Jul.	27	16	33	23	28	21	25	15	28	21
Aug.	28	16	33	23	30	22	24	14	28	21
Sep.	27	14	32	23	26	19	21	12	25	19
Oct.	24	12	29	19	21	13	16	8	21	15
Nov.	23	10	26	14	16	6	10	5	16	11
Dec.	19	8	23	11	11	1	7	2	13	8

Note: Conversion: 0°C = 32°F, 10°C = 50°F, 20°C = 68°F, 30°C = 86°F. Data are based on averages for 24-hour periods, not highest and lowest temperatures within a 24-hour period

park followed in 1983 with the opening of Tokyo Disneyland on a relatively small site just outside the Japanese capital. Despite some initial difficulties, this park, too, became highly popular and a significant financial success for both Disney and the Japanese owners, the Oriental Land Co. However, the Walt Disney Co. had no equity stake, being limited to royalties of 10% on admission revenues and 5% on food and souvenir sales.

In the mid 1980s the company turned its attention to Europe, from which numerous visitors to its California and (especially) Florida parks were drawn. Disney executives evaluated a variety of locations for what was to become Euro Disney, but eventually the choice narrowed to two sites: one outside Paris (pop-

ulation 8 million) in northern France, and the second near Barcelona (population 2.5 million) in eastern Spain.

Barcelona, site of the 1992 Summer Olympics and located on the Mediterranean coast, offered a warmer, drier climate. (See *Exhibit 1* for comparative weather statistics in Paris, Barcelona, Tokyo, Central Florida, and Los Angeles.) However, Paris had the advantage of offering easier access to potential visitors from densely populated areas of Northern Europe (see map in *Exhibit 2*), in addition to being one of the most popular tourist cities in Europe. Disney executives were also influenced by the French government's offer of generous subsidies, tax allowances, and rail and highway improvements, designed to attract some

Exhibit 2 West and Central Europe

12,000 jobs to what was then a depressed agricultural region. The French inducements were successful and Disney purchased a site encompassing almost 20 square kilometers (5,000 acres), located 32 km (20 miles) southeast of the French capital.

Theme Parks in Europe

The size and scope of Euro Disneyland far exceeded that of any existing European theme park. Some parks were relatively compact and urban, such as Copenhagen's famous Tivoli Gardens. Others, like Britain's popular Alton Towers, had been built as adjuncts to an existing attraction (in this case an English stately home). Many amusement parks lacked a coherent theme beyond the appeal of fairground rides promising increasing degrees of stomach-churning thrills. However, Legoland in Denmark was created out of giant versions of the successful children's construction toy. Several European parks promoted the Schtroumpfs (better known as "Smurfs" in English). But these little blue cartoon characters, a big hit on children's television during the early 1980s, had largely disappeared from toy stores, comic books, and the mass media a decade later.

France boasted some 25 theme and entertainment parks, including Parc Asterix, Walibi-Schtroumpf, and Futuroscope (for details, see the *Appendix*). However, two major French parks, Mirapolis and Zygofolies, opened (like Futuroscope) in 1987, had both subsequently closed. Observers ascribed these failures to competition from other entertainment options, including numerous small amusement parks.

Euro Disney

With an investment totaling 21 billion frances, characters drawn from Disney cartoon movies, a site equivalent in area to one fifth the city of Paris, a projected 12,000 "cast members" (employees) on opening day, and a forecast of 11 million visitors in its first year, the Euro Disney project exemplified to its many French critics all that was wrong with American culture—namely size, money, and Hollywood.

As opening day approached, many French intellectuals denounced the park; one described it as "this new beachhead of American Imperialism." Alain Finkelkraut, a philosopher, portrayed it as a "terrifying giant's step towards world homogenization." Jean-Marie Rouart, a novelist, argued that Euro Disney symbolized the transformation of craft into industry. "If we do not resist it," he warned, "the kingdom of profit will create a world that will have all the appearance of civilization and all the savage reality of barbarism."[1]

On the other hand, there was plenty of evidence to suggest that large numbers of French people, especially younger ones, enjoyed watching American movies and TV shows—including those produced by Disney—as well as listening to American rock bands, eating American-style fast food, and wearing American-inspired clothing.

The first phase of the project covered about one-third of the available land area and included the Euro Disneyland park, six hotels with a total of 5,200 rooms, the Festival Disney entertainment and retail area (located between the park and the hotel complex), Camp Davy Crockett with 414 rental cabins and 181 campsites, and Golf Euro Disney, an 18-hole championship golf course. An average occupancy of 70% was anticipated for the hotels. The original plans called for a proposed Phase II to be built in stages and were to include the Disney-MGM Studios Europe (comprising a second theme park plus movie and TV production facilities), initially scheduled to open in 1995. Once completed, these new attractions were projected to attract 5 million guests in the first year of operation and 8 million in the second year, encouraging Euro Disneyland guests to extend their stays. Subsequent stages would eventually add another 13,000 hotel rooms, a major convention center, a water park, a second golf course, and additional campsites.

The design of Euro Disneyland followed the same basic approach as other Disney parks, with some adaptations for northern European weather conditions. Advance press releases described the park as "a giant outdoor stage where guests leave behind their ordinary world and enter lands of memory, imagination, and fantasy." Facing the main entrance lay the complex known as Main Street USA, flanked by shopping arcades offering weather-protected connections to several other attractions. Looping around the boundaries of the park was the Euro Disneyland Express, with stations at Main Street, Frontierland, and Fantasyland. The other two groups of attractions were Adventureland and Discoveryland.

Dominating the park's Central Plaza were the spires of the fairy castle, taller and more lavishly finished than its counterparts in other Disney parks. There was no Matterhorn, but a substantially higher Big Thunder Mountain made up for the former's absence.

Financial Arrangements

To defray the financial risk of this enormous project, of which Phase I alone took several years to complete, the Walt Disney Co. established a separate company, Euro Disney SCA, in which it held 49% of the stock; the balance was sold to investors through public offerings. Though Euro Disney was responsible for operating the Euro Disneyland theme park, it would not own it fully until the end of the 20-year-lease period. The Walt Disney Co. provided management for the company through a wholly-owned subsidiary.

In return for use of the Disney name and logistical support, Euro Disney paid Walt Disney Co. a number of royalties and fees, including a brand name royalty of 10% on all revenues from admissions, sponsorship payments and parking, plus 5% on food, drink, and merchandise sales. There was also a base management fee of 5% of all revenues through 1996, after which the rate increased to 6%. Finally, there was an incentive management fee, levied at a progressive rate on operating income less the expenses needed to maintain the park's existing attractions. Critics felt that the arrangements left the Walt Disney Co. with the upside potential and the European investors with the downside risk.[2]

But Euro Disney had not attempted to avoid all risk. Having seen other real estate developers profit mightily from investments in land for hotels and other purposes in the area surrounding Disney World in Florida, Disney executives hoped that the opening of Euro Disney would lead to soaring values for their huge land investment near Paris. The Phase II plans for a big increase in hotel rooms assumed that visitors would stay longer at the resort. Consequently, to maximize the profit potential of the project, the company decided to own and operate the hotels and other resort facilities rather than lease them to third parties. Also on the drawing board were plans for enormous office developments, shopping malls, golf courses, apartment complexes and vacation homes. The idea was that Euro Disney would control the design, build nearly everything itself, and, at the right moment, sell off completed properties at a big profit.[3]

Catering to a Multinational Audience[4]

For Disney officials, their new European venture represented even more of a challenge than their first foreign theme park, Tokyo Disneyland. Visitors were expected to come from all over Europe (and beyond). At any one time, there might be as many as 50,000 guests in the park. Unlike the California, Florida, or Tokyo parks, no one nationality was expected to dominate at Euro Disney; so handling languages required careful planning.

An early decision, responding to concerns of "American cultural imperialism," was that French would be the first official language at Euro Disney. Some of the attractions would be named in French, others would retain the names used in the American original. Most other signage would be in both English and French (in addition to use of international symbols), and knowledge of two or more languages would

be an important criterion in hiring front-line employees.

Recruitment centers were set up in France and also in London, Amsterdam, and Frankfurt. During 1992, approximately two-thirds of those hired were French nationals; the balance comprised another 75 nationalities, principally British, Dutch, German, and Irish. Some knowledge of French was required of all employees; in the park's opening year, about 75% of them spoke this language fluently, another 75% spoke English, roughly 25% spoke Spanish, and 25% could speak German.

Although Euro Disney retained the basic orientation of other Disney theme parks, some adaptation was made to European culture and languages. The popular "Pirates of the Caribbean" attraction, for instance, acknowledged that it wasn't only English-speaking pirates who enjoyed themselves attacking shipping and coastal ports in a jolly frenzy of looting, burning, and drinking, but also their equally colorful French and Dutch counterparts. So pirate songs were played in three languages. Similarly, "Sleeping Beauty's Castle" recognized the European origins of the popular fairy story and was known instead as *Le Château de la Belle au Bois Dormant*. But "Main Street, USA" remained just that—no one really expected it to be renamed *Rue Principale, États-Unis*.

Many attractions and rides required little explanation, but guests could replace the French commentary in the Visionarium (a 360-degree film theater) by using audio receivers that offered a choice of English, Spanish, German, and Italian. The reservations center catered to people of many tongues, with separate phone lines for each of 12 different languages. The main information center in the park, City Hall, was staffed by cast members speaking a broad cross section of languages.

Special procedures were instituted at the park's medical center to handle emergencies involving guests speaking less commonly encountered languages. With over 70 nationalities represented among employees, there was a high probability that a cast member could be found to interpret in such a situation. Euro Disney could access the language capabilities of every employee by computer (who do we have on duty who speaks Turkish?) and could page them immediately by beeper or walkie-talkie.

Early Operating Experience

The park and resort opened to great fanfare on April 12, 1992. Visitors familiar with other Disney theme parks noted that everything at Euro Disneyland seemed to be larger and more ornate; the hotels, too, were enormous. At FFr 225 for adults and FFr 150 for children, admission prices were not only high by European standards but also higher than at Disney's two American parks.

Despite massive publicity, the first season was not a success. Ignoring much of the glitter and the excitement, the mass media highlighted difficulties and accentuated negative stories, including labor problems. The fiscal year ending September 30, 1992 concluded with an operating loss of FFr 682 million (reduced by other income and exceptional items to a net loss of FFr 188 million). The situation did not improve the following year. Attendance figures were particularly low during the cold, wet winter months, even though many of the rides were weather protected and Disney had organized various seasonal events, including one for Halloween (a popular American children's celebration at the end of October, featuring ghosts, witches, and lanterns made from carved pumpkins).

Among the problems were that attendance at Euro Disneyland had failed to reach target levels, particularly among the local French population which had been expected to form a substantial share of the early market.[5] Average expenditures per visitor, including food and souvenir purchases, were below projections, too. There was also a major seasonality problem, with the lowest levels of attendance a mere one-tenth of those on peak days—a ratio greatly exceeding that of the three sister parks. Finally, occupancy rates in the resort's hotels had proved to be far below projections; for instance, many guests visiting the park for two days would only spend one night in a Euro Disney hotel.

Complicating Euro Disney's financial situation was the company's inability to capitalize on its enormous landholdings. Reflecting falling demand for new commercial developments, land prices fell sharply during the recession that hit France and other European countries in the early 1990s. Worse, interest rates on the billions of dollars in loans and other debt proved to be higher than expected.

Management and Training

In April 1993, a French chairman, Philippe Bourguignon, had replaced Robert Fitzpatrick, the American executive responsible for planning and building Euro Disney. Fitzpatrick, who spoke French and was married to a Frenchwoman, was seen by observers as having spared no expense in constructing the park but had experienced problems in managing day-to-day operations. Bourguignon, president of the park since September 1992, had previously operated the U.S. subsidiary of the French hotel group Accor before taking charge of Disney's property operations in

1988. As chairman, Bourguignon's objective was to ensure that the park adapted itself to European conditions without losing the American feel that he saw as its main draw.[6]

Disney's policy was to have American managers train Europeans who would eventually replace them. However, turnover had been higher than expected. Bourguignon's team was composed of one-third French nationals and one-third Americans, with the balance coming mainly from the United Kingdom, Ireland and the Netherlands. Under Bourguignon, Euro Disney was striving to develop its own managerial culture, neither just a reflection of its American parent nor typically French either.

A key issue involved employee training. Disney had always been known for its strict guidelines. "The Look Book," for example, dictated that female employees should wear only clear nail polish, very little—if any—make-up, and flesh-colored stockings. Men could not wear beards or mustaches and had to keep their hair short and tapered. Guests should be greeted within 60 seconds of entering a facility and helped as needed. The company's 1990 Annual Report announced that "a leading priority was to indoctrinate all employees in the Disney service philosophy, in addition to training them in operational policies and procedures." Euro Disney's goal was to convert the employees, 60% of whom were French, into clean-cut, customer-friendly, American-style service providers. "The French are not known for their hospitality," declared Margot Creviaux, the park's manager of training and development for Disney University. "But Disney is."[7]

However, during the first four months, more than 1,000 employees left. According to management, half quit, and the rest were asked to leave. The women's grooming guidelines were modified because "what is considered a classic beauty in Europe is not considered a classic beauty in America." At Euro Disney, the rules were changed to allow female cast members to wear pink or red nail polish, red lipstick and different colored stockings as long as they "complement [the] outfit and are in dark, subdued colors." Another Disney trademark was to smile a lot. But those familiar with French culture noted that if asked to smile the French were likely to respond, "I'll smile if I want to. Convince me." So Creviaux had to adapt the training to suit Euro Disney's work force. Although Disney stressed total customer satisfaction, in the eyes of some employees the company had imposed controls making that goal impossible to deliver.

To end the labor disputes that had plagued the park, Bourguignon recognized standard French job classifications, set a maximum work week, and annualized hourly work schedules. In doing so, he obtained greater flexibility from his work force. But in response to the poor financial results, 950 jobs were cut from the 11,000-person work force.[8] A Euro Disney spokesperson said the cuts were necessary as the company shifted from start-up to its operating phase.[9] Roger Dupont, a local representative of the CGT union responded, "It isn't the jobs cutting that will improve the image of Euro Disney."

Marketing Concerns

Euro Disney management planned to attract half of the park's visitors from France and the balance from other European countries. The off-season particularly depended on the local population because of reduced travel across Europe in winter. The other Europeans came as expected, but the French comprised only 29% of the attendance. Different reasons were advanced for this shortfall, including the American orientation, the high prices, the weather, and the location. Unlike Americans, Europeans had proved reluctant to take their children out of school for a vacation trip made at the parents' convenience.

Bourguignon blamed the poor financial results in part on Euro Disney's strongly American orientation. "Although most of our visitors come to enjoy an authentically American atmosphere," he noted, "it was just a little too much for them to have to celebrate Halloween."[10] Management therefore decided to place the accent more on events familiar to Europeans. And the American-inspired advertising was changed to a more descriptive campaign explaining what visitors could do at the park.

New policies were introduced to make the park more attractive to Europeans. In June 1993, Disney finally agreed to relax its prohibition on serving alcohol at Euro Disneyland. Four restaurants received permission to serve wine and beer. According to Yves Boulanger, the introduction of alcohol was primarily for non-French visitors from Germany and Britain who wanted wine because it was part of the French experience.[11]

Problems had also occurred with waiting lines, which were noticeably less orderly than in Disney's other parks. "The most often-heard complaint is how unruly and even chaotic the queues seemed to be" reported a *New York Times* correspondent, "even though the lines are not particularly long." Whole families sneaked under ropes and pushed ahead. No Disney employees appeared to be detailed to police the lines, and when guests complained to the offenders, everyone appeared to be speaking a different language and either did not—or pretended that they could not—understand what they had done wrong.

Complaints about high prices for admission and the hotels, combined with substantial seasonal variations in demand, led Bourguignon to break another Disney taboo by introducing cut-rate entry and room rates for the off-season. A lower priced evening ticket, available after 5 pm, was aimed at Parisians.[12] Price reductions were also introduced for school groups, as well as for individuals under 25 years of age or over 60.

Financial analysts continued to blame high prices for many of Euro Disney's difficulties. Disney had forecast that each visitor would buy $33 in food and souvenirs but actual expenditures were averaging 12% lower. Despite the distances involved, many Europeans found that it was actually cheaper to visit Disney World in Florida. The marketing manager of a British travel agency described how, thanks to cheaper accommodations and an Atlantic airfare war, she was able to offer her clients a package price of $115 a day for travel, hotel and park entry, compared to $200 a day for a similar Euro Disney package.[13]

Financial Results for 1993

The full impact of the company's crushing FFr 21 billion debt load became evident with publication of the financial results for the 1993 fiscal year (ending September 30). On November 10, 1993, Euro Disney SCA announced an operating loss of FFr 1.8 billion and a net loss after exceptional items of FFr 5.3 billion (US$930 million). Reflecting a full 12 months of operation, revenues from the theme park and resorts rose from FFr 3.8 billion francs in the previous year to almost FFr 4.9 billion. Although a large loss had been predicted by financial analysts, who had been tracking the company's fortunes closely, the magnitude of the loss was a surprise to many. Euro Disney's financial condition caused the Walt Disney Co. to defer the payment of royalties.[14]

The company changed its accounting policies to charge start-up costs directly to the income statement rather then capitalizing them on the balance sheet. Negotiations were begun with the company's banks to restructure the debt, but rumors began to fly that Euro Disney might have to shut down the park altogether.

The Walt Disney Co. agreed to help fund Euro Disney for a limited period in order to give the latter time to attempt its capital restructuring. Observers believed that while the Walt Disney Co. was anxious to protect its own investors, it could not afford to allow a company bearing the Disney brand name to go under.

Plans were temporarily frozen for the proposed FFr 15 billion Phase II Disney-MGM Studios Park, which was to be a separate operation from Euro Disneyland.[15] Meantime, Euro Disney was attempting to scale down its plan for a 3,400 room hotel and accompanying office complex and to replace it with a commercial complex on the proposed site.[16] This would bring fewer jobs to the region but could reduce Euro Disney's financial burden. The French government, however, might not favor changes of this type.

A Visit To The Park

It was a Saturday morning at the end of the first week of September. The weather had been forecast as overcast and cool, with showers developing in the afternoon, followed by bright periods. Two foreign visitors, who were familiar with both Disneyland and Walt Disney World, decided to see for themselves what Euro Disneyland was like. Noting a poster that promoted sale of Euro Disney tickets at his hotel, one of the visitors went to the reception desk to buy an entrance ticket for the park with his credit card. The following conversation ensued (in French):

Hotel employee: "Sorry, sir, you must pay cash for a ticket here."
Visitor: "Why?"
Employee: "It's a special promotion."
Visitor: "Does that mean tickets here are cheaper than at the gate?"
Employee: "No, but you won't have to wait in line."

The visitor decided to buy his ticket later, remembering a bargain price promotion for a combined RER (regional express metro) train ticket and entry to Euro Disney that he had seen advertised in Paris Metro (subway) stations. At the Châtelet station, bilingual French and English posters advertised the offer, but a clerk in the ticket office declared that the special offer was not available.

The station for Euro Disney was located at the end of the RER line, on a specially constructed extension. Set amid farmland, the new station was named "Marne La Vallée-Chessy" after two nearby towns. Apart from a Mickey Mouse silhouette on the glass exit doors, nothing acknowledged Euro Disney's presence right outside. A left turn from the station and a short walk brought visitors to the entrance to Euro Disneyland. A right turn would have taken them past an entertainment mall offering a variety of souvenir stores and food stands and on to the six hotels of the Euro Disney Resort (see *Exhibit 3*).

It was now around 11:45 am and starting to rain. There were no lines at the entrance booths. One of the visitors asked the ticket seller if he spoke German. The latter said that he did, but subsequently proved unable to carry on a simple conversation in that language. From the entrance, the park appeared to be almost deserted. Main Street, USA, was built to a

EXHIBIT 3 *Euro Disney Hotels and Cabins: Proposed Peak Season Rates, 1994–95*

Disneyland Hotel

500 rooms, very luxurious Victorian theme. Daily room rate, FFr 1,990.

Hotel New York

575 rooms, luxury convention hotel. "Big Apple" theme evoking New York City skyscrapers and row houses. Includes ice-skating rink, convention center, tennis. Daily room rate, FFr 1,025.

Newport Bay Club

1,098 rooms. Elegant theme evoking New England yacht and beach club resort. Includes lighthouse and lakeside verandah with rocking chairs. Daily room rate, FFr 875.

Sequoia Lodge

1,011 rooms, Yosemite/Yellowstone theme based on rustic lodges at U.S. national parks. Fireplaces, year-round outdoor pool. Daily room rate, FFr 775.

Hotel-Cheyenne

1,000 rooms, American West theme. Log fort with lookout tower, corral, covered wagons. Room included double bed and bunk beds, no air-conditioning. Daily room rate, FFr 675.

Hotel Santa Fe

1,000 rooms, American Southwest theme, including American Indian cliff dwellings, adobe style pueblos. No air-conditioning. Daily room rate, FFr 550.

Old West Camp Day Crockett

414 cabins in family-style "wilderness" setting with Old West theme featuring miners, settlers and tavern (plus swimming pool). Daily rate, FFr 770.

All Euro Disney accommodation offered rooms set up for a family of four. Competition was limited within a radius of 4–5 miles (6–8 km) of the park. Offerings in 1994 included Novotel and Days Inn, both of which offered substantially cheaper rates than available at Euro Disney. Other hotel chains, including Accor and Comfort Inn, were constructing inexpensive hotels near the park, due to open in 1995. Visitors to Euro Disneyland could also stay at hotels in the center of Paris or its suburbs.

larger scale than the Disneyland original in California and its theme had been updated from the late 19th century to include reproduction antique cars.

With the rain now falling steadily, the Euro Disneyland Express seemed an attractive option, since the station was weather protected. The line of prospective passengers started well short of the sign which said "30 minutes wait beyond this point" so the two visitors joined the queue with optimism. "It can't take more than 15 minutes from here," said one. However, their optimism proved ill-founded, because the trains were arriving full and only a handful of people were getting off. To compound the problem, the few conductors were failing to fill all the empty seats on the train. Finally, the two visitors decided to wait no longer and headed up Main Street in search of Mickey Mouse.

But there was not a mouse (or other Disney character) to be seen. An earlier discussion with French friends living in a neighboring town had suggested this was an ongoing omission. "It's particularly irritating for my teenage granddaughters to see the TV advertisements full of Mickey Mouse and other Disney characters," the friend had said, "only to go to the park and not to be able to find them. I know they do appear in the parade but that is just for a very limited time in the evening. Another problem for me," the grandfather continued, "is the distance involved in getting around the park. The walk from the parking lot to the gates is bad enough, but when you get inside, the distances are so great that I can only get to a couple of attractions before I am tired out."

Not only were there no Disney characters to be seen on this particular day, there seemed to be an almost total absence of Disney employees, except cleaners. Undeterred, the two visitors set themselves another target: to count the number of Disney paraphernalia—funny hats or other memorabilia—that they encountered. Fantasyland seemed to be a likely place but this proved to be very sparsely populated. So, with the rain getting harder, the search moved on to Frontierland.

Frontierland proved to be the first location with crowds of visitors. Without any success in adding to the number of Disney souvenirs, apart from the yellow Mickey Mouse rain garb, the visitors entered Phantom Manor. "At least it will be dry there," one declared. This haunted house proved to be much more high tech than its California counterpart, containing some dramatic, although not very scary, holograms.

Next it was on to Big Thunder Mountain for the mine train ride. There was a long queue, but patrons could wait under cover. Since there was no entertainment or other distraction to pass the time, the two

visitors struck up conversations with other people in the line. "How has Euro Disneyland met your expectations?" was the question posed to a number of students from southern Germany. "Great!" they said, enthusiastically. "This is much bigger than we had expected." The mine train ride was too fast for umbrellas, so passengers got quite wet (the benefits of the yellow Disney rain gear were becoming clear!). However, everyone gave the ride high marks. On leaving the train, one of the two friends, looking for a men's toilet, accidentally entered one for females; the relevant gender signs were posted low on the exterior wall and were blocked from view by people seeking shelter from the rain.

Lunch was the next order of the day. But in Frontierland the lines were horrendous as guests tried to keep dry. So it was back to Main Street, still relatively deserted, for a pleasant lunch at a Nestlé restaurant. "Let's try the Pirates of the Caribbean next," one of the visitors declared. Unlike *La Cabane des Robinson* or *Indiana Jones et le Temple du Péril,* Euro Disney had chosen to retain the original English as the title for this attraction. "Which way is the Pirates of the Caribbean?" a friendly-looking cleaner was asked. This question received a blank response, even when repeated very slowly. But asking in French for "*Les Pirates des Caraïbes*" brought a warm smile and immediate directions.

There was no queue for the Pirates (which was prominently advertised by a large sign in English). On the boat, instructions were in English and French, but a careful listener could hear strains of sea shanties in English, French and Dutch. It was now over four hours into the visit and still no sign of Mickey Mouse or any other Disney character. Only two funny hats had been spotted, worn by a boy and a girl of about ten years of age.

The next stop was at Star Tours, where professional entertainment helped pass the time while waiting. The two visitors got into conversation with a Belgian family living in Paris. "What do you think of Euro Disney?" they asked. "The cleanliness is extraordinary," one of them responded. "You just don't expect to see that in Europe." Added another, "Overall it's too American, especially the food. It's hard to get an alcoholic drink here. We expect to be able to drink wine and beer with a meal." Afterwards, everyone pronounced The Star Tours ride immensely enjoyable.

Around 6 PM, the rain stopped and the sun came out, creating a dramatic change in atmosphere. Almost immediately, it seemed, the crowds became thicker, smiles broke out, and people became jolly. The flowers and other plantings became more noticeable and the park was suddenly awash with color. During a ride on the *Molly Brown* riverboat, the visitors chatted with a couple from Barcelona; the latter were astounded to learn that the tall trees growing lushly around the lakeshore had only been planted a few years earlier. But they didn't like the climate. "We wanted to have Euro Disney in Barcelona," the man said, shaking his head. "It would have been better there."

With only a short wait required, it was time for a trip on the Euro Disneyland Express. Unfortunately, the recorded announcements were out of synch and the wrong stations announced. Passengers were being told in German, English and French to admire the marvels of the "Grand Canyon" as they passed through totally different scenery.

At 6:35 PM came the first sighting of a Disney character: Alice and the White Rabbit were spotted shaking hands with visitors! Ten minutes later, *Blanche-Neige et les Sept Nains* (alias Snow White and the Seven Dwarfs) could be seen dancing together on stage, but Mickey and Minnie Mouse were never sighted. On returning to Frontierland for a meal, the short lines at the take-out "Cowboy Cookout Barbecue" promised quick service. However, members of the extended family group at the head of the line were unable to work out what they could and could not get for their prepaid food coupons, so purchasing food actually proved to be a very slow process. A request for a beer was turned down—it could only be satisfied at another restaurant—but no one knew which.

Finally, it was time to leave. By 8 PM, the atmosphere was really beginning to feel festive, like that of Disneyland and Disney World. Returning to Paris on the RER, a British couple with a baby in a stroller was asked what they thought of the park. "It was all right. We've already been to the one in Florida," the husband answered. How did Euro Disney compare? "Much the same, I guess." Had they seen Mickey Mouse? "Yes, he was greeting visitors when we arrived at 10 AM. But I expect they sent him inside so that the rain wouldn't spoil his costume."

Planning for the 1995 Season

Euro Disney's financial performance continued to cause alarm during the 1994 fiscal year, which began with 60 creditor banks rejecting a proposed 11 billion franc restructuring of the outstanding debt. Rumors began to circulate that Disney would be forced to close the park. Some months later, however, agreement was reached on restructuring a substantial portion of the debt. A senior French banker familiar with the company described Euro Disney as "a good theme park married to a bankrupt real estate development—and the two can't be divorced."[17]

Philippe Bourguignon had succeeded in achieving some FFr 500 million in cost savings, including laying off 900 staff and placing some 2,000 of the park's remaining 10,000 employees on part-time contracts. Some of the hotels had shut down over the winter months. There were concerns, however, that further cost cutting would lead to a decline in service quality. On the positive side, wait times for many rides had been reduced.

The fiscal 1994 results told a mixed story.[18] After extraordinary items, the net loss fell to FFr 1.8 billion. But revenues were down by 15% to FFr 4.5 billion, including FFr 2.2 billion from the park, FFr 1.6 billion from the hotels, and FFr 0.3 billion from sources such as corporate sponsorship programs. *Exhibit 4* reproduces the financial statements of Euro Disney SCA in U.S. dollars, with the results restated in accordance with U.S.-standard generally accepted accounting principles (GAAP).

Despite some price promotions in the off-season, attendance was down substantially over the previous year:

Period	Fiscal year 1993	Fiscal year 1994
October–March	3.4 million	3.1 million
April–June	3.1	2.6
July–September	3.3	3.1

Disney executives blamed these results on public concerns that the park was going to fail. Still, Euro Disneyland remained Europe's biggest paid tourist attraction. Thanks in part to reduced off-season rates, hotel occupancy rose during the October to March period from 37% in 1993 to 48% in 1994; but between April and September it fell slightly from 72% in 1993 to 71% in the latest year.

Senior management was working to develop a turnaround marketing strategy for 1995. Competition was intensifying, with many European parks, including nearby Parc Asterix, adding dramatic new rides or other attractions. A huge new amusement park, Port Aventura, was scheduled to open near Barcelona, Spain, in March 1995.

Bourguignon told reporters that the company was still undecided on whether to raise or cut admission prices to the park for the coming year. However, he conceded that many French visitors still regarded the park as expensive. Executives anticipated that improvements in European economies would stimulate spending on tourism and entertainment. They looked forward to the much-delayed opening of the Channel Tunnel, linking the French and British rail systems under the English Channel. This link would enhance access to the park via a new Euro Disney station on the TGV high-speed rail line, which also connected to many other cities in France and neighboring countries.

Exhibit 4 *Financial Statements of Euro Disney SCA*

In US$ millions in accordance with generally accepted accounting practices (GAAP) in the U.S.

Balance Sheet	1994	1993	1992	
Cash & Investments	289	211	479	
Receivables	227	269	459	
Fixed Assets	3,791	3,704	4,346	
Other Assets	137	214	873	
Total Assets	4,444	4,397	6,157	
Accounts Payable and Other Liabilities	560	647	797	
Borrowing	3,051	3,683	3,960	
Common Stock		1,042	1,042	
Retained Earnings (Deficit)	833*	(975)	358	
Total Liabilities + Stockholders' Equity	4,444	4,397	6,157	

Statement of Operations	1994	1993	1992	1991
Revenues	751	873	738	—
Costs and Expenses	(1,198)	(1,114)	(808)	—
Operating Loss	(447)	(241)	(70)	—
Net Interest Income (Expense)	(280)	(287)	(95)	76
Income (Loss) Before Income Taxes and Cumulative Effect of Accounting Change	(727)	(528)	(165)	76
Income Taxes	—	—	30	28
Income (Loss) Before Cumulative Effect of Accounting Change	(727)	(528)	(135)	48
Cumulative Effect of Change in Accounting—for preopening costs		(578)	—	—
Net Income (Loss)	(727)	(1,106)	(135)	48
Proforma Amount Assuming the Change in Accounting Method Is Applied Retroactively		(528)	(418)	(87)

Note: Under French GAAP, Euro Disney incurred a 1993 net loss of FFr 5.3 billion (FFr 2.1 billion before the cumulative effect of accounting change), a net loss of FFr1.8 million in 1992 and net income of FFr 249 million in 1991. During 1993, Euro Disney changed its method of accounting for project-related preopening costs. Under the new method, such costs are expensed as incurred, the cumulative effect of the change in method on prior years was a charge against income of FFr 3.2 billion. The effect of the change on the year ended September 30, 1993, was to decrease the loss before the cumulative effect of accounting change by FFr 338 million.
Source: The Walt Disney Company 1993 & 1994 Annual Reports.

New advertising was under development, and a new ride, Space Mountain, was due to open in June. Based on a book by the 19th-Century French science fiction writer, Jules Verne, this indoor roller coaster would give visitors the impression of being fired to the moon from a giant cannon. Even so, Euro Disney would still have about ten fewer attractions than Disney World. And contentious issues remained. Attendance by French visitors remained disappointing, leading some experts to recommend closing the park during the off-season—November through March. There was also a proposal to relaunch the park, changing the name from "Euro Disneyland" to "Disneyland Paris."

Appendix: Details of Three Other Major French Amusement Parks

Parc Asterix

Parc Asterix, located just north of Paris and opened in 1989, was based on a famous French comic book character. Asterix and his fellow characters had their mythical home in a small village in Brittany during

Roman times. Many of their stories concerned their triumphs over the Romans. The history of France played an integral role in the park, and its cuisine was essentially French. Robert Fitzpatrick, formerly CEO of Euro Disney, had declared "Asterix has a better image than any other French park in the minds of kids." Initially costing FFr900 million, the park attracted 1.35 million visitors in its first year, well below its forecast. The first-year deficit of FFr60 million was also very disappointing.

Unlike Euro Disney, Parc Asterix was open only from April to October; however maintaining the park during the winter months still required considerable operational expense. Visitors were attracted to Asterix by its lower prices and the possibility of taking their own food into the park rather than buying it inside. The park was easily accessible by car or bus, being located just off a major autoroute.

Attendance had dropped by 30% following the opening of Euro Disney, but numbers had recovered to 1.3 million in 1993, reflecting a new competitive strategy. Prices were cut, the park design improved, waiting lines reduced, and more signs posted within the park. An 800-seat self-service restaurant and a large new playground were opened, and a children's parade became a daily summer feature. Additionally, a shuttle bus service was introduced to link the park to the nearest RER express metro station.

Many of the attractions at Parc Asterix emphasized French culture and history. Thrills included some traditional fairground rides, such as a giant carousel, as well as "National 7" (the designation of France's most famous highway) which consisted of a tour in antique automobiles through scenes reminiscent of the French countryside and the streets of Paris. There were also several exciting flume rides and the park was constructing Europe's largest roller coaster, featuring five loops and a double corkscrew, due to open in 1995. With a sharp increase in the promotional budget, the park's CEO organized a "Tour of Gaul" (the name given to France in Roman times), involving promotional activities in many several French cities.

Big Bang Schtroumpfs

Opened in Moselle, by the French-German border, in 1988 at a cost of FFr720 million, this park drew only 800,000 visitors in its first year, compared to projections based on US data of 1.8 million. Although the park had a 90% satisfaction rating, only 25% of its visitors were returnees. In 1991, the park was sold to Walibi (Belgium) for FFr50 million.

Walibi management already operated eight amusement parks in Europe and achieved a combined total of some 4.3 million visitors each year in its parks. At FFr 90, the Walibi Schtroumpfs ticket price was only 40% that of Euro Disneyland. Walibi-Schtroumpfs was the third Walibi park in France and the firm had plans to open a fourth park in 1994. By Euro Disney standards, the Walibi operation was a modest one with profits of FFr30 million in 1990. Its new parks reinvested 100% of their revenues and even its established parks reinvested 30%. Every three years, a major new attraction was introduced at each park, for example, in 1993 a "Colorado train" opened at Walibi's park in Brussels, the Belgian capital. Promotion costs were set at about 10% of revenues. Labor costs were minimized: the Walibi takeover of the Schtroumpf park led to labor costs falling from FFr38 million to FFr13 million.

Futuroscope

Futuroscope, the only large new amusement park seen as a financial success, was situated on the outskirts of Poitiers, 380 km (240 miles) southwest of Paris. Focusing on cinema and technology, Futuroscope also served as a laboratory for new experimental techniques. Among the attractions were several theaters with huge screens. In one, the screen extended through a continuous 360-degree circle, while another simulated a "flying carpet" experience through screens at both eye-level and below one's feet; in a third theater, visitors sat in mechanical chairs that moved in synchonization with the film being showed, and in a fourth they watched 3-dimensional films. There was also an interactive media theater and other activities related to media imaging. The orientation was fact, not fiction. With its unusual modern architecture, Futuroscope formed an activity pole for small hi-tech companies, a high school, a college, and a research institute for physics and mathematics. The overall concept promoted education through leisure and attendance was expected to reach 3 million visitors in 1994.

Observers believed that Futuroscope's success lay in its high-technology appeal to parents and children alike. The park had been relatively cheap to build. Its hotels were inexpensive and operated by experienced companies. Marketing efforts for the park had emphasized carefully targeted mailings to schools and colleges, social-events committees, and retirement clubs, thereby avoiding the expenses of a mass media blitz.

References

1. "Only the French Elite Scorn Mickey's Debut," *New York Times,* April 13, 1992.
2. "The Not So Magic Kingdom," *The Economist,* September 26, 1992, p. 87.

3. "Mouse Trap: Fans Like Euro Disney, But Its Parent's Goofs Weight the Park Down," *Wall Street Journal,* March 10, 1994, p. 1.

4. This section is based on material in Christopher Lovelock, *Product Plus* (New York: McGraw-Hill, 1994), pp. 308–309.

5. "Euro Disney Draws Over 1.5 Million in First 7 Weeks," *Wall Street Journal,* June 10, 1992.

6. "Disney's Bungle Book," *International Management,* Jul./Aug. 1993, p. 26.

7. "Mickey Mouse's Source of Manners," *The Washington Post,* Aug. 11, 1992, p. B1.

8. "Euro Disney Giving Investors a Rough Ride," *Boston Globe,* Nov. 27, 1993, p. 94.

9. "Euro Disney Plans," *Wall Street Journal,* Oct. 19, 1993, p. A1.

10. "Disney Goes European," *Marketing,* April 15, 1993, p. 3.

11. "Euro Disney Adding Alcohol," *New York Times,* June 12, 1993, p. A42.

12. "Euro Disney's Off-Season Success Depends on Attracting French," *Washington Post,* Oct. 13, 1993.

13. "The Mouse Isn't Roaring," *Business Week,* Aug. 24, 1993, p. 28.

14. "Euro Disney SCA Company Report," Dean Witter Reynolds, December 31, 1992.

15. "Playing Disney in the Parisian Fields," *New York Times,* February 17, 1991.

16. Ridding, *op. cit.*

17. "Mouse Trap: Fans Like Euro Disney," *op. cit.*

18. "Fears of Closure Haunt Paris Amusement Park," *Financial Times,* November 4, 1994.

Study Questions

1. *What business is Euro Disney in? And what is the market?*

2. *Evaluate Disney's performance at Euro Disneyland: What has the company done well? Where has it performed poorly (and what do you see as the reasons)?*

3. *Evaluate the experience of the two visitors to the park. Create a flowchart of their visit, indicating points at which Euro Disney needs to do better. To what extent do you think that the experience of these two visitors is probably "typical" of many other visitors?*

4. *What are the key factors that Euro Disney must control to improve visitor satisfaction and where should management place its immediate priorities?*

5. *What should be Euro Disney's goals for the 1994–95 season relative to the preceding year? Recommend a strategy for achieving these goals. Be sure to address the pros and cons of:*

   ● *changes in pricing strategy*
   ● *new advertising and promotional strategies (including target audience(s) and message(s))*
   ● *product enhancements*
   ● *a change in name from "Euro Disneyland" to "Disneyland Paris" (or another alternative)*

BT: Telephone Account Management

Christopher Lovelock
Martin Bless

To better serve its small business customers, BT has developed an inexpensive account management program involving telephone contact rather than field visits. The manager of sales development wonders what mix of field and telephone-based channels would be appropriate for managing relationships with larger customers.

"So what would you do in my place, Michael?" asked the regional sales manager.

Michael Tarte-Booth, sales development manager at BT (formerly British Telecom) listened over a pub lunch as his colleague, John Lambert, described the situation. It concerned a small business customer whose telecommunication needs were handled by BT's telephone account management (TAM) program. Tarte-Booth was very familiar with TAM, having been involved with the programme from its early days.

The customer in question had grown in size, and with the addition of a sixth line, now qualified for personal contact with an account executive. But, when informed of what BT viewed as an upgrade in account handling service, the customer demurred, asking to remain with TAM. Said Lambert:

> They wrote us a letter—I've got it here in my briefcase. It was polite but very firm. They don't want to shift from TAM. But now the field sales people are raising hell, claiming these folks as their own. This situation challenges the whole basis of our account management structure for different sizes of business customer.

British Telecommunications

The United Kingdom (UK) was the first European country to depart from the traditional PTT (post, telegraph, telephone) model under which postal and telecommunication services were administered by the same government agency. After being transformed from a government department into a public corporation in 1969, the postal and telecommunications businesses were split apart in 1981. Post Office Telephones became British Telecom. Under the Conservative government of prime minister Margaret Thatcher, numerous public corporations such as British Airways and British Gas were privatized. Soon the government announced its intention to privatize BT and sell up to 51% of the corporation to the public. In November 1984, more than two million people, including 222,000 BT employees, applied for the one billion shares available. A total of £3.9 billion was raised.[1]

As the sole licensing authority for telecommunication operators, the government took the view that competition and choice between operators would be beneficial to customers. In 1984 it awarded a license to provide domestic services to Mercury Communications, owned by Cable & Wireless (a recently privatized operator of international telecommunication services).

The government provided breathing space to BT and Mercury by making clear its intention not to

[1]The value of the pound sterling (£) varied widely against other currencies during the 1980s. Typical exchange rates in 1991 were: £1.00 = US$ 1.70 = C$ 2.25. A second sale of government shares in BT took place in 1991.

license any further fixed network operators for seven years. Separate licenses were awarded to four operators of mobile telecommunication services, including BT and Mercury. To ensure that BT did not abuse its initial virtual monopoly position of fixed network services, an Office of Telecommunications (Oftel) was established to protect the interest of customers. Oftel was widely empowered to oversee and regulate the business conduct and pricing policies of both BT and Mercury. Among other things, it prohibited access by BT marketing personnel to information on customer billing records.

Privatization and the introduction of domestic competition forced a refocussing of BT's activities. Between 1984 and 1991, the company went through two major reorganizations. The second, termed Project Sovereign, was one of the most ambitious attempts to date by a British company to reform its organization, management and culture. These reforms were meant to prepare BT for three challenges. First, the industry's traditional structure—national monopoly operators supplied by national manufacturers—was breaking down throughout the world. Regulatory barriers to international competition were expected to crumble, gradually in some countries, faster in the UK. Second, as companies internationalized, they might prefer to deal with a single telecommunications company worldwide. Providers of telecommunications services would have to tailor their products less to neatly defined geographic markets and more to groups of customers, who could be located globally. And third, more intense international competition and the growing costs of the technology race would lead to concentration of the industry. One manager commented:

> Many people welcomed the changes because of the greater freedom they offered us to respond to evolving market needs and to take advantage of new technologies. But, an equally large group continued to think and act like civil servants, as though we were still a government department. A third group were fence sitters who took a "wait and see" attitude, but were willing to be converted.

During the 1980s, telecommunications had made tremendous technological strides. For many corporate users, data communications became as important as voice communications. The use of fax machines and electronic mail exploded. BT invested heavily in modernization, unconstrained by the public sector borrowing requirements that the government had imposed before privatization. Coaxial copper cables were replaced by fiber optic cables which offered much greater capacity and better signal quality. New electronic exchanges with digital switches not only operated faster and more accurately but also enabled BT to offer a host of extra services such as automatic call forwarding.

In April 1991, the company changed its trading name from British Telecom to BT and adopted a new motto "Putting customers first." The new organization was structured around three customer-centered divisions: Business Communications, Personal Communications, and Special Businesses (including mobile and operator services). Each would deal directly with customers for sales and services, while being supported by other divisions that either managed BT's products and services, operated a worldwide networking capability, or provided development and procurement services. The 31 districts were abolished and only five regions remained of the original geographical structure.

Current Situation

With 1990–91 revenues of £13.15 billion, BT was Britain's second largest company (after British Petroleum plc). Reflecting the growth in both domestic and international markets, plus significant cost cutting efforts, BT's pre-tax operating profit in fiscal 1991 rose to £3.08 billion.

BT operated a technologically advanced network, boasting the highest proportion of optical fiber in its system of any major telecommunications operator. The long distance digital network was complete, while more than three quarters of all customers in the UK were connected to modern electronic exchanges (a few percentage points behind France, which had the highest share of digitalized exchanges of any major country). Further modernization continued at a rapid pace. Britain and Spain remained the only European nations to have privatized their telecommunication services, but a number of others were expected to follow in 1992–93. BT had also invested heavily in international ventures.

Domestically, BT retained a 94% market share. However, Mercury had adopted a strategy of penetrating the business market, starting with the largest customers—which might have thousands of lines. It was not uncommon for big customers to split their telecommunications business between BT and Mercury. At the consumer level, Mercury's presence was minimal except for pay telephones in busy locations—such as city centers and airports. (*Exhibit 1* shows the breakdown of the market by type of subscriber and number of lines.)

Since Mercury had built its network from nothing, it could offer customers state-of-the-art technology

EXHIBIT 1 *BT's Exchange Connections and Calls*			

BT's Exchange Connections in Service in the United Kingdom by Type of Subscriber 1980–1990

Year (at 31 March)	Total Exchange Connection (000s)	Residential Subscribers (000s)	Business Subscribers (000s)
1980	17,353	13,937	3,416
1981	18,174	14,671	3,503
1982	18,727	15,159	3,568
1983	19,186	15,546	3,640
1984	19,812	16,044	3,768
1985	20,528	16,596	3,932
1986	21,261	17,120	4,141
1987	21,908	17,549	4,359
1988	22,857	18,145	4,712
1989	23,946	18,737	5,209
1990	25,013	19,281	5,732

Source: British Telecom

and had pioneered a number of service innovations, which BT was seeking to match. But, Mercury's network was still geographically limited, being focussed on connecting London to Britain's business centers. Broader penetration required connecting customers to its network via BT's local lines, which often still used conventional technology. Mercury planned to spend £500 million annually during the three years 1992–1994 to extend its network and boost its share of the domestic market. It already had 15% of the UK's international traffic and a greater share of private networks. The American telecommunications giant, AT&T (described as the 800 pound gorilla of the industry), was rumored to be eager to invest in Mercury's future.

Additional network competition was expected to come from British Rail Telecom and from a joint venture between US Sprint and British Waterways (which planned to lay cable along the bottom of its canal network). Local competition was seen as coming from cable television operators, many of whom were affiliated with American regional phone companies, and from operators of mobile (cellular) services.

Creating a Pilot Telemarketing Operation

"You are the most difficult people in the world to buy from!" was how a customer described BT to Anna Thomson soon after she joined the marketing depart-

ment of the newly created Thameswey district in 1985. Her colleagues quickly came to recognize Thomson's energy, drive, and enthusiasm for seeking out innovative approaches. Although recruited as network marketing manager, her responsibilities were soon extended to marketing BT's products and services, and she became district marketing operations manager.

Thomson's prior experience had been in the electricity industry, marketing network usage. In her new position, she demonstrated the value of selling customer premises equipment (CPE) as a means of generating network revenues rather than as an end in itself. She adopted an integrated approach to marketing both networks and CPE as complementary products. Thomson remarked that "inevitably the selling of the one would lead to the selling of the other." She emphasized that network sales were far more profitable than CPE sales, but traditionally BT had found it difficult to sell the more intangible product.

While analyzing customer relationships at BT, Thomson singled out small business customers as a neglected market.

> The crux of the whole thing is that effective use of modern telecommunications products and services can make a real difference to the development of any small business today. Use of mobile communication tools, the choice of the right fax machine, installation of a switch that can grow easily and cost effectively to cover extra lines, the use of toll-free numbers and a wide range of datacoms services—all these things help a small business to be flexible as it reorganizes to meet its own customers' changing needs.

> The right telecom choices at the right time can enable a small business to offer new services (like out-of-hours customer service with call redirect), cut operating costs, and steal a march on their competitors. But, small business owners don't have time to research this all alone and so either miss opportunities altogether or make the wrong choices.

In her view, BT had not devoted enough time and energy to building the type of relationship that created loyalty. The only contact BT generally had with these customers was when they called with a problem or a bill was sent out. Typically, BT sales staff were only talking to small business customers once every three to five years, except when the customer initiated contact. Thomson warned that if nothing changed, BT was liable to lose these customers to competition.

Further analysis revealed that some 750,000 inquiries from customers of all types had not been followed up the previous year. The existing sales process, which was almost entirely focussed upon reactive responses to inbound customer calls, was obviously not working. Large accounts (served by field-based account managers) and those that screamed for attention were catered to at the cost of ignoring a huge market of smaller accounts. What was needed, argued Thomson, were telephone-based representatives to look after smaller business accounts.

Recognizing that the most sophisticated applications of telemarketing strategy were to be found in the USA, Thomson convinced headquarters to retain a leading American consultant, Rudy Oetting, to advise on conducting a pilot test in the Thameswey district. This district extended west and south of London, beyond Heathrow airport, along the M3 and M4 motorway corridors. It contained many vibrant business communities, including a significant number of small high-technology firms. The consultant recommended that BT recruit and train telephone-based sales representatives to sell proactively into exactly that market.

Telephone Account Management

A variety of terms were used to describe the use of the telephone as a marketing tool. *Telesales* was often used to describe use of the telephone by salespeople as a communication channel through which prospects could be contacted and a single sales transaction consummated. *Telemarketing* was a broader umbrella term for all types of marketing-related telephone usage. *Telephone Account Management* was defined as proactive contact through the telephone channel to customers who required a continuing personal relationship—but not necessarily face-to-face contact—with skilled sales representatives who could function as communication consultants to small businesses.

Rudy Oetting described such people as bright, aggressive account managers who had been trained to listen carefully to customer needs and ask structured, probing questions about each business and its communication activities. The goal was to build a database of information on each customer which would enable managers to farm a territory systematically without ever leaving the office. In some cases, Oetting declared, they would work jointly with field sales; sometimes they called the shots for the field force, and in other instances, they were the *only* salesforce.

Thomson recognized the potential of such an approach for BT, using its own channel—the telephone—to contact the company's small business customers. She did not accept the traditional view that British business culture would not respond positively to telephone sales contact, being confident it would work well providing the process was oriented towards uncovering and meeting customer needs. But, she saw that the approach would have to be non-threatening and employ well-trained representatives who operated on a much higher level than conventional sales support or customer service personnel.

As the concept took shape, Thomson coined the term *telemanaging* which she defined as:

> Managing the customer primarily through the medium of the telephone, using all the sales, marketing systems and management disciplines of account management.

The TAM Concept

The term TAM came to be used at BT as an acronym for both telephone account management and a telephone account manager. The latter would be a carefully selected salesperson trained to handle a wide portfolio of products and services, working up to 1,000 assigned accounts entirely by telephone. TAMs would be trained to develop specific objectives for each call. During the call, they were expected to update their knowledge of the customer's situation and needs, check whether any problems needed solving, advise on products and services, take orders, and plan a specific date for the next call. The basic goals would be to ensure that the accounts continued buying from BT rather than the competition, and to develop accounts by selling additional products and services. Said Thomson:

> The job of TAMs is to understand the business objectives and organization of their customers and to help their customers make the right investment decisions at the right time—so that we and they become increasingly successful. It's a partnership based on trust, which has to be earned through proven good advice over time. BT believes that this is the way you become a customer's preferred supplier. The basic goal is to continually build and refresh knowledge of the account base, and be the first to address or even anticipate communications needs. This is true relationship marketing but effected within a volume market because the TAM goes through this process a thousandfold. We use our own core product—the telephone—to do the job, because it allows us to manage and market efficiently to hundreds of thousands of customers. You could say we practice what we preach!

Each TAM would endeavor to develop a relationship based on trust. The customer call would remain the focal point throughout the contact cycle. Whether an order was taken or not, the TAM would establish when the next call was to take place and put it on the calendar. All the information collected would be fed into each customer's electronic file.

Thomson emphasized that the value of an account to BT was much more than just line rental charges and fees for network usage. The company also sold a wide range of telecommunications equipment (ranging from individual handsets to private branch exchanges), installation and maintenance, and an array of value-added services (refer to *Exhibit 2* for examples).

When face-to-face contact with the customer was needed, the field sales staff would work together with the TAM. The ultimate responsibility for managing an account, however, would remain with the TAM. Thomson saw teamwork as an essential part of the process. One TAM later described the relationship as follows:

It works on the basis of whoever can close the sale, should close the sale. This means that we have to work as a team; you cannot have a "them and us syndrome." If the TAM is in contact with a customer who wants somebody to pay a visit, it's clear that the sales representative cannot sign the customer up there and then, he or she will pass the case back to the TAM to monitor it. The principle is that if I achieve, we both achieve.

Michael Tarte-Booth

To assist her in implementing the TAM concept, Thomson hired Michael Tarte-Booth, a man with experience in telemarketing on both sides of the Atlantic. Thomson, later insisted that, although the vision was hers, nothing would have happened in the field without her colleague's determination to get it right, day after day. His original career had nothing to do with telecommunications. As he observed, "How I fell into telephone marketing is pure chance."

After obtaining his undergraduate degree from a British university, Tarte-Booth obtained a masters

---

EXHIBIT 2 *Sample Voice and Data Services Offered by BT, 1992*

Voice Services

City Direct provides direct connections between London and the USA offering call facilities such as abbreviated dialling and security safeguards.

SpeechLines is a service for intra-company speech connection.

LinkLine is an automatic freefone service which allows businesses to offer their customers a free inquiry and ordering facility.

CallStream is a service for information providers who sell stored voice or data information via the normal telephone line.

Network services offers call facilities such as call diversion, call barring, call waiting, last number redial, abbreviated dialing and conference call.

Voicecom International provides a 24 hour network of voice mailboxes to send, receive or forward messages from any telephone in the world.

Data Services

Datel is a data transmission service available internationally to over 100 countries.

KeyLine provides analog private circuits for data transmission using moderns.

Leaseline offers analog circuits that enable subscribers to transport voice, facsimile, data and telegraph messages nationally and internationally.

KiloStream and MegaStream provide digital, private circuits between centers at high operating speeds.

PSS is a nationwide public data network using packet switching techniques.

MultiStream enhances access to the public network at local call rates for the business community.

Data Direct is a high speed public data service to the USA and Japan.

Prestel is BT's public Videotex service.

SatStream is a satellite service for business communication with North America and Europe.

Telecom Gold is an electronic mail service with over 250,000 mailboxes in 17 countries.

Integrated Services Digital Network (ISDN) allows customers to transmit voice, data, text or image information at high speeds and assured quality without dedicated private circuits.

degree in geography from the University of Minnesota. Then he went to work in Minneapolis for the American Heart Association, a major nonprofit organization. They needed someone with demographic expertise to analyze census data and pinpoint those geographic locations (down to specific street blocks) where their best potential lay for recruiting volunteer fund-raisers. Tarte-Booth also inherited responsibility for the association's telemarketing operation. He developed the use of the telephone as a primary contact for volunteer recruitment or direct solicitation of donations. One objective was to ensure that the volunteer callers should use their precious phone hours wisely by contacting only the better prospects. The potential power of this marriage between database marketing and the phone as a delivery channel was demonstrated when revenues increased by over 60% during the first year and 90% in the second.

On returning to Britain, Tarte-Booth was hired by a manufacturer of business systems to set up its telemarketing operation. The company was running a large direct field salesforce, but had neglected its customer base for paper-based products, and had disposed of its customer records for this market. The firm's telephone contact strategy was limited to proactive cold calls by sales representatives to new prospects. Thereafter, the channel strategy was simply inbound, waiting for customers to come back by phone or mail with repeat orders. Tarte-Booth's job was to set up a team that would revitalize the business:

> The goal was to re-create the database by acquisition and integration of lists from numerous different sources so that we knew, after telephone contact, who the customers were and who the prospects were. Our initial objective was to derive sales principally through referrals out to the salesforce. But, we had to start out by qualifying our prospects and calling all the names on our list. The response was impressive.

Other groups within the sales organization recognized the value of this activity. Within two years, the company was also targeting other vertical markets in the hospitality, leisure, and car retail and after-sales industries. Said Tarte-Booth:

> The program diversified into new markets and more sophisticated applications. We had truly graduated to an account management operation with a primary focus on repeat purchase. Historically, customers had made repeat purchases roughly once every three years, now they were making them every three months! The whole thing about account management is get-

ting to know and anticipate customers' needs by amalgamating the power of the database, the information you glean from customers, and the immediacy of contact by telephone. We found that customers liked the cloak of invisibility provided by the telephone contact. It gives them greater perceived control. Ultimately, they can drop the neutron bomb and hang up.

Inauguration of the TAM Pilot

After three months' preparation, the new pilot program was inaugurated in November 1986. Almost immediately, BT found that customers demanded a continuing dialog focussed on an understanding of their needs, as opposed to a tactical contact aiming to sell them "the flavor of the month." Customers were also motivated by continuity of contact, wanting to deal with a specific person on a regular basis. They would spend up to 20 minutes disclosing information about their business and needs; but having invested that amount of time, they expected the relationship to be perpetuated.

Thomson's primary mission was to tackle the strategic and political issues related to getting TAM accepted within BT and to develop an overall "Integrated Channel Strategy" to show how all the sales, service and marketing channels (including TAM) should interrelate for BT's objectives to be met. The success of the pilot attracted growing attention. Over the course of the first year, Thameswey achieved a tenfold increase in account coverage and a threefold increase in customer purchasing levels among the pilot customers. These results were achieved at a lower ratio of cost to sales revenues than could have been obtained with face-to-face contact. It also left the field salesforce with more time to talk to larger customers, and enabled them to achieve the high level of consultancy needed in that sector. Tarte-Booth observed:

> The project succeeded strategically because of senior management sponsorship and the interest that Anna generated in the program. It was driven through centrally and had very high visibility within the organization.

National Implementation

Anna Thomson and Michael Tarte-Booth kept in sight the ultimate aim of national implementation. Achieving that goal required careful documentation of the whole process. Other districts would have to be convinced rather than coerced to adopt TAM. In 1987, Thomson left the district to become national telemarketing manager. She saw her role as selling the concept of telemarketing to senior BT managers. Monthly steering committee meetings were held to discuss the progress of the pilot and make tactical changes. Progress reports, detailing success in achieving evolutionary benchmarks, were widely circulated. As Tarte-Booth recalled, Thomson did not try to convince the corporation that TAM was the "greatest thing since sliced bread." Instead, he pointed out:

> We allowed it to prove itself and concentrated on keeping colleagues around the country advised of progress through workshops and seminars. As a result, other districts came of their own accord to inquire about possible implementation. As soon as a district showed serious interest, we followed up with more information in order to gain a commitment. With district autonomy and the fact that TAM was to be implemented on a voluntary basis, the soft sales approach was critical.

In early 1988, Tarte-Booth was appointed national implementation manager. He found that districts whose customer base was dispersed over a wide territory were quick to recognize TAM's value. During 1988, six districts established teams to focus on the small business market. A central development program was created to train the trainers, build the necessary support structure, and develop the database software for TAM. That program provided implementation expertise through a "franchise" package which demanded adherence to the proven methods established in the pilot in exchange for implementation assistance.

By early 1989, districts fell into three distinct categories. In the vanguard were six districts that had already established teams. The second group, described as "the soft underbelly of resistance," was interested but wanted to wait until TAM had proved itself elsewhere. Some sales managers were reluctant to embrace TAM, which was perceived as threatening since it involved a reappraisal of their approach to customers and a reorganization of field sales responsibilities. Strong resistance came from a third group of districts, principally in London and the South East. This hard core was located in the region that not only had the highest customer density but also faced the greatest competitive threat.

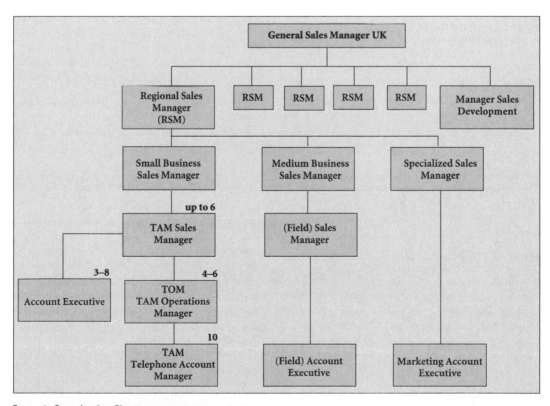

EXHIBIT 3 Organization Chart.

Following the Project Sovereign reorganization, the districts were abolished and field sales territories expanded, thus increasing field reps' travel times. (*Exhibit 3* shows the reorganized sales structure, in which first Thomson and later Tarte-Booth held the position of manager of sales development, operating at the same level as the five regional sales managers.)

Training

Tarte-Booth emphasized that "the TAM program is not about creaming the market. It's about building loyalty and defending against future competition." Given the complexity of the task demanded of a TAM, considerable effort was placed on recruiting the right people. The initial interview with candidates was conducted by telephone, followed by written tests and face-to-face interviews, and concluding with psychometric profiling of each candidate prior to final selection. Recruitment was followed by intensive training. BT built three special training schools to develop a consistent approach to customer care.

Training covered attitudes, as well as skills, ranging from how not to sound like a robot when using a call guide (recommended dialogue) to how to gather and enter relevant information about customers. Training also included hands-on experience with the equipment that TAMs would be selling. Over a twelve-month period, a future TAM would follow five training modules interlinked with live frontline experience at his or her home base. The five modules collectively lasted for 13 weeks. Said Tarte-Booth:

> The training program is designed to be holistic and so embraces the skills, the techniques, the methods, the tools, and the product knowledge integral to the future TAM's job. Their under-standing is tested by rigorous role-playing and coaching sessions. The entire account team is trained together, so all members emerge with a clear understanding of how their jobs interrelate. Before returning to their home units, each team converts theory into practice by making live customer calls from the training center.

Future Plans

By early 1992, BT operated 25 TAM call centers around the UK. Total staffing, including TAMs, TOMs (TAM operations managers) and support personnel, exceeded 450 persons. The annual cost of a TAM was around £41,000, of which 50% was salary (in comparison, field account managers cost £40,000–£60,000 a year, of which about 65% was salary). Anna Thomson had been promoted to a new position, where her task was to develop a global customer service strategy for BT as the company began to expand into a worldwide organization. In this context, TAM was just one part of the jigsaw.

With TAM catering for small business accounts having two to five lines each, Tarte-Booth now turned his attention to other categories of business. His objective was to apply comprehensive account management to the entire customer base, integrating field and phone account management to address the needs of any type of customer. He saw BT's accounts as grouped into slices across a pyramid, with national accounts at the apex and single-line customers at the base. (*Exhibit 4* documents the number of accounts in each group and representative average annual revenues per account.)

In three regions, BT was piloting TAM for medium-sized business customers with 6 to 15 lines.

ExHIBIT 4 *Profile of the Account Management Pyramid at BT*					
			Representative Account Data		
Group	No. of Accounts	No. of Lines per Account	Annual Revenue per Line (Range) £	Annual Revenue from CPE Sales or Revenue[1] £	Annual Revenue from Value Added Network (Range) £
National Accounts	300	100+	1000–3000	100,000	200,000–500,000,000
Key Regional Accounts	3,000	15+	1000–2000	3,000	25,000–200,000
Medium Business Accounts	200,000	6–15	900–1500	500	5,400–22,500
Small Business Accounts	650,000	2–5	600–900	200	1,200–4,500
Very Small Business Accounts	800,000	1	200–600	100	400

[1]CPE = customer premises equipment

Since these customers required an expanded portfolio of products and services, the new program was more complex than the small business TAM. Bigger customers tended to have a more sophisticated approach to decision making. This process had to be reflected in the call guides, the systems, and the training. Tarte-Booth described the new program as follows:

> It's an evolution of TAM and premised on the same channel structure. As such, it shares much of the methodology established for the small business programme, but has evolved to fit the needs of a new market segment.

Further up the pyramid were the key regional accounts, those with more than 15 lines. These customers would continue to be managed on a face-to-face basis through a field salesforce channel. Account managers and specialist executives were in the field to support them, backed by proactive and reactive telephone support. At the top of the pyramid were national accounts—large and lucrative customers with sophisticated communication needs, often international in nature.

Very small business customers with a single line, such as the consultant who worked from home or the small retail establishment, remained an untapped market. BT had experimentally incorporated the top 10% of this group in TAM but quickly learned that the use of TAMs was not a cost effective proposition. The cost of TAMs was viewed by some as prohibitively expensive for very small business (VSB) customers. Tarte-Booth contended that "it's inappropriate to think of TAM in purely cost substitution terms, since BT's objectives are market coverage resulting in account protection and development."

His proposed solution was to test the use of direct mail, designed to generate inbound calls to a VSB account management team. Catalogues of telephone equipment and services useful to very small businesses would be mailed to large numbers of prospects. The goal would be to stimulate the purchase of upgraded telephone products and services. As these single-line customers grew and acquired second lines, they could migrate up the account management pyramid.

Looking ahead, Tarte-Booth envisaged the desirability of creating a more flexible account management structure:

> Developing and implementing account management structures is a fundamentally different task from salesforce management, and the two may well conflict. They also require different skills. What we need is a range of account management options based on different channel configura-

tions. TAM is just one channel within the sales structure at BT. We need a totally integrated and flexible structure for customers, in which their changing needs and preferences will be consistently catered for, whether their need for products and services grows, stabilizes, or shrinks.

The Case of Green & Meakin Ltd.

Green & Meakin Ltd. was a manufacturer of aircraft parts. When the TAM program was first initiated, the firm had three lines and was assigned to Helen Dewhurst, who had exclusive responsibility for its account. As their TAM, she kept in touch with the company on a regular basis and followed through on all its requests, be it for a single socket, a new piece of telecommunications equipment or an additional line. Feedback from the two partners who owned the firm was very positive. They were pleased, they said, with the prompt and efficient way in which Dewhurst handled their business needs. Their experiences with BT prior to the introduction of TAM had been far from satisfactory: hours had been wasted chasing up requests passed from one person who didn't know or couldn't help to another who often proved to be no better.

As the company grew, so did Green & Meakin's use of telecommunication services. One December day, a sixth line was installed. Unknown to the firm, this additional line automatically set in motion the upgrading process. Dewhurst compiled a file on the company which was handed up to the new team. She then contacted Green & Meakin to inform the company that in future it would be handled by a field account executive, reflecting the growing size and importance of the Green & Meakin account. But, the partners were unhappy. One of them called Dewhurst to state that the firm liked the service she had provided and did not view reassigning their account to a new account group as a useful move. Dewhurst responded that, unfortunately, this was company policy, but added that she was sure they would receive excellent service in the future. When the senior partner still expressed dissatisfaction with the proposed move, she suggested that he call her supervisor, the TAM operations manager. Meeting a similar response from this individual and in turn from her superior, the TAM Sales Manager, the senior partner wrote to John Lambert, the regional sales manager, to complain.

The Letter

"Ah, here it is!" exclaimed Lambert, pulling a sheet of paper from his briefcase. "Read it for yourself, Michael."

EXHIBIT 5 *Letter to BT from Green & Meakin, Ltd.*

Green & Meakin, Ltd, 582 Thamesview Centre, Reading, Berkshire

Mr John Lambert   7 January 1992
Regional Sales Manager
BT Southwest Region

Dear Mr. Lambert,

I am writing to you to express my concern over a proposed change in our account coverage status with BT. For the past four years, we have received excellent service through our telephone account manager, Helen Dewhurst. Recently, she informed us that, due to our acquisition of a sixth line, we were scheduled to be "upgraded" in the New Year to a field-based account manager who would make personal visits to us at our offices.

My partner, Jim Meakin, and I phoned Helen (using the new speakerphone we recently acquired from BT) to tell her that we were very happy with the service she provided and did not wish to change to a new account manager. But she told us that the decision was company policy and not hers to change.

Subsequently, I called her superior, Ms Anderson, and got a similar response. Next, the field sales manager called to introduce himself and the account manager who would be taking over from Helen. Jim took the call and said we didn't want to change, but we got the same story about "company policy." We had a similar response when we called the small business manager and the medium business sales manager, respectively. They don't seem to get the point that we are happy being served by Helen over the telephone.

So now I'm writing to you and appealing to your common sense rather than to company rule-books. I know it's your internal policy to reassign customers when they reach a certain size (and we're flattered that you now consider us a "medium-sized company"). But the fact is, we don't need someone to keep coming out to visit us all the time, unless it's to install new equipment or undertake maintenance—which is a technician's job in any case. We feel strongly we're better off remaining with Helen.

We thank you for your consideration and look forward to your response.

Yours sincerely,
/s/ W.F.F. GREEN, Partner

Michael Tarte-Booth unfolded the letter and quickly read it through. It was firm, and to the point (refer to *Exhibit 5*). "This is dated ten days ago," he said. "What's happened in the meantime, John?"

"Well, I simply made copies and sent one each with a covering memo to the relevant TAM operations manager and the sales manager, and told them to sort it out. Neither could agree on a course of action because both claimed Green & Meakin as their own. So they passed the buck to their superiors."

"And then?" queried Tarte-Booth.

"Same problem!" responded Lambert, gloomily. "Neither of those two folks could agree, either. So yesterday it landed neatly back on my desk like a boomerang. What do you suggest I do?"

The waitress came, cleared away their plates and brought them coffee, which gave Tarte-Booth a moment's breathing space to think. "This could well happen again in the future," he said finally, sipping his coffee. "We can't spend all our time deciding when to make exceptions to the rules. I've been working on a plan to restructure the whole account management function at BT. Let me get back with a draft proposal to you in a few days, and I'll tell you then what I think we should do about Green & Meakin, too."

Tarte-Booth swallowed the rest of his coffee, put down the cup and stood up. "Be in touch with you on Tuesday, John. Thanks for lunch. You did say you were paying, didn't you?"

Study Questions

1. *What are the implications for providers and customers of the evolution of telecommunications technology?*
2. *How can the telecommunications market be segmented?*
3. *Compare and contrast mail, telephone, and personal contact as account management strategies.*
4. *Evaluate the way in which BT designed and implemented the TAM program.*
5. *What action should be taken on Green & Meakin's request?*

Museum of Fine Arts, Boston

Christopher Lovelock

Under a new director, a major museum is striving to develop a stronger marketing orientation. An ongoing challenge is how to strike a balance between the need to appeal to audiences and the importance of advancing the mission of the organization.

It was a sunny day in July, 1997 at Boston's Museum of Fine Arts (MFA). Decorative banners promoting current exhibitions rustled in the breeze. Overlooking one entrance, an outsized dragon's head peered down at the people below, its brilliant red and gold colors contrasting with the building's light gray stonework and the green of surrounding lawns and trees. Inside, visitors were entering the Gund Gallery to see the principal exhibition, *Tales from the Land of Dragons: 1000 Years of Chinese Paintings.* Others were attending several smaller exhibitions with an Asian theme or exploring the museum's extensive permanent collections.

Patricia B. Jacoby, deputy director for marketing and development, was lunching with colleagues on an outdoor terrace and reflecting on the progress made in enhancing the museum's marketing capabilities during the past three years. Sipping an iced tea, she reminded her colleagues of the challenges facing the MFA as a new fiscal year began:

> It's not enough to say that we now have a marketing orientation at the MFA. We must live this orientation through our behavior, as part of our everyday operations. We have to maintain the momentum in our dealings with all the museum's stakeholders—members, current and prospective visitors, the local community, staff, trustees and overseers, volunteers and, of course, the media.

Background

Boston's Museum of Fine Arts boasted a permanent collection ranked among the best in the United States. *Connoisseur's World* magazine described it as second in quality and scope only to the holdings of New York's Metropolitan Museum of Art. Many art experts saw the MFA as having world-class collections in such fields as French Impressionist paintings; American paintings and decorative arts; Egyptian, classical Greek, and Asian arts; and European silver. However, its modern and contemporary art holdings were generally held to be less significant.

Founded in 1870, the museum occupied an imposing granite building, one mile west of Boston's fashionable Back Bay area and two miles from downtown. Buses and rapid transit passed by the main entrance on busy Huntington Avenue. Parking was available for a fee but had occasionally proved insufficient to meet peak demand during major exhibitions. Adjacent was the School of the Museum of Fine Arts, which enrolled over 1500 students and offered diploma and degree programs in a variety of fields and art media, including photography. Graduate degrees were offered in association with Tufts University. In addition to its galleries, the MFA's public facilities included two restaurants, a cafeteria, two retail stores, auditoriums for lectures and other events, and two recently renovated outdoor garden courts. Behind the scenes were storage areas, workshops for art renovation and construction of displays, a library, and offices.

Unlike many major American museums, the MFA received no ongoing support from city, state, or federal funds. Government grants were limited to special projects. The basic admission fee was $10; students and senior citizens paid $8, while accompanied chil-

The collaboration of Prof. Stephen A. Greyser, Harvard Business School, is gratefully acknowledged.

Used with permission of the Getty Leadership Institute for Museum Management.

dren aged 17 or under entered free. Wednesday evenings were free to all, but donations were welcomed. An admission surcharge was sometimes imposed for major exhibitions, but museum members—who paid an annual fee—could enter without charge at any time.

Organization and Finances

Like many large nonprofit organizations, the MFA had a complex organizational structure. Its director, Malcolm Rogers, was accountable to the board of trustees, analogous to a corporation's board of directors. The trustees approved the annual budget, controlled the museum's property, and supervised the conduct of its affairs. There was also a board of overseers, which elected both trustees and overseers, and approved any changes to the by-laws proposed by the trustees. Both trustees and overseers served on a variety of museum committees. The museum employed 700 staff members who worked in three broad areas—curatorial affairs, development and marketing, and operations—each of which was headed by a deputy director who reported to Malcolm Rogers.

The MFA's curators, whom some likened to university faculty, worked within departments organized around specific art fields and had both programmatic and project responsibilities. Several of the department heads held prestigious endowed curatorships, although none had tenure. Their programmatic tasks involved knowing, managing, and shaping the museum's collections—a role that involved working closely with scholars, collectors and colleagues and also participating in outside professional activities. Project responsibilities included developing exhibitions, selecting the works of art to display, and deciding how to present them. Curators also presented and interpreted the museum's permanent collection, wrote publications, and conducted lectures and gallery talks.

Reporting to the deputy director for curatorial affairs was the department of education, which presented over 1000 educational programs each year, collectively attracting more than a quarter of all the museum's visitors. Activities included lectures, gallery talks, workshops and demonstrations, family programs, films, music, brochures, audio guides and studio art classes. Education staff were charged with enabling the MFA to achieve what its statement of purpose described as its "ultimate aim to encourage inquiry and to heighten public understanding and appreciation of the visual world" *(Exhibit 1)*.

Some 425 volunteers worked at the MFA. Their activities, coordinated by a full-time staff member,

---

EXHIBIT 1 *Museum of Fine Arts: Statement of Purpose (Adopted by the Board of Trustees, February 28, 1991)*

The Museum of Fine Arts houses and preserves preeminent collections and aspires to serve a wide variety of people through direct encounters with works of art.

The Museum aims for the highest standards of quality in all its endeavors. It serves as a resource for both those who are already familiar with art and those for whom art is a new experience. Through exhibitions, programs, research, and publications, the Museum documents and interprets its own collections. It provides information and perspective on art through time and throughout the world.

The Museum holds its collections in trust for future generations. It assumes conservation as a primary responsibility which requires constant attention to providing a proper environment for works of art and artifacts. Committed to its vast holdings, the Museum nonetheless recognizes the need to identify and explore new and neglected areas of art. It seeks to acquire art of the past and present which is visually significant and educationally meaningful.

The Museum has obligations to the people of Boston and New England, across the nation and abroad. It celebrates diverse cultures and welcomes new and broader constituencies. The Museum is a place in which to see and learn. It stimulates in its visitors a sense of pleasure, pride, and discovery which provides aesthetic challenge and leads to a greater cultural awareness and discernment.

The Museum creates educational opportunities for visitors and accommodates a wide range of experiences and learning styles. The Museum educates artists of the future through its School. The creative efforts of the students and faculty provide the Museum and its public with insights into emerging art and art forms.

The Museum's ultimate aim is to encourage inquiry and to heighten public understanding and appreciation of the visual world.

were organized primarily around the curatorial departments and educational programs. There was also a Ladies Committee whose 70 members were appointed to four-year terms and worked at least two days a week on organizing events, arranging flowers, conducting tours, and staffing the members' desk and information center.

For the fiscal year ending June 30, 1997, the MFA's operating revenues were $85.2 million (including $12.8 million from the Museum School). After deducting operating expenses, the MFA had ended the year with a surplus of $0.7 million which would be applied to rebuilding reserves. *Exhibit 2* provides a 20-year summary of MFA operating surpluses and deficits; while *Exhibit 3* shows a 20-year attendance record.

Recent History

During the past quarter century, the MFA had experienced mixed fortunes. In the late sixties and early seventies it was viewed by some observers as elitist and poorly managed. Higher energy costs and other inflationary pressures contributed to substantial deficits. People accused the MFA of hoarding its remarkable collections, much of them in storage, rather than inviting visitors to come inside and enjoy them. Meantime, the area south of the museum fell into decline, with Huntington Avenue becoming a border between the city's privileged and disadvantaged communities.

During the second half of the seventies, the MFA began to change. In 1976, Jan Fontein, curator of the Asiatic Department, was named director of the museum; he appointed an experienced administrator as deputy director to manage the institution's business affairs. The most visible change at the MFA was construction of the new West Wing, which included the Gund Gallery, designed to house large exhibitions. Many existing galleries were renovated and the Museum School was expanded. At its close in 1987, Fontein's 11-year tenure was described as "a huge success" by *The Boston Globe*, which noted:

> The sleepy, dusty mausoleum of the 1960s today is like a thriving city center, bursting with special exhibitions, lectures, and concerts. The shop and restaurants are packed and the line of cars waiting to get in stretches around the block.

The MFA's financial situation improved sharply under Fontein. Reflecting improved marketing and development efforts (aided by a booming economy), donations rose significantly, membership almost tripled over 10 years to reach 41,049 in 1985–86, and retail and catalog sales leaped from $0.9 million to $11.4 million over the same period. Several "blockbuster" exhibitions fueled the growth in admissions, including *Pompeii: AD*

79 (1978), *The Search for Alexander* (1981–82), and *Renoir* (1985–86). Admission fees rose from $1.75 in 1976 to $4.00 in 1983.

Fontein was succeeded by Alan Shestack, a distinguished art scholar, who served six years before leaving to become deputy director of the National Gallery of Art in Washington. One important achievement was an agreement to establish a sister museum in Japan, the Nagoya/Museum of Fine Arts (due to open in 1999), which would borrow art works from the Boston collection. Another highlight was the exhibition *Monet in the 90s,* which attracted 537,502 visitors, thus becoming the MFA's best attended exhibition. Shestack's directorship also saw the acquisition of three great private collections.

But an extended recession hurt fund raising, leaving the museum heavily indebted from its earlier expansion. Although the *Monet* show contributed to an operating surplus of $2.4 million in 1989–90, the MFA's financial situation deteriorated sharply thereafter. A new deputy director focused on cost cutting—including staff layoffs, shorter visitor hours, and lower spending on development and public information. An important symbol of the museum's straitened circumstances was the 1991 decision to close the original grand entrance on Huntington Avenue. Although this action yielded annual savings of some $100,000, critics charged that the MFA was literally closing its face to the local community and leaving just a single entrance on a side street. Despite such measures, the annual operating deficit rose to over $5 million in 1993–94 *(Exhibit 2).*

Looking back on this period, one administrator noted that the museum's financial difficulties were compounded by poor budgeting. The MFA had failed to develop a base budget that reflected the base number of visitors the museum could attract, so that incremental budgets might then be prepared for specific projects and exhibitions.

A New Director Arrives

In June 1994, the board appointed Malcolm Rogers, 45, an Oxford-educated British art historian who was then deputy director of the National Portrait Gallery in London. Among his many qualities was proven skill as a fund raiser. State support for the arts in the United Kingdom had declined sharply, requiring British museums to cut costs and raise funds from corporate and private donors; Rogers had done this with great success. The National Portrait Gallery was also known for its successful merchandising activities, which had brought in substantial revenues and taken the gallery's name around the world.

Arriving in Boston, Rogers found a dispirited institution. Reflecting financial difficulties and recent

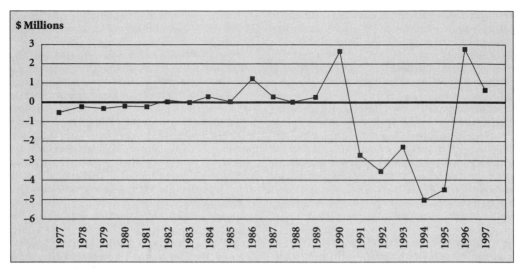

$ Millions

EXHIBIT 2 Museum of Fine Arts: Annual Operating Surpluses (or Deficits), Fiscal Years Ending June 30, 1977–97

staff cutbacks, morale was low. Corporate memberships had slumped and attendance had declined since the heady year of the *Monet* show. The new director lost no time in making his presence felt. One of his first acts was to throw a breakfast for the entire staff. Addressing the crowd, he introduced what would become a central theme:

> We are one museum, not a collection of departments. The museum consists of security guards, curators, technicians, benefactors, volunteers, public relations personnel. We all have our individual professional expertise. And by working cooperatively with colleagues, we all have areas that can be improved.

Rogers' "one museum" theme, repeated at frequent intervals, sent the message that the director's agenda took precedence over that of the traditionally independent curators in terms of setting priorities for acquisitions and exhibitions. Some of the curators disapproved and the curator of contemporary art subsequently resigned.

While quickly recognized for his good humor and friendly, outgoing manner, Rogers also showed that he could be blunt and decisive. To address the deficit, he took a tough line with expenditures and began a program to cut staff size by 20%. Donors evidently liked his style and his message that the museum had to be more welcoming to the community. Two leading supporters of the MFA, Ann and Graham Gund, endowed the director's position with a gift of $3 million.

Developing a Stronger Marketing Orientation

The new director's cutbacks did not extend to services for museum visitors. Said Rogers:

> I'm firmly committed to the idea that museums are here to serve the community, and that's going to be one of the keynotes of my work here in Boston—to encourage the MFA to turn out toward its public and to satisfy as broad a constituency as possible.

Early in his tenure, Rogers reopened the Huntington Avenue entrance, making a major publicity event out of the occasion. To encourage attendance, he reversed the trend of curtailing admission hours. Daily schedules were gradually extended and seven-day operations instituted. On three evenings a week, the museum remained open until almost 10 pm, with the staff working to make Friday nights at the museum a popular venue for a younger crowd. To mark the MFA's 125th anniversary, Rogers initiated "Community Days," opening the museum free of charge on three Sundays each year. The MFA's education department offered free programs throughout the day on these occasions.

In each subsequent year, Rogers undertook high-profile activities to improve the museum's facilities and image. He raised funds to restore a derelict interior courtyard, which was reopened in 1996 as the Fraser Garden Court, featuring sculptures, fountains, flowers, and shrubbery. In 1996–97, new exterior lighting was installed to dramatize the MFA's impos-

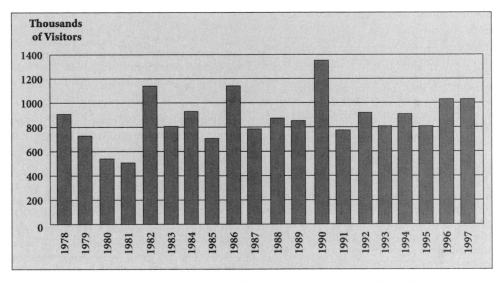

EXHIBIT 3 Museum of Fine Arts: Annual Attendance Fiscal Years Ending June 30, 1978–1997

ing facade and make it more visible after dark to people passing by on busy Huntington Avenue. A second garden courtyard was due to open soon and would be overlooked by a newly expanded restaurant with a rooftop terrace.

Rogers was eager to make the MFA an evening destination of choice, especially for people living in or close to the city. The broader variety of exhibitions (to encourage multiple visits), upgraded restaurants, better lighting, and improvements to the museum's overall atmosphere were all designed to help achieve this goal. The new director enjoyed a much higher public profile than his recent predecessors. As a senior colleague noted:

Malcolm has become something of a personality and that has helped his image of being accessible. He can be funny and irreverent. He likes to do television. He makes himself very available to the media. On the other hand, when it comes to controversy over an exhibition, he can truly hold his own as a scholar. He also recognizes the symbolic power of his office and has chosen to lead the committee on diversity, rather than spinning it off to somebody else. He knows that's important.

Pat Jacoby added: "Malcolm Rogers personifies marketing: He's accessible, he's an advocate of PR, he cares about the visitors, and he believes that the MFA can set the standard for other museums." As director, Rogers sought to pick a mix of exhibitions that combined high scholarly content with popular appeal. He believed that museums of the MFA's size and stature needed to mount accessible and popular shows on a regular basis. His view, shared by the senior staff, was that one show in five should be of a "blockbuster" nature, which meant hosting such an exhibition at least once every two years. But Rogers also recognized the need to display art from the MFA's permanent collection to best advantage, including small revolving shows in a designated gallery.

George Shackelford, recently appointed as Mrs. Russell W. Baker Curator of European Paintings, set out to re-hang all 15 European galleries in innovative ways that were designed to stimulate the audience and engage them more actively. The project included new, user-friendly descriptions of the paintings—the captions were printed in a larger font and used everyday language rather than heavy academic prose. Shackelford, who brought many paintings out of storage and restored them, described the new installation as "a reinterpretation of art for the public." Commenting on the relationship between the permanent collection and blockbuster shows, he observed, "The big shows do bring people to the permanent collection. But the big show is a monster that museums have created. Linking a museum's health to its spectacular exhibitions is a problem."

At the MFA, as at other major museums, curators were sometimes uncomfortable with marketing. As Brent Benjamin, deputy director for curatorial affairs, explained, promotional activities often overemphasized the most popular and familiar objects at the expense of the most artistically significant, thus giving an unbalanced impression of the collection or exhibition:

> In a very real sense, the need to stimulate attendance undercuts the educational message (of course, getting people in the door provides the opportunity to deliver that message). Many curators have a hard time understanding why, at some elemental level, the general public don't perceive the magic in the works of art that they do. The reality that the general visitor brings far less to the interaction with a work of art than a highly trained curator often results in the perception that marketing "dumbs down" the object, the project, and the institution.
>
> At worst, willfulness on each side undercuts the other, and nasty comments all around are the result. By contrast, in the best possible case, communication and involvement from both sides about goals and means of achieving them, and the explicit acknowledgment of criteria used to come to a solution, ought to create understanding and a positive working relationship.

The Marketing Organization

Pat Jacoby, who had joined the museum in 1991 to work in development, held the recently created position of deputy director for marketing and development. Previously, she had been assistant dean for development at the Harvard School of Public Health and had also worked in public television. Jacoby created a staff marketing team to coordinate all MFA communications and to integrate marketing activities throughout the museum. Its members were herself, associate director of marketing Paul Bessire, director of public relations Dawn Griffin, and senior marketing consultant Bill Wondriska, who noted:

> Marketing is more than a narrow set of ideas, expressions, and applications, In its broadest sense, it's everything that carries the signature of the institution, how it presents itself both externally to its guests and internally to its staff. We have to ensure that the external strategy is supported by those who work here. We have a multitude of experiences to communicate, but we're trying to speak with a single voice.

One of Griffin's goals was to create the sense that "there's always something going on here. With the variety of programming that we offer, we can appeal to adults and children: 'There's something for *you!*' " Underlying all this was the element of quality, so that people might expect something worth coming to see. She added:

We try to communicate the feeling of excitement here. With Malcolm, there's also the element of surprise. People locally and nationally are feeling that the museum is changing and that helps to build the excitement. For a lot of our exhibitions, people are feeling that if they didn't come, they missed out.

Griffin saw part of her department's challenge as promoting some of the unique and most exciting elements of an exhibition. This task not only involved working with curators to capture their academic perspectives and insights, but also finding relevant news which might attract the interest of prospective attendees. In her press kits, Griffin included sheets containing "fun facts" about artists and their work. If a popular celebrity visited an MFA exhibition, her staff would get on the phone to ensure that this visit received media coverage. "So far," she said, "the media have responded very positively." Bessire remarked on the past lack of internal confidence in the institution, which extended to its activities and exhibitions. "With all the financial problems," he remarked, "there wasn't a lot of freedom of action for creativity. Under Malcolm, that's changing."

Jacoby and her colleagues were concerned to ensure that the MFA should make itself a welcoming and accessible place. Referring to the need to improve "wayfinding," which involved efforts to help visitors find their way into and around the museum and to locate the art objects in which they were interested, she commented:

> This year, we've established a department of visitor services. We hired the former chief concierge at the Four Seasons Hotel in Beverly Hills to create a commitment to customer service among the guards, the information booth attendants, the ticket sellers, and everyone who works with the customers. He's concerned with everything down to the uniforms, which are going to be changed. We've also hired a new chef and a new general manager for the restaurants.

To promote a consistent institutional identity, the marketing group had commissioned a new logo or "signature" for the MFA to replace the more than 30 different design elements previously used on communications ranging from letterheads to external signage. Featuring the lower case letters "**mfa**" in white, superimposed on a red square, it could be adapted for many different uses, in both small and large scales. In another new departure, the MFA developed a website (*www.mfa.org*) that provided information about the museum and its exhibitions.

In 1995, the MFA commissioned a visitor study involving 100 interviews per month over 12 months. Randomly selected adult visitors were targeted as they exited the museum. Neither school groups nor tour groups (accounting for one eighth of all museum visitors) were included in these surveys. The goals were to obtain baseline information on demographics, reasons for first and repeat visits, what visitors saw and did at the MFA, and how they experienced the museum. The staff planned to compare these findings with those of a 1987 survey and to use the resulting insights in developing a strategy for increasing attendance. Highlights from the findings are summarized in *Exhibit 4*.

The Work of the Marketing Committee

In fall 1996, a trustee marketing committee was formed. Alan Strassman, then president of the board of trustees, stated as a major objective "the inculcation of, and support for, marketing throughout the organization." Other objectives included (1) familiar-ity with museum priorities relating to accessibility, new audiences and the visitor experience; (2) developing a thorough understanding of marketing goals, objectives, strategies, and evaluations; (3) offering advice concerning the marketing program; (4) reviewing the marketing plan and budget and conveying recommendations to the budget and finance committee; and (5) informed advocacy for the marketing program and the MFA itself.

Members included the MFA's chairman, president and three other members of the board of trustees, two members of the board of overseers, senior marketing staff, and representatives from the operations, curatorial, and other areas. To provide outside professional guidance and stimulate fresh thinking, Strassman and Jacoby invited Stephen A. Greyser, a marketing professor at the Harvard Business School who had worked extensively with arts organizations, to serve as chair. Greyser believed that museums should be "mission driven, but market sensitive—blending a strong and clear sense of mission with professional market-

---

EXHIBIT 4 *Museum of Fine Arts: Highlights of Findings from 1996 Visitor Study (Compared against 1987 Study)*

Demographics

- Visitors to the Museum are still predominantly female, White, affluent and older; Asian visitors are still the single largest among minority visitors.
- Sixty percent of visitors continue to be drawn from within Massachusetts; New England states, New York, California, and international remain the largest tourist draws.

Members

- Members are more affluent than the average visitor.
- In terms of benefits, members overwhelmingly continue to value unlimited free admission, discount at the Museum Shop, and subscription to *Preview* magazine.

Time and Money Spent

- Although the median number of visits "in the past 12 months" has gone down from 3.8 to 2 visits, visitors today spend the same amount of time (2.5 hours on average) at the Museum as they did in 1987.
- A high percent of visitors still spend money on things other than admission. Spending levels remain highest at the cafe/restaurant and at the Museum Shop.

MFA Collection

- No one part of the Museum dominates as visitors continue to express an interest in a wide range of the Museum's collection. Their reasons for visiting are as varied as the Museum's collection.

Improvements

- Most visitors, then as now, feel positive about the MFA. However, many are still dissatisfied with signage and the difficulties in finding their way around. Visitors continue to want more benches/seating areas in the exhibit halls and around the Museum.
- Unprompted complaints about parking have increased since 1987.

ing strategy, plans, and programs." He saw effective marketing as a way to help "animate the whole organization" as well as outside target audiences, anticipating that the MFA could reach out to new audiences while also attracting more frequent visits from existing attendees.

Addressing the committee, Pat Jacoby highlighted the contrast between marketing in the recent past and its present situation. Prior to Malcolm Rogers' arrival, she said, the MFA had lacked a central marketing plan and vision, resulting in an absence of direction and continuity. At $900,000, the total marketing budget (including salaries) had been relatively small for such a large institution, resulting in the need to rely on pro bono advertising, which was hard to control in terms of where and when it actually appeared.

She characterized the past attitude towards the media as one of fear, with efforts being made to "protect" the museum from press coverage. News tended to be generated by departments, rather than centrally, often through leaks to the press. The MFA's internal self-image was that of a regional museum, in contrast to the Metropolitan Museum of Art in New York which saw itself as national. Other weaknesses had included inadequate data on visitors, insufficient understanding of sponsors' motivations and requirements, and lack of cohesiveness among the staff.

The present situation was much more encouraging, declared Jacoby. Both the director and the trustees were committed to marketing, and a staff marketing team had been established. The marketing budget had been sharply increased in 1996–97, with some $900,000 allocated for the core marketing and public relations program, plus a further $1.4 million for exhibition-related advertising and PR.

Later, following a curator's presentation of four upcoming special exhibitions, each with an Asian theme, the committee recommended that they be promoted as a group under the umbrella theme, "Asian Spring." However, when one member urged the group to focus on the goal of making MFA exhibitions "fun and exciting experiences" the curator expressed discomfort with the word "fun," although she conceded that some exhibitions might be more entertaining than others. Subsequently, the committee provided timely inputs to staff marketing plans for the 1997 spring and fall exhibitions.

Membership and Other Development Efforts

To attract financial support and encourage more frequent visits, the MFA had developed an extensive membership program. Different categories offered an increasing scale of benefits. For instance, a $50 individual membership provided free admission while a $900 sustaining membership yielded invitations to selected opening receptions, reciprocal membership benefits at 21 major American art museums, special programs with curatorial staff, acknowledgment in the annual report, and copies of certain museum publications. At even higher levels of contribution ($1,800–10,000+), a patron program offered special opportunities to become more closely acquainted with the museum's collections, including invitations to unique events. Membership revenues had risen at a much faster rate than the number of members in recent years (see *Exhibit 5*). In 1996–97, members accounted for 231,000 of the 1.1 million visits to the museum.

A five-year capital campaign was in progress. The goal of $110 million was designed to boost annual operating support and the museum's endowment, rather than finance new construction projects or fund new acquisitions. Support had been broad and the campaign was expected to meet or even exceed its target by the closing date of June 1998. Pat Jacoby noted that revenues from the enlarged endowment would eliminate the structural deficit once the campaign was completed. However, she observed that there was still a lack of understanding among many museum staff, particularly within the curatorial departments, of the importance of funding current positions and programs in order to create more freedom of action for the future.

Rogers was a firm believer in securing corporate sponsorship for exhibitions and other activities. Jacoby observed:

> Malcolm is willing to try new things. He's willing to put a corporate logo on the museum banner, if need be, to underwrite an exhibition. Bell Atlantic is underwriting the Picasso show this fall with a million dollars, while Fleet Bank is underwriting the new Monet show the following year with $1.2 million. As hackneyed as the word "partnership" has become, I think he really understands the concept. He's willing to meet a sponsor half-way, to try to understand their needs as well as the museum's needs and to make things work, rather than saying, "Oh no, we're too pure to display a corporate logo!"

Paul Bessire, the associate director of marketing, added:

> Malcolm immediately created an environment that said companies were welcome at the museum. One of the first things he did was to go out and meet with some of the top CEOs in town and discuss how they might work together. I think that benefited us greatly. He really views it

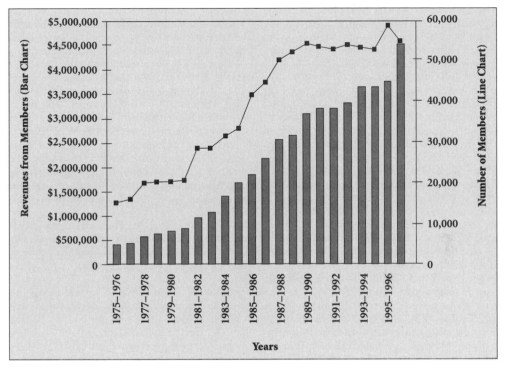

Exhibit 5 Museum of Fine Arts: Membership Totals and Revenues from Members, 1975–76 to 1996–97

as a partnership. It not only paid off in terms of the funding we've received for exhibitions, but also in terms of the assistance we've received from corporations in helping us market these exhibitions. They've been very helpful to us in doing additional advertising and other promotions.

The large bank that supported our recent Winslow Homer exhibition not only offered its customers a credit card featuring a Homer image, but also promoted Homer within its branches and on its ATMs. We probably wouldn't have done that before, because of fears that such actions would smack too much of commercialism. As it was, there were a few who felt we'd gone too far, but that's always going to happen when you push the envelope.

Enterprise Activities

John Stanley, deputy director of operations, oversaw enterprise activities such as merchandising, food service, and parking. He viewed merchandising as central to the MFA's mission. "But if we sell items unre-

lated to our collection," he warned, "we would become liable for unrelated business income tax and would lose our not-for-profit postal rate for mailing items purchased from our catalog." In 1996–97, merchandise sales through the museum shop and other channels amounted to $39.5 million. After deducting cost of goods sold and operating costs, net contribution amounted to $1.9 million. Food service yielded a contribution of $0.8 million on sales of $5.3 million.

Merchandise sales emphasized children's toys, decorative arts (which included posters, pictures, book ends, and vases), books, and paper products such as calendars and note cards. Stanley observed that although books took up a lot of space and were low margin, they were important to the mission because of their educational content, adding that the MFA's main store was the largest independent arts bookstore in New England. Unlike most museums, the MFA developed much of its own merchandise, accounting for some 40% of items (excluding books) and 70% of sales revenues. Items were commissioned from outside vendors, many of whom were located in Europe and Asia.

More than half of all sales came through catalog orders, which were handled through the MFA's distribution center in one of Boston's outer suburbs. About 20% of sales were made through the main museum store, which was being expanded from 5,000 to 6,200 square feet (570 m²). Catering to visitors attending special exhibitions was a small exhibition shop outside the Gund Gallery. Two satellite stores in central Boston—in Copley Square and Faneuil Hall Marketplace—did particularly well because they were in popular tourist locations. Three other stores were located in suburban Boston shopping malls. The MFA had learned from experience that the ideal size for a satellite store was approximately 2,000 square feet (185 m²). The Faneuil Hall store had doubled its sales following its recent expansion from 900 to 1,800 square feet; by contrast, another store was being downsized. There was also an outlet store at the distribution center, where excess inventory was sold periodically at bargain prices.

Unlike New York's "Met," which had 15 stores nationwide (but not in Boston), the MFA had no museum shops outside its principal market area. However, it did sell its own merchandise to wholesalers that supplied other museum stores, thus helping to promote awareness of the MFA's collection to a broader audience. Annual sales through this channel amounted to $3 million, with a gross margin of 30%. Stanley and his staff were always looking for new opportunities and hoped to expand merchandise sales overseas. The agreement for the new Nagoya/Museum of Fine Arts in Japan specified that 75% of the merchandise offered there must come from the MFA's own product line.

In addition to offering desirable products at appropriate prices and displaying them in attractive ways, Stanley saw the secrets of financial success as a combination of realistic margins and "turn" (how quickly items were sold from inventory). For most items, except books, the gross margin was about 54% (meaning that an item that cost the MFA $46 to purchase should be sold for $100). A substantial portion of the gross margin went towards defraying the cost of retail operations and marketing.

The MFA offered no less than 12,000 individual items for sale. Prices ranged from under $20 up to $3,200 for a custom-made reproduction of a 17th century diamond engagement ring, but most items cost between $30 and $50. The enterprise division had learned the need for tight inventory controls after losing money on merchandise operations in 1993–94. A just-in-time inventory policy had been implemented at all stores, with daily deliveries from the distribution center. The current inventory and past sales history of each item (known as a stock-keeping unit or "SKU") was closely monitored through electronic records. Stanley and his staff could check at any time to see what SKUs were selling in what volumes in which stores, as well as checking inventory availability.

Four editions of the catalog were published each year, with a total of ten million copies being distributed. In addition to the MFA's "house file" of museum members and past customers, copies were mailed to prospects on rented lists targeted at people with demographics that matched those of likely purchasers. The busiest sales period was the December holiday season. To complement the catalog, Stanley planned to offer customers the option of a web-based electronic catalog, which would feature a broad array of merchandise that could be ordered through the website.

Developing merchandise related to upcoming exhibitions required a long lead time, since suppliers might require as much as two years' notice to create new items keyed to specific displays. Copyright issues had to be handled very carefully. "We prefer long-dead artists," joked Stanley, "because unless they've been dead for some time, the museum has to seek the right to use the images they created. This task can be time-consuming and expensive."

The Herb Ritts Exhibition

Few major shows at the MFA had generated as much controversy as *Herb Ritts: Work*. It was championed by Malcolm Rogers, who hoped that it would appeal to a wide audience, from newcomers to frequent visitors to the museum. Based in Los Angeles, Ritts, 44, had begun taking pictures in 1980 and had made his name as a photographer of both fashion and celebrities. His images were featured in publications such as *Vogue* and *Vanity Fair* and he had shaped corporate advertising campaigns for many well-known fashion houses and cosmetics firms. Recently, he had begun directing commercials and music videos.

The exhibition—which would also be shown in Ft. Lauderdale, Vienna, Paris and Australia—featured some 230 of Ritts' photographs, all in black and white and ranging in size from intimate portraits to ten-foot murals. It was the first time that a purely photographic exhibition had been featured in the Gund Gallery (the MFA's principal exhibit space), and also the first time that a show had been sponsored by a major fashion house, Donna Karan of New York (DKNY). Commenting on the trend for such firms to support the arts, *The New York Times* observed, "Most designers who support the arts do it as a way of getting their name out to potential customers. For cultural institutions constantly scrambling for money, the fashion world is still a relatively untapped source of support reaching just the kind of affluent visitor they are looking for."

The exhibits included shots of celebrities such as Madonna and other well-known Hollywood stars, images of people, animals, and landscapes from Africa, layouts from the fashion world, and studies of the human form, including both male and female nudes, a few of which displayed frontal nudity or featured gay couples.

The MFA had allocated $450,000 to promote the show, advertising it in a wide array of both general and specialist media, ranging from newspapers and magazines to theater programs and public transit vehicles, as well as in free weekly papers in the city. For the first time, the MFA included national media in the advertising schedule, encompassing both fashion publications and upscale general audience magazines. There was also extensive public relations activity. However, not all went according to plan.

Huge publicity was generated just before the opening in late October 1996, when the management of a major Boston office building ordered that 10 works with elements of nudity, hung in its lobby as part of an AIDS fundraising event and including a photograph by Ritts, be draped in black and then removed. The phrase "Banned in Boston" promptly appeared widely in the media. After a public outcry, the decision was quickly reversed for eight of the offending works, including Ritts'. News stories also reported that the show's preview party was dampened by bad weather, which left Donna Karan and other New York celebrities grounded at La Guardia airport and unable to attend.

Advance reviews of the exhibition were generally unenthusiastic. The *Boston Sunday Herald* review was headlined "Putting on the Glitz." *The Boston Globe* described the show as "fun, all style and little substance, slick and seductive. . . . It's a quick read—art for the attention span of the '90s." Addressing Malcolm Rogers' hope that *Ritts* would lure new, young audiences to the museum, the *Globe's* critic declared, "That might work. . . . But will this show turn young viewers on to *other* art?"

Negative comments continued throughout *Ritts'* 3½-month stay, with critics lambasting it for being commercial in concept and of poor artistic quality. Many stated that Herb Ritts did not deserve the prestige of a major solo show. Rogers felt obliged to defend the show following a *Globe* story titled "The Malling of the MFA," which acknowledged the popu-

---

EXHIBIT 6 *Exhibition Schedule for Gund Gallery, 1994–2000*

Dates		Surcharge (If Any)*
5/94–8/94	Connections: Mark Tansey	none
9/94–1/95	Grand Illusions: Four Centuries of Still-Life Painting	none
2/95–4/95	Ernd Nolde: The Painter's Prints	none
5/95–8/95	John Singleton Copley in America	none
10/95–1/96	Impressions of France: Monet, Renoir, Pissarro and their Rivals	none
2/96–5/96	Winslow Homer	$2 weekday $4 weekend
6/96–9/96	Gauguin and the School of Pont-Aven	none
10/96–2/97	Herb Ritts: Work	none
4/97–7/97	Tales from the Land of Dragons 1000 Years of Chinese Painting	none
9/97–1/98	Picasso: The Early Years	$5
2/98–5/98	A Grand Design: The Art of the Victoria and Albert Museum	$3
6/98–8/98	Edward Weston and Modernism	tbd
9/98–12/98	Monet in the 20th Century	$7.50 weekend $5.00 weekday (reduced rates for seniors, students, and children)
2/99–5/99	Mary Cassatt: A Retrospective	tbd
6/99–9/99	John Singer Sargent	tbd
11/99–2/00	Pharoahs of the Sun: Akhenaten, Nefertiti, Tutankamen	tbd

* In excess of normal admission charge to the Museum (tbd = to be determined)

lar appeal of the exhibition but described many in the Boston arts community as objecting to "the dumbing down, the malling of the museum that Ritts represents." One Boston gallery owner was quoted as saying that "I don't think that quality should ever be sacrificed in the name of new audiences." Commenting on other MFA shows, the critic concluded that with the exception of the earlier Winslow Homer show, recent and planned exhibitions had not been "at an appropriately high level, nor had they been "particularly risky or daring." (*Exhibit 6* lists major shows scheduled from 1994 to 2000.)

When *Ritts* closed on February 9, 1997, it had achieved a total attendance of 253,694, making it the sixth most popular show in MFA history. Overall, the coverage—including local and national television—was the broadest ever achieved by the MFA. By comparison, the previous year's exhibition devoted to the popular 19th century American artist, Winslow Homer, had attracted 270,000 visitors and the *Asian Spring* group of exhibitions had been seen by some 225,000 visitors through the end of June 1997.

As part of its marketing evaluation process, the museum commissioned a visitor study in which self-administered surveys (requiring about seven minutes to complete) were conducted over an eight week period. Visitors (excluding tour groups) were selected at random as they exited the museum. An important objective was to compare *Ritts* visitors to the benchmark research on the museum's audience in general and to its typical winter visitors in particular. A summary of the findings appears in *Exhibit 7*. Summaries of verbatim visitor comments are shown in *Exhibit 8*.

Looking to the Future

The next major exhibition scheduled to be held at the MFA was *Picasso: The Early Years, 1892–1906*. Organized by the MFA and the National Gallery of Art in Washington, it was scheduled to run in Boston from September 1997 to early January 1998 and would include images from Picasso's so-called "Blue" and "Rose" periods. More than 100 paintings, drawings, and sculptures had been selected for display from major collections around the world. The exhibition, projected to attract 350,000 visitors, had been sponsored by a substantial grant from Bell Atlantic, a major telecommunications company serving the eastern United States.

The staff's marketing plan for *Picasso* employed a three-phase approach, each with its own specific

---

EXHIBIT 7 *Summary of Findings from Survey of MFA Visitors Attending the* Herb Ritts: Work *Exhibition*

- Compared to the Museum's winter and general visitors, those visiting the Herb Ritts exhibition were younger and racially more diverse.
- Only 21% visited the Herb Ritts exhibition alone; significantly more (37%) visited in groups of 2 or more compared to the Museum's Winter and General visitors.
- Sixty-three percent of all Herb Ritts visitors were local, which is higher than winter (58%) and General (50%) visitors. More visitors were drawn from outside the Greater Metro Area than in winter.
- Boston residents to the Herb Ritts exhibition were significantly younger (50% under 24 years) and racially diverse (17% minorities) compared to other local visitors.
- More visitors to the Herb Ritts exhibition were non-Members (77%). However, only 20% were first-time visitors. The non-Member repeat visitors were infrequent visitors to the MFA; 65% of the non-Member repeat visitors were local residents.
- The most frequently mentioned source of information on the Herb Ritts exhibition was "Print" (247 mentions), followed by "Friends/Family" (181) and "Banners" (115).
- Half the visitors had planned to visit the exhibition early—either in the past few months or before/as soon as the exhibition opened. The other half made their decision to visit within the past week, the day of, or after they arrived at the Museum.
- Significantly more visitors had positive comments about the Herb Ritts exhibition. Eighty-seven percent said that the exhibition either "Exceeded Expectations" (44%) or "Met Expectations" (43%); and 87% said they would recommend it to "Friends/Family."
- Sixty-two percent planned to see other exhibitions/collections either only on the day of their visit. It appeared that 30% came to see the Herb Ritts exhibition only and did not plan to see other exhibitions/collections that day, but would return within the year.
- Eighty-one percent were aware that DKNY [Donna Karan of New York] sponsored the Herb Ritts exhibition. Of those visitors, 60% had a positive impression of DKNY and 34% had no opinion.

EXHIBIT 8 *Summary of Positive and Negative Comments by MFA Visitors to the* Herb Ritts: Work *Exhibition*

---

(1) What Visitors Liked

Photography (109)
- Wonderful, loved it; gorgeous work; enjoyed very much; exquisite detail of skin; artistic composition; creative.
- Strong images; stark imagery; excellent use of shadows, textures; clear photography.

Photo Content (90)
- Captured beauty of human body, body in motion; essence of personality.
- Particularly liked Denzel Washington, Bono, Bukowski, famous people, Africa, male nudes, images of pop culture, and his use of water.

Exhibit Design (59)
- Powerful exhibit design; visually stunning; excellent lighting.

Large Variety of His Work (25)

Enjoyed Provocativeness without It Being Tasteless; Exciting Stuff (16)

Nice Departure from Traditional Museum Exhibits (12)

Presentation of Different Types of People in Terms of Race, Sexual Orientation and the Physically Challenged (10)

Excellent Artist; Favorite Photographer (4)

---

n = 331
number of mentions in parentheses

(2) What Visitors Disliked

Art Work (27)
- All effect and little substance; the artist seems to be star struck; no depth; poor excuse for art; Ritts is not an artist.

Commercialism (26)
- Very commercial appeal; shameless commercialism.

Exhibit Set-Up (24)
- Did not like exhibit set-up; labels should be larger; would have liked more technical information on the photos; too crowded.
- Overwhelming; too many pictures in one room.

Exhibit Content (20)
- No new pictures; would have liked to have seen more "Africa" pictures.
- Too much emphasis on beautiful people; would have liked to have seen pictures of people like me.
- Did not like homoerotic photos, little too explicit for my taste; inappropriate place (MFA) for exhibit.
- Child pornography; graphic; perverted; self indulgent.
- Disappointing.

---

n = 76
number of mentions in parentheses

Exhibit 9 Museum of Fine Arts, Boston: Expenses Related to the Ritts and Picasso Shows		
	Herb Ritts: Work (actual)	Picasso: The Early Years (budgeted)
Advertising	$377,681	$618,000
Banners	22,000	54,800
Shared costs (MFA portion)	—	880,000*
Matting and framing	145,000	—
Logistics and staging	21,378	1,050,000
Installation	104,568	201,000
Opening	47,836	52,500
Brochures/pamphlets	49,985	135,000
Misc. advertising/marketing	24,398	17,000
Total	$793,348	$3,008,000

* Certain costs of the show, notably insurance and framing, were being shared with the National Gallery in Washington, DC, which would also be hosting the Picasso exhibition.
Source: Museum of Fine Arts, Boston

objectives. Market segments were broken down according to their relationship with the museum, their geographic location, and their demographic category. The pre-opening phase (July 15–August 31) was designed to build awareness and excitement. For the opening phase (September 1–October 31), the staff recommended a campaign that would require more than half the media budget as it sought to reach and attract wide range of audience profiles. Finally, there was a modest allocation for the sustaining or "reminder" phase (November 1–January 4). *Exhibit 9* contrasts marketing and related expenses for the Picasso and Ritts exhibitions.

Pat Jacoby recognized that promoting this exhibition was only one of many challenges in ensuring the museum's continued success in serving its multiple audiences. As she reflected on the future role and responsibilities of marketing at the Museum of Fine Arts, she remembered a recent presentation by Malcolm Rogers, in which he had declared:

Marketing is central to the life of a great museum that's trying to get its message out. It's part of our educational outreach, our social outreach. Unfortunately, certain people don't like the word "marketing." What I see out there—and also to a certain extent inside the museum—is a very conservative culture that cannot accept that institutions previously considered "elite" should actually be trying to attract a broader public and also listening to what the public is saying. But it's all to do with fulfilling your mission.

Clearly part of a museum's mission is guardianship of precious objects, but unless we're communicating those objects to people effectively and our visitors are enjoying them—and the ambiance of the setting in which they are displayed and interpreted—then we're only operating at 50% effectiveness or less. Having said this, I want to stress that the mission comes first and that marketing is absolutely the servant of our mission. I believe that museums stand for a commitment to certain eternal values that they bring to an ever-broadening public. We're not just in the business of finding out what people want and then giving it to them.

Study Questions

1. Define the core product and supplementary services of a large museum like the MFA.
2. Prepare a flowchart of a visit to the MFA by a tourist from out of town who starts by telephoning the museum from her Boston hotel to get information.
3. What differentiates the MFA from a for-profit institution like a department store, a theme park, or a movie theater? How does this distinction affect management priorities and decisions?
4. Evaluate the efforts made by the museum management to make the MFA more marketing oriented. What should be done to create better understanding of marketing among curators?
5. Evaluate the role of Malcolm Rogers. Is he a good leader? Has he been an effective service marketer?

First Direct: Branchless Banking

Jean–Claude Larréché
Christopher Lovelock
Delphine Parmenter

After seven years of operation, the world's first all–telephone bank has built a substantial customer base. However, many financial institutions have followed its lead by adding 24-hour, telephone-based services of their own. The bank's management is debating how best to maintain growth.

In October 1996, seven years after it first opened outside Leeds, England, First Direct was still attracting attention as an innovator that operated a bank with no branches. Intrigued by its success, financial service providers wanted to understand how unseen customers conducted business around the clock over the telephone. An article in the *New York Times* reported:

> Representatives from banks around the world are making the pilgrimage to this industrial city in the north of England for a glimpse of what might be their stagnant industry's equivalent of a miraculous cure. For not only is First Direct the world's leading telephone-only bank, it is the fastest growing bank in Britain. In just six years, it has signed up 2% of Britain's notoriously set-in-their-ways banking subjects, who call its rows of bankers 24 hours a day, seven days a week, to pay bills, buy stock, and arrange mortgages.
>
> (3 September 1996)

Success not only put First Direct in the media limelight but it also helped to maintain high levels of enthusiasm, pride and motivation internally. Fearful that complacency might hinder the bank's ability to uphold growth and success, CEO Kevin Newman never lost sight of the bank's challenges in an increasingly competitive and deregulated environment:

> I believe that in going forward three things need to be developed. We have to be utterly low cost. We must be able to individualize the manufacturing process and recognize that all our customers are individuals. Thirdly, we must build a strong brand as people need to identify with institutions they can trust.

"Kevin," as everyone called the chief executive, sat among the telephone sales staff in First Direct's headquarters on the outskirts of Leeds, 190 miles (300 km) north of London. Newman had installed the information systems that were instrumental in getting the new bank off the ground in 1989. Subsequently, he was promoted to operations director in 1990 and CEO in October 1991. Newman came to the bank from the mass-market retailer, Woolworth's, after having worked at Mars, the candy and consumer goods manufacturer. Although Kevin Newman did not start his career as a banker he was, at 35 years of age, undoubtedly the youngest banking CEO in Britain.

The Birth of the First Direct Concept

In the mid-1980s, Midland Bank, the fourth largest bank in the UK with 2,000 branches, began looking at ways of attracting more affluent and up-market customers. As Peter Simpson, subsequently First Direct's commercial director, remarked:

> If you are losing market share you can do two things: you can grow organically or inorganically. Midland Bank had limited capital, so there was nowhere to go inorganically; its reserves had been spent on the over-priced Crocker National Bank acquisition in North America and with Latin American debt. Organically, the retail banks in the United Kingdom were giving away current accounts for free, and sacrificing their profits in terms of customer value.

Consequently, in June 1988 Midland drafted a team of executives on a project code-named 'Raincloud'. Mike Harris, a former Midland executive, returned as a consultant to lead the top-secret investigation. An examination of consumers' banking habits highlighted that there was a substantial niche of people whose banking transactions were not branch-based. According to a national market research study of British bank customers by MORI in 1988:

- 20 per cent of account holders had not visited their branch in the last month.
- 51 per cent said they would rather visit their branch as little as possible.
- 48 per cent had never met their branch manager
- 38 per cent said banking hours were inconvenient
- 27 per cent wished they were able to conduct more business with the bank over the phone.

This was the beginning of an idea. Rather than reposition the branch network, the taskforce wondered what it would be like to have a bank with no branches. The team discovered that as early as 1981 a Dutch bank, Nederlanse Credietbank had set up Direktbank with a small telephone-staff to cater to the needs of an upscale segment. Since 1986, Bank of America offered an additional service that enabled branch customers to process transactions by pressing buttons on touch tone telephones in response to a voice-activated computer. And in France, several banks allowed customers to make account enquiries via the videotext Minitel screens linked to their home phones.

The Midland team envisioned an entirely new type of bank that would operate from one centre, 24 hours a day, 365 days a year. Employing the UK's 47 million telephones as a low-cost delivery system, it would use human operators rather than a machine to perform all the functions of a traditional bank. Next, Harris's team faced the difficult task of presenting to the Midland board of directors a proposal for a new concept that might compete with its own branch network. Although Midland Bank had successfully retained its customer base with a long list of innovative banking products, it had to acquire additional business to stay afloat. Working with experts in marketing, operations, human resources and technology, Harris was named chief executive of the proposed stand-alone telephone bank. He was given one year to design and launch it.

Developing Operational Systems and Initial Job Design

Rather than incur the delay and expense of obtaining its own bank charter. First Direct was set up as a division of Midland Bank. Short on time—Midland anticipated another bank would introduce a similar telephone service—the team proceeded secretly, working 18-hour days. After much brainstorming the team baptized the new bank 'First Direct' to reflect its pioneering concept of working directly with customers. As far as Midland was concerned, First Direct was a completely new brand and a completely new business. A black and white corporate identity symbolized the simple economical nature of the new bank.

The start-up staff of about 50 worked initially out of London while the operations team evaluated a variety of potential sites for First Direct's one and only office. They were attracted to Leeds as the city offered moderate rental rates and a regional labour pool accustomed to lower salaries than in southern England. Additionally, the Yorkshire accent was recognized as easy to understand, warm and friendly. First Direct leased a modern building in an industrial park outside Leeds that could be modified to suit the bank's needs.

Procedures had to be built from scratch so that any traditional branch transaction could be handled in one telephone call. The planners decided that customers could obtain cash through the Midland automatic teller machines (ATM) network and make deposits electronically, while transactions would be cleared and statements processed at one of Midland's regional processing centres. First Direct would benefit from its parent's massive technology investments of the late 1980s; otherwise Midland played no managerial role.

Next, the team turned to new technology to deliver a portfolio of payment, savings and lending instruments over the phone. A survey of the best call centres in the United States and Canada provided guidance in setting up the systems. First Direct improved upon existing technology to make all customer information accessible by any telephone operator. Furthermore, they integrated the screen and telephone systems so a call could be passed along without the customer having to repeat the entire conversation.

Another group designed job descriptions to meet service standards and the use of high-tech work tools. It was obvious that the new bank's telephone-based staff would have an assignment very different from a traditional bank teller who counted cash, filled out deposit slips, and looked for forged signatures. A visit to Federal Express's Memphis hub provided insight as to how to recruit, train and motivate staff. Kevin Gavaghan, then marketing director of Midland Bank, remembered how the hiring criteria were determined:

> In hiring, First Direct were looking for people that were fast and efficient but more importantly people with warm and engaging personalities. The first flood of applicants showed the way; the first six months proved it. The qualities required were more often than not found in the social professions—teachers, nurses, even firefighters—frequently people working difficult hours under difficult circumstances. Empathy and responsiveness under pressure marked these types out from the traditional bank clerk whose reserve and process-orientation proved at times impossible to reverse.

Initial recruitment advertising gave only sketchy details of employment opportunities in the financial services sector; there was no mention of Midland Bank. As early as May of 1989, First Direct began hiring telephone advisers who were called Banking Representatives (BRs). Training sought to improve the candidate's communication and listening skills so that they sounded friendly, mature and well informed over the phone. By the time of launch, 200 BRs were prepared to answer enquiries and process customer transactions.

Getting Off to a Slow Start

First Direct inaugurated its service at midnight on Sunday, 1 October 1989, in a pointed reference to its seven days a week, 24-hour operation. Although for legal reasons its advertising had to mention that First Direct was a division of Midland Bank, it sought to distance itself from Midland to bring in new customers. First Direct selected a British agency known as a creative hot shop. Howell Henry Chaldecott Lury (HHCL), to orchestrate an aggressive £6 million advertising campaign that kicked off one hour before the bank opened for business.

Traditional banks did not see First Direct as a threat. Sceptics doubted that the concept of telephone banking would ever catch on, or that it would ever be profitable. The competitive spirit within Midland was such that no one anticipated a great deal of cannibalization. Furthermore, as First Direct targeted individuals with relatively high disposable incomes, existing banks never feared it would gain significant market share. Although First Direct was from the outset overwhelmed with telephone enquiries, acquiring new customers proved difficult. Soon the media reported it to be a flop.

Despite its slow start, First Direct began winning a growing number of customers after its first full year of business. By December of 1992, it had almost 250,000 account holders, about 70 per cent of whom had reportedly been attracted from competitors. A year later, Gene Lokhart, CEO of UK Banking at Midland, declared that First Direct had acquired over 350,000 customers, only 20 per cent of whom were formerly Midland customers. The bank lost very few customers, approximately 2 to 3 per cent per year, the majority as a result of natural causes. In 1996, the bank had 640,000 customers and was acquiring about 125,000 new customers a year—the equivalent of opening one new branch each week (*Exhibit 1*).

During the first six years of operations, First Direct's offices adapted to accommodate this phenomenal growth. With the 75,000 square foot (7,000 m²) building in the Arlington Business Centre fully utilized, First Direct unveiled a second purpose-built facility three miles away at Stourton in November 1994. The Arlington location accommodated both back-office operations (foreign investments section, lending services and mortgage underwriters) and the front-office call centre (customer service and new customer department) on a single floor without walls. Besides a second call centre, the 150,000 square foot (14,000 m²) Stourton site housed credit and risk services, investments, new mortgage enquiries, the insurance division, and customer enquiries (Visa, direct debits, standing orders, customer relations). The operations and information technology (IT) staff occupied part of the same trading floor at the centre of the business. The different teams mapped their areas by the signs that hung from the ceiling.

Telephone advisers did not have their own desks but transferred mobile units containing stationery and personal belongings to any desk available during their shift. This hot desking approach enabled full

EXHIBIT 1 First Direct: Estimated Account Data				
Date	Total number of customers	Total number of accounts	Calls/day	Staff
April 1996	641,000	1,100,000	32,000	2,400
December 1995	586,000	800,000	26,000	2,300
December 1994	476,000	700,000	21,000	1,900
December 1993	361,000	500,000	16,000	1,500
December 1992	241,000	350,000	11,000	1,000
December 1991	136,000	200,000	7,000	500
December 1990	66,000	105,000	3,000	300
December 1989	11,000	N/A	N/A	250

Source: Estimates based on Midland Bank Annual Reports and Internal Sources First Direct, 1996

capacity utilization over the non-stop work shift. Kevin Newman was based in Arlington and all the directors sat with their departments at their respective sites—no one had a private office. Richard Rushton, customer services director, had a desk at each site. A mini-van made the ten-minute connection between the two sites every hour.

By early 1996, it was estimated that First Direct served a customer base equivalent to 200 branches. However, the telephone bank employed only 2,400 individuals where a branch network would require a staff of almost 4,000. Its staffing costs were about half those of a typical retail oriented commercial branch. The construction of a third building adjacent to Stourton was scheduled for completion by June 1997.

Efficient information systems were instrumental in keeping costs down. The business required non-stop processing power to perform on-line transactions and to access the bank's mainframe computers. The hub of First Direct's operations, the on-line customer database, used two Sequoia UNIX-based computers at Arlington and Stourton. It also supported and interfaced with the 1,800 personal computers that ran various applications across the two sites. Third parties provided IT support for transaction clearing, card service processing and credit scoring. First Direct used an automatic call distribution (ACD) system to manage one of the largest call centres in the UK. It routed calls to unoccupied operators and bounced calls back and forth between the two centres to balance work loads.

First Direct achieved break-even by the end of the 1994 financial year and in 1995 reported its first full year of profitability. In 1996, Kevin Newman commented on the banks financial performance:

As you know, we have been circumspect about releasing this information for commercial competitive reasons and I do not wish to change this policy. I can, however, indicate that our return on equity is extremely attractive (i.e., 25% plus). Our return on investment is equally attractive, at least as good as that currently being achieved by the UK clearing banks.

Retail Banking in the United Kingdom

Until the 1970s, the so-called Big Four British clearing banks, namely Lloyds, Midland, Barclays and National Westminster, dominated retail banking in the United Kingdom while building societies controlled the mortgage market. Much like the US savings and loan institutions, building societies provided funds for the purchase of homes from a pool of members' savings. No new bankcharters had been issued by Britain's central bank, the Bank of England, since the end of the nineteenth century.

However, in the 1970s the Bank of England allowed banks to provide a more complete range of personal financial services, from share dealing and insurance broking to the provision of financial advice. Additionally, the 1979 Banking Act opened up the mortgage market to institutions other than building societies by formally dissolving the interest rate cartel. In turn, the building societies obtained the right to offer checking accounts and unsecured loans. Abbey National was one of the first institutions to take advantage of this shake-up, becoming a bank in 1989. The early 1980s saw further deregulation, tax incentives and an economic boom in the UK that greatly enhanced personal wealth for many individuals.

By 1993, four of the top ten building societies had obtained bank charters and were competing directly with the Big Four banks in the provision of a broad range of consumer banking services. Consequently, by the early 1990s Britain had an excessive number of banks and branches, difficult to sustain in the face of economic recession and increased automation.

Exhibit 2 *UK Retail Banks—Statistics 1989 & 1995*

Retail Banks	Assets (£ millions)		Pre-tax profits (% of total assets)		Number of branches		Number of employees	
	1989	1995	1989	1995	1989	1995	1989	1995
National Westminster Bank	116,189	166,347	0.3	1.1	2,997	2,215	86,600	61,000
Barclays Bank	127,616	164,184	0.5	1.3	2,645	2,050	85,900	61,200
Lloyds Bank TSB[1]	83,023	131,750	−0.7	1.3	3,722	2,858	87,500	66,400
Abbey National[2]	37,201	97,614	1.3	1.1	678	678	13,600	16,300
Midland Bank[3]	62,619	92,093	−0.4	1.1	2,042	1,701	47,500	43,400
Royal Bank of Scotland	27,436	50,497	0.8	1.2	842	687	20,500	19,500
Bank of Scotland	14,073	34,104	1.3	1.3	527	411	12,100	11,300

Notes:[1] Lloyds Bank merged with TSB in October 1995 and acquired Cheltenham & Gloucester in 1995.
[2] Abbey National acquired National & Provincial in 1995.
[3] Midland Bank was acquired by HSBC Holdings plc in July 1992.
Source: Annual Abstract of Banking Statistics, British Bankers Association, 1996, Vol. 13.

Inevitably, several much-publicized mergers followed. The Hongkong & Shanghai Banking Corporation (HSBC) bought Midland Bank in July 1992. Three years later, Britain's biggest building society, Halifax, planned a merger with Leeds Permanent, the country's fifth biggest. The consolidation process accelerated markedly in 1995 (*Exhibit 2*).

Parallel to this industry-wide reshaping, individual banks and building societies embarked on their own downsizing programmes by closing branches and centralizing transaction processing. The total number of branches fell by 15 per cent between 1980 and 1992, with a loss of over 100,000 jobs. More qualified or senior staff were often replaced by lower-paid, less-qualified workers. The banks and building societies soon attracted unfavourable media attention and criticism for their long queues, high level of errors and exorbitant customer charges. In response to these attacks, Midland Bank was the first to introduce charge-free banking and personal loans. In the late 1980s, the Henley Centre for Forecasting found that customer dissatisfaction remained higher in banking than in any other retail sector in Britain. However, only one in 30 British consumers switched banks in a given year. Despite increased competition, only one person in five could distinguish between the services offered by the various banks.

Many financial institutions saw automation and new technology as ways to replace some expensive branch transactions. Customers' responded enthusiastically and automated teller machines proliferated. Banks made ATM network share agreements and also installed cash machines in non-branch locations like supermarkets. With new technology telephone-based

banking now offered person-to-person, person-to-computer or even computer-to-computer based transactions at an estimated cost as low as one-sixth that of conventional branch-based transactions (*Exhibit 3*).

As early as 1983, the Nottingham Building Society offered Britain's first subscription telephone banking service, known as Homelink. However, the service attracted only 5,000 subscribers. Another pioneer, The Royal Bank of Scotland launched its Home and Office Banking System in 1984 and Direct Line insurance in 1985. By 1996, the use of telephone banking in one form or another was widespread throughout the industry.

The introduction of debit cards and smart cards also favoured the advent of electronic banking. As an alternative to cash, NatWest and Midland Bank piloted the Mondex smart card in July 1995. Positioned as an electronic wallet, it allowed customers to store cash, debit purchases electronically and replenish the card from their accounts at an ATM or through specially equipped telephones. In 1995, Barclays, the largest retail bank in the UK, launched a home banking service accessed through the customer's personal computer.

Acquiring New Customers at First Direct

The majority of First Direct's new prospects called the bank on a toll-free line. Direct mail activity produced high call volume and brought in nearly one half of new customers. More importantly, word-of-mouth recommendations generated about one-third of customer acquisitions. Customer polls showed that 87 per cent of the customer base was either extremely or

---

EXHIBIT 3 *Banking Technology*

- **Automatic Call Distribution—ACD**
  Systems that manage a high volume of incoming calls by routing and placing each call in a queue to the next available operator so that the caller never hears a busy signal.
- **Computer Integrated Telephony—CIT**
  Computer databases are linked to the incoming call, allowing call handlers to quickly access customer files.
- **Calling Line Identification**
  An additional CIT service which shows the number at the source of the call.
- **Interactive Voice Recognition and Response**
  CIT systems can react to the tones entered by telephone, or even recognize certain predetermined voice inputs.
- **Teletext and Videotext-based Access**
  Videotext terminals, with screens and keyboards, provide an interactive access to a bank's computer. The national French Minitel system is the most developed network in Europe; British Telecom offers a similar Prestel network.
- **Multi-Media Kiosks**
  Stand-alone multi-media kiosks may communicate with the customer using powerful interactive digital text, audio, video and animation.
- **PC-based Access**
  A personal computer may access a bank's computer via a modem and telephone network.
- **Internet World Wide Web Site**
  Home banking customers may connect to their bank's proprietary Web site via private dial-up networks and tap into their personal accounts.

Source: Data gathered from various publications.

---

very satisfied with First Direct, compared with an average of 51 per cent for conventional banks; 85 per cent of its consumers actively recommended the bank to friends, relatives or colleagues (*Exhibit 4*). In both 1994 and 1995, First Direct achieved the largest net gain of all UK banks and building societies in customers transferring their checking account.

The new customer team answered enquiries, opened accounts, explained the mechanics of telephone banking and carried out the initial processing

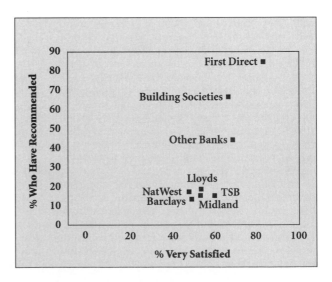

EXHIBIT 4 Customer Satisfaction for UK Retail Bank Customers, Year-End 1995
Source: First Direct Survey conducted between 20 November 1995 and 21 January 1996.

and assessing of the 17,000 prospects that applied every month. They obtained basic customer details (name, address, date of birth) before taking the caller through the application process over the telephone. Then, the computer system automatically generated a preprinted application form for customers to sign and return. Next, First Direct formally processed the application and made various fraud and credit checks. Credit scoring requirements were strict because new customers were instantly issued 25 cheques and a £100 cheque guarantee card that potentially gave access to £2,500 credit. The bank rejected about 50 per cent of applicants.

New customers received a "Welcome" pack and established security procedures to ensure proper identification and confidentiality. Ninety-seven per cent of new customers opened a cheque account; about 70 per cent also transferred their direct salary deposits, 60 per cent opened a savings account, and 40 per cent a credit card account. Although First Direct did not require a minimum balance, the average account balance was about £1,000. After the first three months of activity, First Direct made several mailings and telephone calls to take customers through the "Education" phase in order to build awareness of the range of investment and lending services provided.

Customer Service

The heart of First Direct was the call centre. Regular customers could call at any time of the day or night on a special telephone number charged at local rates, regardless of where the call originated in the UK, or contact the bank from overseas via a special number. First Direct received over half of all calls outside traditional banking hours, many on public holidays. The average customer called First Direct once a month. During peak hours, from 10 a.m. to 12 noon and 6 p.m. to 9 p.m., nearly 800 people worked the phones. That number dropped in the middle of the night to about 40 operators.

Banking reps verified the customer's identity and retrieved the account information on the computer screen. The Customer Information System recorded each customer contact and gave BRs access to all the customer's accounts and business history. Day-to-day transactions such as balance enquiries, electronic payment of bills, or a transfer of funds between accounts could all be completed by the same representative without the customer being transferred. In fact, BRs could handle 85 per cent of the enquiries. Some BRs were accredited to deal with more complicated Visa card or foreign currency requests.

For more specialized information regarding loans, personal insurance, mortgages or investments, BRs transferred customers to telephone advisers within the respective business units. For example, mortgage counsellors were available from 7 a.m. to 12 midnight, seven days a week, for advice on a new mortgage, remortgage or a home improvement loan. A mortgage application could be completed over the phone. Additionally, an experienced group of BRs manned what was called an overnight 'mushroom squad' to answer any type of customer enquiry in any business area.

Telecaster screens suspended from the ceilings in each department signalled the number of calls waiting, the average length of the wait, and the current service level expressed as a percentage. To meet minimum service objectives, 75 per cent of all calls had to be answered within 20 seconds or less. If callers were put on hold for more than two minutes, BRs apologized and arranged a call-back. The bank recorded customer calls to safeguard against transaction errors. As much as possible was done via the phone, but for legal reasons it was sometimes necessary to complete written documents after the phone had been put down.

Although no one at First Direct dealt with customers face-to-face, the employees elected to wear business dress to convey a sense of professionalism. The 1,200 banking representatives (50 per cent of the total staff) formed the customer's overall impression of the company. Bringing with them their own experience as bank customers, BRs strove to be flexible enough to accommodate those customers who complained that the bank's rigid systems did not always meet their needs. When things went wrong, BRs tried to go overboard to recover customers.

At First Direct there was no such thing as a normal workday. Workweeks varied between 16 and 36 hours and there was no premium paid for night or weekend shifts. Full-time BRs worked a 36-hour week with a 10-minute break every two hours and a half-hour lunch break. The 1996 television advertising campaign put pressure on the call centre not only from increased enquiries but also by increasing the average call length of existing customers from three to three and a half minutes. Some telephone advisers were more than willing to work overtime, often putting in 14-hour shifts and taking over 200 calls in a day. (Overtime was paid at one and a quarter times the hourly rate.) Although the staffing was based on sophisticated forecasts, an additional 30 seconds spent with each of First Direct's 32,000 daily callers was likely to jam the call centre. Newman recognized that working in the call centre was a tough job:

Calls come in incessantly, one after another. So, after having answered 150 calls it is difficult to keep the momentum going and to be sincerely friendly on the phone especially when handling tedious transactions. But our business is built on how the next call is answered. The biggest part of my leadership role is to enable a culture which allows people to feel very positive about their contribution to our business so that they may deliver genuine smiles over the phone. This cannot be obtained by *telling* people to do so; they can only do it because they believe it.

The commercial department's principal function was data management geared at building a one-to-one customer relationship. Database specialists fed information to the new product development team and the communications team to jointly determine and optimize marketing strategies. The Management Information Database (MIND) software combined transactional information with behavioral data to predict the next product a customer was likely to purchase. This database prompted BRs to cross-sell other financial services when clients called with routine requests and also helped personalize their conversations with customers:

Sylvia (BR): Hello, First Direct. How may I help you?

Mr Scott (Customer): Good evening, I would like to order some US dollars please.

Sylvia: Your account number, please?

Mr Scott: 58-395-123.

Sylvia: Thank you. Please bear with me while I verify some information for security reasons. Could you please give me the third digit of your password?

Mr Scott: Five.

Sylvia: And the date of your wedding anniversary?

Mr Scott: February 14th.

Sylvia: Thank you, Mr Scott. How many US dollars would you like to order?

Mr Scott: It depends. I'm going skiing in the States. Can you tell me if there is a cash machine in Vail, Colorado please?

Sylvia: I'll need to ask you to hold the line for a minute while I find that information for you sir.

Mr Scott: Thank you.

Sylvia: Hello, yes in fact there is a Cirrus ATM machine at the First Interstate Bank at 38 Redbird Drive in Vail.

Mr Scott: In that case, I'll only take $500 in cash with me and use the cash machine at the resort.

Sylvia: Right. I'll put in an order for $500. Shall I debit your cheque account and have the currency delivered by registered mail to your home address?

Mr Scott: Yes, please.

Sylvia: Thank you sir. You should receive it within three days. We'll include a confirmation of the amount deducted. Have a nice trip!

A few weeks later:

Peter (BR): Hello, First Direct. How may I help you?

Mr Scott: Good evening, I would like to make a payment to British Gas please. My account number with First Direct is 58-395-123.

Peter: Thank you. Please bear with me while I verify some information for security reasons. Could you please give me the first digit of your password please?

Mr Scott: Three.

Peter: And your mother's maiden name?

Mr Scott: Bradford.

Peter: Thank you Mr Scott. I'll be glad to arrange your payment to British Gas. By the way, were you able to find the First Interstate cash machine in Vail when you were on your skiing holiday in Colorado? I hope everything went well.

People and Development

First Direct was the largest private employer in Leeds with over 2,400 employees by early 1996; it projected to add an extra 550 by year-end. Most of the staff were between 20 and 40 years of age; nearly 69 per cent were women and 24 per cent part-timers. Recruitment was carried out continually via a 24-hour phone answering service that provided application information. Two meeting rooms adjacent to the lobby in Arlington were reserved exclusively for interviewing. It was becoming more difficult to recruit telephone advisers because Leeds had become a hub for call centres. (By 1996, there were over 350 24-hour centres within the United Kingdom in the retailing, banking and utility sectors.) The team leaders who interviewed the 60 BRs hired each month looked for people with a positive attitude who were enthusiastic about joining a first-class organization. First Direct also had a reputation for providing comprehensive training and a benefits package that included a mortgage subsidy, a pension scheme and 27 vacation days (*Exhibit 5*).

Recruited from a non-banking background, BRs did not come into contact with customers until they had successfully completed a seven-week training course conducted by 20 in-house trainers. Four weeks were devoted to understanding the bank's products and communication systems. They also practised telephone techniques such as voice projection skills to regulate the pitch and volume vital to create trust and confidence. The last three weeks concentrated on role-playing to build excellent listening skills and the ability to access and input data accurately and efficiently. Only a small part of the customer interaction was scripted for the beginning and end of conversations.

ExHIBIT 5 Banking Representative Recruitment Advertising

Banking representatives were encouraged to use what they thought were the right phrases, given the nature of the rapport. To become a full-fledged BR required passing a total of 54 internal accreditation tests over the first nine months of employment (*Exhibit 6*).

All the BRs were assigned to teams of individuals working the same shift pattern. A team leader acted as a coach and watched the customer service screens to make sure that everything ran smoothly and to identify any members who might need assistance. A lengthy call was a clear signal of a customer problem or complaint. There were over 100 teams in the two call centres with names like "Vernon's Vikings," "JJ and the Dinos," and "Hard Time Lovers." Sales competitions, product awareness sessions and theme days were organized regularly between the teams to bond people together.

The level of basic pay related to the market and to individual acquisition and development of skills rather than to the pay and grading structures of traditional banks. Annual appraisal ratings determined the level of performance bonuses that could go as high as 5 per cent of annual salary. Each year, nearly 30 per cent of the BR staff moved to other departments such

as lending services or mortgages. It took about 18 months to learn the job and to get to know the company before applying for other jobs. Such career opportunities helped keep turnover low at 11 per cent. In 1996, 40 per cent of the employees had been with the firm for at least three years.

First Direct's facilities reflected the needs of a 24-hour workforce. A private security firm manned the entrance to the car parks and reception areas throughout the night. The company restaurant served breakfast, lunch and dinner from 7 a.m. to 9 p.m. seven days a week while vending machines made hot and cold drinks available free of charge around the clock. Daycare centres at both Arlington and Stourton looked after 150 small children.

Marketing strategy

Management did not foresee telephone-only banking as having universal appeal. In fact, First Direct estimated that telephone banking would ultimately attract up to 10 million of the UK's 36 million bank customers. Most First Direct customers were between 25 and 44 years of age, living in metropolitan areas and working as professionals, managers or in high-

EXHIBIT 6 *First Direct Training Programmes*	
Customer service	Duration
Account operating	7 weeks
Back office	1 day
Customer development	1 day
Team leader development programme	Duration
Coaching & feedback	2 days
Motivation	2 days
Effective team leading	3 days
Time and priority management	2 days
Formal training for managers	Duration
Counselling skills	2 days
Developing your team	2 days
Influencing & assertion	2 days
Miscellaneous formal training courses	Duration
Presentation skills	1 day
Written communication skills	1 day
Interview skills	2 days
Appraisal skills	2 days

Source: First Direct, Training & Development Guide, May 1996.

EXHIBIT 7 *Comparative Customer Profiles: First Direct vs. All British Banks*

	First Direct customers	British bank customers
Age		
15–19	1%	9%
20–24	3%	6%
25–34	33%	20%
35–44	32%	17%
45–54	22%	16%
55–64	9%	13%
65+	0%	19%
Sex		
Male	50%	49%
Female	50%	51%
Socio-economic group		
AB	46%	19%
C1	36%	29%
C2	12%	23%
DE	6%	29%

British socio-economic group definitions

Grade	Social status	Occupation
A	Upper middle class	Higher managerial, administrative or professional
B	Middle class	Intermediate managerial, administrative or professional
C1	Lower middle class	Supervisory or clerical, and junior managerial, administrative or professional
C2	Skilled working class	Skilled manual workers
D	Working class	Semi- and unskilled manual workers
E	Lowest level of subsistence	State pensioners or widows, casual or lowest-grade workers

Sources: (1) First Direct NOP Survey, January 1996; Fieldwork November 1995–January 1996. (2)The Financial Research Survey NOP, April–September 1996.

grade clerical positions. Research also showed that about 50 per cent of its customers owned personal computers—twice the market average (*Exhibit 7*). These busy professionals were attracted by the offer of speed and convenience; their extensive use of the bank's services also generated higher profitability. A *New York Times* journalist estimated:

> The average balance is ten times higher at First Direct than at Midland, while the overall costs are 61% less. Overall, First Direct makes money on 60% of its customers, compared to 40% at the average British bank.   (3 September 1995)

First Direct rated several times among the "Best Buys" of *Which?* magazine's consumer reports on retail banking. It also won the 1995 *Unisys/Sunday Times* "Customer Champion Awards" for outstanding customer service in financial services and as overall winner. The First Direct brand seemed to create a service halo; research showed that First Direct customers had a satisfaction level with the ATM system double that of Midland Bank customers, even though they shared the identical network.

Among its full range of traditional banking services (*Exhibit 8*), First Direct featured its interest-bearing cheque account that offered an automatic fee-

EXHIBIT 8 *First Direct Products and Services*		
Type	**Product**	**Features**
Cheque	Interest-bearing cheque account	Interest-bearing, no fees
		£250 automatic fee-free overdraft
		Automatic bill payment
Debt/Credit cards	First Direct Debit Card	£100 cheque guarantee card
		£500 daily cash withdrawals from 7,000 ATMs
		Access to Switch* network
		Access to Cirrus and Maestro ATM network
	VISA Card	No annual fee
		56-day interest-free credit
		£500 daily cash withdrawals
		Membership Visa points programme
Savings & Investments	High interest Savings Account (HISA)	Unlimited withdrawals
	60-day accounts	Minimum deposit £2,500
		60-day notice for withdrawals
	Fixed Interest Savings Account	—
	Money Market Account	£5,000 minimum deposit
	Tax Exempt Savings Account (TESSA)	—
	Personal Equity Plan (PEP)	Medium- to long-term tax-free investment
	Share dealing	Buying or selling on London stock exchange
	Direct Interest Savings Account	High interest rates paid on balances over £1,000
		One free withdrawal or transfer per quarter
	Financial planning	Personal financial planning advice
Mortgages	Variable rate mortgages	25-year financing of 80 per cent of purchase price
	Home improvement loans	—
	Equity release loan	Financing from £3,000 of 95 per cent of home value
Loans	Flexiloan	Rolling loan plan between £500 and £10,000
		Variable interest rate
	Personal loan	—
Insurance	Car insurance	—
	Life insurance	—
	Home insurance	—
Travel services	Foreign currency/Traveller's cheques	Home delivery within 24 hours
	Travel insurance	12-month individual coverage

* Switch electronic debit card was launched in October 1988 by a consortium of three banks: Midland Bank, National Westminster Bank and Royal Bank of Scotland. It enabled purchases to be paid in supermarkets, petrol stations and shops using the Switch network in the UK.
Source: First Direct brochures, March 1996.

free overdraft facility of £250 and cash withdrawals of £500 a day subject to sufficient funds. However, fees accumulated rapidly if customers exceeded the agreed overdraft. First Direct encouraged customers to maximize short-term returns by frequently transferring money between their cheque accounts and multiple savings accounts. There were no transaction charges for any of First Direct's basic services. Advertising claimed that the lack of branches enabled it to pass on savings to customers. Even the Visa card was free of annual charges, offering up to 56 days' interest-free credit as well as free travel accident insurance. First Direct was also known to offer better interest rates on mortgages, personal loans and Visa cards (*Exhibit 9*).

While most UK banks marketed mortgages in the spring or car loans in July, First Direct's approach was

ExHIBIT 9 *Comparative Interest Rates: First Direct and Other British Banks*					
			VISA Card		
	NatWest	Lloyds	Royal Bank of Scotland	Barclays	First Direct
Card	Access/Visa	Access	Visa	Barclaycard	Visa
APR*	22.9%	22%	21.7%	21.6%	19.5%
Annual fee	£12	£12	£10	£10	none

* APR = Annual percentage rate.
Source: First Direct, February 1996.

		Variable Rate Mortgages			
	NatWest	Alliance & Leicester	Halifax	Abbey National	Barclays	First Direct
Interest rate	6.99%	6.99%	6.99%	7.04%	6.99%	6.69%
APR*	7.20%	7.20%	7.20%	7.30%	7.20%	6.90%

* APR = Annual percentage rate.
Source: First Direct, March 1996.

to mail customers information only when they needed it. When First Direct added car insurance in March 1995 to complement the life and household insurance products already offered, it adopted a soft-sell approach. BRs were prompted to collect car insurance renewal dates from customers and to record this information on the customer database. As renewal dates approached, customers received a quotation either in the mail or by phone.

Communications Strategy

The First Direct brand tried to communicate a no-frills, hassle-free approach to banking more in tune with customers' lifestyles. Matthew Higgins, market planning manager, explained:

> People do not see banks as a fundamental part of their lives. We are trying to market First Direct as a background activity. No bank should be at the top of customers' minds. The whole idea with First Direct is that it is efficient, easy, and available when you want it. You simply tap into it and then you go away and do something more interesting.

The purpose of First Direct's initial offbeat ad campaign was to break into a sluggish market by getting people to switch banks. This was a challenging task as it was an industry joke that the British were more likely to change their partners than their bankers. The launch advertising helped First Direct stand out in the crowded financial services market. In 1991, First Direct entrusted Chiat Day, a creative American agency, to invest £3 million in television commercials underlining its customers' extraordinary satisfaction with the new telephone bank. Unfortunately, the resulting campaign did not build the brand and First Direct stayed off the air for three years in search of new solutions. The 1995 television campaign also failed to develop the theme of banking and living in harmony.

Between 1991 and 1995, the press was used almost continuously to attract new customers through offers of high-quality service and no fees. As competition intensified, Chiat Day came out in 1993 with a press campaign to differentiate the pioneer from the new players. Simultaneously, First Direct mailed out brochures explaining the mechanics of telephone banking to a broad upscale audience. The mailing combined with the press ads generated an overwhelming number of customer enquiries. Unable to keep up with the demand, First Direct cut short the campaign so as not to compromise service quality.

Finally, in 1996, First Direct turned to WCRS, a major international advertising network, part of the EURO-RSCG group. Their brief revolved around the necessity of developing a more disciplined approach to building the First Direct brand. WCRS had a solid reputation for image development with clients like BMW cars and Orange mobile phones. Not until 1996 did television advertising demonstrate what it meant to bank with First Direct. Back on the air with two six-week bursts between January and April of 1996, the "Tell me one good thing about your bank" cam-

Tell me one good thing about your bank:

You don't get passed around from person to person when you want to open a new account.

I like the way they are on call 24 hours a day.

I was their first customer, they've got a half a million now.

I can settle my bills over the phone.

They always treat you like a grown-up.

There's no standing in queues.

I can get cash wherever I go.

There are no walls.

I don't have to get dressed to go to my bank.

It's easy.

They never sleep.

Freedom.

EXHIBIT 10 First Direct Television Advertising Slogans, 1996 Campaign
Source: First Direct 1996 television campaign—each spot (from 10 to 20 seconds) featured one of the above slogans as a response to "Tell me one good thing about your bank."

paign underlined the advantages of First Direct to attract dissatisfied customers from competitors. The £7 million television, radio, press and direct mail campaign raised meaningful brand awareness among the target audience from 30 per cent to 45 per cent (*Exhibit 10*).

Management Style, Organization and Culture

In February 1996, Newman restructured the business into five units that operated as profit centres: banking, savings and investments, lending, insurance and mortgages. Product management moved out of the commercial department into integrated operational units at the heart of the business. With this structure each business could eventually acquire customers directly. All the business unit heads reported to Richard Rushton who also managed the banking unit directly—including the call centre, the new customer team, customer service relations and enquiries, customer service support and business planning. All the central support functions such as IT, finance, operations, commercial, credit services and personnel and training were outside this structure.

Known for its leading edge management practices, First Direct attracted top quality managers. Only 50 per cent came from a banking background. Six directors reported to Newman: commercial, customer and financial services, information technology, personnel, finance, and credit services. Their principal task was to develop strategy and people through coaching, while Newman dealt directly with their subordinates on business issues. Thirty distinct roles were key within the organization, where individual accountability and competence were far more important than titles or functions. Although First Direct ran a business around the clock, most managers kept traditional 8 a.m. to 6 p.m. schedules, spending a great deal of time on the floor where they could get firsthand feedback from employees and a feel for service levels. Unlike traditional British banks, everyone was on a first name basis and ate in the same cafeteria. Newman firmly believed in leading by example; the only perk he enjoyed was a company car.

The corporate mission statement greeted all employees as they entered the lobby at each site:

Our mission: to be the best in the world of personal banking
Pioneering: the first 24-hour person-to-person telephone bank
Successful: UK's fastest growing bank
Responsive: the most satisfied bank customers in the UK

First Direct had earlier identified five core business values—responsiveness, openness, right first time, respect and contribution—which were a fundamental part of the training programme and widely shared by employees. This mindset made employees feel part of something special and it was reflected in the image projected to customers over the phone. In 1996 a sixth core value, "*kaizen*," or continuous improvement, was added following the suggestion of a new management hire. To get the entire organization focused on continuous innovation, the internal communications specialist launched a theme day during which the building was decorated in "*kaizen* yellow" and everyone wore T-shirts that they had decorated with coloured pens to express their own creativity.

The Challenges Ahead

In only seven years, First Direct had made a significant impact on the industry and had become a worldwide reference for telephone banking. By 1996, most banks and building societies offered their customers some form of direct access. Direct Line insurance had broadened its offering to include lending, mortgages and savings products to its two million policyholders. Furthermore, competition was now by no means restricted to banks, building societies or insurance companies. Richard Branson's Virgin Direct, launched in March 1995, subsequently introduced savings plans and low-cost life insurance via the telephone. Even the retailing chain Marks & Spencer offered life insurance from early 1995.

First Direct was constantly faced with the predicament of not compromising on service and price so as not to lose those customers who complained that it had grown too quickly. Yet to meet the objective of one million customers by the year 2000, First Direct needed to sign on another 400,000 people. Furthermore, First Direct recognized that its management methods might not necessarily be appropriate in the future. Management wondered how to keep all the strengths of the business and its innovative culture as, over the next five years, it grew to 10,000 employees located at four or five sites.

Critics charged that First Direct had not kept up with banking technology as it did not offer an on-line home banking service. This additional channel would provide increased convenience to customers while further reducing transaction costs. A significant minority of First Direct customers had spontaneously requested PC access to their accounts. Although the HSBC Group signed a deal with Microsoft in late 1995, First Direct did not expect to offer an on-line banking service until 1997. Newman explained his perspective:

> The mode of distribution is changing—at the moment we definitely see it as person-to-person over the telephone. Do we believe that people will bank electronically over the next ten years? We are not fussed about how quickly or by which means our customers choose to access all or part of their banking electronically. The elements for us are: when they do so what is the role of a bank, and how do we deliver competitive advantage in this environment? We must always remember that our "moments of truth" are the telephone contacts with the Banking Representatives. With PC access this disappears, thus limiting our opportunities. Creating value in an electronic world will be a key issue for First Direct. We like to think that we are not really in banking but distribution. We just happen to supply financial products.

Study Questions

1. *What factors enable a company to create and maintain good relationships with its customers? Evaluate First Direct's performance relative to these factors.*
2. *What are the relative roles of information technology and employees in First Direct's relationship building strategy?*
3. *What threats and opportunities face First Direct as it seeks to both retain existing customers and attract new ones?*
4. *What are the pros and cons for First Direct of moving into on-line home banking services? What are the implications for its relationships with customers?*
5. *Consider Kevin Newman's statement that "we are not really in banking but distribution." Do you agree? Why (or why not)?*
6. *What actions should Newman take?*

VerticalNet (www.verticalnet.com)

Das Narayandas

I am in the fastest-growing company that operates in the fastest-growing sector of the fastest-growing media.

These were the words with which VerticalNet CEO Mark Walsh described his job. As of October 1999, VerticalNet was the largest creator of targeted business-to-business vertical trade communities on the Internet (see *Exhibit 1*). The company owned and operated more than 50 industry-specific websites that were being accessed monthly by more than two million visitors worldwide. In addition to its strong balance sheet, VerticalNet had quickly built a strong brand name in the fledgling e-business industry. His company flush with funds raised through a May 1999 IPO and late-summer $115 million convertible debt offering, Walsh was now carefully planning the optimal mix between organic growth and planned acquisitions and alliances.

Walsh did not want his firm to run into the classic management problem of "too much diversification too fast." At the same time, he was keen that VerticalNet parlay its first-mover advantages into a position of strength by expanding the number of vertical communities under its umbrella. "It is very important," Walsh explained, "for us to move into the most attractive business-to-business (b2b) opportunities before anyone else gets in. I am a strong believer in first-mover advantages. But my experience . . . working for AOL has taught me that just getting in is not enough. We also need to leverage the power of numbers and achieve economies of scale and scope."

Walsh wanted also to ensure the success of the recent shift in VerticalNet's strategy, namely, from using content to build communities to trying to integrate e-commerce activities to extract greater value from those communities. "Until recently," Walsh observed,

> it appeared that firms could specialize in a specific area in the Internet space. Look at some of the current leading Internet-based models in the b2b space. We started with building communities using content. Ariba and Commerce One specialized in developing software that enabled large industrial companies to purchase more effectively from their supplier base. Chemdex created a catalog-based exchange in the scientific instruments and equipment industry to serve as a central location for sophisticated buyers and sellers to trade near-commodity products. Tradex got into developing software and systems for others interested in building exchanges. Companies like iMark.com and Adauctions.com used auction models to sell used capital equipment and perishable advertising inventory.

Now, all of a sudden, there is a blurring in the space that most of these firms operate in. Everybody wants to do everything: develop content; aggregate buyers and sellers; facilitate transactions; and build relationships.

Added Blair Lacorte, VerticalNet's senior vice president of corporate strategy:

> The b2b e-commerce world is set to explode over the next three to four years. [See *Exhibit 2* for growth forecasts.] At the same time, we expect that there will be a natural and painful evolution

Professor Das Narayandas prepared this case as the basis for class discussion rather than to illustrate either effective or ineffective handling of an administrative situation.

EXHIBIT 1 *VerticalNet's Communities*

VerticalNet, Inc. (*www.verticalnet.com*) owned and operated more than 50 industry-specific Web sites. These online business-to-business communities, termed vertical trade communities, provided users with comprehensive sources of information, interaction, and e-commerce. They were grouped into 10 sectors.

Advanced Technologies Group

Aerospace online (*aerospaceonline.com*) served engineers, managers, government officials, and consultants in the aerospace industry.

ComputerOEM online (*computeroemonline.com*) was concerned with the design and manufacture of computers and computerized electronics devices.

Embedded technology online (*embeddedtechnology.com*) was concerned with the design and manufacture of systems, computers, controls, software, and devices.

Medical design online (*medicaldesignonline.com*) was concerned with the design, manufacture, and procurement of medical devices.

Plant automation online (*plantautomation.com*) was concerned with hardware and software used in industrial manufacturing, including robotics and automated control systems.

Test and measurements online (*testandmeasurement.com*) was concerned with the design, manufacture and procurement of test, measurement, data acquisition, data analysis, and instrumentation equipment.

Communications Group

Digital broadcasting online (*digitalbroadcasting.com*) served broadcast, cable, satellite, and telco managers, engineers, consultants, and software developers involved in the digital television marketplace.

Fiber optics online (*fiberopticsonline.com*) was concerned with the design and production of fiber optic networks and network components.

Photonics online (*photonicsonline.com*) was concerned with the design and manufacture of lasers, optics, optoelectronics, fiber optics and imaging devices.

RF Globalnet (*rfglobalnet.com*) was the information, bookstore, and educational center for radio frequency, wireless and microwave.

Premises networks (*premisesnetworks.com*) was concerned with the facilities and network infrastructure design and administration.

Wireless design online (*wirelessdesignonline.com*) was concerned with design and development of wireless communications systems and equipment.

Environmental Group

Electricity online (*electricnet.com*) provided comprehensive coverage of transmission and distribution, trading, and convergence of energy services, as well as e-commerce services such as equipment auctions and industrial online purchasing.

Pollution online (*pollutiononline.com*) was concerned with industrial pollution control.

Public works online (*publicworks.com*) serviced public works and municipal maintenance.

Water online (*wateronline.com*) was concerned with municipal water supply and municipal and wastewater treatment.

Power online (*poweronline.com*) was concerned with power generation, electric utility deregulation, emissions control, alternative fuels, and power industry legislation.

Safety Online (*safetyonline.com*) was concerned with industrial and environmental safety.

Solid waste online (*solidwaste.com*) was concerned with the disposal of solid waste.

Pulp and paper online (*pulpandpaperonline.com*) was concerned with the manufacturing, processing, and treatment of pulp and paper.

Food and Packaging Group

Bakery online (*bakeryonline.com*) was concerned with the production and procurement of baking ingredients.

Beverage online (*beverageonline.com*) was concerned with the manufacture and procurement of equipment used in the production of beverages.

Dairy networks online (*dairynetwork.com*) was concerned with the production, procurement, and distribution of dairy products.

Food ingredients online (*foodingredientsonline.com*) was concerned with the manufacture and processing of food ingredients.

Meat and poultry online (*meatandpoultryonline.com*) was concerned with the production, procurement, and distribution of meat and poultry products.

Packaging networks online (*packagingnetwork.com*) was concerned with the production, purchase, design, and marketing of packaging for consumer and industrial products.

Food service/Hospitality Group

E-hospitality online (*e-hospitality.com*) provided travel and hospitality resources for corporate executives, managers, and food and beverage directors of international hotel chains and resorts as well as executive chefs, independent hoteliers, and suppliers.

Food services online (*foodservicecentral.com*) was concerned with food preparation and service.

Health Care Group

Dentistry online (*e-dental.com*) was concerned with dental and hygienist services.

Hospital networks online (*Hospital Network.com*) served professional hospital administrators.

Nurses online (*nurses.com*) served nurses and physicians' assistants.

Manufacturing and Metals

Machine tools online (*machinetoolsonline.com*). *Metrology online* (*metrologyworld.com*).

Surfacing/finishing online (*Surfacefinishing.com*). *Tooling online* (*toolingonline.com*).

Process Group

Chemical online (*chemicalonline.com*) was concerned with the manufacture and processing of chemicals.

Semiconductor online (*semiconductoronline.com*) was concerned with the manufacture, applications, and processing of semiconductor components.

Hydrocarbon online (*hydrocarbononline.com*) was concerned with the processing of hydrocarbons and petrochemicals.

Pharmaceuticals online (*pharmaceuticalonline.com*) was concerned with the development, design, and manufacture of pharmaceuticals.

Adhesives and sealants online (*adhesivesandsealants.com*) was concerned with the manufacture and production of adhesive, sealant, and grout materials.

Food online (*foodonline.com*) was concerned with the manufacture and processing of food products.

Oil and gas online (*oilandgasonline.com*) was concerned with oil and gas production and exploration.

Paint and coatings online (*paintandcoatings.com*) was concerned with the manufacture and production of paint coatings, inks, and thick film printable conductors.

Sciences Group

Bioresearch online (*bioresearchonline.com*)—served bio-research and the life sciences, including drug discovery, research and development and university industry collaborations, worldwide.

Laboratory networks online (*laboratorynetwork.com*) was concerned with the production and manufacture of laboratory equipment, chemicals, and supplies.

Drug discovery online (*drugdiscoveryonline.com*) was concerned with drug discovery and early stage drug development.

Services Group

Property and casualty online (propertyandcasualty.com) was concerned with property and casualty insurance.

Human resources online (*HR Hub.com*) was concerned with human resources.

Source: Company records

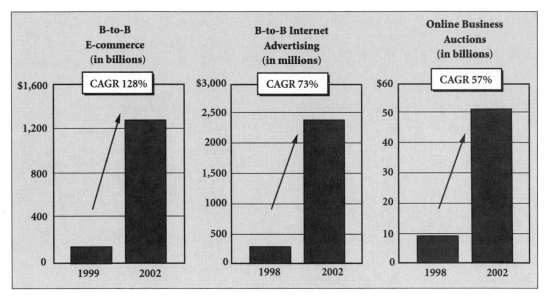

EXHIBIT 2 Projected Business-to-Business Auction and Advertising Growth through 2002
Source: Forester Research

of this nascent industry. Only the strongest and the fittest will survive and we want to make sure that we are one of them. We also want to make sure that we emerge in a strong and healthy position from this attrition game.

Asserted Walsh:

I want us to have the best "3 C" approach, where we combine *content,* editorial content from industry experts; *community,* a network by which professionals from particular industries can access sites to obtain information and search for employment opportunities; and *commerce,* a focused environment by which buyers and sellers can conduct their business. [*Exhibit 3* presents VerticalNet's projected growth strategy.]

In a world where almost any business plan with the words "Internet," "b2b," and "market maker" mentioned in the first three pages will probably receive some sort of funding, we expect to encounter a lot of competition, not all of which understands the complexity of business markets. We all know what happens when one is faced with competitors that are not mature. My job is to work with my management team and make sure that we weather the onslaught of a combination of smart and not-so-fully-baked competitors.

Learning from History

Walsh reflected on the history of early Internet initiatives.

Although the Internet has not been around for long, there are many valuable lessons that can be learned from it. Look at what happened to the old players in the Internet service provider space. Genie, Compuserve, Delphi, and Prodigy were all leaders in their time. They were technically advanced, rich, and complex. They were designed by engineers to be used by engineers. Along came AOL with a friendly GUI, a dumb-it-down approach, simple pricing, and a strong brand name. A look at the survivors tells you which of the two strategies worked. Being simple and building awareness amongst customers is always a winning strategy.

The same thing is now happening in the b2b space. On the buyer's side, early ventures in this world were by the large industrial companies. They used closed proprietary systems to manage their procurements. The objective was classic "command and control." Everything was within a firewall and everything was secured. Systems were designed to prevent a rogue employee from ordering even a dollar's worth of paper clips from unapproved suppliers. We believe that the Internet is not about control. It empowers buy-

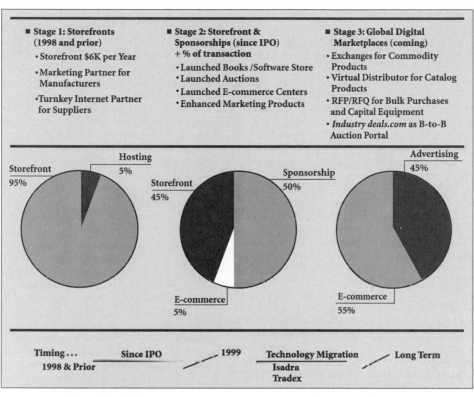

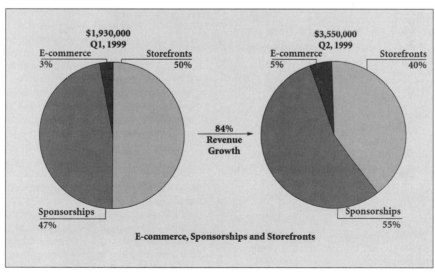

Exhibit 3 VerticalNet's Growth Strategy

Source: Company investor presentation, August 1999.

ers, not chains them. We are focused on creating simple, open, and customizable sites for buyers that are part of our vertical communities.

On the seller's side, the old world was about big companies that did not make the best product per se. It was about getting other things right, which gave these big firms the advantage. They were able to communicate more effectively, reach more customers, and provide better-augmented service. The Internet shatters the clout of big industrial selling organizations. By leveraging the power of the Internet, even small companies can serve global markets. Our communities are open to both large and small sellers. We have used the Internet to level the playing field.

The Beginnings of VerticalNet

The notion that the Internet would be the ideal venue for industrial companies to sell products such as valves and pumps occurred to Mike McNulty in 1995, while selling advertising space for *WaterWorld,* a trade journal that targeted sewage engineers. He and college buddy Mike Hagan, who gave up his job as a Merrill Lynch vice president to come on board, put up a home as loan collateral and used their credit cards to get the idea off the ground. The initial efforts generated sufficient momentum to enable them to secure $7 million from the Internet Capital Group of Wayne, Pennsynvania, and another $9 million from other firms. With this money McNulty and Hagan set up offices in Horsham, Pennsylvania (to be close to key b2b publications based in Philadelphia, New York, and Boston) and began to establish more sites for building communities in other vertical markets.

In September 1977, realizing that the firm's rapid growth necessitated a honed president and leader, Hagan and McNulty recruited Mark Walsh, a Harvard Business School graduate who had previously served as president of General Electric's now-defunct online service, Genie, and founded America Online's b2b division, AOL Enterprise. Respect for Walsh's experience was widespread in the Internet world; a senior executive in the industry acknowledged that Walsh was doing b2b e-commerce well before most of the current crop of Internet startup CEOs.

Under Walsh, VerticalNet continued to grow the number of vertical communities in its fold by extending a handshake to incumbent manufacturers, distributors, and customers in those vertical markets.

The VerticalNet Approach

"In order to succeed in the b2b space," explained Walsh,

it is important for one to understand that this is going to be an "inside out" game and not "outside in." The approach that most Internet age entrepreneurs or market makers have is one of replacing the existing world. In their minds, the current world is made up of dumb manufacturers, dumb distributors, and dumb customers. They think that manufacturers have no customer knowledge, that distributors don't add any value, and that customers have no idea of what they want or what they need. These entrepreneurs have just one maxim: the Internet is supposed to change everything. While there might be an element of truth in this, one needs to be careful about taking this approach . . . too far.

What most people don't realize is that industrial marketplaces have existed for a long, long time. In these worlds, everybody knows one another. It's all one big happy community. Yes, the manufacturers do compete with one another and so do the distributors. But when a new, external threat comes into the picture, there is a closing of the ranks. All of a sudden a common enemy unites all the existing players, who fight tooth and nail to preserve their world. When they close the door, it is all over for the new players. The road to success is to win each of the three constituencies. One needs to be a mini-Yahoo for this community.

In short, it is very important to not get out of the Trojan Horse until you are inside the castle.

Added Lacorte:

Consumer-oriented sites get a lot of hits from viewers who are continuously exploring new sites on the web. It is different in the b2b world. Given the nature of the business, there is a greater amount of self-selection among visitors to a b2b-oriented site. To begin with, it is difficult to imagine an average consumer wanting to visit a site devoted to solid waste even out of sheer curiosity. Further, virtually nobody will go twice by mistake to this site. However, if you are in that business you are very serious about the business and it is usually more than just idle curiosity that leads you to this site.

Imagine that you are an industrial buyer of paints and coatings. You are most likely to visit a site devoted to paints and chemicals with a clear purpose of collecting information and probably making purchases. When you visit such a site you expect to see a place that understands your frame of mind. You want to be in an environment that suggests that people who run the site actually care about the business. There is no doubt in our minds that b2b users are more critical in their evaluation of Internet sites.

There is another difference. In the b2b world transactions are also a lot about information. In addition to knowing how much the product costs and how it can be bought online, an industrial buyer would like to know about the products, the vendors, and the market itself. While in consumer markets it is primarily about price, in b2b markets it is about information, relationship, service, and support.

VerticalNet's Business Model

VerticalNet created, owned, and operated more than 50 vertical business-to-business trade communities on the Internet. It employed stringent criteria for choosing which vertical markets to enter. "The markets we enter need to be large in size, at least $8 billion in annual sales with over $10 million in advertising," explained Hagan.

> Next, the markets need to be fragmented [with] many buyers and many sellers. We don't want a few buyers or sellers to dominate the market. There also needs to be a history of new product/service introductions in the industry. The market should be global in nature with buyers and sellers coming from all parts of the world, North America, Europe, Japan, and other regions. Most of the buyers and sellers should already have on-line access to the Web. Finally, purchases should account for a significant percentage of the seller's revenues.
>
> By being very selective in our entry decision, we avoid the burden of having to educate the market, build critical mass, and then conduct business. We don't want to spend our precious resources creating markets; we prefer transforming ones that are ready for change.

VerticalNet's Web communities acted as comprehensive, industry-specific sources of information, interaction, and electronic commerce (e-commerce). They combined: product information, requests for proposals, discussion forums, e-commerce opportunities, industry news, directories, classifieds, job listings, online professional education courses, and virtual trade shows.

Each vertical trade community was individually branded, focused on a single industrial sector, and catered to individuals with similar professional interests. VerticalNet designed each of its trade communities to attract technical and purchasing professionals with highly specialized product and specification requirements and purchasing authority or influence.

The main objective was to satisfy a developing market not currently being adequately served through traditional channels such as trade publishers, trade shows, and trade associations. This was done by exploiting the interactive features and global reach of the Internet to enable buyers to research, source, contact, and purchase from suppliers (*Exhibit 4* presents details of current and planned features).

VerticalNet's portfolio strategy involved:

- offering a comprehensive, consistent set of features and functionality in its existing, and replicating these offerings in new, vertical trade communities;
- leveraging infrastructure, technology, and marketing and management resources to achieve economies of scale; and
- attracting a greater audience by making individual sites more appealing to a broader array of advertisers and e-commerce-enabled suppliers.

VerticalNet generated most of its revenues from Internet trade advertising, including the development of storefronts, Web pages posted on the vertical trade communities that provided links to advetisers' Web sites (*Exhibit 5* presents details of VerticalNet's storefronts). Advertising customers included more than 150 *Fortune* 500 firms such as Asea Brown Boveri, FMC Corporation, Hewlett-Packard, Koch Industries, Motorola, Schlumberger, and U.S. Filter.

VerticalNet's revenues increased from $965,000 for the six months ended June 30, 1998 to $5.5 million for the six months ended June 30, 1999 (*Exhibit 6* presents a balance sheet, *Exhibit 7* an income statement). Advertising revenues, including those derived from the development of storefronts,[1] accounted for a majority of revenues in both periods. VerticalNet had retained more than 90% of its 1998 advertisers to 1999. Barter transactions, whereby the firm received advertising revenues or other services in exchange for advertising on its Web sites, accounted for approximately 24% of total revenues for the six months ended June 30, 1999. E-commerce accounted for approximately 5% of VerticalNet's revenues.

Operating costs escalated from $1.1 million to $2.9 million during the same period owing primarily to the growing number of personnel and additional equipment required to maintain and operate VerticalNet's expanding base of vertical trade communities. Additional staffing and costs associated with enhancing features, content, and services of the vertical trade communities also drove up product development expenses, from $578,000 to $2.7 mil-

---

[1] During this period, the number of storefronts had grown from 833 to 2,094 *(see Exhibit 8)*.

EXHIBIT 4 *Features of VerticalNet's Online Communities*

Each VerticalNet trade community incorporated the following elements.

Marketplace. A shopping resource that enabled professionals to purchase books, software, and video products via the Internet.

Online Buyer's Guide and Search Engine. A comprehensive buyer's guide fully searchable by product name and supplier. Key word searches displayed companies serving an industry, with storefront advertisers presented first. Links to company storefronts enabled users to research advertisers' products and services and inquire directly about pricing, delivery, and product specifications (i.e., ultimately submit sales leads).

News and Analysis. News and commentary provided by the vertical trade community's editorial team, included feature articles and product case studies, daily updates of press releases, and industry-specific news stories.

Product Center. A comprehensive industry information resource for professionals. Site editors provided objective, third-party analyses of products and their uses.

Community. A suite of interactive features that included real-time discussion forums and bulletin boards for industry professionals and information about trade shows and other industry events.

Resources. "Freeware" and demo-software download library and industry association guides.

Career Center. Resumepostings for job seekers, help-wanted listings, and career support material.

Requests for Proposals/Quotations/Bids. Internationally posted projects open to bid.

VerticalNet had begun to selectively offer additional products and services in some of its vertical trade communities. Among these were:

Education/Training. Products in the continuing professional education, licensing/certification maintenance, and skills upgrade markets, specifically:
- online courses and courseware, including books, software, focused content, and research available for use or purchase in conjunction with courses offered by third party vendors; and
- company-specific: customized intranet or extranet-based education and training services organized by vertical trade community.

Career Center. Career centers active on a number of vertical trade communities offered such services as resume bundling (e.g., selling or offering for a fee groups of candidate types to specific employers) and career planning and assistance (e.g., providing resume software and salary surveys, market reports on companies being investigated by candidates).

"Push" Newsletters. Subscription-based e-mail services, including e-mail-based newsletters with specific content focus.

Electronic Commerce. Commerce-related services that had begun to be offered to advertisers and users included:
- *online stores* (easy-to-use store creation software supported VerticalNet's creation of interactive platforms that enabled advertisers to sell products in easy-to-manage environments);
- *catalog-platforms* that enabled VerticalNet to help advertisers and industry-specific distributors create and populate Internet-based catalogs;
- *classifieds* (launched in several vertical trade communities, these listed individual products and paths to specific sellers);
- *auctions* (launched in several vertical trade communities, these were online listings of new and used industrial equipment; and
- *e-mail service* (free e-mail accounts to be provided to users and registrants in each vertical trade (community by third-party partners were to be supported by the sale of advertising on the e-mail pages).

Source: Company records.

> **EXHIBIT 5** *Features of VerticalNet's Storefronts*
>
> A typical VerticalNet-supported advertiser storefront included the following elements.
>
> **Corporate Profile.** Advertiser background information and product overviews.
>
> **Contact Us.** Supported buyers' and specifiers' e-mail requests for pricing and other product information. Inquiries were often regarded as sales leads by advertisers.
>
> **Career Center.** Listed employment opportunities with advertisers.
>
> **Purchase Online.** Enabled advertisers with electronic commerce capabilities to sell their products online.
>
> **Associated Articles.** Accumulated articles, case studies, and other informational materials about advertisers.
>
> **Product Releases/More Products.** New product announcements.
>
> **Press Releases.** Advertiser-issued press releases.
>
> **Virtual Office.** Enabled storefront advertisers to monitor and evaluate storefront activity (e.g., track numbers of visitors and leads generated by a storefront or banner advertisement) and served as an inquiry management tool.
>
> *Source:* Company records.

lion. Finally, marketing and promotion expenses had jumped from $2.6 million to $9.2 million, reflecting a number of firm-initiated activities. As of June 1999, VerticalNet had accumulated a deficit of $31.7 million, approximately $6.8 million of which had been incurred in the three months ended June 30, 1999.

The Changing Nature of VerticalNet's Revenue Sources

VerticalNet CFO Gene Godick was hoping that within four to five years more than half the company's revenues would be derived from e-commerce transacted at its sites. "We are currently," he explained,

a cross between a trade magazine and a matchmaker that links buyers and sellers that might not have known of each other's existence before the Web [*Exhibit 9* presents screen shots of VerticalNet communities]. One of the benefits of our size is that users can search outside their industry without leaving our site. But this size effect means little if we are not able to also make our communities uniquely attractive.

"Our future success," added McNulty,

depends on our ability to deliver compelling Internet content about various industries that will attract users with demographic characteristics valuable to our advertising customers. Given that Internet users can freely navigate and instantly switch among a large number of Web sites, we have to continuously work hard to distinguish our content and retain our current users while attracting new users all the time. This means that, in addition to our skilled in-house staff, we rely on third parties such as trade publi-

cations and news wires to provide some of the content for our vertical trade communities. It is therefore very critical to our business that we maintain and build our existing relationships with content providers.

We also need to continue to strengthen brand awareness of the "VerticalNet" brand as well as of the brands associated with each individual vertical trade community, for example, *www.wateronline.com*. We believe that brand recognition will become more important in the future with the growing number of Internet sites.

Walsh described the need, from a revenue growth perspective, to broaden VerticalNet's focus from community building and selling advertisements and storefront space. "Currently," he explained,

we base our storefront advertising rates on a variety of factors, including the maturity of the particular vertical trade community, number of storefronts, amount of other advertising purchased, and length of the advertising contract. There is growing support within the firm to move away from this approach to one where advertising rates are based on parameters such as the number of sales inquiries generated or visitors sent from our vertical trade communities to advertisers' Web sites. This move would be a major departure for us since we would . . . change from renting space and charging for ads to taking a percentage of the transactions we facilitate.

The main resistance to this move comes from people who think that most of the transactions will not be completed in our environment. Several industry analysts believe that buyers and

	12/31/96	12/31/97	12/31/98 (proforma)	Six Months Ending 6/30/99
Assets				
Current assets:				
Cash and cash equivalents	$754,716	$5,662,849	$61,984,849	$20,235,068
Short-term investments	—	—	—	12,480,457
Accounts receivable, net of allowance for doubtful accounts of $30,000, $61,037, _____, and $185,947, respectively	607,611	1,806,054	1,806,054	4,446,631
Loan receivable, net of allowance of $80,000 in 1997	84,086	—	—	390,000
Prepaid expenses	145,678	736,625	736,625	2,555,708
Total current assets	1,592,091	8,205,528	64,527,528	40,107,864
Property and equipment, net	491,853	1,072,063	1,072,063	1,816,460
Goodwill and other intangibles, net of accumulated amortization of $282,990 in 1998, pro forma, and $893,459 in 1999, respectively	—	2,451,991	2,451,991	8,159,583
Long-term investments	—	—	—	14,376,407
Deferred charges and other assets	20,143	613,393	613,393	1,809,617[a]
Total assets	$2,104,087	$12,342,975	$68,664,975	$66,269,931
Liabilities and Shareholders' Equity (Deficit)				
Current liabilities:				
Current portion of long-term debt	$150,856	$288,016	288,016	$823,480
Line of credit	2,500,000	2,000,000	—	—
Accounts payable	607,479	1,220,562	1,220,562	1,896,362
Accrued expenses	158,936	1,582,038	1,582,038	2,372,080
Deferred revenues	710,393	2,176,585	2,176,585	5,820,222
Total current liabilities	4,127,664	7,267,201	5,267,201	10,912,144
Long-term debt, net of current portion	399,948	351,924	351,924	517,293
Convertible notes	—	5,000,000	—	
Commitments and contingencies				
Shareholders' Equity (Deficit):				
Preferred stock Series A, B, C, and Preferred stock Series A, B, C, and D: $.01 par value, 40,000,000 shares authorized, 3,247,262, 7,805,667, and 0 shares issued and outstanding in 1997, 1998, and pro forma 1998, respectively	32,473	78,057	—	
Common stock $.01, par value, 40,000,000 shares authorized, 2,526,865, 2,634,379, 16,706,724, 16,946,943 shares issued, outstanding in 1997, 1998, pro forma 1998, and 1999, respectively	25,269	26,344	167,067	169,469
Additional paid-in capital	3,277,344	19,566,368	82,825,702	87,503,466
Deferred compensation	—	(594,033)	(594,033)	(885,405)
Accumulated deficit	(5,698,611)	(19,292,886)	(19,292,886)	(31,662,355)[b]
	(2,363,525)	(216,150)	63,105,850	54,992,481
Treasury stock at cost	(60,000)	(60,000)	(60,000)	(151,987)
Total shareholders' equity (deficit)	(2,423,525)	(276,150)	63,045,850	54,840,494
Total liabilities and shareholders' equity (deficit)	$2,104,087	$12,342,975	$68,664,975	$66,269,931

Source: Company Offering Documents, September 1999.
[a]Includes $1,220,261 of unrestricted cash.
[b]Adjusted for accumulated loss of $132,694 in 1999.

| Exhibit 7 | VerticalNet, Inc. Consolidated Financial Information (Income Statement) through June 30, 1999 | | | |

Annual Reporting, 1996–1998	Year Ending 12/31/96	Year Ending 12/31/97	Year Ending 12/31/98
Revenues	$285,140	$791,822	$3,134,769
Costs and Expenses:			
Editorial and operational	213,544	1,055,725	3,237,971
Product development	213,926	711,292	1,404,557
Sales and marketing	268,417	2,300,365	7,894,662
General and administrative	291,660	1,388,123	3,823,593
Amortization of goodwill	—	—	282,990
Operating loss	(702,407)	(4,663,683)	(13,509,004)
Interest and dividend income	7,491	10,999	212,130
Interest expense	(13,931)	(126,105)	(297,401)
Interest, net	(6,440)	(115,106)	(85,271)
Net loss	($708,847)	($4,778,789)	($13,594,275)
Basic and diluted net loss per share	($0.27)	($1.89)	($5.29)
Weighted average shares outstanding used in per-share calculation (basic and diluted)	2,583,648	2,526,865	2,570,550

Quarterly and Semiannual Reporting, 1998–1999	3 Months Ending 06/30/99	3 Months Ending 06/30/98	6 Months Ending 06/30/99	6 Months Ending 06/30/98
Revenues	$3,551,180	$587,422	$5,484,959	$964,793
Costs and Expenses:				
Editorial and operational	1,688,619	689,644	2,884,756	1,124,977
Product development	1,485,066	385,378	2,694,704	578,258
Sales and marketing	5,546,602	1,679,469	9,176,807	2,614,403
General and administrative	1,970,435	718,734	3,350,071	1,541,893
Amortization of goodwill	335,902	—	610,469	—
Operating loss	(7,475,444)	(2,885,803)	(13,231,848)	(4,894,738)
Interest, net	714,733	14,291	862,379	(61,643)
Net loss	($6,760,711)	($2,871,512)	($12,369,469)	($4,956,381)
Basic and diluted net loss per share	($0.40)	($1.13)	($0.91)	($1.96)
Weighted average shares outstanding used in basic and diluted per-share calculation	16,848,309	2,540,014	13,520,933	2,533,475

Source: Company offering documents, September 1999.

sellers are likely to make contact in our communities, but prefer to transact in the conventional way, face-to-face. They feel that we would have a lot of difficulty enforcing payments in these situations.

On the other hand, a growing segment of managers in VerticalNet thinks that we are leaving a lot of money on the table. Let me give you an example. Let's assume that a valve manufacturer sells valves at $5,000 each to 50 customers that it meets in our communities, buyers that visit its storefront. By charging 5% of the sale value per transaction, we could get as much as $12,500 from this customer.

Currently, we charge about $7,000 to $8,000 per year for firms to have storefronts on our sites.

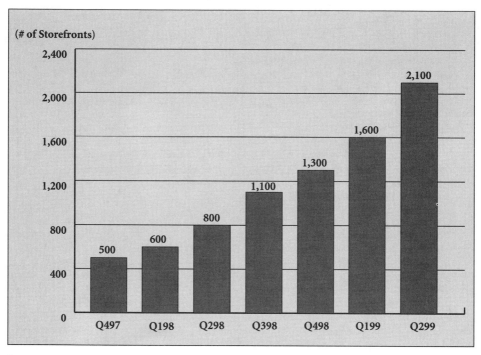

(# of Storefronts)

Exhibit 8 Internet Storefront Proliferation, Q4 1997 through June 30, 1999
Source: Company investor presentation, August 1999.

As you can see from my example, we could charge a small percentage of every transaction that takes place on the storefronts designed by us and still make a lot of money. Manufacturers would also be very happy since we offer them a digital sales arm to get sales that they would never have received otherwise. We have recently set up a higher level storefront, or e-commerce center, that we offer our customers at $15,000 per year. I think this is a very good idea. However, we can do much more in terms of creating and extracting customer value.

By the way, not too many people understand that we have always been an e-commerce play. Each time a buyer visits a storefront they leave rich information on what they want, when, and in what quantities. If we were to consolidate all this information we could create extensive lists of valuable sales leads and sell them. . . . Our customers would love this because they are going to get more bids without having to spend any more effort.

"A few months back," recalled McNulty,

we surveyed a large number of the buyers who visited our web sites. We found that over 20% of the buyers who said they were interested in purchasing specific products or services actually did buy within the next six months or were still actively considering the purchase. Over half of these customers had never done business with the seller prior to the current transaction. The average transaction amount was over $25,000. As you can see, by generating high-quality leads we were facilitating e-commerce even before we formally talked about it.

To manage the migration from content to commerce, VerticalNet had made strategic acquisitions and forged important alliances. McNulty explained.

Recently we bought a company called Isadra, *www.isadra.com,* that is engaged primarily in the development of information technology that integrates sources from multiple locations without regard to the hardware or software environment. This acquisition is going to help us create a search engine that will allow buyers to run "parametric" searches on vendor catalogs in the vari-

EXHIBIT 9 Sample Virtual Communities
Source: Company website.

ous communities in order to find and compare products quickly. Our alliance and equity investment with Tradex, *www.tradex.com,* will allow us to offer our customers the opportunity to create and respond to RFPs and RFQs. Using our relationship with webMethods, *www.webmethods.com* we will be able to provide ERP integration for our buyers and their relationships with their suppliers. We are also able to offer our customers financing vehicles through partners like BancOne and First USA. In the future, we plan to offer letters of credit and other financial services that will further facilitate transactions.

Acquisitions and alliances like this will help us create a friendlier user environment and keep us ahead of the competition. These moves will also help us address some of the industry analysts' concerns that we are too supplier-centric and content focused and that we are not comprehensive enough in our offerings to be a destination for industrial buyers and sellers.

The Changing Nature of Competition

In its current space, VerticalNet competed for a share of customers' advertising budgets with both online services and traditional off-line media, including print publications and trade associations. Although no company had a larger portfolio of vertical trade communities than VerticalNet, a number of companies had begun to offer competitive communities on a standalone or portfolio basis. New York-based Winstar Communications, a provider of telecom equipment to small businesses, had, for example, announced plans to launch Office.com, with more than a dozen categories and an eventual plan to reach professionals in 120 categories, including various engineering specialties, lawyers, doctors, and computer programmers. Cahner's Business Information, a leading trade magazine publisher located close to VerticalNet in the Philadelphia area, had its own b2b portal, 23 Cahners industrial trade magazines collectively termed Manufacturing.Net.

McNulty was cautious about defining VerticalNet's competition. "Given the direction of our firm," he reflected, "it is important to understand that our competition is not just the community builders. We would be shortsighted if we took such an approach. In my mind, we need to view everybody . . . in the b2b e-commerce space as a competitor."

Transitioning the Selling Effort

Because VerticalNet's salesforce comprised primarily seasoned salespeople who had sold in the publishing business, "Our sales reps," maintained Lacorte,

are able to convince marketing managers of small- and mid-sized manufacturers to buy retail and advertising space on our Web sites, something that they have always done in their professional careers. Selling e-commerce solutions is a different ball game. Now they will need to move beyond their comfort zone and start selling to CEOs, CIOs, and MIS professionals, among others. The focus will be on technical issues of how to conduct e-commerce and on strategic issues of why the firms need to supplement their current sales effort using the Internet. We need to make sure that we train them and support them to manage this migration.

Added Walsh:

We have to decide whether we manage the selling effort ourselves or we seek the help of partners. If we decide not to do it all ourselves, the first group of potential partners that comes to mind is the traditional publishing houses. Given their large salesforces these players offer an attractive option for us. There is the issue of whether they would be interested in working with us. The second option is firms like IBM or Oracle that sell e-solutions to industrial companies. We can offer to sell them in bulk storefronts that they can resell individually to their customers.

Issues

Walsh framed the issues VerticalNet faced. "In a way," he explained,

it is a question of doing more of what we do currently versus doing more than what we do currently. As of now we have decided to do both. However, it is important for us to understand that there might be less than expected synergy between these two moves. The "doing more of the same" approach pushes us towards identifying new markets for which we can build vertical communities. This could include focusing on international markets. The "doing more than what we currently do" approach takes us down the e-commerce route. We move away from being focused only on content and facilitating information transfer towards creating and managing transactions and exchanges.

In my mind the only bottom-line consequence is the added value that we bring to the table. I believe that we are rapidly approaching the time when we can turn around and ask our communities to give us a share of the additional value we create for them. We are in a stronger

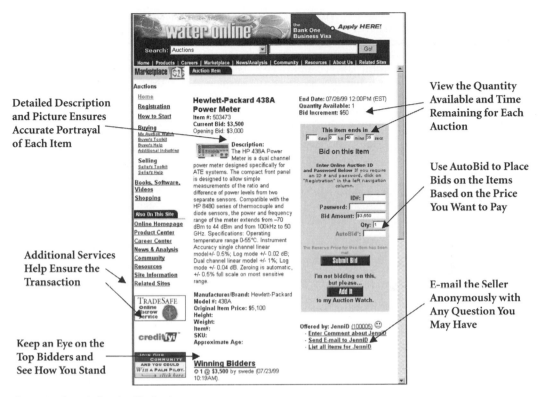

Detailed Description and Picture Ensures Accurate Portrayal of Each Item

View the Quantity Available and Time Remaining for Each Auction

Use AutoBid to Place Bids on the Items Based on the Price You Want to Pay

Additional Services Help Ensure the Transaction

E-mail the Seller Anonymously with Any Question You May Have

Keep an Eye on the Top Bidders and See How You Stand

EXHIBIT 10 Sample Auction Mechanism
Source: Company website.

position than any other player is in the business to harness the benefits of b2b e-commerce. We should be able to move quickly from what we are today to successfully offering a portfolio of services that includes:

- e-commerce centers or transaction-enabled storefronts;
- online auctions where multiple buyers bid on a seller's excess or obsolete inventory;
- electronic marketplaces that aggregate electronic catalogs from suppliers in a vertical market; and
- on-line exchanges or marketplaces for near commodities that enable multiple buyers and suppliers to conduct commerce.

We want to become the AOL-Yahoo-eBAY-Amazon bundle for each of our communities. Let me give you an example of how fast we have been moving. In the span of less than six months we have already deployed auction sites across 25

of our vertical markets. The average price per item is $3,750 and the on-line inventory is around $30 million. I expect this to go to $300 million very soon. We just bought LabX, *www.labx.com,* which has a huge inventory of laboratory equipment that will be available through our auction sites across several of our verticals. Our goal to is to create the biggest b2b auction portal, it is called industrydeals.com. [*Exhibit 10* presents an example of a currently available auction site.]

There is some concern in the industry that size can play against us by reducing our ability to move quickly. Given that there is enormous change, everybody in the Internet space will need to continually adapt to new models that will keep popping up in the b2b e-commerce space. Rather than a concern, I see our portfolio play as a unique competitive advantage. There is no textbook that explains how things are going to evolve in the b2b e-commerce space. Experience is going to win over everything else. With a clear understanding of which of our communities are likely to be more conducive to the e-commerce transition and which are better off being managed with our current, content-laden, community building approach, we can leverage our portfolio to experiment and learn faster than anyone else. We can make mistakes, learn from them, and survive, a risk our more focused competitors can ill-afford.

Conclusion

Walsh observed, reflecting on the issues at hand, "In addition to the external angle of managing markets, customers, and competitors that change at hyperspeed, there is also an internal angle that needs to be understood."

Managing an Internet-related business is not very easy. In the past, one could judge the health of a company by looking at the finished goods leaving the plant every evening or the inventory lying on the shop floor. There was no better way to motivate people than to make a big deal of the turbine that was being shipped out of the plant. The Internet world is very different. Everything is ephemeral. There is nothing else. In this world you need to use other approaches to motivate your people. It's all about celebrations, highfives, and special briefcase awards. It's also about doing new and exciting things all the time.

Being a manager in the new world requires a set of skills that are poles apart from those required to run large companies in traditional industries. In the past managing a firm was like being on the bridge of an oil supertanker. Do you know that it takes these giant ships over five miles to turn around? If you did not anticipate a change in course well in advance, don't even bother, you are not going to be on track anyway. Today, it is more like being on a raft in the Colorado River. There is little or no time to make decisions. There is a new surprise every instant. The name of the game is avoiding the boulders and trying to survive. While each situation has its own challenges, I definitely like the pace of my world.

Study Questions

1. *What do you see as the key factors for succeeding in b2b markets?*
2. *What are the advantages and disadvantages of VerticalNet's portfolio model?*
3. *Does it make sense for VerticalNet to move from content to commerce? Is it realistic to aim to become an "eBay-Yahoo-AOL-Amazon" all rolled into one?*
4. *Walsh is concerned about "too much diversification too fast." Is this concern justified?*
5. *What advice would you give Walsh?*

Menton Bank

Christopher Lovelock

Problems arise when a large bank, attempting to develop a stronger customer service orientation, enlarges the tellers' responsibilities to include selling activities

"I'm concerned about Karen," said Margaret Costanzo to David Reeves. The two bank officers were seated in the former's office at Menton Bank. Costanzo was a vice president of the bank and manager of the Victory Square branch, the third largest in Menton's 292 branch network. She and Reeves, the branch's customer service director, were having an employee appraisal meeting. Reeves was responsible for the customer service department, which coordinated the activities of the customer service representatives (CSRs, formerly known as tellers) and the customer assistance representatives (CARs, formerly known as new accounts assistants).

Costanzo and Reeves were discussing Karen Mitchell, a 24-year-old customer service rep, who had applied for the soon-to-be-vacant position of head CSR. Mitchell had been with the bank for three and a half years. She had applied for the position of what had then been called head teller a year earlier, but the job had gone to a candidate with more seniority. Now that individual was leaving—his wife had been transferred to a new job in another city—and the position was once again open. Two other candidates had also applied for the job.

Both Costanzo and Reeves were agreed that, against all criteria used in the past, Karen Mitchell would have been the obvious choice for head teller. She was both fast and accurate in her work, presented a smart and professional appearance, and was well liked by customers and her fellow CSRs. However, the nature of the teller's job had been significantly revised nine months earlier to add a stronger marketing component (*Exhibit 1* shows the previous job description for teller; *Exhibit 2* shows the new job description for customer service representative.) CSRs were now expected to offer polite suggestions that customers use automated teller machines (ATMs) for simple transactions. They were also required to stimulate customer interest in the broadening array of financial services offered by the bank. "The problem with Karen," as Reeves put it, "is that she simply refuses to sell."

The New Focus on Customer Service at Menton Bank

Although it was the largest bank in the region, Menton had historically focused on corporate business and its share of the retail consumer banking business had declined in the face of aggressive competition from other financial institutions. Three years earlier, the Board of Directors had appointed a new chief executive officer (CEO) and given him the mandate of developing a stronger consumer orientation at the retail level. The goal was to seize the initiative in marketing the ever-increasing array of financial services now available to retail customers. The CEO's strategy, after putting in a new management team, was to begin by ordering an expansion and speed-up of Menton's investment in electronic delivery systems, which had fallen behind the competition. To achieve this strategy, a new banking technology team had been created.

During the past eighteen months, the bank had tripled the number of automated teller machines located inside its branches, replacing older ATMs by

EXHIBIT 1 *Menton Bank: Previous Job Description for Teller*

FUNCTION: Provides customer services by receiving, paying out, and keeping accurate records of all moneys involved in paying and receiving transactions. Promotes the bank's services.

Responsibilities

1. Serves Customers
—Accepts deposits, verifies cash and endorsements, and gives customers their receipts.
—Cashes checks within the limits assigned or refers customers to supervisor for authorization.
—Accepts savings deposits and withdrawals, verifies signatures, and posts interest and balance as necessary.
—Accepts loan, credit card, utility, and other payments.
—Issues money orders, cashier's checks, traveler's checks, and foreign currency.
—Reconciles customer statements and confers with bookkeeping personnel regarding discrepancies in balances or other problems.
—Issues credit card advances.

2. Prepares individual daily settlement of teller cash and proof transactions

3. Prepares branch daily journal and general ledger

4. Promotes the bank's services
—Cross-sells other bank services appropriate to customer's needs.
—Answers inquiries regarding bank matters.
—Directs customers to other departments for specialized services.

5. Assists with other branch duties
—Receipts night and mail deposits.
—Reconciles ATM transactions.
—Provides safe deposit services.
—Performs secretarial duties.

new models featuring color touch screens and capable of a broader array of transactions. Menton was already a member of several ATM networks, giving its customers access to freestanding 24-hour booths in shopping centers, airports, and other high-traffic locations. The installation of new ATMs was coupled with a branch renovation program, designed to improve the cosmetic appearance of the branches. Longer term, top management intended to redesign the interior of each branch; a pilot program to test the impact of these "new look" branches was already underway. As more customers switched to electronic banking from remote locations, the bank planned to close a number of its smaller branches.

Another important move had been to introduce automated telephone banking, which allowed customers to check account balances and to move funds from one account to another by touching specific keys on their telephone in response to the instructions of a computerized voice. This service was available 24 hours a day, every day of the year, and utilization was rising steadily. Customers could also call a central cus-

tomer service office to speak with a bank representative concerning service questions or problems with their accounts, as well as to request new account applications or new checkbooks, which would be sent by mail. This office currently operated on weekdays from 8:00 A.M. to 8:00 P.M. and on Saturdays between 8:00 A.M. to 2:00 P.M., but Menton was evaluating the possibility of expanding the operation to include a broad array of retail bank services, offered on a 24-hour basis.

Finally, the technology team had just introduced home banking via the Internet. This service could be accessed through the bank's Web site, which also contained information about bank services, branch locations and service hours, location of ATMs, and answers to commonly asked questions. All these actions seemed to be bearing fruit. In the most recent six months, Menton had seen a significant increase in the number of new accounts opened, as compared to the same period of the previous year. And quarterly survey data showed that Menton Bank was steadily increasing its share of new deposits in the region.

Customer Service Issues

New financial products had been introduced at a rapid rate. But the bank found that many existing "platform" staff—known as new accounts assistants—were ill equipped to sell these services because of lack of product knowledge and inadequate training in selling skills. As Costanzo recalled:

> The problem was that they were so used to sitting at their desks waiting for a customer to approach them with a specific request, such as a mortgage or car loan, that it was hard to get them to take a more positive approach that involved actively probing for customer needs. Their whole job seemed to revolve around filling out forms. We were way behind most other banks in this respect.

As the automation program proceeded, the mix of activities performed by the tellers started to change. A growing number of customers were using the ATMs and automated telephone banking for a broad array of transactions, including cash withdrawals and deposits (from the ATMs), transfers of funds between accounts, and requesting account balances. The ATMs at the Victory Square branch had the highest utilization of any of Menton's branches, reflecting the large number of students and young professionals served at that location. Costanzo noted that customers who were older or less well-educated seemed to prefer being served by "a real person, rather than a machine."

A year earlier, the head office had selected three branches, including Victory Square, as test sites for a new customer service program, which included a radical redesign of the branch interior. The Victory Square branch was in a busy urban location, about one mile from the central business district and less than 10-minutes' walk from the campus of a large university. The branch was surrounded by retail stores and close to commercial and professional offices. The other test branches were among the bank's larger suburban offices in two different metropolitan areas and were located in a shopping mall and next to a big hospital, respectively.

As part of the branch renovation program, each of these three branches had previously been remodeled to include no fewer than four ATMs (Victory Square had six), which could be closed off from the rest of the branch so that they would remain accessible to customers 24 hours a day. Further remodeling was then undertaken to locate a customer service desk near the entrance; close to each desk were two electronic information terminals, featuring color touch-screens that customers could activate to obtain information on a variety of bank services. The teller stations were redesigned to provide two levels of service: an express

station for simple deposits and for cashing of approved checks, and regular stations for the full array of services provided by tellers. The number of stations open at a given time was varied to reflect the volume of anticipated business and staffing arrangements were changed to ensure that more tellers were on hand to serve customers during the busiest periods. Finally, the platform area in each branch was reconstructed to create what the architect described as "a friendly, yet professional appearance."

Human Resources

With the new environment came new training programs for the staff of these three branches and new job descriptions and job titles: customer assistance representatives (for the platform staff), customer service representatives (for the tellers), and customer service director (instead of assistant branch manager). The head teller position was renamed head CSR. Position descriptions for all these jobs are reproduced in *Exhibits 2–5*. The training programs for each group included sessions designed to develop improved knowledge of both new and existing retail products. (CARs received more extensive training in this area than did CSRs.) The CARs also attended a 15-hour course, offered in three separate sessions, on basic selling skills. This program covered key steps in the sales process, including building a relationship, exploring customer needs, determining a solution, and overcoming objections.

The sales training program for CSRs, by contrast, consisted of just two 2-hour sessions designed to develop skills in recognizing and probing customer needs, presenting product features and benefits, overcoming objections, and referring customers to CARs. All staff members in customer service positions participated in sessions designed to improve their communication skills and professional image: clothing and personal grooming and interactions with customers were all discussed. Said the trainer, "Remember, people's money is too important to entrust to someone who doesn't look and act the part!"

CARs were instructed to rise from their seats and shake hands with customers. Both CARs and CSRs were given exercises designed to improve their listening skills and their powers of observation. All employees working where they could be seen by customers were ordered to refrain from drinking soda and chewing gum on the job. (Smoking by both employees and customers had been banned some years earlier under the bank's smoke-free office policy.)

Although Menton Bank's management anticipated that most of the increased emphasis on selling would fall to the CARs, they also foresaw a limited selling role for the customer service reps, who would

EXHIBIT 2 *Menton Bank: New Job Description for Customer Service Representative*

FUNCTION: Provides customers with the highest quality services, with special emphasis on recognizing customer need and cross-selling appropriate bank services. Plays an active role in developing and maintaining good relations.

Responsibilities

1. Presents and communicates the best possible customer service
—Greets all customers with a courteous, friendly attitude.
—Provides fast, accurate, friendly service.
—Uses customer's name whenever possible.

2. Sells bank services and maintains customer relations
—Cross-sells retail services by identifying and referring valid prospects to a customer assistance representative or customer service director. When time permits (no other customers waiting in line), should actively cross-sell retail services.
—Develops new business by acquainting non-customers with bank services and existing customers with additional services that they are not currently using.

3. Provides a prompt and efficient operation on a professional level
—Receives cash and/or checks for checking accounts, savings accounts, taxes withheld, loan payments, Mastercard, Visa, mortgage payments, money orders, traveler's checks, cashier's checks.
—Verifies amount of cash and/or checks received, being alert to counterfeit or fraudulent items.
—Cashes checks in accordance with bank policy. Watches for stop payments and holds funds per bank policy.
—Receives payment of collection items, safe deposit rentals, and other miscellaneous items.
—Confers with head CSR or customer service director on nonroutine situations.
—Sells traveler's checks, money orders, monthly transit passes, and cashier's checks and may redeem coupons and sell or redeem foreign currency.
—Prepares coin and currency orders as necessary.
—Services, maintains, and settles ATMs as required.
—Ensures only minimum cash exposure necessary for efficient operation is kept in cash drawer; removes excess cash immediately to secured location.
—Prepares accurate and timely daily settlement of work.
—Performs bookkeeping and operational functions as assigned by customer service director.

be expected to mention various products and facilities offered by the bank as they served customers at the teller windows. For instance, if a customer happened to say something about an upcoming vacation, the CSR was supposed to mention traveler's checks; if the customer complained about bounced checks, the CSR should suggest speaking to a CAR about opening a personal line of credit that would provide an automatic overdraft protection; if the customer mentioned investments, the CSR was expected to refer him or her to a CAR who could provide information on money market accounts, certificates of deposit, or Menton's discount brokerage service. All CSRs were supplied with their own business cards. When making a referral, they were expected to write the customer's name and the product of interest on the back of a card, give it to the customer and send that individual to the customer assistance desks.

In an effort to motivate CSRs at the three branches to sell specific financial products, the bank experimented with various incentive programs. The first involved cash bonuses for referrals to CARs that resulted in sale of specific products. During a one-month period, CSRs were offered a $50 bonus for each referral leading to a customer's opening a personal line of credit account; the CARs received a $20 bonus for each account they opened, regardless whether or not it came as a referral or simply a walk in. Eight such bonuses were paid to CSRs at Victory Square, with three each going to just two of the full-time CSRs, Jean Warshawski and Bruce Greenfield. Karen Mitchell was not among the recipients. However, this program was not renewed, since it was felt that there were other, more cost-effective means of marketing this product. In addition, Reeves, the customer service director, had reason to believe that Bruce Greenfield had colluded with one of the CARs, his girlfriend, to claim referrals which he had not, in fact, made. Another test branch reported similar suspicions of two of its CSRs.

EXHIBIT 3 *Menton Bank: New Job Description for Head Customer Service Representative*

FUNCTION: Supervises all customer service representatives in the designated branch office, ensuring efficient operation and the highest quality service to customers. Plays an active role in developing and maintaining good customer relations. Assists other branch personnel on request.

Responsibilities

1. Supervises the CSRs in the branch
—Allocates work, coordinates work flow, reviews and revises work procedures.
—Ensures teller area is adequately and efficiently staffed with well-trained, qualified personnel. Assists CSRs with more complex transactions.
—Resolves routine personnel problems, referring more complex situations to customer service director.
—Participates in decisions concerning performance appraisal, promotions, wage changes, transfers, and termination of subordinate CSR staff.

2. Assumes responsibility for CSRs' money
—Buys and sells money in the vault, ensuring adequacy of branch currency and coin supply.
—Ensures that CSRs and cash sheets are in balance.
—Maintains necessary records, including daily branch journal and general ledger.

3. Accepts deposits and withdrawals by business customers at the commercial window

4. Operates teller window to provide services to retail customers (see Responsibilities for CSRs)

EXHIBIT 4 *Menton Bank: New Job Description for Customer Assistance Representative*

FUNCTION: Provides services and guidance to customers/prospects seeking banking relationships or related information. Promotes and sells needed products and responds to special requests by existing customers.

Responsibilities

1. Provides prompt, efficient, and friendly service to all customers and prospective customers
—Describes and sells bank services to customers/prospects who approach them directly or via referral from custom service reps or other bank personnel.
—Answers customers' questions regarding bank services, hours, etc.

2. Identifies and responds to customers' needs
—Promotes and sells retail services and identifies any existing cross-sell opportunities.
—Opens new accounts for individuals, businesses, and private organizations.
—Prepares temporary checks and deposit slips for new checking/NOW accounts.
—Sells checks and deposit slips.
—Interviews and takes applications for and pays out on installment/charge card accounts and other credit-related products.
—Certifies checks.
—Handles stop payment requests.
—Responds to telephone mail inquiries from customers or bank personnel.
—Receives notification of name or address changes and takes necessary action.
—Takes action on notification of lost passbooks, credit cards, ATM cards, collateral, and other lost or stolen items.
—Demonstrates ATMs to customers and assists with problems.
—Coordinates closing of accounts and ascertains reasons.

3. Sells and services all retail products
—Advises customers and processes applications for all products covered in CAR training programs (and updates).
—Initiates referrals to the appropriate department when a trust or corporate business need is identified.

EXHIBIT 5 *Menton Bank: New Job Description for Customer Service Director*

FUNCTION: Supervises customer service representatives, customer assistance representatives, and other staff as assigned to provide the most effective and profitable retail banking delivery system in the local marketplace. Supervises sales efforts and provides feedback to management concerning response to products and services by current and prospective banking customers. Communicates goals and results to those supervised and ensures operational standards are met in order to achieve outstanding customer service.

Responsibilities

1. Supervises effective delivery of retail products
—Selects, trains, and manages CSRs and CARs.
—Assigns duties and work schedules.
—Completes performance reviews.

2. Personally, and through those supervised, renders the highest level of professional and efficient customer service available in the local marketplace
—Provides high level of service while implementing most efficient and customer-sensitive staffing schedules.
—Supervises all on-the-job programs within office.
—Ensures that outstanding customer service standards are achieved.
—Directs remedial programs for CSRs and CARs as necessary.

3. Develops retail sales effectiveness to the degree necessary to achieve market share objectives
—Ensures that all CSRs and CARs possess comprehensive product knowledge.
—Directs coordinated cross-sell program within office at all times.
—Reports staff training needs to branch manager and/or regional training director.

4. Ensures adherence to operational standards
—Oversees preparation of daily and monthly operational and sales reports.
—Estimates, approves, and coordinates branch cash needs in advance.
—Oversees ATM processing function.
—Handles or consults with CSRs/CARs on more complex transactions.
—Ensures clean and businesslike appearance of the branch facility.

5. Inform branch manager of customer response to products
—Reports customer complaints and types of sales resistance encountered.
—Describes and summarizes reasons for account closings.

6. Communicates effectively the goals and results of the bank to those under supervision
—Reduces office goals into format which translates to goals for each CSR or CAR.
—Reports sales and cross-sell results to all CSRs and CARs.
—Conducts sales- and service-oriented staff meetings with CSRs/CARs on a regular basis.
—Attends all scheduled customer service management meetings organized by regional office.

A second promotion followed and was based on allocating credits to the CSRs for successful referrals. The value of the credit varied according to the nature of the product—for instance, a debit card was worth 500 credits—and accumulated credits could be exchanged for merchandise gifts. This program was deemed ineffective and discontinued after three months. The basic problem seemed to be that the value of the gifts was seen as too low in relation to the amount of effort required. Other problems with these promotional schemes included lack of product knowledge on the part of the CSRs and time pressures when many customers were waiting in line to be served.

The bank had next turned to an approach which, in David Reeves' words, "used the stick rather than the carrot." All CSRs had traditionally been evaluated half-yearly on a variety of criteria, including accuracy, speed, quality of interactions with customers, punctuality of arrival for work, job attitudes, cooperation with other employees, and professional image. The evaluation process assigned a number of points to each criterion, with accuracy and speed being the most heavily weighted. In addition to appraisals by the customer service director and the branch manager, with input from the head CSR, Menton had recently instituted a program of anonymous visits by what was popularly known as the "mystery client." Each CSR was visited at least once a quarter by a professional evaluator posing as a customer. This individual's appraisal of the CSR's appearance, performance, and attitude was included in the overall evaluation. The number of points scored by each CSR had a direct impact on merit pay raises and on selection for promotion to the head CSR position or to platform jobs.

To encourage improved product knowledge and "consultative selling" by CSRs, the evaluation process was revised to include points assigned for each individual's success in sales referrals. Under the new evaluation scheme, the maximum number of points assignable for effectiveness in making sales—directly or through referrals to CARs—amounted to 30 percent of the potential total score. Although CSR-initiated sales had risen significantly in the most recent half-year, Reeves sensed that morale had dropped among this group, in contrast to the CARs, whose enthusiasm and commitment had risen significantly. He had also noticed an increase in CSR errors. One CSR had quit, complaining about too much pressure.

Karen Mitchell

Under the old scoring system, Karen Mitchell had been the highest scoring teller/CSR for four consecutive half-years. But after two half-years under the new system, her ranking had dropped to fourth out of the seven full-time tellers. The top-ranking CSR, Mary Bell, had been with Menton Bank for sixteen years, but had declined repeated invitations to apply for a head teller position, saying that she was happy where she was, earning at the top of the CSR scale, and did not want "the extra worry and responsibility." Mitchell ranked first on all but one of the operationally related criteria (interactions with customers, where she ranked second) but sixth on selling effectiveness (*Exhibit 6*).

Costanzo and Reeves had spoken to Mitchell about her performance and expressed disappointment. Mitchell had informed them, respectfully but firmly, that she saw the most important aspect of her job as giving customers fast, accurate, and courteous service, telling the two bank officers:

> I did try this selling thing but it just seemed to annoy people. Some said they were in a hurry and couldn't talk now, others looked at me as if I were slightly crazy to bring up the subject of a different bank service than the one they were currently transacting. And then, when you got the odd person who seemed interested, you could hear the other customers in the line grumbling about the slow service.

ExHIBIT 6 *Menton Bank: Summary of Performance Evaluation Scores for Customer Service Representatives at Victory Square Branch for Latest Two Half-Year Periods*							
		Operational Criteria[1] (max.: 70 points)		Selling Effectiveness[2] (max.: 30 points)		Total Score	
CSR Name[3]	Length of Full-Time Bank Service	1st Half	2nd Half	1st Half	2nd Half	1st Half	2nd Half
Mary Bell	16 Years, 10 Months	65	64	16	20	81	84
Scott Dubois	2 Years, 3 Months	63	61	15	19	78	80
Bruce Greenfield	12 Months	48	42	20	26	68	68
Karen Mitchell	3 Years, 7 Months	67	67	13	12	80	79
Sharon Rubin	1 Year, 4 Months	53	55	8	9	61	64
Swee Hoon Chen	7 Months	—	50	—	22	—	72
Jean Warshawski	2 Years, 1 Month	57	55	21	28	79	83

[1] Totals based on sum of ratings points against various criteria, including accuracy, work production, attendance and punctuality, personal appearance, organization of work, initiative, cooperation with others, problem-solving ability, and quality of interaction with customers.
[2] Points awarded for both direct sales by CSR (e.g., traveler's checks) and referral selling by CSR to CAR (e.g., debit card, certificates of deposit, personal line of credit).
[3] Full-time CSRs only (part-time CSRs were evaluated separately).

Really, the last straw was when I noticed on the computer screen that this woman had several thousand in her savings account so I suggested to her, just as the trainer had told us, that she could earn more interest if she opened a money market account. Well, she told me it was none of my business what she did with her money and stomped off. Don't get me wrong, I love being able to help customers, and if they ask for my advice, I'll gladly tell them about what the bank has to offer.

Selecting a New Head CSR

Two weeks after this meeting, it was announced that the head CSR was leaving. The job entailed some supervision of the work of the other CSRs (including allocation of work assignments and scheduling part-time CSRs at busy periods or during employee vacations), consultation on—and, where possible, resolution of—any problems occurring at the teller stations, and handling of large cash deposits and withdrawals by local retailers (see position description in *Exhibit 3*). When not engaged on such tasks, the head CSR was expected to operate a regular teller window.

The pay scale for a head CSR ranged from $8.00 to $13.50 per hour, depending on qualifications, seniority, and branch size, as compared to a range $6.20 to $10.30 per hour for CSRs. The pay scale for CARs ranged from $7.10 to $12.00. Full-time employees (who were not unionized) worked a 4-hour week, including some evenings until 6:00 P.M. and certain Saturday mornings. Costanzo indicated that the pay scales were typical for banks in the region, although the average CSR at Menton was better qualified than those at smaller banks and therefore higher on the scale. Karen Mitchell was currently earning $9.10 per hour, reflecting her education, which included a diploma in business administration, three and a half years' experience, and significant past merit increases. If promoted to head CSR, she would qualify for an initial rate of $11.00 an hour. When applications for the positions closed, Mitchell was one of three candidates. The other two candidates were Jean Warshawski, 42, another CSR at the Victory Square branch; and Curtis Richter, 24, the head CSR at one of Menton Bank's small suburban branches, who was seeking more responsibility.

Warshawski was married with two sons in school. She had started working as a part-time teller at Victory Square some three years previously, switching to full-time work a year later in order, as she said, to put away some money for her boys' college education. Warshawski was a cheerful woman with a jolly laugh.

She had a wonderful memory for people's names and Reeves had often seen her greeting customers on the street or in a restaurant during her lunch hour. Reviewing her evaluations over the previous three years, Reeves noted that she had initially performed poorly on accuracy and at one point, when she was still a part-timer, had been put on probation because of frequent inaccuracies in the balance in her cash drawer at the end of the day. Although Reeves considered her much improved on this score, he still saw room for improvement. The customer service director had also had occasion to reprimand her for tardiness during the past year. Warshawski attributed this to health problems with her elder son who, she said, was now responding to treatment.

Both Reeves and Costanzo had observed Warshawski at work and agreed that her interactions with customers were exceptionally good, although she tended to be overly chatty and was not as fast as Karen Mitchell. She seemed to have a natural ability to size up customers and to decide which ones were good prospects for a quick sales pitch on a specific financial product. Although slightly untidy in her personal appearance, she was very well organized in her work and was quick to help her fellow CSRs, especially new hires. She was currently earning $8.20 per hour as a CSR and would qualify for a rate of $10.40 as head CSR. In the most recent six months, Warshawski had ranked ahead of Mitchell as a result of being very successful in consultative selling (*Exhibit 6*).

Richter, the third candidate, was not working in one of the three test branches, so had not been exposed to the consultative selling program and its corresponding evaluation scheme. However, he had received excellent evaluations for his work in Menton's small Longmeadow branch, where he had been employed for three years. A move to Victory Square would increase his earnings from $9.40 to $10.40 per hour. Reeves and Costanzo had interviewed Richter and considered him intelligent and personable. He had joined the bank after dropping out of college midway through his third year, but had recently started taking evening courses in order to complete his degree. The Longmeadow branch was located in an older part of town, where commercial and retail activity were rather stagnant. This branch (which was rumored to be under consideration for closure) had not yet been renovated and had no ATMs, although there was an ATM accessible to Menton customers one block away. Richter supervised three CSRs and reported directly to the branch manager, who spoke very highly of him. Since there were no CARs in this branch, Richter and another experienced CSR took turns to handle new accounts and loan or mortgage applications.

Costanzo and Reeves were troubled by the decision that faced them. Prior to the bank's shift in focus, Mitchell would have been the natural choice for the head CSR job which, in turn, could be a stepping stone to further promotions, including customer assistance representative, customer service director, and, eventually, manager of a small branch or a management position in the head office. Mitchell had told her superiors that she was interested in making a career in banking and that she was eager to take on further responsibilities.

Compounding the problem was the fact that the three branches testing the improved branch design and new customer service program had just completed a full year of the test. Costanzo knew that sales and profits were up significantly at all three branches, relative to the bank's performance as a whole. She anticipated that top management would want to extend the program systemwide after making any modifications that seemed desirable.

Study Questions

1. *Identify the steps taken by Menton Bank to develop a stronger customer orientation in its retail branches.*
2. *Compare and contrast the jobs of CAR and CSR. How important is each (a) to bank operations and (b) to customer satisfaction?*
3. *Evaluate the strengths and weaknesses of Karen Mitchell and other candidates for head CSR.*
4. *What action do you recommend for filling the head CSR position?*

R Cubed

Christopher Lovelock and Reg Price

A small, research-based marketing consulting firm has flourished thanks, in part, to a distinctive culture and working philosophy that make it more productive and position it away from other consultancies. But can it preserve this culture if it opens a second office in another country?

The three founding directors of the New Zealand marketing research consulting firm, R Cubed, faced an important decision in early 2000. Should they open a branch office in Australia? And if they did so, could they hope to maintain the same culture that had served the firm so effectively since its foundation in Auckland in October, 1996?

When Reg Price, Steve Allen, and Donella Parker originally planned their new business, they decided they wanted a snappy, decisive company that would provide good leverage for their individual skills. The three founders had previously worked for a larger marketing research organization whose style and operating procedures had proved incompatible with their own; so by mutual agreement, the company was split into two. Reg, Steve, and Donella took three other employees and about 35 existing clients as the basis for establishing their own research firm. The name, strategy and many of the new firm's "routines" were decided in a single morning of intense discussion. Yet, despite significant growth, there had been little deviation from the decisions made more than three years previously.

But now, market opportunities were broadening as the activities of New Zealand–based clients became more global. At the same time, control of some New Zealand–based companies had shifted to Australia as a result of mergers, takeovers, or more centralized decision making. Steve, Donella and Reg were starting to seriously think about positioning R Cubed for these opportunities by establishing an Australian branch office in either Sydney or Melbourne.

By January 2000, R Cubed employed a total of 12 full-time people (and 4 other contractors), comprised of the three directors (each of whom was active in the business), 6 consultants, and 3 support staff. Revenues for the 12 months ending March 31, 2000 were estimated at $NZ2.3m.[1] Despite the firm's success and growth in New Zealand, R Cubed's owners debated whether the firm's distinctive culture and routines could be stretched beyond a single office structure. "Will further expansion compromise the very essence that has made R Cubed a success to date?" Reg wondered.

The New Zealand Marketplace

Located in the South Pacific and enjoying a temperate climate, New Zealand consists of two large islands (North and South) about 1,300 miles (2,100 km) east of Australia. The country is renowned for its physical beauty, including a magnificent coastline, many thermal areas and inactive volcanoes, and the Southern Alps mountain range which reaches heights exceeding 12,000 feet (3,750m) and is a magnet for both climbers and skiers, depending on the season.

Compared to many other markets, the word best describing New Zealand at the dawn of the twenty-first century was "small." Covering about the same land area as the United Kingdom, but "down under" on the opposite side of the world, adjacent to Australia, New Zealand had a population of only four million. The country had been settled initially by people of Polynesian stock, the adaptable and resourceful Maori, some 600 years earlier. Large-scale European

[1]NZ$1.00 = US$0.52 = C$0.75

settlement, predominantly British and Irish, had taken place since the middle of the nineteenth century, but there had also been some recent immigration from Asia and other parts of the world.

New Zealanders saw themselves as a nation of outward-looking people who were proud of their initiative and industry. The pioneering spirit was still very much to the fore in the population and also in business, where it was evidenced by early adoption and penetration of technology and best practice management thinking. New Zealanders tended to be well-traveled, starting with the "big OE" (big overseas experience), an almost obligatory New Zealand tradition of living in Europe (and perhaps North America) for a year or more after reaching adulthood.

With a population of about 1.3 million, Auckland—where R Cubed was based—was by far the largest city, accounting for almost one-third of the population; the head offices of most national and international companies were located there. By contrast, Wellington, the capital, had only 370,000 inhabitants. Businesses tended to be small (in 2000, 96 percent employed less than ten people) but most multinational corporations had subsidiaries in Auckland and foreign investment was widespread. There was a small, but thriving consulting industry, in which both international firms and local ones competed for clients who sought better information and more effective management approaches combining a mix of "home grown" and imported solutions. The country's size limited the scale and scope of any company that functioned solely in the New Zealand market; so growth-oriented firms often chose to expand overseas, especially to nearby Australia. Asia, North America, and Europe also beckoned.

Nevertheless, New Zealand offered three key attractions for R Cubed's owners. First, because of the country's relatively high standard of living and largely middle class population, a number of multinational companies used it as a training ground in general management for up-and-coming executives. These individuals were sent to New Zealand for a period of two to three years, and many used the opportunity to try to stand out in the hope of achieving future promotions. For R Cubed, executives in this group offered a distinct and attractive market segment. They were seen as hungry for new and innovative ideas that would make a difference, quickly, to their firms' performance. Changing the ways things were done inside a relatively small corporate unit could often be achieved fairly fast.

A second attraction reflected New Zealand's fairly relaxed pace to working. Many professionals worked from 8:30 A.M. to 5:30 P.M., Monday to Friday, but rarely on weekends, and took at least four weeks holi-day a year. For individuals prepared to work at a ramped-up pace, the rewards were high, relative to what could be gained in other local corporate environments. Finally, all three of R Cubed's owners loved living in New Zealand, particularly enjoying the opportunities it presented for an outdoor lifestyle.

R Cubed's Philosophy and Operating Strategy

The firm's name had both internal and external meaning. "Okay," said Steve thoughtfully, when the three founders first discussed their objectives for the business. "Why don't we start with what we each want from our business, and work back from that? I want to work in a place where I can keep learning, where I can get lots of time off, and where I get good rewards." "And I want an environment where I'm stimulated by the work, where we have a group of people who all have a like mindset towards our business, and where the rewards are good," jumped in Donella. "My ideal," said Reg, getting into the swing of it, "is a business where I can work smart, not hard, which remunerates me well, and which I can take a step back from in five years time but still receive an income."

With a bit more teasing out of ideas, the three decided that there were three internal "Rs" relevant for all staff members:

- *Rewards*—immediate via remuneration and in the future through good leverage of people and skills
- *Reflection*—the time to relax and reflect via sufficient time off and a focus on education and learning
- *Recognition*—the reputation needed to attract good quality employees and good quality clients that comes from excellent work and getting results for customers.

"Thinking about internal goals was easy," admitted Donella. "Even though we're quite different people, we're like-minded in terms of what we want. What about the market though? What are our 'Rs' for the market?" Said Reg, "We're in the business of research. We have to achieve results. And we'll do it with the quality of our relationships—Research. Results. Relationships." The other two liked it, but somehow the word "relationships" didn't sit quite right. "It's not the relationships, per se, but the way those relationships are managed which will create the value for our clients," suggested Donella. So, with the help of a thesaurus, the firm was positioned in the market as a research-based consultancy—all about *Results through Research and Rapport*. The name R Cubed was intended to show that the firm was exponentially better.

Strategy and Differentiation

Underlying the positioning strategy adopted for the new firm were the skills of the three directors, who all held Master's degrees. Reg had previously been marketing director for several companies, including an international accounting firm. He taught part-time at the University of Auckland's Graduate School of Business. Steve and Donella were both market researchers with broad practical experience. They all agreed that creating the best results for clients required focusing on the way that research information would be used. However, in their view, most research companies failed to present their findings in a suitable format, typically delivering results in large inaccessible tomes. While their competitors specialised in "quant" and "qual," or promoted products like "stochastic monitors" or "conversion models," or even emphasized work for a specific industry, Steve, Donella, and Reg had discovered that most research users were less than enthusiastic about the performance of these traditional firms.

Steve insisted that to get results for clients, "R Cubed must do a great job of engaging and involving clients, before we even start collecting any information and then make sure afterwards that the research gets to action." Added Donella, "The key people we hire to work with clients can't be researchers . . . they've got to be experienced managers who have an analytical mindset so they can guide people through the information and get the result they need, like a go/no go decision or an agreed way to deal with an opportunity or problem."

Clients

Consistent with the belief that the most value would be created by working with established relationships—emphasizing "rapport"—R Cubed developed what Reg named the "only 20 clients" strategy. His thinking was that the optimal size of the firm in terms of being able to do effective work, generate good rewards, and maintain the self-managing nature of R Cubed encompassed a maximum of 20 enduring clients.

At the time of R Cubed's foundation, the firm had 35 clients with whom it worked at some point during the course of each year. Three years on, there were just 14 clients. R Cubed had one client in nearly all the major sectors: banking, insurance, oil, utilities, auto manufacturing and servicing, government, local government, pharmaceutical, TV, and agricultural products. All were major corporations, the smallest having an annual turnover of NZ$260 million. From R Cubed's perspective, the strategy netted higher revenues and better margins, plus the attraction of working with very good quality clients. In turn, clients reported that they received what they saw as unprecedented attention, responsiveness and quality. Examples of recent R Cubed projects are shown in *Exhibit 1*, while *Exhibit 2* displays year-end figures for the number of employees (excluding the founders), number of clients, and gross annual revenues for that year.

Competition

"It's becoming less and less clear to me who our competitors actually are," observed Donella one day in late 1999. "On the one hand we occasionally encounter one of the five or six large market research firms, but our clients say we are quite different from them." Steve chipped in, "Yes, but we sometimes run into the big accounting-based consulting firms like KPMG or Anderson or the strategic consultancies like McKinsey or BCG . . . but they seem to be in a different market."

What was clear was that R Cubed was winning little of the ad hoc research work that some clients tendered among several research firms. R Cubed had concluded that such clients did not usually put much value on the interaction and consultancy it offered. Further, its marketing-based approach usually excluded R Cubed from the more accounting or technology-driven projects dominated by large consulting firms. Instead, it appealed to relationship-oriented marketing executives dealing with customer issues that required both external information and a process for deciding how to move ahead. This market was growing as managers become more sophisticated in how they used their suppliers and were less inclined to accept a single, superficial answer. As Steve indicated, "We've found a niche that seems to fit between the traditional suppliers; interestingly no one and everyone seems to be our competitor, depending on how you look at it!"

Working Procedures

"Self-managing is the goal. The more we focus on clients, the more valuable this company will be," Reg had stated at the outset. Steve agreed wholeheartedly. "There's not much value in it for anyone if our time is spent managing. We've been there, and it's a terrible distraction." Donella agreed with the principle but believed that more structure was needed: "We still have to have one person with ultimate responsibility for some of the core management tasks. Doing it by committee is cumbersome. Why don't we divide up the jobs?"

"Fine," said Reg. "Why don't you do the people, Steve can do the finance, and I'll do marketing." "That works for me," said Steve. "And for me," agreed

Exhibit 1 *Examples of R Cubed Projects*	
A trading bank	A multi-phase brand development project with facilitated working sessions, a literature search, customer research and interviews with "visionaries" within the Bank and R Cubed's global visionary panel. Uses a "value innovation" approach to achieve differentiation. 4 months duration $NZ120,000 . . . state of the art
A multinational oil company	Developing through facilitated working sessions a "dashboard" of linked key metrics which together form the logic for success in that company. Second phase to find all required information from within or outside the company and then build a predictive model. 3 months duration $NZ100,000 . . . state of the art
An international motor vehicle leasing company	Drawing together all the available information on customers that the company possesses and make it available as a navigable electronic report online and also summarized on one page, called the "big picture." 2 months to develop . . . ongoing $NZ60,000 . . . state of the art
A city council	Using the customer voice to move the local government organization from an "inside out" mindset to an "outside in" one, requiring research and the design of workshop processes. 8 months duration $NZ250,000 . . . state of the art
A multinational car company	Designing a semiautomated customer reporting system that can be operated by the client at the press of a button. Ongoing $NZ120,000 per year . . . typical project
An energy company	Establishing a customer advisory panel to operate at a high level in the company, providing to management advice and feedback on proposed initiatives. Ongoing $NZ60,000 per year . . . state of the art
A trading bank	Research to identify triggers for the defection of customers whose branches are co-locating, so that retention can be improved. 8 months duration NZ$280,000 . . . typical project

Donella. The three owners committed to performing these roles so that neither of the other two would need to think about them. Donella took care of employment contracts, performance reviews, salary reviews, the points system, leave approvals, and recruitment. Steve became responsible for financial systems, meetings with accountants and banks,

expenditure approvals, cashflow planning, and financial reporting. Reg handled directory listings, membership in appropriate industry groups, Christmas cards, client seminars, the Web page, the R Cubed promotional CD, and any advertising the firm undertook. On average, after setting up the different systems, the three found themselves each spending about

Exhibit 2 *R Cubed: Employment, Revenue, and Client Statistics*			
	Gross Annual Revenues for Year Ending 31 Mar (NZ$ million)	Number of Employees (excluding three directors) at Year End	Number of Clients at Year End
1996–1997	0.7 (6 Months)	3	35
1997–1998	1.4	4	33
1998–1999	1.5	5	31
1999–2000	2.3 (estimate)	9	14

one to two days a month on formal company "management."

R Cubed Routines

From the outset, Steve, Donella, and Reg wanted to ensure that there was sufficient internal communication within R Cubed that everyone knew what was happening and had a sense of moving forward, but not so much that the company paralyzed itself through excessive meetings and memo writing. Out of this desire came R Cubed's two key routines.

The Fourterly. The major planning event for everyone was the "Fourterly," a name coined by Reg to describe the firm's four-monthly planning cycle. It signified the directors' belief that a quarterly planning and reflection horizon was too short and six-monthly too infrequent. R Cubed insisted that the three Fourterly meetings held each year would be the only times dedicated to review and future planning; there were no other internal planning and review meetings. So, every four months everyone, including support staff, went off-site (either to a beach or a ski area, depending on the season and the weather) for a day of discussion. Over the years, the agenda of the Fourterly meetings had been expanded to include a half-day's training. The topic selected for this training reflected R Cubed employees' views of what they believed was needed.

The Ops Meeting. The other central routine was the weekly Operations Meeting. Its purpose was to review what was coming up in the week ahead, discuss what had happened during the week just ending, and to bring everyone up to date on administrative business. Various times had been dedicated to this meeting in the past—Monday morning to rev people up, Tuesday morning to ensure more of an information session, or late Friday afternoon followed by drinks. But none of these times had worked that well for everyone. What R Cubed really needed, as Donella said, was "a weekly get-together that no one wants to miss because there's too much to find out and it's just too much fun." And so the decision had been made to hold the weekly "Ops" meeting on Fridays at 12:30 P.M. R Cubed finished its official week after that meeting, at 1:30 P.M. on Friday afternoon. As the directors agreed at the start, "Who wants to work Friday afternoons anyway?"

Working Smarter—Not Harder

R Cubed's owners believed that smart work came from an environment with a learning culture and a structure that gave each individual sufficient flexibil-ity to set his or her own pace. The company's operating procedures were designed to accomplish and reinforce this "smart work" ethic through a number of policies.

Professional education. Formal learning was actively encouraged at R Cubed, with every person, from support staff to directors, having an education budget, set at approximately 10 percent of their gross annual salary. It was noncumulative, operating on a "use it or lose it" basis. The Fourterly performance review system included discussion of appropriate uses of that budget to achieve personal and company objectives. However, much of the initiative for identifying specific courses, conferences, or tuition was taken by individual employee.

Hours of Work. The firm's office hours were 8:00 A.M.–5:00 P.M. Mondays through Thursdays and from 8:00 A.M.–1:30 P.M. on Fridays. However, with the exception of support staff, no employee (including directors) had set work hours. R Cubed did not have timesheets, did not require staff to clock in and clock out, and did not expect any of its people to be present at work at any particular time. But attendance at the weekly Ops meeting and the Fourterly routine was mandatory and was included in everyone's job description. Apart from that, however, Donella, Steve, and Reg believed that staff members could be trusted to use their own discretion and that there were much better measures of productivity than the number of hours spent at work.

Hot Desking. With the exception of support staff, no one at R Cubed had an office or even a cubicle they could call their own. Instead, everyone was assigned a "wheelie" (a file drawer on wheels). R Cubed's office space had been equipped with a long desk that ran along the surfaces of three walls for a distance of roughly 50 feet (15m). When people arrived at the office, they choose where they wanted to sit on this peripheral workbench. Each space had a PC and stationery set. Some PCs were better than others and some spaces were more appealing than others. Because people came in at different times on different days, either because of their own working style or having been at early meetings, it was a case of "first in, best dressed."

The prospect of this arrangement had been unsettling to a lot of people when first proposed in December 1996, as the firm prepared to move to new space in a converted factory. Until then, everyone had been used to having their own "home" in the office, which they decorated with plants, pictures, and personal mementos. To take that away was seen as "scary." The reality, though, proved far different from the prospect. Staff members and directors alike found that the biggest gain was to be had from sitting next to someone different each day. Not only did people develop and cement their personal relationships but there was a learning by osmosis which served to eliminate isolated islands of knowledge. This office layout proved to be pivotal in building the culture of learning. In addition, the practice made good financial sense in a business where people spent a lot of time off site meeting with clients.

When the firm moved to larger offices in October, 1999, a similar workbench was installed in the new building. *Exhibit 3* shows the floor layout in the firm's new offices, which included one private area for small client meetings and a large open area with a moveable wall—that could subdivide the space in two different ways. When focus groups were being observed by clients, two spacious areas were configured so that clients could sit on comfortable sofas, watching two very large TVs next to the pool table and bar, in sight of the quirky R Cubed memorabilia. Other combinations created quiet spaces away from the busy atmosphere of the peripheral work bench. A store room and server room completed the ensemble. Clients walked almost straight into the work area—designed so that there was never a feeling that anything was hidden away.

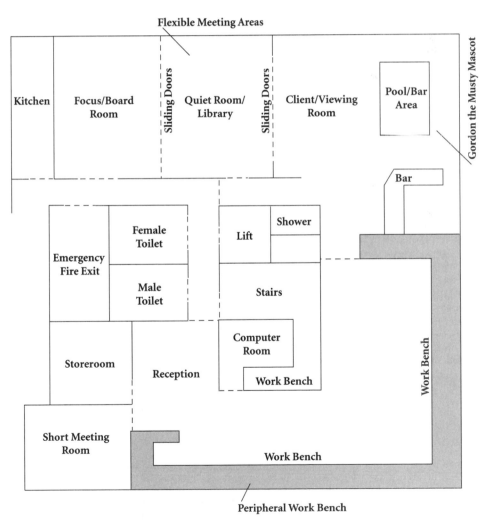

EXHIBIT 3 Floor Plan or R Cubed's Auckland Office

Facets of the R Cubed Culture

Visitors were often surprised at what they encountered, since the physical design and layout of the office bore little resemblance to a traditional, rather staid, professional office. For instance, the "Bad Taste Wall" in the pool room featured an eclectic set of "cubes" and other items; many originated from a "bring along a cube" blitz held soon after R Cubed was established.

"Wouldn't a pool table be a good idea," quipped Steve one day, six months into R Cubed. "It would give us all somewhere to go to have a break, and we've got enough space for it." Coming from the normally frugal VP of Finance and Administration, the idea was jumped upon by all. The pool table soon came to form a central part of the firm's culture. It was the only area where people from R Cubed actively competed against each other; over the years, competition had strengthened. There was a "pool ladder," a system of challenges to rise up the ladder and a complex handicapping system for less-able players. Even the firm's mascot, the musty goat called Gordon (whose stuffed head was mounted on the Bad Taste Wall) had a position on the ladder. Each week someone was chosen to represent Gordon, using the "Random Gordon Generator"—a computer program that randomly selected a person off the pool ladder.

The Mistake of the Week. This was a way for team members to "confess" at the weekly Ops meeting to mistakes they had made during the week. Participants then voted to determine which one had provided the most learning for future improvement. The perpetrator of that mistake won a bottle of wine. The others, however, could still be nominated for the "Brick."

The Brick. This offered a nonconfrontational way for anyone to point out something silly that someone else had done during the week. The winner became the keeper of a real (and dusty) brick and had to wash the tea towels from the kitchen for the following week. The misdemeanors winning the brick had ranged from the most minuscule to the most serious; the rationale for voting traditionally lacked any foundation, thereby adding to the fun and humor.

The Lolly Jar. Voted in similar fashion, out-of-the-ordinary performance and any actions that reinforced the R Cubed "way" were recognized. The winner received a lolly jar containing confectionery, and the contents were usually offered to the rest of the team at the Ops meeting.

The Innovation of the Week. Time was taken during the meeting to recognize and communicate an innovation that had contributed significantly in some way to the well-being of R Cubed. The self-nominated innovation elected by the team won 500 points for that person.

R Cubed Recruitment

Reg summed up the underlying belief that drove R Cubed's recruitment strategy. "If we're going to achieve our personal and company goals, we need people who know what they're doing and who have had enough experience elsewhere to appreciate the work environment here." There were no "juniors" at R Cubed. Because no senior consultant wanted to do the work of juniors, there was a great incentive to think of a smarter and less time-consuming way to do that task or to identify a reason why it did not need to be done at all. Ultimately, the ingenuity required to come up with the solution benefited the client with novel solutions that delivered more value. Most research companies were renowned for their indigestible "telephone book" reports. R Cubed believed that clients didn't value them and knew for a fact that researchers hated writing them. Instead, the firm had replaced such reports by very visual summaries that gave answers instead of just information. Clients indicated that they preferred these summaries to traditional reports. In consequence, R Cubed's senior consultants and directors had, on average, eliminated 40 hours a month from their workload.

Another example of cutting out unvalued work concerned the presentation of monthly monitoring data. Recognizing that clients didn't value them and that researchers hated doing them, R Cubed had adopted a different approach. Contrary to the norm, it set up systems for people to do their own fieldwork (when appropriate) through their call centers and designed wall chart–sized pictures of the results. Clients were able to analyze results and generate their own wall chart at the push of a button using automated (macro-based) computer programs written by a specialist programmer at R Cubed. Such an approach reduced the typical cost of monitoring by an average 40 percent, provided an easy way to disseminate results, but also involved people more in research. As Senior Consultant Cheryl Bouzaid argued,

> Minimizing the amount of repetitive, monitor-type work we do is a clear illustration of a win-win-win situation. Our clients win by getting monitor information in a more cost effective way and by including more staff in the process. R

Cubed wins because people are more effective—spending more time on the parts of the process that we, and our clients, value most highly—designing the right processes and working with our clients to use the information. And R Cubed team members win because we're doing work we enjoy more and working more productively.

The specification for R Cubed's senior consultants was initially coined by Donella as she sought out new hires: "numerate marketers." The underlying belief was that experienced marketers and managers were best placed to help clients get results through research. The experience of unsuccessful hirings in earlier businesses told Steve, Donella, and Reg that researchers recruited from traditional research firms struggled in R Cubed's strong, managerially oriented setting.

There had been a pattern to the three most recent hirings of senior consultants, David Thomas, Catherine Dunkley, and Melinda Gibbon. At least two of the R Cubed directors had worked with each of them—all had previously been clients with whom they had had effective relationships. Melinda described that practice as an effective one for all involved. "Working with R Cubed as a client gave me great insights into what the company did, their values, and routines." Second, each brought a particular set of numerical skills to enrich the firm's blend of capabilities. All were experienced managers in their late twenties or early thirties, possessing the necessary maturity to deal with clients on managerial issues. Finally, each had that "little extra" that impressed the directors: David, reliability and attention to detail; Catherine, people skills; and Melinda, a passion for customer profitability work and one-page reports.

Each candidate had been told early on in the recruitment process that there was a place for them as long as they wanted it. There were no interviews as such but rather discussions about R Cubed and its work. Discussions were based around IFOT ("Information for Our Team")—the R Cubed manual on itself and its approaches that was reviewed and updated at each Fourterly. Efforts were made to explain what the work would be like so that candidates could deselect themselves if they felt unsuited. Afterwards, Catherine remarked that the process was quite different from any that she had previously experienced. "I was more or less told I could choose my own salary, leave, and working hours as I worked within the points system. That concept took a while to get my head around when coming from a traditional employee mindset."

Measuring Results: The Points System

How best to measure results had been a key issue at the time of the firm's formation. Donella had spoken forcefully on this topic: "Just because someone is physically here, doesn't mean they are achieving results. There has to be a better way of gauging someone's value to R Cubed. And it has to be objective, a measure which is completely transparent, beyond personalities."

Unfortunately, examining other businesses for useful insights did not yield anything of great value. In most professional firms, productivity seemed to be defined and measured on the basis of time, sales, or some combination of the two. For R Cubed, however, the time measure seemed irrelevant and the sales measure too small a part of the total business. The directors needed to develop a system that would be relevant for as many people as possible and could be linked directly to the value created for clients. They recognized that they needed to start with the basics, reflecting a deeply held R Cubed belief that simple is best. To the basic question: "What creates value?" the answer was: "Margin."

> But that's not enough on its own, [insisted Steve]. Money in the door is all well and good, but it's money in the door from continuous relationships that creates the most value. The value for the client comes because we get to know that client's business intimately; and the value for R Cubed comes because it costs far less to work with an existing client than to develop a new relationship.

Reg and Donella agreed with him, "Margin, especially from existing clients, should be our indicator of value," declared Reg. "Plus, it's simple to administer."

A system was developed whereby each client-related task earned a certain amount of points, based on the relative importance of that task for creating value for both the client and R Cubed. This allocation had nothing to do with the amount of time a particular function took. For example, the winning of a proposal, which for an existing client might mean a phone call followed by a one-page e-mail confirmation (total time of at most one hour) would be worth 30 percent of the points; the project management function (total time of anywhere between six hours and a week, depending on the project) was worth 10 percent of the points. On any given project, one New Zealand dollar's worth of margin was valued at one point. David Thomas commented:

> We now have a direct and unambiguous link between what each of us does on a job and the

value each member generates for clients—and for R Cubed. As a result we are all highly motivated to work smart, not hard—that is, to spend the least amount of time on tasks that add little value for the client (and are the least interesting for us).

R Cubed Rewards

By recruiting competent and independent people, and backing it up with the points system, the firm sent a strong message to everyone about keeping performance transparent and rewarding performance. R Cubed's owners knew that consulting was an industry where prima donnas flourished. However, while such people tended to do very well for themselves, they often did less well for their team or their company. Yet there were also some very valuable, but self-effacing people to be found in consulting. "We've got to have a reward system that encourages the right behavior," argued Reg from the beginning. "Yes," agreed Donella, "but one that also offers people the flexibility to choose their preferred reward level, without its being part of a formal review process." The outcome of this dialog was a remuneration system with four elements:

1. A *base salary* that was slightly higher than the industry
2. A *team bonus share,* 15% of the net profit each Fourterly was distributed to everyone except directors. Distribution was prorated against the level of a person's base salary. The amount was uncapped and had been as high as 10 percent of an annual salary in one four-month period. This element was designed to allow everyone to share in R Cubed's success.
3. The *individual points bonus* consisted of an annual payment of NZ$1.00 for every 2.75 points achieved over target. This amount, too, was uncapped. It enabled individuals to work at an accelerated pace and be rewarded for it but linked the bonus to the rewards the individual achieved for the company.
4. A *fixed payment* for directorship and functional management responsibilities.

In bad years, R Cubed paid slightly more than the industry average; in good years (or if someone had chosen to work exceptionally hard and well), R Cubed set the industry high.

The Opportunities Internationally

Operating solely in New Zealand, admitted the directors, was a low-risk strategy. But, with few exceptions, the firm's consultants were rarely involved in projects where world-wide decision-making authority was present. This placed a definite ceiling on what could be achieved in terms of internal reward and recognition but allowed a lot of time for the third "R," reflection on what—if anything—to do about this situation.

Early in the firm's history, the directors had recognized the need for themselves and senior consultants to be prepared to travel, not only to develop networks but also to attend international conferences and seminars, particularly to the United States and Britain. The small New Zealand market rarely yielded material at the cutting edge of the research and consultancy fields, hence the decision to establish a substantial education budget. However, when attending international meetings, R Cubed people noticed a lot of material that its presenters claimed as "new" actually employed techniques that their own firm had already tried and discarded; in fact, in a number of areas, R Cubed was clearly ahead of the field in its thinking.

As international interest in their work grew, requests for speaking engagements in Britain and the United States started to appear, as did invitations to write papers and to join more formal networks. All the indicators were that there was a wider market for R Cubed's services beyond New Zealand. Australia was seen as a logical location for a second R Cubed office, because of its geographic proximity, common language, and related culture. With 19 million people, Australia was also a much larger market, with more ties to the Asia-Pacific region.

Auckland was only 3 to 3½ hours flying time from Australia's two largest cities, Sydney and Melbourne, each of which had a population of over three million people. Both were major commercial centers, but Sydney, the state capital of New South Wales, was generally acknowledged to be the city with the most international head offices. However, Melbourne, the state capital of Victoria, had a tighter business community with much local government, energy, and finance—sectors in which R Cubed was experienced—and were businesses where decisions were being made locally rather than by some international parent. The New Zealand time zone was two hours ahead of Eastern Australian time, so it was possible to leave Auckland very early in the morning, spend an entire working day in Melbourne or Sydney, and return to New Zealand late the same night. Some existing projects periodically required such a trip and few staff members at R Cubed were strangers to Australia.

Reg, Steve, and Donella recognized that Australian clients could not be served out of Auckland. Establishing a credible presence in Australia would require R Cubed to set up a local office in one of the two major cities with a full-time staff of its own.

Among the issues was whether to hire an Australian who already had a network of contacts to head up the new office or whether to assign this task to someone from Auckland. If the latter route were followed, it would be necessary to decide whether one of the three directors should go or whether an existing senior staff member should be promoted to director and posted to Australia. Yet another option was to buy an existing consultancy in Melbourne or Sydney and integrate it into the R Cubed family.

The big question was whether it would be possible to replicate R Cubed's approach to doing business in a new location far from the firm's original home. Reg, Donella, and Steve were convinced that R Cubed had been successful and was faced with these wider opportunities precisely because of its carefully planned and nurtured culture. Could this culture be successfully transported to Australia, or would that be a mistake? What would be the implications of giving a new Australian office the freedom to take its own course both commercially and culturally?

Study Questions

1. *Evaluate R Cubed's philosophy of professional work. What do you see as its strengths and weaknesses from the perspective of (a) the owners, (b) senior consultants, (c) clients?*

2. *Is the R Cubed culture sustainable as the firm grows larger? Could it be transferred to an acquired firm in another city?*

3. *From a client's standpoint, what is the relative importance of the process by which consulting firms work versus the output that they produce?*

4. *Should R Cubed make plans for opening an office in Australia? If so, how should it proceed?*

Peters & Champlain

Christopher Lovelock

An international accounting firm is invited by a large client, whose audits it undertakes in seven countries, to submit a competitive proposal for auditing the client's accounts in 53 countries around the world.

Piet de Lesseps studied the fax he had just received from Robert Poirot, audit director of Montini Van Buren (MVB), a major engineering and construction company. De Lesseps, based in Belgium, was a highly regarded client service partner of Peters & Champlain (P&C), one of the major international accounting firms. He was eager to cement the relationship that had united his old firm, Peters & Heinz, with one of its former rivals, ABNZ Stone Champlain. Poirot's company was also the product of a recent merger and was now seeking to consolidate its auditing relationships around the world. De Lesseps scented a great opportunity to raise Peters & Champlain's profile worldwide.

In his fax, Poirot stated that his board wished to cut the number of accounting firms serving MVB worldwide from the current 34 to just one. Proposals were being sought from six leading firms, and MVB intended to select a short list of three from which, after further discussions, a single winner would then be chosen.

Later in the day, de Lesseps met with Jacques van Krabbe, managing partner of the Brussels office, to discuss MVB's request. The two recognized that such an engagement would be of great interest to their firm on an international basis. As de Lesseps declared, "We've had their Belgian business for years. This new request makes them more than just another large

national client and potentially a worldwide gain for P&C." The partners concluded that it would be appropriate to turn to P&C/Europe in Paris for support in developing a suitable proposal.

Van Krabbe took one more look at the fax. "You'd better get cracking, Piet!" he said. "It's already early December and Poirot says here that he wants proposals by January 31."

Montini Van Buren

MVB was an international engineering and construction company. It had been formed in 1990 by the merger of an Italian company, Ing. Umberto Montini SpA of Milan, and a Franco-Belgian firm, Van Buren, Walschaerts, Lesage SA, whose headquarters were in Brussels. Van Buren's traditional expertise had been in tunnelling, hydroelectric and irrigation projects, and port construction. Montini was best known for its innovative work in bridge design and construction; the firm had also been active in building airports, and both firms had had a number of large highway construction contracts. Although Van Buren had been profitable in recent years, Montini had lost money in two of the three preceding fiscal years. The merged company consolidated its headquarters activity is Luxembourg, while also retaining major administrative functions in Brussels, Milan, and Paris.

Montini Van Buren planned and executed major construction projects around the world, sometimes as the consulting engineers, sometimes as the primary contractor, and sometimes as a subcontractor. For really large projects, MVB might enter into consortium agreements with other firms. Significant current activities included work on the Channel Tunnel, preliminary engineering studies for a new transalpine rail tunnel, a deep-water port in Indonesia, building hydroelectric dams in Canada, India, and Argentina, a new subway line in Mexico City, several large bridges on three continents, airport expansion projects in Nigeria, Australia and several European countries, and highway construction around the world, notably in Asian and African countries. Most projects on which MVB worked ran for three to five years or more, although it would sometimes bid on smaller projects that would provide high visibility, entrée to new markets, or exposure to significant engineering challenges. Many projects were commissioned by government agencies and some, such as bridges and dams, extended across national frontiers.

MVB operated in 53 countries, some of which were sales offices working to obtain future contracts. Its accounts were audited on a country-by-country basis by no less than 34 different accounting firms. Local firms held more than 50% of these engagements, with the balance being held by the Big Six—notably P&C, Jones Pittman, and Coulson & Stuart, which also audited the consolidated accounts in Luxembourg. Peters & Champlain were MVB's auditors in seven countries, including Belgium. Many of these relationships extended back a decade or more. In Belgium, for example, Piet de Lesseps had landed the Van Buren, Walschaerts, Lesage engagement as a junior partner 12 years earlier.

Client Concerns

Two days later, de Lesseps travelled to Luxembourg to meet Robert Poirot. He had learned before the meeting that Poirot, who was French, had been recruited by MVB just four months earlier. It was he who had persuaded the board to consolidate the company's auditing relationships. However, de Lesseps had also learned from phone conversations with several P&C partners in different countries that a number of MVB offices were unhappy with the plan, having only recently gone through a similar change due to the merger of formerly separate Montini and Van Buren offices in many countries where both predecessor firms were operating. In fact, P&C had lost the audit engagement for MVB's merged Caracas office to another Big Six firm, Jones Pittman. In three other locations, however, P&C had been the winner, merging with a local firm in two cases and beating out Martin Amundsen, another Big Six firm, in the third instance.

Poirot impressed de Lesseps with his intellect, professionalism, and ambition for both himself and his new company. He came straight to the point, acknowledging his recent arrival at MVB and prefacing his remarks with the comment, "You know more about this organization than I do!" He told de Lesseps that the decision on selection of worldwide auditors for MVB would involve inputs from a number of other senior executives, including the managing director, Mr. Garelli (former chief executive of Montini), the deputy MD, Mr. Brecht (former CEO of Van Buren, Walschaerts, Lesage), the finance director, Mr. D'Amato, and his deputy, Mr. Brugge, and would have to be ratified by the board of directors. Poirot told de Lesseps that he had had some contact with P&C in his previous position with a large chemicals company and had not been overly impressed. 'However, I'm approaching this proposals process with an open mind,' he declared. 'All existing relationships are up for change in the interests of selecting a single firm to conduct our audit engagements worldwide.' Poirot also emphasized that MVB had no interest in follow-on services and was seeking proposals that were strictly limited to audit services.

De Lesseps left Luxembourg impressed by Poirot, but wondering whether other individuals involved in the selection process at MVB would share the audit director's specific expectations for the outcome. From his own experience in serving MVB's Belgian operations, he knew that the firm perceived relatively little difference between competing Big Six auditors and tended to drive a hard bargain on fees. However, he was not sure how firmly this view was held by former Montini executives, such as the managing director, Mario Garelli, or the finance director, Carlo D'Amato (who reported to Garelli).

A few days later, de Lesseps managed to arrange a meeting in Paris between Garelli, who was in town to visit MVB's French office, and Christopher Diebold, P&C's executive partner from the New York office. The meeting at Garelli's hotel was brief but cordial. Garelli told the other two that he had personally commissioned Poirot to organize the process of selecting new auditors worldwide and had been pleased with his presentation to the board. He also emphasized the matrix structure of the firm which was organized both geographically and by major activity groups, such as tunnelling, bridge construction, marine facilities, and so forth.

De Lesseps had known Michel Brugge, the deputy finance director, for several years, since he had formerly been with Van Buren. D'Amato was approaching retirement age, and it seemed likely that his deputy might succeed him within the next two years—or possibly sooner. Brugge had told de Lesseps in the past that he could not envisage replacing Coulson & Stuart as the auditors on the consolidation accounts. Since Brugge appeared to be the strongest person with respect to appointment of new auditors, it was felt unlikely that Garelli would attempt to overrule him.

The Proposal Team Gets Together

Following his meetings with Poirot and Garelli, de Lesseps moved quickly to create a proposal team in Brussels. The European office in Paris provided him with a writer/researcher, Marie-Laure Cot. A partner from the Milan office, Ugo Bianchi, who knew the construction business well, agreed to participate in the team's initial strategy session.

The team's first meeting was held two days before the Christmas holidays. Ms. Cot had prepared a dossier summarizing key information about MVB's operations around the world. This included a table listing MVB's 53 country offices and its current auditors in each one (*refer to Exhibit 1*).

Opening the meeting, de Lesseps declared:

Winning this proposal would be very significant for Peters & Champlain. It's not just the revenues from the worldwide engagement that we're interested in, but also the opportunity for P&C to put into place the 'One Firm, Worldwide' concept that we've talked about so often since the merger. To get this type of business, it's not sufficient to demonstrate that we have a worldwide network of strong local firms—we have to be perceived as truly international in outlook.

We're dealing here with some very distinct differences in culture. On the one hand, there's Van Buren, which is Belgian and where most of top management is Flemish; however, they have given considerable autonomy to their French minority interests, especially in view of all the work they brought in on the Channel Tunnel. The French would never allow themselves to be run by the guys in Brussels! Then there's the old Montini operation based in Italy, but also very strong in Switzerland and Germany, where Van Buren was never able to make much headway. The merger has greatly strengthened the company around the world. Separately, each firm was active in about 35 countries, jointly MVB now operates in 53. And they have a broader array of expertise now; Montini had an outstanding reputation on bridges, highways, and airport construction, while Van Buren was big in dams, tunnelling, and seaports.

From my conversations with MVB it's clear that they see audit work as a commodity—a low price commodity. This was particularly true of Van Buren. Their head office in Brussels would make a short list for their office in each country to choose from. They always claimed that industry knowledge was less important than price.

Poirot told me that he saw all six competitors as fairly equal in quality, but that MVB would be concentrating on global reach, and how each firm would approach the audit and deliver the feedback—the product that they would like to get out of the audit. He said they would concentrate much more on that than on the industry focus itself. What he is interested in knowing is how we propose to approach the audit, how we will manage the audit—how we would organize ourselves, set up our reporting procedures, and so on. He kept emphasizing the end product. He downplayed the opinion on the consolidated financial statements and focused more on the feedback we might be able to offer.

Examining the Audit Process

De Lesseps rose from his chair, walked to the board, picked up a blue marker, and sketched out a rectangle which he divided into four columns. At the top of the first column, he wrote "Planning." The second was headed "Execution," the third, "Reporting," and the fourth "Follow Up." Turning to the group, he remarked:

You could describe the audit process like this. You do your planning based on significant areas that you identify. You can apply this to various things, such as the budget, which is the precalculation of the profitability of an engagement. In the follow up, you can determine whether it was actually profitable or not. My point is that for each stage there are products. The products for the planning stage are the audit plan and the approach plan. For the execution stage, there are audit programs and working papers. Under reporting we have the audit report and management letter. Finally, under follow up, there's the invoice.

With his marker, de Lesseps circled the entire group of products at the bottom of the four columns (*refer to Exhibit 2*). "Some clients consider the whole thing to be a commodity," he declared. "But my point is that a commodity consists of a number of detailed products. And you can differentiate your service by adding value to some of these products." He then underlined "management letter," "audit plan" and "approach plan," adding:

Here's where the big opportunity to add value takes place—the management letter. And the contents and value of that letter are dependent

EXHIBIT 1 *Countries with MVB Operations and Names of Auditors as of December 1991*

Region/Country	Current Auditors[1]
Europe/Near East	
Austria	Local firm
Belgium	P&C (Peters & Champlain)
Cyprus	FBG-WB (FBG-Wills Boswell)
Denmark	JP (Jones Pittman)
Finland	Local firm
France	Local firm
Germany	C&S (Coulson & Stuart)
Greece	Local firm
Hungary	unaudited
Italy	C&S
Netherlands	P&C
Norway	Local firm
Portugal	Local firm
Spain	Local firm
Sweden	JP
Switzerland	DMC (Davis, Miller & Champbell)
Turkey	Local firm
United Kingdom	Local firm
North America & Caribbean	
Bahamas	Local firm
Canada	P&C
Dominican Republic	JP
Jamaica	Local firm
Mexico	Local firm
Trinidad	P&C
United States	C&S
Central & South America	
Argentina	JP
Brazil	MA (Martin Amundsen)
Chile	Local firm
Costa Rice	Local firm
Ecuador	Local firm
Guyana	Local firm
Panama	JP
Venezuela	JP

Region/Country	Current Auditors[1]
North Africa/Arabia	
Egypt	Local firm
Iraq	Local firm (office closed)
Kuwait	Local firm
Morocco	Local firm
Saudi Arabia	DMC
Central & Southern Africa	
Ivory Coast	Local firm
Kenya	C&S
Nigeria	FBG-WB
South Africa	Local firm
Zimbabwe	Local firm
Asia-Pacific	
Australia	P&C
Hong Kong	P&C
India	Local firm
Indonesia	Local firm
Japan	Local firm
Malaysia	C&S
New Zealand	Local firm
Singapore	P&C
Taiwan	DMC
Thailand	Local firm
Consolidation	
(Luxembourg)	C&S

[1] Only Big Six firms are named

EXHIBIT 2 *Framework Sketched by Piet de Lesseps*			

Stages

Planning	Execution	Reporting	Follow up
Significant Issues	Significant Issues	Significant Issues	Significant Issues
Audit Plan Audit Approach	Audit Program Working Papers	Audit Report Management Letter	Invoice

Products

on what you do in the audit plan and approach plan, such as identifying weak spots. You don't start working until you understand what you need to do, you know what the significant areas are and document them to management. You can increase your likelihood of coming up with comments that are likely to be of value to management in terms of how they are running their company.

An audit is much more than adding or taking away numbers. We're talking about understanding the business, risk analysis, and so forth. When you're dealing with multinational clients, it becomes much more important to understand the business in a global sense. With a local client, you can deal with a local environment and focus on local issues, local tax laws, and so forth. In companies like MVB, your primary contacts on the top level are often a small group of managers who have a huge multinational company and feel a little bit uncomfortable in terms of their ability to control the whole system. They look to the

auditors to give them additional comfort with respect to the quality of the international operation—are the numbers reliable, do they have control over their operations, do they know what kinds of assets they have, and do they collect cash on their assets? This is what should be reflected in the management letter.

De Lesseps opened the floor to discussion. One of the senior managers present, Caroline O'Brien, raised an issue:

Mr. Poirot says he doesn't want us to do anything that isn't material to the consolidation. But legal reporting requirements in many countries still have to be observed. He wants us to bring down fees, but I'm not sure he understands that MVB's legal structure requires substantially more audit work than might be necessary for purely business reasons.

"That's a good point," de Lesseps admitted. "I think Poirot still has quite a lot to learn about MVB. But it doesn't alter the fact that the market for audit services is changing from a cost plus basis to a price-led situation."

Study Questions

1. What is the potential value of the MVB business to P&C?

2. What does MVB really want? Why have they decided to go from 34 audit firms to 1?

3. How well-placed is P&C relative to the other competing firms?

4. What is the decision-making unit at MVB, who are its members, and how much influence do they wield?

5. How can auditors add value to an engagement for the client?

6. Recommend a strategy to be included in MVB's short list and then win the second round.

Credits

Chapter 2 p. 48: Used with permission of The Charles Schwab Corporation; p. 49: Used with permission of L. L. Bean.

Chapter 3 p. 58: Courtesy of WingspanBank.com, photo by Steven Bronstein.

Chapter 6 p. 175: Used with permission of Hampton Inns.

Chapter 8 p. 243: Copyright 2000 Sun Microsystems, Inc. All rights reserved. Used by permission. Sun, Sun Microsystems, the Sun logo, Java, Solaris, StarOffice, and all Sun-based and Java-based marks are trademarks or registered trademarks of Sun Microsystems in the United States and other countries.

Chapter 9 p. 276: Used with permission of Priceline.com.

Chapter 10 p. 290: Used with permission of Trend Micro, Inc.; p. 292: used with permission of JP Morgan; p. 293: Used with permission of Radisson; p. 301: Used with permission of Prudential Insurance Co. of America; p. 302: Used with permission of Bank of America; p. 304: Used with permission of Northwest Airlines

Chapter 17 p. 513: Used with permission of Fujitsu Corp.; p. 528: Used with permission of Star Alliance.

Index